MICHAEL SCHMIDT

LIVES OF THE POETS

Michael Schmidt was born in 1947 in Mexico, where he was raised. He studied at Harvard and Oxford and is now director of the Writing School at Manchester Metropolitan University in Manchester, England. He is the editor of *PN Review,* which he established in 1972, and is founder and editorial director of Carcanet Press, which publishes poetry and fiction. His books include collections of poetry, critical books, two novels, and several anthologies. He has translated Nahuatl (Aztec) poetry, and poems and essays by Octavio Paz.

LIVES OF THE POETS

LIVES OF THE POETS

MICHAEL SCHMIDT

VINTAGE BOOKS

A Division of Random House, Inc.

New York

FIRST VINTAGE BOOKS EDITION, OCTOBER 2000

Copyright © 1998 by Michael Schmidt

All rights reserved under International and Pan-American
Copyright Conventions. Published in the United States by Vintage
Books, a division of Random House, Inc., New York. Originally
published in slightly different form in Great Britain by Weidenfeld
& Nicolson, London, in 1998. First published in hardcover in the
United States by Alfred A. Knopf, a division of
Random House, Inc., New York, in 1999.

Vintage and colophon are registered trademarks of Random House, Inc.

The Library of Congress has cataloged the Knopf edition as follows:
Schmidt, Michael, 1947–
Lives of the poets / Michael Schmidt. —1st American ed.
p. cm.
Originally published: London : Weidenfeld & Nicolson, 1998.
Includes bibliographical references (p.) and index.
ISBN 0-375-40624-7.
1. English poetry—History and criticism.
2. American poetry—History and criticism.
3. Poets, American—Biography.
4. Poets, English—Biography.
I. Title.
PR502.S35 1999
821.009—dc21 98-51913
CIP

Vintage ISBN: 0-375-70604-6

Book design by Virginia Tan

www.vintagebooks.com

Printed in the United States of America
10 9 8 7 6 5 4 3

To Charles Schmidt,
Isabel Schmidt
and
Benedict Schmidt, with love

Contents

xii

Contents

LIVES OF THE POETS

The Match

JOSEPH BRODSKY, DEREK WALCOTT,
SEAMUS HEANEY, LES MURRAY

While the Irish football team played the Soviet Union in 1988, four English poets were confined in a radio studio in Dublin—it was the Writers' Conference—to take part in a round-table discussion. English-*language* poets, that is, for none of them accepts the sobriquet "English" and one has vehemently rejected it. In the chair was an anglophone Mexican publisher, me.

First of the four was Russian. Joseph Brodsky, a Nobel Prize winner, was attempting that almost possible Conradian, Nabokovian transition from one language to another, writing his new poems directly in English. Jet-lagged and impatient to return to the soccer, he expressed strong opinions on politics, religion, poetry and sport. In his essays he has argued that, as imperial centers corrode and weaken, poetry survives most vigorously in remote provinces, far from their decaying capitals. One thinks of Rome. Now that the British and American claims to the English language have loosened, the art of English poetry continues to thrive. The *bourse* may still be in the publishing centers of London or New York, but the shares quoted there are in poetic corporations with headquarters in New South Wales, St. Lucia, County Wicklow . . .

There is a triumphalism in this line of argument: emancipation. The postcolonial is as much a fashion in literature as the Colonial is in home decoration. Brodsky might have conceded (he did not) that ethnicity, gender and sexual preference can themselves be provinces or peripheries in which, even at the heart of the old geographical centers of empire, poetry can grow. It is an art that thrives when language itself is interrogated, from the moment John Gower challenged himself, "Why *not* write in English?" to Wordsworth's asking, "Why *not* write a language closer to speech?" to Adrienne Rich's asking, "Why write in the forms that a tradition hostile to me and my kind prescribes?" History and politics can play a part: they propose questions. In poetry the answers come not as argument but as form.

Over a century and a half ago America began to establish its independence, kicking (as Edgar Allan Poe put it) the British grandmama downstairs. Early in this century Scotland began to reaffirm its space, and Ireland too, a space that is firstly political and then cultural. We can speak of sharing a *common* language only when we possess it, when it is *our* language rather than *theirs*. For the Jamaican poet and historian Edward Kamau Braithwaite the English of the educational system in which he was raised, the English of the poetic tradition, is *theirs*. For many black writers in the United States in the 1950s and 1960s, it was *theirs*. For working-class English writers such as Tony Harrison it was *theirs*. When writers interrogate language, they set themselves one of two tasks: to reinvent it, or to take it by storm and (as the novelist Gabriel García Márquez puts it) "expropriate it," give it to the people, often for the first time. "I hate relegation of any sort," says Les Murray. "I hate people being left out. Of course, that I suppose has been the main drama of my life—coming from the left-out people into the accepted people and being worried about the relegated who are still relegated. I don't want there to be any pockets of relegation left."

A time has almost come—the round-table discussion was early evidence of it—to speak unapologetically of a common language, at least for poetry. Instead of affirming separation and difference, we can begin to affirm continuity—not only geographical but historical, analogies and real connections between Eavan Boland and Alfred, Lord Tennyson, Allen Ginsberg and William Blake, John Ashbery and Thomas Lovell Beddoes, Thom Gunn and Ben Jonson, Elizabeth Bishop and Alexander Pope. The story that includes all poets can be told from the beginning.

The second poet in the studio that afternoon was Derek Walcott, born in Castries, St. Lucia, in 1930, of a West Indian mother and an English father.

> I'm just a red nigger who love the sea,
> I had a sound colonial education,
> I have Dutch, nigger, and English in me,
> and either I'm nobody, or I'm a nation.

His was a francophone and Roman Catholic island; he is from an English-speaking Methodist culture. "Solidarity" is not the issue for him that it has become for Brathwaite. He distinguishes between English, his mother tongue, and the form he used at home, his mother's tongue. He might have courted approval had he chosen to affirm himself in terms of race, but he chose instead to identify himself with all the resources of his language. After all, English wasn't his "second language." "It was my language. I never felt it *belonged* to anybody else, I never felt that I was really borrowing it." In a poem about the shrinking back of empire, he writes, "It's good that everything's gone except their language, which is everything." "They" have left it and now it is his. Shakespeare, Herrick, Herbert and Larkin belong to him just as they would to an English person. There's no point in denying the violence and dislocations of colonialism, but if, given what history has already done, a writer responds by rejecting the untainted together with the tainted resources . . .

The third poet at the table was Seamus Heaney. Born in the north of Ireland, he has complained of being "force-fed" with "the literary language, the civilized utterance from the classic canon of English poetry." At school, poetry class "did not delight us by reflecting our experience; it did not re-echo our own speech in formal and surprising arrangements. Poetry lessons, in fact, were rather like catechism lessons."

He has tempered his views since he wrote of the "exclusive civilities" of English. At the round table he declared that the colonial and post-colonial argument is "a theme; it's a way of discoursing about other things, to talk about the language. It's a way of talking about being Protestants and Catholics without using bigoted, sectarian terms, it's a way of talking about heritage. But the fact of the matter is that linguistically one is very adept." He remembers as a child with "the South Derry intonation at the back of my throat" being able to hear, as he read, even though he could not speak it, the alien and beguiling intonations of P. G. Wodehouse. Language can be a medium of servitude; but it can also—properly apprehended—become a measure of freedom. "A great writer within any culture changes everything. Because the thing is different afterwards and people comprehend themselves differently. If you take Ireland before James Joyce and Ireland fifty years afterwards, the reality of being part of the collective life is enhanced and changed."

The fourth poet, the Australian Les Murray, is a witness to the abundance of the English language and to the freedoms it offers. Born in 1938 in Nabiac, rural New South Wales, he was an only child and grew up on his father's dairy farm in Bunyah. His mother died when he was a boy. In solitude he developed a close affinity with the natural world. Australia is a predominantly urban society; Murray is thoroughly rural. In 1986 he returned to Bunyah to farm, to live with the poetry of gossip, what he calls "bush balladry," and to work for "wholespeak." He takes his bearings, emblematically, from Homer and Hesiod: the arts of war and of peace (Hesiod's *Works and Days* embodies the principles of permanence, while the *Odyssey* with its endless wandering and a world subject to strange metamorphoses, and the *Iliad* with its sense of social impermanence and conflict, illuminate the principles of change).

A voice exists for every living creature, human or beast. It is one of the poet's tasks to listen and transcribe: the voice (the diction, syntax and cadence) of the cow and pig, the mollusk, the echidna, the strangler fig, the lyre bird and goose, the tick, the possum, "The Fellow Human." The past is included in the present, and the fuller its inclusion, the less likely relegation will be. Murray works toward an accessible poetry, telling stories, attempting secular and (he is a Roman Catholic) holy communion. An anti-modernist, he might respond to Ezra Pound's commandment "Make it new": "No, make it *present*."

Four writers in English with different accents and dialects, detained in a small recording studio in Dublin, deprived of the big match, all more or less agreeing on the integrity of their art, its place in the world, and on the continuities that it performs. Released at last (the match, alas, was over), the poets returned to Dun Laoghaire for dinner. Their conversation was raucous: a competition of salty tales and limericks ("There was a young fellow called Dave / Who kept a dead whore in a cave"). Neighbouring tables tutted and simmered, and a literary critic from Belfast in her indignation reported the poets' boisterous manners back to the *Times Literary Supplement*.

A time has come to speak unapologetically for a common language and to speak a common language of poetry. Almost.

Our Sublime Superiors

"We all know where we are not at. We all know who our sublime superiors are," says Derek Walcott. I had better declare a material interest in this common language of poetry and give a health warning.

When I was nineteen my father told me to pursue law or some useful vocation, anything I liked, he said liberally, even the Church or the army. What about publishing? Certainly not: speculation, gambling with uncertain futures or merely repackaging the past. When I became a publisher he advised me again: I was not to publish poetry. He echoed the Mr. Nixon of Ezra Pound's "Hugh Selwyn Mauberley": "And give up verse, my boy, / There's nothing in it."

I became a poetry publisher. Mr. Nixon was right—and wrong. The nothing can be very nearly the everything. But my father disowned me. We still exchanged letters, but he no longer took an interest in my future. I had none. I'd made myself a prodigal. I had also made myself free to adopt my own antecedents. I went in quest of them, and they were not easy to find. They survived—if at all—mostly in footnotes, obscure monographs and technical books.

The earliest were called scribes; they later became known as scriveners, printers, booksellers, and finally publishers. They worked in Southwark, then at St. Paul's, in Paternoster Row, Bloomsbury, the Corn Exchange, St. Martin's Lane, Vauxhall Bridge Road. Now we're scattered, like poets, to the round earth's imagined corners: Sydney, New York, Toronto, Jo'burg, Delhi, Wellington. Those who specialize are poor and have been poor for centuries. Why? So that poets—a few of them—can prosper. Publishers get written out of the story and poets live forever. Servants of the servants of the Muse, from the days of scriptoria to the world of desktop publishing, we are dogsbodies of the art: we edit, correct, scribe, typeset or key, print, bind, tout. Are we remembered?

How many of *us* can you name? William Caxton? Good. Maybe Wynkyn de Worde, just about. And after that—ever heard of Tottel,

Taylor, Murray? You might recognize a name, but only because of Wyatt or Clare or Byron. On the whole, as far as readers are concerned publishers are the aboriginal Anon. Gossip about us is sparse and generally unpleasant. If we misjudge a writer or commit a small human or financial irregularity that touches his or her biography, *then* we come alive, villains of the piece, alongside unfaithful spouses and wicked stepparents.

We were the first readers of almost every poem that traveled beyond the charmed circle of a writer's intimates. We said what would go in and in what order, we said change this, drop that (or we silently changed and dropped), we abridged and expanded. We assembled anthologies. We decided when a writer should go public, how long a book should live, how widely it should circulate. We commissioned, gambled, lost and sometimes won. Our childhoods, our money worries, our sexual arrangements, our one-night stands with a promising manuscript and our long nights by taper or sixty-watt bulb *getting it right* for poets, so that they might shine like stars in the perpetual nighttime of your attention, count for very little in the histories.

How a poem arrives at a reader has an effect on how it is conceived and written. The ballad sheet, the illuminated manuscript, the slim volume, the epic poem, the "representative anthology," the electronic poem or performance piece—each makes different demands on the poet and has a distinct technology and market. Poets of the fourteenth century, dreaming of their work passing from hand to hand, have a different sense of their destiny from poets hammering away at word processors or rapping under strobes. Technology is a part of imagination. Parchment elicits one attitude from a writer, paper another. The very textures (not to mention prices) are part of the equation. The cost of eloquence. A quill, a biro and a keyboard download a poet in different ways, at different speeds. Without succumbing to "historical materialism," we can register those differences. The gynecologist William Carlos Williams with quill on parchment would not have responded to the plums in the refrigerator as he did, or written all those little and big poems between patients, swiveling round from his consultancy desk to a typewriter impatient for his attention; and Shakespeare with a word processor might have left better texts and at least have run a spell check. Creative technologies evolve (not always for the better). So does language. So does publishing.

We publishers moved from open-plan scriptoria to stalls in provincial market towns to little bookshops and printers, to small shared offices, to private offices and back to open plan again. So many centuries! We began with Latin. The English we eventually scribed and later printed doesn't immediately strike a modern reader as English.

Only when translated into sound, spoken aloud, does it become comprehensible. If not, our job is to facilitate, to modernize.

And we have a life outside the office, beyond the marketplace. We sit up evenings by a hissing gas fire or under a dozen rugs and read hungrily. Among parchments or manuscripts, or unreeling a document on our screens, we are alchemists looking for gold. By messenger or post or down the line, or over an expensive lunch where we smile and pay, we're receivers of work that's often conceived in sunlight, in repose, in the country, in the jungle, in love's raptures or the rich madness of betrayal, by women and men who live full lives. As for living, our authors will do that for us.

We make choices and reputations, and we are humble. Does a priest feel humble when he hears confession? Does a doctor show humility before a pregnant belly, a head cold or a boil? We have power, yet our authors make us invisible! We legitimize them, then bow to that legitimacy. Just occasionally we emerge from behind the arras, pierced like Polonius by a hundred bodkins shoved into us by poets, biographers and critics. Do we answer back? Can we at least tell a different story?

"Only a poet of experience," Robert Graves says, "can hope to put himself in the shoes of his predecessors, or contemporaries, and judge their poems by recreating technical and emotional dilemmas which they faced while at work on them." A publisher can, too. We turn many a falsehood into truth. Our mishearing or misreading has improved texts. Graves recommends copying out texts by hand, to discover where the weaknesses and strengths are located. "Analeptic mimesis" he calls it. It's grand to have a Greek name for it. Second best is reading aloud: these are still the most efficient approaches to a poem.

I'm not a poet. What am I doing, what can I *know*, I who am worse—my father would have said—than a gambler? "You make books. But you know little. Just as the honey-bottler knows nothing about bees. Why should you be my Virgil, my guide, among the living and the dead?" Because I can read, I can speak, I have ears. I have memory. "But you're entering protected territory. You're no linguist, no prosodist, you're not a historian or a philosopher. Specialists will have your guts for garters. What hope have you of escaping unscathed?"

No hope at all. But we're *all* readers. Being a reader is a worthwhile liberty. I don't doubt I'll make errors—of emphasis, fact, commission, omission. But on the whole we're the lucky ones. Specialists read from a specialism, finding a way through to what they know they'll find. Say they're philologists, literary historians or theorists. They have an agenda, poems slot into it. If *we* stumble across poems they've pinned like butterflies to an argument and try to unpin them so they can fly again, or die, they dismiss us as unlicensed. I prefer to be unlicensed, to read a poem, not a text. Poems, no matter how "difficult" the language when it first sneaks up on us, no matter how opaque the allusions or complex the imagery, no matter what privileges the author enjoyed or how remote his or her learning is from ours—poems because they're there, because they've been published and survived, are democratic spaces. Poetry is language with a shape. It communicates by *giving*. It doesn't conform to a *critical* code. It elicits answering energies from our imaginations—if we listen closely.

We should cultivate techniques of ignorance, C. H. Sisson says, in order to find out what's there, not what we expected to find. Ignorance, if we acknowledge it, is a useful instrument of self-effacement, a way of eluding prejudice, reflex, habitual response. As soon as we're properly ignorant we begin to develop a first rather than a second nature, to question even familiar things in ways that would not have occurred to us before, to hear sounds in poems that eluded our "trained" ears.

A particularly acid but astute biographer (Lytton Strachey) declared: "Ignorance is the first requisite of the historian—ignorance, which simplifies and clarifies, which selects and omits, with a placid perfection unattainable by the highest art." The task is less to explain than to illuminate. We follow a rough chronology because it is convenient to do so, not because we are historicists; and beams of light from the twentieth century shine into the souks and chapels of the fourteenth; the seventeenth century is not extinguished in the twentieth but provides penetrating rays. As we approach a period or a poet in this story, we may feel anticipation as at reaching a familiar town—and surprise that it is not mapped quite as we expected.

Mercator in 1569 published his famous map projection, a vision of the world as the segmented peel of an orange. It took him a long time to get it right; it has been subject to adjustment ever since. How to reduce a lumpy sphere to a plane? Was he the first Cubist? At least his plane is a comprehensible, if not immediately recognizable, image of a sphere at a particular time. The task of drawing a world map of English poetry is like playing three-dimensional chess: you have the growing spaces that English occupies, and three quarters of a millennium during which the poetry has been written in a language gathering into standard forms and then, like Latin at the end of its great age, beginning to diversify into dialects that will become languages in turn. Any account of poetry in English will falsify.

I'm talking myself back to humility, not a virtue with which to embark on an adventure such as this. The best reader needs the seven deadly sins in double measure. *Pride* makes us equal with specialists and professional critics and impervious to their attacks. *Lechery* puts us in tune with the varied passions and loves that we encounter. We feel *envy* when a reader who has gone before preempts our response; this only spurs us on to fresh readings. *Anger* overwhelms us when injustices occur, and it should be disproportionate: when a poet dies in destitution or is lost for a generation or a century. We experience *covetousness* when we encounter poets we are prepared to love but their books are unavailable in the shops, so we covet our friends' libraries or the great private collections. *Gluttony* means we will not be satisfied even by a full helping of Spenser or the whole mess of *The Excursion*; we feed and feed and still ask for more. Finally dear old *sloth* has us curled up on a sofa or swinging in a hammock with our books piled around, avoiding the day job and the lover's complaint. These are necessary vices. The list is found in Langland, Chaucer, Spenser, Marlowe. They knew these vices from the inside, personified and warned against them; don't imagine *they* were innocent. The lavish attention they gave to the vices reveals how much commerce they had with them.

Theorem number one: Wars and revolutions *always* come at the wrong time for poetry; the big possibilities of Gower, Chaucer and Langland, postponed by history and the rise of classical humanism; the lessons of Ben Jonson and the Metaphysicals, dispatched at the Commonwealth; then the appalling ascendancy of French and classical prejudices which eventually drove real talent to madness or the cul-de-sacs of satire and sententiousness; then the French Revolution with its seductions and betrayals wasting another generation of new things, turning it back, as it were, toward the prison houses of the eighteenth century. *Theorem number two:* The French have a lot to answer for, from Norman times onward; and the First World War, its bloody harvest of so much that was new and promised well, impoverishing modernism because it killed Hulme, Rosenberg, Brzeska and also Edward Thomas. There's no straight line, it's all zigzags, like history. Poems swim free of their age and live in ours; but if we understand them on their own terms rather than conform them to ours, they take on a fuller life, and so do we.

The Anthology

One could abandon writing
for the slow-burning signals
of the great, to be, instead
their ideal reader, ruminative,
voracious, making the love of masterpieces
superior to attempting
to repeat or outdo them,
and be the greatest reader in the world.

—Derek Walcott, "Volcano"

Poems swim free of their age, but it's hard to think of a single poem that swims entirely free of its medium, not just language but language used in the particular ways that are poetry. Even the most parthenogenetic-seeming poem has a pedigree. The poet may not know precisely a line's or a stanza's parents; indeed, may not be interested in finding out. Yet as readers of poetry we can come to know more about a poem than the poet does and know it more fully. To know more does not imply that we read Freud into an innocent cucumber, or Marx into a poem about daffodils, but that we *read with our ears* and hear Chaucer transmuted through Spenser, Sidney through Herbert, Milton through Wordsworth, Skelton through Graves, Housman through Larkin, Sappho through H.D. or Adrienne Rich.

Reflecting on poets outstanding today: each has an individual culture. Ted Hughes dwells on Shakespeare, Thom Gunn on the sixteenth century, Donald Davie on the eighteenth. Poets are made of poems and other literary works from a past that especially engages them and of works by near antecedents and contemporaries that embed themselves in whole or in part in their imaginations. Some works stick as phrases, others as misremembered lines. There are also phrases and lines held deliberately hostage, jotted in a notebook for eventual exploitation. Reading T. S. Eliot's *The Waste Land*, we can discriminate between fragmentary allusions that imagining memory provides and those that come from the hostage list. Other poems are less candid in revealing source and resource. Edward Thomas writes, "All the clouds like sheep / On the mountains of sleep"—an amazing image; its source is a poem by Walter de la Mare, and de la Mare's source is Keats. Thomas's genius is in choosing the image and adjusting it to his poem's purposes, not in disguising its theft. There is no theft in poetry except straightforward plagiarism. Every poet has a hand in another poet's pocket, lifting out small change and sometimes a folded bill. It's borrowing, a borrowing that is paid back by a poem.

A poet is a kind of anthologist. Figuratively speaking, John Gower and Geoffrey Chaucer lined up the French poems and classical stories they were going to translate or transpose into English; they marked passages to expand or excise. From secondary sources (in memory, or on parchment) they culled images, passages, facts, to slot into their new context. Then began the process of making those resources reconfigure for *their* poem. Then they began to add something of their own. The scholarly sport of searching out sources and analogues is useful in determining not only what is original in conception, but what is original in mutation or metamorphosis, how the poet alters emphases, changes the color of the lover's hair, adjusts motive, enhances evocations, to make a new poem live. Thomas Gray a few centuries later was making poems out of bits and pieces of classics, the Lego set from which he builds "Elegy in a Country Churchyard," the most popular poem in English, read, for the most part, in blissful ignorance of its resources. "Blissful ignorance" is from Gray as well: "Where ignorance is bliss / 'Tis folly to be wise." Phrases of verse that enter the common language are transmuted in the naïve poetry of speech. Individual speech itself is an anthology of phrases and tags—from hymns, songs, advertisements, poems, political orations, fairy tales and nursery rhymes—the panoply of formal language that form makes liminally memorable. As speakers, each of us is an inadvertent anthologist.

A poet is an inadvertent anthologist working at a different intensity. There is a tingling in the nerves. A poem starts to happen. Selection of language begins in the darkroom of the imagination, the critical intelligence locked out, coming into play only after a print is lifted out of the tray and hung on the wire to dry, the light switched on revealing what is there. The critical intelligence discards blurred, dark or overexposed prints at this stage. Those that survive become subject to adjustment and refinement, unless the poet is one of those who insist on the sacredness of the first take. Preprocessing has occurred: the Polaroid principle.

The greatest reader in the world has a primary task: to set a poem free. In order to do so the reader must *hear* it fully. If in a twentieth-century poem about social and psychological disruption a sudden line of eighteenth-century construction irrupts, the reader who is not alert to the irony in diction and cadence is not alert to the poem. A texture of tones and ironies, or a texture of voices such as we get in John Ashbery, or elegiac strategies in Philip Larkin, or Eastern forms in Elizabeth Daryush and Judith Wright, or prose transpositions in Marianne Moore and (differently) in Patricia Beer: anyone aspiring to be the greatest reader in the world needs to hear in a poem read aloud or on the page what it is made from. As a poet develops, the textures change. Developments and changes are the life of the poet, more than the factual biography. But the "higher gossip" of biography generally distracts readers from engaging the more fascinating story of poetic growth.

A poet grows, poetry grows. The growth of poetry is the story of poems, where they come from and how they change. It begins in the story of language. Where does the English poetic medium begin, what makes it cohere, what impels it forward, what obstacles block its path? The medium becomes an increasingly varied resource; the history of poetry within it is not linear, the rise and fall of great dynasties, the decisive changes of political history; in the eighteenth century it is possible for a Romantic sensibility to exist, for a poet to write medieval poetry, just as in the reign of Charles I poets might still write out of the Elizabethan sensibility, in Elizabethan forms. In the twentieth century the poetry of Pound and Eliot, of Masefield and Hardy and Kipling, of Graves, of the imperialist poets, of Charlotte Mew and Anna Wickham, all occupy the same decades, each anachronistic in terms of the others. William Carlos Williams begins in the shadow of Keats and Shelley and ends casting his own shadows; J. H. Prynne begins in the caustic styles of the Movement and the 1950s and develops his own divergent caustic strategies. There is a history of poetry and, within the work of each poet, a history of poems.

We have to start with language. And to start with language we must also start with politics. The struggle of English against Latin and French is the resistance; the struggle of English against Gaelic, Welsh, Irish and Cornish is a less heroic chapter. Imperial English generates new resistances. At every point there are poems, voice-prints from which we can infer a mouth, a face, a body and a world. A world that we can enter by listening as we move our lips through the series of shapes and sounds the letters on the page demand.

Where It Begins

RICHARD ROLLE OF HAMPOLE,
ROBERT MANNING OF BRUNNE, JOHN BARBOUR

Where do we first experience formal language? In lullaby, nursery rhyme, street rhymes, popular songs, anthems. In church, synagogue, mosque or temple, in hymn and scripture and sermon; in graveyards, on tombstones.

English poets at the start of the fourteenth century were sung to by their mothers or—orphaned by the plague—by foster mothers or relations. They were dragged to church, through churchyards full of individual and mass graves, many inscribed with scripture, others with Latin verses; inside they heard Latin intoned, and sang English, French and Latin. There were sermons in English, the priest pointed to bright paintings of religious events on the walls, or in the stained glass windows, or at statues and images—aids to make visible the truths of faith. Those images expressed a long tradition of symbolism and composition to feed the imagination. Incense clouded from the censers, spreading over upturned faces. The bright images hovered, as if removed, in another, an ideal and lavishly illuminated, sphere, above the reeking congregation.

In such polyglot churches, where shreds of paganism survived in elaborate ceremonial, the children who were to be poets learned that things could be said in quite different languages, and that the language they spoke at home or in the lanes always came last. They learned that there were parallel worlds, the stable Latin world of the paintings, windows, statues, and the world in which they lived, where plagues and huge winds and wars erased the deeds of men. Obviously the earth was a place of trial, hardship and preparation. They wrote out of this knowledge. Knowledge, not belief. Belief came later, when knowledge began to learn its limitation. Belief is an act of spiritual will, born of the possibility of disbelief, born with the spirit of the Reformation. That spirit was just beginning to stir.

Our starting point is fourteenth-century England, a "colonial" cul-
ture subject to Norman rules if not rule, with a Catholic spiritual gov-
ernment answerable to Rome. The people accept the ephemerality of
this world and an absolute promise of redemption for those who prac-
tice the faith. They know that the language of learning is Latin, that the
language of power and business Norman French, and that their English
is a poor cousin. When the Normans took England they saw no merit
in the tongue: an aberration to be erased, just as the English later tried
to erase Irish and Welsh, Scots Gaelic and Cornish, or to impose
English in the colonies. They succeeded rather better than the Nor-
mans did.

By the end of the fourteenth century, the time for English had come,
with the poetry of Sir John Gower, Geoffrey Chaucer, William Lang-
land, the Gawain poet and the balladeers with the dew still fresh upon
it, with an oral tradition alive in market towns, provincial courts and
manor houses. It took most of the century for this to happen, and by the
end some high poetic peaks rose out of a previously almost entirely flat
landscape.

The turbulent middle of the fourteenth century broke the prejudice
in which English was held; it began to flex its muscles. Calamity was its
patron. The Black Death first reached English shores before John
Gower turned twenty, in the twenty-first year of Edward III's reign. In
August of 1348 it arrived from France at Weymouth. It devastated Bris-
tol, and in the early part of 1349 overtook London and East Anglia. It
was still at large in Scotland and Ireland in 1350. Consider what it was
like, to learn each day of dead or dying friends, to see bodies carted
through the streets or heaped in a tangled mess at corners. It was an
especially disgusting illness that started with hard lumps and tumors,
then scalding fever, gray patches on the skin like leprosy. Then the
cough, blood welling from the lungs. A victim had three days: terror,
agony, death.

Langland describes it in a passage that the eighteenth-century critic
Thomas Warton says John Milton may have stored away in his mind (in
Paradise Lost, Book II, lines 475ff). Langland says:

Kynde cam aftir, with many kene soris,	Nature; running sores
As Pockes and Pestilences, and moch	Scabs; destroyed many people
peple shente.	
So Kynde thorgh corruptions, killid ful	
manye:	
Deeth cam dryvyng aftir, and al to dust	dashed to the ground
[pashed]	

Kings and knyghttes, Kaysours, and emperors and popes
popis . . .
Many a lovely lady, and lemmanys of knights' lovers
knyghttes,
Swowed and sweltid for sorwe of Dethis swooned and died; blows
dentes.

All at once there were not enough peasants to work the soil, servants to tend the house, or priests to administer unction and conduct funeral services. No one was immune. Three archbishops of Canterbury and in Norwich eight hundred diocese priests, and half the monks in Westminster, all died in one year. Eight *hundred* priests. The Church was big; the Black Death was bigger. Women toiled in the fields, harvests were left to rust. Parliament was suspended, courts of law were not convened. It was a time of too much loss for sorrow, too much fear for civil strife. There were more dead than graves to put them in: they were piled in plague pits and covered with lime. If the plague made feast of the poor, it was at least democratic. The powerful were not immune: the king's own daughter perished.

Another victim was a big-hearted anchorite who wrote verse, Richard Rolle of Hampole. "Full dear me think He has me bought with bloody hands and feet." He was a man of soul. A poet-martyr. Perhaps he translated the Psalms. It is hard to establish authentic "texts" by an author unless a number of similar manuscripts survive. Most medieval writers formed schools, their works were copied, added to and altered. Much has been assigned to Richard Rolle that may not belong to him. Why was he such a *bad* poet, with only some occasional astonishing lines?

He was born about 1300 at Thornton-le-Dale near Pickering, North Yorkshire. The north of England was the center of English writing—furthest from Norman influence—but it began to lose out to the Midlands. Oxford was becoming focal, especially after the foundation of Balliol College around 1263. Rolle went to Oxford at a time when the friars still led exemplary lives. He learned Latin, disliked ordinary philosophical writers and loved scripture above all else. At nineteen he returned home, anxious about his soul, intending to become a hermit. He preached. The Dalton family set him up as a hermit on their estate. (Hermits were not unusual in the medieval world; they were licensed and controlled by bishops.) He never became a priest but may have been in minor orders. His authority was spiritual. After some years he moved to a new cell close to a hermit called Margaret Kirby; then to Hampole, near Doncaster. Cistercian nuns looked after him. On Michaelmas Day

1349 the Black Death took him. The nuns petitioned for him to be made a saint.

His verses—if they are his—express personal feeling simply. He began in the old alliterative tradition but progressed to rhyme. His followers imitated what was an easy style. What is his, what did he borrow or translate, and what belongs to his follower William Nassyngton? When we think we're admiring Rolle we may be admiring Nassyngton's imitation; but then there is not much to admire in Rolle or his followers. Already poets—even holy poets—are practicing techniques of false attribution: getting their work read by borrowing the authority of a revered name. Publishers began to practice this subterfuge two hundred years later, but it's as well to remember that they learned that deception, and others, from religious poets.

Rolle especially loved the Psalms: "grete haboundance of gastly [ghostly, i.e., spiritual] comfort and joy in God comes in the hertes of thaim at says or synges devotly the psalmes in lovynge of Jesus Crist." He wrote a Latin commentary; then another followed by English versions. It is hard to extrapolate a system of belief from his work, but his doctrine of love is not like other mystics': he is alive to the world he only half inhabits. The good works a man does in this world praise God. Injustice offends *caritas*, and such acts particularly rile God.

His Latin works display, a friendly critic says, "more erudition than eloquence." The surviving verse in English includes a paraphrase of the Book of Job, a Lord's Prayer, seven penitential psalms, and the almost unreadable *The Pricke of Conscience*. It must have been readable once, for it has been widely preserved in manuscript. Warton copied it out and said: "I prophesy that I am its last transcriber." In seven parts, it treats of man's nature, of the world, death, purgatory, Judgment Day, hell's torments and heaven's joys. The verse is awkward to scan: a basic iambic tetrameter measure with six, seven and sometimes (depending on the voicing of the final *e* and how regular you want the iamb to be) ten syllables to the line, and from three to five stresses. It raises the crucial problem of all the old poems: there's so much variation between manuscripts that it's impossible to say what the poet intended.

Miracles occurred at Hampole when the nuns tried to have Rolle canonized. His fame revived just before the Peasants' Revolt, when Lollard influence was increasing. (Lollard, from *lollen*, to loll or idle, was applied to street preachers.) His writings were exploited by reformers. Around 1378 his commentary on the Psalms was reissued with Lollardish interpolations. No one knows who revised it: some point the finger, implausibly, at John Wycliffe. Though not a poet, though his works are as confused in attribution as Rolle's, though exploited, celebrated and reviled for centuries after his death, Wycliffe is one of the tutelary spirits presiding over our history. He made it possible not only for King David to sing in English—there were English versions of the psalter before Rolle—but for Moses and Jesus and God to use our vernacular, for the Bible as a whole to land on our shores in our own language. Suddenly English is good enough for Jesus. It has become legitimate.

The Black Death returned again and again. "Servitude was disappearing from the manor and new classes were arising to take charge of farming and trade." Thus G. M. Trevelyan tells it, making it part of an abstract process, draining it of human anguish and spiritual vertigo. "Modern institutions were being grafted on to the mediaeval, in both village and town. But in the other great department of human affairs— the religious and ecclesiastical, which then covered half of human life and its relationships—institutional change was prevented by the rigid conservatism of the Church authorities, although here too thought and opinion were moving fast." They were provoked by the intransigence of men who governed and profited by the Church. These visionless administrators alienated free spirits and the intellectually dissatisfied. The voice of Wycliffe begins to become audible. Church corruption is attacked by Chaucer, by Langland and (more gently) by Gower; but Wycliffe drives it home from the pulpit and in his writings, forcefully to the lay heart, and to the very heart of the Church. The Church is no *more* corrupt than other institutions, but its corruption is privileged, sanctioned and directed from abroad. The laity is more educated than in the times of Anselm and Thomas à Becket. The Church all the same prefers to ignore discontent and keep its monopolies and privileges intact.

Customs of fiefdom that constrained peasants on the land and preserved the feudal order of society no longer held. Too few men remained to do the work: survivors began to realize their worth, and then their power. They wanted more than they'd had: mobility, food—they even wanted wages. Peasants began to band together, recognizing power in community. The rich grew less secure in privilege. They sensed that *they* were dependents. Up to a third of the population perished in two years. When the plague returned in 1361, it was a plague of children. That year cattle suffered a new disease as well. The fever touched souls: many thought God spoke through that fire.

Reformers found a voice. Some spoke English. Before then, nobles and merchants had taught their children French from the cradle: "And provincial men will liken themselves to gentlemen, and strive with great zeal for to speak French, so as to be more told of"—a kind of social bona fides. But under Edward III change began, accelerating under Richard II. "This manner was much used before . . . and is since then somewhat changed. For John Cornwall, a master of grammer, changed the lore in grammerschool and construction of French into English . . .

so that now, the year of our Lord a thousand three hundred four score and five, of the second kyng Richard after the Conquest nine, in all the grammerschools of England children leaveth French, and construeth and learneth in English, and haveth thereby advantage in one side, and disadvantage on another. Their advantage is that they learneth their grammer in less time than children were accustomed to do. Disadvantage is that no children of grammerschool conneth no more French than can their left heel, and that is harm for them if they should cross the sea and travel in strange lands."

The plague was a catalyst. But transformation was not easy. One version of English could be more remote from another than French was. A northern and a southern man, meeting by chance or for business, would resort to French because their dialects were mutually incomprehensible, as much in diction as in accent. English, a bastard tongue, starts to move in the other direction from Latin. Latin broke up, but English began to coalesce. Dialects started to merge into an English *language* when scribes and later printers got to work and London usage became the idiom for written transactions. Those who made language public and portable, in the form of broadsheets and books, brought it, and eventually us, together. After a hundred years a young maid of Dundee and an old man of Devizes could hold a kind of conversation, not necessarily in limericks.

Much more than half our vernacular literature was northern before that time. Perhaps it still is, except the north has learned to *parler* more conventionally. English in its youth was hungry. The Normans imposed French but English was voracious even before they came, and in the courts of Cnut and Ethelred, when the Conquest was some way off, adjustments took place, influences from the Continent resolving the knots of a congested Old English idiom. We swallowed French (digestion altered us). The Conquest meant that English in its various forms had to gobble up faster. Written texts can be more conservative than speech: there is authority in formality. It is a risk to use the language of the day for important matters because it's in flux and you never know which dialect, which bits of diction or patterns of syntax, will prevail.

Trevisa's translation of the *Polychronicon* reflects how "it seemeth a great wonder how English, that is the birth-tongue of Englishmen, and their own language and tongue, is so diverse of sound in this land," while Norman French, a foreign idiom, is the lingua franca of the islands. In Trevisa's own translation, which makes sense when read aloud, Higden writes: "For men of the est with men of the west, as hyt were vnder the same party of heuene, acordeth more in sounyng of speche than men of the north with men of the south. Therefore hyt

ys that Mercii, that buth men of myddel Engelond, as hyt were parte-
ners if the endes, vnderstondeth betre the syde longages, Northeron
and Southeron, than Northeron and Southeron vnderstondeth eyther
other." But it's the "Southeron" language that prevails. The "Northeron,"
Higden says, is *scharp, slyttyng, and frotyng*—harsh, piercing and grat-
ing. The birthplace of a prejudice.

Foreign affairs continued to be conducted during the plague as if
there was no crisis at home. Skirmishes, battles and wars in France,
Spain and Scotland, cruelty and piracy on every side. There was death
by disease and on the field. England was certainly part of Europe. Sick
at home, Englishmen went abroad to bring back wealth; they were
preparing for their defeat. Edward III died in 1377 and was succeeded by
Richard II, a boy who grew to a colorful, corrupt majority. Demands on
poor and common people grew: demands for tax, service, subjection.
The Peasants' Revolt had urgent causes, though it was too early in his-
tory for the masses to rise successfully against a king. It was high time—
Richard II knew it quite as well as Gower—for the court and the
masters to learn to speak and sing in the language of their people.

Fortunately there was more to build on than Richard Rolle of Ham-
pole. There was *Gawain and the Green Knight, Pearl*, the English bal-
lads and dozens of vulgar translations of French works. There are poems
the scholars will never find, ballads and lyrics, elegies, poems of moral
precept, religious meditations, lives of saints . . . Were they lost because
they weren't worth keeping, or because they were so constantly used
that they were thumbed to pieces? Parchment wasted with the hungry
love of reading eyes, recitation, with handing back and forth between
poets and scholars and minstrels. Were they lost when, at the Refor-
mation, great libraries were burned, or emptied out and sold to the
local gentry—as the wicked and wonderful biographer and gossip
John Aubrey remembers with pain—to be twisted into plugs for wine
casks, sliced into spills to start fires, or cut in convenient sheets as bog
parchment?

Reading English in the first half of the fourteenth century was a
furtive activity, frowned on by authority. When Edward III came to the
throne English was revalued; from being the underdog's tongue it
became the chosen instrument of Geoffrey Chaucer. Robert Manning
of Brunne had used what would become Chaucer's and Gower's tetra-
meters almost fifty years before, with a mechanical awkwardness that
Gower corrected. *Handlyng Sinne* was based on a French work by the
English writer William of Wadington, the *Manuel de Pechiez*—a book
Gower used too. Manning explained his purpose in his *Chronicle of
England*, completed in 1338:

Haf I alle in myn Inglis layd   set it all out in English
In symple speche as I couthe,   could
That is lightest in mannes mouthe.   easiest for men to say
I mad noght for no discours,
Ne for no seggers, no harpours,   not for singers nor harpers
But for the luf of symple men
That strange Inglis can not ken;
For many it ere that strange Inglis   elaborate
In ryme wate neuer what it is,   don't understand it
And bot thai wist what it mente,   unless they know
Ellis me thoght it were alle schente.   it would be wasted

The lines are end-stopped, little breathless runs. One can respond to them but their value is local. Crude stuff, the language not up to much, but it starts clearing a space. The same is true of the Scot John Barbour's vast limping history *The Bruce*, begun in 1372, where the lines do not pause but halt on a proud and assertive (if sometimes approximate) rhyme, often achieved with great violence to the word order. Yet he, too, prepared the way and Scots still have his book in their library of classics, though I suspect few actually read it, apart from schoolchildren who endure their "distinctive heritage" being rammed down their throats.

Tutelary Spirits

RICHARD II AND JOHN WYCLIFFE

Opposite John Wycliffe, England's first European mind, stands Richard II, the other presiding genius of this history. On an impulse he commanded Gower to write in English. He was king when modern (though we call it Middle) English poetry decisively came of age; after his reign darkness again began to fall on poetry.

But first to Wycliffe. Our poetry starts when God and King David, the poet of Ecclesiastes and Job, Jesus and St. Paul speak English with resounding confidence. Rolle and the early Bible translators must take some credit: they first tutored the divine. Reformers and prophets helped locate our distinctive voice. It was Wycliffe who laid the foundation for the English radical traditions, both the liberal and the revolutionary. The light and shadow of his thought play over the work of Gower and Chaucer, of Langland most of all. He is still spiritually and intellectually alive in the age of Milton, still just audible in Shelley. He is not forgotten until our radicalisms become secular and Marx displaces a long Christian socialist and utopian tradition with his materialist literalism.

Like Rolle, Wycliffe was born in Yorkshire, in 1320. Little is known of his career until 1360, when he is described as "master of Balliol" at Oxford. He received ecclesiastical preferments and in 1374 accepted the living of Lutterworth and held it until his death in 1384. His spiritual disciple Jan Hus and Arundel, an archbishop of Canterbury, affirm from different perspectives that Wycliffe translated the Bible himself. Arundel writes to the Pope: "The son of the Old Serpent filled up the cup of his malice against Holy Church by the device of a new translation of the Scripture into his native tongue." In justifying the translation Wycliffe refers to the York mystery plays, which he may have seen in his youth: there the Lord's Prayer and other biblical matter were rendered in English. In *De Veritate Sacrae Scripturae* he argues that scripture is the crucial fact, against which tradition has no weight. His sobriquet was Doctor Evangelicus: why no English Bible when other languages had the Book already? His desire to see it translated was consistent with his desire to spread poor priests throughout England: they should preach from a Bible in their congregation's idiom.

With the passage of time Wycliffe grew combative: frustrated in religious preferment say his detractors, righteous in civic and spiritual wrath say his advocates. "False peace is grounded in rest with our enemies, when we assent to them without withstanding; and sword against such peace came Christ to send." Whether he had a direct hand in it or not, he certainly encouraged work on the Bible and inspired its completion. The institutions of the Church needed to be tested regularly against the word of scripture; laymen had a right to read it in their own language. "It seemeth first that the wit of God's law should be taught in that tongue that is more known, for this wit is God's word. When Christ saith in the Gospel that both heaven and earth shall pass, but His words shall not pass, he understandeth by His words His wit. And thus God's wit is Holy Writ, that may on no manner be false. Also the Holy Ghost gave to apostles wit at Wit Sunday for to know all manner languages, to teach the people God's law thereby; and so God would that the people were taught God's law in diverse tongues. But what man, on God's behalf, should reverse God's ordinance and His will?"

He was patronized by John of Gaunt, the king's uncle, and became deeply involved in political controversies. Employed to negotiate with Pope Gregory XI in 1374, he witnessed a corrupt papacy at first hand. Why should a Pope have the right to make levies in an England already crippled by taxation to finance wars? Why should a Pope appoint foreigners to English benefices? His stance was popular. By means of teaching, sermons and writings, and through his connections and travels, he developed influence at home and abroad. Early on he wrote about "dominion," following Richard FitzRalph, Archbishop of Armagh: the world belongs to God, our "capital lord": only righteousness can justify property; if the church abuses its property or its power, the state must take away its endowments.

And if the state commits abuses? The answer is not far to seek. All secular and ecclesiastical authority derives from God and is forfeit if it is wrongly used. Pope, king, priest, feudal lord: each is subject to this precept. Wycliffe's expression is coarser than FitzRalph's; it is that of a man who accepts rather than teases out a doctrine. His writings escaped from the lecture room and were put to use. He vehemently attacks worldliness and venality, in court and Church. In 1377, when he was summoned before the Bishop of London to answer charges, street riots on his behalf ended the court session. The Pope charged him with heresy, a heresy compounded in 1380 by his work on the Bible. We have to accept, scholars say, that no English writings can authoritatively be attributed to Wycliffe. But no one can say authoritatively that he *didn't* write them. No doubt parts were added, as they were to Rolle; bits were faked. But his spirit informs all but the most extreme distortions of the work.

In 1381, with riots against a poll tax, and tax collectors set upon in many English towns, radicals were not popular with the authorities. The Peasants' Revolt against the 1351 statute of labourers and the new tax frightened court and Church alike. Resistance to popular demands (which were not outlandish except in being popular) hardened. The Kentish rebels chose Wat Tyler as their leader—and there's more than one perspective on him. Essex and Kentish rebels entered London. There was the "Letter to the Peasants of Essex." John Ball combines prose and rough verse in an English remote from that of the court, but not from the alliterative traditions of Old English. It is touched with the radical fraternity implied in some readings—or misreadings—of Wycliffe:

> Iohon Schep, som tyme Seynte Marie prest of York, and now of Colchestre, greteth wel Iohan Nameles, and Iohan the Mullere, and Iohon Cartere, and biddeth hem that thei bee war of gyle in borugh, and stondeth togidre in Godes name, and biddeth Peres Ploughman go to his werk, and chastise wel Hobbe the Robbere, and taketh with yow Iohan Trewman, and alle hiis felawes, and no mo, and loke schappe you to on head, and no mo.

Iohan the Mullere hath ygrounde smal, smal, smal;	John the Miller
The Kynges sone of heuene schal paye for al.	
Be war or ye be wo;	be wary or sorry
Knoweth your freend fro your foo;	friend from foe
Haueth ynow, and seith 'Hoo';	have enough; say "Hold"
And do wel and bettre, and fleth synne,	flee from sin
And seketh pees, and hold you therinne;	seek peace

and so biddeth Iohan Trewman and alle his felawes.

Read aloud, the oddnesses of spelling and word order evaporate. It *looks* very old. But it dates from 1381, more than a decade after Chaucer's *The Book of the Duchess* with its classical allusions, conventionalized landscape and remoteness from the England of miller, carter and plowman. And here is Piers the Plowman, a character out of Langland, or plucked by Langland from popular legend.

Wat Tyler arrived in a London poorly defended. Richard II was holed up in the Tower. On 14 June Simon of Sudbury, chancellor and

Archbishop of Canterbury, was beheaded by the crowd. The next day the king summoned Tyler and his Kentishmen to Smithfield to parley. There Tyler was stabbed by William Walworth, mayor of London, in the king's presence. Leaderless, the rabble dispersed. It was only a matter of time before the king repealed the concessions he'd made under duress. But radical seeds were sown. Wycliffe, discredited at court after the revolt, was already anathema to the Church. He wouldn't shut up. In that fateful year he publicly denied transsubstantiation. In 1382 the secular party in Oxford was compelled (though it resisted) to expel their favorite teacher and his followers. He withdrew to Lutterworth, where, in 1384, he suffered a stroke during mass and died. After Wycliffe's death his "poor preachers"—who founded the Lollard sect—survived, eventually to join the Lutherans in the sixteenth century. His writings establish one of the bases of Puritanism.

The conflict of faith and reason, the hunger for a *reasonable faith*, or for a reasonable institution to transmit the unreasonable core of faith, was not new. Nor did Wycliffe invent controversy. The England he was born into was already awake to religious argument: Occam and Scotus with their inherent mysticism, the reaffirmation of St. Augustine's laws of grace, and other debates were conducted, but generally in the Church. Wycliffe's first controversies were confined to scholastic philosophy: he followed Plato not Aristotle, Augustine not Occam, Bradwardine and not free will. Always an intellectual and not an evangelist, he never became a Protestant who believed in individual grace and revelation. Yet he took hard ideas into the pulpit and shared them with the laity. Proto-Puritans tuned in to him, men who said bad priests should not administer sacraments, men opposed to hierarchy; there was debate over trans- or consubstantiation. More *individual* faith was developing. Wycliffe did not invent doubts. He organized them into a coherent body of criticism. Wycliffe's spirit touched English writers. It inspired John Purvey to complete the English Bible in 1388. After Purvey, there appear to be no new Latin manuscript versions of the Bible. English was official. The Word was out.

Wycliffe's Promethean treachery in aspiring to give people direct access to the Word of God was punished beyond the grave. Over twenty years later, in 1409, the Pope ordered all books by him or attributed to him to be burned. A famous bonfire of his work was built and lit in 1411 at Carfax, Oxford. In Prague, the Wycliffite Jan Hus was excommunicated but continued to preach and defend Wycliffe. In 1415 at the Council of Constance Wycliffe's writings were unanimously condemned and Hus was ordered to recant his heresies, as if on the dead Wycliffe's behalf. He refused and was burned at the stake. Thirteen years later, the

Council of Constance ordered that Wycliffe's bones be dug up, burned, and chucked into the river Swift.

Everyone had a right to the Bible; only a trained few knew what the theologian was up to. Wycliffe was for everyone, not the trained few. He interrogated Church government because it was closed and corrupt. He advocated disendowment, rejected much of the Pope's authority and of papal authority, already weakened by rivalry between Urban VI and Clement VII; he attacked the privileges of bishops and religious orders, the abuse of indulgences, pardons and sanctuaries. His adoption of English rather than Latin is a radical but not a surprising step. A scholar, he regarded Latin as proper for deep thought; as a priest, he believed each soul should have access to the Word. The medieval world in which the educated were connected by Latin and the people divided by dialect was loosening. Nations with distinct priorities, languages, literatures were emerging. Wycliffe used Latin as a scholar of the old order, English as a prophet of the new. The use of English was *political*. It pointed in the direction of democracy, not of nationalism. He did not choose English because it was singularly beautiful or expressive (on the contrary), but because it was the language people used.

We can set aside images of ivory towers. Wycliffe's university *was* democratic, including people from all places and walks of life. Knowledge spilled out, the knowledgeable (like Rolle) spilled out into each corner of the land. Latin came to seem a great barrier to be cast down.

The north of England is more durably Wycliffe's country than the south ever was, and not only because he was a Yorkshireman. The north is where English poetry in its first years remained defiantly English. A native tradition dominated for two centuries. In French there was the vigorous *lang d'oc* which did not prevail against the courtly, smooth tones of the *lang d'oeil*; so the English court, and the city where it lived, in the end provided the orthography, the literary conventions, and to some extent the accent of an English suitable for a verse that aspired to travel beyond its region. The north's *scharp, slyttyng and frotyng* energies remained a resource, and the language of "myddel Engelond" occupied a middle ground. The south imposed conformity and eventually decorum so that Sir Philip Sidney shamefacedly declares in 1581, "I must confess my own barbarousness, I never heard the old song of Percy and Douglas"—the "Ballad of Chevy Chace"—"that I found not my heart moved more than with a trumpet; and yet it is sung out by some blind crowder, with no rougher voice than a rude style; which, being so evil apparelled in the dust and cobwebs of that uncivil age, what would it work trimmed in the gorgeous eloquence of Pindar?" The version of this trumpet call of a poem retrieved in the indispensable *Percy Reliques* of

1765 may have been close to the one Sidney knew. It is certainly in a
"Northeron" language whose rusticity appealed to Sidney's taste even as
it repelled his refined judgment, and is attributed to a blind fiddler:

> The Persè owt of Northomberlande,   Percy
>   And a vowe to God mayde he,
> That he wolde hunte in the mountayns
>   Off Chyviat within dayes thre,
> In the mauger of doughtè Dogles,   despite doughty Douglas
>   And all that ever with him be.

It's hard to see that a Pindar, or a Sidney, could improve on the vigorous
idiom. It was the vulgar tongue, but it became the common poetic
idiom.

Polite society north and south, from the end of the fourteenth cen-
tury until well into the eighteenth, shunned once-popular ballads, as the
Normans had shunned native English. It was a snobbery, a distrust of
the Borders and the Scots, unease at the localizing vigor of dialect and
a distrust of violent feeling and passion. To begin with, tastemakers
(in the monasteries and feudal houses) preferred (if they lacked both
French and Latin) translations of French romances, domesticated in
idiom and occasional imagery, which remained alien to the native tradi-
tion. There should have been nothing wrong with local tradition: it had
served barons and village folk who wanted music and entertainment
well enough. But such verse existed for a locality, and as England was
knitted more tightly together and to other countries by trade, taxation
and war, the privileged and entrepreneurial classes were exposed to
"superior" foreign customs. A gap grew between what the common peo-
ple of a locality liked and what their masters affected. The masters' cul-
ture became a national culture. They were keen to belong to a wider
world, to Europe; to be accepted on the terms that wider world pro-
posed. Serious poets of every land wrote in French or Latin to be under-
stood by the educated in every land.

So in the fourteenth century begins the redskin v. paleface conflict
that pervades English poetry up to our own day and has less to do with
education than with social attitudes. It is north versus south, folk versus
court, Anglo-Saxon versus Norman or Latin, native legend versus clas-
sical myth, plain style versus Petrarchan or aureate style. The Bible is on
the redskin side, not because it is crude but because its subtleties touch
the common nerve, while the decorous courtesies of the classics belong
to the paleface. Yet the scholarship and care that went into the Autho-
rized Version are probably more austere than the scholarship of the clas-

sical humanists, disporting themselves assiduously among Greek and Latin texts.

The dual tension was there even as the language bunched itself into regional dialects and was subjected to rules made from the center, in books, in debate and government: an English spoken in London, Southwark, Westminster, and by extension in Canterbury, Oxford and Cambridge. It was there that the scriptoria prospered and the first rules of writing and copying were agreed upon.

At the center men were educated, and were then exported to the rest of the country as judges, priests and administrators, along with manuscripts and decrees; lords came to the London court and took home London manners and affectations. The south triumphed, with its Norman and Latinate courtly tradition, its classical proprieties a condition for social success. The suppressed tradition simmered, rather as, in the Highlands, the Scots Gaelic tradition survived, or Irish and Welsh. They survived despite repression; the manuscripts were not collected, hand-me-downs of oral tradition wore thin or were forgotten— although so slowly that in the eighteenth century versions of songs five or six hundred years old could still be gathered. The success of southern English was, on a small scale, a foretaste of the success of English in the Empire, a success which retarded native traditions.

"In englesh forto make a book"

JOHN GOWER

S ir John Gower, well into his fifties, the poet who had composed more than 32,000 lines of French verse and 11,000 lines of Latin elegiacs, began—in "the Monthe of Maii" the poem says, in the year 1386(ish) in a high room beside the priory church of St. Mary Overie—to write his first poem in English. Generally he was decorous and quiet as a ghost. Now the scribes felt his physical presence as if for the first time, a kind of sudden storm, though he'd been their master for years. His gray lips were red under his moustache, pursing, shaping sounds. They saw *him*, his long pinched face pleated with age, the acorn head-piece gathering a silky abundance of white hair that, where it escaped, curled upward like the hair of an aging child. He might have been a cleric, a parched disciple of Wycliffe! His mustache and the slightly forked beard—like Chaucer's, except Gower was rounder of face—took on a life of their own; his hand wrote the sounds he did not voice aloud, the fingers danced as if counting beads or syllables. Were his scribes shocked? English was a vulgar tongue, what men like Sir John spoke chiefly to peasants and servants, dressing their better conversation and private thoughts in French. *The Lover's Confession,* or, as he dignified it in Latin, the *Confessio Amantis,* was the poem he embarked on.

Strange matter, you might think, for such a religious old man. *Senex et cecus Iohannes Gower.* Old and almost blind: his eyes froze over completely a few years later. When Sir John regained his composure on that astounding day, he recalled the occasion. After writing so much in the language of the court (French), and of the Church (Latin), he turned to English because he had bumped into King Richard II, still "the boy king" but nearing his majority, on the river Thames. The king invited his poet aboard the barge and asked him to write "some newe thing." Despite ill health, the poet promised to oblige "for king Richardes sake," to provide "wisdome to the wise / And pley to hem that lust to pleye." It was a momentous request. When a poet like Sir John cast aside the sanctioned instruments of his trade, the languages of secular and spiritual power, and took up native clay, took the mess that was English and breathed coherent life into it, the language came alive at last.

English was not foreign to poetry. But it *was* foreign to the great *poeta doctus*, the "learned poet," and it's the learned poet whose works survive. All the early poets were learned but untalented. Sir John was different: he wrote feverishly, under compulsion, and as the work progressed he dictated to his scribes. Those hours of taking down his recitation, the words he'd thought out in the night or translated extempore from French or Latin books, or which he wrested from the air, were exhilarating for his scribes.

He had set up his copying house at St. Mary's. The scribes—French, English, failed students from university, poor clerks earning a crust— were paid to copy his works and any that his noble or church patrons required. There were probably several scribes in 1380. Some prepared the parchments, pinning and lining them, readying the inks. The scribes themselves worked from the poet's dictation, their quills like birds in flight. There was an illuminator who decorated the parchments with color and gilt. The first and best copy was reserved for the king. The other copies were for lesser patrons who needed books to read aloud to provincial courts and convocations, or privately on long winter nights.

When there were errors, they went undetected until a scholar centuries later read over and collated surviving copies. At every point of difference the editor had to make a decision. The creative process continued: a scribe mishearing or inventing silently, a scholar discovering and making new emendations. Always fluid at the edges, the text of a great poem taken down by hand or a poem set in type. Never a final authoritative version.

That's a Renaissance notion: a *final version* of a poem. A poem was never *finished*. Like a cathedral it grew, bits were added or removed to make new space. Even as the poet dictated, scribes might add a bit or, when they grew tired and dozed, miss whole passages. Hovering over them was an ideal poem which the poet almost knew. But even he could change his mind: the poem he made one year might be out of date the next. Sir John wrote his *Confessio* for King Richard; when Richard proved unworthy, he made it over, adding an allegorical record of royal errors. Poems can die—or be killed by fire or neglect—unless the poet refashions and refreshes them. If he learns something new, he has to add it. The aim is to delight, but the purpose is to instruct. Delight without precept is pointless.

In the revised version that he worked on in 1391, Sir John mentions Henry of Lancaster, and the third version of 1393 is dedicated to the future king. Sir John was rewarded with an ornamental collar and when Henry was in due course crowned Henry IV, he allowed him two pipes of Gascony wine a year. Sir John was his laureate and praised him sincerely, not to get patronage—he was a man of means who didn't need support—but because he admired his strength. He deserted Richard who was weak and impressionable. The truths a poet tells alter as the things he sees alter. There are scratchings out, repentances. Marvell and Dryden, Wordsworth and Auden are no different. Hypocrites, their critics say; or perhaps just men changing, growing up.

In 1390—the year after Richard declared he had come of age and took the reins of power in his own hands—Sir John completed his book in its first version. It *was* in the English that the king spoke, that Geoffrey Chaucer spoke, that the clerks used when at leisure. A language not deliberately poetical but precise, easier on the ear than French or Latin, or the rugged English of the north, which is the dialect of the *Gawain* poems, *Pearl* and the ballads. Closer to the dialect of William Langland, that idiom was harsh on the ear.

Sir John's English was accessible rather than ambitious. It is not resonant or inventive like Chaucer's. The lines are for the most part tetrameter couplets, as in Chaucer's early poems. A well-worn French measure that Sir John made supple. He had learned to handle the form skillfully in French: polite, simple, courtly with the unassertive firmness of conversation—a mark of the best French poem. French was his apprenticeship. He understood *extension*, how to play line against sentence and draw the sense out evenly.

A line in the *Confessio* generally has eight syllables, or four iambic feet: teTUM teTUM teTUM teTUM. Because of the rhyme the eye and ear take the line or two lines together—the couplet—as a basic unit. But the reading mind, what Wycliffe called the "understanding," is looking for larger parcels of sense. The ear is satisfied when the meter is balanced and the rhyme struck, but the sentence is incomplete and the mind seeks its satisfaction in resolution of the sense. Sense resolves, but not at the rhyme, so eye and ear move on to their next fulfillment. By the counterpoint—a kind of suspense—created between the arrangement of sounds and the construing of sense, a pace builds and a drama develops that has nothing to do with details of the story or its moral. This drama *in* the language is the *poetry* of the poem. It can bring even the most exhausted tale alive. And that's the thing that never changes, from the time of Homer, or Gower, until today: poetry is *in* language, you can paraphrase the sense but not the *poetry* of an achieved poem.

Confessio Amantis should be read rather briskly and in long runs. Imagine the speaker a man not unlike Sir John at the time, getting on in years, unlucky in love, yet ironically called Amans: Lover. He has complained to Venus that he can't get anywhere with his beloved. The goddess sends him a confessor called Genius to bring him to his senses:

What is a man so long in the tooth up to, looking in the month of May for the love of a young lady? Such love belongs to youth and virtue. Genius interrogates the supplicant, describing one by one each of the seven deadly sins and their subcategories, illustrating them with stories and challenging Amans to confess to one of them. Amans denies the sin of sloth. He tells Genius of his devoted—if fruitless—attention to his beloved:

> I bowe and profre my servise,
> Sometime in chambre, sometime in halle,
> Riht as I se the timès falle.   as opportunity falls
> And whan she goth to hierè masse,
> That timè shal nought overpasse,
> That I naproche hir ladyhede,
> In aunter if I may hire lede   on the chance that I may escort her
> Unto the chapelle and ayein.   back
> Thanne is noght al my weye in vein,   my labor is not in vain
> Somdeil I may the betrè fare,   better
> Whan I, that may noght fiele hir bare,   not feel her
> May lede hir clothèd in myn arm:

This is simple and sensual. It is about desire, which won't let his pulse stop hoping, and her cool indifference. It's hard for the old man; he can't get her body out of his mind:

> Bot afterward it doth me harm
> Of pure imaginacioun;
> For thannè this collacioun   then; reflection
> I make unto myselven ofte,
> And seye, "Ha lord hou she is softe,
> How she is round, hou she is smal!
> Now woldè God I hadde hire al
> Withoutè Danger at my wille!"
> And thanne I sike and sittè stille,   sigh
> Of that I se my besy thoght   busy thought
> Is tornèd idel into noght.   is idle and will come to naught

She controls him; he follows with no will of his own. If she stands he stands, if she sits he kneels beside her. Erotic hope returns, the verse heats up, sentences grow breathless: And, and, and, and . . . He turns his attention to her pets, her pages and chambermaids, anything that is hers upon which he can lavish attention, gain commendation and deflect passion:

And thanne I am so simple of port,   behave simply
That forto feignè some desport   pretend to take pleasure
I pleyè with hir litel hound
Now on the bedd, now on the ground,
Now with hir briddès in the cage;   songbirds
For ther is non so litel page,
Ne yit so simple a chamberere,   chambermaid
That I ne make hem allè chere,   that I am pleasant to them all
Al for they sholdè spekè wel:
Thus mow ye sen my besy whiel,   busy round
That goth noght ideliche aboute.   not idly
And if hir list to riden oute   she wishes
On pelrinage or other stede,   ride
I comè, thogh I be not bede,   I am not bidden
And take hire in myn arm alofte
And sette hire in hire sadel softe,
And so forth lede hire by the bridel,
For that I woldè noght ben idel.
And if hir list to ride in char,   she wishes to ride in a coach
And thanne I may therof be war,   and I am aware of it
Anon I shapè me to ride
Riht evene be the charès side;
And as I may, I speke among,
And otherwhile I singe a song . . .

He plays back and forth between *nakid* and *clothed*, and it's sexy, can-
did, it feels like a true confession of desire heightened by a subtly dis-
closing discretion. The poetry keeps almost concluding, then starting
again in a different key: memory, imagination, strategy, confession. This
is remarkable writing "in character"—a character speaks, acts out his
obsession in the way he constructs and arranges the language. A knight
is reduced by passion to mere temporiser. That's one of love's effects.

What did he feel like, this Englishman already "for my dayes olde . . .
feble and impotent," devoted to an England of which he wrote (in
French), "O gentile Engleterre a toi iescrits," what did he feel, to be
writing verse for the first time in his native tongue? It must have been
like discovering a new world in his own mouth.

But he was not the first. People never stopped writing English, even
if they didn't write it quite so well. The old measures were almost lost,
and new rhymers, because they imitated French without understanding
how it worked, or because they tried to keep alive old forms that had lost
their power over a changing language, might occasionally take off, but
they seldom stayed in the air for long. Still, these verse writers weren't

all flying at Kitty Hawk. But English even in Sir John's time was a language that, shire by shire, borough by borough, was parceled out into mutually obscure dialects.

English verse right up to the end of the fourteenth century was scattered through monasteries, castles and manor houses in manuscript books, each a chaos of orthography and diction, to be read out after a winter supper or as an alternative to scriptural collations. Or it was recited by minstrels who bought verses from monks or dreamed them up for feast days and market days. To speak of such material as a *literature* misstates its purpose and its merit. Sir John was actually a *poet*, not a scribe or a mere versifier.

His king sent him home to write a poem in English, and he wrote 34,000 lines in the end. There's no hesitation in his art. He knew the English poems—the poor crabbed ones that his scribes sometimes had to copy out for clients and patrons; he knew the sweet new style of Chaucer, who in 1385 dedicated to him *Troilus and Criseyde*. It was for "*Moral* Gower and philosophical Strode"—the very Strode with whom Wycliffe conducted friendly logical disputations at Oxford. Some say that Strode wrote the poems *Pearl* and *Gawain and the Green Knight*. It's hard to imagine the logician as a poet: he put such stuff behind him in favor of more sober studies. Strode was eminent for his scholastic knowledge. He may have tutored Chaucer's son Lewis at Merton College, Oxford.

Sir John knew the limping verse histories and romances. But his verse like Chaucer's was fluent, the *Confessio* inspires confidence: here is a man who knows how a voice shapes a sentence, how in verse it can imitate the movement of thought and feeling. Still, it felt strange to write in his daily language. He kept coming back to his unease, now apologetically, now affirming his aims. Chaucer was there for him, making new poems even as Gower composed the *Confessio*. Sir John would not have considered Chaucer a *great* poet: he never wrote great works in Latin or French. All his longer works except for *Troilus and Criseyde* are fragments.

Gower's claims do diminish beside Chaucer, Langland and others. If Chaucer did not write the interminable French lines of Sir John's *Speculum Meditantis* or the Latin hexameters of his *Vox Clamantis*, bravo Chaucer! Think of the sheep whose skins he spared. Yet Gower's claims are large and genuine. The reader who understands him understands his century and gets a handle on the beginning of our poetry—our *real* poetry, not verse in Old English, which is a foreign language, or the limping chronicles and romances that came after. Sir John had suggestive antecedents in English. But his poetry was fathered by French, and after he finished the *Confessio*, French gathered him back to its bosom.

He could only write one further poem in English, for Henry IV, around 1399. It was called "In Praise of Peace." But for seven years—writing and revising—he gave himself up to English, let his scribes' hands shape English words that English ears warmed to. He read in a firm Kentish voice.

Sir John's success was unprecedented in English. *Confessio Amantis* was the first English poem to be translated into the languages of the Continent. This is an ambiguous tribute: it was readily *translatable*. He used a French meter, the conventions of fashionable European verse; much of his poem was adapted from the languages that welcomed it back. Long before Caxton printed it, Spanish and Portuguese versions existed. The *Confessio* is as much a part of the international literature of the "clerks," with Latin and French affinities, as it is of English. Gower's great poetic risk is to choose English: beyond that, he uses accepted forms; intent on conventional matter, the stories he tells, the lessons he teaches. He's not inventive but efficient, a virtue in a moral writer. But if his work illuminates the mind and temper of his age, it casts only a dim light on the social world that lent them substance: the world he lived in.

He is a European although his French and Latin poems are forgotten, along with almost all the French and Latin verse of the first six centuries of our poetry. Nowadays we read Milton's Latin and Italian verses in translation for what they tell us about his father, his early attitudes, his friendships, seldom as *poetry* in their own right. Yet well into the seventeenth century, for some writers—Francis Bacon among them—a book didn't exist until it existed in Latin and belonged to the culture of Europe on Europe's terms, that is, written in a purified classical humanist spirit much like the terms of medieval culture: Latin, though no longer the adaptable and expressive Latin of the medieval church. In the end it isn't Gower's timeless Latin or fashionable French but his English poem that lives. He did something for the pleasure of his king and the kingdom. A labor as much as a pleasure for him. When it was done he felt released back to his natural culture:

> And now to speke as in final,
> Touchendè that I undirtok   undertook
> In englesh forto make a book
> Which stant betwene ernest and game,   labor; pleasure
> I have it maad as thilkè same
> Which axè forto ben excusid,
> And that my bok be nought refusid
> Of lerèd men, whan they it se,   learned
> For lak of curiosite: because it lacks elaboration

For thilkè scole of eloquence
Belongith nought to my science,   I don't know how
Uppon the forme of rethorique   to use rhetoric
My wordis forto peinte and pike,   embellish
As Tullius som timè wrot.   Cicero
Bot this I knowe and this I wot,
That I have do my trewè peine   truly taken pains
With rudè wordis and with pleine,   rough; plain
In al that evere I couthe and mighte,   could
This bok to write as I behighte,   promised
So as silknesse it soffrè wolde;   as far as sickness would allow
And also for my dayès olde,
That I am feble and impotent,
I wot nought how the world is went . . .   I know not; going

Southwark

JOHN GOWER, BOETHIUS, *ROMANCE OF THE ROSE*,
GEOFFREY CHAUCER

Looking today across the river to Southwark you see the recon-
structed Globe Theatre, its pennants rattling in the breeze. South-
wark Cathedral takes you back two centuries further. Sir John
contributed to rebuilding it in its elegant form, a beautiful pattern of the
lighter Gothic; at the same time he founded, at his tomb, a perpetual
chantry. Sir John might recognize his church even today.

Visitors shoulder in past memorials to great men and great names:
Lancelot Andrewes, the divine beloved of T. S. Eliot and, centuries
before, of John Donne and the Metaphysical poets who harkened to his
sermons and learned ways of seeing and expression from him; Edmund
Shakespeare, William's brother, partner in establishing the Globe in
1599; John Harvard, less forgotten because he established a great univer-
sity. The space Gower's scriptorium occupied is now built over a dozen
times, but his tomb survives, gaudily restored. Under a stone canopy
Sir John Gower reclines, overlooked by three allegorical angel muses,
his feet resting on a benign mastiff or lion, his head propped awkwardly
on his three principal works: the French *Mirrour de l'homme* (*Specu-
lum Meditantis*, 1376–79), the Latin *Vox Clamantis* (*c.* 1381) and the *Con-
fessio Amantis*. His hands press together in prayer. The tomb has been
altered substantially and the effigy does not resemble surviving por-
traits. It's taller than in life, more jauntily and tidily bearded, wearing a
long red gown embroidered with gold foliage like a figure out of alle-
gory, a monument fitting for a man of such imaginative and material
substance. He came of a prominent family with estates in Yorkshire,
Suffolk, Norfolk and Kent. Had he not written a word he would have
merited such a tomb, perhaps with a more comfortable pillow.

He was born around 1330 with every advantage landed wealth
affords: security, leisure, education "liberal and uncircumscribed," as
Thomas Warton, that patient historian of our early literature, puts it.
Gower received training for legal and civil office. He grew learned. He

was certainly more than the "burel clerk" or common clerk that his Amans claims to be. Poor William Langland was the burel clerk. Langland had none of Gower's advantages, though some maintain that he had twice his originality and genius. Sir John bought and sold estates, dividing his time between rural and urban abodes until in 1377 he took up residence at what was then St. Mary Overie (Over the River) priory. If he had a first wife, she died before 1380. In 1398 and nearly blind, he married Agnes Groundolf in his own private oratory in the priory. He lived for another decade, then went to his sumptuous rest.

Gower wrote poems specifically for recitation, while Chaucer, the first bourgeois poet, wrote poems to be read silently, in the privacy of one's room, or between two or three people, preferably lovers. His best poems and fragments are too long and richly textured for an audience of monks or courtiers or common folk on feast days. The step from Gower to Chaucer is the step from pulpit or lectern into unbuttoned private comfort.

Gower is complex, of course, and long. But his complexity is old-fashioned allegory. His length as often as not is long-windedness. The *Speculum Meditantis* is allegory and takes itself seriously. Warton says it illustrates the "general nature of virtue and vice, enumerates the felicity of conjugal fidelity . . . and describes the path which the reprobate ought to pursue for the recovery of divine grace": a tidy summary. Gower provides a genealogy of sin, a catalogue of vices and virtues, illustrated with precept, homily and story. In this and other ways it foreshadows the *Confessio*. You might even call it, ungenerously, the French original or first draft.

After writing it he confronted his fear and anger at the events of 1381. His Latin poem *Vox Clamantis*—he chose Latin as befitting a somber occasion, or because he believed he had mastered the medium—is less deliberately conceived than *Speculum*. He had to speak out, about the Peasants' Revolt and, indirectly, about how Wycliffe was in many respects right but in crucial respects misunderstood. *Vox* is a dream fable, a freer form than the *Speculum*, less systematic in argument. The *Confessio*, properly speaking, is an allegorical dream fable, marrying the forms of the first two poems. The Latin elegiacs illustrate the way in which irresponsible action, at both the head and the foot of the body politic, leads to the kingdom's undoing.

Gower is a descriptive moralist rather than an innovator (except in his leniency over incest). He believes what the best had believed for centuries and the poem shapes around those beliefs. He sets out to define and deepen, not to change moral attitudes. Religious belief and a structured and stable society guarantee a common humanity. When church or state fumble, each of us is threatened. English people were once can-

did: "Of mannes hertè the corage / Was shewèd thanne in the vis-
age." In that happy time, words were close to what they named, not dis-
torted by hyperbole and misuse. "The word was lich to the conceite /
Withoutè semblant of deceite."

In 1381 things turn topsy-turvy. Even the Church is at fault.

> In to the swerd the cherchè keie   the key of the church is
> Is torned, and the holy bede   is turned into a sword; prayer
> Into cursinge.

A little radical, but not very. He speaks not with anger like Langland or
sardonically like Chaucer, but with civic and spiritual sorrow.

> For if men loke at holy cherche,
> Betwen the word and that thei werche   their words and their deeds
> Ther is a full gret differance

And

> For now aday is many on   a one
> Which spekth of Peter and of John
> And thenketh Judas in his herte.   thinks like

He keeps distance from an age in which "stant the crop under the rot."
The governing convention of the *Confessio* is courtly love—drawn
from French and other romances about devoted knights and the unat-
tainable ladies they woo and serve. Behind this convention is something
serious, concerned with civic love, order, natural hierarchy. The *Confes-
sio* endorses a pure, old-fashioned feudal order. What alternative was
there—Wat Tyler and his rabble? Besides, such stability is an ideal, not
a possibility. It never truly existed in a sustained form over generations.
The wheel of fortune turns in his tales. The mighty rise, then fall under
it; the poor and unfortunate reap rewards as in the beatitudes. Man is
responsible for his fallen state and needs institution and instruction to
reclaim himself. It's a severe task:

> Who that lawe hath upon hande,
> And spareth for to do justice   scants
> For merci, doth noght his office   in favor of mercy

The *Confessio* is haunted by the poet's studious reading. The ghost of
one writer in particular fascinates him, as it did King Alfred, Chaucer
and Queen Elizabeth I (all of whom translated him or caused him to be

translated into English). That writer was Anicius Manlius Severinus Boethius, Chaucer's Boece, of the noted Praenestine family, the Anicii, born in Rome in 480, consul under Theodoric the Ostrogoth, father of consuls and notables. Boethius fell afoul of Theodoric and got himself condemned to death. In prison in Pavla he was visited—his poem tells us—by Dame Philosophy, to whom he made a confession. She consoled him. He wrote his consolatory poem, only to be cruelly executed in 524. For half a millennium most European poets would have named *The Consolation of Philosophy* one of the great books of all time, for its matter and manner, a mixture of prose and verse. Philosophy does not save Boethius; it reconciles him to his fate. It's a dream, but a dream of truth. The *Consolation* stands behind everything Gower wrote. Behind Boethius, a little hazily, stand the works of Plato and Aristotle, both of whom he set out to translate into Latin; he then tried to harmonize their doctrines. The *Consolation* is *applied* philosophy.

Edward Gibbon, who knew the Romans better than they knew themselves, calls *De Consolatione Philosophiae* "a golden volume not unworthy of the leisure of Plato or of Tully." It was so well known in the dark and middle ages that eight translations in French survive from before the end of the fifteenth century, one by Jean de Meun, author of Part II of the *Romance of the Rose*.

Gower also drew heavily on *that* poem, which Chaucer in part translated. The French poem conventionalized, sometimes tongue in cheek, the ceremonial of courtly love. A large, disorderly masterpiece, it was written by two men of contrasting temperaments. Not a good formal model, perhaps, but Gower like others followed it. He includes too much of it in the deliberately encyclopedic *Confessio*: everything he knows, and then some.

Gower's "Prologue" in general terms passes state, church and commons in review. From that turbulent, plaguey world we retreat to Book One. *Since I cannot put the world to rights, I speak of love.* As in most courtly love poems, the month is May, the world is young. Amans speaks of his condition. "For I was further fro my love / Than Erthe is fro the hevene above." He falls asleep, and who can blame him? Many medieval poets fall asleep to have their vision of truth. It's as though the waking world is a veil that can only be penetrated by means of the symbol structures of dream.

Amans meets Venus, odd for a decidedly Christian poet, but his Venus is a conventional figure rather than a buxom Roman goddess. She summons her priest to hear his confession. No one found it sacrilegious that he made literary play of the sacrament of confession. The poem—paganizing in conceit—is clearly Christian. The deadly sins provide a structure. There's one book for each in its different kinds. Finally Venus shows Amans his wizened face in a mirror and he gets the message, the melancholy at the poem's heart: Amans has been virtuous by default. It isn't "Love cured by Age" or "Passion at war with Time," as C. S. Lewis has it, but more the Virtues of Amorous Ineptitude: Amans knows *all* about love from reading, but his body is outside the equation. Love is in the pulses of the characters in the tales. But Venus and Passion and Genius are insubstantial figures. This is more Will controlled by Resoun, or consoled by Resoun. It's a *cool* poem, whereas Chaucer can be hot, releasing doubtful impulses in the reader. Gower's Amans accepts his fate. At the end of the poem, in the "Epilogue," Amans is delivered back to the waking world of England and the 1390s. It's a mechanical construction, a moral grid. Chaucer outstrips Gower in terms of larger form.

But Gower never overreached himself. He finished all the big projects he started. He was ambitious but did not presume to know *more* than the huge disorderly amount he knew—about science or history or religion. Or about the people in his stories. This is part of his *English* charm: "He thoughte morè than he seide." A long poem thrifty of language. He likes verbs of action. He is sparing with adjectives and adverbs. He focuses on observable fact, the essence of a moral art. He leaves imagery, decoration, the panoply of adjectives, to others—to Chaucer for example.

If we set Gower's "Tale of Florent" beside Chaucer's "Wife of Bath's Tale" we might expect no contest. If we look closely, we find that there is. The two poets, let loose on the same story, work to different ends. Gower wrote his tale first. Florent is set the task of discovering "What alle wommen most desire." Chaucer tells his version in 407 rhymed pentameter couplets as against Gower's 455 rhymed tetrameters. Chaucer narrates in a more complex way than Gower: his story attaches to its fictional narrator, the Wife of Bath, and reflects *her* character. She weaves Arthurian motifs into her story, giving it color and *visual* substance, to painterly rather than dramatic effect. For her Florent's sin against love is rape.

To set the stories justly side by side, we must unplug "The Wife of Bath's Tale" from the *Canterbury Tales*. How different the moral Florent that Gower portrays! He is not a sinner but an epitome of honor tried and tested. Gower spares detail; there's very little gilding. The physical ugliness of the crone Florent must marry to learn the answer to his appointed question and save his honor and his neck Gower does stress, to emphasize Florent's integrity and pluck. His is a drama of motive, conscience and action. The Wife's version is entertainment, and hardly moral. Gower's tale is believable at the level of character, and it is *dramatic*. It reads better aloud than Chaucer's, it is spoken, not literary. It's also less re-readable. But there are incomparable moments. When Gower's Florent reluctantly goes to bed with his hideous wife, before her transformation, the poet renders his feelings in two lines that touched the Shakespeare of *Henry V*.

"For now," sche seith, "We ben both on."   are as one
And he lay stille as any ston.

Where Chaucer makes individual characters, Gower personifies. His tale tends toward abstraction, which is crucial to the boringly universal themes the poem explores.

Had Chaucer finished the *Canterbury Tales*, we might have had occasion to call him mechanical and boringly universal, too—though I doubt it. Because his poem is unfinished he'll always have an advantage over Gower, who completed what he began. Given the allegorical mode, structure *has* to be mechanical. Allegory has meanings that can't be arbitrary but must cohere at different levels. If "the Crown" does something, it means the living person of the sovereign, the institution of sovereignty, and what it contains of the divine within a human order. An image must inevitably contain several meanings. If you're going to write allegory you choose a mechanical structure because figures must connect on many levels. The form is a form of *belief*, unoriginal because belief in a revealed religion cannot be "original." So much—one might suppose—for the poetry being in the language. Beyond literal sense, the situation of the dreamer and the entertaining stories he hears, there's a constant didactic purpose with religious dimensions. What qualifies the mechanical feel is the wry melancholy of Amans's voice and the severity of his confessor. Amans has a tone, close to Sir John's, composed of humility, wry self-deprecation and charity.

Gower's poem might leave a common Londoner or English countryperson cold. It contains little of the living England. It lacks *world*. We acquire instead a universal morality unfolded in tales familiar to readers of romances and a sufficient, if primitive psychology. The poem entertains and instructs in two ways: teaching "facts" (which time has turned to fable—tedious "histories" of religion, royal instruction, astrology) and inculcating "virtue." In its themes, even in the play of metaphor, the explosive politics of the day—Richard's vices, his fate, the Peasants' Revolt, anarchism and barbarity—are hardly a murmur beyond the priory wall. This kind of poem is insulated against real weather. His Latin poem was more topical, direct, troubled by the politics of the day. But it's in Latin and has no readers.

Gower's excellence is evident in discrete parts. Academic critics make a case for the aesthetic wholeness of the *Confessio*. It's an academic, not a poetic case: a pattern can be drawn on the blackboard, but it does not emerge from our experience as we read. A reader prepared to read the work right through comes away as from a vast anthology: one editor has assembled it, but out of such varied materials that the parts exceed the whole. If we focus on passages or stories—"Deianira and Nessus," "Constantine and Sylvester," "Pygmalion," "Demephon and Phyllis," "Ceix and Alceone," "Jason and Medea" or a score of others—and on the words of Amans, the link man, whose disappointment is the poem's occasion, we find the poet there. In the "Prologue" and "Epilogue" briefly you come close to the world he inhabited.

He knew Chaucer personally and survived him. By 1378 their friendship was established. Chaucer left Sir John power of attorney in his affairs when he traveled abroad. He may even have encouraged Gower to try his hand at English. As I have mentioned, Chaucer dedicated *Troilus and Criseyde* "to moral Gower." Gower returned the compliment by dedicating the first recension of the *Confessio* to Richard II and, obliquely, to Chaucer. Later recensions dropped the dedication to Richard and the encomium to Chaucer. Some say the poets fell out, identifying passages in *The Tale of Sir Thopas* as Chaucer's poking fun at some of Gower's beliefs.

For three centuries after his death Gower had champions among poets and critics. Skelton said his "matter was worth gold," praising the content, especially the moral content. He appears as the moralizing chorus in Shakespeare's *Pericles*, and Shakespeare used his tales in shaping plots. Ben Jonson in his *English Grammar* cites Gower more often than any other writer as a model of correctness. But his hold on readers weakened. Now confined to students of Middle English, he deserves to be given back, not whole but in judicious bits, with modernized orthography, to a new audience. If you read aloud, difficulties of diction and prosody resolve themselves.

But Gower's poems didn't come to him as naturally—in Keats's phrase—as leaves to a tree. He approached the language tentatively, advancing with the responsible caution of a prose writer. C. S. Lewis calls him "our first formidable master of the plain style" and, unlike the Augustan poets, "noble rather than urbane." (Chaucer can be urbane and is only intermittently noble.) Taken in large doses he is—monotonous. "It dulleth ofte a mannes wit / To him that schal it aldai rede." He is *easy* in a good sense, much easier to get on with than Spenser or Milton, even when the language is old, because his verse is unpresumingly efficient, his sense of pace well gauged, his moral clear. The *Confessio* illuminates the temper of his social class and intellectual milieu, just as

Langland's *Piers Plowman* illuminates the very world that Gower does not address and excludes the world that Gower's imagination temperately inhabits. To hear and see the age at large, we have to turn to Chaucer. Remember what Venus tells Amans in the poem:

"And gret wel Chaucer whan ye mete,
As mi disciple and mi poete:
For in the floures of his youthe   flower
In sondri wise, as he wel couthe,   as well as he could
Of ditees and of songes glade,
The whiche he for mi sake made,
The lond fulfild is overal.   the land is all filled
Whereof to him in special
Above alle othre I am most holde.   obliged
Forthi now, in hise daies olde,   now he is growing old
Thow schalt him telle this message,
That he upon his latere age,
To sette an ende of alle his werk,   to bring to an end
As he which is myn owne clerk,
Do make his testament of love,
As thou hast do thi schrifte above,
So that my Court it mai recorde."

"And as I lay and lened and loked in the wateres"

WILLIAM LANGLAND

If I postpone Chaucer a little longer, it is because, when he appears, he pushes his contemporaries into the wings. Each deserves attention—a generous man, he might have said as much himself. Each is different from him: he learned from them, reading them in manuscripts, or hearing their verse recited of an evening, at a feast or with a friend. Perhaps he heard these lines:

> "Bi Cryste," quod Conscience tho, "I will bicome a pilgryme,
> And walken as wyde as al the worlde lasteth,
> To seke Piers the Plowman . . ."

Piers Plowman was one of the most popular poems of its time. It survives in over forty manuscripts from the fifteenth century.

When popular works with a religious or political edge are no longer topical they fall into neglect. *Piers Plowman* vanished from sight in the late sixteenth century and reemerged only in the late eighteenth. Thomas Warton helped to restore it to the conscious tradition in the 1770s. It has not lacked readers since. In fact for every reader of Gower, there are a score of Langland readers. Poetic value is not democratically established, but if a work survives with a readership after six centuries, it must have something to recommend it. And in this case it isn't the poet's life. William Langland—called Long Will because he was so tall—is almost anonymous. His name may not even have been William. Warton calls him Robert Longlande, following Robert Crowley who first printed the poem in 1550. His name may not have been Langland. He may have been born about 1331, possibly out of wedlock, in Cleobury Mortimer, Shropshire, or in Shipton-under-Wychwood, Oxfordshire, or in Somerset, Dorset or Devon, where Langland connections exist.

He seems to be claimed by the whole country. E. K. Chambers constructs a plausible biography, diverging from the Reverend Walter W. Skeat's equally credible hypotheses. Warton makes him a secular priest, fellow of Oriel College, Oxford. But Long Will may have received a clerical education at Malvern Priory, where he was made a clerk or scholar. This accommodates the Malvern references in the poem. He was certainly a *poeta doctus*, a learned poet, and his poem is littered with scholastic digressions and embellishments.

The first (A) text of the poem seems to date from 1362. Shortly afterward he settled in London, in Cornhill, with his wife, Kitte, and his daughter, Calote. In 1376 the second (B) text was begun. It's generally held to be poetically the best. The third (C) text, overlong and overembellished, was composed between 1392 and 1398. If all three texts are by the same man, the poem was the work of a lifetime. Warton speaks of other poems written in Langland's manner and quotes them; but the similarities are sparse. True, these other poems alliterate and don't rhyme, but they lack the dense particularity of *Piers Plowman* and are translations or retellings of legend. *Piers Plowman* doesn't do much of that. Its method is not adaptable to continuous historical narrative, partly because the line-by-line dynamic, compressed for social observation, dialogue and allegorical concision, won't "flow" for straight narrative. In 1399 he probably composed the angry poem "Richard the Redeles." Then he vanished.

In the poem we meet the poet, *Lange Wille* (George Gascoigne, also tall, was dubbed "Long George"). If he took minor orders, because he married he failed to ascend the church hierarchy. He was poor, earning his keep by "saying prayers for people richer than himself" and copying legal documents. The poem reveals his knowledge of courts, lawyers and legal procedures. A proud man, he is reluctant to defer to lords, ladies and other social superiors unless he feels they merit deference. His "I" is strong and affirmative—one might say "modern," in the way of Ezra Pound and Wyndham Lewis—compared with Gower's and Chaucer's reticences.

In *Piers Plowman*—its full title is *The Vision of William about Piers the Plowman and the Vision of the Same about Do-Wel, Do-better, and Do-Best*—we must picture Long Will striding in threadbare garb through the streets of London (his principal setting), with eyes wide open, conscience stung and amazed by what he sees. Our first reformer poet, he's visionary but not revolutionary. Calmly, using allegory, he exposes corruptions in church, state and society. He wants people to understand the causes of their suffering and put things right, not to throw the hierarchies down. It was—and is now—fashionable to convert Langland into another sort of radical. But he was as troubled as

most of his contemporaries by the Wat Tyler fracas, even if he was more
in touch with the grievances, having so many of his own. Still, he was a
devout Catholic—the sort Wycliffe would have welcomed heartily
though the Archbishop of Canterbury would have refused to shake his
hand. He believed in the kingdom—of heaven, of this world—and that
virtue and faith could make a road between them. The secular king had
duties and was not above judgment. People who shared his view—like
the anonymous author of "Piers Plowman's Crede"—were more decid-
edly Wycliffite than he was. His poem was used in ways he never
intended. Such a fate can distort a poem: English readers remember
how the Mothers' Union and the Proms misuse Blake's "Jerusalem."

Piers first appears, well into the poem, as a plowman, representing
the common laity, then metamorphoses into a priest, and finally into a
bishop with St. Peter and his papal successors. *Petrus, id est Christus.*"
He is exemplary, his developing example inspires love and respect, or
indicts those who fail to follow him.

Ford Madox Ford's impression of the poem is partial but illuminat-
ing. *Piers* has, he says, "the air of having been written in a place of pub-
lic assembly. As if, while he wrote, individuals came up and whispered
into his hooded ear: 'Don't forget the poor cooks,' or: 'Remember the
hostelers,' or: 'Whatever you do, don't forget to expose the scandalous
living of the lousy friars.' " No one is forgotten: "Kokes and her knaves
crieden, 'hote pyes, hote! / Good goos and grys go we dyne, go we!' " "

You can hear such demotic strains in the eighteenth century, in
Jonathan Swift and John Gay, each vocation acknowledged in its
own voice and idiom. *Piers*'s public tone belongs in the sermon tradi-
tion, explaining the unfamiliar through the familiar. Chaucer has tales,
Gower has legends, Langland has homilies.

Verse form sets Langland apart from Chaucer and Gower. So does
his direct teaching. He draws on the everyday world but writes of types,
not characters. For him more than for Chaucer social conduct is spiri-
tual. He uses the dream convention to cross into a "real" world from the
partial, semblant secular world; to go not into fantasy—a world of ani-
mals, dreams of an old lover, a "house of fame"—but into truth. This is
beautifully symbolized in the "Prologue," where, by a stream, he first
falls asleep:

And as I lay and lened and loked in the wateres,	reclined
I slombred in a slepyng, it sweyued so merye.	dozed; sounded
Thanne gan I to meten a merveilouse sweuene,	dream dream

That I was in a wildernesse wist I neuer   knew
   where;

As I bihelde in-to the est an hiegh to the   high
   sonne,

I seigh a toure on a toft trielich ymaked;   tower; hill; excellently made

A depe dale binethe, a dongeon there-   dungeon
   inne,

With depe dyches & derke and dredful   ditches; dreadful to see
   of sight.

A faire felde ful of folke fonde I there
   bytwene,

Of alle maner of men, the mene and the   poor
   riche,

Worchying and wandryng as the worlde   working; demands
   asketh.

Langland allegorizes by second nature. Men in the fair field make their way either to the tower of truth or to the dungeon of falsehood. His vision includes social, moral and spiritual worlds. A pull of opposites coordinates his poem: between tower and dungeon, Christ and Antichrist, good shepherd and bad. Langland writes in an expansive, digressive tradition. This is the poem's virtue and vice. It includes longueurs as well as arresting detail.

True allegory—Langland's is more true, more antique in feel, than Gower's or Chaucer's—requires intuitive and analytical comprehension from a reader. We don't possess that intuition any longer, and the process of allegorical analysis can be mechanical, its fruits arcane. Unless you're an unreconstructed Roman Catholic, Dante's cosmology is a fiction; Shakespeare's political structures have a varnished, or bloodied, feel, not to mention Blake's angels with sandals on their heads, Wordsworth's burly pantheism and Yeats's silly gyres. Allegory was at least a form universally practiced and figuratively based, an instrument in an age of strict orthodoxies for reading pre-Christian writers like Virgil without getting into trouble. Allegory, the quintessential medieval Christian form, rests on a belief that the Creator can be perceived in his creation, that every created thing signifies in relation to the Creator. The poet witnesses—beyond the particulars of an experience—their significance in a wider scheme, "rendering imaginable what was before only intelligible." Gower's allegory works on two main levels, a "parable sense"—transferring meaning to the present world—and a moral sense, which he will not let us forget. Chaucer's secular allegory works on three levels: a literal, even a *social* level; a "parable-sense"; and a moral sense, more subtly delivered than in Gower. In Langland there's a fourth level, the anagogical, which opens on a spiritual world of being. A consistent allegorical interpretation of the whole poem on four levels should be possible. For medieval listeners, allegory was a way of seeing. They didn't have to unpack a poem like customs officers. They marveled at how it delivered multiple meanings. They *felt* it.

They may not even have understood half of the time, but how many of us understand poetry even half of the time? For them it wasn't a separate category called "the poem," something to stand back from in order to receive an aesthetic *frisson*. It was part of their Christian world.

Taking the B text as our poem, *Piers Plowman* has four parts. First we witness the world of human transactions and meet Piers. Debates and trials are enacted, involving among others Holy Church and Lady Meed, supported by lesser allegorical figures, especially the Seven Deadly Sins. Avarice is especially horrible:

He was bitelbrowed and baberlipped also,	beetle-browed; thick-lipped
With two blered eyghen as a blynde hagge;	bleary eyes
And as a lethern purs lolled his chekes,	purse; cheeks
Well sydder than his chyn thei chiveled for elde;	even lower; chin; trembled with age
And as a bondman of his bacoun his berde was bidraveled.	beard was bedraggled
With a hode on his hed, a lousi hatte above,	hood; louse-infested
And in a tawny tabarde of twelve wynter age,	
Al totorne and baudy and ful of lys crepynge . . .	tattered; dirty; lice

When you say the lines aloud you find your mouth forced by the consonants into all sorts of shapes, and spittle gathers on your lips. You see Avarice: you see and feel what the words mean. He is not seductive: he's an old hoarding hag, cheeks like a purse, beard like a bondman. Visual and moral detail are transmitted simultaneously.

The first part ends with a general decision to make a pilgrimage to St. Truth, and Piers the Plowman offers to serve as guide, provided the pilgrims first help him to finish harrowing his field. After further complications, the poet wakes up. In the second part of the poem he reflects on his vision. Piers returns in the third part, and the poem builds beyond its theological to its spiritual climax, the evocation of God as man in the incarnation, crucifixion and descent into hell. The final part tells of Christ's triumph over sin and death, and our triumph through Him and his authority vested in Peter (now Piers). The poem resolves not in triumph but in a determination to seek the exalted Piers, after Holy Church has been besieged by Antichrist. The *poem* is finished. It has set the reader, or audience, on a path of truth. The unresolved dialectic can be resolved only by individual conscience and effort.

Langland doesn't avail himself of the "improvements" of the English language. Rather than advance the language he deliberately makes it *old*, using the unrhymed alliterative verse of a dying tradition. Is this caprice in a learned man? Having chosen the constraint of strict alliteration, he keeps departing from natural word order. Yet he's often closer to the daily speech of his time than Gower. And unlike Chaucer or Gower he isn't writing in the first person. Langland creates an Everyman for men who warmed to the miracle and mystery plays. He's after general moral truth, not psychology or bourgeois individuality. He addresses a congregation of like-minded souls, not a single reader, certainly not an assembled court. His constituency is the populace.

That is why his manner strikes us as perplexing and perplexed, even obscure. Yet Langland's vocabulary is just as riddled with Norman French and "new words" as Chaucer's. This reveals how wide a currency that vocabulary had, how little Chaucer was the sole inventor of our language. Some suggest that Chaucer knew *Piers Plowman* and used it in "The Summoner's Tale." One thing is certain: if he read Langland he appreciated his comedy. Langland may not display "wit," but there's knockabout and lively jest, as in the street plays of the day.

Still, Langland's form *is* constricting. Gower wrung a variety of paces and syntactical licenses from his couplets. In the accentual alliterative line of Langland, with its varying number of syllables but constant number of stresses, a strong caesura is required around the middle of each line; there is seldom a run-on rhythm or cadence. It's bunched poetry, even when used with Langland's freedom, a line of knots, not a smooth thread. This has some advantages, for instance Langland's ability to vary the register abruptly to excellent effect. Langland's verse accommodates numerous voices, from the cries of street vendors and exclamations of the poor to the honeyed words of Lady Meed and the eloquence of moral lawyers. He tightens the texture on repeated words, using internal assonance and rhyme to rhetorical effect. Despite its seeming rusticity, this most English of poems is in no sense crude. Like Gower, Langland is a moralist who asks us to attend to his matter, not his manner. He seeks to portray not only the world, but the truth: a man speaking not to professors but to men.

If we set Gower alongside Langland (Chaucer stands alone as Shakespeare and Milton do), we can contrast two emerging styles which

become the poles of English poetry in time to come: one rigorously for-
mal, restrained, metrical and rhymed, the other answering a cadenced
norm. Both imitate speech but sing in different ways. One is classical,
the other biblical; one is more artificial and constructed, based, initially
at least, on alien models, the other more "native."

"Go, litel bok"

GEOFFREY CHAUCER

The George Inn in Southwark is photogenic. The neighborhood is pure history. At a pub in White Hart Yard, Jack Cade had his headquarters for the revolt of 1450. It's where Mr. Pickwick met Sam Weller a few centuries later. Chaucer's Tabard Inn was in Talbot Yard. All the coaches set off from here for places south and east. The George is how people imagine Chaucer's Tabard, though it arrived on the site four hundred years after the pilgrims set out on their adventure.

Critics attack Coleridge for not finishing major works (Wordsworth, Byron and others were as bad offenders—all those trunks that never develop legs and arms, or heads that stop short at the neck). They forget that of the great poets the most incomplete is Chaucer, author—as the great literary historian George Saintsbury puts it—of *torsi*. There's unfinished and unfinished, of course. *The House of Fame* is a fragment, but the *Canterbury Tales* is such a huge fragment that we imagine we can infer a whole. Chaucer *did* finish *Troilus and Criseyde*, just as Coleridge finished "The Rime of the Ancient Mariner," not to mention *Biographia Literaria*.

Both men are steeped in literature. But Chaucer is at the start of something. Thus his *envoi* from *Troilus*:

> Go, litel bok, go, litel myn tragedye,
> Ther God thi makere yet, er that he dye,   May God
> So sende myght to make in som comedye!   compose
> But litel book, no makyng thow n'envie,
> But subgit be to alle poesye;
> And kis the steppes, where as thow seest pace
> Virgile, Ovide, Omer, Lucan, and Stace.   Homer; Statius

Modesty, first: "litel bok" for the great English epyllion. This habit of self-deprecation is especially evident in the *House of Fame* and *Canterbury Tales*. After reading even his lesser works we feel we know him. But

who is he? Is Ford Madox Ford right to see him as *im*personal, as much
so as Flaubert? In these lines he recognizes that he has produced a work
different in genre from any he has written, from any written before in
English: a tragedy. The awful truth of the poem makes him long to
write a comedy to follow. He prays for this, and that his book may find
a humble place among authors he considers masters. It aspires at most
to kiss the steps where they pass. Yet it's doubtful that he read Homer,
and who now reads Lucan and Statius?

He prays too that his poem will be properly copied and properly
recited.

> And for ther is so gret diversite
> In Englissh and in writyng of oure tonge,
> So prey I God that non myswrite the,
> Ne the mysmetre for defaute of tonge.   Nor ruin the meter

He knows English is an unstable medium; the copying my scribal ante-
cedents did—they were young, some days lazy, occasionally careless—
filled him with concern. He wrote a poem cautioning his copyist, Adam:

> Adam scriveyn, if ever it thee bifalle
> Boece or Troylus for to wryten newe,
> Under thy long lokkes thou most have the scalle,   a scabby disease
> But after my makyng thou wryte more trewe;
> So ofte adaye I mot thy werk renewe,
> It to correct and eke to rubbe and scrape,   erase
> And al is thorugh thy negligence and rape.   haste

Chaucer led an active life. Compared with Sir John, who pottered
about in his own way at his own pace, Chaucer belonged to the wider
world. He was born around 1340 and survived for sixty years. He died as
the century turned, in 1400. "The English Tityrus," "the well of English
undefiled," Edmund Spenser called him; "O reverend Chaucer, rose of
rethoris [rhetoricians] all," was Dunbar's tribute; and Skelton's:

> Chaucer, that famous clerk
> His termes were not dark,
> But pleasant, easy, and plain;
> No word he wrote in vain.

In one manuscript Thomas Hoccleve leaves a line portrait of him, the
basis for our view of Chaucer in his maturity: a fine two-pointed beard,
wide thin-lipped mouth, long straight nose, eyes of a vivid, calm pale-

ness. His hair, covered in the picture, was covered in life, but where it showed it was pale brown.

He draws himself differently, a small man, hooded, a little beard, eyes used to gazing to the side—eyes, says Robert Graves, that see what, to right or left, you're up to, while, the face averted, you're unaware that he's observing . . . Lydgate celebrates him in his *Life of the Virgin Mary*, as one who used to "amende and correcte the wronge traces of my rude penne." He had foreign admirers. The historian Froissart praised him as a diplomat. Eustache Deschamps wrote a laudatory ballad to him as a translator. In the mid-sixteenth century Lilius Giraldus, the eminent Italian humanist, recognized his accomplishment.

A hundred years later Abraham Cowley described Chaucer as "a dry, old-fashioned wit, not worth reviving." What is our opinion of Cowley? Dryden acknowledges that Chaucer "must have been a man of a most wonderful comprehensive nature . . . because he has taken into the compass of his *Canterbury Tales*, the various manners and humours of the whole English nation, in his age." Dryden "modernized" Chaucer and wrote one of the first great English essays in literary criticism largely about him. He calls him "the father of English poetry," to be venerated as the Greeks did Homer. He remembers how "Spenser more than once insinuates that the soul of Chaucer was transfused into his body; and that he was begotten of him two hundred years after his decease. Milton has acknowledged to me, that Spenser was his original." Wordsworth too "modernized" Chaucer. Matthew Arnold may miss in him the highest poetic seriousness, but he recognizes the value of "his large, free, simple, clear yet kindly view of human life," for he "gained the power to survey the world from a central, a truly human point of view." Few English poets before the First World War were entirely free of a debt to him.

He was born in London, maybe in Thames Street. His father, John Chaucer, was citizen and vintner in London, himself son of Robert le Chaucer who was collector of customs on wine. John Chaucer served Lionel, son of Edward II, later Duke of Clarence. Chaucer's mother, Agnes, outlived John and in 1367 married again. Well placed as the Chaucers were with regard to the court, they remained a merchant family. Despite patronage Geoffrey was never assimilated into courtly life, nor did he—as Gower did—stand aloof from the world. He was a man of affairs first and a poet after.

Was he educated at St. Paul's cathedral school? It's unlikely that he attended university, though he was a member of the Inns of Court. As a young man, some report, he was fined two shillings for beating a Franciscan friar in Fleet Street. In 1357 he received a suit of livery as a member of Lionel's household. In his late teens—it was 1359—he entered

military service, was sent to France and taken prisoner near Rennes or
Reims. By March 1360 he was freed on payment of a ransom: the king
subscribed £16 to it. Some believe that during his captivity he translated
part of the *Romance of the Rose*.

Philippa Chaucer, his wife, was awarded an annuity of 10 marks for
life in 1366. She was born Roet (or Rouet), daughter of Sir Payn Roet, a
Hainault knight, and sister of the third wife of John of Gaunt. This
helps explain, if virtue is not enough, Gaunt's long patronage of the poet
and Chaucer's familiarity with Wycliffe, whom Gaunt fatefully patron-
ized as well.

The king gave Chaucer an annuity of 20 marks in 1367 as *dilectus
valettus noster* (our beloved valet) and by the end of 1368 he was an
esquire. Six years later he was granted a pitcher of wine per day (com-
muted to a money gift). He rejoined the army, and in 1370 went abroad
on public duty of some kind. He must have been successful. In 1372 he
spent a year away, part of it in Genoa arranging the selection of an
English port for the Genoese trade. He went to Florence and perhaps to
Padua. Petrarch died in 1374. It is suggested that in Italy Chaucer was
introduced to Petrarch at the wedding of Violante, daughter of the
Duke of Milan, by the Duke of Clarence: and it is not impossible that
Boccaccio was of the party. It's a tempting but unlikely scenario. Cer-
tainly he took their poetry, like Dante's, to heart. Indeed it may have
helped purge him of French enthusiasms. In *Canterbury Tales* the Clerk
plays a tribute in his Prologue which, if taken literally, gives substance to
the legend of a meeting. It generously records a debt:

> I wol yow telle a tale which that I
> Lerned at Padowe of a worthy clerk,   Padua
> As preved by his wordes and his werk.
> He is now deed and nayled in his cheste,   coffin
> I prey to God so yeve his soule reste!   give
>   Fraunceys Petrak, the lauriat poete,
> Highte this clerk, whos rethorike sweete
> Enlumyned al Ytaille of poetrie . . .   made illustrious; Italy

Back home, Chaucer leased Aldgate gatehouse; he was prospering,
and later in the year was made controller of customs for wools, skins and
hides in the port of London, with an extra £10 pension from John of
Gaunt. How did he conduct his duties and manage to write as well? In
1377 he was back on diplomatic business in Flanders and France. When
Edward III died and Richard came to the throne in 1378, he was in
France once more, then went to Italy, on a mission to Bernabo Visconti.

The controllership of petty customs was added to his duties in 1384,

and two years later he sat in Parliament as a knight of the shire of Kent.
He lived for a time in Kent, where around 1386 he began planning *Can-
terbury Tales*. Then the wheel of fortune turned: during Gaunt's absence
in Spain the Duke of Gloucester rose, Gaunt was eclipsed and Chaucer
lost his controllership. In 1387 Philippa died. The next year he assigned
his pensions and property to someone else, a sign of financial distress.
Then in 1389 the Duke of Gloucester fell, Gaunt was reinstated, and
Chaucer became clerk of works to the king for two years. He was also a
commissioner responsible for maintaining the banks of the Thames. He
was rising again but it was hard. In 1390 he fell among the same thieves
twice in a day and was robbed of public money, but excused from repay-
ing it. In that year and the next he held the forestership of North
Petherton Park, Somerset, and in 1394 his pension was refreshed: £20 a
year from Richard II. But he remained needy. Richard gave him an
additional tun of wine a year, and in Richard's wake his third royal
patron, Henry IV, added 40 marks to the pension Richard restored.
"Envoy to Scogan" and "Complaint to his Purse" suggest that Chau-
cer continued impecunious. Henry gave him a purple robe trimmed
with fur, and he felt secure enough to lease a house in the garden of
St. Mary's, Westminster, close by the palace. He enjoyed it briefly. On
25 October 1400 he died and was buried in the Abbey, in the chapel of
St. Benedict. Poet's Corner came into being, with Chaucer as corner-
stone and first tenant.

Tradition says he lived in Woodstock. Tradition says many things.
He is not above retelling stories of himself and, like all storytellers, he
embroiders. His admirers want him to have more of a life than written
evidence entitles him to. There is a mysterious incident: in 1380 Cecilia
de Chaumpaigne gave him a release *de raptu meo* ("of my abduction or
rape"). It's hard to think of Chaucer as a rapist. This may refer to a more
commonplace matter, an attempt to kidnap a ward or minor and marry
him or her to someone for money.

Did Chaucer have children? The *Astrolabe* is dedicated to "little
Lewis my son," aged ten when it was written. Philosophical Strode may
have tutored "little Lewis" at Oxford. Cancellor Gascoigne, a gene-
ration after Chaucer died, speaks of Thomas Chaucer, rich and well
placed, as Geoffrey's son. This Thomas took the coat of arms of
Rouet—his mother's maiden name—late in life. Gaunt in 1381 estab-
lished an Elizabeth Chaucer as a nun at Barking. She may have been the
poet's daughter.

Why dwell on such a scatter of fact and hearsay? To show at how
many points and in how many ways Chaucer touched his age.

His work divides into three periods, conveniently labeled French,
Italian and English, or mature. Before 1373—he was a "late starter" and

may not have taken up his pen to write English verse until he was almost thirty—he composed the *ABC*, *The Book of the Duchess* (1369–70), early ballads and complaints, his translations of Boethius and of about a third of the *Romance of the Rose*. This is the period of French influence, dominated by the octosyllabic couplet.

Young Chaucer was infatuated with the *Romance*, but abandoned the translation. Maybe Petrarch's emphatic rejection of it affected him. Petrarch, when Guy de Gonzago sent him a copy, received it as a cold, merely artificial and "extravagant composition." Chaucer's version, perhaps only partly by him, runs to 7,700 lines, compared with the more than 24,000 lines of Guillaume de Lorris's and Jean de Meun's composite original. It embodies the lore and literary conventions of courtly romance: dream, allegorical garden, cardboard personification. The latter part of the original includes satire on women, church and the established order. Such satire struck a chord with Chaucer.

The Book of the Duchess shows him almost fully fledged. It's a consolatory romance for John of Gaunt on the death of his first wife, Blanche, and draws on the *Romance*. The octosyllabic couplets foreshadow Gower's fifteen years later; but Chaucer's poem keeps close to a single subject and illustrates a crucial difference between Chaucer and Gower. Gower is encyclopedic by design; Chaucer is inclusive by nature. His verse is integrated because the human and poetic contexts admit more. Allusion and illustration are means, not end. His morality is implicit in the poem, not appended to it. *The Book of the Duchess* hints at what's to come: a dream frame, a garden, personification, confession, allegory, May morning and the hunt. There is also a debt to Ovid's *Metamorphoses*. What makes it Chaucerian is the actual-seeming grief and sympathy, acknowledging the impotence of consolation. The sense of grief depends on the creation of two credible human figures, the poet and the mourner.

> "She ys ded!" "Nay!" "Yis, be my trouthe!"
> "Is that youre los? Be God, hyt ys routhe!"   pitiful

Chaucer alludes abundantly to Blanche, to Lancaster and Richmond (Yorkshire), John of Gaunt's seat. He marries love vision and the traditional elements of elegy. This might argue for a later date: such a deliberated and courtly composition would not answer the needs of immediate, unassimilated grief. But if we read the later love visions, it's clear that this must be the earliest, fresh and complete as few of the later poems are. Some readers are unbeguiled and consider it apprentice work. The weakness is *allegory* and Chaucer's discomfort within its constraints, against which his whole writing life was a struggle.

Did Keats get "La Belle Dame sans Merci" from it? Lines 448–49 and what precedes and follows, the dense wood, the aloneness, the color:

> "Lord," thoght I, "who may that be?
> What ayleth hym to sitten her?"

The poem is so well judged and handled that it's fully expressive: the sleepless narrator, the tale of Ceix and Alcyone, how he at last falls asleep and dreams the hunt, the knight in the forest; his account of the chess game with Dame Fortune, the story of emotional reversals; after the conceits, the knight's confession of his youthful wandering eye, his eventual true love conveyed in physical terms which are a window on the beloved's moral beauty, his courtship, his loss. The interlocutor wakes up. The verse has some of the ruggedness of the accentual tradition but is "correct" when properly voiced.

> "But which a visage had she thertoo!
> Allas! myn herte ys wonder woo
> That I ne kan discryven hyt!   I can't describe it
> Me lakketh both Englyssh and wit
> For to undo hyt at the fulle . . ."

Then the Italian phase, Dante and Boccaccio in the ascendant, when he uses the "heroic" stanza of seven lines and begins to use heroic couplets. This is a wonderful early maturity. It begins (1372–80) with *The House of Fame*, *Saint Cecilia* (which would become "The Second Nun's Tale"), the tragedies used for "The Monk's Tale," *Anelida*, and some lyrics. The defining impact of Italian poetry is made clear and then assimilated in the work of the next six years (1380–86): *The Parliament of Fowls*, *Palamon* (later to become "The Knight's Tale"), *Troilus and Criseyde*, with *Boece* (his translation of the Boethius) probably a bit before, short poems, Boethian *ballades*, *The Legend of Good Women*, and some of *Canterbury Tales*.

Maturity (1386–1400) includes major parts of the *Canterbury Tales*, the Prologues, and work where he is "purely and intensely English." "The figures are all British, and bear no suspicious signatures of Classical, Italian, or French imitation," says Ford; and Warton: "He made England what she was and, having made her, remains forever a part of his own creation."

The *House of Fame* is my favorite torso—unfinished, unfinishable: he bit off more of Dante than he could chew. Pope liked it enough to translate it into his century, out of octosyllabics and into heroic couplets.

Warton didn't like Pope's version: he imitated it, with elegance of diction, harmonious versification, but he warped the story and changed the character of the poem. In correcting its extravagance he overlooked the fact that extravagance was necessary to this kind of poem, that its beauties consisted in extravagances. "An attempt to unite order and exactness of imagery with a subject formed on principles so professedly romantic and anomalous, is like giving Corinthian pillars to a Gothic palace." Chaucer's amazing, amusing eagle vanishes altogether from Pope's version.

Chaucer controls the pace, with a new eloquence learned in part from Dante, chunks of whose *Divine Comedy* the poem swallows as it proceeds. A love vision, it incorporates several love stories, French material, an abridgment of the *Aeneid*,

> "I wol now singen, yif I kan,
> The armes and also the man
> That first cam, thurgh his destinee,
> Fugityf of Troy contree,   fleeing from
> In Itayle, with ful moche pyne   much pain
> Unto the strondes of Lavyne."   coasts; Lavinium

The tone is comic. There's a hint of autobiography in his boredom with routine, his mundane job, and a vivid portrait of a bookish poet who goes home after work, ignores his neighbors and—as the eagle says—

> . . . when thy labour doon al ys,
> And hast made alle thy rekenynges,
> In stede of reste and newe thynges
> Thou goost hom to thy hous anoon;
> Thou sittest at another book
> And, also domb as any stoon,
> Tyl fully daswed ys thy look,   dazed
> And lyvest thus as an heremyte,   hermit
> Although thyn abstynence ys lyte.

He had a big library for his time—perhaps forty books—which he pored over again and again. There is a Breton poem called *Sir Orfeo, Sir Launfal and Lay le Freine*: one of the *Orfeo* manuscripts may ha.e belonged to him. The dialect is Londonish. It is, with "The Wife of Bath's Tale" and "The Franklin's Tale," the most successful lay in English. We do not have an inventory of his library, but he knew the Latin literature current in his century, especially Ovid. He had no scholastic instruction in English (though he had it in French, and in

Italian perhaps). English was unknown in schools even for the modest purpose of construing, until the next century. He made his own path through the untamed—or uncodified—wilds of English.

Metrically *The House of Fame* is similar to the *Book of the Duchess* and uses a love vision (deployed again in the *Legend of Good Women*). A technical advance on the *Book of the Duchess*, it is more learned and has been brushed by the Italian wing—Dante, not Boccaccio. In a sense it's our first great comic poem. How *visualized* the fantasy is, clear as a painting by Hieronymous Bosch: the architecture, the "science" that underpins it, the sense of heat and cold, and the narrator's fear, effort, exhaustion and exaltation. Love is the theme, but Chaucer turns to fame, the fame of lovers. His ostensible motive is to escape the routine of life and visit a place of extraordinary persons, stories and events. Allegorical readers try to attach it to his disappointment at lack of recognition; others tie it to court events. It may be simple entertainment. Unlike the *Tales*, it's drawn from books, not from life.

The narrator, like Ganymede who was "mad the goddys botiller," is plucked up by an eagle and swept off in one of the earliest English dreams of nonspiritual and nonmechanized flight. But he isn't going to Olympus to mix martinis for Jove. This isn't transcendental or mystical in that way; and the eagle keeps "articulating" as they fly. His first word is "Awak!"—a squawky word in "the same vois and stevene / That useth oon I koude nevene"—perhaps Mrs. Chaucer. The eagle reassures him, but when he opens his eyes he's scared out of his wits. Does Jove want to make him into a star? He is not Enoch or Elijah or Romulus or Ganymede. But Jupiter is rewarding him for his laborious, bookish research into love and for his writing. Jupiter knows his man, a customs officer, a solitary even in the social world. The eagle takes him to the House of Fame for instruction and distraction. He calls his passenger "Geffrey," becomes philosophical, explains the natural order, how sound works, and much else. As they ascend, the world dwindles below. Looking up the poet sees enlarged the Milky Way and the stars.

The invocation in Book One is to the god of sleep, in Book Two to "every maner man / That Englissh understonde kan." Book Three invokes Apollo, and Chaucer lets the rhyme carry the reader from the invocation into the dream. In the invocation he wryly sets himself in the same relation to Apollo as Apollo is to Daphne. Reflecting on the vanity of Fame, he climbs a crystal hill: "A roche of yse, and not of stel." The ice image is developed: the words and names are so melted he cannot read them (as gravestones are in old churchyards). On the other side of the hill the names are unmelted: true fame, protected from heat by the shadow of the castle. He can't describe the castle, it's too beautiful. But he can tell the "substance" of what it contained, so big, seamless and

precious: "and ful eke of wyndowes, / As flakes falle in grete snowes."
He evokes the musicians he hears:

And many flowte and liltyng horn,	flute; clarion
And pipes made of grene corn,	
As han thise lytel herde-gromes,	shepherd boys
That kepen bestis in the bromes.	broom bushes

This is the poetry that shaped Spenser's voice in *The Shepheardes Calender*.

Finally he goes inside the house, having seen more than he can tell, and sees still more. Abundance of vision makes it hard for him to finish his work. Inside he finds a huge lady, Fame, enthroned, her head touching the sky, her feet the earth. She's covered with eyes, like Virgil's Rumor. He evokes the Apocalypse, but here a secular, or classicized, version: an interesting marriage of Roman and biblical divinity.

In the poem he does not distinguish among historical, legendary and mythical figures. They're an equal resource for the poet; his audience will expect all three kinds. Josephus, Statius, Virgil, Ovid, Lucan, Claudian, the chroniclers of Troy do the same, and disagree—some favor Troy, some Greece:

Oon seyde that Omer made lyes,	
Feynynge in hys poetries,	
And was to Grekes favorable;	
Therfor helde he hyt but fable.	he regarded it as fictitious

As in Dante, parties of the damned and blessed appear, petitioning Good Fame. The lady is fickle and disappoints. Then comes Aeolus, god of wind, whom she gets to blow Bad Fame abroad. Images of coprology and farting hover near the surface. The poet witnesses the wronging of right reputation, the unjust whims of Fame, how it is louder the further away it gets from Aeolus's smelly trumpet. A third party of good petitioners arrives and she promises better fame than they deserve. Aeolus blows his golden horn. Again, the poet responds to smell more than sound. The black trumpet is all stink, the gold trumpet's mouth is balm in a basket of roses. Another group asks that their deeds remain unknown. A fifth group asks anonymity, but she refuses since their good deeds, known, will breed good deeds. A sixth group of semiwastrels gets good fame. The lazy and covetous get the thumbs down. Then come traitors, "shrews," men who have been utterly bad and courted fame for fame's sake.

Geoffrey gets into conversation. Why is he there—as petitioner?

Certainly not, says the poet. He is led out to the labyrinth, Dedalus's construction. The quaint house spins and is never still: the dizziness of fame. Lightly built of twigs, with holes to let sound escape, it's an ever restless, sleepless place. The poet sees his eagle perched nearby, asks leave to visit the spinning labyrinth, and the eagle agrees, but points out that he needs a guide—otherwise he won't get in (or out again). The poem stops.

Though the figures are literary, the world imagined is concrete, particular, the voices "real": it was a short step to put real characters into a world seen rather than visualized. At the end of the poem the rush of people eager to gain a view of the "man of gret auctorite" is especially clear: they "troden fast on others heles, / And stampen, as men doon aftir eles."

In *The Parliament of Fowls* we meet the mature Chaucer. Another love vision, it is also a bird and beast fable, pointing toward "The Nun's Priest's Tale." Again a gormless poet, who knows not love "in dede" but from books, is reading. He dozes, dreams: a supernatural guide conveys him through an allegorical vision. What is the poem's occasion? A valentine entertainment? No better explanation has been offered. There is more social satire than Chaucer practiced before, rising out of a conflict between the "gentil" and the "cherles," or common birds. The opening lines are among his best-known. The craft he speaks of in the first line is not poetry, but love:

> The lyf so short, the craft so long to lerne,
> Th' assay so hard, so sharp the conquering,   attempt
> The dredful joye, that alwey slit so yerne,   slides away so quickly
> Al this mene I by Love . . .

His professed ignorance of love-craft, his desire to learn from books and dreams rather than action in the field of love, add to the humor. The volume he reads before his dream is the apocryphal Ciceronian *Somnium Scipionis*, a classic attributed to Scipio Africanus, neglected today but with an importance for medieval writers second only to that of Boethius's *Consolation*.

> For out of olde feldes, as men seyth,
> Cometh al this newe corn from yer to yere,
> And out of olde bokes, in good feyth,
> Cometh al this newe science that men lere.   learn

Night falls on his reading and "Berafte me my bok for lak of lyght" so "to my bed I gan me for to dresse," depressed because he has what he doesn't want and lacks what he wants. In sleep Scipio Africanus calls on him. The dream is wish fulfillment, as a hunter in dream revisits the wood, a barrister dreams successful cases. Scipio takes him to a garden, and the first inscription over the gate is a reversal of Dante's *Inferno* lettering (the second is bleak, for failed love):

> "Thorgh me men gon into that blysful place
> Of hertes hele and dedly woundes cure;
> Thorgh me men gon unto the welle of grace,
> There grene and lusty May shal evere endure.
> This is the wey to al good aventure.
> Be glad, thow redere, and thy sorwe of-caste;   cast away sorrow
> Al open am I—passe in, and sped thee faste!"

He stands affrighted till Scipio shoves him through, assuring him that as he has no taste for love he's in no peril: he can gather useful subjects for his writing. He is led into a forest of immortal trees. An idyllic river flows, flowers bloom: the superb description again foreshadows Spenser and early Milton. Each tree and creature is assigned an attribute from a human world: "The sayynge fyr," "the dronke vyne," "The victor palm" and so forth.

Cupid and his daughter Will are preparing arrows. All the courtly virtues are personified. "I saw Beute withouten any atyr." Venus. The Goddess Nature. And here is the hierarchy of birds for mate choosing, and a quite wonderful catalogue of birds that prefigures Skelton's lists. Nature holds on her hand a loved female formel eagle, the catalyst for the courtship debate. Nature insists that the female has to consent to being chosen. A tersel eagle claims the formel and declares terms and conditions of perfect courtly servitude. Other tersels of lower condition interject and the debate commences.

In *The Parliament* Chaucer *visualizes*. He attributes this power to his reading and stresses the derivative nature of his work: he's a reteller of tales. But he is no regurgitator. He assimilates and retells past knowledge in present terms. Selection and collation are preliminaries to creation. In *The Legend of Good Women* he makes the point the other way around: "And if that olde bokes weren aweye, / Yloren were of remembrance the keye." Translation and creation go hand in hand. He chooses, participates in the text, adapts, prunes and patches it.

Troilus and Criseyde, his great finished poem, is the outstanding verse narrative in English, the more remarkable for standing so near the threshold of our poetry. Sidney marveled at it: "Chaucer, undoubtedly, did excellently in his *Troilus and Criseyde*; of whom, truly, I know not whether to marvel more, either that he in that misty time could see so clearly, or that we in this clear age go so stumblingly after him. Yet had he great wants, fit to be forgiven in so reverent an antiquity." It goes with "The Knight's Tale," his second great narrative, and like it is rooted in Boccaccio. He claims to be translating and asks pardon for aught amiss: "For as myn auctor seyde, so sey I." This is a way of borrowing authority, the authority of a classic text. But he is not translating: he is adapting. "The Knight's Tale" condenses a huge story, *Troilus* expands a small story in the *Filostrato*. The characters are different from Boccaccio's. Though the structure is allegorical, Chaucer's characters outgrow the figurative and take on dramatic life; he lets them, he makes them real. Warton conjectures from certain images in the poem that it may have been composed on Chaucer's travels: had he composed it at home other metaphors and images would have occurred to him. Or is it based more closely on an original than we suppose?

Chaucer's telling of *Troilus* in five books improves on the plot and characters of Boccaccio and provides philosophical and dramatic coherence and a visualized setting. Saintsbury calls Chaucer a hermit crab, crawling into someone else's shell, this time Boccaccio's, and making it his own, a common medieval practice. The woodenness of Chaucer's allegorical figures softens here into a kind of realism we do not find again in our poetry before Marlowe. Characters may be representative; they are not stylized.

The poem begins with Calkas's treacherously going over to the Greeks. He has read the oracles. He leaves his daughter Criseyde in Troy. Hector forgives her when she seeks mercy for herself. It is April, a month fatal for lovers, who repair to the temple for their ceremonies.

> Among thise othere folk was Criseyda,
> In widewes habit blak; but natheles,
> Right as oure firste lettre is now an A,
> In beaute first so stood she, makeles.   matchless

Chaucer alludes to Anne of Bohemia, Richard's queen. Troilus is cruising in the temple and teasing his friends for falling in love. Then he sees Criseyde. He resists but at last allows himself the full rein of love. He sings his love song, then burns for her volubly, but she is ignorant of his love; her nonresponse he takes for indifference or an indication that she has another beau.

Pandarus arrives. He courts Troilus's confidence with banter and concern. The language moves into courtly love gear. He offers to help—how the devil can you help me, says Troilus, you who never prospered in love yourself? (In this Pandarus recalls the narrators of *The House of Fame* and *The Parliament of Fowls*.) Keeping to courtly rules, Troilus resists naming his beloved. Pandarus tells him that unknown she will despise him if he dies and she knows no cause; besides, he's making himself unlovable. "Unknowe, unkist, and lost, that is unsought." Pandarus evokes Boethius's wheel of fortune. At last Troilus confesses, repents to the god of love for past cynicism, and Pandarus goes to work. Troilus has the fervent zeal of the convert. His indolence is turned to action, his vices to virtues, he returns to the field of battle and all are delighted to look into his face.

The second book shifts to Criseyde. "Owt of thise blake wawes for to saylle, / O wynd, o wynd, the weder gynneth clere . . ." April is gone. It is May, mother of happy months. Procne awakes Pandarus with her sad song and he hies to Criseyde's. He finds her listening to a maid reading from the tales of the siege of Thebes, one of Chaucer's unsettling anachronisms. Pandarus pricks her curiosity, and women, we know from Pandora, cannot resist temptation. He starts praising Troilus. Criseyde attends. At last she persuades him to come clean and he drops his bombshell; if she doesn't respond, Troilus will kill himself and so will he. He weeps. Criseyde hears him out but doesn't immediately respond. He gives advice. She accuses him of letting her down. He starts to kill himself; she slyly humors him. He lies about how he found out Troilus's love. He goes, she repairs to her closet "And set hire doun as stylle as any ston." Then Troilus rides below her window, returning from battle.

> Criseÿde gan al his chere aspien,
> And leet it so softe in hire herte synke,
> That to hirself she seyde, "Who yaf me drynke?"

Her love is not sudden: a sinking in, she talks herself into it. She is concerned first for her own *estaat*, then for his *heele*. In sleep she dreams that a bone-white eagle removes her heart. As she sleeps, Chaucer takes us back to Troilus. Pandarus persuades him to write a letter, then persuades Criseyde to reply. They meet and declare fidelity.

It cannot last. Book Four invokes the furies, the end of the affair. The focus of the Proem is on Criseyde. After a day of battle, a truce for the exchange of prisoners is declared. Calkas asks that Criseyde be sent over in exchange for Antenor. Troilus, a courtly lover, can't name his love. Hector says the Trojans don't sell women and she is no prisoner. The people resist, with perhaps an allusion to 1381 and Jack Straw:

> The noyse of peple up strite thanne at ones,
> As breme as blase of straw iset on fire;   fiercely; blaze
> For infortune it wolde, for the nones,   misfortune
> They sholden hire confusion desire.

"Ector," quod they, "what goost may yow enspyre,
This womman thus to shilde, and don is leese   allow us to lose
Daun Antenor—a wrong wey now ye chese— . . ."   Master

The political irony is not lost on Chaucer: Antenor later turned traitor.
The common will is not to be trusted.

At moments of special tension Chaucer resorts to heavy alliteration:

And as in wynter leves ben biraft,
Ech after other, til the tree be bare,
So that ther nys but bark and braunche
    ilaft,
Lith Troilus, byraft of ech welfare,   bereft of all happiness
Ibounden in the blake bark of care,
Disposed wood out of his wit to   disposed to go out of his mind
    breyde,
So sore hym sat the chaungynge of
    Criseyde.

Troilus laments hugely and long. Pandarus comes and bucks him up.
First he argues that Troilus has had his love: let her go, seek out another.
But Troilus, doggedly faithful, accuses Pandarus of playing racket, "to
and fro, / Nettle in, dok out, now this, now that." Pandarus urges
Troilus to ravish her (with her consent) before she goes. Criseyde mean-
while is raising her own moan, reading her will and testament to the air.
Pandarus comes and talks her round.

Pandarus summons Troilus from the temple, lectures him in a
Boethian spirit, then takes him to Criseyde. Their meeting is touching:

Soth is, that when they gonnen first to mete,
So gan the peyne hire hertes for to twiste,
That neyther of hem other myghte grete,
But hem in armes toke, and after kiste.

Briefly, they are too full of feeling for language. She puts her head on his
breast and faints. He thinks her dead and designs to kill himself. He
finds his voice and makes another speech, she comes around and cries
out his name, he is overjoyed and kisses her some more, to this effect:
"For which hire goost, that flikered ay on lofte, / Into hire woful herte
ayeyn it wente." Seeing the sword she chides him for considering sui-
cide. She suggests they go to bed and discuss matters further since day
is drawing nigh. And thus in Romeo and Juliet haste they make their
way to consummation. In bed they plan secret meetings. She has a low

opinion of her father and thinks to bribe and corrupt him. She unfolds
her plot, and Chaucer comments, as if to absolve her from what comes
later:

> And treweliche, as writen wel I fynde,
> That al this thyng was seyd of good
>   entente;
> And that hire herte trewe was and kynde
> Towardes hym, and spak right as she
>   mente,
> And that she starf for wo neigh, when   was nearly dead of sorrow
>   she wente,
> And was in purpos evere to be trewe

Troilus comes round to her point of view, recovers, gets excited and
"Bigan for joie th'amorouse daunce." Speech has cleared their hearts as
birdsong makes a morning. She swears and swears fidelity with huger
and huger oaths. Note: She does not doubt his faith for an instant.

Like the fifth act of a Shakespearean tragedy, the Parcas or Fates
begin the last book. Diomede comes to take Criseyde away. He senses
Troilus's love. As he leads Criseyde among the Greeks he chats about
the Greek world and how she will feel at home there. He takes her to
Calkas's tent and declares his new love for her. Back in Troy Pandarus
tries to distract Troilus, but he wants to see his beloved. Criseyde's house
is shut up. He remembers, then reverts to grief. "Men myght a book
make of it, lik a storie."

We return to Criseyde, busy being courted by Diomede and pushed
by her father into his arms, until she falls. After a couple of months she
has forgotten Troilus. Diomede is virile and eligible. She is beautiful,
with only one fault: her eyebrows join. Troilus is more a paragon than
Diomede, but he is no longer there. Diomede pleads with Calkas,
with her. She gives him hope, and having given him hope, she must
in time give the rest. She does so with diminishing reluctance, calcu-
lating her need, forgetting her troth. She laments her infidelity, know-
ing what it is and deliberately turning—laments, but does not repent.
The author can't say how long it took her to turn. His sources are un-
clear. He suggests the time was brief, but gives her the benefit of the
doubt.

Troilus and Pandarus are on the walls, straining their eyes for a
sighting of Criseyde. They keep gazing, conversing and japing. Troilus
imagines he sees her but it's a distant cart. Night falls. After some days,
Troilus is overcome by jealousy. He weakens and everyone, from King
Priam down, is concerned. One night he goes to bed and dreams of a

wood with a large sleeping boar, in whose arms lies Criseyde, kissing it. Pandarus counsels him to write a letter, which he does eloquently. She replies, her reply not transcribed for us, but she promises to come in due course. Troilus asks Cassandra to interpret his boar dream, which she does, relating it to Tideus who was Diomede's father. Her interpretation is long, its conclusion merciless: "Wep if thow wolt, or lef! For, out of doute, / This Diomede is inne, and thow art oute." No one believes Cassandra, that's what she's famous for. Troilus keeps his hope just a little longer.

When Hector is slain, Troilus becomes chief warrior. He sneaks out to try to glimpse Criseyde in the night, in vain. Then she writes again, this letter quoted in the poem. At last Troilus understands. Deiphobus in battle has rent from Diomede Criseyde's brooch, which Troilus gave her. He still loves but knows he cannot have or trust her ever again. He refers to her as "bright Criseyde," an epithet that recurs seventeen times in the poem. He goes to battle and triumphs over all but Diomede.

Chaucer begs pardon from his lady readers. They will find elsewhere, in other sources, that Criseyde proved false. It isn't his story, he is just the teller of an historical tragedy.

He must release Troilus's soul. Slain by Achilles, he ascends to heaven and looks down on the little spot of earth, embraced by the sea; he despises earth's vanity, gazing at where he was slain. He laughs at those who lament his passing. Chaucer urges readers to set their young minds on higher things, to love God and Christ who died and rose. *He* will not betray. Finally Chaucer condemns the pagan world and its rites, its gods, its (and our) appetites. The classical gods are rascals. There is a final, gracious hand-washing in the dedication:

> O moral Gower, this book I directe
> To the and to the, philosophical Strode,
> To vauchen sauf, ther nede is, to correcte,
> Of youre benignites and zeles goode.
> And to that sothefast Crist, that starf on   steadfast; died on the
>   rode,   cross
> With al myn herte of mercy evere I preye . . .

And he prays, he prays with Dante of the *Paradiso*, in a key that changes the key of his whole poem. The prayer rounds up the tone from passion to a kind of transcendence, a change of key that is not overextended so as to destroy the impact of the poem but that brings it from the treacherous brink of the erotic and subversive back into the realm of courtly and divine love.

In *Troilus and Criseyde* the plot holds no surprises. The poet tells us the outcome in the opening passages: "The double sorwe of Troilus," "Fro wo to wele, and after out of joie," and as early as line 55 we are prepared for Criseyde's bad faith: "the double sorwes here / Of Troilus in lovynge of Criseyde, / And how that she forsook him ere she deyde." It is not the working of plot but the philosophical process of predestination and the motive and development of character we watch. In the fifth book the poet insistently intervenes, to hold our sympathy at bay so that we can judge characters fairly. They've grown too big for the moral clarity he seeks. Criseyde is too beguiling. Yet we do keep a certain distance. Chaucer insists, even as he makes Troy visible, that it is remote in time, a different world altogether. Facts are foreknown and static. Narrative need not be linear. It can turn back on itself, allow gaps in sequence. Chaucer stops and starts action, accelerates and brakes, lingers when we would have him hurry and hurries when we would have him stay. It's a technique he uses in "The Knight's Tale" too, leaving Palamon and Arcite "ankle deep" in blood while he visits another part of the story. Our perspective becomes all-inclusive, as Troilus's does when his "lighte goost" escapes his body and ascends to the highest sphere.

There are two time schemes, historical and symbolic. It is April in the first book, May in the second and third; Book Four takes place three years later, in autumn; Book Five passes in a cold season. This poetic chronology provides images and a satisfying cycle, an additional unity. With autumn the tone begins to change.

The philosophical theme is proved by facts in the narrative. Dreams never lie: Troilus's dream of the boar and Criseyde's of the eagle are symbolically true. Pandarus, who, like Criseyde's turncoat father, is an astrologer, foresees what is to be and catalyzes it. His foreknowledge is great. At one point the poet tells us, "But God and Pandarus wist al what this ment." Only the lovers cannot see ahead.

Criseyde, when she falls in love, is natural and passionate, her virtue pragmatic. We learn little of her past except that she has been widowed. Her father's treachery made her presence in Troy precarious. Pandarus advises her to love Troilus in part to protect herself. All these facts tend a little to exculpate her. If she is natural and active once aroused, Troilus, the knight and warrior, in matters of love proves phlegmatic and philosophical. Just when we expect his heart to break, he launches into Boethian lectures on predestination: "For al that comth, comth by necessitee, / Thus to ben lorn, it is my destinee." When he first falls in love his response is not virile and eager but passive and reflective. The word "think" is associated with Criseyde. Talking (at length) is the prerogative of Troilus. Action characterizes Pandarus. These are, despite particular characterization, their modes of being. To this extent Chaucer's characters are thematic clauses in an argument.

It is the narrator (not "Chaucer himself") who alters most during the course of the poem. An innocent servant of the servants of Venus—a sort of Pandarus himself—he is overcome by what he has to tell. He tries to draw a positive moral; it defeats him. He interrupts the story to preempt our objections. In the end, with tender pity, he lets Criseyde go. He condemns reluctantly but absolutely: "Men seyn,—I not,—that she yaf hym [Diomede] hire herte." His effort to keep us at a moral distance from the story has snared him in it.

Chaucer makes emotional abstractions accessible to the senses through homely metaphors. When Troilus loves, his heart like a loaf of bread begins to "sprede and ryse." Epic simile behaves this way, likening great with familiar things. Bayard the horse remembers his horsiness after a moment's abandon to feeling; there is the snail, lyming of bird feathers, a snare; "Now artow hent, now gnaw thin owen cheyne!"; a whetstone, or

> But also cold in love towardes the
> Thi lady is, as frost in wynter moone,
> And throw fordon, as snow in fire is soone.   destroyed

Criseyde's memory of Troy is a knotless thread drawn painlessly through her heart. The language is fully transitive. Characters fight, touch, kiss, embrace. Dialogue is credible, even dramatic. Pandarus reports to his niece from the battlefield: "There nas but Grekes blood,—and Troilus." That pause sparks the best hyperbole in the poem.

Chaucer develops an architecture, balancing scene against scene, linking by echo and reiteration passages in different books. This patterning begins in the stanza form. Normally the pivot of the stanza is in the fourth line, the center. The language builds to it, then changes tone or direction into the final couplet. The pivot can be the line, a word, or a subject and verb carefully placed. In Book Two, we read Pandarus's subtle exhortation:

> Now, nece myn, the kynges deere sone,
> The goode, wise, worthi, fressche, and free,
> Which alwey for to do wel is his wone,   custom
> The noble Troilus, so loveth the,
> That, but ye helpe, it wol his bane be.
> Lo, here is al! What sholde I moore seye?
> Do what your lest, to make hym lyve or deye.   you please

There at the stanza's heart is "Troilus, so loveth," preceded by his virtues and followed by his desires. There is also Chaucer's mastery of the enjambement. One example, Troilus's declaration:

> But fro my soule shal Criseydes darte
> Out nevere mo . . .

Is "darte" a noun? "Out" comes at the head of the line with the emphasis of a verb. It becomes a preposition only in retrospect. It is "darte out," no talk of darts but of mingled souls; yet the dart hovers at the edge of metaphor.

After *Troilus and Criseyde*, Chaucer's next production, *The Legend of Good Women* (*c.* 1385) is minor: a penance exacted by the God of Love for his defamation of women in *Troilus and Criseyde*. He must write of "Cupid's saints." Another love vision (all the love visions have the word "of" in the title, emblematizing possession), it is most original and interesting in the "Prologue," where the daisy undergoes her memorable metamorphosis into that most faithful of Trojan women, Alceste. The poet worships the daisy on the first of May. The "Prologue" is a sort of palinode, a poem of celebration. Here Chaucer uses for the first time the rhymed decasyllabic couplets, which become heroic couplets. The poem has a secure place in the history of English prosody.

Apart from minor and miscellaneous work, his last great poem, largely from his mature period, is *Canterbury Tales*. As Dryden comments in his preface to *Fables Ancient and Modern*: "Here is God's plenty!" Dryden "modernized" some of the *Canterbury Tales*. "All the pilgrims in the *Canterbury Tales*, their humours, their features, and the very dress, [I see] as distinctly as if I'd supped with them at the Tabard in Southwark." The breadth of Chaucer's direct knowledge and observation is formidable. "He is a perpetual fountain of good sense; learned in all sciences; and therefore speaks properly on all subjects. As he knew what to say, so he knows also when to leave off; a continence which is practised by few writers." In particular, few medieval writers. The accuracy of detail impressed Dryden. "Chaucer followed nature everywhere; but was never so bold to go beyond her." In their scope the *Tales* reveal "a most wonderful comprehensive nature," learning and social vision, despite what the Roman Catholic Dryden sees as Wycliffite blemishes in his thought—evident especially in "The Parson's Tale," though certainly not strident.

Canterbury Tales is an anthology of stories of many kinds set in the framework of a pilgrimage, the medieval equivalent of a vacation, with spiritual overtones. The tales are told by individuals, the first such *characters* in English literature, passing the time on their journey from

Southwark to the tomb of St. Thomas à Beckett at Canterbury. Our first interest is in the pilgrims, introduced one by one in the "Prologue," Chaucer's most original verse, evoking season, place, a motive for the gathering, then the pilgrims themselves, in order of social eminence: a knight at the top, a plowman at the bottom, and in between representatives of the Church in its various manifestations, also a shipman, a cook, a franklin, a widow, and so on. The host of the Tabard becomes master of ceremonies and accompanies them on the journey.

The sequence of tales was to include four by each pilgrim, but exists only in extended fragments. Rivalries and friendships are suggested; surrounding the drama of each tale is the drama of the storytellers revealed in their prologues. A tale can provide a window on their enthusiasms and hostilities. Friar and Summoner expose one another in their true colors. By savagely criticizing the Church from the mouths of members of its corrupt and privileged classes, Chaucer "made it true" and wryly distanced himself from controversy. "The Knight's Tale" is obliquely answered by the Miller's coarse, delightful tale, which in turn gives offense to the Reeve and provokes from him a further low tale.

"The Knight's Tale" introduces the dominant themes: love, marriage, justice, predestination, the wheel of fortune—a courtly, civic and philosophical opening of a pilgrimage that concludes with the tedious theological didacticism of "The Parson's Tale." Chaucer finally recants all but his moral works: the translation of Boethius, the legends of saints, homilies, moralities and devotions. Between Knight's and Parson's stretch the other tales, twenty-four in all, not all complete.

Chaucer's women are among his best creations. Criseyde, his completest and most complex woman, is a triumph. In the *Tales* we meet others. The Prioress faints at the sight of blood, mothers her puppies and swoons if one dies. She combines courtliness with an easy religious vocation: *amor vincit omnia* is her motto. She suffers a frustrated desire to be a mother. Hence her dogs and her tale about the murder of a child. Chaucer makes her physically and psychologically present. Her hypocrisies charm, but they remain hypocrisies.

The Wife of Bath's prologue and her tale express rather than reflect her character. Her syntax, her face, her clothes, her stars, her past, all particularize her. Her dress is out of fashion: it is the fashion of her youth, her better years. She introduces her five husbands. Her vitality makes us overlook her numerous peccadilloes. Opposite and hostile to her is the repugnant Pardoner; she, the insatiable, throbbing but sterile woman faces in him the bitterly impotent man.

Chaucer is the father of English poetry for two reasons. The first is technical: adapting continental forms he evolves a relaxed and distinctly English style; he enriches the poetic vocabulary; and he introduces through translation and adaptation the great Latin, French and Italian poets into English *poetry*. The second reason relates to the first. In his powerful and original style Chaucer provides a formal and a thematic model. He brings *England* into the new English poetry. Langland portrays London, but his is a moralized, allegorical metropolis, in the spirit of didactic documentary. Chaucer introduces the diversity of English character and language, of English society at large. He has themes, not polemics or moral programs. His eyes are mild and unclouded. Gower writes from books. Chaucer starts writing from books, but the world takes over his verse.

Of the poems doubtfully attributed to Chaucer, one, "Merciles Beaute," a triple roundel, touched Ezra Pound to the quick:

> Your yen two wol slee me sodenly;   two eyes will slay
> I may the beautee of hem not sustene,
> So woundeth hit thourghout my herte kene.

Doubtful attribution in the centuries after his death meant that almost any unattributed poem of merit (and some that were attributed) were put on Chaucer's account, as it were, and his oeuvre grew and grew, until Thomas Tyrwhitt (1730–86), Chaucer's first great editor in the eighteenth century, stripped the body of work down to what could definitely be identified, from internal evidence, as the poet's own work. In 1775 he published an edition of *Canterbury Tales* with prefatory matter and glossary. Not a theorist, just a learned scholar of classical and medieval literature who had enjoyed legal training and possessed an impeccable ear, Tyrwhitt first realized that Chaucer's metrics depended on the voicing of the "feminine 'e.'" This "discovery" reopened the ear to fourteenth- and fifteenth-century prosody. Indeed, it even affects how we can read Thomas Wyatt in the sixteenth. Tyrwhitt is one of those rare scholar-critics who merits an honored place in Poet's Corner, along with all the great printers and publishers.

"Sing cuccu!"

ANON.

Anon. is a poet without dates, parents or gender. Anon. appears in the fourteenth and in the twentieth centuries, in Britain and Australia and Africa, always with a song in the heart. Often the song is sad, as though something important—perhaps the author's identity—has been lost. "Reverdie" is Anon.'s, subtitled "Rondel." Two lines precede it:

> Sing cuccu nu! Sing cuccu!
> Sing cuccu! Sing cuccu nu!

"Rondel" means round in form; the poem circles back on itself with a refrain, like a cuckoo's woodland repetitions. The poem feels like a fragment of a longer piece:

> Summer is icumen in,
>> Lhudè sing cuccu;
> Groweth sed and bloweth med
>> And springth the wodè nu.
>>> Sing cuccu!
> Awè bleteth after lomb,
>> Lowth after calvè cu;
> Bulluc sterteth, buckè verteth;
>> Merie sing cuccu.
>>> Cuccu, cuccu,
>> Wel singès thu, cuccu,
>> Ne swik thu never nu.

That's all there is. The language isn't hard if you listen: Summer is coming in, the cuckoo sings loudly. The seed grows, the mead blows and the wood springs anew. Sing, cuckoo. The ewe bleats after the lamb, the cow lows after the calf, the bullock leaps, the buck—verteth? has it something to do with green, the *vert* that the French brought with them? Or is the *v* pronounced *f* as in German, and is the buck making another sort of sound?—sing merrily cuckoo, cuckoo, cuckoo, you sing well cuckoo; then the sting of the poem, that word "swik" which means cease or give up—*never stop singing*.

It celebrates, like the opening of the *Canterbury Tales*, a change for the better; knowing that spring gives way to summer, autumn to winter, it asks—it prays—to the cuckoo, spirit of the wood, that this new beginning remain new, that the cuckoo never cease its song. Modernized, the poem evaporates, but the original, with strange accent and vocabulary, is necessary, full of feeling. It's small, whole and complex. This ancient piece moves us the way a good song does. After the immense allegories of Gower and Langland and the hectic world of Chaucer, this strikes us with the freshness of nursery rhyme and goes straight into memory. Artful it is, not artificial. It isn't trying to be anything but itself. Who wrote it? It was copied in the margin of a manuscript, which is how it survives. Was Anon. man or woman? Our instinct is to call the medieval Anon. "him." Perhaps the name is forgotten because Anon. was a woman, and the society of poets was virtually all male at the time.

How many poems of this virtue got lost because people didn't value their own language? Welsh, Scots Gaelic and Irish, Cornish and Manx, all the little languages on which English played the colonial trick, had such verse. Some survives, though the language of power prevails, and if power stays in place for a few centuries, summer will never icum in again on a rural tongue. A surviving poem from Ireland, not in Irish, is in love with its land and its saints:

> Icam of Irlaunde,
> Ant of the holy londe
> > Of Irlande.
> Gode sire, pray ich the,
> For of saynte charitè,
> Come ant daunce wyt me
> > In Irlaunde.

Behind strange spellings our language is thinly veiled: I am of Ireland, and of the holy land of Ireland. Good sir, I pray you, for the sake of holy charity, come and dance with me in Ireland. Said like that it flows away like sand through the fingers: what holds it, all that *can* hold it, is its original sounds, which are inseparable not from the sense but from the experience of that sense.

Here is another poem by Anon. What does it *do* to us, with four little lines?

Western wind, when will thou blow,
    The small rain down can rain?
Christ, if my love were in my arms
    And I in my bed again!

The copyist can standardize spelling—the poem does not depend on quaintness. It strikes us as more "modern," despite a folk feeling. It is not about our experience. It is about open space, longing and love, with an oath that is at once a prayer.

Anon. is the greatest of the neglected English poets.

Entr'acte

CHARLES OF ORLEANS, THOMAS HOCCLEVE,
JOHN LYDGATE, JULIANA BERNERS

Why does vernacular poetry falter in the fifteenth century? The Renaissance, which that century ushers in, is soon mired in classical humanism. Petrarch, the embodiment of this new spirit, urged the use of Latin in preference to the coarse vernacular; languages just gathering confidence were rolled back before the universal claims of Latin. Even champions of vernacular reneged. They incorporated their experience into that of classic writers, remote from the street cries, lullabies, ballads and working songs of the oral tradition, and remote too from the new literature of the previous century.

An absolute requisite of Renaissance humanism was authority and precedent, elements that resided in the almost sacred authoritative text. It was the heyday of the editorial scholar, not the editor. When vernacular literature crept out again, it found readers in the market for masters, canonical classics and those who sounded like them. Anon. has no place at the high table; writers like Langland are beneath contempt. The classics are found among the Italians, or at home—apologetically— in Chaucer and Gower, then later and proudly in Sidney, Spenser, and preeminently in Milton. Shakespeare is a bit too near the ground, too profuse and varied to be a fountainhead, too anarchic. After all, he broke most of the rules of dramatic (and poetic) form, extended syntax and muddied diction in preposterous ways, and the plays are suspect because he never saw them through the press. Few writers in the fifteenth century dared to ask: What is a natural language? Is it what we daily speak, what we write in and pray in, or is it an old-newfangled Roman idiom with cold purities, marble outline? We have learned to forget the English Latin poets, even the good ones. We forget most of the English poets who wrote in French—and the French forget them.

An exception is Wace, born in Jersey in the twelfth century. His *Le Roman de Vrut* was a sort of translation of Geoffrey of Monmouth's Latin *History of the Kings of Britain*, which he finished in 1155 and presented to Eleanor of Acquitaine, Henry II's queen. Also in the twelfth century there's Thomas d'Angleterre, who must have been English—his *Tristram* survives in bits and pieces. But who reads Wace? Who reads d'Angleterre? We forget, or we *almost* do, the French poets who wrote in English. Charles of Orleans (1394–1464/5) is usually left out of account. Aristocratic, with an easy directness, he deserves attention. He's like a Tudor poet born a century too early, an eager daffodil blasted by frost.

Few Frenchmen (indeed, few Englishmen) mastered English as well as he did in the shadows of an English court where he was held prisoner for years, just as, earlier, Chaucer (more briefly, with a modest ransom on his head) was imprisoned in France. Detention was an important part of education. A grandson of Charles V of France, Charles of Orleans's son by his third wife, Marie of Clèves, became King Louis XII. His cousin Isabel at the age of seven became the wife of King Richard II and was kept in custody after the king was killed because his successors did not wish to repay her dowry. She married Charles when he was twelve; she was so distressed to lose the title of queen of England that she wept through the ceremony. His cousin Catherine became the wife of Henry V and a character in Shakespeare's play. He was himself a possible heir to the French crown.

His pedigree is full and complex and would have fascinated a man like Proust. Born in Paris in 1394, he was the eldest son of mad King Charles VI's only brother. At thirteen he became head of his house and faction when his father was assassinated. His first mission was to avenge his father. His wife died in childbirth, leaving a daughter. He married Bonne d'Armagnac, who was twelve, and continued pursuing his family's enemies. He signed a marriage contract between his daughter, nine months old, and the six-year-old Duke of Alençon, who later fought beside Joan of Arc. Defeated, excommunicated, he struggled back to grace and was restored in 1412 (he was eighteen), his father's reputation cleared, the Duke of Burgundy discredited. Then at Agincourt the English found him under a heap of dead Frenchmen. They took him and held him for ransom. In Canterbury he was paraded through the streets and endured a cathedral service of thanksgiving for his defeat. His brother too was a hostage. They were held in various prisons—the Tower, where James I of Scotland was also interned; Pontefract, where Richard II was murdered; Fotheringay; Ampthill; Windsor. The ransom was too much for his estates, beggared by war. The Clarences and Somersets were greedy. Prisoners were chattels to be sold, milked and bequeathed in wills.

His brother had the *Canterbury Tales* copied out and the brothers read it to one another, getting to know the characters and the language.

They read Boethius, consolation in the circumstances, and composed prayers. Henry V in his will recommended that they not be released until Henry VI—who inherited the thrones of England and France when he was nine months old—should come of age. Charles was eventually freed in 1440 at the age of forty-six. He married Marie of Clèves—then fourteen—and worked for peace between England, France and the factions, retiring to Blois after a few more bloody noses. There he gave himself up to the arts, including literary gatherings and the competitions between poets that he sponsored.

"Ther nys leef nor flowre that doth endewre / But a sesoun as sowne doth in a belle." Sometimes he translated his own French poems, allegories and amorous pieces, but half his poems in English were composed in the language of his captors and a few of the French poems are translated from English originals. It's hard to tell whether a poem is an English chicken or a French egg. Writers in other centuries have done this—Samuel Beckett, for example, and James Joyce in the twentieth.

Some said he couldn't have done the English poems: no *Frenchman* could have. But where versions of a poem exist in French and English you see the differences: they're in his personal manuscript. His detractors ignore the quality of the versions, and of the originals that they reject: English is closed to foreigners, even foreign prisoners held for twenty-five years. This linguistic hubris reflects a common fear of the alien, though the English had no difficulty in believing that their poets could write in French (or Latin) according to their degrees of skill. Like Gower, Charles wrote Latin religious poems as well as French and English. His manuscript book—he was a royal scribe, a noble predecessor, as it were—shows how, as he learned the language, he found his (metrical) feet. There is a rondel he composed, remembering—he had time to remember ("When I am hushed it marvel is to me / To hear my heart, how that he talketh soft")—a beloved.

The smylyng mouth and laughyng eyen gray	laughing gray eyes
The brestis rounde and long smal armys twayne	breasts; two
The hondis smothe the sidis streiyt & playne	smooth hands; straight sides
Yowre fetis lite what shulde y ferther say	your light feet
Hit is my craft when ye are fer away	
To muse theron in styntyng of my payne	assuaging my pain
The smylyng	
The brestis	
So wolde y pray yow gef y durste or may	if I dared and were allowed
The sight to se as y haue seyne	

Forwhi that craft me is most fayne   desirable

And wol ben to the howre in which y day   will be until the day I die

       The smylyng

       The brestis

The reprise lingers, with sadness, with desire. Wyatt may have known his verse: he seems to remember him, as he remembers Gower and Chaucer.

A chief person in his poems is Heart, now clad in black, now in a dungeon, occasionally thrilled by the lady's beauty, then cast down again by her *hauteur*. Heart has moods, Heart speaks, counts money and tears, counsels, despairs of counseling, complains, hopes, celebrates. He's part of the allegory of love and, in the end, of faith. Charles isn't Heart, the poems are not anecdotal confessions. The ladies, like Dame Philosophy in Boethius, are representative, not specific, figures. They are not one of his three wives, the queen or any lady of the English court. The poems do not arise from a passing carnal passion. Charles wrote lyric poems of subtlety a century before the Tudor poets got going, in the tedious age of those interminable, yawning poems by Hoccleve and Lydgate.

What of Thomas Hoccleve? Was he so very bad? Warton says he is "the first poet that occurs in the reign of Henry the Fifth." His verdict is peremptory: "Occleve is a feeble writer, considered as a poet." Considered as a man, he was little better. But he took into a new century and reign improvements of language that Chaucer and Gower effected. Hoccleve is the first—there's hardly another until Wyatt and Gascoigne—to speak in his poems not only *as* himself but *of* himself. His candor is excessive: he lays himself open without a sense of irony, the *ur*-confessional. His Amans is not a papery fiction but a man in need of psychiatric attention. Even so, his poetry is deficient in "world," in the colored, scented, sounding particulars that confront and affront him.

Hoccleve was born around 1368 and vanished from view around 1426. He may have come from Bedfordshire. For years he worked as a clerk in the office of the lord privy seal but seems not to have distinguished himself. He had a modest pension, was always poor and sometimes loopy. If he indulged in dissipation, he did it in taverns and without much style. In 1409 his pension increased to £13 6*S*. 8*d*. (All we know for sure about our early poets has to do with money: what they got paid. Even now, when poets get together, money and sex are what they tend to talk about.) Around 1411 he married. Five years later he was quite mad. In 1424 he got a benefice (or a *corrody*, or charge on a monastery).

Hoccleve is the first large-scale poet for whom we have several manuscripts in his own hand. They reveal the writerly habits of the day. He also left autobiographical lines which, Saintsbury says, "make him

(in a very weak and washed out way, it is true) a sort of English and
crimeless Villon, to the actual picture of his times that we have in *Lon-
don Lickpenny*." Saintsbury refers to "La Male Regle," in which the poet
petitions for his salary to be paid and unfolds a mildly vicious nature.

The state of his texts is unstable: many manuscripts remain un-
printed. His most important piece is a version of Aegidius's *De Regi-
mene Principium*, which he calls *The Regiment of Princes* and addresses to
Henry, Prince of Wales. It runs to 5,500 lines. Much is commonplace,
but the first 2,000 lines, a dialogue between the poet and a beggar, are
interesting, with autobiography and the address to Chaucer. In the
"Prologue" (not printed at the time) he apostrophizes his master:

O mayster dere, and fadir reverent,	father
My mayster Chaucer, floure of eloquence,	
Mirror of fructuous entendement,	fruitful understanding
O universal fadir in science,	knowledge
Alas that thou thine excellent prudence	
In thy bed mortel mightest not bequethe . . .	

These lines, written just after Chaucer died, were worked back into the
"Prologue." His poems swallow material from different periods without
embarrassment.

After the *Regiment* in importance are the verse stories from *Gesta
Romanorum*: "The Emperor Jereslaus's Wife" and "Jonathas," "La Male
Regle" with its confessions, and the "Complaint" and "Dialogue" (largely
autobiographical), "and a really fine *Ars Sciendi Mori*" says Saintsbury,
which one critic describes as (uncharacteristically) "manly." Somehow
he attracted a great patron of the age, Duke Humphrey, who around
1440 gave the University of Oxford one of the finest libraries of the
day—six hundred volumes. "They were the most splendid and costly
copies that could be procured," says Warton, "finely written on vellum,
and elegantly embellished with miniatures and illuminations." Most of
the books were removed as "popish" under Edward VI and destroyed or
scattered. Duke Humphrey was also Lydgate's patron and a friend of
European scholars and writers in the arts and sciences.

Hoccleve was an unpalatable man of the world. John Lydgate being a
myopic monk—he was among the first English poets to wear spectacles—
had acres of time after prayers and was turned into a verse machine by
his superiors, churning the stuff out by the yard. In 1800 Warton's vig-
orous and rather mad foe the literary antiquary Joseph Ritson described
him as a "prosaick and driveling monk." The bulk of his work is
huge, yet little is known of his life: not much of it is invested in the

verse. There must be more than 140,000 lines. Longer than Words-
worth. Longer than Milton. Longer than Milton and Wordsworth put
together. There's occasional humor. But Lydgate is not consistently
funny as Chaucer can be. He has little control of tone and veers toward
prosodic incompetence and prolixity. Saintsbury sees it as an overem-
phatic caesura with discord at both ends of the line: "Even in rime royal,
his lines wander from seven to fourteen syllables."

Born around 1370, Lydgate died in 1450 or thereabouts. He reached
his highest eminence under Henry VI, around 1430. He'd become a
monk at the big Benedictine abbey of St. Edmund's Bury in Suffolk at
a young age, after being educated at Oxford and in France and Italy,
from where he returned a master of the languages and literatures of both
lands. So proficient was he that he opened a school in his monastery to
teach sons of noble houses the elegancies of composition. Like Gower,
he set himself apart: his acquisitions were those of study, not derived
from the world of affairs. His *Miracles of St. Edmund* and other huge
devotional poems emerged from his cloister.

Robert Graves tells how he "was forced (apparently against his
will) to become a sort of scholarly *Versificator Regis*. The rules of his
Order compelled every monk to unthinking obedience; so Henry V
commissioned Lydgate, through his superior, to translate Giovanni
delle Colonne's 30,000-line *Historia Trojana*, which took eight years;
then the Earl of Warwick called him to Paris in 1426 to turn into
English a French poetical pedigree proving Henry VI to be the rightful
King of France. In the same year the Earl of Salisbury set him another
translation task: the 20,000-line *Pélerinage de la Vie Humaine*—an alle-
gory. Next, the Duke of Gloucester commanded him to translate Boc-
caccio's 36,000-line *De Casibus Illustrium Virorum* (*Fall of Princes*), an
even more formidable commission." Graves quotes these lines:

> Thus my self remembyring on this boke
> It to translate how I had undertake,
> Ful pale of chere, astonied in my loke,
> Myn hand gan tremble, my penne I feltè quake.
>
> I stode chekmate for feare when I gan see
> In my way how littel I had runne.

His horror at the size of the task does not translate as Hoccleve's would
have done in self-pity. He chooses metaphorical expression in the lan-
guage of chess.

Lydgate is mired in his age, if not in the age before, yet he points forward. His *Fall of Princes*, *Siege of Troy* and *Destruction of Troy* stand reading. The *Fall of Princes* is a "set of tragedies," a prototype for the *Mirrour for Magistrates* that so entertains and instructs the sixteenth century. Characters appear before the interlocutor Bochas and report on their downfalls. The best copy of the poem has a portrait of Lydgate. When Adam arrives he greets his interlocutor as "Cosyn Bochas."

Lydgate's *Siege of Thebes* pretends to be an additional Canterbury tale. The narrator arrives in Canterbury, chances on the pilgrims, goes back to their inn, is welcomed by the host, who comments on his threadbare outfit, and the next day on the return from Canterbury Monk Lydgate is enjoined to tell his enormous tale, interrupted by a steep descent near Broughton.

Warton finds some delight in *The Life of Our Lady*, and Saintsbury says the best way in is via *The Complaint of the Black Knight*. Gray and Coleridge valued him; he is worth a patient attempt. Shortly after his age William Dunbar pays tribute to Chaucer, Gower and Lydgate in "The Goldyn Targe," as though they could justly inhabit a stanza together:

> Your angel mouthis most mellifluate   honeyed
> Oure rude langage has clere illumynate,
>   And fair ourgilt oure spech that   gilded over
>   imperfyte
>   Stude, or your goldyn pennis schupe   remained;
>   to write;   before your pens prepared
> This ile before was bare and desolate
>   Off rethorike or lusty fresch endyte.   writing

He was one of the first English writers "whose style is cloathed with that perspicuity, in which the English phraseology appears at this day to an English reader." And what a range of forms, themes and tones he displays—it's his prolixity that makes Lydgate a problem for modern readers. Excerpted he shines, and Warton finds lines of miraculous compression and originality. From *The Life of Our Lady* he singles out a passage in which Lydgate argues the virgin birth against unbelievers. His argument is clinched in metaphor:

> For he that doth the tender braunches sprynge,
> And the fresshe flouris in the grete mede,   flowers; meadow
> That were in wynter dede and eke droupynge,
> Of bawme all yvoyd and lestyhede;   balm; emptied; energy
> May he not make his grayne to growe and
>   sede,   grain; seed

Within her brest, that was both mayd and
    wyfe,   virgin
Whereof is made the sothfast breade of lyfe?   true

The grain is transformed into bread *within the virgin*, an amazing con-
sistency of metaphor working at every level, emerging in incarnation
and the transubstantiated Host. Conceit gathers force and finally bursts
to the surface in a literal meaning.

Warton isolates other instances, more lyrical, less metaphysical
in character: "Like as the dewe discendeth on the rose / With sylver
drops . . ." and

When he of purple did his baner sprede
On Calvarye abroad upon the rode,   rood (cross)
To save mankynde . . .

Lydgate is easy to read, easier than Chaucer, but his language is less pre-
cise, less thrifty. He's easy but smooth. He soon bores. Moments of
reward, which in Chaucer occur in almost every line, are scarce. Lan-
guage is in excess of its occasion, and Lydgate is a rhetorician in both
the good and bad senses: he is absolute master of the figures of rhetoric,
but he also spins out, often a very thin thread, sometimes no thread
at all. His verse will admit anything, and the rest is prosaic structure
and prosaic movement. Yet he was popular for a couple of centuries.
Henry VIII got Richard Pynson to print *The History Siege and Destruc-
tion of Troye* in 1513. Another, more correct edition was printed in 1555 by
Thomas Marshe.

When Chaucer and Gower and Langland were about, it seemed that
English poetry had a center that would hold and grow stronger as the
language cohered and poetic skills evolved from good examples. But in
the powerful south the fifteenth century belonged to fat language, pro-
lixity. The growth of pedantic humanism in Europe and in England, the
hunger for authority that drove poets and scholars back on the classics,
made English appear as unserviceable as it had when the Normans sup-
pressed it. Hoccleve isn't substantial enough to rebut the humanists by
example; Lydgate was the equivalent to a modern journalist, churning
out matter for a market, in his case a court wanting history and verse
delivered in easy form. And Henry V was not enthusiastic about pane-
gyrics, or about English poetry. Patronage for him was more a custom
than a choice; in the troubled times of his successors it was a cus-
tom often honored in the breach. There was a more concise talent, that
of the first English woman verse writer, Juliana Berners, born around
1388. She contributed (it is believed) "advice literature" to *The Book of*

St. Albans (1486). Her succinct and unabashed definitions of hunting terminology and her advice to hunters may have been translated from prose originals, but they have an original feel. Practical verses—no one would claim they are poetry—yet more pleasurable, instructive and *concise* than much that passed for poetry at the time, pointing the way for Thomas Tusser a century later.

"Merely written for the people"

Shunned by the court and the universities, vernacular literature returned where it had survived during the suppression of English; in ballads, street cries, street poems, it drifted from centers of influence—London and Oxford—to the Marches, the Borders, into Scotland, where a different king reigned with another court. Indeed James IV or V of Scotland composed "The Gaberlunzie Man." Three centuries later Bishop Percy puts it this way: "As our southern metropolis must have been ever the scene of novelty and refinement, the northern countries, as being most distant, would preserve their ancient manners longest, and of course the old poetry, in which those manners are so peculiarly described."

True ballads are nobody's property. Anon.'s, they exist in various versions, depending on when and by whom they were first written down. The most wonderful of them, "The Ballad of Sir Patrick Spens," has the name of Sir Patrick substituted in some versions with the name of the famous Scottish admiral Sir Andrew Wood. Where scansion allowed, ballads could be taken off the peg for quite different occasions from those originally celebrated.

> O lang, lang, may the ladies stand
>> Wi' thair gold kems in their hair,   combs
> Waiting for thair ain deir Lords,
>> For they'll se thame na mair.

Sung in a minor key, usually with "tragic" or savage endings, the ballads' chief concerns are battle, love and death. If careless singers or printers struggling with unfamiliar dialect claimed the right to exploit and spoil them (some of my predecessors lived off the back of ballads that were hugely popular), who can deny us the right—Robert Graves asks—to guess how the originals went? More than any other form of literature, ballads emancipate scholar and poet: the text is not sacred; creative involvement can take place. In Graves's case invention goes too far, but as he accounts for his adjustments we learn about his techniques of composition, and about the ballad form itself.

Some English ballads survive by historical chance. Antwerp printers issued work for English readers, filling in gaps left by Caxton. Adraien van Berghen around 1503 printed Richard Arnold's *Chronicle*, a miscellany that, between a list of the tolls of Antwerp and the differences between English and Flemish coinage, includes the ballad "The Nut Brown Maid." Some survived through plays, or were gathered with "real" poems into books. But the ballad, when confined to the page after printing came in, usually traveled as a single or folded sheet and was sold for half a penny. In 1520, a man who bought two halfpenny ballads could have used the same money for two pounds of cheese or a pound of butter; for 2d. he could have bought a hen and for 6d. a pair of shoes. Printed ballads were cheap to produce and popular even before publishers learned the art of titling and packaging. In 1595 title pages gave no author or author's credentials unless that author was already well known. Early printed ballad titles were unwieldy and unmemorable. "The Norfolk gent his will and testament and howe he commytted the keepinge of his Children to his owne brother whoe delte moste wickedly with them and howe God plagued him for it" came to be known in later times as "The Babes in the Wood."

Ballads were especially hard for the authorities to control. They sprang up of their own accord and traveled from mouth to mouth without benefit of the censor. When they were printed they might be monitored and controlled. In 1586 the Star Chamber decreed an end to provincial printing or "imprinting of bookes, ballades, chartes, pourtraictures, or any other thing, or things whatsoever, but onelye in the cittie of London"—plus Oxford and Cambridge (one printer each). With the approach of the Civil War vigilance relaxed. Ballads needed to be controlled because they contained news, sometimes in biased or subversive form, and city people were hungry for information. With the ballad journalism is born.

It was 1622 before news report publications, called *Corantos*, first appeared, relating mainly foreign news and none of it dangerously new. From 1632 to 1638 the *Corantos* were suspended by the Star Chamber after complaints from the Spanish ambassador. In 1641 home news was permitted in the first of the *Diurnalls*, followed by *Weekly Accounts*, *Mercuries*, *Intelligencers* and accounts of the progress of the Civil War. The first publication that was recognizably an ancestor of our newspapers was the *London Gazette* (1665). With censorship, inevitably, news was disseminated in the form of fiction. Ballads outnumbered all other forms of publication, though "prognosticating almanacs" became for their publishers "readier money than ale or cakes," Thomas Nash recalls. Many high-minded individuals (Puritans especially) were against the "sundrie bookes, pamfletes, Poesies, ditties, songes, and other workes . . . serving . . . to let in a mayne Sea of wickednesse . . . and to no small or sufferable waste of the treasure of this Realme which is thearby consumed and spent in paper, being of it selfe a forreign and chargeable comoditie" (William Lambarde). Already in the seventeenth century killjoys of the press were present, with economic arguments against importation on the grounds that it is unpatriotic, and moral arguments against information on the grounds that it provokes wickedness.

We cannot establish relative prices in the early period: nothing in manuscript is comparable to the halfpenny ballad sheet; there is no direct comparison between manuscripts and printed books. Printed texts were clearly cheaper than scribal texts, and readership developed— for ballads, a broad popular readership. The ballad sheets passed from eager hand to hand. After the Great Fire of London in 1666, book and ballad prices shot up because stocks were destroyed.

It may at first seem ironic that the eighteenth century, with stiff manners, powdered wigs and slavish decorum, was the great age for rediscovering and preserving ballads. Their apparent rusticity and simplicity appealed to poets, scholars and readers so long gagged by proprieties that any coarseness, any deviation from good taste with the sanction of antiquity was tonic. The work of poets like Robert Burns and Sir Walter Scott, and the scholarly transcription and exposition of the Bishop of Dromore, Thomas Percy (1729–1811), mean that we have a substantial morsel of oral literature, especially from the north, and a "literary" ballad tradition that grows directly from "folk" roots.

The Scot James Macpherson's forgeries of the ancient poems of the Gaelic poet Ossian (1760) and his later fabrications inspired many poets, including Thomas Gray. With its apparent formal freedom (the translations are in highly charged, mannered prose), the "primitive" music boomed across the restraints and politenesses of a caustic Cambridge: for Gray it hinted that poetry might one day breathe fresher air, as it had in earlier centuries. Johnson declared: "Sir, a man might write such stuff for ever, if he would abandon his mind to it." It was precisely abandon that the poets impressed by Ossian desired, an abandon they found too in the more authoritatively sanctioned verses that Bishop Percy put in the *Reliques*. Ossian's "Songs of Selma" conclude:

Such were the words of the bards in the days of song; when the king heard the music of harps, the tales of other times! The chiefs gathered from all their hills, and heard the lovely sound. They praised the voice of Cona! the first among a thousand bards! But age is now on my tongue, my soul has failed!

And so on. It is the Celtic twilight over a century before it officially fell, and the authentic voice of the old poems, which sounds in English in the ballads, is here muffled under a pillow of inhibition. Hazlitt takes the Ossianic poems seriously, as indeed they should be taken, despite Macpherson's subterfuge, because they touch a chord with his age. He says: "As Homer is the first vigour and lustihead, Ossian is the decay and old age of poetry." From that decay William Blake took some of his zanier bearings.

For Bishop Percy, who, whatever he felt for the old poems, was keen to demonstrate his descent from the noble Percys of Northumberland and to celebrate his family (quite a few of the ballads bring his ancestors' deeds into focus), Macpherson was a catalyst. He based his forgeries— remotely, perhaps—on the Scots Gaelic oral traditions of his childhood, embroidering and extending them in English. Macpherson was compelled to forge the originals when his deceit was suspected. In 1765 *Percy's Reliques of Ancient English Poetry*, with no hint of scandal and with exhaustive editorial probity, brought a refreshing blast of genuine popular poetry (and some literary imitation) into the neoclassical drawing room. He was not above including work of known authorship—by Skelton, Marlowe, Ralegh, Shakespeare, Queen Elizabeth, Beaumont and Fletcher, Samuel Daniel, James I, Lovelace, Suckling, Jonson and others. His purpose in combining literary and popular was to reveal a coherent strand in poetry, perhaps to show how anonymous ballads could hold their own in more refined company. Some of the anonymous ballads, with their unstable texts, existing as they do in dozens of versions with different endings and emphases, began in literary texts but were taken over by the people and made malleable to their needs, like the Spanish ballads of Antonio Machado and Federico García Lorca, which in the 1930s were adopted by the people and sung or recited in taverns in Spain, the authors unacknowledged and unknown.

Yet in the *Reliques* literary ballads and anonymous popular ballads prove different in kind. Percy's old friend Doctor Johnson was not impressed. He parodied the meter of "The Hermit of Warkworth: A Northumberland Ballad" in memorable quatrains, including:

I put my hat upon my head
And walked into the Strand;
And there I met another man
Whose hat was in his hand.

He found distasteful the way many ballads parceled out prose matter in tidy, risible quatrains—risible, that is, if you stand back from quaintness and archaic language and look meaning in the face. And if you are unable to imagine the music that the poems shed in passing into print.

Sir Walter Scott read the *Reliques* in 1782 and they determined the course of his literary life. His three-volume *Minstrelsy of the Scottish Border* is, with F. J. Child's four-volume *The English and Scottish Popular Ballads*, the place to look for great ballads. Percy, much earlier and with clouded motive, was a reasonable scholar: he discovered an old folio manuscript from the middle of the previous century that belonged to Humphrey Pitt of Shifnal, in his native Shropshire. It included ancient material and ballads from the seventeenth century. "As most of them are of great simplicity, and seem to have been merely written for the people, he was long in doubt, whether, in the present state of improved literature, they could be deemed worthy the attention of the public." Encouraged by Joseph Addison, Lord Dorset and others he undertook the project with an unlikely colleague, the poet William Shenstone (1714–63), famous for the artificiality and "prettiness" of his work, and for his "improvements" to his estate near Halesowen. He died before *Reliques* was complete, but perhaps his influence opened the book out to poems that are ballads only by extreme extension of the term.

Augustan gentlemen reading the *Reliques* may not always have reflected that popular ballads voice opposition, celebrate resistance, lament defeat. There are poems from the time of Chaucer (who alludes to the old poems and knew them at first hand) to the Civil War, "but not one that alludes to the Restoration." Either by that time popular and oral traditions no longer functioned as previously, or the men from whom this literature emanated did not identify with the Restoration.

The word "ballad" is from Norman French, spelled "*ballet*," a song to which people danced. Dance and song are now as separate as ballet and ballad, but it's worth recalling that they shared a cradle. Ballads were originally a record and reenactment of deeds; later, by a strange analepsis, the term came to refer to any kind of poem, homespun, old- or ill-fashioned. Early English dance-ballads are now often called folk songs. The "Song of Songs" was known as the "Ballad of Ballads," suggesting a confluence between the ballad, the vernacular Bible (with the politics that it implied) and the hymn, which often adapts ballad forms. The Puritans, hostile to lascivious balladry, purged and converted many of them into religious songs.

Old ballads are tied in with pre-Christian lore. Robert Graves stresses the pagan witchiness of surviving ballads. He classifies ballads under four heads:

1. Festival songs
2. Songs to lighten repetitive tasks: spinning, weaving, grinding corn, hoeing, etc.; "occupational ballads"
3. Sea shanties
4. Entertainments to pass an evening

Another category of ballads exists to keep in memory historical events, which, with the passing of time, are refined to legend. And there are savage and satirical ballads to avenge an ill or pillory a wrongdoer. Scurrilous poems and satirical ballads may have led to the first statute against libels in 1275, under the title: "Against slanderous reports, or tales to cause discord betwixt king and people." Later satirists and libelers managed to "publish" their poems to advantage, "although they did not enjoy the many conveniences which modern improvements have afforded for the circulation of public abuse." One poem, in the time of Henry VI, was stuck on the palace gates while the king and his counselors were sitting in Parliament. A few years earlier, when Henry V returned after Agincourt, ballads celebrating his deeds were pinned to the gates, but he discouraged this cult of personality.

Ballads were originally a minstrel's job, working to a lord ("minstrel" means "a dependent"). In *Piers Plowman* one monk knows the ballads and rhymes better than his paternoster. Monasteries for a fee provided minstrels with fresh, or reheated, songs and stories and themselves used them for holy days. Some abbeys and monasteries supported a resident minstrel. Welsh abbeys occasionally sustained a Welsh-language bard and were repositories for the poetry of the Britons. But as time passed minstrels were fired by employers, or grew bored with the court or monastery, or were set loose by military defeat (especially in Scotland and the north), and began to wander like mendicants, but singing rather than preaching or selling indulgences. The invention of printing dealt them a final blow—a printed ballad became common property: "The many good Bookes, and variety of Turnes of Affaires, have putt all the old Fables out of doors: and the divine art of Printing and gunpowder have frighted away Robin-good-fellow and the Fayries." Strolling minstrels disappear in Elizabeth's reign, arrested as vagabonds or displaced by the circulation of "town literature": the ballad seller on his rounds. For two centuries after Shakespeare's death broadsheet ballads kept printers alive. Inn-walls displayed them, they appeared in public places. Not until Dickens's time did they too begin to fade out. In *The Winter's Tale* Clown announces a ballad seller and Mopsa says: "Pray now, buy some! I love a ballad in print o' life, for then we are sure they are true."

Their truth is of course not of an historical order. Detecting bits of the old religion is a fascinating activity with ballads; so is filling in the scene, imagining the full plot, when the history is missing. The point at which they are written down may have been a point beyond which their literal sense still resonated for the common ballad hearer. For the first audiences, too, there may have been mysteries (we need not call them obscurities). Graves reminds us that a coven is a group of thirteen. " 'Robin' was a title often given to the male leader of a witch coven, the female leader being called the 'Maid'—hence 'Maid Marian.' " Pagan and Christian marry, but another element is history, valuable to a poet less as fact than for the types and tales it throws up. Graves demonstrates the historical reality of Robin Hood through his employment (documented) by Edward II to train up good archers in the royal army.

The ballad-minstrel tradition thrived most and survived longest in Scotland and the Borders. Indeed, says Graves, it never quite died in the "chimney corners of English and Scottish farmhouses, as also in the hills of Virginia, Kentucky and Tennessee." Wordsworth's "Solitary Reaper" is doing nothing less than warbling a ballad when the poet beholds her single in the field. Because most minstrels and balladeers were from the north of England or Scotland, there is a "prevalence of the northern dialect" in their work. Percy stresses that real minstrels did not write down their poems. By that token, the *Reliques* is the echo of an echo. Some of the fifteenth century can be heard in it.

"Not as I suld, I wrait, but as I couth"

ROBERT HENRYSON, WILLIAM DUNBAR,
GAVIN DOUGLAS, STEPHEN HAWES

Scotland provided more than ballads in the fifteenth century. Here the major English poetry was composed by writers whose anonymity is almost as complete as that of the ballad makers.

Robert Henryson was probably born around 1425. His death is a guess too: 1508? It is alluded to in William Dunbar's "Lament for the Makaris." He is the first and greatest of the so-called "Scottish Chaucerians."

> To cut the winter nicht and mak it schort,
> I tuik an quair, and left all uther sport,   book
> Written be worthie Chaucer glorious,
> Of fair Crisseid, and worthie Troylus.

The unknown author of the beautiful love vision *The Kingis Quair* (possibly James I, king of the Scots, who may have written it around 1424, concerning his time in prison in England twenty years before—his cell near Charles of Orleans's—and his love for Joan Beaufort), William Dunbar and, less generously, Gavin Douglas acknowledge debts to "worthie Chaucer glorious." They invite the now-resented title "Scottish Chaucerians" and to an extent deserve it. Chaucer's spirit moves in Scottish literature well into the sixteenth century. "Chaucer was the 'rose of rethoris all,' the 'horleige and regulier' for the future movements of poetry," Edwin Morgan reminds us. But "their references to Chaucer's 'sugarit lippis,' 'aureate termis,' and 'eloquence ornate' rather than to his pathos, his simplicity, or his narrative gift help to betray the background of their eulogies." Chaucer is undeniably behind them, but not too close. He is a legitimate authority, an accessible classic.

These poets are truer to Chaucer's spirit than his immediate English heirs. They are true, too, to a Scottish tradition, alliterative and intensely formal, a tradition that includes narrative of sophistication and passion. If Scottish critics stress the Scottish sources of Henryson and Dunbar, English critics as often disregard them. Though their different languages admit elements of dialect, none of these poets adopts an historical, spoken Scottish idiom. Each employs "an artificial, created, 'literary' language, used, for almost a century, by writers of very different locality and degree, with an astonishing measure of uniformity." Chaucer is crucial, especially to Henryson: his most important poem is a postscript to *Troilus and Criseyde*. Only Douglas finds it necessary to call the language he uses "Scots," to distinguish it from the tongue of the "Inglis natioun." Before his time, "Scots" was used with reference to the Gaelic language of the Highlands, the language Macpherson's Ossian would have sung in had he sung at all.

Henryson's fame rests, first, on his *Testament of Cresseid*. It "completes" Chaucer's *Troilus and Criseyde* and is the great moral romance of the fifteenth century. Sir Francis Kinaston in 1640 gave a sour account of Henryson's purpose: "He learnedly takes upon him in a fine poetical way to express the punishment and end due to a false inconstant whore." The poem is more humane and moral than this suggests. Henryson was as fond of Criseyde as Chaucer had been, as troubled as he by her inconstancy and fate. Henryson wrote other poems, notably the *Morall Fabillis of Esope*, which set him among the few great fabulists in our literature.

Little is known of his life, less even than of Langland's. Kinaston calls him "sometime chief schoolmaster in Dunfermling" (at the Benedictine abbey grammar school) and adds that he was "a learned and witty man." Already "licentiate in arts and bachelor in decrees," he may have attended the University of Glasgow in 1462 (it was established in 1451). He may have studied in France. Of all the Scottish poets of his time, only he was not connected with the court—a humble schoolmaster with a divine gift. Kinaston records the only anecdote we have about the poet: "Being very old he died of a diarrhoea or flux," to which he appends a "merry" if "unsavoury" tale. When the physician despaired of his cure, an old witch came to the bedside and asked Henryson if he would be made better. She indicated a "whikey tree" in his orchard and instructed him to walk about it three times, repeating the words: "Whikey tree whikey tree take away this flux from me." Henryson, too weak to go so far, pointed to an oak table in his room and asked, "Gude dame I pray ye tell me, if it would not be as well if I repeated thrice theis words oken burd oken burd garre me shit a hard turd." The hag departed in a rage and in "half a quarter of an hour" Henryson was dead.

H. Harvey Wood prepared the 1933 edition of Henryson's *Poems and*

Fables. He claims his poet to be the greatest of the Scottish *makars*, a judgment many non-Scottish readers share. Henryson isn't so startling a technician as Dunbar, though he is every bit as expert within his range. He lacks Dunbar's eccentricity. He possesses a humanity well beyond Dunbar's, and a wealth of particular observation of detail and human conduct equal to Chaucer's. Dunbar is "A Poet," always anxious to prove it; Henryson is a moralist who writes poems. Dunbar is literary; he has a following among poets. Henryson is an illustrator of common truths, a storyteller using verse as his medium, and appeals to the common reader. Dunbar is a poet of abrupt changes of tone. Henryson can manage such changes, but is capable of subtler modulations as well.

Modulations take various forms in his work. In the *Testament*, they are emotional: the progress of Cresseid, of her father Calchas and of Troilus himself correspond to changes in the moral argument that rhythm and diction underpin. A clearer example is to be found in the fable entitled "The Preaching of the Swallow." The seasonal stanzas move from a spring of lush, latinate and aureate diction to a thoroughly native diction, bristling with consonants, as the year moves into winter. Henryson is closer to the alliterative tradition than is sometimes acknowledged. In descriptions and in passages of action he will employ the *rim ram ruf* with gusto, normally adopting a vocabulary almost without Latinisms, largely monosyllabic. To his Chaucerian techniques he adds resources from an older alliterative tradition. Chaucer, a crucial resource, was not an invariable model.

The tradition of allegory lived on in fifteenth-century Scotland. Henryson is a better moral allegorist than Gower because, though he appends a moral to his fables and other poems, the poetry substantiates and embodies the lesson drawn. You feel again and again the informing presence of Dante in his verse. Sometimes the tone is so unmistakably Dantesque that you wish he had done for the *Commedia* what Gavin Douglas does for the *Aeneid*. Take, as an example, the prologue to the fable of "The Lion and the Mouse." The poet in sleep is visited by his master Aesop. He is at once inquisitive and respectful:

> "Displease you not, my gude maister, thocht I   though
> Demand your birth, your facultye, and name,   profession
> Quhy ye come heir, or quhair ye dwell at hame?"   why; where

> "My sone" (said he), "I am off gentil blude,
> My native land is Rome . . ."

Nothing could be clearer: voices talking. And like Dante, Henryson selects his metaphors exactly, and his diction can be mimetic, as in "The

Harrowis hoppand in the saweris trace." This is language in the spirit of William Barnes.

We can't but think of Dante in "Orpheus and Eurydice." Henryson sends Orpheus to an underworld not pagan but very like hell. Orpheus allows himself (as we sometimes wish Dante would) certain merciful liberties with the damned. He plays his instrument so that the waters are still and Tantalus can drink; briefly Tityrus is relieved of agony. Though it's a hell where all are dying "and nevirmoir sall de," Orpheus performs acts of charity, the same charity that Henryson evinces in the *Testament* both for Cresseid and for Troilus.

The *Testament* grows out of Chaucer's poem, an extraordinary fact since *Troilus and Criseyde* is so complete and so Chaucerian. Henryson's temper is different, but the gap is no greater than that between Marlowe's and Chapman's passages in *Hero and Leander*. In the midst of winter Henryson, who presents himself as an old man, takes down Chaucer's poem to while away the night. Both the season and the narrator's age suit the theme. What happened to Cresseid, he asks. He answers: Diomede cast her off, she went home to her father Calchas, who received her with love as a returning prodigal. She visited Venus's temple to pray, but in her prayer she railed against Cupid and Venus. She fell asleep and dreamed that those gods summoned their peers to try her. Saturn, the judge, an old, repellent figure, found her guilty and Cynthia, the moon, struck her with a leprosy. Waking, Cresseid finds the dream to be true. She departs, disfigured and lamenting (in nine-line stanzas that contrast with the Chaucerian seven-line stanzas of the rest of the poem), drawing a partial moral:

> Nocht is your fairnes bot ane faiding flour,
> Nocht is your famous laud and hie honour   reputation
> Bot wind inflat in uther mennis eiris.
> Your roising reid to rotting sall retour.   rosy-red (cheeks); return

In the sequel she learns a fuller moral lesson. Urged by a leper lady to "mak vertew of ane neid" (make virtue of necessity), "To leir to clap thy clapper to and fro, / And leir efter the Law of Lipper Leid," she goes begging by the roadside. Troilus passes that way,

> And with a blenk it come into his thocht,
> That he sumtime hir face befoir had sene.
> Bot scho was in sic plye he knew hir nocht.   she was in such a state

He recalls but does not recognize her, feels a spark of love, and empties his purse into her lap. Cresseid does not recognize him either, but another leper announces the knight's name. Cresseid swoons, recovers, and comes to a full recognition of her guilt. She writes her testament and dies; the ruby ring Troilus had given her is returned to him. Henryson hints that he may have built for her a marble monument and rounds off the poem with a moral for the women in the audience.

On the strength of this poem alone Henryson would have a place well above the tree line on Parnassus. But there is more: the eclogue "Robene and Makyne," and "The Garmont of Gud Ladeis," "The Bludy Serk," "Orpheus and Eurydice," and especially the *Fables*, all of which contribute to our sense of his achievement, which includes allegorical satire. The animals in the fables represent classes and types of men, the fable form liberates them from a specific milieu into a general significance.

There are thirteen fables. Henryson pretends they are translations of Aesop, though the best—"The Country Mouse and the Town Mouse"—is from Horace, and others belong to the profusion of *fabliaux* current at the time. With further modesty, he claims to be ignorant of rhetoric and promises to write "in hamelie language and in termes rude." Though the low style prevails, the rhetoric is impeccable. Unlike other fable writers, he does not tell and moralize at the same time but keeps the moral for the end of the poem.

The fable of the mice, "The Taill of the Uponlandis Mous, and the Burges Mous," is the most achieved, vivid in visual detail, corresponding closely to social types, and full of good humor and good sense. His narrative is dramatic as well. The town mouse sets out to seek her sister:

> Bairfute, allone, with pykestaf in hir hand,
> As pure pylgryme scho passit out off town,   she left
> To seik hir sister baith oure daill and down.   over both dale

Speech—mouse speech married to common speech—is rendered. When, back in town, the mice are first surprised at their dinner by a servant, the country mouse falls and swoons. Her sister calls, "How faire ye, sister? cry peip, quhair ever ye be." The arrival of "Gib hunter, our jolie Cat" (Gilbert—a common name for cats well into the sixteenth century), who catches the country mouse, is full of suspense:

> Fra fute to fute he kest hir to and ffra,   tossed
> Quhylis up, quhylis doun, als cant as
>   ony kid;
>   sometimes; merry
> Quhylis wald he lat hir rin under the
>   stra,

Quhylis wald he wink and play with hir
    buk heid.   play hide-and-seek with her
Thus to the selie Mous grit pane he did,   innocent; distress
Quhill at the last, throw fortune and   through fortune and
    gude hap,   good luck
Betwix ane burde and the wall scho crap.   she crept

As in the *Testament*, so in the *Fables* trial and confession motifs add to the Chaucerian tone. Patrick Crutwell, comparing Henryson and Chaucer, comments that Henryson's "picturesque detail owes its effectiveness to the solidity and seriousness of what it grows from." Picturesque and transparently allegorical: the frog is frog and more than, or other than, frog:

    . . . hir fronsit face,   wrinkled
Hir runkillit cheikis, and hir lippis syde,   wrinkled cheeks; wide
Hir hingand browis, and hir voce sa hace,   hoarse
Hir logerand leggis, and hir harsky hyde . . .   dangling; rough

There emerges from the *Fables*—by analogy—a more or less complete human world, to be appraised in moral terms.

Gavin Douglas (1475?–1522) acknowledges his debt to Henryson more generously than he does his debt to Chaucer. In reading his *Eneados*, the translation of Virgil's *Aeneid*, we sense the nature of that debt in Douglas's control of his couplets and his skill at writing directly, especially in his original prologues, which preface each book of translation. He knows the huge challenge he's set himself:

Besyde Latyne our langage is imperfite,
Quhilk in sum part is the caus and the   which is partly the cause and
    wyte   reproach
Quhy that of Virgillis vers the ornate   why
    bewte   beauty
Intill our tung may nocht observyt be.   may not be seen in our tongue

He is harsh on his own language: it lacks variety of tone, inflection and diction.

Betweyn "genus," "sexus" and "species"
Diversyte in our leid to seik I ces.   language I cease to seek
For "objectum" or "subjectum" alsswa   also
He war expert couth fynd me termys twa,   could; two terms

Quhilkis ar als ryfe amangis clerkis in scuyll   which; common; school
As evir fowlis plungit in laik or puyll.   plunged; lake; pool

But his language brings a kind of rough energy to Virgil that the Latin poet would hardly have recognized. Douglas is blisteringly harsh on Caxton's prose version of the *Aeneid*—as close to the original, he says, as the devil is to St. Augustine: "I red his wark with harmys at my hart," he declares, that Caxton's book should even share a title with the divine Virgil's. His assault is a brilliant essay on the art of translation and on Caxton's literary shortcomings.

Douglas was the third son of "Bell-the-Cat," fifth Earl of Angus, a nobleman without prospects. After a good education he was caught in the political struggles of the day on the "other side" (the victorious side) in the Battle of Flodden and its aftermath. He entered St. Andrews University in 1490, took his master's degree in 1494, and in 1501 was provost of St. Giles, Edinburgh. He probably studied in Paris as well. He took orders and ultimately, after much controversy, became Bishop of Dunkeld (1515). He died, out of favor, of the plague in London in 1522. Almost a decade earlier his poetic labors had come to an end. When he completed the *Eneados* he wrote, "Thus up my pen and instrumentis full yor / On Virgillis post I fix for evirmore." He would wait "solitar, as doith the byrd in cage," his youth over. It took him some eighteen months to translate Virgil. The *Eneados* is the first important complete translation into English of a major classical poem. His other works include the "Palice of Honour," a substantially original dream allegory. Some of his poems and translations, notably his version of Ovid's *Art of Love*, have not survived.

Douglas's working text of Virgil was hardly perfect; appended to it was a full commentary. He translated keeping close to the original but interpolating matter from the commentary. He also included Mapheus Vegius's apocryphal thirteenth book (1428). His poem is almost twice as long as Virgil's, yet close to it in spirit. Renaissance humanists in their passion for pure latinity divorced the poem from its wide audience by academicizing it. Douglas was on the common reader's side.

Ezra Pound declares, "Gavin Douglas re-created us Virgil, or rather, we forget Virgil in reading Gavin's *Aeneid* and know only the tempest, Acheron, and the eternal elements that Virgil for most men glazes over." This tribute to Douglas's directness reflects Pound's own sense—many readers share it—that the Virgil we read is filtered through centuries of scholarship and exegesis, so that we can hardly see his face. Douglas could, and in reading him we experience Aeneas's adventures afresh.

Reflecting on the work of Chaucer, Gower, Henryson and Douglas, we can understand what Dryden meant when he wrote of Chaucer, "The genius of our countrymen in general" is "rather to improve an invention, than to invent themselves; as is evident not only in our poetry, but in many of our manufactures." Translation nourishes a native literature. "Improvement" is too strong a word to apply to Douglas's Virgil, but his transposition of the poem into courtly idiom with a peculiarly Scottish flavor is characteristic of the writing of the age. Douglas achieved much with few decent models to work from. His modesty remains genuine: "Not as I suld, I wrait, but as I couth."

He uses roughly one couplet per Latin hexameter: twenty syllables for sixteen, with numerous poetic auxiliaries and doublets to plump out his measure, giving roughness to its rightness. He is naturally most himself in the prologues, where he experiments in alliterative verse (Book Eight) and he states his mind. Warton praised particularly the prologue to Book Twelve: the lines "are effusions of a mind not overlaid by the descriptions of other poets but operating, by its own force and bias, in the delineation of a vernal landscape, on such objects as really occurred." Douglas loved to write (the excesses of "The Palice of Honour" attest to this), and he was clear in his mind about style and genre. This he reveals in the prologue of Book Nine:

The ryall style, clepyt heroycall,	royal; called heroic
Full of wirschip and nobilnes our all,	above all
Suldbe compilit but thewhes or voyd word,	without clichés; empty
Kepand honest wys sportis quhar thai bourd,	true to jests where they occur
All lowus langage and lychtnes lattand be,	loose; lightness let stand
Observand bewte, sentens and gravyte.	
The sayer eik suld weil considir thys,	speaker
Hys mater, and quhamto it entitilit is:	his matter; whom it is addressed to
Eftir myne authoris wordis, we aucht tak tent	watch out
That baith accord, and ben convenient,	suitable
The man, the sentens, and the knychtlyke stile,	meaning; knightly style
Sen we mon carp of vassalage a quhile.	speak; courage

He develops principles of poetic decorum functional and far less restricting than those Renaissance humanists promoted. He is modest again when he says, "Guf ocht be weill, thank Virgil and nocht me." The faults are his fault, since he is unequal to his original's "ornat fresch endyte." If he has "pervert" Virgil, he has also caught the movement and spirit of the *Aeneid*, and woven into the poem his prologues, which we can read as northern eclogues.

More famous than Henryson and Douglas is William Dunbar. His credit this century has risen thanks to Hugh MacDiarmid's attempt to "re-create" a distinctively Scottish literature with the cry, "Not Burns— Dunbar!" The masculinity of Dunbar's verse, its formal skill and verve, its effective malice, its variety, set him apart from his contemporaries, English and Scottish. He wrote allegories such as "The Golden Targe"— the poet puts in an appearance at the sumptuous court of Venus—and occasional poems. The occasional pieces address a variety of subjects in many forms and can't usefully be described as Chaucerian. They are his major achievement. Bumptious, overbearing, unbridled, he knows no taboos. A friar? Not in his verse, which abounds in everything but charity. "Tidings from the Session" lays into the courts; "Satire on Edinburgh" tells the truth about conditions in a then-disgusting city. "The Dance of the Seven Deidlie Synnis" and the "General Satire" say things not previously said or sayable in English verse, in tones not previously heard. He is a flayer, a Juvenalian satirist. Never gentle, he can be "elfin." "At first it may seem absurd to try to recover at this time of day," Mac-Diarmid says, "the literary potentialities of a language which has long ago disintegrated into dialects. These dialects even at their richest afford only a very restricted literary medium, capable of little more than kail-yard usages, but quite incapable of addressing the full range of literary purpose." MacDiarmid builds his polemic almost exclusively on Dunbar, his chosen ancestor, and only nods *en passant* at Douglas and Henryson. "Dunbar is in many ways the most modern, as he is the most varied, of Scottish poets." Dunbar lends himself to MacDiarmid's nationalist argument. He marries a moribund but still viable alliterative tradition to a French syllabic tradition. There is none of Henryson's transparency of language or Douglas's directness. The sound surface of Dunbar's poem calls attention to itself: we are required to admire the often astounding technique. He is the closest thing we have in English (and MacDiarmid might not like to hear it called English) to the candor, self-exposure and excess of Villon. He may have been in France when Villon's poems were published posthumously in 1489. He is more like Villon than like Skelton, though he has been called "the Scottish Skelton." In 1500 he was back in Scotland, no longer a Franciscan friar of the strict Observantine but a court priest with a royal pension. In 1501 he received ten marks from Henry VII of England for his poem with the refrain, "London thou art the floure of Cities all," and two years later he wrote his celebrated "The Thristill and the Rois" to celebrate the marriage of James IV of Scotland and Margaret Tudor. Thus he came to be admired on both sides of the border.

Dunbar (1460?–1520?) worked in the courtly tradition, friar and courtier in one, busy about other people's lives and secrets. He chafed under the restraints of his order and seems to have enjoyed wandering, perhaps as far as Picardy and other parts of France. His poems "are fundamentally and exclusively Scottish." They are not nationalist, and it's an irony that the radical nationalist and Communist Hugh MacDiarmid built so much on an apolitical poet enamored of romance, engaged in the ephemeral scheming of courtly life. He may have graduated from the University of St. Andrews as a bachelor of arts in 1477. He survived and lamented the defeat of Flodden in 1513. His verse is part of the decisive, brief flowering of aristocratic culture that finished there. James IV was a responsive patron, though less so than he has been portrayed. He was among the last great princes of chivalry, as his death proved. Learned, a linguist in as many as eight tongues, he cultivated the arts and sciences in his court and in his country. All this Dunbar celebrates. He also shows a dark side.

His love of ceremony and pomp emerges in several poems, even in the organization of imagery, much of it in heraldic colors, especially in "The Thristill and the Rois" and "The Golden Targe." The aureation he learned from Chaucer contributes to the surface of his verse, but he also deploys the coarse colloquial diction of his day. His style is an amalgam of literary English and the demotic, mingling registers, passing from sublime to grotesque in a single sentence. He is a master of parody, a rogue, at times a scurrilous rogue, especially in the "Flyting of Dunbar and Kennedie"—his rival Walter Kennedy, whom he later celebrates in the great "Lament for the Makaris," where he first laments Chaucer.

Rime royal, short stanzas, couplets, alliterative forms: the technical range dazzles. And he's at home in many modes: allegory, dream vision, hymn, prayer, elegy, panegyric, lyric, comic narrative, satire and flyting. Edwin Morgan writes, "His first mark is a certain effectual brilliance that may commend him more keenly to the practising poet than to the ordinary reader—an agility, a virtuosity in tempo and momentum, a command of rhythm." Warton says, "I am of opinion, that the imagination of Dunbar is not less suited to satirical than to sublime allegory: and that he is the first poet who has appeared with any degree of spirit in the way of writing since *Piers Plowman*." Sadly, Warton did not have access to the work of Henryson. On Dunbar, he continues: "The natural complexion of his genius is of the moral and didactic cast." And yet he has not Langland's social scope or conscience, nor Chaucer's bemused humanity. Ungenerosity of spirit mars the poems; it vanishes only in the elegies and religious poems. He flays his foes, his greatest pleasure is in the flyting, the bawdy, the grotesque. His longest poem, and one of his best, "The Tretis of the Tua Mariit Wemen and the Wedo," combines bawdy satire and moral censure in a single unrhymed alliterative parody of the romantic mode.

His is a poetry without intimacy—in that respect like Langland's; feelings, when it has them, attach more to the subject and the chosen form than to the poet's candid emotion. It's not that the poems are insincere: sincerity is beside the point. He invests emotion only in his elegies. His religious poems, C. S. Lewis writes, are "public and liturgical" rather than devotional. He brings an equal lucidity and professional polish to flytings and elegies. One does not look for psychological depth or perceptual accuracy beneath the polish. It is as though for all his courtliness, his political and diplomatic activity, and the potency of his technical arsenal, he were a poet local to a time and place: James IV's court. There is no wide world, though the narrow world compels.

In "Dregy of Dunbar" he parodies liturgical form, presenting the king's stay in Stirling as purgatory, his return to Edinburgh as a return to heaven. "Requiem Edinburgi dona eis, Domine," he says. The interweaving of Latin among other language registers can be parodic or, in the somber poems, can add ritualistic emphasis. He appears to have been born a technician: there is an even excellence of composition and we cannot detect development or establish chronology. Throughout, comedy tends toward the grotesque, the nightmare. Primary colors, little shading, nothing overheard. Edwin Morgan points to his "startling indifference to theme in poetry." He is a poet one cannot but admire; yet it is hard for the non-Scot to do more than admire. Sir Walter Scott regards him as "unrivalled by any which Scotland ever produced," and it is tempting to think that MacDiarmid agreed with him, but MacDiarmid, so similar in spirit but so immensely copious, tends to use Dunbar as a weapon with which to beat poor Robert Burns and Burns's admirers over the head. Whatever we say in Dunbar's favor, he is limited to the courtly. He is brilliant and narrow, a medieval poet with more economy of expression than the English Chaucerians, greater formal resources, and wry humor. He has been touched by the new French poetry. In his work the old elements are made serviceable one last time—vivid, real, fully expressive.

And what had England to show for itself at this time, on the cusp of the Tudor century? Stephen Hawes, the archetypal "transitional figure." His situation was especially hard in terms of the language he had to use. It's important to recall that throughout the fifteenth century difference in dialects made it hard for people from one shire to understand those from another, and literature of the past became incomprehensible to the ear: the voiced final *e* was vanishing gradually and unevenly, area by area, word by word. People in Henry VII's reign couldn't understand each other, much less the past. Henry VII made his laureate a French poet, the blind Bernard André of Toulouse, preferring the French to the chaotic native Muse. Scottish poets were less diverse in dialect, or the language was evolving less briskly; they had a chance while the English ear was still listening out for itself.

Much of the readable early fifteenth-century verse is to be found in the Chaucer apocrypha. Like a great magnet his oeuvre attracted not only corruptions introduced by scribes, but the verse of any genuinely competent poet. It's worth hunting down *The Floure and the Leaf, The Cuckoo and the Nightingale* and others. In fact, it's rather sad that Chaucer's act has been so scrupulously cleaned up by later scholar-editors, since, in the end, the work that they excluded has almost vanished.

Printing was finding a place and promised to bring eventual conformity to the language. My predecessors—those who didn't became jobbing legal copyists, frightened of new technology—"retrained." Scribes turned into type designers, rubricators. They discussed patterns and rules, letter forms and how a poem might best be accommodated on the page. Medieval English poetry was more or less over. There was in every area an oral tradition of poetry in dialect, and the morality plays were still around. But for literary poetry, a settled prosody was unthinkable, unless one froze poetic language at a certain point and declared: *this* is it, *these* are poetic sounds; Stephen Hawes seems to have done something of the kind.

He stands at the door of a new age, but—still a medievalist in his digressive, allegorical approach and in the value structure of his verse— he does not pass through. His chief innovation is inkhorn terms, the invention of new and compound words that smell of the lamp and, with his awkward word order, make him sound peculiar and even comic. He stands between Chaucer and Spenser. The *Passetyme of Pleasure* is a kind of poor uncle, though not a parent, of *The Faerie Queene*. W. Murison shows a number of parallels and perhaps analogues or direct debts. But Spenser's poem lives because for him La Bel Pucel of Hawes is embodied in the Queen of England and everything acquires a specific political as well as a chivalric meaning. Spenser writes from an actual, an attestable occasion, even when his allegory wanders off down elaborate avenues.

Hawes (1475?–1523/30?) regarded himself as the last, lonely "faithful votary of true poetry." In the 5,800-line rime royal *Passetyme* (Wynkyn de Worde says it was written in 1505–6) he laments his uniqueness, abandoned by a departed culture, and displays considerable learning. He was educated at Oxford and visited several foreign universities. He

entered Henry VII's household as a groom of the chamber. His life
was an example of virtue. He was a great reciter of verse, especially
Lydgate's. He did produce a few remarkable pieces, not least a shaped
poem against swearing. Like his fifteenth-century predecessors, he is
best in extract, but the good extracts are even fewer than are to be found
in Hoccleve and Lydgate. Even so, there's something fine and firm in
his simple, reactionary devotion to his art; he is not content to be a job-
bing poet, a translator by the yard. "Accordingly," comments C. S. Lewis,
"his failure excites sympathy rather than contempt."

The Watershed

WILLIAM CAXTON

Though William Caxton was a man of medieval taste and temperament, he introduced a sea change in our culture, in the dissemination of works of literature and ways of literacy. He contributed no theories to the intellectual world. His writings are largely forgotten. He invented nothing. But the impact of his entrepreneurial work has proved more radical than the ideas of Wycliffe, Latimer, Cromwell or any other Englishman. He fathered what was to become an informed democracy. That democracy spread through the decay of empire.

Humanism was well begun by the time Erasmus first visited England late in the fifteenth century. The Greek scholar William Grocyn had established principles of critical scholarship; John Colet was lecturing on the Pauline Epistles and setting them into an historical context. "Pure," or classical, Latin was being reestablished at court "for diplomacy and historiography." Against this background Caxton's activity seems to propose a different program, as though English printing would run in the teeth of the universities and their specialisms. The books Caxton printed between 1475 and 1491 answered to medieval tastes. The new elements in popular literature are the books of fools or follies, *The Ship of Fools*. Just as "cutting-edge" writers were slow to rise to the challenge of electronic publishing, so humanists and printers, even when they approched the classics, were differently impelled. In our tradition, entrepreneurial and intellectual cultures never make comfortable bedfellows.

It's almost an accident that Caxton occupies the place he does. Had it not been him, another enterprising expatriate returning home might have brought the technology he acquired, though another would have pursued different editorial ends. The key to the invention of printing lay in movable type. Johann Gutenberg of Mainz, born at the end of the fourteenth century, is credited with the introduction of the craft. His Latin edition of the Bible, known as the Mazarin Bible (1450–55), was the first book to be printed in Europe and is still one of the most beautiful. Printing was perfected and it spread, as journeymen left masters and set up for themselves. Printed works appeared in Italy (1453), Basel (1466), France (1470), Hungary (1473), Spain (1473), Poland (1474), Bruges (1474), England (1476), Sweden (1483) and Mexico (1539). By the end of the fifteenth century, as many as 40,000 items had been issued. Books usually appeared as quartos bound between wooden boards and decorated copiously with woodcuts. Print runs were small, averaging fewer than five hundred, with some notable exceptions. The vernacular gained ground, but most fifteenth-century productions were religious or legal works in Latin.

The earliest printed books are called *incunabula*, from the Latin for "swaddling clothes," publications from the infancy of printing. An incunabulum, or incunable, is any printed book, booklet, or broadside from the fifteenth century. Incunabula resemble the manuscripts they supersede. They do not sport a title page; instead, author, title, printer, place, and date of publication are provided in a final paragraph, a "colophon." Some printers devised a woodcut for identification, and the word "colophon" gradually transferred to that emblem. During the Reformation and Counterreformation many incunabula were destroyed; those that survive are prized, some more so than the labored manuscripts of my scribal predecessors.

Caxton was hard-working, an artist in his craft, a dedicated writer-printer (the term "publisher" gained currency in the eighteenth century). Few men of the time possessed his taste or his range of interests, those of a cultured dilettante with only himself and his patrons to satisfy. He shows style in his judgment and his writing. About a third of the more than one hundred books he printed were his own translations. When moved to be emphatic, he is "almost as vigorous as Latimer himself. In his power of writing with a naïve vivacity, while deliberately striving after a more ornate manner, Caxton belongs to his age. He provides, as it were, a choice of styles for his readers." His most popular book is *The Golden Legend*.

Born in Kent around 1422, he lived almost to the age of seventy. The English of his childhood he describes as "broad and rude," colored with idioms and accents of the large Flemish community that lived in Kent. He received—we don't know where—a good education (though he never trusted his Latin) and began as did many of his class, both English and Flemish, as a cloth merchant. By 1463 he was governor of the merchant-adventurers in the Low Countries. Six years later he gave this up and entered the service of the Duchess of Burgundy, turning to literary work. In 1471 he made a visit to Cologne, saw a printing press at work, and there the prosperous mercer settled down and learned to print.

In 1474 he acquired two fonts of type. They were cut in imitation of ordinary scribal hand. He founded a press in Bruges before returning to England. His first book was *Recuyell of the Historyes of Troy*, dated 1475—the first of his own translations that he printed. It had been popular and much in demand in manuscript. He tired of having it copied and went for print. His versions generally carry a prologue or epilogue—sometimes in verse—that reveals his sense of humor and due modesty.

In 1476 he returned to England, and the next year his press "in a house with the sign of the Red Pale" at Westminster produced *Dictes or Sayengis of the Philosophres*, the first dated book printed in England. He printed pamphlets: Lydgate's *Temple of Glass*, Chaucer's *Anelida and Arcite* and others. His edition of the *Canterbury Tales*, a massive undertaking, appeared at this time, as did *The Moral Proverbs of Christine de Pisan*, the first book by a woman printed in England. He went on to print more than ninety editions.

Only 370 books of all kinds were printed in Britain before 1500, and this includes different editions of the same work. But because English printing started late and impecuniously, it was largely a *vernacular* publishing culture. The classics had to be imported because the cost of acquiring fonts was so high. And because the publishing culture was vernacular and Caxton was Caxton, the literary values were generally high.

What else did he print? In 1482, Higden's *Polychronicon*, with Caxton revising Trevisa's 1387 English version and updating it to 1467. This continuation is the one major original work by Caxton that we possess. In 1481: three of his own translations including *Reynard the Fox*. In 1483: more Lydgate, plus a new edition of *Canterbury Tales*, with his prologue showing the esteem in which he held Chaucer. He placed a memorial tablet to his poet in Westminster Abbey. About this time he also published *Troilus and Criseyde*, *House of Fame* and, in September 1483, Gower's *Confessio Amantis*. In 1485: Sir Thomas Malory's *Morte d'Arthur*. In 1489: *The Fayttes of Arms*, generally attributed to Christine de Pisan. In 1490: *Eneydos*, not a translation but a romance based on the *Aeneid*—the book that so irritated Gavin Douglas. Caxton in his preface reflects on the speed of change in English: "And certaynly our langage now used varyeth ferre from that wgiche was used and spoken when I was borne." He comments on variety of dialect and declares: "And thus bytwene playn, rude, and curious I stande abasshed, but in my judgemente the comyn termes that be dayli used ben lyghter to be understonde than the olde and auncyent englysshe." John Skelton helped revise the book for the press, so Douglas's blame should be spread between Caxton and the first great English poet of the sixteenth century.

In 1491 he died, having just completed translating St. Jerome's *Lives of the Fathers*, which Wynkyn de Worde, his foreman who became his successor, published in 1495, declaring that the version was completed on the last day of Caxton's life.

Given his background and his independence of means, Caxton never printed for a market but consulted his own taste, leading rather than following his readers. His editions were small. He edited with care, a custom his immediate successors did not honor. Wynkyn de Worde and Richard Pynson were printers more than publishers. Pynson published a *Canterbury Tales* among the law books that were his specialty. Three years after Caxton died Pynson printed Lydgate's *Fall of Princes*, translated from Boccaccio. He also first published *Mandeville's Travels* and in 1509 Barclay's translation of *The Ship of Fools*. His most durable literary text appeared betweeen 1523 and 1525: Froissart's *Chronicle*, translated by John Bourchier, Lord Berners. But he suffered from lack of type, especially Greek. Scholars sent their work abroad when English manufacturers were unequal to the typographical challenge.

When a manuscript of a printed text survives, often the printed version shortens or abridges the original—especially with Pynson (whose English was poor). Owing to lack of type and the cost of composition in time and resources, such truncations were published and may have displaced original texts. Scribes had drowsed from time to time, or—unable to keep up—dropped a line here and there. But what Pynson did was more cynical. One scribe may err while another gets it right. But 500 copies, all identically corrupt, do damage. Technology replicates cheaply; it can also spread corruption.

Wynkyn de Worde was more interested in poetry than Pynson. But his 1498 *Canterbury Tales* shows his carelessness: the text was hardly edited at all. He did not always date his books, but many of them were literary, including Skelton's *The Bowge of Court*. Wynkyn printed at least 640 books, 150 poems and romances. Robert Copland was his chief translator and could be a good editor. In 1581 he wrote the poor play *The Castell of Pleasure*, in which a skeptical exchange between author and printer occurs:

AUTHOR   Emprynt this boke, Copland, at my request,
                And put it forth to every maner state.

COPLAND   At your instaunce I shall it gladly impresse,
                But the utterance, I thynke, will be but small.

Bokes be not set by: there tymes is past, I gesse;
The dyse and cardes, in drynkynge wyne and ale,
Tables, cayles, and balles, they be now sette a sale.
Men lete theyr chyldren use all such harlotry,
That byenge of bokes they utterly deny.

Like publishers down the generations, he laments the demise of the printed book as a force to be reckoned with. His lament is issued before the art of printing in England has had even half a century's innings.

After 1521, new English books were fewer, but not for the reasons Copland adduced. The revival of learning meant a concentration on educational works and classical texts. Erasmus was not good for English-language publishing. The English printers were poor and growing poorer; Continental printers targeted the English market: the Dutch, Belgians and French especially. When in 1525 at Worms an edition of Tyndale's *New Testament* was issued, a change began: thereafter many foreign publications were controversial or subversive, works by exiles, refugees and "unsettlers." The Stationers' Company, incorporated 1557, was granted a national monopoly on printing. The issue was one of control: stemming the flood of foreign imports and limiting the independence of native printers.

Gentlemen in England were contemptuous of books made by machine. So great was the prejudice that scribes sometimes copied from print for the "authentic" reader. Early typecasters designed letters that imitated scribal practice. The new crept in under the guise of the old. If prejudice was pronounced in England, it existed on the Continent as well. The Abbot of Spanheim's letter *De laude scriptorum manualium* urges continuance of parchments and manuscripts as more durable, more appropriate than printed books. Durability, the long term; and, of course, the importance of the monasteries in scribal work. If the reproduction of texts became a secular activity, the Church would lose control—which it did. Some English and many German monasteries got presses.

Caxton's revolution was decisive but not dramatic. It took a long while for its effects to work their way through the literary system. The author might have been expected to derive some benefits; and he did, three hundred years later. Until the eighteenth century, there was close commerce, but not equal dealing, between authors and printer-publishers. Some relationships were exemplary. Erasmus lived at his printer-publisher Frobe's house. Gabriel Harvey was maintained by his printer. Authors might be professional servants or employees of the publisher. They called regularly at their printers to correct proofs—part of the agreement. The printer considered himself absolved from all errors: the author was responsible. (Caxton was the exception: he had been a scrupulous proofreader. Wynkyn de Worde was content with a lower standard than his master. Proofreaders were costly professionals, often too costly.)

Printing took place near the markets where manuscripts were available for sale. Cathedral precincts were most popular, Paternoster Row at St. Paul's, the Red Pale near Westminster—Caxton's almonry. Oxford, Cambridge, Southward, St. Albans, York, Tavistock: wherever there were strong ecclesiastical interests or major civic institutions. A few bootleg printers emerged, servicing the outlawed religious groups—to begin with, the Puritans. One such dissident ended up publishing from Manchester.

Printing grew during the fifteenth century. When the sixteenth dawned, though the old scribal arts survived, and the taint of "trade" made publishing distasteful to gentlemen, the multiply produced text was a fact of life to which readers and writers were learning to adjust, just as today there is an adjustment between producers, readers and publishers to new technology: electronic publishing. Caxton provided crucial texts and an even more crucial example. After his return from Bruges in 1476, things would change, and keep changing. The way a poet conceives and then visualizes a poem, the way a reader sees it disposed on the page, the change of feel to the fingers from vellum to paper, the loss of contact with readers, the emergence of middlemen between writer and audience, the greater authority of a multiply produced text, the development of rules and consistencies of usage: all these considerations weighed with every person, writer or reader, for whom a poem was a creative space. The architecture of that space was adjusted to something less flexible, as though language were under arrest and enduring the disciplines that would bring it to classical stability and perfection.

Motley

JOHN SKELTON

Dunbar looks back at the medieval world and seems to draw a line under the fifteenth century. The center of gravity, after the decisive Scottish poetic flowering and subsequent military defeat, shifts back to the south. Ford Madox Ford calls the Tudor and Stuart years the Spacious Age. How much our writers owe to the Mediterranean, especially to Boccaccio and Petrarch! He adds: "With the sixteenth century the art of letters had become essentially a matter of movements rather than one of solitary literary figures." English begins to acquire a coherent *literature*. Classical humanism was in part responsible; so was the development of the popular theater, but also the growth of printing.

At the beginning of the century, the constant in English poetry was rhyme, meter being irregular because the language had not been stabilized, the status of the final *e* unresolved right through the reign of Henry VIII. John Skelton depends on rhyme to an unusual extent: his "Skeltonics" are based on little else: "a poetical barbarism." It was not just because of his apparent formal crudeness that Alexander Barclay, the monkish Scot, calls him a "rascolde poet": he *was* something of a rascal in fact. But an unusual one: classically educated, he could "forget his Classics when looking at the countryside and not see Margery Milke-Ducke as Phyllis and Jolly Jacke as Corydon, or find 'behind every bush a thrumming Apollo' (John Clare's criticism of Keats)"— says Robert Graves, approvingly. Dunbar's contemporary, he stands like Janus at the threshold of the English Renaissance, facing both ways. He teases the tired old courtly traditions and discharges satire without mercy. He writes astonishing religious poetry, but his poems of celebration, social comment, parody and praise, and those headlong "Skeltonics," are what make him alive. His is the first modern English: we read him without recourse to a glossary.

No Englishman more relished the Scottish defeat at Flodden than

Skelton. He gloated in his indecently chauvinistic poem "Against the Scots." He played for a time in the Tudor court a role comparable to Dunbar's in the court of James IV. Like Dunbar he was a man of the cloth and a courtier with royal duties. He tutored the Duke of York, later Henry VIII. He commented wryly on the pleasures and vices of the royal milieu. With Dunbar he shared a certain public heartlessness, but he was never a convincing courtier. He kept getting into trouble. He wasn't convincing as a priest, either, though he was rector of Diss, Norfolk, where his diocesan bishop punished him for "having been guilty of *certain crimes* AS MOST POETS ARE."

Milton agreed with the bishop: "I name him not for posterity sake, whom Henry the 8th named in merriment his vicar of hell." Milton declines to understand the king's jest: the rector of Diss, the rector of *Dis* (Latin for hell). Milton calls him "one of the worst of men, who are both most able and most diligent to instil the poison they suck into the courts of princes, acquainting them with the choicest delights and criticisms of sin." The poet of *Paradise Lost* and the author of the classic tract against censorship *Areopagitica* would gladly have censored the anarchic, joyous laureate, as though he single-handedly had derailed the future king. Alexander Pope dismissed him as "beastly Skelton." This had nothing to do with the fact that Skelton was a kind of editor, assisting Caxton with his Virgil. Had Pope known this, he might have disparaged him even more vehemently.

Skelton isn't formally competent in the way Dunbar is; instead of a diverse skill he possesses a distinctive style, with certain affectations: those insistent and surprising rhymes, a refusal to stay still before his subject. His poetry is in touch with the spoken language of the day. He is not, of course, a reporter of court or gutter speech, but his language includes what he heard from highly placed and humble people alike. His pastoral work took him among wool merchants, farmers and clerics, all with different accents and ways of talking; and new religious notions flowed in at the port.

He is capable like Dunbar of savage flytings; he spares no foe. But his best work is compassionate and moral in a new manner. In his time allegory was no longer an entirely viable mode. The new humanism found it crudely scholastic. Skelton drew upon it to exaggerate and satirize, driving it to the extreme by individual idiosyncrasy.

Born probably in 1464, possibly in Cumberland, he was first known to the world as a classical humanist. He studied at Cambridge, went to "Oxforth," where he was made Poet Laureate and took a further degree in 1488, a degree which "implied a diligent study of mediaeval grammar and rhetoric, though the *Poeta Laureatus* need not have written any poems—except perhaps a hundred Virgilian hexameters, and a Latin comedy, both eulogizing Oxford, to prove that he had mastered Latin prosody and the Aristotelian unities." He translated Diodorus Siculus's *History of the World* (c. 1485) and the *Epistles* of Tully (Marcus Tullius Ciceronis, a.k.a. Cicero). In 1489 he was laureate of Oxford and Louvain, a scholar of international repute. Erasmus called him *Britannicarum literarum decus et lumen*. He compiled *A New English Grammar*, now lost with much of his other work. In 1489 he was admitted laureate of Cambridge. In 1498 he took religious orders and wrote a bitter satire, *The Bowge of Court*. The next year he was tutoring the future king, Henry VIII: "I gave him drink of the sugared well / Of Helicon's waters crystaline."

His Latin verses were praised even by Warton, who finds little to praise in the rest of his work. The verses on refusing to return a borrowed palfrey are in character; other verses express his doubt about the real presence in the sacrament. There is a frailty in his theological poems which contrasts with the imaginative force of his devotional writing ("Woefully Arrayed," for example). It makes sense to distinguish between theological poems, which examine tenets of faith, and devotional problems, which respond to Christian verities, especially the Crucifixion.

Skelton was first rewarded for his labors as tutor to Prince Henry by the future king's mother: she gave him a curacy "to reward his conscientious tutorship and good influence on the unruly boy." *Good* influence, Milton take note. His praise for her father, Edward, is undoubtedly sincere. It was 1504 when he removed to Diss, where his vernacular poetry came into its own. No record survives of the shock his fresh and extremely "low" verses provoked in humanist erstwhile colleagues. *Phyllyp Sparowe,* which includes the first mention in English poetry of some seventy species of bird, *The Tunnyng of Elynour Rummyng,* celebrating a seriously unlicensed publican, and other pieces did his reputation as a scholar no good. His conduct as rector did him no credit either. He was said to keep "a fair wench in his house." When the bishop instructed him to expel her through the door, Skelton obeyed, only to receive her back again—legend has it—through the window. But his faith was almost orthodox, however unorthodox his character as rector.

By 1509 he was back at court. The king pardoned him for an unrecorded offense. Advanced in years in 1512, after being created *Orator Regius,* a sort of Latin secretary, by his former pupil, he made—Graves reports—"a startling public avowal of devotion to the Muse-goddess, when he appeared wearing a white and green Court dress embroidered with the golden name CALLIOPE. He chose Calliope ('lovely face') rather than any of the Goddess' eight other names because, as he writes in an *amplificatio* of Diodorus Siculus' *History*, Calliope combines 'incomparable riches of eloquence with profound sadness.' " In 1516 he wrote *Magnificence*, his one surviving interlude and not a negligible contribution to the development of secular drama. Some of the passages call Blake to mind: "To live under law it is captivity: / Where dread leadeth the dance there is no joy nor pride."

By 1519, living in a house within the sanctuary of Westminster, he expressed his freedom by launching a campaign, with bleak and comic consequences, against Cardinal Wolsey as traitor to king, church and people in *Collyn Clout* and other work. He was a "cur and butcher's dog." The next year, *Why come ye nat to Courte* brought the conflict to a head. The king could no longer protect his orator. Skelton was abandoned to the cardinal, who sent him to prison. He earned his liberty by a penance and a jest. Kneeling before Wolsey, he suffered a long lecture, and at last said, "I pray your grace to let me lye doune and wallow, for I can kneele no longer."

"Speke Parrot" was composed in 1521. He enjoyed the patronage of the Howards in Yorkshire, wrote his self-staged apotheosis in *The Garlande of Laurell*, and returned to London, where he now flattered Wolsey in the hope of receiving a prebend. It was not granted. In old age he called himself the "British Catullus." He died in 1529, the year before Wolsey fell, leaving several children by a marriage he confessed to upon his deathbed. He was buried at St. Margaret's, Westminster, and his stone reads *Joannes Skelton, vates Pierius, hic situs est.*

There is a strong case against Skelton. In *The Arte of English Poesie* (1589) Richard Puttenham called him "but a rude railing rhymer, and all his doings ridiculous; he used both short distances and short measures, pleasing only the popular care." Francis Meres in his invaluable *Palladis Tamia, Wit's Treasury* (1598) branded him "buffoon." Warton states the case most fully: "Skelton would have been a writer without decorum at any period," his humor "capricious and grotesque." Not only his subjects but his manner Warton finds objectionable: "He sometimes debases his matter by his versification." But Caxton claimed that Skelton improved the language. How could this be so, asks Warton (forgetting that Caxton died in 1491, before Skelton had begun to give offense), for Skelton "sometimes adopts the most familiar phraseology of the common people." About the style he is emphatic. It is an "anomalous and motley form of versification." "Motley": Skelton as jester once again.

Warton describes fairly; but we reach a different verdict. Our prejudice favors "the most familiar phraseology of the common people," the spoken language. Not that anyone ever *spoke* Skeltonics, but his diction draws on the demotic of various classes. Warton does not mention the large number of invented and obscure words that are also found in the poems, a literariness that derives from Skelton's master Lydgate and from Chaucer. Sufficient evidence of artistry exists to make us trust even his most apparently off-the-cuff verses. Graves and Auden find in him the English poet of the transition between the Middle Ages and the Renaissance. Graves insists that "a study of the *Oxford English Dictionary* will show that Skelton enriched our vocabulary more than any other poet before or since, even Chaucer."

The taproots of his English work go deep into the fourteenth century and beyond. The rhyming Goliardic tradition of medieval Latin verse attracted him. He called his poems "trifles of honest mirth," which aligns him with the Goliardic, though he preferred accentual to syllabic prosody. If his Latin elegiacs were free of monastic phraseology, as Warton says, his English verses often include monastic Latin tags, developing a macaronic style of mixing English and Latin and sometimes French, which has been practiced in English for centuries, usually in carols, hymns and religious compositions, seldom in so lighthearted and witty a fashion, even by Dunbar. Skelton is a renegade humanist who recognized—having contributed to the movement—the spiritual and linguistic impoverishment that doctrinaire humanism implied. He came to relish elements in language that humanism tried to extirpate in its frenzy to purify Latin and, in a different sense, English.

His first English poem is an elegy on Edward IV. It's less elegy than meditative monologue, spoken by the king reflecting on ephemerality, fortune (with "sugared lips"), and "mutability." The complex verse form includes Latin refrains and an effective use of the *ubi sunt* ("where have they gone") motif, celebrating deeds even as it acknowledges their passing. The poem is not all wooden; it suggests what is to come. The accentual verse, with a marked caesura, falls into two short, phrased lines, with a truncated Anglo-Saxon feel. Though not systematically alliterative, it has the pondered emphases of alliterative verse, with short syntactic phrases.

In his next poem, also an elegy, he asks Clio to help him "expel" his "homely rudeness and dryness." "My words unpolished be, naked and plain, / Of aureat poems they want illumining." But nakedness and an individual plainness were to be his hallmarks, until the exuberance of the late poems. With *The Bowge of Court* he came of age. "Bowge" (*bouche*) means "rewards." In this secular allegory a dreamer takes ship and experiences the comradeship of courtly Disdain, Riot, Dissimulation and other perilous personifications. Boarding in innocence, he is reduced to paranoid dread. Chaucer is Skelton's master: the stanza form is that of *Troilus and Criseyde*, and when the language is most achieved, we feel Chaucer in the very movement of the verse. Riot is described in these terms:

> His cote was checkerd with patches rede
>   and blewe,
> Of Kirkbye Kendall was his short
>   demye;   Kendal cloth; gown
> And aye he sang *in fayth decon thou*
>   *crewe:*
> His elbowe bare, he ware his gere so   his clothes were threadbare
>   nye:
> His nose droppings, his lippes were full
>   drye:
> And by his syde his whynarde, and his   short sword
>   pouche,
> The devyll myght dance therin   the Devil could dance in an empty
>   for any crouche.   pouch—no cross (coin)

Entering on his forties (an older age then than it is today), living in the provinces, perhaps intellectually uncompanioned, driven upon himself, Skelton changed his style of life and writing. The eccentric poet hinted at in earlier poems came into his own in *Phyllyp Sparowe*. He used Goliardic verse, parodying the sacred rituals of the Church, to celebrate Jane Scroop's sparrow eaten by the convent cat. The first line reads *"Pla ce bo,"* the first word of the Office of the Dead, divided into three mock-solemn syllables that set the rhythmic pattern: short-lined, three-stressed. The first part of the poem is spoken by Jane, lamenting the bird. The elegy develops to ranging parody and satire. The famous catalogue of birds is not just a list: it evokes some of Philip's cousins, "The lark with his long toe," "And also the mad coot, / With balde face to toot" and more. An erotic subtext gives the poem its force: Jane laments her sparrow as a lover:

> It had a velvet cap,
> And wold syt upon my lap
> And seke after small wormes
> And somtyme white bred crommes
> And many tymes and ofte
> Betwene my brestes soft
> It wolde lye and rest
> It was propre and prest   pretty and neat
>   Somtyme he wolde gaspe

Whan he sawe a waspe
A fly, or a gnat
He wolde flye at that
And prytely he wold pant
When he saw an ant

Jane pleads her simplicity and ignorance, then entertains with a show of erudition and an enormous reading list. Finally Skelton's voice takes over and praises her. She loved the bird, the poet loves her. A Catullan syndrome, a very English poem.

The Tunnyng of Elynour Rummyng is certainly not charming: a poem in seven "fits," it's indebted to *Sir Gawain and the Green Knight*. Elynour's obnoxious "tunnyng," or alcoholic brew, luridly described in its vat, attracts fallen women of all sorts. Elynour herself, based on an actual publican who traded near Leatherhead, Surrey, is Skelton's most repulsive creation. Her face was "Like a roast pig's ear, / Bristled with hair." The poem is the quintessence of his "motley" verse, which he describes in *Collyn Clout*:

For though my ryme be ragged,
Tattered and jagged,
Rudely rayne-beaten,
Rusty and mothe-eaten,
Yf ye take well therwith,
It hath in it some pyth.

The "pyth" is that of satirical moralist. In the poems against Wolsey he satirizes with equal verve ecclesiastical corruption and the faithless laity. He is an establishment man, opposed to those who use rather than serve it. Skeltonics, a helter-skelter measure bordering on doggerel, suit the helter-skelter social world he mocks.

When, late in his career, he chose to use a long line, a more relaxed syntax followed and greater depth. "Speke Parrot" is—even in the corrupt texts we have—his masterpiece. The years of learnedness laugh at themselves in obscure references and allusions. He shifts attention from immediate effects to a more integrated poetic language that reflects a mind that, to begin with, seems abandoned to eloquent mania. The parrot who speaks is a Polly-glot, stuffed with knowledge, all of it—given the situation of the bird, a pet and a captive, caged—garbled and useless.

My lady mastres, Dame Phylology,   mistress
Gave me a gyfte in my neste when I lay,
To lerne all language . . .

"Speke Parrot" celebrates language and, in the same breath, acknowledges its impotence in the world of action. The poem slides away from mock allegory and rhetorical and linguistic jollity, until we're left with a bold, unmasked indictment of the state of learning, morality, the Church, the judiciary.

In Skelton's later work there is a constant pull toward dramatic form. The poems employ dialogue and idiomatic speech and develop character. In this as in other ways Skelton is a poet of transition, still dignified with the authority of the Middle Ages, yet expert in the new learning and the new forms. In *The Garlande of Laurell* occur those lyrics— "With marjoram gentle," "By Saint Mary, my lady," "Merry Margaret" and others—that crown the medieval lyric tradition and are at the same time among the finest celebratory lyrics of the early Renaissance.

Petrarch Comes to England

SIR THOMAS WYATT, HENRY HOWARD EARL OF SURREY

"Great lyrics" in the conventional sense are not to be found in Skelton. We have to look beyond him to someone conventionally greater, a man who belongs entirely to the Renaissance, whose blood has been warmed by the Mediterranean. Sir Thomas Wyatt (1503–1542) is the first great English lyric poet. "But here I am in Kent and Christendom / Among the Muses where I read and rhyme."

Almost all of his lyrics are dramatic. The reader plunges in medias res, usually into a complaint against an unregarding or unattainable lady. The poems can be located on a map of passion. They are thrifty, with little but telling detail and a minimum of physical evocation. Like other poems in the song tradition, their imagery is conventional.

Wyatt used over seventy different stanza forms, many of which he invented. At times he taxes himself beyond his technical skills. Critics disagree about his meters, and until the middle of the twentieth century it was fashionable to regularize them by actually changing his words and word order. Are the irregularities poetic flaws, manifestations of peculiar genius, or proof that his language is still in a state of accentual transition? Meter apart, one can't argue against the *rhythm* of the best poems, the variations—less numerous than is normally thought—on a metrical norm. They ensure his poetic superiority over Surrey and even Sidney, whose smoothness can be cloying. Violations of metrical decorum answer—or seem to answer—to modulations of emotions.

Sir Thomas involved himself in the king's affairs (in every sense) more deeply than Skelton did. A courtier, soldier and gentleman, not a priest, he was born at Allington Castle, beside the Medway in Kent, in 1503. His father, devoted to the Tudors, presented his son at court when he was thirteen. He attended St. John's College, Cambridge. At seventeen he married Lord Cobham's daughter. She bore him a son and a daughter, then proved unfaithful. Wyatt refused to have her under his roof.

At twenty-three he began actively serving his king. He accompanied an embassy to France, and the next year another to the Pope. Captured by Spanish troops, he managed to escape. In 1528 he became marshal of Calais, a post he held for four years. When he returned to England he held prominent posts in Essex and was chief ewer (in his father's place) at the coronation of Anne Boleyn.

Legend has it that he was in love with Anne. It's likely; and that his confession to the king before the marriage on 1 June 1533 saved him his head when she lost hers on 19 May 1536. He was imprisoned in the Tower that year—but as a result of a quarrel with the Duke of Suffolk. It had none of the sinister overtones that Roman Catholic propagandists and romantic critics suggest. Wyatt was soon back in favor. He became sheriff of Kent and in 1537 ambassador to Spain. He returned from Spain in 1539, on his father's death.

> Tagus, farewell, that westward with thy streams
> Turns up the grains of gold already tried:
> With spur and sail for I go seek the Thames
> Gainward the sun that sheweth her wealthy pride
> And to the town which Brutus sought by dreams
> Like bended moon doth lend her lusty side.
> My King, my Country alone for whom I live,
> Of mighty love the wings for this me give.

The lines speak honest zeal on the king's behalf. Wyatt had detractors at home, and a trial at which he was acquitted of charges of treason and immorality. He returned to his post at Calais, later served as MP for Kent, then as vice-admiral of a new fleet under construction. He died suddenly in Sherborne in 1542, of a fever, on his way to accompany a Spanish envoy from Falmouth to London.

Wyatt's poems were first published in *Tottel's Miscellany* (1557). Richard Tottel—one of my most distinguished Tudor predecessors, who worked from the Hand and Star in Temple Bar from 1553 until his death in 1594—loved metrical regularity rather too much, and he was the first to regularize Sir Thomas's meter by altering his language. The poems were thus misprinted from the outset, but—as you expect of a good publisher—with the best intentions: Tottel, and his collaborator the translator and cleric Nicholas Grimald, knew that the poems would not please readers if they were irregular. Wyatt's work presents serious textual difficulties even now (I have modernized the spelling). What we read today was collected largely by G. F. Nott in 1816 and revised and improved by A. K. Foxwell in 1913, with some later adjustments. Our Wyatt is not the Wyatt that the sixteenth century read.

Some verse forms Wyatt invented, others he imported. From Italy he brought terza rima, ottava rima and the sonnet. Though he was the first great English sonneteer, the sonnets he translated and composed had little effect on his smooth-mannered successors, who went to the fountainhead in Petrarch rather than to Wyatt's efforts. He failed to domesticate terza rima, which he used with mixed effects in his three satires. They tend toward blank verse, with enjambements so frequent that the rhymes appear accidental rather than elements of form, except in a few passages. One is the opening of the first satire, on court life:

> Mine own John Poins, since ye delight to know
> The cause why that homeward I me draw,
> And flee the press of courts whereso they go,
> Rather than to live thrall, under the awe
> Of lordly looks, wrapped within my cloak,
> To will and lust learning to set a lawe . . .

The theme is familiar from Skelton, but the added note of personal seriousness in line six is an important development. The tone is intimate, not public, the image "wrapped within my cloak" quick, vivid, part of the subject, not decorative.

If Wyatt sometimes failed to acclimatize his imported forms, he did add to the resources of our poetry. His immediate legacy to his successors was "poulter's measure," an alexandrine followed by a rhyming four-teener. C. S. Lewis finds it hard to forgive him this invention, though Surrey, Turberville, Gascoigne, Golding and others used it with a kind of authority.

Wyatt and Henry Howard, Earl of Surrey, are bracketed together as fathers of English Petrarchanism. Richard Puttenham saw them as "the two chief lanterns of light to all others that have since employed their pens upon English poesy: their conceits were lofty, their styles stately, their conveyance clear, their terms proper, their metre sweet and well-proportioned, in all imitating very naturally and studiously their master Francis Petrarcha." This is more true of Surrey than Wyatt, whom Puttenham read in Tottel's polished text. Certainly Wyatt's imitations of Petrarch are neither studious nor merely Petrarchan.

The introduction of Petrarch into England was not an unalloyed good. He taught two lessons, one of form and one of subject. The formal lesson provided dangers for native syntax and diction, requiring adjustments and mannerisms against the grain of the language. The thematic lesson imperiled lesser talents. Petrarchan love conventions recast courtly conventions in a new age, and their chief novelty for

English poets depended on their disregarding elements latent in the native tradition. Petrarch required not so much translation as transposition into English. This Wyatt did. Those who followed were less successful.

Wyatt found the refined, spiritual love of Petrarch uncongenial—even incredible. He was a man of flesh and fiery blood and his best poems are decidedly un-Platonic, arising out of carnal passion. He avoids the aureate style that later Petrarchans developed. In Petrarch's sonnets the octave normally establishes a specific occasion—a thing perceived, an emotion felt. The sestet generalizes from that occasion. Wyatt saw Petrarch's skill in structuring an idea, a structuring more allusive and concise than the mechanical procedure of allegory, but not unrelated to it. His own poems structure emotions: the generalizations that emerge relate to physical passion and hardly seek to transcend it. He is forthright, clear in outline, colloquial, undecorated. Shakespeare was able to use Wyatt's poems familiarly in, for example, *Hamlet* and *Twelfth Night*. Surrey and Sidney bring orthodox Petrarchism to England; in Wyatt the energy of an old tradition, mediated through imported models, remains alive.

The best illustration of Wyatt's freedom with Petrarch is his imitation of *"Una candida cerva"* (*Canzoniere*, poem 190), which he renders in "Whoso list to hunt." In Petrarch's sonnet the speaker sees a doe and follows her, coveting her as a miser covets gold. Around her neck he notices a diamond and topaz collar that says *"Nessun mi tocchi."* She is Caesar's. He follows half a day and falls exhausted. She disappears. Wyatt takes the poem and rearranges the halves of the sestet. *"Nessun mi tocchi"* he translates with superb blasphemy into Christ's words, *"Noli me tangere."* He does away with the miser image and from the outset presents the lover as a tired hunter. He heightens the hunting image—not in Petrarch at all—with the words "Yet may I by no means my wearied mind / Draw from the deer," suggesting an arrow (a Cupid's arrow, too) that has hit its mark without slaying it. Wyatt imparts dramatic unity, with a fitting climax in the last three lines. The poem lacks Petrarch's intellectual clarity, but it has been transmuted into Wyatt's manly, less reflective idiom. The doe may be Anne Boleyn.

Most of his poems develop a single theme. Statements of feeling are tight-lipped and masculine, not overstated or ironized. He uses rhetorical devices with restraint: means of expression, not ends in themselves. An older native tradition survives in him, despite Petrarch, and it helps to explain his prosody. He combines meter with the older accentual verse. Unless we read him with a metronomic ear, we must expect to hear at times a regular iambic pentameter line followed by a line from the accentual tradition, with a marked caesura and probably two strong stresses (and perhaps a secondary stress) in each half line. His best-known poem, with verbs and adjectives suggesting animal passion, reflects this:

> They flee from me that sometime did me seek
>> With naked foot stalking in my chamber.
> I have seen them gentle, tame and meek
>> That now are wild and do not remember
>> That sometime they put themselves in danger
> To take bread at my hand . . .

It includes the most prosodically contested of Wyatt's lines, "But all is turned thorough my gentleness / Into a strange fashion of forsak-ing," which Tottel amended for regularity, as he did the first passage. It is futile to force Wyatt to scan, as, for example, by voicing the *e* in "strange." The two accented syllables, followed by two unaccented, "stránge fáshion of," force a brief pause and then an acceleration not substantiated by syntax or meter, an irregularity with dramatic aural rightness if we listen with both ears.

The persona of the unhappy lover, like a glum Hilliard miniature, becomes repetitive and tiresome. He has little to celebrate. Occasionally he risks a female voice, but the effect is not striking. The poems vary greatly in quality, from the twenty or so masterpieces, among the best lyrics in English, to conventional works in which wordplay, so cherished by sixteenth-century poets, displaces thought and experience, or where a poem develops by accretion rather than progression.

Much ill is spoken of Wyatt's *Penitential Psalms*. One critic declares that the real penance is to read them at all. Yet they are among the first and certainly among the better of the modern metrical versions. A com-parison between Wyatt's uneven efforts and those of Sternhold and Hopkins, or Archbishop Parker, proves that, though they do not crown his achievement, they do him no discredit. He is the first of a *type*—the noblest type—of poet in English literature: a man of action, servant of his king, his God and of his Muse, like Surrey, Ralegh, Sidney, Fulke Greville, Lovelace and others. Surrey defines the type in his elegies to Wyatt. They fall short of Wyatt's achievement but have the merit of sincerity.

Henry Howard, Earl of Surrey, having outshone Wyatt until this century, has now been eclipsed. He is still a magnificent poet, a great inventor, not least of a modern English Virgil and of blank verse.

> I call to mind the navy great
> That the Greeks brought to Troyè town,

And how the boisterous winds did beat
Their ships, and rent their sails adown,
Till Agamemnon's daughter's blood
Appeased the gods that them withstood.

His virtues tell against him: prosodic skill, formal competence. He contributes more to the development of poetry in his century than Wyatt does. He develops the unrhymed iambic pentameter (blank verse), his sonnets are influential, while Wyatt's are only admired. He is a thoroughgoing Petrarchan. He may be essentially a stepping stone from Wyatt to Sidney, but that's a worthy fate.

He was born in Kenninghall Palace, Norfolk, in 1517. From the outset he had advantages. His father was the third Duke of Norfolk. The learned, widely traveled tutor John Clerke took his education in hand and made him an exemplary linguist. He mastered Latin, Italian, French and Spanish. As a boy he was close to the young Duke of Richmond, illegitimate son of Henry VIII, and stayed with him at Windsor. He recalled this happy period later in life, after Richmond's death and during his detention in the castle,

Where each sweet place returns a taste full sour,
The large green courts, where we were wont to hove,
With eyes cast up unto the maiden's tower,
And easy sighs such as folk draw in love . . .

He recalls the ladies, the dances, the tales, games, tournaments and confidences:

The secret thoughts imparted with such trust,
The wanton talk, the divers change of play;
The friendship sworn, each promise kept so just,
Wherewith we past the winter night away . . .

In a sonnet he remembers those years with unusual physical particularity, more like Gascoigne than conventional Surrey in its realization: "When Windsor walls sustain'd my wearied arm, / My hand my chin, to ease my restless head."

In 1532 he married the Earl of Oxford's daughter, enhancing his position. He progressed as courtier and warrior, fighting on land and at sea. In 1545 he was given command of Boulogne, but the next year he was arrested and charged with high treason: conspiring against the succession of Edward VI. Henry resented the popularity of his knight—a man ostentatious and ambitious, though not for the Crown. He was a blood relation of Catherine Howard, and this too the king held against him. In January 1547 Surrey was beheaded at the Tower.

He passed into legend on a slightly lower plain than Sidney was to do. Thomas Nashe fictionalized him, exaggerating his qualities, in *The Unfortunate Traveller*. One speech Nashe attributes to Surrey is certainly in character: "Upon a time I was determined to travel, the fame of Italy, and an especial affection I had unto poetry my second mistress"— the first being Elizabeth Fitzgerald, the Geraldine of the sonnets, who had doubtful Italian origins—"for which it was so famous, had wholy ravished me unto it." Geraldine was to Surrey what Laura was to Petrarch, an incarnate Muse, a pretext for poems, an ideal. Warton calls her "a mistress perhaps as beautiful as Laura," and describes Surrey's achievement in Petrarchan terms: "At least with Petrarch's passion if not his taste, Surrey led a way to great improvements in English poetry, by a happy imitation of Petrarch and other Italian poets." He was more imitative, even in love, than Wyatt, and most of his poems concentrate on love's anxieties. He returned from his first journey to Italy, Warton tells us, "the most elegant traveller, the most polite lover, the most learned nobleman, and the most accomplished gentleman, of his age." He would have seemed a bit out of place at Hampton Court. Excess of accomplishment contributed to his undoing. It was rumored that he had designs to wed Princess Mary.

A not altogether native grace characterizes his lyrics. There is little of the suggestive awkwardness of Wyatt but instead an acquired facility. The poems please rather than move us. Warton approved: "Surrey, for justness of thought, correctness of style, and purity of expression, may justly be pronounced the first English classical poet. He unquestionably is the first polite writer of love-verses in our language." Correct, pure, classical, polite: also, a little dull. The poems can have a metronomic regularity, though the syntax is extended and complex. From Wyatt he learned poulter's measure (couplets consisting of a twelve-syllable iambic line alternating with a fourteen-syllable iambic line) and could write well in it:

> I know to seek the track of my desirèd foe,
> And fear to find that I do seek. But chiefly this I know:
> That lovers must transform into the thing beloved,
> And live (alas, who could believe?) with sprite from life removed.

Poulter's measure is best used for serious statements or for burlesque. It can undermine the tone of a sober poem: "And when I felt the air so pleasant round about, / Lord, to myself how glad I was that I had gotten out!" The lighter tone mars with human warmth an otherwise chilly poem. His best-known poem in poulter's measure, "In winter's just return," succeeds despite rather than because of the verse form he has chosen.

Surrey developed what came to be known as the Shakespearean sonnet and—most important—the blank verse of his translations of Books Two and Four of Virgil's *Aeneid*. Grudging respect has been paid this work, yet it is subtly conceived and executed with exemplary plainness, a verse direct and transparent, displaying its matter rather than its manner. Roger Ascham approved his attempt to write without what Warton called the "gothic ornament" of rhyme. It was part of a humanist strategy. In the hands of Surrey's successors, it proved to be much more. A passage from his version of Book Two illustrates the virtues of his form. The Greek fleet withdraws behind Tenedos.

> There stands in sight an isle, hight Teneden,   called
> Rich, and of fame, while Priam's kingdom stood;
> Now but a bay, and road unsure for ship,
> Hither them secretly the Greeks withdrew,
> Shrouding themselves under the desert shore.
> And, weening we they had been fled and gone   thinking
> And with that wind had fet the land of Greece,   reached
> Troyè discharged her long continued dole.   gave vent to; grief
> The gates cast up, we issued out to play,
> The Greekish camp desirous to behold,
> The places void, and the forsaken coasts . . .

Though rhyme has gone, the sound structure within each line, and between consecutive lines, is tight; assonance and alliteration, inner rhyme and half-rhyme, keep the verse taut. It lacks the verve of Gavin Douglas's translation, but it is direct and faithful to the original. It moves at a pace at once dignified and speakable. Surrey attempts to approximate Virgil's means as well as his meaning, and in this he reveals himself to be the first English poet thoroughly in the humanist tradition promoted in England by scholars such as Roger Ascham and Sir John Cheke. By following rather than dragging Virgil into English, Surrey extends English verse technique. Douglas, who was after the meat of his original, served it up according to a medieval recipe.

Forty of Surrey's poems appeared, alongside Wyatt's, in *Tottel's Miscellany*—their first publication. A decade had passed since his death, but his reputation was still fresh. He was the only poet singled out by name on Tottel's title page. It is hard to summon up much enthusiasm for the lyrics. "The soote season, that bud and bloom forth brings" recalls Langland in phrase and alliteration, and in the not entirely conventional particularity of its images:

> The hart hath hung his old head on the pale;   fence
> The buck in break his winter coat he flings;
> The fishes flete with new repairèd scale;   float
> The adder all her slough away she slings . . .

But in a poem with preponderantly end-stopped lines and only two rhymes, the effect is of accretion, not progression, a common vice in Surrey: his poems draw on conventional tropes but do not integrate them into statement. "Brittle beauty" and even "Set me whereas the sun," each poem in its way memorable, are assortments of image and allusion, not coherent structures.

"Alas, so all things now do hold their peace," "When raging love," "O happy dancer," "Laid in my quiet bed," "Epitaph on Thomas Clere" and "Sardanapalus" possess as poems some of the virtues of his blank verse, but in rhymed forms, where thought and image develop together. They are among the best poems of the time. Those that record personal experience are often the most memorable. And Surrey can be memorable. Thomas Hardy echoed lines of Surrey's, such as "Now he comes, will he come? alas, no, no," and who can deny that the poet who wrote "I Look into My Glass" did not have deep in memory Surrey's lines, "Thus thoughtful as I lay, I saw my wither'd skin, / How it doth show my dinted jaws, the flesh was worn so thin"?

Surrey's debt to Wyatt is occasionally apparent in style and image. "Wrapt in my careless cloak" recalls Wyatt's first satire; a poem with an extended chess conceit has a Wyatt-like lightness of touch; there are poems of mere wordplay, too; and verses spoken by women. But Surrey's four elegies for Wyatt bear witness to the fact that the older poet was for him an inspiration rather than a model. Surrey was more ambitious and sophisticated than Wyatt, and though a fine poet, a lesser one.

The Green Knight

THOMAS LORD VAUX, THOMAS TUSSER,
THOMAS SACKVILLE EARL OF DORSET, GEORGE GASCOIGNE,
EDWARD DE VERE, ISABELLA WHITNEY

In the sixteenth century the native tradition of lyric poems builds on and away from medieval traditions of grammar and rhetoric. A line can be drawn from Skelton to Sir Thomas More, Wyatt, Lord Vaux, George Gascoigne, and then Barnabe Googe, George Turberville, Sir Walter Ralegh. (The language is so close to current English that I take the liberty of adopting modern spelling from this point onward, except where archaic forms are intended.) Here is Thomas, Lord Vaux, from a poem published by Tottel the year after his death.

> My lusts they do me leave,
>   My fancies all be fled,
> And tract of time begins to weave
>   Grey hairs upon my head.
>
> For age with stealing steps
>   Hath clawed me with his crutch,
> And lusty life away she leaps
>   As there had been none such.

Each stanza explores a set of figures: metaphor does not decorate but carries the argument.

> The harbinger of death,
>   To me I see him ride;
> The cough, the cold, the gasping breath
>   Doth bid me to provide
>
> A pickaxe and a spade,
>   And eke a shrouding sheet,

> A house of clay for to be made
>> For such a guest most meet.

A poetry austere and rich at once, true without a hint of sentiment, wise with the wisdom of a life lived in the world and not merely by the grace of literature.

These poets explore broad, generic themes of permanent significance and moral importance. Personal experience, stripped of contingency and universalized, is an ingredient. Reasonable men address reasonable readers with wit, with passion. Their structures are argumentative or cumulative, the purpose didactic, cautionary. Metaphors revive the force of allegorical figuration: they affect us as *meaning* on several levels, but they need not be "construed" according to an interpretative code in the way that allegorical figures do. A fashion for the Petrarchan drove native poetry underground; it resurfaces at the end of the century in another form.

Bad native poetry is immediately recognizable. It has nothing to hide behind. The most obvious is the "useful," or "instrumental," poem. Thomas Tusser's *Hundreth Good Pointes of Husbandrie* (1557) is full of instruction on farming, housekeeping and gardening, charming we may think at first, but soon tedious and flat: Rudyard Kipling made an edition of this "serviceable" verse; contemporary poets like C. H. Sisson enjoy it because the age's customs and habits are unfolded before our eyes from the irregular little pleats of Tusser's couplets. Bad in another way is the queen's cousin Thomas Sackville, Earl of Dorset's "Induction" and "The Complaint of Buckingham" for *The Mirror for Magistrates* (1563 edition)—one of the most popular volumes of the time, printed and reprinted, revised and re-revised—and his (assumed) contributions to the last two acts of Thomas Norton's *Gorboduc*. Verbose, labored, he is mechanical in unpacking the nuances of conventional metaphor. If Tusser charms with awkward aphorisms, Sackville is merely pedantic. The fall of Troy provides him with a tremendous, conventional canvas. What's Hecuba to him?

> Not worthy Hector, worthiest of them all,
>> Her hope, her joy; his force is now for nought.
> O Troy, Troy, Troy, there is no boot but bale;
>> The hugy horse within thy walls is brought;
>> Thy turrets fall, thy knights, that whilom fought
>>> In arms amid the field, are slain in bed,
>>> Thy gods defiled and all thy honour dead.

The closing couplet is not remote in cadence from Pope's in "Eloise to Abelard": a moment of prosodic definition in a standard mess of language. Sackville, like Edward de Vere, Earl of Oxford, wrote verse early and fell silent in later life. Wyatt, Surrey and Sidney died young. Lyric poetry was a young man's art. Here is the plain, figurative, logical, wonderful voice of the young Edward de Vere:

> Were I a king, I could command content;
>   Were I obscure, hidden should be my cares;
> Or were I dead, no cares should me torment,
> Nor hopes, nor hates, nor loves, nor griefs, nor fears.
>   A doubtful choice, of these three which to crave,
>   A kingdom, or a cottage, or a grave.

Plain diction, general equivalence between metrical and syntactical units. It declares, a verse of bold subtlety, choosing characteristic detail, universal images, and is uninterested in the nuanced concreteness of image, the tentativeness of feelings. The native style at its best beguiles because it is clear in intention and lucid in execution.

Isabella Whitney, the first woman to publish a volume of her verses, *A Sweet Nosegay or Pleasant Posy, Containing a Hundred and Ten Philosophical Flowers* (1573), flourished in the decade after 1565. She adopted the plain style with prosaic confidence and a kind of tripping energy that tends to fall over its feet in its eagerness to close a rhyme. Her fictional "Wyll and Testament: on having to leave London" is less predictable and derivative than her aphoristic, Senecan *Philosophical Flowers*: a lively doggerel, almost rising to satire.

George Gascoigne exemplifies the plain style as no one else does, and because he is a "transitional poet" (falling between the stools of "silver" and "golden" poets, between Wyatt and Spenser, between the first and second halves of the century) he is often forgotten.

> My worthy Lord, I pray you wonder not
> To see your woodman shoot so oft awry,
> Nor that he stands amazèd like a sot
> And lets the harmless deer, unhurt, go by.

His neglect is one of the not uncommon outrages in English poetry: Donne and Herbert were overlooked and misvalued for centuries; Smart and Cowper are only now being brushed down. Gascoigne for centuries has been more a footnote than part of the living text. He deserves as much celebrity at least as Surrey, as Ralegh—maybe even as Sidney.

The American poet Yvor Winters considers Gascoigne to be "one of the great masters of the short poem in the century." Winters loves "sentence" in poetry: the concise, sometimes aphoristic expression of general truths (taken to excess "sentence" becomes "sententious"). Gascoigne's best poems are extraordinarily good. No wonder he was among Ralegh's favorites. Ben Jonson admired him, and Shakespeare was touched by him: there are echoes in the language of the plays. He takes up the original qualities of Wyatt—and his vices, especially facile wordplay and poulter's measure, which he puts to good use. He advances the native tradition, occasionally dusted but ungilded by Italian influences. He advances it because he understands it.

Born in 1530 in Cardington, Bedfordshire, George was descended from Sir William Gascoigne, Henry IV's chief justice. His father, Sir John, was a man of substance. Gascoigne studied at Trinity College, Cambridge, and in 1555 entered Gray's Inn, London and represented Bedfordshire in parliament. At Gray's Inn he produced two plays. One, *Supposes*, out of Ariosto's *Suppositi*, is probably our first English prose comedy. It provides Shakespeare with the subplot of *The Taming of the Shrew*. The other is a translation of an Italian version of Euripides, the first classical Greek play to appear on the English stage.

A prodigal, Gascoigne was disinherited. To mend his finances, and perhaps for love, he married in 1562 Elizabeth Breton, a widow and the mother of the poet Nicholas Breton. Debt continued to dog him. He fled from his creditors to Holland, where he served the Prince of Orange (1572–74) and was imprisoned by the Spanish and released. On his return to England he discovered that some of his poems had been issued in unauthorized versions—not by a predecessor I would acknowledge. Printers and publishers have been scrupulous (for the most part) with the living, whatever liberties they have taken with the dead. He contacted another printer and together they published authorized versions in the laboriously entitled *An Hundred Sundrie Floures bound up in one Poesie*. This included the first linked sonnet sequence in English (an example of the form is "Gascoigne's Memories IV") and the prose narrative *The Adventures of Master F. J.*, which, if not translated from an Italian original, has claims to being the first English "novel," or roman à clef. In 1575 he issued *The Posies*, in which he scored another first by including "Certain Notes of Instruction," a treatise on the writing of English verse derived from Ronsard's 1565 treatise. James I (James VI of Scotland) later based his *Reulis and Cautelis of Scottish Poesie* on it.

The next year Gascoigne produced *The Glass of Government* (a "prodigal son" play) and *The Steele Glass*, the first use of blank verse for nondramatic original composition. His *Complaint of Philomene*, also in 1576, set the pattern of Ovidian narrative verse that Shakespeare follows in *Venus and Adonis* and *The Rape of Lucrece*. When he died in 1577, he had been an MP, courtier, soldier, farmer, writer and friend of writers,

including Spenser. He has as many "firsts" to his credit in poetry as
Christopher Columbus does in geography. Yet by his own account,
especially in "Gascoigne's Woodmanship" and "The Green Knight's
Farewell to Fancy," he failed in all he attempted.

In his time he was not regarded as a failure. Indeed he was the best-
known writer of his day. *The Steele Glass*, a satire on the debasing effect
of Italian manners in England, provoked Ralegh's first surviving poem.
His plain-speaking style appealed widely. Yvor Winters calls it "almost
an affectation of plainness, even of brusqueness." His "I" talks in the
diction of the day ("like a sot"); it is not refined like the constructed "I"
of polite writers. Gascoigne makes no secret of his circumstances,
incompetence and failure; he plays them up, jokingly exaggerates them.
There's candor in his confessions, without the self-pity and self-regard
of Hoccleve's heart-on-sleevery or the poised disappointment, moaning
and bellyaching of Wyatt and Surrey.

An advantage of a plain style is that good poems stand out from bad;
no figured veil obscures the faults. And from the weak poems good pas-
sages float free with the force of aphorism:

> If so thy wife be too, too fair of face,
> It draws one guest too many to thine inn;
> If she be foul, and foilèd with disgrace,
> In other pillows prickst thou many a pin.

The thought is commonplace; but tone, diction, conciseness bring the
commonplace to life. What is good in Gascoigne, and there is consider-
able and varied good, has an abrupt clarity and a positive verbal impact.

Elegy—serious and satirical—is his natural mode. He memorializes
failure and loss in a tone without resignation. An almost physical sense
of the material reality and the desirability of what he has lost or failed in
is captured in the accentual and alliterative lines of his "native" poems.
His most delicate achievement is his humor: bittersweet without bur-
lesque, without loss of poetic seriousness.

In "Certain Notes of Instruction" Gascoigne emphasizes poetic
"invention": find the right word or phrase to illustrate and amplify;
avoid "*trita et obvia*," the merely conventional and familiar. Verbal dis-
covery, surprise: he revives convention in new structures, new meta-
phors. The alliteration that binds many poems together produces, not
the archaic effect we might expect, but a colloquial tone, a sense of unre-
finement. In writing about failure his mastery is clearest. "The Lullaby
of a Lover," who puts his youth, his eyes, his will, his sex, to sleep, is in
metrical verse, heightened by alliteration and assonance. Here he sings
his youth to sleep:

First lullaby my youthful years;
It is now time to go to bed,
For crooked age and hoary hairs
Have won the haven within my head.
With lullaby, then, youth be still;
With lullaby content thy will;
Since courage quails and comes behind,
Go sleep, and so beguile thy mind.

He advances naturally, from image to image. Other poems, for instance the religious "Gascoigne's Good Morrow," are less alive, accumulating imagery, repeating a theme, but not developing a poetic argument.

In "Gascoigne's Memories III" he celebrates spiritual and material failure:

> The common speech is, spend and God
>   will send;
> But what sends he? A bottle and a bag,   a beggar's possessions
> A staff, a wallet, and a woeful end,
> For such as list in bravery so to brag.   fine clothes

Is this Thomas Tusser at court, proffering the hackneyed advice he could not follow himself? It's similar in kind, yet different in effect. One begins to hear, not fancifully I think, the tones of the Ben Jonson of *Timber*, even suggestions of the colloquial Shakespeare.

In "Gascoigne's Woodmanship" he confesses to his lord that he has failed in hunting, philosophy, everything. He is luckless, ill-starred. A quiet, persistent line of satire accompanies his confession: he is not the sole object of his irony. "The Green Knight's Farewell to Fancy" shows him at his most accomplished. Another account of failures, it is his most original and witty production. Here he gardens:

> To plant strange country fruits, to sow such seeds likewise,
> To dig and delve for new found roots, where old might well suffice;
> To prune the water-boughs, to pick the mossy trees—
> Oh, how it pleased my fancy once! to kneel upon my knees,
> To graft a pippin stock when sap begins to swell;
> But since the gains scarce quite the cost, *Fancy* (quoth he) *farewell*.

The "Green Knight" is a version of Gascoigne: the visor does not hide him. His one hope is divine grace, for on earth he is doomed, in each vocation, to fail. Coming to Gascoigne after reading Surrey is like stepping out of a library into the wide open air, a thoroughly English air.

Only he could have written off his own Muse so disarmingly, and only a dull reader would believe him:

> A fancy fed me once, to write in verse and rhyme,
> To wray my grief, to crave reward, to cover still my crime:
> To frame a long discourse, on stirring of a straw,
> To rumble rhyme in raff and ruff, yet all not worth a haw:
> To hear it said there goeth, the *man that writes so well*,
> But since I see, what poets be, *Fancy* (quoth he) *farewell*.

"A little man with little hands and little cuffs"

EDMUND SPENSER

If ever there was a poet reared in a library, it is Edmund Spenser. There's something a bit monstrous about him. Queen Elizabeth valued, though she could not like, this "little man with little hands and little cuffs." John Aubrey reports at second hand that he was "a little man, wore short haire, little band and little cuffs." His allegorical epic *The Faerie Queene* celebrates Elizabeth; she features, always idealized, elsewhere—everywhere—in his work. He was an eager poet of the established order: monarchy, court, the English church, powers that sustained and rewarded him. His was not a critical but a celebratory commitment. He never got quite enough thanks for his labors: portraits show, beneath his domed brow and emphatic nose, lips a little petulant, and the eyes gaze coldly back. Tetchy. And he could speak with forked tongue: his shepherds unburden themselves, allegorically, of some harsh truths about Spenser's world.

His books sold steadily until the latter half of the twentieth century. Poets especially warm to him. Keats pays him the tribute of imitation in his apprentice work and draws nourishment from him throughout. He calls him the "elfin poet." Coleridge said: "In Spenser . . . we trace a mind constitutionally tender, delicate and . . . I had almost said effeminate." He might well have used the term: there are in *The Shepheardes Calender* and at other points in the poetry moments of sexual and erotic ambiguity. Over a century earlier than Coleridge, Milton (who would not have permitted himself to perceive such irregularities) regarded Spenser as a great poet and a moral teacher: his own work is full of direct debts to Spenser's poems. Blake, Wordsworth and Thomas Hardy imitated him at the outset of their careers. His formal influence is felt in the early poems of Byron and, preeminently, in James Thomson's *The Castle of Indolence*. Well into the twentieth century, poets pay him tribute.

Walter Savage Landor sounds a lonely dissenting note a century before. He wrote to Wordsworth, "Thee gentle Spenser fondly led, / But me he mostly sent to bed." The present age agrees with Landor.

Spenser says he is Chaucer's heir, a claim it is hard to take seriously unless we consider an archaizing style to be Chaucerian. The differences between Chaucer and Spenser are more striking than any similarities. Chaucer "makes it new"; Spenser deliberately antiquates, not least in reverting to systematic allegory, whereas Chaucer had rumbled, in his middle years, the bankruptcy of that mode. Chaucer's poetry moves from allegory toward a world of real people rather than personifications. Spenser moves back, deserting the ground Chaucer helped to prepare, in which Marlowe, Shakespeare and other writers of the time took root. Chaucer reached into the literal world, Spenser back into the figurative and ideal. They do share a sensuous imagination. Chaucer makes the world visible and tangible. Spenser at his best exploits the senses to make ideas imaginable.

But when Spenser calls himself Chaucerian, it is more than a gesture. By the latter half of the sixteenth century Chaucer's music was muted. His language could hardly be heard. Waller judged that he could only boast "sense," "The glory of his numbers lost." We are back to the voiced final *e*, which history silenced. Poets who could not hear saw Chaucer as awkward and faulty, a man whose numbers didn't add up. Spenser read him somehow, perhaps inspired by Gascoigne's cogent enthusiasm, and sensed the equal length of lines, perhaps even allowing himself to voice that treacherous *e*. He wrote a conclusion to Chaucer's unfinished *Squire's Tale* that found its place in *The Faerie Queene*. Certainly the example of Chaucer was monitory to the classical humanists. If language could change so radically over a century and a half, it needed to be stabilized, given an Augustan fixity, and from the labor to "stabilize" it emerged strict laws, and rules of decorum.

Many a radical poet—Milton, Pope and Eliot spring to mind—have a strategy in the markers they put down in their critical writings. The intention is to be a great poet and to be received as a great poet, and their prose work clears a space for them, showing how and what they read and how they might be read. In Spenser the art is not lacking, the scholarship or dedication; nor is the politicking. Chaucer and Virgil give an equal light. Spenser wanted to be read by the same eyes that read the *Eclogues*, *Georgics* and *Aenied*, *Troilus and Criseyde* and *Canterbury Tales*. He wanted the transition from the classic poems to his own to be smooth and clearly understood.

In his age political and social ideas had a peculiarly potent embodiment. Elizabeth would preside over a recovery of classical learning and discipline, the reestablishment of true religion, the growth of power. The virgin queen embodied a new start, she was the just Astraea, the English Augustus, "fair vestal, throned by the West," bringing back (as Sir John Davies declares in one of his "Hymns" to her) "the golden days, / And all the world amended." Such optimism survived the first decade of her reign. *Semper eadem* (Always the Same) was her motto, the Phoenix her symbol, suggesting her red hair and England's recrudescence. Surrounding her was unprecedented pomp and ceremony, at court or when she went on her spectacular progresses to the castles, palaces and the new "prodigy houses" of her noble subjects (Wollaton, Burghley, Holdenby, Theobalds, etc.), and that pomp spread through the institutions of her rule: church, the law, the universities all developed formality and ceremony. Portraits and tomb effigies from her period display a new magnificence. The fronts of houses become heraldic statements and define the character and status of the master and his family. Poems, too, share in this "refacing." New decorum, rhetorical propriety, generic correctness are practiced, rule books written. The queen, even as she grows old, is never portrayed as aging, ill, or bald: she always embodies splendor, a vigorous young England.

Born in London around 1552, Spenser was the son of a gentleman, but one who also worked as a journeyman in cloth making. Later in life the poet claimed a not impossible kinship with the noble Spencers of Northampton. Some of his childhood he spent in Burnley, Lancashire, where he may actually have experienced the unrequited love that "Colin" laments in *The Shepheardes Calender*. He was educated at the Merchant Taylors' School under the headmastership of Richard Mulcaster, a humanist deeply interested in singing and instrumental music and in the English language. Memorably he declared: "It is our accident which restrains our tongue, and not the tongue itself." Spenser was already writing verse, translating from the French sonnets of Joachim Du Bellay (1522–60)—"Bellay, first garland of free poesy"—and probably studying the Platonists who were to direct his philsophical imagination.

He went up to Pembroke Hall, Cambridge, in 1569. Lancelot Andrewes was his contemporary, but Spenser took up instead with Gabriel Harvey, an opinionated young Fellow senior to him, who advocated the modish humanist and Puritan prejudices of the day, and a man so close to his bookseller (his publisher) that he was sometimes subsidized by him. *The Shepheardes Calender* Spenser entrusted for printing to Hugh Singleton, who a year before had published a tendentious Puritan tract called *The Discovery of a Gaping Gulf* that resulted in the author's, John Stubbs's, having his right hand chopped off. The printer was still in prison. There is more Puritan sentiment and argument in the poem than we see today. Like the young Milton, young Spenser was bold, cheered on by Harvey, who held him in thrall for some time.

Harvey's dogmatic revulsion from the medieval made him hostile to Spenser's eventual plans for *The Fairie Queene*. He wanted his protégé to write English in classical meters, and they debated the adaptability of Latin and Greek prosodies to English. Spenser obligingly experimented, but Harvey's arguments were to have more, though not a radical, effect on Sir Philip Sidney.

In *The Shepheardes Calender* Spenser tried to make pastoral a more serious mode. He mingled the pastoral of *Colin Clout* (from Skelton) and *Piers Plowman* (from Langland) with Arcadian and English flora and fauna. Formal "pastoral" diction he laced with rustic terms and archaisms. His first notable poem, it consists of twelve eclogues that exploit thirteen different meters and forms. Colin Clout, Spenser's bucolic self, speaks the first and last eclogues lamenting frustrated pastoral love. The other ten poems are dialogues with recognizable characters. Hobbinol, for example, is Harvey. One poem celebrates Eliza, the queen. Four are about love, four are religious and moral allegory in pastoral disguise, one is an elegiac lament, and one, "October," is devoted to a perennial theme: the low regard and reward for the art (and artist) of poetry. The swain called Cuddie exclaims:

> They han the pleasure, I a slender price;
> I beat the bush, the birds to them do fly:
> What good thereof to Cuddie can arise?

His friend Piers consoles him: "Cuddie, the praise is better than the price." But it never feels that way (and the publisher is usually blamed).

Spenser's art takes shape here in an archaic diction and vividly representative images and metaphors. Though in a "low style," the eclogues do not sound *spoken*. The rusticity is posed, the aphoristic truths rehearsed:

> To kirk the nar, from God more far,   the nearer to church
>   Has been an old-said saw,
> And he, that strives to touch a star
>   Oft stumbles at a straw.

Such neat commonplaces he may have gleaned from his days in Burnley. He has glimpsed the natural world through the veil of literary pastoral, and the verse sometimes sees with amazing clarity: "Keeping your beasts in the budded broom" is a line Keats must have valued, or this:

See'st how brag yond bullock bears,   boastfully
So smirk, so smooth, his prickèd ears?   neat
His horns bene as broad as rainbow bent,
His dewlap as lithe as lass of Kent.

We will not respond to the poem with the surprise, delight and pride
of its first readers. Here they discovered the new poetry in English,
unprecedented and fully fledged. E.K. (whoever he was) provided notes
which drew attention to every detail of rhetoric exploited with a delib-
erate intent. E.K. reveals not only what Spenser wants him to say but
how a particularly alert Elizabethan might have read, construed, or even
deconstructed, the poem, by means of an understanding of its rhetorical
elements, so judiciously deployed.

Harvey secured Spenser a place in the Earl of Leicester's household.
He was there when *The Shepheardes Calender* was published in 1579, a
momentous year for our literature because the new poetry is established.
It appeared anonymously, but Spenser was generally known to be the
author. He met Sir Edward Dyer (author of "My mind to me a king-
dom is") and befriended Sir Philip Sidney, to whom the *Calender* is
dedicated. Indeed the poem exemplifies the rules and qualities that Sid-
ney and his circle had been advocating. Spenser was original and brave.
He learned from every source, yet copied hardly at all. From the classics
he sought legitimacy, transposing their terms to his setting and situation
rather than merely translating them.

Aubrey gives an amusing, if not dependable, account of Spenser pay-
ing court to the noblest of the knight poets. He was at work on *The
Faerie Queene* and brought Sir Philip Sidney a copy. Sidney was busy
and did not peruse it immediately. Spenser departed tetchily. When
Sidney did begin to read, he was impressed and called the poet back,
"mightily caressed him, and ordered his servant to give him so many
pounds in gold . . ."

With Sidney, Spenser formed a literary club called the Areopagus,
devoted to naturalizing classical meters in English. Was this the first
English poetry society, devoted to promoting a movement? It chose an
aloof name: the Areopagus is the hill of Mars in Athens, near the Acropo-
lis, where the "Upper Council," the city's supreme judiciary, convened.

In 1580 Spenser was appointed secretary to Lord Grey of Wilton,
new Lord Deputy of Ireland, and left old friends for Ireland, where he
made new ones, including Sir Walter Ralegh. He may have seen action
during the Desmond Rebellion (though it is hard to imagine him as a
soldier), and in 1586 was awarded as one of the "undertakers" an estate
including the ruined castle of Kilcolman in County Cork, with 3,000
acres of land. The first poem he wrote there was prompted by Sir Philip

Sidney's death: his fine elegy "Astrophel" (1586), with its circular rhetoric and repetitions. And there he prepared *The Faerie Queene* for press. Ralegh encouraged him to return to England and publish the first three books of his epic.

In Ireland he saw some brutal sights, including "the execution of a notable traitor at Limerick, called Morrogh O'Brien. I saw an old woman which was his foster-mother take up his head whilst he was quartered, and sucked up all the blood running thereout, saying that the earth was not worthy to drink it; and therewith also steeped her face and breast and torn hair, crying and shrieking out most terribly." His matter-of-factness implies, not so much that he was unmoved, as that the scene was one among many extreme scenes.

In 1589 Spenser was in London to entrust the text to the printer. Ralegh, in favor with the queen, presented him at court and she gave him a £50 pension. By the time the first part of the epic appeared in 1590, the Earl of Essex had succeeded the late Earl of Leicester as Spenser's patron. The poet reluctantly returned to Kilcolman in 1591. He wrote *Colin Clouts Come Home Againe* and dedicated it to Ralegh (1591, published 1595). In 1594, to lessen his solitude, he married Elizabeth Boyle. His great "Epithalamion" (1595) followed, and the eighty-eight sonnets in the *Amoretti* may be attributable to the same sacrament. In 1596 he completed the next chunk of *The Fairie Queene* and it was published in 1597. The following year his castle at Kilcolman was burned in the insurrection. His youngest child perished in the fire and his work-in-progress on *The Faerie Queene* burned too. It's possible that Spenser completed, or nearly completed, the last six books of his poem. He returned to London and died destitute in 1599. He was buried at the Earl of Essex's expense and lies near Chaucer in Westminster Abbey.

Beside the sonnets of Sidney and Shakespeare, Spenser's *Amoretti* appear, for all their accomplishment, uninspired. The best is sonnet LXXV, "One day I wrote her name upon the strand." But his praise of marriage and the courtly sentiment—lacking the ambivalent vigor of *The Shepheardes Calender*—seldom rises above convention. Courtly sentiment is best expressed in *The Faerie Queene* itself. One sonnet admits a personal note, referring to the epic and to his exhaustion:

> After so long a race as I have run
> Through Faeryland, which those six books compile,
> Give leave to rest me being half foredone,   finished
> And gather to myself new breath awhile.

The "Epithalamion" is superior in conception and execution. Following in the tradition of classical marriage odes, it displays in pure form that idealized sensuality which animates parts of *The Faerie Queene*, and like the epic is meticulous in organization, taking the twenty-four hours of the wedding day. A stanza of introduction is followed by ten stanzas in which the procession gathers and leads the bride in to the ceremony. The two central stanzas tell of the ceremony itself, then a group of ten more stanzas brings home the bride and beds her, and a final stanza rounds out the whole. Within this horological architecture are other symmetries: the words "day" and "night" are repeatedly counterbalanced as part of the device. It might seem to us a cold thing, to structure a love and marriage poem so deliberately; yet part of the passion of an Elizabethan poem is a passion of intelligence; deep feeling elicits the deepest art of which he is capable. Much of the pleasure a poet seeks to impart to a reader is of an intellectual kind. Whether or not we are aware of structural features, we cannot but respond to the declared feeling. Eager for the bridal night, the poet exclaim:

> How slowly does sad Time his feathers move!
> Haste thee, O fairest planet, to thy home,
> Within the western foam.

When in Book Four of his epic he came to adapt Lucretius's invocation to Venus from *De Rerum Natura*, it was with this refined passion that his chorus of lovers is made to exclaim:

> Great God of men and women, queen of the ayre,
> Mother of laughter, and welspring of bliss,
> O grant that of my love at last I may not miss!

The "Prothalamion" (1596), written for the marriage of others, is less intense. But its refrain, which echoes strongly in Eliot's *The Waste Land*, "Sweet Thames! run softly, till I end my song," and the control of rhythm over long sentences in a complex stanza form, make it unforgettable in its virtuosity. Coleridge enjoins us to "mark the swanlike movement of his exquisite Prothalamion. His attention to metre and rhythm is sometimes so extremely minute as to be painful even to my ear, and you know how highly I prize good versification."

Spenser follows, as Milton was to do, the Virgilian pattern for becoming a Great Poet. First you write your eclogues, then your georgic, then your epic. In his patriotic and moral epic *The Faerie Queene* he translates qualities of *The Shepheardes Calender* into a "high style" where they acquire an enhanced allegorical dimension. He retains sensuous directness, for instance in the catalogue of trees in the first canto of Book One, especially:

The Eugh, obedient to the bender's will: yew
The Birch for shaftes; the Sallow for the mill;   arrows; shrub willow
The Mirrhe sweet-bleeding in the bitter
    wound.

The first three books of *The Faerie Queene* are prefaced with an
explanatory letter to Ralegh. Of the projected twelve books, the first
six and fragments of the seventh, the "Mutability Cantos" from the
Legend of Constance, survive. Spenser declares that his purpose is
moral: "to fashion a gentleman or noble person in virtuous and noble
discipline." Milton took Spenser at his word, presenting him as a moral
teacher in the *Areopagitica*. Nineteenth-century admirers lost sight of
the moral teaching, disregarded the system of allegory and appreciated
the poem's "beauty." Coleridge wrote: "The whole of the *Faerie Queene*
is an almost continued instance of beauty." This is true, but incomplete.
It became the general view, and the poem was emancipated from its
moral and historical purpose. The morality was archaic, the allegory
obscure; the poem survived by virtue of images, techniques and inci-
dents, not its intentions: in short, by virtue of its poetry, not its instru-
mental aim.

Borrowing from Tasso's discourses on epic poetry and from Ariosto,
in his prefatory letter Spenser distinguishes between the historian's and
the poet's perspectives: "An historiographer discourseth of affairs
orderly as they were done . . . but a poet thrusteth into the midst, even
where it most concerneth him, and there recoursing to the things
forepast, and divining the things to come, maketh a pleasing analysis of
all . . . The beginning therefore of my history, if it were to be told by an
historiographer should be by the twelfth book, which is the last; where
I devise that the Faery Queene kept her annual feast twelve days; upon
which twelve several days, the occasions of the twelve several adventures
happened, which, being undertaken by the twelve several knights, are in
these twelve books severally handled and discovered." There follows a
description of how the completed poem would have worked. The
description does not fit the poem we have, and of course the twelfth, key
book was burned.

"A gentle Knight was pricking on the plain," the poem starts. Book
One belongs to the Red Cross Knight, who defends Una from
Archimago and Duessa, or, in the allegory, Anglicanism defends truth.
Sir Guyon (temperance) destroys the Bower of Bliss in Book Two. Book
Three is dominated by Britomart and Belphoebe (chastity); in Book
Four Triamond and Cambell exemplify friendship, and we encounter
Scudamour and Amoret. Artegall, knight of justice, appears in Book

Five, and Spenser devotes much of his allegory to events in recent English history. Sir Calidore, in Book Six, embodies courtesy.

The projected twelve books would have contained twelve cantos each, presenting twelve virtues and twelve exemplary knights. Prince Arthur, who symbolizes magnificence, the perfection of all the virtues, sets out after a vision to seek the Faerie Queene (Elizabeth, variously figured by Belphoebe, Gloriana, Mercilla and others). Arthur is to seek her for twelve days, encountering each day one of her knights and assisting each to triumph. The poem was to end in Arthur's marriage to Gloriana (Glory). Spenser hoped by the device of Arthur to give the poem unity, without forfeiting the freedom to develop each romantic book as a largely self-contained unit.

So mechanical a conception of form and allegory, arbitrarily conceived, not rising out of an integrating action, accounts for most of the difficulties. In part the allegory derives from legend and convention; in part it is devised to shadow Spenser's ideas. It works like a code, while traditional allegory functions at best as an accessible common language based on accepted "readings" of accepted figures. Spenser, with a humanist education, returned to the Middle Ages for his form, but he took only part of what he found there, leaving behind necessary substance. And he only partly archaized his language, giving it an antique patina. His allegory is overcharged with moral and conventional elements. Britomart is not only chastity: she stands for aspects of the queen, and for the religious figure of St. Catherine. Artegall recalls Achilles in action and dress, if not temperament. Arthur contains some of Aeneas, Guyon some of Odysseus. These literary dimensions are apposite up to a point, but they complicate figures who lose rather than gain expressive value when they come to act.

Spenser "characterizes" allegorical figures in varying degrees. Some are cardboard, only just two-dimensional, such as "Despair." More particularized, often with emblematic names—"Sansfoy" and his brothers, for example—are those who act, but in a limited area. Amoret belongs to a more differentiated category, type more than figure; recognizable flesh on stylized bones. Central to the poem are the vital actors representing virtues: developed as characters, their virtues are vulnerable. When such almost-real representations move among static figures of allegory, dramatic interest is low. The moments of tension in the poem are not when a dragon appears or a battle is fought, but the seductions in which human motive and action are recognizable. A special moment is when Paridell woos the miser's wife with his eyes, speaking not a word.

Spenser's condensed history of the British kings in Book Two is expository verse of a high order. He moralizes the story of King Leyr (Lear) even as he tells it:

> But true it is that, when the oil is spent,
> The light goes out, the weeke is thrown away: wick
> So, when he had resign'd his regiment,
> His daughter gan despise his drouping day,   declining
> And weary wax of his continual stay.

This is psychology on a par with Gower's, not Chaucer's; but the verse moves with transparent ease.

For this poem Spenser invented his own "Spenserian Stanza," comprising eight iambic pentameter lines and a final hexameter, rhyming a-b-a-b-b-c-b-c-c. It is slow-moving, the hexameter giving a finality to each stanza. Compared with the natural expressive flow of Chaucer's stanzas in *Troilus and Crisyede*, with its central climax, Spenser's dignified, ceremonial measure retards the narrative. It works best in description or where the poet expresses motion rather than action. A rich passage occurs in the fourth canto of Book Three, where Cymoënt speeds over the sea to the side of wounded Marinell:

> Great Neptune stoode amazèd at their sight,
> Whiles on his broad round back they softly slid,
> And eke him self mournd at their mournful plight,   even
> Yet wist not what their wailing meant; yet did,   knew
> For great compassion of their sorrow, bid
> His mighty waters to them buxom bee:
> Eftsoons the roaring billows still abid,
> And all the grisly monsters of the sea
> Stood gaping at their gate, and wondered them to
>   see.

> A team of dolphins rangèd in aray
> Drew the smooth charett of sad Cymoënt: chariot
> They were all taught by Triton to obay
> To the long raynes at her commandement:
> As swifte as swallows on the waves they went,
> That their broad flaggy fins no foam did rear,
> No bubbling rondell they behind them sent.
> The rest, of other fishes drawen were,
> Which with their finny oars the swelling sea did
>   shear.

By contrast, action is magnified and slowed down; the procession is impressive rather than exciting.

We miss "human interest" in Spenser's mature work. And the poetry works by extension rather than concentration, a medieval feature he gets from Gower, Lydgate and Hoccleve. One must take *The Faerie Queene* in large doses: the impact is cumulative. The best effects are so much a part of the overall verbal context that they do not detach as aphorism or vivid image.

The Spenserian tradition includes Milton, Keats, Byron, Tennyson, Hardy and others. But his spell is now broken. He has been called a poets' poet. In the latter half of this century he has become an academic's and a theorist's poet. Numerologists find him especially satisfying (one need only note how often the word "twelve" has appeared above). His work does not merit so reductive a fate. For ease and lucidity of language over long stretches of narrative he has no superior but Chaucer. Ignorance of Spenser is ignorance of a fountainhead of English poetry.

Aubrey records a final piece of fascinating misinformation—or is it? Are the last books of *The Faerie Queene* one day to be discovered? "Lately, at the college,"—Pembroke Hall—"takeing-downe the Wainscot of his chamber, they found an abundance of Cards, with stanzas of *The Faerie Queene* written on them."

"Of love, and love, and love"

SIR WALTER RALEGH, SIR PHILIP SIDNEY, MARY SIDNEY
COUNTESS OF PEMBROKE, QUEEN ELIZABETH I

It's chiefly Sir Walter Ralegh, whose year of birth is supposedly 1552 (like Spenser's), who tempts us to hope that great poems may be rediscovered centuries after they vanish. Of all the sixteenth-century poets' lives his is the most intriguing in its adventures and mishaps. If anyone understood the wheel of fortune, it was this Edmund Hillary of social and political climbing, this indomitable adventurer, lover and explorer.

"He was a tall, handsome and bold man; but his *naeve* [. . .] was that he was damnable proud," Aubrey tells us. Later he embellishes "handsome" in ways that make us wonder at Queen Elizabeth's taste: "He had a most remarkable aspect, an exceeding high forehead, long-faced and sour eie-lidded, a kind of pigge-eie. His Beard turned up naturally." He kept his Devonshire burr and had a small voice. In his age the effortlessly aristocratic Sidney was loved and revered; Ralegh was feared and despised by all but his close circle. Both were legends alive—and dead. Sidney was born with the silver spoon, but Ralegh's spoon was merely plated. He had to make his way by talent, wit, chicanery and strength.

Born in East Budleigh, Devon, Ralegh was the son of a not particularly distinguished gentleman. In his midteens he went up to Oriel College, Oxford, and then to the Middle Temple. Anthony à Wood reports that he was "worthily esteemed" there, and we know that Francis Bacon, his friend, walked arm in arm with him around the gardens of Gray's Inn. By 1576 he was writing verse.

His life as a soldier included service with the Huguenots in the French wars of religion. He was active in Ireland and his name is associated particularly with Smerwick and Youghal and the suppression of Irish resistance. In 1582, an army officer aged thirty, he came home from Ireland. Already known at court, instantly he climbed the north face of royal favor. Sir John Harrington recalls Elizabeth in a letter: "When she smiled, it was pure sun-shine, that every one did choose to bask in, if they could; but anon came a storm from a sudden gathering of clouds, and the thunder fell in wondrous manner on all alike." Ralegh experienced both weathers. Did he really spread a cloak over a puddle for her? He became her favorite because he exceeded all the other courtiers in the inventiveness and extravagance of his courtesies. He understood the codes of sentiment to which she responded and sported her favors in all the right ways. It cannot have been easy. Spenser in *Colin Clouts Come Home Againe* reflects on the hollowness of court love, so different from the courtly love of Chaucer:

> For all the walls and windows there are writ,
> All full of love, and love, and love my dear,
> And all their talk and study is of it.
> Ne any there doth brave or valiant seem,
> Unless that some gay mistress' badge he bears:
> Ne any one himself doth aught esteem,
> Unless he swim in love up to the ears.

Ralegh enjoyed such play, having the parts for it more than Spenser did. He became a knight in 1584, was appointed captain of the guard in 1587, and received other preferments. The queen granted him a monopoly in connection with wine trading and a patent to conquer and colonize in her name. For a decade he was generally in favor. Ralegh re-sealed her affection when he gave her *Ocean's Love to Cynthia*, and when he presented to her Edmund Spenser with the first three books of *The Faerie Queene*. Ralegh wore Elizabeth's favors ostentatiously and did not prepare for, though he prepared, his fall.

He fell because he got Elizabeth Throckmorton pregnant. She was the queen's maid of honor. He married her secretly in 1592 and that was that. After a spell in the Tower he was released to live in Sherborne, Dorset. Aubrey, who knew the places Ralegh lived, evokes the splendors both of his London residence Durham House on the Thames and of Sherborne Castle. His provincial exile was not long. He served the queen again in naval action against Spain and later in his apparently unsuccessful voyage of exploration to Guiana. It did have some long-term consequences: the potato returned with him, and, Aubrey says, "Sir Walter was the first that brought Tobacco into England and into fashion." This is another of Aubrey's embroideries: it was John Hawkins (initiator of the slave trade between Sierra Leone and Hispaniola) who introduced tobacco into England in 1565, though Ralegh may have made it fashionable. As early as 6 December 1492 Europeans were raking their lungs with New World smoke: Columbus landed in Hispaniola (Quisqueya) and Luis de Torres y Rodrigo first records smoking tobacco (describing natives who "drink smoke"). Rodrigo de Jerez was the first European to take up the habit. More credible is Aubrey's statement that Ralegh took a trunk of books on his travels to study and that he was a "chymist" (an alchemist). "He was no Slug; without doubt he had a wonderful waking spirit, and a great judgment to guide it."

The queen—"a Lady whom Time had surprised"—died in 1603. The accession of James VI of Scotland (James I of England) did not enhance Ralegh's fortunes. The poet made James "laugh so that he was ready to beshitt his Briggs" at some coarse verses, but the suspicious new monarch was not long beguiled. He worked quickly: Ralegh was tried for treason, condemned to death, reprieved and detained in the Tower for thirteen years. In 1615 the king released him unpardoned to pursue the royal interest in further exploration of Guiana, where Ralegh claimed to have discovered a gold mine. He went under impossible conditions and lost his son on the expedition. He returned broken and dying to a pitiless king, who—urged on by his relative the Spanish king, who "proved" the gold mine was a fabrication—in 1618 had him beheaded (ostensibly still on grounds of treason) for what he'd done long before in the struggle against Spain. On the scaffold Ralegh revealed his true colors. Aubrey is surely a dependable witness here. "He was an a-christ, not an atheist." He spoke there of and to God, never mentioning Jesus. Even within the supposed symmetries of the Trinity he detected, and directly addressed, the angle at the top.

Ralegh did not entirely die. Izaak Walton in *The Compleat Angler* recalls a wonderful moment some years after his death. In a field (like Wordsworth two centuries later) he beholds "a handsome milk-maid that had not yet attained so much age and wisdom as to load her mind with any fears of many things that will never be, as too many men too often do: but she cast away all care, and sung like a nightingale: her voice was good, and the ditty fitted for it: it was that smooth song which was made by Kit Marlow, now at least fifty years ago: and the milk-maid's mother sung an answer to it, which was made by Sir Walter Ralegh in his younger days." Thus Marlowe's "The Passionate Shepherd" ("Come live with me and be my love") receives a timeless rebuff, the commonplace wisdom of the flesh speaking:

> But time drives the flocks from field to fold,
> When rivers rage and rocks grow cold,
> And Philomel becometh dumb;
> The rest complain of cares to come . . .

> Thy gowns, thy shoes, thy bed of roses,
> Thy cap, thy kirtle, and thy posies,

Soon break, soon wither, soon forgotten,
In folly ripe, in reason rotten.

Thy belt of straw and ivy-buds,
Thy coral clasps and amber studs,
All these in me no means can move
To come to thee and be thy Love . . .

The lines "But Time drives the flocks from field to fold, / When rivers rage and rocks grow cold . . ." release literal weather on Marlowe's ideal landscape and show the cast of Ralegh's imagination. He writes not out of habit but necessity. Satire, parody, elegy, lament and lyric are the product of occasions or experiences that demand expression. He speaks for and as himself. At his trial in 1603 he declared he was "wholly gentleman, wholly soldier." This man wrote the poems.

Gascoigne was his first poetic mentor. His tribute "In Commendation of George Gascoigne's *Steel Glass*" reveals Ralegh's preference for plain style and brusque, masculine utterance. Two sententious lines may have come back to him during his trials and imprisonment: "For whoso reaps renoun above the rest, / With heaps of hate shall surely be opprest." Gascoigne literalizes convention, planting Petrarchan flowers in English soil. Ralegh, first by logic and later in a passion of disappointment, reduced the conventional to the absurd, as in the reply to Marlowe, or distorted and personalized it. His verse, fragmentary, formally flawed, bears the impress of an imagination more agitated and powerful than Gascoigne's. Gascoigne took failure with wry grace. Ralegh had to swallow disappointment after success and endure the punishments of very different monarchs. He has no distinctive style: now he resembles Surrey, now Gascoigne, Sidney or Spenser. He succeeds on their terms, he has no poetic terms of his own. But he has a distinctive voice.

"Epitaph on Sir Philip Sidney" is his first reckonable work. The poem follows roughly the chronology of Sidney's life; it informs, celebrates and laments all at once. It is superior to Surrey's elegies to Wyatt, which, equally sincere, lack the courage to particularize.

Ralegh's sonnet "Farewell to Court" prefigures in its three quatrains the verse form and tone of the *Ocean to Cynthia*. It must have been important to him since in the later "Conceit Begotten of the Eyes" he alludes back to it, and he quotes it outright in the *Ocean*. The original passage is among his best.

As in a country strange without companion,
I only wail the wrong of death's delays,

Whose sweet spring spent, whose summer well nigh done;
Of all which past, the sorrow only stays.

In the *Ocean to Cynthia* he recalls:

Twelve years entire I wasted in this war;
Twelve years of my most happy younger days;
But I in them, and they, now wasted are:
"Of all which past, the sorrow only stays"—

So wrote I once, and my mishap foretold,
My mind still feeling sorrowful success,
Even as before a storm the marble cold
Doth by moist tears tempestuous times express.

The presence of transcending, spiritual love even in the frustration of
worldly love raises some complaints to the level of devotional poetry.
"True love" is not "white nor brown"; she is a form, angel and nymph.
"As you came from the holy land / Of Walsingham," about the Queen
of England, includes the Queen of Heaven. The human queen "likes
not the falling fruit / From the withered tree." The pilgrim has seen her,
the aging poet's true love:

Such an one did I meet, good Sir,
     Such an angelic face,
Who like a queen, like a nymph, did appear
     By her gait, by her grace

The poise of the last line, a semantic surprise anticipated by the repeti-
tive construction Ralegh favors, places him not where C. S. Lewis does,
in an archaic school, but in the company of his metaphysical successors.
In another poem he writes, "She is gone, she is lost, she is found, she is
ever fair": the extra four syllables in his line are inevitable: pressure of
experience overrides prescriptions of form.

But the pressure is not always high, and Ralegh can sometimes bind
a poem together by a specious logic, using "or" and "but" to pretend con-
nection. The underlying principle is contrast or juxtaposition. Disconti-
nuity is only intellectual, since images develop consistently over gaps in
argument. By sequential discontinuity and subversion—deliberate or
inadvertent?—he sometimes defeats his great foe, time, and gains free-
dom within memory. But memory itself embitters the present, history
offers frail consolation: "On Sestus' shore, Leander's late resort, / Hero

hath left no lamp to guide her love." Marlowe was a friend, and Marlowe's poems were deep in his memory.

Among Ralegh's poems are tributes to Spenser's epic (he was dedicatee of the first three books). The sonnet appended to the first part of *The Faerie Queene* out-Spensers Spenser and strikes a beautifully Petrarchan note new to Ralegh, even as it sets Spenser as a "celestial thief" above Petrarch (and Homer).

> Methought I saw the grave where Laura lay,
> Within that temple where the vestal flame
> Was wont to burn, and passing by that way
> To see that buried dust of living fame,
> Whose tomb fair Love and fairer Virtue kept,
> All suddenly I saw the Faerie Queene:
> At whose approach the soul of Petrarch wept;
> And from thenceforth those Graces were not seen,
> For they this Queen attended, in whose stead
> Oblivion laid him down on Laura's hearse.
> Hereat the hardest stones were seen to bleed,
> And groans of buried ghosts the heavens did pierce;
> > Where Homer's spright did tremble all for grief,
> > And cursed th' access of that celestial thief.

Spenser compliments Ralegh more modestly as "the summer's Nightingale," and in *Colin Clouts Come Home Againe* evokes Ralegh fallen from royal grace:

> His song was all a lamentable lay,
> Of great unkindness, and of usage hard,
> Of Cynthia the lady of the sea,
> Which from her presence faultless him debarr'd.

"A lamentable lay" describes those poems reflecting on fortune, ephemerality, fate. Resigned at last, he meditates on the pilgrimage through death toward judgment. "Give me my scallop-shell of quiet," said (doubtfully) to have been written by Ralegh while awaiting execution in the Tower, is penitence in a man so wedded to this world, finding religious hope. "Go, Soul, the body's guest" is less resigned. From the point of death it turns and regards the world. A cumulative, incantatory indictment follows: not argument but an envenomed series of specific condemnations, with a modulated refrain. This is a poem after experience, not after thought.

Say to the court, it glows
  And shines like rotten wood;
Say to the church, it shows
  What's good, and doth no good:
    If church and court reply,
    Then give them both the lie.

Tell potentates, they live
  Acting by others' action,
Not loved unless they give,
  Not strong but by their faction:
    If potentates reply,
    Give potentates the lie.

Shakespeare's Antony and Ralegh have much in common: great gifts, passionate disposition, impulsiveness, influence, great friends and foes. Each is undone in service of a queen.

Poetry was a small part of Ralegh's activity. He took few precautions to preserve his poems. His principal literary undertaking was to write while in the Tower, with what books to hand we do not know, his vast digressive *History of the World*. Ironically, the prose he's remembered for today is letters and miscellaneous works. Even in his own day he found it hard to interest people in his *History*, though it lived after him and touched later writers, most decisively Milton. Aubrey recalls the author's frustration with his readership and his bookseller: "His Booke sold very slowly at first, and the Booke-seller complayned of it, and told him that he should be a loser by it, which put Sir W. into a passion, and sayd that since the world did not understand it, they should not have his second part, which he tooke and threw into the fire, and burnt before his face." Volume one ends with the death of Prince Henry, who would have been his patron had he survived.

Also in the Tower, that gloomy incubator of poetry, he composed— or recomposed—his longest and most ambitious poem, of which "The 21st (and last) Book of the Ocean to Cynthia" survives, together with some twenty lines of the "22nd Book," a fragment of what may have been an essentially autobiographical epic romance. The manuscript was lost until 1860, when it turned up among the Cecil papers at Hatfield House. It was first published in 1870. Apart from this large fragment, fifty-odd other poems survive, about a dozen more doubtfully attributed, and some sixty metrical translations of passages from Latin and Greek authors scattered through the *History*. Ralegh's work, like Wyatt's, was in no useful sense available until the later nineteenth century.

The *Ocean to Cynthia* is not the poem Ralegh presented to the queen: that went missing. Did the queen see through Ralegh's attempt to curry favor, after the "betrayal" of his marriage to her lady-in-waiting, and destroy it? She released him from prison at the end of 1592 less because of a poem than because his expedition returned to England with a rich prize ship—one of the most bullioned of those brought into English ports—and he bought himself out. His restoration to favor was late and partial. Did James discard it when he swept out the palace on taking up residence in London? Our *Ocean* is a sequel of sorts.

Addressed by a lover to his mistress in the figure of the Ocean addressing the Moon, there can be no doubt of the relationship or its occasions. The Moon is the queen, the court, England, whose service commanded Ralegh's entire commitment. Reason says his struggle isn't worth the candle, but it is powerless against his fixed will to serve and "her" cyclic, irresistible influence.

> To seek new worlds for gold, for Praise, for glory,
> To try desire, to try love sever'd far,
> When I was gone, she sent her memory,
> More strong than were ten thousand ships of war.
>
> To call me back . . .

The poem can be read as "modernist" *avant la lettre*; we're tempted to suppose the discontinuities and gaps are deliberate, but the manuscript suggests it was a draft, or—what seems more likely to me—an attempt at recollection or reconstruction, made in prison, to reclaim from memory a text, with no copy taken, given to the queen and now, with the queen, lost.

Something odd is at work, beyond the problematic nature of the manuscript. It is the sounds the poem makes. Ralegh has moved beyond the aphoristic style, pithy and spare, to an elaboration brushed by the wings of Spenser and Petrarch, rich in verbal texture and in metaphor extended sometimes to "metaphysical" lengths. Like other longer poems, it mixes styles and, like some of his short poems, lacks progression. But the trajectory of this poem, and of the work as a whole, traces English poetry's transition from plain to aureate style. When the ax was to fall on his nape, the plain style asserted itself in the most amazing confrontation with death in English verse:

> And this is my eternal plea
> To him that made heaven, earth, and sea:

Seeing my flesh must die so soon,
And want a head to dine next noon,
Just at the stroke, when my veins start and spread,
Set on my soul an everlasting head.
Then am I ready, like a palmer fit,
To tread those blest paths which before I writ.

Ralegh was flesh and blood, no doubt about it.

But Sir Philip Sidney, to judge from the purity of his diction, the conventionality of his writing, the elevation of his sentiment, was pure spirit. "Reason, look to thyself! I serve a goddess." He is the first major English poet-critic, a model of correctness, clarity and measure. A man with enviable social advantages, he put them to full use and excelled in all he did. He has been portrayed as the most unambiguously attractive English writer, a Renaissance *uomo universale* without Surrey's ambition or Ralegh's hubris. He was all of a piece, a bit brittle, with a carefully acquired polish, but noble and consistent in thought and action. Fulke Greville—a lifelong friend, editor of the 1590 *Arcadia*, and his first biographer—called him "the wonder of our age" in his "Epitaph."

Salute the stones, that keep the limbs, that held so good a mind.

Sidney, the hope and the patron of English poetry, died at the age of thirty-two, in 1586, of wounds received at Zutphen in the Netherlands campaign.

Most of his contemporaries elegized him. Ralegh retells the life:

A king gave thee thy name; a kingly mind,
That God thee gave, who found it now too dear
For this base world, and hath resumed it near,
To sit in skies, and sort with powers divine.

Kent thy birth-days, Oxford held thy youth;
The heavens made haste, and stay'd nor years nor time,
The fruits of age grew ripe in thy first prime;
Thy will, thy words; thy words the seals of truth.

Great gifts and wisdom rare employ'd thee thence,
To treat from kings with those more great than kings . . .

Ralegh's first stanza calls Sidney "Scipio, Cicero, and Petrarch of our time." On the tombstone of one of his contemporaries appear the words "friend of Sir Philip Sidney." It was a sufficient distinction for the eternal record.

He was born in 1554 at Penshurst Place, Kent, the estate Ben Jonson celebrated in "To Penshurst." The king who gave him a name was Philip of Spain, his godfather. He entered Shrewsbury School, Shropshire, on the same day as Fulke Greville. From there he went up to Christ Church, Oxford, but left on account of the plague. He spent time at Elizabeth's court, writing a masque in her honor in 1578 to mark her visit to Wanstead—with modest music, recorders and cornets—and went on missions to the Continent. He spent time as well with his beloved sister Mary, later Countess of Pembroke, in Wiltshire. In every page of his life, he seems to have lived up to the prescriptions and advice of Castiglione's influential textbook *The Courtier*, even down to the matter of writing verse—not in the expectation of becoming a great writer but because "at the least wise he shall receive so much profit, that by that exercise he shall be able to give his judgement on other men's doings." So too he should know music and painting.

His travels began early. At the age of eighteen he was in Paris during the St. Bartholomew's Day Massacre. He traveled on to Germany and to Italy, where at Padua his portrait was painted by Veronese. He also visited Ireland and Wales with his father, deputy of Ireland and president of Wales, and ably defended his conduct of Irish policy. He received from Spenser the dedication of *The Shepheardes Calender*, and from Richard Hakluyt the dedication of the *Voyages*. In 1580 he briefly forfeited the queen's favor by opposing her proposed marriage to the Duke of Anjou. That cloud past, he served as an MP, was knighted in 1582, and in 1583 married the daughter of Sir Francis Walsingham. He made preparations to accompany Ralegh and Drake to the West Indies in 1585, but he was sent instead to the Netherlands, where in 1586 he died. As he lay wounded he called for music, "especially that song which himself had entitled *La cuisse rompue*." His was a musical family.

Another book dedicated to Sidney was Stephen Gosson's famous attack on writers, *The School of Abuse, Containing a Pleasant Invective against Poets, Pipers, Players, Jesters, and such like Caterpillars of a Commonwealth* (1579). The young poet did not find it "pleasant" and in reply composed his *Apology for* (later *Defence of*) *Poesy* (probably 1581, published 1595). Sidney doesn't refute Gosson with invective but writes an urbane, reasoned argument. Without originality of thought but with clarity he distills the literary criticism of the Italian Renaissance. In the words of J. E. Spingarn, "so thoroughly is it imbued with this spirit, that no other work, Italian, French, or English, can be said to give so complete and so noble a conception of the temper and principles of

Renaissance criticism." Sidney's original sources were the critical treatises of Minturno and Scaliger. What his essay lacks in novelty it makes up for in conviction, unity of feeling and elegance of style.

For Sidney poetry is the first art, the light bearer. Following Aristotle (as mediated through his disciples) he defines art as imitation, mimesis: poetry is "a speaking picture" whose end is "to teach and delight." Sidney's aesthetic is inseparable from his general view of life. The idea of imitation was crucial. The artist is a second creator producing a second nature. He imitates the ideal, showing what may or should be rather than merely copying what is. This moral art frees the will from the trammels of nature, draws it to virtue. The astronomer looks for stars and sees only stars, the geometer and the arithmetician look for shapes and numbers and find shapes and numbers. Musicians, too, are constrained by their discipline and inclination. The natural philosopher and the moral philosopher teach according to their subjects, the lawyer follows his books and precedents and the historian is bound by what men have done. The grammarian "speaketh only of the rules of speech," and the rhetorician and logician are similarly trammeled. The metaphysician too must "build upon the depth of nature." Only the poet is free to marry precept and example, "disdaining to be tied to any such subjection, lifted up with the vigour of his own invention." He "doth grow in effect another nature, as the Heroes, Demigods, Cyclopes, Chimeras, Furies, and such like: so as he goeth hand in hand with nature, not enclosed within the narrow warrant of her gifts, but freely, ranging only within the zodiac of his own wit." Where philosopher, historian and the others address the learned, the poet addresses all men.

The liberality of Sidney's sense of poetry emerges in passage after passage, but chiefly when he reflects on the purpose of the art: "this purifying of wit—this enriching of memory, enabling of judgment, and enlarging of conceit—which commonly we call learning . . . the final end is to draw us to as high a perfection as our degenerate souls, made worse by their clayey lodgings, can be capable of." The poet is "the least liar" among writers: "He nothing affirms, and therefore never lieth. For, as I take it, to lie is to affirm that to be true which is false." The poet has thus a boundless freedom to invent and the sanction of inspiration.

The *Defence* remains a living text. It makes a case now seldom heard, and the more interesting for that reason. Sidney knows that the poetic art is unique, enfranchising, and at the same time limited if not limiting. Nature's "world is brazen, the poet only delivers a golden." So in *Astrophel and Stella*, when the Muse—echoing Petrarch—says, "Look in thy heart and write," or when Sidney criticizes in other poets "a want of inward touch," he is not after vulnerable candor or breaches of convention, but a creative power that animates an imaginative world, different from this world but consistent with it and, in that specialized Platonic sense, "real." Why, one is tempted to ask, this insistence on a wholly autonomous world for poetry, a world parallel to the real world, with its own laws, patterns and values? The reply to Gosson is more than a justification of poetry. It is a justification of the freedom of language, exploration and concern that poetry might enable. The strategy Sidney adopts, which is not to answer the attack but to advocate "in parallel," is a rhetorical approach rarely used. In recent years Eavan Boland, trying within Irish poetry to clear a female space, employs the same kind of unaggressive, reasonable and reasoned strategy. It is hard to answer because it adjusts the counters of argument in an unexpected way.

A century after Sidney's death Aubrey apostrophizes him thus: "Sir Philip Sydney, Knight, whose Fame shall never dye, whilest Poetrie lives, was the most accomplished Cavalier of his time. He was not only an excellent witt, but extremely beautiful: he much resembled his sister, but his Haire was not red, but a little inclining, viz. a darke ambor colour. If I were to find a fault in it, methinkes 'tis not masculine enough; yett he was a person of great courage." There is a hint of ambivalence in "not masculine enough." Later in his brief life of Sir Philip's sister Mary, the incomparable translator of the Psalms and (after Queen Elizabeth, who mastered four languages, translated Boethius, and passed her time in prison and in court with making verses) the first noticeable English woman poet, he lets certain real or tittle-tattle cats out of the bag. As John Lyly said in quite another context, "Appion, raising Homer from Hell, demanded only who was his father; we, calling Alexander from his grave, seek only who was his love."

Certainly Sidney today attracts interest, not for what his poetry and fictional prose say, but for what they don't quite say, what they imply, what they withhold even as they twitch the curtain over it. And for what his too-celebrated life does not disclose. We might do worse than start with his sister, whose saintly reputation as a translator of the Psalms is perhaps as partial as her brother's knightly fame. Mary Herbert, Countess of Pembroke (1561–1621), was raised at Ludlow Castle, where Milton's *Comus* was first performed a century later. Her father, Sir Henry Sidney, was president of Wales. She was well educated (Latin, Greek, Hebrew) and loved learning and learned people. Philip was her constant companion in her early years. Queen Elizabeth made her a member of the royal household in 1575 and she accompanied the sovereign on progresses. That same year she became the third wife of Henry, Earl of Pembroke. The Earl of Leicester (then in favor) advanced part of her dowry, since her father was not well heeled at the time. It was she who proposed *The Old Arcadia* to Philip, who then revised and added to it as the never completed *Arcadia*, instructing on his death—as Virgil did with the *Aeneid*—that his friends should destroy it. His friends were no more obedient than Virgil's. In dedicating the first text to Mary he recalls how he wrote it at her house in Wilton, "in loose sheets of paper, most of it in your presence, and the rest by sheets sent unto you as fast as they were done." Not a collaboration, but a creative intimacy as close as that between Dorothy and William Wordsworth. Her *annus horribilis* was 1586: her mother, father and brother died in that year. Piously, she followed up Philip's projects (including the psalter and *Arcadia*) and became, as he had been, patron of various poets, including Spenser, Samuel Daniel, Nicholas Breton, Thomas Nashe, Donne and Jonson. Her version of Psalm 57 begins:

> Thy mercy, Lord, Lord now thy mercy show,
>> On thee I lie
>> To thee I fly;
> Hide me, hive me as thine own,
>> Till these blasts be overblown,
> Which now do fiercely blow.

The very movement of her Psalms can be heard in the mature work of George Herbert.

There is no reason to *believe* Aubrey, but it is hard to resist listening to him. When Mary was engaged to Pembroke, we're told, the earl's father feared she would "horne his sonne" and urged the earl to keep her in the country. Aubrey goes the full length of slander: it may be that Philip and Mary were closer than brother and sister ought to be and that "Philip Earle of Pembroke" was *their* issue. "She was a beautifull Ladie and had an excellent witt, and she had the best breeding that that age could afford. Shee had a pritty sharpe-ovall face. Her haire was of a reddish yellowe." She liked in spring to watch the stallions mounting the mares ("She was very salacious"). Having watched the horses she would horse about herself. "One of her great Gallants was Crooke-back't Cecill, Earl of Salisbury."

"In her time, Wilton House was like a College, there were so many learned and ingeniose persons. She was the greatest Patronesse of witt and learning of any Lady in her time." Alchemy was one of her enthusiasms: her resident adviser was Adrian Gilbert, Sir Walter Ralegh's half-brother. It was a kind of proto-Bloomsbury.

In place of a saintly, noble brother and sister we have an image of talented individuals in love with life, with one another; people who under the excessive clothing of the day had bodies with the cravings and needs that all but saintly bodies can't avoid. It is not hard to believe this of Skelton, or Wyatt, or Gascoigne, or Ralegh. But *Sidney*? Like Surrey before him, he seems above all that. The seeming comes from the hagiography—as patron and friend he was revered—and from the poems, which are fictions, in contrast to Ralegh's, which wear historical occasions on their sleeves even when most conventional. The sentiments are not real, or are not necessarily those expressed. Something is missing in Sidney's poems. Is this absence what the poems are about? Or are they politenesses, accomplishments like horsemanship or fencing or singing or playing the spinet? Or have they if not attestable occasions, then personal motives? *The Old Arcadia* exists, we suppose, to entertain: Mary proposed it and he wrote it. But what did he write? A complicated tale of strange ambivalences, sexual and emotional confusions, "happily" resolved but still puzzling. In this century, they caught the eye of Thom Gunn. Early in his career, fascinated by Elizabethan and Jacobean poets and not yet able to inscribe his homosexuality openly in his poetry, he begins to pick at the idyllic tapestry in "A Mirror for Poets," its title echoing *A Mirror for Magistrates*, where against the sordid, violent reality of Elizabethan England he evokes "Arcadia, a fruitful permanent land":

> The faint and stumbling crowds were dim to sight
> Who had no time for pity or for terror:
> Here moved the Forms, flooding like moonlight,
> In which the act or thought perceived its error.
> The hustling details, calmed and relevant.
> Here mankind might behold its whole extent.
>
> Here in a cave the Paphlagonian King
> Crouched, waiting for his greater counterpart
> Who one remove from likelihood may seem,
> But several closer to the human heart.
> In exile from dimension, change by storm,
> Here his huge magnanimity was born.

It's only within the stabilities of a fiction, set apart from a world of political, religious and moral custom, that characters, themselves fictional, are free to enact instinctive relationships and desires. But even there constraints are beamed in from the social world. In Elizabethan times—how different the Jacobean age, before the theaters were closed!—fiction, whatever the complications of sexual desire and impulse, had to end by affirming the norm. If a man desires a youth, that youth must be a girl disguised or have a twin sister who elicits the same response from the man when she's produced in the nick of time. We're given complications—real complications traced through fiction— and we're given a fictional resolution, real in terms of the environing culture.

It would be foolish to suggest that Sidney was homosexual: the cate- gory is only defined in the latter half of the nineteenth century. There were in Sidney's time specific sexual acts proscribed, principally sodomy, and effeminacy was satirized, but close relations between men were commonplace, and it was not considered disreputable for a man to praise the physical charm of another or of a youth. A social stigma might attach to effeminacy and a moral and legal stigma to "disclosure," and in the seventeenth century the stigmas became more acute. But Marlowe in his translations of Ovid, in *Hero and Leander* and the plays, Shakespeare in his *Sonnets* and some of the plays, Donne in his *Holy Sonnets* and other writers seem to accept (without in-your-face empha- sis) elements in their nature or in the nature of their characters that were to become attenuated or inexpressible later on. They find ways of saying that are not confessional or penitential or hortatory. They weave the subject in among others, and they resolve it into an unexceptionable dominant narrative.

The love that dared not speak its name could only not speak it once it had been named. Unnamed it was ambiguously privileged. "The one salient fact about homosexuality in early modern England, as in early modern Europe generally, is the disparity that separates the extreme punishments prescribed by law and the apparent tolerance, even positive valuation, of homoerotic desire in the visual arts, in literature, and ... in the political power structure," states Bruce R. Smith, in *Homosexual Desire in Shakespeare's England*. "What are we to make of a culture that could consume popular prints of Apollo embracing Hyacinth and yet could order hanging for men who acted on the very feelings that inspire that embrace?"

Weaving a subject in was perhaps a less compromising task for writ- ers of the "newer" writing classes than for those who breathed the scented air of the court. A knight, still habituated to courtly convention and aspiring within its confines, would be less keen, one suspects, to write "Was it the proud full sail of his great verse" or others of Shake- speare's vulnerable sonnets, assuming his desire inclined that way, than one of Sidney's plaintive, almost bodiless poems of desire or rejection. The very position of Sidney in the public scheme of things checked his pen. No matter how private, how personal, a poem recited or written or printed is a public act. He could read the work of friends and protégés, talk and carouse, but his own written record was prepared with caution. However cautious he was, he was a man of integrity: his concerns emerge in prose as part of larger concerns, and can be sensed elsewhere in his writing.

If, in Ford's Spacious Age, "The art of letters had become essentially a matter of movements rather than one of solitary literary figures," excepting of course Shakespeare (though he too is a collaborator and in some of his works a collaboration), poets didn't earn a living *as* poets, unless they had a patron. "There was as yet no publishing system to make this possible"—booksellers were working at it but needed a sufficient market before they could remunerate poets—"and when finally the stationer (a publisher-cum-bookseller) set up shop, no copyright law at first protected the author. A poem was not a physical object of agreed value, liable to be stolen in the usual sense. Unless the author could prove theft of a manuscript book of poems (an obvious felony, because vellum had value, and copyists' fees were high), he had no cause for complaint if someone memorised and printed his poems." Part of the importance of Elizabethan and Jacobean dedications to noble and powerful people resided in this: they were symbols of security, demonstrating endorsement and connection, proving the writer was not a hack and suggesting the possibility of protection.

Tottel set a fashion for anthologies. He was canny: he knew that the printer and bookseller, not the poet, *could* profit; after the Charter of 1566 to the Stationers' Company (granted as a means for effecting censorship as dissent was spread by print), the bookseller, not the poet, held the copyright. When Thomas Thorpe got hold of Shakespeare's sonnets from the mysterious Mr. W.H., and recorded them at Stationers' Hall, Shakespeare could neither legally prevent their publication nor profit from their success. Nor indeed had he a right to correct the proofs, guard against deliberate corruption, or assert his moral right. It was fortunate that in Thomas Thorpe he had a responsible printer.

A few fine lyrics did not entitle a man to be called a poet. Nor did plays. Sonnet clusters and sequences, or epyllions, epistles and epics were necessary. Many men wrote a few fine poems and did not have the effrontery to regard themselves as poets. Many wrote bad long sequences, epyllions and epics and did. Sidney could regard himself as a poet. *Astrophel and Stella* (published first in 1591, six years after his death), the first major sonnet sequence in English and the model for later sequences, the poems from the *Old Arcadia*, and a few additional pieces constitute his *oeuvre*. Within a small body of work he proves himself as inventive in form and meter as Spenser. The sonnets have a linguistic and intellectual thrift and an emotional control that place them in a class of their own. Petrarchan in manner, but with an overall unity of theme and image and, though without plot, a progression of feeling, *Astrophel and Stella*, written between 1581 and 1582, the period of his courtship but not about his wife, is his masterpiece. Astrophel is lover, Stella the beloved. The names ("lover of stars" and "star") correspond nicely to the theme, like Ralegh's Oceanus and Cynthia. Astrophel both is and is not Philip, and Stella both is and is not Lady Penelope Rich, whom he met when she was a girl of fourteen and he a successful soldier of twenty-one. If only, he reflects, his heart had shown more foresight! There is no hint that the two ever had anything beyond social dalliance. Possibly later poems in the sequence are addressed to his wife-to-be, who as his widow married the legendary Earl of Essex, that other worshiped knight of his age.

When he sets a sonnet in time, it is usually night. Images of light and dark insistently remind us of the relationship. In the sequence the poet first labors to express his love, then to win its object. He gets her at last, then circumstances part them. There are 108 sonnets and eleven "songs" in the sequence. The tone changes from poem to poem: the reader must continually adjust expectation. We are not directly involved. We witness rather than participate in the emotion.

Many individual sonnets are dramatic in structure. "What, have I thus betray'd my liberty?" deriving from Catullus's *"Miser Catulle, desinas ineptire,"* declares his liberty from Stella—and his thralldom:

> I may, I must, I can, I will, I do
> Leave following that which it is gain to miss.
> Let her go! Soft, but here she comes . . .

Another sort of drama develops in "Be your words made, good Sir, of Indian ware," in which he demands of his interlocutor "whether she did sit or walk; / How cloth'd; how waited on; sigh'd she or smil'd." We're put in mind of Cleopatra demanding news of Octavia. Sidney addresses his heart, desire, absence. He debates with a sage whose wisdom is powerless against love. Poems develop logically, but often a last line or couplet trips logic by declaring emotional fact. In more than one sonnet he debates with himself.

> Come let me write. And to what end? To ease
> A burthened heart. How can words ease, which are
> The glasses of thy daily vexing care?
> Oft cruel fights well pictured-forth do please.
> Art not ashamed to publish thy disease?
> Nay . . .

Passion can reduce the poet to a flow of sounds as near a cry as sense allows: "I. I. O I, may say that she is mine" is a line of astounding vocalic values. "No, no, no, no, my dear, let be."

"Come, Sleep, O Sleep, the certain knot of peace" made its impact on Shakespeare; "As good to write, as for to lie and groan. / O Stella dear"; "I am not I: pity the tale of me"; and Herbert's line "Let me not love thee if I love thee not," has a source in Sidney's "That I love not without I leave to love"; and Herbert may have been touched by the line "But ah, Desire still cries: 'Give me some food!' " The spell is often achieved by simple repetition: "Do thou then—for thou canst—do thou complain / For my poor soul." The non-sonnets that punctuate *Astrophel and Stella* advance the narrative, relieve the tension, and have merit beyond smoothness. The first printer altered the interspersing of sonnets and songs, and in arranging a continuous sequence solely of sonnets, with the songs at the end, ruined the progression and set the trend for "pure" sonnet sequences, which was never Sidney's intention. His aim was to invent a tale of love, clean of allegory; as Nashe said: "The argument cruel chastity, the Prologue hope, the Epilogue despair." These are love poems in lieu of love. Giles Fletcher says in *Licia*—and we must agree with him if we are to read the Elizabethans at all—: "A man may write of Love and not be in love; as well as of husbandry and not go to the plough; or of witches and be none; or of holiness and be flat profane."

Sidney wrote his *Old Arcadia* between 1578 and 1580. The first version was an "idle work" for Mary at eighteen, a young wife expecting her first child. He revised the first part radically, sending the revision to Greville. This became the basis of the first edition (1590), which Greville broke into shorter chapters within the larger books and provided with part titles. Incomplete as it was, readers and piety demanded that the revised part be wedded with the unrevised first version (the *Old Arcadia*) in 1593. This too proved unsatisfactory—as usual the printer was blamed—and a more cogent third version was published in 1613. It became the most popular English prose narrative of its period and for a long time after, finally displaced by Samuel Richardson's *Pamela* a century and a half later. *Arcadia* after its two false beginnings substantially profited publishers. It also influenced poets and prose writers in Britain and on the Continent. Shakespeare and Milton made it a resource for their work. Lady Mary Wroth, the poet's niece, wrote a romance inspired by it, and Anne Weamys composed a sequel. The Queen of France, Marie de Médicis, sent Jean Baudoin to England to translate it for her. Its fame comes down to our century, Virginia Woolf making use of it ("as in some luminous globe, all the seeds of English fiction lie latent") in *Orlando*. Now it is less read even than *The Faerie Queene*, yet anyone wishing to get a purchase on the poetry of the time cannot afford to ignore it.

The first version was novelistic, while in revised form it is more in the spirit of Spenser, or Ovid's *Metamorphoses*, a romance to be sure but always tending toward allegory. Sannazaro instructed Sidney in romance: from him he learned to alternate prose and verse. Prose supplies a context—plot and setting—for the verse. Despite pastoral trappings, *Arcadia* is a heroic romance.

Much of the metrical verse in *Arcadia* is smooth, oversmooth, the impulse diffuse, the content thin. There are lapses of taste. "The lively clusters of her breasts" recalls the sonnet where Sidney promises in future to kiss, rather than bite, Stella's nipples. But there are triumphs: "Reason tell me thy mind, if there be reason," "Phoebus, farewell . . . ," "My true love hath my heart," and the long invective "The lad Philisedes." There are a few fine lyrics on age and love, including "My sheep are thoughts, which I both guide and serve." One senses here and in the sonnets a religious spirit that, given time, might have written more than the one great religious poem "Leave me, O love, which reachest but to dust," a resolution of carnal in metaphysical desire, of human in divine love.

Sidney's brand of integrity is not fashionable. Nor does his verse appeal widely as it did in the past. "So good a mind," Greville said, and so it is. Sidney's verse, like his prose, like his official life, is exemplary, like a statue: handsome, evocative of an age, an intelligence, even if the stone is cold. Yet it is not so cold, or so white as it has come to seem. There is more of Ralegh, and perhaps of Marlowe, in Sidney than the record has admitted; and perhaps in Ralegh more of Sidney than his blustery history leads us at first to acknowledge. Yet on Elizabeth's poems—she was after all an accomplished writer—his imprint is firm. Her poem "On Monsieur's Departure" has some of her fallen knight's nice delicacy:

> Some gentler passion slide into my mind,
> For I am soft and made of melting snow;
> Or be more cruel, love, and so be kind.
> Let me float or sink, be high or low
>> Or let me live with some more sweet content,
>> Or die and so forget what love e'er meant.

Substance with and without Rites

GEORGE CHAPMAN, CHRISTOPHER MARLOWE,
WILLIAM SHAKESPEARE

George Chapman in his early work confuses obscurity with profundity. It is in his translations of Homer and in the four sestiads he wrote to complete Marlowe's *Hero and Leander* that his gifts are seen to full advantage, following as it were in the wake of preceding clarities. T. S. Eliot tried to put his finger on a specifically Elizabethan-Jacobean quality, a quality he associates more with Donne than Chapman: "In common with the greatest—Marlowe, Webster, Tourner, and Shakespeare—they had a quality of sensuous thought, or of thinking through the senses, or of the senses thinking, of which the exact formula remains to be defined." When the poet-critic Edgell Rickword praises Chapman and draws attention to the end of the third sestiad of *Hero and Leander* as prefiguring Donne, he has something similar in mind. He singles out the lines "Graceful Aedone that sweet pleasure loves, / And ruff-foot Chreste with the tufted crown," revealing Chapman's skill and proving it equal, at least some of the time, to Marlowe's. He might have looked at Chapman's syntax, too. Chapman unfolds a sentence further than almost any other poet in English, and does it without obscurity of effort, like a singer with amazing lungs, who never needs to catch breath, yet keeps the flow of words, the flow of sense and of feeling, unbroken. *De Guiana* is a classic instance. Rickword, writing in 1924 of *Hero and Leander*, declares: "What an example for our distracted poetry, which so often now strikes at the absolute and achieves the commonplace! These poets [Chapman and Marlowe] lived life from the ground upwards."

George Chapman is capable of some of the strangest writing of his age as well, as though Thomas Lovell Beddoes had an ancestor in the sixteenth century:

Kneel then with me, fall worm-like on the ground,
And from th' infectious dung hill of this round,
From men's brass wits and golden foolery,
Weep, weep your souls, into felicity.

In the dedicatory letter to *Ovid's Banquet* (1595) he writes, after Horace, "The profane multitude I hate." He consecrates his "strange poems to those searching spirits, whom learning hath made noble and nobility sacred." If he wrote plainly it would "make the ass run proud of his ears." After Sidney's classical, aristocratic clarity, we meet a self-indulging mind at work. Ideas become unstable, vapory. *Ovid's Banquet,* at moments vivid, is mechanical in progression. It doesn't add up. Decoration passes for development of thought. The poem is intellectually complicated, not poetically complex. Chapman's thought processes, Rickword says, "are nearer the surface, and interfere with its crystallisation, first into imagery and then into formal expression."

The fault is not peculiar to Chapman. As the dedicatory letter suggests, he is a man who stands apart, "positions" himself: he thinks things out, and the act of thinking is involved in the act of making. A colorful theory, now generally discredited, suggests that there existed, centered on Ralegh, a "School of Atheism" (as its detractors called it) or a "School of Night," perhaps the butt of the chaste college in Shakespeare's *Love's Labours Lost.* It included Marlowe and a few notable scientists and thinkers as well. The School of Night might have taken as its anthem Chapman's lines:

Sweet Peace's richest crown is made of stars,
Most certain guides of honoured mariners;
No pen can anything eternal write
That is not steeped in humour of the Night.

Chapman was born of gentleman-farmer stock in or near Hitchin, Hertfordshire, around 1559. Little is known of his early life. He may have attended Oxford, though by his own account he was self-taught. He may have seen service in the Netherlands: there is lived vigor in his Homeric battle scenes. His first published poems were "The Shadow of Night" and a companion piece (1594). In both he developed a theory of false and true dreams. The poems mix eloquence, obscurity, and dull comprehensibility. The matter was not so deep as he thought. He grew away from but never outgrew his clouding aesthetic.

In 1595 his first play was produced. He was admired by Spenser, Samuel Daniel, Shakespeare and others. Some associate him with the "rival poet" in Shakespeare's *Sonnets*, the one who lures away the beloved. "Was it the proud full sail of his great verse, / Bound for the prize of all too precious you." If so, there are no answering poems. Chapman became a sonneteer with the elegant "Coronet for his Mistress" appended to *Ovid's Banquet*. In 1596 he wrote *De Guiana*, supporting Ralegh in his troubles with the queen. The poem did not influence Elizabeth but includes a fine evocation of Chapman's figure of Hero, a figure often encountered in his plays, a man of intellect and passion:

> But you patrician spirits that refine
> Your flesh to fire, and issue like a flame
> On brave endeavours, knowing that in them
> The tract of heaven in morn-like glory opens;
> That know you cannot be the kings of earth,
> Claiming the rights of your creation,
> And let the mines of earth be kings of you;
> That are so far from doubting likely drifts,
> That in things hardest y' are most confident;
> You know that death lives, where power lives unus'd,
> Joying to shine in waves that bury you,
> And so make way for life e'en through your graves . . .

This is a portion of an immensely spacious single sentence, a whole verse paragraph. *De Guiana,* his one poem in blank verse, is a *carmen epicum* (epic song) without narrative plot, an oration addressed to the queen, dramatic in rhetoric.

His hero, like many of Shakespeare's, has some affinities with the heroes evoked in one of the great translations of his age, Sir Thomas North's rendering of Plutarch's *Lives of the Noble Grecians and Romans* (which replaced the *Lives of the Saints* and was in turn replaced, a couple of generations later, by John Foxe's *Book of Martyrs* as inspirational reading). This was the period in which the indomitable Bess of Hardwick cut the faces of saints out of the copes from Lilleshall Abbey, which she acquired to hang at Chatsworth, and stitched in classical faces, embroidering their names above them. Plutarch taught action, civic responsibility and devotion to the larger order now embodied in the queen. North says as much.

In 1598 Chapman completed *Hero and Leander* and began to publish his translations of Homer. In 1609 *Euthymiae Raptus*, a philosophical poem subtitled "The Tears of Peace," was published. In it Homer as guide reveals to the poet the figure of Peace in tears. The poem is dedicated to James I's son, Prince Henry, a patron of his translation work and an ally of Ralegh who died two years later. Chapman composed the "Epicede on Prince Henry." The loss of his noble patron was a disaster to him and his purse. Chapman was impecunious: he was first arrested for debt in 1599, and the last ten years of his life were plagued by creditors.

He saw prison, too, after the accession of James I. With his then friends Ben Jonson and John Marston he was locked up for staging the comedy *Westward Hoe*. It included ill-timed jests at the expense of the Scots. Chapman turned hostile to Jonson, resenting his arrogance and success. In 1634 he died in poverty and probably bitterness. He was buried in St. Giles-in-the-Fields, London, and Inigo Jones (who also fell out with Jonson) provided a monument.

It is de rigueur to criticize Chapman's four sestiads of *Hero and Leander*. Warton long ago commented on the "striking inequality" between Marlowe's and Chapman's parts of the poem. Edward Thomas said: "Marlowe died, and Chapman knew not the incantation." The tide against Chapman should turn. Edgell Rickword pointed to the crucial line in the transition to the third sestiad. "Love's edge is taken off"—the moral must follow. Marlowe enacted the consummation; Chapman, temperamentally suited to the task, had to enact the consequences. Chapman is a thinker. Some of his best writing is expository—and so is some of his worst.

He understands from the outset his task in *Hero and Leander*: "New light gives new direction, fortunes new." The poem finds an altered register, and intensity. There are moments of Marlovian physicality. Of Leander he says: "Now (with warm baths and odours comforted) / When he lay down he kindly kiss'd his bed." Hero treats her bed with similar sexual piety. Chapman's sestiads abound in small transformations, preparing for the culminating metamorphosis of the lovers into birds. He has a sense of the whole poem, his *and* Marlowe's parts. The parallelisms are not mechanically but poetically and dramatically right, the characters develop; there's nothing static in how they recognize the consequences of their actions.

The lovers have sinned against Ceremony, furtively committing an act for which they should have sought religious sanction. Leander is visited by Thesme, goddess of Ceremony. She appears

> . . . with a crown
> Of all the stars, and heaven with her descended,
> Her flaming hair and her bright feet extended,
> By which hung all the bench of deities;
> And in a chain, compact of ears and eyes,

She led Religion; all her body was
Clear and transparent as the purest glass:
For she was all presented to the sense;
Devotion, Order, State, and Reverence
Her shadows were; Society, Memory;
All which her sight made live; her absence die.

For C. S. Lewis this is the classic evocation of the Elizabethan world order. Chapman's Ceremony is what Concord is to Spenser and Degree to Shakespeare: it is that ordained, hierarchical proportion that provides institutions with legitimacy and authority. Ceremony draws a human and divine meaning from mere nature. To offend against her is to offend against her shadows, Devotion, Order, and State and Reverence; it is to deny society's custom, ignore the past, usurp authority. Ceremony admonishes Leander. She

Told him how poor was substance without rites,
Like bills unsign'd, desires without delights;
Like meats unseasoned; like rank corn that grows
On cottages, that none or reaps or sows . . .

That final humble metaphor, suggesting an abandoned village, has the rustic precision of Homeric simile. The drama of two lovers broadens out into an interpretation of all human experience. Hero is compared with a city surprised and pillaged: thoughts are invading troops. So broad a simile would seem absurd in another context. Chapman makes it work. The development of their reactions—Leander's decision to act, Hero's to accept—is realized with a psychological aptness that recalls *Troilus and Criseyde.*

There is the other Chapman. His name is best remembered because of Keats's sonnet "On First Looking into Chapman's Homer":

Much have I travelled in the realms of gold,
    And many goodly states and kingdoms seen;
    Round many western islands have I been
Which bards in fealty to Apollo hold.
Oft of one wide expanse had I been told.
    That deep-browed Homer ruled as his demesne;
    Yet did I never breathe its pure serene
Till I heard Chapman speak out loud and bold:
Then felt I like some watcher of the skies
    When a new planet swims into his ken;
Or like stout Cortez when with eagle eyes

He stared at the Pacific—and all his men
Looked at each other with a wild surmise—
    Silent, upon a peak in Darien.

Keats—ridiculed by his educated contemporaries for being unable to
read Homer in the original and for confusing Balboa with Cortez—
was right: Chapman "speak[s] out loud and bold." If his boldness is dif-
ferent in complexity from Marlowe's, there is a similar vigor and a
livelier intelligence. He made Homer integral to English literature. His
Iliad and his *Odyssey* are—alongside Golding's translation of Ovid's
Metamorphoses—neglected masterpieces, like most translations.

Chapman's notion of the "great man" hardly squared with the
Homeric hero, and he distorts to some extent. For him Homer is "learn-
ing's sire." He makes him didactic, seeks a deep sense in each phrase and
action, interpolates, moralizes. Prefacing the *Iliad*, Chapman writes, "It
is the part of every knowing and judicious interpreter, not to follow the
number and order of words, but the material things themselves, and
sentences to weigh diligently." Sentences are "meanings." The prescrip-
tion is thoroughly Horatian. It accounts for the virtues and flaws of his
versions. Warton is harsh: Chapman forfeits dignity and simplicity,
writes redundantly, impoverishes where he cannot "feel and express."
Warton calls the fourteeners used in the *Iliad* "awkward, inharmo-
nious, and unheroic." Pope, himself a notable translator of Homer, was
less dismissive. Chapman, Pope noted, covers his defects "by a daring
fiery spirit that animates his translation, which is something like what
one might imagine Homer himself to have writ before he arrived at
years of discretion." Pope had arrived at years of discretion, and per-
fected the precise couplet that clicks shut like a latch.

Homer was Chapman's destiny—"angel to me, star and fate." He
completed the *Iliad* in 1611, the *Odyssey* in 1616, and the *Hymns* in 1624.
"The work that I was born to do, is done," he says. Whatever its flaws,
it is a triumph. It can be appreciated only *in extenso*. I offer a sample, the
death of Hector from the *Iliad*:

    . . . Then all the Greeks ran to him,
    To see his person; and admired his terror-stirring limb:
    Yet none stood by, that gave no wound, to his so goodly form;
    When each to other said: O Jove, he is not in the storm
    He came to fleet in, with his fire; he handles now more soft . . .

The verse is plain, the syntax loose but clear and dramatically phrased to
the climax, and the choice of words as right as it is unexpected.

Chapman was prolific. He did not suffer academic critics gladly, especially when they attacked his Homer. His purpose was "with poesy, to open poesy." In translating Homer he became a form of his own notion of the hero. There are four hundred pages of his poetry and about a thousand of his translations. More than many neglected Elizabethan and Jacobean poets, Chapman is worth persisting with. There are always rewards—seldom a whole poem, but passages so fine that they outshine, however dull their context, some of the classic lyrics of the age. Yet he will never be forgiven for daring to complete Marlowe's *Hero and Leander*.

That is why it is best to praise Chapman before cuing Marlowe on stage. Marlowe's first two sestiads of *Hero and Leander* are uniquely wonderful in English: witty, easily erotic in a dozen ways, the language unaffected, riveting. No wonder ten editions of the poem appeared in the forty years after its first publication: after Sidney's *Arcadia* it was the best-seller. Few copies survive: it was so popular that it was "read to rags." Linley's 1598 edition was the second, the first to contain Chapman's "completion." (There are other "completions," the first by Henry Petowe, who prefaces his with a panegyric on Marlowe: "I being but a slender Atlas to uphold and undergo so large a burden." His happy ending turned the lovers into pine trees.) The irony is that Marlowe stops at the point beyond which he would have lost interest: fulfillment. In lighter mood, the great tragedian leaves it to the stage hands to deal with the consequences and clean up the psychological, moral and metaphysical mess he created.

In his plays as here, Marlowe's characters exist at the perilous brink of caricature. In *Hero and Leander* his "over-reaching" sweetens with a hint of comedy. Michael Drayton—author among much else of the great topographical poem *Polyolbion* and of memorable sonnets (including "Since there's no help, come let us kiss and part"), heroic verse and the "Ballad of Agincourt" ("Fair stood the wind for France")—loved Marlowe's verse, and in his "Elegy of Poets and Poesie" Marlowe appears "bathed in the Thespian springs." He

Had in him those brave translunary things,
That the first poets had: his raptures were
All air, and fire, which made his verses clear:
For that fine madness still he did retain
Which rightly should possess a poet's brain.

Like all his contemporaries Marlowe is a borrower. Eliot demonstrates how he borrows from that very different poet, Spenser. The evidence is in *Tamburlaine*, and less nakedly elsewhere: Spenser showed him a way of being lyrical, importing into his vigorous verse strange and complementary tones. Marlowe, like Spenser, repeats line and passages, recycling, sometimes improving as he goes.

His first important borrowing is from Ovid, the undervalued *Amores*, wonderfully simple, the language transparent.

> In summer heat, and mid-time of the day,
> To rest my limbs upon a bed I lay;
> One window shut, the other open stood,
> Which gave such light as twinkles in a wood,
> Like twilight glimpse at setting of the sun,
> Or night being past, and yet not day begun.

Christopher Marlowe the poet achieves quite different effects from Kit Marlowe the playwright. The playwright evokes ambition and power, but the poet is a younger man, creating a world of balance and proportion. The poems lack the exaggerated action, the grandiloquence of the "mighty line." Puttenham disparaged Marlowe's hyperbolic dramatic style—"the over reacher, otherwise called the loud liar"—and Nashe commented on "the specious volubility of a drumming decasillabon." The poems aren't vulnerable to these strictures. They neither overreach nor drum. None of his "monstrous opinions" (unless you consider sexual frankness monstrous) disfigures them. They are thrifty of language and serious in content, though the tone is light.

Marlowe, born in Canterbury in 1564, was the son of a shoemaker. He became a scholar at the King's School, Canterbury, and afterward at Corpus Christi College, Cambridge. He took his BA in 1584, his MA three years later, by which time he had probably completed *Tamburlaine*. He was the first of the university wits to employ blank verse. It's generally thought that most if not all of his small surviving body of nondramatic verse—*Hero and Leander,* "The Passionate Shepherd," and the Ovid and Lucan translations—were written in his university years, the fruit of youth and relative leisure. The six years that elapsed between his taking his MA and his shadowy death—possibly as a result of drink, or low political intrigue, or a romantic entanglement with a rough character "fitter to be a pimp, than an ingenious *amoretto*," or perhaps a tussle over the bill ("le recknynge")—at the hand of Ingram Frisar in a Deptford tavern on 30 May 1593 were busy ones. He wrote plays, was attacked for atheism, was associated (if it existed) with Ralegh's "School of Night," and lodged with Thomas Kyd (author of *The Spanish Tragedy*), who later brought charges of blasphemy against him. These he had to answer before the Privy Council in 1593, the very council that secretly employed him to spy on English Catholics on the Continent. He achieved much in a short life.

Had Chapman not brought it to a competent end, Marlowe's *Hero and Leander* might almost be taken as a whole poem. Completion, or moral conclusion, was not necessary. If Marlowe wrote it at Cambridge, he could have moralized it himself had he felt the need. The absence of a moral is moral statement enough, and characteristic of this poet. The poem is an epyllion or miniature epic, a form common in the sixteenth century, deriving from Theocritus, Catullus and Ovid. Marlowe knew his Ovid, and his poem is Ovidian mythological-erotic verse of a high order.

It provides a contrast with Shakespeare's efforts in the same genre, *Venus and Adonis* and *The Rape of Lucrece*. Shakespeare begins in action. In the earlier poem, "rose cheek'd Adonis" is at chase by line three, laughing love to scorn in line four, and being loved in line five. *The Rape of Lucrece* begins with the lustful Tarquin off hotfoot, "Borne by the trustless wings of hot desire." Conventionally dramatic, both poems awkwardly accommodate the reflective laments that, excellent in themselves, like static arias interrupt the dramatic pace.

We cannot judge Marlowe as a tragic poet in *Hero and Leander*. He portrays consummation: *desunt nonnulla* ("the rest is lacking") leads into Chapman. But it's not absence of tragedy that makes his poem superior to Shakespeare's: it's a difference of procedure and tone. Shakespeare's six-line pentameter stanzas rein in his natural pace and hobble narrative continuity, much as the sonnet form can distort thought and weaken emphasis in his great sequence. The stanzas are conclusive with the resolving couplet at the end, a tonal sententiousness or closure just when fluid movement is required. Marlowe chose the more versatile pentameter couplets, which move swiftly when they must and can be used for reflection and description too. They carry a voice, its passions and ironies, lightly modulating from register to register.

Marlowe avoids, or deflates, the heroic exaggeration that vitiates other epyllia, humanizing his protagonists in the process. They are, in the end, girl and boy. The mission of the poem is to get them to this natural end. When Hero first appears in the temple, she wears a gaudy veil of artificial flowers and is covered from head to foot in leaves. She looks rather like a pot of ivy. In seeming to praise her, Marlowe defines the unnatural conventions that overlie the natural girl. He praises her chastity but does not condemn her for letting drop her fan. Only her eyes and hands are plainly visible. He thwarts idealization by ironizing ideality and by simple satire. The truth he presents boldly: "Love is not full of pity, as men say, / But deaf and cruel where he means to prey." The word "prey" is at one with the animal images running through the poem: animal desire, not courtly refinement, drives the action. The animal images are natural, not censuring. Love is stripped of mystique. Hero is finally naked. Leander's argument against chastity does not convince; his desire does. He speaks "like a bold sharp sophister" with borrowed arguments, for he is (like Hero, but in a different sense) "a novice." " 'My words shall be as spotless as my youth, / Full of simplicity and naked truth.' "

The core of his argument is charming: I shall be faithful to you as you are more beautiful than Venus. With such logic Satan prevailed upon Eve. The indictment of virginity, " 'Of that which hath no being do not boast, / Things that are not at all are never lost,' " can indict all metaphysical belief. The poem is wedded to the physical world. The images metamorphose, making the poem more sensually vivid. Hero has "swallowed Cupid's golden hook / The more she striv'd, the deeper was she strook." Neptune fondles Leander's swimming body, making it exquisitely real. Gods too are lusty.

The love of Hero and Leander is not consummated in the temple. Hero will not let Leander so much as touch her sacred garments. She bids him "Come thither" to her turret set squarely in the natural world:

> Upon a rock, and underneath a hill,
> Far from the town, where all is whist and still
> Save that the sea, playing on yellow sand,
> Sends forth a rattling murmur to the land,
> Whose sound allures the golden Morpheus
> In silence of the night to visit us,
> My turret stands . . .

The deferred subject and verb and the dramatic unpleating of the syntax demonstrate the flexibility of Marlowe's handling. The drama is in language and character, not action.

Metamorphosis is the heart of the poem: Hero's change is richly Ovidian. She is the first and last character we see, her transformation complete. At the start she's Leander's opposite. Her wreath and veil "shrub her in," her costume and scent are hyperbolically described, she exists only as a figure. Leander, by contrast, is "beautiful and young." "His body was as straight as Circe's wand." It was with her wand that Circe transformed men into beasts.

Their first encounter is in Venus's temple, among portrayals of "heady riots, incests, rapes," the loves of the gods, especially those in which they became animals—bulls or swans. In this place Hero sacrificed turtledoves. The mythological pictures amuse and affect us; their significance is ironic. Hero's change is complete at last:

Thus near the bed she blushing stood upright,
And from her countenance behold ye might
A kind of twilight break, which through her hair,
As from an orient cloud, glims here and there.

In the very completeness of his two sestiads, Marlowe suggests that no lessons can be drawn from love, only about it.

His versions of Ovid's *Amores*, the *Elegies*—the first translated into English—deserve more attention than they receive. For his contemporaries his translation of Lucan may have been more important. For us that labor has lost its force, but the Ovid remains fresh, with an expressive range almost as wide as that of *Hero and Leander*. Jonson, Donne and other poets owe him a debt for the *Elegies*. "Elegy" was originally the generic term used for a song of mourning in alternate hexameters and pentameters. The elegiac meter was later adopted for the expression of personal feelings. For Ovid, as for Jonson, Donne, Marvell, Carew, it was a language of reflection, exhortation, tribute, varied in subject matter and tone, often amorous.

Marlowe condensed Ovid's *Amores* from five into three books. This exercise sharpened his prosodic skill with the couplet and the Ovidian manner. There are direct echoes of *Hero and Leander* or, if the *Elegies* came first, in *Hero and Leander*, a similar variety of emotion and allusion. We find the arguments against chastity, the quest for pleasure as an end, and the "atheism" ("God is a name, no substance, fear'd in vain").

"The Passionate Shepherd," Marlowe's best-known poem, attributed to a range of poets, including Shakespeare, is the more memorable by the number of replies it inspired, among them Ralegh's and, perhaps indirectly, Marvell's "To his Coy Mistress." Marlowe's poems and translations make a small body of work. He may have given up writing poems at the age of twenty-three, but the Marlowe who is lamented in *As You Like It* as the dead shepherd is the poet of *Hero and Leander*, "The Passionate Shepherd" and the *Elegies*.

Bad Feelings

WILLIAM SHAKESPEARE, EMILIA LANYER

When drama began to be printed, blank verse was an ugly medium. Printers did their best to set it out prettily but got little enough thanks for their labors. Not wholly unconnected with this, some of my predecessors harbored bad feelings about William Shakespeare. About the work and the way it broke upon the world. Not about the man, born in the same year as Marlowe yet somehow seeming his junior and his apprentice. The great painter William Turner once said of Thomas Girtin, who died at twenty-seven, "Had Tommy Girtin lived, I should have starved." But Girtin died, Marlowe died; and Turner lived, Shakespeare lived. Laurels are awarded accordingly. When the First Folio of the complete plays was planned, Richard Field, who had printed the bard's *Venus and Adonis* in 1593 and *The Rape of Lucrece* in 1594, stood aside because he didn't like the theater (the audiences were so unruly and the weather at times inclement); besides, he reflected, the texts of the plays proposed were so corrupt that it would have been dishonest to serve them up; it was not Shakespeare. So much for the wages of integrity: the plays *were* served up, and he was not at table to savor a portion of the profits. When I see the text of a Shakespeare play I think of Richard Field, getting by on pamphlets and jobbing printing, while a series of corruptions in the name of his friend the poet spun out in unstoppable circulation, to benefit his competitors.

The First Folio was published by a temporary syndicate in 1623. Two printers produced it, William and Isaac Jaggard. Three publishers were responsible, Smethwicke, Aspley and Blount, working with the acting company that owned Shakespeare's manuscripts. The price was high at 20s., but the book consisted of nearly 1,000 pages, and prices were rising at the time. Shakespeare had been dead seven years. His widow and family saw no benefit from what was to be, after the Bible, the greatest book ever published in English. If only they had done a better job with the editing! When I see the tomes in libraries I want to get them out from under the glass and mark in the corrections: misprints, poor formats, even erroneous attributions.

The greatest poet of the age—the greatest poet of all time, for all his corruptions—inspires in publishers and in other writers a kind of vertigo. For Donald Davie Shakespeare represents "a vast area of the English language and the English imagination which is as it were 'charged,' radio-active: a territory where we dare not travel at all often or at all extensively, for fear of being mortally infected, in the sense of being *overborne*, so that we cease to speak with our own voices and produce only puny echoes of the great voice which long ago took over that whole terrain for its own." This is true of the plays. But had Shakespeare produced only the epyllia, the *Sonnets* and the occasional poems, we'd have a more proportioned view of him, smaller in scale than Jonson, Donne, Spenser and Marlowe. The poems are excellent, but it is the language and vision of the plays that dazzles. The slightly absurd scenario of *Venus and Adonis*, the excesses of *Lucrece* and the uneven brilliance of the *Sonnets* would not by themselves have changed the world. *Venus and Adonis* was, it's true, Shakespeare's most successful poem. By the time he died, ten editions had been published, and six followed in the two decades after his death. There was money in that large, bossy, blowsy goddess almost eating alive the pretty lad. Nowadays it is read because it is by Shakespeare. And *Lucrece*, with its cruel eloquence, its harsh tracing of one of the most brutal tales of rape in the classical repertory, while better balanced and constructed, touches unreflectingly on matters that require a less restrained psychology than the poet can provide. The movement from sublime to ridiculous is swift, as in the stanza where Lucrece's father and husband vie with one another in hating Tarquin the ravager:

> Yet sometime Tarquin was pronouncèd plain,
> But through his teeth, as if the name he tore,
> This windy tempest, till it blow up rain,
> Held back his sorrow's tide, to make it more.
> At last it rains, and busy winds give o'er,
>   Then son and father weep with equal strife,
>   Who should weep most for daughter or for wife.

In Ted Hughes the epyllia have a passionate modern advocate and expositor, who reads them as a key to Shakespeare's work. But there are problems in the poetry that no amount of explication can resolve. Not least of these is the closing couplets in the different stanza forms of *Venus* and *Lucrece*, each stanza rising to epithetic closure. Concluding couplets, like the refrain or tag phrase in a ballad, are an *automatic* "release"; such formally predictable "releases" can cease to be effective because they are expected. In narrative poems they can seriously impede the progress of the story.

The epyllia are poetry made out of poetry. The *Sonnets*—though they employ many conventions—are poetry apparently made out of the life, much as the plays are written out of the life of England and London at the time. Aubrey takes us to the heart of Shakespeare's London. "Near [the Bear Garden] was a Theatre, known by the name of the GLOBE Play-House, to which Beaumont, Fletcher, and Philip Massinger belonged and wrote for; and though the most eminent Place for Tragedies, Comedies, and Interludes, was, because of its Situation, only used in the hot Summer Months." He takes us by the arm and steers us on: "Not far from this Place were the Asparagus-Gardens, and Pimblico-Path, where were fine walks, cool Arbours, &c. much used by the Citizens of London and their Families, and both mentioned by the Comedians at the Beginning of 1600; 'To walk to Pimblico' became Proverbial for a Man handsomely drest; as these walks were frequented by none else." Much nearer the playhouse another form of entertainment was available. "Next the Bear-Garden on this Bank was formerly the Bordello, or Stewes, so called from the severall licensed Houses for the Entertainment of lewd Persons, in which were Women prepared for all Comers. The Knights Templars were notable wenchers." The "Stewes" had various privileges confirmed by the court and numerous regulations honored more in the breach than the observance. They were occasionally closed down. In 1506 there were eighteen houses; Henry VII closed them and they were reopened with twelve. In 1546 they were shut again "by Sound of Trumpet"—"by King Henry VIII, whose tender Conscience startled at such scandalous and open Lewdness." Henry, tutored by John Skelton, may have overcome his aversion. "These Houses were distinguished by several Signs painted on their Fronts, as, a Boar's Head, The Crane, the Cardinal's Hat, the Swan, the Bell, the Crosse-Keys, the Popes Head, and the Gun." In Shakespeare's day the neighborhood was not Mayfair, that's certain. The stewes were owned by the church.

This is a story about poetry, not drama or *literal* prostitution; the plays I'll leave to someone else. I'm concerned with "the rest," a handful of works that the poet took most seriously: the epyllia Richard Field published, the 154 *Sonnets* and "The Phoenix and the Turtle." I could add songs from the plays, but once you dip into a drama, where do you stop? A monologue is like an aria, a description can be like a whole pastoral or satire. And which songs are Shakespeare's, which did he pull out of Anon.'s bran tub? *Two Gentlemen of Verona, Love's Labours Lost, A*

Midsummer Night's Dream, *The Merchant of Venice*, *Much Ado About Nothing*, *As You Like It*, *Twelfth Night*, *Hamlet*, *Measure for Measure*, *Cymbeline*, *A Winter's Tale* and *The Tempest* all include detachable songs, but the plays snared them and that's where they belong.

Shakespeare is so much at the heart—is the heart—of this story that even by skirting around him we take his measure. Apart from his genius, Shakespeare had some real advantages. The world for him was new, as it had been for Chaucer. There were the navigators' discoveries, there was the rising power of the monarch, new industry, new learning. The daily world was fuller, too: Aubrey tells us how cherries came to England under Henry VIII (from Flanders); but not until Elizabeth's time did hops arrive in Kent. Beer of a sort came in under Henry VIII, along with turkeys: "Greeke, Heresie, Turkey-cocks, and Beer, / Came into England all in a year." No fishmongers existed inland; most estates had fishponds or kept fish in the moat for fasting days. Carrots "were first sown at Beckington, in Somersetshire," and turnips in the early seventeenth century came from Wales; early on all cabbages were imported from Holland. The catalogues of flora and fauna that occur not only in Shakespeare but in the works of other writers are records as much of novelty as heritage. And new things kept coming in the seventeenth century: "clovergrass" was brought in out of Brabant or Flanders; pines and fir trees were first planted in England in the 1640s, and the first canals were built. Tabby cats came in and replaced "the common English Catt," which "was white with some blewish piedness: sc. a gallipot blew. The race or breed of them are now almost lost." Also the modern brown rat supplanted the black rat, which had carried the plague. Under Charles II gardens bloomed in England. Jasmine and laurel were added to our shrubberies.

To the advantages of a new world, Shakespeare could add the advantages of a singularly complicated personal libido. "The Phoenix and the Turtle," a lament and metamorphosis first published in Robert Chester's *Love's Martyr* in 1601, sounds a little like the incantations of *A Midsummer Night's Dream*:

Let the bird of loudest lay
    On the sole Arabian tree,
    Herald sad and trumpet be,
To whose sound chaste wings obey.

But thou shrieking harbinger,
    Foul precurrer of the fiend,
    Augur of the fever's end,
To this troop come thou not near.

From this session interdict
    Every fowl of tyrant wing,
    Save the eagle, feathered king:
Keep the obsequy so strict.

Nothing should mar the melancholy requiem of turtle dove and phoenix, perfect but ill-assorted in their love:

So they loved, as love in twain
    Had the essence but in one;
    Two distinct, division none:
Number there in love was slain.

It is as if Shakespeare was toying with a mystery like the Trinity, in which three are one and one is three.

Hearts remote, yet not asunder;
    Distance, and no space was seen
    'Twixt the turtle and his queen:
But in them it were a wonder.

So between them love did shine,
    That the turtle saw his right
    Flaming in the phoenix' sight;
Either was the other's mine.

Property was thus appalled,
    That the self was not the same;
    Single nature's double name
Neither two nor one was called.

The love is immortalized, but without issue, as between two whose different natures are overwhelmed by an *almost* metaphysical affection. The poem, like Marvell's "My love is of a birth," does not develop: it grows by accretion, assertion. So strange is the subject, so strange the affection, that it can only be affirmed. Language is uneasy with it: "Either was the other's mine."

This passionate disparity is at the heart of all of Shakespeare's poems and some of the plays. The *Sonnets* have attracted a critical literature second in vastness only to that on *Hamlet*, and so various that at times it seems the critics are discussing works entirely unrelated. They contain a mystery, and the critic-as-sleuth is much in evidence. Unlike sonnets by his contemporaries, none of these poems has a traced "source" in Italian or elsewhere; most seem to emerge from an actual occasion, an occasion not concealed, yet sufficiently clouded to make it impossible to say for sure what or whom it refers to. Setting these veiled occasions side by side can yield a diversity of plots: a Dark Lady, a Young Man, now noble, now common, now chaste, now desired, possessed and lost. All we can say for sure is that desire waxes and wanes, time passes. Here certainly, the critic says, are hidden meanings; and where meanings are hidden, a key is hidden too. Only, Shakespeare is a subtle twister. Each sleuth-critic finds a key, and each finds a different and partial treasure. A. L. Rowse found his key, affirming that Shakespeare's mistress was the poet Emilia Lanyer (1569–1645), illegitimate daughter of an Italian royal musician and also an intimate of the astrologer Simon Forman, who gives a brief picture of a brave, cunning operator. Her 1611 volume of poems includes ten dedications and cleverly celebrates the Dowager Countess of Cumberland, the poet's particular quarry, in company with Christ and biblical heroines. The words she attributes to Eve are the first clear glimmer of English feminism in verse. Eve may—*almost* innocently—have handed Adam the apple; but Adam's sons crucified, in the bright light of day and reason, Jesus Christ. "This sin of yours hath no excuse, or end."

There is a further mystery: Who is "the only begetter of these ensuing sonnets Mr. W.H." to whom the poet (or the publisher?) wishes "all happiness and that eternity promised by our ever-living poet"? The T.T. who signs the dedication is Thomas Thorpe, publisher-printer in 1609 of the poems: W.H. may have been his friend, who procured the manuscript, or Shakespeare's lover, or a common acquaintance—William Herbert, Earl of Pembroke? Henry Wriothesley, Earl of Southampton (dedicatee of the two epyllia)? William Hervey, Southampton's stepfather, getting the poet to encourage his stepson to marry? Much passionate energy is expended on a riddle without a definitive answer. Thomas Thorpe was a mischievous printer. I suspect he knew what he was doing: no title page in history has been more pored over.

In 1598, Francis Meres compiled a catalogue of English writers of the day and lists Shakespeare's "sugred sonnets among his private friends"—kept private, perhaps, because of their subject matter. Two of the sonnets, 138 and 144, were printed by William Jaggard in 1599 in *The Passionate Pilgrim*, a miscellany erroneously attributed to Shakespeare. After three editions the error was corrected. The whole sequence was published by one G. Eld for Thomas Thorpe in 1609. Only thirteen copies of this remarkably reliable quarto survive. Did Shakespeare see it through press? Was it withdrawn from circulation? We can assert no more than what survives on paper. Are the poems written early or late? W. H. Auden believes them early; it seems more likely, given that so many refer to the youth of the young man and the age of the courting poet, and given the theme of time and competition for the beloved between established writers, that they are in large part the product of the poet who was edging his way through *The Merchant of Venice*, *Julius Caesar* and *Twelfth Night* (1596–1600) to *Hamlet* (1601).

There is not a linear plot to the sequence of the sonnets. There are "runs," but they break off; other "runs" begin. Is it a series of sequences, or a miscellany of them? Some editors reorder the poems without success. Sonnets 1–126 are addressed to a young man or men; the remainder to a Dark (-haired) Lady. There may be a triangle (or two): the beloveds perhaps have a relationship as well. The poems are charged with passionate ambiguities.

Those who read the poems as a sonnet sequence were for a long while baffled. The *Sonnets* were neglected, or virtually so, until 1780, when they were dusted down and reedited. They did not immediately appeal, but gradually, during the nineteenth century, they caught fire— fitfully, like wet kindling. Wordsworth, Keats, Hazlitt and Landor failed to appreciate them. Those who love them properly are fewer than those who enjoy them. Those who love them properly are fewer than those who enjoy arguing about them. W. H. Auden argues (credibly) that "he wrote them . . . as one writes a diary, for himself alone, with no thought of a public." T. S. Eliot suggests that like *Hamlet* they are "full of some stuff that the writer could not drag to light, contemplate, or manipulate into art. And when we search for this feeling, we find it, as in the sonnets, very difficult to localise." Now the public clambers over them, prurient, with several dozen authoritative guides.

Shakespeare's life is so nearly erased that it is no help in elucidating the verse. Aubrey, writing only a couple of generations after his death, misinforms us that Shakespeare's "father was a Butcher, and I have been told heretofore by some of the neighbours, that when he was a boy he exercised his father's Trade, but when he kill'd a Calfe he would doe it in a high style, and make a Speech." He contrasts the excellence of Shakespeare as an actor with Jonson, who "was never a good Actor, but an excellent Instructor."

Drama could be profitable: this discovery coincided with "the coming into the field of the first pupils of the new grammar schools of Edward VI," men who did not resent or distrust commerce and entrepreneurship. A new class of "mental adventurers," the classically educated sons of merchants, made the running. Marlowe was the son of a cobbler, Shakespeare of a prosperous glove maker of Stratford-on-Avon, where the poet was born in 1564. Both were provincials, one educated at the grammar school at Stratford, the other at King's School, Canterbury. They were harbingers of the social change that would culminate in the Commonwealth.

One of Shakespeare's advantages was an apparent disadvantage. He was not university-trained. "When Shakespeare attempts to be learned like Marlowe, he is not very clever." That is part of the problem with his epyllia. But Ford Madox Ford reminds us that he had "another world to which he could retire; because of that he was a greater poet than either Jonson or Marlowe, whose minds were limited by their university-training to find illustrations, *telles quelles*, from illustrations already used in the Greek or Latin classics. It was the difference between founding a drawing on a lay figure and drawing or painting from a keen and delighting memory." Sidney advises: "Look in thy heart and write." In the *Sonnets*, Shakespeare takes Sidney's counsel without the pla-tonizing the great courtier intended. The heart he looks into is singu-larly complex and troubled, and the poems he writes from this impure "I" are as full of life as the plays.

Words Strung on Air

THOMAS CAMPION

Shakespeare happened; he towers so high that most who shared the world with him are dwarfed by his sheer scale. The poets that suffer least are the most specialized. Beside the Giant, I set one of the smallest perfections in the tradition.

"The world," wrote Thomas Campion, doctor, poet, and musician, "is made by symmetry and proportion, and is in that respect compared to music, and music to poetry." Campion's poetry was liked at court and circulated beyond its confines. In the middle of the seventeenth century it dropped out of sight. It was not recovered until 1887, when A. H. Bullen issued the first collected edition. Campion hadn't played his immortality cards very cleverly. A disciple of Sidney, fascinated by classical meters, he published his *Observations in the Art of English Poesie*, attacking rhyme and experimenting in classical forms, in 1602, a decade after the controversy had blown over (the cause defeated). He wrote masques, the most transient of literary forms. (Apart from *Comus*, how many masques can you name?) His art does not *require* music, but it seems to: the poems are songs, many of which he set himself, and as musical styles changed, they too disappeared.

One is put in mind of the miniature art of Nicholas Hilliard, the Elizabethan goldsmith turned painter whose tiny, brilliant images brought noble contemporaries intimately alive. Hilliard evolved his art of "limning" out of the residual medieval art of manuscript illumination, a source of our portrait art. His is not art for common men, it is not useful—you cannot hang his pictures or integrate them into tapestries. It's an art to be valued in aesthetic terms alone. One must hold it close to the eye, or wear it about the neck: art as token. Campion's best songs are more "public" than that: they are not made exclusively for intimate occasions. But they are *useless*: they do not satirize, render thanks, flatter or praise. The love they invoke is unattributable, their seasons archetypal.

The publication in 1613 of Campion's "Songs of Mourning" for the death of Prince Henry (of whom every poet seems to have had high hopes), was preceded by *Two Books of Ayres*, the first of *Divine and Moral Songs*, the second *Light Conceits of Lovers*. In 1614 appeared his treatise on music, *A New Way of Making Fowre Parts in Counterpoint*. He expended much effort on masques, and the images in his verse have some of the brittle sharpness of masque properties. The poems are sparse in physical particularity: their effect depends on prosodic virtuosity. Few poets used a greater variety of stanza forms to such effect, within a narrow range of diction, allusion and theme.

Campion requires close attention; his work vanishes if you stand at a distance from it. Anyone reading him should try to hear at least some of the airs and consider the precision of his musical structures; in performance he organizes the musicians like syllables in an elaborate stanza. The masque he wrote for Lord Hays's wedding in 1607, presented before the king in Whitehall, used all the resources of the King's Music. He arranged the musicians carefully in groups: "On the right hand were consorted ten musicians, with bass and mean lutes, a bandora, a double sackbut, and an harpsichord, with two treble violins; on the other side . . . were placed nine violins and three lutes; and to answer both the consorts (as it were in a triangle) six cornets and six chapel voices were seated almost right against them, in a place higher in respect of the piercing sound of those instruments." He marshals syllables with similar consideration and precision.

In his Latin poems he acknowledges a debt to Chaucer. More tangible debts are to Wyatt, Surrey and Sidney, and to the Latin poets. The poems fall into four general categories: amorous laments (and rare celebrations of love); (not very) wanton and witty fancies; devotional poems; and frank declarations of love. His natural world is not the world of nature: it is Arcadia, a masque setting with nymphs and shepherds. We must accept this convention; if we do, we hear a clear personal note and sometimes glimpse a solid reality. Invention in sound, balanced syllables, manipulation of rhythm and rhyme, attempts to give vowels "convenient liberty," juxtaposition of stanzas with similar syntax and rhythmic progression but contrasting emotional content—such techniques create the effects. Many lines have an odd number of syllables and begin with a stress, an effect required by the music.

The enjambement serves the meticulous craftsman well. Yvor Winters singles out one example to illustrate a general point:

> Now winter nights enlarge
> The number of their hours

> And clouds their storms discharge
>   Upon the ayrie towers.

The suspension of syntax at the end of the first and third lines suggests two possible directions for the meaning. The following line takes up one meaning, but the second remains active in our mind—and in the poet's. He takes it up later. "Enlarge" can mean increase in number or increase in space. It is number the poet means, but space is suggested and developed in the last stanza. Such effects give the poem aural and intellectual point. It is on a small scale, but carried out with the assurance of a craftsman, one of the most brilliant in the language.

At the opening of the *Fourth Book of Ayres* (1617), Campion describes his lyric art: "The apothecaries have books of gold, whose leaves being opened are so light as that they are subject to be shaken with the least breath and yet rightly handled, they serve both for ornament and use; such are light ayres." It would be hard to find poems more perfect in form than "When to her lute Corinna sings," "Follow thy fair sun," "The man of life upright," "To music bent is my retired mind," "Fire, fire, fire, fire!," "There is a garden in her face"—with or without music. Even in his day Campion must have seemed a bit archaic and refined. Marlowe, Jonson and Donne were contemporaries. Their world was beyond his grasp—or his interest. In his field, however, Campion is nearly incomparable.

Singing School

BEN JONSON, LADY MARY WROTH

Campion is only *nearly* incomparable. Ben Jonson—another man described as "the first poet laureate"—compares with any poet of his age and the next. He's the most versatile writer in the history of English poetry. He can almost out-Campion Campion and he fathers Robert Herrick's lyrics and those of other "Sons of Ben," Jonson's followers, who climb near to Campion's heights:

> Drink to me only with thine eyes,
>   And I will pledge with mine;
> Or leave a kiss but in the cup,
>   And I'll not look for wine.
> The thirst that from the soul doth rise
>   Doth ask a drink divine;
> But might I of Jove's Nectar sup,
>   I would not change for thine.
> I sent thee late a rosy wreath,
>   Not so much honouring thee
> As giving it a hope, that there
>   It could not withered be.
> But thou thereon did'st only breathe,
>   And sent'st it back to me;
> Since when it grows, and smells, I swear,
>   Not of itself, but thee.

He can set himself on a par with the satirists of the generations that followed his own, with a greater fluidity in his use of the couplet:

> At court I met it, in clothes brave enough,
>   To be a courtier; and looks grave enough,
> To seem a statesman: as I near it came,
>   It made me a great face, I asked its name,

A lord, it cried, buried in flesh and blood,
    And such from whom let no man hope least good,
For I will do none: and as little ill,
    For I will dare none. Good Lord, walk dead still.

Or he writes "On English Monsieur":

Would you believe, when you this Monsieur see,
    That his whole body should speak French, not he?
That so much scarf of France, and hat, and feather,
    And shoe, and tie, and garter should come hither,
And land on one, whose face durst never be
    Toward the sea, farther than half-way tree?
That he, untravelled, should be French so much,
    As French-men in his company should seem Dutch?
Or had his father, when he did him get,
    The French disease, with which he labours yet?
Or hung some monsieur's picture on the wall,
    By which his dam conceived him, clothes and all?

The common elements in these poems and the epistles, elegies and plays are balance, construction and proportion (except in flattery). Even at his most intemperate, his art brings disparate elements into tight control. The fireworks hang suspended in the air, a promise, a pleasure even at their harshest.

And since our dainty age
    Cannot endure reproof,
  Make not thyself a Page,
To that strumpet the Stage,
    But sing high and aloof
Safe from the wolf's black jaw, and the dull
    Ass's hoof.

His epitaph in Westminster Abbey reads: "O rare Benn Johnson." Cutting the stone, Aubrey tells us, cost 18*d.*, paid by Jack Young, later Sir Jack. He also tells us that the living poet had a certain peculiarity of face: "Ben Jonson had one eie lower than t'other, and bigger, like Clun the Player; perhaps he begott Clun." If there is dirt to be dished, and even if there isn't, we can trust Aubrey to dish it.

Jonson suffers one irremediable disability: Shakespeare. Alexander Pope underlines the point in his *Preface to the Works of Shakespeare* (1725): "It is ever the nature of parties to be in extremes; and nothing is so probable, as that because Ben Jonson had much the more learning, it was said on the other hand that Shakespeare had none at all; and because Shakespeare had much the most wit and fancy, it was retorted on the other, that Jonson wanted both. Because Shakespeare borrowed nothing, it was said that Ben Jonson borrowed everything." In the plays the proximity of Shakespeare does Jonson most harm, though he writes plays so different from his friend's that they seem distinct in kind and period. Part of that difference is Jonson's poetic balance, deliberate artistry: he knows what he wants to say and has the means of saying it, no more or less. He reaches a conclusion and stops: no discovery leads him beyond his destination. He speaks for his age, while Shakespeare speaks for himself. Jonson's art is normative, Shakespeare's radical and exploratory. In Jonson there's structure and gauged variegation, in Shakespeare movement and warmth. Coleridge disliked the "rankness" of Jonson's realism and found no "goodness of heart." He condemned the "absurd rant and ventriloquism" in the tragedy *Sejanus*, staged by Shakespeare's company at the Globe. At times Jonson's words, unlike Shakespeare's, tend to separate out and stand single, rather than coalesce, as though he had attended to each individual word. His mind is busy near the surface. He is thirsty at the lip, not in the throat.

It's true, but it is not the whole truth. Jonson's attitude to the very sound of language can seem casual. Except in songs from the plays ("Queen, and huntress, chaste and fair," for instance) and a few lyrics, words are chosen first for their sense and accent, second for their sound value: *meaning* is what Jonson is about—not nuance but sense. So there are clumps of consonants and a sometimes indiscriminate collocation of vowels. Swinburne called him "one of the singers who could not sing." Dryden pilloried him as "not only a professed imitator of Horace, but a learned plagiary of all others; you track him everywhere in their snow." It is the kind of poetry Jonson writes that irritates his critics: they disapprove of what he's *doing*. When he isn't singing, he speaks, an art Swinburne never learned. If his poetry is "of the surface," he has made his surfaces with a special kind of care, and to effect. If he borrowed from classical literature, he was no different from his contemporaries, except that he had a deeper knowledge of what he was quarrying than many did (and did not always acknowledge the debt—though this was not yet the custom). He translated Horace's *Ars Poetica*. Many poems borrow lines, but he integrates them into his verse. He is of a stature with Martial and Juvenal: collaboration, not plagiarism, is the term for what he does. Eliot concedes that Jonson and Chapman "incorporated their erudition into their sensibility." So, too, did Eliot.

Dryden's criticism is telling at one point: Jonson "weaved" the language "too closely and laboriously" and he "did a little too much

Romanise our tongue, leaving the words he translated almost as much Latin as he found them." Dryden ends with the inevitable verdict: "I admire him, but I love Shakespeare." Yet Jonson, not Shakespeare, paves the way to Dryden and Pope.

Shakespeare—who, as Pope insists, "lived on amicable terms" with Jonson, and "was introduced upon the stage," and encouraged by him—does not overshadow Jonson's nondramatic verse. It stands as a model to two subsequent generations of writers and includes poems so distinctively his own in kind that we could confuse them with the work of no one else. Most notable among these are the "country house" poems, elegies and epigrams.

In classical times an "epigram" was the inscription on a tombstone, usually in elegiac verse. But like the term "elegy," "epigram" outgrew its original sense. For Jonson it named the short and not so short occasional poem with a single mood or idea: satirical, amatory, dedicatory or elegiac. He and the "sons of Ben" developed it to high perfection. His long poems tend to "epigram" in the newer sense of "pithy brief statement": couplets and other passages detach themselves and catch like burrs in the mind.

If not a consistent master of mere "music" in verse, Jonson is a master of stress. His poems are regular, with the authority of speech, even in his most intricate forms, an intricacy at times of alternation between a constant and a variable line length, as in "Her Triumph":

Have you seen but a bright Lily grow,
    Before rude hands have touched it?
Have you marked but the fall o' the snow,
    Before the soil hath smutched it?
Have you felt the wool o' the beaver?
    Or swan's down ever?
Or have smelt o' the bud o' the briar?
    Or the nard i' the fire?
Or have tasted the bag o' the bee?
O so white! O so soft! O so sweet is she!

These lines spoke to Ezra Pound: the more we read Jonson the more we see him as an enabling figure comparable to Pound. Clarity of expression is matched by intellectual and perceptual rigor. His aesthetic is expressed in an aphorism: "Language most shows a man. Speak that I may see thee." In the poems we hear and see the man. He addresses a variety of subjects with equal variety of feeling. He doesn't save poetry for moments of crisis or climax. It is a natural language that answers any occasion. Edmund Bolton, writing in his *Hypercritica* in 1722, comments, "I never tasted English more to my liking, nor more smart, and put to the height of use in poetry, than in the vital, judicious, and most practicable language of Benjamin Jonson's poems." Smart, vital, judicious, practicable. Jonson wrote with feeling, tempered thought and wit, a language close to speech: comprehensive, colloquial.

His ability to catch the tone of each situation, class and calling was due in part to his background. He was born in London in 1572, probably a month after his father's death. His mother married again, a bricklayer, and he spent his boyhood working with his stepfather, Aubrey tells us, "particularly on the Garden-wall of Lincoln's Inne next to Chancery Lane," where a passing nobleman, hearing him reciting Greek as he worked and discovering his wit, had him given an exhibition (minor scholarship) to Trinity College, Cambridge. This pretty story may be untrue; but we know he was educated at Westminster School under William Camden ("Camden, most reverend head, to whom I owe / All that I am in arts, all that I know"). Like Marlowe and Shakespeare, he was the new kind of writer, from the new classes. In 1588 he left school and began bricklaying, a fact that later enemies used against him. After military service in Flanders, he married in 1594. Two children were born; both died and were lamented in elegies: "Here lies to each her parents ruth" and the harrowing, resigned "On my First Son," Benjamin:

> Farewell, thou child of my right hand, and joy;
> My sin was too much hope of thee, loved boy,
> Seven years thou wert lent to me, and I thee pay,
> Exacted by thy fate, on the just day.
> O, could I lose all father, now. For why
> Will man lament the state he should envy?
> To have so soon 'scaped world's, and flesh's rage,
> And, if no other misery, yet age?
> Rest in soft peace, and, asked, say here doth lie
> Ben Jonson his best piece of poetry.
> For whose sake, henceforth, all his vows be such,
> As what he loves may never like too much.

In 1597 he was acting and writing for the Admiral's Company of Players. His first work for the stage may have been additional scenes for Thomas Kyd's *A Spanish Tragedy*. In that year he was imprisoned for his part in *The Isle of Dogs*, a seditious play of which he was probably part author. During his spell in prison he became a Roman Catholic, a faith he held for twelve years. In 1598 he killed a fellow actor with a rapier and narrowly escaped hanging. (Aubrey reports with wild implausibility that he killed Marlowe, "the Poet, on Bunhill, coming from the Green-curtain play-house"—"a kind of Nursery or obscure Play-house"). He was branded on the thumb. *Every Man In His Humour,* in which Shake-speare played a part, was staged at the Globe in 1598. Jonson made progress as a playwright and was soon established as a leading tragic and comic dramatist. He was a heavy drinker: "Canarie was his beloved liquor," Aubrey assures us. He would carouse, go home to bed, and after a good sweat get up to study. "I have seen his studyeing chaire, which was of strawe, such as olde woemen used."

In 1612–13 he completed the first book of *Epigrams.* The next year he traveled abroad with Ralegh's son and wrote a fine commendatory poem for Ralegh's *History.* In 1616, the year of Shakespeare's death, Jonson's "first folio" was published—the only first folio to be seen through the press by its author. It was a crucial book, its success paving the way for Shakespeare's First Folio seven years later, in which Jonson had a finan-cial stake and for which he composed his famous elegy "To the Memory of my Beloved, the Author, Mr. William Shakespeare: and what he hath left us," one of the most eloquent blurbs ever written.

After 1616 begin what Dryden calls Jonson's "dotages," a string of unsuccessful plays. But Jonson was far from doddery. He made his leg-endary journey on foot to Scotland to visit William Drummond of Hawthornden, with whom he stayed for three weeks until Drummond's wine cellar was drunk dry. Drummond gave an account of his conversa-tions with Jonson and, since he as a *poeta doctus* was vain of his achieve-ments, took pleasure in commenting on Jonson's ignorance. In effect, he says that Jonson had little French and less Italian. Certainly Jonson was not in the contemporary European swim. He took his bearings from the classics.

In later years he may have been a deputy professor of rhetoric at Gresham College, London. Such an appointment would explain the pedagogic relations he has with the Sons of Ben. He earned respect as a technical master, as Pound was to do. He was venerated by younger poets, those who knew him and those who knew only his work, notably Herrick, Carew, Lovelace and Suckling: the Cavaliers. Jonson was *the* poet to emulate: he serves the language, he does not inscribe it with his "own character" or weave it in accordance with personal myth. The most classical of poets, he nourished himself on the classics and imparted classical virtues. His "school," "tribe" and Sons affirm something as salu-tary as it is strange to our age, when poets are required to have "a voice." He and his followers were masters, with meanings to convey. In their art there is an element little valued now: self-effacement before the rigors of form and the challenge of subject. They don't lack "subjectivity," yet what interests us is not subjectivity, eccentricity or individuality, but their centeredness, a sense of sanctioned authority, the legitimacy of the classics. Rejecting the false, fatuous excesses of the stage in its decline, Jonson says in "Ode to Himself":

> Leave things so prostitute,
> And take the Alcaic lute;
> Or thine own Horace, or Anacreon's lyre;
> Warm thee by Pindar's fire:
> And though thy nerves be shrunk, and blood be cold,
> Ere years have made thee old,
> Strike that disdainful heat
> Throughout, to their defeat:
> As curious fools, and envious of thy strain,
> May blushing swear, no palsy's in thy brain.

The poem ends conventionally flattering the king, but before that (how reluctant we are to accept praise of kings, while we admire the cult of Elizabeth) he ventures successfully as near to the complexity and purity on Pindarics as any English poet has done. He received an MA from Christ Church, Oxford, in 1619.

He works like Campion in the ephemeral mode of masques and draws images from masque conventions, for instance in the elegies that end in staged apotheoses. He collaborated with the architect and designer Inigo Jones, but as Jones grew more self-important, they fell out. Jonson resented the superior success of friends and juniors, and they rounded on him. Jones certainly did, and Jonson's satires on his onetime friend are brutal and distasteful. His later years, in which he suffered from palsy and paralysis, were especially bitter. He was neglected by King Charles upon his accession (James paid him attention). Six petitions of debt were filed against him. Charles eventually realized his value and the poet found new aristocratic patronage: he did not die, as Chapman did, in want. He was buried in 1637 in Westminster Abbey, with Chaucer and Spenser his only peers in that poetic afterworld.

Two modern poets, Yvor Winters and Thom Gunn, insist that Jonson is the man from whom we learn most not only about his age, but about our art. Winters places Jonson at the heart of what he calls the "native tradition," heard in the plain-spoken poems of Wyatt, Gascoigne, Greville and others. From Marlowe he learned that the best verse integrates images rather than using them decoratively. He could control rhetoric for complex tone. Expository rather than persuasive, he has, Winters says, a *specific* morality, and the poems apply it to a social world: relations between people and the people and God.

Gunn suggests that Jonson chose classical models to balance a personal tendency toward extremes—a credible reading, given what we know of Jonson's life and what we sense in the controlled vehemence of the satires, as from the dark world of the comedies. Gunn senses a problem of "willed feeling," which modern readers dislike, especially in poems of flattery that protest that they're not flattering. Those to King James, King Charles and noblemen of various stations are fulsome and repetitive. "How, best of Kings, do'st thou a sceptre bear!" (the Earl of Rochester found a distinctly disrespectful way of depicting that scepter.) Jonson's flattery only works when it's indirect, as in "To Penshurst" and "To Sir Robert Wroth," where he praises patrons by celebrating their estates and style of life. The sincere tributes to Camden, Shakespeare, Donne, Drayton and others are in a different league of seriousness.

All poetry, Gunn reminds us, is occasional, and a good poem remains true to its occasion, its subject. It can be the death of a prince or a boy actor ("Weep with me all ye that read"); it can be a moment of anger at social affectation; a thank-you letter or an impulse to translate a classical poem ("Drink to me only," "Come, my Celia," "Follow a shadow"). It can be a large-scale social indictment ("On the Famous Voyage"), the publication of a book, a sickness or a journey. It can be a weekend at a country house. Such poems are "works of a diverse nature," united by a sensibility to some extent typical of the best of its age. The religious verse has its occasions, too: "A Hymn to God the Father" is utterly chaste and precise:

> Who more can crave
> > Than thou hast done:
> > That gav'st a Son,
> To free a slave?
> > First made of nought;
> > With all since bought.

Only in the love poetry does Jonson descend to the commonplace, but even there with a command that makes it readable. Aubrey reports: " 'Twas an ingeniose remarque of my Lady Hoskins, that B. J. never writes of Love, or if he does, does it not naturally." Best are the elegies in which an old man addresses a young mistress:

> Alas, I have lost my heat, my blood, my prime,
> Winter is come a quarter ere his time,

My health will leave me; and when you depart,
How shall I do sweet mistress, for my heart?

In the elegy "Let me be what I am" there is less resignation. We see one
face of the speaker in such work. The poems that moralize give a certain
solidity to their moral categories by their setting. They take off from a
specific point. In "To John Donne" he writes:

> . . . those that for claps do write
>   Let pui'ness', porters', players' praise delight,   novices'
> And, till they burst, their backs, like asses, load:
>   A man should seek great glory, and not broad.

In another poem, "He that departs with his own honesty / For vulgar
praise, doth it too dearly buy."

Jonson is a moral critic of literature and society. Even personal prob-
lems, the elegies for his children, the "Execration upon Vulcan" (after a
fire destroyed his manuscripts and library), the "Ode to Himself," have
general point and reference; they don't exist for themselves. Poetry is
occasional and *applied* writing. Development in Jonson is moral, not
formal; we follow from poem to poem a mind that sometimes runs deep.
The work should be read *in extenso*, taking the *Epigrams*, *The Forest*, *The
Underwood* and *Miscellany* whole, prose aphorisms along with verse.
The best poems have a tone of just approval or censure, this justice a
product of formal control, balance and conclusion, and equitable wis-
dom. It is important to remember that poetry feigns; the tone and tex-
ture can say one thing while the poet is keen for us to infer something
else. "Rare poems ask rare friends," "A good poet's made, as well as
born," "In small proportions, we just beauties see; / And in short mea-
sures, life may perfect be." Pithy rightness is his hallmark. He is our
greatest epigrammatist.

"To Penshurst" and "To Sir Robert Wroth" are original in ways we
have to remind ourselves how to appreciate. Notions of "landscape"
took shape rather late. Among the first painted landscapes were Inigo
Jones's idealized scenarios for Jonson's masques. "Such are the distin-
guished beginnings of the kind of painting in which Englishmen have
excelled." Such too were the beginnings of a literary tradition that takes
pastoral convention into the actual countryside and finds in the har-
mony between nature and nurture a civilizing theme. The "country
house" poems are occasional, responding to external events. "To Pens-
hurst," in pentameter couplets, "To Sir Robert Wroth," in pentame-
ter/tetrameter couplets, progress with tidy conclusiveness, each detail
moralized and added to the tally, developing broader themes of order,

proportion, natural hierarchy. "To Penshurst" is the finest "country house" poem, celebrating a place associated with Sir Philip Sidney. Jonson first praises its lack of affectation and deliberate grandeur, its healthy naturalness. In classical terms he evokes the park and generalizes its qualities by subtle use of the definite article and the possessive pronoun with collective and plural nouns, much in the manner that Pope was to perfect:

> The lower land, that to the river bends,
> Thy sheep, thy bullocks, kine, and calves do feed:
> The middle grounds thy mares, and horses breed.
> Each bank doth yield thee conies; and the tops,
> Fertile of wood, Ashour, and Sidney's copse,
> To crown thy open table, doth provide
> The purpled pheasant, with the speckled side:
> The painted partridge lies in every field,
> And, for thy mess, is willing to be killed.

This is more alive than Pope's "Windsor Forest" because the *kind* of pastoral language is new. The past participles "painted" and "purpled" suggest the hand of nurture. The word "open" unostentatiously marks the host's hospitality as much as nature's. Jonson presents less an artificial than a cultivated and compliant landscape, a refiguring of Eden. It's a distinction worth bearing in mind. It is Pope, in "Windsor Forest," who artificializes. "To Penshurst" celebrates responsible hierarchy, natural proportion: praise justly and gratefully rendered, not flattery.

"To Sir Robert Wroth," with its diminishing couplet, sounds a similar note of just praise. Sir Robert is the natural squire, hunter and farmer, with fields, livestock and fruit trees. The natural cycle is contained in the simple couplet: "The trees cut out in log; and those boughs made / A fire now, that lent a shade!" Jonson evokes a golden age, cultivating landscape with classical tools, avoiding pastoral idealization. "Strive, Wroth, to live long innocent," he urges. Others can be soldiers, merchants, usurers profiting from their victims' distress, or sycophantic courtiers. Wroth leads a life of service: he serves God, his country and his neighbors. And he earns the friendship, gratitude and service of one of the great poets of his age.

It's worth remembering that, from Jonson, he also earned a degree of obloquy. Wroth's wife was Lady Mary, Sidney's grandniece (or granddaughter, if we credit Aubrey), a poet of merit "unworthily married to a jealous husband" (the words are Jonson's, and Jonson, who did not like sonnets, liked hers) to whom she dedicated *A Treatise on Madde Dogges*. She wrote the first English sonnet sequence by a woman ("Pamphilia to

Amphilanthus") and built on her great-uncle's prose romance one of her own, scandalously publishing it under her own name. Wroth died in 1614 leaving her with a baby and numerous debts, and she fell into a relationship with her cousin William Herbert, Earl of Pembroke, bearing him two bastards. Jonson's praise of her husband in his great poem, qualified by dispraise in his prose, underlines a paradox at the heart of his enterprise. He is a poet not quite in the court and thus not secure in patronage, though not yet wedded to Grub Street, its disciplines and treacheries. The world of such a man is unstable, and part of Jonson's greatness is to have survived in it and to have made it survive in his verse.

Jonson makes us guests at great houses and lets us hear the age's mannerly speech and savor its hospitality. We hear his songs, too; and we meet, through his eyes, friends and foes as real as any in poetry. He was among the first great poets to take an active interest in publishing, to seek fortune and solace from the printing of his own work in book form. He is the grandfather, or godfather, of Grub Street.

"The world's a bubble"

JOHN DONNE, SIR FRANCIS BACON

In 1608 John Donne wrote to Sir Henry Goodere regretting that he had allowed his "Anniversaries" to be printed: "The fault that I acknowledge in myself is to have descended to print anything in verse, which, though it have excuse, even in our times, by example of men which one would think should have little have done it as I; yet I confess I wonder how I declined to it, and do not pardon myself." Not only were the poems ill received (by Ben Jonson among others); he felt exposed and ridiculous. He'd fallen to Grub Street level. Unlike Sidney, he *acquiesced* in publication. No blame attaches to his printer. A contemporary described him: "Mr John Donne, who leaving Oxford, liv'd at the Inns of Court, not dissolute but very neat; a great Visitor of Ladies, a great Frequenter of Plays, a great Writer of conceited Verses." Such a summary Donne found unpleasing.

In his age privacy and "nicety" were finding language and an art: the portrait and portrait miniature, like Hilliard's: easel paintings for private appreciation, for sharing in a gallery with select friends, or for secret appreciation—like the composer's chamber-sized airs, or the courtier's lyrics and elegies, each encoding a specific occasion. Privacy implied that a picture or poem had meaning only, or only in full, to the recipient, the dedicatee, and those in the know. A great violator of such privilege and privacy was the often inaccurate Aubrey, poison-pen portraitist, whose prurience evokes a century of large and little lives. In Donne's court years the age of vast allegorical tapestries and historical canvases was giving way to a human scale. There were inadequate antecedents for such an art. No wonder that in a poem to Goodere Donne writes:

Who makes the Past, a pattern for next year,
　　Turns no new leaf, but still the same things reads,
Seen things, he sees again, heard things doth hear,
　　And makes his life, but like a pair of beads.

The subject is spiritual: the fortifying of the soul. But religious and secular, soul and body, are so intertwined in Donne, his thinking and feeling so of a piece, that what he says of one sphere remains true of another. That's why his religious and devotional poems affect with force even readers who disbelieve or detest the vexed Anglican faith they arise from. C. H. Sisson invokes him in "A Letter to John Donne":

> I understand you well enough, John Donne
> First, that you were a man of ability
> Eaten by lust and by the love of God . . .

Sisson goes on to contrast Donne with modern men of ability:

> That you should have spent your time in the corruption of courts
> As these in that of cities, gives you no place among us:
> Ability is not even the game of a fool
> But the click of a computer operating in a waste
> Your cleverness is dismissed from this suit
> Bring out your genitals and your theology.
>
> What makes you familiar is this dual obsession;
> Lust is not what the rutting stag knows
> It is to take Eve's apple and to lose
> The stag's paradisal look:
> The love of God comes readily
> To those who have most need.

Donne intended to speak to a few, but in the complex clarity of his speaking he engaged, three centuries later, a far wider readership than any of his public-voiced contemporaries.

He allowed his poems to circulate in manuscript among special friends. One of them might copy out a piece for private pleasure, another make a secret record, but the public that knew Donne at court or later heard his sermons in St. Paul's was generally ignorant of his poetry. He, like George Herbert, Andrew Marvell, Henry Vaughan, Richard Crashaw, Thomas Traherne and others, did not welcome the sobriquet "poet." Did Doctor Johnson misvalue him and his fellow "Metaphysicals" because they didn't *say* they took themselves seriously as poets? It's not that they insisted on amateur status, only that they did not see writing poems as imparting a status or constituting a recognizable identity. They lived off their wit, but in a wider world.

Struggling with his religious vocation in 1608, Donne writes to

Goodere in depression and indecision; at no point does he consider becoming a *writer*: "I would fain do something, but that I cannot tell what is no wonder. For to choose is to do. But to be no part of anybody is to be nothing. At most, the greatest persons are but great wens and excrescences, men of wit and delightful conversation but as moles for ornament, except they be so incorporated into the body of the world that they contribute something to the sustentation of the whole." Here, in the intimacy of a letter, we hear in subtler voice the man who would one day deliver the great "No man is an Island" sermon. He has yet to act, but he knows he can't contribute—or not sufficiently—to "the sustentation of the whole" by being a poet. Besides, he had only a limited appetite for reading the stuff: "His library contained little poetry, and he confessed that he was 'no great voyager in other men's works.' "

One man's works he did voyage in: Francis Bacon's. Among the papers he kept by him until he died was a copy of Bacon's then famous poem "The World."

> The world's a bubble, and the life of man
>   Less than a span,
> In his conception wretched, from the womb,
>   So to the tomb;
> Curst from the cradle, and brought up to years
>   With cares and fears.
> Who then to frail mortality shall trust,
> But limns on water, or but writes in dust . . .

The poem led to a debate in 1597 that harked back to the ancient debate preserved in the classic Greek Anthology: Which life is best, the court, the country or the city? The church is not offered as an option. Bacon's poem is more than a philosopher's curious reflection. Formally accomplished, it uses metaphor suggestively, enough indeed to have affected the twenty-year-old Donne, whose "Satires" date from around the time "The World" was circulated among friends, 1592.

Bacon's poem affirms the vanity of life, the fact of death and the need to prepare for it. These were urgent themes for Donne in later years. Nowhere is the Jacobean way of death better illustrated than in Donne's preparations. Most men allowed their survivors to bury them as they thought appropriate. Donne took his death into his own hands. The rehearsals as much as the memorial tell us more about him than we could learn from the rooms he lived in. His single aim was to die and remember death appropriately, leaving an adequate monument to commemorate the spiritual struggle and teach others to consider their fate, a sermon in action leading to a sermon in stone. Izaac Walton in his

wonderful "Life of Donne" tells the story. "Dr Donne sent for a carver
to make for him in wood the figure of an urn, giving him directions for
the compass and height of it; and to bring with it a board of the just
height of his body. These being got, then without delay a choice painter
was got to be in readiness to draw his picture, which was taken as
followeth.—Several charcoal fires being first made in his large study, he
brought with him into that place his winding-sheet in his hand, and,
having put off all his clothes, had this sheet put on him, and so tied with
knots at his head and feet, and his hands so placed, as dead bodies are
usually fitted to be shrouded and put into their coffin, or grave. Upon
this urn he thus stood with his eyes shut, and with so much of the sheet
turned aside as might show his lean, pale and deathlike face." He kept
the picture by his bed "where it continued, and became his hourly object
till his death." Before he prepared for death, however, he lived life to the
full, first outside, then inside the Church.

Only a little over a decade separates Marlowe's *Elegies* and Donne's
love poems, yet the differences are startling. Set Marlowe's thirteenth
elegy from Book One ("To Dawn, not to hurry") beside Donne's "The
Sun Rising." Both are in the same genre and draw on similar conven-
tions. This is Marlowe:

> Now o'er the sea from her old love comes she
> That draws the day from heaven's cold axle-tree.
> Aurora, whither slidest thou? down again,
> And birds for Memnon yearly shall be slain.
> Now in her tender arms I sweetly bide,
> If ever, now well lies she by my side.
> The air is cold, and sleep is sweetest now,
> And birds send forth shrill notes from every bough:
> Whither runn'st thou, that men and women love not?
> Hold in thy rosy horses that they move not.

Donne, by contrast, must have seemed to his friends rawly impassioned
and possessed of new energies:

> Busy old fool, unruly Sun,
> Why dost thou thus,
> Through windows and through curtains call on us?
> Must to thy motions lovers' seasons run?
> Saucy pedantic wretch, go chide
> Late schoolboys, and sour prentices,
> Go tell court huntsmen, that the King will ride,
> Call country ants to harvest offices;

Love, all alike, no season knows, nor clime,
Nor hours, days, months, which are the rags of time.

Between Donne and Marlowe there are obvious formal differences, and consequently stark contrasts: between the cadenced couplets of Marlowe and the harsh, spoken lines of Donne. Marlowe's language of convention (no less expressive for its conventionality) has been replaced by an "unpoetic," dramatic handling of the conventions themselves. The main difference is conceptual. Marlowe's elegy, with the tenderness of lines five to seven, creates with each image a specific scene of love. Donne, by line four, is dealing with generalities. His attention has been distracted from his beloved onto the image of the sun, and thence to the street and the world. We lose sight of the ostensible subject in a poetry of extension, until the third stanza, when the poet's mind returns to bed, and his relationship, a microcosm, swells to the proportions of a macrocosm. "She is all states, and all princes, I, / Nothing else is." Donne's attitude to the sun changes from rancor to charitable pity. Yet the reader remains unenlightened about the relationship that occasions such superb arrogance. Donne's poem has wit, but one is undecided whether it has an actual subject or is a pretext for developing poetic conceit.

Robert Graves notes how Donne's opening inspirations wear out after two or three lines, and mere wit propels him forward. There is fitfulness, a counterpoint between imagination and artifice. This is a virtue for a casual reader whose delight is continuously rekindled; but if the poems are reread, delight diminishes. Graves remarks: "Donne is adept at keeping the ball in the air, but he deceives us here by changing the ball."

A juggler who, unperceived, changes the balls as he juggles was bound to appeal to the modernists. After centuries of relative neglect, Donne found in T. S. Eliot an advocate. But even as he celebrates Donne, Eliot suggests that the work will speak to the first half of the twentieth century more eloquently than to the second. The case—or cases—against Donne and the Metaphysicals are of long standing, and it is worth remembering the terms in which they were made and—Eliot suggests—would be made again.

Jonson, after initial reservations, admired Donne above most of his contemporaries, but "for not keeping number" he deserved hanging. Donne incorporates the energy of speech in his meters and his phrased verse is effective, though we have to agree with Yvor Winters that there are examples "more of rhythmic violence than subtlety." He lacks Marvell's metrical agility. "It was as if, impatient as he was of women, love, fools and God, he was impatient too of the close steps of metre." His satire consciously roughens the surface and defies scansion. Take a passage from the second satire: having pilloried different kinds of writers, he lights on plagiarists:

> But he is worst, who (beggarly) doth chaw
> Others' wits' fruits, and in his ravenous maw
> Rankly digested, doth those things out-spew,
> As his own things; and they are his own, 'tis true,
> For if one eat my meat, though it be known
> The meat was mine, th' excrement is his own:
> But these do me no harm, nor they which use
> To out-do Dildoes, and out-usure Jews

In this coarse manner he speaks after Juvenal, harshly departing from meter without quite abandoning the norm. Yet the first half of the second line is very nearly unsayable.

Dryden's case against him goes beyond prosody. Even in the amorous poems Donne is, he says, "metaphysical"; he "perplexes the minds of the fair sex with nice speculations of philosophy, when he should engage their hearts." For Dryden, he's a great wit, not a great poet. The force of this case is felt by those who, in the brilliance of Donne's word-play, his spinning out of startling analogies and conceits, find at work deliberate intelligence, not imagination: a talent of the surface rather than the depths, for which dalliance with language is more erotic than dalliance with the beloved. He moves us by surprise rather than by truth. Marvell and Herbert deliver a kernel of experience, while Donne might seem to deliver the husk that held it. We're aware of a person delivering the poems in various voices. "The vividness of the descriptions or declamations in Donne, or Dryden," says Coleridge, "is as much and as often derived from the forced fervour of the describer as from the reflections, forms or incidents which constitute their subject and materials. The wheels take fire from the mere rapidity of their motion." Having hoisted Dryden on the same petard, Coleridge offers an epigram on Donne:

> With Donne, whose muse on dromedary trots,
> Wreathe iron pokers into true-love knots;
> Rhyme's sturdy cripple, fancy's maze and clue,
> Wit's forge and fire-blast, meaning's press and screw.

"Self-impassioned": that's Coleridge's verdict and "Valediction Forbidding Mourning" justifies it. Metaphor and conceit develop by association of idea or semantic nuance, not appropriateness of physical form. The image of the dying man suggests the lovers' separation. Stoically, the poet prays that it be without tempests (tears); tempests suggest sky and moving earth, an image detailed without reference to preceding images. Astronomy follows naturally and is developed until, on the word "refined," Donne's mind turns to metals and alchemy: gold is the next image. The expansion of hammered gold suggests attachment in separation, and in come the famous compasses. Double meaning or intellectual (but not logical) association lead from stanza to stanza. A powerful pseudo-argument develops, convincing because of the *sense* of logic, and the spell holds for the duration of the poem. As Winters says, the "rational structure" is used to "irrational ends." Donne elaborates and decorates at the expense of theme, sometimes so for that he displaces it altogether.

Doctor Johnson's is the most concise case against Donne. In his *Life of Cowley*, Johnson says the poet specialized in what he calls "enormous and disgusting hyperboles," a bad habit contracted from Donne. "Who but Donne," he asks, "would have thought a good man was a telescope?" Applying Dryden's term "metaphysical" to Donne and other poets of his time, he calls them "men of learning" whose "whole endeavour" was "to show their learning." They wrote verse rather than poetry, "and very often such verses as stood the trial of the finger better than the ear." Dryden, Johnson says, ranks below Donne in wit but surpasses him in poetry. For Johnson wit is what is "at once natural and new," not obvious but "upon its first production, acknowledged to be just," so we wonder how we ever missed it. In Donne the thought is new, but seldom natural; it is not obvious, but neither is it just.

Yet if we define wit as *discordia concors*, sensed similarity in things dissimilar, then Donne and the Metaphysicals have that—at a certain cost: "Their courtship is void of fondness, and their lamentation of sorrow." They are neither sublime nor pathetic, they evince none of "that comprehension and expanse of thought which at once fills the whole mind." They replace the sublime with hyperbole, "combinations of confused magnificence, that not only could not be credited, but could not be imagined." An example from "Twickenham Garden":

Blasted with sighs, and surrounded with tears,
  Hither I come to seek the spring,
  And at mine eyes, and at my ears,
Receive such balms, as else cure every thing;
  But O, self traitor, I do bring
The spider love, which transubstantiates all,
  And can convert Manna to gall,
And that this place may thoroughly be thought
  True Paradise, I have the serpent brought.

What have we here? A storm-tossed wandering lover—a self-traitor, an alchemist, a god and an Adam. We have a serpent and a spider. We have various levels of experience and metaphor woven in a resonant, affective, but meaningless stanza—or meaningful to the exegete, who patiently teases out sacramental themes and recognizes the dramatic inversion of religious images in service of carnal passion.

Johnson does not set out to dismiss the Metaphysicals but to characterize them. Herbert and Marvell he overlooks. For Johnson, the best poems are true from any angle of approach, and Donne's are true from only one angle. Each word is restricted by context to a single significance. Joan Bennett makes this into a virtue in her account of Donne: he impresses words and images into service in a specific way; they appear clean of conventional association, without nuance or ambiguity.

Johnson's most telling criticism is that Donne's allusive strategy points always away from the poem's occasion, it does not refer back and concentrate. Readers must bring various bits of information to their reading, where ideally "every piece ought to contain in itself whatever is necessary to make it intelligible." Again it's clear why Eliot and the modernists fell for Donne.

The thematic concerns and radical procedures of Donne's poetry reveal a personality as complex and controversial as the verse itself. Born in London in 1572, he was a city creature. When he had to reside outside London for a time he complained bitterly. He has in his heart no place for the pastoral. His father was an ironmonger who prospered but died when the poet was four years old. Images of metallurgy and alchemy had a special resonance for him. His mother was the daughter of John Heywood, poet, playwright, and a descendant of Sir Thomas More; it was a Roman Catholic family with, in his great-uncle Thomas Heywood, a Catholic martyr. Two uncles were Jesuit priests. Donne received a Roman Catholic education and was reared a firm recusant. For a decade, from the age of twelve, he studied at Hart Hall, Oxford, with his brother Henry; then both proceeded to the Inns of Court, referred to at the time as the "third university." Henry gave refuge to a seminary priest and both brothers were arrested. Henry died of the plague in Newgate Prison before he came to trial. The priest was hanged, taken down and disemboweled before an appreciative crowd.

Though he harbored a dislike for the Jesuits, Donne found the transition to Anglicanism hard. To achieve preferment, he had to abandon a faith that blocked his progress. But the struggle between faith and family loyalty on the one hand, and burning ambition on the other, made him a writer different in kind from his contemporaries, more like the poets of the Continent. As Ford says, "The greatest of all these great ones have invariably about them a note of otherworldliness: they have seen Hell, they have wrestled with God, they have sounded horrors superhuman and inconceivable." In Dante, Villon, Isaiah, St. Augustine, we find this "greatest." And sometimes in Donne. *Amour* is bleached out of him, his very gender changed, by the blast of faith and the hunger and doubts it brought him. Other Metaphysicals are more or less comfortable in conscience and in their material circumstances. Donne was virtually compelled against a recusant conscience to turn Anglican and, in order to put food in his family's mouth, to live a kind of partial truth, to take orders from the king in a church he regarded as in a sense heretical, to give sermons on themes and occasions where political interests claimed the right to use him.

Following his heart, he made certain crucial miscalculations. After military service with Essex at Cadiz, and an expedition to the Azores, as well as diplomatic missions, he was secretary to the shrewd and influential Sir Thomas Egerton, Lord Keeperone. It was a good job that gave him insights into the devious workings of court and the state machine. At twenty-nine he fell in love with Anne More, daughter of a rich Surrey landowner whose sister was Egerton's new wife. By the time of their clandestine marriage he had composed the *Satires* (1593–98), the majority of the *Elegies* and many of the *Songs and Sonets*. He had completed *The Progress of the Soul* and had become a member of Parliament. Egerton drove him out and they were never reconciled. For fifteen years Donne struggled to support a growing family. "John Donne, Anne Donne, Un-done," he wrote when he was dismissed. And for a long time it seemed he was right.

He was briefly imprisoned. Forced to live off the generosity of friends, he pursued his study of canon and civil law to provide himself with a livelihood. His depressions were acute: he contemplated suicide. He wrote *Biathanatos*, a partial justification of suicide, in 1606. In that year he removed with his growing family to Mitcham, where living might prove cheaper than in London, retaining for himself lodgings in the Strand. He made a number of valuable friends, among them Mrs. Magdalen Herbert, mother of the poet George and of Lord Herbert of Cherbury, the Countess of Pembroke, and the Countess of Huntingdon. Several of them received tributes of verse.

By 1609, drawn by Dean Thomas Morton's anti-Jesuit pamphleteering, he contributed to the debate his *Pseudo-Martyr*, an incitement to papists to take the oath of loyalty to the Crown. This and other pamphlets attracted the king's attention. In the next two years the king urged him—some say, ordered him—against his secular ambition into the church. During the period of his resistance to the king he wrote the *Holy Sonnets* (1609–1611), an expression of faith and of his doubt of vocation. He continued to resist through 1614, when he was able briefly to return to Parliament. In 1615, after a final attempt at secular preferment, he took orders and completed his *Epicede and Obsequies*, probably begun in 1601. They are Donne at his most fantastic and "public." The bulk of his religious verse was by then completed as well.

Having taken orders, he was made a royal chaplain, preaching to king and court, and his talent for sermons was such that some are still read today. He dealt too with diplomatic correspondence (a form of secular work more to his taste). He traveled. In 1617 at Paul's Cross, outside the old St. Paul's, which was destroyed in the fire of 1666 and replaced by Wren's defiant thimble, he ascended to the outdoor pulpit to deliver a Sunday forenoon sermon, the commendatory sermon on the anniversary of the death of Queen Elizabeth (who had reigned for the first thirty-two years of his life). His audience that day included Sir Francis Bacon (the Lord Keeper), the Earls of Arundel and Southampton, the Archbishop of Canterbury, and a throng of Londoners, from merchants to tramps, from great ladies to whores. He was a catch for the English church. Four years later he was appointed dean of St. Paul's. Between 1619 and 1623 he wrote his three "Hymns," almost the last of his verse; and in 1623, as a result of serious illness (he expected death), he composed the *Devotions*. But he survived another eight years. In 1630 he began to weaken. In 1631 he preached the sermon he knew would be his last, now known as *Death's Duel*, and died in just the way he had rehearsed.

During his life, his verse circulated—it is impossible to determine how widely—in manuscript. Two years after his death the poems were published. The publisher may have felt a slightly indecency in handling the work, "so difficult and opaque it is, I am not certain what it is I print." But the book sold rather well, running through six editions before 1670. Here, the dean—celebrity, monster of eloquence, performer, eccentric—is discovered as a man with a body that felt lust, pain and love, and a mind whose attunement to circumstance was not always easy. The American poet Allen Tate has the effrontery to speak of him as "a contemporary," perhaps because of his lusts and religious uncertainties, and proceeds to misread him in this light. With Donne, if one misunderstands the man one misreads the poems. T. S. Eliot wanted to draw him back into the mainstream of English verse and his attempt involved a little critical distortion. But Eliot did not misread the man. Donne's skepticism is unlike our own. His religious struggle was due to an uncertainty about the terms, not the fundamentals, of faith. His problem was not in believing, but in believing rightly, and having accepted right belief, to behave accordingly. We do Donne no justice by loading on him our doubts; nor does he (as Herbert does) offer us help with doubt. His struggle in the secular poems was to determine and resist the finitude of man's nature; in the religious poems it was to establish finite man's relations with an infinite God manifested in the Incarnation and celebrated in the Mass.

The poems seem logical but work by association. Mario Praz reflects on the baroque quality of the verse. Donne's "sole preoccupation is with the whole effect": not so much a quest for truth as for effectiveness. The poems *enact*, rather than argue or explore. Imagery is imported into rather than implicit in the situation. Analogies with modern techniques can be drawn, but poets who claim kinship with him do not pursue his formal ends or share the philosophical and theological verities that underpin his work. "A thought to Donne was an experience; it modified his sensibility," wrote Eliot. True, but Donne had a consistent sensibility secured by a consistent faith that provided him with an *identity*, how-ever tormented. The difference between his sensibility and those of modern poets who learn from him (Eliot and Edgell Rickword excepted) is the difference between a poet turning an idea into poetry and a poet ruminating poetically on an idea. Donne's poems generate ideas. They are concentrated, dramatic and realized.

He is inevitably the dramatic center of his poems, as actor or acted upon. He detaches himself from the experience in order to set the self in the dramatic frame. Even in the religious poems he presents a self strug-gling. But at times we doubt the actual—if not the dramatic—intensity of the struggle. Rickword sees it as Donne's "intense preoccupation with the individual at the extreme tension of consciousness"; we might regard it, less charitably, as a form of posturing. Technique favors the ungener-ous reading, given Donne's unwillingness to focus long on an actual subject. His wit hops off at a tangent; he can't resist a grandiloquent phrase or its suggestions, peripheral drama or subplot. Often the tan-gents are memorable.

It is worth making the case against Donne because his actual achieve-ment has been obscured by those who praise his eccentricities, paint him as a contemporary and deprive him of his authority as a rich, even an alien, *other*. Donne, lover and divine, apprehends ambivalence in himself and fastens it to objects outside himself, keeping his love but forfeiting the object of his love until he finds the greater object, and in it finds self-doubt.

In the physical world he experiences now ecstasy, now disgust, an ecstasy as intense as disgust. A love of timeless pleasure in one poem becomes in another a bitterness at the ephemeral nature of all attach-ments. On the spiritual plane he knows both exalted joy and a deep sense of unworthiness. Idealism is checked by realism and spiritual pes-simism. The city, love affairs, longing for secular preferment and later for religious grace produce a profoundly ambiguous poetry. Such perplexity occasions that "forcing of congruities" which is responsible for the best and worst in his work. Where the Augustan solves the perplexity in one way and the Romantic in another, Donne, like Crashaw, Vaughan and Herbert, leaves it unresolved, laying it with a reluctant trust on the altar of a living faith. He wrestles with idea and reality at once, and cannot lie in a single rapture in bed with his beloved the way that Marlowe can in his "Elegy."

Songs and Sonets and *Divine Poems* contrast principally in dramatic form. The persistent wooer becomes the penitent object of divine wooing. As a lover Donne can be passionate and sometimes cruel, but seldom tender. In "The Jet Ring" he writes, "Circle this finger top, which didst her thumb," revealing how small her hand, how large his own, a relative power in the relationship. In the *Divine Poems* the tables are turned; he experiences such treatment from his God. He is amazed that God should look his way, is "drawn to God by the mystery of his condescension" in the Incarnation. In the first of the "Holy Sonnets" he writes,

> Despair behind, and death before doth cast
> Such terror, and my feeble flesh doth waste
> By sin in it, which it toward hell doth weigh . . .

giving us the sense of a man hemmed in before and behind, and like Faust weighed downward by his own guilt. God is a magnet drawing him to heaven. As in the love poems, emotion—in this case, fear born of a sense of unworthiness—stimulates thought; it is not a drug pleasing to the senses. Emotion accentuates his egotism: there is no broad typicality about his struggle, as about Herbert's. It is too extreme. This is its dramatic virtue and its poetic bound, a bound he can transcend, as in the meditative ninth elegy, "The Autumnal," so infused with affection and regard that it is rapt, adjusting in a tone of appreciative banter its bizarre elements into a series of aphoristically precise statements. It is also transcended in the best religious sonnets and poems, especially in "Thou hast made me," "I am a little world," "This is my play's last scene" (with the "I" acquiring a sort of typicality), and in the hymns. It is found more rarely in the *Songs and Sonets*. "Donne's muse ranged through almost every mood save Herbert's and Crashaw's serene belief in the Saviour who saves . . . or Marvell's serene, almost cavalier indifference." Yet who before Donne so weds piety and wit? The witty preacher, "He punned even with God, and inserted wit among the attributes of divinity." And he lay prostrate before Him like a bride.

Pastoral Care

ROBERT HERRICK, GEORGE HERBERT, HENRY VAUGHAN

> The bed is ready, and the maze of love
> Looks for the treaders; everywhere is wove
> Wit and new mystery; read, and
> Put in practice, to understand
> And know each wile,
> Each hieroglyphic of a kiss or smile,
> And do it to the full; reach
> High in your own conceit, and some way teach
> Nature and art one more
> Play than they ever knew before.

Donne celebrates his own love, Robert Herrick the love of others. His poetic antecedents can be traced to "rare arch-poet Jonson," but his poems have a complete polish only seldom found in the archpoet's. He concentrates less on argument than elaboration. Swinburne was hard on Jonson, but he calls Herrick the "greatest songwriter ever born of English race." Coming from the deliriously melodious Swinburne, this alerts us to certain verbal qualities: a concentration on sound, even at the expense of sense.

Figurative language, delightful conceit, revived conventions: these are parts of Herrick's small, intimate poetic arsenal, developed far from the urban commotion that surrounded Jonson's verse. Even his epigrams seem leisurely. He expects us, after hearing a poem, not to judge or act, but to reflect and savor. His is a generally benign universe, with some of the charm of Marvell's, though only a little of its latent violence and lacking its intellectual qualities. For Herrick, the natural order is rural. He gave up seeking the aristocratic patrons who drew writers such as Marvell into the turbulent politics of the day. History broke in on Herrick's life with the English Civil War, and like other Cavaliers (those loyal to Charles I) he was cut to the quick by the execution of his king, but as a poet he was remote from affairs: pastoral in every sense.

Herrick was born in London in 1591. His father was a goldsmith and banker from Leicestershire, his mother a mercer's daughter. The year after his birth, his father fell out of an attic window, leaving a sizable estate of £5,068, which was initially attached by the Crown because the dead man was presumed a suicide. Suicide was a felony, the estate was forfeit. After an anxious time, Juliana, the widow, saved the estate. Robert, his three brothers and two sisters were raised in Hampton, Middlesex, far enough from London for him to enjoy the river eyots, meadows and chalk hills, and Hampton Court with its stately to-ing and fro-ing.

It's uncertain where he was educated, but he certainly mastered the Latin classics. In 1607 he was apprenticed as a goldsmith to his rich uncle. After six years he'd had enough of his overbearing relation, though his head was filled with the intricacies of his craft and a feeling for the fine ladies for whom his handiwork was destined. He went up to St. John's College and, later, Trinity Hall, Cambridge, to study law, and there—despite a continual duel with his uncle to get funds from his inheritance—he secured a BA in 1617 and an MA in 1620. Three years later he was ordained along with his college friend John Weekes, to whom (under the name of Posthumus) he dedicated "His Age," a long poem grounded in Horace. His formal mastery is nowhere clearer than in the fourth stanza, on his favorite theme of ephemerality. The fifth and sixth lines contain the essential quality of Herrick's art:

> But on we must, and thither tend,
> Where Anchus and rich Tellus blend
>   Their sacred seed;
> Thus has infernal Jove decreed;
>   We must be made,
> Ere long, a song, ere long, a shade.
> Why then, since life to us is short,
> Let's make it full up, by our sport.

The last couplet offers feeble consolation.

There is a biographical blank for a time: probably the young poet lived in London, earned the patronage of Endymion Porter, a friend of the Duke of Buckingham, and joined the Sons of Ben at the Apollo Chamber of the Devil and St. Dunstan in Temple Bar. His first (brief) recognition as a poet came in 1625 with verses on the death of James I. He must have started writing earlier, two or three years before he went to Cambridge. He was a perfectionist, a goldsmith even in his verse, and revised, compressed and rendered smooth with great dedication. Some of his epigrams are in poor taste, but few are flawed in execution.

In 1627 Porter secured him a place as chaplain to the Duke of Buckingham during the ill-starred expedition to the Isle of Ré in the Bay of Biscay to support the French Huguenots. Weekes went with him. The next year the duke was murdered. Herrick's mother died, and he inherited far less than he had hoped. After the double setback—loss of patron and of expectations—he was given the living of Dean Prior, Devon.

Situated on the road between Exeter and Plymouth, on the edge of Dartmoor, it was a small and manageable parish and in some weathers and some frames of mind it seemed idyllic. The larger landscape finds no place in his poems, but the detail of blossom, river and meadows is there in full. The parishioners were rural folk, small landowners and farm workers, and maybe a handful of weavers—a far cry from the Devil and St. Dunstan. He was not in a hurry to become a parish priest: he did not settle there until 1630, maybe reluctantly. He expresses a dislike:

> More discontents I never had
>   Since I was born than here,
> Where I have been and still am sad,
>   In this dull Devonshire.

It may be more than imitation of classical dissatisfaction; but he wrote contented poems as well. Notable among them is "A Country Life: To his Brother," which in form and moral resembles Jonson's "To Sir Robert Wroth." The difference is of class. Wroth was an aristocrat, Herrick's brother a less exalted being. Herrick calls him to a life of paternity and good husbandry. "A Panegyric to Sir Lewis Pemberton" follows Jonson's poem more closely, to good effect.

Herrick was ejected from his living in 1647 by the Parliamentarians. After some years in London, where in 1649 he published his *Hesperides* and *Noble Numbers*, without success for himself or his printer, he was reinstated at the Restoration and held his living from 1662 until his death in 1674. He had his devoted servant, Prudence Baldwin, and many friends. Most of his surviving poetry—over a thousand poems—was written before 1649.

He was a Cavalier, and loyalists said they liked his book, but few others did. A hundred and fifty years went by before a reprint. Abraham Cowley and Edmund Waller found readers, but Herrick, whose work is not unlike theirs in some respects, didn't appeal. He wasn't asked to contribute with other Sons of Ben to the Jonson memorial volume of 1638. He may have stopped writing because no one read him. It's possible that a growing fashion for Donne's poems, which hindered the reception of the work of Michael Drayton and others, had the effect of casting Herrick as an anachronism. A long time must pass before an anachronism is released back into time.

For Herrick the execution of Charles I ended a natural social order; he never adjusted to the new world. His best poem on the subject, "The bad season makes the poet sad," speaks through convention with a profound personal conviction:

> Dull to myself, and almost dead to these
> My many fresh and fragrant mistresses;
> Lost to all music now; since every thing
> Puts on the semblance here of sorrowing.
> Sick is the land to th' heart; and doth endure
> More dangerous faintings by her desp'rate cure.
> But if that golden Age would come again,
> And Charles here rule, as he before did reign;
> If smooth and unperplext the seasons were,
> As when the sweet Maria lived here:
> I should delight to have my curls half drown'd
> In Tyrian dews, and head with roses crown'd;
> And once more yet (ere I am laid out dead)
> *Knock at a star with my exalted head.*

The note is Horatian, intense feeling contained and heightened by technical skill. Herrick doesn't judge. Perhaps the state was sick, but the "cure" was "desperate" and destroyed as much as it cured. Little work survives from the years after the death of the "brave Prince of Cavaliers." Herrick, losing his England, lost his voice as well.

Like other Cavaliers, he is an "agreeable" writer, "consciously urbane, mature, and civilised," as F. R. Leavis notes. He owed debts to Donne as well as Jonson, but his real masters were the Latin classics. Leavis overstates the "close relation to the spoken language" of the Caroline lyric. Herrick's language is remote from the English spoken in his Devon parish, or the language of the merchant class from which he came. His is the language of the wits, old-fashioned even for the times. It is *clear*, but that's not to say it is close to speech. On the contrary, had it been idiomatic it would have dated as much as the language of Jonson's coarser comedies.

The poems abound in transitive verbs, suggesting movement if not action, and Herrick rejects the Spenserian manner *tout court*. He rejects, too, the refined Arcadian landscape. Literal experience underlies his pastoral. One might regard it more properly as rural, for nymphs and shepherds are replaced with figures very like his parishioners. It is England and Devon he writes of. At the opening of *Hesperides* he lists his subjects:

> I sing of brooks, of blossoms, birds, and bowers:
> Of April, May, of June, and July-flowers.
> I sing of Maypoles, hock-carts, wassails, wakes,
> Of bride-grooms, brides, and of their bridal-cakes.
> I write of youth, of love, and have access
> By these, to sing of cleanly-wantonness.

Youth, love, and that wonderful phrase "cleanly-wantonness"; weather, luxuries, ephemerality, myth, fairyland, dreamland, heaven and hell: the "Argument of his Book" accurately advertises its contents. Generally the poems address a single or imagined hearer. Sometimes he talks with himself, or with "Prew" (Prudence, his housekeeper). His words emerge from a shared solitude, as though to answer a rural silence. There is no public authority about them. His lived pastoral, enhanced with classical allusion, includes a good deal of practical wisdom and close observation. The earthy influence of Thomas Tusser's verse advice to farmers is felt, but Herrick keeps his hands clean, his prosody under control.

Although he was a clergyman, it is striking that his poetry is almost totally innocent of the Fall. He is classical to such a degree that most of his poems are pagan in attitude. His "many fresh and fragrant mistresses," preeminently Julia, but also Anthea, Perila, Sappho, Electra, Lucia, Corinna, Amarillis and others, are not virginal, are not Dante's Beatrice or Petrarch's Laura. They are courtable girls without metaphysical pretension. The poems can be erotically frank and joyful. When he celebrates a wedding, it is to enjoin the couple (notably his dear college friend Sir Clipseby Crew) to enjoy lawful bliss. The bed itself he animates enthusiastically:

> And to your more bewitching, see, the proud
> Plump bed bear up, and swelling like a cloud,
>   Tempting the two too modest; can
>   Ye see it brustle like a swan,
>   And you be cold
> To meet it, when it woos and seems to fold
>   The arms to hug it? Throw, throw
> Yourselves into the mighty over-flow
>   Of that white pride, and drown
>   The night, with you, in floods of down.

He urges consummation in those amazing pillows, his theme: *carpe noctem*. Frankness within a refined, conventional style gives it authority. He's seldom solemn, always a wooer or a sad (though not bitter) elegist of happiness. In his "Farewell" and "Welcome" to sack he speaks with a whole voice, as if to a wife or mistress.

He suggests, with a few paradoxical adjectives, actual passion or disruption underlying a formal statement. The poems are perfect but celebrate the conscious or unconscious imperfections or relaxations of rule that beguile the heart. "A sweet disorder in the dress," "an erring lace," "bewitch" him more than "when art / Is too precise in every part." He is delighted with the way Julia's petticoat transgresses. A phrase such as "harmless folly" in "Corinna's going a-Maying" provides a key. Or in "Upon Julia's Clothes," his most famous poem, the unstated, underlying image of fish and hook livens a brittle conceit. And in "To Music," "the civil wilderness"—a phrase met with elsewhere in his poetry—is one of those expressions bordering on oxymoron. Some of the elegies—for example, the one on the death of Endymion Porter's brother, or on his own dying brother—and poems such as "To Live Merrily, and to Trust to Good Verses" address the dark realm of passion and ephemerality. But usually the bright surface is unclouded. There are hints, sufficient to recommend present pleasure. "Gather ye rosebuds while ye may," "Fair daffodils, we weep to see"—such poems are suasive and in no sense morbid.

So generous, so pagan a poet at Dean Prior, with his cure of souls, made little impression on the poetry of the time. He was an anachronism, the last Cavalier, the man in whom the Elizabethan tradition of songwriting reaches—too late—its perfection. In the nineteenth century his verse was revived. In this century, his work and that of other Cavaliers has been overshadowed by the Metaphysicals. Herrick is as charming as Marvell, though he lacks his intelligence; technically he's a peer of Donne, though without his scope. He speaks in many tones of a range of human experience. He does not get lost in Arcadia and is free too of the extremes of attitude, the posturing, which mar much Metaphysical verse. He does not display his learning: he uses it. His work is not, in Doctor Johnson's phrase, "singular," but general in application and normative in effect—a "moral" art, like Jonson's, only gentler, more temperate, more pagan, and as durable.

Herrick made a poem—not a particularly good one—in the shape of a cross. George Herbert made poems in shapes too: an altar, Easter wings. This ingenious form of poetic devotion had to be appropriate and decorous. It traced its ancestry to the *Technopaegnia* of the Alexandrians, who insisted that shape must be relevant to content. The "corona," or linked sonnet sequence, the acrostic poem that embedded the name of the queen, the beloved, or a religious figure (for example Sir John Davies's *Hymns of Astraea*, which build around the acrostic ELISA-BETHA REGINA), are part of the classically sanctioned spiritual and secular play of poets who give themselves an additional formal challenge, on top of meter and rhyme, to try their skills. Such experiments prefigure the more arbitrary experimentation of Auden in suppressing the use of articles in certain poems, or the OuLiPo writers, or John Ashbery, in *The Tennis Court Oath*, setting himself challenges that baffle, then enhance, sense. Only poets in love with their language and their virtuosity set themselves such tasks.

There are analogies with music, the ways in which composers develop a "lettered" theme, or restrict themselves to a narrow range of notes and combinations in order to "say" something. George Herbert, like his brother Lord Herbert of Cherbury, was a musician, and when he was rector at Bemerton used to walk into Salisbury to make music with friends. In the slight poem "Church-Music" there is a wonderful movement of gratitude, expressed with natural, unforced synesthesia:

> Sweetest of sweets, I thank you: when displeasure
> > Did through my body wound my mind,
> You took me thence, and in your house of pleasure
> > A dainty lodging me assigned.
>
> Now I in you without a body move,
> > Rising and falling with your wings:
> We both together sweetly live and love,
> > Yet say sometimes, *God help poor Kings*.
>
> Comfort, I'll die; for if you post from me,
> > Sure shall I do so, and much more:
> But if I travel in your company,
> > You know the way to heaven's door.

God help poor Kings. When Charles I awaited execution, he read Herbert's *The Temple* for consolation.

Born in 1593 in Montgomeryshire, Wales, George was the fifth son of Richard Herbert, scion of a distinguished Anglo-Welsh family, and Magdalen, a woman of parts and friend of Donne, who in her widowhood dedicated his celebrated, conceited "Autumnal" to her: "No spring, nor summer beauty hath such grace / As I have seen in one autumnal face . . ." Richard Herbert died in 1596, leaving ten children. After three years the family removed to Oxford, and two years later to London. From twelve to sixteen, Herbert attended Westminster School; Lancelot Andrewes, then dean of Westminster, taught there during his first year, introducing the boys to a style of elaborate and trenchant expression. At the age of twelve he was writing satiric Latin verses against the Presbyterian polemicist Andrew Melville. He started his music studies and became proficient, especially (like Campion) as a lutenist.

After a decade of widowhood Magdalen married Sir John Danvers, a man twenty years her junior, in 1609, the year George went up to Trinity College, Cambridge. She continued to influence her son until her death in 1627. To her, when he was sixteen, he wrote from college a new year letter reproving "the vanity of those many love-poems, that are daily writ and consecrated to Venus," and lamenting "that so few are writ, that look towards God and Heaven." He enclosed two sonnets (quoted by Walton in his indispensible *Life*), one of them good, foreshadowing the Metaphysical aesthetic of "Jordan (i)," and resolves, "that my poor abilities in poetry, shall be all, and ever consecrated to God's glory."

> My God, where is that ancient heat towards Thee
> Wherewith whole shoals of martyrs once did burn,
> Besides their other flames? Doth Poetry
> Wear Venus' livery? only serve her turn?
> Why are not sonnets made of Thee, and lays
> Upon Thine altar burnt? Cannot Thy love
> Heighten a spirit to sound out Thy praise
> As well as any she? Cannot Thy Dove
> Outstrip their Cupid easily in flight?

Milton is gently prefigured here; also Herbert's mature verse. His eldest brother, Lord Herbert of Cherbury, poet, diplomat and Neoplatonist, was urbane, worldly; he abandoned religion. George began on a similar path but took a different turning, from secular to divine vocation, particularizing his language as he went. He wrote these lines as much to please his mother as God. Yet all of his surviving English poems are devotional, despite his early secular ambitions and his reluctance—like Donne's—to enter religious orders.

From this beginning he is a figurative writer: flame (faith), livery (the secular court), altar, song, dove. These are not counters to decorate an idea. Through development and contrast they extend meaning. Paraphrase cannot displace them. Ornamental metaphor merely glosses essentially prose meaning; conceit tends to displace meaning altogether.

(For a vivid chain of conceits, one need look no further than Donne's "Autumnal.") Herbert's figures, adapting familiar religious matter, *are* the argument, moving with inherent logic.

In 1613 he took his BA, became a minor fellow of Trinity College and wrote two Latin elegies on the death of that most elegized of men, Prince Henry. Despite delicacy of health, he took his MA and a fellowship in 1615–16. He was required to take orders within seven years, which he failed to do. At this time he was friendly with Donne, who had just taken orders himself.

He took the first step toward a secular career in 1618 when he became reader (praelector) in rhetoric at Cambridge. The next was in 1620 when he was elected public orator of the university. His friendships with Bacon (who let him read his works before submitting them for publication, and whose *Advancement of Learning* he helped translate into Latin), Donne and Lancelot Andrewes flourished. Lord Herbert, appointed ambassador to France in 1619, dedicated his treatise *De Veritate* to George and to William Boswell. In 1623–24 he served as MP for Montgomeryshire; a fellow MP was his Cambridge contemporary Nicholas Ferrar, who plays a crucial part in his immortality. In 1624 he was at last ordained deacon. Thus he debarred himself from further secular preferment.

The deaths of friends and patrons—including James I in 1625, Bacon and Andrewes in 1626 and his mother in 1627 (Donne preached her funeral sermon)—and the influence of Donne and Nicholas Ferrar sobered him. He was installed a canon of Lincoln Cathedral and received the living of Leighton Bromswold in 1626. Many poems of discontent and uncertainty date from this period. In 1628 he resigned his oratorship. He married (happily) Jane Danvers, a relation of his stepfather's, after a three-day courtship and in 1630 received the living of Fugglestone with Bemerton, near Salisbury. In September of that year he was ordained priest at Salisbury Cathedral. Aubrey reports that the Earl of Pembroke "gave him a Benefice at Bemmarton (between Wilton and Salisbury) a pittifull little chappell of Ease at Foughelston. The old house was very ruinous. Here he built a very handsome howse for the Minister, of Brick, and made a good garden and walkes." Donne died in 1631 and Herbert's last firm link with London was severed.

His last three years were marked by devotion and unostentatious charity. In 1633 he died of consumption. At Bemerton, Aubrey tells us, "He lyes in the Chancell, under no large, nor yet very good, marble grave-stone, without an Inscription." Shortly before his death he sent a manuscript of his poems, *The Temple,* to Ferrar at his religious community of Little Gidding, urging him to publish or burn the book as he saw fit. Ferrar published. Before the year was out two editions had appeared.

Ferrar is a key figure. Herbert was his friend and they must have discussed together, at Cambridge and later, issues of faith. Ferrar was more assertive than Herbert. At Little Gidding he maintained among his family a strict devotion to the Book of Common Prayer, to the forms of worship, and especially, in an age when Communion occurred in many parishes at most twice a year, a devotion to the central sacrament of the Anglican Church, which was celebrated at least every month (as it now is every Sunday). Vocal prayers drawn from the prayerbook and a thorough knowledge of the Psalms were the keys of Ferrar's simple discipline. It is possible that Herbert, whose poems are, for all their freshness, a tissue of allusion to and expansion on scripture, shared this view—this vision—though within a parish, not a specialized community. Both men steered a perilous course between Puritanism and papism. What Herbert shares with Ferrar is a sense of the joy of faith when grace is present: as Maycock says in his *Chronicles of Little Gidding*, "It was a note that had not been heard in English devotional writing, a quality that had not been displayed in English religious life, for something like a hundred years." Ferrar was not attempting to reestablish monasticism: his was a private venture, an attempt to live truly, according to scripture, with his family, and to bear witness through his and through their life. Herbert's approach to his vocation and family, if less rigorously structured, was not unlike Ferrar's.

In his short time at Bemerton Herbert revised poems and composed more than half of *The Temple*. The collection begins with "The Church Porch," an extended moral and stylistic preparation for what follows.

> Harken unto a Verser, who may chance
> Rhyme thee to good, and make a bait of pleasure.
> A verse may find him, who a sermon flies,
> And turn delight into a sacrifice.

The short poems he described as "a picture of the many spiritual conflicts that have passed betwixt God and my soul." There is throughout the book a continuity of tone, yet each poem represents a single experience.

His tone and phrasing affected Henry Vaughan. Indeed Vaughan echoes lines and forms, not as an imitator but as one whose imagination, poetic and spiritual, Herbert helped to constitute. Less directly, Richard Crashaw is Herbert's debtor. Herbert had a number of near contemporary imitators and his book went through several profitable editions.

Then, late in the seventeenth century, he went out of fashion. Addison, the most mechanical versifier of his age and a maker of fashion, pilloried him as a "false wit." The error of Herbert's early champions—men of faith—was to sell the poet on the strength of his piety, not his poetry (as Wilfred Owen's advocates sold him, taking him at his word, on the strength of his pity, not his poetry). Even Ferrar's advertisement for the first edition attests to this. Herbert's form of piety became unfashionable even before the Enlightenment was in full swing.

Yet piety contributed to his reemergence. John Wesley, in the eighteenth century, adapted several poems as hymns, adjusting their prosody to suit the form, and published a selection without alteration. It remained for Coleridge, in his *Biographia Literaria*, to revalue Herbert's poetry. In a letter he confessed that at one time he had read Herbert to chuckle over quaint, obscure passages with indecorous diction. The mature Coleridge saw the matter differently: he praises the "style where the scholar and the poet supplies the material, but the perfect well-bred gentleman the expression and arrangements." He perceives complex and fantastic thought expressed in a clear, plain language. With this he contrasts those later poets whose fantastic and complex language conveys trivial thoughts. "The latter is a riddle of words; the former an enigma of thoughts."

Edgell Rickword says: "A writer survives in each generation, otherwise than as a figure in literary text-books, precisely to the extent that he interests us as a contemporary; one of the qualities of the classics is a perennial modernity." This is wrong. A "classic" can emerge into different modernities and be eclipsed between times, as Jonson, or Langland, or Blake demonstrate. Or Donne, or Spenser, now occluded, or George Herbert.

It is in his development of syntax that Herbert resembles Donne. Otherwise, they have less in common than is normally supposed. Donne fills the canvas with himself and his drama; Herbert keeps proportion, retaining in his poems a sense of the context of his experience. A context can be natural, temporal or spiritual. He looks through or beyond manifest nature toward God. His eye never stops on mere detail. In this way he is the most *transitive* of the Metaphysical poets, passing from the finite and particular to the eternal, or recording a longing—or failure—to do so. He had what Charles Cotton described in 1675 as "a soul composed of harmonies." Images are at times far-fetched, but generally suitable. Such qualities—the transitive nature of prayer, the surprising appositeness of image and diction—appealed to the imprisoned Charles I, and to William Cowper in his depression. The poems travel to extremes of experience but are shot through with consolation.

His spiritual struggle puts our different struggles into form; this is part of the universality of his poems. Another part is the pleasure they give, the surprise at each rereading of finding not the same poem but something different, some new semantic nuance that takes us into an area of the verse we had not felt before, or a metrical effect that surprises us, or an image that suddenly comes clear. Like Donne, he gives his poems a dramatic cast. Many begin in medias res, addressing, cajoling, lamenting. But he shies away from Donne's attitudinizing. His poetic logic develops correctly; not Donne's pseudo-logic but the strict logic of Sidney. A medieval quality, different from Donne's new scholasticism, survives in the work. His allusions, his direct use of scripture and traditional imagery, his natural reversion to parable and allegory, imply that the Anglican devotional poet cannot but return to time-proven processes of spiritual imagination and response. A dependence on scripture takes the brittleness out of his erudition. He takes his bearings from a common source of wisdom. The esoteric he introduces either to make it familiar or to debunk it. Critics can attend too closely to the personal nature of his spiritual struggle, undervaluing the universal and didactic elements of poems spoken out of faith by a priest—a priest who is not above direct, sermony didacticism from time to time.

Herbert is a formal genius. Stanza shapes visually corroborate meaning or process. There are the picture stanzas, the *technopaegnia*. In a more subtle sense, in a poem such as "Mortification," the stanza contracts and expands, a process that depends on syllabic length and indentation and imitates breathing:

> When man grows staid and wise,
> Getting a house and home, where he may move
> Within the circle of his breath,
> Schooling his eyes;
> That dumb inclosure maketh love
> Unto the coffin, that attends his death.

Each stanza enacts an identical rhythmic and visual process, as the baby grows into an old man bound for death. Life in all its ages is a rehearsal for the final verity. The shape is an emblem of mortification and finally of grace. The poem has an appropriate dwelling, an architecture, in this case heightened by the repeated "breath" and "death" rhymes in each stanza. "Denial," "The Star" and "Frailty" are among the poems in which form itself is an object of meditation.

In "Love bade me welcome," as Christopher Ricks points out, we sense an unstated, underlying pun on the word "host." It is the structural occasion of the poem: God is the soul's host at the table; he is also the consecrated host of which the sinner partakes at the holy table.

Similarly, in "The Temper (i)," the word "temper" takes on a comple-
ment of meanings, including the tempering of steel.

The colloquial tone of the best poems is sustained by an undecorated
diction. "Jordan (i)" advocates plainness, though in itself it is so complex
that it is at odds with its statement. In general Herbert rejects verses
that "burnish, sprout and swell, / Curling with metaphors." His imagery
includes stars, trees, food, wine—each with symbolic value but a firm
literal sense. Objects begin as themselves, then cast a shadow beyond
themselves, tracing a pattern of grace. Herbert works from small clauses
and word clusters, advancing an idea or emotion by stages, control-
ling nuance to achieve a consistent metaphorical and literal meaning.
"Prayer (2)" begins:

> Of what an easy quick access,
> My blessed Lord, art thou! how suddenly
> May our requests thine ear invade!

The simple words are simply arranged. Yet "quick" means "speedy" and
"vital"; "access" and "invade" carry military overtones. These suggestions
corroborate literal meaning without distorting or displacing it. "Thou
can'st no more not hear, than thou can'st die." God is all-powerful, yet
constrained by his own nature to be accessible and eternal. The paradox
is contained:

> Of what supreme almighty power
> Is thy great arm, which spans the east and west,
> And tacks the centre to the sphere!

Even at the height of cadence, Herbert contrives to bring God's action
to simple comprehensibility by the verb "tack." It makes solid the vast
motion of God. A minimal verb, it magnifies the agent and the action.
Often, when he develops a rhetorical description, he magnifies the
effect by reducing the terms of action.

Herbert can be as personal as Donne, but we focus less on him than
on the experience he tells of. "Affliction (i)" is directly autobiographical
but presents a general type, despite allusions to university, illness,
incumbency, private frustrations: a type for the development of faith.
Grief instructs him: 'grief did tell me roundly, that I lived.' Learning is
of little use:

> Now I am here, what thou wilt do with me
>   None of my books will show:
> I read, and sigh, and wish I were a tree:

> For sure then I should grow
> To fruit or shade: at least some bird would trust
> Her household to me, and I should be just.

The man afflicted longs for purpose, a tree's purpose to give fruit and shade, a tree's foundation, its roots. If he were a tree, he would stand in the same relation to a bird as God stands to him; only (by implication) unlike God he would be just to his tenant. This oblique blasphemy heightens a contrast in the following stanza and highlights the poet's longing for a *sign*, even a negative proof. Colloquial diction builds to a metaphysical paradox suggested by Sidney's love poems, used with an urgency beyond Sidney's scope. Each monosyllable calls for a stress: "Let me not love thee, if I love thee not."

> Yet, though thou troublest me, I must be meek;
>   In weakness must be stout.
> Well, I will change the service, and go seek
>   Some other master out.
> Ah my dear God! though I am clean forgot,
> Let me not love thee, if I love thee not.

When the poet dares to speak in the voice of Christ, it is with reversed affliction: Christ unable to comprehend the conduct of man, just as man is perplexed by God's conduct, both His grace and His with-holding of it. Herbert's Christ is always in the garden or on the Cross.

His verbs, like Herrick's, are usually transitive. A catalogue of verbs in any of the better poems proves him to be a poet of moral action rather than gesture. There's movement even when thought is static. This quality we relish the more when we come up against the assured, elegant verse of Dryden and the brittle century for which his refinements paved the way. The simple drama of Herbert's sonnet "Redemption" is unequaled in English poetry before or since. A new parable, worthy of the old:

> Having been tenant long to a rich Lord,
> Not thriving, I resolved to be bold,
> And make a suit unto him, to afford
> A new small-rented lease, and cancel th'old.
> In heaven at his manor I him sought:
> They told me there, that he was lately gone
> About some land, which he had dearly bought
> Long since on earth, to take possession.
> I straight return'd, and knowing his great birth,
> Sought him accordingly in great resorts;

In cities, theatres, gardens, parks, and courts:
At length I heard a ragged noise and mirth
Of thieves and murderers: there I him espied,
Who straight, *Your suit is granted,* said, and died.

The Temple, or Sacred Poems and Private Ejaculations appeared with Nicholas Ferrar's authority in 1634; *The Country Parson* (1652) and *Jacula Prudentium* followed. Walton says that 20,000 copies of *The Temple* were sold in a few years.

The Eccentric

JOHN MILTON, ANNE BRADSTREET,
MARGARET CAVENDISH

"Milton, with the possible exception of Spenser, is the first eccentric English poet, the first to make a myth out of his personal experience, and to invent a language of his own remote from the spoken word." Thus W. H. Auden, forgetting Chaucer who "invents" the language Milton was to use, the self-involved excesses of Hoccleve, the wild candor of Skelton stepping across the threshold into modern English, the witty and plainspoken candors of Gascoigne, the erotic and spiritual adventures of Donne. No: Milton is not the first or even the second eccentric poet. It is in the nature of the poetic vocation—if we contrast it with a vocation for verse—to be eccentric, to work at a slight or a sheer tangent to prevailing conventions, to invent a language that speaks or sings in ways that "the spoken word" does not aspire to. The spoken word, in Auden's sense, is generally instrumental, conveying instructions, information, feelings. The words that poems speak may do those things, but they have another dynamic, which is to honor one another, to exist together as a whole entity that, while it has an occasion, *becomes* an occasion, autonomous at once of the events that give rise to it and of the poet who utters it.

Yet Auden's view of Milton is not eccentric. Milton was revered through two and a half centuries. Before Eliot tried to knock the bust off its plinth, only Doctor Johnson had expressed damaging misgivings, and he tempered criticism with grudging respect. Milton became a spiritual and literary duty, a task and test, a measuring stick, and a rod to every poet's back. Shakespeare was monumentalized, but he remained engaging, inspiring, inimitable; Milton furrowed the brow of most readers. Walter Savage Landor looked up and saw:

Milton, even Milton, rankt with living men!
Over the highest Alps of mind he marches,

And far below him spring the baseless arches
Of Iris, colouring dimly lake and fen.

The "fen" recalls Cambridge, where Milton, a beautiful youth with long
locks, studied. "His harmonicall and ingeniose Soul," writes Aubrey,
"did lodge in a beautifull and well-proportioned body. He was a spare
man . . . He had abroun hayre. His complexion exceeding faire—he was
so faire they called him *the Lady of Christ's College*. Ovall face. His eie a
darke gray." For Landor, Milton's poetry and prose constitute a huge
stone arch, compared with the ephemeral rainbows of other poets. For
Wordsworth, in one of his great sonnets, it is Milton the radical who
demands attention. There's that fen again:

Milton! thou should'st be living at this hour:
England hath need of thee: she is a fen
Of stagnant waters: altar, sword and pen,
Fireside, the heroic wealth of hall and bower,
Have forfeited their ancient English dower
Of inward happiness. We are selfish men;
Oh! raise us up, return to us again;
And give us manners, virtue, freedom, power.
Thy soul was like a Star and dwelt apart;
Thou hadst a voice whose sound was like the sea;
Pure as the naked heavens, majestic, free,
So didst thou travel on life's common way,
In cheerful godliness; and yet thy heart
The lowliest duties on itself did lay.

Yet Wordsworth was one of the few English poets of his time to strug-
gle out from under the burden of Milton and write back into English.
Milton leaves his mark less on the diction and more on the syntax and
cadence of his verse and the wonderful way he handles line endings.

On one thing Robert Graves and T. S. Eliot, often at loggerheads,
agree. They do not like Milton. Graves dislikes him as a man, and finds
in his verse the very faults his life demonstrates. His book *Wife to Mr
Milton* is savagely judicious. In an essay he cast aspersions on the moral
integrity of this most high-minded of authors, on the Milton Words-
worth invokes. "By the time he had been made Secretary of State for the
Foreign Tongues to the Council of State (a proto-Fascist institution)
and incidentally Assistant Press Censor—why is this fact kept out of the
text-books when so much stress is laid on the *Areopagitica*?—he had
smudged his moral copybook so badly that he had even become a 'crony'
of Marchmont Needham, the disreputable turncoat journalist."

This says much about Milton, and about Graves. Eliot is less ad hominem, though as an Anglican and latter-day Royalist he can't have felt comfortable with so vehement a man. "In Milton the world of Spenser was reconfigured and almost unrecognisable . . . What had been reasonable and courteous, a belief in the *fact* that men of culture and intellect will be able to engage in rational discussion and agree to disagree, had been displaced by faction and sometimes violent intolerance. The moderate had stood down and the fanatic had taken his place, in the pulpit, in Parliament, and on the very peaks of Parnassus." Eliot focuses on the impact of such changes on prosody. During the Elizabethan and Jacobean periods, blank verse was a fully expressive medium; "After the erection of the Chinese Wall of Milton, blank verse has suffered not only arrest but retrogression."

The Lady of Christ's College is a protean figure and no critic has been able to hold him satisfactorily for long. If you grapple with his marvelously complex language, you lose sight of its place within his elaborate and allusive forms; if you try to characterize his politics, you find the texture of the verse often running against the structure, as though his imagination was correcting what his partisan mind wanted to say. Can we believe even the simple sentiment of these Panglossian lines that close *Samson Agonistes*?

All is best, though we oft doubt
What th' unsearchable dispose
Of Highest Wisdom brings about,
And ever best found in the close.

Can *he* believe them, or only within the context of his artifact?

John Milton was born on 9 December 1608, "half an hour after 6 in the morning," Aubrey says, "in Bread Street, in London, at the Spread Eagle, which was his [father's] house (he had also in that street another howse, the Rose; and other houses in other places)." Milton *père* was a well-to-do scrivener and money lender who had attended Oxford, rebelled against his own father's Roman Catholicism, and been disinherited when an English Bible was found in his chamber. He was, Aubrey says, "an ingeniose man; delighted in musique; composed many Songs now in print, especially that of *Oriana*." He died in 1647 and was buried in Cripplegate Church.

He instilled in his son a taste for music and encouraged his ambition to be a writer. If Milton as a boy of nine or ten wanted to read late, his father made sure that a maid sat up with him until midnight and after. According to Aubrey, by the age of ten Milton was already a poet. "His school-master then was a Puritan, in Essex, who cutt his haire short."

By the time he went to St. Paul's School, it had begun to grow back. There he studied under the excellent Alexander Gill. Gill used English verse in his lessons and Milton may have had his first exposure to Spenser there. He learned Latin, Greek and Hebrew and wrote what was regarded as exemplary Latin verses. In his last year at St. Paul's, at fifteen, he wrote a poem with which any churchgoer is familiar from the hymnal, a paraphrase of Psalm 136:

> Let us with a gladsome mind
> Praise the Lord, for he is kind
> For his mercies aye endure,
> Ever faithful, ever sure.

Less successful but still dazzling is his paraphrase of Psalm 114, in couplets, including the beguiling lines:

> The high, huge-bellied mountains skip like rams
> Amongst their ewes, the little hills like lambs.

Metaphor here, and later in his work, has a different function from the one we recognize: the awkward juxtaposition of "huge-bellied" and "skipped," the strange figuring of the mountains and hills, creates a tension of unlikeness remote from "all the clouds like sheep / On the mountains of sleep" that Edward Thomas gives us. Milton's imagination incorporates the suggestive Hebrew usage into his largely classical culture. If we deplore mixed metaphor we will find much to cavil at in Milton.

When he went up to Christ's College, Cambridge, in 1625 he found the place disappointing, the curriculum dry and narrow. He craved a broader, more liberal education than was offered. He composed Latin poems in the manner of Ovid and Horace, epigrams, a Latin mock epic on the Gunpowder Plot, Italian sonnets, more English paraphrases of the Psalms, and the eleven stanzas "On the Death of a Fair Infant Dying of a Cough." His Latin elegies are in some ways his most personal utterances, including details of his life and thought not recorded elsewhere. He was at this time as much at home in Latin as in English verse.

"On the Death," for a nineteen-year-old poet, is a remarkable production, Elizabethan in manner, full of conceits that attest to his mastery of convention. It is notable for its finish, not its feeling. In the seventh stanza there is a hint of things to come:

> Wert thou some star which from the ruined roof
> Of shaked Olympus by mischance didst fall;

Which careful Jove in nature's true behoof
Took up, and in fit place did reinstall?
Or did of late Earth's sons besiege the wall
    Of sheeny heav'n, and thou some goddess fled
Amongst us here below to hide thy nectared head?

Images of falling, rebellion, and the pagan gods are here with the delicacy (marred by archness) of the poet of *Comus*: accomplishment awaiting a subject.

After taking his BA in 1629, Milton stayed on at Cambridge. It was the period of his three religious poems, "On the Morning of Christ's Nativity," the incomplete "The Passion" and "Upon the Circumcision." The nativity ode is his first important English poem, celebrating the birth as an event without losing sight of its theological and cultural consequences. The central paradox is crucial to all his verse: human child and Son of God. The poet, like one of the Magi, arrives at the manger. Four introductory stanzas are followed by a hymn. He evokes the cold weather, not Mary or Joseph. Nature, humbled and bared before the swaddled infant, almost displaces the Virgin in the poem. Those who expect an imperious Messiah stand in awe before the helpless infant who becomes a focus for the whole natural world. The image of musical harmony acquires force. It is not, however, the Millennium:

But wisest Fate says no,
This must not yet be so;
    The Babe lies yet in smiling infancy,
That on the bitter cross
Must redeem our loss,
    So both himself and us to glorify;
Yet first, to those ychained in sleep,
The wakeful trump of doom must thunder through the deep.

These lines are so powerfully elliptical that the image is of the *babe* crucified. Into a hymn of joy flows the future, the somber truth that the dragon is not dead. The pagan gods depart, and we lament them: this babe is a swaddled Puritan. In the last stanza babe and Virgin are left together, one asleep, the other watching, protected by angels.

Milton took his MA in 1632. By then his career was well begun. Not only the great sonnet "On Shakespeare" (1630) but "L'Allegro" and "Il Penseroso" had been completed (1631). The latter two, delicate and clear, use the tetrameter coupled with complete assurance and achieve, in prosody and syntax as well as diction, a distinction of *tone* between the voices of the happy and the melancholy man. The thoughtful man

lingers in our company (176 lines) longer than the happy man (152). Both
poems refer to the same conventionally visualized world, rather as
Blake's "Innocence" and "Experience" offer two perspectives upon the
same material. Milton evokes distinct temperaments, or humors, "L'Al-
legro," pastoral, "Il Penseroso," elegiac. "Il Penseroso," with his passion
to know the secrets of the dark and his concern with death, is a little
silly, with the gentle self-mockery we hear in Chaucer, an unusual note
in Milton. Chaucer is directly referred to in lines 109–20 and echoed
in lines 8–9. "Il Penseroso" is scholastic; meanwhile "L'Allegro" is less
reflective, a Renaissance sort of fellow, patronizing "sweetest Shake-
speare, Fancy's child," who will "Warble his native woodnotes wild." He
mentions *en passant* Jonson's "learned sock." Milton was young enough
to encompass both moods. History had yet to instruct him in the
somber facts of political life, and his religious faith, though firm, was
not yet hard.

After Cambridge, he retired for six years to his father's Bucking-
hamshire estate—having written one of his ambitious and certainly his
most respectful and flattering Latin poems to him, "Ad Patrem"—in
order to complete his poetic training. "I take it to be my portion in this
life, joined with a strong propensity of nature, to leave something so
written to aftertimes, as they should not willingly let it die." He pre-
pared himself more systematically than any other English writer has
ever done: he wanted to know *all* that a man could know. He wrote
three significant works at this time. *Arcades,* a diminutive masque for
the Dowager Countess of Derby, was the fruit of his musical interests
and brought him into contact with his father's friend the composer
Henry Lawes. *Comus* (1634), his great masque, was produced by Lawes.
And there is his elegy "Lycidas." Other work included a sonnet on the
flight of youth ("How soon hath Time, the subtle thief of youth"),
marking his twenty-fourth birthday, and three poems based on Italian
madrigals.

Arcades shows Milton's command of Elizabethan idiom and his skill
in addressing an aristocratic audience. Lawes was confident to commis-
sion *Comus,* to celebrate the inauguration of the Earl of Bridgewater as
Lord President of Wales. It was performed at Ludlow Castle, Shrop-
shire. Milton, it is conjectured, played the part of Comus, seductive
prototype for Satan.

Comus is not dramatic but ceremonial. The theme of chastity brings
both elements into play. Here Milton again fuses Platonic and Christian
thought. The Lady rejects Comus's very specific advances and is freed
into a universal love of the good. The allegory is simple: the Lady, lost
in a wild wood, is tested, and in the end is found, and found virtuous.
The Earl of Bridgewater's three children were shown off to advantage

and received instruction from the masque: on the first night they played the Lady and her two brothers.

A mélange of styles is tried in *Comus*, a transitional work, the fruit of retired studies in philosophy, theology and poetry. Little of the contemporary world finds its way in. Some of the writing is richly Elizabethan; some can't but remind us of Dryden. Spenser and Shakespeare are nearby. Matthew Arnold speaks of Milton as being at the "close" of Elizabethan poetry. If this is so, *Comus* must be the last Elizabethan poem, already an anachronism when performed. It resists the excess of metaphysical wit, yet opens out, beyond that, to the drier regions of the late seventeenth and early eighteenth centuries, when language began to hover above its subject and to regard itself; when, as Arnold puts it, expression took precedence over action.

The character of Comus is a triumph. He not only tempts but embodies the temptation he promotes, a corrupt corrupter who exclaims of her vocal ravishments, when he hears the Lady sing:

> How sweetly did they float upon the wings
> Of silence, through the empty-vaulted night,
> At every fall smoothing the raven down
> Of darkness till it smiled.

The word "wings" belongs to silence, but prepares the way for "down"; silence and darkness are smooth-feathered birds. These overlaid images establish expectations of texture and movement, which Comus bears out in verbs of flight and in specific phrases: "the winged air darked with plumes"; "smooth-haired silk," which "spinning worms" weave "in their green workshops." It is almost the voice of his friend Marvell, only it is *not* a voice, shrinking away from the coarseness of common speech.

The tone of the poet of *Paradise Lost* is audible too:

> But he that hides a dark soul and foul thoughts
> Benighted walks under the mid-day sun;
> Himself his own dungeon.

These lines belong to the Elder Brother, a priggish character, who echoes (to refute) an earlier speech by Comus. Milton was unsuccessful with protagonists. Christ, God and Sampson repel us in different ways; what they represent they do not recommend. His antagonists can be admirable. They are given much of the best verse. Comus and Satan are attractive villains. Blake could claim Milton as "of the Devil's party" and John Middleton Murry branded him a "bad man" on these grounds. Robert Burns declared, "I have bought a pocket Milton, which I carry perpetually about with me, in order to study the sentiments—the dauntless magnanimity, the intrepid, unyielding independence, the desperate daring, the noble defiance of hardship, in that great personage, SATAN." Milton's unequal skill in moral characterization is inevitable. Goodness and virtue cannot be particularized without limiting or containing them. Virtues are flimsy, tend toward abstraction when they aspire to be comprehensive. Evil, however, *has* to be particularized. Fallen men fall in different ways. Evil acts in a world of characters we recognize. The devil has the best, because the most diverse and seductive, tunes. A marriage between virtue and character, between pure qualities and mundane objects, is beyond most art, even his. Or is it beyond our comprehension? Is there a modern prejudice that finds the individual invariably more real, more attractive, than the universal?

"Lycidas" was composed for a collection of elegies dedicated to Edward King, a fellow undergraduate of Milton's at Cambridge, who was drowned. King was not intimate with Milton, but the poet knew him as a Latin versifier and a candidate for holy orders. A pastoral-elegiac mode, lamenting a fellow "shepherd-poet," was appropriate. King's intended vocation, pastoral in another sense, provided a pretext for introducing the religious strain; and the manner of his death, by water, supplied a wealth of classical references suitable to the idiom.

Although there are verbal echoes and borrowed motifs from Spenser's *Shepheardes Calender*, "Lycidas" is a very different kind of poem. Johnson condemned it for its diction, rhymes and prosody, but he disliked pastoral and found distasteful the introduction of criticism of the Church into such a context. He also comments that "where there is leisure for fiction there is little grief." The grief in the poem is no more or less real than that of other pastoral elegies. The poem is not lament but elegy in a wider sense, like Milton's Latin elegies. King's death provoked in the no-longer-so-young Milton (he was twenty-nine) reflections on his own mortality, his limited achievement, and on the Church for which he himself had been destined. Bitter at the loss of so promising a life, he asks why the just and good should be squandered.

Each element in the poem belongs to a baptized tradition of pastoral elegy. The procession of mourners, the catalogue of flowers, the lament to nature, were off-the-peg. How he combines conventions, what he puts into them, is what matters. They're part of a classically sanctioned framework. Something else, specifically Protestant and highly developed, is there too.

We should be surprised that Doctor Johnson was deaf to the kinds of feeling that inform and unite the poem, which moves from apprehension of death, through regret, to passionate questioning, rage, sorrow and acceptance. The poem begins in a minor key but progresses to a

larger music, of divine justice and human accountability. The poem's
climax is a harsh attack on the clergy: "shepherds" corrupted by self-
interest. Beside this indictment is set the catalogue of flowers, a superb
tonal contrast. Lycidas has drowned: there is no hearse on which to
place the flowers, so Milton evokes the body afloat in the sea. Beside
this emblem of nature's impersonal force he places the affirmation of
resurrection. Order returns to the pastoral world ("Tomorrow to fresh
woods, and pastures new"). "Lycidas" more than *Paradise Lost* justifies
God's ways to man, and is the finest elegy in the language. Not all agree.
Graves complains that "the sound of the poem is magnificent; only the
sense is deficient." The sense is deficient only to those who wish to limit
the kind of sense poetry can make. Graves cannot forgive Milton for
being the man he was; he cannot forgive the poem for not being lyrical.
Most of the misreadings of "Lycidas" proceed from a lyric expectation.
From a lyric we tend to expect a single, stable perspective on a specific
area of experience; we expect integration and singleness of effect. "Lyci-
das" is a chain of effects: argument, lament, doubt, celebration. Single
passages are "lyric," but the poem as a whole is in another mode. It's the
most complex and the last poem of Milton's youth.

In 1638 he traveled to Italy. He was away from England for fifteen
months, recalled only upon the outbreak of the Civil War. On his return
he memorialized in his best Latin elegy, the "Epitaphium Damonis," his
only intimate friend, Charles Diodati, whom he met in Geneva. Sir
Henry Wotton, ambassador at Venice, had also delighted in his com-
pany. On his return he became a private tutor and began to plan an epic.
It was to be Arthurian, celebrating the English nation. He describes it
in the "Epitaphium."

The Civil War drew him into political life. He began pamphleteer-
ing. If, as he says, he wrote prose with his "left hand" and poetry with
his right, the left hand produced four fifths of the surviving opus. His
whole endeavor was to see the Reformation through. For him the true
reformers were, in England, "the divine and admirable spirit of Wyclif,"
the Lollards, Marian martyrs and suppressed sectaries who followed
him. Wycliffe was a necessary martyr, one to be revered both for what
he did and wrote, and for what he represents in English and European
radical and reformist history.

In 1642 Milton, the learned and formidably accomplished poet,
married. He chose a sixteen-year-old Roman Catholic girl. It was a
disaster. Aubrey is kind about the first Mrs. Milton, and Graves wrote a
book giving her side of the miserable story. So troubled was Milton
by the whole affair that he wrote his pamphlet on divorce, which was
censored. Censorship provoked his best-known prose work, the *Are-
opagitica* (1644), an attack on official censorship, though he would have

been inclined to censor poems he found obnoxious, and indeed he became a censor under Cromwell. When we consider the calculated adjustments—or hypocrisies—in Dryden's spiritual and political career, we should remember Milton, who embodies the same kinds of compromise with circumstance, though he ended up on the Anglican, Dryden on the Roman, side of the fence.

The sonnets of 1642–58 are very different from the seven Italianizing sonnets of his youth. Written in the gaps between his substantial prose writings, they divide between the polite and the public. It is the trumpet call of the public sonnets that astonished Wordsworth: "Cromwell, our chief of men" (his only Shakespearean sonnet, where he asks the leader to "save free conscience from the paw" of Cromwell's extremist followers, "hireling wolves whose gospel is their maw") and, especially, "Avenge, O Lord, thy slaughtered saints," the great English poem of rage and revenge. Others might have been astonished by his vehement little translation from Seneca's *Hercules Furens*, for *The Tenure of Kings and Magistrates*:

> There can be slain
> No sacrifice to God more acceptable
> Than an unjust and wicked king.

It was 1649, the year of Charles I's execution.

In 1646 Milton's first volume of *Poems* appeared. It included Latin, Greek, Italian and English work. In 1649 he waded deep into politics, defending the regicides in print. He was appointed secretary for foreign tongues to Cromwell's council of state, a post he held for ten years. He had no say in policy but was required to compose official propaganda. This he did with skill and conviction. Blindness overtook him in 1652. He wrote his famous sonnet, "When I consider how my light is spent," but he did not stint in his secretarial labors. During this period he suffered another loss. In 1656 (his first wife having left him long before) he married a second time, Katharine Woodcock. This marriage was happy, but Katharine died in 1658. For her he wrote his last sonnet, one of the most moving in English:

> Methought I saw my late espousèd saint
> > Brought to me like Alcestis from the grave,
> > Whom Jove's great son to her glad husband gave,
> > Rescued from death by force, though pale and faint.
> Mine, as whom washed from spot of child-bed taint
> > Purification in the old Law did save,
> > And such as yet once more I trust to have

Full sight of her in heaven without restraint,
Came vested all in white, pure as her mind.
Her face was veiled, yet to my fancied sight
Love, sweetness, goodness in her person shined
So clear as in no face with more delight.
But O as to embrace me she inclined,
I walked, she fled, and day brought back my night.

Robert Graves has nothing to say about this poem. It would have been hard for him to dismiss: it conforms to the rules of the lyric and, oddly, more even than "Lycidas," to the expectations of elegy. Milton was to marry once again, in 1662. His third wife, Elizabeth Minshull, survived him. He married her "the year before the Sicknesse"—"a gent. person, a peaceful and agreable humour."

We think of the poet, going blind, his cause (the Commonwealth) coming undone, as being of a melancholy disposition. Aubrey, a contrary witness, makes him out to have been a congenial chap. "He would be chearfull even in his Gowte-fitts, and sing." He adds, "He pronounced the letter R (*littera canina*) very hard—a certaine signe of a Satyricall Witt—*from John Dryden*." And reflecting how after the Restoration he was visited by foreign admirers, "He was much more admired abrode then at home."

The Restoration put an end to his pamphleteering. It seemed, indeed, that he might be punished. But several of his friends, among them Andrew Marvell and Cavalier poets in whose corner he had fought behind the scenes, secured his safety, though he was briefly imprisoned. The Commonwealth extracted from him, beyond the sonnets, little verse. In his remaining years he made up for lost time, completing three major works upon which he had been engaged before: *Paradise Lost* (published 1667 in ten books, revised 1674 in twelve), *Paradise Regained* (1671) and *Samson Agonistes* (1671). His revised *Poems* appeared in 1673. Internationally known, he was invited abroad but stayed at home. In 1674 he died.

"My mind," wrote Coleridge of the later Milton, "is not capable of forming a more august conception than arises from the contemplation of this greatest man in his latter days: poor, sick, old, blind, slandered, persecuted: 'Darkness before and danger's voice behind,' in an age in which he was as little understood by the party for whom, as by that against whom, he had contended, and among men before whom he strode so far as to dwarf himself by the distance; yet still listening to the music of his own thoughts, or, if additionally cheered, yet cheered only by the prophetic faith of two or three solitary individuals, he did nevertheless

> . . . argue not
> Against Heaven's hand or will, nor bate a jot
> Of heart or hope; but still bore up and steer'd
> Right onward."

Does Coleridge overstate the case? Milton had the slave labor of his daughters, who read to him and scribed for him (the first women scribes thus recorded, who earned as meager a keep as the apprentice scribes in the old scriptoria), he had his plague of visitors who brought gifts, and it's doubtful that he was so weak as to find "slander" and "persecution" more than the buzz of gnats. He was busy; he had become the Oliver Cromwell of his little world.

It was long assumed that the sequence of publication of the three last great works reflected the sequence of their composition. But a different chronology has been proposed. W. R. Parker suggests that *Samson Agonistes* was begun in the late 1640s and pursued in the 1650s. By 1655 Milton had probably written the dialogues of *Paradise Regained*—about three quarters of the poem. This places *Paradise Lost* at the end rather than the beginning of the last period. Poetically, this makes sense. *Samson Agonistes* is the thinnest-textured of the three, not because it is a drama but because Milton's mature style was in formation. Images are switched on, as it were, and then switched off when they have done their illumination: they do not inter-qualify and build, they exist for their moment. Intellectual and moral aridity; the uncompromising and obnoxious coldness in the words of Samson's father on hearing of the destruction of the theater, the foe (and his son), "Come, come; no time for lamentation now"; undigested debts to Shakespeare; the intensity of Samson's lament on blindness, which implies that the poet had contracted the disability recently (later he accepts it calmly enough): these things suggest not a culmination of his work but a transition toward the largely dialogue form of *Paradise Regained*. *Samson Agonistes'* magnificent passages are well known: the description of Delilah, the lament on his blindness, arias in a Puritan opera. But the tragedy as a whole is intolerable. It is a political, not a moral poem.

Paradise Regained refers *back* to *Paradise Lost* in its opening lines, but this does not confirm a chronology of composition. In conception it is much more modest than *Paradise Lost*: the poetry lacks the style and lushness of epic. Spenser, after the model of Virgil, proceeded from pastoral eclogue to epic. Did Milton follow the same prescribed route? E. M. W. Tillyard noted the similarities between *Paradise Regained* and Virgil's *Georgics*. If one prefers to argue for *Paradise Regained* as a dramatic poem, one must apologize for its shortcomings in every aspect, from characterization to dialogue and action: a conflict in the mind of

Christ, it deals exclusively with his temptations in the wilderness. We observe not the mind's processes, but stylized temptations. There is a continuous parallel between Old Testament history and Christ's New Testament development. The poem is epic neither in style nor manner: it sings inaction, not action—refusals of temptation that are action only on a moral plane. Read as a Puritan georgic it makes formal sense, converting "the modes of classical poetry into the service of Christianity." A georgic is a poem about the cultivation of the spirit, not the soil. Simple phrasing, lack of decoration, a general plainness, set it apart from *Paradise Lost*. The diction and style of the closing passages of each poem register their radical difference. In *Paradise Regained*, "characters" exist solely as clauses in Christ's self-discovery.

Paradise Lost deals with the Fall, from which Christ redeems us. By the middle of the Commonwealth Milton's social optimism and desire to celebrate England in Arthurian epic had faded. Christian epic was the highest form to which a poet could aspire. Its scope was cosmic, timeless, its moral purpose clear. Other forms of poetry were trivial by comparison. He began writing in 1658 and finished it around 1663. He defended his choice of blank verse on aesthetic and political grounds: his authority was Homer and Virgil. He advanced the usual arguments against "trivial" rhyme: "True musical delight," he says, "consists only in apt numbers, fit quantity of syllables, and the sense variously drawn out from one verse to another." The key implement is supple and clear syntax, mimetic in some passages, analytic in others. Milton is expert at this drawing out, spreading his meanings, as Spenser does, sometimes over more than a dozen lines. Each sentence, every image, every word, has a number of functions to perform on literal and moral levels. Latinate syntax and diction allow flexibility and through echo or etymology create complex harmonies inaccessible in a simpler style. In using blank verse Milton claimed he was recovering an "ancient liberty" for English, long confined to the bondage of rhyme. Arnold praised Milton above all for this style, the poet's "perfect sureness of hand": nothing could be changed without violence to the prosodic or intellectual content.

Along with Latinate syntax and diction comes a panoply of classical and biblical allusion. The use of particular geographical names gives the poem enormous scope in space. The forward narration of the angels makes it possible for him to include all historical time, and in portraying the godhead he incorporates eternity. *Paradise Lost* positively bristles with learning. It is deliberate in plan, development and decoration. Despite the design, the poetry transcends its formal conception; characters are real, stand up and speak with some independence. They have distinct idioms: each fallen angel who joins in the great debate in hell speaks with a different inflection. Satan has as many voices as forms.

The poet, who intrudes in the first person at several junctures, establishes a voice and orientation of his own: we can attribute the narrative. Autobiographical matter adds authority. There are, too, the perspectives. Scenes are presented through the eyes of particular characters, so that we see not only what but *as* they see. Satan's vision of Paradise is more vivid than an "objective" vision could be. He sees with the eyes of resentment and revenge.

Milton integrates the levels of meaning. There is literal story, moral drama, political argument. Images of natural process substantiate the action or figure the movement of the poem, most poignantly in Book Nine, when nightfall and the human Fall are expressed side by side. "Earth felt the wound" of the Fall: the act changed not only the human condition but nature itself.

The twelve books move from the defeat of the rebel angels, their expulsion and fall, to the Fall of man and his expulsion from the Garden. There is "architecture" in the parallelism of scenes, and in the development of clusters of imagery connected with the several themes. But is there too *much* design? Has Milton done more than revive the medieval mode of allegory? Johnson was not alone in objecting to the "want of human interest" in the poem. Adam and Eve—apart from the archangel Michael's prophecies—are the only *people* we meet, and they're remote in innocence and in their earth-shattering guilt. We observe, standing apart. Coleridge distinguishes between the epic and the dramatic imagination. Both discover unity in variety, but the epic discovers unity by throwing its subject into the past, regarding it from a distance, while the dramatic brings it up close. A useful distinction, it illuminates both the failure of *Samson Agonistes* and the success of *Paradise Lost*. Our human access to *Paradise Lost* is, initially, through the realized character of Satan. Milton progressively diminishes him, through animal imagery and transformations, until he is a mere serpent. Thereafter we follow a sensuous argument, a symbolic enactment of our Fall. The longueurs of a poem whose action is so simple and whose telling so majestic and gradual come especially in the long conversations of Adam with Raphael and Michael. Expression exceeds occasion. We may agree occasionally with Yvor Winters's criticism of the "pompous redundancy" of the verse, the rhetoric working as it were in spite of and away from the subject, "a dependence on literary stereotypes." But whole books of the poem, notably the first, second, fourth and ninth, survive such criticism, and none of the books is wholly unastonishing.

For *Paradise Lost* Milton received an initial payment—generous in a way, given the length of the poem, Milton's fall from grace, and the uncertainty of its success—of £5 and a further £5 when the first edition of 1,300 copies was sold through. The edition of 1674 broke Books Seven and Ten in two, bringing the epic to the appropriate twelve books. That was the year of Milton's death. Six years later his widow sold out the rights for £8. That particular arrangement was shrewd on the printer's part.

The case against Milton is largely a case against his effect on the eighteenth and nineteenth centuries. It was universal in Britain, and not confined to these islands. Milton is strictly inimitable: a radical and an anachronism. T. S. Eliot delivered telling blows, some of them against the moral content. The poem's moral purpose, like that of *The Faerie Queene*, has become muted and remote. We read it for reasons other than edification. It fell to F. R. Leavis to square his shoulders before the master and try to knock him down. Leavis attacks first *Paradise Lost* and the grand style. He finds it predictable: "routine gesture," "heavy fall," "monotony." He speaks of Milton's "sensuous poverty"—the language is self-regarding, not turned to "perceptions, sensations, or things." Elevation and remoteness impoverish rather than enrich our experience. Milton is "cut off from speech . . . that belongs to the emotional and sensory texture of actual living." His style is "an impoverishment of sensibility." Milton had "renounced the English language." Having finished with *Paradise Lost*, Leavis turns to the other poems and makes short work of them.

Many of his charges are in part true. There is monotony; the grand style does compel an attitude in the reader (it has designs on us), the language is cut off from speech—except when it is speaking. But such facts need not be incriminating. The poem answers the more serious case. It is far from "sensuous poverty": only a reader deaf to Milton's complex forms of integration could level such a charge. It is richly imagined and in part richly realized, *imaginable*. There is subtle and delicate life in the verse, and a variety of subtleties and delicacies. In dismissing Milton, Leavis assaults the wide area of English poetry which he affected; and his effect is still felt. The prejudice of our age, as much an unwritten rule as the rules of decorum were in the eighteenth century, is contained in Leavis's declaration that Milton's language is "cut off from speech." His sin is his language.

Yet for two and a half centuries—even for a "speaker" like Wordsworth—Milton's virtue was this language, which engaged and developed subjects difficult to combine, moral verities and the created world. The language of speech is not the only, or first, language of poetry. To criticize work in terms strictly irrelevant to it is of little value: a critical act of "brute assertive will," or a prejudice so ingrained as to be indistinguishable, for uncritical readers, from truth itself. With the decline of literacy, Milton, like Spenser, becomes a more difficult mountain to scale, more remote from the "common reader." Yet Chaucer and

Shakespeare, the only poets in the tradition who are Milton's superiors, both grow and recede in the same way and are not dismissed. They *seem* more accessible. In the end Leavis's hostility, like Empson's and Richards's in other areas, is to the Christian content of the poems, and in Milton it *is* obtrusive and central. We read Herbert's and Donne's divine poems even if we are unbelievers: there is their doubt to engage, and the framed drama of specific situations. But Milton will not allow disbelief to go unchallenged: his structures and narratives are not rooted in individual faith but in universal belief. The question of revealed *truth* raises its head as in no other poet in the language. Readers who resist have to make do with Satan and Comus.

Difficult, too, is the first poet of America, Anne Bradstreet, a woman who shared the rigors of Milton's faith, and who stands at the threshold of a new tradition but is too reticent to force her foot in the door. Her verse for the most part looks back to her native England for form and diction and tells an English story even as it speaks from a new continent. She was born in Northamptonshire around 1612 into the highly placed Dudley family. She was a great reader in the well-stocked library of her Puritan father. At eighteen she married a Cambridge graduate nine years her elder, and under Governor Winthrop, crossing in the *Arbella*, they joined the Puritan emigrants in Salem, Massachusetts, becoming pioneers and moving out to Ipswich and North Andover. She bore eight children there ("I had eight birds hatcht in one nest, / Four cocks there were, and hens the rest . . .") and wrote verse on myriad subjects, including long works on English history and on biblical subjects—"the fruit of some few hours, curtailed from her sleep and other refreshments." She is remembered for her more domestic pieces, as though—she being a woman—this were her proper sphere. Yet there is energy and spiritual force in her large-scale work. In 1652 *The Tenth Muse lately sprung up in America* was published in England. She died in 1672 and her book appeared in revised form in Boston in 1678—the first volume of verse to be published there and "most vendible." Her widower became governor of Salem during the witch-hunt trials.

There was little encouragement for her writing in the Puritan severity of the New World, where women had a specifically secondary role, a role her poems acknowledge even as they make their anxiously modest claims. Governor Winthrop wrote ruefully of "a godly young woman" who had given herself up to a kind of madness: to reading and writing "many books." She kept her writing to herself and her circle, but her brother-in-law had it published without her knowledge in London.

She had absorbed Ralegh, Sidney and Francis Quarles, and she was passionately drawn to a translation of the French Calvinist Guillaume du Bartas's compendious poem that Joshua Sylvester translated as *The*

Divine Weeks and Works. Du Bartas is her problematic Muse. She was writing, but she was also writing against, no matter how readily she accepted her situation and circumstances. Her literary culture was arrested in 1630 when she set sail. One of her most celebrated poems is an encomium for Elizabeth I, long deceased. Milton's Puritan wing never brushed her; in a culture of denial she was giving, humane, even ambitious, and out of the extreme exigencies of motherhood she wrote—as Adrienne Rich says—"the first good poems in America." The best of these are poems to her husband, her father, and a poem on the burning of her house in 1666, which includes the brutally self-punishing Puritan lines:

> Then, coming out, beheld a space
> The flame consume my dwelling place.
> And when I could no longer look,
> I blessed His name that gave and took,
> That laid my goods now in the dust.
> Yea, so it was, and so 'twas just.

Milton would applaud the sentiment but find the crude end-stopping of lines and the awkward rhyming rebarbative.

John Berryman's first major poem, *Homage to Mistress Bradstreet*, gives her a more flexible voice. His imaginative advocacy turned attention back to her. The fact that she wrote with such candor and competence under the circumstances remains a miracle. Yet her poems cannot be made any better than they are.

Set her beside Margaret Cavendish, the eccentric Duchess of Newcastle (1623–73) and they both come into clearer focus. "The crazy duchess" was childless, was not Puritan, was probably less deeply but more broadly read than Anne Bradstreet, but enjoyed the society of cultured men, including her poet husband. With him she endured exile in poverty during the Commonwealth, returning with the Restoration. Her wily couplets share the selfish energies of Rochester and Sedley; they have a social tone. Her attempt to bring Metaphysical style into the second half of the seventeenth century is brave and not altogether unsuccessful. In Bradstreet we admire the poet's enormous pertinacity, but the value of the poems depends upon our knowledge of a self-denying life. The duchess's verse contributes to the better verse of her age, and by being slightly antiquated it has—paradoxically—an air of originality in its conceits. She does not somehow *seem* serious, but when we read "A Woman drest by Age" and others of her conventionally spiritual poems, we realize how serious she is, though her verse does not run deep.

An End of Delicacy

RICHARD LOVELACE, RICHARD CRASHAW,
SIR JOHN SUCKLING, THOMAS CAREW, ANDREW MARVELL,
EDMUND WALLER, HENRY VAUGHAN

Milton marks a beginning more than an end, gathering the energies of the Elizabethan age, reconfiguring the poetic, political and religious trends in a way that closes off the past. After Milton, certain forms and styles are out of bounds. But poets grew alongside him on whom his shadow did not fall. Old-fashioned Anglican survivors, they wrote what they had to write regardless of him.

Richard Lovelace, "the most amiable and beautiful person that ever eye beheld," "a most beautifull Gentleman," "loved Adonis," inherited substantial estates in Kent, went from Oxford to court, served in the wars, was imprisoned for supporting the king and wrote the poem "Stone walls do not a prison make." He rejoined the king in 1645. As he was reported dead, his beloved Lucy Sacheverell, the Lucasta of his verse—"So you but with a touch of your fair hand / Turn all to saraband"—married elsewhere. His return from the dead was a mistake. In 1648 he was back in prison, preparing his book of poems *Lucasta* for publication. His entire fortune was invested in the Royalist cause. Disappointed, consumptive, he became a threadbare object of charity. "Obiit in a Cellar in Long Acre, a little before the Restauration of his Majestie." This pell-mell life epitomizes the heroic and tragic careering of a young Cavalier, final heir of Wyatt, Surrey and Sidney, exemplary, anachronistic, a cautionary tale from the *Mirrour for Magistrates*, which no one much read anymore. Even the verse is, at first glance, something of an anachronism.

Andrew Marvell's poem commending *Lucasta* (1649) abounds in insect images. It also predicts a harsh reception for the thirty-one-year-old Cavalier's first book.

The barbed censurers begin to look
Like the grim consistory on thy book;

And on each line cast a reforming eye,
Severer than the young Presbytery.

Lovelace's situation was already vexed: Parliament had sequestered his remaining fortune while he was in prison. Marvell looks back to happier days. The poems were composed by a royal favorite, loved by the court and by the wits. Now, "Our Civil Wars have lost the civic crown. / He highest builds who with most art destroys." *Lucasta* appeared in the year of the king's execution and belonged to the fallen order. Marvell's prediction was not far of the mark.

Lucasta achieved small success. Lovelace is remembered now chiefly for "To Althea, from Prison" ("Stone walls . . .") and "To Lucasta, Going to the Wars" ("I could not love thee (dear) so much, / Loved I not Honour more"). But there's more to him than a couple of anthology pieces. His misfortune was to appear in print in the very year his cause was lost. His style was out of fashion, demanding as it does intellectual and prosodic control, conscious devising. Some poems are marred by a preciosity which in Herrick appears charming, but in Lovelace indicates a failure of tact. Formal lapses, gaps in argument, an occasional lack of prosodic energy, weaken his poems. But the best, perhaps thirty, are accomplished works.

Lovelace, eldest son of a Kentish gentleman, was born either in Holland or in Kent in 1618. His creature poems reflect rural roots, where, for example, "The Grasshopper" invites the elder Charles Cotton to carouse:

Up with the day, the sun thou welcom'st then,
    Sport'st in the gilt plats of his beams
And all these merry days mak'st merry men,
    Thyself, and melancholy streams.

But ah, the sickle! Golden ears are cropped;
    Ceres and Bacchus bid good night;
Sharp frosty fingers all your flowers have topped,
    And what scythes spared, winds shave off quite.

Poor verdant fool! And now green ice! Thy joys,
    Large and as lasting as thy perch of grass,
Bid us lay in 'gainst winter rain, and poise
    Their floods with an o'erflowing glass.

The moral is rural-courtly, the creature emblematic. "The Ant" ("Thou, thine own horse and cart, under this plant / Thy spacious tent") and

"The Snail" ("Compendious snail! thou seem'st to me, / Large Euclid's strict epitome") are emblematic too, but more tied in to specific social occasions than "The Grasshopper." A happy confluence of Aesop and Tusser? The pastoral of Spenser with the unattenuated voice of Gascoigne? The wit of Donne with the formal tact of Herbert? Or simply an individual figuring of rural realities that body forth the larger social and political realities of the day? These poems, and "Aramantha," with which *Lucasta* concludes, are Lovelace's chief legacy. "Aramantha" introduced Marvell to the notion of the political pastoral in tetrameter couplets, Gerald Hammond notes in his introduction to Lovelace's *Selected Poems*, "in which the local landscape comes to represent the whole of England, its flora and fauna emerging as types of the factions which fought out the civil war, and which is presided over by an heroine who gradually develops from a vision of Arcadian innocence into a complex figure of national and personal salvation."

Lovelace's father was not only a gentleman but a soldier, killed at the siege of Groll when his son was nine. Lovelace became his mother's ward. In 1629 he was admitted to Charterhouse school, possibly on the king's nomination, at the same time as Richard Crashaw, son of an anti-Catholic pamphleteer and Puritan preacher, who was to become a notable recusant poet. Crashaw went to Cambridge and eventually (in every sense) to Rome, Lovelace to Oxford, each to a separate destiny.

In 1631 the king made Lovelace Gentleman Waiter Extraordinary. His adolescent comedy *The Scholars* was played "with applause." His accomplishments seem a shadow of Sidney's. Charles Cotton wrote in his memorial verses:

Thy youth, an abstract of the world's best parts,
Enured to arms, and exercised in arts;
Which with the vigour of a man became
Thine, and thy country's pyramids of flame;
Two glorious lights to guide our hopeful youth
Into the paths of honour, and of truth.

Among his other deeds, he was the first literal translator of Catullus into English. In 1636, at Gloucester Hall, Oxford, he was made an honorary MA on the occasion of a visit by the king and queen. The next year he received a Cambridge MA and went to court.

When Charles I's serious troubles began, Lovelace served him, first as an ensign in the Bishops' Wars (1639–40), along with the equally ill-fated poets and fellow Cavaliers Sir John Suckling and Thomas Carew. During 1640 he wrote *The Soldier*, a tragedy now lost. He was arrested and committed to the Gatehouse at Westminster for leading the men of

Kent in presenting to Parliament the Kentish petition, seeking the retention of bishops and the Book of Common Prayer and supporting the king's authority. (In what a different cause the men of Essex and Kent marched behind Wat Tyler.) He was released on condition that he cease actively supporting the royalist cause. A condition he did not meet: from that moment on he began his lavish spending on the king's campaign.

He was with Charles in Oxford in 1645, then traveled abroad and was arrested on his return. The execution of his king changed everything. He had no future in Cromwell's England. For eight years he survived, writing with a different tone and purpose. In 1656 he composed "The Triumph of Philamore and Amoret" for the marriage of Charles Cotton the younger, the poet who memorialized him. It was his last outstanding poem. He died probably in 1657. *Lucasta, Postume Poems* was assembled and published in 1659 by his youngest brother, unprofitably.

Donne and Jonson were the Cavalier poets' chief models. Carew leaned more to Jonson, which leaves him often stiff and wooden. Lovelace followed Donne, and the flaws in his work might have been remedied had he attended more to Jonson. But he preferred brilliance and surprise to clarity. Thus in "Ellinda's Glove" he wrote:

> Thou snowy farm with thy five tenements!
>   Tell thy white mistress here was one
>   That called to pay his daily rents;
> But she a-gathering flowers and hearts is gone . . .

Pure conceit, carried to extremes: the opening surprises and charms, but surprise passes and deliberate charm outstays its welcome.

Donne is echoed in several poems, notably "The Scrutiny" and "Night." This is not the spirit in which Vaughan echoes Herbert, whom he took spiritually to heart, but something less subtle, for Lovelace is Metaphysical by design, not by nature. "Gratiana Dancing and Singing" is wildly implausible: when she ceases dancing, "The floor lay paved with broken hearts." We hear in Lovelace Continental echoes, too, of writers who were to be important to the Restoration poets, especially Rochester.

Just over a hundred poems by Lovelace survive. Even in so small a body of work, the formal variety is enormous. There are poems connected with war and prison; complaints and love and antilove conceits; poems about creatures; poems on painting (for Lovelace, a friend of Peter Lely, was learned in the art); occasional poems including elegies, epithalamia and anniversary celebrations; pastorals such as "Aramantha" and "Amyntor's Grove"; a formal satire; meditations; dialogues . . . the range is wider than Herrick's, though the final achievement is not so great.

Lovelace's trajectory illuminates the trends in English poetry at the time. His early verse is intimate, even private in its concerns, written for a friend or circle of friends, wits and courtiers. When that world crumbled his address became more public: favored courtier become outcast and fugitive.

John Suckling's poetry is wryly cynical on the surface, with an embittered wit. In Lovelace, cynicism is thematic, irony is not a technical device but a thematic verity. He is not so obviously accomplished as Carew, but he is more memorable, his development more interesting in its typicality. He survived a great loss and endured the aftermath.

> I would love a Parliament
> As a main prop from heaven sent;
> But ah! who's he that would be wedded
> To th' fairest body that's beheaded?

An ungainly stanza, the awkwardness proceeds from and mirrors feeling.

The best Restoration poets resemble Lovelace. Yet even a casual reading shows the coarseness of their work compared to his, how ready they are to be satisfied with mere effect. History has started again and in its new, or renewed, light shadows are shorter and less opaque. Their view of poetry is at once more precise—they have come home from France, after all—and narrower. Though many are courtiers, they are not Cavaliers. Ideals of devotion and service are a thing of the past. Charles I's was the last courtly court. Lovelace embodies older virtues: an *uomo universale*: courtier, scholar, soldier, lover, musician, connoisseur of painting, latter-day Sidney, devoted to king, mistress and art. "To Althea, from Prison" is the quintessential Cavalier statement, passionate, *lived*. He was the last of the knight-poets; his death in poverty rather than service proved that the age of Wyatt, Surrey, Ralegh, Sidney and others of their stamp was over.

The transition was not abrupt: a line cannot be drawn. A poet like Andrew Marvell spans three ages like a delicate but serviceable bridge. The first length spans Charles I's reign and fall, the second spans the Commonwealth, the third the Restoration. "He was of middling stature, pretty strong sett, roundish faced, cherry cheek't, hazell eie, browne haire. He was in conversation very modest, and of very few words: and though he loved wine he would never drinke hard in company, and was wont to say that, he would not play the goodfellow in any man's company in whose hand he would not trust his life. He had not a generall acquaintance." Marvell is a poet whose political readjustments in times of turmoil have not told against him. There is something honest-seeming about everything he does, and running through his actions a constant thread of humane concern. The king loved him even when he leaned toward the Puritan cause; at a perilous time he wrote verses commending both Lovelace and—the only other time he wrote commendatory verse—Milton's *Paradise Lost*. Even when he celebrated Cromwell, his praise was temperate. He possesses transparency of conscience to an unusual degree. Poetry is a delight in language, image and truth. Through poetry balance is restored even when the world is off its axis.

> And now to the abyss I pass
> Of that unfathomable grass,
> Where men like grasshoppers appear,
> But grasshoppers are giants there:
> They, in their squeaking laugh, contemn
> Us, as we walk more low than them;
> And, from the precipices tall
> Of the green spires, to us do call.

His grasshopper shares much with Lovelace's. Marvell's origins, however, were less distinguished. His father was a Low Church clergyman, "facetious, yet Calvinistical." Marvell was born in Hull in 1621. The town boasted a good grammar school, which he attended. Then he went up to Trinity College, Cambridge, at the age of twelve, during the poetic ascendancy of Cowley and Crashaw. He received his BA in 1638–39 and was briefly a convert to Roman Catholicism. He left the university in 1641 without taking a further degree. Well trained in languages, he composed his earliest verses in Greek and Latin on the death of Princess Anne. Aubrey declares, "For Latin verses there was no man could come into competition with him."

When the Civil War came he was noncommittal. He went abroad for four of the seven years 1642–49, spending two years in Rome. He may have traveled as a tutor in preparation for his later posts. By 1649 he was keeping Royalist company. As well as contributing to *Lucasta*, he wrote verses on the death of Lord Hastings:

> Go, stand betwixt the morning and the flowers;
> And, ere they fall, arrest the early showers.
> Hastings is dead . . .

Already the garden is there. In a poem full of Donne and generalization, the mature Marvell stirs.

His Royalist sympathies, though attenuated, had not entirely faded in 1650 when he composed his "Horatian Ode upon Cromwell's Return from Ireland." It is the most complex and the best directly political poem in the language. It retains a radical balance in the terms of its celebration and commendation. Here is how Charles dies on his "tragic scaffold":

He nothing common did or mean
Upon that memorable scene:
　　But with his keener eye
　　The axe's edge did try;
Nor called the gods with vulgar spite
To vindicate his helpless right,
　　But bowed his comely head
　　Down as upon a bed.
This was that memorable hour
Which first assured the forcèd power.

Like the great historian Edward Hyde, Earl of Clarendon, Marvell can't quite bring himself to watch as the ax cleaves the royal nape. Cromwell, the "forced power," is by contrast with the ceremonious king all movement, agitation. He has an "active star," seeks glory and adventure—in more senses than one. The poem lives because of Marvell's sense of loss—and gain, and because of the pivotal vision of "A bleeding head," from which the eventual blessing of a strong government flows. Charles embodies right. Marvell, it is recorded, declared that the "cause was too good to have been fought for," and "men should have trusted the King." He respects Charles, he admires Cromwell. Cromwell's forced victory was "To ruin the great work of time":

Though justice against fate complain,
And plead the ancient rights in vain:
　　But those do hold or break
　　As men are strong or weak.

Might has prevailed. Marvell, never cured of his royalism, at one moment looked forward to a dynasty of Cromwells. It was not to be.

He found favor with the moderate elements of Cromwell's party and became tutor to Mary, daughter of Lord Fairfax, a distinguished retired general in the Parliamentarian cause who had wished—but not quite dared—to save the life of the king, and to whom Milton dedicated a fine sonnet. Marvell spent two years in Fairfax's household at Nunappleton, Yorkshire. Poetically it was a fruitful time. He wrote to praise and please his patron, celebrating Appleton House and the park and creating those poems whose charms are as real as they are hard to define.

In 1653 Milton recommended Marvell for the post of assistant Latin secretary. Four years later it was awarded him. Meanwhile, residing at Eton, he tutored a ward of Cromwell's and became more firmly a supporter of the Commonwealth. He was intent to serve his country and the de facto government and to make progress himself. In 1655 he published anonymously "The First Anniversary of the Government under O.C."

He was elected MP for Hull in 1660 and held the seat until his death. He supported the Restoration and seems to have been accepted as a man whose loyalty (unlike Milton's) was not in question. In any event, he helped secure Milton's safety and release. He served the Crown in embassies abroad, campaigned for religious toleration and became a satirist against the court party. He died in 1678 in London. His *Miscellaneous Poems*, including much of his best work, was published in 1681, though the "Horatian Ode upon Cromwell's Return . . ." was canceled from all but one copy and was first reprinted in 1776.

Marvell was not a professional writer. Most of his poems are in one way or another "flawed." The tetrameter couplets he favored prove wearying: the form can dictate rather than receive the poetry. The excessive use of "do" and "did" auxiliaries to plump out the meter mars many lines. Some of the conceits are absurd. Many of the poems, even "The Bermudas," fail to establish a consistent perspective: it is not always easy to visualize. Other poems are static: an idea is stated and reiterated in various terms but not developed. This is the case even in "The Definition of Love," which says memorably in eight ways that his love is impossible, but does not specify why or how, does not supply the "occasion"; or in "A Dialogue between the Resolved Soul and Created Pleasure," which despite its form is not dialogue: voices bump against each other. Intellectual development is often, as in Donne, by sleight of hand, pseudo-logic, false syllogism. There are thematic inconsistencies. In "Upon Appleton House" he suggests the natural order is superior to artificial order, but describes nature in terms of artifice. He condemns Palladian architecture in stanza six, but fifty-eight stanzas later evokes the woods, approvingly, in Palladian images. Moral value is sometimes assigned to rather than discovered in his images. And Marvell is not usually dramatic in presentation, unlike Donne or Herbert.

Yet because of some spell he casts, he is a poet whose faults we not only forgive but relish. Beneath an inadequate logic the poetry follows its own habits of association and combination. Two modes of discourse are at work, a conscious one, and something unwilled yet compelling. We cannot decide which of a poem's effects are deliberate, which casual or accidental. They seem products of a not altogether untroubled leisure at Nunappleton. T. S. Eliot contrasts Marvell with Donne. Donne would have been "an individual at any time and place"; Marvell is "the product of European, that is to say Latin, culture." The difference is in the use of the "I." Donne's "I" demands attention, Marvell's directs it. In Marvell the flaws do not disappear beneath gesture; inconsistency and uncertainty are aspects of a mind concerned with subject. That subject is not self. However distinctively he appropriates a landscape or scene, it never becomes a *paysage intérieur*. The macrocosm is never displaced by the microcosm.

In "To his Coy Mistress" the poet begins with a cool, reasonable proposition. From the temperate beginning the poem gathers speed, rushing to a cruel resolution. Image follows image with precise brevity; each extends and enriches the idea. The imaginative center holds together a varied development. Marvell doesn't always discriminate between the fresh and startling and the merely odd, yet what is odd is often delivered with such effective phrasing that it disarms us even in its absurdity, for instance the salmon fishers who "like Antipodes in shoes / Have shod their heads in their canoes."

Marvell's verse delivers sharp surprises in part because of its quietness. Surprises emerge, they are not insisted on. He seems always to be *recognizing* significance in what he sees. His whole mind is engaged, along with his senses. His intensity is *awareness*; even as he speaks he is aware of things he *might* have said. The classics shaped his poems, but scripture is never far away. He doesn't discharge his poems but launches them quietly. They run less smoothly than Herrick's but they run further and deeper. If drama is generated, as in "To his Coy Mistress," it is by control of pace and imagery, not by situation. His verse is urbane, detached, with recurrent motifs and words and a recognizable tone that distinguishes it from the work of other Metaphysicals. He has his own themes, too. Wise passivity marks some poems, which leads to closeness with the natural world as his imagination relaxes and receives. Other poems strive for contact through passion or activity, a kind of contact in which individuality is lost in the teeming variety of the world. Underlying these themes is the knowledge that in love or action time can't be arrested or permanence achieved. A sanctioned social order can be ended with an ax, love is finite, we grow old. Political reality drove the theme deep in him. We feel it obliquely in "The Nymph Complaining for the Death of her Fawn." For an intelligence such as his, the lived experience of a crucial historical event was more powerful than any accident of private biography. Perhaps he is naturally a poet of aftermath.

Like Herrick, he came late in his "literary period" and was overlooked by those who might have profited from reading him. Contrasting Marvell with Edmund Waller (his contemporary, but more a man of what was to come than of what then was) we can feel the difference. Except in his best poems Waller delivers us finished ideas; Marvell happens upon ideas. He has no settled opinions, except the fundamental ones. His poems balance particulars of which he is certain with conflicting generalities of which he is unsure, as in the line "courteous briars nail me through," which dissolves the word "courteous" on the cruel verb and brings into its ambience "court" and crucifixion. Such lines, quietly delivered, lead us not to admire his wit but to apprehend his subject. It was already the age of Dryden, and Dryden took wit in a different direction. The age of Dryden: an age in which writers took up the pen to set down what they knew, not in order to explore the unfamiliar; an age of communication rather than discovery.

Devotional poets resisted the force of Dryden's example longest. Aubrey was cousin of Henry Vaughan (162?–95) and his twin brother, Thomas. Aubrey settles an old score in his account. "Their grandmother was an Aubrey: their father, a coxscombe and no honester than he should be—cosened me of 50s. once." The sons, unlike their father, were not temporal schemers. Their eyes were generally fixed on higher things. Henry provides "authentic tidings of invisible things." His chief collection of poems, *Silex Scintillans* (*Sparks from the Flint*, 1650, enlarged 1655), was the mature work of a man led to passionate faith by bereavement, illness and the poems of George Herbert. The book's title he explains: "Certain divine rays break out of the soul in adversity, like sparks of fire out of the afflicted flint." His hermetic imagination is rarefied compared with Herbert's, and comparison with Herbert is inevitable: as Henry declared, Herbert's "holy life and verse gained many pious converts (of whom I am the least)." He frequently echoes in phrase, syntax and development specific poems by Herbert. Edmund Blunden sets them side by side in his poem "The Age of Herbert and Vaughan":

> In close and pregnant symbol
>   Each primrosed morning showed
> The triune God patrol
>   On every country road,
> In bushy den and dimble.

Blunden is truer to Vaughan than Herbert. Herbert knows an immanent God; Vaughan's God is less immediately present. The poet approaches him through symbol but cannot readily perceive him in natural imagery:

Some love a rose
In hand, some in the skin;
But cross to those,
I would have mine within.

Marvell is the poet of green, a "green thought in a green shade," his eye
on a fruitful garden; Vaughan is the poet of white in its implications of
moral and spiritual purity, skyscape, cloudscape: "a white, Celestial
thought," the white light of stars, or in his translation of Boethius's
"that first white age." The most rapt English devotional poet, the most
spiritually attentive, he lived in a spectrum between the pure white of
infancy and a recovered whiteness of eternity:

I saw Eternity the other night
Like a great ring of pure and endless light,
All calm as it was bright,
And round beneath it, Time in hours, days, years
Driven by the spheres
Like a vast shadow moved . . .

"The World" does not sustain intensity throughout, dwindling to delib-
erate allegory. It examines the shadow, "The fearful miser on a heap of
rust," a vivid moment. The poem has the virtue of describing Vaughan's
chosen territory for discovery: areas beyond the senses, accessible only
to intuition. "Invisible things," things he evokes in "Faith" ("Bright, and
blest beam!"), "The Passion" ("O my chief good!"), "Peace" ("My Soul,
there is a country") and elsewhere. His achievement is to bring the tran-
scendent almost within reach of the senses.

There's not a wind can stir,
Or beam pass by,
But straight I think (though far),
Thy hand is night;
Come, come!
Strike these lips dumb:
This restless breath
That soils thy name,
Will ne'er be tame
Until in death.

Such obliquity doesn't obscure the material world; it illuminates what
exists beyond it. Through human love it ascends to the divine, with the

light of faith. Images of darkness belong to the world. Images of light—
starlight, pure light—belong to the fields of heaven and eternity.

"My brother and I," Henry wrote, "were born at Newton in the
parish of St Brigets in the year 1621." Vaughan's father was a second son
of a family in the old Anglo-Welsh gentry. Henry's twin became a her-
metic philosopher ("Eugenius Philalethes," lover of forgetfulness) whose
works were familiar in the next century even to a skeptical Jonathan
Swift. A priest, Thomas was ejected from his living at Llansantffraed
after the Royalist defeat in the Civil War. He died of mercury poisoning
in an alchemical experiment in 1666.

More certain knowledge survives about Thomas than about Henry.
Henry called himself "Silurist" to acknowledge his roots and his land-
scape, because his native Breconshire was once inhabited by the Silures.
It is supposed that he went to Jesus College, Oxford, around 1638, took
no degree, and turned up in London to study law in 1640. He became,
we do not know by what steps, a medical doctor, and spent his later
years practicing in his Welsh neighborhood. In the Civil War he proba-
bly served with Royalist forces and tasted their defeat, which coincided
with personal bereavements. His first book, *Poems, with the Tenth Satire
of Juvenal Englished* (1646), was not very distinguished work by a Son of
Ben. Their conventional "Amoret" has more literature than flesh on her
bones. His second book, *Olor Iscanus* (*Swan of the Usk,* 1651), revealed
deepening seriousness. It begins in Wales, his true territory. London, its
styles and concerns, are less than an echo. Almost best in the book are
his translations of some of the verses from Boethius's *Consolation of Phi-
losophy,* especially "Metrum 5," with its rhythmic and thematic foretaste
of two of his great poems, "The Retreat" and "Childhood":

> Happy that first white age! when we
> Lived by the earth's mere charity,
> No soft luxurious diet then
> Had effeminated men . . .

More than translation, this is a comm. .ted Royalist looking to a lost age.
It *was* lost, and irrecoverable. He turns his attention elsewhere and sud-
denly finds "a country / Far beyond the stars." The choice of the word
"country" is significant. His imagination naturally turns to allegory; he
is among the last Boethians, seeing into a spiritual future through a lens
that most of his contemporaries found clouded and archaic. Remote
from London and the hub of fashion, he was free to take bearings with
his own instruments.

Silex Scintillans (1650) contains his best poetry. The debt to Herbert
is great, but when an experience is sufficiently intense Vaughan's own

idiom, rhythm and themes make their own space in Herbert territory. His style is thick with biblical echo and allusion: for Christians steeped in scripture each poem has an immediate sense of familiarity, a resonance as intense as any in Herbert's poems. Vaughan prefaces many pieces with biblical epigraphs, to underline their source and allegiance. His faith is fresh, the product of an abrupt spiritual conversion and notably lacking in doubt. The dramatic openings and developments, whether simple allegory, allegorical journey or emblem, relate it to and distinguish it from other Metaphysical work. His revelation is certain. At times he experiences a triumphant sense of election, demanding no proof beyond his own. The conversion came from reading Herbert. Vaughan was surprised by grace.

After 1655 he composed little durable verse. *Thalia Rediviva* (1678) revisits the secular world of his first books and adds little to his credit. What happened to his assured genius? Faith may have cooled, conscience (endlessly pining over past sins and excesses) may have smothered the holy Muse. Perhaps work as a doctor overtaxed him, or his brother's death destroyed a crucial stability, or physical frailty undermined his imaginative resolve. Later in life he suffered litigation within the family and squabbles over property. The claims of a secular world clouded the spiritual sky. It was not to be a quiet old age. When he died in 1695, he had written no verse of moment for forty years. His interesting if derivative prose book, *The Mount of Olives,* dates from 1652. His memorable prose and verse belong, at most, to a decade in a life of seventy-odd years. Even that work, by an obscure Welsh doctor buried near the river Usk, was forgotten until the nineteenth century. First for his piety and then for his poetry, he was taken off the shelf and reedited. Since then his reputation has grown.

Silex Scintillans, C. H. Sisson says, is best read as a whole book. The best poems are set in the context of the uneven imagination that produced them. Private experience is communicated in the language of Anglican Christianity. Along with images of light come those of water—baptism, cleansing, rejuvenation. If light is far and starry, water is close, physical and metaphysical or mystical. Vaughan brings us "authentic tidings of invisible things" but also skillfully presents a created world in which he participated and lived a difficult life. It is not surprising that one of Sisson's finest poems, "The Usk," is rooted in the landscapes and concerns of Henry—and Thomas—Vaughan.

Vaughan died on the brink of the eighteenth century, the very last voice contained entirely within what many regard as the great century of English poetry, the crucial century of English history, in which the old order was finally violated, and the Restoration, rather than reestablishing continuities, produced a new dawn.

New Pilots

JOHN DRYDEN, JOHN WILMOT EARL OF ROCHESTER,
KATHERINE PHILIPS, APHRA BEHN,
ANNE FINCH COUNTESS OF WINCHILSEA, EDWARD TAYLOR

In the new dawn the great eagle of English poetry is fit, sleek and well fed, but its wings have been clipped—tastefully and painlessly, of course, but the bird finds flight difficult. It will never again convey in its talons a plump and struggling poet like Geoffrey Chaucer to the House of Fame. Next time a poet really flies in the flesh, it will not be on "viewless wings of poesy" but in a machine.

It is hard for a reader arriving at his work in the sequence of English poets not to think ungenerously of John Dryden. Dryden opens verse to a popular readership, what in more cynical moments we call a market. His books sold well. Jacob Tonson—who bought *Paradise Lost* for £8 from Milton's widow—says as much; he was willing to pay real money to keep Dryden on his list. Tonson published Addison, and Rowe's edition of Shakespeare, and an edition of Beaumont and Fletcher (he understood how money could be wrung from drama). Between 1684 and 1708 he published *Miscellanies*, which Dryden edited until his death in 1700 and which included work by Pope, Swift and Ambrose Philips. He was the secretary of the immortal Kit-Cat Club, which brought together writers and others of a Whig persuasion—Steele, Congreve, Addison, and Vanbrugh among them—to meet at the house of the distinguished pastry cook Mr. Christopher Katt, in Shire Lane (off Temple Bar), whose mutton pies were called kit-cats. Later meetings were held *chez* Tonson at Barn Elms. Godfrey Kneller painted the club members at less than half-length because the low ceiling of Jacob's dining room could not accommodate half-size portraits. The portraits are in the National Portrait Gallery, where they look sociable but a little stunted. It was clever of Tonson to draw writers around him in a social way. He could control them and pick off works as they were completed, without danger of losing them to competitors. It is not impossible that he enjoyed the company of writers, and they his.

Dryden was generally a professional and not a troublesome author. He was hugely accomplished, one of the most confident and resourceful poets in the language. Still, he fills the modern reader with misgivings. Something is missing, something that even a minor poet of the earlier age, and some of his minor contemporaries, possess. That impalpable something is palpably lacking in Dryden. We find him more than a symptom of change: he is also a cause.

He held court at Will's Coffeehouse, as Ben Jonson had done at the Apollo Room; he was sought out by poets and poetasters who wanted to be legitimized. Dryden was more like the despotic French composer Rameau than Jonson. Jonson taught a various discipline, Dryden taught rules by example and precept. "From his contemporaries," Doctor Johnson remarked, Dryden "was in no danger. Standing therefore in the highest place, he had no care to rise by contending with himself; but while there was no name above his own, was willing to enjoy fame on the easiest terms."

As the century turned, "a delicate precocious boy" was taken to Will's and introduced to Dryden. Inspired by Dryden's clear eminence, the young Alexander Pope wanted it for himself. The quest was for recognized correctness which led to power in a tinpot literary world. Poets were now in competition with one another; there was a pecking order, with rewards according to perceived eminence. There were "objective" yardsticks of propriety, decorum and form. How gentle by contrast the rule of Jonson: a bibulous, cantankerous but generally benign enabler who inspired younger poets and encouraged their verse, as against the severe, mannerly, powdered, snuff-snorting, cosmopolitan poetic pontiff. The characters of both Jonson and Dryden are oversimplified in summary, but there is undeniably a new tone.

Does something happen to the English imagination in the latter part of the seventeenth century, something radical and irreversible? T. S. Eliot thinks so and calls it a "dissociation of sensibility." It is plausible to locate it in the complex historical events that led to the Commonwealth and the Restoration: a break with cultural and spiritual continuities and political certainties; a wave of influence from the Continent, especially France, from where a king returned; a new spirit of skepticism, new codes of decorum and politeness, that Enlightenment which cast such murky darkness on the world of instinct, intuition and spontaneity. Something happens to the English mind to create the immense gap between Donne and Pope, between poets who feel thought and poets who think. For Donne a thought had a context and an occasion; it modified him, it magnetized other thoughts, it was volatile and in process. For Dryden a thought was something to be tidied up and refined for presentation. Poetry's function as a *synthesizer* of experience is first attenuated, then virtually banished in the age Dryden in his maturity inaugurates.

Graves pays him an ambiguous tribute. "He earned the doubtful glory of having found English poetry brick and left it marble—native brick, imported marble." He recalls Doctor Johnson's comments on Dryden's *need* to flatter: "The inevitable consequence of poverty is dependence. Dryden had probably no recourse in his exigencies but to his bookseller." It is true: Dryden was compelled to get money from Tonson, his bookseller, and to supplement it from those to whom he dedicated his poems and their relations. His bookseller-publisher had his own fish to fry. A writer could expect a limited income from the printing of his work: like modern poets, he earned real bread from flattery.

> Th' unhappy man, who once has tailed a pen,
> Lives not to please himself but other men:
> Is always drudging, wastes his life and blood,
> Yet only eats and drinks what you think good . . .

A rule evolved that poets were not to write "low" any longer. A low style is unsuitable for serious subjects, as for serious patrons. Poets could not write English in the way Chaucer and Skelton and Shakespeare and Jonson had done. An unofficial but pervasive censorship developed. It was called decorum.

In his preface to *Fables Ancient and Modern*, Dryden reflects on the permanence of Chaucer's characters: "Mankind is ever the same, and nothing lost out of nature, though every thing is altered." A confident Augustan sentiment, learned from Lucretius, characterizes the father of the eighteenth century, the man Eliot sees as dividing with Milton the heritage of seventeenth-century poetry into two narrower channels. "In Dryden, wit becomes almost fun, and thereby loses some contact with reality." Dryden's mature language is prodigiously efficient. It lacks subtlety, intimacy, doubt and fear. It is a language for discourse and definition, not physical evocation or personal statement. Ford is harsh about his legacy: "It is really to Dryden, writing wholly within the seventeenth century, that the eighteenth owes the peculiar fadedness of all its adjectived nouns and latinised cliché phrases."

Readers describe his qualities in other than poetic terms. For Johnson he is the "father of English criticism" and speaks in a "tone of adamantine confidence." Arnold calls him "a classic of our prose." Through Dryden later ages define their priorities. There are many things he's not, many things he doesn't do and can't do. But there are things he does incomparably well: his place in English poetry, visited grudgingly by new readers but gradually increasing in charm and attraction as they revisit, is a place of lucidity, analysis, critical insight, general "truth." Coleridge says, "Dryden's genius was of that sort which catches fire by its own motion; his chariot wheels *get* hot by driving fast." The best way to read him, especially the dramatic poems and translations, is not at a student's dogged pace but headlong. Gerard Manley Hopkins called his nature "masculine": "his style and his rhythms lay the strongest stress of all our literature on the naked thew and sinew of the English language." Wyndham Lewis pairs him with Daniel Defoe as a "tongue that naked goes."

Dryden was born at the vicarage of Aldwinkle, Northamptonshire, of Puritan antecedents, in 1631. Educated at Westminster School under the great Richard Busby (who included John Locke and Matthew Prior among his pupils), he wrote and published at eighteen his first notable poem, "Upon the Death of Lord Hastings." It is flawed, combining memorable lines with strained—not to say mixed—metaphors and ill-judged effects: the smallpox spots on the diseased lord are compared to

> . . . rose-buds, stuck i' th' lily skin about.
> Each little pimple had a tear in it,
> To wail the fault its rising did commit.

The work is full of promise, a suggestive confusion. A Metaphysical impulse runs through it; a courtly instinct, too. Most effective are the moral conclusions, tightly drawn in efficient couplets.

He went up to Trinity College, Cambridge, where he did not distinguish himself but took his BA in 1654. He attached himself to his rich cousin Sir Gilbert Pickering, chamberlain to Cromwell, and in 1658 wrote his elegy on Cromwell's death. The metaphors are used decoratively, turned on and off like bulbs to give local illumination, and the matter is uncontrolled in its emotional flow, so that Johnson could declare that Dryden had "a mind better formed to reason than to feel." With the Restoration, reason told him to get in the front row of flatterers. In "Astrea Redux" he praises the king and Sir Robert Howard, whose daughter he married later. Charles II made him Poet Laureate in 1668. An active dramatist from 1663 onward, he pilloried the king's foes in plays and satires.

He was made historiographer royal in 1670, a reward for service and for his impressive but overmeticulous *Annus Mirabilis*, the year of wonders, 1666. He prided himself on accuracy in his description of naval encounters and the great fire of London. This is his first poem with the full authority of the mature style:

Our dreaded Admiral from far they threat,
>   Whose batter'd rigging their whole war receives.
All bare, like some old oak which tempests beat,
>   He stands, and sees below his scatter'd leaves.

The move from conventionality to the effectively Homeric simile is masterly: the serene remove of the "old oak" (which is still the ship's oak mast), in its forest, surrounded by bereaving autumn, is philosophically poised and affecting. His patriotism is of a novel, imperial stamp, and Shakespeare touches his language:

Yet, like an English gen'ral will I die,
>   And all the ocean make my spacious grave.
Women and cowards on the land may lie,
>   The sea's a tomb that's proper for the brave.

One of the distinctive qualities of Dryden, who seems at times to belong to the following century, is that he is so different in kind from Milton. His English roots are in Chaucer and Shakespeare rather than Spenser.

In 1681 *Absalom and Achitophel* appeared, the first of our great political satires. It attacked Shaftesbury and the party opposed to the court. A bald, less oblique assault on Shaftesbury, *The Medal*, followed in 1682. It was Dryden's most fruitful period. In the same year he published the Anglican *Religio Laici* (*A Layman's Faith*). The allegorical *The Hind and the Panther* attempts to vindicate his later (1687) turn to Roman Catholicism.

Much has been made of Dryden's opportunistic shifts of religious and political allegiance. Doctor Johnson justifies the poet's religious sincerity as a Catholic by pointing to the letters and the life. Dryden's sons were all unquestionably devout Roman Catholics, two of whom served the Church. As to his political opportunism, Ford Madox Ford makes the case for him: "It is difficult to see what other course a man writing on public matters could have taken if he set the peace of a sufficiently tormented country above all other matters." When James II was dethroned, Dryden was fifty-seven. He'd found his faith, remained a Catholic, and lost both his royal appointments under William III. In bitter poems he satirized new time servers, famously Thomas Shadwell in *MacFlecknoe*.

He published two *Poetical Miscellanies* in 1684 and 1685, which include important poems. Johnson called "On the Death of Mrs Killigrew" "the noblest ode that our language has ever produced." It is masterly, but must strike a modern reader as a coldly deliberate tribute:

Art she had none, yet wanted none:
    For nature did that want supply,
    So rich in treasures of her own,
    She might our boasted stores defy:
Such noble vigour did her verse adorn,
That it seem'd borrow'd, where 'twas only born.

Convention is refined but not animated. Dryden makes play with the language of virtue; the poem celebrates his subtlety more than it celebrates the unfortunate Mrs. Killigrew.

Pope spent his early years in translation, an apprenticeship. Dryden turned seriously to translation only later in life. With collaborators he rendered Ovid's *Epistles*. He was the kind of poet who could maintain an atelier because it was in the nature of his poetic language that it was imitable, a social mode of discourse. In 1692 his outstanding *Satires of Juvenal and Persius* appeared. Three years before his death, in 1700, *The Works of Virgil* was published. Some regard this as Dryden's masterpiece. Pope calls it "the most noble and spirited translation I know in any language." His last major work, published in 1700, was *Fables Ancient and Modern*, an anthology of translations from Ovid, Boccaccio and Chaucer, including one of his most celebrated prose prefaces. Tonson ordered verse by the yard, originally asking for 10,000 lines and receiving more than he bargained for. Dryden wrote for money: Tonson's fee, a patron's largess. He was an occasional poet in an even more literal sense than Jonson.

Even the plethora of his critical detractors would agree that Dryden is one of those rare writers, like Spenser, Milton, Wordsworth and Eliot, who by example and critical writing redirected the current of English poetry. Without an understanding of his techniques and concerns, it's hard to make sense of the eighteenth century, on the eve of which he died. Its achievements and *longueurs*, its stylizations, its manners and mannerisms, are figured or prefigured in his writing. He was the architect of that Augustan mansion in English literature which demands more effort from the modern reader than any other. We must adjust to well-proportioned rooms in which familiar things are rendered unnaturally real in definition and made typical; or to satires in which a familiar world is mercilessly turned topsy-turvy. If we judge him by the effect he had, he is great. If we judge the work itself, we can't deny him greatness, unless on grounds of limited tonal range (on such grounds Milton himself would fail). Dryden's technical and formal assurance have few parallels. He is a civic, public, social poet. Our age has a distaste for such work and its values, but if we dismiss Dryden, we dismiss the clearest English poet, and the most accomplished of public poets.

Unlike the Earl of Rochester, who went a certain way with reason, then discarded it in favor of instinct because reason led to a dark dead end, Dryden stuck with reason as a sufficient means of exploration and discourse, leading to the portal of faith. "A man is to be cheated into passion, but reasoned into truth," he writes in the preface to *The Hind and the Panther*. Reason has limits, and beyond it faith opens out the way. He evokes the process in one of the most resonant passages in *Religio Laici* (*A Layman's Faith*):

Dim, as the borrow'd beams of moon and stars
To lonely, weary, wand'ring travellers,
Is Reason to the soul: and as on high,
Those rolling fires discover but the sky
Not light us here; so Reason's glimmering ray
Was lent, not to assure our doubtful way,
But guide us upward to a better day.
And as those nightly tapers disappear
When day's bright Lord ascends our hemisphere;
So pale grows Reason at Religion's sight;
So dies, and so dissolves in supernatural Light.

Reason in the civic sphere reveals the need for order and authority. It's worth remembering that his three important early poems praised or celebrated figures of authority and power: Hastings, Cromwell, Charles II.

Reason is the root of his aesthetic, its formality audible even when the tone is informal. He is seldom grandiloquent or assertive; a vein of wit runs through even his most sober work. He concurs with Hobbes about the place of fancy and judgment in the creative process. "Time and education beget experience; experience begets memory; memory begets judgment and fancy, judgment begets the strength and structure, and fancy begets the ornaments of a poem." Wit is in the interplay of judgment and fancy. Fancy perceives similitude in things dissimilar, judgment perceives distinctions in things similar. Rhyme, he argues, helps to keep fancy under control.

Such a concept of poetry compels a poet to be exact in his use of image and metaphor in order to illuminate and instruct. The truth of a figure—literal, allegorical or satiric—must be maintained. Implied, too, is a propensity to work toward general truths. This produces an impersonal tone, so that one can hold Dryden responsible for the whole argument of a poem without always being certain of his personal attitude to particulars.

The gap between Donne and Dryden could not be wider. Descartes and the new philosophy—and Hobbes—come between them. So does Cromwell and the Restoration, with French habits acquired in exile. Poetry as a serious exercise was called into question. Three modes principally appeal to Dryden, all of them deliberate, public and, in one way or another, "useful." First are prologues and epilogues, comical, critical, expository or hortatory. Dryden's comic epilogues are among his best. Mrs. Ellen, "when she was to be carried off dead by the bearers" at the end of *Tyrannick Love* (1670), exclaims, "Hark, are you mad? you damn'd confounded dog, / I am to rise, and speak the Epilogue." She addresses the audience courteously as the ghost of the character she has played. She berates the poet:

> O Poet, damn'd dull Poet, who could prove
> So senseless! to make Nelly die for Love,
> Nay, what's yet worse, to kill me in the prime
> Of Easter-term, in tart and cheese-cake time!
> I'll fit the fop; for I'll not one word say
> T'excuse his godly out of fashion play.
> A play which if you dare but twice sit out,
> You'll all be slander'd, and be thought devout.

Presumably, having delivered her epilogue, she is carted offstage to general applause.

The second acceptable mode of verse is the consciously decorative, rhetorical poem, usually occasional and celebratory. The "Ode on St Cecilia's Day" and "Alexander's Feast" display the virtuosity of the poet honoring an occasion. Third comes the heroic or religious epic, on a large scale, with ceremonious action, contemporary reference, and didactic intent. The obverse of this is the satire, which Dryden develops with a metrical virtuosity and clarity of diction unlike Donne's, rejecting *asprezza* and harsher tones. In *Absalom and Achitophel* satire is cruel and direct, but the prosody impeccable: Achitophel's human deformity is not spared, but it does not distort the surface of the verse:

> A daring pilot in extremity;
> Pleased with the danger, when the waves went high
> He sought the storms; but for a calm unfit,
> Would steer too nigh the sands, to boast his wit.
> Great wits are sure to madness near allied,
> And thin partitions do their bounds divide;
> Else, why should he, with wealth and honour blest,
> Refuse his age the needful hours of rest?

> Punish a body which he could not please;
> Bankrupt of life, yet prodigal of ease?

Figurative language is not Dryden's forte. Often it is not integrated with the argument but runs alongside, decorating and heightening but not collaborating with it at a deeper level. Milton exemplifies another mode. In "lik'ning spiritual to corporeal forms" Milton begins with figure and metaphor and attempts a realization that itself carries moral significance; Dryden teases prose meanings into metaphor. In each case a partial process is enacted. Pope, by contrast, thinks in shapes and forms, exploits reversals, contains his meanings in the figures themselves but works as it were with atomized forms and metaphors, divorced from the expected context and releasing new meanings in an original context. His poetry tends to fragment into brilliant shards. Milton's procedure comes closest to the "organic" concept of poetic form enunciated by Coleridge and exploited by the Romantics. Dryden's procedure is remote from this. He distrusts antithesis, paradox and disjunction and is wary of placing excessive confidence in plain narrative, at least for didactic purposes.

His satires are conceived in a different spirit from Pope's. For Pope the ideal order is no longer tangibly embodied, there is no "right" party, no legitimate order: his satiric exaggerations do not always suggest a norm, his distortions contain more malice than instructive justness. Dryden accepts the *status quo* as the norm, accepts necessary authority, placing facts rather than values first. This "philosophical actualism" he learned from Hobbes. Fact has more authority than traditional sanction, in politics as in literature: a king's authority is a formal, not a sacred one; to be of value a poem must be of use. The tendency to stylize material in order to draw its morals, the way attitudes replace passions and figures replace characters, is due in part to Charles II's own taste. From his French exile he brought back a preference for rhymed, formalized dramas. The king was patron: though he did not call the tune, no doubt he tapped out a rhythm with his foot. Dryden obliged his king and his publisher. Flattery is his worst vice, yet he is so assured that he retains, or regains, his integrity.

Doctor Johnson's assessment of Dryden is still the most concise and judicious. Dryden rather than Sidney is "the father of English criticism," especially on the strength of the *Essay on Dramatic Poesy* (1668). Johnson criticizes the inconsistent approach in Dryden's essays, the occasional marring casualness and partiality. But these faults don't imperil a broader achievement, which (unlike Milton's or Cowley's) is at root not scholarly but critical. His art is to express clearly what he thinks with vigor. Before Dryden there was "no poetical diction, no system of words at once refined from the grossness of domestic use, and free from the harshness of terms appropriated to particular arts."

The advent of "diction" was a mixed blessing. Dryden intended refined diction to make language transparent, unobtrusive, capable of general statements of truth without obscurity or vulgarity: hence the excellence of his theory and practice of translation. But for some of his followers, diction came to mean refinement of manner, affectation, not efficient, unencumbered expression. When Johnson claims that he refined the sentiments of poetry, he wishes to praise the public manner and the absence of individual quirkiness. Yet it is the element of individual tone, of apprehensible character or "voice," that we miss in Dryden. It is overstatement to say that he "tuned the numbers" of English poetry. He refined the heroic couplet and handed it as a vital instrument to his successors. His prosodic virtuosity in the songs from the plays, in odes and elegies, is not in doubt: but he had equals among his predecessors, not least Jonson. When Dryden "refined" language, he rid it of dross, but also of much expressive power. He retuned his instrument to certain harmonies but it was incapable of some older and deeper strains. The loss is felt not so much in his own work as in the work of his heirs.

Efficiency, his chief virtue, he perfected from his stage writing. What Homer was for Pope, theater was for Dryden. It gave him a public: there he discovered and perfected a "popular" style. He was not "much inclined" by genius to write for the stage, but necessity took him there and instructed him. The many plays contain little of his best writing. One of them, *All for Love,* based on Shakespeare's *Antony and Cleopatra*, retains theatrical appeal today. But the stage was his pacing ground. Without that experience I doubt that he could have sustained *Absalom and Achitophel*, the best political satire in the language. The satires, full of the political and literary life of the time, retain a wider reference. The prologues and epilogues are not remote from common speech. The allegories, too, reflect his age's intellectual and spiritual concerns. Eliot's tribute to Dryden is partial and paradoxical: "Dryden appeared to cleanse the language of verse and once more bring it back to prose order. For this reason he is a great poet." It would be better to say that Dryden suggests an order for poetic language different from his predecessors'. What is prosaic in Dryden is his ideas, not his language. When Eliot suggests that he "once more" brings the language of poetry back to prose order, we are inclined to ask: When in the history of English poetry up to Dryden's time had the language of poetry followed prose order? Dryden did not take English poetry back but inexorably forward to a new phase. His verse rejects as much as—perhaps more than—it discovers.

Dryden had virulent enemies in his time. His satires and the king's favor enraged John Wilmot, Earl of Rochester, who legend says had him mugged one night in a dark passageway off Garrick Street, near Covent Garden. Did Rochester see Dryden as an upstart? Was he troubled by his religion? Did he fear that Dryden might persuade the king out of his patient affection for his troublesome courtier? Or was he simply jealous of the skills and dogged industry of the greatest poet of his age? We are back to *competition* between poets. "Mr Andrew Marvell (who was a good Judge of Witt) was wont to say that he [Rochester] was the best English Satyrist and had the right veine. 'Twas pitty Death tooke him off so soon." Marvell was not alone in speaking up for Rochester, a man by turns in and out of favor at court: volatile, brilliant and unpredictable. Also, at his best, philosophical:

Nothing! thou elder brother even to Shade:
Thou had'st a being ere the world was made,
And well fixed, art alone of ending not afraid.

During his poetic apprenticeship two generations later, Alexander Pope wrote "Upon Silence" in imitation of Rochester's "Upon Nothing": "Silence! Coeval with Eternity; / Thou wert ere future's self began to be." His piece is a respectful exercise, while Rochester's is one of the few necessary masterpieces the poet wrote. The young Pope took Rochester to heart as a master. Rochester attempted to think in verse, to think even the darkest thoughts, a feat he performed with appalling lucidity in "Upon Nothing." He lays bare the philosophical basis for his notorious libertinism. What had seemed vice becomes an expression of something more fashionable in our time, an accepting nihilism.

The poem explains what many see as the saddest squandering of authentic genius in English poetry. When Pope, forty years after his imitation of Rochester, came to sleep in the same bed Rochester had graced at Atterbury, he was "With no poetic ardours fir'd." No wonder: Rochester left a small oeuvre to suggest what he might have been capable of. The work is formally conservative and eccentric in theme and subject. Pope came to see him and other poets of Charles II's court—including Charles Sackville, Earl of Dorset, the beguilingly cheerful and erotic Sir Charles Sedley, Sir George Etherege, William Wycherley and Henry Savile—as a "mob of gentlemen who wrote verses." Marvell, more amused and forgiving, called his wry and waggish contemporaries a "merry gang." Merry in company they must have been: Samuel Pepys, on 30 May 1668, joined them: "And so to supper in an arbour: but Lord! their mad bawdy talk did make my heart ache! And here I first understood by their talk the meaning of the company that lately were called

Ballers: Harris telling how it was by a meeting of some young blades, where he was among them, and my Lady Bennet and her ladies; and their there dancing naked, and all the roguish things of the world. But, Lord! what loose, cursed company was this, that I was in tonight, though full of wit; and worth a man's being in for once, to know the nature of it, and their manner of talk, and lives."

Charles II's court was hospitable to wit and culture of an aristocratic and Frenchified kind. It was the Indian summer of "court culture." F. R. Leavis finds the poets lacking in "positive fineness" and "implicit subtlety." The country house is supplanted by the coffeehouse, the "fine old order" gone. But something is gained in the way of forthrightness, certain social tones that had not been heard before in "polite" circles irrupt into the verse, soon to be snuffed out by strict preceptors for whom purity and propriety of diction were an unbreachable rule.

The Restoration court frolicked in the austere shadows cast by the Commonwealth: a continuity had been broken, an old order perished. Court writers and politicians experienced an ambivalent euphoria; the stability that empowers poet or statesman to take, as a matter of course, a long view or undertake a long work, would not return for decades. Idealism of a powerful, defeated sort—the moral high ground—seemed to be occupied by the other party. Divine sanction gone, there was less a sense of right than of success in the air. Hobbes, not Filmer or Hooker, was the philosopher of the day. Hobbes affected Rochester (as he did Dryden) deeply. As a courtier, the poet's chief allegiance was to "pleasure" conceived in a narrow range, and nihilistic atheism.

Charles II's court continued its connections with France. The circumstances of his restoration contributed alien elements to his reign. Court writers were inevitably self-absorbed in ways it had never occurred to their predecessors to be. The decline in civic courtesy and the frail imperatives of duty and service, and the apparent liberality of the court milieu attracted the great French philosopher Voltaire. And Voltaire found Rochester's work congenial. In *Lettres philosphiques* he says, "All the world knows Lord Rochester's reputation"; he will introduce the other Rochester, not just a libertine but a man of genius, *"le grand poète,"* with his "ardent" imagination. Voltaire celebrates the satires, which, whether the ideas expressed are true or false, possess real energy. Boileau, with Cowley, was among the earl's favorite authors. His satire belonged to a contemporary European tradition.

Rochester experimented on his life as his contemporaries experimented in science. It is fashionable to see him as "essentially serious," a "radical critic" of his time, even a moral visionary. On the evidence of the verse, apart from "A Satire Against Mankind," he is neither socially

radical nor penetratingly serious. His seriousness of theme emerges in
only a few poems, and there more as statement than exploration. Hos-
tile to reason, he denied himself the main avenue of philosophical
exploration. Yet this hostility to reason is itself a theme, as in "Tun-
bridge Wells":

> Ourselves with noise of reason we do please
> In vain; humanity's our worst disease.
> Thrice happy beasts are, who, because they be
> Of reason void, are so of foppery.

Given this view—and despite his power as a rhetorician—Rochester
can't get far beyond satire. Indeed, within satire he goes only a certain
way. He denies himself the scope of the long poem and works within the
confines of received forms. His temperament and antecedents make it
hard to imagine what other strategy he could have devised.

He was born in Ditchley, Oxfordshire, in 1647. His father, a Royalist
general, led an abortive rising in Yorkshire in 1655 and died in exile two
or three years later. Rochester's mother was of a family with Puritan
connections. At the age of twelve he went up to Wadham College,
Oxford, a center of the new scientific and intellectual developments that
led to the foundation of the Royal Academy. In 1661 the precocious
young nobleman was made an MA by the incomparable historian Lord
Clarendon himself. The restored king granted him a pension in 1660, in
recognition of his father's service. Under such favorable stars, Rochester
toured France and Italy and returned to England in 1664. He made him-
self visible at court. His feelings for Charles II were ambiguous, almost
those of a young man for a forceful stepfather. Some of his scathing
satires are directed against the monarch. In 1665 Rochester was confined
to the Tower for attempting to abduct a Somerset heiress, whom he
married two years later ("I'll hold you six to four I love you with all my
heart," he wrote to her later, during one of his infidelities). Thanks to
the plague, he was released from the Tower, joined the fleet, and gave
intrepid service, though there is evidence that he was less stalwart
ashore.

Always in and out of favor, he became a gentleman of the king's bed-
chamber in 1666, an honor more than a duty. The remaining fourteen
years of his life passed in a series of unsettled and rash acts, with periods
of study and work. If he wrote the notorious play *Sodom*, it was around
1670. Between 1673 and 1676 his best satires and "Upon Nothing" were
composed. In 1675 he was appointed keeper of Woodstock Park. Later in
life he claimed to have been drunk for a five-year stretch—country life
cannot have been too agreeable. He died, after a dubious conversion

exhaustively chronicled by his spiritual monitor, the egregious Gilbert Burnet, in 1680.

We can choose between two versions of Rochester. Sir George Etherege in his play *The Man of Mode* presents him as the charming, inconstant and self-involved Dorimant. We can embellish this image with the story of the smashing of the sundials in the Priory Gardens and the "murderous affray" at Epsom. On the other hand we have the scholar (on the evidence of Anthony à Wood and of the fragments of his translation of Lucretius). Burnet, who negotiated his reconciliation with God and was at best a Whig rascal, wrote of his good looks, his civility, his intelligence: "He loved to talk and write of speculative matters, and did so with so fine a thread, that even those who hated the subjects" were charmed by his treatment of them. But, Burnet adds, physical led to intellectual dissipation, "which made him think nothing diverting which was not extravagant."

The real Rochester is closer to Etherege's version. Johnson praises the "vigour of his colloquial wit"; but "The glare of his general character diffused itself upon his writings." The very shortness of his pieces reflects the shortness of his periods of sobriety and study: nevertheless, the dots of brilliance in the writing, taken together, add up to a reckonable star.

He works in four "kinds"; extended satire, libel or squib, racy anecdote, and love poem. Some of the love poems are spoken by women ("I could love thee till I die" and "Ancient Person" being among the best). Love is of a resolutely carnal nature. "Leave this gaudy, gilded stage," " 'Tis not that I am weary grown," "Absent from thee I languish still" and "The Mistress": these works rank high in English love poetry. Forthright, they have an air of sincerity. The anecdote poems, too, have a forceful, grotesque bawdiness and can be erotic and startling. "Fair Chloris in a pigsty lay" is the best known. We might consider them downmarket eclogues. The squibs and libels marry wit and malice and do some damage to their subjects, notably the king.

In imitating Ovid ("O Love! how cold and slow" and "The Imperfect Enjoyment") he moves toward satire. It is useful to compare his imitations with Marlowe's (*Elegia*, book 2, elegy 9, and book 3, elegy 6). Less than a century separates them. Marlowe's versions are visualized, and governed by vivid metaphor undeflected by wit. Rochester argues rather than evokes, idea is developed at the expense of metaphor. His language is more conventional and polite than Marlowe's. In Marlowe there is a sultry, ambiguous sexuality; in Rochester forthrightness, without undertones—what Eliot, writing of Dryden, called "lack of suggestiveness." Compare Marlowe's:

Dost joy to have thy hookèd arrows shakèd
In naked bones? Love hath my bones left naked.
So many men and maidens without love!
Hence with great laud thou may'st a triumph move.

with Rochester's:

On men disarmed how can you gallant prove?
And I was long ago disarmed by love.
Millions of dull men live, and scornful maids:
We'll own love valiant when he these invades.

Rochester is the more correct; Marlowe, despite—or because of—his
awkwardness, the more satisfying. The second line focuses the different
genius of each writer, the third epitomizes the radical change in sensi-
bility that has occurred.

Age, "beauty's incurable disease," is the key apprehension of Roch-
ester's harsh vision. He satirizes affectation and the social forms that
lead to a squandering of possible or actual pleasure; and he satirizes
excesses that themselves foreshorten pleasure and in which he, as much
as the king, indulged. He cannot stop attacking reason, that *"ignis
fatuus,"* a contrived and distracting sixth sense: "Huddled in dirt the rea-
soning engine lies, / Who was so proud, so witty, and so wise." This
sense of mortality is unredeemed by religious certitude. The one virtue
Rochester celebrates is love. In "A Letter from Artemisia in Town to
Chloe in the Country" he writes,

Love, the most generous passion of the mind,
The softest refuge innocence can find,
The safe director of unguided youth . . .

It is "That cordial drop heaven in our cup has thrown / To make the
nauseous draught of life go down."

Love a "passion of the mind"? Marlowe would not have understood
that Rochester's satire seeks to free the impulse of love from inhibition
and convention. Rochester is the apologist for "sex" rather than courtly
or romantic love. Yet underlying even this theme is the pervasive truth
presented in "Upon Nothing":

Great Negative, how vainly would the wise
Inquire, define, distinguish, teach, devise,
Did'st thou not stand to point their blind philosophies.

His satire is directed at court and society at large, in the manner of Juvenal, but the objective of his satire is not social. Unlike Dryden's, Rochester's satire is informed by metaphysical despair, not social optimism. The best way of dealing with despair is to laugh, and some of his wicked poems, like those of Sir Charles Sedley, provide a salacious delight not to be found elsewhere in English.

Aubrey chronicles the death of Lord Rochester, with which Burnet filled many sanctimonious pages, in three rapid, telling sentences. "In his last sickness he was exceedingly penitent and wrote a letter of his repentance to Dr Burnet, which is printed. He sent for all his servants, even the piggard-boy, to come and hear his palinode. He died at Woodstock Park, 26 July 1680; and buried at Spilsbury in the same county, Aug. 9 following."

Among the female poets of their age, Dryden favored "the Matchless Orinda," Katherine Philips (1632–64), wife of James, who at Cardigan Priory, their Welsh home, set up a kind of intellectual circle called the Society of Friendship and entertained the intelligentsia. "Orinda," a celebrated translator of Corneille's plays, wrote her poems to other women, in particular Anne Owen, the Viscountess of Dungannon, with whom she maintained an intense platonic friendship. She can be simperingly sentimental; she also rises to mild satire, though she lacks the vigor of the Duchess of Newcastle. She died of smallpox at thirty-two and became a mildly tragic figure of legend.

Aphra Behn (1640–89) is more Rochester's kind of poet, feisty and self-reliant, the first English woman to become a professional writer. He was her friend and patron, but irregular in patronage as in everything else. Her colorful life—starting, when she was sixteen, with an eight-year trip to Surinam and beyond with her father, the appointed lieutenant governor, who died en route; her experience of the New World, of a slave rebellion and other adventures that may or may not be true—gives her exotic appeal. She returned to England in 1664, married a merchant and was bereaved probably in the plague of 1665. She became a spy in Antwerp, did her work well but was never properly paid. She saw the inside of a debtor's prison in 1668 and resolved never to return. So she became a writer. The theater was her main market and she wrote fourteen plays. When this market dried up she started writing fiction, or "faction," including *Oroonoko* (1688), with its not altogether believable basis in her early experiences. She died the next year, poor again and in considerable pain, and, like earlier female writers, was forgotten.

Some of her poems are songs uprooted from her plays. Some are lascivious entertainments that pull no punches and are as erotic—in a different key—as Sedley's. Indeed some of her poems share lines with his. It would be wrong to claim technical originality for Aphra Behn as a poet. But as a woman poet, and as a woman writer, she clears an important space; she breaks as many taboos as Mary Wroth did, and possesses more substantial gifts. Against polite Dryden, impolite Rochester, against proper "Orinda," the matchless Aphra Behn.

Anne Finch, Countess of Winchilsea (1661–1720), sourly pondered "the situation of the woman writer." Her imagination was shaped by the seventeenth century, though it was in the eighteenth that her voice was finally heard. Alexander Pope, who rather liked her, also derided her (with his friends Gay and Arbuthnot) in a play, *Three Hours after Marriage*, in which she appears as Phoebe Clinket, the loopy lady poet. (Sylvia Plath played the part of Phoebe in a Cambridge University production of the play.) Many of Finch's contemporaries shared Pope's ambivalence. The only book she published in her lifetime appeared anonymously when she was fifty-two. She had "the skill to write, the modesty to hide." Wordsworth prepared a selection of her verse and since that time she has never sunk entirely from sight. He liked her poem "Nocturnal Reverie," which, he said, contained in its descriptions of groves and meadows at night the only new images of "external nature" between the poetry of Milton and Thomson.

> When darkened groves their softest shadows wear,
> And falling waters we distinctly hear;
> When through the gloom more venerable shows
> Some ancient fabric, awful in repose,
> While sunburnt hills their swarthy looks conceal,
> And swelling haycocks thicken up the vale;
> When the loosed horse now, as his pasture leads,
> Comes slowly grazing through th'adjoining meads.
> Whose stealing pace and lengthened shade we fear
> Till torn up forage in his teeth we hear . . .

It is a vision closer to nature than Pope's aestheticizing in "Windsor Forest"—a series of observations, not of epithets and qualities.

She is read today for her poems on the friendship of women and on the situation of women, and for the poems of conjugal contentment. No other woman poet of the time so bitterly reflects upon the circumstances that inhibited women from expressing themselves in print.

Another strange voice, new and yet with old and tested tonalities, is Edward Taylor, born around 1642 of prosperous Puritan yeoman stock in Leicestershire during the Civil War. Unable to subscribe to the Act of Uniformity after the Restoration, cast out of his job as a schoolmaster, forbidden to go to Oxford or Cambridge, forbidden to preach or worship, he emigrated to Boston when he was twenty-six. He was already a passionate admirer of Francis Quarles and of the Metaphysical poets—not only Donne and Herbert (whom he echoes) but Vaughan, Traherne and Crashaw as well. And Du Bartas. Like Anne Bradstreet's, his literary culture suffered a kind of positive arrest on his departure. He attended Harvard College and became a pastor (and physician) in the frontier hamlet of Westfield, a hundred miles west of Boston, retiring in 1725, the father of numerous offspring by two wives and in possession of a library, remarkable for its time, of some two hundred books.

On his death he left a 400-page manuscript of religious poems, composed as part of his spiritual preparation for administering the Lord's Supper, and including two substantial sequences. In 1937 they were discovered in a library and America had another substantial early poet, a Puritan nourished on the great Anglican Metaphysicals, who began to carve out his own kind of poetry on a physical and spiritual frontier. His nonexistence in American poetry for the two centuries after his death makes it hard to set him in the American frame: his work is sadly without issue until this century, when poets such as Robert Lowell take apprentice bearings from him. To English readers he seems at first an anachronism, his conceits at times outlandish and mechanical. ("Shall Spirits thus my mammularies suck?" or "Be thou my Lilly, make thou me thy knot: / Be thou my Flowers, I'll be thy flower pot.") Yet he is a figurative thinker, he has a deep sense of evil and of man's fallen nature. He uses verse as an instrument of redemption, not—as Milton does—of instruction. He can surprise us into a sudden vision of the divine order, a sense of how we might attain unity with God through the created world. "Shall I not smell thy sweet, oh! Sharon's Rose?" Or, "Lord, blow the coal: thy love enflame in me." It is as though his Anglican mentors have leavened his spirit, made him not less severe but more humane, accepting of the forms of grace that pass through the human senses. He is one of those rare Puritans who will risk saying yes to right pleasure.

How sweet a Lord is mine? If any should
      Guarded, engarden'd, nay, imbosomed be
In reeks of odours, gales of spices, folds
Of aromatics, Oh! how sweet was he?
He would be sweet, and yet his sweetest wave
Compar'd to thee my Lord, no sweet would have.

Three Friends

JONATHAN SWIFT, JOHN GAY, ALEXANDER POPE

If writers are friends in the eighteenth century, it is best that they plow different furrows or live in different cities. A prose writer and a poet might be friends, but men active on the same patch might fall out over a patron, a reward, an error of emphasis. Yet some of the great writers of the early eighteenth century knew and applauded one another. *Gulliver's Travels*, *The Threepenny Opera* and *The Dunciad* are cousin works by men who had one another's interests—to some extent—at heart.

Jonathan Swift's mother was a Leicestershire Herrick, of Robert Herrick's family—so it happens that the savage satirist and the gentle Cavalier grow on a single family tree. They also share, in different centuries, a religious vocation and a politics. Yet their poetic imaginations belong on opposite sides of the divide that was the Commonwealth and Restoration. Swift is a brilliant savage who understands—though he cannot control—the political and literary jungle in which he lives.

> If on Parnassus' top you sit,
> You rarely bite, are always bit:
> Each poet of inferior size
> On you shall rail and criticise ...

His reputation as a poet stands higher in this century than ever before. Several modern poets identify original virtues in his verse, long regarded as peripheral to his major prose work. Robert Graves considers the verses "trifles," "but these trifles, though darkened by a morbid horror of man's physical circumstances, demonstrate the proper use of English: they are clear, simple, inventive, pungent, unaffected, original, generous, utterly outspoken."

Born in Dublin in 1667, Swift insisted on his Englishness. He was of Yorkshire stock. His father died before Swift was born. His education was paid for by an uncle, first in Kilkenny and later at Trinity College, Dublin, where he did not distinguish himself. He traveled to England

and became secretary to Sir William Temple at Moor Park in Surrey. There, among other studies, he labored at verse, subjected his work to endless revisions, and fell under the influence not of Milton, whose religion and politics were anathema to him, but of Abraham Cowley, whose Pindaric odes appealed (disastrously) to many young poets. Swift's odes are negligible. His first significant poem, "Mrs Harris's Petition," was not composed until he was thirty-four (1701), by which time he had put Cowley aside and opened his ears to the spoken language of the day, the new eighteenth century. The "Petition" is thoroughly colloquial, in irregular long-lined couplets that assume the tone of a woman speaking at great speed. Undecorated, it displays what De Quincey called Swift's "vernacularity."

When he composed the "Petition" he had left Temple, abandoning his very promising secular career, and had taken holy orders (1694). He was to rub shoulders with men of power and in his prose writings to make a mark on English affairs, but he was not destined to be a man at court. His first living, in Kilroot, Ireland, displeased him. He returned briefly to England but in 1699 was back in Ireland as chaplain to the Earl of Berkeley, a post from which he was ousted by private intrigue. He became vicar of Laracor. Deeply embroiled in religious and political affairs, he eventually became dean of St. Patrick's, Dublin. With the death of Queen Anne, the Whigs, his enemies, came to power. There was to be no further preferment for him.

In his later years he became a political enigma, "with the Whigs of the State and the Tories of the Church," Doctor Johnson said. His treatment by parties and patrons provoked a healthy distrust of men in power and intensified his sense of personal grievance. He considered life in Ireland exile. Yet he did much for the Irish, earning their respect if not their love. Through correspondence he maintained his friendship with Pope and Gay, with Dr. John Arbuthnot, Henry St. John Viscount Bolingbroke and others in England, but his mind ran on Irish affairs. He was aware of conditions at every social level; his Toryism was of that particularist kind which will not tolerate exploitative corruption from any quarter.

His vexed relations with women, especially "Stella" and "Vanessa," and his disgust with physical functions, have given much latitude to Freudian interpreters. Disgust informs much of the prose and verse, but so does a real interest in common people, their language, actions and concerns. The verse opens on this area of his genius, and on his darker musings. It possesses the satiric virtues of the prose with an additional element: the "I" speaks, speaks *as itself*, with an uncompromised acerbity that few poets have mastered. When he died in 1745, Ireland and

England were in his debt. The topicality that limits the appeal of some of his prose is itself the appeal of the verse: it catches inflections and remembers small actions now lost—the voices of gardeners, street vendors, laborers, which we hear refined in Gay; the tone of a cryptic man of conscience speaking of his world, his bitter life, his wary loves. He is commemorated by a great epitaph: he lies *"ubi saeva indignatio ulterius cor lacerare nequit. Abi, viator, et imitare, si poteris, strenuum pro virili libertatis vindicatorem."* Yeats translates it thus:

> Swift has sailed into his rest;
> Savage indignation there
> Cannot lacerate his breast.
> Imitate him if you dare,
> World-besotted traveller; he
> Served human liberty.

Boswell found Johnson's "Life of Swift" too harsh. In thirty pages, the poems receive three succinct paragraphs. In the poems "there is not much upon which the critic can exercise his powers. They are often humorous, almost always light, and have the qualities which recommend such compositions, easiness and gaiety." Their diction, prosody and rhyme are correct, conforming to Swift's own notion of good style: "proper words in proper places." Johnson's highest praise follows: "Perhaps no writer can be found who borrowed so little, or that in all his excellences and all his defects has so well maintained his claim to be considered as original." He is original in part because—in his mature poems—he's so spare. As Johnson says, his thoughts were "never subtilised by nice disquisitions, decorated by sparkling conceits, elevated by ambitious sentences, or variegated by far-sought learning." In this he resembles his contemporary the novelist Daniel Defoe, never shirking a difficult subject or elaborating for elaboration's sake.

Trifles and bagatelles, Johnson tells us, were necessary to Swift. Many of the poems are occasioned by little more than a love of language as it is differently spoken, and a fascination with people. The activity of humble folk provides substance: to represent is at times a sufficient end. There are the "Descriptions" of "Morning," "A City Shower" in particular, which realizes a peopled scene with slight satirical coloring:

> Brisk Susan whips her linen from the rope
> While the first drizzling show'r is borne aslope,
> Such is that sprinkling which some careless quean
> Flirts on you from her mop, but not so clean.

Bustling verbs animate scene and metaphor. Human actions rather than natural phenomena arrest attention. Ford comments on his "most unusual power of conveying scenes vividly . . . scenes rather of the sensibility than of material objects and landscapes." Coleridge calls Swift—he has the prose more than the verse in mind—"*anima Rabelaisii habitans in sicco,*—the soul of Rabelais dwelling in a dry place."

In the more ambitious pieces Swift challenges his reader. F. R. Leavis indicates the paradoxical nature of his approach: "Lacking the Augustan politeness, he seems with his dry force of presentment, both to make the Augustan positives . . . look like negatives, and to give the characteristic Augustan lacks and disabilities a positive presence." Without "Augustan urbanity," "spiritual poverty" and "hollowness" are underscored. There is a unique irony at work, not normative, like Dryden's, but radical: thematic rather than stylistic. This is why his poems, even the most topical, retain force today. "I take it to be part of the honesty of poets," he wrote, "that they cannot write well except they think the subject deserves it." The subjects he chose he approached as if for the first time, as if we stepped from the chill, clear world of reason into a world of men. Bolingbroke was not quite fair when he suggested, "If you despised the world as much as you pretend, and perhaps believe, you would not be so angry with it." Swift is a vigorous hater, but with a hatred rooted in disappointed expectation. He is merciless not to those below him on the social ladder but to those above, the empowered, and to the vain who persist in self-deception. Flattery is the grossest sin, chastised in the satirical "On Poetry: A Rhapsody."

Edgell Rickword and later C. H. Sisson took Swift's verse to heart. In a crucial essay, "The Re-Creation of Poetry" (1925), Rickword describes a "poetry of negative emotions, of those arising from disgust with the object." "Swift is a great master of this kind of poetry. His verse has no pleasure-value beyond that of its symmetry and concision, but it is the most intricate labyrinth of personality that any poet has built around himself, not excepting Donne." Rickword loves Donne, which makes his point compelling. Donne makes the labyrinth beguiling; Swift undecorates as he goes. The narrow, narrowing power of the verse is great. "The Progress of Beauty" and "The Furniture of a Woman's Mind" exemplify the voice of "negative emotion." So does "The Progress of Marriage" or "Verses on the Death of Dr Swift," where he directs satire at himself. His imitation of Horace's *Odes*, book 2, poem 6, with wry self-knowledge and a canny understanding of the world, evokes the man and those who use him. Conventional love is remote from this verse.

Swift is hard to recommend as a poet because he is hard to quote out of context. There are few purple passages, detachable maxims; the poetry is drawn evenly through the poem in ways that out-of-context quotation violates. The epitaphs, the spoofs, the eclogues, the anecdotes spoken by various voices, the ironic love poems, the first-person poems, will not be broken up into tags like the rich couplet bric-a-brac of Pope. In Swift we come upon a writer who might have preferred to be called versifier rather than poet. There is a difference in kind in his work from that of his predecessors; and he is not "polite" enough to have beguiled his contemporaries into imitation. He stands alone, he doesn't sing, he never ingratiates himself. He speaks, and he understands how the world wags.

The most brilliant poet of the eighteenth century would have been a composite figure made up of the three poet-friends, Swift, Pope and John Gay. Swift's savagery rooted in a concern for common people, Pope's verve and imaginative profligacy, and Gay's gentle good cheer might, taken together, have given us a writer of Shakespearean—or at least Chaucerian—proportions. Genius was parceled out, not combined, in the eighteenth century, and Gay was fortunate to have been given gentle, beguiling elements. "Tell me, ye jovial sailors, tell me true, / If my sweet William sails among the crew." His epitaph reads, "Life is a jest; and all things show it, / I thought so once; but now I know it." It is as true as Swift's epitaph is to him.

For Pope and their circle Gay was a "play-fellow" rather than a "partner." Pope reports that he was treated "with more fondness than respect . . . He was a natural man, without design, who spoke what he thought and just as he thought it." This isn't quite fair. Gay is a great parodist. His satirical method is different from Pope's. He is an ironist rather than a satirist. Gay lacks the sure moral voice of Pope and the firm orientation of Swift: he will not be tied to an opinion. Amused and alarmed by human fallibility, vanity and self-deceit, he does not rise to that rage which makes and mars the satires of his friends. Evil is unclear to him; he avoids moral absolutes.

He was born in Barnstaple, Devon, in 1685. His father, who died when Gay was ten, was a Nonconformist man of affairs from established Devonshire stock. The boy was educated at the local grammar school, then apprenticed to a silk mercer in London. He disliked the job, secured his release and returned to Devon, where he began writing verse. In 1707 he went back to London to become a writer, and the next year published *Wine*. It celebrates wine in Miltonic parody: "Of happiness terrestrial, and the source / Whence human pleasures flow, sing heavenly Muse." Of a Muse that failed another poet, he writes as of the fallen angel Lucifer:

> Now in Ariconian bogs
> She lies inglorious floundering, like her theme
> Languid and faint.

He parodies the debate of the fallen angels. Closing time is like the departure of Adam and Eve from the Garden. He parodies not only Milton's language and style, but his plot and structure, a trivial subject handled in a grand manner. The moral: water drinkers cannot be successful writers. It's clever and sustained but, as Doctor Johnson dourly opines, inconsequential: an exercise that any decent versifier might perform. It lacks the purpose of his later parodic satires. Yet it shows how deeply embedded Milton is in the eighteenth century, how the choice of Milton over Cowley was almost complete. In Gay there are no vestiges of Swift's first master.

In 1711 he met Pope and found himself in the best possible literary milieu, with a friend and critic who, though younger than he, could help and advise, a warrior eager to exploit his talents in his own literary vendettas. If Pope did not fully appreciate Gay's benign genius, he valued his friendship and helped him in times of need. Gay's nicest tribute to Pope, "Mr Pope's Welcome from Greece," celebrates the translator of Homer as himself a Homeric hero upon concluding his famous translation.

Gay's talent for eccentric, accurate observation and his sense that the established literary modes were vulnerable to real experience and needed to open out toward an actual world inform all his verse. He could deflate epic, georgic, eclogue and dramatic modes by literalizing rather than ridiculing them. He laughed them back to a more inclusive life. In his "low style" he did things Swift must have appreciated, wrote ballads and burlesques. In two of his several attempts he was a considerable dramatist. He had an instinctive, if not an infallible, sense of his public.

During his two years of service as secretary to the Duchess of Monmouth (1712–14) he wrote his first notable poems and began contributing to Sir Richard Steele's *Guardian*. It was his friend Pope and not a noble patron who was honored with the dedication of his first major poem, *Rural Sports* (1713), based on *Windsor Forest*. The overall form leaves much to be desired, but the detail lives. Johnson called it "realistic pastoral." It prepared the ground for *The Shepherd's Week* (1714), Gay's best "pastoral." *Rural Sports* exploits the pathetic fallacy to effect. Fish and worms behave in such a way as to suggest the animal fable, a genre he later practiced. An uninsistent religious strain sounds through the poem. Country streams are "Sweet composers of the pensive soul."

The Shepherd's Week, a sort of truncated *Shepheardes Calender*, was part of Pope's campaign against Ambrose Philips, whose pastorals had been praised in preference to Pope's own. Gay imports into the polite, idealized world of swains and shepherdesses some of the rollicking Devonshire peasants of his youth. Spenser and Virgil, as well as Philips, are among his targets. Convention is invaded by flesh and blood. In "Monday" he footnotes his own lines eighty-three to eighty-eight and refers to their source in Virgil:

> *Populus Alcidae gratissima, vitis Iaccho,*
> *Fermosae Myrtus Veneri, sua Laurea Phoebo.*
> *Phillis amat Corylos. Illis dum Phillis amabit,*
> *Nec Myrtus vincet Corylos nec Laurea Phoebi.*

Johnson says the pastoral can only be burlesqued into life. Gay adapts these lines as:

> Leek to the Welsh, to Dutchmen butter's dear,
> Of Irish swains potato is the cheer;
> Oats for their feasts the Scottish shepherds grind,
> Sweet turnips are the food of Blouzelind.
> While she loves turnips, butter I'll despise,
> Nor leeks nor oatmeal nor potato prize.

This form of traduction into common diction and experience marks Gay's parodies, especially his dramatic masterpiece *The Beggar's Opera* (1728), a "Newgate pastoral" composed at Swift's suggestion. It sets out to discredit the Italian opera that had held the stage in London for ten years. This "ballad opera," as Johnson called it, was an unparalleled success. The sequel, *Polly*, banned by Walpole, sold well when it was published (1729). Swift commented on the predominance of humor over wit in these works; the rules are parodied and satirized—marriage and honor for example—but finally upheld. Despite having parodied opera, Gay became Handel's librettist for *Acis and Galatea* (1732) and *Achilles* (1733)—staged after his death.

He had left the service of the batty Duchess of Monmouth in 1714 and served under the Duke of Clarendon at Hanover. Queen Anne's death brought this brief appointment to an end and he experienced no courtly preferment thereafter. Like Swift, he felt disappointment: his sense of the social world clouded, his poetry matured. In 1713 he'd published *The Fan*; but in 1716 he published *Trivia*. The change is remarkable. *The Fan* follows too closely on the heels of Pope's *The Rape of the Lock*. It is weak because it is unsystematic and unsubtly overstated. It does not grasp the real firmly enough to mythologize it. It is literary, in the spirit of *Wine*. But *Trivia: or the Art of Walking the Streets of London* is the great evocation of London in verse. It originates in Juvenal's third satire, as Johnson's "London" does, but it is gentler and, though less powerful, more complex than Juvenal's poem. The parodic target is Virgil's *Georgics* and the fashionable georgic tradition. An ironic contrast between the rural order, which the form imposes, and the disorder of city life, which is the subject, provides the humor. In an even georgic tone he describes bizarre and terrible incidents. The Great Frost, evoked in the second section, includes an account of the death of an apple vendor:

'Twas here the matron found a doleful fate:
Let elegiac lay the woe relate.
Soft as the breath of distant flutes, at hours
When silent evening closes up the flowers;
Lulling as falling water's hollow noise;
Indulging grief, like Philomela's voice . . .

Doll, the fruit vendor, is decapitated as she falls through the ice, her voice dying in the "pip-pip-pip" of her pippin cry. The incongruity between manner and matter is a measure of Gay's ironic power. The reader remains uncertain of the poet's tone.

"Nothing about *Trivia* is straightforward," says Marcus Walsh, "not even the title, which means primarily crossroads, but is also a Roman name for the goddess Hecate." Not only the title, but words, parodic passages and scenes are equally complex. A bootblack is begotten by immaculate conception; Vulcan visits Patty and makes her patterns. As in a good georgic, we receive advice, but here it is about our dress for walking the London streets: suitable shoes, coat, walking stick, hat; about the weather and the sights to see. We hear creaking shop signs, wagons and carriages rumbling by, street cries. There is mud, a street fight, pickpockets, whores, chairmen, vendors, watchmen, rakes. The values that inform georgic poetry are parodied and rejuvenated.

In 1720 Gay published his *Poems on Several Occasions* with success. He lost the money he made, however, in the South Sea Bubble fiasco and was so disappointed that, had Pope and his circle not come to the rescue, he would have died. He became commissioner for the public lottery in 1722, and spent his later years at various houses, especially with the Duke and Duchess of Queensberry, who took his chaotic affairs in hand. In 1725 he published "To a Lady on her Passion for Old China," a sustained polite moral satire: "What rival's near? a China jar." Two years later *The Fables* appeared, written for Prince William, later Duke of Cumberland. In 1738 sixteen posthumous *Fables* were published, more overtly moral and satiric than the earlier pieces, and in epistolary form after the manner of Pope. Gay died in 1732 and was buried in Westminster Abbey.

The *Fables* proved popular, running through fifty editions before 1800, a poetry bonanza for his publisher, along with Thomson's *The Seasons* and Pope's work. The *Fables* were illustrated by Thomas Bewick and later by William Blake. Gay uses his animals to illuminate human nature, either by contrast or caricature, varying the tone and approach. Some are serious, others simply comic. The moral, as Johnson says, cannot always be drawn. When he adopted fable form, he found literary parody difficult, since fable itself is parody. Gay is compelled to neglect one of his best skills and modern readers feel its absence. "The Elephant and the Bookseller," "The Butterfly and the Snail," "The Two Monkeys," and the fox fables stand out from the rest. But they are less entertaining than *Trivia*. They are frail compared with Henryson's fables. Yet no one has written a poem to vie with *Trivia* as living verse documentary and brilliant parody. Pope wrote Gay a fuller epitaph than the one he provided for himself, and it touches on the paradox of Gay's innocent integrity:

> Of Manners gentle, of Affections mild;
> In Wit, a Man; Simplicity, a Child;
> With native Humour temp'ring virtuous Rage,
> Form'd to delight at once and lash the age;
> Above Temptation, in a low Estate,
> The uncorrupted, ev'n among the Great;
> A safe Companion, and an easy Friend,
> Unblam'd thro' Life, lamented in thy End . . .

"A safe Companion": Pope had few of those. Ford's account of him is not inaccurate, though it is peremptory and unkind. "It has well been said of Pope that his work divides itself into three periods which correspond to the three reigns under which he wrote. Under Queen Anne he was a personal pastoral English poet; under George I he was a translator and 'made much money by satisfying the French-classical taste of his day with versions of the *Iliad* and the *Odyssey* and with bitter-sweet poems of the bag-wig and sword-knot type' . . . The heavy materialism and gross agnostic alcoholism settled on the country that had driven out the Stuarts and forgotten the piety and music of Herbert and Donne; so Pope turned his mind to the problems of his age. And in a series of poems that were 'serious' and censorious enough he made his muse sing his day."

Unkind, not inaccurate, to say that Pope is one of the first verse

businessmen, setting out to make a living free of any patron except pub-
lic esteem; among the first to flatter for a living not a nobleman or mon-
arch (though he does both) but a party. He writes with assurance and
authority which set at nothing the animosity his character arouses. He
wrote even his letters for publication; in his privacies (there are few *inti-
macies*) he felt himself to be on show, accountable to his idea of himself.

Developing Dryden's measure, the heroic couplet, Pope recovers
complexities of the poetic process that Dryden had refined away. He
thinks in metaphor, shape and form; he does not decorate a line of
thought. Thought matters less in his work than in Dryden's. There are
none of those spiritual crises which matured Dryden's ideas and gave
them abiding weight. For Pope the crises were not religious or political
but social and literary. If as a man he was crudely ambitious, in some
respects dishonest, in love with his role as a poet and with material
profit as a writer above all else, he did command deep friendship from
discriminating men—Swift and Gay, but also Bolingbroke, Arbuthnot
and others. That is so much to his credit that bad report is partly
answered. At the heart of his work an unresolved philosophical contra-
diction provokes much of the best verse. Of twentieth-century poets
W. H. Auden most resembles him in his omnicompetence, ambivalence
and social character.

Alexander Pope was born in Lombard Street, London, in 1688.
His Roman Catholic father was a merchant, and both parents were
advanced in years when the little misshapen poet came into the world.
From a protective home he acquired not religious certainties, but the
instincts of an entrepreneur. In the year of Dryden's death, when Pope
was twelve, the family joined a Catholic community in Windsor Forest.
Soon the young Pope was writing imitations of Waller, Cowley, Roches-
ter, Chaucer and Spenser, and translating from Thomas à Kempis,
Ovid, Statius and Homer.

At the age of twelve he contracted the first of a series of illnesses
that, with his physical disability (a hunched back), left him *nearly* an
invalid for the rest of his life. He read eclectically and was encouraged to
write. In the year when illness beset him, he wrote a poem imitating
Cowley and indebted to Horace, "On Solitude":

> Happy the man, whose wish and care
> A few paternal acres bound,
> Content to breathe his native air,
> > In his own ground.

> Whose herds with milk, whose fields with bread,
> Whose flocks supply him with attire,

Whose trees in summer yield him shade,
                    In winter fire.

Blest! who can unconcern'dly find
Hours, days, and years slide soft away,
In health of body, peace of mind,
                    Quiet by day,

Sound sleep by night; study and ease
Together mix'd; sweet recreation,
And innocence, which most does please,
                    With meditation.

Thus let me live, unseen, unknown;
Thus unlamented let me die;
Steal from the world, and not a stone
                    Tell where I lie.

Like the voice of an inmate of Gray's churchyard, its resignation (a literary stance) is credible because the form is so astonishingly achieved, phrases building precisely, now gathering evidence, now deploying it, so that the conclusion is not only just but inevitable. The second stanza anticipates the future poet: fields yield bread and sheep clothing, the images translated into a market value: it matters less what they are than what they provide.

When he was nineteen, his *Pastorals* appeared in Tonson's *Poetical Miscellanies, Part VI*. Pope insists more than once that he wrote the poems when he was sixteen, along with "A Discourse on Pastoral Poetry," in which he sets out, in a short space, to summarize the critics' conflicting accounts of the mode: "You will also find some points reconciled, about which they seem to differ, and a few remarks which I think have escaped their observation." His adolescent hubris is beguiling and a little intimidating: Dryden is a guide, Spenser a model, but in both he finds faults that he sets out to remedy as much in his prose discourse as in the poems themselves. The poems are of little interest today: they are stiff with eager correctness. But the poet's accomplishment was auspiciously welcomed. In 1711 perhaps his best nonsatirical composition, *An Essay on Criticism*, appeared and the *Spectator* and the *Guardian* took up the young prodigy. He was twenty-three.

Pope attributed the virtues of his *Pastorals* not to observation of nature but "to some old authors, whose work as I had leisure to study, so I hope I have not wanted care to imitate." Here is literary—entirely literary—eclogue. In the first lines, along with classical echoes, we hear

Spenser, Milton and Waller. The syntax is classicizing and at times silly. "Two swains, whom Love kept wakeful, and the Muse / Poured o'er the whitening vale their fleecy care." The Muse appears to be both wakeful and a shepherdess—until we realize that she is a second cause for insomnia after love. Lapses of syntactical clarity are common in Pope. Thomas De Quincey sees the problem as "almost peculiar to himself. It lay in an inability, nursed doubtless by indolence, to carry out and perfect the expression of the thought he wishes to communicate. The language does not realise the idea: it simply suggests or hints it." Pope *indolent*? Surely not, surely not at the age of sixteen. Injudicious, inexperienced perhaps, but never indolent. De Quincey is talking about the mature work. Pope is a treacherous "model of correctness."

Yet couplets from the *Pastorals* reveal the virtues of his writing, too: "their fleecy care" is a roundabout way of saying "sheep," but it has the effect of stressing the shepherds' responsibility (an abstract meaning) and physically evoking sheep (and their use). It combines pictorial and moral elements. The technique is deployed in *Eloisa to Abelard* (1716), a romantic "heroic epistle" unique in his work.

> In these deep solitudes and awful cells,
> Where heav'nly pensive, contemplation dwells,
> And ever-musing melancholy reigns;
> What means this tumult in a Vestal's veins?

"Deep" and "cells" are apprehensible to the senses; "solitudes" and "awful" are abstract. Parallel construction mingles the terms: hermitage and state of mind. Within solitude a hierarchy is proposed: melancholy reigns, contemplation dwells: a pensive, ever-musing kingdom, shaken by earthly desire. "Vestal's veins" is oxymoronic in effect. Pope attaches shapes and scenes, most vividly in the passage in which tears distort the visible world for Eloisa, the speaker:

> Can'st thou forget what tears that moment fell,
> When, warm in youth, I bade the world farewell?
> As with cold lips I kiss'd the sacred veil,
> The shrines all trembled, and the lamps grew pale . . .

This miracle of a passage suggests the poet Pope might have become with different priorities, other admirers. *Eloisa to Abelard*, undramatic yet gripping because of its close-textured, consistent evocation—developing imagery of lips, eyes, tears, pallor, coldness and burning—can lay claim to being the last achieved English epyllion, just as his *Pastorals* provide the last, almost asphyxiated gasp of Spenserian eclogue. The subject is human nature and passion at their most paradoxical. Pope never tried the mode again, perhaps because it gave him only limited scope for what De Quincey described as his "talent for caustic effect." Besides, the subject was "unwholesome"; it may have shaken him.

"Windsor Forest" suggests another might-have-been. He observes nature less through "old authors" than through his own eyes; we see (stylized) something like the Forest itself. The scene is brittle, natural detail presented in terms of artifice and carrying a moral or interpretative weight. Transitive verbs energize the verse, fusing concrete images and abstract qualities:

> Oft, as in airy rings they skim the heath
> The clam'rous lapwings feel the leaden death.
> Oft, as the mounting larks their notes prepare,
> They fall, and leave their little notes on air.

"Leaden death" for "shot" or "bullet" suggests the physical weight of ammunition and checks the skyward movement of the previous line. Mounting larks are shot and fall, their music left suspended.

In 1712 Pope was getting to know Swift, Gay, the neglected poet Thomas Parnell and the genial physician and polemicist Dr. John Arbuthnot, who invented John Bull. They became pillars of his social world and collaborators in works for stage and page, and they began inventing the Scriblerus Club. *The Rape of the Lock* was published by Barnaby Bernard Lintot in his *Miscellany*. (In *The Dunciad* Pope later compared Lintot to "a dabchick," which was ungracious since Lintot had printed his work and was an honorable publisher.)

Two years later an extended version of *The Rape* appeared. This chief of English mock-heroic poems, the verse masterpiece of Queen Anne's reign, grew out of an actual event but, in a satirical spate against polite ladies, pursued a social foible to absurd lengths, into "the moving toyshop of their heart." The lady's very boudoir is displayed, her ritual of social preparation disclosed. The drama of her stolen lock of hair is delicious, trivial, the satire tart rather than corrective—and it charms. Pope is at home in the world he describes, half seduced by its opulence, and if not willing to forgive, reluctant to chastise excesses, which he pushes in his poem to further excess. Yet at the fringes of his poem a cruel social world peeps in:

> Meanwhile declining from the noon of day,
> The Sun obliquely shoots his burning ray;
> The hungry Judges soon the sentence sign,
> And wretches hang that jury-men may dine;

> The merchant from th' Exchange returns in peace,
> And the long labours of the *toilette* cease—

We skitter merrily past the "wretches," but they stay suspended incongruously above a world of "Puffs, powders, patches, Bibles, billet-doux." A politician reading these lines might have foreseen what the little poet would do on a different scale.

In 1713 Pope issued proposals and started to raise subscriptions for his translation of Homer's *Iliad*. It appeared between 1715 and 1720 and profited him greatly, despite a spoiling effort by Thomas Tickell, who published the first book of an *Iliad* two days after Pope's *Iliad*, books 1–4, appeared, and numerous critical attacks. All publicity proved good. In 1725–26 the *Odyssey* less successfully followed, produced with two assistants (by then, like a painter, he had an atelier to prepare the huge Homeric canvases: his minions primed them and he added a verbal stroke here and there and called them his, as indeed the contracts for them were). In his *Iliad* Pope fully mastered the couplet, with a finality at times glib, for the form forces parallelisms and imposes rigid pattern on the matter. It is suited more to aphorism and satire than narrative. Yet he made the couplets—intermittently—flow. Johnson's estimate of the translation is as high as Pope's estimate of Dryden's Virgil: "the noblest version of poetry which the world has ever seen." Less generous and less successful Grub Street residents dubbed him the "poetical undertaker." In 1725 his six-volume edition of Shakespeare was published: he was almost as much of a literary factory as Johnson.

His Shakespeare was not good and its numerous errors and inconsistencies were exhibited by Lewis Theobald in *Shakespeare Restored*, a timeless error on Theobald's part since he earned for himself the role of principal butt in the original *Dunciad*, and even his admirable 1734 edition of Shakespeare, a model for later editors, did not restore his name. Pope was not a man to cross. Fortunately Colly Cibber offended Pope even more severely than Theobald had done, for Cibber, whose life as an actor and writer was remote from Pope's experience, was made poet laureate in 1730. In the 1743 four-book version of *The Dunciad* Cibber replaces Theobald.

When I say Pope profited from his writings, I can be specific. Patronage was at its height under Queen Anne, and there was a settled market price: five to ten guineas for the dedication of a play, less for the dedication of a poem. With the accession of George I this changed. Writers became too proud and independent to sue for patronage. From Lintot Pope got £16 2s. 6d. for the first book of Statius (1712); £7 for *The Rape of the Lock*; £32 5s. for "Windsor Forest." Homer was published by subscription; Lintot paid Pope £200 for each of six volumes. In the end

Pope realized £5,324 4s. on this work. Johnson estimated that the cost of living, about 1730, was in the region of £30 per annum. Thus Pope's little epigram "On Authors and Booksellers" is a little harsh: "What Authors lose, their Booksellers have won, / So Pimps grow rich, while Gallants are undone." The best printer-booksellers dealt more or less honorably with their better authors, as dairy farmers deal with good cows. A sense of the economics of the trade emerges when full records exist, and of course for a businessman of letters like Pope, records survive.

On the proceeds of his writing, Pope was able to settle in Twickenham in 1718, in his famous house with a grotto, with his recently widowed mother. There he lived until his death in 1744. He practiced a frugality that rivaled Swift's, but without Swift's excuse. Success did not spoil him, but the pleasures of prosperity induced him to undertake projects he should have left alone, especially the Shakespeare.

The substitution of Cibber for Theobald in the *Dunciad*—poet for scholar—is arbitrary and tells against the virulent generality of the satire. That the substitution required so little adjustment to the text shows how removed from its targets, how merely scornful, and how unintegrated it is. Pope attended to the surface of the work, but the satire only occasionally deepens and tells. The four books progress toward the triumph of eternal Dullness ("born a Goddess, Dullness never dies") and exploit different modes of humor from book to book. First Pope deploys literary satire and parody, advancing through coprological, sexual and even sadistic forms of humor. The fourth book remains most vital, scourging habits and institutions of education. But the verve of the language exceeds its occasions, a kind of overkill. In all but the fourth book the satire, unlike Dryden's, lacks a moral norm which, by contrast, it endorses. Where is Pope firing from? He did not dislike the society in which he found himself, though he did at times dislike himself. De Quincey calls the rage "histrionic," for effect, and goes further: Pope was a hypocrite, his insincerity spilled over into his nonsatiric work.

He translated Horace's satires with his usual skill, but even there we're tempted to agree with De Quincey. We should fight temptation: Pope is morally uneven but eludes categorical condemnation or endorsement. He is often at his best with borrowed anger. In 1735 he wrote his "Epistle to Dr Arbuthnot" (later called "The Prologue to the Satires"), combining satire with personal statements of intense candor. His skill in composing whole poems is intact, even after the *Essay on Man* (1733–34) which, despite memorable aphoristic passages, fails as didactic and philosophical verse. It was attacked and defended for its morality; now it is excerpted for its good passages but neglected as a whole. Johnson's

verdict is just: "Never was penury of knowledge and vulgarity of senti-
ment so happily disguised." Technically a tour de force, it is hollow at
the center. De Quincey asks, which *should* have been Pope's greatest
poem? The *Essay on Man*. And which was in fact his worst? The same.
It "sins chiefly by want of central principle, and by want thereof of all
coherency amongst the separate thoughts." Compared with the *Essay on
Criticism*, written twenty-two years before, it looks still more inverte-
brate. Pope became professional in the worst sense.

His techniques can deal with almost any theme; but his sense of
structure and his ability to present consecutive, consistent thought are
limited. Johnson remarks on his "poetical prudence": "He wrote in such
a manner as might expose him to few hazards. He used almost always
the same fabric of verse; and, indeed, by those few essays which he made
of any other, he did not enlarge his reputation . . . By perpetual practice,
language had, in his mind, a systematic arrangement; having always the
same use for words, he had words so selected and combined as to be
ready at his call." A dangerous facility: "His effusions were always vol-
untary." For De Quincey his satiric rages were similarly factitious. In the
Essay on Man he bit off not more than his style could chew, but more
than his intellect could digest.

Pope's intellectual incompleteness can be attributed in part to his
age, for much more than Dryden he was a man of his time. He's been
called a "cosmic Tory," a social optimist (though closer to Hobbes in his
evaluation of the individual), believing "whatever is, is right" and con-
verting the status quo into a universal ethic. In such an approach there
is a cool, impersonal arrogance that he shares with some of his journal-
ist contemporaries—a new breed—who couldn't quite bring themselves
to choose between deism and Locke's psychology, but felt confident in
rejecting traditional theology as outmoded. Pope remains intellectually
"between." He distrusts empirical inquiry as strongly as Swift did, but
without Swift's reasons. For such a mind the appeal of authority should
be great; Pope is wary even of authority.

The imagination "gilds all objects, but alters none." Such an aes-
thetic is a world away from the Sidney of the *Apology*. Pope wants not to
expand imagination and understanding but to formulate and give per-
manent expression to thought and experience; not to particularize but to
establish general truths. That nature conceals, under its varied surface, a
basic pattern or harmony, is a worked-up belief, as willed as the lan-
guage itself. He was able in the *Essay on Man* to change the description
of nature as a "mighty maze, and all without a plan" to a "mighty maze
but not without a plan" when it was suggested that his vision was too
negative. So radical a change, casually made, reveals the shallow current
of his thought. Thus Theobald and Cibber, scholar and poet, were inter-

changeable in the *Dunciad*. His rancor was arbitrary. The closing lines
reflect on the themes of the poem, but perhaps also on its willful struc-
ture or *construction*.

> Lo! thy dread empire, Chaos! is restor'd;
> Light dies before thy uncreating word:
> Thy hand, great Anarch! lets the curtain fall;
> And universal darkness buries all.

The best of Pope is wonderful, but excellence is found *in extenso* only
in the earlier poems, translations and satires. Later it emerges locally:
the shiny surface of his philosophical disquisitions yields like thin ice
when we walk out upon it. His best writing depends on the elusive way
he makes solid an abstract or moralizing passage by combining unex-
pected words, and by rhyme that seals the "conjunction disjunctive"
(Coleridge's phrase) of the couplets. Dryden's couplets tend to be self-
contained; Pope's contain at their best a paradox, an irresolution, which
compels us to read on. They create suspense. He makes whole poems
when he avoids the temptation to try for a total statement.

Dead Pastoral

JAMES THOMSON

One of the most successful British poets of all time—in Pope's terms of unit sales and vast editions—is James Thomson, the man who momentarily reinvented pastoral and is now read primarily by scholars who prefer dust to living dirt and by students puzzled by the reputed tedium of the eighteenth century. In English poetry nothing today is more enigmatic than Thomson's huge and long success. Contemporary neglect of Spenser and Milton does not diminish them; the neglect of Thomson is eloquent.

Once he was the poetic equivalent of the Gideon Bible; his poems were to be found in every inn and cottage in the land. The verse was reassuring and instructive but never taxing.

> What, what is virtue but repose of mind?
> A pure ethereal calm that knows no storm,
> Above the reach of wild ambition's wind,
> Above those passions that this world deform,
> And torture man, a proud malignant worm!

His one immortal poem is "Rule Britannia," though few remember to attribute it to him. He inspired respect from men as different as Doctor Johnson and William Wordsworth. His poetic antecedents—Milton above all—and his adoption of the fashionable scientific and philosophical thought of his time confine him to his age. Self-conscious modernity dates. Miltonic blank verse does not liberate but muffles his peculiar genius. His novelty is his subject matter: literal seasons, actual countryside, seen through wholly eighteenth-century eyes. His contemporaries did not sense this disparity between style and matter. Oliver Goldsmith reflects on these lines:

> O vale of bliss! O softly swelling hills!
> On which the power of contemplation lies,
> And joys to see the wonder of his toil.

"We cannot conceive a more beautiful image than that of the Genius of Agriculture, distinguished by the implements of his art, imbrowned with labour, glowing with health, crowned with a garland of foliage, flowers, and fruit, lying stretched at his ease on the brow of a gently swelling hill, and contemplating with pleasure the happy effects of his own industry." Donald Davie suggests that Oliver Goldsmith was adding very little to Thomson's actual intention: it was natural for his readers to tease out—to unpack—meaning in this way, translating out of metaphoric code. Modern readers hardly recognize a happy peasant at all.

Thomson was born at Ednam, in the Borders, in 1700, the year of Dryden's death, and reared in Southdean, a neighboring parish to which his father, a minister, was transferred. Educated at Jedburgh and at Edinburgh University, he studied divinity. He published poems in Edinburgh journals, and when his prose was deemed "too ornate" for the pulpit by his instructors, he left Edinburgh for London to become a writer. He was tutor to the son of the Earl of Haddington and was introduced into Pope's circle. In 1726 he published a poem partly completed before he reached the capital. It was *Winter*, first of *The Seasons*, which were published together in 1730 and in various updated and revised forms between then and his death in 1748. The book was part of a program he enunciated in 1726: poetry should free itself from social satire. He abandoned heroic couplets, accepted what he took to be Milton's disciplines, and looked for subject matter beyond the city gates.

Before 1730 he published shorter poems and *Sophonisba*, an ill-fated tragedy. He traveled to the Continent and received a sinecure on his return. In 1735 he published the poem *Liberty*, and thereafter composed plays and collected a further sinecure and a pension from the Prince of Wales. A bachelor, he settled comfortably in Richmond. In 1745 he wrote his most successful play, *Tancred and Sigismunda*. Three years later he composed *The Castle of Indolence*. He died of a fever and was memorialized in William Collins's superb ode, the best thing Thomson ever occasioned:

> In yonder grove a Druid lies,
> Where slowly winds the stealing wave!
> The year's best sweets shall duteous rise
> To deck its poet's sylvan grave!

Doctor Johnson describes Thomson as of "gross, unanimated, uninviting appearance." He admired the work and gave Thomson high marks for his original "mode of thinking, and of expressing his thoughts." "His blank verse is no more the blank verse of Milton, or of any other poet . . .

His numbers, his pauses, his diction, are of his own growth, without transcription, without imitation. He thinks in a peculiar train, and he thinks always as a man of genius." What is more, he possesses "a mind that at once comprehends the vast and attends to the minute."

Proximity to the subject and an enthusiasm for the novelty of Thomson's subject matter in an age poor in novelty lead Johnson to this— what must seem to us—misvaluation. Thomson's language in *The Seasons* owes debts to Milton in almost every line. *The Castle of Indolence* is indebted to Milton and Spenser for language and manner. His originality of form consists of reviving the georgic—which had been done by several of his immediate predecessors. He includes new science and new attitudes not original to him. His poetry reflects fashionable thought and springs from the discursive experimental activity of his time. He is skillful in handling blank verse, there are notable passages, but even Johnson had to admit, "The great defect of *The Seasons* is want of method." Formal failure is masked by verbal exuberance. It's hard at times to see through the adjectival undergrowth to a subject. Thomson continually revised his verse, both to perfect it and to keep it abreast of new scientific findings. To the original 4,000 lines Thomson added roughly 1,400 in successive revisions.

The Seasons, like Gower's *Confessio Amantis*, is encyclopedic, a compendium of the wisdom, knowledge and *bien pensant* prejudice of the age, including zoological, botanical, meteorological and geological information, political and moral reflection, sentimental tales. It reflects a dissatisfaction with decorous and stylized poetry, but reacts without the radical passion of Smart, Blake or Wordsworth. Thomson plays acceptable music in a different key, with different themes, not new music. Milton was responsible for the change of key. Thomson did not adopt the dynamics of Milton's language: he borrowed from the surface. He vulgarized Milton as he vulgarized new science. It suited his ends to blend the discoveries of Newton with the optimistic deism of Lord Shaftesbury.

Coleridge disliked the style but saluted the poet. "The love of nature seems to have led Thomson to a cheerful religion; and a gloomy religion to have led Cowper to a love of nature. The one would carry his fellow-men along with him into nature: the other flies to nature from his fellow-men. In chastity of diction, however, and the harmony of blank verse, Cowper leaves Thomson immeasurably below him; yet still I feel the latter to have been a born poet." Thomson's originality was to present a version of nature itself as subject. Wordsworth owes him a verbal and thematic debt. He *can* be convincing in the detail of his writing. In *Winter* the movement of birds foretells a storm:

Retiring from the downs, where all day long
They picked their scanty fare, a blackening train
Of clamorous rooks thick-urge their weary flight,
And seek the closing shelter of the grove.
Assiduous in his bower, the wailing owl
Plies his sad song. The cormorant on high
Wheels from the deep, and screams along the land.
Loud shrieks the soaring hern; and with wild wing
The circling sea-fowl cleave the flaky clouds.

There is also a delicious luxury in some of his *Summer* effusions:

Bear me, Pomona! to thy citron groves;
To where the lemon and the piercing lime,
With the deep orange glowing through the green,
Their lighter glories blend. Lay me reclined
Beneath the spreading tamarind, that shakes
Fanned by the breeze, its fever-cooling fruit.

But, by ascending from sensual observation to generalization, he forfeits our attention. In his optimism there is an aloofness that grates. Unlike Swift, he is not eager to rouse others—the humble, for example—to a sense of their potential. In *Summer* he reflects: "While thus laborious crowds / Ply the rough oar, Philosophy directs / The ruling helm." Here is a poet Hobbes has left unmarked. He celebrates commerce, enterprise, ambition, in ways that would have been impossible half a century later. His is the Whig epic. He prefigures Walter Bagehot.

Thomson's verse lives in its descriptions and in odd lines. He is a poet of fragments. His nature appears fragmentary because he celebrates a first cause through it, not—as Wordsworth does—a force latent within it. He lacks Wordsworth's engagement. His is an enthusiasm of the various senses, but the whole man is withheld. Wordsworth's imagination is continuous with the experienced world, Thomson's tangential to it.

He tries to find poetic epithets for scientific terms and this mars the verse; and obsolete science disrupts certain passages. Even his most particular definitions answer no necessary poetic purpose. He screws his language up by heightened diction and elaborates syntax to produce the *effect* of poetry, but the poetic occasion remains at best nebulous. Gilbert White's prose portrays a clearer nature than Thomson's verse does. White addresses a subject, Thomson an audience. His most useful contribution—to William Cowper, George Crabbe and Wordsworth among others—was to show how landscape might be used for emotional projection, to reveal an observer's mind as much as the thing observed.

In *The Castle of Indolence* he adopted Spenserian form and diction and wrote what some regard as his finest poem. Formally it is more coherent than *The Seasons*. The old wizard Indolence speaks persuasively. The poem is a smoothly satirical record of temptation overcome, with knights and witty transformations. Each sense is tempted in turn. Thomson pillories various human types and espouses various causes. There are memorable figures—for example, "A little, round, fat, oily man of God" with "a roguish twinkle in his eye," who is a bit of a lecher and might be at home in a poem by Crabbe. We meet members of Thomson's circle, which, in his later years, was distinguished chiefly for the presence of the occasionally incomparable poet William Collins. The poem's Spenserian form imposes on Thomson tautologies, ill-considered similes and solecisms, but they do not destroy altogether the effect. In the allegory, Art and Industry in knightly form destroy the castle and its wizard lord. As in *The Seasons*, here is the verse of Whiggery, which, set beside Goldsmith's or Johnson's, remains rooted in period, class and place. No wonder it sold. It is the sort of verse that was modern in its time.

Doctor Johnson

Doctor Johnson is a natural poet born into the age of prose, condemned to develop skills that were unnatural to him and to write, at great length, in the wrong medium. Edmund Wilson, the most Johnsonian of American writers, is harsh: "For all of Johnson's vigorous intellect and his elaborate brilliance, he is a figure of secondary interest: it is not altogether that he is prejudiced and provincial but rather that his prejudices do not have behind them quite enough of the force of the creative mind." Hazlitt's view: "He has neither ease nor simplicity, and his efforts at playfulness, in part, remind one of the lines in Milton:—'—The elephant / To make them sport wreath'd his proboscis lithe'. . . This want of relaxation and variety of manner has, I think, after the first effects of novelty and surprise were over, been prejudicial to the matter. It takes from the general power, not only to please, but to instruct." He adds, "The structure of his sentences, which was his own invention, and which has been generally imitated since his time, is a species of rhyming in prose, where one clause answers to another in measure and quantity, like the tagging of syllables at the end of a verse; the close of the period follows as mechanically as the oscillation of a pendulum, the sense is balanced with the sound; each sentence, revolving round its centre of gravity, is contained with itself like a couplet, and each paragraph forms itself into a stanza."

His age tended to distort natural impulse, driving it to madness in the case of Christopher Smart or to "specialism" in the cases of Swift, Gay and Pope. Such distortions were givens. Ford declares, "The language used by the eighteenth century—and Samuel Johnson—was a translation." He itemizes stock phrases. "The eighteenth century retired from life that was coarse into a remoter region where individuals always became types and language more and more rarefied itself." Writers came obsessively to use the definite article: "the poet," not "a poet"; "the hill," not "a hill"—until "we arrive, then, at Johnson, the most tragic of all our major literary figures, a great writer whose still living writings are always ignored, a great honest man who will remain forever a figure of half fun because of the leechlike adoration of the greatest and most ridiculous of all biographers." This was the strange, respectful, attentive microscopist James Boswell, whose biographical subject was "a man who loved truth and the expression of truth with a passion that when he spoke resembled epilepsy and when he meditated was an agony. It does not need a Boswell to tell us that; the fact shines in every word he wrote, coming up through his Latinisms as swans emerge, slightly draped with weeds, from beneath the surface of a duck pond. His very intolerances are merely rougher truths; they render him the more human—and the more humane." If he was released from bondage to a prescribed language and the values that determined it, it was through becoming a conversationalist and learning to deploy a rhetoric that was not constructed upon the page, a rhetoric for the ear. The development in his style from the latinizing of his amazing little novel *Rasselas* to the terse directness of *Lives of the Poets* is decisive. He brought his prose back toward the language of *his* considered speech.

Doctor Samuel Johnson: novelist, lexicographer, biographer, critic, editor, pamphleteer, conversationalist, moral and critical center of his age, point of reference and illumination for later ages, he represents with broad wisdom and authority of style the radically English intelligence, its power of generality and of discrimination. The poems, often neglected, are a fragment of his huge work. In them, as T. S. Eliot says, he has contrived "to be original with the *minimum* of alteration," a feat "sometimes more distinguished than to be original with the *maximum* of alteration."

Born in Lichfield in 1709, the son of a bookseller in the modern sense, he took an interest in his father's wares. Educated at Lichfield Grammar School and later at Stourbridge Grammar School, when he was nineteen he went up to Pembroke College, Oxford, where he felt acutely out of place because of his poverty and class. Friends clubbed together to buy him shoes. He left the university in 1731 without taking a degree. He did not enjoy his year as a schoolmaster or "usher," being unable to keep order or to convey his learning or his dogged enthusiasms. He was a phlegmatic man who, if moved by need or passion, was capable of heroic labors and surprised even himself with his powers. He undertook as his first literary job a hack translation of Father Lobo's *Voyage to Abyssinia* (published 1735), useful to him when he composed *Rasselas* twenty-four years later, in the evenings of one week, to defray his mother's funeral expenses and to pay her debts. His memory was orderly and encyclopedic, even if he tended to surround himself with disorder.

He married in 1735 and the next year opened a private school in Edial, Staffordshire, where he looked after a handful of pupils. They are said to have found their master fascinating and a little strange; they spied on him and Mrs. Johnson, a woman considerably older than himself, on whom the Doctor doted. Among his pupils was David Garrick, his theatrical protégé. With Garrick he went to London in 1737 and took root there. It was not—at the beginning—an easy transition, for success came slowly. In "London," an imitation of Juvenal's third satire, written the year after he arrived, he evoked an unregenerate, hostile environment: "This mournful truth is everywhere confess'd, / *Slow rises worth, by poverty depressed.*" The poem is spoken by a man preparing to leave the city. Johnson may have been tempted to follow the voice but London was his destination.

He worked on his tragedy *Irene* and began writing pieces, and later reporting parliamentary debates, for the *Gentleman's Magazine*. His friendship with Richard Savage at this time bore fruit in the celebrated *Life of Savage*, finest of his indispensable *Lives of the Poets* (1779–81). In 1745 he published his plan for an edition of Shakespeare, and two years later his preliminary plan for the great *Dictionary of the English Language*. His poetic activity, always fitful, culminated in 1749 with "The Vanity of Human Wishes," an imitation of Juvenal's' tenth satire, and his first signed work. In the same year *Irene* was produced and published, without much success.

Independent periodical work on the *Rambler*, of whose 208 issues he wrote more than 200, occupied him from 1750 to 1752, when his wife died. Despite this loss and his natural indolence, the projects he had initiated carried him along with their momentum and came to fruition, the *Dictionary* in 1755, the Shakespeare ten years later. He also contributed to the *Idler*. In 1762 he was awarded a royal pension.

The next year James Boswell descended like a benign Scottish parasite on his life, and thus began the biography—a monologue with commentary and digression—and much of the legend of Doctor Johnson. Boswell stands between readers and the Doctor. Johnson presided over the Literary Club from 1764, and in his circle were Sir Joshua Reynolds (who left a striking portrait of him), Edmund Burke, Oliver Goldsmith and many others. In the same year he met Mrs. Thrale, who tended him devotedly in his extended difficulties.

After his Shakespeare was published, his literary activities diminished. In the nineteen years before his death in 1784 he published political pamphlets, *A Journey to the Western Islands of Scotland* (1775), where Boswell had conducted him two years earlier, and *Lives of the Poets*, begun in 1777, which he struggled to complete for publication in 1779–81. He was awarded the degree of doctor in civil law at Oxford in 1781, exactly half a century after he had left the place with no degree at all.

An account of his evolving literary manner does not reflect the turbulence of mind that his prayers, letters and actions suggest. Literary work was not a place to explore subjective impulse and distress; it was where fact, critical discrimination and imaginative and moral insight were called for, a place of self-effacement and thus of relief. Pessimism and acerbity color much that he wrote and intensify the imaginative work. The comments on poets and on Shakespeare are those of a man matured by untold—but not all unrecorded—torments, who understood weakness and failure because he recognized the human paradoxes in himself. It's hard to understand his hostility to Swift the man, for only Swift of his near contemporaries was his equal in imagination, integrity and inner turmoil.

Johnson's severe Augustan perspective, when he came to appraise works, must have appeared a bit old-fashioned in its standards and expectations even in his own day. Donald Davie insists that "it is the mind which knows the power of its own potentially disruptive propensities that needs and demands to be disciplined." This is true of Swift and Cowper and, in the twentieth century, of A. E. Housman and Yvor Winters, but especially so of Johnson with his heavier burdens and larger projects. He chooses poetic forms for this reason. His couplets, for "gravity, sheer weight," are unprecedented; if not "personal" in a modern sense, they are fraught with personal consequence.

He condemns "the cant of those who judge by principle rather than perception." Yet "principle" seems to turn him off Milton, and he misreads "Lycidas" for this reason. But perception, especially in his reading of *Paradise Lost*, overrides principle. Reason is strong; strong reason knows limits beyond which it cannot be trusted. Beyond those limits one must make do with feeling or faith. Johnson on Shakespeare confirms the power of perception, even in passages where Shakespeare most violates Johnson's cherished principles.

Particularism is at the heart of Johnson's conservatism. His Tory stance was a matter of orientation, not party affiliation: indeed he criticized parties with severity. He hated Whiggery, however, from his earliest years in London. In "London," Thales cries out as he leaves the city:

> Here let those reign, whom pensions can incite
> To vote a patriot black, a courtier white;
> Explain their country's dear-bought rights away,
> And plead for pirates in the light of day;
> With slavish tenets taint our poison'd youth,
> And lend a lie the confidence of truth.

Political skepticism guarantees that his declarations are disinterested.

His comprehensive knowledge of past literature gave him the means with which to measure the work of his day. His versions of Juvenal and Horace take for their ground the efforts of earlier translators and writers, but he follows Horace's advice and, in rendering an "original," gives it to his own age. He updates references where he can, evoking London rather than Rome. At the age of fifteen he had translated Horace's *"Eheu fugaces,"* a suitable preliminary to "London" and "The Vanity of Human Wishes":

> Your shady groves, your pleasing wife,
> And fruitful fields, my dearest friend,
> You'll leave together with your life,
> Alone the cypress shall attend.

It's not literal translation, even here. In his *Life of Shenstone* he describes the nature and pleasure of "imitation" as a creative mode: "The adoption of a particular style, in light and short compositions, contributes much to the increase of pleasure: we are entertained at once with two imitations, of nature in the sentiments, of the original author in the style, and between them the mind is kept in perpetual employment." The reader who knows no Juvenal, Horace or Latin will experience half, or less than half, the poem, but will still find something of weight. This product of Johnson's teenage pen does not compare in accomplishment with Pope's "On Solitude."

When he was seventeen he wrote "Upon the Feast of St Simon and St Jude," interesting chiefly for its skillful rather than spirited use of the stanza form Christopher Smart was to adopt in "A Song to David." Despite early prosodic precocity, Johnson came to rely upon the heroic couplet for serious poems. Some of the ephemeral pieces do live. Although "An Ode on Friendship" expresses conventional sentiment in conventional quatrains, it has the authority of conviction. The "Epitaph on Sir Thomas Hamner" is civic verse of a high order. His "Prologue" composed for Garrick is a verse essay on the English stage with notable observations on Shakespeare, Jonson, the Restoration poets ("Intrigue was plot, obscenity was wit") and the effect of excessive rule and refinement: "From bard to bard, the frigid caution crept, / Till declamation roar'd, while passion slept." He conjures the "vicissitudes of taste" from which he, arriving in London a mature man of twenty-eight, stood aloof. His sense of merit is one with his sense of cultural history: there can be no compromise with tradition. Modern excellence must measure itself against proven excellences of the past.

As a reader and critic, he appreciates *sensually* both overall form and realized subject matter. No critic before him so often uses the word "image." Donald Davie has commented on the power of *verbs* in the best Augustan writing. Johnson's verbs are strong. For him wit (the "constant presence of critical intelligence") fuses idea and image to convey truth. He condemns Pope for reducing strength of thought to felicity of language. Wit is seeing what is not obvious but what is seen to be just in all its parts when first produced. He distinguishes between intrinsic and extrinsic forms. It is intrinsic form we perceive in the best works. In his *Life of Cowley* he writes, "Words being arbitrary must owe their power to association, and have the influence, and that only, which custom has given them. Language is the dress of thought." The dress must fit not only the thought but the dignity of the speaker or occasion. Decorum proves crucial in discrimination. The complex association of words with thought, image, speaker and prosody we call form, intrinsic form; it may include conventional external form like the sonnet, which we recognize, but we respond only if intrinsic form is correct.

Johnson looks for certain qualities in verse. First: generality of reference. Natural detail should suit thought, not distort or displace it. Like most of his contemporaries, he overuses the definite article. "The Vanity of Human Wishes" tries for universality but instead tends toward abstraction. He also seeks to instruct. A poem should detect order and suggest moral direction, even if it reminds the reader of a known truth rather than discovering a new one. He seeks to make a work pleasing, sensuous gratification deriving from sound, imagery and organization and the moral and intellectual pleasure of its rightness. Poetry is the "art of uniting pleasure with truth." Genius is "a mind of large, general powers."

T. S. Eliot regards "The Vanity of Human Wishes" as the most accomplished satire in the language. Some readers see it as a work—like *Samson Agonistes*—in which the extremity of the moral is intolerable and reduces the artistic achievement. And the epigrammatic completeness of many of the heroic couplets militates against its overall integration. Continuity of argument and imagery, however, ensure unity. The imagery in particular is worth attention. It can remain implicit in allusive verbs or adjectives. Theater, pageant (with fireworks) and performance recur. In line sixty-four he mentions "scene," followed by "solemn toys" and "empty shows," "robes and veils," until we come to the word "farce," which draws the allusions into coherence, connecting "stage" images in an emblem of vanity. In line seventy-four he uses the word "burning," then "call," but not until line seventy-six do we surmise fireworks. The suggested image remains unstated. The evaporation of the "call" connects with earlier images of mist, phantoms, the unreal masquerading as the solid. Johnson qualifies concrete nouns with abstract ajdectives. Such techniques coordinate and connect the couplets. Pope achieves much the same verbal alchemy, though often for rhetorical effect; Johnson uses it to integrate the elements of the poem.

Johnson owes Pope a big but not uncritical debt. The moral and intellectual concentration of Johnson's couplets exceeds Pope's. Johnson is the more serious: "His warrant for public utterance," Leavis says, "is a deep moral seriousness, a weight—a human centrality—of theme. It is a generalising weight." His abstractions concentrate meaning, do not gesture at it. In his generalizing imagery, half remains static and located, the other half is in motion or acts: "The *steady* Roman *shook* the world." Connection between mutable and immutable (sometimes ironically reversed) or between the physically stable and the evanescent, releases the general truth. There is no other poet in English with Johnson's specific gravity.

Methods and Madnesses

THOMAS GRAY, CHRISTOPHER SMART, OLIVER GOLDSMITH

It is not surprising that Thomas Gray's "Ode to Adversity" appealed to Doctor Johnson. It is a poem about endurance, and the Doctor admired the efficiency of the writing and Gray's "sentence," or meaning. It is not a poem characteristic of Gray who, though he can be solemn, never smells of dust and dirty linen.

As boys at Eton, Gray (Orozmades), Celadon (Horace Walpole), Favonius or Zephyrus (Richard West) and Almanzor (Thomas Ashton) established the Quadruple Alliance, coming together in mutual hatred of the sporting fraternity and a shared love for classical poetry. Gray, often ill at ease in general company, found fortitude and self-assurance in subgroups. Shrill-voiced, witty and playfully inventive among friends, to the world at large he presented an austere façade. At seventeen, soon after he went up to Peterhouse, Cambridge, he sent Celadon a poem he says he got off the ghost of John Dennis after a visit to the Devil Tavern. Poet, dramatist and critic, Dennis had been sent up by Pope in *The Dunciad*. He had died earlier in the year and his memory was warm enough to kindle mild satire. Gray's conceit is that Walpole conjured the ghost, who gives an echo account of his worldly existence.

> That little, naked, melancholy thing,
> My soul, when first she tried her flight to wing,
> Began with speed new regions to explore,
> And blundered through a narrow postern door.
> First most devoutly having said its prayers,
> It tumbled down a thousand pairs of stairs . . .

The casual nature of the composition is clear: the soul is "she" then "it," ungendered in a careless transition. At last it arrives in a weird metropolitan Elysium: "Here spirit-beaux flutter along the Mall." Dennis tires, abandoning description, but adding a lewdly adolescent *postscriptum*:

> Lucrece for half a crown will show you fun,
> But Mrs Oldfield is become a nun.
> Nobles and cits, Prince Pluto and his spouse
> Flock to the ghost of Covent-Garden House:
> Plays, which were hissed above, below revive;
> When dead applauded that were damned alive . . .

There's no solemnity in sight; and though the poem achieves at its best an impeccably decorous manner, the figure who shaped it, not a happy man, was capable of deep friendship and lighthearted good cheer.

Not a happy man: such a verdict supposes that modern readers can glean from the facts of a life something of its subjective quality. If that quality is not patent in the poems, have we a right to presume? Surmises about poets of the eighteenth century are especially hard because their hearts, when worn on their sleeves, were usually frilled with lace, and as often as not decorously disguised. Direct expression is what many of them, and Gray in particular, longed to risk: some way of naming objects in the world and passions in the heart. Hence his attraction to all the experiments and forgeries that claimed to emanate from a world of feeling and language beyond the confines of Augustan diction and received form.

> In climes beyond the solar road,
> Where shaggy forms o'er ice-built mountains roam,
> The Muse has broke the twilight-gloom
> To cheer the shivering native's dull abode.

The *ignis fatuus* he pursued was the pseudo-primitive; in it he found space—however spurious—to breathe a different air. For Coleridge he seldom breathed real air at all; most of his lyrics are "frigid and artificial." Coleridge has a point and should be answered, "Yes, but . . ."

Doctor Johnson's best poetry is imitation of Juvenal and Horace. It is improper for the poet to pretend to originality. He prefers transposition, restatement in a new context of proven, especially classical, work. Other Augustan poets took "imitation" differently, in the spirit that led T. S. Eliot to weave his verse out of new thread mingled with strands from other works. Eliot, often in ironic spirit, borrows to define his themes. Gray, without programmatic irony, "imitated" in this spirit. His critics and the poet himself annotated the "sources" of many lines. Roger Lonsdale, a great editor of our time, writes, "One seems at times to be confronting a kind of literary kleptomania, such is his dependence on the phrasing and thoughts of other poets." He's most original in the extent of his derivativeness, his tactful borrowing, from Greek,

Latin, English and other writers. William Collins runs him a close
second.

Gray turns in his early verse less to Pope and Dryden and more
to Spenser, Shakespeare and Milton for metaphor and organization.
This underlines a dissatisfaction with the narrow frontiers of Augustan
verse.

> But not to one in this benighted age
>   Is that diviner inspiration given,
> That burns in Shakespeare's or in Milton's page,
>   The pomp and prodigality of heaven.

His enthusiasm for Thomson's *The Seasons* (in which he sensed, as we
no longer can, an actual nature alive), for James Macpherson's Ossianic
forgeries, for the "primitive" Celtic poets, and his longing to infuse pri-
mal energy into the effete literary tyrannies of his day, his interest even
in the absurd Pindaric mode, all reflect dissatisfaction, a casting about
for a way through and *out*. Some of his poems, including "The Fatal Sis-
ters," "The Descent of Odin" and "The Bard," imitate Welsh and Norse
poetry. He could not make the break: he strove to regenerate poetry only
from poetry. He never wrote, he said, "without reading Spenser for a
considerable time previously." His best poems are not those labored
"original" compositions, but the thoroughly Augustan pieces, above all
the elegies.

A *poeta doctus*, or learned poet, he translated passages of Statius,
Tasso and Propertius. Most of his waking hours were spent in study. He
attempted a blank-verse tragedy in *Agrippina*. In all, he produced rela-
tively little poetry, some of it in Latin and Greek. His debt to Dante,
whom he imitated in the opening of the "Elegy Written in a Country
Churchyard," is great: he understood the Florentine better than any
other Augustan and went so far in his early twenties as to translate the
cruel, moving Ugolino passage in which a father devours his own chil-
dren. He employs not Dante's *terza rima* but a blank verse that recalls
now Milton, now Spenser. The story itself touched a deep nerve in him,
the sole survivor in a family of twelve children: the drama and grim
pathos are communicated in something like a speaking voice.

He was born in 1716 in Cornhill. His father was a scrivener—in an
earlier age he might have been a scribe—and his mother and aunt kept
a milliner's shop. They prospered and gave him the best education their
money could buy. In 1735 he was admitted to the Inner Temple. His
intention was to pursue a legal career. In 1739 he embarked on a tour of
France and Italy with Walpole. A falling out with his friend hastened
his return to England in 1741. They remained estranged for four years

but then became faster friends than ever. Walpole commissioned a portrait of Gray at thirty-one. He holds the manuscript of the Eton poem: a fair likeness, the lips tight, gentle almost smiling eyes, a handsome straight nose; the collar open, casually disarranged—a boyish Gray, the person Walpole held dear from school days.

Several bereavements marked him deeply, and his father's death in 1741 left him financially insecure. The law lost its attraction. He settled back at Cambridge, first at Peterhouse, later at Pembroke College, and apart from a few absences—in London for research, Stoke Poges for relaxation with his family, York and the Lakes for rambles—he remained in Cambridge until his death in 1771. In 1768, after a long campaign, he was appointed Regius Professor of Modern History. He engaged in university politics and stooped to partisan satire in "The Candidate," a poem that distressed his admirers by its vulgarity. He rhymed the word "bitches" with "stitches" (a term for lying with a woman).

Shortly before his return to Cambridge his poetic energies were released, possibly by the force of bereavement. In 1742 he completed the "Ode on the Spring," his first important composition, a confident mastery of pure convention. The verse, as Roger Lonsdale says, is entirely self-conscious, moralizing the subject *and* moralizing the moralizing convention as well, as if to undercut itself. "Ode on a Distant Prospect of Eton College" is a finer poem, his first to appear in print, full of the anxiety personal losses induced (including the death of Richard West). The intricate ten-line stanza form in tetrameters and trimeters is taut and understated. It is a "topographical poem," relating to an actual prospect—from his uncle's summer house in Stoke Poges he could look across the Thames to Windsor and Eton—but the poetic prospect is across time, into the past. The view provokes elegy, not without bitterness. This is the most transparently subjective of his poems. The pessimism of a worldly-wise man surveying innocent youth leads to a final stanza whose terrible force Keats and Wilde were to echo:

> To each his sufferings: all are men,
> Condemned alike to groan;
> The tender for another's pain,
> The unfeeling for his own.
> Yet ah! why should they know their fate?
> Since sorrow never comes too late,
> And happiness too swiftly flies.
> Thought would destroy their paradise.
> No more; where ignorance is bliss,
> 'Tis folly to be wise.

So negative a view receives correction in the "Ode to Adversity:"

> Thy form benign, oh Goddess, wear,
> Thy milder influence impart,
> Thy philosophic train be there
> To soften, not to wound my heart.
> The generous spark extinct revive,
> Teach me to love and to forgive,
> Exact my own defects to scan,
> What others are to feel, and know myself a man.

Solemn, certainly. He struck other notes from his classic lyre. Walpole's cat drowned in a goldfish bowl, an accident that produced one of the best animal fables, or elegies, in English, "Ode on the Death of a Favourite Cat," satirizing the character of woman. Walpole superintended Gray's publications from his Strawberry Hill Press, whose chief activity was to publish Walpole's own works, *The Castle of Otranto*, a gothic novella, and his writing on painting and history. The Strawberry Hill books are the product of a kind of vanity, Walpole's desire to control not only language but its dissemination. He didn't distribute them widely. He was a make-believe publisher, some of whose dreams survive.

Walpole was available for consultation on the "Elegy Written in a Country Churchyard," which Gray completed in 1750 at his uncle's house in Stoke Poges. The success of this great poem became irksome to him. He was after another sort of originality, yet his later work was criticized in the light of the definitive Augustan achievement. He married in this poem two incongruous but mutually attractive styles: the sedate, tidy elegiac and a Miltonic rhetoric.

We may at first balk at the welter of present participles—more than ten in the first twenty-one lines—or at Gray's tendency to define by negatives, but participles suggest continuation in time and evoke a natural process; definition by negatives implies what they specifically exclude, so the poem evokes what is *not*, even as it portrays what is. The quatrains function rather like extended couplets: most of them have the finality of epigram.

The "Elegy" animates the conventional with actual observation; a literal and a formal world come together and agree. If his success is, in Leavis's words, "of taste, of literary sense" rather than "of creative talent," what good sense, what good taste! The distinction is hardly relevant to the poem we have. It is invidious to suggest that taste and sense at such a level of achievement are not a form of "creative talent." Johnson's judgment, that the poem "abounds with images which find a mirror in every mind, and with sentiments to which every bosom returns an echo," is borne out by the popularity of the work and the number of passages and lines that have entered common speech. Robert Wells calls it "many poems in one. I admire the way that it unfolds and surprises itself. The strong wayward current of its rhetoric is exploratory. Just over half-way through (with the stanza 'Yet ev'n these bones . . .') Gray veers away from the conclusion he had originally planned, and re-enters his subject, to discover the unwritten poem standing at the edge of the one he has been writing, a preoccupation at variance with his conscious theme." The concerns that hover at the edge of the "Elegy" are personal: Gray is a man of homosexual temperament inhabiting a world rich in all things, not least denials. His feeling for what Wells calls "suppressed potential" has personal resonance, the "preoccupation which steals up on [his] first theme, changing the course of the 'Elegy,' is the need for answered affection and the presence of a 'kindred spirit,' for the knowledge that a real meeting has taken place this side of the grave." It is the theme of the Eton poem more subtly and fully developed, more consolingly accepted.

Gray, Johnson says, "thought his language more poetical as it was more remote from common use." The odes are vitiated by "a kind of cumbrous splendour which we wish away . . . glittering accumulations of ungraceful ornaments . . . they strike, rather than please; the images are magnified by affectation; the language is laboured into harshness. The mind of the writer seems to work with unnatural violence." This is the case with Gray's experimental works and can be explained by his desire to suggest energy where he felt none, to drum up a passion but without motive force. Donald Davie identifies the fault: "Gray seems to have been distinguished by low vitality." He does not pour forth his verse, even in his vatic poems. He labors line by line.

Low vitality meant that major schemes were abandoned: the projected "History of English Poetry," for which he composed "The Progress of Poesy," a species of *translatio regni* of poetry from classical cultures to England, with due praise for English liberty, though not in the complacent tones of Thomson. To Thomas Warton he handed on his plan and notes for the "History," and Warton incorporated much of Gray, though he went his own way and achieved his own incomplete book. Later Gray wrote "The Bard," a poem whose lack of inner dynamic produces effects similar to those in Blake's most eloquent visions, where an *excessive* dynamic fragments the work and leads to ill-judged absurdities. Inevitably Gray returned to translation, to recharge his batteries.

He was indebted to earlier poets, but he is a creditor to many successors. Wordsworth owes him some debts in phrasing, image and theme, especially in "Hymn to Ignorance," and a negative debt, for Gray was a poet against whom he could react in formulating his own practice and theory of poetic diction. Goldsmith owes Gray specific debts. "The Alliance of Education and Government" is not generically remote from Goldsmith's much better poems, "The Traveller" and "The Deserted Village." Goldsmith's verse is less preconceived than Gray's, less careful, more impassioned.

T. S. Eliot says that the second-rate among eighteenth-century poets were those who, disaffected with conventional modes, "were incompetent to find a style of writing for themselves." Gray tried, but lack of energy let him down. His formidable conventional skills do not suggest that he could have been other than he was. What he is—as a letter writer as well as a poet—attests to the positive, learned virtues of an age, but also to its limitations. There is no acceptable space for such a man to live a full life. The "Elegy" remains, and anyone who cares for poetry will enjoy it. Read in the light of his life, it reveals as much about him as *The Waste Land* does about Eliot. The most "impersonal" poets, those who borrow voices and wear elusive masks, regarded attentively are often terrifyingly candid.

On Margate sands.
I can connect
Nothing with nothing.

Christopher Smart, Robert Graves tells us, "wrote *A Song to David* in a lunatic asylum, and when his collected poems were published in 1791, it was omitted as 'not acceptable to the reader.' This poem is formally addressed to David—Smart knew that he was no madder than King David had been, and a tradition survives that he scrabbled the verses with a key on the wall of his cell." However they were written, they remain a wonder and a mystery, begotten of the Bible, of broad and deep learning, and of some catalyst that made a confusion that the poet resolved, against chaos as it were, to put in some sort of order.

For the word of God is a sword on my side—no matter what other weapon a stick or a straw.
For I have adventured myself in the name of the Lord, and he hath marked me for his own.
For I bless God the Postmaster general & all conveyancers of letters under his care especially Allen & Shelvock.

For my grounds in New Canaan shall infinitely compensate for the
flats & maynes of Staindrop Moor.
For the praise of God can give to a mute fish the notes of a
nightingale.

Is it nonsense? Yes. Is it nonsense? No. "It is not impossible that when
Smart is judged over the whole range of his various productions—
conventional in form as well as unconventional, light and even ribald
as well as devotional, urbane or tender as well as sublime—he will
be thought of as the greatest English poet between Pope and Words-
worth." Is his apparent madness a reaction to the severities of the
Augustan Muse? Can a mad poet be, as that strictest of modern critics
Donald Davie suggests, "the greatest English poet between Pope and
Wordsworth"? There are such poets in other languages, notably Fried-
rich Hölderlin in German, though his poetry and his madness are of
another order.

Smart's originality is the product not of a candid, puzzled, anxious
personality like William Cowper's, nor the lucid, nostalgic and humane
sensibility of a Goldsmith. It's the product of a distinctly *poetic* imagi-
nation, using that term in a classical sense. Smart seldom composes
verse: he is a poet rare in any age, most rare in the eighteenth century, a
spiritual enthusiast and a consummate verbal artist. He might resemble
Blake, only he has greater formal tact, a better ear, a better (that is, a
less didactic) nature. His poems exist to celebrate God, not to cajole,
instruct and persuade us.

The more we know about Cowper's life, the more we appreciate his
verse. With Smart the case is different. Biography obscures his achieve-
ment because it seems to apologize for it. He is regarded for his mad-
ness (so much more colorful than Cowper's or Collins's) at the expense
of the poems. Wilfred Owen famously said, "The poetry is in the pity";
the apologist for Smart says, "The poetry is in the madness." It is and
isn't. We readily assume that he wrote in madness, that what he wrote,
in its forms and themes, partakes of his derangement. Or we divide the
work into sane and "insane" and judge the parts by distinct criteria. But
his madness can be seen not so much as disorder as *alternative* order, his
religious vision not as eccentric but as direct, comprehensive. To say an
artist is "mad" is to say very little. What matters is what he makes of lan-
guage. Smart makes passionate poetry. Doctor Johnson gives a memo-
rable account of Smart's illness: "I did not think he ought to be shut up.
His infirmities were not noxious to society. He insisted on people pray-
ing with him; and I'd as lief pray with Kit Smart as anyone else. Another
charge was that he did not love clean linen; and I have no passion for it."

A Song to David was not, as far as we know, composed in madness. It was certainly not composed in confinement. Structurally rigid, it comes alive in its astounding prosody, not in its theological content. *Jubilate Agno* (*Rejoice in the Lamb*), though produced in confinement, deserves to be read as celebration, too. Recent critics and editors who follow Smart's own order for it claim that it is based on a clear scheme, the "antiphonal structure of Hebrew poetry," as Davie says, the prosodic principles described by Robert Lowth: lines beginning with "Let" run parallel (ideally on a facing page) to lines beginning with "For": responses. It gives a sense of having been extemporized, written at speed. It was in fact composed at the rate of between one and three lines a day, almost as though it was a devotional journal. Erudite and allusive, the psalmodic lines are deployed with considerable rhythmic versatility. Because Smart did not prepare the *Jubilate* for press, much of its obscurity and difficulty may result from the way editors have presented it, not quite understanding his intention and without his manuscript before them. There will never now be a "definitive version." It is doubtful that Smart himself could have overseen one.

No known cause in his upbringing can be adduced as the cause of what he called the "peculiarity" of his imagination. He was writing verse at the age of four. He fell in love with a girl three times his age who used to cosset and caress him. A man pretended he would wed her; when the child told him he was too old, the man threatened to send his son in his place. Terrified at the prospect, Kit wrote eight lines to preempt his imaginary rival:

> Madam, if you please
> To hear such things as these.
> Madam, I have a rival sad
> And if you don't take my part it will make me mad.
> He says he will send his son;
> But if he does I will get me a gun.
> Madam if you please to pity,
> O poor Kitty, O poor Kitty!

Pretty, irregular, pathetic: already in infancy insecure in love, already subject to the teasing and treachery of the adult world.

Smart was born in Shipbourne, Kent, in 1722. Peter, his father, was steward of the Vane family establishment of Fairlawn. After his father's death when he was eleven, he spent his youth in Durham under the supervision of the Barnard branch of the Vanes. He may have experienced another frustrated passion there. He spent his holidays at the

Vanes' Raby Castle in Staindrop. They helped him to Cambridge, where he was a sizar at Pembroke College and distinguished himself as a scholar and poet. In 1745 he was elected a fellow of Pembroke. While at Cambridge he translated Pope's "Ode for Music" ("Ode on St Cecilia's Day") into Latin, won Pope's approbation, and composed tripos verses. He also wrote secular poems, amorous and otherwise. He became a friend of the organist and composer Charles Burney, from whom he learned about music; through him he got to know Johnson's circle.

Despite his academic success, he was not an ideal student or college fellow. Overfond of drink and something of a spendthrift, in 1747 he was arrested for debts to his tailor. In 1749 he went to London to try his hand in Grub Street. He wrote ballads and fables for London periodicals. He became a competent editor. In 1752, the year of his marriage to Anna Maria Carnan, stepdaughter of his own publisher, *Poems on Several Occasions* was published. It included a georgic, "The Hop Garden," a tribute to hops and to his native Kent. Between 1750 and 1755 he won the Cambridge Seatonian Prize five times for religious verse, Miltonic in manner. "On the Goodness of the Supreme Being" (1755) is the best of these, invoking "Israel's sweet Psalmist," David, one of Smart's peculiar muses: "thy tuneful touch / Drove trembling Satan from the heart of Saul, / And quelled the evil Angel." Music remained a solace to him, as to Saul. He translated Horace into prose and later turned the versions into verse. Horace was his other muse. David and Horace, an odd but, as it proved, a fruitful combination.

Between 1756 and 1763 he was confined for insanity, brought on in part by religious fervor, in part by financial improvidence (by now he had a wife and two daughters and had not learned good husbandry). Doctor Johnson and others did what they could to alleviate his difficulties. He saw the inside of St. Luke's Hospital for the Insane and of Mr. Potter's madhouse in Bethnal Green (in 1758 his wife retired to Dublin and his marriage was at an end). He worked hard after his release, but six years later was again imprisoned for debt. He died, aged forty-nine, in 1771 in the King's Bench Prison. Most of his best religious poetry dates from 1759–63. The *Song to David* was completed and published in the year of his release from asylum. The *Psalms, Hymns and Spiritual Songs*, published in 1765, date from this period. *Hymns for the Amusement of Children* appeared in 1770.

"Pope's 'Messiah' is not musical, but Smart's 'Song to David,' with its pounding thematic words and the fortissimo explosion of its coda, is a musical *tour de force*," says Northrop Frye. From the first stanza there's a relentless but never monotonous regularity, syntax urging the reader on across stanza endings, creating expectation and suspense; and a taut sound organization, with strong alliteration and assonance, cunning deployment of monosyllables and polysyllables almost as though they came from different language registers, and concentrated climaxes in three-word sequences, usually expressing progression, as in the final stanza, which picks up the word "glorious" from the stanza before:

> Glorious, more glorious is the crown
> Of Him that brought salvation down
>   By meekness, called thy Son;
> Thou at stupendous truth believed,
> And now the matchless deed's atchieved,
>   DETERMINED, DARED, and DONE.

Smart returned to this form as suitably ecstatic for some of his psalm translations. Two lines of tetrameter tauten into trimeter, and the rhyme scheme is made rigorous by Smart's preference for assonance and approximation between the rhymes. It was among the strictest forms he could choose, especially over a span of eighty-six stanzas; he proved his versatility, from the opening invocation of David and Christ to that concluding stanza. The first three stanzas—the treble construction is especially significant for him—initiate the music and establish the themes:

> O Thou, that sit'st upon a throne,
> With harp of high majestic tone,
>   To praise the King of kings;
> And voice of heav'n-ascending swell,
> Which, while its deeper notes excell,
>   Clear, as a clarion, rings:
>
> To bless each valley, grove and coast,
> And charm the cherubs to the post
>   Of gratitude in throngs;
> To *keep* the days on Zion's mount,
> And send the year to his account,
>   With dances and with songs:
>
> O Servant of God's holiest charge,
> The minister of praise at large,
>   Which thou may'st now receive;
> From thy blest mansion hail and hear,
> From topmost eminence appear
>   To this the wreath I weave.

Such verbal weaving combines with a structure of schematic rigidity. R. D. Havens pointed out in 1938 (when the slow process of dusting down the enigmatic poet began in earnest) how the stanzas are bunched in "threes, or sevens or their multiples—the mystic numbers." Donald Davie summarizes the structure: "After three stanzas of invocation come two groups of seven describing David, then three sets of three describing David's singing, and a further set of three describing the effects of his singing" and so on. The alternation between longer and shorter stanza runs and the syntactical and rhythmic parallelism and repetition within the "bunches" creates an aurally beguiling progression.

The power of rhythm combined with the inventive accuracy of his diction set Smart in a class of his own. Had Gray taken the poem to heart, he might have found a way out of his poetic congestion. Here, learning and artifice do what Gray wanted pseudo-primitivism to do for him. Early in his career Smart achieved uncluttered and unabstract poetic *impressions*, if not images; in his mature work even obscure and recondite allusions have a direct impact, not visual so much as sensual. David was master of Smart's rhythms, both taut and expansive; Horace taught him "the curiosity of choice diction." Marcus Walsh quotes Smart's preface to Horace: "the beauty, force and vehemence of *Impression* . . . by which a Genius is empowered to throw an emphasis upon a word or sentence in such a wise, that it cannot escape any reader of sheer good sense, and true critical sagacity."

Behind the language and structure of the *Jubilate Agno* stand the examples of the Old Testament in the King James Version, the Book of Common Prayer and, more remotely and distortedly, Milton. Smart allegorizes detail but not overall design. Each line has a various significance revealed in punning and contrived parallelisms, which Addison described as "false wit," a wit aurally rather than analytically recognized to be right. "Let Jotham praise with the Urchin, who took up his parable and provided himself for the adversary to kick against the pricks." It is the old adversary, the devil, whose spell is deflected by continually, musically praising creation and Creator. The rightness strikes us over long passages, cumulative, as in the famous evocation of Jeoffrey, the cat, which Benjamin Britten set to music:

> For he keeps the Lord's watch in the night against the adversary.
> For he counteracts the powers of darkness by his electrical skin and
>   glaring eyes.
> For he counteracts the Devil, who is death, by brisking about the life.
> For in his morning orisons he loves the sun and the sun loves him.
> For he is of the tribe of Tiger.
> For the Cherub Cat is a term of the Angel Tiger.

The devil in the heart of Saul, the madness in the mind of Smart, provoke the psalms of David and the *Jubilate*, exorcisms, charms against chaos, celebrations of a divine force. Works of nature and art ("For flowers are peculiarly the poetry of Christ," "For the TRUMPET of God is a blessed intelligence and so are all the instruments of HEAVEN") are aids against the adversary.

Smart goes where Gray could not: enthusiasm and vaticism overflow from a full if troubled spirit. He is not an imitator even in his translations, which hold the original in a form and language that make no concessions. He feels and conveys the force of the poetry he admires. His intuition is attuned to a broad tradition, not caught in the rut of convention. Marcus Walsh calls Smart's mature style "mannered, religiose and self-conscious"—and each becomes a positive critical term, for together they produce a "homogeneous" style that "unifies"—the crucial word—"a number of divergent influences." It is the paradoxical combination of influences, biblical and classical, and the disruptions his imagination registers, that make him outstanding and eccentric. Learning and accidents of biography deliver him from the bondage of Augustan convention into the sometimes anarchic, vertiginous freedom of *Jubilate Agno* and the originality of the *Song to David*. He has few heirs; in the context of his century his work is a symptom more than a resource. How could it be a resource when the definitive editions belong to the twentieth, not the eighteenth, century?

Beside his world, that of Oliver Goldsmith looks comfortable and consoling. "All the motion of Goldsmith's nature," writes Thomas De Quincey, "moved in the direction of the true, the natural, the sweet, the gentle." He had an "unpretending mind": a fair judgment. Versatile he certainly was; his literary activity was almost as varied—though not so copious—as Johnson's: poet, novelist, dramatist, journalist, nature writer, essayist, correspondent. Like Johnson's, his reputation as a poet rests on a few fine poems.

He was a remarkable Anglo-Irishman, like his friend Edmund Burke, the statesman, whose roots remained deep in Ireland, yet who flourished in England. His "Irishness" is different from Burke's, as their milieux and destinies were to prove. But their concerns and values are similar.

Yes! let the rich deride, the proud disdain,
These simple blessings of the lowly train;
To me more dear, congenial to my heart,
One native charm, than all the gloss of art . . .

Probably in 1730, Oliver, fifth child and second son of the Reverend Charles Goldsmith, was born in County Westmeath. His father became

curate of Kilkenny and moved to Lissoy, where the boy spent his child-
hood. He went to Trinity College, Dublin, at the age of fifteen as a sizar.
Two years later his father died. The young Oliver, who did not distin-
guish himself academically, was publicly reprimanded for participating
in a student riot. In 1750 he managed to take a degree. When he failed
to get ordained, he became a tutor, perhaps toyed with the possibility
of emigration to America, and at last, in 1752, settled into medical stud-
ies, supported by his family, first at Edinburgh and later at Leyden.
He traveled widely in Europe, where he conceived and developed *The
Traveller, or a Prospect of Society* (1764), the germ of *The Deserted Village*
(1770).

In 1756 he was in London, pursuing medicine as an apothecary and
as a physician in Southwark. He may have served as a proofreader in the
novelist Samuel Richardson's printing house and as an usher, or under-
schoolmaster. So many jobs suggest that he prospered in none. His lit-
erary aspirations grew; journalism and translation work began to find
him. He nearly sailed to India as a physician with the East India Com-
pany at Coromandel, but it was not to be. Writing began to feed him. In
1759 *An Enquiry into the Present State of Learning in Europe* was pub-
lished. He became known as Dr. Goldsmith and numbered among
friends and associates the novelist Tobias Smollett, the poets Edward
Young, Edmund Burke and Doctor Johnson.

His essays, "letters"—satirical epistolary essays by imagined for-
eign travelers—and other writings found a market and a price. But like
Smart he was impecunious. He made the acquaintance of bailiffs. A
new waistcoat swallowed up the money another man might have saved
for accommodation or food. Goldsmith was sociable beyond his means.

His *Essays* (1765) and the novel *The Vicar of Wakefield* (1766) set him
in the first rank among his contemporaries. But his immediate circle
failed to take him seriously—much as Gay was undervalued by his
friends. There is condescension in their banter, and in their criticism of
his political analysis in "The Deserted Village." Johnson said bluntly,
"Goldsmith had no settled notions upon any subject; so he talked always
at random. It seemed to be his intention to blurt out whatever was in
his mind, to see what would become of it." Goldsmith's incomplete
"Retaliation" (1774) is said to have been composed in response to Gar-
rick's extempore "Epitaph": "Here lies Nolly Goldsmith, for shortness
call'd Noll, / Who wrote like an angel, but talk'd like poor Poll." The
"Retaliation" savors a little of resentment. There is, however, nothing
resentful in the tone of his plays and lighter poems, notably "The
Haunch of Venison" (1770), or in the sheer unpedantic readability of his
prose, which has not the gravity of Johnson's nor the orotundity of
Burke's, but is full of the virtues of character that De Quincey admired.

No wonder he commanded an audience and had a market for his prose and plays.

Of the plays, *She Stoops to Conquer* (1773) has proved most memorable. His themes in all his works were serious even though the tone was often light: regret for a vanishing rural order (which he idealized); impatience with the Whiggery that was replacing ideals of patrimony with the practice of investment and profit, with appalling social consequences. Goldsmith is the poet of Burke's prose, catching the essence if not the logic of Toryism. By the time he died in 1774, he had witnessed poignantly the end of a social order almost as decisive as the earlier end that came with the execution of Charles I.

Like Gray and Collins, Goldsmith the poet was a great borrower and imitator; unlike them, his chief resource was his own prose works. There is an almost linear continuity between prose and verse, rather as in the work of Thomas Hardy, Rudyard Kipling and Edward Thomas. His poems, like most in the eighteenth century, were preplanned and pursue a discursive rather than "imaginative" development. But as Donald Davie writes of *The Deserted Village*—and it goes for *The Traveller* as well—though it is "an example of poems consciously planned like essays," it appeals "through a hidden imaginative continuity." The poetic process functions not in the argument but in the natural imagery, presented as frail and subject to change, exploitation and destruction. "The natural," Davie says, "which we think of as robust, is thus associated with what is vulnerable and fugitive."

Most of Goldsmith's surviving verse is the work of his maturity. The earliest pieces include translation and epigram, proofs of wit and formal skill, and exercises in social and literary irony. La Monnoye's "Ménagiana" provided a model for his satirical elegies, where a fourth line in each quatrain undermines conventional sentiment with "the truth." Typical is a stanza from "An Elegy on that Glory of her Sex, Mrs. Mary Blaize":

> She strove the neighbourhood to please,
>> With manners wondrous winning,
> And never followed wicked ways,
>> *Unless when she was sinning.*

"On the Death of the Right Honourable—" follows the same pattern. Satire is only accidentally social: its object is to ridicule a sentimental literary mode, most wittily in "On the Death of a Mad Dog." Goldsmith could serve up poetry of the very sort he parodied, a sentimental mixture favored at the time, as in his touching romance "Edwin and Angelina." T. S. Eliot's judgment is fair: Goldsmith had "the old and the new in such just proportion that there is no conflict; he is Augustan and also sentimental and rural without discordance."

"The Double Transformation: A Tale," the first largely original poem he wrote, owes a debt to Swift, though he is more temperate than the Dean:

> Jack sucked his pipe and often broke
> A sigh in suffocating smoke;
> While all their hours were passed between
> Insulting repartee or spleen.

The moral of this tale is general, contrasting beauty and vanity, exploring what a wife owes a husband. By contrast, "The Description of an Author's Bed-chamber" smacks of autobiography: poverty was a condition well known to the poet. Scroggen lies in his room, safe from the bailiffs under a rug:

> A window patched with paper lent a ray,
> That dimly showed the state in which he lay;
> The sanded floor that grits beneath the tread,
> The humid wall with paltry pictures spread

Evoking cold, hunger and thirst, the poem is rueful rather than angry. Scroggen's condition is an unhappy given of his vocation. One is put in mind of Hogarth's engraving *The Distrest Poet*, and the verb "grits" runs our own shoe soles across the unswept floor.

The Traveller owes something to his own prose and to Samuel Johnson, who contributed a number of lines and urged the lethargic poet to complete the work. Goldsmith drew on Montesquieu's *L'Esprit des Loix* in formulating the ideas: the poem was patiently conceived and exhaustively revised. He drafted it first with wide gaps between the lines, filling them with deliberations and deletions. He exploited the popular topographical genre: the physical suggests a moral panorama; natural detail acquires moral weight as in Gray's Eton poem, but on a grand scale. It proceeds from Italy through Switzerland, France and Holland, to Britain. It started in a letter Goldsmith wrote to his brother, and perhaps for this reason there is a frank directness of address in its couplets, which have little of the stiff formality of Johnson's or the decorousness of Pope's. The argument often stretches across couplets: they are not emphatically end-stopped and can hardly be called "heroic." Intellectual expansiveness loosens the form and reflects an imagination concerned more with the process of thought than with ripe, polished conclusions.

He judges the virtues and faults of each nation he surveys. It is strik-
ing how he evokes nations, their cultures and temperaments, through
landscape, insisting on a continuity between man and environment.
Lord Macaulay thought this work the noblest and most simply planned
philosophical poem in the language. There is novelty in the way he
introduces, as Roger Lonsdale shows, his own "predicament and sensi-
bility as matters of interest and importance" at the beginning and end.
Here (and more so in "The Deserted Village") Goldsmith repeats
words, not as Pope does locally for special emphasis, but throughout the
poem—words that are pivots of thought and mood, whose reiteration
adds to the meditative tone. We have arrived at the very frontier of
Romanticism.

But we are not ready to cross over. In the epistle dedicatory to his
brother, Goldsmith attacks blank verse, Pindaric odes and metrical
experiments. "Every absurdity has now a champion to defend it, and he
is generally much in the wrong, so he has always much to say; for error
is ever talkative." He promises wholesome formal conservatism. Worse
than poetic is political partisanship: "Party entirely distorts the judg-
ment and destroys the taste. When the mind is once affected with this
disease, it can only find pleasure in what contributes to increase the dis-
temper." For himself, "Without espousing the cause of any party, I have
attempted to moderate the rage of all." Goldsmith is a moderator, but
not a pragmatist. He has his own orientation. "At gold's superior charm
all freedom flies, / The needy sell it and the rich man buys." His praise
of liberty puts Thomson to shame. In *The Traveller* he rails against
party:

> O then how blind to all that truth requires,
> Who think it freedom when a part aspires!
> Calm is my soul nor apt to rise in arms,
> Except when fast approaching danger warms:
> But when contending chiefs blockade the throne,
> Contracting regal power to stretch their own;
> When I behold a fractious band agree
> To call it freedom, when themselves are free;
> Each wanton judge new penal statutes draw,
> Laws grind the poor and rich men rule the law;
> The wealth of climes, where savage nations roam,
> Pillaged from slaves to purchase slaves at home;
> Fear, pity, justice, indignation start,
> Tear off reserve and bare my swelling heart;
> Till half a patriot, half a coward grown,
> I fly from petty tyrants to the throne.

He laments rural depopulation, enclosure, the decay of the countryside. Thus the Industrial Revolution was recorded in poetry not in itself, but in its effect on the principles of permanence. Few poets experienced the industrial cities. They witnessed change almost entirely in terms of its impact on rural England. Cowper, Crabbe, even Hardy, observe the decay of the established order, but perceive the new order and its vicissitudes only from a distance.

The Deserted Village focuses initially on one "place," Auburn, which Goldsmith idealizes and generalizes: it comes to represent all such communities. The poem, drafted in prose, was then corseted into couplets, which disciplined and condensed expression, but always with reference to an initial design. The idealization of Auburn, possibly the Lissoy of his childhood, is not excessive. If it is sentimental, it is not falsely so; it serves as the ground against which he develops his meditation, without the argument of *The Traveller*. Place and thought give way to elegiac feeling, a sense (not just an idea) of irrevocable loss: organic, traditional communities sacrificed to the inconstant will of commerce, enclosure, exploitation. For him this represents a loss of personal roots, yet his lament is comprehensive because his is by extension a general experience. The blisses of village life—"charm" and "sweet" recur too frequently in his evocation—are so pervasive as to be almost abstract. The general judgment is appealingly simple and just:

> Ill fares the land, to hastening ills a prey,
> Where wealth accumulates and men decay:
> Princes and lords may flourish or may fade;
> A breath can make them, as a breath has made;
> But a bold peasantry, their country's pride,
> When once destroyed, can never be supplied.

Times "When every rood of ground maintained its man" are over. Trade is the undiscriminating instrument of change. In the past, the peasant crowned "A youth of labour with an age of ease." The lines about the man who "Bends to the grave with unperceived decay, / While resignation gently slopes the way" are often cited for the appositeness of their verbs, the exact fit of language with image and moral content. Such usage gives the lie to those who say Goldsmith has an "essentially prosaic" imagination. He is the author of *The Vicar of Wakefield*, admittedly—the vicar himself is invoked in lines 133–92. But the imaginative procedures of poet and novelist are distinct, even if the poem took off from a prose draft. The verb "slope" is a measure of the poet.

Satire is too weak a word for Goldsmith's passionate sorrow at the effects of the deeds of those who would replace modest happiness with egotistical splendor, displace the organic and vital with the formal, monumental and ornamental ("The country blooms—a garden and a grave"). They compel common men—their countrymen—to leave their native soil and emigrate to unknown lands; the humble have no redress against the power of wealth. Johnson contributed the poem's final quatrain. We are moved by the poem; but we are resigned, for the poet seems to know that what he elegizes is gone beyond recall, that Whiggery is the order of the day. As in the early poem about the poet's threadbare room, this poem does not resist: it accepts what is. This is the source of its aesthetic wholeness (it is not "instrumental," it does not advocate change) and its political inadequacy.

"The stricken deer"

WILLIAM COWPER, CHARLOTTE SMITH

William Cowper wrote some of the best-known hymns and poems in English—so well known that they travel incognito, having acquired the authority of anonymity, like the ballads "Rule Britannia," "Drink to me only" and "The Passionate Shepherd." Such a fate never overtook a Romantic poem. Cowper is not quite a Romantic, though his hand is on the latch. He is the *other* poet with a claim to being the "greatest" between Pope and Wordsworth. As mad as Smart, though with a different kind of madness, he broke through to God in his hymns, and in "social" and "normative" verse discovered the social language, if not the society, of his time.

His poetry proved of value to Coleridge and Wordsworth. Coleridge's original lectures on English poetry define three periods, the third running from Cowper to "the present day." For him something important begins with Cowper, a poet who read the poems of George Herbert with delight when Herbert was almost forgotten, who knew Milton's work as few before him had, and developed a personal, discursive, blank-verse style that in directness and variety of tone foreshadows Wordsworth's. He loved Robert Burns and regretted only the dialect, not because it was inexpressive but because English readers gave up on it too easily ("His candle is bright, but shut up in a dark lantern"). De Quincey often joins Cowper's name with Edward Young's and Wordsworth's as meditative poets of a kind, always allowing to Wordsworth the greenest laurel.

Cowper's spiritual and secular unhappiness were of a piece with those of other poets of his century. But he dwells insistently on his own guilt, with the hubristic humility of a Protestant who knows himself to be the most abject of all sinners: such exaggeration guarantees him the attention, even if derisive, of God.

> Your sea of troubles you have past,
>   And found the peaceful shore;

I, tempest-tossed, and wrecked at last,
　　Come home to port no more.

Critics are reluctant to make the claims for Cowper that he deserves. There's something about him: the self-obsession of Hoccleve, the variable copiousness of Thomson, the excellence of the hymns, which are a genre not *quite* polite . . . In one anthology the head note for Cowper begins, "Of all the poets in this selection, Cowper is perhaps the smallest in poetical stature. He would probably have counted himself lucky to figure in such grand company."

In important ways Cowper is original, and the emotional and intellectual range of his poems is wide. A "milder muse" dominates, but there are reasons for this: Cowper had to court that Muse more intensely than any poet in the language, because for him poetry was a means of talking himself back from the edge, not—in the fashion of the 1960s and 1970s—of coaxing himself over it. Acquaintance with his darker verse makes the "milder muse" a formidable and healing figure. Cowper's work gains in definition when we understand his motives in writing. His Augustanism is illuminated when we realize, as Donald Davie does, that the poems "were written under the shadow of psychosis."

Cowper was born in 1731 at Great Berkhamstead, where his father, a grand-nephew of the first Earl Cowper and onetime royal chaplain, was rector. On his mother's side he could claim remote kinship with John Donne. His first trauma was his mother's death when he was six, a loss consolingly weighed in the remarkable poem "On the Receipt of my Mother's Picture out of Norfolk," written after his earliest experience of madness. "Oh that those lips had language! Life has pass'd / With me but roughly since I heard thee last . . ." Intense pathos, untouched by sentimentality. At his first school he was bullied. He went on to Westminster School, where he was happier and able to excel. Among his classmates was the satirist Charles Churchill. Cowper read Homer, Milton and Cowley deeply. He translated Homer and the Latin poems of Milton.

At the age of eighteen he entered the Middle Temple and in 1754 he was called to the bar. He fell in love with his cousin Theodora, whose father, sensing Cowper's instability and poor prospects, opposed the match. It was another blow to him. His "Delia" poems, addressed to Theodora, though not his best work, attest to his devotion. He came to expect failure—even, at times, to court it. He began to withdraw from the world, and his father's death, leaving him only a modest inheritance, precipitated his decline. He was a commissioner of bankrupts (1759–65). His family exerted itself to secure him a better post, but when it was offered he was unable to accept it. He attempted suicide and was confined to an asylum. He was not surprised by his breakdown: it was part of the pattern he expected.

Recovery coincided with an evangelical conversion. Later he could write, "The path of sorrow, and that path alone, / Leads to the land where sorrow is unknown." He was lifted up by reading a biblical text in Romans. Tenuously "cured," he went to live in Huntingdon with the Reverend and Mrs. ("My Mary") Unwin (1765–67). The Unwins, Anglican evangelicals, supported him, and after her husband's death Mrs. Unwin tended Cowper in his illnesses. His love for her was the subject of several poems more mature and memorable than the "Delia" poems:

> Thy indistinct expressions seem
> Like language uttered in a dream;
> Yet me they charm, whate'er the theme,
> > My Mary!

This was written in the twentieth year of their friendship; she is fading, and he believes himself (as usual) responsible for her decline. They had almost married, but desisted at a recurrence of Cowper's malady. She fell ill in 1791 and he helped look after her until her death in 1796. He died, miserable and ill, in 1800, having composed his harrowing poem "The Castaway" two years earlier:

> No voice divine the storm allayed,
> > No light propitious shone;
> When, snatched from all effectual aid,
> > We perished, each alone:
> But I beneath a rougher sea,
> And whelmed in deeper gulfs than he.

The "he" was mercifully drowned; the "I" survives to suffer. Images of storm, shipwreck, drowning and isolation are leitmotifs through the poetry, even in unexpected humorous contexts. Shipwreck and drowning epitomize human vulnerability. Theological and psychological elements coexist in the images: they come at points when Cowper is peculiarly, darkly, himself. "Alexander Selkirk," ostensibly about the human prototype for Robinson Crusoe, is a personal vision: Cowper as castaway. "The Loss of the Royal George," a superb dirge, comes fraught with personal cargo. The ship sank in calm water, unexpectedly.

> Toll for the brave—
> The brave! that are no more:

> All sunk beneath the wave,
> Fast by their native shore.

Happy or at least contented times precede his miserable end. With Mrs. Unwin he moved to Olney. There they encountered a rather dreadful Calvinist, the Reverend John Newton. Whatever else he may have done, he elicited from the poet the *Olney Hymns* at a time when Cowper was again suffering mental and spiritual torment. His faith revived, but he still doubted his own election for salvation. He dreamed that God had damned him and the hymns are heavy with a hopeless hope. Davie suggests that Cowper's depressive madness was connected with the extreme Calvinism of the evangelicals. He recovered from the dream of damnation, resigned worldly ambitions, accepted his fall from grace. In nature he found external solace. Tending leverets and birds gave purpose to his retirement. The nature he describes in his verse with minute and loving particularity appealed to those caught up in the vogue for the picturesque. Unlike them, he came to nature directly, not through art.

His earliest attempts at extended verse were the eight *Moral Satires*, suggested to him by Mary. He worked best when someone requested poems from him. Newton catalyzed the hymns, Lady Austen provoked *The Task*, the roistering ballad "John Gilpin" and other poems. Occasions for poems were offered by those solicitous for his health and keen to prevent him from reflecting on his spiritual condition. The verse is much more than therapy. It has the mild urgency of a man intent to look abroad, away from himself, to attach his vision to the created world. At least nature won't condemn or rebuff him. What he writes is strenuously normative, judiciously moralized: self-doubt in quest of certitude. The tenuous structure of the long poems reveals the uncertainty of his control, but it is hard to fault the surface. Coleridge praises above all the "clarity of diction" and "harmony" of the blank verse.

Cowper translated widely. His blank-verse Homer is not a masterpiece: set beside Pope's couplet version it shows how much even late Augustans abandon when they abandon rhyme. But his Horace, Virgil and Ovid are variously excellent. He translated from French and from the Greek Anthology, displaying technical competence in epigrams, hymns, anthems, elegies, lyrics, pastorals, discursive poems and epistles (in verse and prose: he is among the best letter writers in the language).

Norman Nicholson concentrates on the paradoxical nature of the poet: "a recluse who became the spokesman of a great popular religious and democratic movement; and an oddity, an eccentric, a refugee from society, who, perhaps more than any other English poet, expressed the aspirations of the average man of his time." The poems have "the merit of good conversation," an intimacy with their readers. Normative verse is powerful when it is hard won, when the troubled poet willfully achieves normality.

Conversational verse is uncommon in an age still overshadowed by Pope, whom Cowper admired with reservations, and under the spell of Milton. Cowper's Milton is not mediated through Thomson: it is Milton himself, whose Latin he translated, whom he set out to edit in 1791. He avoids Milton's grandiloquence because he is aware of having particular readers, concerned with specific issues and images. He has a defined *personality*, and he selects in *The Task* a loose associative form over a narrative structure. His debt to Milton is not, like Gray's and Collins's, to the shorter poems, but to *Paradise Lost* and *Paradise Regained*. His other master is Homer; he doubts only the morality of devoting so much time to a pagan poet. The absence of Shakespeare is evidence of how essentially literary a poet Cowper was in his earlier work.

D. J. Enright compares Cowper with Herbert. Cowper asks that we assent to his presentation of faith, while Herbert's representations are of faith as experience. Cowper teases out his morals, Herbert as often as not leaves the moral implicit. Cowper is didactic where Herbert is devotional, with the immediacy of prayer and not the remove of sermonizing. Coleridge admires in *The Task* the "vein of satire which runs through that excellent poem, together with the sombre hue of its religious opinions." "Opinions" is the right word, opinions argued and affirmed, only seldom conveyed to the pulse. Yet the opinions must have been widely held, for between its publication in 1782 and 1800 eleven editions of *The Task* appeared.

In "Table Talk," the first of the *Moral Satires*, Cowper modestly presents his claims as a poet. "I play with syllables, and sport in song." The understatement goes too far. This poem begins with philosophy and politics and, like good table talk, takes much else in its stride, most memorably the halcyon poetic genius. His literary firmament includes Homer, Virgil and Milton.

In 1783, the year of Crabbe's *The Village* and Blake's *Poetical Sketches*, Cowper began *The Task*. Lady Austen requested an epic about a sofa. "I sing the Sofa. I, who lately sang / Truth, Hope and Charity." Soon enough he gets back to Truth, Hope and Charity. After a history of seats, a comment on the suitability of sofas for sufferers from the gout, he expresses a desire that he may never experience that illness. Why?

For I have loved the rural walk through lanes
Of grassy swarth, close cropped by nibbling sheep,

And skirted close with intertexture firm
Of thorny boughs . . .

The sofa establishes a tone: drawing room, comfort, conversation. It inaugurates, too, what is virtually a theme: the rich texture of things in the world, physical sensations, and the theme of illness and enforced repose. The poem connects not by argument or narrative but through tone. It develops by association an interchange between particular observation and moral generalization. Cowper's blank verse suggests the tone and subject matter of Wordsworth:

Nor rural sights alone, but rural sounds,
Exhilarate the spirit, and restore
The tone of languid Nature.

"Languid" may not be Wordsworthian, but more than a common debt to Milton associates the poets in our minds. They partly share a vision of nature. Of the cacophonous birds, Cowper writes that they

. . . have charms for me,
Sounds inharmonious in themselves and harsh,
Yet heard in scenes where peace for ever reigns,
And only there, please highly for their sake.

Cowper is less elemental, more comforting than Wordsworth.

Abstracted from the poetry, the thought of *The Task* is not distinguished, but in context it is realized and vivid. Only the positive moral exhortations, against slavery and blood sports, for example, or in favor of certain religious views, weary the reader. In promoting reform Cowper prefers exhortation to satire. Yet in poetry, satire is generally the more effective.

One of the triumphs of Cowper's art and vision comes in the third book, "I was the stricken deer," evoking the function of Christ and the true nature of redemption, which for an exalted moment sets Cowper almost on a par with Herbert.

I was a stricken deer, that left the herd
Long since; with many an arrow deep infixt
My panting side was charg'd, when I withdrew
To eek a tranquil death in distant shades.
There was I found by one who had himself
Been hurt by th' archer. In his side he bore,
And in his hands and feet, the cruel scars.

With gentle force soliciting the darts,
He drew them forth, and heal'd, and bade me live.
Since then, with few associates, in remote
And silent woods I wander, far from those
My former partners of the peopled scene;
With few associates, and not wishing more.

This is oblique autobiography. Other vivid descriptive passages, about cucumbers, greenhouses, animals, the winter landscape and the hearth, add a documentary interest to the poem, but always animated by a spiritual and a psychological interest. One need only compare *The Task* with Thomson's *The Seasons* to see how the Augustan imperatives were being questioned and eroded by a first-person singular coming to terms with its singularity.

In "John Gilpin," "Epitaph on a Hare" with its accuracy and gentle humor, "The Poplar-Field" which meant a great deal to both Coleridge and Hopkins, and "Yardley Oak"—the majestic unfinished moral poem—readers find the readiest access to Cowper. They first hear him (without proper introduction) in church when they sing his *Olney Hymns*, "Oh! for a closer walk with God" and "God moves in a mysterious way." In the poems it is the same voice, and a music not of organs but of intimate speech.

Eighteen years after Cowper's birth, in 1749, an unaccountably neglected poet, Charlotte Smith (half remembered as a novelist) was born. If Cowper had his hand on the latch of Romanticism, her foot was firmly in the door. Wordsworth read her: Dorothy Wordsworth recalls his turning the pages of her *Elegiac Sonnets, and Other Essays*—the fifth edition, for she was popular in her time; and he visited her in Brighton. She treated him politely, introducing him to other women writers in the town. In London at the end of the century she dined with the young Coleridge. A recurrent footnote, doggedly represented in anthologies by a sonnet that is wonderful ("Pressed by the moon, mute arbitress of tides") and to which few attend closely, she is a key poet of the transition to Romanticism.

Among women writers she is, after Mary Sidney, the first substantial poet. The sonnets resemble Cowper's verse in tone, but without his specific anxieties. Meditative, judicious, Smith also has a clear, unconventional vision. Her language seeks out representative detail; too many exclamations and vocatives irrupt into the verse, yet scene and sensibility are sharply delineated:

The wild blast, rising from the western cave,
  Drives the huge billows from their heaving bed,

> Tears from their grassy tombs the village dead,
> And breaks the silent sabbath of the grave!
> With shells and seaweed mingled, on the shore
>   Lo! their bones whiten in the frequent wave;
>   But vain to them the winds and waters rave;
> *They* hear the warring elements no more:
> While I am doomed—by life's long storm oppressed,
> To gaze with envy on their gloomy rest.

Gothic, yes: but beneath or despite the gothic, astonishing in visual, prosodic and *tonal* precision. Her coy description of herself as "an early worshipper at Nature's shrine" sells her short. It is true that she observes nature, walking out on the hills and along the shore, but her "worship" is more "witness," her nature is not transcendent, despite her rhetoric. What distinguishes her as a writer is her formal assurance. In the much-anthologized "Thirty-Eight" she masters with wit and wisdom a difficult form and develops a crucial theme, that of growing older, with tact, feeling and wit.

She was born Charlotte Turner at Bignor Park in Sussex and enjoyed a privileged childhood, though her mother died when she was three. Terrified at the prospect of her father's remarriage, she herself disastrously married Benjamin Smith, profligate son of a West India merchant, when she was sixteen. He spent them into debt and then debtors' prison. She bore Mr. Smith ten children, eight of whom survived; she left him, and began—having already started in 1784 with the *Elegiac Sonnets*, which had success—to make her way as a writer. She wrote on average a book each year for two decades. Mr. Smith remains, in various fictional guises, the villain of her life and occasions some of the gloomy skies in her poems. But she had read Rousseau and was inspired by the French Revolution. Her poetic imagination emerges generally at night; in the dark, shapes are larger, lights brighter, the landscape takes on an alternative, accepting definition. In her major poem, *Beachy Head,* she does not appropriate, colonize or look through nature to an absolute. She witnesses and celebrates with gratitude to nature rather than, through nature, to God.

What makes her neglect unaccountable is that she achieved, *avant la lettre,* so much that is celebrated in the work of Wordsworth in particular, as well as the Coleridge of "This Lime Tree Bower" and the blank-verse narratives. *Beachy Head* evinces, beyond its assured tone, a mastery of blank-verse meditation and a compelling, complex syntax that mimes the movement of thought. Clearly she is rooted in the eighteenth century, but emancipation has taken place, she has created first a distance from the stylistic vices and reflexes of the age, and then a space for her own sensibility to identify a physical world and a physical and spiritual self.

> The high meridian of the day is past,
> And Ocean now, reflecting the calm Heaven,
> Is of cerulean hue; and murmurs low
> The tide of ebb, upon the level sands,
> The sloop, her angular canvas shifting still,
> Catches the light and variable airs
> That but a little crisp the summer sea
> Dimpling its tranquil surface.

Pure description, and from its purity something more comes, as though we are returning to a literal uncomplicated world after the packed diction and decorum of the "social century." Charlotte Smith is not, like Smart and Cowper, an exception, someone set apart as a consequence of illness or the estrangements of genius. She is propelled forward by Milton, Thomson and Pope. There are the epithets, the rhetorical bric-a-brac, the large abstractions, yet in the foreground a literal vision is trained upon an actual world. And she has a landscape quite as specific as Wordsworth's, the Sussex of her unimpeded childhood. Her personal hardship is there in tone, but seldom in the frame; celebration and reflection are given in judicious measure:

> Ah! hills so early loved! in fancy still
> I breathe your pure keen air; and still behold
> Those widely spreading views, mocking alike
> The Poet and the Painter's utmost art.
> And still, observing objects more minute,
> Wondering remark the strange and foreign forms
> Of seashells; with the pale calcerous soil
> Mingled, and seeming of resembling substance.
> Though surely the blue Ocean (from the heights
> Where the Downs westward trend, but dimly seen)
> Here never rolled its surge. Does Nature then
> Mimic, in wanton mood, fantastic shapes
> Of bivalves, and inwreathed volutes, that cling
> To the dark sea-rock of the wat'ry world?
> Or did this range of chalky mountains once
> Form a vast basin, where the Ocean waves
> Swelled fathomless?

Such blank verse, with its variable enjambements, creating the kinds of syntactical suspense that urges us on, so that description is vibrant, unpredictable and alive in the verse reflection, is unusual in any century. The diction is assured and "modern" in the manner of Thomson, using a precise, scientific register, yet naturally, as an informed person would. If the verse were anonymous, would we be inclined to surmise that it was written by a woman? I think we would, especially if we knew the date of its composition. *Beachy Head* was published in 1807, the year after Charlotte Smith died. It is the work of an unsung maturity: at times humorous, full of a love of specific nature, marked too by longing, less for youth and romance than for that lost world when imagination was unconstrained, the world before Benjamin Smith and children and the labor of sustaining a family as a single parent. The world before she, like some of her intimate friends and some of the Romantics she prefigures, was an opium addict. Yet these circumstances are not adduced in the poems. They inform only the tone.

Charlotte Smith's poetry may have been delivered from the trammels of the eighteenth century by means of her fiction writing: the verse is wonderfully efficient, in its disclosure of scene and theme, evenly measured, rising to grandeur, scaling down to microscopic observation. Her fault in the longer poems is formal: extension rather than structure. Yet if we read her as we tend to read Cowper, Pope or Thomson, in extract, she is not out of place. Her work was once popular, but it was not absorbed into the critical culture of the day; its claims were not made. We can say that she was appreciated by Wordsworth, but his appreciation was not eloquent. We can say that her example empowered Elizabeth Barrett Browning. But Charlotte Smith is not a footnote to Romanticism. She deserves to be read today.

Youth and Age

Thomas Warton wrote a judicious account of Thomas Chatterton in the decade of the "marvellous boy's" death. It is a tribute to the success of the legendary forger that, though some critics believed they had rumbled him, others sat on the fence. In Thomas Rowley's poems, Warton declares, the fifteenth century will be vindicated: "A want of genius will no longer be imputed to this period of our poetical history, if the poems lately discovered at Bristol, and said to have been written by Thomas Rowlie, a secular priest of that place, about the year one thousand four hundred and seventy, are genuine." His indecision is on poetic rather than scholarly grounds; the poems "possess considerable merit," he declares; there were still grounds for regarding them as genuine. In the end Warton, on the evidence of parchments and handwriting, and of spelling conventions, comes down on the side of the disbelievers. Yet he is reluctant to do so. He is enchanted: "This youth, who died at eighteen, was a prodigy of genius; and would have proved the first of English poets, had he reached a maturer age." Which was more marvelous: that a fifteenth-century poet of real moment should be rediscovered, or that a teenager from the provinces should create so plausible and sustained a poetic work? In the end the spell Chatterton cast was broken. "He was an adventurer, a professional hireling in the trade of literature, full of projects and inventions, artful, enterprising, unprincipled, indigent, and compelled to subsist by expedients."

> Begin, my Muse, the imitative lay,
> Aonian doxies sound the thrumming string;
> Attempt no number of the plaintive Gray,
> Let me like midnight cats, or Collins sing.

Chatterton survives for what he meant to the Romantics more than for anything he wrote. Much of his (false) work is outstanding, all of it provides evidence of genius that did not give itself time to mature fully, though mature it certainly is. His writings fill three volumes; there are longueurs. He was not Arthur Rimbaud. To the Romantics he symbolized genius untutored, misunderstood, misprized by "the ingrate world" (Keats). Keats used to intone the magnificent lines from the minstrels' song in the play *Aella*:

> Comme, wythe acorne-coppe and thorne,
> Drayne mie hartys blodde awaie;
> Lyfe and all yttes goode I scorne,
> Daunce bie nete, or feaste by daie.
>> My love ys dedde,
>> Gon to hys death-bedde,
>> Al under the wyllowe tree.

To Chatterton's memory Keats dedicated an indifferent sonnet, and then *Endymion*, the poem he described as "a feverish attempt, rather than a deed accomplished." Keats sets his hero "among the stars / Of highest Heaven." In a letter to Reynolds he confides, "I always somehow associate Chatterton with autumn. He is the purest writer in the English Language. He has no French idioms, or particles like Chaucer—'tis genuine English idiom in English words." In a letter to his brother he adds, "Chatterton's language is entirely northern. I prefer the native music of it to Milton's cut by feet." Chatterton's "pure" English proved useful in Keats's emancipation from Milton. He loved the "Rowley poems" in "Middle English," not the precocious but otherwise unexceptional English poems.

Wordsworth refers to Chatterton in "Resolution and Independence" and carries the poet's name further in time and space than any other tribute does: "I thought of Chatterton, the marvellous Boy, / The sleepless Soul that perished in his pride." Coleridge was behindhand in his tribute. For over thirty years he tinkered with his "Monody on the Death of Chatterton," spoken figuratively at the poet's grave (as a pauper suicide, his grave was unmarked). The life and death of the poet detained him. The poems that he praises in passing are the "Rowley poems." Coleridge's significant poetic debt to Chatterton is in the metrical organization of "Christabel."

What, apart from the life, was the appeal of Chatterton? Why do some claim him as "the first Romantic"? There are undeniably fine poems and stanzas, especially among the forgeries. Best are certain passages of *Aella*, "An Excelente Balade of Charitie (As wroten bie the goode Prieste Thomas Rowley 1464)," and "Eclogue the Third." The authority of his "language" is felt in the amusing and, in tone at least, plausibly medieval quatrain:

> Theere was a Broder of Orderys Blacke
>   In mynster of Brystowe Cittie:
> He layd a Damoisell onne her Backe
>   So guess yee the Taile of mie Dittie.

Remarkable for its oddity, such verse also has a separable *quality*. The best passages in *Aella* do not lose their imaginative force when translated back into modern English (Chatterton drafted them in English, then medievalized the language).

He remained popular until the middle of the nineteenth century as a Romantic legend, a lesson in resisting to the death literary and social convention. From his setting forth he was marginal. He was born in Bristol in 1752. His father, a schoolmaster and subchanter at the Church of St. Mary Redcliffe, died before the boy was born. Chatterton's mother supported him, working as a seamstress and running a "dame school." It was she who, one day disposing of some antique documents, aroused in the hitherto listless child an enthusiasm, first for the illuminated letters, then for the old words. She taught him to read. Later he busied himself studying at home and at St. Mary's (where he claimed to have gained access to a mysterious box containing Rowley's manuscripts).

When he was seven he was sent to a grim Bristol school, Colston's Hospital. He kept himself to himself, writing occasional satirical poems about his schoolmate-tormentors to keep his spirits up—poems such as "Sly Dick," "in arts of cunning skilled." At the age of ten he began to write more earnest poems. "On the First Epiphany," written when he was eleven, was published. He composed more satirical as well as religious verse, revealing a precociously informed (or cleverly imitative) skepticism in matters of public morality. In 1764 he presented a pupil-teacher with a forged medieval poem. His first gull was duped.

In 1767 he was apprenticed to an attorney. He composed further forgeries. Most of the "Rowley poems" were completed in 1768–69. He persuaded several Bristol burghers, some of his friends, and for a time he succeeded with the great Horace Walpole. Ambition to be a writer took him to London. Pride forbade him to return home a failure. In 1770, in his eighteenth year, starving and in despair, he poisoned himself with arsenic in a rented room in Holborn.

His ambition, talent and pride were frustrated at each endeavor, perhaps because he started off on the wrong, borrowed medieval foot: his own feet would have carried him far. He could find no peer in Bristol to converse with. There his forgeries were admired as antique manuscripts, not as poems. He could find no patron. Grub Street exploited his energy but not his genius. Yet he achieved the "Rowley poems." Was he a "native," or "born," poet? Romantic writers needed to believe in such creatures. Coleridge pointed out in a note on "Resolution and Independence" that Wordsworth could name only two: Chatterton and Burns.

Chatterton's invention of Sir Thomas Rowley, fifteenth-century "Secular Priest of St John," was not perverse. His truly perverse forgeries consisted in providing "authentic" pedigrees for drab notables or convenient documents for local historians. Rowley by contrast was a serious enterprise. He has character and a tone of his own quite distinct from Chatterton's in his modern English verse. He lives in an idealized medieval Bristol. Rowley's rank, religious vocation ("The Church of Rome [some Tricks of Priestcraft excepted] is certainly the true Church," Chatterton wrote in his "Articles of Belief"), his erudition, all extended Chatterton beyond the cramped, commercially evolving Bristol of the slave trade in which he existed without wealth, status or prospect, and was compelled to observe a faith he found colorless and hypocritical. Rowley was necessary to him; his best poems partake of that necessity.

"Forgery" was a device for escaping the conventions that checked the genius of Gray and disoriented the work of Smart and Cowper. Macpherson's Ossian, and Walpole's own *The Castle of Otranto*, which pretended to be translated from an Italian original, were two of the best-known forgeries. A harking back to pre-Renaissance culture, a hankering after "native" roots and styles kept writers such as Gray and Warton active. An interest in philology and earlier versions of the language was developing.

Chatterton's dramatic instinct allows him not only to describe but to enter the world of Rowley. He owes debts to Shakespeare, and *Aella*, his most sustained Rowley work, though unstageable, is dramatic. His language derives most from Chaucer, but his imagination is at home in the sixteenth century. The forgeries are not mosaics of philological plagiarism, any more than Gray's poems are mosaics of poetic plagiarism. They make a solid structure of old- and new-baked bricks. Behind Chatterton's English poems stand Pope, Gay and Swift. Without Rowley, Chatterton would have remained a minor Augustan, unless Grub Street had provided him more than crusts. With Rowley he became an original, a proto-Romantic, using the past as a way of apprehending the world and rejecting the conventions of a narrowed culture.

Keats in the preface to *Endymion* speaks of himself and of adolescence in terms applicable to Chatterton. "The imagination of a boy is healthy, and the mature imagination of a man is healthy; but there is a space of life between, in which the soul is in ferment, the character undecided, the way of life uncertain, the ambition thick-sighted." It was in this space that Chatterton perished in a sordidness to which the Romantics imparted a tragic glamour.

A story stranger even than Chatterton's, and in its ending sadder, is that of Phillis Wheatley, who—born around 1753 somewhere in Africa (perhaps Senegal) and under a name entirely lost—was transported into slavery in America. She was bought as a child on her arrival in Boston by a tailor, John Wheatley, and reared by him and his wife, whose servant she became. Phillis learned English quickly, then Latin. Her masters introduced her to the poetry of Pope and Gray and at the age of thirteen she was writing religious verse. Her first published poem was an elegy on the death of an evangelical minister, composed when she was seventeen. A prodigy of imitation rather than invention, she traveled to England in 1773, where her first book, *Poems on Various Subjects, Religious and Moral,* was published, with a preface signed by various American men of substance, including John Hancock. The Countess of Huntingdon entertained and patronized her in London. In America she met with George Washington, to whom she addressed a poem. Her celebrity ended here: returning to Boston, she watched her masters die, and married a freed slave who succumbed to debtors' prison. She had three children, one of whom survived. She drudged to support it and herself, then died in 1784; the last child followed soon after. Poetry abandoned her in her hardship or, it is safer to say, any poetry she wrote in her later, sketchily charted years has not survived. Those who supported and sponsored her in her early success lost sight of her or perhaps averted their eyes.

Her poems disappoint those seeking—in the first substantial black poet in English, and the first black woman writing in the language— evidence of her circumstances as a slave, as a woman, as a freed woman. Indeed the poems belong to a tradition more English than American: there is less of her world in her verse than of Anne Bradstreet's in hers. She does refer to her origins, addressing a poem to another black artist, a painter; and a letter of thanks to the Earl of Dartmouth; an epigram on her origin affirming that "Negroes, black as Cain / May be refined and join the angelic strain"; but her heroic couplets march along in terms of such generality as to make them at most points indistinguishable from the conventional work of the day. Indeed her poem to George Washington, which concludes with the couplet "A crown, a mansion, and a throne that shine, / With gold unfading, WASHING-TON! be thine" shows how conventional language could betray an enthusiastic sensibility, how an ideology can inhere in imagery and form when they are not tested against the particulars of experience. Phillis Wheatley is a harbinger.

For particulars we turn to another Romantic precursor, glamourless George Crabbe, who, unlike Chatterton and Wheatley, survived well into the nineteenth century and, having influenced Wordsworth, lived to learn from him in turn. Wordsworth imitated him in *The Excursion* and Crabbe attempted Wordsworthian blank verse and explored his childhood (*Infancy, A Fragment,* 1816), though by then his best work was done. He very nearly attained the age of eighty. His remorseless vision of human nature and society makes Thomas Hardy seem almost cheerful. His poems chronicle the human condition—or predicament—mercilessly, like a sort of Suffolk Zola. His place in the genealogy of Romanticism is assured because of *how* he portrays that condition, and the landscapes through which his characters are led by their lives.

Hazlitt puzzled over his work. "Mr Crabbe's style might be cited as an answer to Audrey's question—'Is poetry a true thing?' There are here no ornaments, no flights of fancy, no illusions of sentiment, no tinsel of words. His song is one sad reality, one unraised, unvaried note of unavailing woe. Literal fidelity serves him in the place of invention; he assumes importance by a number of petty details; he rivets attention by being tedious." He continues, with a degree of wry appreciation: "The world is one vast infirmary; the hill of Parnassus is a penitentiary, of which our author is the overseer: to read him is a penance, yet we read on! Mr Crabbe, it must be confessed, is a reclusive writer. He continues to 'turn diseases to commodities,' and make a virtue of necessity." Then, again: "Mr Crabbe gives us one part of nature, the mean, the little, the disgusting, the distressing . . . He does this thoroughly and like a master, and we forgive him all the rest." We *do* read on; once we develop a taste for his characters, his world and its somber tonalities, we do forgive him.

Doctor Johnson was able to admire him, even against the grain of his natural prejudice against plain style. Crabbe kept more or less to the style he devised early *because* it was admired: approbation atrophied and to an extent impeded him. But he could describe nature (not Nature) at every stage of his work with a minuteness and inwardness that set him above Thomson: "Even Thomson describes not so much the naked object as what he sees in his mind's eye, surrounded and glowing with the mild, bland, genial vapours of his brain:—but the adept in Dutch interiors, hovels, and pig-styes must find in Mr Crabbe a man after his own heart." And indeed Crabbe, given his Suffolk, given the Dutch trade, is the most Dutch of English poets in terms of depiction, with a rich palette of dark colors, intoxicating variegations on a small scale, the humble, the apparently trivial. His sourness and misanthropy we make allowance for. "The situation of a country clergyman is not necessarily favourable to the cultivation of the Muse. He is set down, perhaps, as he thinks, in a small curacy for life, and he takes his revenge by imprisoning the reader's imagination in luckless verse." So he says, "Lo! the gay lights of Youth are past—are dead, / But what still deepening clouds of Care survive!" In the twilight of Augustanism Crabbe was doomed to tend a parish remote from the metropolitan heart. He commanded a large readership. Byron declared him "Though nature's sternest painter yet the best."

"A provincial Pope" or "Pope in worsted stockings" are accepted versions that rouse F. R. Leavis to an extravagant defense of a writer who combines novelistic virtues with those of a poet. He praises Crabbe's use of couplets in dialogue. They're not evidence of "awkward elegance clothing an incongruous matter": the couplet "represents, one might say, 'reason's self.' " Leavis goes further: "In the use of description, of nature, and the environment generally, for emotional purposes he surpasses any Romantic." Here he goes too far. Crabbe *is* a master storyteller, and it is more useful to see him in the poetic narrative tradition of Chaucer than in the novel tradition of his century. In "Peter Grimes," "Procrastination," "The Frank Courtship," "The Lover's Journey" and elsewhere, the verse connects individual and communal experience, the weathers of the heart and of the world, mental and physical landscapes. There is humor if not wit in some of the portrayals. His originality is dramatic and psychological, accomplished not by formal or stylistic invention but by conventional skills.

He was born in Aldeburgh, Suffolk, in 1755, son of a collector of salt duties. His background was not privileged. For his early schooling he went to Bungay and Stowmarket, Suffolk. When he was thirteen he was apprenticed to an apothecary and farmer for three years, then for another three to a surgeon-apothecary. He started writing poems. When he was seventeen he became engaged to Sarah Elmy, but did not marry for eleven years. At the age of twenty-one, after working briefly as a laborer, he set up as an apothecary and was appointed surgeon to the poor in Aldeburgh. *Inebriety,* a moral poem modeled on Pope, was his anonymous debut. At twenty-two he went to London to advance his medical training, returning again in 1780 with £5 in his pocket, to make his way as a writer. It was a struggle, and in the unsettled years there he witnessed the antipapist Gordon Riots. He secured Edmund Burke's patronage: Burke attempted to "civilize" or "Londonize" the poet but remodeled only the surface: Crabbe was not able to change his spots or willing to disguise his nature. *The Library,* another long poem in the manner of Pope, appeared. Burke introduced him to some of the great men of the day. He was ordained deacon and returned to Aldeburgh as curate in 1782. Shortly after, he was ordained priest and appointed chaplain to the Duke of Rutland at Belvoir Castle.

The Village, his first major work, appeared in 1783. Doctor Johnson read, corrected and praised it. It reveals a skilled poet with broadly social concerns and a documentary technique. It's no surprise that Henry Fielding was Crabbe's favorite novelist—a moralist teaching through laughter, his moral categories corresponding to psychological types. Crabbe is a literalist, a portrayer and interpreter rather than a visionary. He does not conceal rural ills "in tinsel trappings of poetic pride." His poetry is richer in social detail than Cowper's because his range of experience and human involvement was greater. A conservative when faced with needless change, he was radical in one respect: he showed what was, before suggesting what ought to be. What was being destroyed— by individuals and by political and commercial interests in the life of the community—was of greater value than what was replacing it. Social issues interested him less than social verities:

> . . . cast by fortune on a frowning coast,
> Which neither groves nor happy valleys boast;
> Where other cares than those the Muse relates,
> And other shepherds dwell with other mates;
> By such example taught, I paint the cot
> As Truth will paint it, and as Bards will not . . .

Of the poor he asks, "Can poets soothe you, when you pine for bread, / By winding myrtles round your ruined shed?" In the first book of *The Village* he expresses firmly, if repetitiously, a poetic commitment to which he remained true, by and large, in his later work. His craft improved, his concerns became more profound as they became more particular, but his orientation was constant. He can be "old fashioned" but seldom nostalgic.

In 1785 he became curate of Strathern, Leicestershire, was doctor to the poor of the parish, and studied botany and entomology, work useful in his later poetry. In 1789 he moved to the living of Muston, Leicestershire, where he stayed for three years before moving back to Suffolk; he kept the Muston living until 1814, returning in 1805, when laws against absentee clergy were passed. About 1790 he began taking opium on doctor's orders to control vertigo and continued the practice for the rest of his life, whose length and general health he attributed to the virtues of the "medicine." His wife's manic-depressive illness, the death of his third son and other troubles afflicted him. He went through a period of abortive activity, wrote and destroyed three novels, began work on *The*

Parish Register (1807) and *The Borough* (1810). In *The Parish Register* he found the voice that distinguishes his best work. In *The Borough* he went further, writing twenty-four "letter" poems about the life of a country town. The twenty-two-year gap in poetic publication was not time wasted. After so many false starts he found his pace and manner: *Tales* (1812), including twenty-one stories in various tones on various subjects, is his masterpiece.

After the death of his wife (1813) and with the growing success of his books, his remaining years were active but not fruitful. He met other writers, including Wordsworth (to whom Francis Jeffrey had preferred him in the *Edinburgh Review*), Southey and Scott. He traveled, he wrote further poems and tales, but even the once-popular *Tales of the Hall* (1819) is inferior to *Tales* (1812). In 1832 he died in Trowbridge. His son George was his excellent biographer, his account now unaccountably neglected.

Crabbe's final years were passed in a world remote from the one that had shaped his imagination. Leavis declares he was "hardly at the fine point of consciousness in his time." C. H. Sisson responded, "What an excellent thing not to have been! How many false hopes did this solid and pertinacious observer decline to share!" Thomson was the sort of poet who kept "at the fine point of consciousness" doggedly and forgettably. Crabbe's provincial conservatism no longer requires apology. The ills he recognized have worked themselves into human consequences that writers "at the fine point" fail to register. Crabbe was no prophet, but in Suffolk he could see before his eyes depopulation, enclosure, grinding poverty, corruption among the gentry and by the gentry of the poor, mental illness, breakdown in community, the triumph of Methodism (which ate into his own congregation). It was a world against which John Clare contended, at a different level. Crabbe was a witness, honest and uncompromised.

He was born in the same decade as Blake and Burns; his first writings appeared five years after the publication of Goldsmith's *The Deserted Village*; his verses were adjusted and blotted by Johnson; he met, influenced, and was influenced by Wordsworth; he survived Keats by eleven years. The only other English poet who provides so impressive a time bridge is Michael Drayton (1563–1631). Drayton remade his art with each change of fashion. Crabbe did not.

Novelists admired Crabbe. Jane Austen and E. M. Forster championed him. But the connection between his and a novelist's art is tenuous. The general scope of the *Tales* is novelistic but the individual scope of each tale is not. Each is different in manner and intention; they share a landscape, but that landscape alters from tale to tale. In the mature tales, morality is explored through plot, and in several it is less morality than psychology that interests him. The consequences of action are social or personal, in any event moral, tending to particular rather than general resolutions. In his compressed style, his affinity with Chaucer and his distance from the novelists of his time clearly emerges. Lovers pass through a landscape that smiles, each detail illuminating an aspect of their happiness; when love founders, they return through the same landscape as through another world, altered, frowning. Crabbe's precise correspondences are the essence of his originality. In "Procrastination," the objects with which people surround themselves define their characters; moral abstraction acquires physical weight:

> Within that fair apartment, guests might see
> The comforts culled for wealth by vanity:
> Around the room an Indian paper blazed,
> With lively tint and figures boldly raised;
> Silky and soft upon the floor below,
> Th' elastic carpet rose with crimson glow . . .

The objects blaze, rise, glow—animated, as in Keats's "The Eve of St Agnes"—while the inhabitants, surrounded by the spoils of empire, are almost inanimate. Most vivid is the timepiece above the heiress's head:

> A stag's-head crest adorned the pictured case,
> Through the pure crystal shone th' enamelled face;
> And while on brilliants moved the hands of steel,
> It click'd from prayer to prayer, from meal to meal.

The device in the final line recalls Pope, but the effect is purely Crabbe's. Elsewhere a hostess of the new breed (though "a pale old hag"—Crabbe does not mince words) "carves the meat, as if the flesh could feel." Such observation lays character bare. In one of the best poems in *The Borough*, "Peter Grimes," on which Benjamin Britten based his opera, changing seascapes figure the changes in the protagonist's troubled mind, without ever ceasing to correspond to the actual world. In a tale such as this, motive is always clear: Peter Grimes's cruelty to the boys he kills is his vicarious attempt to punish the waywardness of his own youth. His actions are not abstract sadism: they have a psychological source. Crabbe's is a poetry of consequences.

He did not achieve the best tales easily. He advanced from an early Popelike rigidity of narrative and description to a more relaxed, comprehensive manner. His concerns, at first documentary, became social and then individual—a movement toward character, but always from a firm apprehension of a given, common world. The moralizer becomes a moralist as the tales learn to contain, in a single statement, morality and psychology. Sequence gives way to careful parallelisms, and within a single tale verbal, syntactical and rhythmic repetitions prepare the way for climaxes, reversals and conclusions as in "Peter Grimes": "And hoped to find in some propitious hour / A feeling creature subject to his power," or, "He'd now the power he ever loved to show, / A feeling creature subject to his blow."

Crabbe's *Tales* are described by Howard Mills as a "mixture of inertia and originality." The language is at times off the peg. We do not look for purple passages or honed couplets. We look through, rather than at, the language, which is efficient, not flashy. We see a Suffolk world through its transparency, not heightened with Augustan decorum but very nearly literal in its drizzle, or dust, or simple twilight.

Killing Doctor Johnson

WILLIAM BLAKE

"I do not condemn Pope or Dryden because they did not understand imagination, but because they did not understand verse," says the peremptory William Blake. Robert Graves shares his impatience with the decorous couplet tradition from which Blake vigorously wriggled free. He praises Blake's early *Island in the Moon* (1784, composed when the poet was twenty-seven) as worth "a thousand prophetic books"; he quotes with relish the cruel lines on Doctor Johnson and the whole Augustan crew. "The prophetic robe with its woof of meekness and its warp of wrath was forced on [Blake] by loneliness and his modest station in life." Edward Thomas is more judicious: "In his youth, [Blake] had a gift of simple and fair speech; but he lost it. Although he could always catch the heavenly harmony of thoughts"—and here Thomas chooses to ignore the rigors Blake believed he had transcended—"he could seldom mount them on a fitting chariot of rhythm and rhyme. His fine passages were the direct gift of the Muse, and are followed by lines of other origin."

Blake is not often *judiciously* read. He polarizes readers, eliciting ecstatic enthusiasm from Allen Ginsberg and severe antipathy from poets repelled by the visionary and the Beats. Blake confuses poets—and readers. T. S. Eliot responds in a puzzling way. Speaking of Blake's honesty, a quality peculiar to great poets, he declares: "It is an honesty against which the whole world conspires, because it is unpleasant." Well, the *whole* world does not conspire against Blake. For more than half a century the world has seemed to take his side, parroted his aphorisms, adopted the simplifications with which he ridicules traditional discipline, scholarship and the fought-for (as against the asserted) truth. Blake's visionary poems have pumped up their muscles with steroids into a pulsing simulacrum of moral and spiritual health. If we accept their terms we can cast out whole centuries of art and literature and revel in the dubious freedoms of our unbridled century.

Blake's apprenticeship in a manual profession and his self-education, the fact that he was not lured into journalism or into the painting academy, secured his freedom. There was "nothing to distract him from his interests or to corrupt those interests," says Eliot. Nothing except the limitation of those interests themselves, scorn for a culture that bred a different kind of intelligence, a different—was it a lesser?—order of imagination. Eliot makes a sentimental case against formal education. He distrusts "the conformity which the accumulation of knowledge is apt to impose." He portrays learning in this context as corrupting, Blake as an innocent. He humors the tendentious naïf. In the *Songs of Innocence* and *Songs of Experience*, Eliot says, "The emotions are presented in an extremely simplified, abstract form. This form is one illustration of the eternal struggle of art against education, of the literary artist against the continuous deterioration of language." Equally curious is Eliot's claim: "He is very like Collins. He is very eighteenth century."

Eliot praises the early work and the first mature work but can't overcome his distrust of the excesses, the "automatic" writing of the later work. "We have the same respect for Blake's philosophy . . . that we have for an ingenious piece of home-made furniture: we admire the man who has put it together out of the odds and ends about the house." This condescension to a poet whose claims he is trying to advance sets the critic on a superior plane. He patronizes with the refinement of an education whose clutch he praises Blake for having eluded. There is more confusion to come. Blake is praised as a free spirit but also as a poet condemned in his freedom. "What his genius required, and what it sadly lacked, was a framework of accepted and traditional ideas which would have prevented him from indulging in a philosophy of his own, and concentrated his attention upon the problems of the poet." Eliot is eloquently off-beam, and this last point is the most telling. In the end Blake lacks concentration: without stable givens, each idea, each constituent intellectual and imaginative element has to be asserted, set down, before a poem can begin to move. When a musician abandons tonality, he finds his scope altered, but what seems a freedom *from* leads into drastically narrowed technical terrain. Eliot compares Blake implausibly with the luminous Friedrich Nietzsche of *Also Sprach Zarathustra*.

The visionary poet commences his career with electrifying clarity.

For Mercy has a human heart,
Pity, a human face:
And Love, the human form divine,
And Peace, the human dress.

This is the best of him, archpoet of embodiment who strives to bring abstractions before our eyes as manifest, just as he allows us to glimpse, all too fleetingly, the streets and green places of a London undergoing dramatic change, the London where he spent all but three years of his life.

He was born there in 1757, and there seventy years later he died. His father was a haberdasher. What formal education he received was in art: he became an engraver's apprentice and studied at the Royal Academy of Art. His graphic work is integral to his literary activity, and his literary activity invariably has spiritual dimensions, or pretensions. Even as a child he had visions. "Ezekiel sitting under a green bough" and—in Peckham—"a tree full of angels." These figures stayed with him. And he became a vision for later poets.

In America in the late 1940s Allen Ginsberg, interested in Supreme Reality, alone and suffering a "dark night of the soul sort of," his lover Neal Cassady having sloped off, and having himself just masturbated, with a volume of Blake before him—"I wasn't even reading, my eye was idling over the page of 'Ah, Sun-flower,' and it suddenly appeared—the poem I'd read a lot of times before." He began to understand the poem, and "suddenly, simultaneously with understanding it," he "heard a very deep earthen grave voice in the room, which I immediately assumed, I didn't think twice, was Blake's voice." This "apparitional voice" became his guiding spirit: "It was like God had a human voice, with all the infinite tenderness and anciency and mortal gravity of a living Creator speaking to his son." On Ginsberg this "anciency" fathered *Howl*, though the Blake simulacrum was aided by the hallucinogens popular at the time, the recipe for Part II of the poem including peyote, just as for *Kaddish* he was assisted by amphetamine injections. "The amphetamine gives a peculiar metaphysical tinge to things, also. Space-outs." Blake managed his visions without substance abuse. Ginsberg's appropriation of the poet of innocence and experience did much to promote Blake to the alternative culture of the 1950s and 1960s. This is not the Blake who visited William Butler Yeats and gave him—a canceled line—"a terrible beauty." For William Blake, as for Yeats, there were few serviceable shortcuts to wisdom. Spirits spoke to them, they did not doubt them for a moment; but they spoke to stimulate the spirit, not because the spirit had been pricked with a syringe or had swallowed a salad of grass.

The young Blake pursued his own passions in reading; he never followed a decorous Augustan curriculum. When he was twenty-four he married the illiterate Catherine Boucher, daughter of a market gardener. He taught her to read and she became his assistant in etching and binding. His first book was *Poetical Sketches* (1788). He etched, watercolored and bound most of his other books: *Songs of Innocence* and *The Book of Thel* (1789), *The Marriage of Heaven and Hell*, *The Gates of Paradise* and *Visions of the Daughters of Albion* (1793), *Europe* and *Songs of Experience* (1794) and *The Book of Ahania* (1795) and others. Later large ventures were *Milton* (1804–18) and *Jerusalem* (1804–1820).

At the suggestion of his painter friend John Flaxman, William Hayley invited Blake and his wife to Felpham on the Sussex coast in 1800. Hayley, the autobiographer and poet-biographer of Milton and Cowper, gave him three years' work as an illustrator. The arrangement went badly wrong. Hayley chose an artist of greater imaginative integrity than he had bargained for. He tried to bring Blake to heel artistically in various ways—after all, he was paying the bills—but Blake could not oblige for long. Whatever the Blakes eventually came to feel about Hayley, a friend of Cowper and Southey, they enjoyed Felpham and the sea: it was their one extended stay outside the metropolis. In 1803 an infamous soldier turned up in the Felpham garden and sealed their fate. The gardener asked the soldier to cut the grass. Blake disliked soldiers and ordered him off, cursing (among others) the king, and speaking of Napoleon in terms insufficiently hostile. When he was tried on a charge of high treason at Chichester in 1804, he was acquitted thanks to Hayley's testimony. Thus ended the Blakes' not entirely unhappy seaside idyll.

As poet-illustrator Blake was too startlingly original to attract many admirers at the time. The neglect of his poetry became virtual oblivion after his death in 1827, and only Alexander Gilchrist's *Life*, completed by his wife, Anne, and published two years after his death (1863), revived interest. (Anne wrote essays on Whitman's poetry, too: her ears were open to the new cadences.) Since the *Life* Blake's reputation has burgeoned.

In his last twenty-odd years, when he had occasional acolytes but no settled readership, intellectual isolation may have determined the development of his writing. F. R. Leavis remarks, "He had no public: he very early gave up publishing in any serious sense. One obvious consequence, or aspect, of this knowledge is the carelessness that is so apparent in the later prophetic books. Blake had ceased to be capable of taking enough trouble." This isn't quite right. Judging by the manuscripts, Blake took considerable trouble; but trouble of an odd sort; Leavis rightly points to "the absence . . . of adequate social collaboration." He's also right to say that Blake's "symbolic philosophy is one thing, his poetry another." The more pronounced the philosophy, especially in the prophetic books, the more opaque and poetically inert the symbolism. Blake's best poems work despite his symbolic philosophy.

Yet his genius produced that philosophy which hates the word "philosophy"; it generated what Leavis calls "a completely and uncompromisingly individual idiom and technique," rendering the poet "individual, original, and isolated enough to be without influence"—in his own age, in any case. This genius limited his large work. For all but the aficionado, Eliot's verdict on the prophetic books rings true: "You cannot create a very large poem without introducing a more impersonal point of view, or splitting it up into various personalities. But the weakness of the long poems is certainly not that they are too visionary, too remote from the world. It is that Blake did not see enough, became too much occupied with ideas." Eliot perceives in Blake a loss of cultural and philosophical bearings, an eccentricity that ends in solipsism. Crabbe, a lesser poet, is a better teacher, at least about the world we *actually* inhabit. Crabbe's ghost would never have strayed into Ginsberg's postmasturbatory reverie or answered the call of Dexedrine: he would have been in the street outside, doggedly observing the lives of passers-by.

Blake's prophetic and biblical pretensions are clear from his titles: "The Book of" this or that, and even "Songs," suggest Old Testament prophets and King David. Biblical reference, allusion and cadence inform his work even when he tilts at conventional religion. Disillusion schooled him. Like Wordsworth, he regrets the direction the French Revolution took. Between *Songs of Innocence* (1789) and *Songs of Experience* (1794) his social optimism faltered. Innocence speaks with a voice all transcendence, experience with a voice incapable of transcendence. Behind Blake's poems is an apprehended social reality; he is conscious of evils and injustices in the ways of man to man. When he approaches such themes directly, as in "London," he is among the first and fiercest poets of the modern city. In his prophetic books he translates perceived reality away from direct presentation, into a symbolism that sets out grandly to effect a process of regeneration. But the regeneration is itself symbolic: the actual world above which it hovers is perplexed but untouched by it. Blake, when he is "timeless," becomes oblique, a poet demanding exegesis. His earlier work possesses immediacy that the older Blake forfeits for a brocade of symbols.

From his earliest *Sketches*, he has his own tone and method. In rejecting "imitation" of form and perception he established his originality. "An Immitation of Spenser" is quite un-Spenserian. He experiments with an archaic mode, looking for a way out of the eighteenth century: "That wisdom may descend in faery dreams." The imitation fails because mythology and archaized language do not answer his needs. Eliot overstates the affinity between Blake and his eighteenth century. There are common epithets and strategies, but what is striking is Blake's original formal imagination and his freedom from conventional diction.

Imitation is the shadow of a shadow; art for Blake is *creation*. What the eye sees as real *is* real, whether simple rain cloud or the weeping child within the cloud. Blake's best poetry is a seeing and seeing into, with unconventional eyes. He does not describe, he projects. Man's divine part is his ability to create, a faculty Blake exercised for over half a century. He sees what is and what is implicit. He rejects prescribed forms as part and parcel of his rejection of social institutions. In *The Book of Thel* he declares that Wisdom cannot be contained or simplified in "a silver rod" nor Love in "a golden bowl," both ecclesiastical and sacramental allusions. The lines from *Thel* were originally included in *Tiriel*, a cry against the tyranny man imposes on man.

Remarkable among the early *Sketches* ("the production of untutored youth, commenced in his twelfth, and occasionally resumed by the author till his twentieth year") is "To Autumn." Here he proposes a collaborative relationship with Nature:

O Autumn, laden with fruit, and stained
With the blood of the grape, pass not, but sit
Beneath my shady roof, there thou may'st rest,
And tune thy jolly voice to my fresh pipe;
And all the daughters of the year shall dance!
Sing now the lusty song of fruits and flowers.

The conventional pastoral of a city boy becomes original poetry in the wonderfully paced second line. Autumn becomes a figure, walking, stained with autumnal juice. Is it sacrificial or Dionysian? The fifth line suggests the latter. The poem continues:

"The narrow bud opens her beauties to
The sun, and love runs in her thrilling veins;
Blossoms hang round the brows of morning, and
Flourish down the bright cheek of modest eve,
Till clust'ring Summer breaks forth into singing,
And feather'd clouds strew flowers round her head.

The spirits of the air live on the smells
Of fruit; and joy, with pinions light, roves round
The gardens, or sits singing in the trees."
Thus sang the jolly Autumn as he sat,
Then rose, girded himself, and o'er the bleak
Hills fled from our sight; but left his golden load.

Autumn sings through a young poet. Love, a substance flowing in the veins of flowers, is contained in imagery, not abstracted from it. Nature has an aspect: "brow," "cheek." The clouds are "feather'd" and active, strewing not rain but (the effect of rain on plants displaces the rain itself) flowers, and the "singing" of the line before turns clouds into birds. No simile is used: Blake evokes equivalences, connections, a natural wholeness. What in another poet would be abstraction in Blake breathes the air, though it would be impossible to paraphrase or draw a diagram of the scene. The images are visionary and transparent.

If the poem is conceptually impressive, prosodically it could hardly be more interesting. The enjambements throughout, but especially in the first line of the second stanza, dramatically affect ear and eye, enhancing the surprise of the vision. Other *Sketches* suffer from an excess of adjectives. Here adjectives pull their weight. Parallel syntax and rhythms from stanza to stanza produce the effect of rhyme, though the poem is unrhymed. There is "through rhythm" but no metrical regularity, despite the blank verse norm it plays away from.

Soon after completing the *Sketches*, Blake annotated Swedenborg's *Divine Love*. We love what contains us most, what is most human, a dog more than a wolf. The poet leads the reader to love, the end of the golden chain that leads to Eden. "Think," Blake writes, "of a white cloud as being holy, you cannot love it, but think of a holy man within the cloud, love springs up in your thoughts, for to think of holiness distinct from man is impossible to the affections. Thought alone can make monsters, but the affections cannot." Around this time he put a child in a cloud in the introduction to *Songs of Innocence*, a poem that recalls the procedure of "To Autumn." When the child in the cloud weeps, with pity rather than sorrow, we are a little disconcerted by such rain; and the cutting of the reed or pipe and the making of a pen are equally perplexing. The poet forfeits a measure of independence when he consents (it is consent, unlike the introduction to *Songs of Experience* with its imperative "Hear the voice of the Bard!") to write. In *The Marriage of Heaven and Hell* Blake says, "The Poet is Independent and Wicked; the Philosopher Dependent and Good." The poet should be his own law, creating the world in which he walks. For him the world is an extension of the senses; he proceeds from sense to vision. The grandest poetry, Blake says, is immoral, as are the greatest heroes: Iago, Satan, Christ "the wine bibber." When he set Milton in the devil's camp he was praising the poet who outshone the theologian, his Satan over his God.

Annotating Wordsworth, Blake gives further evidence of the process of his imagination. Physical objects, he says, are at variance with the imagination: objects do not exist apart from perception. When we adapt this statement to Blake's imagery, we resolve a problem. Many of his images are deflected from particularity into abstraction. In the opening of *The Marriage of Heaven and Hell*, however, his imaginative process is vividly demonstrated:

> Once meek, and in a perilous path,
> The just man kept his course along
> The vale of death.
> Roses are planted where thorns grow,
> And on the barren heath
> Sing the honey bees.

The first three lines are figurative, moral language; the three that follow are images. Figurative and particular correspond rhythmically; rhyme connects "vale of death" with "barren heath"; and parallelism connects the rose and the meek man, the honey bees and the just man. The images body forth the figurative language. Here Blake does not deflect image into abstraction: he segregates two registers of language, bodiless and embodying. His language enacts the division between heaven (the word) and hell (the substance). In the stanzas that follow he mingles and then resegregates registers in pursuit of the theme.

In his best work he avoids simile unless its point of reference is contained in the poem. For example, in "The Echoing Green" he writes in line twenty-six, "like birds in their nests," recalling "skylark and the thrush" earlier in the poem. He distrusts similes because they single out qualities—moral or otherwise—from a subject and the thing to which it is compared. Simile *disembodies* and is at variance with his vision. "The Sunflower" and "The Rose" are not referred back to human experience: they include it. Lamb and Tiger are not equated with Christ, though they include him.

Blake's allegiance to the plain language of the King James Bible, his innocence of eighteenth-century diction and convention, and his social vision made it possible for him to write balladic lyrics ("The Little Black Boy," "The Chimney Sweeper" and others) in an idiom more direct than Wordsworth's in his deliberate, studied ballads. The effortlessness of *Songs of Innocence* and *Songs of Experience* proceeds from a sensibility untroubled by decorum, and from a rhythmic tact that takes his poems directly to the pulse. They work at the deep level where "Lycidas," *The Song to David*, "Kubla Khan" and very few other poems reach us.

In both sequences subject matter is similar. Tone, emphasis and conclusions differ. Innocence does not understand beyond its innocence (though what is beyond hovers near, as in "A Blossom," "The Echoing Green," "The Chimney Sweeper"); experience is melancholy because it remembers but no longer possesses innocence. Yet in the experience poems positive powers are at work in the gloom, as in "Holy Thursday" and "The Lily."

Auguries of Innocence carries Blake's aphoristic wisdom to extremes in a couplet monotony unrelieved by effective enjambement. The couplets, separately, are striking paradoxes; taken together they detract from one another. The poem asks to be read as a polemical creed, with all that that implies of willful devising. There is none of the transparency of the *Songs*. No couplets were ever less Augustan, despite meter and paradox. The paradoxes are (intentionally) discontinuous.

Among the prophetic books, *The Book of Thel* is most poetically lucid. It too considers innocence and experience from an original perspective. The unborn soul foresees her life and looks back from her grave. She travels through various states of creative innocence, symbolized successively by lily, cloud, worm and clod. Each, with its limits, terrifies free unborn Thel. She rejects such life, unable to comprehend the "curb upon the youthful burning boy" and the "little curtain of flesh on the bed of our desire." But *The Book of Thel* is not satisfactory. It demands exegesis in terms of Blake's symbolic philosophy. So does *Urizen*, which enacts a process of reduction, from unlimited potential to human and natural bondage. "Like a human heart, struggling and beating, / The vast world of Urizen appeared"—but that world is by stages constrained, dwindling to the one-dimensional world of Ulro. Part of the concluding section is powerful and succinct:

> They lived a period of years;
> Then left a noisom body
> To the jaws of devouring darkness.

The giants themselves diminish, their progeny are pygmies—in short, philosophers:

> And their children wept, & built
> Tombs in the desolate places,
> And form'd laws of prudence and call'd them
> The eternal laws of God.

They became the creatures of "non-entity" frequently evoked, particularly in *Los*.

For Blake, liberty, a state of mind and spirit, entails the ability to create. His philosophy connects with this belief. There are four states of perception, the highest with four dimensions, in descending order: Eden, Beulah, Generation and Ulro. Four antitheses rule the development of the prophetic books: imagination and memory; innocence and experience in religion; liberty and tyranny in society; outline and imitation in art—each pair, as Northrop Frye notes, is a variation on the antithesis of life and death. Yet knowledge of Blake's scheme, or explication of figures, does not improve the poetry. If a poem lives on a primary level, knowledge and explication perfect understanding; without communication to the mind or senses, a poem becomes a game for exegetes.

Like the philosophies he rejects, his own philosophy obscures what was visible before and distorts the real. *Milton* opens with four of his best and best-known quatrains, sung by the Women's Institute and by the nation: "And did those feet in ancient times . . ." He urges "mental fight." Yet the prophetic chapters that follow are a poetic disappointment, quite apart from their philosophy. We feel the same disappointment in *Jerusalem*, despite electrifying lines, for example, "Trembling she wept over the space and closed it with a tender moon." The later prophetic books are scattered with such moments but undercut by a rhetorical and philosophical scheme that corresponds remotely to the world it would illuminate. Failure of clarity is a failure of thought. Did Blake despair of an audience and write to expand his own consciousness, or that of his friends the angels? These works have served the careers of many critics and scholars. "In a Commercial Nation impostors are abroad in every profession." They have answered to a number of modern causes because they will accommodate a variety of contradictory interpretations. "Thought alone can make monsters." Blake forgot that early wisdom.

Humble Truth

JAMES MACPHERSON, ROBERT BURNS

The achievement of the Scottish Chaucerians was almost out of memory when James Macpherson (1736–96), inventor of the Gaelic poet Ossian and the most successful forger in British poetry, burst on a jaded eighteenth-century world. The apparent energies of his translations seemed to mark a new beginning for a distinctly Scottish literature. Twenty-three years after his birth, and without his social or material advantages, a genuinely new force emerged, speaking and singing not in pseudo-Gaelic but in English and in the dialect of his part of Scotland. This poet lived hard and died poor at thirty-seven—the same year that Macpherson's remains were ceremoniously deposited, at his request, in Westminster Abbey.

Of the eighteenth-century poets, Robert Burns is most out of place. He belongs among the Romantics, not because they romanticized him but because he emancipated himself from Augustan language and decorum as decisively as Blake did, not by means of madness or through the agency of angels but by listening to the traditional songs and poems of common people and daring to write in their language. "By our own spirits are we deified," to follow Wordsworth a line further. He and his sister, Dorothy, visited Burns's last home and his grave in a spirit, to judge from Dorothy's letter, of tutting melancholy. The poet, only six years dead and as yet undeified, lacked a respectful headstone.

For Coleridge, Burns was "Nature's own belovèd bard," and "*always-natural* poet." Edward Thomas quotes a poem of his and says: "It is as near to the music as nonsense could be, and yet it is perfect sense." His poetry is a relief because he uses language according not to rules but to deeper laws. "Spirit and body are one in it—so sweet and free is the body and so well satisfied is the spirit to inhabit it." The poems "seem almost always to be the immediate fruit of a definite and particular occasion." They remain true to their occasions by remaining true to their speakers.

Burns was so successful (though he tasted few material fruits of his success) that for many he stands for the whole of Scottish poetry. With

Burns Nights to celebrate his memory each year in Scotland, Moscow
("That Man to Man the warld o'er, / Shall brothers be for a' that") and
Chicago, with a Burns industry that has (it is not his fault) cast a tar-
tan haze over the literature of his country, it's no surprise that Scottish
writers keen to revive their literature this century, after the abyss of the
nineteenth, should lay so many literary and cultural ills at his door. His
most vehement detractor is Hugh MacDiarmid. "The highest flights of
[Burns]—from any high European standard of poetry—may seem like
the lamentable efforts of a hen at soaring; no great name in literature
holds its place so completely from extra-literary causes as does that of
Robert Burns." It is true that Burns has been appropriated by the heri-
tage industry. He is sanitized, bowdlerized, sentimentalized. If we turn
away from this, and from MacDiarmid's corrective verdict, to the
poems, we do not need to reserve judgment. This is not the work of a
chicken Icarus:

> O wert thou in the cauld blast,
>   On yonder lea, on yonder lea,
> My plaidie to the angry airt
>   I'd shelter thee, I'd shelter thee.

Keats had a more complex view of Burns than Wordsworth did and
was more generous than MacDiarmid. In "On Visiting the Tomb of
Burns" he writes:

> All is cold Beauty; pain is never done
> For who has mind to relish, Minos-wise,
>   The Real of Beauty, free from that dead hue
>   Sickly imagination and sick pride
>   Cast wan upon it! Burns! With honour due
>   I oft have honour'd thee. Great shadow, hide
> Thy face; I sin against thy native skies.

Writing to Reynolds from Scotland Keats says, "One song of Burns is of
more worth to you than all I could think of for a whole year in his native
country. His Misery is a dead weight on the nimbleness of one's quill . . .
he talked with Bitches—he drank with blackguards, he was miserable.
We can see horribly clear in the works of such a Man his whole life,
as if we were God's spies." Yet neither misery nor joy characterizes
the work. He is sufficiently of his century to find more interest in man,
his foibles, his institutions, his ballads, than in mere personal revela-
tion or natural description. Byron, less drawn to the accidents of his
biography, valued the lucid pathos of the poet, and something more.

"What an antithetical mind!—tenderness, roughness—delicacy, coarseness—sentiment, sensuality—soaring and grovelling, dirt and deity—all mixed up in one compound of inspired clay!" Matthew Arnold in 1880 wrote a warm appreciation of his comic and satirical work, criticizing the sentimental poems. His assessment was crucial in the reappraisal of Burns's merits. The modernists—MacDiarmid excepted—generally ignored him.

There is a political version of Burns. Radicals English, Scottish and European have set up a bronze bust, emphasizing the anticlerical satires, the tilting against hypocrisy and rank, the "egalitarianism." Burns's life attracts them: it does little credit to the Scottish bourgeoisie and gentry. His sympathy for the American and French revolutions adds to his *usefulness*. His appeal in the Soviet Union was partly explained by this. In "Scots Wha Hae" he wrote:

By Oppression's woes and pains,
By your sons in servile chains,
We will drain our dearest veins,
    But they shall be free!

In more familiar manner he says, in "For a' that,"

Is there, for honest Poverty
        That hings his head, and a' that;
    The coward-slave, we pass him by,
        We dare be poor for a' that!
    For a' that, and a' that,
        Our toils obscure, and a' that,
    The rank is but the guinea's stamp,
        The man 's the gowd for a' that.   gold

The version of Burns that irked MacDiarmid, who led the Scottish renaissance with the cry "Not Burns—Dunbar!," was the one that read the poet in narrow chauvinistic terms. Scottish expatriates and nostalgic Scots at home championed him with what Arnold called "national partiality." And in MacDiarmid's view Burns's rural and ballad poetry in Scottish dialect set a disastrous example for a century of dialect poets who imitated what had become an outmoded idiom and subject matter, producing a linguistic and cultural caricature. Burns answers to each partial description and includes rather more than their sum. He wrote more than six hundred poems; his formal, tonal and thematic range is greater than that of his Scottish predecessors and of most of his English contemporaries.

He was born in Alloway, Ayrshire, in 1759, into the family of a tenant farmer, an event the poet later commemorated in "There was a lad was born in Kyle." The gossip in the poem predicts, "He'll be a credit till us a' "—and he'll have a lively future among the ladies (which he did). Burns's father and neighbors, though poor, had a respect for education and hired a tutor to see to their children's schooling. Later, the father himself undertook to teach them. At the age of fifteen, working on his father's farm, Burns wrote his first verses. His Latin was indifferent, but he was well-read in the English poets and understood French enough to read Racine. The Scots poetry of Allan Ramsay suggested to him the possibilities of dialect. Robert Fergusson's Scots verse proved the eventual catalyst: after reading it, Burns began his "demotic" career in earnest, but he was already that way inclined. At sixteen he wrote,

> O once I loved a bonnie lass,
>   An' aye I love her still,
> An whilst that virtue warms my breast
>   I'll love my handsome Nell.

Nell was Nelly Kirkpatrick, and he noted: "For my own part I never had the least thought or inclination of turning poet till I got once heartily in Love, and then Rhyme and Song were, in a manner, the spontaneous language of my heart." He had a native tradition and a native tongue. To Fergusson he addressed three poems, largely about that poet's (and perhaps his own) hardships and neglect: "Curse on ungrateful man, that can be pleas'd, / And yet can starve the author of the pleasure." Burns's English poems have merit, but pale beside the Scots writing. He knew this himself: "These English songs gravel me to death," he wrote. "I have not the command of the language that I have of my native tongue. In fact, I think that my ideas are more barren in English than in Scotch." His attempts to "translate" his poems were fruitless.

The key year in Burns's poetic career was 1786, when the Kilmarnock edition of *Poems Chiefly in the Scottish Dialect* was published. In the years before the poet watched his father's death in 1784, a year after his bankruptcy. Burns was now provider and head of the family. His mother's servant, Betty Paton, gave him his first child out of wedlock in 1785, a daughter.

> Tho' now they ca' me fornicator,
>   And tease my name in kintra clatter,   country gossip
>   The mair they talk, I'm kend the better;
>   E'en let them clash!

> An auld wife's tongue's a feckless matter   worthless
>   To gie ane fash.   trouble

He also composed "The Fornicator. A New Song." "The rantin dog the
Daddie o't" is a song put in the mouth of Betty. Throughout his work we
find songs of a sexual frankness and jollity as outspoken as some of the
poems of the Restoration, and yet a good deal more down-to-earth than
those. Eighteenth-century Scotland was an unlikely environment for
them.

   In 1785 Burns met Jean Armour, whom he married in 1788 after
she had borne him two sets of twins. His brilliant satirical attacks on
Calvinism begin at the time of her pregnancy. In the same month in
which *Poems* was published the Calvinists took revenge and exacted
from him a public penance for fornication with Jean. He was tempted
to emigrate with another girl, composing poems about his planned
departure. The gossips were right; he had a complicated and thorough
love life.

   Poems proved a success; the next year a second, enlarged edition was
published. Both versions omitted the church satires and included
instead more general satirical pieces. Apart from the church satires, the
Poems contain the core of his original work. Most of it was composed in
1785 and early 1786—a remarkable production, including "To a Moun-
tain Daisy," "Halloween," "The Address to the Deil," "To a Mouse," "To
a Louse," "The Cottar's Saturday Night," the best epistles, "The Twa
Dogs" and many others: satires, pious pieces, dramatic monologues,
mock elegies, songs, lyrics and flytings. The poet was twenty-six. Four
years later he wrote "Tam O'Shanter," completing his important origi-
nal work. He wrote more poems, but his chief labor thereafter was to
collect and publish Scottish folk songs and ballads.

   Literary Edinburgh took him up—no doubt as one who "walked in
glory and in joy / Behind his plough," a role he found it hard to sustain
without big doses of alcohol and the camaraderie of low types. As a
result, literary Edinburgh in general put him down again. Sir Walter
Scott as a boy of fifteen saw the poet and recalled his "manners rustic,
not clownish," his "massive" countenance, his shrewd look: "The eye
alone indicated the poetical character and temperament. It was large,
and of a dark cast, and literally glowed when he spoke with feeling and
interest." Lord Glencairn and Mrs. Dunlop became his patrons and
friends. His admirers secured him a post in the Excise Division in
Dumfries and rented a farm for him. He worked hard, investing his
imaginative energy in collecting and revising material for *The Scots
Material Museum* (1787–1803) and the *Select Collection of Original Scottish
Airs* (1793–1818). He traveled, gave up farming, was promoted in the

Excise Division. His work took him out in all weathers. He caught rheumatic fever and died in 1796, leaving a wife and a large progeny. Jean was not his only current love. There were Betty, Mary Campbell, Mrs. McLehose ("Clarinda") and others.

Perhaps he died bitter. Though he had friends and advocates, he'd certainly been ill-used. He had foibles, could be curmudgeonly and difficult, held firm and outspoken opinions, did not suffer fools. But he scarcely deserved the hardships that befell him, or the hostility. Carlyle in his essay gets the proportions right: "Granted the ship comes into harbour with shrouds and tackle damaged, the pilot is blameworthy ... but to know how blameworthy, tell us first whether his voyage has been round the globe or only to Ramsgate and the Isle of Dogs."

Burns's place in Scottish culture is very different from his place in English. Debts to the Augustans are few: the polite tradition of Edinburgh, with few exceptions, was an echo of Dryden and Pope, a world of fixed rules of diction and form. We can see him in connection with English Romanticism. But as Donald Davie reminds us, he was "adopted posthumously." In reading Wordsworth's and Keats's tributes, do we recognize any but a simulacrum of Burns? Only Byron—another Scot "mad, bad and dangerous to know"—heard him more or less clearly. F. R. Leavis goes too far when he suggests Burns "counts for much in the emancipation represented by the *Lyrical Ballads*." He counts for something: a comparison between Burns's and Wordsworth's ballads reveals how much and also how little. Arnold precedes Leavis when he writes, "Wordsworth owed much to Burns, relying for effect solely on the weight and force of that which with entire fidelity he utters. Burns could show him." Wordsworth's "At the Grave of Burns" and other poems written on Burns and about his neighborhood borrow one of the Scottish poet's forms, but not his energy. Wordsworth records a debt:

> He has gone
> Whose light I hailed when first it shone,
> And showed my youth
> How verse may build a princely throne
> On humble truth.

A pious moral more than a poetic lesson learned. Burns might have grimaced at such sanctimony.

Arnold stripped away some of the sentimental gloss: "Let us coldly say that of much of this poetry, a poetry dealing perpetually with Scotch drink, Scotch religion, and Scotch manners, a Scotchman's estimate is bound to be personal." Burns's world is "often a harsh, a sordid, a repulsive world"—part of its attraction and also its limitation. Much of the bacchanalian verse is "poetically unsound," vitiated by a factitious bravado, written in reaction, to shock and amuse, but not to extend or interpret experience. He often lacks "the high seriousness which comes from absolute sincerity" (which is just as well). One feels this in the poems about fornication and those about drink: defiance in verse is rare, especially difficult to achieve when the poet defies an audience without questioning his own position. Yet there is a great poet in Burns: Arnold compares him to Chaucer: "Of life and the world, as they came before him, his view is large, free, shrewd, benignant—truly poetic, therefore; and his manner of rendering what he sees is to match." Unlike Chaucer, he has "a fiery, reckless energy" and "an overwhelming sense of the pathos of things." After all, his great poems were written when he was a young man.

Arnold directs attention to a poem central to Burns, but until then generally neglected, "The Jolly Beggars." It has "hideousness," "squalor," "bestiality"—"yet the piece is a superb poetic success. It has a breadth, truth, and power which . . . are only matched by Shakespeare and Aristophanes." Other good poems possess "archness and wit" as well as "shrewdness." These include "Duncan Grey," "Tam Glen," "Whistle, and I'll come to you my lad," "Auld Lang Syne"—and, no doubt, "A Red, Red Rose," "Green Grow the Rushes," "The Banks o' Doon" and a score of others.

After reading a lot of Burns, we reluctantly agree with Gerard Manley Hopkins, who wrote in a letter to Robert Bridges of "a great want" in his utterance. Hopkins defined this a little imprecisely: "He had no eye for pure beauty," a lack he shares with another poet equally versatile: Dunbar. There is little repose in Burns. The closest he comes to it is in a few lyrics and the epistles, where he addresses one or two and speaks with the candor Arnold described in his essay. In "Epistle to Davie, a Brother Poet" Burns confesses how sour he is about his own wants, and the unequal distribution of wealth (it is no wonder that he was immensely popular in the old Soviet Union: he was easy to politicize). But he finds consolation in the open air:

What tho', like Commoners of air,
We wander out, we know not where,
     But either house or hal'?
Yet *Nature's* charms, the hills and woods,
The sweeping vales, the foaming floods,
     Are free alike to all.
In days when daisies deck the ground,
     And blackbirds whistle clear,
With honest joy, our hearts will bound,

To see the *coming* year:
    On braes when we please then,
        We'll sit and *sowth* a tune;   to try a tune with a
    Syne *rhyme* till 't, we'll time till 't,   low whistle
        And sing 't when we hae done.

Liberty Versus Legitimacy

WILLIAM WORDSWORTH, DOROTHY WORDSWORTH,
SAMUEL TAYLOR COLERIDGE

In Burns, William Wordsworth admired what seemed to him the spontaneity and the sense of a common life to which he aspired. What is second nature to Burns is cultivated by Wordsworth. His wholeness of vision is deliberated. In the old poet it evolves into a kind of rueful dogma. When real emotion intrudes, as in the "Lucy" poems lamenting the loss of an innocent and of innocence, his visual imagination blurs as if with tears; he resorts to conventional tropes. The poems are popular because they are moving; yet are they not also moving because they are sentimental?

The trajectory of Wordsworth's work in the nineteenth century is like T. S. Eliot's in the twentieth. He shakes the age awake with a freshness of language and vision, then changes tack; it is as though Moses led his tribe out of the eighteenth century and then turned around and tried to go back again. Tinkering with his early poems to make them more correct, writing verses of reaction and recantation, he does what Eliot does in the later essays and in *Four Quartets*. He abandons a new faith to embrace the old. It is no longer serviceable. He settles into a winter of "long and piteous complacency" beside an ecclesiastical Tory hearth. Hazlitt considered his later philosophic works "a departure from, a dereliction of his first principles." Readers can choose among his several phases, but it is hard for the lover of the young Wordsworth to love the old. Hazlitt declares: "Liberty (the philosopher's and the poet's bride) had fallen a victim, meanwhile, to the murderous practices of the hag, Legitimacy. Proscribed by court-hirelings, too romantic for the herd of vulgar politicians, our enthusiast stood at bay, and at last turned on the pivot of a subtle casuistry to the *unclean side*: but his discursive reason would not let him trammel himself into a poet-laureate or stamp-distributor, and he stopped, ere he had quite passed that well-known 'bourne from which no traveller returns'—and so has sunk into torpid, uneasy repose, tantalised by useless resources, haunted by vain imaginings, his lips idly moving, but his heart for ever still, or, as the shattered chords vibrate of themselves, making melancholy music to the ear of memory!" Hazlitt's vehemence is that of a man disappointed in a great enthusiasm and hope.

He remembers his first visit to Alfoxden, just after the French Revolution, a time when "the mind opened, and a softness might be perceived coming over the heart of individuals, beneath 'the scales that fence' our self-interest." Wordsworth is more succinct: "Bliss was it in that dawn to be alive . . ." Hazlitt recalls that "Wordsworth himself was from home, but his sister kept house, and set before us a frugal repast; and we had free access to her brother's poems, the *Lyrical Ballads*, which were still in manuscript, or in the form of *Sybilline Leaves*. I dipped into a few of these with great satisfaction, and with the faith of a novice. I slept that night in an old room with blue hangings, and covered with the round-faced family-portraits of the age of George I, and II, and from the wooded declivity of the adjoining park that overlooked my window, at the dawn of day, could '—hear the loud stag speak.' " The novitiate was neither brief nor casual. Hazlitt grew close to Wordsworth, Coleridge and their circle, he witnessed their estrangements, how friendship turned to formal acquaintance, intimacy to legend. On first meeting, Wordsworth seemed to him "gaunt and Don Quixote–like. He was quaintly dressed (according to the *costume* of that unconstrained period) in a brown fustian jacket and striped pantaloons. There was something of a roll, a lounge in his gait, not unlike his own Peter Bell. There was a severe, worn pressure of thought about his temples, a fire in his eye (as if he saw something in objects more than the outward appearance), an intense high narrow forehead, a Roman nose, cheeks furrowed by strong purpose and feeling, and a convulsive inclination to laughter about the mouth, a good deal at variance with the solemn, stately expression of the rest of his face . . . He sat down and talked very naturally and freely, with a mixture of clear gushing accents in his voice, a deep guttural intonation, and a strong tincture of the northern *burr*, like the crust on wine." His native Northumberland did not leave his voice.

Even at this period, in dress as in his contradictory manner and inflection, he is not quite in focus. There remained something incomplete about him, as about his radicalism: he always left a road open to the past. Robert Graves says he "even deigned to apostrophise a spade. He had been lending a hand in a neighbour's potato patch; but though he called a spade a spade he could not bring himself to call a labourer a labourer, or a potato patch a potato patch. The title is: 'To the Spade of a Friend (an agriculturist). Composed while we were labouring together in his Pleasure Ground.' " Burns had touched (albeit intensely) only the tips of his nerves. Hazlitt says "his poetry is founded on setting up an opposition (and pushing it to the utmost length) between the natural and the artificial; between the spirit of humanity, and the spirit of fashion and of the world." He explains the political impulses behind this innovation: "The political changes of the day were the model on which he formed and conducted his poetical experiments . . . His Muse . . . is a levelling one."

So Wordsworth's last four decades were an aftermath: he wrote copiously and competently, but in the main dully. When he was seventy-three he became poet laureate. "Daddy Wordsworth," the translator and poet Edward Fitzgerald called him. Rossetti's quip was, "Good, you know, but unbearable." For Tennyson he was (metaphorically) "thick-ankled." The poems that confronted the prejudices of his age and challenge, even as they provide, some of the prejudices of ours, were for the most part written before 1807. Then he began to recognize a paralyzing truth with which his direct plainspeaking verse could not readily deal. "The deeper malady is better hid, / *The world is poisoned at the heart.*"

He came into the world "trailing clouds of glory" but with a hint of the winter that would overtake him, in the year of Chatterton's death, 1770, at Cockermouth in Cumberland. His beloved sister, Dorothy, was born the next year. By the time he was thirteen he was an orphan. His feeling of isolation stemmed in part from the loss of his parents: the family is for him a recurring image of stability, security and continuity. Also, of a special kind of sadness.

Educated at Hawkshead Grammar School, he began writing verse half in, half out of the manner of Pope. At the age of sixteen he composed the lines

> Calm is all nature as a resting wheel.
> The kine are couched upon the dewy grass;
> The horse alone, seen dimly as I pass,
> Is cropping audibly his later meal.

The first two lines are literary, the latter literal. Within a conventional apprentice piece, the original mind of Wordsworth is at work on perceived nature. The poem, about memory and the image of home, isolation, and resentment at the officious care some people lavished on him, hints at themes he would explore exhaustively later.

At St. John's College, Cambridge, he failed to distinguish himself. In 1790 he went to France and Italy, crossing the Alps on foot. The next year he returned to France and became involved with the revolutionary movement and with Annette Vallon, a Frenchwoman who bore him a daughter. He did not marry her and an unattested remorse followed from this as from the defeat of his political idealism.

His first interesting published poems appeared in 1793. "An Evening Walk" and "Descriptive Sketches" relate to some of his experiences on the Continent. The first, in couplet form, is full of Augustan abstractions and observed physical detail, with little connection between the two levels of language and perception: he renders sight and thought, not integrated vision. "Descriptive Sketches" includes excellent writing and he used it when he came to write "Cambridge and the Alps" in *The Prelude*. His politics are eloquent, but born of thought rather than observation:

> Once, Man entirely free, alone and wild,
> Was blest as free—for he was Nature's child,
> He, all superior but his God disdained,
> Walked none restraining, and by none restrained:
> Confessed no law but what his reason taught,
> Did all he wished, and wished but what he ought.

The optimistic ideology of the time identified the reasonable—hence noble—savage, the natural man. The French Revolution declined into the Terror and its aftermath. Wordsworth's enthusiasm died. He wrote *The Borderers* (1795–96), an unperformable Shakespearean tragedy replete with a rational anarchism borrowed from William Godwin, and the poem "The Convict," in anapestic measure, in which he examined the physical and emotional nature of a man isolated and in fear.

Wordsworth met Coleridge in 1795. They became neighbors in Somerset and collaborated on *Lyrical Ballads* (1798). They traveled to the Continent and Wordsworth and Dorothy spent the winter together in Goslar, Germany. The poems written in Goslar are among his best. A winter landscape, the encouraging presence of his loving sister, the recent memory of his conversations with Coleridge, which clarified his own poetic processes: such factors brought him to maturity. The poems are personal and include the first book and other passages of *The Prelude* (written at Coleridge's suggestion), "Nutting" and the "Lucy" poems. The verses composed in Somerset still bear—apart from the magnificent "Lines Written Above Tintern Abbey"—eighteenth-century affinities. The Goslar poems belong to the nineteenth, to his own voice. In the "Lucy" poems he struck briefly a tone and manner that he never repeated and that none of his imitators or disciples, not even Arnold, approached, try as they might. It is not possible to relate the poems to specific incidents or a specific person, despite the theories that have been advanced. The loved and lamented one may be emblematic. The physicality of the devotion and the sense of loss, the mysterious courtship and hinted characterization, and most poignantly the vision of death, bring these poems closer to ballads than the *literary* ballads Wordsworth had composed before.

In 1799 he moved with Dorothy to Grasmere in Cumberland, where he spent most of his remaining years. He wrote his rustic short epic of hope and isolation, "Michael," in 1800. A new, enlarged edition of *Lyrical Ballads*, including the brilliant and provocative "Observations," appeared in the same year. Later he added his note on "Poetic Diction." From this period date some of the best sonnets. Like Milton, whom he invokes in "Milton! thou should'st be living at this hour," he uses the form most effectively for civic subjects: a call to arms, an exhortation, a concise statement of principle, a broad observation. His best-known sonnet, "Upon Westminster Bridge," is a love poem addressed to a city.

He married Mary Hutchinson in 1802, much to Dorothy's discomfiture. Hazlitt found Dorothy, herself a remarkable diarist and an unremarkable poet, distressing to watch. "Her eyes were not soft, as Mrs. Wordsworth's, nor were they fierce or bold; but they were wild and startling." Deep she seemed, but with a depth Hazlitt found repellent, as he did the monomania of her devotion to William.

Loss—his brother's death, Coleridge's physical decline, Dorothy's troubles, political developments in France—sobered him. The first version of *The Prelude* was completed in 1805. It was not published in his lifetime but in 1850, the year of his death, by which time he had altered it significantly, not always for the better. The year 1807 marks—with the publication of "Intimations of Immortality," "Miscellaneous Sonnets" and "Sonnets Dedicated to Liberty"—the end of Wordsworth's most fruitful time.

He wrote on—and on—however, freed by a sinecure of £400 per annum. He traveled. In 1814 *The Excursion* appeared. It incorporated "The Story of Margaret" ("The Ruined Cottage"), his first major attempt at blank verse, which so impressed Coleridge in 1797. *The Excursion* is a poem in nine books. *The Prelude* was to lead into it; and it was to be succeeded by a third extended poem, the three under the general title *The Recluse*. Coleridge helped him map it out as a philosophical poem about man, nature and society, recounting in *Table Talk* his precise advice on the structure. "I think Wordsworth possessed more of the genius of a great philosophic poet than any man I ever knew, or, as I believe, has existed in England since Milton; but it seems to me that he ought never to have abandoned the contemplative position which is peculiarly—perhaps I might say exclusively—fitted for him. His proper title is *Spectator ab extra*." He returns to this theme, comparing

Wordsworth and the great German poet Goethe in their "peculiarity of utter non-sympathy with the subjects of their poetry. They are always, both of them . . . feeling *for*, never *with*, their characters."

But Wordsworth was not Coleridge's kind of philosopher. Coleridge—who helped his friend in many ways toward his best verse—bears some responsibility for giving Wordsworth a distorted sense of his gift. Hazlitt shows no mercy: "Mr Wordsworth's mind is obtuse, except as it is the organ and the receptacle of accumulated feelings; it is not analytic, but synthetic; it is reflecting, rather than theoretical." More specifically, "The personages, for the most part, were low, the fare rustic: the plan raised expectations which were not fulfilled, and the effect was like being ushered into a stately hall and invited to sit down to a splendid banquet in the company of clowns, and with nothing but successive courses of apple-dumplings served up. It was not even *toujours perdrix*!"

According to Wordsworth, *The Recluse* was to have "for its principle subject the sensations and opinions of a poet living in retirement." The sensations were within his range, the opinions were less distinguished and less readily accommodated. In *The Prelude*, ideas rise out of experience; in *The Excursion* they are applied to it. *The Excursion* depends on a flimsy narrative. It tries to develop extended debates on religious faith. A pastor illustrates the effects of faith by adducing examples from the people planted in his churchyard. This is not the epitomizing spirit of Gray but the expansive moralizing of Gower. The poet draws general conclusions; the final books reflect on social themes, particularly the Industrial Revolution, its effect on the poorer classes, and the need for proper educational institutions for the children of the poor. An enormous essay, civically admirable, the verse never quite delivers the sense of right truth that we get from Pope, or from Crabbe.

Other poems take plots from legend and classical mythology. Wordsworth became enslaved to narrative and argument. A few early poems appeared in later years, "Peter Bell" (1798) and "The Waggoner" (1805) as late as 1817. But they feel out of place, their freshness dulled by context. Of the later poems, "Yarrow Revisited" is among the best, an occasional piece that draws on the experience of two earlier poems. But it is slight compared with what came before. His conversion in his later years was complete. A young radical became a tetchy foe of liberalism. Edmund Burke, the incomparably eloquent Tory, became a hero. The author of *The Prelude* composed *Ecclesiastical Sonnets*; the pensive solitary became a comfortable talker.

Coleridge kept faith with the Wordsworth he valued, the pre-*Excursion* poet. The earlier poems reveal, he says, a "union of deep feeling with profound thought, the fine balance of truth in observing, with the imaginative faculty in modifying, the objects observed; and above all

the original gift"—he shares it with Spenser and Milton, incidentally—
"of spreading the tone, the atmosphere, and with it the depth and height
of the ideal world around forms, incidents, and situations, of which,
for the common view, custom had bedimmed all the lustre, had dried up
the sparkle and the dew drops." We quarrel with the word "ideal"; it
introduces a Coleridgean distortion. Otherwise the account is hard to
better.

Wordsworth develops his concerns simply. Nature was a first pas-
sion. He became a radical enthusiast with a social vision that the French
Revolution seemed to realize but, as it happened, betrayed. From the
brotherhood of man he turned to particular men, solitaries in known
landscapes, and the expression of nature in relation to these men, the
correspondence between a given world and the inner life—a synthesis
of his earlier concerns. His development through the three phases
occurred over a decade. After 1807 religious faith overcame him and was
either the cause or effect of his loss of imaginative certainty. Adjusting
to orthodoxy, he was no longer a discoverer.

A poem such as "Resolution and Independence" in its very title
records a debt to the eighteenth century, the age of Johnson, of moral
and psychological categories. Wordsworth's poetry remains normative,
not aberrant or extreme. He portrays extremity only to celebrate survival
and endurance. Even the relative absence of "poetic diction" in *Lyrical
Ballads* is a radical response to conventions of the eighteenth century,
deliberate strategy, not originality in the spirit of Burns, Blake or Smart.
The title *Lyrical Ballads* announces to readers with Augustan expecta-
tions that distinct genres, lyric and ballad, were to be fused, in disregard
of the rules.

"Ballad" misleads readers as to Wordsworth's attitude to the lan-
guage of poetry. "Ballad" suggests "popular" verse in a popular idiom.
But "We Are Seven" was the only *Lyrical Ballad* published as a broad-
sheet. None has an especially dramatic narrative line. Narrative of action
was never one of his special talents. His language avoids off-the-peg
diction; it is a language men might *speak*—they would hardly be likely
to sing it. The poems address not the vulgar audience to which Burns
appeals but the audience that read Crabbe and Cowper, the audience
whose language Wordsworth, with a Cumberland accent, actually spoke.
In *Lyrical Ballads* only Coleridge's "The Ancient Mariner" achieves
consistent balladic effects.

Wordsworth set down his intentions in the famous preface to the
1805 edition. Against the "gaudiness and inane phraseology of many
modern writers," he proposed "to choose incidents and situations from
common life, and to relate or describe them . . . in a selection of lan-
guage really used by men." He does not mean pseudo-rustic, but natu-

ral language without decoration or conventional formulas. "A selection of language" precisely defines "diction." He chooses an alternative diction, but diction nonetheless. It may approximate at times to the language of unaffected countrymen, "because such men hourly communicate with the best objects from which the best part of language is originally derived," but he "purified" it of defects repugnant to reason. Arnold called it (approvingly) writing *without* style. For Wordsworth "voice" is the language people really use, something they share, not—as it has become—something specific to an individual, identifiable from the "voice-print" of distinctive or eccentric usage. He would have had little truck with Hopkins, none at all with Sylvia Plath.

Beyond his poetic aims he had a philosophical and psychological purpose: to trace through incidents and situations "the primary laws of our nature: chiefly as far as regards the manner in which we associate ideas in a state of excitement." The terms derive from his reading of the philosopher David Hartley, who refuted the idea of innate moral instincts and proposed theories of association and inference.

Wordsworth speaks to and of men. His solitaries achieve dignity in spite of suffering and loss, especially in "Michael" and "The Old Cumberland Beggar." Their suffering is a part of them, much as they are a part of the landscape in which they move. He best delineates character when he concentrates on aftermath. If he seems to dwell, to the point of relishing, on the suffering of others, he is drawn to it as a purifying force, a force that isolates and defines essential integrity.

In the "Preface" he formulates his view of the poetic process. "I have said that poetry is the spontaneous overflow of powerful feelings; it takes its origin from emotion recollected in tranquillity; the emotion is contemplated till by a species of reaction the tranquillity gradually disappears, and an emotion, kindred to that which was before the subject of contemplation, is gradually produced and does itself actually exist in the mind. In this mood successful composition generally begins." It is the least understood of Wordsworth's statements. He does not say that poetry is "emotion recollected in tranquillity": that is the point of departure. Poetry re-creates primary experience. "I wandered lonely as a cloud" (1804) reads almost as a paradigm of this belief.

The two versions (1805, 1850) of *The Prelude*, Wordsworth's most remarkable work, differ. The old poet strengthened weak phrases, drew texture in more tightly, omitted some of the interjections, changed to transitive verbs many "to be" constructions. He subtly altered emphases, making the poem more literary. There is thematic change too. He plays down his early radicalism, his antagonism to Cambridge; he blames himself for his French enthusiasms; he adds fine passages, among them a tribute to Burke. Nature he regards more meekly, God becomes an orthodox figure. "Feeling"—essential in the early version—becomes contemplative, "observing," "pondering." For all the "literary" gains, there is a loss of immediacy.

The thirteen books (fourteen in 1850) of *The Prelude* trace the "Growth of a Poet's Mind" in Hartleyan terms, from first consciousness to his disappointment with the French Revolution and his return to nature in an altered mind. The poem is dedicated to Coleridge and in its direct address has at times the candor of a verse epistle, directed to a single recipient, not a wide audience. We seem to overhear. He deploys blank verse with such freedom and spoken assurance that it is hard to decide whether to call it iambic pentameter or quantitative measure. *The Prelude* is philosophical rather than visionary. Wordsworth's literal imagination required that he establish scene or incident before he could release a meaning. Blake is consistently visionary, while for Wordsworth there are "in our existence spots of time / Which with distinct pre-eminence retain / A vivifying virtue." He requires a "real solid world / Of images." His imagination was for the most part "Subservient strictly to the external things / With which it communed." Nature, as we learn from the Tintern Abbey poem, he went to first "more like a man / Flying from something that he dreads than one / Who sought the thing he loved." The first books of *The Prelude* provide a fuller account. Nature becomes a force with which the isolated imagination is attuned:

> For I, methought, while the sweet breath of Heaven
> Was blowing on my body, felt within
> A corresponding mild creative breeze,
> A vital breeze which travelled gently on
> O'er things which it had made, and is become
> A tempest, a redundant energy
> Vexing its own creation.

Such energy *must* issue in creation.

Fear (danger) and beauty (desire) are fundamental; he exposes them in various incidents: when he waits for the horses, or sees a gibbet, or rows out on Lake Windermere; when he violates a copse. If he responds to nature destructively he *feels* footsteps following, or the mountain itself in pursuit. This is part of the reciprocity with nature which formed his imagination, the loss of which depleted his poetry. In Book Three the dissociation from nature begins. Cambridge, that *multum in parvo* of so much that repelled him, quickened his temporary alienation. But in Book Four, above Hawkshead, his consecration to poetry occurs: he triumphantly regains his sense of nature. "I made no vows, but vows / Were then made for me." He begins to observe the inhabitants of the landscape, the old soldier for example: "a desolation, a simplicity."

In Book Five he considers liberalism and education. Formal teaching renders youth intellectually precocious but unfeeling. He recalls himself as a boy hooting on the banks of Windermere, answered by terrifying silence. In Book Six the Winander boy, now an adult, crosses the Alps on foot and experiences definitively the permanent forms and the transitory content of nature. The heart of his vision: it is one of the most electrifying moments in English verse, not so much for what it sees as for the way in which the syntax carries the cadence deeper and deeper into the reader's pulse:

> The immeasurable height
> Of woods decaying, never to be decayed,
> The stationary blasts of water-falls,
> And every where along the hollow rent
> Winds thwarting winds, bewildered and forlorn,
> The torrents shooting from the clear blue sky,
> The rocks that muttered close upon our ears,
> Black drizzling crags that spake by the way-side
> As if a voice were in them, the sick sight
> And giddy prospect of the raving stream,
> The unfettered clouds, and region of the heavens,
> Tumult and peace, the darkness and the light
> Were all like workings of one mind, the features
> Of the same face, blossoms upon one tree,
> Characters of the great Apocalypse,
> The types and symbols of Eternity,
> Of first and last, and midst, and without end.

Against this amazing insight with its liturgically charged climax, Book Seven, an external portrayal of the city and its corrupting powers, seems thin, a conventional contrast with what has come before. Wordsworth is seldom poetically comfortable when he goes to town. After the "Retrospect" in Book Eight, Books Nine and Ten take us to France, and Eleven and Twelve describe how reason impaired his natural sympathies and instincts. He became in his French enthusiasms more a foe of falsehood than a friend of truth. But on his return those "spots of time" from the past renew their "vivifying virtue." His imagination is restored. In the moonlit landscape, the last book confirms this recovery:

> A meditation rose in me that night
> Upon the lonely Mountain when the scene

Had passed away, and it appeared to me
The perfect image of a mighty Mind,
Of one that feeds upon infinity,
That is exalted by an underpresence,
The sense of God, or whatso'er is dim
Or vast in its own being . . .

Often epiphanies occur when, from a great height, he surveys the world before him, and from what he sees or surmises flows a meaning he *feels*: in the Alps, above Tintern Abbey, and here.

"Lines Composed a few miles above Tintern Abbey" preceded the completion of the 1805 *Prelude*. Here he insists on natural "connection," recurrence ("again" is used several times in the first verse paragraph), and on presence ("this" and "here"). He experiences the power of memory and of what is to come, himself set firmly in the present, among particulars. In condensed form, this poem contains the substance of *The Prelude*.

Most memorable of Wordsworth's poems is "Intimations of Immortality," an ode written between 1802 or 1803 and 1806. Technically it is a tour de force. A few readings fix it in memory: not as argument, rather as a developing mood or emotion, an apprehension, distilling as experience the wisdom of *The Prelude*. It is a less positive formulation, less intellectually resolute in its attempt to find "strength in what remains behind," as though the "real world / Of images" and those "spots of time" were already losing force. And so they were, a sense of that "mighty Mind" was overcoming the sense of the particulars of its creation. Hazlitt is at our elbow with a sour comment: "Lord Byron we have called, according to the old proverb, 'the spoiled child of fortune': Mr Wordsworth might plead, in mitigation of some peculiarities, that he is 'the spoiled child of disappointment.' " Before disappointment, by questioning poetic convention, with a powerful and original vision of nature, and by developing an inclusive personal style, Wordsworth— with Coleridge now beside, and now beyond him—extended the language and thematic range of English poetry into the new century. After the great poems and especially *The Prelude*, we forgive the Wordsworth who was all fresh growth and bright foliage for turning to bark and wood and winter, and we defend him against his numerous detractors who included Landor: "Dank, limber verses, stuft with lakeside sedges, / And propt with rotten stakes from broken hedges."

Wordsworth's poems cured Locke of terrible depression in the illness that came over him from excessive study as a youth. Arnold elegized him with a need and passion as intense as that which Wordsworth on a different occasion felt in conjuring Milton. Arnold's father befriended Wordsworth, who supervised the building of the Arnolds' house at Fox How while Dr. Arnold was headmastering at Rugby ("What beautiful English the old man speaks!" the Doctor declared). It is no accident, given Wordsworth's change of political and artistic direction, that Matthew Arnold speaks of him in couplets. Couplets without the humor or wit of Pope: from Wordsworth he sucked unsmiling earnestness, sincere, moving, a little portentous.

> Ah, since dark days still bring to light
> Man's prudence and man's fiery might,
> Time may restore us in his course
> Goethe's sage mind and Byron's force;
> But where will Europe's latter hour
> Again find Wordsworth's healing power?
> Others will teach us how to dare,
> And against fear our breasts to steel;
> Others will strengthen us to bear—
> But who, ah! who, will make us feel?
> The cloud of mortal destiny,
> Others will front it fearlessly—
> But who, like him, will put it by?

Well, Samuel Taylor Coleridge for one. If Wordsworth kept in his cupboard the emotional skeleton of Annette Vallon and an illegitimate child, Coleridge's cupboard is poor in intimate skeletons (his secret sin is plagiarism). He believes in words, they have a compelling reality for him: he believes in naming more than in the objects named. He takes delight in thinking: it is a sensuous experience for him, and talk itself is one of his intensest pleasures. "The pith of my system is to make the senses out of the mind—not the mind out of the senses, as Locke did." It's an impulse he communicated to Wordsworth, as he recalls in *Table Talk*. "The present is an age of talkers," Hazlitt says, "and not of doers; and the reason is, that the world is growing old. We are so far advanced in the Arts and Sciences, that we live in retrospect, and doat on past achievements."

Coleridge trusted friends—he did not suspect Wordsworth's secret—and believed the best of them. "When friends failed him," Graves remarks, he "was always lost." And they generally failed him. At the time of his break with Wordsworth he wrote: "I have loved with enthusiastic self-oblivion those who have been well pleased that I should, year after year, flow with a hundred nameless rills into their main stream."

Things were patched up, but Coleridge no longer trusted his friend or himself. And Robert Southey sold out to journalism. Hazlitt makes savage prose of his disillusion with the brotherhood. "If Mr Coleridge had not been the most impressive talker of his age, he would probably have been the finest writer; but he lays down his pen to make sure of an auditor, and mortgages the admiration of posterity for the stare of an idler."

Coleridge's life is one of the saddest in English poetry. Full of intelligence and promise, he was disappointed on every front. "[Coleridge's] mind is (as he himself might express it) *tangential*. There is no subject on which he has not touched, none on which he has rested." Hazlitt is as just as he is cruel. Coleridge hungered for new beginnings, for an impossible America and a Pantisocracy he conjured up as a young man, with friends willing to entertain the notion of a community of the elect in a new world. The image of an America of new beginning recurs long after the project collapsed. It is there in the poems of dejection and betrayal. Hazlitt gets close to the man he began by respecting and even loving above all others.

At the age of twenty he was intrigued to hear of Coleridge. "A poet and a philosopher getting up into a Unitarian pulpit to preach the Gospel, was a romance in these degenerate days, a sort of revival of the primitive spirit of Christianity, which was not to be resisted." In 1798 he went on a vast winter walk to hear him speak. "When I got there, the organ was playing the 100th psalm, and, when it was done, Mr Coleridge rose and gave out his text. 'And he went up into the mountain to pray, HIMSELF, ALONE.' As he gave out his text, his voice 'rose like a steam of rich distilled perfumes,' and when he came to the last two words, which he pronounced loud, deep, and distinct, it seemed to me, who was then young, as if the sounds had echoed from the bottom of the human heart, and as if that prayer might have floated in solemn silence through the universe . . . The preacher then launched into his subject, like an eagle dallying with the wind." It was a sermon—tending to pacifism—about the gap between Christian and secular visions of war. From a distance in church "there was to me a strange wilderness in his aspect, a dusky obscurity, and I thought him pitted with the smallpox." In fact, close up, "His forehead was broad and high, light as if built of ivory, with large projecting eyebrows, and his eyes rolling beneath them like a sea with darkened lustre . . . His mouth was gross, voluptuous, open, eloquent; his chin good-humoured and round; but his nose, the rudder of the face, the index of the will, was small, feeble, nothing— like what he has done." That conclusion is filled with Hazlitt's later disappointment.

Coleridge walked crooked and kept crossing Hazlitt's path as they went along. Hazlitt walked straight and deferentially. His verbal portraiture is vivid: physiognomy and temperament illuminate each other, his first impressions unblurred by aftermath. Indeed there is piquancy in the distance he records between youthful impressions of youthful men and the transformations time and history wrought upon them— Coleridge as well as Wordsworth—when they turned to the "wrong" patrons and retreated from their first, embodied imaginings. Contrasts of voice and approach are neatly recorded. "Coleridge has told me that he himself liked to compose in walking over uneven ground, or breaking through the straggling branches of a copse-wood; whereas Wordsworth always wrote (if he could) walking up and down a straight gravel-walk, or in some spot where the continuity of his verse met with no collateral interruption."

It is not that Coleridge went off: he went wrong, lost direction because he lost friends. "All that he has done of moment, he had done twenty years ago: since then he may be said to have lived on the sound of his own voice." Hazlitt portrays him at Christ's Hospital thronged with friends, including Lamb, walking about the quad in earnest disquisition, especially on Greek tragedy. Then, infatuated with Hartley, "he busied himself for a year or two with vibrations and vibratiuncles and the great law of association that binds all things in its mystic chain, and the doctrine of Necessity (the mild teacher of Charity) and the Millennium, anticipative of a life to come—and he plunged deep into the controversy on Matter and Spirit, and, as an escape from Dr Priestley's Materialism, where he felt himself imprisoned by the logician's spell, like Ariel in the cloven pine-tree, he became suddenly enamoured of Bishop Berkeley's fairy-world, and used in all companies to build the universe, like a brave poetical fiction, of fine words . . ." Hazlitt builds his single sentence on and on, stuffing it with Coleridge's vast learnings for two full pages before we arrive at a full stop, ". . . but poetry redeemed him from this spectral philosophy, and he bathed his heart in beauty." After the epic sentence he concludes: "Alas! 'Frailty, thy name is *Genius!*'—What is become of all this mighty heap of hope, of thought, of learning, and humanity? It has ended in swallowing doses of oblivion and in writing paragraphs in the *Courier*.—Such, and so little is the mind of man!"

Hazlitt's verdict on the Lake Poets is chilling: "But the poets, the creatures of sympathy, could not stand the frowns both of king and people. They did not like to be shut out when places and pensions, when the critic's praises, and the laurel-wreath were about to be distributed. They did not stomach being *sent to Coventry*, and Mr Coleridge sounded a retreat for them by the help of casuistry, and a musical voice." Fortunately, they had been young before they reached their mature accommodations, and even when accommodated there is in their dullest utterance the fascination of echo, more compelling than the indignity of self-betrayal. For Hazlitt, living with and then against them, what mattered was where their lives took the wrong turning. For us what matters is the poems they wrote and where they might lead us.

> O happy living things! no tongue
> Their beauty might declare:
> A spring of love gushed from my heart,
> And I blessed them unaware

Along with Doctor Johnson, Coleridge is the great critical intelligence among English poets, but a very different kind of intelligence from the Doctor's. His interests extend beyond poetry to society, philosophy and religion, but poetry is the heart of wider concerns with language and the power of imagination and ideas. Unlike Johnson, he had no settled opinions; he was a man in search of truth, perplexed by personal, philosophical, political and aesthetic indecisions. We find consistency of principle, uncertainty of application. His mature political thought is lucid, but he cannot—for example in *On the Constitution of Church and State*—bridge the gap between idea and implementation in practical, institutional forms. Yet Hazlitt is wrong: Coleridge does *not* indulge in casuistry to get out of an intellectual corner.

Uncertainty has aesthetic consequences. Unlike other Romantic poets, he never establishes a personal mode. He writes Augustan verse of little distinction, discursive poems, then the handful of meditations and nature poems in which he is most himself, and finally three great poems that defy classification: "Christabel," "Kubla Khan" and "The Rime of the Ancient Mariner." Of these poems, two are ostensibly unfinished. Throughout his work there are fragments, including "The Destiny of Nations." Other poems he worked on for years and remained dissatisfied. His "Dejection: An Ode" adopts a fragmentary form, juxtaposing verse paragraphs that are thematically but not logically sequential. Formal fragmentation reflects the theme: like a modernist, he breaks it to make it whole. He did not complete his vast projected philosophical work. His attempt to schematize transcendental philosophy distorted the ideas imagination could apply but analysis unraveled.

Self-doubt and indecision began early. Born in 1772 in Ottery St. Mary, Devon, Coleridge was the youngest son of the local vicar. His father, who understood and indulged him, died when the boy was nine. No one replaced this benign figure of authority. Coleridge's mother did not know what to make of him; when he came to marry in 1795 he chose a woman too like his mother, setting in train the difficulties of his later years.

He attended Christ's Hospital School in London as a bright charity boy. Charles Lamb was a junior classmate. He had excellent masters, read the classics and modern literature, grew interested in the literature of travel, and excelled in a sympathetic environment. In 1791 he went to Jesus College, Cambridge. He was too well prepared for university: the curriculum bored him, no one paid him serious intellectual attention, he grew idle, got into debt (which for one so ill provided was easy), and suddenly on impulse enlisted in the 15th Dragoons, from which his family had to rescue him. He returned to Cambridge but did not complete a degree.

He and Southey met in 1794. Both were enthusiastic about the French Revolution and Coleridge admired Southey's poems. They became friends, planning to found what Coleridge christened a "Pantisocracy," a commune on the banks of the Susquehanna. This pipe dream had one practical consequence: Coleridge married Southey's sister-in-law. Already he was taking opium—to alleviate toothache.

In 1793 he had his first published poems, in the *Morning Chronicle*. In 1796 he started his own politically and religiously nonconformist newspaper. *The Watchman* ran for ten issues before it folded. By the age of twenty-four he had failed to complete his Cambridge course, contracted a disastrous marriage, and seen two cherished projects run aground. He had written unsuccessfully for the theater. But he had a new enthusiasm: Wordsworth. They first met in 1795. As with Southey, so with Wordsworth: Coleridge was immediately impressed with his work. In 1797, when Wordsworth settled near Coleridge in Somerset, they collaborated on *Lyrical Ballads*. Coleridge contributed "The Rime of the Ancient Mariner." His poetry developed rapidly as a result of their intimacy. Between 1795 and 1802 he composed his best poems and poetic torsos, starting with "The Aeolian Harp" (1795) and including the flawed but interesting poems "Reflections on Having Left a Place of Retirement" (1795) and "The Destiny of Nations" (1796). There followed "This Lime-Tree Bower My Prison" and "The Rime of the Ancient Mariner" (1797); "Christabel" (1797, Part II 1800); "Frost at Midnight," "Kubla Khan," "Fears in Solitude" and his recantation "France: An Ode" (1798); the fragmentary "Hexameters" to Dorothy and William Wordsworth (1798–99); "The Keepsake" (1800)—the falling off was noticeable in those two poems; and his final masterpiece, "Dejection: An Ode" (1802). The Muse became fitful in her attentions. Coleridge's major poetic achievement was complete: he was thirty years old.

His interest in German transcendentalist philosophy—he did much to advance the ideas of Kant and Schelling in England—grew out of his early Neoplatonist studies. In "The Destiny of Nations" he had expressed his essential vision:

> For all that meets the bodily sense I deem
> Symbolical, one mighty alphabet
> For infant minds [. . .]

"Sense" in the singular defines his view of the interdependence of the senses, a fusing perception we meet in the "swimming sense" he feels before the manifold spectacle of nature; or in the line describing synesthesia, "A light in sound, a sound-like power in light"; or "to see is only a language." In the 1796 poem we also visit Plato's cave:

> Placed with our backs to bright Reality,
> That we may learn with young, unwounded ken
> The substance from the shadow . . .

After visiting Germany in 1798–99, he returned to England and settled near Wordsworth in Cumberland to continue his studies. He fell hopelessly in love with Wordsworth's sister-in-law, but he was already married. He wrote journalism, lectured, traveled, suffered further financial hardship and grew increasingly dependent on opium. In 1810 he quarreled openly—conflict had been brewing—with Wordsworth. It was one of the great losses of his life. They were reconciled, but the original friendship was over. His reputation grew as his powers declined. In 1817 his prose masterpiece *Biographia Literaria* was published. His mature political writing is the quintessence of that English Toryism rooted in Sir Robert Filmer and Richard Hooker, adhered to by Swift, Johnson and Goldsmith, and richly proclaimed by Edmund Burke. Its expression is elegiac: that moment in English history was over. Coleridge died in 1834.

He set down his poetics mainly after the poems were written. Intellectual energy and creative power he portrayed as wrestlers locked in combat. Intellectual energy won, he was a critic, and he took issue with Wordsworth. Wordsworth declared that there was no essential difference between the languages of prose and verse. The inessential difference was meter, which in verse bridles emotion, creates associations, and balances the "commonplace" with intense emotion. It protects the reader from too direct an assault by the poet's feelings. Coleridge argues that prose and verse are languages distinct in construction and effect. Meter is not a negative force, a bridle, but part and parcel of the statement, the vehicle for emotion itself, a positive power. Each passion dictates a pulse and form of expression. Meter harmonizes by unifying the parts. Instinct or imagination elects and judges meter: "Could a rule be given from without, poetry would cease to be poetry, and sink into a mechanical art."

The instinctive and involuntary play a greater part in Coleridge's conception of poetry (and in the best of his poems) than in the work of his predecessors. He first defines what Romanticism is and does: organic form, intuitive formulation. From these follows the essential "suspension of disbelief": we judge a poem first by asking what it sets out to do, then by appraising how well it does it, and only then do we ask whether it was worth doing. Coleridge evolved his controversial theory of imagination, secondary imagination and fancy. The first he describes as the "living Power, Prime Agent of all human Perception"; the second as an "echo of the primary, coexisting with the conscious will, yet still identical with the primary in the *kind* of its agency, differing only in *degree* and *mode* of operation"; and the third as "a mode of memory emancipated from the order of time and place, blended with and modified by that empirical phenomenon of the will, which we express by the word 'choice.'"

Unlike Wordsworth, he never succumbs to the power of physical objects. His early work is full of transitive verbs, while Wordsworth deploys the verb "to be" more than most great poets, assuring himself of the otherness and actual presence of objects. Coleridge explores connection: the life of imagination can be more vivid than the life of the senses themselves. In "This Lime-Tree Bower My Prison," with the colloquial directness of a blank verse epistle, the power (who has injured his foot and is unable to accompany his friends—notably Lamb, just down from the city—on a walk) gives them directions, then relaxes in his lime-tree bower. In imagination he sees what they will see in reality, his perception heightened by the fact that he sees through the eyes of Lamb, on release from city life. The extended syntax of the sentence describing the friends' descent is mimetic language at its best. They see particulars and then the wider panorama. Passive in his bower, Coleridge experiences the immediate sensuous pleasure of his place, the memory of the route his friends take, their pleasure as he imagines it, and an additional, integrating sense of wholeness and well-being, despite his injury. He draws a moral:

> . . . Henceforth I shall know
> That Nature ne'er deserts the wise and pure;
> No plot so narrow, be but Nature there,
> No waste so vacant, but may well employ
> Each faculty of sense, and keep the heart

Awake to Love and Beauty! and sometimes
'Tis well to be bereft of promis'd good,
That we may lift the soul, and contemplate
With lively joy the joys we cannot share.

He concludes, "No sound is dissonant that tells of Life." Written in the same year as "The Rime of the Ancient Mariner," this poem proposes the themes of the greater poem. Nature, even in desolate circumstances, can waken the alert heart. When the Mariner understands this, his redemption begins. Perception is for Coleridge an ever-active faculty: it detects a large continuity, then assimilates the data of perception into that continuity, that organism. "I regulated my creeds by my *conception*, not by my *sight*," he says. Images are the materials of which conception builds its edifice: he is after unity, not causal process.

In "The Aeolian Harp," his first remarkable poem, Milton, Gray and Cowper, early mentors, stand a little off and let the young poet speak. He begins with particularity, addressing his new wife, who leans on his arm. His senses move from the cottage to the vines that deck it, then outward to the clouds; the scent of the bean fields reaches him, and the "stilly murmur of the distant sea / Tells us of silence." All the senses are engaged. Then the Aeolian harp, placed on a casement where the breeze can draw harmonies from it, sounds. Its strain draws the poet's mind away to a world of imaginative suggestion and romance, until his wife's rebuke recalls him. The poem moralizes in conversational blank verse, at once gentle and joyful. The instrument is an important image, releasing imaginative energy by its harmony. Here it foreshadows the "dulcimer" in "Kubla Khan." In form and tone it prepares the way for "Frost at Midnight" and, more remotely, for "Dejection: An Ode."

"The Frost performs its secret ministry / Unhelped by any wind," "Frost at Midnight" begins. With conflicting emotions of paternity, solitude and unfulfillment, the poet hears how "the owlet's cry / Came loud—and hark, again! Loud as before." Agitated by the stillness, to him the fluttering "film" on the grate suggests a stranger who may come. The place where he sits musing becomes an extension of his mind, the frost itself an agent, transforming nature as his imagination transforms memory. He returns to childhood, then turns to his child, contrasting his past and Hartley's present. The poem ends with a blessing on his son. The earlier discursive poems are concerned with existence in space, with landscape and panorama. "Frost at Midnight" and "Dejection" are about time. They are nocturnal, reflective, profoundly personal and intensive rather than expansive.

In "Dejection: An Ode," Coleridge confronts the failure of his life and vision. His marriage decays, he is hopelessly in love with someone else, he is unwell. The wry opening gives way to despair. We hear the Aeolian harp and tones of "Christabel" and "The Ancient Mariner." A storm rages but does not now, as it would have done before, arouse imagination: only "A grief without a pang." Stars and moon: "I see, not feel, how beautiful they are!" He echoes Wordsworth, Milton and his own earlier verse. This poem too ends with a benediction—on his beloved. Beyond grace, he could make one great poem at least of his failures.

The discursive poems cast light on his chief poetic achievement, the three "great unparaphrasables." "Christabel," his longest poem, is a fragment of ghostly romance which by a technique of rapt questioning and breathless images establishes dramatic tension: "Is the night chilly and dark? / The night is chilly but not dark"; "Is it the wind that moaneth bleak?" These passages prepare for Christabel's interrogation of the mysterious Geraldine. Nothing is defined. We know it is "a month before the month of May," and May is the month of romance. Poor Christabel will not savor its fruits. A gothic atmosphere, the eerie simplicity of the accentual form with variable rhyme scheme, delights for almost seven hundred lines. Geraldine, a supernatural creature, by a spell silences Christabel. Rendered mute, Christabel observes and suffers the beginning of Geraldine's evil designs. *Desunt nonulla.* No Chapman has come along to complete what Coleridge began.

"The Rime of the Ancient Mariner" achieves what no other literary ballad of the period did: the tone of folk ballad. In an impersonal ballad singer's voice, Coleridge explores in dramatic ways a theme developed in the discursive poems. The Mariner chooses one of three young men bound for a wedding feast. He tells his story: his ship, ice-bound near the pole, the albatross of good omen, his gratuitous act of slaying it, the punishment wrought on the whole crew; his individual penance and regeneration when in his heart he blessed the creatures about the becalmed ship. Released, he travels the world teaching reverence, love of God and his creatures. For six hundred and twenty-five lines Coleridge touches our deepest interests. The poem works on us like a dream: questions of belief or disbelief never arise: we attend. Passages have entered common language; the images draw back to consciousness folk elements and hermetic symbolism. Wordsworth wrote privately to the publisher urging that the poem be dropped from future editions of *Lyrical Ballads* as being out of key with the other poems in the book. He was uncomfortable with its dimensions and themes: Did he sense, too, how much more powerful, durable and *inevitable* it was than the other poems in the book?

Rudyard Kipling quoted two lines of Keats and three of Coleridge from "Kubla Khan":

A savage place! as holy and enchanted
As e'er beneath a waning moon was haunted
By woman wailing for her demon lover!

"These are the pure Magic. These are the clear vision. The rest is only poetry." It is sacrilege of sorts to "interpret" the magic. Like "Christabel," "Kubla Khan" is, some believe, a fragment, a poem that emerged from a half-drugged dream interrupted in composition by the famous arrival of the person from Porlock. Many interpretations are possible, each partial. More valuable are the formal studies, attending closely to images and how they relate. Interesting but not very useful is the search for sources. What the poem means is inseparable from the words and rhythms it uses. Paraphrase hardly gets a toehold. It is not until the second half of the poem that the "I" appears: "A damsel with a dulcimer / In a vision once I saw . . .":

Could I revive within me
Her symphony and song,
To such a deep delight 'twould win me,
That with music loud and long,
I would build that dome in air . . .

The first half of the poem evokes the "stately pleasure dome." In the second half the "I" wishes to retrieve it. Could he hear the music he once heard in a vision, he could re-create in air "That sunny dome! those caves of ice!" He would be like Kubla Khan, himself sacred and exalted. The dulcimer recalls the harps we hear elsewhere in Coleridge's work, instruments that harmonize the world of ideas and the world of the senses, and liberate imagination from the constraints of literal vision. In "Kubla Khan" the poetry achieves an intensity unprecedented in the discursive poems. The dulcimer's sound would recreate not things perceived but imagined. Contemplation authenticates; it can even transform and generate objects of contemplation, as in "Frost at Midnight." "Could I revive within me": it is a conditional clause. In fact he cannot. He cannot even "complete" the poem. If he could, he could complete *himself*, become one with "flashing eye" and "floating hair." Yet from its partial disclosure we can infer the vision. The poem is about desire, not the failure of desire. In this thwarted hope resides its power. It belongs near the end of his greatest creative period. His next and last major poem is about failure: "Dejection: An Ode."

Marble into Flesh—and Spirit

WALTER SAVAGE LANDOR, GEORGE GORDON LORD BYRON,
FELICIA DOROTHEA HEMANS, PERCY BYSSHE SHELLEY

Walter Savage Landor possessed a powerful intellect deflected by few doubts. He is ice beside the turbulent spates and droughts of Coleridge. He saw clearly, even radically, in social terms, but never pretended to "vision." To step from the quicksilver and quicksand of Coleridge into the calmed world of Landor is to move out of living dream and nightmare into a stable, artful or artificial world, in which a classical order displaces the shifting reality in which the poet lived. "Manners have changed, but hearts are yet / The same, and will be while they beat."

The minor poet and man of literary fashion Aubrey de Vere called Landor "proud, not only of his style, but of the pains he took with it. That care, he said, should be only in part concealed; light touches of the chisel should remain on the marble." His art does not conceal the fact that it is art, or that it is wrested from language and tradition. It *displays* skill. Limpidity contains even as it attests to the formal struggle. He is not unlike Ben Jonson among his predecessors, and Thom Gunn among his heirs. "What is it," muses Coleridge, "that Mr Landor wants to make him a poet? His powers are certainly very considerable, but he seems to be totally deficient in that modifying faculty which compresses several units into one whole. The truth is he does not possess imagination in its highest form,—that of stamping *il più nell' uno*." Is Coleridge doing anything more than lamenting that Landor is not a Romantic? He's right to say that in the poetry, "You have eminences excessively bright, and all the ground around and between them in darkness." There is no sense of oeuvre, of a unified body of work, despite stylistic continuity from poem to poem and decade to decade of the poet's work.

Landor is best known today for two or three lyrics and for Dickens's genial caricature of him as Boythorn in *Bleak House*, where Mr. Jarndyce reflects, "There's no simile for his lungs. Talking, laughing, or snoring, they make the beams of the house shake . . . But it is the inside of the man, the warm heart of the man, the passion of the man, the fresh blood of the man . . . that I speak of . . . His language is as sounding as his voice. He is always in extremes; perpetually in the superlative degree. In his condemnation he is all ferocity. You might suppose him to be an Ogre, from what he says; and I believe he has the reputation of one with some people." The shorter poems, almost caustic in their reserve, seem the product of quite another sort of man; the long narratives entirely lack the vigor of the socially more taciturn and passionate Byron. Landor wore his Romanticism on his sleeve, reserving composure for his writing.

His large and once popular production of prose, *Imaginary Conversations* (1824, 1828, 1829), is now little read. His long poems, despite the enthusiasm of Southey, De Quincey, Shelley and others, are neglected. Posterity overlooks him, though a few of the best poets, Yeats, Pound and Robert Frost among them, steer by his lights. It is no wonder that he appealed to them. His is the most classical pen of his day: the remote past was ready and serviceable in the present. His radicalism has to do with roots, primarily Greek and Roman ones.

He was born at Ipsley Court, Warwickshire, in 1775. His mother was of an old family, his father a successful doctor. The fractious boy was withdrawn before being expelled from Rugby (before Dr. Arnold's time), where he had excelled in classics and written fine Latin poems. He was rusticated from Trinity College, Oxford, where he had a reputation as a wild Jacobin. His active romantic life soon got under way and provided him with pretexts for poems. He prefigures Robert Graves, though he never had the challenge of a Laura Riding, or a White or a Dark Goddess. His libido did not require theory to justify its waywardness. It certainly did not seek out among its objects an intellectual equal.

He suppressed his first book, *Poems* (1795), in part for its simplistic and fashionable political enthusiasms. The first poem in the collection declares his settled literary passion for Sappho, Anacreon, Ovid and Catullus. They remain guides. *Gebir: A Poem in Seven Books* (1798, Latin translation by himself 1803) and *Poetry by the Author of Gebir* (1802) gained him the admiration of a few contemporaries but hardly a readership. In 1805 his father died and he came into the family estate. He made Southey's acquaintance in Bristol in 1808. Later in life he met the leading writers of the day, but Southey remained his closest literary friend, even the Southey who sold out to journalism and whom Hazlitt regarded as a renegade.

He married in 1811 and spent much of the rest of his life in flight from this unfortunate match. *Count Julian,* an undramatic tragedy, appeared in 1812. In 1814 he left England for eighteen years, spending much of that time in Italy. The historical trilogy *Andrea of Hungary,*

Giovana of Naples and *Fra Rupert* occupied him until around 1840. Publication of the two volumes of *Hellenics* (1846, 1847), *The Italics* (1848), *The Last Fruit off an Old Tree* (1853)—perhaps his best book—and his *Heroic Idyls* (1863), including Latin poems, complete his bulky, uneven output. A few fine poems appeared in this last book, notably "Ye who have toil'd," which proves that his senility was not so complete as some critics suggest. He died in Florence in 1864. His long life may or may not have been largely happy, but there is intellectual and temperamental consistency in it, from his troubles at Rugby through his polemical activities on a larger social stage.

The poetry, too, has consistency. If we describe him as a neoclassicist, it is not to associate him with the Augustans but to distinguish essential parts of him from the Romantics. His intense, unquestioning commitment to poetry, his belief that the poet is by nature more alive than other men, his often careless and insensitive enthusiasms, set him among the Romantics. So does an occasional sentimentality, his emotive intent. Yet his program was distinct from theirs from the outset.

Gebir is a heroic poem and a political allegory in blank verse. It tells the story of two brothers. Gebir is prince and conqueror, his conquests stayed by love, his life destroyed by treachery. Tamar is a pastoral figure who wins the love of a sea nymph and is transported beyond the world of mortals. *Gebir* was not a poem expecting an audience. It confronts rather than invites readers; the challenge is accepted by few today. Superbly crafted, it is deliberate and cold in execution, the action slow, Miltonic, as of monumental figures in a land of heavy gravity. Milton deals with huge Christian themes on his large canvas; Landor projects the intimate dynamics of love and betrayal. Anthologists rescue choice passages but rarely the poem itself. Much later Landor addressed to reluctant readers his excellent "Apology for *Gebir*."

Throughout his career he produced poems that related to it in form and theme, among them "Crysaor" and "The Phocaeans." The plays and "scenes" and his historical trilogy share the large faults and local virtues of *Gebir*. Landor's penchant for remote events to illuminate present social and political problems was artistically misjudged, imposing anachronism and distortion on subject matter. The neoclassicist resembles in some ways a late medieval allegorist adjusting a subject on a Procrustean bed. He commands long forms in intellectual rather than imaginative ways. Landor the poet is visible in certain passages, where he seems to congratulate himself on his ambitious enterprise.

Better to turn to the shorter poems and lyrics. They are remote, but in another way. In the *Hellenics* his classical imagination proves Greek rather than Roman, despite his skill in Latin versification and his debts to Ovid and Catullus. In "On Classick and Romantick" he writes,

Abstemious were the Greeks; they never strove
To look so fierce; their muses were sedate,
Never obstreperous: you heard no breath
Outside the flute; each sound ran clear within.

When he's abstemious, his lyric and elegiac art achieves such distilla-
tion. He contains and generalizes his subject, whether landscape or
images of human perfection or relationship. Measure, balance, fidelity
and form are the classical qualities he pursues. Here is "Dirce":

Stand close around, ye Stygian set,
    With Dirce in one boat conveyed!
Or Charon, seeing, may forget
    That he is old and she a shade.

This, by the author of *Gebir*: the contrast exemplifies the larger paradox
of his imagination. Romantic and classicist, radical and conservative
coexist, producing divergent voices. In a poem such as "Fiesolan Idyl"
Landor writes with emancipated, guiltless sensuality, even sexuality. His
style when it refines also intensifies. He is among the most quietly sen-
suous of English poets. Were our age not so unbuttoned, this part of
his poetry would have a devoted readership. Unlike Burns, he never
explores the senses for effect. They open into relationship.

In *Hellenics* the verse has some of the plainness of Catullus. The
poems to Ianthe and Rose Aylmer are among the finest lyrics in the lan-
guage. Landor was alive to diction, if not register, in his language. The
short poems conform to a single plan and tone. It may not be the lan-
guage people actually speak, but we instantly recognize it, just as Ben
Jonson would have done. Such language does not date: secure within
tradition, it is timeless, which means also that it is static. His passion
ends in "a night of memories and of sighs."

The Greek Anthology, with themes of love and the erosions of time,
spoke intimately to him. His verse learns thrift from the short Greek
poems. It can be as devastating in epigrammatic lampoon as in sus-
tained lyrics. How can so few words carry so much moral weight, like an
ant shouldering a boulder? His much anthologized "I strove with none"
is an example: a biography in four lines, with a moral asperity that a
lesser author would dissipate over several stanzas. The fact that Landor's
themes are age-old and commonplace does not render them less true.
His forms, too, are traditional. His originality is in the fact that he uses
them, and uses them so well, in the nineteenth century. One can be an
"innovator," as the American poet Robert Pinsky demonstrates in his
account of Landor's poetry, by reviving, adapting and developing tradi-

tional forms, quite as much as by invention. His program guarantees against excess, untruth, treacherous experiment. After all, "Thoughts when they're weakest take the longest flights, / And tempt the wintry seas in darkest nights."

Not least among Landor's poems are those addressed to members of his family (for example, the excellent "To My Child Carlino"), to his friends (Wordsworth, Browning, Dickens and others) and to poets he admired but never met (Keats, Burns). They observe life and literature judiciously, they praise, celebrate, advise. To Browning he writes, as of himself:

> There is delight in singing, though none hear
> Beside the singer: and there is delight
> In praising, though the praiser sit alone
> And see the prais'd far off him, far above.

"Landor," says Pinsky, "not only wrote well, but he also had a peculiar, extreme concern for the idea of writing well, and this concern modified every subject he touched." He places Landor exactly: "Landor's career seems especially pertinent to the definition of two kinds of poetry: poetry which emphasises the discovery of content"—as Wordsworth's does—"and poetry which emphasises the discovery of tone." If we probe a lyric by Landor, we may find that its effect is well in excess of its "content," that the experience of it flees from analysis. It is not that the poems lack meaning, but the meaning is largely *effect*, a product of tone.

Landor has left his impression on other poets. Later in his century Swinburne and Hopkins read him attentively. Pound is his most eloquent modern champion. If Pound makes excessive claims for him, they have helped to generate new interest in a writer who brought into English poetry qualities—local rather than fundamental or formal—that were tonic in his time and remain so in ours.

Byron is a different nature: he "discovers content." He also discovers a range of tones. Yet he was not content with what he did. He wrote to his publisher, John Murray, in 1820: "*All* of us—Scott, Southey, Wordsworth, Moore, Campbell, I—are all in the wrong . . . we are upon a wrong revolutionary poetical system, or systems, not worth a damn in itself . . . and that the present and next generations will finally be of this opinion . . . I took Moore's poems and my own, and some others, and went over them side by side with Pope's, and I was really astonished (I ought not to have been) and mortified at the ineffable distance in point of sense, harmony, effect, and even *Imagination*, passion and *Invention*, between the little Queen Anne's Man, and us of the Lower Empire." Byron as usual is direct and trenchant. He might have traced the decline in detail down a century, through Thomson's labored nature, Cowper's lax blank-verse Homer, Crabbe's prosaic couplets. Had he done so he would have noted a specific gain—the development of distinctive human voices, individual tones. The loss, the change, for good or ill, was decisive. So decisive that for many readers today the bulk of the eighteenth century remains terra incognita. It demands an effort they are reluctant to make, an effort of construction; and it posits a social culture and a discipline that poets no longer value.

Notably absent from Byron's list of poets is Coleridge, who remarked of Byron in *Table Talk*: "It seems to my ear, that there is a sad want of harmony in Lord Byron's verses. Is it not unnatural to be always connecting very great intellectual power with utter depravity? Does such a combination often really exist *in rerum naturâ*?" There is a kind of *legitimate* depravity in Pope; he observes so skillfully the rules of the age that he takes command of them. Byron is depraved on his own terms, like Auden, who admires him, and with his "very great intellectual power" he makes great art of his waywardness, yet an art confined within its own borders. Pope's is a social, "universal" voice; Byron in his mature poetry establishes intimate complicity with a sympathetic reader and leads each of us individually into his zones of depravity, like a schoolboy taking us behind a shed to show us something delicious but not altogether proper in the adult world. His wickedness is beguiling—and constraining. Coleridge laments the failure of Byron's "art of versification," yet he praises the *Don Juan* Lambro passages as "the best, that is, the most individual, thing in all I know of Lord B.'s works. The festal abandonment puts one in mind of Nicholas Poussin's pictures." His enticing "festal abandonment" is compared not to music or dance but to the most sensuous and suggestive work of a great graphic artist. Here we have a measure of the distance from Pope: Byron is interested in setting and in scene as presentation, not moral representation. He is less interested in abstract qualities, more in textures, scents, *actualities*.

We can acknowledge from the outset that there is a tawdry excess in much of Byron, a satirist's knack of simplifying for effect, but only sporadic satirical consistency. "Byron knew and regretted the colossal vulgarity, which he shrouded by a cloak of aloof grandeur," Robert Graves suggests. "It was a studious vulgarity: cosmetics and curl papers tended his elegant beauty; an ingenious, though synthetic, verse technique smoothed his cynical Spenserian stanzas. But he had unexpectedly come into a peerage and an estate while still 'wee Georgie Gordon with the feetsies'—whom his hysterical and unladylike mother used to send limping round the corner from her cheap Aberdeen lodgings to buy two-penny-worth of 'blue ruin'; and whom, at the age of nine, a nymphomaniac Calvinist housemaid had violently debauched." "Lord

Byron is an exceedingly interesting person," Shelley wrote to the novelist (and poet) Thomas Love Peacock, "and, as such, is it not to be regretted that he is a slave to the vilest and most vulgar prejudices, and as mad as a hatter?"

Already, inevitably, the poet's life obtrudes, the legend exaggerated but always with more fact in it than most legends contain. His is the British Romanticism that was exported to Europe where the Lake poets are all but unknown and Burns, Sir Walter Scott (as novelist) and Byron constitute our Romantic tradition. With Scott he shares narrative skills and a firm sense of audience and how to exploit it. With Burns he shares verbal directness—in poems such as "To Thomas More" and "So, we'll go no more a' roving"—and certain political sympathies: peer and plowman were in different centuries radicals. All three were sons of Scotland. "Thou shalt believe in Milton, Dryden, Pope; / Thou shalt not set up Wordsworth, Coleridge, Southey," Byron says. He has the alternative measure of his century.

He divides poetry readers into those who love and those who despise him. W. H. Auden, after describing the peculiar and extraordinary life, then scales him down, reassuring us, "He had no unusual emotional or intellectual vision, and his distinctive contribution to English poetry was to be, not the defiant thunder of a rebel angel, but the speaking voice of the tolerant man-about-town." Ford doubted whether Byron had an intellect at all and knew he had no heart (a fact that doesn't trouble Auden). The word "tolerant" is at least debatable in so thoroughgoing an egotist. Auden proposes Byron as a model for those young poets, presumably without vision, who wish to write with "speed, wit, and moral seriousness combined with lack of pulpit pomposity." Ford disagrees: "To an Anglo Saxon concerned for his poetry and his language, both verse and language of Byron are odious." He is repelled by the vulgarity—not the honest vulgarity of a writer like Burns, but a profound vulgarity of sensibility, a moral dishonesty that is part and parcel of Byron's heartlessness. Byron is, certainly, tactless, but not wholly undiscriminating. His attacks on Southey, Wordsworth, Coleridge and Keats are more than the effusions of prejudice, even if they are less than the fruit of cool judgment. He hated Southey's change from radical to Tory: it condemned the older poet *tout court*. But Byron was too young to have experienced the euphoria and subsequent trauma of betrayal that was the French Revolution. His politics were not *lived* until he went to Greece to fight for freedom and died. Those of a Whig aristocrat, his politics were more the product of certain social aversions and personal pique than of pondered experience: politics from the outside. He chose Greece as his theater of political action, not Britain. His civic heart beat more vigorously abroad than at home.

He was possessive of Greece. When another popular poet of the time, Felicia Dorothea Hemans, wrote of Greece—her poems often accessed historical material, applying to it familiar sentimental templates—he attacked her. Her kind of vulgarity was an extreme form of his: child of a successful Irish merchant, not a peer, she looked up—and down—the social ladder and caught precisely the middle voice, without even a hint of dissent. Born in 1793, she married and had five sons, and was abandoned. Even so she wrote as if God were in His heaven. She wrote for a living and therefore wrote to sell. When William Rossetti pilloried her "cloying flow of right-minded perceptions of moral and material beauty," he praised the very skills in packaging popular sentiment that made her such a best-seller. Byron's "flow" was deliberately of "wrong-minded perceptions," almost as deliberate as her establishment ventriloquism. Why mention her in the same breath as Byron? Because they both pursue, in different ways, parallel strategies in capturing readers, and establishing a market. Her development of the figure of long-suffering, pure, intelligent and sensitive woman helped determine Victorian stereotypes. The Hemans heroine and the Byronic hero are, in a sense, complementary figures—caricatures, simplifications for an audience hungry for simplification and easy uplift or ready entertainment. She remained a wholesome cultural-spiritual fixture well after her death in 1835, and throughout the Victorian age. If we could take Mrs. Hemans seriously—her most famous poem "The Homes of England" has been forever stolen from her by Noël Coward's famous parody—we would have to read her in the light of her life quite as much as we do Byron.

For biography is a *necessary* concern when we approach Byron's verse. His most original invention is the Byronic hero, and we must determine the degree to which this creature, his attitudes and gestures, correspond with Byron, and to what degree they amount to a *persona*, a consistent mask from behind which he enacts his views or discredits the views of others.

He was born with an ill-formed foot in London in 1788, son of a profligate Scottish aristocrat and officer and an emotionally volatile and unstable heiress. His parents separated in 1790, when Byron's father had spent most of his wife's fortune. The son idealized his absent father, a violent and—like his son—an egotistical man. He also suffered from a possessive and dubious Calvinist nanny who filled him with forebodings about damnation and indications of how best to make his way to hell.

He came obliquely into the family title in 1798, went to Harrow and then in 1805 to Trinity College, Cambridge. His disability made him aggressively eager to excel in anything that tested courage and prowess, and he was a man of enormous energy in love and other exercises. At Cambridge he published his first book, *Fugitive Pieces* (1806), and then republished it the next year in two revised, enlarged and retitled versions. Hardly a remarkable debut, it did not merit the contempt it received in 1808 in the *Edinburgh Review*. The attack was productive: in 1809 appeared Byron's first substantial poem, his satire *English Bards and Scots Reviewers*, over a thousand lines of invective and justification, in which the poet assumes a superior tone belied by the length and the obvious rancor of his piece. He connects his name with those of Pope, his chief idol, and Dryden. In defending himself he attacks everyone else in sight, including Southey, Wordsworth and Coleridge. The poem, a rhetorical essay, evinces scant justice either to his own work or to that of his contemporaries.

He left England and spent the next two years in Portugal, Spain, Greece and the Levant. He swam the Hellespont, addressing wry verses to Leander. And he started composing *Childe Harold's Pilgrimage*, a fictionalized account of his travels. The narrator is not the emphatic Byron known to his foes and friends, but the kind of man he liked to imagine himself to be: morose, enigmatic, bitter, dashing, cultured, with certain social ideals and an eye for the picturesque. If he were less nebulous he would be fascinating. He travels and reflects. More substantial than his reflections is the question: Why is he so gloomy? Byron was not quick to deny that Childe Harold and George Gordon were the same chap. Was this his darker side? Inspired by his nurse's Calvinism, perhaps, or his love for his half sister? In fact the narrator isn't *Byron*. He is an early manifestation of the Byronic hero. The poem struggles toward dramatic monologue. Lack of design, a chronicle progression, a unity depending entirely on the narrator, point toward the picaresque mode of *Don Juan*, his masterpiece.

He returned to England in 1811 to find his finances in disrepair. To repair them he wrote. Books One and Two of *Childe Harold's Pilgrimage* appeared in 1812. To his publisher's delight Byron was "famous overnight," outselling Murray's other authors, who included Jane Austen, George Crabbe and George Borrow. Byron began to capitalize on his success, writing a series of verse narratives, popular adventure novellas. *The Giaour* (1813) went into eight editions in one year. There were *The Bride of Abydos, The Corsair, The Prisoner of Chillon* and others. These works are poems by virtue of the fact that they are in efficient verse. They do not interpret experience but escape into adventure, with bold characterization (the heroes usually have a secret and undergo hardship), some violence and romance. Money and fame found him out. Fortunately there was more to him than verse adventurer, things beyond picaresque epic and satire, narrative and squib. He wrote lyrics, the visionary "The Dream," elegies and plays. His best dramas—which are not his best work—are *Cain* (in particular), *Manfred* and *Sardanapalus*.

Following in his father's footsteps, he married an heiress in 1815. He left her the next year for reasons never satisfactorily explained, after the birth of a daughter. There was a scandal and the poet responded to what he took to be social hypocrisy. He left England for Italy and never returned. But his writing continued to prosper his publisher and him. The third and fourth books of *Childe Harold's Pilgrimage* (1816, 1818) were successful. *The Lament of Tasso,* rather less so, was a dramatic monologue spoken by Tasso to his beloved, in prison. In a similar spirit he later put words about Italian independence into the mouth of Dante. In 1818 he began the first five of the sixteen books of the unfinished *Don Juan* and, as if to warm up for that task, composed *Beppo*. He became friendly with the Shelleys and in 1822 joined with Leigh Hunt—Skimpole in Dickens's *Bleak House*—and Hunt's brother to produce *The Liberal,* a periodical that ran for four issues and carried his most famous attack on Southey and his most effective personal satire, *The Vision of Judgment.* In 1824 he joined the Greek army in the struggle for independence from the Turks. He died of a fever in Missolonghi the same year.

Byron hated "sentimental and sensibilitous" people. His dismissal of Keats is only the most damaging aspect of this hatred, which became an assertive, sometimes aggressive expression of virility in his work, masking his sexual ambivalences. Everywhere we sense an impetuous, unresting nature, a personal amorality of a sort that became more common, if less *macho* and exuberant, later in the century: "The great object of life is sensation—to feel that we exist, even though in pain." The spirit of Lord Rochester lives, not only in Byron's moral outlook but in the way he stresses "Nothing," and echoes Ecclesiastes in "Vanity of vanities." The chief difference between the two peers is intellectual. Rochester had ideas and developed them; Byron had opinions and prejudices that, as Auden suggests, were commonplace, certainly not "unusual," and expressed them vehemently.

Among the shorter poems, some of the passionate "Hebrew Melodies" excel as lyrics with, at times, balladic power. There are passages in *Childe Harold's Pilgrimage* that anthologists cannot resist—for example, "Roll on, thou deep and dark blue ocean" from Canto IV. Those entrusted with selecting from Byron face a difficult choice. Swinburne includes big chunks; Arnold, principally purple passages. Swinburne chooses for sonority and extension, Arnold for shape and content. Swinburne is just to the poet: Byron's effects are cumulative. Arnold is just to the poetry, refining a sharper formal intelligence out of the formal extension of the work. Local felicities become lyrical, but divorced from their narrative context they lose the poet's intent.

Byron conceived both *Beppo* and *Don Juan* after reading a pseudo-Romantic Arthurian poem by John Hookham Frere, a collaborator of Murray's in the *Quarterly Review*. He borrowed Frere's ottava rima—he had used it before, but never in satirical spirit—and his poetic plan was to have no plan, to write an open-ended, picaresque work, reminiscent in some ways of Laurence Sterne's *Tristram Shandy*. In *Beppo* Byron mastered the measure; in *Don Juan* he mastered a digressive manner. He chose for his mise-en-scène nothing less than the entire world.

Don Juan, the great Italian poet Eugenio Montale says, is Byron's only *readable* poem. It records six major and several lesser adventures of the hero, a passive man whom circumstances and women draw into love and risk. Adventure begins in the boudoir of Donna Julia in Spain, and includes cannibalism in an open boat, and the famous love affair with Haidée, the high point of Byron's art. The amusing scenes in Turkey, where Juan is sold into slavery and encounters the sexually voracious Sultana Gulbayes ("Christian, canst thou love?") give way to the Russian court and Catherine II's colorfully original sexual inclinations. The poem does not end: it is discontinued, in the midst of Juan's diplomatic mission to England, where three ladies pursue him. Amid satire and frivolity are passages of impassioned writing, especially in the third canto, where Byron writes "The Isles of Greece," declaring his commitment to Greek liberty.

> The mountains look on Marathon—
>   And Marathon looks on the sea;
> And musing there an hour alone,
>   I dream'd that Greece might still be free;
> For standing on the Persian's grave,
> I could not deem myself a slave.

It rises to passion, but ends with a vision, not of popular freedom, but of a hero.

> Fill high the bowl with Samian wine!
>   Our virgins dance beneath the shade—
> I see their glorious black eyes shine;
>   But gazing on each glowing maid,
> My own the burning tear-drop laves,
> To think such breasts must suckle slaves.

Place me on Sunium's marbled steep,
    Where nothing, save the waves and I,
May hear our mutual murmurs sweep;
    There, swan-like, let me sing and die:
A land of slaves shall ne'er be mine—
Dash down yon cup of Samian wine!

The *Don Juan* narrator is his artistic triumph, a voice urbane and amusing, of a droll cynic who can speak with tact and delicacy, as in the Haidée episode, but is also capable of virulence, good humor, mischief, bathos and vulgarity. Byron deflates many portentous stanzas with an absurd rhyme, the silliest including "Euxine" / "pukes in" and "intellectual" / "hen-pecked you all." The narrator can talk on any subject; he indulges digression more and more as the poem proceeds, and responds in whatever way a subject requires. He is responsible for the poem's limitations as well. What Landor wrote of Byron's work as a whole touches *Don Juan* particularly. Byron "possesses the soul of poetry, which is energy; but he wants that ideal beauty which is the sublimer emanation, I will not say of the real, for this is the more real of the two, but of that which is ordinarily subject to the senses." In short, he provides progression without unity. Each incident stands isolated from the one before. There are parallels and contrasts, but as often as not they're accidental. Picaresque writing tends to forget one adventure as soon as another begins.

From the outset tone proves a problem. "And if I laugh at any mortal thing, / 'Tis that I may not weep . . ." Yet there is little in the poem for tears. Serious subjects are seriously treated—the question of Greek freedom, for example. Byron calls the poem "Epic Satire," but comedy more than satire fills it, no firm perspective is established, no consistent target assaulted. Wellington and the court come in for effective direct attack at various points; critics find other correspondences. But Byron switches political satire on and off as the spirit moves him. He abandons the formal singularity of his master Pope. He laughs at his manipulation of language more often than he chastises particular evils. In scope, the epic includes Europe, Africa and Asia Minor in the action. But it's epic without gods. It has elements of satire, but satire without firm design.

The theme of *Don Juan* is reversal or transformation—metamorphosis—in language and action, a movement from what seems to what is. At the outset, Juan's parents appear as paragons of beauty and virtue. Each is undermined with telling details, until we know Donna Inez to be a doting hypocrite (based on Byron's mother). Every possible relationship is thwarted, every remote fear actualized. The moral of the poem, if it has one, seems to be the need to break down self-deception:

Byron betrays us, too, time after time, as Sterne does, in what we desire from the narrative.

We lose interest in the story after the first five books and concentrate on sexual, alimentary and travel images, on incident and digression, and finally on the narrator himself. He takes over from his hero, reminisces, cajoles, jests. The poem becomes journal more than narrative; the increasing casualness of the author after the relative narrative wholeness of the early books underlies the absence of overall conception. *Don Juan* loses momentum in proportion as the narrator plays with our expectations. His cleverness becomes mannerism, repetitious and willful. "My tendency is to philosophise / On most things, from a tyrant to a tree."

Byron's creative life divides into two periods: 1805–17 (before *Beppo*) and 1817–24 (after *Beppo*). When he discovered a new use for ottava rima he found his vehicle. He could write "moral satire" without a morality of his own. He became a judge working, as it were, without laws, attacking hypocrisy but not from a perspective of self-knowledge or higher knowledge. The savvy tone invites our complicity and stands in for deeper integrity. The language is efficient without delicacy or "effeminacy." In *Don Juan* the narrator becomes almost indistinguishable from Byron himself. What was it Graves said? "I pair Byron and Nero as the two most dangerously talented bounders of all time."

W. H. Auden distrusted Percy Bysshe Shelley almost as much as he loved Byron. In the course of a review of Herbert Read's book on Shelley he declares: "I cannot believe . . . that any artist can be good who is not more than a bit of a reporting journalist . . . To the journalist the first thing of importance is subject . . . In literature I expect plenty of news . . . Abstractions which are not the latest flowers of a richly experienced and mature mind are empty and their expression devoid of poetic value." The young Auden speaks from a settled prejudice common to his generation and the ones before and after. Graves declares: "Shelley was a volatile creature of air and fire: he seems never to have noticed what he ate or drank, except sometimes as a matter of vegetarian principle. Keats was earthy, with a sweet tooth and a relish for spices, cream and snuff, and in a letter mentions peppering his own tongue to bring out the delicious coolness of claret . . . When Shelley in *Prometheus Unbound* mentions: 'The yellow bees in the ivy-bloom,' he does not conjure up, as Keats would have done, the taste of the last hot days of the dying English year, with over-ripe blackberries, ditches full of water, and the hedges grey with old man's beard. He is not aware of the veteran bees whirring their frayed wings or sucking rank honey from the dusty yellow blossoms of the ivy."

He is right in one respect: Keats is not Shelley. But Shelley does things that Keats never attempted. He does things no other English poet has achieved. Perhaps he is, as Graves suggests, a spiritual her-maphrodite. Perhaps his philosophy is, in some respects, off the wall, though not so zany as Blake's. Yet when William Carlos Williams was in his last illness he asked Robert Lowell, "Tell me honestly, Cal. Am I as good a poet as Shelley?" When Williams was a boy Shelley was *the* poet. He was that for a reason that Williams understood, utterly differ-ent though their aesthetics were.

> Walk upon the winds with lightness,
> Till they fail, as I am failing,
> Dizzy, lost, yet unbewailing.

Perhaps he heard the wonderful vocalic modulations, so mechanically imitated by Swinburne, or the effortlessness of the rhyming, or the intellectual delicacy and complexity of thought that underpins even his most conventionally Platonic images.

"Wordsworth, Scott, and Keats," wrote Matthew Arnold, "have left admirable works; far more solid and complete works than those which Byron and Shelley have left. But their works have this defect—they do not belong to that which is the main current of the literature of modern epochs, they do not apply modern ideas to life." So much the better, we might think. But Arnold continues, "They constitute, therefore, minor currents," and so, he claims, does the work of their followers. By con-trast, Shelley and Byron will be remembered "long after the inadequacy of their actual work is clearly recognised, for their passionate, their Titanic effort to flow in the main stream of modern literature; their names will be greater than their writings." The last part of Arnold's prophecy has come true for Byron. If Shelley is not quite so effective a name to conjure with, if his biography and beliefs—in free love, revolu-tion and so on—are less celebrated, it is because Shelley had a better mind, capable of exploring ideas as well as expressing memorable opin-ions. He did not pay court to an audience. He did not pose at the heart of his best poems. There is no equivalent to the Byronic hero in Shelley. He was a poet first and last, and if a man of vision, a man of specifically *poetic* vision. He is, as C. H. Sisson has said, "The last English poet to write as a gentleman." What blurs his work are in fact the "modern ideas" Arnold attributes to him, ideas that are no longer modern and no longer apply; and a conscious distance from what Arnold means by "life."

Shelley's roots in specific landscape and community are as shallow as Byron's were. Perhaps we should say that the aristocratic milieu into which he was born could not contain him. It did provide him with a voice, but at heart he is a disciple of Goethe, a European. The Mediterranean irresistibly called to him. He learned from classical philosophy and literature, Italian and Spanish culture. Dante was his master and he translated some of the *Divine Comedy*. He translated passages of Homer, Euripides, Virgil, Cavalcanti, Calderón and Goethe.

Byron and Shelley are part of a dynamic surface of English poetry, a "major current" that more or less flowed away, their language and sentiments so successful that they have been trivialized. To read them now, we must cross that trivializing barrier. If we do, we recognize in Shelley the greater poet. Both men, who became friends, share, beyond class and opinions, certain formative experiences. But there are basic differences in their poetic programs. Shelley's political and philosophical formulations result from positive thought and desire rather than reaction. In aesthetic terms Byron is frumpily old-fashioned; Shelley advances the art of English poetry by an original approach to language and an original—if fanciful—view of poetic vocation and character.

He was born in 1792 at Field Place, Horsham, Sussex, the family seat. His father was a baronet. He attended Eton, where he concentrated on scientific studies. He was already writing, and reading the fashionable literature of the time. In 1810 he went to University College, Oxford. There he read Godwin's *Political Justice*, which fired his imagination. The next year he was sent down for writing a pamphlet entitled *The Necessity of Atheism*. In the same year he married the sixteen-year-old Harriet Westbrook, whom he left after three years. She drowned herself in the Serpentine, Hyde Park, in 1816.

Shelley entered upon a correspondence with Godwin and carried his radicalism into a wider arena in 1811. Southey influenced the verse of *Queen Mab*, though when Shelley met Southey, the older poet's conservatism repelled him. He admired and befriended Leigh Hunt for his more or less consistent liberal outspokenness. More fruitful was his friendship with Thomas Love Peacock. In 1821 he answered Peacock's *Four Ages of Poetry* with his well-known *Defence of Poetry*, a quintessential Romantic document in which the centrality of the poetic vocation is affirmed in Platonizing terms that have much in common with Sir Philip Sidney's, though Shelley's claims for poetry are less circumscribed.

In 1814 he called at Godwin's house and met Mary, Godwin's daughter by Mary Wollstonecraft, and they eloped to the Continent. In 1816, Harriet's suicide having left him a widower, they were married. She as much as her father inspired him. *Alastor: or The Spirit of Solitude* was composed in 1815–16. He describes this Miltonic poem "as allegorical of one of the most interesting situations of the human mind," namely, "a youth of uncorrupted feelings and adventurous genius"—a projection of

Shelley himself—"led forth by an imagination inflamed and purified through familiarity with all that is excellent and majestic, to the contemplation of the universe." So much for the impact of Harriet's suicide. The "Preface" is a catalogue of abstractions. The poem is better than the description. It ends when Alastor, frustrated in his search for the embodiment of the ideal, "descends to an untimely grave." It is a Platonist's *Prelude*, floating free of the informing world and existing in an eloquent void. To this period also belongs the "Hymn to Intellectual Beauty."

In 1816 the Shelleys were with Byron on the Continent, and returning made the acquaintance of Keats. Keats and Shelley became friendly rivals. Shelley wrote *The Revolt of Islam* (1817) in "competition" with *Endymion*. He left England again in 1818, disaffected with a social world he saw in part through the eyes of the embittered Byron, in part through his own political disillusion. He translated Plato's *Symposium* and steeped himself in Greek literature. In 1819 he wrote *Prometheus Unbound*, a masterwork of prosody and construction. He allegorizes liberty of imagination in Prometheus and develops his philosophy of endurance and creation:

> To suffer woes which Hope thinks infinite;
> To forgive wrongs darker than death or night;
>   To defy power, which seems omnipotent;
> To love, and bear; to hope till Hope creates
> From its own wreck the thing it contemplates;
>   Neither to change, nor falter, nor repent;
> This, like thy glory, Titan, is to be
> Good, great and joyous, beautiful and free;
> This is alone Life, Joy, Empire, and Victory.

He composed his Shakespearean play *The Cenci* around this time, a piece more dramatically successful than the Elizabethanizing plays by his contemporaries: it can actually be made to work on stage.

His first year of sustained creation was 1819. In response to the Peterloo Massacre in Manchester, out of which the trade union movement was born, he composed *The Mask of Anarchy*, passionately addressing an imagined constituency and adopting a plain, forceful form of address. The soaring poet here hovers near to the actual earth and its events, delivering a direct and suasive statement about political fear and violence:

> I met Murder on the way—
> He had a mask like Castlereagh—

Very smooth he looked, yet grim;
Seven blood-hounds followed him.

The corrupt oppressors are simply and vividly drawn, as in a cruel
caricature. This is less satire than polemical allegory. Hope addresses
the oppressed in lines that float free of context, becoming effective
slogans:

"Rise like Lions after slumber
In unvanquishable number,
Shake your chains to earth like dew
Which in sleep had fallen on you—
Ye are many—they are few!"

This is not the language of ballad. Ballad was beyond the aristocrat
populist. He can write directly, but on his own terms, which are—in his
view—universal. Ballad is rooted in the tribal and rural; this poem
addresses an urban populace, a proletariat. The narrative is not docu-
mentary but symbolic. Abstractions moralize action, which is itself
translated into abstract form. The allegory is clear, provoked by specific
incidents: even if we did not know the occasion, it would be effective in
its urgency of utterance and its unambiguous solidarity.

Personal loss occasioned his celebrated "Ode to the West Wind."
Both his children by Mary died, he was homesick for England and
politically disappointed. "To a Skylark" and "The Cloud" belong to this
reflective period, and "The Sensitive Plant" and "Letter to Maria Gis-
borne" followed. Toward the end of 1819 Shelley met Sophia Stacey, for
whom he wrote "The Indian Serenade" ("I arise from dreams of thee"),
"To Sophia" ("Thou art fair, and few are fairer") and other poems. To a
later love, Emilia Viviana, he wrote *Epipsychidion* (1821). It was fortunate
that Mary had her own life and concerns.

Unlike Byron, Shelley valued Keats ("a rival who will far surpass
me") and invited him to Italy. Keats declined, though he made his final
journey to Rome with Joseph Severn later in the year. Upon Keats's
death ("Lost Angel of a ruined Paradise!") Shelley composed "Adonais,"
his greatest elegy—some say it is more about Shelley than Keats, as
"Lycidas" is more about Milton than Edward King, or "In Memoriam"
more about Tennyson than Arthur Hallam—but it is perhaps his best
poem. The tonal modulations he achieves are magnificent:

He will awake no more, oh never more!—
Within the twilight chamber spreads apace
The shadow of white Death, and at the door

Invisible Corruption waits to trace
His extreme way to her dim dwelling-place ...

Shelley referred to it as "the least imperfect of my compositions." It is
one of the clearest expressions of his Platonism, outshining his deter-
minedly philosophical *The Witch of Atlas* because it has an actual occa-
sion and engages the poet's whole sensibility in each of its fifty-five
stanzas. The fifty-second stanza declares:

The One remains, the many change and pass;
Heaven's light forever shines, Earth's shadows fly;
Life, like a dome of many-coloured glass,
Stains the white radiance of Eternity,
Until Death tramples it to fragments.—Die,
If thou wouldst be with that which thou dost seek!
Follow where all is fled!—Rome's azure sky,
Flowers, ruins, statues, music, words, are weak
The glory they transfuse with fitting truth to speak.

When the Greek war of independence began, Shelley wrote *Hellas*
(1821). His later poems are increasingly occasional in character. He sati-
rizes Wordsworth in "Peter Bell the Third," a long and eventually dole-
ful jest against Wordsworth's subject matter and manner. In 1822 some
of his finest lyrics, including "O, world! O, life! O, time!" and "When
the Lamp is Shattered," appeared. He worked on the unfinished *Tri-
umph of Life* and joined Byron and Hunt in planning *The Liberal*. In
July, sailing to Lerici, Shelley drowned when his boat, the *Don Juan*,
foundered in bad weather. He was thirty.

Had he not died, what direction would his work have taken? He had
moved toward a clearer structure in his poems, a more direct relation-
ship between imaginative concerns and the world his imagination was
constrained to occupy. The power of specific impulses already motivated
the mature poems; the more specific, earthbound image might have fol-
lowed. Had he returned to England, his politics might have evolved at
home rather than among the less pressing, less intractable crises of other
people.

Might have ... The most memorable characterization of Shelley's
work is Arnold's: "a beautiful and ineffectual angel, beating his wings in
a luminous void in vain." George Santayana defended him: "Shelley
really has a great subject matter: what ought to be; and ... he has a real
humanity—though it is a humanity in the seed, humanity in its internal
principle, rather than in those deformed expressions of it which can
flourish in the world." This is as much as to say, with Arnold, that the

angel beats its wings not in the world but in a luminous void. It sees "what ought to be" but has no strategy for bringing the ideal into being. Leavis writes, "Shelley, at his best and worst, offers the emotion in itself, unattached, in the void." T. S. Eliot found he could read Shelley when he was fifteen, but not later on, for Shelley's ideas required assent or dissent, belief or disbelief.

Shelley draws some of his figures from his early scientific studies. Edmund Blunden tells us that "many of the poet's strangest and most seemingly superficial figures are his presentations of scientific fact as it was accepted in his day." This is interesting but not helpful to a modern reader. More to the point, he shows how recurring figures in the long poems—few are without eagles, serpents, sunrises, storms—do not possess consistent value. Now a specific man is an eagle, now the eagle embodies a vision or idea. One thing is certain: Shelley's eagle is never an eagle. And he uses certain adjectives time after time not to clarify the sense but to impart a tone, a coloring.

He has, if not two voices, two processes. The one urges on into the void, with large statements whose applicability eludes us. Here the poet is—as the *Defence* portrays him—"unacknowledged legislator of mankind," also unelected and without constituency. The other process tends to particularize emotion: love poems, elegies, statements of disappointment and resignation. Often the abstracting technique is at work, but the poems have a determined effect, as in "Stanzas Written in Dejection Near Naples" or "Lines Written Among the Euganean Hills." Between these two processes a crucial difference exists: the first constructs, the second interprets, experience. Shelley's most popular poems are in the latter category. He sees himself as a moral, not a didactic writer, seeking to "awaken" and "enlarge" the mind, and this he does best through experience, not through projection.

F. R. Leavis attacks. The poet requires a suspension not of disbelief but of critical intelligence. His figurative language is at fault; there is "a general tendency of the images to forget the status of the metaphor or simile that introduced them and to assume an autonomy and a right to propagate, so that we lose in confused generations and perspectives the perception or thought that was the ostensible *raison d'être* of imagery." When Leavis speaks of Shelley's "weak grasp upon the actual," we demur. Several poems come to mind in which the actual is recognizably rendered: "Music, when soft voices die," "Ozymandias," "Sonnet: England in 1819," "Lines to an Indian Air," passages in *Prometheus Unbound*, "Song to the Men of England":

Wherefore feed, and clothe, and save,
From the cradle to the grave,

Those ungrateful drones who would
Drain your sweat—nay, drink your blood?

It depends on what we understand by "actual." Shelley proves that
an idea can be as actual and poetically viable as an image: what matters
is its realization. Certainly metaphor generates metaphor in his verse,
a poem can speed away from its occasion. Often this is part of tech-
nique, creative disorientation in order to release ideas from the tram-
mels of what *is*. Static images work against this process; hence image
and metaphor are interrelated but not related outward to specific points
in the world, which would distort the Platonic reality of his ideas.
Emancipated from the actual, his language is a self-referring structure.
Swinburne, without Shelley's serious philosophical sanction, carries this
strategy beyond sense.

Shelley rejects a rationalist tradition of normative and conventional
art. He stresses emotional fluency, the mystical source of poetry (the
dying coal); he believes in the centrality of the poet. Such views have not
been popular in England since the First World War, though they have
retained or gained currency in other anglophone lands. That poetry is
"not subject to the control of the active powers of the mind," that there
is no "necessary connection" between it and "consciousness or will"—
such views can cause offense if taken seriously. We do well to distrust
Shelley. But within the vast realm of his poetry, plays and prose exist,
apart from masterpieces to be valued, lessons to be learned, even if only
by reaction. His imaginative strategies cannot be borrowed, any more
than Milton's can, but they remain in a deep sense exemplary. A young
poet keen to attract a popular audience can ask Byron for a master class.
A serious and questing poet will recognize in Shelley a more challeng-
ing mentor, and one who will give only private instruction.

"Touch has a memory"

JOHN CLARE, WILLIAM CULLEN BRYANT, JOHN KEATS,
THOMAS LOVELL BEDDOES

In John Clare's poems we are back in a world of physical objects and processes, the minutiae of soil, season, natural and human creatures, the daily impressions of rustic life and rural hardship, yet also a world of shrewd discrimination. Modern readers can get distracted by romantic notions of Clare as untutored, a natural growth misvalued and destroyed by his age. Yes, but he belongs to his literary milieu as much as to his landscape. He watched the funeral cortège of his beloved Byron pass; he understood the genius and the waste of Chatterton; he lamented the cutting through his favorite marshland of the Manchester–London railway line.

Between his birth in Helpston, Northamptonshire, in 1793 and his confinement in the General Lunatic Asylum in Northampton in 1841 he paid four extended visits to London and spent a few months in Epping Forest, though he remained for the most part in or near his native village, much of the time under his parental roof. His is a landscape of actual heathland, fen, sheep pasture and hamlets, linked by rutted tracks and roads to the market towns. He lived under what Philip Larkin would have called a "tall sky." So remote, even the upheavals of enclosure touch him less as a social issue than as a personal sadness, a further erosion of the glowing world of childhood that counterpoints his vision of the adult world. Whatever critics make of him as a political symptom, he is not a political poet: he draws few large conclusions about rural change. What exists for his imagination is what is actually before him, so that even categorical words like "beauty" attach to his specific senses. The afflatus of Shelley is entirely alien to him.

He is impatient of Pope's verse: its smoothness tires him. Keats said that in Clare's poems "the Description too much prevailed over the sentiment." Of Keats, whom he pitied and revered and to whom he sent messages through their mutual publisher, Clare said, "He often described Nature as she appeared to his fancies and not as he would have described her had he witnessed the things he described." Clare witnessed everything from ground level.

"Clare, a labourer's son," Graves says, "was mouse-poor and quite without influence or connections. Though his first book of poems (1820) proved immediately successful, it sold well only because poetry happened to come all at once into fashion, for dubious reasons." He was not quite so without connections as Graves says. Billed as an "English peasant poet" by John Taylor, his canny publisher (who also published Hazlitt; Henry Francis Cary, the translator of Dante; Keats and Landor), he became more than a nine-day wonder, but his success was the temporary result of astute marketing. His reputation faltered. Visitors to his dwelling at Helpston didn't pay for the privilege of his company, any more than Milton's guests did. Because of his weeklong rhyming fits and his growing popularity as a lionized socioliterary aberration, he ceased to get day-laboring jobs from farmers, who found him undependable. He had seven children by his illiterate wife, Patty Turner, whom he married to make an honest woman of her. In 1830 he gave up trying to please others and, Graves declares, commenced his service to the White Goddess.

Graves, like many other poets, appropriates Clare; and yet Clare remains intractable. He can be dressed up in a dozen interpretations but each of them remains partial. What matters is the language with which he sees and makes connection. "No, not a friend on earth had I / But my own kin and poesy." "The golden furze-blooms burnt the wind," "hollow trees like pulpits," "the velvet of the pale hedge-rose": he sees, touches, hears, smells and tastes precisely, effacing himself in loving contemplation of his subject. His pathos, unheard of elsewhere in English poetry, draws on his sense of the vulnerability of natural things, of the rural order, and, obliquely, his own vulnerability. In the nature poems he is reluctant to speak of himself. "In spite of his individual manner," says Edmund Blunden, "there is no poet who in his nature poetry so completely subdues self and mood and deals with the topic for its own sake." He expresses himself in his choice of subject and diction, but such self-expression is not the poem's purpose. There are few storms in his poems, little embellishment of natural processes. The external world remains external. He chooses insects for their distinctive otherness: "These tiny loiterers in the barley's beard, / And happy units of a numerous herd / Of playfellows," or birds, flowers, streams, fields, meadows. "Fairy Things" is characteristic. Most of his work comes into focus in the present tense: "He gives no broad impressions—he saw the kite but not the kite's landscape," wrote Edward Thomas. Yet taken together the poems reveal the Northamptonshire countryside that was his world.

From birth he was ill placed for poetry. His father, the bastard son of a wandering fiddler-schoolmaster and the parish clerk's daughter, worked as a farm laborer. Though poor, he did his best to educate the boy. Clare interspersed farmwork with study. At the age of seven he was tending the geese; before his teens he was helping at the plow. Sundays he spent in the fields, and at sixteen he was writing poems. He was also early in love—with Mary Joyce, whose father eventually forbade their friendship. Later in his madness he came to regard Mary as his first wife, his Muse to whom he addressed his poems. He conversed with her in his head long after she died a spinster.

The poet farmed, gardened, became a soldier, even spent time among gypsies. He read what he could: Thomson's *The Seasons* helped him find direction. He was "itching at rhymes" (a favorite expression). When he was twenty-seven Taylor brought out his first book, *Poems Descriptive of Rural Life and Scenery*. It was a great success, running through four editions in one year, the same year he married. Within a month of the wedding, his first child was born. He visited London and was exhibited in literary and aristocratic circles. The label "peasant poet" limited his scope in ways he came to regret. Success raised his expectations and estranged him from his community, a disaster when his fame proved ephemeral. He hoped for a financial security he never achieved.

The Village Minstrel was published with less success the following year. Clare visited London again, met Charles Lamb and the lively poet Thomas Hood, and began contributing verse and prose to periodicals on a regular basis. His prose articles and letters have a character of their own, natural (or homespun) and frank. His editors had the task of correcting and punctuating his unconventional prose. Verse was his natural medium. They had to correct its orthography and punctuation as well.

In 1823 he began to suffer periodic illnesses connected with his later mental troubles. The next year he spent more than two months in London and met Coleridge and De Quincey, who held him up as an example: here was a man who, without advantages, rose on genuine merit to literary achievement. "His poems were not the mere reflexes of his reading. He had studied for himself in the fields, and in the woods, and by the side of brooks." His defect as a poet was his assiduous accuracy, which according to De Quincey (and Keats) displaced the emotion. De Quincey notes how Clare was drawn not so much by "the gorgeous display of English beauty, but the French style of beauty, as he saw it amongst the French actresses in Tottenham Court Road." He recalls Clare's "rapturous" enthusiasm for Wordsworth, whom he initially resisted reading, and who "depressed his self-confidence."

The Shepherd's Calendar appeared belatedly in 1827 and failed. In seven years Clare had experienced his rise and fall. He was breadwinner for nine dependents, including his parents. The strain told on him. The years 1828–29 were almost stable. In 1830 illness returned; he grew haggard and weak. Lord Milton provided him with a new cottage three miles from Helpston, to which he reluctantly moved. His madness began in earnest in 1833. *The Rural Muse* (1835)—his best book, though it appeared in a form very different from the one he intended—failed, despite good notices. It was the last book published in his lifetime. *The Midsummer Cushion*—a vast, uneven collection of later work—was not published until 1979. He was committed to an asylum in Epping Forest in 1837. Some months later he ran away, making the four-day journey home on foot with considerable hardship. Eventually he was shut up in the Northampton asylum. The charge was "years addicted to poetical prosings." There he spent his remaining twenty-three years, dying in 1864.

Early readers compared Clare unfavorably with Burns, whose work he had not read. But Edward Thomas contrasts the two: "Unlike Burns, he had practically no help from the poetry and music of his class. He was a peasant writing poetry, yet cannot be called a peasant poet, because he had behind him no tradition of peasant literature, but had to do what he could with the current forms of polite literature." Modern critics can forget that fundamental fact. Clare's work owes little to his class, though scansion, diction and pronunciation are true to his accent. His sense of social issues—unlike William Barnes's—is parochial. He is harsh on those better placed than he is, who misunderstand and misprize poetry and poets. "An Effusion on Poesy" addresses a "genteel opinionist in poetry":

> Labour! 'cause thou'rt mean and poor,
> Learning spurns thee from her door;
> But despise me as she will,
> Poesy! I love thee still.

In "Impromptu on Winter" he identifies the "petty gentry" with the chilling weather.

Enclosure distressed him for personal reasons. The plight of the peasants is not his concern in his lament for the loss of Swordy Well, where he had played and tended cows. "The Fallen Elm," on the same theme, is one of his best poems; and "Remembrance," written during his illness, returns to the theme again:

> Enclosure like a Buonaparte let not a thing remain,
> It levelled every bush and tree and levelled every hill

And hung the moles for traitors, though the brook is running still
It runs a naked stream cold and chill.

Such poems *include* a general loss but stand clear of the people, apart
from those close to him. Poetry, like nature, is a space away from men:
"Thou light of the world's hermitage," an art that illuminates solitary
contemplation.

Clare's poetic models were literary, his Muse homely,

> . . . who sits her down
> Upon the mole hill's little lap,
> Who feels no fear to stain her gown,
> And pauses by the hedgerow gap.

This precious figure is out of place in his literal world, one of many con-
ventional blemishes, which include borrowings in diction from Thom-
son, an excessive use of epithets and superfluous adjectives, a tendency
to overwrite, all faults that became less numerous in his later work. They
hardly blur the visualization and presentation in such poems as "Eve-
ning Schoolboys," "Hares at Play," "Rural Scenes," "The Shepherd's
Tree," "My Schoolboy Days" or the autobiographical nightmare "The
Return" (1841): "So on he lives in glooms and living death, / A shade like
night, forgetting and forgot." In diffuse form this poem expresses the
same anguish as "I Am," his best-loved personal poem, in which isola-
tion is heightened by tempest and sea images, until he witnesses "the
vast shipwreck of my life's esteems." The poem stands without apology
beside Cowper's bleakest work.

Clare's poetic foe was his facility. He could write poem after poem
without blotting a line. Some poems come merely from a joy at utter-
ance. His reluctance to revise means there are many effusions that go on
too long, without shape or cogent development. Some open arrestingly:

> Leaves from eternity are simple things
> To the world's gaze—whereto a spirit clings
> Sublime and lasting. Trampled underfoot,
> The daisy lives, and strikes its little root
> Into the lap of time . . .

But this initial precision soon dissipates in prolixity. Clare repeats
images and whole lines that he especially likes.

He often starts a poem with "I love"—the leaves, the gusts; or to
walk, to hide, to hear. The act of loving description is the poem. If it

succeeds, we know why he loves. His primary achievement is nature poetry. The poems that reveal the tensions of mental illness are more popular today, often for other than poetic reasons. The accomplishment of the poet who wrote "The fish were playing in the pool / And turned their milk-white bellies up" is visual and verbal. Clare came to imitate his earlier in his later work. His range of statement is not wide, and he was so prolific as almost to exhaust his subject matter. There is a sameness of tone about his writing—no wonder he loved the wider freedoms traced by Byron, or the more peopled world of Robert Bloomfield, like him a laborer and later a shoemaker in London, whose *The Farmer's Boy*, published in 1800, sold 26,000 copies in three years. Clare is not, as some claim, a "great poet." But his best writing—not his best poems, for the best writing is often contained in uneven poems—his best writing is in a class of its own. Only Edward Thomas, of later poets, learned its abiding lessons.

A new nature and landscape at this time were struggling to find their way into verse forms that the eighteenth century had left full of moral and philosophical starch, the nature of a land that had hitherto been for the most part content to live on imported forms and diction. William Cullen Bryant's poetic career began when he was ten, with versifications of the book of Job; at thirteen he was writing satire about Thomas Jefferson; but his vocation began in earnest with a meditation on death entitled "Thanatopsis." It begins:

> To him who in the love of nature holds
> Communion with her visible forms, she speaks
> A various language; for his gayer hours
> She has a voice of gladness, and a smile
> And eloquence of beauty . . .

The mood soon darkens. If the terms seem precociously to mingle the eighteenth century ("Pope's celestial fire" and touches of Cowper) with elements of Southey and themes analogous to those of Coleridge and Shelley, the poem is largely original in its combination of strains.

Bryant, born in America of severe Pilgrim stock in Cummington, Massachusetts, in 1794, was the first poet to make a point of his Americanness. In essays and lectures he considered what a specifically American literature might look like. Landscape and character deserved a place of their own, and he lamented the fact that "transatlantic approbation" was required before a writer was endorsed at home. European Romanticism itself eased the way for American literary emancipation, the move from Puritan priorities to transcendentalism.

Bryant was a sickly baby with a tyrannical grandfather (the formidable Calvinist-federalist Ebenezer Snell). The baby poet had a huge head, and his father, a doctor, would plunge it into icy water each morning to shrink it. When the boy began to grow up, his father made him work in the fields and take long constitutionals. The cure worked: he lived to be an old man. It was on such walks that he began to *see*, and what he saw of nature had yet to find a poetic language. Ebenezer stood between him and the education he desired—Harvard or Yale—and his poems developed in a thwarted solitude. On his own terms Bryant attracted an English readership. Arnold thought "To a Waterfowl," his most anthologized piece, one of the best short poems in the language. He actually saw the bird in flight: it was no figment, no figure, but a flapping creature whose literal motion elicited literal feeling and thought. The poet is making the transition in it from the crabbed world of Ebenezer Snell into the freer realm of nineteenth-century nature (Emerson is just around the corner). The poems of nature and description abandon the deliberate universalizing of his models and acknowledge the actual world. The diction retains its European varnish until gradually and insistently he introduces the American words, effectively in "The Prairies," with its poised precisions.

Bryant became a big noise in American journalism, a champion of liberal causes and a catalyst. When Dickens arrived in New York, he is reported to have asked on coming down the gangplank, "Where's Bryant?" It was he who made certain that Central Park and the Metropolitan Museum of Art were established. He became a Unitarian. He opposed slavery and advocated free trade and trade unionism. He continued publishing verse, but it is the earlier work, in which he began to discover American priorities, and his essays and lectures, that had abiding impact. In Britain the fact that he was recognized at all is significant: the first American-born poet to be accorded relatively uncondescending recognition. In 1878 he was still in harness: the eighty-four-year-old, having delivered a speech at the unveiling of a statue of Mazzini in Central Park, tripped as he left the podium and died of concussion. Just as he helped to create Central Park, he had also begun to lay the foundations for American poetry.

John Keats's short life—in span a third of Bryant's and less than half of Clare's—passed in a rage of passionate activity. He is a world away from both, yet they share a fascination with the natural world. Clare and Bryant had the task of rendering things seen and loved in a recalcitrant, Augustanized medium, adjusting and extending the medium for their purposes. Keats starts with the medium and brings it to bear on nature.

One evening when he was eighteen he met his friend Charles

Cowden Clarke, son of the headmaster of Clarke's School, which Keats had left to undertake a medical apprenticeship. Clarke read him Spenser's "Epithalamion," the poem that caused Coleridge such delicious prosodic pain. Astonished, Keats took home the first volume of the *Faerie Queene*, which (Clarke says) he "ramped through . . . like a young horse turned into a Spring meadow." One of his earliest poems, "Imitation of Spenser," begins "Now Morning from her orient chamber came" and groans with adjectives. The third stanza presages the Keats to be:

> Ah! I could tell the wonders of an isle
> That in that fairest lake had placèd been,
> I should e'en Dido of her grief beguile;
> Or rob from aged Lear his bitter teen:
> For sure so fair a place was never seen,
> Of all that ever charmed romantic eye:
> It seemed an emerald in the silver sheen
> Of the bright waters; or as when on high,
> Through clouds of fleecy white, laughs the cerulean sky.

His chief concern in his poetry was poetry itself, and, as with many other young poets, "the imagery he chose," Robert Graves insists, "was predominantly sexual. Poetry for him was not a philosophical theory, as it was for Shelley, but a moment of physical delirium"—a delirium that releases the poet, and the poem, even if only for a moment, from the flow of time.

> What can I do to drive away
> Remembrance from my eyes? for they have seen,
> Aye, an hour ago, my brilliant Queen!
> Touch has a memory. O say, love, say,
> What can I do to kill it and be free
> In my old liberty?

The language is ambivalent. "Although he was male-minded enough in ordinary sexual business," Graves notes, "as his letters to Fanny Brawne, and his song 'Give me women, wine and snuff,' show, the critics were right: he did mix the sexes in his poems." The language of sensuous and emotional excess, especially in *Endymion* and *Hyperion*, repelled critics who found it mawkish and said so. When Keats died, Byron, referring to a savage review, wrote: " 'Tis strange the mind, that very fiery particle, / Should let itself be snuffed out by an article."

Keats's early descriptions are unsatisfactory. In his essay "How Poets

See," Graves tells us: "Keats was short-sighted. He did not see land-scapes as such, so he treated them as painted cabinets filled with inter-esting objects . . . His habit was to allow his eye to be seduced from entire vision by particular objects . . . He saw little but what moved: the curving, the wreathing, the slanting, the waving—and even then, it seems, not the whole object in motion but only its edge, or highlight." This "mind-sight" depends less on vision than on a composite impres-sion of the senses and memory. It comes into focus irregularly, with sur-prising sharpness. Such "mind-sight" could not be conveyed in what Keats mockingly calls "the rocking horse" of the heroic couplet. The eighteenth century is over. We are back with an earlier poetry, the vivid-ness of Chaucer, the allegorical sweetmeats of Spenser.

"Milton had an exquisite passion for what is properly, in the sense of ease and pleasure, poetical luxury," wrote Keats, "and with that, it appears to me, he would fair have been content, if he could, so doing, preserve his self-respect and feeling of duty performed." But Milton had other passions, religious and social, and thus "devoted himself rather to the ardours than the pleasures of song." Keats, for his part, was almost content in his passion for poetic luxury. "Keats as a poet is abundantly and enchantingly sensuous," Arnold says, but, "the question with some people will be, whether he is anything else." Arnold sets out to prove that, though he lacked fixed purpose, Keats in pursuit of Beauty was heading for something moral and wholesome: the "ardours" of song. He quotes from the "Epistle to Reynolds": "But my flag is not unfurl'd / On the Admiral-staff, and to philosophise / I dare not yet." The virtue of Keats's poetry is precisely that he does not emptily "philosophize." Unlike many of his contemporaries, he evades the systematic distortion of a worldview that, when it recognizes itself, adjusts the world to fit.

Louis MacNeice fancifully calls Keats a "sensuous mystic." The cate-gory blurs into impressionism. Arnold is closer to the truth: Keats's "yearning passion for the Beautiful" (his own terms) "is not a passion of the sensuous or sentimental poet. It is an intellectual and spiritual pas-sion." Keats claimed that, had he been strong enough, he would have lived alone and pursued his quest for Beauty through particular experi-ments: "I have loved the principle of beauty in all things."

He was born in London in 1795, son of a livery-stable manager who died when the boy was nine, leaving Keats, his brothers Tom and George, and his sister Fanny to the care of their mother. She remarried and sent the children to live with her mother at Edmonton, then a vil-lage, now part of London. Mrs. Keats died six years later of consump-tion, the illness that killed Tom in 1818 and Keats himself three years later. His father's estate was left in the charge of managers of doubtful integrity: when Keats most needed money, none was to be had.

He attended school at Enfield from 1803 to 1811 and studied Latin, French and history. He began to translate the *Aeneid*, but only started his "serious" reading after he left school. Apprenticed to a surgeon, when he was twenty he entered Guy's Hospital as a student and dresser. His poems began to appear in print. Around his twenty-first birthday he composed "On First Looking into Chapman's Homer." The plan for *Endymion* (1818) took shape. He met Leigh Hunt, who introduced him to artists and writers and directed his taste. Hunt, though he encouraged Keats's aestheticism, showed his young protégé connections between poetry and the other arts. Keats's best work often finds its pretext in art rather than nature. Hunt introduced him to Hazlitt and the painter Benjamin Robert Haydon, complementary intelligences, the one acerbic and strict, the other expansive and enthusiastic. He met Shelley and Wordsworth.

With Shelley's help he published his first book of poems in 1817 and followed it with *Endymion* the next year. *Endymion* received killing reviews in *Blackwood's Magazine* and the *Quarterly Review*. Keats came to accept that some of the censure was just. But hostility, we now know, resulted from reviewers' ill-will to the liberal Hunt: Keats was caught in the crossfire. Some poets were quite as hostile as the reviewers, however. Byron at a later date described Keats as "this miserable self-polluter of the human mind." He despised what he took to be the poet's effeminacy, passivity and nostalgia. Keats's sonnet "Byron! how sweetly sad thy melody!" might have deserved a warmer response.

Keats's poetic maturity begins in 1818. He composed "Isabella, or the Pot of Basil," saw his brother George off to America, nursed his brother Tom through his final consumption, traveled to Scotland (where he visited the tomb, cottage and landscapes of Burns and poured forth lamenting praises) and Ireland, contracted his own consumption on the Isle of Mull in July, and met Fanny Brawne, with whom he fell precipitately in love and to whom he wrote those love letters that Arnold described as "underbred and ignoble." They are not his best letters. He also began the composition of *Hyperion*.

In 1819 he composed the body of work on which his claims on our attention rest: "The Eve of St Agnes," "La Belle Dame sans Merci," the great odes, "Lamia," and much else. He completed *Hyperion*. At the beginning of 1820 his consumption took hold. He sailed to Italy with his friend the painter Joseph Severn in September. On board ship he wrote the final version of the sonnet "Bright Star." In November, from Rome, he wrote the last of his famous letters. He died on 23 February 1821 and was buried in the Protestant Cemetery in Rome, where Shelley's mortal remains joined him the following year. On Keats's grave appear the words "Here lies one whose name was writ in water."

His last five years brim with human experience; he decided to abandon medicine for poetry and his world opened out. His writing matured in a matter of months. The earliest surviving work reveals skill in phrasemaking: he uncannily snares an image in a memorable phrase or line. "I look upon fine phrases as a lover," he wrote. "I stood tiptoe upon a little hill" displays this early power and its faults. Volleys of adjectives and occasional mixed metaphors give way to lucid visualizations. The clouds are "pure and white as flocks new shorn" sleeping "On the blue fields of heaven"; we hear "A little noiseless noise among the leaves, / Born of the very sigh that silence heaves." He decrees himself a poet of praise who watches "intently Nature's gentle doings"; and if, as Edward Thomas believes, we are given no sense of actual setting, we do experience particular natural phenomena: minnows, flowers, breezes. We meet Apollo, a presiding spirit; images of looking upward to heaven and the gods, of ascent and final soaring are crucial to several poems. In "I stood tiptoe" emotion spills over images but does not fuse with them. In later mature work he contains emotion *in* particulars: indeed emotion unifies them. The father of poets may still have been the "dear delight / Of this fair world." But nature he apprehended as isolated phenomena; the countryside was a vast natural gallery; its underlying processes, which Clare and Wordsworth witnessed, were invisible to the casual walker.

"On First Looking into Chapman's Homer" is his first great poem. The sonnet defines a response through analogies: how he felt on reading Chapman's translation. He responds like an astronomer looking up at a new planet or like a conquistador (a modern Odysseus, a warrior-hero) looking down on a new ocean. Planet and ocean are actually old, but are seen for the first time. "Sleep and Poetry," also in the 1817 volume, is over four hundred lines long. It defines his "poetics," such as they were at the time. Apollo glows in his firmament, and there is much concrete imagery. In rather unruly couplets Keats rejects Augustan convention: "musty laws lined out with wretched rules," the tendency to "inlay, and clip, and fit" till "the verses tallied." Certainly his verses, with many feminine rhymes, enthusiasm and no clear progression, owe few debts to the eighteenth century. "A drainless shower / Of light is poesy," he declares.

In *Endymion* Keats's rapid development begins. Written in a short time, it is, he concedes, "a feverish attempt" and not "a deed accomplished." He asks at one point, "Muse of my native land, am I inspired?" Probably not: what is striking, apart from the remarkable anthologized passages, is the evidence of a transition from a poetry that praises to a poetry that feels; from the poet who describes from the outside to the one who employs "negative capability," effaces his identity and writes as it were from within his images, "becoming" the sparrow on the gravel. *Endymion* explores the ways in which beautiful forms and figures, myths richly told, might clarify and strengthen the minds of men, not merely for a moment, but for good. Poetry expands and deepens awareness:

> Nor do we merely feel these essences
> For one short hour; no, even as the trees
> That whisper round a temple become soon
> Dear as the temple's self, so does the moon,
> The passion poesy, glories infinite,
> Haunt us till they become a cheering light
> Unto our souls, and bound to us so fast,
> That, whether there be shine, or gloom o'ercast,
> They alway must be with us, or we die.

This is not portentous: it is *true*, but a truth expressed without a wink or nudge of irony. What was before mere aesthetic exploration overflows here into a general verity. Such resonance is limited, however, to a few passages. *Endymion*'s besetting faults are structural. The verse is so delighted with details of setting, nuances of look and movement, its theme and its self-intoxicating cadences, that the narrative is slow. Spenser is partly responsible for the faults, as for the virtues. The weakness is the mode, which also condemns *Hyperion* and *The Fall of Hyperion* to survive as unsatisfactory contexts for some of Keats's most brilliant passages.

The narratives "Lamia," "The Eve of St Agnes" and "Isabella" are compact and dramatic and, despite gothic and magical elements, enact human dramas, romantic in nature but comprehensive in emotional range. The gods move off. Keats ceases to moralize the poem as it progresses and becomes instead an implicit interpreter. In "Lamia" he takes a story from Robert Burton's *The Anatomy of Melancholy*, one of his favorite books. Lamia, a sorceress, loves Lycius. She is transformed into a beautiful girl whom he courts and wins. At the wedding, the sage Apollonius, Lycius's old tutor, recognizes Lamia and names her. She vanishes, and with her all of Lycius's expectations and dreams. Lycius was deceived but joyful. The sage, representing truth, rescues him from deceit, but kills him.

> Philosophy will clip an Angel's wings,
> Conquer all mysteries by rule and line,
> Empty the haunted air, and gnomèd mine—
> Unweave a rainbow, as it erewhile made
> The tender-personed Lamia melt into a shade.

"Lamia" enacts without resolving the disparity between feeling and fact, which fascinated Keats. It is the metaphor of an emotion, like most of the poems of his maturity. It explores dream in the context of fact. "The Eve of St Agnes" sets passion in the context of passing time, a theme of urgency for a poet aware of his impending death; and "Isabella" portrays love thwarted by social circumstances.

"The Eve of St Agnes" and "Ode on a Grecian Urn" approach Keats's main themes from opposite directions. At the opening of "The Eve of St Agnes" he distances us from the narrative, giving a long view, then panning in. The story is enacted; then, in the way that Chaucer taught him to do, he throws it back into the long view: the lovers escape in time, but not from it. Madeline, like Lycius, finds reality inferior to the dream: "And those sad eyes were spiritual and clear; / How changed thou art! how pallid, chill and drear!" By contrast, in "Ode on a Grecian Urn," we are brought up close to the contemplated object from the very first line, in which it is personified and sexualized as the "still unravished bride of quietness"—both "still" and "still unravished." The poet would animate the marble figures. But they have escaped time altogether and can anticipate only eternal anticipation without fulfillment. We're left in the urn's presence: not distanced or contextualized, it is its own context and fills our perception.

"The Eve of St Agnes" underlines the lovers' vulnerability: forces from outside penetrate the rooms. Storm beats against inner warmth, moonlight falls ghostly on a closed scene, draughts waft the furnishings. These elements intensify and accelerate passion, only to absorb it when the lovers step out into the night and go to the reality that a realized dream becomes. Age is the backdrop of the drama: old Angela and the beadsman depict youth's inescapable future. Through the poem we follow the contours of unresolved emotion, not the progression of an idea. The lover Porphyro knows, without acknowledging, the truth of passion: he sings Madeline an "ancient ditty, long since mute" from Provence: *"La belle dame sans mercy."* Keats's poem of that title, written in 1818 but not printed until 1848 in *Literary Remains*, relates to all the narratives, though it is far more condensed and mysterious.

The three great narratives, rich in detail, idealized characterization, and gothic elements, inspired poets, painters and musicians later in the century. The Pre-Raphaelites in particular drew sustenance from them. "The Eve of St Agnes" radically reconfigures resources of tone and characterization that Keats adapted from Chaucer and Shakespeare. *Romeo and Juliet* was not far from his hand when he wrote the poem. And his phrasing owes Shakespeare a debt. *Cymbeline* suggests the way Madeline's bedchamber is made solid before our eyes. Keats does not imitate his masters: he has assimilated them.

The odes—"To a Nightingale," "On a Grecian Urn," "To Autumn," and the lesser "To Psyche" and "On Melancholy"—are incomparable. The charge that he "lacked experience" is fatuous; nor are they "merely sensuous." They are the step beyond moral romance to the romance of feeling itself, feeling as subject, the "true voice."

Intoxication precedes the song of the bird in "To a Nightingale"; its voice is not heard until the fifth line, and the creature is never seen. Announced by its effect, it remains effect, a dryad of the trees. The first stanza introduces thematic ingredients: joy, sorrow, music, death, and the rapture that frees the poet into the world of sense. A conflict of desires develops: first, the desire to vie with and equal the dryad in eloquence; then, the desire to die at the height of the ecstasy its song inspires. Every sense apart from sight is engaged: in the darkness there is no light "Save what from heaven is with the breezes blown / Through verdurous glooms and winding mossy ways." We see what we cannot see, the green, the gloom, the moss, the path winding in darkness. None of his poems equals this one for evocation, sense drawn to focus by birdsong and night, away from a sordid world the dryad has never known:

> The weariness, the fever, and the fret
>> Here, where men sit and hear each other groan;
> Where palsy shakes a few, sad, last grey hairs,
>> Where youth grows pale, and spectre-thin, and dies . . .

Age and death: the death of his brother informs that last line. Recollection of the actual world breaks his reverie. How is he to escape—through poetry? His mind holds back, though imagination is "already with thee" in the light of heaven. Twice his emotion rises to the bird, twice it is recalled, first by the reality of the human condition, then by a sense of his inadequacy. He considers death, but the thought corrects itself with the reflection that in death he would be deaf to the bird's "high requiem." The word "forlorn"—like a bell, contrasting with the bird's song—calls him back again to the world. The bird flies at the word's tolling, a knell to the feeling and its cause. "Fled is that music: Do I wake or sleep?" Keats's deepest feelings weave themselves into the texture of the poem, itself elicited by an actual nightingale the poet heard in a garden. "O for a life of Sensations rather than Thoughts!" he had declared. The odes achieve that life. Thoughts are subservient to the tone of feeling and remain potent because unresolved.

"Ode on a Grecian Urn" provides teachers and schoolchildren with an inexhaustible paradox in its closing lines. It is well to remember that the urn, not Keats, declares, "Beauty is truth, truth beauty." Keats adds, "that is all / Ye know on earth, and all ye need to know." Is it a statement of faith? Or is the "ye" the human images on the urn? Is he reflecting on its knowledge rather than ours? The way he presents images, the repetitions of "happy" and "ever" and "forever," with their mournful effect (like "forlorn" in the "Nightingale"), and the poem's tone balance without contradicting the categorical conclusion. Is the poem different in kind from the other odes and narratives? The conclusion *means* only in the context of the poem itself.

Each stanza proposes a paradoxical contrast between static portrayal and the activity portrayed. The "still unravished bride of quietness," child of "silence" and "slow time" is a poignant personification. The poem examines the images on the urn: "maidens loth," "mad pursuit," "struggle to escape," "pipes and timbrels," "wild ecstasy." The serene object gives way to the violent passion of its decoration. Sexual tension is strong throughout the first three stanzas, beginning with the "unravished bride," "panting," fear and desire—arrested at a point before release. Actions that find fulfillment only in time are translated to a timeless context.

In the fourth stanza Keats turns to the sacrificial procession and the village, which, emptied of its populace, will "evermore" be silent, and never know *why* it is "desolate," only that it is. In the last stanza the urn becomes a "Cold Pastoral," an oxymoron. Having brought the urn to life, revealing through the play of imagination his own intense ambivalence about time and the nature of beauty, he delivers the final lines with a conclusive air that only qualifies the experience of the poem itself.

"Poetry should surprise by a fine excess, and not by singularity." In the odes what is dazzling is the fine excess, the wealth of apposite images that, in stanzas of impeccable prosodic development, answer to the poet's deepest concerns. If Keats lacked the intellectual resources of Coleridge or Shelley, he still came close to solving the same problems of poetic form they wrestled with. The odes indeed appear to the reader as the wording of his own highest thoughts, "almost a remembrance." And they answer more than sufficiently the doubts that Clare expressed. "Touch has a memory," for Clare of the particulars of Northamptonshire, which was his world; for Keats in the odes, where memory brings his whole life into play.

Beyond the charmed circle of poets in the canon is a rather monstrous and melancholy figure, a little absurd and generally overlooked: Thomas Lovell Beddoes, born in Shropshire in 1803, and dead (a suicide after several attempts) in 1849 at the Cigogne Hotel in Basel, Switzerland. Son of a physician—who, legend says, brought home bodies to dissect in the parlor after dinner, and who discovered laughing gas and administered it to Coleridge—Beddoes became a physician himself. He wrote verse from an early age, some of it ghoulish, foreshadowing the manner of his later work. He published very little during his lifetime, certainly not his most important work, *Death's Jest Book*, which he began at twenty-two, when he left England, and kept revising until death put an end to blotting and it was published in 1850. His most celebrated poem is "Dream Pedlary," perhaps devoted to his companion of one year, a Russian Jewish student called Bernhard Reich. John Ashbery suggests he may have been the "loved, longlost boy" of the poem. His later years he spent with a young baker called Konrad Degen.

Beddoes misbehaved—at Oxford, in Göttingen, in Zürich—and his life was mysterious, peripatetic, unobserved. The "poems" that exist are generally fragments, plucked out of his plays and from *Death's Jest Book*, which imitate, though not in a spirit of forgery, the Jacobean drama, taking images that unfold in a hugely extended syntax. Death is his theme: "Death is the one condition of our lives," he says, earning from Ezra Pound the sobriquet "prince of morticians." His verse pulls up "a mass of algae / (and pearls)." His most eloquent contemporary advocate is John Ashbery, a poet whose syntax is as various and unpredictable as Beddoes's own, and who revels in the Firbankian elements of the verse. Beddoes is a figure unaccountably omitted—apart from "Dream Pedlary," "one of the most seamlessly beautiful lyrics in the English language"—from the general feast. It is not only isolated images and cadences that astonish us: "Within the myrtle / Sits a hen-robin, trembling like a star, / Over her brittle eggs"; "If there were dreams to sell / What would you buy?"; "Where in their graves the dead are shut like seeds"; it is the strange exchanges between strange characters. In the *Jest Book* the Duke asks Isbrand: "How? Do you rhyme too?"

ISBRAND: Sometimes, in leizure moments
                And a romantic humour; this I made
                One night a-strewing poison for the rats
                In the kitchen corner.

DUKE: And what's your tune?

ISBRAND: What is the night-bird's tune, wherewith she startles
                The bee out of his dream and the true lover,
                And both in the still moonshine turn and kiss
                The flowery bosom where they rest, and murmuring
                Sleep smiling and more happily again?
                What is the lobster's tune when he is boiled?
                I hate your ballads that are made to come
                Round like a squirrel's cage, and round again.

> We nightingales sing boldly from our hearts:
> So listen to us.

Another madness, hanging over from the Augustan age? Or is this the Romanticism we never quite had, more extreme than the gothic that was yet to come, more candid in its obliquities than many of his great (unknown) contemporaries? Thomas Kelsall, a friend and admirer, wrote a life and published some of the poems.

Kelsall corresponded with Robert Browning and it was hoped that Browning would make a selection of Beddoes's work. Kelsall upon his death left Browning the manuscripts and other material in a box which, as Browning's interest cooled, was referred to as "that dismal Box." Fortunately James Dyke Campell, another partisan, copied the manuscripts around 1886, before they vanished. Edmund Gosse finally edited the texts, which have since been put in rather better order but are hard to obtain. Browning missed his chance to adjust our sense of his century and to make public one of the most curious and still misprized voices of his time, a poet who belongs with Shelley on the one hand, and with Wilde on the other, as a radical presence who gradually gets language on his own terms. Is this, perhaps, in the voice of Isbrand, Beddoes himself?

> How I despise
> All you mere men of muscle! It was ever
> My study to find out a way to godhead,
> And on reflection soon I found that first
> I was but half created; that a power
> Was wanting in my soul to be a soul,
> And this was mine to make ...

Long Gray Beards and
Glittering Eyes

WILLIAM BARNES, ALFRED LORD TENNYSON,
RALPH WALDO EMERSON

Fanatics have their dreams, wherewith they weave
A paradise for a sect . . .

The lines from *The Fall of Hyperion* evoke Keats's century, its disappointed political and social ideals. History proved autonomous of the human will: it would not succumb to prediction, logic or control, and even more brutally in the next century it proposed and then disproved the prophecies of Karl Marx. In the provinces, on a local scale, a few writers set out on heroically doomed ventures. In his "Dissertation on the Dorset Dialect of the English Language" (1844), William Barnes identifies with what he hopefully calls "that increasing class who wish to purify our tongue and enrich it from its own resources"—the resources of dialect. He swims hard against a tide in which "the spread of school education among the lower ranks of the people" (the fruit of an idealism) seems destined to erase the abundance of local usage and reduce the expressive resources of language. Barnes's Dorset dialect, he believes, is the purest and most authentic in Britain, and one of the most expressive. He devotes his efforts to advocacy and exemplification, providing a varied and coherent dialect poetry. If he lacks the folk roots and molten libido of Burns, if he seems to be constructing a dialect poetry in the way that Hugh MacDiarmid was to do in Scotland less than a century later, it is not the hopeless enterprise we judge but the poetry. Hardy, Barnes's devoted advocate, aligns him with Collins, Gray and Tennyson, rather than with "the old unpremeditating writers in dialect. Primarily spontaneous, he was academic closely after; and we find him warbling his native woodnotes with a watchful eye on the predetermined score, a far remove from the popular impression of him as the naïf and rude bard who sings only because he must." Hopkins, too, in correspondence with Robert Bridges and Coventry Patmore, valued Barnes's enterprise.

"To write in what some may deem a fast out-wearing speech-form," says Barnes, using an entirely Anglo-Saxon diction, "may seem as idle as the writing of one's name in snow on a spring day . . . [but] . . . I cannot help it. It is my mother tongue, and it is to my mind the only true speech of the life that I draw." There is no useful point of comparison between Barnes and Burns. If Burns lacks repose, Barnes lacks urgency, extremes of feeling, flights of rhetoric, social and sexual abandon, satiric sting. Burns was a Scots poet in the tradition of Dunbar; Barnes, an English poet in the main tradition, who happened to write—or had to write— in dialect. He tends a narrower patch and ponders it at greater leisure— he lived to eighty-five. He is a wise poet, but a poet almost by chance. He wrote poems "as if I could not help it, the writing of them was not work but like the playing of music." Few poets are as inextricably rooted in their place as he. Hopkins said: "Barnes is a perfect artist. It is as if Dorset life and Dorset landscape had taken flesh and blood in the man." This is as true of the eclogues as of the lyrics and elegies. Hardy commented on this quality, the "closeness of phrase to vision." "Come, Fanny, come! put on thy white, / 'Tis Woodcom' feäst, good now! tonight."

Barnes was born at Rush-Hay, Bagber Common, near Sturminster Newton, Dorset, in 1801. His father was a not very prosperous tenant farmer. When Barnes was five his mother died; he was sent to the Vale of Blackmore, where his aunt and uncle reared him. The rural life he evokes was a lived, not an artificial experience. A poem in "common," or "national," English tells of his early years:

> We spent in woodland shades our day
> In cheerful work or happy play,
> And slept at night where rustling leaves
> Threw moonlight shadows o'er our eaves.
>   I knew you young, and love you now,
>   O shining grass, and shady bough.

This nostalgic, conventional language does not get into the dialect poems, though the subtle prosody does. In "The Leäne" ("The Lane")— one of his best poems—he contrasts *was* and *is*:

> Years agoo the leäne-zides did bear grass,
>   Vor to pull wi' the geeses' red bills,

That did hiss at the vo'k that did pass,   folk
    Or the bwoys that pick'd up their white
quills.
But shortly, if vower or vive   four or five
    Ov our goslens do creep vrom the agg,
They must mwope in the geärden, mwore dead
than alive,
    In a coop, or a-tied by the lag.

The poem considers the consequences of the enclosure of the common land.

The vicar and the schoolmaster took an interest in young Barnes. He learned Greek and Latin. When he was thirteen his uncle went bankrupt and Barnes became a solicitor's clerk in Dorchester. When the solicitor who had furthered his education died, the eighteen-year-old Barnes moved to another clerkship. He progressed gradually. He met and decided to marry Julia Miles, and did so—nine years later. At the age of nineteen he printed *Poetical Pieces*, including a translation from the Greek of Bion. He became an engraver and at twenty-two was appointed headmaster of a school in Mere, Wiltshire. Ten years later he became a headmaster in Dorchester. He was a fine schoolmaster—original and erudite, adept at languages. His poems attest to a knowledge of classical, Persian ("Woak Hill") and Welsh forms, among others. His *Philological Grammar* reveals him to be at least on nodding terms with more than sixty languages, which influenced his "principles and forms." *The Glossary of the Dorset Dialect* (1844, 1863, 1886) was his most valuable contribution to philology and lexicography.

His first real collection, *Poems of Rural Life, in the Dorset Dialect*, with a dissertation and glossary, appeared in 1844. Further collections followed in 1846 and 1868—this last in "common English." As well as poetry, he wrote books on mathematics, currency, social questions and archaeology. E. M. Forster criticizes his prose intelligence as "provincial." He might equally have said rooted in community and language, and deeply learned. "Provincial," in Barnes's case, is not pejorative. If he pursues his intellectual program to purge English of Latinisms and to Saxonize it too far, it does not mar the verses.

He became a bachelor of divinity (Cambridge) after ten years' study and was given his first curacy at Whitcombe, near Dorchester, in 1848. His wife's death four years later occasioned some of his finest verse and began a decade of difficulty. Beyond the emotional was a practical bereavement: Julia managed his affairs, a task for which he had no talent. In 1862 he was given his first and only living, that of Winterbourne Came. He was again secure and remained so until his death in 1886. For twenty-four years he was an exemplary parson. Hardy knew him as the "aged clergyman, quaintly attired in caped cloak, knee-breeches, and buckled shoes"—the shoes are on display in Dorchester Museum today—"with a leather satchel slung over his shoulders, and a stout staff in his hand." A "little grey dog" followed at his heels. Hardy memorialized Barnes in his fine poem "The Last Signal" and later edited and introduced a selection of his verse.

Barnes loved the lives around him. His anger at the enclosure of common land and the consequences for poor farmers (his own uncle was bankrupted) informs many pieces. In "The Common A-Took In," an eclogue, Thomas and John exchange views on the common land. Thomas says,

> 'Tis handy to live near a common:
> But I've a-zeed, an I've a-zaid,
> That if a poor man got a bit o' bread,
> They'll try to teäke it vrom en.

He suggests that "they" might rent out "bits o' groun" that by rights belong to the poor: a further indignity.

The eclogue form that relies on dialogue appealed to Barnes because, as C. H. Sisson writes, "it suited his sense of the plurality of lives about him." He catches variety of inflection, tone and character. He takes as model the *Idylls* of Theocritus in preference to Latin or English imitations. "The dialogue," Sisson says, "is remarkable for being so ordinary. What other poet of mid-Victorian times has presented us with speakers of such solid actuality?" Meter and speech are matched. And, Sisson adds, "The resonances of the ancient speech carry with them more of the physical presence of the speaker, of the gestures and facial expressions and turns of mind and emotion. Speech is a physical thing, and poetry draws deeply upon the physical personality." Among the best eclogues are "A Ghost," "The Väiries," "The Lotments" and "The Heäre."

The dialect elegies for Julia speak of a particular grief but generalize the griever into a representative rural figure. To have spoken otherwise would have been, for Barnes, self-pity and in bad taste. Related poems of resignation at once celebrate and lament things lost. "The Happy Days when I were Young" and his last outstanding poem, "The Geäte a-vallen to" are in this mode.

In emphasizing dialect poems, we might overlook the English writing. There are moments of fine visualization: a rider records "My mare's two ears' white tips"; there's the "ribby bark" of trees; nightfall, when "The mill stands dark beside the flouncing foam"; "A Winter Night" may have inspired some of Hardy's *Satires of Circumstance*. Of the

English poems, "Black and White" is among the best. Its metrical dexterity, internal rhyme and alliteration "in the Welsh manner," and the modulated refrain (Barnes's use of refrains is always masterly) place it on a par with Hardy's best work and the best of Barnes's dialect poetry. It reports on experience and celebrates:

> At the end of the barton the granary stood,
> Of black wood, with white geese at its side,
> And the white-winged swans glided over the waves
> By the cave's darksome shadows in pride:
> Oh! the black and the white! Which was fairest to view?
> Why the white became fairest on you.

William Allingham remembers visiting Alfred, Lord Tennyson, when Barnes was also a guest. The two poets were immediately "on easy terms, having simple poetic minds and mutual good-will." The talk was of "Ancient Britons, barrows, roads," and during dinner they exchanged stories of "Ghosts and Dreams." Afterward in the drawing room Tennyson took port, while Barnes declined to drink. They withdrew to Tennyson's top room, where Darwinism raised its head. Tennyson expressed an aesthetic pantheism, and Barnes made his excuses and went to bed. Barnes, Tennyson surmised, was "not accustomed to strong views theologic."

For Barnes, theology was a question of revealed truth, not of "strong views." Tennyson was more a man of feeling than of ideas or beliefs. He could—and did—*entertain* possibilities; his poetry is diverse in invention, formal and thematic, and less of a coherent piece than Barnes's, Hardy's or Browning's. It has a recurrent set of feelings and a recurrent kind of setting. In "An Ancient to Ancients" Thomas Hardy—a bit reductively—evokes it.

> The bower we shrined to Tennyson
>   Gentlemen,
> Is roof-wrecked; damps there drip upon
> Sagged seats, the creeper-nails are rust,
> The spider is sole denizen;
> Even she who voiced those rhymes is dust,
>   Gentlemen!

Tennyson's settings and emotions could seem artificial and trumped up, just as for modern readers, after long infatuation, the concerns of T. S. Eliot's *Four Quartets* can come to seem factitious. "Do you know, a horrible thing has happened to me," Hopkins wrote to a friend in 1864. "I have begun to doubt Tennyson." He began to doubt after reading *Enoch Arden* (1864). He found competent, interesting verse, but without the steady excitement of Tennyson's earlier work. Hopkins chose the right time to record a doubt. Much of Tennyson's weaker work dates from the last thirty years of his long life; and most of the strongest was written between 1830 and 1835.

Of his contemporaries, only Barnes enjoyed a longer working life than he did. Tennyson was first moved to verse at the age of five and began writing three years later when "I covered two sides of a slate with Thomsonian blank verse in praise of flowers." Thomson was at the time the only poet he had read. A couple of years later Pope's *Iliad* became his passion; he wrote "hundreds and hundreds of lines in regular Popeian metre, nay even could improvise them," as could his brothers, to the delight of their poet father. He moved on to writing a 6,000-line epic in Scott's octosyllables. Brevity and condensation were never his strong suit. "I wrote as much as seventy lines at one time, and used to go shouting them about the fields after dark." His first poems appeared in book form when he was eighteen; his last poems, in the year of his death, 1892: sixty-five years of writing, and perhaps fifty of those with only Browning as a serious rival, and that not until the 1860s.

Tennyson built his huge poetic edifice on a narrow base. A wordsmith, he went for extension but was unable to sustain extended form; he did not master narrative but kept setting himself narrative challenges. He did not welcome criticism, except from his friend Arthur Hallam (1811–33), whose early death affected the course of his life and art.

Alfred Tennyson, later first Baron Tennyson, was born in Somersby, Lincolnshire, in 1809, son of an aggressively melancholy country rector-versifier from whom he inherited temperamental gloominess and received an early education in the well-stocked rectory library. It was there that he and his brothers began to write. In 1827 he and his elder brother, the far from negligible but neglected Charles Tennyson Turner, issued *Poems by Two Brothers*. In 1828 Alfred went to Trinity College, Cambridge, where he met Hallam. To Hallam he paid attention. They discussed the nature of poetic language. In 1830 *Poems Chiefly Lyrical* was published and received hostile attention. Another book, *Poems*, followed in 1833. Hallam sent the first of these books to Leigh Hunt, who—having backed Keats, Shelley and Byron—set about "discovering" Tennyson: "We have seen no such poetical writing since the last volume of Mr Keats," wrote Hunt. There *was* a flavor of Keats in the volume that included "Mariana," "Claribel," "The Lotus Eaters," "The

Palace of Art," "The May Queen," "Oenone" and "The Two Voices," a debate on suicide. "Tithonus," one of Tennyson's most powerful poems, dates from this period, though it was not published until 1860.

When Hallam died in Vienna in 1833, Tennyson lost not only an intimate friend and collaborator but also a brother, for Hallam was to have married his sister. For nine years he published little. He may have been distressed by a savage notice in the *Quarterly Review*, which had trodden so heavily on Keats and Shelley before him. But he was also grieving and writing *In Memoriam*, the best of his long works; and he was courting his future wife and making heavy weather of his finances. *Poems* (1842) brought him back into the public eye. It included early work but also "Locksley Hall," "Ulysses," "Morte d'Arthur"—the prototype for *Idylls of the King*—and other important work. In 1847 *The Princess: A Medley* appeared, memorable for its great lyrics, which include "The splendour falls," "Tears, idle tears" and "Now sleeps the crimson petal." The blank verse narrative tide advances on these islands of lyric poetry, but they can be rescued without damage to their integrity.

In 1850 Tennyson received public laurels and fulfilled a private desire. He was married after a courtship whose length reflected not reluctance but lack of money. He published *In Memoriam*. And he became poet laureate, succeeding Wordsworth. The "Ode on Wellington" and "The Charge of the Light Brigade" are masterpieces of laureate art. Few laureates are so transparently sincere, prompt and prosodically competent in the execution of their duties. "The Charge of the Light Brigade" entered the common memory.

Fame came to weigh on him. He moved to Farringford on the Isle of Wight. *Maud: A Monodrama* (1855) and the first four *Idylls of the King* (1859) confirmed his hold on the English poetry of the day. *Enoch Arden* registers the effect of too strong a sense of audience. Hopkins says it is Tennysonian rather than Tennyson. The Representative Voice sounded, and some readers recoiled. Sentimental rendering of a tale with dramatic potential—a tale like one of Crabbe's—and a failure of subtlety were clear. The volume included "The Northern Farmer, Old Style," a dialect poem that, beside Barnes's, merits harsh attention. In 1869 *The Holy Grail* appeared. The Arthurian romance grew.

More than two decades remained to him. He'd made a second home near Haslemere, Sussex, and from there issued his unhappy verse plays. Shakespeare provided his model, but Tennyson was a poet of lyrical reflection; his narrative skill was slight, his dramatic talents slighter. Nowhere are his limits clearer than in *Maud*. Madness here is mere rant in comparison with Lear's wild wisdom. Lear's language breaks and resolves in connotative and accidental combinations (controlled remotely by the wider imaginative logic of the play). His madness is dramatically integrated because it is syntactically and semantically disintegrated. In *Maud*, the poet raves in long lines that are dramatically unconvincing because too lucid: not a condition of mind but a state of feeling, or a statement about feelings, a passion against social and other ills. It is not the character who speaks—or if he speaks, it is not in character. The poetry is powerful, but the monologue form fails the poet.

During his years of dramatic enterprise he published *Ballads and Other Poems* (1880). *Tiresias, and Other Poems* (1885) salvaged some old and added new work. *Demeter, and Other Poems* (1889) included "Crossing the Bar." *The Death of Oenone* coincided with his own in 1892.

Even excluding the plays, it is a vast body of work: poems of feeling and of sentiment, poems of thought and of received opinion. When Browning acquired an audience, he turned garrulous. Tennyson turned sententious. But the Representative Voice does not merely entertain doubts, he actually feels them; his politics, like his religion, are rooted in memory of the past and fear of the future. A liberal, he distrusts progressivism even as he acknowledges the injustices and evils that make it necessary. Tennyson is an intellectual enigma, which is why many take him to be a philosopher speaking for their own indecision and doubt.

Arnold knew better, writing to his mother in 1860: "The real truth is that Tennyson, with all his temperament and artistic skill, is deficient in intellectual power; and no modern poet can make very much of his business unless he is pre-eminently strong in this." Arnold, right in his analysis, is wrong in his conclusion. Had Tennyson possessed "intellectual power" or a real "philosophy," he would hardly have improved his best lyrics, though he might have avoided some fatuities. His *poetic* weakness is not intellectual: it is narrowness of register. He tries every genre, masters a number of verse forms, but whole registers of language are inaccessible to him. When he tries consciously to elude his refining style, he turns out poems such as "Dora," arch and affected, talking down, quite unlike Wordsworth's voice in similar circumstances. Or he adopts dialect, without conviction or authority.

Tennyson's poetic vices stem from an ignorance of the limits of his talent, leading him to undertake vast poetic expeditions kitted out with the wrong equipment. He maintains, even in dull poems, prosodic interest. His instinct for appropriate rhythm is unmatched among the Victorians. And it *is* an instinct. But a passion for open vowels can grow monotonous, an aspect of his mimetic theory of language. He believes sound and syntax can create equivalents to motion and image. In "The Palace of Art" he draws syntactical portraits. "The Lotus Eaters" is a mimetic exercise. He's said to have regarded "The mellow lin-lan-lun of evening bells" as his best line. He was keener at the start to shape a language adequate for experience and image than to create a vehicle suitable for ideas. He often salvages lines from forgotten poems and plugs them into new contexts. Such lines come from the past and have special virtue. The past is a place of certitude. Early in his career he begins constructing Camelot and never substantially improves—in the whole of the *Idylls*—on "The Lady of Shalott" and "Morte d'Arthur," despite the slow eloquence of "The Passing of Arthur." His Arthurian world is a dream place that nurtures lyrics, where "The Lady of Shalott" loses romantic innocence. As a background for action and heroic narrative it is too brittle and brightly painted to contain large figures without a degree of ironic adjustment and lightness, and Tennyson was not an ironist.

He has another past to call on, a stratum of myth and legend of more intimate concern from which he retrieves two great poems, "Ulysses" and "Tithonus." Out of these characters he coaxes complete monologues: they answer to his voice. "Ulysses" was composed shortly after Hallam's death. The young Tennyson assumes a mask of age, in tune with the character and its inaction. Ulysses' Ithacan landscape is also a state of mind, the detail symbolic. The speaker forces value from the very sense of partiality and fragmentation: the past indeterminate and lost, recalled in shards of memory; the future unknowable. This condition generally leads Tennyson to compose lyrics of despair. But Ulysses pilots him toward an unsurrendering hope: isolated, separated from his subjects (hoarders, feeders, sleepers) who "know not me," far from old comrades, from youth. "I am become a name."

The poem proves psychologically plausible because of the inconsistencies in Ulysses' reflections, his glossing over of motive. His son Telemachus will "make mild / A rugged people, and through soft degrees / Subdue them to the useful and the good." He projects upon his son unproven qualities of leadership and transfers to him a responsibility *he* has no stomach for. He wants knowledge and adventure—elsewhere, not in the present but *through* the past, to re-meet his peers. The mask of age is revitalized by a force from youth, driving him toward a receding horizon: the hero's and the artist's undying quest. Arthur Hallam encouraged in life and inspired in death the indirect, condensed and evocative style of "Ulysses." One is tempted to call the mode symbolist.

Hallam's death inspired *In Memoriam, A.H.A.*, a sequence of elegies in taut quatrains with cyclic a-b-b-a rhymes, simple and expressive in the redistribution of conventional rhyme emphases. The debt to the Greek poets, to Horace and to other classic writers, is clear in the images and conventions such as the garden of Adonis. The suppressed sensual—even sexual—feeling has a strange potency. There are phrasal echoes of the full-fleshed classical elegies. Those models helped him imbue personal loss—physical, emotional and spiritual—with universal reference. The widowed Queen Victoria took solace from the poem; it was read by soldiers and widows as though written out of their own grief. In the sixth elegy he writes, "Never morning wore / To evening but some heart did break." He invites readers to attach their own grief to his. With Virgilian tact he touches the deep sentiment of the age: helpless sadness of loss, fear of a shrouded future, a generalized guilt and religious doubt. The poem enacts a "ritual of recovery"—moving from despair by stages not to happiness but to a wan wisdom, metaphysical rebirth, a meeting beyond the grave, "soul in soul."

The plot is mere chronology: a cycle of seasons which first counterpoint and later corroborate the feelings of the poem. Easter and Christmas have an evolving significance. Dream, memory and desire are checked and at last controlled by duty, dogma and moral steadfastness. Tennyson called *In Memoriam*, with its steady ascent from the depths, a "Divine Comedy." He struggles free of grief first by way of personification. "Sorrow" becomes a figure, then "Love" and "Faith" detach themselves. Thus, *ideas* divide from *feelings*, they gain force and at last ascendancy, until Tennyson can write, " 'Tis better to have loved and lost / Than never to have loved at all." Religion finds a toehold and helps in the recovery. But T. S. Eliot points out that "it is not religious because of the quality of its faith, but because of the quality of its doubt." Tennyson acknowledges as much: "There lives more faith in honest doubt, / Believe me, than in half the creeds." He illustrates it, too:

> . . . but what am I?
> An infant crying in the night;
> An infant crying for the light:
> And with no language but the cry.

Or the totally unknowing, more haunting, "What hope of answer or redress? / Behind the veil, behind the veil." There is a plain language of despair as well: "On the bald street breaks the blank day"; and "A weight of nerves without a mind." The use of religious images may be distasteful, as in "They call me in the public squares / The fool that wears a crown of thorns," or in the identification of Hallam with Christ and his elevation to the status of Victorian hero (a parallel between Carlyle and Tennyson is often drawn), but religious metamorphosis is necessary to the theme.

Tennyson spoke to and for his age in *In Memoriam*. Its success as a long poem depends on its fragmentariness. The sections are elegiac idylls, assembled into a sequence. Like *Maud*, the sequence hangs together thanks to what Eliot called "the greatest lyrical resourcefulness that a poet has ever shown." Elegies and poems of aftermath were Tennyson's forte. He was a gray beard from the beginning.

The idyll, a brief poem that describes an idealized incident or scene, suited him well in "Ulysses" and "Tithonus." The *Idylls of the King*, despite—or because of—the labors Tennyson expended on them, fail. They are not idylls in the generic sense but static chunks of Arthurian epic, large and a bit vulgar, like those Victorian paintings that glitter with thick paint and seem to reflect the light rather than reveal themselves. The verse emerged at low pressure, with deadly deliberation and calculation and none of the urgency that lends *Maud* and *In Memoriam* a compelling readability, a sense of discovery.

Among his juvenilia is a poem called "Song" ("A spirit haunts"), which contains in miniature many of the qualities Tennyson later perfected. Keats may have touched the young poet but he has been assimilated into Tennyson's style: formally complex, vivid in image and mimetic in language, answering at once to an actual scene and to a subjective mood. The words evoke and enact in a single process:

> The air is damp, and hushed, and close,
> As a sick man's room when he taketh repose
>   An hour before death;
> My very heart faints and my whole soul grieves
> At the moist rich smell of the rotting leaves,
>   And the breath
>   Of the fading edges of box beneath,
> And the year's last rose.
>   Heavily hangs the broad sunflower
>   Over its grave i' the earth so chilly;
>   Heavily hangs the hollyhock,
>   Heavily hangs the tiger-lily.

In 1838 Ralph Waldo Emerson persuaded his American publisher to issue a volume of Tennyson's poems, but the publisher reneged. The American and the English writer met in 1848, when Tennyson, returning from Killarney in Ireland, stayed at Coventry Patmore's house, where Emerson was visiting on his way to France. Tennyson was rather anti-American, owing in part to the fact that British writers were mercilessly pirated in the United States. Emerson, on the first night, found Tennyson "cultivated, quite unaffected" and lively in recounting tales of his Irish journey. He had "the air of one who is accustomed to be petted and indulged by those he lives with." It was suggested that Tennyson might accompany Emerson to France, but Tennyson wanted to go to Italy. When Emerson visited him in London in his lodgings, he came away disappointed by the poet he had so staunchly advocated a decade before.

Just as Tennyson at the time was the Big Name in British poetry, so Emerson was the giant among American writers, the first to be successfully exported, the first with an enormous European reputation. Emerson the poet is altogether smaller and less compelling than Emerson the thinker, preacher and writer. Yet he was a poet and he wrote, in those large ambiguous sentences that mean all things to all (liberal) men, essays that opened America to American poets.

The poems did not find favor with English critics. Arnold, lecturing in America and not ingratiating himself with his audience, remembers how Milton said poetry should be simple, sensuous, or impassioned. "Well, Emerson's poetry is seldom either simple, or sensuous or impassioned. In general it lacks directness; it lacks concreteness; it lacks energy." The grammar is "often embarrassed." He is poor even in single lines, though Arnold quotes those lines and brief passages with amazement. Emerson's *Essays*, on the other hand, are for Arnold as central to the prose of his day as Wordsworth's verse to the poetry. Yet—and his verdict is on the *Essays*—"He cannot build; his arrangement of philosophical ideas has no progress in it, no evolution; he does not construct a philosophy." Readers who first catch their breath at Emerson's astounding sentences eventually stifle a yawn: they are vertical rather than horizontal, each standing upright and refusing to bend into the next sequentially, to make a circuit, to make a path for reason.

Born in Boston in 1803, Emerson was a cradle Unitarian (his father was a liberal Unitarian pastor), and himself became a pastor in 1829, eight years after he graduated from Harvard. His father died when he was a boy, but a Calvinist aunt, Mary Moody Emerson, steered his attention to Shakespeare, Bacon, Milton and to Burke, and, despite their differences, he revered her and learned from her a candid straightforwardness.

What he lacked then, and for all his days, was—as William Butler Yeats observed of him, Thoreau and Whitman—the sense of *evil* that was so real for Nathaniel Hawthorne and Herman Melville. "Put in something about the Supernal Oneness," said Edgar Allan Poe sardonically; "Don't say a syllable about the Infernal Twoness." There was bad and there was good, but *evil*? It was an outmoded category; his temperament could never make much of it, even when he lost his young wife, abandoned the pulpit and went to Europe for the first time to reflect on his future. He met Landor, Carlyle and Coleridge—whom he promoted in America on his return, since Coleridge had helped him to discriminate between the logical and the intuitive routes to truth—and was encouraged to study the German idealist philosophers. Whole areas of human experience elude him, and from the vantage point of a later century his benign, generous optimism looks almost like willful sentimentality. He is a learned prophet of dawn, not of night and nightmare, providing a no longer plausible resource except in his tolerance. Even that has been stigmatized as mere passivity: "Active passivity" was his retort.

Bryant had a take on nature that Emerson took much further: "The whole of nature is a metaphor of the mind." In such a vastly digestive statement resides the solipsism of Emerson at his most rapt. In his attacks on orthodoxy, his insistence on inherent understanding, he broke the colonial mold and became a figure of controversy. Or he *seemed* to break the mold. Poe adds, "Above all, study innuendo. Hint everything—assert nothing." Eastern religious forms had found out Emerson and liberated him from *specific* meaning.

He had moved to Concord, Massachusetts, and produced at the Old Manse the essays that gave shape to a new American identity. He established himself as a philosopher, lecturer and essayist at the heart of the Transcendentalist community, a revolutionary group in the area of civic reform. This was all very well except that it did not provide an adequate base for poetic imagination. The poet was a seer, with access to the oversoul via nature. It was not so much his willful ideas about the poet but his more general reflections on the art of poetry, his advocacy of new and open forms, and his endorsement of Whitman that set him at the heart of the new poetry. He lived almost as long as Barnes, dying in 1882.

The poems require a suspension of prosodic expectation. They seldom sing, and when they do it is in small bursts. We are expected to engage with their meanings. A poem, for Emerson, is a more condensed and allusive form of essay, or an illustration.

> "Pass in, pass in," the angels say,
> "In to the upper doors,
> Nor count compartments of the floors,
> But mount to paradise
> By the stairway of surprise."

"The stairway of surprise" is a little miracle, but no wonder Arnold had trouble with the grammar: What are the second and third lines doing, exactly? Are the angels, is the poet, garbled?

In his belief that line lengths and rhythms, and phrases, are determined by breath—an organic connection between the poem and the poet—he foreshadows the theories of Charles Olson a century later. But his physiology and Olson's are different in kind: Emerson's body is curiously disembodied, missing or suppressing certain vital bits. Yet when we get to his "Ode: Inscribed to W. H. Channing," we can forgive him much in the light of the first few lines, which are so open, so American: a new note of utter freshness, as brilliant and convincing as those first demotic runs of John Skelton's were, Skelton's harbingers of a new beginning:

> The God who made new Hampshire
> Taunted the lofty land
> With little men;—
> Small blat and wren
> House in the oak:—
> If earth-fire cleave
> The upheaved land, and bury the folk,
> The southern crocodile would grieve.
> Virtue palters: Right is hence;
> Freedom praised, but hid;
> Funeral eloquence
> Rattles the coffin-lid.

It is not fanciful to hear in this not only some of the taut, phrasal qualities of Emily Dickinson but, more especially, the strange portioning out of sense that we get in Marianne Moore's "What are Years?" All Emerson had to do was to abandon meter, not for the long cadences of Whitman but for short, intense phrases, for his beloved abstractions married to concrete images. What the English Augustan poets had done, merging moral and physical categories, he could do, when the spirit (or oversoul) moved him, with philosophical ideas and the actual creatures and objects of his world. Not a new world any longer, but the possibility of a new poetry. *Leaves of Grass*, "The Raven" and Miss Dickinson are just around the corner, each awaited by a different kind of cruel neglect.

Snapping Asunder the Leading-Strings

HENRY WADSWORTH LONGFELLOW, EDGAR ALLAN POE, HENRY DAVID THOREAU, HERMAN MELVILLE

Emerson surprised British readers, but—judging from Arnold—enthusiasm turned to a more temperate response, bordering on distrust. He was a persuasive speaker, he seemed on a level with Carlyle; but was he not also too protean, too one-size-fits-all with his baggy sentences and capacious ideas? Henry Wadsworth Longfellow, on the other hand, could sing. He could tell stories about America. Maybe his forms were imported, but they were tempered and transformed by his fantastic world. He provides an alternative to the gothic even as he shares in some of its preposterous attitudes and posturings.

> All solemn Voices of the Night,
> That can soothe thee or afright,—
> Be these henceforth thy theme.

He became a best-seller. Is it true that ten thousand copies of *The Courtship of Miles Standish* were sold in London on one day? Judging from stock in second-hand bookshops today he was bought and cherished for a few generations, then turned out. *The Song of Hiawatha* was in vogue in all the languages of Europe, even translated into Latin by the brother of Cardinal Newman. For Europeans, American poetry *was* Longfellow.

He was born in 1807 in Portland, Maine, and in "My Lost Youth" he evokes the trees, the black wharves, the ships and sailors, the fort, and that sense of loss we all experience returning to a place once dear to find the spaces we thought were ours have closed over:

Strange to me now are the forms I meet
    When I visit the dear old town;
But the native air is pure and sweet,
And the trees that o'ershadow each well-known street,
    As they balance up and down,
        Are singing the beautiful song,
        Are sighing and whispering still:
        "A boy's will is the wind's will,
And the thoughts of youth are long, long thoughts."

That native air moves the boughs to "balance," momentarily suggesting the movement of Wallace Stevens's "The Idea of Order at Key West." Only Stevens in later American poetry is musical in the ways that Longfellow at his best can be.

He attended the then-new Bowdoin College at Brunswick, Maine, where he shone. He graduated in the class of Nathaniel Hawthorne. Bowdoin offered him a new chair of modern languages, freeing him from his father's proposed course, that he should follow him in the law. Longfellow was already being published and acclaimed, especially for his translations. He visited Europe before he began his university job: France, Spain, Italy and Germany were on his itinerary, and on his return he wrote textbooks for his courses and prepared further translations.

He married (for love) and took a professorship of French and Spanish at Harvard. He visited Europe with his wife, who lost their child and died in Holland. He returned alone to Harvard and entered the famous rented lodgings at Craigie House in Cambridge, his final home. There he wrote *Hyperion*, about a youth who travels to forget sorrow. *Voices of the Night* was his first book of poems. It appeared in 1839. "The Psalm of Life" grits its famous teeth with fortitude:

Tell me not in mournful numbers,
    Life is but an empty dream!
For the soul is dead that slumbers,
    And things are not what they seem.

"And now I long to try a loftier strain, the sublimer Song whose broken melodies have for so many years breathed through my soul in the better hours of life, and which I trust and believe will ere long unite themselves into a symphony not all unworthy the sublime theme, but furnishing 'some equivalent expression for the trouble and wrath of life, for its sorrow and its mystery.' " Two years later, *Ballads and Other Poems* put him

firmly in the frame. It was what the public wanted and it makes us won-
der why Whitman so admired the poet as a "counteractant" to the mate-
rialism and egotism of "an age tyrannically regulated with reference to
the manufacturer, the merchant, the financier, the politician." The spirit
of the age may have wafted through Longfellow; but there must have
been an element of calculation in the rumbustious, the tight-lipped and
heroic figures he traced in "Excelsior" and elsewhere. He seems to com-
bine the assured rhetoric of the Tennyson of the *Idylls*, with the exuber-
ance of Browning on one hand and of the Borders balladeers on the
other. It's a heady mix: popular and folk poetry tailored for the wide-
eyed bourgeoisie.

A third visit to Europe included a stay with Dickens, another writer
who knew how to assess and work an audience. They went slumming
together one night in 1842, shortly after Dickens's own return from the
New World, which had so beguiled and puzzled him. Dickens and oth-
ers helped inspire the *Poems on Slavery*, which Longfellow composed on
his way home.

In 1843 he married again and his new father-in-law gave them
Craigie House. His wife gave him six children; he wrote, published and
was happy, growing more popular with each book, even his verse drama.
For him the language of verse was an aloud language, and sound counted
as much as—or more than—sense. In the toils of sound he sails near to
nonsense—too near, perhaps. Yet also in the toils of sound he will, much
to Arnold's annoyance, break the rules of his chosen prosodies, espe-
cially hexameters, when his ear tells him to. He privileges his ear over
the form, and some of his finest prosodic effects are in the unexpected
variations that possess an inexplicable rightness. It was *Evangeline*, the
first substantial poem of real length from America, published in 1847,
whose hexameters beguiled and irritated Arnold. Rhapsodic but stiff,
the music cannot trace the subtleties of feeling, though it answers the
theme of natural recurrence almost too well.

> So came the autumn, and passed, and the winter,—yet Gabriel
>   came not;
> Blossomed the opening spring and the notes of the robin and
>   bluebird
> Sounded sweet upon the wold and in wood, yet Gabriel came not.

He knew the risks he was taking, and they were worth taking *at the
time*. It is a risk comparable to poulter's measure in the sixteenth cen-
tury, and equally treacherous. He deployed it again in *The Courtship of
Miles Standish*.

In 1849 he published *The Seaside and the Fireside*, in 1851 *The Golden*

Legend and four years later the immortal (and some would say unbearable) *Song of Hiawatha*. Hiawatha lives and dies, a figure out of legend translated into the rhythms of the great Finnish national poem, the *Kalevala*, with which Longfellow the philologist was familiar.

> Should you ask where Nawadaha
> Found these songs so wild and wayward,
> Found these legends and traditions,
> I should answer, I should tell you,
> "In the bird's-nests of the forest,
> In the lodges of the beaver,
> In the hoof-prints of the bison,
> In the eyry of the eagle!"

Abandoned to his meter, which is a kind of inverted iambic tetrameter, TUM-te-TUM-te-TUM-te-TUM-te, each line end-stopped, the poem proceeds on its irregular, repetitive way: a literary poem pretending to belong to the oral tradition and guaranteed, when read aloud to small children, to fill them briefly with wonder and then with sleep.

Critics are harsh. An early Boston review disliked the subject matter, "silly legends of the aborigines." Poor didactic verse, perhaps—that may be its merit. Few understood the magic of the meter. In the end that is what matters here, and a diction ushering into verse, as if for the first time, a whole new tribe of words. It is not epic, neither is it ethnography. It is a poem of origins and the discovery of new starting places: in Finland, in the wigwam, with the beaver and the bison.

Longfellow resigned his chair in 1854 in order to write more. But his second wife, also dearly loved, died suddenly. While she was sealing a letter with wax, her dress caught fire from a taper. Longfellow himself suffered severe burns in trying to save her. He was changed, physically and spiritually. He undertook a translation of Dante's *Divine Comedy*, completing it in 1867 and working on other poems as well, many addressed to his huge readership, but keeping the best for himself.

In 1872 his trilogy, *Christus,* appeared. He thought it his best work, though few today would agree with him. He was unstoppable and the verse kept flowing until 1881, when he began to fail. The next year he died, at the age of seventy-five. He was at the height of his popularity, dividing the age with Tennyson, and his influence on other poets (often unacknowledged because an enthusiasm for his work is not quite proper) was and perhaps still is great: on Kipling, on Swinburne and Hardy—and on Stevens? On the Philip Larkin of "The Explosion"? That busybody Amy Lowell was too close to the reputation to appreciate the work: she saw it as her mission to purge poetry of his bad effects.

She would have to rid the world of Edward Lear and Charles Dodgson (Lewis Carroll), whose nonsense verse strays into the musical zones that Longfellow mapped with his self-propelling meters.

In England he had received doctorates *honoris causa* from Cambridge and Oxford and the queen had granted him an audience, but the greatest honor was conferred two years after he died. He was the first American poet to find himself, in bust, in Poets' Corner with Chaucer, Dryden and the rest.

If Longfellow had modern readers, they would easily recognize his faults. He writes with excessive fluency, the poem sometimes gets away and romps on its own, and he can be cloyingly sentimental (as can Tennyson and Hardy). Excessive concentration on sound can actually degrade metaphor and sense. Incongruity of metaphor is often as striking as congruity. In *Evangeline*:

> On the river
> Fell here and there through the branches a tremulous gleam of
>   moonlight
> Like the sweet thoughts of love in a darkened and devious spirit.

It won't do. Nor will the high-sounding metaphor whose resonance has no context—the famous "Footprints in the sands of time," for example. He can seem to be sending himself up, but he was an earnest man, capable of broad humor though not of wit. He never takes an ironic glance at himself in the mirror. Like those of other poetic high priests of the Victorian age his poems may start in his experience but they borrow the wings of narrative or legend. Sometimes in a sonnet or a short lyric we meet another poet—for instance in "The Cross of Snow," published posthumously and seeming real, though drawn from a book of pictures:

> In the long, sleepless watches of the night,
>   A gentle face—the face of one long dead—
>   Looks at me from the wall, where round its head
>   The night-lamp casts a halo of pale light.
> Here in this room she died; and soul more white
>   Never through martyrdom of fire was led
>   To its repose; nor can in books be read
>   The legend of a life more benedight.
> There is a mountain in the distant West
>   That, sun-defying, in its deep ravines
>   Displays a cross of snow upon its side.
> Such is the cross I wear upon my breast

> These eighteen years, through all the changing scenes
> And seasons, changeless since the day she died.

Octave and sestet, rhyme, the discipline of meter, impose a passionate clarity on this poem of abiding grief. He suffered excessive popularity; he has now suffered three quarters of a century of critical neglect. But this does not mean he is unread. Even poets will occasionally, furtively, find themselves speechless before a poem such as "The Tide Rises, The Tide Falls."

It is the same furtive impulse that leads them to that other great anathema, Edgar Allan Poe. He never suffered in his lifetime, as Longfellow did, from popularity or prosperity. When Poe died, the egregious Rufus W. Griswold, who did his utmost to douse the flame of memory, wrote in the *New York Tribune*: "Edgar Allan Poe is dead. He died in Baltimore the day before yesterday. This announcement will startle many, but few will be grieved by it." James Russell Lowell allowed him to be three-fifths genius, the balance fudge. As a critic Poe is five-fifths genius, the first great American theorist of verse and, in an entirely untub-thumping way, the first to declare independence: "We have snapped asunder the leading-strings of our British Grandmamma."

At the age of fourteen Poe regarded poetry as instrumental, writing verses to woo girls, or miserable verse when he failed to do so. The mother of his friend Robert Stannard inspired his most perfect poem when Poe was fifteen or sixteen. He saw her standing by a window niche: "The light falling upon her, caught in her dark ringlets crossed by a white snood, glowed in the classic folds of her gown, and flowed about her slenderly graceful figure." (The prose occasion is vivid, like something out of Flaubert—Charles Bovary observing Emma early in their courtship, for example.) This became the three-stanza poem "To Helen," one of the most beautiful in the language:

> Helen, thy beauty is to me
>   Like those Nicéan barks of yore,
> That gently, o'er a perfumed sea,
>   The weary, way-worn wanderer bore
>   To his own native shore . . .

The poem is brief, intense, the diction precise and chaste, the meter carefully gauged, the sound values as important as they are in Longfellow but less raw, less superficial. The poem has no message: it is not *about* experience, it *is* an experience; and the closing lines recall "Kubla Khan" in their unparaphrasable certitude.

The didactic repelled him. So did extended narrative in verse. So did allegory. "In defence of allegory (however, or for whatever object, employed) there is scarcely one respectable word to be said," he writes in a review of Hawthorne. He was impatient with Emerson and the Transcendentalists, who seemed to him unlikely to produce verse of any moment. They were too burdened with certainties and metacertainties, too passive, too full of self-respect. An oversoul could have little truck with a Muse. She is a particularist. Natural, metaphysical and aesthetic realms do not connect in a way convenient to the philosopher-poet.

"For the fullness of Poe's vision," says the poet Richard Wilbur, "one must go to the prose, but certain poems are partial distillations of it." He selects, with his customary unerring taste, "Evening Star," "Sonnet to Science," "Fairyland," "To Helen," "The City in the Sea," "To one in Paradise," "The Haunted Palace," "The Conqueror Worm," "Eldorado" and "Annabel Lee" as the crucial Poe. No "Raven," no "Ulalume," no "Bells"? Certainly a great deal of death and afterlife, ghosts, other-worlds. Poe wrote in "The Philosophy of Composition," "I asked myself—'Of all melancholy topics, what, according to the universal understanding of mankind, is the *most* melancholy?' Death—was the obvious reply. 'And when,' I said, 'is this most melancholy of topics most poetical?' . . . 'When it most closely allies itself to *Beauty*': the death, then, of a beautiful woman is, unquestionably, the most poetical topic in the world." Poetry is, Poe says, "a wild effort to reach the beauty above," and the poems move away: to the past, the future, another realm or star.

Poe's lucidity as critic and (at his best) as poet is willed, not the fruit of an orderly upbringing. His parents were actors when he was born in Boston in 1809. By the age of three he was an orphan. His drinking, gambling father abandoned ship shortly after his birth; his mother moved to Richmond, Virginia, and died. The boy became the foster child of a Scottish merchant, John Allan (who provided Edgar's middle name), and his wife. The Allans moved to England (1815–20) and Edgar went to school in Stoke Newington. They returned to Virginia. His foster parents quarreled interminably and the boy was not happy.

Poe fell in love at the age of seventeen with Sarah Elmira Royster and she responded. But when he went up to the University of Virginia, her parents stood between them and she married a Mr. Shelton. (In the last year of Poe's life, when she was widowed, he again asked for her hand and was denied.) At university he did well in classics and French, but he drank, gambled and withdrew in 1826. It is hard to reconstruct his life: he left his literary estate to Griswold, who energetically rewrote the poet's history, forged letters and invented episodes. The legends he set in motion are still repeated as fact. We do know that Poe and Allan fell out; Poe ran away to Boston and arranged for the publication of *Tamer-*

lane and Other Poems (1827), meanwhile working as a clerk. Later that year he joined the army, and when Mrs. Allan died in 1829 he went home to Richmond and published another book, *Al Aaraaf, Tamerlane and Minor Poems*. The word "Aaraaf" says it all: a wonderful, impossible succession of vowels. Mr. Allan helped him get a place at the military college of West Point. His book got favorable notices and he left West Point to write. Then began his serious depressions and bouts of heavy drinking.

Poems: Second Edition appeared in his twenty-second year, and its critical introduction was a foretaste of the major essays to come. He wants a poetry with three primary qualities: indefinition, music and symbolism. "A poem, in my opinion, is opposed to a work of science by having, for its *immediate* object, pleasure, not truth; to romance, by having for its object an indefinite instead of a *definite* Pleasure, being a poem only so far as this object is attained; romance presented perceptible images with definite, poetry with indefinite sensations, to which end, music is an *essential*, since the comprehension of sweet sound is our most indefinite conception. Music, when combined with a pleasurable idea is poetry; music without the idea is simply music; the idea without the music is prose from its very definitiveness."

From the outset Poe seeks out the extreme and intense. His verse is certainly extreme in its prosodic strategies and its "music." He is extreme in the pressure he places on feeling over intellect, and on the way he plays the senses "all at once" by a kind of synesthesia. The "indefinition" is not the absence of content that we get from Swinburne but a fullness that cannot be paraphrased. The combinations of concrete and abstract words do not come from Augustan moral categories but from modulations of feeling and fear. He was hostile to Emerson in verse, chiding his universal oneness:

> Yes, Heaven is thine; but this
>> Is a world of sweets and sours;
>> Our flowers are merely flowers,
> And the shadow of they perfect bliss
>> Is the sunshine of ours.

His own Israfel emanates from somewhere else, from where he can see this world without being implicated in it.

Things began to improve for the poet. In 1832 he was living in poverty with an aunt. His stories began to have a vogue, he won a prize; in 1836 he married his cousin Virginia, and became editor of the *Southern Literary Messenger*, in which appeared several stories and two important poems—"To One in Paradise" and "The Coliseum." His pen was said to employ "vitriol for ink" and his critical writings began to be read. He did not suffer fools, or those he thought were fools (Longfellow, for example), but he was a strong advocate. In 1837 he went to Philadelphia as editor of *Burton's Gentleman's Magazine* for a year, and some of his best stories were published. In 1841 he edited *Graham's Magazine* and published "The Murders in the Rue Morgue."

Success of a kind. But he stayed poor. His wife was dying. In 1844 he was in New York, and the next year "The Raven" came out, first in a paper and then in the book *The Raven and Other Poems*, the key volume. His foes took the opportunity and avenged themselves in reviews. He brought out the essay "Philosophy of Composition," describing how "The Raven" came to be, but he was critically maimed. In 1847 his wife died and he returned to the bottle.

"Ulalume," in 1848, was a masterpiece. But he knew his end was approaching. To a friend he wrote: "I am constitutionally sensitive—nervous in a very unusual degree. I become insane, with long intervals of horrible insanity. During these fits of absolute unconsciousness I drink, God only knows how often or how much. As a matter of course, my enemies referred the insanity to the drink rather than the drink to the insanity." "Eureka: A Prose Poem" was the last work he saw published. His sense of unity was unlike Emerson's: "We should aim at so arranging the incidents that we shall not be able to determine of anyone of them, whether it depends from anyone other or upholds it." A year later he died.

In "The Poetic Principle" he sets out his famous argument, that a long poem is a contradiction in terms: "A poem deserves its title only inasmuch as it excites by elevating the soul"; a poem of length will not be able to keep up the excitement. It will fall into didactic mode, and that is the greatest heresy.

The body of his poetic work is small, but its impact was great—great not where it might have been expected to detonate, in America, or in an England sliding inexorably toward Swinburne, but in France. His essays, poems and fictions were hugely admired; he was in France what Longfellow was in England: the great American poet.

The French were getting symbolism together. They warmed to Poe's idea of the poem as *itself*, noninstrumental, nondidactic, something that cannot be paraphrased, appropriated, analyzed. The questions a poem raises are of form, not of content; of process, not of product. Any scene that is painted will not be literal, any geography adduced will be imaginary. The poem will be comprehended, but that comprehension will be nontransferable. The rhythm of meanings in "The Raven"—despite attempts to misread it thus—is not allegorical. The raven derives its meaning from the poem and means only within the poem.

A poem says nothing, it means nothing, but it *does* something. It was to this that Charles Baudelaire responded, translating the writings into French and fueling the Gallic passion for the storyteller and poet. Poe is crucial to the emerging definition of symbolism, of a poetry that will not describe but instill feelings, emotions. What matters is the ways in which sounds and images, whole and fragmentary, come together. His poetry and stories—dubbed "evil" by his detractors—do open out into dark areas of experience and feeling. He writes, "Through the prompt-ings of perverseness we act without comprehensible object . . . Through its promptings we act, for the reason that we should not." André Gide called it the *acte gratuit*; like the poets, he loved Poe as a writer and exemplar, misreading him as a moral (because amoral) teacher. He seems to ignore the centrality of guilt in the stories, as crucial as the sense of loss in the poems. Fyodor Dostoevsky is nearer to Poe in his fic-tion than any American successors. For a time it was not only France (Debussy and Ravel as well as the poets) and Russia (Chekhov and Tur-genev too) that welcomed him, but England: Conan Doyle, H. G. Wells, Aubrey Beardsley. It was a short step from Poe's sense of art's autonomy to the fin-de-siècle "art for art's sake." In Poe rather than in Emerson and Longfellow, whose roots still fed back into Chaucer, Shakespeare and Milton, American literature becomes *original* in ways that he him-self defines. "We have at length arrived at that epoch when our literature may and must stand on its own merits or fall through its own defects." Like Longfellow, Poe is in eclipse and has been for quite a spell. Yet like Longfellow, he too has furtive readers. Those who read his poems atten-tively will have rhythms and phrases lodged in memory for good, so infectious is the near-nonsense magic of his language, so delicious the melancholy he induces. Unless we read in an ironical mood, in which case the poems become merely preposterous.

Not so preposterous, however, as the poetry of another great prose writer, Henry David Thoreau, whose importance is less as a poet than as a man who cleared a few more acres in the American forest for a native poetry to be seeded. His sense of what a poet must be is larger and more amorphous than Shelley's even. He borrowed some of his prose tech-niques from Emerson, though his phrasing is more succinct. "He must be something more than natural—even supernatural. Nature will not speak through but along with him. His voice will not proceed from her midst, but, breathing on her, will make her the expression of his thought." This is all familiar Transcendentalist stuff. What follows might seem more attuned to Poe: "He then poetises when he takes a fact out of nature into spirit. He speaks without reference to time or place. His thought is one world, hers another." Then he reverts to Emerson-izing: "He is another Nature—Nature's brother. Kindly offices do they perform for one another. Each publishes the other's truth." Such intel-lectualizing exists at the level of theory. What a poet must be and must do exist at some distance from what poems are and do.

Born in 1817 in Concord, Massachusetts, Thoreau had a severe upbringing. He went to Harvard, became enthralled by the classics and tried to translate Aeschylus. He intended to earn his living as a surveyor. In his first book, *A Week on the Concord and Merrimack Rivers,* he alludes widely to classical literature, quoting also from Gower, Shakespeare, Quarles, Milton, Byron, Tennyson—and Emerson. Emerson invited Thoreau to live with him, discovered he wrote verse, and encouraged him in Emersonian measures. The arrangement did not work. Thoreau's temperament was oppositional: he disliked Puritanism, the state and the social order. His essay "Civil Disobedience" remains his most influential prose work—or his most influential *title*, since few now take the trouble to consult the excellent essay. "That government is best which governs least . . . I quietly declare war with the State after my fashion, though I will still make use and get what advantage of her I can, as is usual in such cases." There are other essays, and there is *Walden* (1854), read now generally in extracts, about his attempted life of self-sufficiency and individual husbandry at Walden Pond, on land that Emerson owned. During this time he refused to pay tax because his country was waging war against Mexico. The gesture was less eloquent than it might have been: his aunt Maria bailed him out after only one night's incarceration. He found it difficult to forgive her.

Tubercular, he caught a chill while surveying tree stumps in 1860 and never recovered. In 1862 he died. His journals were published post-humously and *Poems on Nature* appeared in 1895. The poems—most of them the work of his youth—lack the virtues of the prose, which has a spoken feel, homespun in its metaphors, astute in its moralizing. The poems also moralize. He is oracle and witness at the same time, so that he raises his voice before he has much to say. There are some wonderful moments when the volume is kept steady and the tone approaches con-versation, as in "Conscience is Instinct Bred in the House":

Conscience is instinct bred in the house.
Feeling and thinking propagate the sin
By an unnatural breeding in and in.
I say, Turn it outdoors
Into the moors
I love a life whose plot is simple . . .

But what does he go on to say?

And does not thicken with every pimple,
A soul so sound no sickly conscience binds it,
That makes the universe no worse than 't finds it.

Meter and diction run out of control and are curbed by a willful violence, to sound and sense. More consistent is "Smoke," where in an almost Poelike spirit the image is conjured but (by its very nature) left undefined:

Light-winged Smoke, Icarian bird,
Melting thy pinions in thy upward flight,
Lark without song, and messenger of dawn,
Circling above the hamlets as thy nest;
Or else, departing dream, and shadowy form
Of midnight vision, gathering up thy skirts;
By night star-veiling, and by day
Darkening the light and blotting out the sun;
Go thou my incense upward from this hearth,
And ask the gods to pardon this clear flame.

This is the translator of Aeschylus at work. He has read Emerson and Longfellow (that "nest") but the rhythms are his own. They work well again in "Haze":

Woof of the sun, ethereal gauze,
Woven of Nature's richest stuffs,
Visible heat, air-water, and dry sea,
Last conquest of the eye . . .

He has the courage to leave an image lean, even incomplete, so that we bring it into being, supplying part of the matter. As in the prose of *Walden*, there is sometimes a sense of collaboration as we read. A poem addresses its subject, like Herbert addressing "Prayer," and it contains its meanings. In "Sic Vita" the poet works toward a kind of metaphysical note.

I am a parcel of vain strivings tied
        By a chance bond together,
    Dangling this way and that, their links
        Were made so loose and wide,
            Methinks,
        For milder weather.

Even the conventions of indentation belong to the seventeenth century, the long lines with most accents ranged left, the shortest furthest indented. The poem almost succeeds, and this is a tribute to Thoreau's formal skills, which he was ready to abandon too soon.

His is an individual voice, but the individuality has more to do with his personality and what he writes about than with his formally defined voice. He avoids Emerson's syntactical solecisms and he flies closer—generally—to our material world. Emerson remarked of his poems: "The thyme and marjoram are not yet made into honey."

Emerson, Poe, Thoreau—great prose writers who are also poets. And then Herman Melville. "I am like one of those seeds taken out of the Egyptian pyramids, which, after being three thousand years a seed, and nothing but a seed, being planted in English soil it *developed* itself, grew to greenness, and then fell to mould," he wrote to Nathaniel Hawthorne in the midst of composing *Moby-Dick*, filled with self-wonder and self-doubt.

He wrote a great deal of verse, much of it published posthumously, so that he only becomes properly available in the mid-twentieth century, and the jury remains divided. Randall Jarrell declares: "Whitman, Dickinson, and Melville seem to me the best poets of the nineteenth century here in America . . . Melville's poetry has been grossly underestimated." "Some critics," says the poet Robert Penn Warren, "would place his name among the most important American poets of the nineteenth century, or even today." Some wouldn't.

The American Civil War brought his poetry to a topical head, though he had written verse before. *Battle-Pieces* appeared in 1866. The initial impulse was almost journalistic, but the poetry of such a writer, with his definite sense of evil and good (in that order), and his feeling for his own nation and the people involved at all levels in its murderous turbulence, took the poetry beyond its initial impulse. A Unionist strongly opposed to slavery, he was able to foresee, as Walt Whitman did, some of the bad consequences of just action. "But the Founders' dream shall flee." In "The March into Virginia" he shows the jollity of confidence—carriages accompanying the soldiers to watch the sport—in all its stupid innocence; and the consequences of battle itself. The wind blows one way, he says, but always with unpredictable backcurrents. "It spins *against* the way it drives." This is history's way too, apparently possessed and driven by ideas and reaching resolutions, but never more than miasmically under control.

Readers of *Moby Dick* know how richly Jacobean Melville's writing can be, how erudite in reference and allusion, but the erudition is that of a man of culture and of action, not a scholar or critic. On the decks of his ships a Portuguese sailor will recite Camões and no one will bat an eye. Dante and Homer, King David and Milton, Virgil and Shakespeare are living presences in the language. The poetry is less deliberately poetical than the prose, generally more economical and direct and, like the prose, often based on actual experiences of travel, of politics and religion, with a genuine urgency of engagement.

He was born in New York in 1819. His father, a prosperous business-man, went bankrupt and mad, dying before Melville was thirteen and leaving a large family. Melville and his siblings worked hard. He was a clerk, a teacher, a farm worker, and then at eighteen he signed on as a ship's boy. He sailed widely, deserting his ship the *Acushnet* in the Marquesa Islands, where he lived for a time with the "cannibal" Typee. Escaping on board a whaling ship from Australia, he was detained in Tahiti as the member of a mutiny. He finally returned to Boston in 1844. He married a woman of means and in 1847 settled in New York, where he found his way into a vigorous literary world. He wrote his early, successful prose books *Typee* (1846) and *Omoo* (1847). Their subject matter was sensational: adventure and cannibalism. The allegory on political and religious themes *Mardi* (1849) was rejected as too abstruse. He went back to straight storytelling in *Redburn* (1849) and *White-Jacket* (1850), realizing that he could only succeed when he provided what the market demanded. He began to uncover the cruel reality of life and law at sea.

Moby Dick proved hard and exhausting to write. But he knew it was original and he understood that it was good. Published in 1851, it was not a success; until the first quarter of the twentieth century it was neglected. Ambitious later books were rejected. The failure of *Moby Dick* helped turn his primary attention to verse. *Battle-Pieces* (1866) was welcomed as peripheral work by a man who had once been famous for his prose. Seriously disturbed in his mind, he made a trip to the Holy Land (meeting with Hawthorne in Southport en route), and out of this visit emerged his most ambitious if not his most accomplished poem, the 18,000-line *Clarel*, twice as long as *Paradise Lost*, and in the octosyllabic couplets of Gower's *Confessio Amantis*. Eventually, Melville—after working as a minor customs officer in New York—was reduced to dependence on his wife's money: she gave him an allowance to buy books and to print his later works in small editions for the tiny readership he retained. He died in 1891, quite forgotten, with the manuscript of the prose work *Billy Budd* completed but unpublished. His reputation was at such a low ebb that even this masterpiece went unpublished until 1924. More poems appeared in the same year.

Some of Melville's poems relate to the novels and can be read in

conjunction with them, as extensions or distillations. The themes over-
lap. Prose and verse are in his view closely related, as he suggests in
"Art":

> But form to lend, pulsed life create,
> What unlike things must meet and mate:
> A flame to melt—a wind to freeze;
> Sad patience—joyous energies;
> Humility—yet pride and scorn;
> Instinct and study; love and hate;
> Audacity—reverence. These must mate,
> And fuse with Jacob's mystic heart,
> To wrestle with the angel—Art.

The poet's challenge is to synthesize from diverse and discrepant mate-
rial, to move from the passivity of response to the activity of creation,
what T. S. Eliot calls "the intolerable wrestle with words and meanings."
In a single action the wound is made, the bow is acknowledged. Oppo-
sites and contrasts are not resolved but held in tension.

It is hard not to feel, with Whitman so very near at hand, that
Melville's tragedy was formal: had he been able to find a form less
constraining, less distorting of his natural impulse, more responsive to
the kinds of cadence and natural vigor that find a way into his prose,
he might have been a radical presence in his nation and century. But the
Augustan legacy and his own educational culture weighed upon his
verse intelligence. His pilgrimage to the Holy Land was intended to
rediscover his faith and to expose the ambivalences of his heart to a land
of austere clarities. In *Clarel* he tries to be didactic but has no certainties
to impart: he challenges himself spiritually but does not rise to the chal-
lenge. He raises more questions than he can answer: like us he is learn-
ing, feeling his way. Clarel is a pilgrim, an American student of theology
in search of faith who dos not reach his destination. Clarel neglects the
heart, and a man cannot reach truth or understanding unless his heart is
wholly with him.

Melville's poems, less sumptuous in semantic nuance than the prose,
less second nature to him than his fiction, are worked at and worked up,
yet the difficulty of the restraining forms remains central. So does the
rumor of an "unspeakable" theme, unacknowledged at times, at times
veiled from himself, which has to do with a radiant sexual irresolution.
More insistently even than Conrad, Melville depicts a male world in
prose and verse, a world in which intimate relationships and erotic expe-
riences are between men and types of men: at sea, in the army and else-
where. He celebrates, laments, touches—and he occasionally foresees,

not with the huge and benign vision of Walt Whitman, but with narrowed eyes, looking further than the future. His is not the optimism of Emerson but something more serious: he sees beyond a bad age, he sees to the other side of evil; nature consoles, but it also remembers and comments.

> We elms of Malvern Hill
>> Remember every thing:
> But sap the twig will fill:
> Wag the world how it will,
>> Leaves must be green in Spring.

It is not necessary to look into the "facts" of Melville's life, to which it would be presumptuous for us to assign specific weight among the other known—and unknown—facts: his affection for Hawthorne, his strained marriage, the suicide of one of his sons and the loss of another. What we have unarguably before us is the writing: what it says and what it does not say. In verse as in prose, seriousness deepens with imaginative candor (especially in his late fictional masterpiece *Billy Budd*), certain elements progressively gain definition, elements that may have contributed to his eclipse as critics and readers turned away from something they could not quite comprehend or countenance. And this, too, is a new world.

"They lived once thus at Venice" and in Camden

ROBERT BROWNING, ELIZABETH BARRETT BROWNING,
WALT WHITMAN

Back in the Old World, in 1841, Tennyson met Robert Browning—three years his junior—at one of Richard Monckton Milnes's celebrated breakfasts. Aubrey de Vere hardly notices Browning, but he gilds the memory of Tennyson's "large dark eyes, generally dreamy but with an occasional gleam of imaginative alertness, the dusky, almost Spanish complexion, the high-built head and the massive abundance of curling hair like the finest and blackest silk"—handsome if a bit frayed. Tennyson and Browning did not immediately hit it off, though a few years later at the publisher Edward Moxon's dinner table (three months before Browning's elopement with Elizabeth Barrett) they became friends, and though not intimate they remained friends—meeting in France, Italy and England—for the rest of their lives. Tennyson had not relished Browning's consonantal cacophony since he read *Sordello* in 1840. But both men swallowed hard and spoke well of one another's verse, dedicating poems to each other. Browning liked Tennyson's verse better than Tennyson liked Browning's.

In *The Victorian Age* G. K. Chesterton speaks of Thomas De Quincey's sentences "that lengthen out like nightmare corridors, or rise higher and higher like impossible eastern pagodas." This well describes Robert Browning's verse, with its novelistic plots: "The obscurity, to which he must in large degree plead guilty, was, curiously enough, the result rather of the gay artist in him than the deep thinker. It is patience in the Browning students; in Browning it was only impatience." Readers who spend a few hours with the poet can come to feel, after the rich amusement and opulence of the worlds he creates, an impatience, that what attracted the poet was a character rather than a person, a setting and a historical period rather than abiding emotions that attach to his usually fictional experiences.

One impatient reader is Matthew Arnold, who finds the sugary optimism and gaiety of Browning's graybeards particularly specious.

> Grow old along with me!
> The best is yet to be,
> The last of life, for which the first was made

writes Browning. He entertains ideas, attitudes, sentiments. It is hard to judge when he's being serious, when he's being himself. Scattered through his monologues, he makes us watch for him with a prismatic eye. Our impatience reveals two things: a prejudice in favor of a stable, or relatively stable, poetic perspective, an identifiable "I," and a desire for poetic accountability. Browning's characters say doubtful things, but the poet can bow aside and insist that they are *personae*, that the monologues belong to characters who speak, whom he creates as Shakespeare did characters in a play or Chaucer did a pilgrim.

The Ring and the Book (1868–69) is variously claimed as Browning's masterpiece, as a splendid failure and as an enormous and enormously tedious poem marking the transition between the poet's good work and the garrulous, unsatisfactory verse of his last twenty years. It is certainly long, recounting a seventeenth-century Roman murder from various points of view and in various voices that fill twelve books. It anticipates Umberto Eco's *The Name of the Rose*. Browning describes it as "truth broken into prismatic lines." He got the facts from a "square old yellow book" picked up for eight pence; he swears he never deviated from the facts it described. The impulse behind this as behind some of the dramatic monologues is that of a novelist or storyteller; but verse is his medium. Part of his achievement was to write verse that often outsold the prose of his contemporaries and was read with the same eager prurience as novels are.

Before his critics, Browning becomes that "square old yellow book." There are as many versions of him as there are solutions to his murder story. Was he a sublimated anal-erotic, an ordinary entertaining chap, a deep thinker, a charlatan? Such variety illustrates his view that individual imaginations deal individually with a given reality. This individuality and human diversity he explored, so some contend. Or were his dramatic monologues simply a trying on of a succession of insubstantial masks? In either case, Browning declares: "Art remains the one way possible / Of speaking truth, to mouths like mine at least." It is a point of departure: What was that mouth like? What truths does it tell?

He was born in Camberwell, London, in 1812, the son of a well-to-do bank employee who provided him with an education as a weekly boarder at the Reverend Thomas Ready's school in Peckham, but more particularly at home with private tutors supervised by Papa. His father also provided, eventually, a private income. Father and mother—she a sensitive, devout lady—encouraged the boy's writing. When he was twelve they tried in vain to get his first volume of poetry, *Incondita,* published. He later destroyed the manuscript. At the age of fourteen he wrote the rather remarkable poem "The Dance of Death," in which Fever, Consumption, Madness, Ague and Pestilence dance around and each one tries to prove that it is the fiercest foe of mankind. This may be his first set of dramatic monologues: he'd begun to tire of Byron and was reading Shelley, and his appetite for Shelley was never satisfied.

When he went up to the University of London he did not quite complete the first year of his course. He led a relatively uneventful life, cultivating an interest in the theater. In 1833 he published his first book, *Pauline,* anonymously, which was fortunate because it was not well received and did not sell. Some suggest that because of its reception he preferred afterward to wear a metaphorical mask rather than to expose himself directly. *Pauline* owed a large debt to Shelley: it was vulnerable verse, but it lacked, as derivative verse usually does, a necessary energy. In 1834 he flirted with the notion of entering the diplomatic corps and traveling to St. Petersburg with the Russian consul general. The next year his father paid for his second book, *Paracelsus,* to be published. Thomas Carlyle, Wordsworth and others were generous about it, but it was not a success. He wrote plays. These too fared badly (*Strafford,* with the great T. N. Macready starring, lasted only five nights at Covent Garden).

Nor did he improve his fortune with *Sordello* (1840), a poem that baffled readers and was a substantial failure, making his name a byword for willful obscurity for years to come. It tells of a young poet who fails to discover his art when he withdraws from the world. Ezra Pound was the first poet to derive real benefit from it and to understand the nature of its originality. Shelley's *Alastor* may be its generic cousin, but Shelley's is the better poem. His second play, *Pippa Passes* (1841), is the one that is remembered, thanks to the famous detachable songs. He claimed to have the "perfect gallows" of theater production. Certainly his talents did not lie in that direction. His drama does not hold a mirror up to nature: it is a projection of the spirit. Characters rather get in the way or suffer from garrulity. He wrote other plays and the first of his prose essays, on Chatterton, a poet-ventriloquist (or forger) after his own heart. The *Dramatic Lyrics* (1842) and *Dramatic Romances* (1845) pointed the way to his best work.

In 1845 he wrote his first letter to the consumptive Elizabeth Barrett in Wimpole Street ("I love your verses with all my heart"). Eluding the eye of her jealous father, they eloped in 1846 to Italy. Between their arrival and her death in 1861 he wrote *Men and Women* (1853) and *Dramatis Personae*, published after his return to England as a widower in 1864. This is the book that began his huge and durable success. *The Ring and the Book* followed and was a best-seller. Thereafter he produced abundantly: *Balaustion's Adventures* and *Prince Hohenstiel-Schwangau* (1871), *Fifine at the Fair* (1872), *Dramatic Idyls* (1879–80) and *Jocoseria*, which includes the engaging "Christina and Monaldeschi" (1883). He died in 1889 at his son's house in Venice. Ten years later, his correspondence with Elizabeth Barrett Browning was published.

His work found an English audience only slowly. America proved more permeable than Britain. His fame, based eventually on poems written between 1842 and 1864, increased at home as his writing became more expansive and diffuse. A life that had been a solitary quest, undisturbed by too much attention—indeed, troubled by negative criticism and neglect—became a life of celebrity. His fame rivaled Tennyson's. Were greatness measured by influence, he would be held the greatest of Victorian poets. His effect on Pound, T. S. Eliot, Auden and many writers of our own day is a matter of record. He perfected the dramatic monologue, the "persona" poem; he insisted on something like a speaking voice in verse of great physical particularity; he lacked a systematic philosophy or worldview. A beguilingly incomplete figure, sufficiently original to instruct and yet not so uniquely original as to intimidate, he epitomizes the derivative Victorian aspirations evident in the architecture, music and painting of the age.

He developed dramatic monologues from various sources. Writing for the stage may have defined the genre for him. He knew Byron's personae poems, Shelley's veiled personal statements, Landor's *Imaginary Conversations* and other contemporary work. His original stroke was to make the form his primary instrument for exploring the world or, rather, past worlds—Italian, Provençal, English, anything with a lustrous varnish on it. His work seldom intersects the present in which he lived.

He finds a form, an order and design within the variousness of reality, which affirms that variousness. The important task, he says, is to avoid imposing a priori values and forms on experience. He aims to detect, and to a limited extent he succeeds. But as Arnold wrote to Arthur Hugh Clough in 1848–49, "Browning is a man with a moderate gift passionately desiring movement and fullness, and obtaining but a confused multitudinousness." Had Arnold written that after reading *The Ring and the Book*, his judgment would have been harsher. In that work there is a comprehensive organization, but it is an organization of artifice, not of imagination, a conscious patterning not detected but imposed, not thematic but mechanical. It is the kind of organization that appeals to academic critics: it gives them something to describe and explicate. George Santayana—a little brutally, perhaps, but the Browning bandwagon was rolling very fast in 1910—pointed to the inconclusiveness of Browning's poetry, its gesturing at wholeness, and the limited scope of his comprehension. He possesses a "truncated imagination," his art is "inchoate and ill-digested," the personae "always displaying traits of character and never attaining character as a whole." It is hard to disagree; nor is it necessary to do so. There is much to admire in Browning, without demanding wholeness of vision or of conception. Detail, felicities of rhythm, the occasional masterly vignette are what anyone can value. Idolatry is not compulsory. Nine tenths of the poetry can be read once and not read again. That leaves one tenth, a huge amount of durable work.

From Byron, Browning picked up a tourist's easy vulgarity. The materialism of his "historical" characters, the concerns they express at moments of crisis, are Victorian and English concerns. His sentiments, too, can be cloyingly Victorian. He selects the eccentric, the morally deformed, the man with a grudge, guilt, secret or crime to his credit. He chooses them for effect. His vulgarity is a kind of journalistic prurience in love with opulent detail: he is wide-eyed. The Italy he evokes is not that of Dante or Michelangelo, as Santayana says. One learns more from the poems about his prejudices and tastes than about his ostensible subjects. His monologues are less explorations of character than stories obliquely told. Soliloquy lays bare a mind or conscience; but Browning's monologues inform and entertain, face always toward an audience. "Though lyric in expression," he writes of his 1863 poems, they are "always Dramatic in principle." They are "utterances of so many imaginary persons, not mine." This is disingenuous: the imagination is his, after all. His "persons" may have "pasts," unique gestures, but they are not distinguished by diction. They speak a similar language, choosing different forms and faces.

The shorter poems he called "lyric in expression," spoken from a single perspective and sensibility. Their dramatic nature is evident if we consult the index of first lines: " 'Ay, but, Ferishta,' a disciple smirked"; "Boot, saddle, to horse, and away!"; "Escape me?"; "Going his rounds one day in Isphahan"; " 'Heigho,' yawned one day King Francis"; "Hist, but a word, fair and soft"; "You'll love me yet!—and I can tarry." Like Donne, whom he admired, Browning plucks at our sleeve with a startling phrase, plunges us in medias res, ignites our curiosity time and again. He satisfies our curiosity. His syntax can be effectively mimetic, scurrying in breathless clauses to a climax, or pacing with dignity, or deliberating ponderously, as the action, rather than the character, requires.

Many of the monologues address an imagined interlocutor: we get two personae for the price of one, the interlocutor inferred from the tonalities and attitudes of the speaker. The poems confess. In "The Laboratory" the speaker gleefully chuckles with a Jacobean relish, "To carry pure death in an earring, a casket, / A signet, a fan-mount, a filigree-basket . . ." Women reveal secret acts, men secret desires. Some speakers frankly address a large audience ("How They Brought the Good News from Ghent to Aix"); some, apparently mumbled into a beard, are overheard. "Soliloquy of the Spanish Cloister" has a jealous monk railing against his brother in God, Father Lawrence. A master-piece of malice, uncannily complete in its delineation of the monk's own deadly vices, it is charged with bitter, relentless eroticism:

> *Saint*, forsooth! While brown Dolores
>   Squats outside the Convent bank
> With Sanchicha, telling stories,
>   Steeping tresses in the tank,
> Blue-black, lustrous, thick like horse-hairs,
>   —Can't I see his dead eye glow,
> Bright as 'twere a Barbary corsair's?
>   (That is, if he'd let it show!)

The actual speaking aloud of lines three, four and five causes the reader to salivate. The poem is an anthology of malicious expressions, seeming to condense all the variety of Byron into a little span. Other poems respond to one another. Best are the pair "Meeting at Night" and "Part-ing at Morning": in the first a man arrives (evoked at speed, verbally thrifty), in the second a woman experiences his departure.

Browning's themes are the big ones: desire, love, religion (if not belief), time and sometimes death. Desire is largely a matter of the lower passions: it does not exalt but taxes its subjects. Religion is a world of color, ceremony and dark desire: not where the physical world is tran-scended, but where its material qualities are heightened. Time and the isolation of the individual provoke memorable statements, redolent of Hardy's bleak view, but entertained less earnestly than Hardy's. "Never the time and the place / And the loved ones all together," a late poem begins. Unfulfillment: Hardy quotes the lines and owes much to Brown-ing. The right moment passes; a chance of fulfillment, in love or in action, is overlooked. Each lost moment drives one further into isola-tion. Browning's couples are separated by incompatibility, by a third party's jealousy, by death. "My Last Duchess" expresses the duke's desire for unmolested solitude. His last duchess has been reduced to a painted likeness, the human form retained as an unresponsive, unbetraying artifact. Characters on the point of death express final isolation and individuation: they become luminously single and particular as their lives, lusts or worries pass before them in review. Few are noble in thought, sentiment or deed: we deal with the middle-range of mankind, each unique, none transcendent. Even aristocratic and humble speakers are imbued with bourgeois individuality. Browning was inescapably the son of a prosperous bank employee. When he speaks, or seems to speak, for himself, a tempered and credible voice sounds, as in "By the Fire-side." Its setting and comforts are those of a man with a private income, at home and petulant and spoiled, like the older Auden.

The technical delight and brilliant urgency of image and voice of such poems as "A Toccata of Galuppi's" and "Two in the Campagna" draw even a skeptical reader back to Browning. Poems that merely tell a story are exhausted in a couple of readings; those more than conventional in sentiment ("Infinite passion, and the pain / Of finite hearts that yearn") or brilliantly conceived and executed are more enduring. One of Browning's inexhaustible poems is "Childe Roland to the Dark Tower Came," a dark quest, an allegory with but a vague connection to the common world, a nightmare (indeed, it is based on a dream) in which action alone seems to save the knightly protagonist. From the opening stanza . . .

> My first thought was, he lied in every word,
>   That hoary cripple, with malicious eye
>   Askance to watch the working of his lie
> On mine, and mouth scarce able to afford
> Suppression of the glee, that pursued and scored
>   Its edge, at one more victim gained thereby.

. . . to the thirty-fourth and last . . .

> There they stood, ranged along the hill-sides, met
>   To view the last of me, a living frame
>   For one more picture! in a sheet of flame
> I saw them and I knew them all. And yet
> Dauntless the slug-horn to my lips I set,
>   And blew. *Childe Roland to the Dark Tower came.*"

. . . the spell is maintained, even over patches of uncompelling writing and awkward rhyme. The theme is unspecified, *individual* triumph over strange forces and in the face of the defeat of others. This nebulous, not quite disclosed (perhaps not fully apprehended) theme draws from Browning his best poems: something not deliberate but sought in a deep region of the mind. The mask becomes transparent, so much is concentrated in language and urgent rhythm. His purpose may have been, as a character says in "Old Pictures in Florence," "To bring the invisible full into play." He does so not when he renders the invisible visible, but when he deepens the visible, giving psychological verity to a vivid surface. Browning is no more or less a realist than Dickens: realists can, at their best, be fantasists. Walter Savage Landor had something like this in mind when he wrote "To Robert Browning":

There is delight in singing, though none hear
Beside the singer; and there is delight
In praising, though the praiser sit alone
And see the prais'd far off him, far above.
Shakespeare is not *our* poet, but the world's,
Therefore on him no speech; and short for thee,
Browning! Since Chaucer was alive and hale,
No man hath walk'd along our roads with step
So active, so inquiring eye, or tongue
So varied in discourse. But warmer climes
Give brighter plumage, stronger wing; the breeze
Of Alpine heights thou playest with, borne on
Beyond Sorrento and Amalfi, where
The Siren waits thee, singing song for song.

Robert looms so large that he occludes Elizabeth Barrett Browning. She deserves limelight, not as the object of his romantic attention but as a significant poet herself. In her time she was prolific and very highly thought of; he lived rather in her shadow, whatever adjustments posterity has made. Virginia Woolf described her as one of those "rare writers who risk themselves adventurously and disinterestedly in an imaginative life." Woolf's novel *Flush* is the story of Elizabeth up to her elopement, told by the dog to whom the poet devoted a witty, sentimental poem. Flush was a real canine and the gift of the famous (and forgotten) essayist, Elizabeth's friend Mary Russell Mitford. An anthology of poets' dogs would feature the plucky and eloquent Flush (Woolf's version) alongside Pope's Danish dog, Bounce; William Cowper's spaniel, Beau; Wordsworth's Music; Scott's Maida; Byron's Boatswain; Thomas Hood's (and later Charles Lamb's) Dash; Arnold's Geist (how integrated his vision was, extending even to the domestic pooch);

Emily Brontë's bulldog, Keeper; and Landor's Pomeranian pair, Pomero and Giallo. Dogs reveal their masters.

Elizabeth Barrett was born in 1806, the eldest of a large and prosperous family, at Hope End, Durham, Hertfordshire. The family fortune derived from extensive Jamaican sugar-cane plantations. She wrote her first poem in her sixth year. Her father, an affectionate autocrat, encouraged her, as Robert's parents had encouraged him, publishing her epic *Battle of Marathon* when she was fourteen. She was a sickly child with bad lungs and suffered a kind of nervous collapse in her midteens, becoming invalid and dependent on opiates. Tucked away in a dim room at 50 Wimpole Street, London, she was cherished by her severe, doting father. She became famous there, publishing her translation of Aeschylus's *Prometheus Bound* and in 1838 *The Seraphim and Other Poems*. That was the year that her favorite brother was drowned swimming at Torquay, and she entered her strict reclusion and determined grief. By the time *Poems* appeared in 1844 (the American edition with an introduction by Edgar Allan Poe), she was a well-known poet and scholar. It was this book that in 1845 drew Robert to her like a magnet. Six years her junior, he courted her; they eloped in 1846, and her father never forgave her.

They went to France, where Elizabeth paid her intense respects to George Sand ("Thou large-brained woman and large-hearted man . . ."), then to Italy, settling in Florence in the Casa Guidi; there Elizabeth gave birth to a son. She wrote in the years following *The Casa Guidi Windows*, about the Italian risorgimento, and her successful and controversial "epic" verse novel, *Aurora Leigh,* in which she considers the situation of a woman and the role of the poet. She was spoken of at one time as a possible poet laureate when Wordsworth died. The job went to her admirer Tennyson. In her later years, political and spiritual concerns affected what had been the subtly nuanced and very particular texture of her verse: ideas took command of her feelings and imagination.

She was quite rapidly forgotten after her death in 1861, apart from the *Sonnets from the Portuguese* (1850) which she dedicated to her husband and in which the traditionally male preserve of the love sonnet became a new kind of instrument, capable of quite unexpected tonalities.

> When our two souls stand up erect and strong,
> Face to face, silent, drawing nigh and nigher,
> Until the lengthening wings break into fire
> At either curvèd point,—what bitter wrong
> Can the earth do to us, that we should not long
> Be here contented?

Those tonalities sound in many of the love poems. Who—male or female—before her wrote in this manner?

> We paled with love, we shook with love,
>> We kissed so close we could not vow;
> Till Giulio whispered "Sweet, above
>> God's ever guaranties this Now."
> And through his words the nightingales
>> Drove straight and full their long clear call,
> Like arrows through heroic mails,
>> And love was awful in it all.
> The nightingales, the nightingales!

Published posthumously by her bereaved husband, this poem ("Bianca among the Nightingales") with its modulation from joy to bereaved betrayal, and others equally dramatic in trajectory, point up a fundamental difference. How much more than her husband she trusts in the value of vowels, how much closer to Tennyson her music; yet Giulio's seductive sophistries, which the speaker wishes to believe and we believe too, are the sophistries of a shared love and not of a seducer. There is a sexual complicity in the joy of her love poems, as though the man and the woman understandingly in love are on the same side of the language. "Let us stay / Rather on earth, Beloved." And of course the favorite, "How do I love thee? Let me count the ways."

Elizabeth Barrett Browning is being revalued by feminists and general readers. Her political concerns—as an abolitionist (remembering her father's Jamaican plantations), an advocate of Italian unification, an *ur*-feminist—render her more alive to the tensions of her age than many of her celebrated male contemporaries. But it is the poems by which she will revive, if she does, and in them she is more vigorous and defined than is the soft-focus woman drawn (and then erased) by the Victorians whom her husband subsequently beguiled. The claims that can be made for her are real claims, if not far-reaching.

Ezra Pound loved Browning as only poets love—with jealousy and disappointment. "And half your dates are out," he exclaims,

> . . . you mix your eras
> For that great font Sordello sat beside—
> 'Tis an immortal passage, but the font?—
> In some two centuries outside the picture.

An "immortal passage" founded on a factual error, like Larkin's monumental couple holding hands in "An Arundel Tomb" (the gesture was a

Victorian sentimental emendation to the medieval tomb sculpture). One cannot withhold response to a great poem just because it is factually out of true, but having responded one can come back with indignation, feeling a little cheated by the false authority, which one then forgives.

What Pound loves in Browning is Italy and the play of voices (which Pound learns to weave together in the *Cantos*). "Sordello" is the threshold over which Pound passes, at last, into his great, contested work. It was in part Browning who made it possible for Pound to make peace with another voice of which he is made, his American precursor Walt Whitman. He resented and resisted Whitman; he read again, and resisted, but at last he makes a pact: "Let there be commerce between us."

> I make a pact with you, Walt Whitman—
> I have detested you long enough . . .
> It was you that broke new wood,
> Now it is a time for carving . . .

For good or ill, Pound was made of Whitman, the American cadences rang in his ears. In 1909 he wrote, "What I feel about Walt Whitman": "He *is* America. His crudity is an exceeding great stench, but it *is* America. He is the hollow place in the rock that echoes with his time. He *does* 'chant the crucial stage' and he is the 'voice triumphant.' He is disgusting. He is an exceedingly nauseating pill, but he accomplishes his mission." Whatever pain he causes, Pound concedes that "when I write of certain things I find myself using his rhythms." And, "Mentally I am a Walt Whitman who has learned to wear a collar and a dress shirt." Whitman is his "spiritual father" and he cannot conceal the fact. "I think we have not yet paid enough attention to the deliberate artistry of the man, not in details but in the large." And "His message is my message." Twenty-five years later he closes his *ABC of Reading* with Whitman (and Thomas Hardy). There are thirty well-written pages in Whitman, but he can't now find them. Yet his "faults are superficial, he does convey an image of his time, he has written histoire morale, as Montaigne wrote the history of his epoch." Because history is not only the facts retold but the style of address, the attitude of mind. The problem with Whitman, says Pound, is not that he broke the rules but that he sometimes obeyed them, and the moments of obedience undercut his expansive originality: "Certainly the last author to be tried in a classroom."

Out of his reflections on Whitman came Pound's general thoughts on the teaching of poetry. The best it can do is "expose counterfeit work, thus gradually leading the student to the valid." But "it is only maturer patience that can sweep aside a writer's honest error, and overlook unaccomplished clumsiness or outlandishness or old-fashionedness, for the sake of the solid center."

It is Whitman's solid center that appeals to composers, notably Vaughan Williams in the *Sea Symphony* and Delius's setting of "Sea Drift," finding in the flow of Whitman's richly vocalic cadences a superb musical aria. Charles Ives responded, setting some of the poems as songs. Franz Kafka regarded Whitman as a supreme formal innovator, and he had more impact abroad, on the free verse of the Continent, than he did at home. Van Gogh admired him as one admires a healer who promises "a world of healthy, carnal love, strong and frank" under a benign starlit sky (a sky depicted in some of Van Gogh's paintings). Henry James, Melville and Swinburne responded to him; rather tetchily Tennyson nodded in his direction, and then the Rossettis, and Yeats. He touched William Carlos Williams and, very differently, Hart Crane. E. M. Forster takes the title *Passage to India* from Whitman, a deliberate encoding of a crucial unstated sexual theme. Also the Spaniards and Latin Americans, most notably Federico Garcia Lorca, for whom the old poet's beard was "alive with butterflies." And then there was the Russian futurist Vladimir Mayakovsky, who fathered a whole movement on the threadbare visionary American. There are those who respond to his technical experimentation and those who warm to his political and sexual vision. "He occasionally suggests something a little more than human," said Thoreau to a friend. For Emerson he was "a Minotaur of a man." The wonderful poet-critic Guy Davenport says: "I like to think that eventually he will shame us into becoming Americans again." Whitman declared himself "Walt Whitman, an American, one of the roughs, a kosmos, Disorderly fleshy and sensual . . ." He touched T. S. Eliot *and* Williams, D. H. Lawrence *and* Thomas Mann (for whom *Song of Myself* was "a great, important, indeed holy gift"). Allen Ginsberg makes use of him almost as often as he uses William Blake.

Born in 1819, Whitman was seven years Browning's junior and outlived him by three years, dying (as Tennyson did) in 1892. Yet they are so wholly remote from one another that they seem to exist in different languages.

Leaves of Grass, Whitman's principal work, is huge. The title suggests individual growth and common growth together, a political and comradely image. If the sections of the poem are read as a sequence, there is a narrative: the progress of a man among men, his soul growing and opening out on a journey of immense moment and magnitude, which ends in a fulfilled vision. Whitman began the book when he was thirty-six and worked on it for the rest of his days. He published the first edition of *Song of Myself* in 1855 but kept adding and adjusting until he was seventy-two and the last edition was published.

Born in West Hills, Long Island, he came of farming stock. His father, a small-town carpenter in Brooklyn (Brooklyn was then little more than a village) was volatile and intemperate, so the boy turned for love and security to his mother:

> The mother with mild words, clean her cap and gown, a
> > wholesome odor
> > falling off her person and clothes as she walks by,
> The father, strong, self-sufficient, manly, mean, anger'd, unjust,
> The blow, the quick loud word, the tight bargain, the crafty lure . . .

The surviving correspondence between the two reveals how close their bond was.

Whitman became apprenticed to a printer. Then, at nineteen, he set up his own newspaper, *Long Islander*. He became a schoolteacher, wrote a temperance tract, stories, conventional verse. He could not hold down journalistic jobs because he *would* be radical. His life was gathering shadows and secrets, not least of which was his motive for going in 1848 to New Orleans to work on the *Crescent* newspapers, and what happened there. This journey of a few months, his notebooks make clear, effected in him a complete transformation. The Bohemian dandy was a prophet, the voice of the single man was ready to speak for America. *Leaves of Grass* was conceived. What happened? Was it the grandeur of the landscapes that he saw, the variety of people and scenes (he returned via the Great Lakes, Niagara and the Hudson), or was it a love affair with a woman (the "Children of Adam" sequence in *Leaves of Grass*)— or a man (the "Calamus" poems)? Was it a religious reckoning? There is a kind of joyful mysticism in the verse, to which Emerson responded. A compelling image relating to this period, written in 1860 and published seven years later, comes in this astounding poem:

> I saw in Louisiana a live-oak growing,
> All alone stood it and the moss hung down from the branches,
> Without any companion it grew there uttering joyous leaves of dark
> > green,
> And its look, rude, unbending, lusty, made me think of myself,
> But I wonder'd how it could utter joyous leaves standing alone
> > there without
> > its friend near, for I knew I could not,
> And I broke off a twig with a certain number of leaves upon it, and
> > twined

around it a little moss,
And brought it away, and I have placed it in sight in my room,
It is not needed to remind me as of my own dear friends,
(For I believe lately I think of little else than of them,)
Yet it remains to me a curious token, it makes me think of manly
      love;
For all that, and though the live-oak glistens there in Louisiana
      solitary in a
            wide flat space,
Uttering joyous leaves all its life without a friend or lover near,
I know very well I could not.

Many stories are contained in the uncircumstantial candor of his state-
ment here. Mark Strand speaks of the poet's "democratic" syntax, by
which he means "the nonsubordination of the clauses," and this is surely
the key to his poetry's even, accruing power and to the way it repels
poets reared in the Browning school of dramatic climax. Whitman is all
about access: to experience, to language, to each other. He spreads in
space and into new vistas. The isolating monologue would have chilled
his blood. Shortly after he returned to New York, in 1849, he stood
behind the other mourners at the funeral of Edgar Allan Poe.

Instead of his name, in the first edition of *Leaves of Grass*, Whitman
placed a daguerreotype: the poet in proletarian garb. He required a big
page for his long lines, eight by eleven inches. A thousand copies or so
were issued, and only one shop, Fowler & Wells of New York and
Boston, was willing to take stock. Naturally it didn't sell, but the poet
sent copies to people who might be of use to him, including Emerson.
The poet John Greenleaf Whittier burned the copy he received, no
doubt revolted by the unexpected candor. "Copulation is no more rank
to me than death is," wrote Whitman. The lines were of biblical verse
length, and there were apparent improprieties in the diction and in the
images of bathing, and women watching men bathe. "They do not think
whom they souse with spray." Even before Freud, there is no mistaking
what the poem *says*, though what it means is rather more complex.

No sales, critical neglect, despite the great prose "Preface," as central
in American poetry as Dryden's in British. "The direct trail of him who
would be the greatest poet is today. If he does not flood himself with the
immediate age as with vast oceanic tides . . . and if he does not attract
his own land body and soul to himself and hang on its neck with incom-
parable love and plunge . . ." Whitman dives headlong and makes no
apology. He is there: "I celebrate myself." He beckons and he repels, like
the prophet or priest of a new religion less particular than Thoreau's,
more full-bodied than Emerson's, "the great psalm of the republic." "This

is what you shall do: Love the earth and sun and the animals, despise riches, give alms to every one that asks . . . read these leaves in the open air in every season of every year of your life . . . dismiss whatever insults your own soul, and your very flesh shall be a great poem." The poem happens before us, giant and inclusive. We ride as much as read the long-cadenced lines. There are the great lists that itemize America, the continuous repetitions of phrase and syntactical structure, the unhallowed liturgy of love and desire. There is the man himself:

> Camerado, this is no book,
> Who touches this touches a man,
> (Is it night? are we here together alone?)
> It is I you hold and who holds you,
> I spring from the pages into your arms . . .

Upon receiving his copy of *Leaves of Grass*, Emerson alone responded: "I am not blind to the worth of the wonderful gift of *Leaves of Grass*. I find it the most extraordinary piece of wit and wisdom that America has yet contributed . . . I find incomparable things said incomparably well, as they must be. I find the courage of treatment which so delights us, and which large perceptions only can inspire." Of course, without Emerson's permission, Whitman reproduced his commendation at every opportunity. He had been recognized by a great man of letters. The 1856 edition had a preface that was a kind of declaration of independence from British poetry. In the third edition, 1860, he added—against Emerson's advice—the poems in which sexual concerns are more directly dealt with and changed the title to *Song of Myself*. It was banned in Boston, and in Britain an edition appeared omitting the newly added work.

For Whitman, as for Melville (and for Henry James), the Civil War gave serious shape to his imagination. Before he finished the collection of new work for the fourth edition of *Leaves*, the war began. Like the rest of America, he was anxious and excited at the outset. The national emotional trajectory was comparable to that in Britain in the First World War: hope and optimism—

> Beat! beat! drums—blow! bugles! blow!
> Through the windows—through doors—burst like a ruthless force
> Into the solemn church, and scatter the congregation,
> Into the school where the scholar is studying . . .

followed by a recognition that the forces released had run out of control. Whitman did not enlist, but hearing that his brother was wounded he set off in search of him and became a bearded, attentive Florence Nightingale figure, comforting men, writing their letters, helping to dress wounds, listening and writing prose and the verse that became *Drum-Taps* and *Sequel to Drum-Taps*, later published in *Leaves of Grass*.

Compassion became his keynote. He stayed in Washington to help in the wards. President Lincoln on horseback passed him in the street and raised his hat. It was the soon-to-be-assassinated Lincoln who elicited his famous elegies "O Captain, My Captain" and "When Lilacs."

> When lilacs last in the dooryard bloom'd,
> And the great star early droop'd in the western sky at night,
> I mourn'd, and yet shall mourn with the ever-returning spring.

Whitman was not a poet of despair: he rises above grief to celebration, through nature. For Swinburne this poem was "the most sweet and sonorous nocturne ever chanted in the church of the world."

Whitman stayed in Washington from 1865 until 1873, holding down a clerk's job. He suffered a stroke and retired to Camden, New Jersey, where—looked after by young friends—he worked on his evolving, reforming book, which did not finally please him until the last "death-bed edition," of 1891. In the later years of his life Whitman's most devoted readership was English, not American; and they read him not for his prosody or formal invention but for his matter, his "exuberant homo-eroticism," as Gregory Woods puts it. He "sent shock waves through the furtive gentility of Britain's Uranian community," transforming their aesthetic, classicizing homosexuality into something forward-looking and visionary: a modern sensual world with a place in it for them. When Wilde was thirteen his mother had read him passages from *Leaves of Grass*. At Oxford during his exams, one of the questions asked was what Aristotle might have made of Whitman. Whitman was in his blood, and four years later, visiting and lecturing in America, he went to call on him in Camden, New Jersey. The old poet and the young man regarded one another with respect and misunderstanding. Whitman found Wilde "frank and outspoken" as well as "manly."

Upon being asked in a convoluted way in a letter from one prominent British Uranian admirer whether, perhaps, sometimes, a bit of sex was implied in Whitman's great psalms and paeans, he replied unambiguously, *no*, and further insisted that he had fathered six children and had a grandchild. None of these relations has been traced. Wilde, who had met the man face to face, insisted that he made no secret of his homosexuality. "The kiss of Walt Whitman is still on my lips." That, too, sounds implausible. The poems are quite clear about the matter and take it as far as we have any right to go.

Winter Is Good

CHARLOTTE BRONTË, EMILY BRONTË, EMILY DICKINSON,
CHRISTINA ROSSETTI, DANTE GABRIEL ROSSETTI

The Brontë sisters, Charlotte (1816–55, a.k.a. Currer Bell and, married, as Charlotte Nicholls), Emily (1818–48, a.k.a. Ellis Bell) and Anne (1820–49, a.k.a. Acton Bell), shared a poetic project. When they were girls Emily and Anne composed the Gondal sagas. Charlotte and her brother, Branwell, composed the Angria sagas, and these fantasies continued to engage them well into their early adulthood. Poems attached to the stories, and the figures of the sagas, with their wild passions, never quite died. The poems are often the fruit of their big gestures, their brimming hearts and earthquake heartbreaks. This does not mean the three women are a composite creature, what R. E. Pritchard calls a Brontësaurus. In their verse, though Emily is by far the best of the three, there are differences of emotional intensity and of prosodic and formal skills.

All three are gothicized Romantics. Their settings are often nocturnal, wintery—the long dark winters of the Yorkshire Moors around Haworth, where they were born and lived through a litany of bereavements (two elder sisters, their mother), and where they received their education and wrote tirelessly and voluminously. The weathers and settings reflect extreme states of mind and emotion, and the forms are somber: balladic and hymn stanzas for the most part. The diction is restricted if not restrained, the range of intense emotions is confined.

Their world was not wide. Charlotte went furthest, becoming a teacher and in 1842 traveling with Emily to Belgium, where both attended a finishing school and Charlotte endured an unhappy romance. They came home in 1843 and three years later, with Anne, published *Poems by Currer, Ellis and Acton Bell*, of which two copies were sold in the first year. The names were chosen to neutralize their genders in the public world. The critical and commercial failure of the verse impelled all three young women into fiction.

In 1848 Emily ("stronger than a man, simpler than a child," according to Charlotte), and their brother, Branwell (a promising artist who fell into dissolute ways), died. In 1849 Anne—as a poet the most rueful and miserable of the sisters—succumbed to tuberculosis in Scarborough. Charlotte lived on, married her father's curate in 1854, but died nine months later. Three short lives, all of which have become legendary, the parsonage where they lived a place of pilgrimage, their novels among the most popular in the tradition as much on celluloid as on paper.

Most of the poems that were collected in the book were written between 1844 and 1846. Anne's verse can largely be discounted. It is competent, self-involved and miserable with an exaggerated, self-dramatizing misery. There are exceptions, in particular the anthologized poem "We know where deepest lies the snow." Charlotte wrote more than half her poetry between her thirteenth and twentieth years. "Once indeed I was very poetical," she declares, "when I was sixteen, seventeen, eighteen and nineteen years old—but I am now twenty-four approaching twenty-five—and the intermediate years are those which begin to rob life of its superfluous colouring." It is a terrifying commonplace: that poetry is the product of "superfluous colouring" and ceases as the world turns to its natural, adult grays. At fifteen, in "The trumpet hath sounded," she marries the hymn voices that rise to heaven with images of fairyland: "And, mingling with stern giant forms / Their tiny shapes were seen . . ." This is a fairyland remote from Spenser's. It modulates out of the hymn quatrains into curiously tripping eleven-syllable lines. "Mute, mute are the mighty, and chilled is their breath . . ."

Her mature verse seldom escapes its conventions. Solitary, she begins: "Again I find myself alone"; "What does she dream of, lingering all alone?" She strives, in will and dream if not in action. There is a beloved who does not respond, there is a dream of response, but the dream and the literal will not be reconciled. The poems are restrained in melody, a play of shadows that never solidifies into natural forms. The contingent world, even a fictional version of it, does not emerge as it sometimes seems to do, fitfully, from Anne's poems.

After the rueful passivity of her sisters' poems, Emily's have an emotional vigor of quite another order. They emerge from the sagas of childhood (almost two hundred of Emily's Gondal poems survive) and relate to the big events and emotions of heroic characters. At nineteen she wrote:

Lord of Elbë, on Elbë hill
The mist is thick and the wind is chill

And the heart of thy Friend from the dawn of day
Has sighed for sorrow that thou went away

More ballad than hymn, the landscape is almost real, but then we meet a gothic forest and a conventionally "desolate sea." Emily, like her characters, loved liberty and the open spaces of the moors. She insisted on her own patterns of life. Having nursed Branwell through his last illness, she caught cold at the funeral service and began her own two-month decline to death. Yet even on the day she died she insisted on rising in the morning, getting dressed and beginning her daily duties, as if the will could force its dying vehicle to live on. The will is the force her poems celebrate, a will that knows its limitations, as in the poem "I am the only being whose doom":

First melted off the hope of youth,
Then fancy's rainbow fast withdrew;
And then experience told me truth
In mortal bosoms never grew.

'Twas grief enough to thank mankind
All hollow, servile, insincere;
But worse to trust to my own mind
And find the same corruption there.

The third line ending, pointing as it does in two possible directions, is masterly; the acid recognition of the first stanza is as harsh as Arnold at his most unforgiving. The best-known and best of her poems are "Cold in the earth, and the deep snow piled above thee!," written for the heroine of the Gondal saga for her dead beloved, and the last lines of verse she wrote:

No coward soul is mine
No trembler in the world's storm-troubled sphere
I see Heaven's glories shine
And Faith shines equal arming me with fear

This poem ends with lines that hover somewhere between the hymns of Isaac Watts and the dense lyricism of Emily Dickinson. It is a faith that comes into clear focus late and in extremity:

There is not room for Death
Nor atom that his might could render void

Since thou art Being and Breath
And what thou art may never be destroyed.

There is intense life in the verse of Emily Brontë, the kind of life that strains the forms and breaks them into new configurations. As in her fiction, so to a lesser extent in her verse, form is a means and not an end. Her technical versatility is in no way exemplary. Another poet could learn only one valuable lesson from what she does, and that is the ways in which form *lives* when it is driven urgently by powerful impulses, and how when that urgency ends a poem should stop.

When Emily Dickinson was nineteen she was mired in convention: "Awake ye muses nine, sing me a strain divine, / Unwind the solemn twine, and tie my Valentine!" The uncertain fourteener couplets now gallop, now stumble, to their end-stop. Lines seldom run over, though they have a strong caesura and can be read, taken in pairs, as prototypes for her later quatrains. "Thou art a *human* solo, a being cold, and lone, / Wilt have no kind companion, thou *reap'st* what thou hast *sown*." From the age of fourteen she was full of optimism for herself. "I am growing handsome very fast indeed!" She expected to become "the belle of Amherst when I reach my seventeenth year." And at nineteen she was part of a lively community, with dances, charades, dinners, and a Valentine tradition that she honored in prose and verse. Hers was a polite world. To a friend she wrote of Whitman, "I never read his book—but was told that he was disgraceful."

How was it that out of this conventional and cheerful young woman emerged the reclusive, prolific, miraculous Emily Dickinson, not the belle but—as Mabel Loomis Todd wrote in 1881—"the *Myth*"? "She has not been outside of her own house in fifteen years," Todd declares, and then evokes the legendary lady dressed all in white:

The Soul selects her own Society—
Then—shuts the Door—
To her divine Majority—
Present no more—

Dickinson wrote 1,775 poems, letters that fill three volumes, as though in writing she invested a life first offered on the altar of convention and then snatched back before the quotidian gods had a chance to make her into another charming American wife and mother.

Five years after Dickinson died, Todd brought out the first volume of her verses, edited and improved by her and Thomas Wentworth Higginson so as to bring them almost within the bounds of convention. Only a handful of the poems had been published (also edited and "improved") in the poet's lifetime. It was a lifetime uneventful on the surface, and those events we know have fueled a conflagration of supposititious biography. The original take on her was sentimental: she had fallen in love with a man—a married man, perhaps—(various candidates were proposed) and been rebuffed. Or had she succumbed to agoraphobia? Or had some other emotional trauma affected her? Her poems both dramatize and conceal whatever it was. We were not to know and, in the end, we never will. Adrienne Rich says, "More than any other poet, Emily Dickinson seemed to tell me that the intense inner event, the personal and psychological, was inseparable from the universal; that there was a range for psychological poetry beyond mere self-expression." We have the legend, but the crucial facts in the recorded life are absent. Dickinson's reticence seems part of her poetic strategy: if we could assign the poems to specific emotional events, we would ground them. As it is, they are a miracle and a mystery of language.

Born in Amherst in 1830, she was the second child of the lawyer Edward Dickinson and his reticent wife. They were one of the better families. Austin was her elder brother, Lavinia her younger sister. It was apparently a happy home. She was educated at Amherst Academy and then sent to Mount Holyoke Female Seminary, where she distinguished herself unostentatiously. The evangelical movement reached the institution while she was there and claimed some of her contemporaries. Emily withheld herself, even when her family succumbed to the fashionable fervor. (At twenty-four she declined to be a church member, though sometimes she attended for pleasure. It cannot have been easy to go against the will of her father, but she could place no trust in the efficacy of emotional conversion.)

Her father withdrew her from Mount Holyoke after a year in which her religious resistances had already become manifest, and she returned home. Her reclusion began. She became increasingly agoraphobic, and the girl who had visited Boston and Worcester and even, with her congressman father, had spent a couple of months in Washington and Philadelphia, chose to stay at home. To the editor of the *Atlantic Monthly*, Thomas Wentworth Higginson, to whom she wrote many letters and who never quite took her poems on board, she confessed that she never left home. So reticent was she that, when a doctor was called to her in her last illness, she allowed him to examine her only from a distance as she walked up and down behind a partly open door. She became deeply attached to her sister-in-law Susan Gilbert Dickinson, her beloved companion. She died of Bright's disease (nephritis) in 1886 and at last left home.

Her literary favorites she seems to have regarded as an alternative

family, hanging their portraits in her room: Carlyle, Elizabeth Barrett
Browning, George Eliot. She admired Emily Brontë's "No coward soul
is mine," and Higginson read it at her funeral. She read *Jane Eyre*,
Middlemarch, Aurora Leigh. Skirting around Whitman, she read the
Transcendentalists. She read the King James Bible and the Book of
Common Prayer; she knew the hymns, she loved Webster's *Dictionary*,
she knew the poets of the sixteenth and seventeenth centuries: some of
them were family too.

Life, time, nature and eternity are the big counters she moves about
the rapid little quatrain squares of her verse, but each counter she makes
her own through metaphor and her vivid subversions of expectation.
"Her wit is accuracy," says the poet Alison Brackenbury, but "She is the
spider, not the fly." Not being the fly: perhaps that was her strategy of
withdrawal from a world in which she saw women snared in the strict
geometries of the social web, and decided that for her the freedom of an
elected solitude—not of a spinster only but of a recluse—was preferable,
even *necessary*. So she can write,

> My life closed twice before its close—
> It yet remains to see
> If Immortality unveil
> A third event to me
>
> So huge, so hopeless to conceive
> As these that twice befell.
> Parting is all we know of heaven,
> And all we need of hell.

There is in her resignation a willed acceptance: not sorrow but some-
thing harder and wiser, that takes off from pain into the deeper dark-
ness. The impulse is religious but the consolations, like the abstractions,
are not orthodox. Nor is the tone: it is wry, it plays with images, the
comedy and cruelty of the bird hopping unobserved along the walk, of
the bee in its fuzzy bonnet, or the incongruous sound that breaks in on
rapture or grief. Sometimes she is merely charmingly whimsical:

> Bee! I'm expecting you!
> Was saying Yesterday
> To Somebody you know
> That you were due—
>
> The Frogs got Home last Week—

She signs the poem as though it were a letter: "Yours, Fly." On an entirely different scale, she writes in a letter: "You mention Immortality! . . . That is the Flood subject." The minute and the boundless have a place in her taut stanzas, where they are interrogated. She is seeking proof and disproof, but can find neither satisfactorily in received religion or in settled materialism. She wants a faith that she can hold, even if only in language, and taste and smell, even if only through the grace of words. An immanence. And she does sense it at times, and then loses it and herself with it. "And God at every gate," one poem promises:

O Sacrament of summer days,
Oh Last Communion in the Haze—
Permit a child to join.

Thy sacred emblems to partake—
Thy consecrated bread to take
And thine immortal wine!

Not First but Last Communion, autumn, the emptiness of winter to follow. If there is a mystical note in her verse, it is rooted insistently in particulars of this world, where His life, His wounds, His love can be inferred. Such mysticism never resolves in an affirming faith. It inheres in what she perceives and cannot be detached. In her white—wedding? Communion?—dress, in her seclusion as absolute as any nun's in a closed order, we might have expected a more resolute spiritual conclusion to her life of meditation than the reality. She sewed her poems into little books and put them away, one after another, in a box, where after her death her sister found them, nine hundred poems "tied together with twine" in "sixty volumes." And it's not an untenable theory that the beloved whom she mourns, departed, may be Christ, the soul's lover, rather than a particular man—or a particular woman.

    She rejected conventional religion, she withdrew from the world, and in 1862 as the pressure of her verse built up in her, she contacted Higginson. Thirty-two, with over three hundred poems already to her credit, she was not conversant with the ways of the literary world. She had responded to Higginson's "Letter to a Young Contributor" in the *Atlantic Monthly*. He was well known as a lecturer concerned with women's rights and women writers. "Are you too deeply occupied to say if my verse is alive? . . . The mind is so near itself it cannot see distinctly, and I have none to ask." Higginson responded, as his critics say, pompously, "without understanding." It would have been difficult for any American reader in the midst of the Civil War to "understand," on the strength of a handful of curiously punctuated poems, what lay behind them. In responding he gave her a sufficient initial encouragement, and he continued to correspond. It is easy to patronize a man like Higginson in retrospect for his "lack of vision." What was remarkable about him was that *he* did not patronize. He sensed, if not strongly enough, that he was dealing with an authentic spirit. Many an editor would have left Miss Dickinson's letter unanswered.

His advice was not helpful: she must make the poems more regular, she must punctuate them more conventionally. She did not comply; seeing her poems tidied up upset her: they lost expressiveness and definition. Ironically, his advice made her more resolute in her originality. It is hard to define her originality. I first experienced it when Robert Frost came to my school. In a lecture he called "The Pan-Handle of Poetry" he recited eight lines of verse:

The heart asks pleasure first,
And then, excuse from pain;
And then, those little anodynes
That deaden suffering;

And then, to go to sleep;
And then, if it should be
The will of its Inquisitor
The liberty to die.

I was fourteen at the time and had always found her mawkish in textbooks: "I heard a fly buzz when I died" and "I like to see it lap the miles." After Frost's recitation in that slow dismissive voice of his, I knew the poem word-perfect and have never forgotten it. But it was not *her* poem, and it was not word-perfect. This was the version Mabel Loomis Todd published, shaking out the loose straw of the poet's dashes, taking down her capital letters and, where a word seemed ominously suspended by a definite article, assigning it by a possessive pronoun: "its Inquisitor," not "the Inquisitor." "Liberty," not the paradoxical and troubling "privilege." What Dickinson needed was a good dose of logic and correctness, à la Higginson. The Todd-Higginson volume of 1890 was a success, and the next year 166 more poems were published, as well as the letters, and further poems edited by Todd in 1896. An edition by Emily's niece and heir Martha Dickinson Bianchi came out in 1914 under the title *The Single Hound*, the text based more closely on original manuscripts. In 1929, 1935 and 1945 editions appeared, and finally, in 1955, a collection of all the extant poems, restored by Thomas H. Johnson, with variant readings and fragments, reproducing closely the original punctuation. Dickinson could speak again—or for the first time—in her own voice. The version Frost should have recited (though, an old man, he stuck with the one he had known for years) was this one: different diction, punctuation, rhythm:

The Heart asks Pleasure—first—
And then—Excuse from Pain—
And then—those little Anodynes
That deaden suffering—

And then—to go to sleep—
And then—if it should be
The will of the Inquisitor
The privilege to die—

Here is her originality, unmuffled after eight decades of propriety, an irregularity that answers to the darting, tentative process of the poet's sight and feeling, the rapid transformations that follow an unfolding argument or feeling. Dickinson's poetry is the drama of *process*; "The Heart asks Pleasure" is nothing less than an essential autobiography. And this poem revealing as much of the afterlife as we can be sure of:

I died for Beauty—but was scarce
Adjusted in the Tomb
When One who died for Truth, was lain
In an adjoining Room—

He questioned softly "Why I failed"?
"For Beauty," I replied—
"And I—for Truth—Themself are One—
We Brethren, are," He said—

And so, as Kinsmen, met a Night—
We talked between the Rooms—
Until the Moss had reached our lips—
And covered up—our names—

What are we to make of "Themself"? Do we change it to "themselves" or "the two" as editors did, or do we acknowledge that this is the very *kind* of her originality, what drew that meticulous, savagely austere poet of the German language, Paul Celan, to translate her alongside the Russian Osip Mandelstam? The language is not *literary*. It enacts heard experience. Kinsmen, unexpectedly met, chatting late into the night from their different places: it brings beauty and truth into intimate focus. Strange: These are the same great terms of Keats's "cold pastoral."

Enactment at its best occurs in a powerful portrayal of physical dying and its effect on those who keep vigil when death permits the final breath to flow:

> The last Night that She lived
> It was a Common Night
> Except the Dying—this to Us
> Made Nature different
>
> We noticed smallest things—
> Things overlooked before
> By this great light upon our Minds
> Italicized—as 'twere.
>
> As We went out and in
> Between Her final Room
> And Rooms where Those to be alive
> Tomorrow were, a Blame
>
> The Others could exist
> While She must finish quite
> A Jealousy for Her arose
> So nearly infinite—
>
> We waited while She passed—
> It was a narrow time—
> Too jostled were Our Souls to speak
> At length the notice came.
>
> She mentioned, and forgot—
> Then lightly as a Reed
> Bent to the Water, struggled scarce—
> Consented, and was dead—
>
> And We—We placed the Hair—
> And drew the Head erect—
> And then an awful leisure was
> Belief to regulate—

The penultimate stanza must be among the most perfect in her work, corresponding to every element in the experience together and by turns, and the metaphor uncannily apposite. The poem is deliberate in its deployment of capital letters, a kind of formal dress which at the proper time is set aside. In 1886 she too consented, and was dead.

English critics tend to set Christina Rossetti in the frame alongside Emily Dickinson. Dickinson, says C. H. Sisson, "has to be read with, and judged against" Rossetti. He implies a superior "purity" in Rossetti's language, and no doubt he is right: her diction is refined and largely conventional, her measures more on the Higginson model, and she can be very good. But the two are different in kind even when they touch upon the same themes. The Englishwoman is a poet not of thought or ideas but of emotions, while the American engages with ideas and the feelings they generate and command in the same breath. Religious faith for Christina Rossetti was much more a matter of adjustment than of fundamental struggle. She regarded poetic form as something given and received, to be practiced with skill and originality, but again without fundamental questioning or adjustment. Hers is a measurable and verifiable quality, of a kind unusual at her time. Ford saw her as a harbinger of where poetry would go in coming generations, and he was not wrong: the poems point in the direction that poetry always goes: after radical shakeups, it falls back into familiar channels, with the clarity of reaction and relief.

Beside the poetry of her formidable and sometimes vulgar artist brother, Dante Gabriel Rossetti, her verse shines brighter than against Dickinson's. It is indeed at once more precise and firmly conceived, he being (in Ford's words) a mere "impressionist." "Occasionally," he says, "[Dante Gabriel] displayed a sense of words. Look at these for the loss of the White Ship in the ballad of the same name: 'And the ship was gone; / And the deep shuddered; and the moon shone.' " His admirers are overwhelmed; they "insist that he write four hundred lines more of bilge, never blotting a line. None of them ever blotted a line." And while this adulation occurred, "all the while, up in the fireless top back bedroom on the corner of the cracked wash-stand, on the backs of old letters Christina Rossetti sat writing." For Ford only Browning and Christina Rossetti in their period were worth rereading.

It is the simple directness of Christina Rossetti's language that draws poets of a later generation, like Elizabeth Jennings. She admires, and learns from, what C. H. Sisson calls "the intimate falls of her rhythms." Rossetti is available to any reader: subtle in form and those thoughts that take the shape of feelings, direct in emotional charge.

She was born "with a pen in her hand" in London in 1830. She started composing early, her first story when she was too young to write. Her first poem she dictated to her mother: "Cecilia never went to school / Without her gladiator." Her early mature poems (a few in Italian) have some of the merits of her best work, and she continued writing almost to the end. If her life is not full of the biographical interest of the major Pre-Raphaelites, it was marked by deep human commitments, friendships, two intense but not turbulent or successful courtships ("My heart is breaking for a little love"), fears and regrets. It was also fueled by a faith that felt wonder, doubt and moments of intense penetration of religious mystery, of a kind not common among her contemporaries. The religion of the later poems has not the flashes of the earlier—like Wordsworth, she lost something as time closed in on her. She becomes doctrinaire, catechistic. The large body of her poems is narrow in range, but there are moments of mastery. Her very quietness is a source of strength. She is the Gwen John to Dante Gabriel's Augustus, the one we turn to when the artful and the artificial weary us and we seek a true voice of feeling. She died after a severe and disfiguring illness in 1894. In the weeks before her death she disturbed the neighbors each night with her unaccountable screaming.

The first book appeared in 1862, *Goblin Market and Other Poems,* including the eponymous poem, the first by a Pre-Raphaelite to gain attention. It has, in the words of the poet-editor and anthologist David Wright, "a vitality and sensuousness allied to simplicity, clearness and intellectual coherence, in notable contrast to the lushness of most of the poetry of the period." The poem has been regarded, despite its intense sexuality, as proper for children. Several books followed, with love poems and religious verse for adults, for children poems bordering on nonsense, beautiful without the humor of Lear or Carroll. She was interested (a sign of her professionalism) in "my dear Copyright." She knew what it meant materially to be a professional writer of essays, religious meditations and poems.

The poems that have become embedded deep in the tradition are "In the bleak midwinter," the unbearably plangent "When I am dead, my dearest," the almost cloying "My heart is like a singing bird," and "Remember me when I am gone away." For C. H. Sisson one poem, "Memory," essentializes her, and indeed her handling of form is so quietly tactful, her diction so plain and preponderantly monosyllabic, the contingent facts so quietly cleared away, that it stands (despite its conventional look) unique in its century for unexaggerated candor:

> I nursed it in my bosom while it lived,
>> I hid it in my heart when it was dead.
> In joy I sat alone; even so I grieved
>> Alone, and nothing said.

I shut the door to face the naked truth,
    I stood alone—I faced the truth alone,
Stripped bare of self-regard or forms or ruth
      Till first and last are shown.

I took the perfect balances and weighed;
    No shaking of my hand disturbed the poise;
Weighed, found it wanting: not a word I said,
      But silent made my choice.

None knew the choice I made; I make it still.
    None knew the choice I made and broke my heart,
Breaking mine idol: I have braced my will
      Once, chosen for once my part.

I broke it at a blow, I laid it cold,
    Crushed in my deep heart where it used to live.
My heart dies inch by inch, the time grows old,
      Grows old in which I grieve.

Her mind, as Sisson says, is resolute: she knows what she is doing, the pain she causes and its consequence: yet she acts.

Her brother, Dante Gabriel (1828–82), has been eclipsed even as her star has risen. Only his most famous poems, "The Woodspurge" and "The Blessed Damozel," are tenuously held in popular memory. The whole Pre-Raphaelite *thing*, at the hub of which he stands, with its attitudinizing, its excesses, its wild and sometimes lunatic palette, is less popular in literature than in the galleries. His poems do not partake of the charged excess of the paintings. In form and diction they are more chaste (whatever their occasions may have been); they are not dated except in their hankering after allegory, a trace of medievalism that does not mar the diction, though it provides us with personifications of a curiously varnished type. Formally, in sonnets and narratives and inventive lyrics, he is a master—of enjambement, of cunning irregularity in prosody—who approaches "voice" with a diction remarkably unliterary and uncluttered for a man of his coterie. Ford is excessively unkind to him, though for Ford perhaps his sin was to have cast so long a shadow on his sister, who now glows with such a steady light of her own.

The Phantom of Ourselves

MATTHEW ARNOLD, ALGERNON CHARLES SWINBURNE,
GERARD MANLEY HOPKINS

Writing in 1848 to his dear friend the poet Arthur Hugh Clough, the author of the witty and beguiling verse novel *Amours de Voyage* (1858), Matthew Arnold dismisses Browning as "a man with a moderate gift passionately desiring movement and fullness, and obtaining but a confused multitudinousness." Browning's ideas are not sufficiently strong: the world's multitudinousness prevails and imposes fragmentation. To his mother he wrote twenty years later: "It might be fairly urged that I have less poetical sentiment than Tennyson, and less intellectual vigor and abundance than Browning; yet, perhaps because I have more of a fusion of the two than either of them, and have regularly applied that fusion to the main line of modern development, I am likely enough to have my turn, as they have had theirs."

But Arnold never quite had his turn as a poet, partly because of the deliberate way he conceives his role, partly because Arnold the critic frightens readers off. The faint praise even of so sympathetic a reader as Robert Graves sells him short: "He was so capable, honest and humourless a monumental mason that he deserves more honour than most of his energetic and vainglorious contemporaries—the Brownings, Tennysons and Rossettis." Max Beerbohm realized that there was a less somber, less grandiloquent side—not only the man who elegized his dogs and a canary along with Wordsworth and Goethe, but a man whose good humor occasionally bursts forth in the letters. Auden early in his career takes the measure of Arnold's moral *feeling*—what sets him apart from his contemporaries is a sense that ideas matter, actions are to be judged by motive rather than effect. A hunger for order is part of his hunger for truth. But this diminishes him in Auden's eye to being something of a ventriloquist's dummy for the values of his father, the educationalist.

His gift knew what he was—a dark disordered city;
Doubt hid it from the father's fond chastising sky;
Where once the mother-farms had glowed protectively,
Stood the haphazard alleys of the neighbours' pity.

—Yet would have gladly lived in him and learned his ways,
And grown observant like a beggar, and become
Familiar with each square and boulevard and slum,
And found in the disorder a whole world to praise.

But all his homeless reverence, revolted, cried:
"I am my father's forum and he shall be heard,
Nothing shall contradict the holy final word,
Nothing." And thrust his gift in prison till it died,

And left him nothing but a jailor's voice and face,
And all rang hollow but the clear denunciation
Of a gregarious optimistic generation
That saw itself already in a father's place.

This is near Lytton Strachey's cruel verdict, which makes Arnold (also through paternal legacy) provincial, repugnant to that assertive commissar's cosmopolitan morality, and rather risibly unsophisticated. From his shrill perch Strachey misreads the real achievements of the father and forgets that the impact of father on son was not the impact of just any teacher and preacher, but of a very particular one, on a son who was able to write "Dover Beach" and "Sohrab and Rustum."

Lionel Trilling gets a proper purchase on Arnold. Against the mellifluousness of his Victorian contemporaries, "Arnold breaks into melody only occasionally, but through all his verse runs the grave cadence of the *speaking* voice . . . His very colloquialism . . . is one of Arnold's charms; it is the urbanity of the ancient poets . . . which assumes the presence of a hearer and addresses him—with a resultant intimacy and simplicity of manner that is often very moving." Arnold is set beside the more copious, less earnest, Landor, as central to that other nineteenth-century line, which seemed to perish in the 1890s but emerged once more in the teens of the next century.

Though Swinburne later changed his tune, he wrote of Arnold's *New Poems* (1867): "The majesty and composure of thought and verse, the perfect clearness and competence of the words, distinguish this from other poetry of the intellect now more approved and applauded." He had in mind Tennyson's and Browning's intellectually unburnished instruments beside Arnold's antique lyre. Swinburne's rhetoric is not altogether empty: *New Poems* included "Thyrsis," "Heine's Grave" and "Rugby Chapel." The best work shows composure, if not "majesty": a dignity suited to Arnold's moral seriousness. He balances feeling and thought—feeling not in *excess* of thought. Arnold has the seriousness, if not the certainty, of Johnson. Virgil's *Aeneid* is pervaded—he says— by a brooding melancholy, "the haunting self-dissatisfaction" of the poet's heart. Arnold in his lyrics, elegies and poems of action is self-dissatisfied: with his poetry, his life, his society, his sense of time—a universalized pathos, a vision of the human condition in his century that combines the negative clarity of an Old Testament prophet with the manners of a classical patrician: resignation tempers vehemence. He sees things as they are and will be. In "Dover Beach," the greatest single poem of the Victorian period, a moment of happiness regards itself in the context of history. Gazing at the sea, the poet calls his beloved to watch and listen with him. He hears the tide on the shingle. Sophocles heard in that sound "the turbid ebb and flow / Of human misery." He finds thought there too. The Sea of Faith is ebbing, and with it the certainties of faith. He hears

> Its melancholy, long, withdrawing roar,
> Retreating, to the breath
> Of the night-wind, down the vast edges drear
> And naked shingles of the world.
>
> Ah, love, let us be true
> To one another! for the world, which seems
> To lie before us like a land of dreams,
> So various, so beautiful, so new,
> Hath really neither joy, nor love, nor light,
> Nor certitude, nor peace, nor help for pain;
> And we are here as on a darkling plain
> Swept with confused alarms of struggle and fight,
> Where ignorant armies clash by night.

Negative vision emerges from a particular situation: "Come to the window, sweet is the night air." Beside Browning's dramatic monologues this grows even taller in its technical and intellectual accomplishment. Tidally, the lines contract and expand; enjambements heighten the tone, counterpoint the rhythms, which have the variety and hesitancy of a speaking voice, rising to the open cadence of the concluding lines.

Arnold was not invariably so intimate, severe or good a writer. Many poems are drab or sententious. If his best are sober in tone and elegiac in manner, so are his worst. There are reasons for this, not all of them personal. Tennyson and Browning enjoyed relative financial independence; Arnold, son of the educationalist Thomas Arnold, headmaster of Rugby, had to earn a living conventionally. Work took him away from writing. The world he moved through as a schools inspector—and he knew more at first hand of conditions in the social and political world than any of his Victorian contemporaries—was hard to square with the cultural world he possessed. His social criticism and his poetry flow from this gaping disparity between the actual and the potential. His criticism suggests that change is possible, while his verse acknowledges—in its classical and heroic subjects and elegiac mode—a steady decline from the past to the materialist, philistine Victorian present he inhabits. In his own life, there was a decline as well, a fall from grace. He never achieved the great poem he believed he could write.

He was born in Laleham, Surrey, in 1822. He had crooked legs and spent two years in leg braces to correct the deformity. The family moved to Rugby in 1828. Arnold's early education was, unhappily, at Laleham for two years, under his uncle's supervision; then at Winchester; and finally at Rugby itself, where he made friends with Clough, and with Thomas Hughes, author-to-be of *Tom Brown's School Days*. Fox How, near Grasmere, close by the Wordsworths', was the family holiday retreat and remained Arnold's bolt-hole for the rest of his life.

He won a scholarship to Balliol College, Oxford, in 1840 (as did Clough) and a year later his father became Regius Professor of Modern History at the university (while remaining headmaster of Rugby). He wrote poems, won prizes, developed his friendship with Clough, attended John Henry Newman's (still Anglican) sermons, and got a reputation as a not-over-the-top dandy and dependable student. His father died suddenly of heart illness in 1842, and this bereavement cast a shadow over Arnold's thought. He took the Newdigate Prize for poetry and in 1844 received a second-class degree. He taught briefly at Rugby and in 1845 was elected fellow of Oriel College, Oxford. Friends and family considered him a dilettante and were unprepared for the seriousness of his poems published anonymously in 1849. *The Strayed Reveller, and Other Poems* contained "The Forsaken Merman" and the famous sonnet to Shakespeare. By this time he had traveled to France and Switzerland and was on his way to becoming a modest man of the world.

In 1851 he was appointed inspector of schools, responsible for the primary and secondary establishments run by nonestablished Protestant denominations. On the strength of this employment he got married. The next year, again anonymously, *Empedocles on Etna, and Other Poems* appeared, as did his first son. Among the "other poems" was "Tristram and Iseult." In 1853 *Poems, A New Edition* (this time with his name on it) was published, with a selection from earlier books and "Sohrab and

Rustum," "The Scholar-Gipsy" and "Memorial Verses to Wordsworth," one of the best elegies in the language. *Poems: Second Series* (1855) includes the disappointing poem of action, "Balder Dead." *Merope: A Tragedy* (1858) was unsuccessful. His final collection, *New Poems* (1867), was hardly new. Apart from "Thyrsis," dedicated to the memory of Clough and composed in 1864–65, most of the work dated back to his best years as poet between 1845 and 1857, but particularly 1848 and 1852. He resembles the great Romantics in that he is essentially a young poet, composing his best work in his late twenties and early thirties, the force of his gift then slackening. He suffered a series of appalling bereavements, culminating in 1868 when he lost his eldest and youngest sons. In 1869 a two-volume edition of collected poems appeared.

Arnold was elected Oxford Professor of Poetry in 1857. He was reelected and served until 1867. Critical activity may have curbed his poetic impulse, though *Merope* shows the impulse already in decline. He had the will, but no longer the integrating imagination: middle age belongs to the great prose work, on translating Homer, the *Essays in Criticism*, and his best-known work of social criticism, *Culture and Anarchy* (1869). He was promoted to senior and later chief inspector of schools. He engaged in educational campaigns, and the range of his criticism is wide. He made a lecture tour of the United States and retired from the inspectorate in 1886. In 1888, on his way to meet his daughter on her arrival from America, he died in Liverpool.

The last thirty years of his life he spent preeminently as critic and public man. He did not like the role. The bitterness of "Growing Old" is an oblique reply to Browning's dewy-eyed "Rabbi Ben Ezra," for whom old age is a time of rich fulfillment. "What is it to grow old?" Arnold asks. He lists the answers, the last containing a "self-dissatisfaction" turned on the world:

> It is—last stage of all—
> When we are frozen up within, and quite
> The phantom of ourselves,
> To hear the world applaud the hollow ghost
> Which blamed the living man.

"The Last Word" is equally uncompromising. The terrible distance between youthful hope and the reality of age also provides the dramatic tension in *Empedocles on Etna*. The young poet Callicles confronts Empedocles: he *has been* young. In "Youth and Age" the theme is reenacted: age acquires calm as its crown—that is certainly not the crown youth hankered after.

"In *Culture and Anarchy*, in *Literature and Dogma*," writes T. S. Eliot,

"Arnold was not occupied so much in establishing a criticism as in attacking the uncritical." Eliot understands better than any reader what cultural and intellectual isolation mean to a critical mind: it is compelled to affirm the value of criticism, to seek resistance and opposition in order to fortify and define itself. For Arnold, with few intellectual and imaginative peers, the activity became like shadow-boxing. Elsewhere Eliot says, "Arnold—I think it will be conceded—was rather a propagandist for criticism than a critic, a populariser rather than a creator of ideas."

If Eliot is right about the social essays, his strictures do not apply to Arnold's writings on literature. Or to his poetry. He evolved a theory of the art so exacting that—except in "Sohrab and Rustum"—he could not live up to it himself. He undervalues lyric and elegy—modes natural to him—and stresses the importance of a suitable, large subject, preferably heroic. "Action" he strives for: excellent actions appeal "to the great primary human affections," which do not change. He comments, "It is a pity . . . that the poet should be compelled to impart interest and force to his subject, instead of receiving them from it." There are few common subjects to turn to in an age whose art wanted sanity. The classics teach balance and proportion: sanity is the virtue of ancient writers, its lack the vice of the moderns. Arnold's is a normative, civilizing aesthetic, at a time when the wasting modern "dialogue of the mind with itself has commenced." "To Marguerite," from the "Switzerland" sequence, answers Donne: each man *is* an island; even love cannot change that condition:

> Who order'd that their longing's fire
> Should be, as soon as kindled, cool'd?
> Who renders vain their deep desire?—
> A God, a God their severance ruled!
> And bade betwixt their shores to be
> The unplumb'd, salt, estranging sea.

This is not spoken from behind a mask or by a persona, but by the poet's own voice. He does not contrive a metaphysical apotheosis, the way Tennyson does in *In Memoriam*. He does nothing to deflect the apprehension: not "God" but "a God." It is bold, uncompromising verse, the truest written in the Victorian period.

No wonder Algernon Charles Swinburne fell out of love with Arnold's poems. They ask too much, and—from Swinburne's point of view—exclude too much. Swinburne is another kind of phantom. In his work we look in vain for truths of the Arnoldian variety—indeed, for truth of any kind at all. His poetry is art and artifice, going out of its way to lose its occasion in prosodic extension and excess. "Look, you, I speak not as one light of wit, / But as a queen speaks, being heart-vexed . . ." T.S. Eliot is persuaded that a not quite namable something inheres in the melodious mush of the language. "We may take it as undisputed that Swinburne did make a contribution; that he did something that had not been done before, and that what he did will not turn out to be a fraud." Eliot's "something" and his double negatives back his sentence as far away from affirmation as it can go; but it affirms. Many argue that Swinburne is a fraud, using Eliot's tempered advocacy to define that fraudulence, the sort we suspect in Edith Sitwell, in some of Dylan Thomas, and less certainly in the Louis MacNeice of *Autumn Sequel* and in Ted Hughes. Not that any of them sets out to deceive readers; they deceive themselves. They let the machine of rhythmic language run, it uses them to make poems; they abdicate to a treacherous dynamic which ought to require scrupulous control. Eliot, the master of concentration, celebrates—with reservations—Swinburne's diffuseness.

He insists that Swinburne cannot usefully be called musical: there are sound values, but the poems are neither singable nor setable. Image and idea are unimportant: sound matters, sound in the vowels especially, sounds in the weave and cross-weave, the rhyme and dissonance of syntactical construction. Shelley is Swinburne's master: he has "a beauty of music and a beauty of content." "Now, in Swinburne the meaning and the sound are one thing. He is concerned with the meaning of the word in a peculiar way: he employs, or rather 'works,' the word's meaning. And this is connected with an interesting fact about his vocabulary: he uses the most general word, because his emotion is never particular, never in direct line of vision, never focused; it is emotion reinforced, not by intensification, but by expansion . . . It is, in fact, the word that gives him the thrill, not the object." And here is Eliot's decisive reservation. "Language in a healthy state presents the object, is so close to the object that the two are identified." Unhealthy though Swinburne is, Eliot praises him: "Only a man of genius could dwell so exclusively and consistently among words as Swinburne."

There is something absurd about the image of Swinburne, aged thirty, kneeling before the Italian leader Mazzini and reading him "A Song of Italy." There is much that is absurd about him: his enthusiasms, his life, his poems.

Swallow, my sister, O sister swallow,
    How can thy heart be full of the spring?
        A thousand summers are over and dead.

That first line is one of the more curious errors of taste in English poetry. In the Mazzini episode, so like a painting by one of his Pre-Raphaelite friends, we can read a great deal about the man: his passion for liberty and his desire for subjection; his ostentation; his naïve political and poetic idealism. Gesture! Gesture! Swinburne had every social advantage: education, access to the notables of his day, money, devoted friends. There were compensating psychological and social disadvantages, for it was late in the day to be a Romantic; the fin-de-siècle began well before the *fin*; gesture became what action had been for earlier poets. Vague thought and sentiment were confused with profound sensibility.

Swinburne reacted against the rigorous moral code of the time. His visit to Mazzini was an aspect of this reaction, his eager prostration before hired flagellants another. He was piqued when critics questioned the morality of his verses. There can be little doubt about his personal morality. A group of French writers gathered at Flaubert's house one evening in 1875 to gossip about Swinburne. Alphonse Daudet mentioned that he was homosexual: "There are the most extraordinary stories told about his stay at Étretat last year . . ." Guy de Maupassant chipped in: it was he who *almost* saved Swinburne from drowning (a boat arrived first) and was invited to lunch the next day. "It was a strange place where they lived, a sort of cottage containing some splendid pictures . . . and a big monkey gambolling around inside." His hosts would not name the meat he ate. There was no wine, only spirits. "As for Swinburne," Maupassant added, "picture a little man with a forked chin, a hydrocephalous forehead, and a narrow chest, who trembled so violently that he gave his glass St Vitus's dance and talked like a madman." He spoke excellent French and was hugely, if diffusely informed. After lunch Swinburne and his friend got out "some gigantic portfolios," including collections of obscene photographs taken in Germany, "all full-length and all of male subjects." In Oscar Wilde's view, expressed to the Goncourt brothers some years later, Swinburne set out to shock and prove himself a homosexual and bestializer without ever having *done* anything about either vice. It was merely a gesture, a plea for attention.

There is another Swinburne, articulate lover of the Elizabethans, of Landor, of the strict intellect and language of Johnson, of Blake (whom he did much to restore to favor), Whitman, Baudelaire, the Marquis de Sade. He stands opposite Hopkins. Hopkins is all decision and the human consequences of decision, Swinburne all indecision and its inconsequentiality. Each poet developed a language, two extreme approaches to syntax, diction, rhythm and form. Their successes and failures are complementary.

Swinburne was born in London in 1837, his father an admiral, his mother a cultured and titled lady. There were ancestral estates, holidays on the Isle of Wight, and in general a pampered childhood. Then Eton. He was presented to Wordsworth when he was twelve, and by his late adolescence he could take great poets in his stride. He was indulged, encouraged, and his emotional development was arrested in adolescence. There was promise in his poetic beginnings. At the age of twelve—already besotted with the Elizabethan playwrights and the sixteenth century generally—he wrote a four-act verse play based on Cyril Tourneur's *The Revenger's Tragedy*. In memory he embroiders even his worst excesses of imitation: "I had contrived to pack twice as many rapes and about three times as many murders as are contained in the model, which is not noticeably or exceptionally deficient in such incident." He exaggerates: his play has only one rape and a modest death count. Its limpid verse makes perfect sense and is often beautiful in effect, especially the extension of syntax and the amazingly deft use of enjambements. "I am torn / From Life to happiness . . ." All that remains of this precocity in the later work is the prosodic skill.

The themes of the poetry hardly developed after 1866. Once it got into gear it stayed in that gear, uphill and down, for forty years. There is good writing and bad, but rhythms and approach remain constant, apart from increasing facility: acceleration, and a decrease in tension with the years. His earliest work is often best, the description of love from the verse drama *Atalanta in Calydon*, for example:

Thou art swift and subtle and blind as a flame of fire;
Before thee the laughter, behind thee the tears of desire;
And twain go forth beside thee, a man with a maid;
Her eyes are the eyes of a bride whom delight makes afraid;
As the breath in the buds that stir is her bridal breath:
But Fate is the name of her; and his name is Death.

Here are the fleeting themes: love, death, fate, fear, pain; the incantatory rhetoric, the end-stopped lines, the semicolons, the evanescent image. We seem to see, but it is the passage of phantoms in a hurry. They are not the "phantoms of ourselves."

At Eton he fell in love with Sappho, Victor Hugo, Walter Savage Landor and Mary Queen of Scots. Later he wrote three plays about Mary. He left Eton for unspecified reasons and went on to Balliol College, Oxford, where he met the Pre-Raphaelites and fell under the spell of Dante Gabriel Rossetti and William Morris. He left Oxford without a degree and in London met, among others, Ruskin, Browning and Arnold. In 1864 he met Landor in Florence. His first book, *Atalanta in Calydon* (1863), is in classical tragic form. The choruses include many of his best-known poems. Ruskin called the whole effort "the grandest thing ever done by a youth, though he is a demonic youth." Ruskin was forgetting recent history. There was, after all, Keats and before him Chatterton.

In 1866 his best collection, *Poems and Ballads*, appeared. Its prosodic range is formidable. The book was severely criticized on moral grounds and occasioned from the author the pompous and inconclusive "Notes on Poems and Reviews," in which he characterized his book as "dramatic, many-faced, multifarious," and stressed the overall unity of organization, refusing personal responsibility for any single statement wrenched from context. Most passionately he defends "Anactoria," his adaptation of Sappho's ode, as "the supreme success, the final achievement, of the poetic art." He sought to "express and represent" the poet herself, not translate the poem. He played variations upon the sapphic theme, and the musical analogy is in place, for the poem follows a logic of the ear, as it were, not of thought. Still, the moral objection to Swinburne retains some force. Poems such as "Laus Veneris" cannot but raise qualms, and his later work asks to have a moral light turned upon it, not because it is immoral in subject matter and treatment, but because in aestheticizing experience it impoverishes moral and artistic judgment.

In 1871 *Songs Before Sunrise* appeared, poems about liberty that share a dullness with *Songs of Two Nations* (1875). There was another collection of moment still to come, *Poems and Ballads: Second Series* (1878). His life was increasingly disorganized and libidinous. His friend Theodore Watts-Dunton took him under his wing in 1879. They moved to Putney and lived there until the poet's death in 1909. There were several later collections of poems, notably the third series of *Poems and Ballads* (1889). Swinburne wrote verse up to his death, but his imagination died young: the later work—including novels, plays and criticisms—came from a different zone of his imagination, or played at echo with the accomplished earlier work.

His originality of taste must be celebrated. To have read and appreciated Whitman in England in the 1860s was remarkable. To have admired and imitated Baudelaire during the poet's own lifetime was even more so:

> I know not how this last month leaves your hair
> Less full of purple colours and hid spice,
> And that luxurious trouble of closed eyes
> Is mixed with meaner shadow and waste care

His enthusiasm for Blake reveals an original sensibility. He could be an excellent advocate. None of his contemporaries had a better sense of the

Elizabethans than he. But from this we turn back to the verse. Ezra Pound valued his translations of Villon. Whatever their merits as translations, they were among the best verse he wrote. He had a substantial original to work from. In his own verse he is a poet of natural and unnatural forces, not of nature. He attempts to cast a spell with hypnotic repetition and exaggerated cadence. We are washed by a flow of words—not thought or evocation of image, but enchantment. There is seldom any *specific* content; emotion dilates over a wide area. It is hard to quote because the effect depends on taking large doses.

Edmund Wilson disliked the language: monotonous, without the vigor of speech, preponderantly monosyllabic. Swinburne's is a language of disorientation. Words float free of their expected sense, serving an attitude or sentiment, losing reference. Nouns have no gravity, adjectives relate not so much to nouns as to the pervasive tone. "Sweet," "light" and other filler words do overtime, but little work. Smooth rhythm neutralizes the natural force of language. Mixed metaphor, the heaping up of lush verbiage point to an alternative poetic order. Eliot showed how intellectually loose and metaphorically unconsidered the verse was. It can—the moral question again—make a corpse momentarily erotic in "The Leper." A scribe's necrophiliac passion impels him to fondle, kiss and otherwise molest a body, reflecting (in a monologue in Browning's manner):

> Nothing is better, I well know,
>> Than love; no amber in cold sea
> Or gathered berries under snow:
>> That is well seen of her and me.

Something must be wrong with a style that can aestheticize and morally neutralize such a scene.

> Six months, and I sit still and hold
>> In two cold palms her two cold feet.
> Her hair, half grey half rusted gold,
>> Thrills me and burns me in kissing it.

Where tension exists, it is between simple polarities: pain and pleasure, life and death, love and death, love and time, youth and time. The enactment of such conflicts can hardly be called a poetry of ideas. It is a poetry of moods. Synesthesia, or the mixing of senses—audible sights, visible sounds and so on—is part of a reductive process, owing a superficial debt to the profound art of Baudelaire. Fingers, lips, the "pores of sense," do the work eyes do in other verses. In a sense we ingest

Swinburne, rather as the sea, a favorite image of his, ingests (as it were maternally) the swimmer and the shipwreck.

He raises fundamental questions about poetic language. How far can schemes of rhythm be usefully carried? What is the effect of sound patterning when intellectual control is in abeyance? What value has a poetry without ideas, with no specific content beyond mood and feeling—even when the subjects are ostensibly intellectual, like "liberty," and the content almost perceptible? Can poetry hope in any valid sense to approach the condition of music *in the terms* of music? Was Swinburne struggling (like Arnold and Hopkins) at the end of an exhausted tradition, seeking in technical facility an energy not naturally his? The choruses from *Atalanta* and poems such as "Tristram of Lyonesse," "Dolores," "A Forsaken Garden," "The Triumph of Time," "Laus Veneris" and "A Nympholept" raise these—and the moral—questions. They do not answer them. Perhaps the power of the choruses from *Atalanta* is that they have a context and touch a specific theme at a specific season:

> . . . winter's rains and ruins are over
>   And all the season of snows and sins;
> The days dividing lover and lover,
>   The light that loses, the light that wins;
>
> And time remembered is grief forgotten,
> And frosts are slain and flowers begotten,
> And in green underwood and cover
> Blossom by blossom the spring begins.

Even here, all-purpose "all" is at work, adding nothing, the overtaxed "and," the facile word spinning in lines four and five, behind which we grope for sense. Either readers have a taste for this sort of "magic," or they stand back in mute astonishment. Yet when we read this and other choruses, we hear Swinburne's effect on poets to whom his work was read in their infancy, Edward Thomas, Edgell Rickword, Charlotte Mew, Sylvia Townsend Warner and W. H. Auden among them. There was a magic in Swinburne, and the enchantment held, even against critics, for half a century after his death.

Not yet quite fixed on his religious vocation, Gerard Manley Hopkins saw Swinburne at Oxford when he returned to take his degree. Walter Pater, who had been Hopkins's tutor, arranged to introduce him to Swinburne's intimate friend, the exuberant painter Simeon Solomon. A month later he visited Solomon's studio in Pater's company. Solomon was an outspoken homosexual associated with the Pre-Raphaelites. In

1873 (well before Oscar Wilde) he was charged with buggery. His career destroyed, he became an alcoholic and died in a workhouse in 1905. Hopkins does not describe his visit to Solomon's studio or his response to the painter's later fate, but his own temperament at the time was unresolved and Solomon's evident talent and lifestyle represented a kind of final siren call to the young poet about to become a novice in the Jesuit order. At Oxford Hopkins had fallen in love with a young poet called Digby Mackworth Dolben—Robert Bridges introduced them— and they exchanged poems. "It was probably from Dolben that Hopkins caught the habit of thinking of the manhood of Jesus Christ in distinctly physical terms," writes Gregory Woods. In 1867 Dolben drowned, "and his influence on Hopkins became all the more lastingly intense in the refining fire of grief." The influence was less on his poetry than on his spirit. He too "belonged to that culture of sentimental and erotic male friendships shaped by both Greece and (Catholic) Rome to which Newman and Faber had belonged before him." His spirituality was carnal; was perhaps a way of dealing with and rendering transcendent what in a different man would have been a carnal choice, a spiritual abdication.

For Hopkins, sound and rhythm are quite as important as they are for Swinburne, but Hopkins develops areas of imagination and intelligence that Swinburne neglects altogether. His Paterlike aestheticism transcended itself into religious faith; his sexual ambivalence honed his chastity, so that at times his posture in relation to God is comparable to Donne's, though his sense of the literal surrounding world, through which grace is manifest, is more solid than Donne's, less deliberately dramatic. His faith breaks with the Anglican tradition; so too his poetry breaks with much that came before. His intolerable wrestle with the nature and language of verse is real, of a seriousness altogether deeper and more coherent than that of the poets of the Rhymers' Club or of his major contemporaries.

He was not to be *their* contemporary: his poems were first published in book form twenty-nine years after his death. He is, in effect, a twentieth-century poet. Robert Bridges, the poet laureate who consistently supported, encouraged and misunderstood his work, took it upon himself to correct the poems in layout, diction and syntax for the 1918 edition. It was another thirty years before his texts were fully restored.

Hopkins left a small body of poetry. A handful of juvenilia escaped the fire; forty-eight mature and more or less finished poems, and a number of fragments survive. Letters, notebooks, sermons and other prose completed the oeuvre. Had he been published in his lifetime, as a younger contemporary of Tennyson, Browning, Arnold, Swinburne, what might his work not have done to the disoriented final decade of the century? But had it been published, what would the pressure of a readership have done to him? As it is, he belongs to the nineteenth but his poetry to the twentieth century. Bridges's 1918 edition appeared a year after *Prufrock and Other Observations* by T. S. Eliot. Bridges's endorsement did little to recommend this unknown Jesuit to a modernist generation of writers and readers that might have understood him. Or not, given modernism's secular bias.

Hopkins was born in Stratford, Essex, in 1844 into a well-to-do family. His mother was pious, his father wrote verse and encouraged his children to play music and draw. Hopkins never abandoned these pursuits. His first ambition was to be an artist. Ruskin and the Pre-Raphaelites prescribed his early world. Human figures are idealized and refined into representative types. Female figures generally embody purity and vocation. Male figures can be treated with greater freedom and ambiguity. Hopkins's verse never outgrows what at first seems an adolescent sensualism but is in fact a chaste homoeroticism. He wrote "The Bugler's First Communion" when he was a priest in his thirties; he evokes a communicant straight out of one of the more sentimental canvases of the time, charged with an energy quite alien to a man of the cloth and unsettling when he evokes it on such an occasion: the "Breathing beauty of chastity in mansex fine," "limberliquid youth, that to all I teach / Yields tender as a pushed peach," and so on. Yet this "witness" to manly beauty is of a piece with his other celebrations of the created world. It would have been prurient and dishonest for him *not* to have included it, whatever the properties of its inclusion. In 1882 he wrote to Bridges: "I might as well say what I should not otherwise have said, that I always knew in my heart Walt Whitman's mind to be more like my own than any other man's living. As he is a very great scoundrel this is not a pleasant confession. And this also makes me the more desirous to read him and the more determined that I will not."

From a brilliant performance at Highgate School, Hopkins went to Balliol College, Oxford (in the wake of Arnold and Swinburne), in 1863. He secured a first-class degree in Greats (Classics) four years later. It was a time of intellectual activity and crisis. He struck up his friendship with Robert Bridges. He ruminated on language, setting down in a notebook that "the onomatopoeic theory," as he calls it, "has not had a fair chance. Cf. Crack, creak, croak, crake, graculus, crackle." The concerns of the mature poet start here. He progresses in a healthily assertive way toward the mimetic language he developed in later poems. He asks not only *what* language means but *how* it means to the senses, how it contains—in order to convey—what it signifies.

Walter Pater marked him. So did Arnold, then professor of poetry. Pater and Arnold spoke languages so different in style and earnestness as to be virtually antithetical. Dissatisfied with conventional Anglicanism and drawn by a love of ceremony and ritual in an Oxford where the Oxford Movement was in increasing disarray, Hopkins turned to the ceremonialism of the Anglo-Catholics and then succumbed to the Church of Rome. He was received into the Church in 1866 by John Henry Newman, who took a particular interest in him.

At university Hopkins's discipline began: self-denial in the interest of the self. He evokes the effect of religious faith on the imagination. Imagine, he says, the world reflected in a water drop: a small, precise reflection. Then imagine the world reflected in a drop of Christ's blood: the same reflection, but suffused with the hue of love, sacrifice, God made man, and redemption. Religious faith discovers for a troubled imagination an underlying coherence which knows that it cannot be fully or adequately explained. In its liberating, suffusing light, Hopkins could relish out loud the uniqueness of things, which made them "individually distinctive." This he called "inscape"—an artist's term. "Instress," another bit of individual jargon, refers to the force maintaining inscape. Inscape is manifest, instress divine, the immanent presence of the divine in the object.

As he progressed further, he attended to the thirteenth-century Franciscan Duns Scotus, *Doctor Subtilis,* as it were, whose thinking went against the grain of Thomas Aquinas and orthodox Jesuit discipline. Scotus, in philosophy an extreme realist who rejected common notions of "natural theology" and questioned the possibility of a harmonious relationship between faith and reason, confirmed Hopkins's version of particularism in his "principle of Individuation," or *haecceitas* ("thisness"). Scotus licensed him to affirm his own individuality and gave him confidence and the philosophical sanction to write poems, one of them addressed to Scotus himself. The stress falls on the "I," which Scotus (the "he") had empowered him to use in this way:

> Yet ah! this air I gather and I release
> He lived on; these weeds and waters, these walls are what
> He haunted who of all men most sways my spirits to peace;
> Of realty the rarest-veinèd unraveller; a not
> Rivalled insight . . .

Veins—the unseen lines of inscape—Scotus unraveled, approaching "realty," not "reality." The old abstraction is elided into a new, unique term. Hopkins valued in his remote mentor precisely those qualities that had led the humanists to reject him, and religious reformers in the fifteenth and sixteenth centuries to follow suit: his discrimination of unique entities and his insistence on *distinction.* Our word "dunce" derives from the vilification of the Dunsmen, or Dunces, a fact that may have amused Hopkins, who—Jesuit or not—insisted on retaining a mind of his own. The poem to Scotus, in its procedures and cadences, calls to mind the work of later isolated poets, David Jones and Geoffrey Hill in particular, who have attended to Hopkins with an analogous seriousness and spiritual integrity.

Taken together, a suffusing faith and particularism emancipated Hopkins from the panoramic, intellectualizing and abstracting Romantics and Victorians. Objects do not evoke nebulous sentiment. They point in a single direction, eliciting feeling not for themselves but for God. In this vertical vision things relate not among themselves but through God. The sonnets that express concern for social ills—"God's Grandeur" and "The Sea and the Skylark"—suggest no political solution but see through or beyond industrial landscape to nature, through nature to God. "God's Grandeur" makes original use of images of industrialism to magnify, by contrast, nature, which "is never spent," despite what people have done to the environment. In his prose these experiences bring him near to utopian socialism; in his poems they bring him close to God:

> And for all this, nature is never spent;
>   There lives the dearest freshness deep down things;
> And though the last lights off the black West went
>   Oh, morning, at the brown brink eastward, springs—
> Because the Holy Ghost over the bent
>   World broods with warm breast and with ah! bright wings.

The adjective "bent" relates back to the octave of the sonnet, its metal images contrasting with images of the natural and human worlds.

After Oxford and some traveling, Hopkins was accepted into the Jesuit novitiate in 1868. He burned all his verse that he could find, though from his Oxford years three poems of interest survive: "Let me be to thee as the circling bird," "The Habit of Perfection" and "Heaven-Haven." They suggest that the poet accepted the Ignatian discipline in his imagination before the soul curbed itself. They are limpidly clear and simple compared with some of Hopkins's later work.

Seven years passed before he wrote another poem. He mastered Welsh and Welsh prosody in that time, but vowed not to write original verse unless his superiors asked him to. In 1875 they consented to his memorializing a shipwreck in which a number of nuns perished. "The Wreck of the Deutschland" is dense with seven years' concentration of religious experience and inevitable ruminations on language and poetic form. The poem is complex and forbidding. Bridges could not stomach

it. He suggested that poetry requiring a "conscious effort of interpreta-
tion" was bad if that effort was expended on unraveling, not complexity
of image, idea or metaphor, but syntax, syntax arranged in such a way as
to distract from, rather than lead through, the poem. Bridges was right
in general terms, but in poetry there are no valid general rules, and he
simply could not respond to the essential dynamic of his friend's verse.
When he quoted a stanza of "The Wreck of the Deutschland" in his
anthology *The Spirit of Man*, he smoothed out the syntax, did away with
complexities of diction, and scrapped Hopkins's scrupulous indenta-
tions, which are meant to indicate stress patterns. It is commonplace to
sneer at Bridges, but it is worth remembering that he was a critic whose
word Hopkins took to heart, and without his encouragement and effort
the poems might never have reached us at all.

If we put ourselves in Bridges's place and try to read the poem as if
for the first time, we may agree with Hopkins that syntax is the line or
vein of the poem's "inscape," making a unique object. But is anything
gained by calling Christ "Mid-numbered He mid three of the thunder
throne"? Is it not intolerable circumlocution? When the poem ends with
a line containing six genitive cases, unpronounceably expressing depen-
dent relations and coming perilously near mixed metaphor ("Our hearts'
charity's hearth's fire, our thoughts' chivalry's throng's Lord"), the effort
required of the reader is analytic, not imaginative—or imaginative in a
scholastic sense.

The poem is in two sections, the first largely personal, the second
dealing with the wreck and allowing digression. The singer in the first
section reflects on the nature of and his relation with God, on faith and
on nature. The fourth stanza is wonderfully achieved. It begins:

> I am soft sift
> In an hourglass—at the wall
> Fast, but mined with a motion, a drift,
> And it crowds and it combs to the fall . . .

God punishes—and grants grace: the storm at sea—and salvation.
Man—the poet, the ship battered by the storm—learns by suffering to
recognize grace. The ten stanzas of the first section possess remarkable
unity of imagery. The ship makes haste to Christ the Host for succor.
The force of individuation comes from Christ, God as man, and not
from God Himself. Christ is "lightning and love": first lightning, then
love.

The second section recounts the events of the shipwreck in a verse
full of mimetic sound and fury. There are digressions on Luther, on the
poet's stay in Wales. The initial conflict of sea and ship is narrowed

down to Gertrude, the nuns, the sailors. But the concentration of the first part is inevitably dissipated. Hopkins's mind is too full after seven years' silence. "The Wreck of the Deutschland," new in so many ways, has the air of having been unpacked rather than written.

In his verse Hopkins mixes two basic forms. The first is accentual—syllabic, or, as he calls it, running rhythm: a strict number of syllables and regularly placed stresses allow some variety of stress but little syllabic variation. The other form is what he calls "sprung rhythm," in which the number of syllables varies but the number of stresses in each line remains constant. "Sprung Rhythm," he writes, "is measured by feet of from one to four syllables, regularly, and for particular effects any number of weak or slack syllables may be used." He develops the definition at length and applies the form with originality.

The influence of Welsh poetry on his alliterative and assonantal writing cannot be denied. He develops an English *cynghanned*, a patterned repetition of consonants. This provides another vein holding a poem together, and harmonizes often remote images through sound organization. The best example of this is "Pied Beauty." "The Starlight Night," too, with its Nativity scene, depends on close sound organization. Only controlled cadence resolves the difficult and perhaps technically incorrect syntax of "The Windhover." Some poems, notably the unspectacular but good sonnet "The Valley of the Elwy," have more conventional virtues, the syntax unfolding smoothly, the sonnet form held in tension with the spoken rhythm of the statement. It was necessary for him to ungarble his style in order to achieve the assured control of the "dark sonnets." As he wrote to Bridges, "No doubt my poetry errs on the side of oddness . . . I hope in time to have a more balanced and Miltonic style." The triumphs of the odd style at its oddest are "Peace," "The Leaden Echo and the Golden Echo" and "Spring and Fall" ("Márgarét, are you grieving"), a poem that stays whole in memory after a couple of readings. We pardon Bridges for his unsympathetic handling of "The Wreck of the Deutschland" in his 1924 anthology, but what he did to "Spring and Fall," altering diction and making substantial omissions, is a crime.

Neglect preceded the dark sonnets. "The Wreck of the Deutschland" was not printed. Nor, in 1877, was "The Loss of the Eurydice," a lesser work, which is clearer than the earlier memorial poem. "And you were a liar, o blue March day," and the last line, "Prayer shall fetch pity eternal," show development toward a clearer voice, a more headlong approach to narrative and to God. In 1879 he wrote a letter to Bridges that puts his verse—its intentions, in any case—in an unexpected light: "It seems to me that the poetical language of an age shd. be the current language heightened, to any degree heightened and unlike itself, but not (I mean normally: freaks and graces are another thing) an obsolete one. This is Shakespeare's and Milton's practice and the want of it will be fatal to Tennyson's *Idylls* and plays, to Swinburne, and perhaps to Morris."

There were poetic aberrations, like the sonnet to Purcell. Still he was unpublished. It is hard to determine the unsettling effect that neglect had on his poetry. Nervous and physical illness, which began in 1874 and never left him, probably aggravated it. He prepared a preface for his poems. He wanted, he *needed*, more than a couple of readers so that his words would have context and provoke an echo. They are sacramental in nature, and Communion is a sacrament, sharing out and giving back. It was not to be. The poems accumulated in shadow. In 1884 he was appointed professor of Greek at University College, Dublin. In 1885–86 he wrote the dark sonnets, expressing a religious doubt far more bleak and self-searing than any before in English poetry. He profoundly disliked Dublin. In 1889 it killed him with typhoid from the polluted water supply.

The dark sonnets are his most astonishing work, for here ruptured syntax, inversions and sound patterning answer a violence of negative spiritual experience. In the work of George Herbert, which Hopkins loved, Christ is the wooer, the soul the wooed. In Hopkins, the soul, painfully aware of its own fallen nature, desperately woos Christ. There is almost despair, for a beautiful and vigorous Christ has withdrawn, grace is withheld. The earlier ease of loving faith—"I say that we are wound / With mercy round and round / As if with air"—is gone. After the dark sonnets there is silence.

Underlying one sonnet, "Carrion Comfort," is the metaphor of eating; storm underpins the language of "No worst"; "I wake to feel the fell of dark" dwells on the disgusting nature of the body, its taste and smell. Whatever the psychological and spiritual motives of the poems, they are powerful statements of love and loss, of a desire that grace has not yet satisfied, of unfulfillment. The poet who step by step "individuated" himself here at last stands apart from even his God. To have become a Catholic against the wishes of his family; a Jesuit against the advice of his friends; a disciple of Scotus against the orthodoxy of his order: he had made himself alone. In his poetry, too, he developed a solitary, inimitable idiom. He aimed to create phrases from which the meaning would "explode" on the reader, and in the dark sonnets he achieves such phrases. His crisis came, by transposition, to mean a great deal to the audience he began to acquire thirty years after his death:

I wake to feel the fell of dark, not day.
What hours, O what black hours we have spent
This night! what sights you, heart, saw; ways you went!

And more must, in yet longer light's delay.
　　　With witness I speak this. But where I say
Hours I mean years, mean life. And my lament
Is cries countless, cries like dead letters sent
To dearest him that lives alas! away.

A Beginning of the End of Victorian Poetry

THOMAS HARDY, CHARLOTTE MEW, EDWIN ARLINGTON
ROBINSON, EDGAR LEE MASTERS, STEPHEN CRANE

Robert Bridges probably sent Thomas Hardy a complimentary copy of Hopkins's poems in 1918, but Hardy makes no reference to it. The work of an obscure Jesuit is unlikely to have made an impression on the seventy-eight-year-old atheist. With Swinburne Hardy maintained a cordial and mutually admiring correspondence. But he is remote from both men, having more in common with Arnold. He tetchily disagrees with him from time to time. The question of influence hardly arises. But with Browning it's a different matter.

Hardy, more famous as a poet now than ever before, has suffered a sorry fate since the Second World War. This private, discontented man, author of great novels and a huge body of mainly melancholy poetry, has been stiffened by polemicists into a kind of totem, a talisman against alien American and Irish modernism, a vindicator of the Palgrave's *Golden Treasury* principle of nice or pretty English lyric poetry. Those who dislike the real and imagined legacy of Hardy heap contrary coals on his head. Provincial, (inventive) traditional formalist, pragmatist and pessimist, even misogynist, Hardy is drafted into service for a range of causes, a play of longer and longer echoes. The poet Gottfried Benn, speaking of German *Geist*, or cultural spirit, said that when you try to define it, it dies: it exists, like time in a clock, unexplained and informing. Once history or national politics demand that it be codified, it loses creative force and becomes an instrument of tyranny. What once nurtured now constrains: writer, reader and critic repair to it, not as a resource but as a legitimizing ideology. There are two Hardys, both intriguing: the living writer and the dogmatic critical construction. We're concerned here with the former, though it's necessary to allude to the latter, if only to cut the poet free of the strangling patristics that have ivied him over.

Robert Louis Stevenson visited Hardy in Dorset in 1885, thirteen years before Hardy's first collection of poems appeared. He saw "a pale, gentle, frightened little man, that one felt an instinctive tenderness for, with a wife—ugly is no word for it!—who said 'Whatever shall we do?' I had never heard a human being say it before." Stevenson took away a vivid impression of Emma Hardy, but only sympathy for the "little man," her husband, already a celebrated and controversial novelist. Even at that time the label "pessimist" had attached to him; it was only a few years before he was stigmatized for "immorality" because of *Tess of the d'Urbervilles* (1891) and *Jude the Obscure* (1896) and abandoned prose fiction in favor of verse.

The wife Stevenson found rebarbative is Hardy's unlikely Muse. Anyone who reads the poems and novels might sympathize with Mrs. Hardy: her husband was not—as his success grew—a barrel of laughs. A joyful, tempestuous courtship and marriage subsided into dogged vocation, a sense of faded days for her, and an increasing unease at her husband's fame and his developing themes, not to mention his not necessarily innocent, and certainly not infrequent flirtations with admiring younger women. Stevenson saw the ash of a real fire of love, the human embodiment of Hardy's theme of disappointment and the subject of his best poems, the failure of love under time's unforgiving dial.

Hardy was born in Bockhampton, Dorsetshire, in 1840, the third year of Victoria's reign. His father was a builder and a musician. Hardy partly acquired both skills. His mother regarded herself as socially a cut above her husband (Emma later regarded herself as a cut above Thomas). She had ambitions for her son and he received the best education his family could afford, studying in Dorchester and later at King's College, London. Articled as an ecclesiastical architect from 1856 to 1861, he became a specialist in the Gothic Revival and a more than competent draftsman. His poems and fiction include architectural images, and he is persistently preoccupied with visual perspective. The crafts associated with building, wood- and stoneworking also appear.

For five years he worked in London at an architect's office and became a prizeman of the Royal Institute of British Architects. During this period he wrote the earliest of the poems he was ultimately to collect decades later in *Wessex Poems* (1898). In 1870, by inclination and encouraged by his friend Horace Moule, he began a career as a novelist with *Desperate Remedies*, published in 1871.

From childhood he exercised in verse and regarded himself as a poet. He attempted to translate the biblical book of Ecclesiastes into Spenserian stanzas—a project he (perhaps fortunately) never completed, though he deploys biblical images and subject matter and echoes the rhythms of the King James Version by second nature in prose and verse; certainly the glum vision of Ecclesiastes affected him.

He was always musing about poetry, defining and redefining, thinking in terms of poems, developing his craft in the spirit of a joiner or stonemason perfecting skills in preparation for the big work—a rood screen, a spire, *The Dynasts*. Some of the early poems Hardy turned into prose and used in descriptive passages in his fiction. Later he translated them back into verse. It is possible to see the impact of his poetic concerns throughout the fiction, in the shaping of scenes, the obliquity and economy of satirical and tragic payoffs, and most of all in the highly organized rhythms of the prose at points of lyrical or dramatic heightening. The impact of the fiction on the verse is also clear: he is a storyteller. His first surviving poem, "Domicilium," written when he was seventeen, about his paternal grandmother, a figure central to his boyhood, reveals how things were when she first came to live in her new house at Higher Bockhampton. The opening could almost be by Robert Frost:

> It faces west, and round the back and sides
> High beeches, bending, hang a veil of boughs,
> And sweep against the roof. Wild honeysucks
> Climb on the walls, and seem to sprout a wish
> (If we may fancy wish of trees and plants)
> To overtop the apple-trees hard by.

A number of his critical opinions are provident and—if we take into account the literary milieu of Victorian and Edwardian England—radical. Sometimes wry asides, observations on the practice of criticism or the craft of writing, issue in aphorism. "My opinion is that a poet should express the emotion of all the ages and the thought of his own." "My opinion is . . .": his useful opinions emerge from long practice in prose and verse; the doubtful ones are the fruit of ingrained prejudices and disappointments. Both true and false are put forward as undeniable verities.

In 1887 he writes, "I begin to feel that mere intellectual subtlety will not hold its own in time to come against the straightforward expression of good feeling." But his poetry grew in intellectual range and ambition, if not in subtlety, culminating in *The Dynasts*. Hardy is never technically straightforward. He sets himself exacting challenges in almost every poem. Still, he claims his mission to be to show "the other side of common emotions." "The business of the poet . . . is to show the sorriness underlying the grandest things, and the grandeur underlying the sorriest things," bringing opposites and contrasts into controlled tension, without resolution. "To find beauty in ugliness is the province of the poet." Such dicta are an index of his practice and can be applied to the work of many of his successors, but not all, and not necessarily the best. Like Philip Larkin's critical declarations in more recent times, Hardy's are adduced by his partisans as gospel, though they emerge from and refer back to his own accomplishment. Some of them are deliberately mischievous.

Out of this program—if you line up his statements they draw parameters within which "the poet" functions—comes a specific poetic style. "The whole secret of living style and the difference between it and dead style, lies in it not having too much style." In dealing with "the other side of common emotions," style must grow out of the commonness. Language must correspond in register to the subject matter and be appropriate to the occasion: a rustic plot demands plain diction; a poem on the loss of the *Titanic* ("The Meeting of the Twain") a more developed, contrived language, appropriate to the subject, drawn from the technological age whose skills and overreaching pride produced the doomed liner. The language must finally be subtle enough to contain the "beauty" and "ugliness," and containment is a function of meter and form. This is a suggestive view of poetic tension: some poems—"The Man He Killed," for example—state one thing ("quaint and curious war is") but in hesitant syntax, metrical disruption, contradict what the speaker seems to be saying.

"A certain provincialism of feeling is invaluable," writes Hardy. "It is the essence of individuality, and is largely made up of that crude enthusiasm without which no great thoughts are thought, no great deeds done." This view, too, has become an item of faith for some (including Lawrence), who reject cosmopolitan modernism and the formal pretensions of writers who seem to them to practice "mere intellectual subtlety." In the British context this issues in a narrowing chauvinism, a refusal to engage with work that does not conform to what became the Georgian prejudices that abide, in a decayed form, in the "provincial" and local enthusiasms of our time.

Hardy can't be held responsible for what posterity makes of him. At Max Gate, sour and retiring, he did not feel like a pope; as new generations of writers (novelists and poets) came up behind him, he may have felt bewildered. A temptation in an age overwhelmed with literary options, as ours has been since the teens of the twentieth century, is to sacralize a substantial poet and draw laws out of his work, rather as, in the two centuries after Milton, he was the Anointed, and Spenser the Baptist.

Much that later critics take as Hardy's fixed opinions are his passing attempts to justify himself to real and imagined critics. "Poetry is emotion put into measure. The emotion must come by nature, but the measure can be acquired by art." One of his ambitions was to write a handful of poems worthy of inclusion in a good anthology. Even when he speaks of other writers, he responds to virtues that he imagines their works share with his. He highlights in one writer "the principles that make for permanence": "the value of organic form and symmetry, the force of reserve, and the emphasis on understatement, even in his lighter works"—a concise description of a Hardyesque, conventional English temperament. Ironic that it emerges from his reading—or misreading—of a French writer, Anatole France. Odd too that he of all writers should apostrophize "organic form": not since the Augustans has there been such a *constructor* of poems as Hardy. The "art that conceals art" does not mask his effortful mastery: his poems are constructed, not grown. Whatever the bucolic trappings, he's a craftsman.

From other writers he picks up tags and phrases to applaud: "Incidents in the development of a soul! Little else is worth study" (Browning); the poet "should touch our hearts by showing his own" (Leslie Stephens). Illumination falls on what Hardy wanted his poetry to be. The poems both exceed and fall short of these aspirations.

In 1874 Hardy married Emma Gifford, who so alarmed Stevenson eleven years later. Emma was the sister-in-law of a parson whose church in Cornwall Hardy helped to "improve" in the Victorian manner of marring with commendable intent. The first two years of their marriage were apparently happy, but passion cooled. Hardy may never have behaved badly to her, but his gallantry became formal and aloof, endurance replaced love, and more than thirty-five years' unhappiness elapsed before Emma died. It was at her death that she became the faded Muse of his great poems, the elegies of 1912–13, and a few others that came later. On her death, his mind flooded by recollections of their happy years, he experienced remorse for his part in the decades of hostility. He wrote her poems not at the age of thirty, when he was courting, or at thirty-four, when happily married, but in 1912, at seventy-two, when death did for his heart what life had failed in.

The elegies are poems of guilt as much as love. They lament not the death of Emma but the squandering of love. She died suddenly, and the first elegy ("The Going") expresses urgent recrimination as well as guilt:

> Never to bid good-bye,
>   Or lip me the softest call,
> Or utter a wish for a word, while I
> Saw morning harden upon the wall,

> Unmoved, unknowing
> That your great going
> Had place that moment, and altered all.

The materiality of the language ("saw morning harden") heightens the harsh paradox of her "deed." The alteration it effected was devastatingly simple. Emma, in dying, denied Hardy the chance to atone for his part in their unhappiness. She rendered the present hard, the past unalterable:

> Well, well! All's past amend,
> Unchangeable. It must go.
> I seem but a dead man held on end
> To sink down soon . . . O you could not know
> That such swift fleeing
> No soul foreseeing—
> Not even I—would undo me so!

If he forgives her in this stanza, in the breaking syntax of loss, he also accuses her. The nature and scale of his loss become clear in the poems that follow. They entail his entire past, bringing to an intimate personal climax a theme that in the novels and poems sometimes seems contrived, the almost systematic unfulfillment of promise. There are twenty-one poems in the final sequence, "Poems 1912–13" (the first eighteen are the original run), and they progress from immediate apprehension of loss to a kind of stoical acceptance—not the religious consolation of Tennyson's movingly if implausibly resolved *In Memoriam* but something more rueful and certainly unredeemed.

In 1914 Hardy married again, a much younger woman, Florence Dugdale, who had long been his amanuensis. With her—she must have been a patient woman—he revisited places where he had stayed with Emma in their happy years. Later he went alone. Poems came from these revisitings: "Beeny Cliff: March 1870–March 1913," "At Castle Boterel," "St Launce's Revisited," and "Where the Picnic Was." Emma in turn revisits him as the "hauntress," and when he employs so poignant a ghost, the verses acquire an intensity he seldom achieved before. "The Voice" is among his few flawless poems, opening with the lines:

> Woman much missed, how you call to me, call to me,
> Saying that now you are not as you were
> When you had changed from the one that was all to me,
> But as at first, when our day was fair.

Three stanzas of this fluent, desolately monosyllabic, powerfully nostalgic cadence are arrested on a final variant quatrain. Fancy deceives no more; it gives way to the unmitigated reality of isolation:

> Thus I; faltering forward,
> Leaves around me falling,
> Wind oozing thin through the thorn from norward,
> And the woman calling.

The sequence originally appeared in *Satires of Circumstance* (1914). Its emotional veracity, quite as much as its technical variety and assurance, set it in a class apart from the other *Satires*. Elsewhere Hardy's insistent predisposition to pessimism borders on the comical. Here we have something qualitatively different, a vulnerable candor, an insistence on going deep, without mercy to self and without "constructing something upon which to rejoice."

In Hardy's early poems the syntax is often obscure and full of inversions. He needs at times to reverse into a rhyme or displace a polysyllabic word from its natural position in syntax in order to adjust it to the meter (so much for the organic metaphor). But there's little development—except in deftness—through his poetry. Themes of nature's indifference and hostility, lost or thwarted love, and time, are developed with mournful insistence. Many poems are organized in a similar way, the plot working to an unexpected climax, as in a verse fable. But we come to expect the would-be unexpected turn of plot; the element of surprise, as in the stories of Maupassant, becomes mechanical.

In *The Life of Thomas Hardy*, Hardy says, "The world does not despise us; it only neglects us." In his poem "Neutral Tones" he evokes nature's neutrality. Objective and subjective worlds do not correspond. Tragedy is beyond his range: there are no gods to offend or serve. There is no sin against a given rule, only the sin, repeated day after day, against self, the failure to choose rightly and to act in pursuit of a noble happiness. There is guilt, to be sure: "hid from men / I bear that mark on me." There is a sense of responsibility for others. But the dominant theme is always individual unfulfillment in time. Where Wordsworth's past contains the lost childhood, the infant "trailing clouds of glory" gradually diminishing into impoverished man, and Tennyson's past is an idealized world of order, Hardy's vision is of a past not idealized but *unrealized*, a past that was full of potential, when "everything glowed with a gleam"— but "we were looking away." A past with a wide range of choices is placed beside a present that wrong choices have impoverished. What *is* stands juxtaposed, implicitly or explicitly, to what might have been.

Death plays a leading role. Hardy chooses situations where death—or the dead, always equipped with ironizing memory—watch life, or life watches death. In almost every poem death or ephemerality is present. "I rose up as my custom was"—the speaker of the poem gets out of his grave to go visit friends. In "Channel Firing" the dead sit up and comment on the futility of their lives, of war, of faith, the foolishness of God, the featurelessness of the future. In other poems the poet seeks out ghosts or old people and talks with them or makes them talk. Resignation gives them all a similar voice.

There is frequently a problem of tone in the poems. Apart from inadvertent humor in an ill-judged phrase, or the overinsistent lugubriousness, there are poems where he varies the manner deliberately. Humorous poems are interspersed with decidedly serious ones. At times he leaves a poem hauntingly suspended between seriousness and humor. "Transformations" is one of his best short poems, revealing the "other side of common emotions." He is writing about a graveyard, but the poem presents no image of decay. On the contrary, he celebrates *life*—admittedly, vegetable life—with such imaginative force that the graveyard alters into something unexpectedly generative. Man is resurrected, but not as the church promises.

> And the fair girl long ago
> Whom I often tried to know
> May be entering this rose.

There's an erotic charge in the triplet, the rose bearing a complement of symbolic association, the verb its sexual overtones. Through the rose—someone admired but unattained—the speaker relates to the graveyard and what it implies. But how real is the consolation? The line that throws doubt on the tone is "So they are not underground . . ." It strikes a comic note, a kind of proto-Lawrencian "Look, we have come through—in flowers." The poem continues a little further, heightening the images of growth with "nerves" and "veins," "the growths of upper air." The pathetic fallacy is at once proposed and subverted; the tone remains tantalizingly unresolved.

Other graveyard poems are less positive in imagery and unambiguous in tone, for example "Rain on a Grave," "Voices Growing from a Churchyard" and "Drummer Hodge." But nature absorbs the dead here, too. Hardy appreciates natural objects without any sense of metaphysical content—as objects. He may long for religious faith and the community and communion it brings, but he is "outside, prayer denied," and he finds little comfort in religion, except in its artifacts. His ghosts are seldom meant to be more than stage properties, illusions. No gothic horror trails them from the grave. Their news is of failure in life—and afterlife. "Death's inviolate halls" don't let real souls go. Nor will he romanticize objects in nature. Shelley's "Skylark" is a poem in which he concedes to the bird power to make a song that might throw men into ecstasies—but the creature is not immortal. Hardy is saying, "Hail to thee, blithe bird! Spirit thou never wert." His "Darkling Thrush" is a real bird, too, growing old, still singing. The song does not fill the poet with joy; it accentuates his grief. There is no romantic certainty, only the concession of a possibility, as tenuous as that expressed in "The Oxen."

His habit of setting past and present experiences side by side amounts to more than a dramatic strategy. When newlyweds are about to consummate their marriage, a street musician plays a tune that, for one of them, conjures a past love, and their mutual rapport is destroyed. This is like the world of Proust, in which dormant memory stirs in the midst of a new relationship and disrupts it. Memory and desire are in tension, but memory is the more powerful. Hardy's refrain is that individuals are finally sealed in the particulars of their own biography, that they can never communicate or share themselves fully with another. There is an implicit, universal alienation between individuals; they cannot progress beyond a limited intimacy. Shakespeare will "remain at heart unread eternally." So will each of us.

Isolation causes unfulfillment, and there's no remedy. Memory cannot be controlled, it bursts into the room of the present like an unwelcome guest or a messenger. God himself—the God of Hardy's childhood—like the ghosts, appears as a memory to accentuate isolation. Expressing joy, the darkling thrust confirms sorrow. Life becomes— life *is*—"a thwarted purposing." The past is clarified only as the present reveals what we have missed and lost. In one poem an old lady lives willfully in the past: "Past things retold were to her as things existent. / Things present but as a tale." In the elegies to Emma, the past, rich with potential, is juxtaposed with the present, too. But the world of memory is invariably more complete:

> Nay: one there is to whom these things,
> Which nobody else's mind calls back,
> Have a savour that things in being lack,
> And a presence more than the actual brings;
> To whom today is beneaped and stale,
> And its urgent clack
> But a vapid tale.

The present, hinted in the fleeting sound of the train—"urgent clack"— is flattened by "vapid tale," which corresponds to it rhythmically and syllabically, but which in its different sound and sense values destroys the urgency. Things in memory are vivid and disrupting to the individual largely because they are so private, like the "savor" of food, and not to be shared.

Accused of willful pessimism, Hardy called himself an "evolutionary meliorist," quoting the line from "In Tenebris ii:" "If way to the better there be, it exacts a full look at the worst." The "satires" teach us not to make the same mistake twice, or not to repeat the errors others have made. Yet since every poem is about error, the suggestion must be that, even if we do not repeat we will find our own strategies of unfulfillment. There is in Hardy's notion of time and memory something that no evolution could ameliorate. The world might become as he urges in the late novels and in some poems that startled his late-Victorian audience ("The Christening" and "A Wife to Another," for example), more tolerant and hence more tolerable. But the individual condition is hardly improved. Social optimism is balanced by psychological pessimism. He calls it realism and the poems are didactic, "applications of ideas to life." But he is not a philosopher. He presents "a series of fleeting impressions I have never tried to coordinate," "unadjusted impressions." It is fruitless to look for system or myth. There is only repeated "process," an insistence on returning—like one of his beloved dogs so piously buried at Max Gate—to the same thematic bone.

The poems were written by a novelist, but they are different in kind from fiction, whatever they learn from its forms; the impulse, structure and effect are insistently lyric, the style original without being particularly idiosyncratic. He uses (and discovers) a wider range of rhymed and metrical forms than any other modern English poet, including Auden. His oeuvre amounts to almost a thousand poems. Whereas the novels bring background into focus—landscape, community, the intrusions of history—the poems generally take setting for granted. Unlike Kipling, who has to establish a setting before his poem can get going, Hardy takes location as implicit and plunges in medias res, thriftily giving only necessary information in a phrase, a tone of voice suggested by metrical pause or variation. We're seldom engaged by the character of the speaker; it's a situation that arrests us, its moral or psychological typicality. His "voice," unlike the individuating and unique "voice" of the modern poet, is Wordsworth's common voice, "a man speaking to men" in a common language of experience.

The Dynasts, his epic verse "drama," reveals most of his stylistic skills and weaknesses. It appeared in three successive volumes (1904, 1906, 1908). Written "in three parts, nineteen acts, and a hundred and thirty scenes," largely in verse, about the wars with Napoleon, it covers the action of ten years (1805–1815), shifting between England and the Continent, and culminating at Waterloo. On a Tolstoyan scale it is his account of "The Human Tragedy"—not only of heroes and generals but of common men, with backing from a chorus of lugubrious "phantom intelligences." The central fact of the poem is Napoleon's isolation, which causes his downfall. Hardy conceived the poem as early as 1882. He noted down: "Write a history of human automatism, or impulsion— viz., an account of human action in spite of human knowledge, showing how very far conduct lags behind the knowledge that should really guide it." Twenty-two years later he published the first part. It is the *summa* of Hardy's thought, but as he himself noted, he is not a thinker but a man of deep intuitions. Intuition serves the lyric imagination, but the epic imagination requires more comprehensive skills, a more various emotional culture. The burden of *The Dynasts* is borne much better and with real economy in fine short poems—"The Man He Killed" or "In Time of the 'Breaking of Nations' "—than in the lumbering development of *The Dynasts*. Structure lets it down. The "phantom intelligences" have no poetic valency. The best parts of the poem relate the thoughts and preoccupations of common people, with the simple diction of their speech.

Many poems contain invented words: nouns turned to verbs, positive words made negative, and so on. In the wonderful short poem "Thoughts of Phena: at news of her death," the following invented or archaic words appear: "unsight," "enray," "enarch," "disennoble" and "upbrimming." He uses odd epithets—"aureate nimb," for instance— and a sense of ghostly musing is conveyed in words of spectral quality, suggesting meaning without containing it, unfamiliar but comprehensible. This poem, without images, remains clear through a consistent use of negatives; it deals in thoughts, not pictures. It is a poem of "unsight."

He is capable of unfortunate coinages—"stillicide" and "cohue" are two—but when he invents, or borrows from Dorset usage, the word "unhope" at the end of "In Tenebris ii," we forgive his less happy inventions. He is also capable of writing grotesque lines, with the comic effect of unresolved syntax or sentimental twaddle. In one poem he writes, "While her great gallied eyes through her hair hanging loose . . ." In a piece composed for a charitable cause, he evokes the "frail human flowerets, sicklied by the shade," a line to touch the heart of Madeleine Basset.

Hardy, sixty years old at the turn of the century, is the first essentially twentieth-century poet, familiar with Darwinism, acquainted with Einstein's work, caught between a new scientific approach and old religious dogmas. He conceived his moral role as "interfusing" essential religion, stripped of superstition and dogma (and, much to Emma's dismay, godhead) with scientific rationality. But it was not this, or his ideas about time and the individual, that made him "the most far-reaching influence, for good or ill . . . in British poetry of the last fifty years," as Donald Davie calls him. It is more his approach to craft and subject matter that in certain crucial ways illuminates the path for others. Davie writes, "Hardy has the effect of locking any poet whom he influences into a world of historical contingency, a world of specific places at specific times." Here as much as in Jonson we have a sense of the poet's "occasions," which has been developed by Thom Gunn and those who learn from him. We have, as in Geoffrey Hill, the sense of places "enghosted" with echoes, events and voices that attach to them, belong to them as much as the stones and trees do: history *inherent*. Here is the limited world of provable experience which contains Larkin's tight-fisted Muse. Poetry detects order and expresses it. It is not the function of the poet to project order or to accept, even rhetorically, untenable consolations. He makes the real world more accessible, more *real*. If the truths of that world are hard little pellets of disappointment, so be it. The truth is told. The poet's task is not to posit an alternative world, even though behind the satire and its merciless ironies is the might-have-been.

Many of Hardy's early critics lament a lack of technique; rusticity was seen as naïvete or faulty craft. Strachey spoke of "the gloom . . . not even relieved by a little elegance of diction." But this want of "elegance" is original, in the way Wordsworth's was original in *Lyrical Ballads*. It delivers poetry back to an inclusive, less class-bound tradition, in which the poem's language is not prescribed but new-made in the light of its subject.

Ford says that Hardy "showed the way for the Imagists"—a suggestive note, coming from an editor and friend of the Imagists. In two ways particularly he may have affected them. His direct language, sharing the quality of speech, stood out sharply against the poised, literary idiom of Robert Bridges, the metrical drubbing of Kipling at his most popular, and the polite ruggedness and "picturesque" of the Georgians. Another perhaps more important example Hardy set the Imagists was of the power of juxtaposition, showing how two incidents, images or plots can "interfuse" one another. Ezra Pound wrote of his poems, "Now *there* is clarity. There *is* the harvest of having written twenty novels first."

Hardy, like Housman, is an ironist. But irony in their poems is different in kind from the ironies that permeate modern verse and the dominant literary and critical idiom in England. Donald Davie writes, "The older poets do not recommend irony as a secure or dignified stance from which to confront reality, rather it is the stance of reality as it confronts *us*. Their irony is cosmic, where an Auden's is provisional and strategic." When Hardy writes of "life's little ironies," the ironies are inherent in "life," not in the poet's approach to it. They are thematic, not strategic. This sets Hardy apart from poets who have learned lessons at his knee; cosmic irony and guilt are the acid residue of failed faith.

Another attraction to later poets is his unsentimentality, unless we take his insistent pessimism to be a sort of blurring of categories, an automatic or easy habit of response. Lionel Johnson commended the "primitive savor" of his work, its "earthy charm," but more emphatically stated, "He is among the least sentimental of writers." For this quality Auden was drawn to him. But Auden especially admired his "hawk's vision, his way of looking at life from a very great height . . . To see the individual life related not only to the local social life of its time, but to the whole of human history . . . gives one both humility and self-confidence."

The very faults in Hardy make him a good teacher. His followers do not imitate his techniques but perceive in the way his poems work and fail to work what problems of form and subject matter he was grappling with. He clarifies in his poems many of the modern poet's problems. No serious writer since the turn of the century has written in ignorance of him. In one way or another, the substantial writers of the last eighty years acknowledge a debt. When Robert Graves visited him at Max Gate, the house he built near Dorchester, where he died in 1928, Hardy said, "All we can do is write on the old themes in the old styles, but try to do it a little better than those who came before us." It's an extraordinarily modest statement for the man who brought English poetry forward, unpretentiously and irreversibly, into the twentieth century. Modest too is the claim:

> I am I
> And what I do I do myself alone.

Why has Charlotte Mew never found the larger readership her work merits? She was among Hardy's favorite women writers. I first heard of her from Elizabeth Jennings in 1970: she wanted to edit a selection of the work. Mew was republished in 1953 by her friend and champion Alida Monro, then again in 1979 when her *Collected Poems and Prose* were issued for the first time, with an introduction by Val Warner. Even after a biography that anatomized her eccentricities, and a novel that suggests she had a romance with Hardy, poetry readers are likely to ask, as I did in 1970, "Charlotte who?"

In 1953, before Sylvia Plath altered the map of English poetry, Mew must have seemed a sad, rebarbative figure. Alida Monro's edition of her poems looked like an act of piety. In 1979 readers must have been more ready for the poems, but in a chunky volume with all of her stories they were buried under the weight of prose. Her originality of form and theme, her electrifying uniqueness, mean that one day she will find a constituency, without special pleading.

Her life was not easy or happy. She was born in London in 1869 into a moderately well-to-do family. Her father was an architect who had come to London and married his boss's daughter. She, a petite, apparently cosseted Victorian lady, was one for keeping up appearances. Had she married beneath herself? When financial hardship beset the Mews, she insisted on maintaining a genteel front. Eventually it became necessary to let out rooms to lodgers, but this was kept secret from all but the most intimate friends.

Charlotte enjoyed the education of a Victorian lady, was taught no skills and never went—in formal education—beyond the Lucy Harrison School for Girls in Gower Street. Her home was not particularly literary. She confessed that she never learned the rules of punctuation. Monro regularized the punctuation of her poems.

If her mother was painfully particular, her father took family responsibilities less seriously, and when he died—she was twenty-nine and still living at home—he left almost nothing. Charlotte and her sister Anne (her dearest companion) and their mother suffered to remain "proper," indeed, to survive. Anne was an artist specializing in furniture restoration. Charlotte could teach. The anguish of earning their way became a permanent torment: they had not been reared to this. In the year of her death, through the good offices of John Masefield, Walter de la Mare and Hardy, Charlotte was awarded a Civil List pension—but it came too late.

Charlotte had another sister, and a brother, both of whom suffered acute mental instability and were placed in asylums. There seemed to Charlotte and Anne to be a taint of madness in their family, and each vowed never to marry lest the illness be handed down. This decision may have been prompted as much by inclination as by conscience. Charlotte's most anthologized, though not her best, poem, "The Farmer's Bride," tells the story of a country marriage where the bride refuses to be touched, much less possessed, by her groom. The stair—an image that recurs in several poems—separates man and wife for good:

> She sleeps up in the attic there
> Alone, poor maid. 'Tis but a stair
> Betwixt us. Oh! my God! the down,
> The soft young down of her, the brown,
> The brown of her—her eyes, her hair, her hair!

Her aversion to the farmer is equal in intensity to his desire.

Charlotte's early travels, to northern France especially, impressed her deeply. When she reached the peak of her poetic powers in the years 1909–1916, writing at last with confidence and urgency, she set several poems in France. She is temperamentally an urban poet, a poet of characters in cities, rooms, passageways, a poet of confined spaces. Even the poems set in the English countryside have this enclosing quality. She knew rural England as a visitor, seeing it through the eyes of the pastoral poets she admired, notably Hardy.

Despite her intense reticence she urgently needed to express something, the nature of which she herself did not completely grasp. Given the hardships she experienced, her emotional nature and her educational background, it is astonishing that—after the unpromising early prose romances—she did not create a fantastic, escapist world. Instead, she began to develop a prose style that engaged with her reality at its most vulnerable and exposed. From this style it was a small step to poetry. The rhythms of her verse are present in her mature stories. Those stories belong to their period and have little to offer modern readers, except as a context for her verse.

Communication in the best stories is by gesture, facial expression, or through symbols. Conversation is always secondary to *how* things are said. The ordering of images is more expressive than the plot itself. Later, in the poems, the form is of crucial importance. There is as much eloquence in the disrupted, dramatic syntax, the long fluent line, the rhythmical emphasis and the quality of the objects rendered, as in plot and explicit statement, if these are present at all.

When Mew was writing her best poems, Alida, wife of Harold Monro, the poet, publisher and manager of the Poetry Book Shop, read her work in a magazine. She invited Mew to a reading at the shop and later arranged for the publication of her two books, *The Farmer's Bride* (1916) and *The Rambling Sailor* (1929), which appeared posthumously. Alida's memoir was for many years the only source of biographical information on the poet.

A letter Charlotte wrote to a friend tells us about her mode of composition and her idea of form. She writes of "In Nunhead Cemetery" (note the dashes): "The last verse which you find superfluous is to me the most inevitable—(and was written first)—being a lapse from the sanity and self-control of what precedes it—the mind—the senses can stand no more—and that is to express their failure and exhaustion." She does not write the poem straight out: she assembles it, fits it together. The artistry is in organization. Content, under sufficient emotional pressure, will violate form if the poem is to be true. We often look in vain for formal roundedness and perfection in her work, regularity of meter or consistency of stanza: form is servant, not master. The emotional content elbows the form out, or draws it in. To very different ends she allows herself precisely those freedoms that Edward Thomas demands, but her poetry is more deeply subjective, more private, than his. Its power is in the physical veracity of observation, the astonishing metamorphoses of imagery, and a speaking quality of voice, all indexes of the speaker's intense response.

Her review of Emily Brontë's poems brings us a little closer to her notion of form. She has been compared with Emily Brontë, but apart from a shared intensity, the comparison does damage to the integrity of each. They differ as much in their use of form as in the quality of passion they convey. Mew remarks that Emily Brontë's forms are "curiously deficient": "They are melodies, rather than harmonies, many of a haunting and piercing sweetness, instinct with a sweeping and mournful music peculiarly her own . . . Everywhere, too, the note of pure passion is predominant, a passion untouched by mortality and unappropriated by sex." Mew's own poems, in a determined and unusual way, aim at harmonic effect—in other words, the combining of a variety of elements in a single phrase or rhythmic run. She achieves opacity, the poetry paced phrase by phrase (the phrases of different lengths) rather than through extended cadences, even in the long-lined passages. Each phrase draws elements—sometimes contradictory or conflicting—from several registers of human sensation and emotion, together with qualities of voice, tone and inflection. It is not a poetry of developing thought but of developing emotional recognition in a physical world. We find little sweetness: her poems are everywhere infected with mortality, lament the passing of beauty, passion, people and things loved. There is a profound, troubled sensuality about all her poems and an explicit sexuality in some. It is the *impure* passion, longing for purity, usually expressed in religious imagery (she was drawn to Roman Catholicism but never crossed over) since there is no earthly permanence.

Mew's early poems dwell on religious suffering (in the form of martyrdom), punishment, death, sorrow, loss and love, a cheerless panoply of the big themes. There is one poem of misanthropic humor, "Afternoon Tea," but the others, occasionally sparking with wit, are dramatic and elegiac. Images of the stair, the rose, red petals, dreams and hair recur, so that the poems seem to interqualify and illuminate each other. Traditional images are heightened and made strange by her peculiar physicality of response.

It was in "Poems from France" that she established her voice. "The Fête" was her first outstanding poem. A boy in a French school experiences the fair—and love. His dramatic monologue ends with an expression of loss—loss, in effect, of purity, innocence, something intangible:

All my life long I shall see moonlight on the fern
    And the black trunks of trees. Only the hair
Of any woman can belong to God.
The stalks are cruelly broken where we trod,
    There had been violets there,
      I shall not care
As I used to do when I see the bracken burn.

The pain and loss implicit in pleasure are conveyed in an exacting verse form; the response is uncomprehended, coming in phrases that relate to physical particulars but do not, for the speaker, cohere, though for the reader they build a mood and story. The same power of expression characterizes "Madeleine in Church," her largest achievement, uneven but powerful. It too is a dramatic monologue and also a prayer, of 140 lines, spoken by a woman who fails to reestablish religious faith after a life of sensuality. The printer first entrusted with the task of typesetting the poem returned the manuscript, solemnly declaring it blasphemous.

"Madeleine" reminds us of Mary Magdalene, whose redemption was made possible only by the physical person of Christ. "She was a sinner, we are what we are: the spirit afterwards, but first the touch." The poem is about "the touch," and the inability of the person—without incontrovertible, personal revelation—to credit anything beyond the physical world. Christ cannot, surely, understand the darkness of her soul. She tries to explain herself to Him:

We are what we are: when I was half a child I could not sit
Watching black shadows on green lawns and red carnations
    burning in the sun,
      Without paying so heavily for it
That joy and pain, like any mother and her unborn child were
    almost one.
            I could hardly bear
    The dreams upon the eyes of white geraniums in the dusk,
        The thick, close voice of musk,
      The jessamine music on the thin night air,
    Or, sometimes, my own hands about me anywhere—

Her materialism is not intellectual but emotional. It longs for and cannot comprehend the metaphysical. "We are what we are" is the refrain. She asks God, "If it is Your will that we should be content with the tame, bloodless things." The poem is celebration as much as lament. She laments the ephemerality of the physical experiences which seem all-important, and yet she relives and celebrates. The power of the poem is in the ambiguous way she at once prays to and rejects Christ, and in the astonishing formal risks she takes with line length and pace. "If there were fifty heavens God could not give us back the child who went or never came." She cannot accede to Christ:

> Oh! He will take us stripped and done,
> Driven into His heart. So we are won:
> Then safe, safe are we? in the shelter of His everlasting wings—
> I do not envy Him His victories, His arms are full of broken
>   things.

It is hard not to hear the probing, unappeasable voice of Hopkins in the penultimate line, but how remote are their two worlds, except in physical intensity and spiritual hunger. For Madeleine, as for Mew, if we can trust the evidence of the poems, the world is too real to allow belief in anything beyond the power that bodies and objects and their mute attraction have over the mind and heart—and soul: "the spirit after-wards, but first the touch."

There are echoes in Mew—of Browning, inevitably, but also of Hardy and others—but "influences" are assimilated to her own ends. With Hardy she shares some themes, for instance the unalterability of past experience, memory, and their effect on the present; ephemerality of passion, regret, the difficulty of sustained love. Heaven is not "to come" but in the past, in youth and its spent intensities. The future is merely a termination of possibilities, a putting out of candles one by one. "I remember rooms that have had their part / In the steady slowing down of the heart." It is a difficult, unredeemed vision, thoroughly materialistic: her pseudo-mystical stair leads to a physical landing. Refusing the Christian heaven in "Not for that City" she defines the stair:

> And if for anything we greatly long,
> It is for some remote and quiet stair
>   Which winds to silence and a space of sleep
>   Too sound for waking and for dreams too deep.

"Things that kill us seem / Blind to the death they give," she wrote in "The Quiet House," a poem she reckoned her most subjective. In it the physical imagination is sharpened to a degree unprecedented even in "Madeleine in Church":

> Red is the strangest pain to bear;
> In Spring the leaves on the budding trees;

In Summer the roses are worse than these,
> More terrible than they are sweet:
> A rose can stab you across the street
> Deeper than any knife:
> And the crimson haunts you everywhere—
Thin shafts of sunlight, like the ghosts of reddened swords have
> struck our stair
As if, coming down, you had spilt your life.

Mew's sister Anne died in the winter of 1927. The loss weakened the poet and she was taken to a sanatorium. She entrusted to Alida the copy Hardy had taken in his own hand of her poem "Fin de Fête." She bought some disinfectant and drank it. When her death was reported in the local paper, she was identified as "Charlotte New, said to be a writer." It is no wonder Hardy admired her: had he written a sequel to *Jude the Obscure*, it might have been the story of her life, which enacts so many of his cruel themes.

In American poetry a transitional figure comparable to Hardy in all but scale and stature is Edwin Arlington Robinson (1869–1935), whose name is often coupled disadvantageously with that of Robert Frost. They both, Frost says, "stayed with the oldfashioned way to be new"— itself a Hardyesque strategy—pouring the new wine of their subjects into old bottles burnished for the purpose. Robinson is more artful than Hardy, more coy than Frost. His New England is domestic and some-times a little like a picture postcard: "Here where the wind is always north-north-east/And children learn to walk on frozen toes . . ." Yet in double measure he is the poet of "life's thwarted purposing," of what might have been. On his mother's side he was descended from Anne Bradstreet—another life of "thwarted purposing."

Hardy invented Wessex, a landscape with towns and villages parallel to his native Dorset. Robinson invents a New England town, Tilbury, and peoples it with voices. Browning is behind his monologues, and Robinson seems to talk to himself through them:

> "Well, Mr. Flood, we have the harvest moon
> Again, and we may not have many more;
> The bird is on the wing, the poet says,
> And you and I have said it here before.
> Drink to the bird."

"The bird is on the wing." Mr. Flood, who speaks the poem, rather implausibly nods to Robert Browning.

His people live "Like a dry fish flung inland from the shore," or pursue, with almost no hope of discovering, the vanished land of past potential. He wrote the sprawling trilogy of poems *Merlin* (1917), *Launcelot* (1927) and *Tristram* (1927), his magnum opus comparable in ambition to Hardy's *The Dynasts*; but like Hardy, it is for his poems on a smaller scale that he is remembered, like the treacherously self-revealing "Miniver Cheevy":

> Miniver loved the days of old
>   When swords were bright and steeds were prancing;
> The vision of a warrior bold
>   Would set him dancing.
>
> Miniver sighed for what was not,
>   And dreamed and rested from his labors;
> He dreamed of Thebes and Camelot,
>   And Priam's neighbors.

In "Isaac and Archibald," a long poem, a child watches two old men, "And wondered with all comfort what might come / To me, and what might never come to me . . ." This is the sort of world (but on a smaller scale) George Crabbe inhabits in Suffolk and makes real in the *Tales*. Robinson in 1896 wrote a sonnet to Crabbe:

> Give him the darkest inch your shelf allows,
> Hide him in lonely garrets, if you will,—
> But his hard, human pulse is throbbing still
> With the sure strength that fearless truth endows.
> In spite of all fine science disavows,
> Of his plain excellence and stubborn skill
> There yet remains what fashion cannot kill,
> Though years have thinned the laurel from his brows.

Crabbe is the flame of unattenuated wisdom beside which, Robinson suggests, the lights of current poets are but flickers. In this he includes his own unstable light.

Born in Maine, Robinson was brought up in Gardiner, the prototype for Tilbury. He thought of himself as "a tragedy from the beginning." His parents were old and couldn't make sense of him; he did not follow his brothers into the commercial paths prepared for him. He was sickly and sensitive, and his love of literature was not approved of. He spent two years at Harvard but was recalled when his father's health and fortunes went into decline. His romantic life was equally vexed: his first love rejected him and married one of his more solid brothers; when that brother died, she still refused his overtures. Easier than speaking in his own voice, which might have been marked by self-pity, he channeled his feelings through characters, parceling himself out (for each is an aspect of his own disappointments or, when winged, a vehicle for his own aspirations) among them.

He paid for the publication of his first book in 1896, *The Torrent and the Night Before,* revising and republishing it a year later as *The Children of Night.* Theodore Roosevelt admired it. Then Robinson moved to New York, where he lived in poverty, drinking heavily. In 1902, assisted by friends, he brought out a novel in verse, *Captain Craig.* Roosevelt secured Robinson a clerkship in the New York Custom House in 1905. His first book to be commercially published was *The Town Down the River* (1910). He began each summer to stay at the MacDowell Colony, a composers,' artists' and writers' residence in Peterboro, New Hampshire. His 1916 collection, *The Man Against the Sky,* was his breakthrough. He went on to win three Pulitzer Prizes and publish extensively. *Tristram* was a best-seller. Robert Frost wrote the introduction to his posthumous volume—his twenty-ninth book—in the year of his death from cancer and alcoholism. "His theme was unhappiness, but his skill was as happy as it was playful."

Robinson's pessimism was more pathological than philosophical. He speaks of many people, invoking Everyman, allegorizing, fictionalizing, refracting, but in the frame is always "I," however masked, however recondite. The "playful" skill that prefers to deliver a compelling effect rather than a compelling truth, that gives elegance and finish precedence over the authority of subject, is characteristic of many poets who "stayed with the oldfashioned way to be new." The received forms imposed received expectations *of* form. In "New England" he writes,

> Passion is here a soilure of the wits,
> We're told, and love a cross for them to bear;
> Joy shivers in the corner where she knits
> And Conscience always has the rocking-chair,
> Cheerful as when she tortured into fits
> The first cat that was ever killed by Care.

It's elegant, the personifications made domestic and fleetingly concrete in a tissue of received ironies. He is a brilliant writer of sonnets. His brilliance is homespun but not in the tonally and formally adroit way of Frost: the air of contrivance and prettification hovers about his poems; there is pain, but pain witnessed rather than endured. Given that the life was as it was, we might have anticipated a greater formal radicalism, a break with the constraints that, in literature, echoed the constraints of the rigid culture he was born of. He comes close sometimes. In "Richard Cory" he writes,

> So on we worked, and waited for the light,
> And went without the meat, and cursed the bread;
> And Richard Cory, one calm summer night,
> Went home and put a bullet through his head.

His little tragic characters are on a scale with Arthur Miller's in, for example, *Death of a Salesman*. Yet Miller's characters bear the weight of the history and politics of a cruel and reductive economic model. Robinson's characters cannot gain that purchase on themselves. They are creatures of emotional failure, psychological ciphers who touch us and move us, but not deeply or very far. In the end Robinson is *literary*, so that the literal "facts" that disrupt his poems, that are supposed to ground them in a real world, are effects on a par with the plangent prosody, the irony, the choice diction. "Miniver Cheevy," his most celebrated poem, is almost autobiographical. Miniver was "born too late." Like his author, he longs for a "Vanished Land."

More prolific than Robinson was Edgar Lee Masters (1869–1950). He wrote fifty books, one of which, *Spoon River Anthology*, is still widely read—like the poems of John Betjeman—by people who have little taste for Poetry with a capital P. His Spoon River is a Midwestern version of Tilbury, but the people who live there, in personality, intrigue and tragedy, are more credible than Robinson's—like smaller-scale, poetic versions of Sherwood Anderson and Sinclair Lewis characters (the presence and the controversial success of *Spoon River* is said to have inspired them).

Masters was a lawyer in Chicago for twenty-five years (starting at the age of twenty-two). Born in Kansas, he was raised in rural Illinois. An independent boy out of sympathy with his father, in tune with his quiet, artistic mother, he earned his own living by the age of sixteen, attended Knox College in Illinois, and wrote poems. Before he was twenty-five he had written four hundred poems in a variety of styles, most of them nineteenth-century. Swinburne and Shelley, Poe and Whitman all had their impact on him. In 1915 he stumbled upon a Whitman-derived free-verse line, on the whole shorter-breathed than Whitman's and full of particulars of voice and circumstance. His goal was concision, the authority of the epigram. Like those novelists who, from the compelling sprawl of Proust, learn to write briefly, so from the immense abundance of Whitman he learned to condense his style. *Spoon River Anthology* includes more than two hundred epitaphs, each spoken by the dead of Spoon River. They sit up and essentialize themselves, then return to a recumbent posture and await Judgment Day. What they tell of their community and their tight-fisted, tight-hearted world is satire and realism in equal measures. The introduction promises us a cast of characters as vivid and rooted as those that appear in Hardy's *Satires of Circumstance* and *Life's Little Ironies*. These are life's little people.

The problem with the collection—what makes it popular and what very nearly confines it to the world of prose—is the two-dimensionality of the characters created. They stand for various forms of failure and unfulfillment, and the ironies that emerge from each are similar in valency. Yet, unlike Robinson, Masters does elude the merely literary. If his figures are thin, they also convince. This must be a function of the free verse, used with immense discretion, the rhythms throwaway, casual.

Those of my generation reared in America on New Critical anthologies had reason to resent Masters. His poem "Petit the Poet," a kind of parody (we did not sense it at the time), summarized everything we disliked about the art of poetry—what made us impatient with Dickinson and Poe and Bryant and the great Joyce Kilmer, author of "Trees," and all the rest. Masters's poem begins:

> Seeds in a dry pod, tick, tick, tick,
> Tick, tick, tick, like mites in a quarrel—
> Faint iambics that the full breeze wakens—
> But the pine tree makes a symphony thereof.
> Triolets, villanelles, rondels, rondeaus,
> Ballades by the score with the same old thought:
> The snow and the roses of yesterday are vanished;
> And what is love but a rose that fades?

What was he doing, alluding to Villon in the snows of yesteryear, and to Whitman and Homer at the poem's conclusion? Masters was creating the poet that he wanted *not* to be, the small-minded poet whose eyes were closed to his world even as they opened on all the resources of his art. It is in inclusive poems like "The Hill" (where all the Spoon River dead are buried) and "The Lost Orchard" that we might have come to love him, as we learned unaccountably to love Carl Sandburg because there was no varnish on him. It is those poems rather than "Petit" that sent the book through nineteen printings in its first edition and caused a great stir of controversy because of the "negative" picture of provincial life it painted.

Masters was part of the "Chicago Renaissance"—or "Naissance"—working with Harriet Monroe at *Poetry*, aware of the work of Ezra Pound and H.D., among others. In the end, propelled by the success of

Spoon River, he moved in 1920 to New York and spent his last few years at the Chelsea Hotel among other writers. The provinces when they succeed gravitate to the metropolis as if to home—to Chicago, to New York or London—and are translated out of themselves. From 1915 to his death in 1950, only *The New Spoon River* of 1924 made any mark, and that mark was nine years familiar. Fame liberates and fame confines. He was an unlikely heir of Whitman. *The New Spoon River* attacks urbanization, but a bitterness that seems put on, an anger that rings hollow, deflect his earlier insight. He was far from his characters, his "Hill" and his relations and their lives.

If we are looking for unalloyed "truth" at this time of day, we must turn to a prose-writer poet who died young: Stephen Crane (1871–1900). He is more modern than Robinson and Masters, indeed, in some respects, more modern than Frost—like Isaac Rosenberg, with a spirit touched by the Old Testament and uncomforted by the New. "God is cold," says a refrain to a late poem, discovered long after his death. It is his directness that is so astonishing, the absence of "literary" definition. Like Hardy, he was a novelist. He has many stories and six novels to his credit, the best-known being *The Red Badge of Courage*. He also wrote two volumes of verse before he died of tuberculosis in a German sanatorium. He was twenty-nine.

Crane's father, a Methodist minister in New Jersey, died when he was eight. He studied at Lafayette (military) College, and then Syracuse University, rejecting every one of his father's values. He was drawn to journalism as a career, and—a quiet and gentle man—he was fascinated by poverty, violence and war. His first novel was infatuated with sordid realism, more Hardyesque than Hardy in its deterministic pessimism: "It tries to show," he says in a dedicatory note, "that environment is a tremendous thing in the world and frequently shapes lives regardless. If one proves that theory, one makes room in Heaven for all sorts of souls (notably an occasional sweet girl) who are not confidently expected to be there by many excellent people." In Jacksonville, Florida, he married such a girl, Cora Taylor, a brothel madam, whom he brought to England in 1897. They settled at Brede Place, Sussex. Like gun running and being a war correspondent, it was an adventure to which he committed himself in earnest.

The writer Hamlin Garland, meeting Crane, was curious about some papers he saw sticking out of his pocket. "Upon unrolling the manuscript," he reports, "I found it to be a sheaf of poems written in blue ink upon single sheets of legal cap paper, each poem without blot or correction, almost without punctuation, all beautifully legible, exact and orderly in arrangement." Crane had more "up here"—tapping his head—"all in a little row." He could draw them off complete. He published *Black Riders* in 1895. In his final year a second volume of poems, *War Is Kind*, appeared.

Joseph Conrad, Henry James and H. G. Wells admired his prose. The poems were slow to catch on. John Berryman, largely responsible for revaluing Anne Bradstreet, also shone a light on Crane. The poems are like the prose in one way: they depend upon a Hardyesque irony, the irony of life, not of style. There is something cold and archetypal about the poetry, as about Rosenberg's early biblical verse, and something that seems more of the twentieth than the nineteenth century: a poetry of bones without flesh, of acid resignation without hope.

> A man feared that he might find an assassin;
> Another that he might find a victim.
> One was more wise than the other.

Untitled, numbered like entries in a verse journal, often staccato, the poems have an essential, un-literary urgency about them. They seem to have been written out of a pressure of content, and not because Crane imagined himself to "be a poet."

> Fast rode the knight
> With spurs hot and reeking
> Ever waving an eager sword.
>   "To save my lady!"
> Fast rode the knight
> And leaped from saddle to war.
> Men of steel flickered and gleamed
> Like riot of silver lights
> And the gold of the knight's good banner
> Still waved on a castle wall.
> A horse
> Blowing, staggering, bloody thing
> Forgotten at foot of castle wall.
> A horse
> Dead at foot of castle wall.

What do we make of such a poem? What do we make of Rosenberg's "Dead Man's Dump"? Crane's poems are allegorical anecdotes, jottings that seed in us and provoke reflection. They require that we add to them our own ironies:

> The impact of a dollar upon the heart
> Smiles warm red light,

Sweeping from the hearth rosily upon the white table,
With the hanging cool velvet shadows
Moving softly upon the door.
The impact of a million dollars
Is a crash of flunkeys,
And yawning emblems of Persia
Cheeked against oak, France and a sabre,
The outcry of old beauty
Whored by pimping merchants
To submission before wine and chatter.

There has been nothing like this in English poetry before. It owes debts to the Bible, perhaps to Whitman, to the discipline of responsible journalism, and to an eye for hard truths. It is verse entirely free of class bias, national bias, but not of an informing tradition that makes him write "Cheeked against oak" and "the gold of the knight's good banner." Berryman declares that he "was not only a man with truths to tell, but an interested listener to this man. His poetry has the inimitable sincerity of a frightened savage anxious to learn what his dreams mean." This is wrong: he wants to understand his waking hours and what happens when he witnesses a battle, or a love, or a cruel sunset. The linguistic range is narrow, the themes chillingly repetitive but always in a subtly different key. Yet he teaches a modern poet more than Masters and Robinson can do, and he anticipates many of the radical departures that awaited English poetry when Victorian verse at last finished dying.

"The land of lost content"

A. E. HOUSMAN, RUDYARD KIPLING, ISAAC ROSENBERG,
WILFRED OWEN, SIEGFRIED SASSOON, RUPERT BROOKE

How artful and artificial Alfred Edward Housman seems, set beside Stephen Crane. For a long time it was considered a bit *de trop* for people with literary taste to love, or even to like, Housman's verse. It belonged to self-pitying adolescence and after that to the mass of readers who don't like *real* poetry—whose taste will encompass John Betjeman, Charles Causley and Dylan Thomas but stop short at Hardy, Auden and W. S. Graham. Housman: solitary, sour, homosexual, without a lover, without God. Today it is again possible to confess a liking for his work, though it still hardly figures on the academic syllabus. The unmade bed of Stephen Crane is more critically acceptable than the passionate, cold pillow of Housman.

Yet from the day *A Shropshire Lad* was published until now he has been a best-selling author. The silence of critics has not affected popular taste. The poems are taken to heart and learned by heart, despite the now mercilessly documented character of the harsh, opinionated professor, the sometimes vindictive classical scholar, the tensely repressed homosexual. The voice of the poems is of an uncannily refined classless purity. He sings—for he seldom speaks in the way of modern poets—the ageless themes of mortality, thwarted love and sacrifice.

He touches two exposed poetic nerves: the nerve that responds to popular ballads, for his poems, in strategy, theme and tone often resemble the anonymous elegiac ballads of the Borders; and the nerve that responds to hymns, though his hymnlike stanzas celebrate no god. We find in his pastoral nostalgia something more than bittersweetness, in his melodies something more than mere song. The poems are above all memorable. Phrases and stanzas come to mind at times of stress, or simply when one is out walking and a landscape or memory suddenly appropriates a stanza. Composers including George Butterworth in 1913 and Ralph Vaughan Williams in 1914 recognized excellent *Lieder* texts in the poems. (Benjamin Britten, surprisingly, kept his distance, perhaps warded off by Auden.)

What some modern poetry readers look for—grit, real hearts on imaginary sleeves, a deliberate roughening of diction and meter—they do not find in Housman. Formal conservatism and the repetitiveness of mood and tone leave them cold. The raw imperialism of Kipling or the authentic pastoral of Hardy say more to them than the poise of Housman. He is a poet different in kind, his affinities more in the eighteenth and early nineteenth than the twentieth century, yet his poems are not archaic, old-fashioned or conventional. He does something new, yet it has the huge authority of classical and English antecedents. He defines in practice the difference between traditional and merely conventional verse. It would be foolish to pretend that he is a major poet: he has too limited a repertoire, his achievements are in one genre. But he is undeniably a great poet, since he did what he did with genius, finding impersonal idioms to express his deepest hurt.

He was born in 1859 in Fockbury, Worcestershire. His comfortable, conservative, middle-class background was conducive to the development of an interest in literature, which matured into a passion for classical studies. He seems to have enjoyed escaping into the countryside for walks. The eastern horizon of these childhood outings was Shropshire.

He was educated at Bromsgrove, Worcester, and then at Oxford. His university career included impressive achievements and failures. He became an outstanding textual critic, so single-mindedly involved in his texts that he omitted to mug up his ancient history and philosophy and—under severe emotional strain—failed to take even a pass degree. He went down and entered a civil service job in the Patent Office. After a decade there (1882–92) his classical achievements earned him a chair of Latin at University College, London, where he worked for the next decade. From there he published his first collection of poems, *A Shropshire Lad* (1896). In 1911 he became professor of Latin at Cambridge, a post he held until his death in 1936. His editions of Manilius, Juvenal and Lucan are magisterial; his acerbity in critical debate and his passion for accuracy made him something of a terror to his professional colleagues.

A Shropshire Lad achieved for Housman wide and almost immediate fame as a poet. In its expressions of frustration and futility and in its measured, traditional voice, the book answered needs like those Tennyson's *In Memoriam* had answered two generations earlier. It was twenty-six years before Housman published another collection, called simply *Last Poems*. This was followed, as "last poems" sometimes are, by *More Poems*, a collection issued in 1936, shortly before he died. A few poems (including some very funny parodies) have since been appended to the oeuvre, but the *Collected Poems* is slim for a poet who reached the age of seventy-seven. Its thinness is manifest in various ways. Though all the work was assembled by a mature man—his books appeared when he was thirty-seven, sixty-three and seventy-seven—the mood and content are stuck in a groove that seems adolescent. The poems lack formal and linguistic development and seem self-imitative, not only revisiting themes but redeveloping earlier phrases and images. If, as his biographers suggest, he came to terms, to some troubled extent, with his sexual and emotional nature, the poems touch on this resolution only obliquely. Unless, that is, we read them as encoded expressions of a secret odyssey.

Housman expressed his *public* attitude to poetry most fully in a lecture, "The Name and Nature of Poetry," delivered in Cambridge in 1933. He condemned the "difficult" poetry of the Metaphysicals, in vogue at the time, and by implication discredited much of the new poetry of the century, especially the poets who had brought the Metaphysicals back into currency. Poetry, both composition and reading, was for him less an intellectual than a physical experience. It took hold of him, engaged him, at a level he could not intellectually plumb. A poem's effect had to do with music, rhyme and emotional direction, less with teasing out *meaning*. His theories drew on his own practice, not on an assessment of modern poetry; they answered a deep prejudice in his audience. If they signify primarily as they relate to his verse and the classical verse he liked best, his admirers gave them wider credence. Here was an unanswerable—because instinctive and unanalyzable—case against those odd, rebarbative experiments that threatened the coherence of English poetry. The young poet-critic I. A. Richards left the lecture muttering, "Housman has put the clock back thirty years!"

And indeed his attitudes and his poems in several ways recall the purer poets of the Rhymers' Club, though without the taint of decadence. Whatever Housman's emotional turmoils, his poems are remote from the indulgences of the Decadents. After Oscar Wilde's trial and punishment, whole areas of experiment and sensibility were sealed off, as if radioactive. Only a close reader (with or without knowledge about the poet's life) will note Housman's connection with the Decadents and take a subversive moral meaning from the poems. Housman's perennial appeal has something to do with the accretions of biography, which "open out" the poems to unexpected readings, the very readings they may have been intended to be proof against. Just when he might have begun to fade, biographical fashions of the day broke open his privacies to prurient light.

The poems are not argumentative. They are metaphors for emotions. Because of their formal and tonal predictability, they can be parodied, their pessimism is at times forced, at times sentimental. Not infrequently the expression is convoluted and banal. His passions—for the Greek Anthology, Heine, Wordsworth, Arnold, Kipling and others— did not imbue him with the power to *think* in verse. Indeed he did not wish to do so. Though an atheist, he is often ambivalent in his use of religious images and themes and—like Hardy—seems frequently to acknowledge a malignant deity, calling him "whatever brute or blackguard made the world." Unlike Hardy, he never hankers after communion or community. What *thought* there is in his poems engages only the surface: it edits, while he lets emotion hold the depths—often distressingly unchecked. A classical concern with surfaces yields some coy circumlocutions, as in the famous stanza:

> Now, of my threescore years and ten,
> Twenty will not come again,
> And take from seventy springs a score
> It only leaves me fifty more.

He's saying that one is young only once and life is brief. In another poem he has a peculiar way of saying that the lads found and picked a lot of daffodils: "And home at noonday from the hills / They bring no dearth of daffodils." The parodies of Housman that many, including Ezra Pound, have attempted are not nearly as amusing as Housman's inadvertent self-parodies.

For him, the pastoral is a literary world. The intensely English feeling of his poems derives less from a closeness to landscapes and rural communities than from a nostalgic deployment of place-names and a strong sense of traditional value in his chosen forms. A real Shropshire milkmaid or lad lost in one of his landscapes would recognize little but the flowers. This is part of the late nineteenth-century heritage that Housman, like Kipling, Hardy, Elizabeth Daryush and to some degree Yeats, brought into the twentieth.

Housman's was a more modern temperament than Kipling's, willing to let go, to wave a rueful rather than a rhetorical farewell to things. But he was less modern than Hardy, resorting to gauged plangencies, never deliberately ruffling up his meters or alloying his diction with contemporary idiom. His choice of subject matter too defines him. He elects for himself what Hardy was elected *by*, the pastoral. It would be better to speak of Hardy as "rural" rather than "pastoral." For all Housman's use of English names and his ruddy lads and lasses, his debt is to classical masters, to Theocritus, Horace, Virgil, to the condensed and aphoristic poems in the Greek Anthology.

His insistent rhymed quatrains (almost all his poems are in a single basic measure, though he wrings remarkable variations from it) have a haunting authenticity of movement. His furtive desires helped to fence him into the world where his poems exist, and also intensified his expression around an emotional core. The poems could not be forthright about his theme at the time; they take advantage of the necessary obliquity in various ways, not least in their apparent universality of application. They are not, as Christopher Isherwood declares homosexual writing generally to be, propaganda; or if they are, they are arcane. A knowledge of the poet's life refocuses attention on the homoerotic element within the poems, but it cannot translate the poems into gay poetry in any meaningful sense, any more than a sense of Gerard Manley Hopkins's sexual nature radically revises our response to any but two or three of his poems.

As with Hopkins, however, the poet's sexuality contributes to the pessimism that makes the poetry poignant. Housman's condensed language and instantly memorable rhythms are a different strategy from Hopkins's resolute, baroque impurities. To Housman, poetry was "a morbid secretion, like the pearl in an oyster." He would often conceive a stanza whole, sometimes an entire poem, and write it out in almost a final draft. At other times part of a poem would come easily while another part might demand from him superhuman concentration and numerous drafts and redrafts. Sometimes a phrase appears in his notebooks and is lost sight of for years, to emerge later in a poem. He usually composed when depressed or unwell. Great bouts of creativity are followed by long gestating vacancies.

All of his poems work together, thematically and formally, almost as a sequence or, more correctly, a series. The *Collected Poems* add up to a sort of preemptive elegy—not for things lost but, more melancholically, for things never attained. They look back on no emotional or physical fulfillment, anticipate no trumped-up theological consummation. Youth did not recognize the urgency of self-fulfillment; age muses wryly that, had youth made its choice, a different anguish would have ensued. The situation is that of classical tragedy: any choice condemns the chooser. When, in later years on holiday in Italy, he found a native friend or friends with whom he could engage in intimacy, he was locked as much by age as habit into a poetic idiom that could admit fulfillment only as a brief respite intensifying the sense of ephemerality and loss. Given the moral world he lived in, to act out a homosexual passion had destructive consequences. Wilde's fate paralyzed men like Housman.

Yet sublimation had real consequences too, blighting his life. Retrospective desire prompts some of the best poems, epitomes of "the wound and the bow" vision of art:

> Here dead lie we because we did not choose
>   To live and shame the land from which we sprung.
> Life, to be sure, is nothing much to lose:
>   But young men think it is, and we were young.

In another poem he writes, "But he that drinks in season / Shall live before he dies." Housman missed his season: when he came to drink it was toward sunset.

We cannot conveniently label Housman's verse: the forms are classical, the content Romantic; the forms are simple, the content at times sophisticated; the forms are derivative, the content, masked, as it sometimes must be, feels original. He is a classical poet and like Gray a classicist of accomplishment, for whom the classics are a source of imaginative life; but like Gray he has a romantic temperament. The world to which his romanticism is confined confronts him, as it does Hardy, with teeming paradoxes, inscrutable irony. He writes from personal apprehension of this, but when he says that his verse with its sad and "narrow measure spans / Tears of eternity, and sorrow / Not mine, but man's," he is guilty of partial deception—whether he deceives himself we cannot say. He acknowledges in other poems that his is a specific suffering; the mass of others are more or less content, if not happy, ignorant of the ironies that impale him.

The poets of this century whose distinctive mood is pessimistic seem often to be the tautest formalists: Hardy, Housman, Elizabeth Daryush, Philip Larkin and Geoffrey Hill. They are also impersonal writers, expressing negative vision without direct recourse to autobiography. The inability to find objects for authentic commitment makes them elect a self-contained, effective form of statement, larded with negatives, setting off the darkness with a deeper darkness, confronting chaos with sharply formed fragments. They bear torches like Lawrence's gentians, which radiate darkness, not light. Form is a solid thing, a stay in a world of flux with no revealed order and no inherent structure, in which projected order is recognized as nothing more than projection.

Housman's poems often begin in apparent optimism: day breaks, the heart identifies a new object of love. But they seldom maintain good cheer. His ballads—among the most achieved literary ballads in our literature—reveal his skill in dramatic reversal. "Farewell to barn and stack and tree" and "The Carpenter's Son" are faultless, timeless, and each time we read them the emotional impact is deeper. There is drama, bordering on melodrama, in some of his recurrent situations: a man committing suicide, a man hanged, a soldier dying gratefully. The still nullity of the grave—"the nation that is not" he calls it more than once—is peopled by the multitude at last released from passion, and also from the social convention of marriage:

> Lovers lying two and two
>   Ask not whom they sleep beside,
> And the bridegroom all night through
>   Never turns him to the bride.

In the last half of the poem from which the stanza comes, five negatives appear: *"not," "nothing," "never"* and *"no,"* four prominent steeds in Housman's apocalypse. Vainly he tries to escape this world by fancy. In one poem he gazes at pure reflections on water, longing for that other world, until he perceives a face looking back at him with the same discontent and longing. There is no Echo in sight.

When anguish borrows a historical perspective, Housman's poems take on magnificent authority. The particular anguish is seen to recur down the ages; the men who have suffered it are together in the commonwealth of death. When wind frets Wenlock Edge, the poet stands where a Roman soldier stood when Uriconium was a settlement:

> 'Tis the old wind in the old anger,
>   But then it threshed another wood.

> Then, 'twas before my time, the Roman
>   At yonder heaving hill would stare:
> The blood that warms an English yeoman,
>   The thoughts that hurt him, they were there.

Recurrence is inevitable and harshly consoling, conferring legitimacy on a profound anxiety: "The tree of man was never quiet: / Then 'twas the Roman, now 'tis I." He comforts himself with oblivion: "Today the Roman and his trouble / Are ashes under Uricon."

Soldiers are the principal actors in the poems. The Shropshire Lad enlists and is wounded and killed all over the Empire, responding to each fate with much the same resignation. Soldiers inhabit the poems even when they are unseen, "drumming like a noise in dreams." The noise is constant though the dream changes.

Nostalgia for the shire where, in sadness, "homely comforters I had" is an occasional consolation, though usually it heightens unfulfillment. "The land of lost content": Housman has no peer this century for evoking the ambivalent contents of the past, the ambivalent bourn of the future, and a present diseased with longing for both a past that cannot be relived and a future death that, when it comes, will render him insentient, will not even be apprehended as relief.

> Into my heart an air that kills
>   From yon far country blows:
> What are those blue remembered hills,
>   What spires, what farms are those?
>
> That is the land of lost content,
>   I see it shining plain,
> The happy highways where I went
>   And cannot come again.

Joseph Rudyard Kipling—nostalgic too for lost content—shares more with Housman than the year of his death, 1936. He was born in Bombay in 1865. "Rudyard" refers to Lake Rudyard, Staffordshire, where his mother and father had courted. His father was a talented teacher of sculpture at the Bombay School of Art and later curator of the museum at Lahore, responsive to the rich multitude of cultures in which he and his family lived. His mother was sister of Lady Burne-Jones and of Stanley Baldwin's mother. Thus one of his backgrounds was intellectually lively and socially privileged. The other shared in different and older cultures. India in his early years was real to him, not as something inferior or dominated but as something mysterious and compelling. It helped constitute his imagination and memory. As a young child he was under the care of an Indian nurse, and he became proficient in Hindustani as well as English. This was more than a "below stairs" experience of the Raj. When as a little sahib he returned to England with his sister, he stood at an awkward angle to the colonial world; the country he came to lacked the warmth, color and easy intimacy of the one he had left. When he returned to India as a young man, he had changed, but it was India that seemed different, no longer second nature to him. He invests much of his writing in reclaiming the first India for himself, and for others—children and adults.

He was six when he was packed off to England for his education, first to the home of an elderly evangelical relation in Southsea. His miserable six years there ("the House of Desolation") were relieved by occasional visits to the Burne-Jones establishment near Brighton. There William Morris became his Uncle Topsy. Sir Edward Burne-Jones was at work on illustrations for Morris's Kelmscott Press edition of Chaucer's *Canterbury Tales*. Apart from these oases of warmth and jollity, the boy endured a life of solitary unhappiness, moving in 1879 to a minor public school, the United Services College, Westward Ho!, in Devon. There he began writing verse. The experiences of those early years frame much of his later writing.

His first book was a collection of poems, privately printed in 1881: *Schoolboy Lyrics.* The next year, at sixteen, he returned to India and served on the staff of the Lahore *Civil and Military Gazette*, contributing articles and poems. In 1889 he became foreign correspondent for the Allahabad *Pioneer* and began traveling—to China, Japan, America, Australia and Africa. Work as a correspondent made him a keen observer. He saw deeply into Indian—and not only Indian—affairs, with the complex perspective of one who understands his own British tribal needs and priorities, but also the needs and priorities of a loved other world. He gives the impression of a writer with inside information—about the British Army, India and other subjects. Accuracy of detail and a public tone are results of his journalistic training.

The light verse he wrote for newspapers was collected in *Departmental Ditties* (1886), a book that reached an English audience. But it was *Plain Tales from the Hills* (1888) that made a real mark in England and paved the way for the writer's return. He arrived in London in 1889 with a reputation. He was fêted by editors and fellow writers but generally stood apart, a plain man among the literati, preferring the company of men of action, of public deeds—Stanley Baldwin, Lord Milner, Max Aitken (who became Lord Beaverbrook). This was the period of his greatest popularity. Until 1902 he was the most eloquent literary spokesman for a Tory populism that was patriotic, imperial and—above all—responsible. The privileges of being English entailed real duties, duties that were imperatives.

When we say he was popular, we can quantify what we mean. By 1918, *Departmental Ditties,* his least achieved book, had sold 81,000 copies; by 1931 it had sold 117,000 copies. *Barrack-Room Ballads and Other Verses* remained his most popular book, selling 182,000 copies by 1918 and 255,000 by 1931. The *Definitive Edition* of the poems, published in 1940, had gone through sixty impressions by 1982. Like Housman, even when his shares were no longer quoted on the intellectual *bourse,* and critics turned their backs on him, he remained popular with readers.

His first major success, *Barrack-Room Ballads* (1892, 1896), contains many of his best-known poems. Hymns, music-hall songs, ballads and public poetry lay behind his instantly popular verse. Popularity did not earn him the obloquy of fellow writers that it tends to engender today. It was not considered culpable or vulgar that he fixed his eye on an audience. He developed his demotic Cockney dialect, experimental forms, and mastered traditional metrics in long and short measures as no poet apart from Auden has since done. He fails when skillful technique betrays inadequate ideas, when a poem has no intellectual or emotional necessity and is a mere exercise or pretext.

Such was his reputation that, after Tennyson's death, he was offered the poet laureateship. He refused. This was the first of several honors he declined. In later years, for example, he would not accept the Order of Merit, and when his remains finally came to rest at Westminster Abbey, his name was "unenhanced."

Kipling married the American Caroline Balestier (Carrie), lived for five unpleasant years on her family estate in Vermont, and in 1897 returned to England for good, settling first at The Elms, Rottingdean, Sussex, and then in 1902 acquiring Bateman's, Burwash, Sussex, from which he stirred abroad only occasionally in the last thirty-four years of his life. He was still a relatively young man, but he had wearied of travel. The unsuccessful American experiment blurred his later work, producing a vein of anti-American sentiment, a coarse misogyny, a distaste for extreme forms of democracy and a renewed sense of the mission and the values of Empire. There was more in this than the growing conservatism of a successful man growing old, wanting the world to stay the same. For Kipling there was an urgent duty in arguing the case for the Empire in its irreversible decline.

After all, he had seen so much of it from so many angles, he had understood its cultures and potentials, and he foresaw the consequences of its decline not only for England but for the subject nations. His reporting during the Boer War was brilliant, presenting "news events" that showed an understanding of the underlying causes. In retirement at Bateman's, observing from a distance rather than reporting from the fray, and, often alone with his disappointments, he was beset by serious melancholy. The relentless themes of duty, sacrifice and devotion were elicited particularly by the First World War, in which his only son John was killed in 1915 at the Battle of Loos (the body was never found). "The Children" is about his and other parents' loss:

These were our children who died for our lands: they were dear in
  our sight.
    We have only the memory left of their home-treasured sayings
      and laughter.
    The price of our loss shall be paid to our hands, not another's
      hereafter.
Neither the Alien nor Priest shall decide on it. That is our right.
    But who shall return us the children?

It is as though the biblical cadences gradually lay hold of his verse: he speaks from a moral height in a voice that contains all the voices he has spoken in before.

In Kipling as in Hardy we find a poetry from the turn of the century without traces of poetic weariness, without the rhythmic overemphasis of Swinburne, the esoteric qualities of Arthur Symons, or the twilight of early Yeats. He was a plain-speaking poet, nowhere more pithily than in his "Epitaphs of the War." These brief, uncompromising last words illustrate his skill in poetry of summary declaration, tough yet humane. "The Coward" is the best of them: "I could not look on death, which being known, / Men took me to him, blindfold and alone." His most famous epitaph has the same epigrammatic conciseness; few talents of this century have been given to epigram, a form more difficult to master—for it demands pure content and direct expression—than discursive forms. "If any question why we died / Tell them, because our fathers lied."

This bald, concise style does not dominate Kipling's work. But it reaches its finest development in the poem "The Way Through the Woods," which seems at first different in kind, but which is similarly declarative, summary and unclouded by sentiment. The movement is of pensive speech:

> They shut the road through the woods
> Seventy years ago.
> Weather and ruin have undone it again,
> And now you would never know
> There was once a road through the woods
> Before they planted the trees.

There are a few poems of comparable, quiet directness. "The Runes on Weland's Sword" is another one, gnomic but equally resonant.

The completeness of Kipling's experiences—of the Raj, where he knew the Indian and the colonial; of England, where he was insider and outsider; of the Empire, where he was apologist and elegist—give him an aloofness or apartness, even when he pretends to be familiar. It also contributes to the impersonality of his writing, an unwillingness to dwell on subjective experience, a preference for the hard completeness and truth-telling of the "Epitaphs," for example. The death of his son informs "My Boy Jack," but it is a poem of general loss. Such impersonality is, however, usually accompanied by certain thematic obsessions—they are the subjective element, forcing the verse toward particular meanings, or celebrating certain virtues and chastising certain vices.

The opinions and preoccupations attributed to the soldier and the "lower" classes—indeed the very terms in which Kipling has them express themselves—are not as authentic as they seem. He does not exactly *appropriate* them, but he does at times assign to them a character and opinions that he infers rather than *hears*. The personae in the dramatic monologues and ballads can seem like journalist caricatures, forfeiting authenticity to authority, for an effect of easy resonance. There is inadvertent satire even in his most earnest ballads.

Kipling's ambition to achieve an "irrefutable prose statement," as C. H. Sisson puts it, means that poems often end on a specific effect, not a general one. Background, setting, tones and accents of voice become more important than the integrity of poetic statement. The storyteller will not let the poet loose. Where in Hardy's *Satires of Circumstance* the background is implicit, in Kipling it is made explicit and often dominates the foreground. He has to define a context through his speakers before he can wrest from them the poem he wants.

We're often uneasy reading Kipling. The poems, when one has grasped what they say or has been cudgeled by it, seem better than their meanings—as though the communication of meaning is an excuse for something else, perhaps the fulfillment of a technical or dramatic challenge the poet sets himself; yet, because the meanings are bluntly present, because they coordinate that "something else," they are bound to them and lack autonomy. T. S. Eliot stresses that Kipling is, to begin with, a ballad maker, that we do not defend him against charges of obscurity but of "excessive lucidity": "People are exasperated by poetry which they do not understand, and contemptuous of poetry which they understand without effort." Obscurities occur in Kipling, but not in his meanings so much as in his motives. Eliot makes another valuable point: Kipling's use of language in verse differs little from his use of it in prose.

Setting Kipling's verse alongside his prose, we feel that there is simply too *much* language, too many words in many of the poems. When he sets out toward a rhetorical effect, as in refrain poems and narrative pieces, we see the destination a mile off, and the remainder of the journey can be tedious. In prose Kipling is not sidetracked: it relates to, and relates, a story and setting efficiently and faithfully. When he interposes a poetic form between himself and his subject, he is tempted to elaborate, to test the form he's created almost as though this testing were the purpose of the poem.

Kipling is indebted, among his contemporaries, to Browning for his dramatic monologues, to Swinburne for some of his rhythms, to the Pre-Raphaelites; towering behind his work is the King James Version of the Bible. But ballad, hymn and short story remain his chief *poetic* determinants. He is a public poet first and last, despite formal inventiveness. His work develops thematically, but the style remains spry, unrepetitive, essentially stable. Eliot sees his development as a shift from "the imperial imagination into the historical imagination"—from geography and the present to history and the sources of and analogies for the present. There's a change, too, from a concern with the limbs of Empire—India and the army, principally—to a concern with the imperial heart, with England, with Sussex in particular as its emblem. He pursues imperial responsibilities home.

His ballads are either narrative, with a plot and often dialogue, or dramatic monologues. He writes topical poems, occasional verse, sometimes "hymn-ballads" such as "Ave Imperatrix," celebrating Queen Victoria's escape from an assassination attempt in 1882. Eliot praises his hymn writing, stressing the extreme poetic objectivity necessary for this mode. And Kipling writes prophecies as well, with remarkable prescience as to events, though his imperial perspectives can seem archaic. In later years he translated Horace with his customary directness, and throughout his life he was a parodist: *The Muse Among the Motors* is a delightful, neglected sequence in which he parodies Chinese, Greek and Latin poems, the *Rubáiyát*, Middle English, Shakespeare, Donne, Wordsworth, Emerson, Longfellow, the Brownings, Clough and others, setting them the task of writing about the motor car. "The Idiot Boy" parodies Wordsworth's "Lucy" poems:

> He went alone, that none might know
>   If he could drive or steer,
> Now he is in the ditch, and Oh!
>   The differential gear.

Housman is a poet of fixed emotions, Kipling, of fixed ideas. He knows what most of his poems will say before he begins. They are not essays in discovery but expositions and iterations. The idea—which can be dramatic, political or satirical—is generally introduced in the first stanza and repeated or decorated as the poem progresses. In the dedication to *Barrack-Room Ballads* he promises us poems about "such as fought and sailed and ruled and loved and made our world." "Our" world is England and its Empire: Kipling's verse does not readily lend itself to translation. And yet Bertolt Brecht translated *Barrack-Room Ballads* into German—implausible, given their political differences. But Brecht found in Kipling a quality of directness, a concern with "actual" speech, that he needed in shaping his own verse and drama.

In Kipling's dedication he describes the sort of man he admires, the man who "had done his work and held his peace and had no fear to die"—a preference he shared with Joseph Conrad, whom he resembles in various dark ways. In the subtle "Sestina of the Tramp-Royal," written in the quasi-Cockney dialect devised for his rustics, his chosen man speaks out:

> Speakin' in general, I'ave tried 'em all—
> The 'appy roads that take you o'er the world.
> Speakin' in general, I'ave found 'em good
> For such as cannot use one bed for long,
> But must get 'ence, the same as I'ave done,
> An' go observin' matters till they die.

This is the "trail that is always new" of "The Long Trail"; a mood of acceptance, of dutiful, cheerful resignation, dominates.

"The Vampire" and "Harp Song of the Dane Woman" are in Kipling's more mysterious ballad vein. The "Harp Song" begins,

> What is a woman that you forsake her,
> And the hearth fire and the home-maker,
> To go with the old grey widow-maker?

The "widow-maker" is the sea. The other poem, never specifying its meaning, evokes the fool who prayed "to a rag and a bone and a hank of hair." Several poems are charged with a cruel mystery, suggesting sometimes a revulsion from sexual intimacy. They are as much about death and sexual uncertainty as about vampires and Danish women.

The political and prophetic poems are at once the most popular and unpopular of his works. At times he turns against his own political stance, writing "The Fabulists 1914–18" with a bitterness that lends power to the public statement. The rhythmic and syntactical echoes of his most popular poem, "If . . . ," add a vehemence to the irony:

> When desperate Folly daily laboureth
>   To work confusion upon all we have,
> When diligent Sloth demandeth Freedom's death,
>   And banded Fear commandeth Honour's grave—
> Even in that uncertain hour before the fall,
> Unless men please they are not heard at all.

Despite misgivings about democracy, Kipling celebrates England and English institutions. The psalmodic "A Song for the English," full of Biblical cadences in a strictly rhymed form, has attracted various parodies. "Fair is our lot—O goodly is our heritage!" he says. After five introductory stanzas he presents "a song of broken interludes . . . of lit-tle cunning." The songs are essentially dramatic narratives of England's relations with the sea, Empire, and the duties of the present to those who died in making that Empire. Kipling praises the virtues of severity, resistance, strength, taciturnity and loyalty. He is at pains here and else-where to alert the English at home to their responsibilities. He does this most powerfully in "The Islanders." "The Dykes," a later poem, dra-matically laments irresponsibility. "All that our fathers taught us of old pleases us now no more." The exhortation to "Take up the White Man's burden— / Send forth the best ye breed" comes in a poem that tends to prophetic satire, not jingoism. The responsibility the burden imposes, the reluctance of those who are ruled, the conceit and deceit of admin-istrators, are conveyed in it.

Everywhere in his poetry we are confronted by formidable skill. Though he wrote few fine lyrics, few lyric writers could achieve his bal-ladic forms. In "The Ballad of East and West" his aptitude with long lines is unmatched: "There is rock to the left, and rock to the right, and low lean thorn between, / And ye may hear the breech-bolt snick where never a man is seen." This is the natural, expressive style Kipling evolved: it can deal with surface reality, it can name things—anything, the style is inclusive—and it can suggest depths without damaging the surface. Though it has the veracity of speech, it also has the authority of song.

"The Benefactors," a poem that opens with a parody of Landor, goes on to question the usefulness of art in confronting reality:

> And what is Art whereto we press
>> Through paint and prose and rhyme—
> When nature in her nakedness
>> Defeats us every time?

It is the nakedness Kipling is after. Using popular rhythms, from music hall for instance, the poet approaches a *common* poetry. "Bobs" can be sung to the tune of "She'll Be Coming Round the Mountain"; "Danny Deever," "Fuzzy-Wuzzy," "Tommy," "Gunga Din" and "Mandalay" have the lilt and verve of music-hall turns. Other poems march, others have a pulpit feel about them. "Natural" expression includes humor, a quality in which the early poems abound and which critics tend to overlook.

Insider and outsider: Kipling was an innovator from within a tra-dition, inventing forms, developing rhythms, pursuing a poetry that instructs as it entertains. The instruction is of its period; it repels read-ers with the experience of the Second World War behind them, and young readers who cannot abide incorrect notions. Insistence on racial superiority, on "the Blood" that binds the English, and the paternalistic note reserved for the people of the colonies, grate. But Kipling also wrote *Kim*. His critics deduce his politics selectively, finding in him a crude consistency of thought that the major works themselves belie. Hardy is a pessimist, but not a programmatic one, any more than Kipling is a thoroughgoing racist, sadist, protofascist or feudalist—all terms his critics have applied to him. Each poem aspires to consistency and truth to *itself*. But the poet is neither philosopher nor politician. He retains the essential freedom to change, to start a new book, a new poem, to find a new path or an old path through the woods. As an epitaph for journalists killed in the First World War Kipling inscribed, "We have served our day." This is what he did, in a day when journalism was not merely a job but a vocation, and when ideals of service were not held suspect.

Was he an interpreter of popular will or the inadvertent advocate of a new barbarism, the barbarism inherent in the imperial ideal? Robert Buchanan, a Gladstonian Liberal, characterized him as "the voice of the hooligan," and —yes—we can agree, but beyond the hooligan there is the deep believer, who knows what he has seen and deduces from it what might be, against the current of what actually was happening: the Empire's overextension and eventual decline. "Recessional" is the great poem of Empire, discursive rather than dramatic, expressing anxiety at imperial hubris, the pride before the fall. Like Edward Elgar's music, so Kipling's verse was appropriated by the jingoists. At the victory ceremony for the Boer War outside the Transvaal Parliament, 10,000 soldiers sang "Recessional." Kipling became less popular as he began to question and to stigmatize those who had become his chief admirers. He insisted on the hard truths underlying his—and their—ideology. His popular poems, Eliot says, elicit a *single* response: they shape that response, conforming readership as hymns and prayers conform a congregation—a common language, the vulgar tongue. This instrumentalism would be a profanation of poetry, but Kipling's muse speaks with conviction; she is not bought or compelled, and she is not complacent. "The Islanders" did much to estrange his devoted audience; it was a poisoned chalice he presented them.

> Arid, aloof, incurious, unthinking, unthanking, gelt,
> Will ye loose your schools to flout them till their brow-beat
>   columns melt?
> Will ye pray them or preach them, or print them, or ballot them
>   back from our shore?
> Will your workmen issue a mandate to bid them strike no more?

Will ye rise and dethrone your rulers? (Because ye were idle both?
Pride by Insolence chastened? Indolence purged by Sloth?)

Angus Wilson declares that it "takes each sacred cow of the clubs and
senior common rooms and slaughters it messily before its worship-
pers' eyes." Magisterial, with vehement sarcasm, he turns to the flag
wavers, the lazy, the malingerers, and shows them where they are likely
to fail. They serve false gods, like the chosen people who, in the Bible,
suffer the scourge of the angry prophets. Despite his formal variety, he
always sounds a hectoring note; he *insists* in the way that Marlowe's dra-
matic verse or the Old Testament insists, with severity.

Out of the Old Testament, not the King James Version, but rather
the Hebrew, emerges the first major Jewish voice in English poetry.
Isaac Rosenberg is another poet for whom authority is a central theme,
but who never had a land of content to lose. His rhythms have no
precedent in English verse; his poems are as original as Stephen Crane's,
but in scope and accomplishment much greater. And yet not one of
Rosenberg's poems is *entirely* successful. For him writing poems was a
necessity, and the struggle to find a serviceable idiom very nearly an
agony.

> The troubled throng
> Of words breaks out like smothered fire through dense
> And smouldering wrong.

T. S. Eliot was one of his first advocates. "Let the public ask itself," he
wrote in 1920, "why it has never heard of the poems of T. E. Hulme or
Isaac Rosenberg, and why it has heard of the poems of Lady Precocia
Pondoeuf and has seen a photograph of the nursery in which she wrote
them." Well, for one thing, the poems of Hulme and Rosenberg were
not generally available. More to the point in Rosenberg's case, for all his
promise, he was killed in action before that promise was fulfilled. He
lacks the formal polish, the conventional authority of Owen and Sas-
soon. He had none of their social advantages. From a very different
background, he was feeling his way toward another kind of poetry, a
goal he did not attain, and he left his uneven attempts. But he was the
only poet involved in the First World War who consciously set out to
devise a language to engage with the experience directly, veering neither
into Owen's public rhetoric nor Sassoon's ironizing. He is distinguished
in the canon not only by his exceptional imagination, but also by his
unusual background.

He was born in Bristol in 1890 into a family of Russian Jewish émigrés. At the age of seven, he went with his family to London, moving from relative poverty to actual poverty. He was sent to elementary school in Stepney. When he was fourteen he was apprenticed as an engraver to a firm of "art publishers" and attended evening classes at the Arts School of Birkbeck College. He wanted to become a painter.

In 1911, after his apprenticeship, three ladies from his community provided the wherewithal to send him to the Slade. His graphic work has as many startling qualities as his verse—careful heightenings, subtle distortions, some intentional and some the result of a technique not quite mastered. His boldness at times recalls the line-work of the young Wyndham Lewis, and his portraits are powerful.

When very young he began writing verse and circulated it, attracting some attention. The earliest surviving piece, composed when he was fifteen, is indebted to Byron (including the unusual Byron of the *Hebrew Melodies*); it draws too on his Jewish background, the source of much of his early thematic material. "Ode to David's Harp," with its archaisms, vocatives and unironized enthusiasm, is the work of a boy with natural if unshaped skills. It concludes:

So clearly sweet—so plaintive sad
More tender tone no harper had.
O! when again shall Israel see
A harp so toned with melody?

In 1912 he published privately the first of three pamphlets, *Night and Day,* including principally poems of his adolescence. *Youth* (1915) and *Moses: A Play* (1916) followed. The total extent of his pamphlets, including preliminary matter, is sixty-eight pages. His reputation rests not on these works so much as on the war poems, which were not collected and published in full until nineteen years after his death, by Gordon Bottomley and Denys Harding. Siegfried Sassoon provided an introduction. An inadequate *Selected Poems* had appeared in 1922.

In 1914 Rosenberg traveled to South Africa for his health, but returned the next year, having been unable to make his way as a teacher or portrait painter. He delayed enlisting as long as he could, for he was physically and temperamentally ill suited for military service. Driven by poverty, he finally enlisted, and in 1916 he was sent to France, where he fell in action two years later.

Introducing the *Collected Works*, Sassoon raises several important points. "I have recognised in Rosenberg," he writes, "a fruitful fusion between English and Hebrew culture." Sassoon himself was of Jewish ancestry. He speaks of a "racial quality, biblical and prophetic." With a few exceptions, notably "The Jew," the poems are not about *being* Jewish. The biblical imagery and the strange accent of the poems bring new tonal elements into English.

Sassoon finds the poet "scriptural and sculptural"—he "*modelled* words with fierce energy and aspiration." Rosenberg did not readily accept words as they came to him. He interrogated them, meditated on them, and combined them in startling new ways. The English he uses does not come to him by second nature, as a given. The poet controls his medium, as best he can, at every point. Here is the real "wrestle with words and meanings" that Eliot writes of in *Four Quartets*, a wrestle enacted between the poet and his language, and in the war poems, between the language and the intractable material with which it must deal. What are received diction and form for his Georgian contemporaries are simply inexpressive for him. Language remains dynamic, resistant. Paying little attention to punctuation, concentrating on cadence and image, he never shies away from mixed metaphor or questionable and archaic usage. When he had a war image to convey he did so with resolute objectivity, neither blurring nor heightening the literal. In "Dead Man's Dump" we read, "A man's brains spattered on / A stretcher-bearer's face." He doesn't dwell on the image for effect: the image suffices. The use of the indefinite article suggests generality, and the poem goes on drawing the wider context. This detail takes its place among others, many horrific, others strange or neutral. Rosenberg is not a rhetorician, a photographer or journalist. He's a soldier, his eyes wide with wonder turned on the world that bursts around him. When, describing the dead, he uses in the same poem the image "a lid over each eye," he suggests decomposition, the isolation of the twinned organs of sight in death. Though they decay, the dead are united as well, but not in a sentimental way:

> The grass and coloured clay
> More motion have than they,
> Joined in the great sunk silences.

The sparse hard images are sparked alive by verbs: bones "crunch" under wheels. But his most powerful effects depend on a psalmodic lengthening and shortening of cadence and on words that, without specifying single meanings, carry a burden of suggestion, integrated in the firm but uneasy cadence. Freed from mere description, freed too from prescriptive meaning and association, they find new significance. In "Dead Man's Dump" one stanza wavers between image and symbol, between experience and response:

None saw their spirits' shadow shake the grass,
Or stood aside for the half used life to pass
Out of those doomed nostrils and the doomed mouth,
When the swift iron burning bee
Drained the wild honey of their youth.

There is none of Owen's sugar in that honey. Rosenberg presents time
in war not as a chronology but as an unrelenting present: "The shells go
crying over them / From night till night and now."

In the war poems Rosenberg came close to achieving the kind of
verse his early writings cleared the ground for, though there is an
incompleteness about them which is part of their power. Though they're
more accomplished than his early work, there is continuity between the
apprentice pieces of *Night and Day* and his last poems. In the first pam-
phlet, the poet muses: Is he a god finder or a sin bearer for man? He
wakes in the morning with "a larger capacity to feel and enjoy things";
having "communed with the stars, his soul has exalted itself, and become
wiser in intellectual experience." The burden of the early poems is that
"by thinking of higher things we exalt ourselves to what we think
about." Prophetic and didactic voices dominate. His early poems are
striking not for their achievement but for their oddness, even in the
transitional decade of the 1900s:

Sing to me, for my soul's eyes
Anguish for these ecstasies
And voluptuous mysteries
That must somewhere be,
Or we could not know of them.

There are, too, strange images from vertiginous perspectives of the sort
we get in David Jones:

Sudden the night blazed open at my feet.
Like splintered crystal tangled with gold dust
Blazed on my ear and eye the populous street.

The only stylistic affinities that come to mind are with Blake. The
archaisms are piled on: "starven," "'gainst," the "en-" prefix is used to
make verbs intensive. Language is under pressure, forging its own
resources. Rosenberg, like Lawrence, does without stylistic irony. He
writes because he has something to say, and only poetry will do.

His early poems reject notions of a benevolent God. He comes to
realize that compassion and endurance are not enough. The struggle

against a bad god, against evil generally, even if it is rooted in the maker, is worth undertaking if it effects "realignments" in individual ways of seeing and in social attitudes. Critics note the radical tendencies in his verse and consider his radical approach to prosody and diction, his very openness to experience, to be a political dimension. They may be right, but the radicalism is not necessarily "democratic." There is more in his verse of the seeds of "vorticism," more affinity with the Imagists and modernists than with liberal writers. For him poetry is not instrumental: it is a language of exploration and record, not a suasive tool. Rupert Brooke, Sassoon and Owen write a poetry different in kind from his.

His main theme is power: of god, of evil, or of man. Biblical allusions charge the poems with a volatile energy. He casts himself in the role of Absalom and God in the role of David, and in "Chagrin" describes the inexplicable, unexpected and apparently malevolent power at work, snaring him:

> From the imagined weight
> Of spaces in a sky
> Of mute chagrin, my thoughts
> Hang like branch-clung hair . . .

The formal imagination, peopling empty air with forms, concretizing thought but avoiding apostrophe, is "sculptural," aware of space and its potentialities:

> We ride, we ride, before the morning
> The secret roots of the sun to tread,
> And suddenly
> We are lifted of all we know
> And hang from implacable boughs.

Power includes responsibility—to past and future as well as the present. This is Kipling's theme translated to a metaphysical realm. Irresponsibility has consequences: first causing suffering, then reaction. In "The Dead Heroes" he declares, "Strong as our hurt is strong / Our children are." In a potentially sensational subject matter, there is no sensationalism. He can define through indefinition, as Edgar Allan Poe does, or Milton in hell—and his refusal to make pretty or ugly what is neither pretty nor ugly, what simply *is*, confirms his integrity of purpose. He is always thinking in his poems, especially about language. "Snow is a strange white word," one poem begins. Elsewhere he would "bruise the air" with words. They have magical power, shadowing the things and qualities they denote.

There is humor—sometimes black humor—too. In "Break of Day in the Trenches," his best-known poem, he addresses a rat: "Droll rat, they would shoot you if they knew / Your cosmopolitan sympathies." It has brushed the hands of men in opposing trenches, it has scrabbled among the dead. Later in the poem he plucks a poppy and with careless insouciance places it behind his ear. The tone of the poem wavers but holds, yet in its wavering is the whole force of Rosenberg's art:

Poppies, whose roots are in man's veins
Drop, and are ever dropping;
But mine in my ear is safe—
Just a little white with the dust.

The rhythm of the last two lines, unresolved, observing, is entirely his own. It belongs to the moment of the experience. Rosenberg does not step back or draw a moral. The poem stays in a present tense that will not relinquish its immediacy, that will not release us with a reassuring cadence. Edwin Muir characterized Rosenberg's achievement in these terms: "He gives above all a feeling of power which is not yet certain of itself, which is sometimes tripped up by its own force." At his best he conveys the power of the events that snared him—in the trenches, for example—and will not allow poetic conventions to let him, or us, off that immediate hook. We don't weep at his poems as we do at Owen's; he doesn't deliberately stir up anger like Sassoon. He brings an individual human situation up close, he *exposes* us by evoking his own exposure as calmly as the dawn will allow. When Lawrence was looking for "the urgent, insurgent now," he might have found it in Rosenberg at his best, suspended in the perpetual present of his unchosen circumstances. It is no wonder that in the next world war Keith Douglas, a comparable poet of presence, wrote, "Rosenberg, I only repeat what you were saying."

The First World War was for Housman and for Kipling *another* war. They had lived through earlier ones, and the difference this time was one of scale, of proximity, and of immediate loss—of friends, of a son. Yet for Rosenberg the war was his maturity, the whole of it. And for Rupert Brooke, who died in 1915, it was the canonization. All the younger poets who fell in the war experienced it as something horribly new and unprecedented. Those who fell before the end of 1915 were able to imagine that their endeavor was heroic. Those who survived into the later years of the war, experiencing the camaraderie, bereavement, cold, mud, cruel authority, gas, rats, and the incomprehension of the civilians back home, came to understand its real cost and the vanity of that cost as it seemed to them. Brooke wrote poems—most famously "If I should die"—that were of use to the war effort. Rosenberg wrote poems that could not be put to such use. Sassoon and Owen wrote poems that could be turned against the war, instrumental poems that by shrewd selection and heightening of detail and vivid word magic might be used against the conflict, or at least used to make the civilian population understand the reality—or rather the surreality—of it.

For Owen it began with word magic, a Keatsian program: "Escape? There is one unwatched way: your eyes, / O Beauty! Keep me good that secret gate." His Keats was diluted with early Yeats. He borrowed epigraphs from Yeats, he followed his lushly adjectival example. Yeats did not reciprocate the admiration. When he came to edit the *Oxford Book of Modern Verse* in 1936, he excluded Owen, later describing him as "all blood, dirt, and sucked sugar-stick . . . He calls poets 'Bards,' a girl a 'maid,' and talks about 'Titanic wars.' There is every excuse for him, but none for those who like him." This summary dismissal has at best a grain of truth in it. Did Yeats read beyond the effusive, lush, energyless early poems? Whenever Yeats uses the word "all," it's best to take what he says with a pinch of salt.

But it is also important to approach Owen with as clear a head as possible. His poetry is so closely linked with his death, his sentiments, and the almost sacred cloak that posterity has draped around his ghost, that an assessment of his actual achievement and contribution is hard. Sylvia Plath is the only other poet whose life, death and work are so closely interfused. Martyr-poets both. Rosenberg, T. E. Hulme and Edward Thomas were not martyrs in the same sense. They belonged to the wrong set.

Owen's poems answer certain preconceptions about poetry and war: for those reared on Palgrave's *Golden Treasury*, they are reassuringly traditional, even in their formal innovations. They seem true, even if they do not extend but rather endorse and clarify what the *bien pensant* already believe or feel. Owen's work helped to shape postwar beliefs and feelings as, early in the war, Rupert Brooke's helped to stimulate the patriotic nerve. Do Owen's poems *now* evoke experiences, or merely feed preconceptions? A naïve reader is drawn to the appealing naïveté of Owen's changing passions as he is exposed to war and the issues it raises, to Sassoon and the issues he raises. Owen attracts serious artists too, notably Benjamin Britten, whose *War Requiem* expanded Owen's audience and added a haunting extra element to the poems. Britten's choice of texts was political: his pacifism found in the elegiac, the sardonic and the vatic Owen the words it needed, their authenticity heightened by the poet's death. Britten chose the poems for other reasons, too. There is a challenging prosody, and a clear development yielding a mighty emotional charge.

Owen was born in 1893 in Oswestry, Shropshire, where he spent a pampered childhood. At the age of ten he visited rural Broxton by the Hill and—in Wordsworthian fashion—his poetic vocation was affirmed. There, "First I felt my boyhood fill / With uncontainable movements; there was born / My poethood." He wrote copiously in his early years. His education was conducted at the Birkenhead Institute, at the Shrewsbury Technical College, and at London University. Edmund Blunden recalls that Owen tended to choose his friends for what he could get out of them—intellectual stimulus, principally. His first master was Keats, whom he celebrated and to whose shrines he made pilgrimage. His early devotion to the beautiful is often expressed in a Keatsian spirit. Gray, Shelley, Tennyson, Arnold and Swinburne colored his imagination, too: it was steeped in elegiac Romanticism.

In 1913 he wrote half seriously of his plan to publish "Minor Poems—in Minor Keys—By a Minor." The early writings are little more. Sharp, sensuous passages do occur, but set in a relentless tide of assonance and alliteration. The "music" of poetry drew him: sounds generally but especially the sounds of instruments are mimed:

I have been gay with trivial fifes that laugh;
And songs more sweet than possible things are sweet;
And gongs, and oboes.

Ineffable "sweetness" and "music" made him overfond of adjectives, which clot the verse and steal the limelight from perfectly adequate nouns. The adjectives often draw out qualities already implicit in the verbs. "Pale flakes with *fingering* stealth come *feeling down* our faces" is perilously close to tautology. Sound, not sense, dictates unhappy epithets even in the major poems: "dull rumour" and (Yeats is responsible for this one) "the poignant misery of the dawn" in "Exposure," for instance. Agony treated in this way becomes mellifluous, aestheticized. The language betrays its occasion into mere pretext. In the first eight lines of the sonnet "The Seed," another fault appears: the seven-times repeated syntactical construction, "the—of the—." Dylan Thomas learned some of his less convincing strategies from such redundant rhetoric.

Owen may have been entranced by the poetic "music" of the French poet Paul Verlaine. He spent two years teaching English in France (1913–15) and made some literary friendships. He read Baudelaire, and through him turned his attention back to English poetry and Swinburne, Baudelaire's first English advocate. He realized how the French writers he admired were all transgressors, men who got in trouble with the police, who went to and beyond the limits of convention, as their admirer Oscar Wilde had done. Verlaine cast a salutary gloom over Owen's early exuberance, though the melancholy tone does not entirely suit him—until he has a suitable subject. Love might have been such a subject: the 1916 sonnet that begins "Three rompers . . ." refers back to a time of innocent male love and ends with the line "The sea is rising . . . and the world is sand"; in "To Eros" of the same year, he casts himself in the role of Psyche. These unposturing, almost direct expressions of sexual perspective have the candor of Shakespeare's disappointed sonnets. They strike a note unlike the decadent strains of the fin-de-siècle. But they strike it only a few times, unassertively, and until recent years it has been a polite convention to look the other way when passing by these poems.

In 1915 Owen enlisted in the Artists' Rifles. Under intolerable stress he was invalided out in 1917 and convalesced for a time near Edinburgh. There he became friendly with the already established and dissident poet Siegfried Sassoon. They discussed poetry and other topics and Owen's admiration knew no bounds. His letters were always fulsome, but those he wrote to and of Sassoon achieve absurd adolescent intensity. He calls Sassoon his "Keats + Christ + Elijah + my Colonel + my father-confessor + Amenophus IV, in profile." No doubt Sassoon's enthusiasm for the promising work of an attractive young man helped bolster Owen's confidence. Sassoon was a poet of considerable accomplishment, undervalued today. In 1917 Owen was able to report proudly to his mother: "I am held peer by the Georgians."

Sassoon talked about the war and war in general—and the Christian duty of passivity before violence, as well as other problems of conscience. Owen agreed—even his letters from the front echo Sassoon's sentiments. He became less a poet than a "war poet," his mission to tell those at home, in the clearest terms, what the trenches were like, how fear of death and the presence of suffering numbed the sensitive men or drove them mad. This was Sassoon's theme and mission, too: to make the civilian population sensible to its responsibilities (Kipling's mission, with a new twist). Home on leave, Owen carried photographs of the war injured to illustrate his point.

Psychologists have got to work on the biographical material. Owen has been characterized—reductively—as an "injustice collector." A sense of duty coupled with a gnawing masochism sent him back to the front, and after writing more poems and enduring the worst of the last campaign, he was awarded the Military Cross but was killed the week before the Armistice, in 1918. Edith Sitwell and Siegfried Sassoon published the first collection of his poems in 1920.

In some ways he resembles the once equally idolized Rupert Brooke. Unlike Brooke, however, he was not known by his trench comrades as a poet and thus preserved a receptive anonymity. Like Brooke's, his poetic approach was rhetorical; his aim, to adjust the new subject matter to the old forms. For him poetry was instrumental, a form of witness and also of propaganda. It must be suasive, not only evocative: it must contain the experience but also, implicit or explicit, a moral conclusion. Though he reverses Brooke's "noble heroics," his attempts at realism are parallel to Brooke's. Brooke had the audacious gumption to describe seasickness in a satiric poem—an experience not celebrated in English poetry since Byron's *Don Juan*. Owen, who lived through most of the war, takes harder risks, describing for example the effect of gas on soldiers. Brooke's poems were used to advance the war cause; Owen's, no less emotive, would have served pacifism had they been collected during his lifetime, and did so after his death. Each poet put his rather different new wine in old bottles.

"The new material, if it could be presented at all, needed a profound linguistic invention," C. H. Sisson has written. Owen lacked that originality. He did experiment effectively with what Edmund Blunden called "para-rhyme"—off-rhymes such as "head" / "lad"—and Blunden praises the effect. Less successfully he experimented with internal rhyme, strong assonance and alliteration. Such experiments developed or refined common poetic techniques. His approach is not formally radical, his blend of irony and pity not new—we have it in Hardy, Housman and Kipling, and earlier in Landor, Arnold and Clough. Only the subject matter is wholly new, and his fascination with the detail of physical suffering.

At heart Owen is less a realist than an idealist. He is drawn to the ugly and sordid *because* he is attracted to the beautiful. His passion for poetry is not, and never could have been, overwhelmed by pity. Others among the Georgians face the same problem; masked as realists, they follow beauty down urban alleyways and into the trenches. Adapting to "the ugly" the rhetoric attached conventionally to "the beautiful," they elicit a plangent irony from the misalliance of language and subject matter. Rosenberg and Edward Thomas are exceptional, discerning in extreme experience the convention-purged, unique language and forms it requires.

When Owen realized how poignantly the hideous can be conveyed in terms previously reserved for the beautiful, his work developed suddenly and decisively. But traditional poetic diction, traditional meters and forms, particularly Keatsian, entail a certain neutralizing moral effect. They depend on balance, proportion and perspective, qualities that, since they are absent from the war experience, the poet has to fabricate, resorting to irony and to those forms that, with a final couplet, nudge away the immediate, rhetoricize or sentimentalize it. Pain does not groan or scream and break the form open; poise is never violated.

The resonance is in understatement, an accepting irony, a very English tone. This is why Owen's poems are susceptible to musical setting where Rosenberg's are not: the expression can be left to the music, since the unspoken anguish in the vivid reportage *remains* unspoken—that is its force. In Rosenberg form and language answer to content: they do not neutralize but realize it. Owen can express intense love and describe intense physical agony in the same forms. The maimed man and the pastoral landscape are given in the same rhythms. Owen sensed this neutralizing effect and tried to overcome it by moralizing. In "Disabled" he displays his war photographs, and with grotesque sexual overtones dwells in fascinated detail on wounds.

What makes Owen a war poet, while Thomas and Rosenberg, both victims of the war, have a broader remit, is the biographical accident that Owen was very young and inexperienced when he went into the trenches. Thomas and Rosenberg had endured a life of hardship; the war was for them an extreme experience in a life of experiences. The war was Owen's big experience, his one theme. It supplied its own absolute context.

In the famous "Preface" to the poems—rough notes, not a finished, gnomic essay—he is naturally dominated by the immediate experience. He promises a rhetorical and moralistic collection. The youthful arrogance—"This book is not about heroes. English poetry is not yet fit to speak of them"—is pardonable only in the light of the achieved poems. "Above all," he writes, "I am not concerned with Poetry." In fact—unlike Rosenberg—he is so concerned with "poetry" that the force of much of his war experience is excluded from the poems.

Poets of the Second World War turned to models other than Owen. Keith Douglas turned to Rosenberg, Alun Lewis to Edward Thomas. The reason is clear: Douglas and Rosenberg are concerned with power, with the moral and psychological issues of human motive, and the lasting transformations that war effects in men. Owen's concern is with phenomena, vivid externals, and the poems are in the end didactic rather than psychologically or, indeed, morally penetrating. His models are taken over from the nineteenth century, his grotesques are romantic, his beauty is late romantic.

The achievement of Owen's poems is considerable, and Rosenberg, from whom one can learn so much, left no poem as finished, as solidly made, as the best of Owen's early or mature work. Owen's poems not directly about the war contain a violence of a different kind. "Shadwell Stair" is a fanciful, disturbing "spirit of the place" poem:

I am the ghost of Shadwell Stair.
    Along the wharves by the water-house,

> And through the dripping slaughter-house,
> I am the shadow that walks there.

Other pieces are less felicitous. In "Fragment: 'Cramped in the Funnelled Hole,'" he overwrites. In nine lines, the possessive runs rife: "yawn *of* death," "middle *of* his throat *of* phlegm," "one *of* many mouths *of* Hell," "teeth *of* traps," "odour *of* the shell," and so on. In "Arms and the Boy" the overwritten insistent alliteration issues in bathetic, weirdly erotic sentiment: "Lend him to stroke these blind, blunt bullet-heads / Which long to nuzzle in the hearts of lads." We can contrast this with the entirely appropriate word choice in "Conscious": "The blind cord *drawls* across the window-sill." That subtle, disorienting synesthesia drew Edith Sitwell to the poems.

The authority of his command of traditional forms makes for dramatic climaxes and conclusions. "The Parable of the Old Man and the Young" retells, with a savage twist, the story of Abraham and Isaac. Religion, tradition, leadership, are pilloried. "Greater Love" and "Dulce et Decorum" are driven by an even more vigorous rhetoric. As indictments of war they cannot be surpassed. The specific historical reality that has given rise to them, their occasion in the history of conflict between nations, pales into insignificance. Nations, their values and institutions, disappear in the blinding light of Owen's irony. It is this that gives them their durability as poems of use. But we can see—when rhetoric breaks down—just how intellectually thin his characters are, how psychologically unrealized his monsters of authority. In "The Dead-Beat" a doctor laughs at the death of a supposed malingerer: "That scum you sent last night soon died. Hooray." In "The Next War" a similar tonal miscalculation occurs.

Subject matter apart, Owen's great originality is found in certain spare, carefully worked passages where movement from line to line is heartrending: at once surprising and in retrospect inevitable. Some of the best lines occur in "Asleep," constructed for the most part of monosyllables:

> After the many days of work and waking,
> Sleep took him by the brow and laid him back.
> And in the happy no-time of his sleeping
> Death took him by the heart.

The few adjectives are simply chosen. If in the lines that follow he forfeits the force achieved here, these lines are a satisfactory climax in a less than satisfactory poem.

Owen finished few poems to his absolute satisfaction. They exist in several drafts, and the invidious task of piecing together authoritative versions has fallen to his editors. We may imagine, from the passage above, that Owen would have pared down his overwriting, further adjusted his forms, and extended the best of the longer poems, "Strange Meeting." The perfection of "Futility"—which does not once specifically mention the war—shows what finality he could achieve. And "Anthem for Doomed Youth" mingles pastoral and war imagery to the point of resigned heartbreak.

"Hospital Barge at Cérisy"—a sonnet of late 1917, not much anthologized—achieves in the sestet (after a labored octave) an effect as rare in Owen's work as it is in modern English poetry: a sudden fusion, in a moment of broken quietness, of allusions from various areas of experience, a poetic rather than a rhetorical resonance. "Her" in the second line quoted here refers to the barge.

> One reading by the sunset raised his eyes
> To watch her lessening westward quietly,
> Till, as she neared the bend, her funnel screamed.
> And that long lamentation made him wise
> How unto Avalon, in agony,
> Kings passed in the dark barge, which Merlin dreamed.

The echo of Yeats's version of Ronsard, "When you are old," may be heard in the first two lines. But Owen moves on to a momentary transformation here well beyond the scope of Yeats's early style. It is a natural grandeur of statement, intuitive and unanswerable.

"A language not to be betrayed . . ."

W. B. YEATS, THE RHYMERS' CLUB,
EDWARD THOMAS, ROBERT FROST

When Wilfred Owen was a boy Yeats was already camped above the snow line on Parnassus. He was active on many fronts, in England, Ireland and America; he communed with the spirit world, with his own mythologized past, and with the legends of Ireland. Through the Rhymers' Club he knew the latest French poetry. When Owen was an adolescent, Yeats was running out of puff, but help was on its way, crossing the high seas: the young Ezra Pound, bound for Europe.

William Butler Yeats's life is a tangled complex of fortuitous meetings, chance influences, intellectual inconsistencies, a sequence of dramatic public and private conflicts played out in a personality that was in crucial ways very simple: his docile vanity, the sincerity of his political vacillations, his human devotion. A man alive in his time, he never stood still but built and built on what had come before—not a coherent Palladian edifice but a Disneyland castle of halls and turrets and pinnacles and buttresses. The late poems follow the same thematic concerns as the earlier, but the poet of the fin-de-siècle is different in kind from the engaged twentieth-century poet. From 1887 to 1939 he moved from a deliciously resigned passivity to tense engagement, from adjectives to verbs. His more than half a century of verse constitutes an *oeuvre* more exemplary and, in the end, more coherent than any other poet's of his time except for Eliot and Stevens. How much more "intolerable struggle with words and meanings" there is in late Yeats than in late Eliot; how much less tinsel even in the over-decorated poems of the fin-de-siècle than in Stevens's luminous constructions.

Yeats was born in Dublin in 1865. His father, John Butler Yeats, was an accomplished painter. His mother, Susan Pollexfen, was a member of an old Anglo-Irish family that Yeats liked to consider aristocratic. The Anglo-Irish background—Protestant in religion, yet guardedly Republican in sentiment—was characterized by strongly held and hotly debated opinions on various topics, not least art and literature.

Much of his childhood he spent in London, where his parents moved in 1867. They lived off income from family lands in Kildare until 1880, when the Land War put an end to it. In 1875 Yeats entered the Godolphin School in Hammersmith and visited Ireland during the longer school vacations, when he stayed with the Pollexfens in County Sligo. An early poetic impulse was to change the name of his toy yacht from *Sunbeam* to *Moonbeam*. It was a decisive act.

In 1880 the Yeats family returned to Dublin, and until 1883 William attended the High School in Harcourt Street. Then he entered the School of Art. The first of his verses were published in 1885. This precocious apprentice work was shown to Father Gerard Manley Hopkins, then serving in Dublin. The priest described the work in a letter to Coventry Patmore as "a strained and unworkable allegory about a young man and a sphinx on a rock in the sea (how did they get there? what did they eat? and so on; people think such criticisms very prosaic, but common-sense is never out of place anywhere . . .) but still containing fine lines and vivid imagery." It was a long time before Yeats and common sense reached some sort of accommodation. In a review of William Morris written late in 1896, Yeats foresaw a time when William Morris, not Shelley, would become "the type of the poet: for he more than any man of modern days tried to change the life of his time into the life of his dream." His review plays with the giant counters of beauty and the age, hovering some distance above its subject and saying volubly almost nothing at all. He was repaying a debt to a poet he admired, who had expressed admiration of his work. It was a rhetorical gesture of piety.

Fatefully, in 1886 Yeats attended his first séance. His passion for spiritualism and magic was already far advanced: whatever voices he heard on that occasion exacerbated his enthusiasm and he set up regular rendezvous with the spirits, who generously provided him with occasions for verse. A passion for things Irish developed too, and he read Irish poetry and the Gaelic sagas in translation. He began to question the motives of the Anglo-Irish. In 1887, a resolute Irishman, he moved back to London and became a Theosophist.

In London he was active in literature and politics. One particular event in 1889 proved crucial: he met and fell in love with the fiery Republican who haunted him for the rest of his days, Maud Gonne. His biography, from 1889 until Maud Gonne's marriage, is punctuated by the statement, "Yeats proposed to Maud Gonne."

It was 1891 when he became involved with the Rhymers' Club, a group of poets who met regularly at the Cheshire Cheese, Fleet Street, and discussed everything—especially poetry. Lionel Johnson and Ernest Dowson became his close friends. Johnson instructed him in philosophy. Arthur Symons, the outstanding poet-critic of the 1890s, frequented the club and Yeats shared rooms with him in 1895. Symons laid out European literature before him, directed his attention to Mallarmé, Calderón, St. John of the Cross and others. Unlike the Rhymers, who, apart from the harsh and impecunious John Davidson (a substantial figure), practiced an aesthetic of "art for art's sake," Yeats came to feel that "literature must be the expression of conviction, and be the garment of noble emotion, and not an end in itself." Perhaps his Irish convictions made him proof against the feathery seductions of aestheticism, but he never denied his debt to the "Poets with whom I learned my trade, / Companions of the Cheshire Cheese . . ."

Blake and Shelley, too, alerted the young Yeats to the fact that there was more potential in poetry than was dreamed of in the Rhymers' philosophy. With Edwin Ellis, he prepared an edition of Blake's poems (1893). Blake and Shelley had more impact on his beliefs and sentiments— his sense of the poet's identity, social function and imaginative scope— than on his poetic techniques, though he may have learned from their grandiloquence, and he was not above borrowing a phrase or two when he needed it. Blake opened a wider highway toward symbolism than the French poets Symons set before him.

London and Paris were his meccas at the time. In Paris he encouraged the dramatist John Synge. In 1896 he met Lady Augusta Gregory (1852–1932) and formed a courtly and devoted friendship with her which proved durable and creative. In succeeding years he spent time at Coole Park, her estate, studying folklore and plotting an Irish renaissance. In 1897 they invented the Abbey Theatre, which opened in Dublin in 1904. Yeats wrote many of his verse plays for the Abbey. Indeed, it exercised his patience, rhetoric and spleen for years and helped to modify his naïve social idealism because of the politics it elicited.

In 1908 his *Collected Works* were issued in eight volumes. He was forty-three, a poet of established reputation, a dramatist and prose writer, a lecturer at home and abroad. He felt drained of energy. He had reached the end of his first period of creative activity. It was to this period that Owen was indebted.

Critics lay insufficient stress on the effect Ezra Pound had on Yeats's development. Returning from the funeral of Synge, he met the young Pound in 1909, and Pound, who had admired his work since his school days, was often with him from that time until his death, at one time an intimate friend who acted as best man at his wedding and witnessed his will. Pound entered Yeats's life when Yeats seemed played out, his way forward unclear. He was reading Ben Jonson, he was trying to *speak* in verse, to find new energy. In Basil Bunting's terms, he was trying to escape from the aesthetic to the documentary tradition.

Yeats had never encountered a character like Pound: American from the Midwest, not New England, passionately devoted to his art, hugely well read (without scholarly inhibitions), opinionated, free of the English burden of tradition, willing to consider poetic resources from far afield. From the time of their acquaintance, new particularity and concreteness enter Yeats's verse. The change is not in the approach to content only, but in diction as well. Pound, the younger man, almost in the role of apprentice, must have discussed corrections and revisions with Yeats, bringing out tendencies already implicit in his style. We can imagine him hacking away at the lush undergrowth of adjectives, resisting the passive voice and weak verbs, as he was to do so decisively when, later, T. S. Eliot gave him the typescript of *The Waste Land*.

In 1913 Yeats was awarded a Civil List pension and in 1915 refused a knighthood, the Irish in him strengthening against institutional seductions. In 1917 he bought his "castle" in Ballylee—near Coole Park and Lady Gregory. Little more than a broken tower and cottages, it was to Yeats replete with legendary resonances. This was altogether an active year. It included three proposals of marriage to three different women. The last accepted, and at fifty-two Yeats was married.

The Nobel Prize for literature came his way in 1923; later he was a senator in the Irish Parliament. His health began to deteriorate and, in 1924, suffering from high blood pressure and respiratory problems, he repaired to Sicily, where he was enthralled by the Byzantine mosaics. In his illness he entered an intensely creative period, composing *The Tower* poems and some of *The Winding Stair*. His friends' deaths, his own slow physical deterioration, the political turmoil of Ireland and Europe, bore in upon him. His most heartfelt loss was Lady Gregory, who died in 1932. He wrote her a heroic and tender elegy. Certainly, without her he would have been a very different poet.

Taking practical steps to retain his sexual potency, he subjected himself to the Steinach operation in 1934. But he was unarguably old. Spending more and more time in the congenial climate of southern France, he died in 1939 and was buried at Roquebrune. His body was returned to Sligo and reinterred there in 1948.

Yeats was haunted by the idea of the great *poet* more than the great *poem*. Poetry was a mode of identity; the poems often divert attention back to the poet as a kind of *vates*, or priest. He works toward an irrefutable art, evanescent, mysterious, hermetic, which only yields up its content fully to the initiate. Art defends and defines the self. He takes a cue from the Irish bards, but at the same time aligns himself finally with the dwindling Anglo-Irish aristocracy. In "Coole Park and Ballylee, 1931" he writes, "We were the last romantics—chose for theme / Traditional sanctity and loveliness," embattled in a world hostile to art. "My poetry is generally written out of despair," he reports. "Like Balzac, I see increasing commonness everywhere, and like Balzac I know no one who shares the premises from which I work." That conscious identification with great writers of the past is characteristic. He seeks a lonely legitimacy by association with other solitary geniuses. The autobiography to which he treats us is never quite *true*. The lines are boldly traced, but significant details are omitted. Pure reality withers him. He fails to understand psychology, to credit causal relationships. His eye is always on the larger form and on its effect, what it tells and how the teller appears in it. This helps to explains the simplicity of his political and social views: at points of crisis they define themselves in tendentious ways. The reluctance of Irish people to accept his or his friends' art—at the Abbey, or at the Art Museum—soured his political optimism. Though he thought he despised bourgeois interests, he voted as a senator with peers, bankers, lawyers and businessmen against the representatives of the humbler classes. Many poems develop the theme—notably "Upon a House Shaken by the Land Agitation" and "To a Wealthy Man who Promised a Second Subscription to the Dublin Municipal Gallery if it were Proved the People Wanted Pictures."

Early on he had a political ambition to reconcile the courteous Protestant with Ireland's martyred, repressed Roman Catholic heritage. One vehicle for this, he thought, might be the recovery of Irish legend and poetry. Yet he did not want his writing to become local to Ireland. "I thought we might bring the halves together if we had a national literature that made Ireland beautiful in the memory, and yet had been freed of provincialism by an exacting criticism, a European pose." Later he wrote, "All literature created out of a conscious political aim in the long run creates weakness by creating a habit of unthinking obedience. Literature created for its own sake, for some eternal spiritual need, can be used for politics. Dante is said to have unified Italy. The more unconscious the creation, the more powerful." It was not a *new* Ireland Yeats was prophesying. First he sang the ancient, and then the moribund, apparently heroic Anglo-Irish aristocracy. But the people who were Ireland's present and future, by their actions and through their representatives, disappointed him.

He craved mystery rooted in the "unconscious." In his parlance this is not a psychological term but something larger, a place of unalloyed (if unacknowledged) commonality. In an extravagant moment he claimed that he could believe in all that has ever been believed—the onus of disproof is on the unbeliever. The impulse toward the unknown led him to hermetic pursuits, yet his ideal worlds are—like his vision of the past—materialistic and literal, even when moonlit: this world made better, more heroic and powerful, more ceremonious, emancipated from old age and other human disabilities, but perceptible and rewarding to the five senses. Out of the desire to give form to mystery, and an inability to give it form except in images of our world, grew his interest in communication with other regions, even with the dead.

He evolved a pseudo-geometry, a system of gyres, lunar phases, degrees of subjectivity and objectivity. A desire for conceptual order complements a desire for mystery. He was, after all, an admirer of the eighteenth-century Anglo-Irish writers Burke, Berkeley, Goldsmith and Swift, whom he loved: their solidity and cogency attracted him. Fortunately his elaborate theories, elucidated at length in *A Vision* (1925), are not crucial to an appreciation of the poems, though Yeats found them enabling. The critic and classical scholar C. M. Bowra, who knew the poet during his time at Oxford, once told me that these airy constructs were as real for Yeats, "as a Christian's faith is real." Each aspect of them drew legitimacy from some hermetic antecedent, so that Yeats could claim to be not a discoverer but a rearranger and interpreter of received wisdom.

His systems certainly enabled him to externalize inner conflicts. From 1909 to 1911 he was intimate with the spirits. He discovered his spiritual opposite, Leo Africanus, and they corresponded: that is, Yeats wrote him letters to which he (through Yeats) replied. Leo helped him to a kind of self-knowledge. This self-clarification is apparent in several poems, notably "Hic et Ille," a dialogue that Pound nicknamed "Hic et Willie." To find himself, the poet had to discover an image of himself, through opposites.

Opposites provide a constant tension in Yeats's work. He swings between extremities: spontaneity versus craft, laughter versus seriousness, mask versus face, spiritual excitement versus sexual agony. The poems set out to bring into tension and retain in tension contrasts or opposites, chiefly that between Leda and Lethe, physical love and death. He declared that "sex and death are the only things that can interest a serious mind." Certainly his best poems are those written in expectation of death, with the joys of physical passion still agitating him.

From the outset he had two stylistic impulses in his writing: a highly cadenced style for shadows and mystery; and a stark, phrased, declarative style, with precise images for specific meanings. His development is in the shifting balance between the two styles in response to changes in his ambitions and passions. The early poems, rooted in romanticized Celtic legend, full of abstract emotion, are governed by the first style. In his middle period, where the poems draw on biographical, historical and local particulars, ideas and emotions become more specific and the two styles come into an unsatisfactory balance. The final period is characterized by a stark, precise and spoken style, the poems based on biographical and local particulars, but now with a specific emotional and intellectual content. Naturally in each period there are poems that foreshadow later developments or reecho earlier achievement.

In the early writing his evasive symbolism depersonalizes the poems. In the later work it becomes a probing instrument. But even those symbols drawn from life in *The Tower* have meanings ascribed to them. The meanings do not inhere in the objects in a particular context. In his middle and late poems Yeats frequently explicates symbols within the poem, for fear that we might miss their meaning. In "A Prayer for my Daughter," for instance, we are reminded in the unsuccessful final explication, "ceremony's a name for the rich horn, / And custom for the spreading laurel tree." This is the problem of essentially arbitrary symbolism. Early symbols, the rose for example, tend to humanize the ideal. Later symbols, especially the mask, tend to idealize the human. His early attempt to draw the numinous and mysterious into his symbols becomes an attempt to transform what is crudely human into something numinously heroic or ceremonious, sanctified and mysterious.

The poetry is always heard, not overheard. It is a poetry of all but social evasion. There is little intimacy about Yeats. Richard Ellmann, his best reader, writes that his "mastery seems almost excessive" at times, bordering on "overmastery." This is not the huge competence of Auden, at play in the toy shop of poetic form, but *mastery*, the possession of a unique rhetoric for use on a real but limited range of themes. It is a mastery so complete that it can occlude the genuinely problematic, ride over the potholes of nonsense without even sensing them. Late in life he recognizes the evasiveness of his symbols, the tendency of his verse to turn away or inward, and in the concentrated intensity of the late poems he tries to remedy this. But he has an imperfect sense of generality; he is willing to plump out a truism as truth. As his mastery increases, his art becomes less truthful. But his main concern is not—until the later poems, and even there in an attenuated spirit—truth, but the house of myth and legend, where he can become a principal tenant, where it is his voice we hear casting the spell, and where real men are reduced—or, in his mind, enlarged—to masks, figures and types useful to myth, regardless of the human reality they had. If he assumes a mask, so must they. "In Memory of Major Robert Gregory" falsifies by masking the real characters of Lionel Johnson, John Synge and George Pollexfen. He does not epitomize: he caricatures. Real persons, events and occasions are trimmed to serve his rhetorical purposes. Yet the poems speak with the authority of a truth teller. The disparity between the quality of statement and the quality of witness weakens our trust in the poet, a fact that for some readers devalues the poems.

While Hardy's sense of the individual's isolation is based on memory (accidents of biography make us utterly distinct), Yeats's sense of isolation derives from his self-consciousness. Aware of his otherness, he knows that others project different roles on him. He accepts the projections and assumes masks, building several myths around himself. The poems continually refer back to the poet. In "The Indian to his Love" Yeats writes, "A parrot sways upon a tree / Raging at his own image in the enamelled sea." The only experiences powerful enough to deliver us from self-consciousness are sexual love and the apprehension of death.

In the early collections *Crossways* (1889) and *The Rose* (1893), the poems are of mood rather than feeling. He later referred to their "unmanliness." The rose was a useful symbol. Crucified, it suffered with the sufferer. It hung upon the cross of time. It carried its traditional symbolic meanings from religion, but in Yeats's early poems came to stand for Ireland and Maud Gonne as well: "Red Rose, proud Rose, sad Rose of all my days!" How like Valéry's later cadence, in *"Le Cimitière Marine," "Vrai ciel, beau ciel, regardez mois, qui change!"* But to what a different end the symbolism works: for Valéry the passion is intense and exploratory, a bodied longing; for Yeats it is nostalgic, rueful, courtliness without hope of consummation. Yet it bears a large weight of association for the poet. The rose is never *real*. Gertrude Stein might have said of his early verse, "A rose isn't a rose isn't a rose."

These poems are peculiarly unimpassioned in their passionate, tricked-out romantic sentiment, deliciously affecting but ineffectual. Yet there is an impression of almost classical control:

Rose of all Roses, Rose of all the world!
The tall thought-woven sails, that flap unfurled
Above the tide of hours . . .

"The Lake Isle of Innisfree" is popular in part because in it a romantic theme is treated in a fully romantic idiom.

The sense of control results from Yeats's insistent use of intransitive verbs, participles, and "to be" constructions, especially in the shorter lyrics; and from his partiality to the genitive construction, "the—of—," rather than the simple possessive. Such habits of language extend and loosen the rhythms. The intransitive verbs are a pseudo-"classical" element, stilling the romantic noun and adjective content. The rhythms flow, while the images and symbols suffer from a strange inertia. In "The Pity of Love" and "The Sorrow of Love" he holds back the transitive verbs to good effect, deploying them at the climax. But generally the intransitive verbs, so at odds with the rhythm, suggest passivity and dream.

In the Seven Woods (1904), Yeats's worst collection, marks a transition. The poems are coldly made. In "The Ragged Wood" one noun, for instance, carries a burden of adjectives and one prepositional phrase: "that sliding silver-shoed / Pale silver-proud queen-woman of the sky . . ." This is the excess that seduced the young Owen's ear, an excess picked up like a virus from Swinburne. It was six years before Yeats published his next collection, years spent writing plays, working for the Abbey, and reconsidering his diction. *The Green Helmet and Other Poems* (1910) shows him grown more lean and supple, having learned something from composing poetic dialogue for the stage and hearing actors making sense and nonsense of his verse. But still the poetry is statuesque, static through intellectualized emotion, verbally intransitive. Emotion prompts the questions, intellect shapes them and their implicit or explicit replies. Yeats had still to learn his own lesson: "The more unconscious the creation the more powerful."

Responsibilities (1914) was published two years after Pound had sought Yeats out as a master and taken him in hand. Pound's influence may be felt in the Chinese dedicatory couplet, but more in a new tautness, the way ideas are realized not by moralizing, but in the symbols themselves. There is a new containment, a different kind of authority in the public tone he adopts in some of the poems. When he attacks bourgeois philistinism and chastises the misled humbler classes, he experiments with the severe satire of the bardic poets. He contrasts Renaissance patrons and audiences with the boorish, penny-pinching public servants, the unresponsive public. The jingling of the till now exceeds in sweetness the plucking of the poet's harp. In "September 1913" he laments, "Romantic Ireland's dead and gone, / It's with O'Leary in the grave." It hardly matters that such an Ireland never existed: for Yeats it did. The Irish heroes and martyrs perished to make way for a pusillanimous bourgeois order:

> What need you, being come to sense,
> But fumble in a greasy till
> And add the halfpence to the pence
> And prayer to shivering prayer, until
> You have dried the marrow from the bone?

"Come to sense": a loaded phrase. Such calculating "sense," without mystery, a world away from the Augustan tradition he admired, is to Yeats base sterility. Scornfully he adds, "For men were born to pray and save." In a later poem, "The Seven Sages," he defined the Whiggery he detested:

> ... What is Whiggery?
> A levelling, rancorous, rational sort of mind
> That never looked out of the eye of a saint
> Or out of a drunkard's eye.

Responsibilities is full of beggars, hermits, outcasts, people whose gifts are rejected and whose sacrifices are vain. Men should be responsible to the heroes and patriots, true to the constituency whose sacrifice cleared a space for Ireland. The new vigor of the verse is reflected in precision and concreteness of imagery, in the more real-seeming passions, and in the active verb forms. "The Mountain Tomb" is full of active verbs—a poem in motion, purger of the "unmanly" passive voice. Anger and disillusion shake the dreamer awake.

The Wild Swans at Coole (1919) is Yeats's first great modern collection, a book that is of a piece and touches his world at every point. The wild swans sail on the lake in Lady Gregory's estate. They're natural, beautiful, powerful; most important, they return, they have a noble freedom and a noble permanence. "That crowd, that barbarous crowd" are the antagonists. "In Memory of Major Robert Gregory" reveals Yeats's subtle sense of poetic organization. He sets out to recall "the friends that cannot sup with us": first, Lionel Johnson, a recluse too learned for this world; then Synge, recluse too, dedicated not to scholarship but to social observation; last among the ghosts, George Pollexfen, a horseman and withdrawn observer of the stars. Major Gregory, an active man and an artist, embodies the virtues found singly in the other ghosts. "Soldier, scholar, horseman, he": a Renaissance man. The poem works to its climax by progression through great men to the Great Man, the occasion of the poem. The effect is broad-brush: the various ghosts are simplified, the word "all" as a vague, gesturing stroke occurs more than fourteen times.

Yeats is fascinated by the possibility of modern heroism, in an age in which the causes one might wish to fight and die for are hopelessly vitiated. "An Irish Airman Foresees his Death" calls up a pilot (Major Gregory again) motivated by no social or religious commitments, but by "a lonely impulse of delight"—a sufficient motive for heroic action in a spiritually impoverished world.

In *The Wild Swans at Coole* the poet begins to age rapidly. The mythologized autobiography is potent—an "I" myth replaces the "we" myth of earlier poems. Yeats begins to explore and enlarge unique, individual experience. "To a Young Beauty" is a trifle arrogant, "The Scholars," excessively scornful. But he can be scornful of himself—or the self he presents to us—as well. In "Lines Written in Dejection" he laments the passing of magic, the lunar vision, and accepts the "embittered," "timid" sun. He craves—or says he craves—simple rustic readers, "the wise simple man." In "The Fisherman" this reader resembles an idealized version of his own youth:

> . . . "Before I am old
> I shall have written him one
> Poem maybe as cold
> And passionate as the dawn."

He reworked his poems tirelessly. Sometimes he began from a prose draft and turned it into verse. The care that went to the writing of "The Fisherman" is invisible, an art that conceals art, for the poem speaks and is only slightly marred by rhetorical inflation. Humor and ribaldry more readily enter the poems, and do so more convincingly.

Michael Robartes and the Dancer (1921) includes, as well as the famous poems "Easter 1916," "The Second Coming" and "A Prayer for my Daughter," "Solomon and the Witch," one of his most persuasive expressions of the theme of self-consciousness and its dispelling (for good or ill) in love:

> Maybe the bride-bed brings despair,
> For each an imagined image brings
> And finds a real image there . . .

The "real image" becomes his quarry. Throughout this book, in the anthologized poems especially, Yeats handles verbs with cunning. "The Second Coming," raw and visionary with political and religious overtones, like the Byzantium poems that followed, cannot be pinned down to one occasion and will not yield to paraphrase. The poems, without settling into the merely literary, are autonomous and self-contained, shaped in what Edward Thomas calls "a language not to be betrayed."

"Sailing to Byzantium" appears in *The Tower* (1928). Here, an old man rejects, as he is rejected by, the sensuous world of youth, ephemerality and the natural cycle. He travels, in quest of the "Monuments of unageing intellect," to Byzantium—where art arrests change but in so doing transforms it into something other. There he wills himself to be transformed, freed of human passions and the body, that "dying animal." He wills himself to be absorbed "into the artifice of eternity." A powerful intellectual passion animates the poem, as powerful as the sexual passion of the later poems of desire and lust. "The Tower" itself is one of Yeats's finest long poems, exploring further the theme of age. His self-mythologizing has a bardic aspect: the mad poet's task is to drive others mad. In this collection Yeats settles finally for a less tentative statement of the artist's predicament. "Ancestral Homes" and the first section of "Meditations in Time of Civil War" recall the stately homes commissioned by bitter, angry men, built to express sweetness, harmony, civilizing qualities. What if the house lacks the *power* of its sweetness? What if art is, in the end, intransitive or passive, in a time of civil war itself affected by events, but without effect on them? These questions burn at the center of his political poems, troubling him more than the events that give rise to them.

Sato's sword is placed beside the pen and paper. The overriding perception is that hate is more powerful than love because it leads to action. "Among School Children" examines the fate of hope, faith and love with a terrifying, intimate pessimism. It also suggests, in the famous closing lines, that form and content, action and actor, are ideally inseparable: "How can we know the dancer from the dance?" The perceived ideal can rise out of an accurate presentation of the real.

Three collections were published after *The Tower: The Winding Stair and Other Poems* (1933), including "Words for Music Perhaps" and "A Woman Young and Old"; *A Full Moon in March* (1935); and *Last Poems* (1936–39). Death and love are the dominant themes. The celebrated "Crazy Jane" sequence, with the wit, pathos and passion of Yeats's later years, and "Byzantium," the culmination of the sequence of poems that began in *The Tower* and of his hermetic idiom, are a large part of the achievement of the later books. His declining years were marked by a continuing development, an acceleration and intensification that took hold of his rhetoric and filled it out with authentic matter: fear, doubt, longing for new beginnings. In search of an authentic theme he rejects (as he has been deserted by) the "masterful images." His magnificent poem "The Circus Animals' Desertion" proposes a new odyssey, more taxing than any he has undertaken hitherto; and if the challenge, which grows out of a self-recognition more authentic and harrowing than any that has come before, occurs too late, the fact that it occurs at all, throwing in question the whole of his life's work, is as heroic an act of integrity as Pound's in the last fragmentary *Cantos*, when he concedes, "It's a botch," and "I cannot make it cohere," his "errors and wrecks" lying about him. But Yeats is not talking of his formal experiments; rather, of his moral quest. He acknowledges his evasions, the price of his "overmastery." His decision to begin again is the more powerful coming from one for whom there have been so many beginnings. This one is different in kind from the others—not a new turning on the lavish old roads, but a determination to strip away the masks, to find the naked "I." Far from being a denial of the heroic ideal, this is the most heroic act of all:

> ... Now that my ladder's gone,
> I must lie down where all the ladders start,
> In the foul rag-and-bone shop of the heart.

In 1909 Edward Thomas reviewed Yeats's *Collected Works*. He had reviewed Yeats before, deploying the terms he used for Swinburne, Doughty and Davies. Now he reaches a conclusion that is just, whether we take it positively or not: "The heavy voluptuous splendour of much of his work has yet a ghostliness as of the palace made magically of leaves. Even his heroes and beautiful women are aware of this . . . He never leaves us, any more than Crashaw, content with the glory alone. It calls our attention to a spirit behind and beyond, heaping high lovely, invisible things that it may show the greater beauty that can survive their crumbling into dust." Thomas assigns the "palace of leaves" to this spirit, or what T. E. Hulme might later, less generously, have called "the circumambient gas." Thomas, that most devoted reader and serious poet, did not read Yeats's later work. He was killed in April 1917 by the blast of a shell before Arras. It was the year that Yeats, dreaming of heroes, was negotiating the purchase of his "castle," two years before *The Wild Swans of Coole* was published.

When Thomas died, the American poet Robert Frost wrote to Helen Thomas, his widow, "Who was ever so completely himself right up to the verge of destruction, so sure of his thought, so sure of his word?" If this was true of Thomas, then both Frost and Helen were in part responsible.

Thomas's life, though desperately busy, was not full of incident. The three crucial events in his life gain significance in retrospect. First was his meeting with Helen Noble in 1894. This led to virtual marriage when he was still an Oxford undergraduate. She provided him, sometimes a little insistently, with an emotional and practical mainstay, but also—rather earlier than either of them intended—a family. Having published his first book while at Oxford, he decided to become a writer. He followed his vocation for twenty-two years, preparing hundreds of book reviews, compiling anthologies and editions, and writing over thirty prose books on subjects ranging from the countryside to tourist guides, from literary criticism to stories, biographies, autobiographies and an autobiographical novel.

Robert Frost was the second crucial event, first the poems and then the man. In 1914 Thomas reviewed *North of Boston* no fewer than three times, saying in the first review, "This is one of the most revolutionary books of modern times, but one of the quietest and least aggressive. It speaks, and it is poetry." That was the quality he admired most in Frost, the proximity of the language of verse not to the constructions of prose but to the dynamic of speech. Frost, for his part, liked Thomas's nature writing and during their "year of friendship" pointed out prose passages that he felt Thomas might attempt in verse. From Frost he derived the confidence to compose poems. In August 1914 he wrote to his intimate friend Eleanor Farjeon, "I may as well write poetry. Did anyone ever begin at thirty-six in the shade?" Reading poetry had been his passion and vocation; now he set about writing the fewer than 150 poems that constitute his *oeuvre*.

War was the third event. In 1915 he enlisted in the Artists' Rifles, was made a map-reading instructor and was promoted the next year to second lieutenant. Army service freed him from financial worry and the labor of freelancing. It gave him a formal, disciplined existence away from Helen's devoted demands, away from the responsibility of a growing family, where he could write his poems. Helen saw his enlisting as a kind of surrender, but for the poet in him it was an act of emancipation.

Philip Edward Thomas was born in 1878 in Lambeth, London, the eldest of six sons. His parents were of Welsh extraction and he felt affection for Wales, though his distinctive landscape is the south of England, especially Wiltshire, Kent and Hampshire. He attended St. Paul's School, Hammersmith, and went to Lincoln College, Oxford. In 1897, when he was nineteen, *The Woodland Life,* his first prose book, was published. Already he and Helen were living together; they were married in 1899. Their three children were born in 1900, 1902 and 1910. They lived in Kent and then in Hampshire. Between 1910 and 1912, driven by financial necessity, Thomas wrote no fewer than twelve of his prose books. He suffered a mental breakdown in 1911 and contemplated suicide.

The prose of Edward Thomas, written under pressure and at speed, generally for money, is often dismissed by critics or considered only in its direct relation to the poems. But in his quiet, unprogrammatic way, he was one of the most percipient literary critics of his time, the rare kind who reads his contemporaries and appraises them with assurance and gravity. He was among the first reviewers to appreciate Frost; he also recognized Ezra Pound's achievement in *Personae*, which he reviewed in 1909, though his pompous friend Gordon Bottomley talked him out of that enthusiasm. Throughout his mature prose there are passages of criticism and descriptive writing which merit attention.

When Thomas began writing prose, his style was haunted by the ghost of Walter Pater. It is poised, poetical, coldly conceived, more an architecture of language than an expressive instrument, remote from the natural voice. As more demands were made on his time, he wrote more briskly and fluently. In a letter to Eleanor Farjeon he said he was "trying to get rid of the last rags of rhetoric and formality which left my prose so often with a dead rhythm." Prose and verse rhythms are early concerns of his criticism.

Ironically, after his passion for Pater had passed, he was commissioned to write a book about him. It proved to be one of his best critical studies. He takes Pater to task in these terms: "Unless a man write with his whole nature concentrated upon his subject he is unlikely to take hold of another man." Swinburne had been another of his favorites. Again, when his love for Swinburne was over, he was asked to write a book about him. Of Swinburne's vocabulary he says: "The words have no rich inheritance from old usage of speech or poetry, even when they are poetic or archaic or Biblical. They have little variety of tone. The blank verse changes and does everything but speak." He reacted against the one-dimensional, unresonant quality of Swinburne's vocabulary, subsumed under the flood of monotonous rhythm, as he had against the studied, arch, deadening artifice of Pater.

An attitude, indeed a coherent critical approach to poetry, can be deduced from his criticism and reviews. He draws a distinction between reality and realism: the style that attempts "reality" imitates the proportions and rhythms of nature, while the "realist" style concentrates on reproducing detail. He prefers the former and in his poetry practices it. But he is pragmatic in his approach to new work, as to unfamiliar form, assessing it on its own terms first, and his taste encompasses Charles Doughty as well as Frost.

In a review he wrote, "The worst of the poetry being written today is that it is too deliberately and not inevitably English." In his Pater book he extends this argument. "Only when a word has become necessary to him can a man use it safely; if he try to impress words by force on a sudden occasion, they will either perish of his violence or betray him." And in an obituary review of Rupert Brooke, the point is taken further. "He did not attain the 'Shelleyan altitude' where words have a various radiance rather than meaning." Such succinct observations are worth more than a dozen essays of exegesis. They were crucial to Thomas's own eventual poetic development. His two poems entitled "Words" extend the ideas. In poetry, Thomas seeks a diction that is at one with the poet's normal, daily use, that does not deploy poeticisms or words that the author forces into service. In effect, the "Shelleyan altitude" he speaks of means that the best poetry is unparaphrasable, self-justifying and self-contained. The words exist, beyond their denotative relationships, in a more richly and truly connotative structure. He clarifies the point finely in another review. "The important thing is not that a thing should be small, but that it should be intense and capable of *unconsciously symbolic significance*" (my italics).

Natural rhythms are extensions of natural vocabulary. Thomas wrote to a friend about Frost's "absolute fidelity to the postures which the voice assumes in the most expressive intimate speech." How much truer this is of his own verse than of Frost's in the early books that Thomas lived to read. His instinctive grasp of form is best expressed in his analysis of Richard Jefferies's essay structure: "Even if it were all nightmare, the very truthfulness of the agitated voice, rising and falling in honest contemplation of common sorrows, would preserve it, since it is rarely given to the best of men to speak the truth. Its shape is the shape of an emotional mood, and it ends because the emotion ends. It is music, and above, or independent of, logic." So in the poems it is a truth instinctively apprehended, not intellectually grasped, that we look for.

If we contrast Frost's with Thomas's approach to what is similar subject matter, the nature of Thomas's originality becomes clear. Unlike Thomas's English country people, Frost's rural characters have prejudices but no traditions—they seem without roots in their landscape. Thomas's are extensions of a landscape with a history; they possess a native wisdom and humanity we usually look for in vain in the more competitive, untrusting characters of Frost's poems. Formally, Thomas's poems are more subtle than Frost's early work. Frost used archaisms, and the iambic regularity contributes to the sometimes monotonous movement of his poems. Thomas wrote lines of variable length, many of them neither metrically nor syllabically regular but purely stressed in rhythm. He seldom chose a prescriptive form: the pressure of content, the experience or occasion, determined line lengths, pauses, rhythm and extent. Even his sonnets are irregular. Thomas is most subtle in his line endings. A poem's rhythm and syntax may seem to indicate a direction of development which, at the beginning of a new line, unexpectedly alters: syntax and line ending are counterpointed. We do not linger over a literary effect; we are surprised deeper into the experience. Take the lines ending in "might" and "beautiful" in this passage from "October":

> The rich scene has grown fresh again and new
> As Spring and to the touch is not more cool
> Than it is warm to the gaze; and now I might
> As happy be as earth is beautiful,
> *Were I some other* or with earth could turn
> In alternation of violet and rose,

Harebell and snowdrop, at their season due,
And gorse that has no time not to be gay.

The reversal of sense, especially in the words I have italicized but also earlier in the poem, and the tension of rhythm straining our expectation in one direction, while syntax deftly goes in another, creates a unique resonance.

The "I" of Thomas's poems we must usually take to be the poet himself. If he adopts a persona (he occasionally uses "the child" as speaker) he places the persona's words in quotation marks. Frequently the "I" is not presented at all, the poem exists with the speaker implicit only in the rhythm. He refuses to deflect his voice through a mask. The theme of solitude is conveyed in an authentic speaking voice—authentic because undecorated. His solitude is cleaner than Walter de la Mare's: the older poet always has a burden of poetic language and antecedent choking his voice. In "Melancholy" Thomas writes, ". . . if I feared the solitude / Far more I feared all company." In "That Girl's Clear Eyes," the isolation of the individual in the sealed, unbreachable world of personal experience, which he can never fully share, is expressed, not as in Hardy, as a reductive isolation, but as a solitude brimming with a vain desire to share:

> . . . Every one of us
> This morning at our tasks left nothing said,
> In spite of many words. We were sealed thus,
> Like tombs.

The poems are located in Thomas's experience, which, if more generous than Hardy's, is no less solitary.

His most powerful effects are achieved when he contrasts a clearly visualized external world and a tenuously apprehended inner world. His evocations of nature have the vividness not of an internal but of an external landscape. Thomas often locates a poem in a season, in a specific place. The experience is anchored in time and on the map. His daughter Myfanwy recollects actual walks with her father that then became poems. He is concerned with names and naming and, in poems such as "Adelstrop" and "Old Man"—which explore the distance between the name and the thing named—the inadequacy of words to what they name. External and internal worlds coexist, the name (however inappropriate) and the thing named, and both in their coexistence and in the distance between them the resonance of the poems is achieved. "A gate banged in the fence and banged in my head," one poem says. The experiences elicit and confirm one another.

Thomas's favorite time setting is a period of transition: twilight, the point of change between seasons, or the present rendered vivid as the point between past and future, one felt as history, the other as potential. The poems mark transitions between emotions as well—the almost dark and almost light, the almost lost and almost found. "Interval" specifically evokes the point of transition:

> Gone the wild day:
> A wilder night
> Coming makes way
> For brief twilight.

"The Thrush" is more subjective:

> And April I love for what
> It was born of, and November
> For what it will die in,
> What they are and what they are not ...

This is winter, viewed from either end.

To approach the truth of a thing, Thomas sometimes strengthens a simile in order to transfer our attention from the thing described to what it is compared with. The effect is Wordsworthian—"The cataracts *sound their trumpets* from the steep." The trumpet image is stronger than the image of the cataract and displaces it. Thomas does this with powerfully evocative effect: "The swift with wings and tail as sharp and narrow / As if the bow had flown off with the arrow." In another poem he conjures "all the clouds like sheep / On the mountains of sleep." Thomas takes metaphor back to the landscape: it ceases to be a conceit, finding its place in a larger structure. The nuances of such strong comparisons are always controlled to make us aware of what he calls "unconsciously symbolic significance."

Thomas, like a cameraman, adopts various spatial perspectives to express a whole experience. We see things from two or three vantages. In "The Watcher," a man in a hotel looks out at a horse and carter by a ford. He is in turn watched by "stuffed fish, vermin, and king-fishers" in a glass case within. He stands, sealed off by glass both from the living world and a nature artificially preserved. In "Thaw," perspective provides the central tension. The poem is set between seasons:

> Over the land freckled with snow half-thawed
> The speculating rooks at their nests cawed
> And saw from elm-tops, delicate as flower of grass,
> What we below could not see, Winter pass.

The rooks' and our own perspectives are contrasted. They "speculate"—both look and prognosticate. The word assumes its fullest sense, including etymology. It stands out as an item of diction because it is Latinate and polysyllabic, because it is drawn from a register quite different from the descriptive, largely monosyllabic register of the rest of the poem. The elm-tops become, to the rooks, a seeding meadow; since the tops of the elms are first to renew, the rooks are seeing spring, while those below, still in winter, can only draw an inference from the birds. Thomas will reverse perspective to emphasize an emotion: "a poor man of any sort, down to a king," he writes, or in another poem, "The clay first broke my heart, and then my back; / And the back heals not."

Few of Thomas's poems are without birds; several have the names of birds as their titles. It is birds' voices ("A pure thrush word") and flight that most attract him. Another recurrent image is rain and storms, which wash clean and alleviate tension, sometimes suggesting tears. Though Thomas wrote only a handful of war poems, images obliquely suggesting war and conflict are frequent and integrated into a personal rather than a public utterance. His most characteristic image is of roads, paths, lanes. He praised Hardy for his sense of roads and their poignant significance, how they connect people even when they are apart. He declares: "This is an imaginative fact."

> Roads go on
> While we forget and are
> Forgotten as a star
> That shoots and is gone.

"If" and "as if" in Thomas's poems suggest a world of similarities parallel to the real world: it may be an inner world, or the past, or some possible future. It is never a fantastic or fabulous world, and if at times it seems a refinement, it is not an escape. *Seeming* parallels observed *being*. The world of seeming is conveyed also by a deft use of negatives. Thomas describes or states what is *not* the case, and thus conveys what could be or what has been, as well as what is. A complex use of explicit and implicit negatives occurs in "Old Man." Musing on the flower —clematis vitalba—called "old man" and "lad's-love" (and also "traveler's joy"), out of the jungle of memory and of sensuous recollection he discovers:

> I have mislaid the key. I sniff the spray
> And think of nothing; I see and I hear nothing;
> Yet seem, too, to be listening, lying in wait

For what I should, yet never can, remember:
No garden appears, no path, no hoar-green bush
Of Lad's-Love, or Old Man, no child beside,
Neither father nor mother, nor any playmate;
Only an avenue, dark, nameless, without end.

While Hardy is obsessed with what the mind remembers, how memory and the past impinge on the present, Thomas is troubled by what is forgotten, or half remembered. "I can remember much forgetfulness," Hart Crane says—each thing forgotten is a loss, since the missing experience could enrich, or interpret and resolve, the present:

All lost, as is a childless woman's child
And its child's children, in the undefiled
Abyss of what will never be again.

"The past is the only dead thing that smells sweet," he writes. He recalls not *what* he has forgotten, only *that* he has.

Perhaps the most original aspect of his art, after the rhythms, which are so supple and subtly *un*metered, is his control of diction, especially verb tenses. His mind can engage an experience whole; the tenses draw together various times scales:

Just hope has gone for ever. Perhaps
I may love other hills yet more
Than this: the future and the maps
Hide something I was waiting for.

When, in the first seven lines of "The Glory," he wishes to convey complete peace, he withholds the main verb until the eighth line, giving an impression of the bustling stability of nature. In "The Green Roads" he devises a couplet stanza where the first line of each couplet ends with the word "forest," and the second has an internal rhyme and is end-stopped. The form grows out of a repetitive syntax and the effect is, like the paths themselves, suspended, without apparent origin or destination.

We would need to look to the best of George Herbert's poetry to find in English a more direct voice, resistant to paraphrase; or poems made of words so totally second nature to the speaker. The lucid, self-contained quality of Thomas's language and vision, unliterary, uncontrived, are exemplified in the conclusion of "I Never Saw that Land Before":

I neither expected anything
Nor yet remembered: but some goal
I touched then; and if I could sing
What would not even whisper my soul
As I went on my journeying,

I should use, as the trees and birds did,
A language not to be betrayed;
And what was hid should still be hid
Excepting from those like me made
Who answer when such whispers bid.

Writing to Helen after Edward Thomas was killed, Robert Frost said, "I want to see him to tell him something. I want to tell him, what I think he liked to hear from me, that he was a poet." It was a friendship that, later in life, Frost tended to play down. Thomas had been a friendly critic who helped to establish Frost, and he was grateful; and no doubt he quite liked Thomas's verse, though Frost felt it was too irregular, too obedient to the voice, and in subject matter too narrow, too narrowly English, too insistently dark, like the dark talk of the letters Thomas wrote to Frost from France. Thomas's poems were not collected until after his death, and it was not until well after the Second World War that they became popular.

Like Thomas, Frost got started rather late as a poet. In 1912 he sailed to England with his wife and four children, without a book to his credit, and with a list of frustrations and disappointments behind him. In 1915 he sailed back, an established poet. But his early unsuccess colored his sense of himself and his achievement. He was left with besetting doubts.

Born in 1874 in San Francisco, his father was a New Englander, his mother a Scot. At the age of eleven, on his father's death, he was taken to New England. He went to Dartmouth College but hated the academic world and took a job in a mill. He started his undergraduate course again in 1897, at Harvard. In 1899 he left, tried shoemaking, editing a local paper, then farming. At thirty-six he traveled to England, taking a house in Beaconsfield, Buckinghamshire, where he met Thomas.

An English publisher took his first book, *A Boy's Will*, in 1913. It is a very English-seeming book, full of archaisms, recognizably poetic forms (it opens with a couplet-sonnet and includes several sonnets) and themes, an unexceptionable Georgian sensibility. What Thomas recognized here was an absence of rhetoric, a plainness, and (wonderful phrase) "a calm eagerness of emotion" which raised the plainness to unique harmonies. This is the language men might use in speaking to men, without eccentricity, occasionally crystallizing in an aphorism. " 'Men work together,' I told him from my heart, / 'Whether they work together or apart.' " He has read Hardy, but his poems are more regular than his. He has read Arnold, but his spirit is less philosophical. He has read de la Mare, but his verse is more real than his. The poem that immediately catches in the reader's memory is the peculiar sonnet "Mowing":

> There was never a sound beside the wood but one,
> And that was my long scythe whispering to the ground.
> What was it it whispered? I knew not well myself . . .

Taken out of context, the third line could belong to a poem by Thomas; in context the meter takes hold of and transforms it into the dominant music. In Thomas rural activity is always part of a rural culture; the activities in Frost's poems are isolated. Whether it is mending a wall, sharpening saws, swinging birches, the activity is singular. When he mows, the action is sufficient in itself, the hay is almost irrelevant. What matters is the body inside action.

In *North of Boston* Frost has found his own way. The book begins with "Mending Wall," "Something there is that doesn't love a wall," with its homely aphoristic ending, "Good fences make good neighbours." The second poem is the long eclogue "The Death of the Hired Man," voices mulling over a rural event.

> "Warren," she said, "he has come home to die:
> You needn't be afraid he'll leave this time."
>
> "Home," he mocked gently.
>   "Yes, what else but home?
> It all depends on what you mean by home.
> Of course he's nothing to us, any more
> Than was the hound that came a stranger to us
> Out of the woods, worn out upon the trail."
>
> "Home is the place where, when you have to go there,
> They have to take you in."
>
>   "I should have called it
> Something you somehow haven't to deserve."

There is a hypnotic veracity about the poem, the way it moves, spinning about words like "home," "pride," "night," "us" and "him," inclusion and exclusion. The spell is broken by the dramatic closing line. This poem and the other eclogues, including "Home Burial," are powerfully original, their formal precursors (perhaps not influences) to be found in the poems of Crabbe and in Wordsworth's "Michael," their thematic cousins in the ironies of Hardy the novelist as well as the poet. It is a verse that puts much of the Georgian enterprise in the shade: a pastoral that is wholly human, and human in all its tragic diversity of life, love and death.

In his third book, *Mountain Interval* (1916), several of his famous poems appear, lyric this time as well as eclogue: "The Road Not Taken," the sonnet "The Oven Bird," the incomparable "Birches," and "Out, Out." The poems avoid the literary. They are wry and wise, not folksy but full of aphorisms. Quiet events and terrible events take place in the daily lives and seasonal cycles of rural New Hampshire. There is loneliness in every poem, and Frost himself lived in fear of madness, his circumstances curiously similar to those of Yvor Winters, whose formalistic wisdom is wrung from the deepest personal anguish. Frost's biography is a contradictory story, the generous man and the selfish, the jealous and the loving. The craggy old man, windswept, reading a poem at the inauguration of President Kennedy, the nation's favorite poet, and the man who lived the real life and wrote the letters as well as the poems, hardly seem to coincide. The poem he read at the inauguration, however, tells us who he is *as a poet*, which is what matters. It was called "The Gift Outright":

The land was ours before we were the land's.
She was our land more than a hundred years
Before we were her people. She was ours
In Massachusetts, in Virginia,
But we were England's, still colonials,
Possessing what we still were unpossessed by,
Possessed by what we now no more possessed.
Something we were withholding made us weak
Until we found out that it was ourselves
We were withholding from our land of living,
And forthwith found salvation in surrender.
Such as we were we gave ourselves outright
(The deed of gift was many deeds of war)
To the land vaguely realizing westward,
But still unstoried, artless, unenhanced,
Such as she was, such as she would become.

The poem "lectures," it speaks of "us" and "ours." It speaks of a nation and the relationship between colonists and a land, citizens and the land. In this poem most clearly, but in many of the eclogues, many of the lyrics, too, the poet is speaking and speaking *for*. Frost, in his grasp of his vocation, is the purest of the heirs of Walt Whitman. He has lost the glow of optimism that marks Whitman, he lives in a declining century, but he retains unalloyed his patriotism and his sense of commonwealth. Whitman had personal secrets, and so did Frost, who fostered a public image of himself as the sage, goodhearted farmer-poet. He was more than that, brighter and darker in his heart. The Frost icon was painstakingly demolished in Lawrance Thompson's three-volume biography, a veritable dump truck full of paydirt. After the outrage at Thompson's "treachery" it is true that the poet was reconsidered and demoted. Slowly his reputation has been rebuilt.

Whatever his failings as a man, as a poet he was "made out of democracy," and one of his popular lectures, which I heard as a schoolboy in Pennsylvania, was called "The Panhandle of Poetry" and was meant to help those of us who didn't like verse to get a purchase on it. He presented himself as a facilitator: Could we find a way into poetry through "Stopping by the Woods on a Snowy Evening"? We could, we did.

But the verse we found our way into was not quite as we imagined it would be. It is easy at one level, but once you are inside, the world it makes is full of sinister shadows, unredeemed, unforgiving. There are voices talking, the poet transcribing, trying to be faithful to what he hears and at the same time faithful to his art. To remain faithful to the voices, he has to give them space and range, he has to honor their diction; to remain faithful to his art he must select, perfect, finding rather than imposing order. Aware of things and creatures, with their divergent wills, the poet in the end affirms nothing apart from the fact that nothing can be affirmed. Meaning remains latent. "The figure a poem makes. It begins in delight and ends in wisdom." When Frost says "delight," he means the delight of sound, and of recognizable context, not the delight of affirmation or jollity. When he says "wisdom" he means not moral lesson but human insight. Wisdom understands what is, it does not judge, it does not generalize. "Like a piece of ice on a hot stove the poem must ride on its own melting"—a wonderful image for the making of the poem and for the reading of it. The good poem takes the poet over, uses the poet to get itself written, surprise by surprise. The good poem is inexhaustible. "Read it a hundred times: it will for ever keep its freshness as a metal keeps its fragrance."

Frost's pessimism is harsher than Hardy's. The later poems settle into the blackest moods and, in Randall Jarrell's words, make "pessimism seem a hopeful evasion." Though there is no coherent meta-physical structure sustaining Frost's human vision, there is a sense of evil so ingrained that it is our condition. The poet resigns himself to it. Calm, without heightening of language, without rhetorical exaggeration, he tells it as he believes it to be: the lives, the night skies, the winter weather. The natural language and the self-effacement of the speaker are what make the poems cut so deep, seem so inevitable in their movement. They are uttered by a voice, but not by a defined subjectivity. They have the appearance of objective statement, as though they simply occurred in the language, where we find them.

Frost loved books about isolation: *Walden, Robinson Crusoe,* essays and fictions in which men live and survive alone, sufficient in themselves. This is a self-centeredness, but the self that he centers on is not a psychology, not a bourgeois "I" but a self that believes it stands for every man—every American man. The Mexican poet Octavio Paz visited Frost in his Vermont cabin—a long walk uphill. "With his white shirt open—is there anything cleaner than a clean white shirt?—his blue eyes innocent, ironic, his philosopher's head and his farmer's hands, he looked like an ancient sage, the kind who prefers to observe the world from his retreat. But there was nothing ascetic in his looks, rather a manly sobriety." He had withdrawn "not to renounce the world but to see it more clearly." He told Paz that he had written his first poem at the age of fifteen. It was about *la noche triste*, the night Hernán Cortez fled from the Aztec capital laden with gold: human conquest, greed, defeat.

> The Montezumas are no more,
> Gone is their regal throne,
> And freemen live, and rule, and die,
> Where they have ruled alone.

"In each verse," Frost said to him, "a decision awaits us, and we can't choose to close our eyes and let instinct work on its own. Poetic instinct consists of an alert tension." In this sense poetry is "the experience of liberty. The poet risks himself, chances all on the poem's all with each verse he writes." Most important, if the poet is to remain free, he must not abandon himself to style. Once a language has been found, the poet must continually fight against it.

Paz visited Frost when the poet was seventy. He lived another nineteen years. He kept reading poetry, his favorite form of understanding, as he said, and the best way of thinking. In an interview he remarked, "Too many poets delude themselves by thinking the mind is dangerous and must be left out. Well, the mind is dangerous and must be left in." Readers who imagine Frost is an emotional writer misunderstand his pessimism and his wisdom. They have not heard in him, more clearly than they do in William Carlos Williams or Pound or the Projectivists, Whitman's wise child.

In his last book, published in 1962, the year before he died, he includes "The Gift Outright," originally published in the 1940s; it had a new pertinence in the age Kennedy's election seemed to promise. He also included new poems that, coming from one so near extinction, joked perilously with metaphysics. In "Away!" he chooses to die:

> Don't think I leave
> For the outer dark
> Like Adam and Eve
> Out of the Park.
>
> Forget the myth.
> There is no one I
> Am put out with
> Or put out by.
>
> Unless I am wrong
> I but obey
> The urge of a song:
> "I'm—bound—away!"
>
> And I may return
> If dissatisfied
> With what I learn
> From having died.

It is hard to detach the poem from the memory of his slow, dismissive voice. He did not laugh at his jokes, yet through his work runs a dark and not unwholesome humor, not to be confused with wit. It is an aspect of his stoicism and a proof of his conditional solidarity.

"The lighting of the lamps"

T. E. HULME, D. H. LAWRENCE, T. S. ELIOT,
EZRA POUND, H.D. (HILDA DOOLITTLE)

The big outdoors of Thomas and Frost, peopled by common men and women rooted in a landscape, is an increasingly rare scenario in the urban worlds of the twentieth century. There is landscape, but unpeopled; and there is the thronging city. Also increasingly rare is a poetry that is not concerned with itself, a poetry not about poetry, pretending to be process but actually being *about* the process. The "decadent," experimental legacy of the fin-de-siècle, deflected by the Wilde affair, began to emerge from the shadows. Yeats never made any bones about it: poetry was not a civic activity. Art began the process of understanding by understanding itself, and this could involve the singling out of its own resources and techniques, bringing them forward, experimenting with them. Swinburne—undervalued as he currently is—was the most successful experimentalist, obsessively fascinated with the properties of meter and rhythm. He is less a Victorian than an early modernist. So, too, Aubrey Beardsley: fascinated with line, and not only with line but with line on paper, the medium never allowing the viewer to forget it, even as the image struggled in its louche web. And Henry James, building a syntax more and more nuanced, extended, each extension delving into smaller and smaller crannies of character and motive, action in a patient catalepsy.

Experiment was not intended to foreground the artist, and yet because the art contrived—in its exaggeration of certain elements, its exclusion of others—to reveal its contrivance, the artist became a focus of curiosity. Experiments in different mediums were received by consumers—the age of the consumer had arrived—without new understanding. Critics voiced outrage and gave the new work a kind of notoriety, but the poet or artist was denied a critical context. Criticism did not try to extend understanding but to limit it: the word "no" replaced "how" and "why." What the poet intended literally was read in the old symbolic way. The weird narratives of Swinburne were taken in the same spirit as the narratives of Crabbe or Wordsworth and found morally obnoxious (well, they *are*). And were not the inspirations for such things foreign, especially French? Were the lives of our Bohemian artists not based on a deplorable foreign model? Was there not rather too much of the love that dares not speak its name in their circles, too much moral liberality? The critics, some of them remarkably astute and eloquent men (all of them men) missed the joke and missed, too, the serious investigation that was under way. For them art and morality were indissoluble; art for art's sake was immoral. No doubt art and morality *are* indissoluble; yet the moral and the orthodox are not synonymous. On the day that Oscar Wilde was sentenced, Richard Garnett, editor of the British Museum catalogue, predicted that British poetry would be dead for fifty years. Respectability and poetry were never comfortable bedfellows. Poetry was doomed to be what it already largely was in Britain, a minor art: the Rhymers and then the Georgians, with only Hardy, Yeats, Kipling, and arguably Housman to suggest that it might be something more. And only Yeats had time for the experimentalists.

Change and renewal would have to insinuate themselves subtly, would have to come from unexpected places, undefended flanks. A Trojan horse. And so they did: a Cambridge philosopher-mathematician, a Midland lad from the working classes, a gang of Americans. The seeds of change were very curious.

> . . . I was bound
> Motionless and faint of breath
> By loveliness that is her own eunuch.

Minor poetry and singularly unpromising, almost comical in the absence of tone: self-parodying. Thomas Ernest Hulme is an enigma. For T. S. Eliot he was "the author of two or three of the most beautiful short poems in the language." Was it two or three, and which were they? All of his very few poems were very short. Michael Roberts, the great modern-verse anthologist, admired Hulme's critical and philosophical work and extended many of his ideas, writing an excellent study of him. Modern readers consider him more in the light of his thought and influence than of his poetry. The poems he wrote are "beautiful" in Eliot's sense, though very much the fruit of their period. They illustrate his critical arguments but remain peripheral, where his thought is central to any serious consideration of modern poetry, as it is to the reappraisal of the poetry of the past.

Hulme was born in 1883 at Gratton Hall, the family home, in Endon, Staffordshire. In 1901 he went up to Cambridge on a scholarship to study mathematics. In 1904 he was sent down suddenly for unspecified reasons—something to do with libidinal adventures. He tried a course in biology and physics at University College, London, commuting to Cambridge to attend philosophy lectures. Impatient of authority, he dropped out and left England in 1906, taking a cargo boat to Canada. There he experienced—on "the flat spaces and wide horizons of the virgin-prairie of Western Canada"—the "necessity or inevitableness" of verse. He sensed the "chasm" between man and God, "the fright of the mind before the unknown." The sheer weight, the tall abundance of those northern spaces, compacted his language: it tried to become hard, definite, resistant like stone.

He returned to Europe in 1907 and studied in Brussels with the philosophers Henri Bergson and Jules de Gaultier and the critic Rémy de Gourmont. In 1908, with the pressure of his Canadian experience and the suspiciously foreign perspectives and skills he'd acquired on the Continent, he arrived back in London and founded the short-lived Poets' Club, a convivial discussion group. His next club did not have a name. It met at the Eiffel Tower Restaurant in Soho. There, in company with F. S. Flint, Edward Storer, Ezra Pound and perhaps Wyndham Lewis, among others, he read poems and discussed his theory of the "image" in poetry.

His ideas were derivative—of Bergson, de Gourmont, de Gaultier and others. He was a lucid assimilator and proselytizer. In 1911 he published a series of essays on Bergson, and in 1912 the "Complete Poetical Works of T. E. Hulme" were published in January in the *New Age* and again (more this time) as an appendix to Pound's collection *Ripostes*. Hulme's actual collected poems—there were so few, he is like a poet of ancient Greece whose work survives in fragments—were published in 1960 in A. R. Jones's *The Life and Opinions of T. E. Hulme*. As well as the poems and essays, he published translations of Bergson and Georges Sorel. *Speculations* and *Notes on Language and Style*, collections of fragments and short essays, were published posthumously. He planned many further works but fell in action in Flanders in 1917.

He was not academically trained in literature: he was an outsider in the literary milieu he chose—or created—in London. It needed a clear-headed outsider to begin diagnosing the infirmities of British poetry (and British culture more widely) and to propose remedies. He reacted most passionately against the facility of the 1890s poets, their self-indulgence; he was equally unfriendly to much of the "new" verse of the day, the emerging Georgianism. He and his friends discussed Oriental forms, the tanka and haiku, *vers libre* ("free," or unmetered verse) and "poems in a sacred Hebrew form." They countered prolixity with precise brevity, refuted the "vacuity" of their contemporaries with what they conceived as vivid, tight-lipped images. F. S. Flint recalled that much of their discussion was about poetic craft, one *point de repère* being French writers such as Jules Laforgue, a particular influence. Hulme insisted on "absolutely accurate representation and no verbiage." What at first seems a refreshing naïveté in his attitude to language in relation to the world proves to be the fruit of a deep radicalism, his sense of that world inferred through language itself.

The Continental and historical models Hulme chooses, and his rejection of Romanticism, are part of a wider mission. With Wyndham Lewis he rejects a man-centered worldview and repudiates the principle of continuity. This principle is so prevalent a preconception, informs so many of our institutions and beliefs, that we believe it describes reality, when in fact it is but one way of conceptualizing it. We tend, because we are conditioned to believe in continuity, to draw back from gaps and jumps in nature, and between ourselves and nature. Hulme posits discontinuity between various realms of thought, the possibility of creating new kinds of connection, new forms. In this context "image" means that things not normally associated can be brought together into significant relationship; that relationships independent of normal ideas of continuity and logic can be resonant. This is the core of the Imagist revolution at its most pure, a revolution Hulme catalyzed, though he did not contribute to the Imagist anthologies or participate in their polemics. He seems to have stood back to watch his mischief take effect. Imagism stresses that poetry communicates metaphorically, not logically.

His program was for a neoclassical poetry: free to find or make associations without reference to "continuous contexts": accurate and hard, intellectual, precise, and pessimistic, for man is small (those vast Canadian spaces had shown him how small), an animal, and fallen. These ideas or orientations develop differently in Eliot and Lewis.

Lecturing in 1914, Hulme argued against meter: "It enables people to write verse with no poetic inspiration, and whose mind [*sic*] is not stored with new images." The word "inspiration" has the aspect of an unpurged residue from the very ideologies he set his cap against, but what he says of meter is crucial. Meter is a facilitator; poetry is not a facile art. Meter and the rhetorics that go with it can take over and inflate a poem, can impose a lax diction and deform ideas if it is unskillfully handled. The unit of significance in the poem, he argues, is not the word but the phrase or sentence; a poet, he argues, should consider the effect of the whole poem, not its local felicities. *Vers libre* had a crucial attraction for him and those who learned from, or with him. Here is the kernel of William Carlos Williams's "variable foot" and of Charles Olson's "breath" theories. If not the word, if not the "continuity" of syntactical units, then the *line* becomes the crucial unit, and a poem is a construction made less of words than of lines, each with a dynamic that harmonizes or contrasts with those that precede and follow. Rhythm in short and long measures displaces meter, and the appraisal of rhythm becomes a matter of acute instinct and discrimination. The metronome can be thrown away.

Hulme rejected Romanticism largely because of what he saw as its grandiloquent optimism, its inherent faith in progress, or what Hardy called "evolutionary meliorism." He saw man as "a fixed and limited animal whose nature is absolutely constant. It is only by tradition and organisation that anything decent can be got out of him." Though temperamentally hostile to authority, he proposes an authoritarian ethic. The new classical poet knows he is made of clay, that he's physically and perceptually finite. "He may jump, but he always returns back; he never flies away into the circumambient gas."

Bergson taught him distinctions (he might have learned them from Coleridge) that he introduced back into English poetic discourse: between intellect and intuition. Intellect analyzes and is the language of prose; intuition, the language of poetry, places the artist "back within the object by a kind of sympathy and breaking down . . . the barrier that space puts between him and his model." The model, the object, is what the poet sets out to evoke in the image. Implied in this is a rigorous suppression of personality. Pound's famous dictum "Make It New" comes from Hulme, too, who takes from de Gourmont the notion that language is constantly nearing extinction, shedding resonance, and must be regularly reinvigorated with a stock of new metaphors.

"Thought," says Hulme, "is prior to language and consists in the simultaneous presentation of two different images." This was an early formulation of Pound's definition of the image: "that which presents an intellectual and emotional complex in an instant of time." It was not a new idea, but it had not before been singled out and made the basis of a doctrinaire poetics. Previously it had been taken as one ingredient among many in the complex thing called poetry. Coleridge, in *Biographia Literaria*, defined it: "It has been observed before," he wrote, "that images, however beautiful, though faithfully copied from nature, and as accurately represented in words, do not of themselves characterise the poet. They become proof of original genius only as far as they are modified by a predominant passion; *or when they have the effect of reducing multitude to unity, or succession to an instant;* or lastly, when a human and intellectual life is transferred to them from the poet's own spirit" (my italics). Despite the Romantic implications, this defines better than Hulme or Pound did what an image isn't and is, what it can and cannot do. Coleridge's definition comes in the context of an argument about language and the scope of poetry broader than Hulme envisaged. Coleridge, in his middle years, was trying to set down insights he had drawn from a lifetime of reading, meditating and writing. His intention was not prescriptive but deductive from the best examples he had available. The fact that Hulme's and Pound's dogmatic teaching started a *school* of poets reveals how some of the outstanding creative forces in our century have lost the wide perspective that earlier poets possessed and took for granted, have been reduced by metaphysical doubt and innate pessimism to programmatic reform. Pound's irrepressible imagination and formal hunger extended his theories so that, over a long life, the trajectory of his prose and verse moves well beyond the early definitions. But Hulme's life was short.

Hulme's poems "Autumn" and "City Sunset," both published in 1909, have the distinction of being the first Imagist poems. "Autumn" is the better of the two:

> A touch of cold in the Autumn night—
> I walked abroad
> And saw the ruddy moon lean over a hedge
> Like a red-faced farmer.
> I did not stop to speak, but nodded,
> And round about were the wistful stars
> With white faces like town children.

The poem observes. Two images fuse: skyscape and human faces. Moon becomes farmer, stars *town* children. The poem humanizes a skyscape and etherealizes a landscape. There is, too, implicit celebration of the rural at the expense of the urban—a Romantic, or a distinctly English, residue.

In "Images," one poem reads in its entirety, "Old houses were scaffolding once and workmen whistling." Two aspects of the same thing are juxtaposed, a past and a present. The effect is more resonant than in much strictly Imagist verse because it has a time context; it does not exist (as the earlier poem does) in a perpetual present or on a timeless plane. William Empson writes that Imagist poetry is poetry that has lost the use of its legs—it does not move (in any sense), it does not evoke time sequence, existing only in space. This is one way in which it resists the tyranny of continuity, of cause and effect. Committed to the image, it disregards the contexts of the image. It has no conscience beyond artistic perfection. Hulme escapes Empson's stricture occasionally, when he humanizes, or reduces, nature. His poems arise out of observation, not (as often with later Imagists) out of literature. In his poems he takes some liberties with his doctrines. For example, "The Man in the Crow's Nest":

> Strange to me, sounds the wind that blows
> By the masthead, in the lonely night.
> Maybe 'tis the sea whistling—feigning joy
> To hide its fright
> Like a village boy
> That trembling past the churchyard goes.

As in "Autumn," nature is brought down a peg or two. The poem possesses dramatic eeriness, due partly to the rhymes, which create a tenuous stability. The precise syntax is wholly effective, and when the poet speaks in the last line of the boy not as "who" but "that," he effects a subtle depersonalizing even there.

Hulme was a passionate man who knew he needed discipline and containment, intellectual control. His fellow modernists were similarly passionate and ambitious but less philosophical, less intellectual. The in-turned passions of Eliot, the extrovert passions of Pound, the classical purity of H.D. and the bald ambition of Amy Lowell are related qualities of a generation of American writers who made it their business to create new spaces in English poetry, who believed that they could break through the conventionality of the host literature and access the empowering tradition. One Englishman identified with their diverse program. He was as much an outsider as they were.

David Herbert Lawrence was not a *pure* radical. He contributed verse to the Georgian anthologies edited by Edward Marsh and to the Imagist anthologies—not those edited by Pound, for whom he was not rigorous enough, but those edited by Amy Lowell. Conflicting voices are heard in his early writing. The more popular is dramatic, telling stories, interposing moral comment, loosely formal in approach. The Georgians could take such verse on board, though its presence in Marsh's staid compilations highlights the power of Lawrence's apprentice work and the emotional and technical conventionality of much of the poetry that surrounds it. Marsh included "Seven Seals" and "Snake," the closest he came to publishing erotic verse.

Amy Lowell chose for her Imagist book terse, imagistic and unmoralized poems. They are less immediately appealing. She published "Green" in 1915:

> The sky was apple-green.
> The sky was green wine held up in the sun.
> The moon was a golden petal between.

This verges on surrealism *avant la lettre*. In another poem Lawrence wrote, "The street-lamps in the twilight have suddenly started to bleed." He may have been writing to order for the Imagist anthology, but as he gained confidence in the power of clearly constructed images to convey feeling, he retreated from the received formal modes he had mastered only uncertainly. He moved toward a personal and eventually a vatic idiom. Eventually he came to sound like the Nietzsche of *Also Sprach Zarathustra*, big-voiced and assertive, with an inevitable loss of delicacy and precision. Yet he never settled entirely into one particular mode: his travels, his prose writing and reading always affect the supple, unstable style. Yet each poem bears his voice-print: it is hard to mistake his writing for that of any other poet, no matter what formal option he is exploiting.

His development through the *Collected Poems* is fascinating. It is the gradual evolution, or modulation, of a voice becoming more idiosyncratic and personal, declaring independence of traditional means, driven by emotional and intellectual predispositions that come to dominate his writing. There is a pressure of *content* behind all he writes. The germ of his mature style is present at the outset: he develops by disencumbering himself. Some of his best poems are achieved in the period just before his formal emancipation was complete, when there is still tension between the pull of tradition and the anarchic, recreative forces of his temperament. He emancipated himself because poetic theory and precedent exerted limited authority over him. Present emotion, present experience, demanded their own form; each image required unique articulation.

Lawrence was born in Eastwood, Nottingham, in 1885, the fourth child in his family. His father was a coal miner, his mother a former schoolteacher who came to despise her not always sober, sometimes uncouth husband. The tension between his parents is evoked in the poem "Discord in Childhood": "Outside the house an ash-tree hung its terrible whips." Inside, the disputatious voices rose and fell. Lawrence found initial security with his mother, but their relationship proved emotionally ambiguous, inhibiting his later relations with women. His background is full of contradictions: between his father's insistent working-class attitudes and values and his mother's middle-class hankerings; between the rural and industrial landscapes that coexisted around him; between sexual and moral obligations that often seemed, in those early years, at odds. A further complication in his childhood was the diagnosis of a lung infection, which, in 1930, was to kill him.

From the local council school he gained a scholarship to attend Nottingham High School. At the age of sixteen he began work as a clerk in a surgical appliances firm at thirteen shillings a week. He left to follow in his mother's footsteps by becoming a pupil teacher in Eastwood and later in Ilkeston. Then at eighteen he went to University College, Nottingham. Until 1912 he taught at a school uncommittedly, exasperatedly, all the while working on his first novel and writing poems. Much of his teaching career was spent in Croydon, Surrey, among different landscapes and accents from those he knew in Nottinghamshire. "How can I answer the challenge of so many eyes?" he asks in one poem. The challenge of eyes later on, when he was invited to read his poems at Harold Monro's Poetry Bookshop in London, made him read with his back turned to the audience, a form of modesty that riveted attention even more narrowly upon him.

His social and intellectual background set him apart from the writers of the day. Without academic and financial advantages, emerging from the turbulent household of Mr. and Mrs. Lawrence with their irreconcilable values and contrasting ambitions for him, he was possessed by a dogged earnestness that he never lost. Not for him the socialized, ironic tones of Oxbridge writers, the mild experimental luxuries of Bloomsbury, busy with itself. Even today the absence from his prose and verse of what might be called social graces or social vices— which, applying familiar templates to unfamiliar subjects and feelings, habituate readers, deliberately setting them at ease—challenges those of us accustomed to the more mannerly or deliberate pathos and savagery of some of his contemporaries. For Lawrence is direct, *in* his writing, and makes no bones about it. He can write humorously, but he does not play with his medium or caricature subject matter or character for effect. We find, in his novels, stories, essays and poems quite as much as in his erratic and often brilliant correspondence, a man for whom writing is not so much an art as an act, an act with radical moral import and consequence. As his illness took firmer hold and he began to seek friendly climates to prolong his summers and defer death, his writing accelerated in urgency. He asks readers to invest more of themselves in his work than most writers require, and it is possible to balk—for some it is impossible not to balk—at the large ethical demands of his early and late work in particular, which often occlude the considerable artistic risks he takes. Perhaps the largest artistic risk was to take his art in such deadly earnest, and to ask us to do so too. This, quite as much as the vigor and consistency of his work, drew so perceptive and sour a critic as F. R. Leavis to admit Lawrence to the upper reaches of a Parnassus that he so severely guarded against lesser mortals.

But Leavis's encomia came later. In the early years, teaching pupils who were reluctant to learn and whom he found it difficult and unsatisfying to motivate, irked him. He began to suffer the emotional and physical strain of a vocation for which he had no vocation. The death of his mother in 1910—after which he wrote several elegies, including "Sorrow," "Brooding Grief" and, in a different vein, the wonderful "Piano"—left him worn out and near despair. These experiences provided plot, images and themes not only for *Sons and Lovers* (1913), his most autobiographical novel, but also for *The Rainbow* (1915) and *Women in Love* (1921), books many regard as his masterpieces.

In 1911 his literary career began to take shape. Without his knowledge a friend—his first devoted lover—sent some of his poems and the story "Odour of Chrysanthemums" to Ford Madox Ford. Ford invited Lawrence to meet him, which the poet did with superb shyness and reluctance. Ford remembers (or reinvents) the meeting brilliantly in *Portraits from Life* (1937), recalling how "he had come, like the fox, with his overflood of energy—his abounding vitality of passionate determination that seemed always too big for his frail body." Ford included the work in the *English Review,* talked up the new writer, and handed on his first novel, *The White Peacock,* to Messrs. Heinemann. It duly appeared, and in 1912 Lawrence wiped the chalk from his fingers, abandoned the classroom and traveled abroad for the first time.

Most of the poems Lawrence had written up to this time were far from assured. They are silted with abstractions, forced rhymes and weak auxiliaries; sometimes the syntax has to reverse to obey the constraints of meter or rhyme scheme. Some of the poems are obsessed with a physicality that falls short of carnality. "Virgin Youth," for instance, a poem he later revised to highlight the erotic element, is a paean to frustration. And frustration is—not surprisingly, given his dislike of school mastering and his impatience for large literary success, for £2,000 a year—a dominant theme, disclosed unintentionally in the flawed forms. "Monologue of a Mother," "Cherry Robbers" and other poems are tentative in expression if not content. The power of these poems is in evocative imagery, painterly vision. There is an adolescent tone in much of this writing, a desire to shock without the necessary bravado, which persists, though the bravado becomes commensurate in later poems. In *Nettles* (1929) and much of the later work there is unripeness, immaturity of sentiment and thought, and the occasional marring petulances, of the vestigial brat. These elements are at odds with the serene assurance of the very last poems and of the best animal and flower poems.

Self-discovery involved Lawrence in running away with Frieda von Richthofen, the wife of a distinguished Notthingham professor, in 1914. This romance has become legendary, though the legend sometimes omits the fact that Frieda lost contact with her children, that she and her lover had a volatile and reposeless love. Together they traveled, sustaining one another in flight from critical and moral opprobrium at home, and in flight from death. Unstable their love may have been, but it was sustaining. Had it not been, Lawrence could hardly have braved the difficult years of rejection and illness. His novel *The Rainbow* (1915) was confiscated and banned. In the same year he was forced with Frieda to abandon their home in Cornwall. They were thought to be German spies. He began to feel persecuted—he *was* persecuted. These pressures contributed to his least successful poetic veins: of satire and apocalypse.

After the First World War, Lawrence and Frieda, tired of an England that was hostile to his artistic mission, traveled widely. He wrote travel books, essays, introductions, novels and poems. He painted. Much of his most stimulating prose occurs in essays briskly written for a specific occasion; the ideas retain an alarming freshness and challenge. Large-scale aphorisms trigger a wealth of subsidiary ideas as we read. These detonations of sense are the product of sharp, partial insights which dazzle one part of a work at the expense of the rest. Lawrence is always right, though never entirely right. Yet the essays, more than his poems themselves, have effected fundamental changes in later writers— encouraging a greater sense of presence and presentness, a sense that the language of poetry (as of prose) is *enactive*, making its subject in a complex mimesis of syntax, rhythm and diction.

Wherever he traveled—to Italy, Australia, New Zealand, the South Seas, California, Mexico and New Mexico—he strove to *be present* in the place, not seeing it as a visitor with a Kodak but apprehending it through its landscape, art and literature. In 1926 he was back in Italy. He spent his last four years traveling through Europe trying to retard the development of the illness he refused to acknowledge was tuberculosis. In 1930 he died in a sanatorium in the South of France.

His achievement as a poet is overshadowed by his achievement as a novelist, though his poetry has never lacked admirers and is increasing in presence as his prose writings are buried under academic study. The poems explore the themes of the prose fiction, but where the novels concentrate on relationships between people, the poems explore the relationship between individual and a given world, recreating those states of mind which exist, subjectively, apart from human contact. They complement the fiction. If, in *Women in Love,* the character of Birkin is unsatisfactory because exaggeratedly subjective and infuriatingly dominant, in the poems, Birkin—so like Lawrence himself— speaks directly, freed from the constraint of plot. At a time when his contemporaries were donning masks and inventing personae in order to speak, Lawrence's mature poems belong, for the most part, unabashedly to the first person, a first person who can sound angry, vatic or lyrical, a first person "alive in the language."

At the outset there are a number of poems of relationship. *Love Poems and Others,* his first collection, appeared in 1913 and includes his relations with his mother and his first and second lovers. These poems, written guiltily ("as if it were a secret sin"—they are autobiographical) are marred by deliberate literary effects. He distinguishes between two sorts of poems, those written by his "demon" and those composed by a more conscious hand. He will revise and tamper with the latter; but the former are final and irrevocable.

He is continually thinking about poetry, how it differs from prose in construction and objective, and his letters and essays are full of distinctions enormously enabling to later writers and readers. In 1913 he wrote to Edward Marsh that he saw his poems in spatial rather than temporal or rhythmic terms, more "as a matter of movements in space than footsteps hitting the earth." There is still an emphasis on movement, but it is a movement away from the regular footfall of prescriptive meter toward the expressive cadences and suspensions of conversation, and later the incantatory, often biblical movement that Whitman helped him achieve. "It all depends on the *pause*," he wrote, "the lingering of the voice according to feeling—it is the hidden *emotional* pattern that makes poetry, not the obvious form." Soon he rejected the sense of balance that characterizes Georgian work. On the other hand, he could not depersonalize or aestheticize experience in the Imagist manner.

Later he called for a poetry of "the immediate present," where "there is no perfection, no consummation, nothing finished": *open* poetry. "Consummation" is a key word, suggesting that his poems deliberately defer or avoid dramatic climax: such climaxes set the artist outside the artifact, casting him inevitably in the role of constructor, orchestrator. He acknowledges Whitman as the master poet of the "present," a writer whose poem has neither beginning nor end—this, Lawrence reminds us, does not mean that he has no past and future. The voice of the "present" tends to be rhapsodic, celebrating "the urgent, insurgent Now," the "instant present"—if, that is, the demon dictates it. From Lawrence's general statements about poetry, which add up to something like a theory, it would not be unreasonable to have expected from him a long poem or long poems like Blake's or Whitman's, or—among his successors—Olson's or Robert Duncan's. But for all that he learned from American poetry, his sensibility remained decidedly English, his runs seldom exceed the lyric. There are sequences and series, but few attempts at sustained long poems. The longer runs are to be found in the prose fiction, and often the prose writings are truer to the spirit of his poetic theory than the poems themselves.

Free verse is essential, he believes, to poetic utterance. A poetry without preconceived meter, stress patterns or syllabic count, articulated by "the whole man," expressing his passions, conflicts and contradiction, is a voice of integrity, and poetry must be a language of integrity. He does not see free verse as finally *un*free because ultimately subjective in its movement. Subjectivity, the willful ascription of significance to certain words, images and rhythms, is his principal limitation. Yet unlike his imitators who strive to achieve a voice unique to themselves, there is the Wordsworthian legacy still at work in Lawrence, a man speaking to men. What matters is not the idiosyncrasy of voice, the mannerisms of expression, but the suasive authenticity of movement.

Free verse compels a revolution less in prosody than in diction. Traditional diction, formal, tending toward archaism, off-the-peg for a poet working at half energy, is quite unserviceable in free verse. It sounds ridiculous. And after the revolution of free verse, it is rendered less serviceable for traditional metrical verse as well. Ironically, the modernist revolution in prosody revivified diction even for those writers—like Frost, like Larkin—who stand aloof from it. Lawrence took the revolution further than Hulme and the Imagists, writing an accessible poetry that was immediately appealing, recognizably experiential, a kind that, with different tools, the Georgians were crafting in conventional ways.

Lawrence sloughs off clichés and deploys a fresh language, new wine for his new bottles. He tells us, in a weirdly eroticized phrase, that in free verse "we look for the insurgent naked throb of the instant moment." We are to expect "no satisfying stability, satisfying to those who like the immutable." The "pure present" is a realm, he says, which we have never conquered. And he, too, fails to conquer it, for there *is* a stability in his poems—though not always "satisfying." It is not the stability of the moralist who asserts meaning, though often Lawrence is intrusively didactic in awkward places, where the imagery has contained the very message he delivers in paraphrase. It is a stability of language, predictable rhythmic phrasing within a poem. His free verse is never as free as he claims; in many poems a cadential pattern is repeated with minimal variation. Free verse can be accompanied by a shortened syntactical measure (the short sentence being thought, perhaps, appropriate for the "urgent insurgent now"), which entails a shortening of the rhythmic measure. To achieve longer cadences it is necessary to bank up repetitions, or to create series.

Like Blake, Lawrence preempts his readers' misgivings by acknowledging the faults in his writing and identifying them as necessary virtues. The poet James Reeves writes of Lawrence: "He had not the craftsman's sense of words as living things, as ends in themselves. Words were too much means to an end." And so they were. Lawrence would have said: And so they should be. This is why he sits uneasily alongside the Georgians, whom Reeves admires and advocates. He was never a "craftsmanly" writer. In his perceptive and not altogether sympathetic study, Reeves adds, "He can seldom have conceived a poem as a whole before he sat down to write it. It grew under his pen." So did William Carlos Williams's and—we may guess—some of Ezra Pound's. The freedom of free verse has something to do with tolerating surprise, even with inviting it into the process. There is an analogy between the form of some of Lawrence's poems and "the musical impromptu," a "series of loosely connected variations."

The famous *Pansies* (1928)—Lawrence once referred to them as "rag-poems"—are named after the flower, but the title suggests too *pensées angliciées*. The verb *panser* comes to the poet's mind as well, "to dress or soothe a wound." Each "pansy" is "a true thought, which comes as much from the heart and genitals as from the head." *Pansies* are the closest Lawrence came to developing his own poetic form. That it is inadequate to all but the statement of image or opinion—without the compression or memorability of epigram, though it claims the authority of that form—implies the limitation of his formal imagination in verse. But when he allows an image to shape the form, as in the animal poems, or when he lets rhythm take hold, as in "The Ship of Death," questions of analyzable form are beside the point.

The precision he learned from Imagism makes a poem such as "Baby Running Barefoot" strong, keeping it free of sentimentality and cliché. But he can write such Georgian waffle as "The first white love of youth, passionless and vain." We know from external evidence that he was writing of real experiences, those described fully in *Sons and Lovers*. Encumbered by poetic diction, the poems fail. A lesson he never wholly learned: authenticity of emotion does not guarantee authentic poetry. In "Snap Dragon," a poem about the same experiences, he revealed latent powers that eventually produced the animal and death poems; nevertheless, it is technically marred. Its loosely rhythmic form demands that he interpose "did" auxiliaries to plump out the measure; he forces the rhyme. Yet the flaws corroborate a tone of tentative innocence. Something of the poem's troubling eroticism carries over into other love poems, particularly the Imagist "On the Balcony" and the Georgian "A Youth Mowing."

He wrote political poems. In "Now It's Happened," he chastises the Russian Revolution, its betrayal of the great Russian artists of the previous century, with political and poetic naïveté. In "Hibiscus and Salvia Flowers" he chides left-wing demonstrators in Sicily, ostensibly because they pluck beautiful flowers to plug their churlish buttonholes, but also because he despises egalitarianism and the despotism of the crowd. Like Pound's, his politics emerge from his aesthetics, though—he not having lived as long as Pound, and having distinct priorities—his political errors seem less noisome than the American's.

The animal poems find natural form in free verse, forms that answer the images. "The Mosquito" erratically alternates long and short lines, attacks and retires. A similar process occurs in "Bat," and in "Snake" the sinuous and the darting lines complement one another. These poems prefigure the Australian poet Les Murray's celebrated collection *Translations from the Natural World*, in which an appropriate language is found for animals to speak. Murray takes the experiment beyond rhythm and syntax into diction itself.

In "Snake" the speaker finds himself guilty of the Fall, attempting to kill a dark angel that inspires terror and fascination, the serpent visiting the water trough defining in its movement, shading and self-contained purpose another world. Lawrence would cross over into this purposeful, innocent world. When his human nature does not impede him, he can do so, as in his finest poem, "Bavarian Gentians," where he risks the dark and its indefinitions. In "Snake" he observes, attacks, laments. The snake, as an image, hovers between reptilian, human and divine. For an instant its drinking reminds him of a cow drinking, but it ascends in his observation by stages to being godlike. As the snake unfolds its meanings, the poet reveals himself in the terms he applies to it and eventually in his instinctive response, violence, and its withdrawal into the "dreadful," the "horrid black hole." As he hurls a log, the snake reverts to being merely a snake, the man becomes that limited creature, that fallen angel:

> And so I missed my chance with one of the lords
> Of life.
> And I have something to expiate;
> A pettiness.

There is an entirely colloquial humor—clean of irony—in the animal poems. In "Tortoise Family Connections" the baby tortoise is portrayed:

> Wandering in the slow triumph of his own existence,
> Ringing the soundless bell of his presence in chaos,
> And biting the frail grass arrogantly,
> Decidedly arrogantly.

The furniture and the cadence of the first three lines recall those of Ted Hughes's animal poems, yet the grace that illuminates Lawrence's animal world, accepting and unthreatening, celebratory, a grace of tone and witness, belongs to no other poet this century. Lawrence writes: "Man cannot live in chaos. The animal can. To the animal all is chaos, only there are a few recurring motions and aspects within the surge." Those recurrences are our points of access; and having gained access, the poet presses back toward chaos, to subject himself to the animals' environment, not to destroy himself but to extend his understanding. The real artist, he urges, will see things *in* chaos.

"The Ship of Death" braves dark, unknown waters. It's one of the outstanding, and certainly the most ambitious, of his dark poems. The images evoked remain suspended, isolated within a powerful, incantatory cadence. Unlike most of his poems, "The Ship of Death" is memorable not for its shape or cadence, but for the actual phrasing. "We Have Gone Too Far" is in the same vein, with a cadential intensity, like rhapsodic keening and, triumphantly, a celebration. This is the world of "Bavarian Gentians," where the flowers radiate darkness as a torch does light. The poet does not draw back: he embraces the experience.

As revealed in the poems and the prose around them, Lawrence can be read as a sometimes shrewd diagnostician, a revolutionary *avant la lettre*, who saw what poetry might do and how his contemporaries were selling it short. But because his prose work took precedence, or he lacked sufficient formal imagination, or because the time was not quite right, he did not write the poems his criticism proposed. His best poems and writing about poetry, like Cézanne's pictures and letters, promise much that was to come, much that is still to come. Like no other poet of his century apart from Pound, Lawrence remains insistently, insultingly, undeniably contemporary, a demanding enabler whom writers follow as often to perdition as to a promised land.

At Cambridge in the 1940s, where F. R. Leavis was making a critical talisman of Lawrence and Eliot (minus his objectionable piety), the young lecturer Donald Davie remembers tutoring the equally young poet and would-be filmmaker Charles Tomlinson. Tomlinson was interested in the *visceral*, in Henry Miller and Lawrence, whose work engaged the whole body, with special reference to the libidinal bits. Davie's task was to steer his charge onto a more disciplined path, not by insisting, as Leavis did, that Lawrence was the moral teacher, but by creating a context in which Lawrence's temperature might be credibly taken. Lawrence represents a zigzaggy middle way between the revolutions of Pound and Eliot and the counterrevolution based on Hardy. Lawrence admired Hardy but went another way: a kind of prophet but no idealist, he suffered "constant guilt and horror at what the English had done to England." Davie, having identified serviceable elements in Lawrence (but not in his poetry), defined the Lawrence mystique, the kinds of license issued in his name. He gets him clear in the frame, and in getting Lawrence clear he redefines Hardy—and Eliot.

Eliot, like Hardy, is at the heart of Donald Davie's concerns. The American modernist is so deeply a part of Davie's imagination, and of another *echt* English writer from another landscape, C. H. Sisson, that they are sometimes not wholly aware of the debt, as if Eliot is part of their second nature. They are made of Eliot (and Pound) quite as much as they are of Hardy. The tension within their poetry and criticism is generative. A vigorous modernism has taken root in them, but in an inhospitable and always skeptical English soil. It was Davie's task to bring Eliot into play in Tomlinson's creative world, as in those readers who feel the contrary pull of Hardy or Lawrence.

After their deaths, writers tend to suffer a revaluation, first (in the immediate aftermath) overvalued, and then knocked down a few pegs. Eliot's reputation has undergone a serious and excessive devaluation since he died in 1965. His politics, usually presented in a form so simplified he would not have recognized them, have told against him. There are shadowy areas in the biography into which prurient critics point their torches. The poetry and the criticism remain controversial in much the way they were when they first appeared, as if the paint had not yet dried on them. Eliot effected a radical change in the ways in which the intelligentsia thought about poetry and literature generally, but the change—in Britain at least—was not as fundamental as it once seemed. There are forces of reaction, the most potent being those that present themselves as the most "liberal" and democratic.

Whereas Lawrence is inscribed in each of his poems, Eliot insists on the poet's impersonality. Hugh Kenner terms him "the invisible poet." Marianne Moore saw him as "a master of the anonymous." Eliot is largely responsible for such critical rhetoric. It does not fit him as poet, critic or dramatist. His work is immediately recognizable as his. It would be hard to confuse even the least-known of his lines with that of another poet. His images, cadences and tones are distinctive.

Why did he so stress "impersonality" and recoil at the idea of a biography? Did he harbor dark secrets? The biographies he was adamant should not be written reveal a man unhappy and discontented by nature, but no more monstrous than most and, even in his success, more vulnerable than many. His insistence seems to have been a strategy to protect the poems from the higher gossip which reads the work as a camouflaged commentary on specific occasions in the life and thus, just as a crudely historicist approach confines the work within its period, kills the poem as poem, reading it as document or text. He was right to fear the worst. His first marriage is the subject of a play and a film. Speculation abounds about his early years. What are we to make of his racial attitudes?

But what are we to make of his *poems*? His description of the creative process is lucid, but relates most pertinently to the early poems. He says "the emotion of art is impersonal." The writer experiences "a continual surrender of himself as he is at the moment to something which is more valuable. The progress of an artist is a continual self-sacrifice, a continual extinction of personality." The language borders on the religious and mystical, and these terms Eliot employed before he became a committed Anglican. What occurs in his work is an extinction of biographical referents; but the personality in all its reticences is a palpable presence in every line. His poems are the more personal for carrying the sometimes heavy burden of the various cultures he has assimilated.

For Eliot, tradition is a matter of accretion. Each new work of literature relates to and subtly alters the work that has come before. A writer acquires tradition by dedicated reading, study and a sharpening discrimination. Writers and readers develop an instinct for both the pastness and the presence of tradition. All literature is finally contemporary, no writer can be judged outside the context of the living tradition. But some resources are no longer, or not just now, serviceable; forms, registers and elements of diction can belong specifically to their period, and though the works still speak, their resources are unavailable today.

Eliot developed among poets seeking a modern idiom, trying to renew poetic forms and accommodate new material. He learned something from the vivid social poet of the 1890s John Davidson, particularly about subject matter. The essays of Davidson's contemporary Arthur Symons directed his attention (as they had Yeats's before him) to French poets such as Jules Laforgue and the symbolists. The poet's mission was to discover analogy and unity in disparate elements of experience and to hold them in expressive tension. Eliot took this to mean discovering a stable, independent "set of objects, a situation, a chain of events which shall be a formula of that *particular* emotion; such that when the external facts, which must terminate in sensory experience, are given, the emotion is immediately evoked." This is the famous "objective correlative," a term widely misused in criticism. Eliot viewed it in terms of imagery, implicit plot and the organization of sound.

By coordinating the sound qualities of words the poet elicits meanings from areas of consciousness that language does not generally penetrate, but where meanings are latent. It is the auditory imagination which performs these "raids on the inarticulate," by placing words in a context, using them in full knowledge of their semantic value, their cultural associations, and then maximizing their rhythmic and aural effect, fusing several levels of speech and thought in a single experience. Though he mastered traditional meter, Eliot developed stress rhythms as distinctive as they are inimitable (though they lend themselves to parody).

The idea of an "auditory imagination" is haunting. Eliot—and some poets after him, including Louis Zukofsky and Ted Hughes—have entertained the idea that a poem read to people ignorant of the language it is written in will elicit a response, perhaps a correct response, simply through its sound values. It is a seductive notion, but those who have sat through poetry readings in unfamiliar languages know that the "music" of a language eventually becomes monotonous, and a hunger for sense, or for recognizable referents, asserts itself after a few minutes.

Thomas Stearns Eliot was born in St. Louis, Missouri, in the United States, in 1888, the seventh child of Henry Ware Eliot. His father was company secretary and ultimately chairman of the Hydraulic Press Brick Company. He provided a prosperous home and a good education for his offspring. The family was Unitarian in religion, devoted to good works, taught to believe in human perfectibility and to distrust ritual. Piety without sacrament, a certain moral severity, and a materialist bent gave the young Eliot a host of elements against which to rebel.

He seems to have enjoyed a happy, if formal, relationship with his parents. He studied at Smith Academy in St. Louis, where he wrote a number of poems, some of which survive. The earliest, written when he was nine or ten, were about "the sadness of having to start school again every Monday morning." Four years later he wrote "some very gloomy quatrains in the form of the *Rubáiyát*." At sixteen he wrote "A Fable of Feasters," which reveals a love of Byron and genuine prosodic skill. His mother, Charlotte, ambitious to be a poet, encouraged her son. When she read his early, cloying imitation of Ben Jonson, she esteemed it as better than anything she had written, which shows less humility than foresight and a discriminating ear.

Eliot attended Harvard College between 1906 and 1910 and wrote the "Ode" for Class Day in 1910. He cut his editorial teeth on the Harvard *Advocate*, the literary journal to which he also contributed poems. Boston and Cambridge, Massachusetts, left a deeper impression on his early poems than St. Louis had. It was the land- and cityscape of his imagination, much as New Hampshire became Frost's chosen landscape, though he was a Californian by birth.

Greek and Latin were central to Eliot's studies at Harvard, and he attended a course on Dante, about whom he later wrote a suggestive, influential and largely wrong-headed essay. He also read French, German and some philosophy. French poetry attracted him, especially Laforgue. He imitated the Frenchman in "Humoresque," which he published in the *Advocate*, and another poem, "Spleen," in which alleys and cats get their first look in on his verse, along with signs of balding and the excessive fastidiousness that Prufrock more fully displays. In "The Death of St. Narcissus," another early piece, the first stirrings of *The Waste Land* sensibility are heard. The poem's mannered eroticism combines the legend of Narcissus and the story of St. Sebastian, mingling them with material from Arthurian romance. In 1909 and 1910, when he began his graduate work, Eliot wrote "Portrait of a Lady" and "Preludes

I and II," and began work on "The Love Song of J. Alfred Prufrock." It was startlingly assured and precocious work for a young man of twenty-one, steeped in the classics and European culture, and with Henry James as a kind of tutelary spirit.

Eliot responded to Laforgue's tonal suppleness, his precise imprecision, the way character is created not by plot and external detail but by hesitancies of voice, peculiarities of detail, by playing off the familiar and subverting expectations. It is a kind of clarity that eludes paraphrase, whose logic is not constructed but inferred. The earlier symbolists had tended—as Donald Davie describes it—to set images at a certain distance from each other, letting the unspoken sense emerge from the spaces between. Individual images were made expressive beyond the physical sense to which they were addressed; sounds became visible and smells palatable—the synesthesia that infatuated Edith Sitwell. Individual images become symbols, points at which disparate meanings are drawn together and expressed all at once. For the later symbolists the poem itself, as a whole, is the symbol. It might have a plot, all the elements of which work toward a complex symbolic meaning or meanings. Laforgue achieves suggestiveness by developing plots, or pseudo-plots, which give a poem continuity without limiting its particular significance—drawing, as it were, a grid-map that relates differently to different land masses. Organization becomes symbolic, and fragmentation is a crucial strategy.

Eliot visited France in 1910, attending lectures at the Sorbonne, and returned to Harvard to pursue his doctorate on European and Indian philosophy in 1911. Among his teachers were George Santayana and Irving Babbitt. In 1914 he traveled to Marburg to pursue his studies, but with the First World War he turned up in London, gravitating to Merton College, Oxford, where he continued working on his doctoral thesis on the philosophy of F. H. Bradley. It finally dawned on him that he was not cut out to be a philosopher and in 1915 he left university and married for the first time. He tried his hand at teaching in a junior school in London, but soon moved on to work at Lloyds Bank. London at the time was strewn with literary groups and cliques. Bloomsbury was at work, and so were the Sitwells. Eliot reviewed books and wrote articles. He came into contact with Ezra Pound and with Imagism. If he spent most of his adult life in England, he never ceased to regard himself as an American poet. In 1959 he declared, "My poetry has obviously more in common with my distinguished contemporaries in America than with anything written in my generation in England."

Though never an Imagist, Eliot understood the Imagist program and, as a fellow traveler, profited from it. He wrote later that Imagism was the *point de repere* for any consideration of modern English poetry.

His association with Pound, like so many other writers', was energizing: he began to pare down his language, to economize for impact. He learned how important juxtaposition was as an organizing instrument, that the setting side by side of images or vignettes not obviously or logically related could be used to precise effect, without explication or moralizing.

Robert Graves met the youngish Eliot in 1916, while on leave. He describes him as "a startlingly good-looking, Italianate young man, with a shy, hunted look, and a reluctance (which I found charming) to accept the most obvious phenomenon of the day—a world war now entering its bloodiest stage . . . I was due to return to the Somme any day, and delighted to forget the war too in Eliot's gently neutral company."

In 1917 Eliot, together with H.D. (Hilda Doolittle), took over editorship of the *Egoist* from Richard Aldington. He needed the formal authority and the responsible freedoms an independent editor enjoys in order to develop a literary environment, with collaborators willing to take risks in appraisal and reappraisal. In 1922 he founded his most influential magazine, the *Criterion*, which, with Edgell Rickword's short-lived *Calendar of Modern Letters*, established a new standard of critical and creative writing. His years as a magazine editor coincided with his early success as a poet. In 1917 *Prufrock and Other Observations* appeared, and *Poems* (1920, published by Leonard and Virginia Woolf and the Hogarth Press) widened his readership. In 1922 came *The Waste Land*, which seemed to change English poetry for good. Eliot became at first the most controversial, and then the most respected avant-garde writer of his day. *The Hollow Men* (1925) did little to extend his reputation, for despite the poems' merit, Eliot seemed to be pastiching or parodying the novel strategies of his earlier work.

In 1927 he became a British subject and joined the Church of England. *Ash Wednesday* (1930), the first substantial production of the English Eliot, was received without enthusiasm, its religious concerns anathema at a time of increasing social tension and its poetic strategies too demanding for new readers. The dramatic fragments *Sweeney Agonistes* (published in book form in 1932) have only in recent years attracted the attention their originality merits. In 1944 his last major poetic work, *Four Quartets*, was published (*Burnt Norton*, 1935; *East Coker*, 1940; *The Dry Salvages*, 1941; *Little Gidding*, 1942). After that, most of his flagging poetic energies were directed to dramatic verse.

Eliot's later career took him into the thick of publishing. It cannot be denied that the task of editing other people's work, appraising manuscripts for publication, engaging in the actual trade, diverted him from his own work, much as they did Edgell Rickword from his. He became part of an establishment he was instrumental in creating. He won various awards, including the Nobel Prize and the Order of Merit in 1948, and was canonized as "the poet of the century"—rewards for the major poet of *The Waste Land* and the critic of *The Sacred Wood, Tradition and the Individual Talent,* and the other major books and essays, not the editor or the minor dramatist of the verse plays.

His forcefulness as a critic, the patrician authority of his style, defined one possible way for English literature this century to go; but when he was established, he began a gradual recantation, manifested in his plays, later poems and criticism, and in the poetry list he published at Faber and Faber with its notorious sins of omission and commission. He qualified and undermined the radical challenge he threw down in his early works. He changed ground subtly on Milton and on Goethe, poets he had earlier criticized with stupendous severity. The change was dictated by the occasions for which the later appraisals were prepared, and yet change there was, of a kind that smacks of disingenuousness. The later Eliot hardly diminishes the early firebrand. Prufrock may have grown into the elder statesman, but it is Prufrock who is our contemporary, while the elder statesman of Eliot's last two decades is unreal. Eliot was assimilated into the culture he adopted.

Elder Eliot bears much of the responsibility for deflecting modernism in Britain, for lessening its impact on English poetry and critical thought. The apparent climax of his poetic writing, *Four Quartets,* for all its obliquity, rejects the intensity of *The Waste Land* and his earlier modernist work. *Four Quartets* is discursive and in places prolix. Though intellectually taxing and rhythmically resourceful, a work of undeniable magnificence in nineteenth-century terms, it has as much in common with late Auden as with early Eliot. The poet is expatiating before an audience, exploring rather than discovering his meanings. He becomes a complex but explicit moralist. The subtle erotic undertones of his best writing have vanished. A lax discursiveness makes too many concessions—particularly in *The Dry Salvages*—to the merely poetic, and the organization, similar in each quartet, is to some extent arbitrary. Discoverer becomes missionary. When a poet of Eliot's stature in his later work rejects the exacting practices of his youth, his foes can say "I told you so," his followers can participate in the rejection, sitting at the feet of the comfortable elder, avoiding contention with the serious young man.

Eliot's situation as an expatriate twice over—from Unitarian St. Louis to agnostic Boston, from New England to England—taken with his social and religious concerns, his hunger for a natural home, make his development comprehensible. E. M. Forster wrote of his religion, "What he seeks is not revelation but stability." The epigraph to "Burbank with a Baedeker, Bleistein with a Cigar," reads with an irony that in retrospect cuts both ways, *"nil nisi divinum stabile est; caetera fumus"* ("only the divine stands firm; the rest is smoke"). In *Ash Wednesday* he "constructs something upon which to rejoice," accepting the forms of faith in the hope, or belief, that by grace faith will follow. This is the "grammar of assent" of the Catholic and Anglo-Catholic nineteenth century. A quest for stability is central in Eliot's work, and the early poems evoke the very instabilities and discontinuities from which the later writings seek to extricate him. The social and personal agony of *The Waste Land* and the individual agony of "Prufrock" are responses to instability, and the poet could not have stayed in that place for long without self-destructing. The power of the religious poetry is not in its faith but in the desire to believe, to find something believable, in the forms, liturgies and dogmas quite as much as in the deity. Religion is an instrument of acculturation for him: Anglicanism and Englishness are intertwined.

When stability is entirely beyond his reach, as in "Prufrock," the tone becomes elegiac, or satirical in the "Sweeney" poems. Desire for stability results in his radical conservatism as a critic, an impersonal dealing in "certainties" and his technical experimentation as a poet. Poems and prose fulfill complementary functions; in time the prose was destined to triumph over the tense anxieties of the verse. Craving stability based on the old order, a writer has to discover what forms are viable in the present. The great innovations—often the work of conservative imaginations—generally occur in our literature in the elegiac mode and spread out from there. The Prince in Giuseppe de Lampedusa's great novel *The Leopard* declares the strategy: to stay the same we must change. Adjustments of form, of surface, protect the deeper dispositions and divisions of a culture.

When Eliot began writing for the theater, he saw the poles of dramatic language as being ceremonial and liturgical at one extreme (the chorus, the dance) and realistic, social, demotic at the other. His poems are enacted between these extremes, tending first toward one, then the other. They are often dramatic (more dramatic than the plays). Dramatic monologues are among his best work; like Pound, he owed a debt to Browning as much as to Laforgue. Many of the poems' epigraphs are drawn from plays, classical as well as English.

In *Ash Wednesday* Eliot began to dramatize not voice but content. The "speaker" here, not self-defining as in Prufrock, not a figure as such, becomes morally implicated in what he says, expressing not generalities but particular experiences. The question arises: Is he posturing, is the internal conflict real *in the way he suggests*, is he gesturing at religious meanings? The impact of this poem seems to me a sufficient answer, but more insistently the same question arises with *Four Quartets*. When he speaks of "the intolerable wrestle with words and meanings," the "wrestle" is not felt in the exposition to which he treats us. He appears to be constructing something with which to wrestle. The poet becomes visible, personae dwindle. Eliot, when he pauses to reason or puzzle out an idea, lets the poem go. Pound knew this and put his pencil through such passages in *The Waste Land*. He didn't perform the same surgery on the *Quartets*—he would have been temperamentally incapable of doing so, the themes and procedures being so remote from those he and Eliot had developed two decades earlier.

Eliot is not at his best as a philosopher, mingling discursive with allusive poetry, except when he shatters the former with a decisive intrusion of the latter, or when he reports speech and is not himself speaking. So long as the impersonal experiencing is maintained, the poetry is safe. This "impersonality" disappears not when we read actual biographical data—Eliot is reporting a nervous disorder: "On Margate Sands. / I can connect / Nothing with nothing"—but rather when we read, "After such knowledge, what forgiveness?" in "Gerontion" and feel the images, moralized, have been left lifeless. Eliot reaches a degree of experiential intensity unparalleled in modern poetry; it is natural, if regrettable, that he had to retreat into cogitation.

Illness, fever, delirium, nervous disorientation—like half-sleep—he believes allow a freedom of association within the poet's mind. Images, long incubated, flow free under the vertiginous release of mental and physical disorientation. If they find language, poetry may occur. This appears to have been the case with the rapid composition of *The Waste Land* and *Sweeney Agonistes*. For Eliot, this is not inspiration but something ambiguously negative, "the breaking down of strong habitual barriers" that "re-form very quickly." One is tempted to say that this, precisely, *is* inspiration, clearly defined. But most critics take inspiration to be a positive impulse.

"The Love Song of J. Alfred Prufrock," completed when Eliot was twenty-three and published in a book six years later, is his most striking early achievement. Discontinuous and fragmentary in plot, the poem is continuous only in rhythm and tone. Without specifying a location, Eliot vividly evokes a series of places. The title contains the governing irony: this "love song" is in fact an elegy, and an elegy not for what has been but for what might have been had the eloquently inadequate speaker been more equal to the social challenge of his world and more complete in himself. Juxtaposing fragments of conversation, observation, experience, Eliot creates a mosaic, a characterization that does not stop at character but realizes a particular social class that Eliot knew well. It is at once inner and external landscape, a state of mind and a flickering narrative. The poem becomes a symbol, a form through which a multitude of tentative meanings flows; it is successful in the mode to which the more overtly symbolic and less accomplished "Gerontion" also belongs.

"Portrait of a Lady" is "Prufrock" 's companion piece, though it was completed earlier and, because more specific in plot and the relationships it evokes, it is more limited in its resonance than the more famous poem. The title comes from Henry James's great novel, the epigraph, from Marlowe's play *The Jew of Malta*: "Thou hast committed— / Fornication; but that was in another country, / And besides, the wench is dead." These words contrast sharply with the contained, dry tone of the poem, suggesting another country and another age in which sexual desire is acted on. The quiet, proper and cultured lady serving tea, the equally proper Prufrockian visitor, are illuminated by the title and the epigraph, which propose two models of selfish, self-destructive or destructive action. In the world of Eliot's lady, nothing actually happens: manners and custom have dried out the protagonists, who gradually brim with self-disgust. As in "Prufrock," manners and attitudes that govern communication make the expression of anything important virtually impossible. It is a culture of obliquity. "That is not what I meant at all . . ." complains a voice in "Prufrock." Failed communication as a theme recurs even in Eliot's most assured and least successful later work. These constraints he portrays so well in part because he was himself constrained and never entirely escaped, at least not in daylight. The bizarre nighttime and no-time of the "Sweeney" poems, less oblique, has the candor of madness.

In "Preludes" Eliot was exploring the same theme indirectly, with reference to other social orders of which he had less experience:

I am moved by fancies that are curled
Around these images, and cling:
The notion of some infinitely gentle
Infinitely suffering thing.

The verse turns on the word "thing." Against the anguish of almost recognition, the poet savagely counsels:

Wipe your hand across your mouth, and laugh;
The worlds revolve like ancient women
Gathering fuel in vacant lots.

These are the separate "worlds" of social classes, isolated worlds of individual men and women, as solitary in Eliot's cityscape as in Hardy's unforgiving rural setting.

The image of music plays through the poetry. In poem titles we read of songs, rhapsodies, preludes, quartets, "Five-Finger Exercises." Music suggests a certain kind of organization, an attitude to language, certain intended effects. In *The Waste Land* it is a tragic music; later it becomes the painful, redeeming Shakespearean music. Images of architecture, painting, and of course a constant flow of literary allusions, inform the poetry. Being an urban writer, Eliot has no nature to fall back on: it is all nurture, his poems are made of made things, on a ground entirely given over to human projects, passions and tragedies. A figure wandering through much of the poetry is old, sexless Tiresias, who has achieved a numb, knowing stability.

Eliot and Pound rebelled together against what they saw as the mis- use of free or unmetered verse. A mannered acerbity enters Eliot's blackly humorous and suggestive "Sweeney" poems and the other work in rhymed quatrains. Though style and tone change, the organization remains the same. The "Sweeney" poems possess the same precise im- precision, the same sudden juxtapositions and transitions of imagery. They draw on the English Metaphysical poets—Donne in particular— as much as they do on the late symbolists, and they are dense with liter- ary allusion. Where they are less supple than the poems that precede them is in tone. The quatrain form is chosen for a polemical purpose, to stand against the failures of the free-verse writers. Used with the verbal intensity Eliot requires of it, the quatrain is incapable of those sudden shifts of mood and tone that occur in earlier poems. It is only here, how- ever, that Eliot achieved a thoroughgoing impersonality of manner.

Sweeney Agonistes, fragments of a verse play, was published, one imagines, with some trepidation by the writer. He certainly kept it in his drawer for rather longer than even Horace would have advised. Eliot composed it at great speed and without premeditation. The rhythmic brio of the near-nonsense verse is dazzling. Despite the brevity of the fragments, characters and unanchored situations are suggested. These fragments reveal what originality Eliot *might* have achieved as a drama- tist had he premeditated verse drama less and let his turbulent imagina- tion write the plays, for the turbulence in *Sweeney* is unprecedented in English verse. These are not the affluent classes of his finished plays, the society whose voices he never quite managed to register accurately. Here the characters are rootless, leading their hectic lives in an urban world ignorant of country houses and the Church of England. Telephone con- versations, unexpected arrivals and departures, Tarot readings, intru- sions of characters from other poems—including Mrs. Porter and Sweeney himself—and undisguised sexuality and cruelty, make it unique in Eliot's work and central to it: a potent "might have been." This is the dramatic genius that Eliot suppressed (or lost) in order to write the ceremonious plays, from *Murder in the Cathedral,* with its moral pretensions, to *The Confidential Clerk.* Eliot in his plays tried to make the verse unobtrusive, to communicate subtle and sometimes esoteric meanings. He achieves flatness rather than conversational fluency, relieved by a few memorable scenes in which the poetry is given its head and the action ritualized.

In *The Waste Land* he demanded to be read differently from other poets. He alters our way of reading for good, if we read him properly. The poem does not respond to analysis of its meanings—meanings cannot be detached from the texture of the poetry itself. The idiom is synthetic, fusing (or collaging) voices, each with its own allusions and images and implicit life story. The shifting voices and tones of voice are not signaled by marginal directions but in alterations of cadence and diction within the "flow." Though the poem cannot be said to be "organic," it does enact a process, stage by stage evoking people, places and cultures, their fullness impoverished and laid waste. The downward movement of the poem is turned, in the final section, toward potential regeneration. Before this point, the pattern is of decline: historical and legendary figures of the past, sharply evoked, are succeeded by the lackluster, passionless, unregenerate "present," its classes and concerns evoked in sterile female figures and emblematic voices. Cleopatra, Desdemona and Ophelia give way to the neurotic lady, the typist and the women in the pub, their relationships cursory, inarticulate, incomplete.

Eliot's apt literary and cultural allusions—to Spenser, Dante, Baudelaire, Wagner, Shakespeare and others—have a particular force when redefined in terms of *The Waste Land.* The past in its most achieved forms is implicated and degraded in the present; the poem is enhanced by our recollection of the works from which the allusions are taken. We might be tempted to read *The Waste Land* against the grain of *Tradition and the Individual Talent,* for in the poem Eliot suggests that cultural addition adjusts the past indeed, but also degrades it.

There is more than manipulation of allusion and narrative at work in *The Waste Land.* In the opening lines of "The Burial of the Dead," the first section of the poem, Eliot uses five present participles: "breeding," "mixing," "stirring," "covering" and "feeding." Each occurs at a line ending, with the emphasis of enjambement, suggesting ongoing process, organic and natural. In the first eight lines of the poem, spring, summer and winter are suggested. Memory and desire (past and future) are latent in the cruel rebirth of the year.

The natural progression is juxtaposed to the nattering recollections of Marie. Her voice is displaced by the dark tones of, perhaps, Tiresias, "for you know only / A heap of broken images". . ."I will show you fear in a handful of dust." The longing strains of Wagner's *Tristan und Isolde* are silenced by the hopeless refrain, *"Oed und leer das Meer"* ("Desolate and empty the sea"). The cruelty of false starts—Marie curtailed by Tiresias, memory by the present—leads to the sham hope that spiritualism may hold the answer, and Madame Sosostris, the clairvoyant, is visited. Her turning up of cards that are sequences of images is in emblematic form what the poet is doing, turning up and setting side by side before us a sequence of voice images, from which we can draw conclusions about the present, past and future. The relationship between card and card, the sense of sequence, must be inferred. The Tarot cards provide a correlative for the discontinuous technique of the poem. They offer no revelation. The future cannot be confidently predicted; the present is without direction.

"A Game of Chess" pursues the process of degeneration into the intimacies of relationship. The opening passage compels us to recall Shakespeare's Cleopatra, Virgil's Dido, and (degeneration already setting in) the heroine of Pope's *The Rape of the Lock*. The verse breaks off suddenly in a jazz tune, the cheapness and accuracy of which recall the verve of the songs in *Sweeney Agonistes*. In "The Fire Sermon," the third section of the poem, Marvell's "To His Coy Mistress" degenerates into an insalubrious ballad, and Sweeney himself puts in a brief appearance. The Buddha's "Fire Sermon" was preached against the fires of lust, envy, anger and other destructive passions. It too is put to work in this altering context. A suggestive eroticism is at play. There are hints of perversion in Mr. Eugenides's advances, of impotence in Tiresias, of loveless sex and infecundity. But the section is not satirical in intent—rather, it is painfully elegiac. It is a verse that enacts the process of decay, most aptly when it introduces the theme through allusion to great art and artists, historical personages, and the history of a particular river, the Thames, at the heart of a particular urban society just after the Great War.

"Death by Water," the fourth section, evolved out of Eliot's own French poem, *"Dans le Restaurant."* The passage intensifies and alters the recurrent image of water, with its normally curative and baptismal powers. This particular image of drowning is an emblem of futility, fulfilling Madame Sosostris's prophesy but to no purpose: the futility of worries over profit and loss, youth and age, the elements, all forgotten in the once-and-for-all transformation of death, a bleak stability without suggestion of rebirth (though the allusion to Shakespeare's redemptive play *The Tempest* sows seeds to which the final section at last adds water).

"What the Thunder Said" concludes the poem in what is the most difficult, and least successful, section. As the drought breaks and the thunder speaks, various elusive suggestions of hope occur—the fleeting image of Christ at Emaus, for example. We move east from the Thames to the great holy Ganges. But despite the thunder's advice to "give, sympathize, and control," the speaker of the closing lines is the mad prince, without inheritance and without posterity, snared in the present. This final juxtaposition, of hope and the man incapable of grasping it, is the most tragic and telling in the poem.

The Waste Land is inexhaustible because of the way in which it evokes a particular social, moral, historical and aesthetic moment, freighted with an abundant past, wrecked on a sterile present. To ask for a coherent "solution" to the poem is to misread the very technique. There is a solution, but there is a cultural and historical gap between the mad prince and the thunder's counsel. The thunder speaks to the mad prince, but the mad prince cannot act upon its advice. The generous philosophies of the East, and the Christian faith, which begins to seem possible, demand an open ear, a heart prepared. The poem is incomplete because the poet is too truthful to "construct something upon which to rejoice."

In *Ash Wednesday* the subjective element dominates more than in any of the other poems. The idiom is neither discursive nor committedly allusive and spare. It hovers. Liturgical allusions, used in the spirit in which Eliot deploys literary allusions, weaken the overall effect. Something of the subjectivity is to be felt in "The desert in the garden, the garden in the desert"—internal and external landscapes are interchangeable because constructed, not given. The "I" is more powerful here than the correlatives through which it works. A psalmodic cadence is employed, as though the poet chooses liturgical music in order to persuade himself. "Journey of the Magi" and "Marina" pursue similar themes and come up with more tentative answers, inviting rather than compelling assent. "Marina," one of Eliot's most perfect poems, is brief, intense and sensuous: desire based on memory, not working against it.

Four Quartets are more comprehensible—or paraphrasable—than Eliot's earlier poems. They include much subtlety and fine verse. Considered as poems, their discursive and finally monotonous progression between points of achieved poetry can disappoint readers resistant to Eliot's meanings. *Four Quartets* is a poem of meanings, detachable meanings. His thoughts change course, not for dramatic effect or to suggest fragmentation as in earlier poems, but simply because he can go no further with them. He plays them out. Having accepted at Oxford that he was no philosopher, he returned to philosophical verse. A flatness of diction and rhythm, a prosaic plumpness of phrase, these occur, but no "intolerable wrestle / With words and meanings." The battle was over well before that phrase was neatly turned round its enjambement. Of the four, *Burnt Norton* is the outstanding quartet, including some of his most quoted lines. Yet the *poem* is not memorable. Eliot has simplified his technique, if not his discipline, to appeal to a wide audience, not in order to clarify his meanings.

He had grown older; history had taken various turns since the challenge of *The Waste Land* and the technical precocity of the *Prufrock* poems. If one is critical of *Four Quartets* it is only by the standard Eliot set in his early poems. They are disappointing—not at first reading, but when they have been lived with for a few years. They lack the intensity and eloquence of unspoken meanings. They are "full of high sentence" and not quite *true*—worked up, too reasonable, too sociable, the product rather than the process of thought. Edgell Rickword got the early Eliot right, noting the two sharp impressions the poems make: "urgency of the personality, which seems sometimes oppressive, and comes near to breaking through the so finely spun aesthetic fabric," and "technique which spins this fabric" and issues in an economy of expression which sets the slim *Poems, 1909–1925* on a different plane from "the bulky monsters of our time." He adds, "It is by his struggle with technique that Mr Eliot has been able to get closer than any other poet to the physiology of our sensations . . . to explore and make palpable the more intimate distresses of a generation for whom all the romantic escapes had been blocked."

Eliot's poetry has a comparable importance within the tradition to Dryden's and Wordsworth's in earlier centuries, effecting a renewal in poetic language. Even today, "Prufrock" and *The Waste Land* are more challenging and "contemporary" than much work produced last year or last decade. They are *contemporary*, present in the way great poetry remains present and available, entering our aural memory and lodging there. It is with Eliot and Pound that our poetic and critical language, our sensibility, are thoroughly shaken out. If the dust has settled again, if the challenge of modernism has not been accepted in the longer term, it is our loss. Against the formal rigor and wholeness of Eliot's oeuvre the fiddlings of postmodernism have a facile and fudged look. The cold hand of convention grips firmly; those radical intelligences which turn our eye back to the informing tradition and help us to pry ourselves free are few. To take them seriously involves disciplines and revaluations that are hard to sustain in a conformist literary culture. Even Eliot, in the end, breathed the same air as lesser poets.

But Ezra Pound didn't. When Robert Graves met him at All Souls', Oxford, in T. E. Lawrence's rooms, he was surprised: "From his poems, I had expected a brawny, loud-voiced, swashbuckling American; but he was plump, hunched, soft-spoken and ill-at-ease, with the limpest of handshakes." Pound hadn't much time for the Georgians, and at this point Graves was associated with them and with all that Pound had set his cap against.

Born in Hailey, Idaho, in 1885, Pound grew up in Wyncott, Pennsylvania, and became a student, ultimately at the University of Pennsylvania, of Romance languages. His contemporaries included William Carlos Williams and H.D. (who attended Bryn Mawr), and he became a close friend of each—indeed he courted H.D., but her father thought him a poor match. After graduation in 1906 he taught briefly, but was dismissed as too bohemian for Wabash College, Indiana. He traveled to Venice, publishing his first book, *A Lume Spento,* at his own expense. He was besotted with Swinburne and Dante Gabriel Rossetti and Browning. Whitman was in his blood. He was translating the poetry of the troubadours, Provençal and Anglo-Saxon verse. "The Seafarer," included in 1912 in *Ripostes,* is his first major poem and foreshadows the opening of the *Cantos.* Indeed everything he read and translated at this time was "laid down" for eventual decanting into his great work. It was in *Ripostes* that he included Hulme's poems. The Imagists were invented, with their list of rules: "Direct treatment of the 'thing' whether objective or subjective; to use absolutely no word that did not contribute to the presentation: as regarding rhythm, to compose in sequence of the musical phrase, not in the sequence of the metronome." He busied himself about his career and about H.D.'s—she too was in London—and Richard Aldington's, who married her. Pound sent their verse off to *Poetry* (Chicago)—he was acting as foreign correspondent for the journal— and it was he who persuaded Hilda Doolittle to call herself H.D. Imagiste (the frenchified ending signifying her Continental affinities), later abbreviated to H.D. Pound also promoted the work of Williams, Flint, Ford, James Joyce and Amy Lowell (the last of which he rather regretted). In *Poetry* he published "A Few Don'ts by an Imagist"—Moses' commandments for modern verse—including "Go in fear of abstractions" (which he abbreviated as "GIFOA" in the margins of *The Waste Land*) and "Don't chop your stuff into separate iambs." One thing we don't look for in Pound's prose is polite correctness of expression. He writes prose the way he talks—emphatically, without embellishment, and in a definite tone of voice.

He took his own medicine. A thirty-one line poem he ran through the Imagist wringer came out as two very famous lines, the poem called "In the Station of the Metro"; alongside H.D.'s "oread" it is the paradigmatic Imagist poem that fuses two images without interpretative fuss: "The apparition of those faces in the crowd; / Petals on a wet, black bough." Defining what he meant by the image, Pound evoked "the precise moment when a thing outward and objective transforms itself into a thing inward and subjective."

Imagism was not enough—and besides, the rich and always forthright American poet Amy Lowell, with her mauve Rolls Royce and, legend says, a cigar clenched between her teeth—usurped his place as editor of the Imagist anthologies. With her it became tennis without the net: in Pound's view she did not understand *vers libre* or what genuine Imagism was (even though she did admit Lawrence to the club, and Lowell wrote some creditable verses of her own). Pound renamed the group the Amygists and took his ball elsewhere. He invented a new game with Wyndham Lewis, a game more dynamic than Imagism and encompassing the graphic and plastic arts as well as poetry. They called it Vorticism and together produced two impressive issues of the magazine *Blast*. Such movements were polemical groupings, launchpads for some of the most significant talents of the century. The modest beginnings with their dictats and papal bulls would be absurd were it not for the fact that Pound, Williams, H.D., Marianne Moore, Lewis, Joyce, Lawrence and others all subscribed in one way or another early in their careers.

For Pound, more important than the movements was his personal engagement with other languages. Ernest Fenollosa, an American working in the Orient, had left notes on *The Chinese Written Character as a Medium for Poetry*. His widow entrusted to Pound the editing of the manuscript, and it was a crucial task in his development. Already in *Lustra* there were Oriental touches. From Fenollosa he learned something of the dynamic of a language entirely different in construction from those he already knew, a language whose writing was ideogrammatic, and whose ideograms, he believed, included image elements. The Japanese *Noh* plays, which he edited and translated from Fenollosa's versions, were also of interest to Yeats. *Cathay* (1915) includes Pound's seventeen translations or imitations of Chinese verse, his most compelling versions of any poetry apart from *Homage* to *Sextus Propertius*. The "Song of the Bowmen of Shu" is called "Ode" in the *Classic Anthology of Chinese Verse*. There is nothing conventionally "songlike" about it. Donald Davie, Pound's best English reader, says that it recalls no preexistent English form. It may have a touch of plainsong about it, but otherwise it is something new, a resource invented out of another language and literature. Pound has "internalized" the "music." In his versions one line of Chinese characters often becomes a single sentence, the punctuation relaxed to ease the flow, with commas where we would expect full stops. Punctuation *dictates* the pace and is used unconventionally. Pound's Chinese measure is not the syllable or stress count, but the fulfillment of the grammatical movement of the sentence—a contained rhythm of syntax. "To break the pentameter, that was the first heave," he said elsewhere. Certainly in the poems in *Cathay* the pentameter is no longer in control. The finest of the Chinese poems is in the voice of a woman: "The River-Merchant's Wife: A Letter."

What was the common denominator between the score of cultures with which he was on more than nodding terms by his early thirties? The search led him toward the *Cantos*. A crucial stepping stone was *Homage to Sextus Propertius*, which he published in 1917, working on this classical project at the same time as the Chinese. He develops an idiom that is full of parodic elements. It is a "translation" that at every point tells the reader it is translation: deliberate awkwardnesses, classroom translationese and some of the finest and most poised of his writing are juxtaposed in a work that conjures up an ancient and a modern world, a classical and a modern sensibility, in the same breath.

It was in *Hugh Selwyn Mauberley*, published in 1920, that—in variable rhymed quatrains—he managed to slough off the last tatters of the 1890s. Eliot read the poem as "a document of an epoch," and it deserves to be placed beside *The Waste Land*, with which it shares certain themes and techniques. The quatrains break down in the fourth section, and in *vers libre* Pound writes one of the great war poems, vividly prefiguring the clarity and anger of the *Cantos*:

These fought in any case,
and some believing.
                    pro domo, in any case ...

Some quick to arm,
some for adventure,
some from fear of weakness,
some from fear of censure,
some for love of slaughter, in imagination,
learning later ...
some in fear, learning love of slaughter;

Died some, pro patria,
                    non "dulce" non "et decor". ...
walked eye-deep in hell
believing in old men's lies, then unbelieving
came home, home to a lie,
home to many deceits,
home to old lies and new infamy;
usury age-old and age-thick
and liars in public places.

Daring as never before, wastage as never before.
Young blood and high blood,
fair cheeks, and fine bodies;
fortitude as never before

frankness as never before,
disillusions as never told in the old days,
hysterias, trench confessions,
laughter out of dead bellies.

Mauberley is more closely focused than *The Waste Land* on the European, and specifically the English, political, cultural and spiritual world after the war, the poverty of spirit, the coarse materialism and the hollowness of those who make and those who promote "value." It is a poem of bankruptcy, and after seeing *Mauberley*'s world it was only a matter of time before Pound abandoned England for good as a world that could not be repaired. *Mauberley* is the last poem by Pound which English readers at large will tolerate. Many seem to part company with the poet after this point, seeing the later work as a wild aberration in its form, language, allusiveness, and in its politics. The theme of usury appears in *Mauberley*. It becomes an eloquent ("With usura hath no man a house of good stone," Canto XLV) and then a poisoned strand in the *Cantos*, the strand upon which he hangs his notorious anti-Semitism. In 1966 the Russian poet Yevgeny Yevtushenko refused to share a podium with Pound. When Robert Lowell read one of the *Pisan Cantos* at New College, Oxford, in 1968, half the audience walked out in protest.

In 1945 the poet, in a prison cage at Pisa, under arrest by the American military for his collaboration with the Italians in the war, took savage stock of what he had said and how he had behaved, of what had happened, discriminating what was and what was *not* vanity in what he had done and made.

"Master thyself, then others shall thee beare"
    Pull down thy vanity
Thou art a beaten dog beneath the hail,
A swollen magpie in a fitful sun,
Half black half white
Nor knowst'ou wing from tail
Pull down thy vanity
    How mean thy hates
Fostered in falsity,
    Pull down thy vanity,
Rathe to destroy, niggard in charity,
Pull down thy vanity,
    I say pull down.

But to have done instead of not doing
        this is not vanity

To have, with decency, knocked
That a Blunt should open
        To have gathered from the air a live tradition
or from a fine old eye the unconquered flame
This is not vanity.
        Here error is all in the not done,
all in the diffidence that faltered,

Canto LXXXI ends with a comma. *Dessunt nonulla.*

In 1914 Pound married Dorothy Shakespear. In 1920 they moved to Paris and in 1924 to Italy, where they settled in Rapallo. There he stayed for much of the rest of his life. Before he left England he had begun the *Cantos*, and they were developing into a long poem, a work which was all-consuming. In 1925 he revised and published *XVI Cantos*, and five years later a further thirty *Cantos* followed. In the end there were 117 complete or almost complete *Cantos* (the last seven as *Drafts and Fragments*, published in 1968, four years before the poet, who had fallen silent, died). The books and essays that came out while the *Cantos* were being composed were political and economic polemics expounding his monetarist and fascist views, essays (notably *How to Read* and *ABC of Reading*) and translations.

As Donald Davie says, for those who value the *Cantos* the poetry must "survive a self-evidently and perilously wrong understanding of history, and hence of politics." It must also survive the huge wealth of reference, of disparate-seeming traditions, that inform it: Chinese ideograms, quotes from Thomas Jefferson, Provençal, Italian, Greek and a host of other cultural "zones." Pound more clearly than any of his contemporaries illustrates the complete change in attitudes to "tradition" that occurs when the center no longer holds, when the English that was exported to the colonies comes home with its own luggage, not the luggage that was exported with it.

Pound's life changed after he arrived in Italy. It became more concentrated. There were no longer regular casual meetings with groups of friends. If someone came to see him, they visited, sometimes for weeks at a time. Young poets stayed near him in Rapallo, just as they stayed near Laura Riding and Robert Graves in Mallorca. He established informally what he called the "Ezuversity." Concentrating on his studies, he developed his anticapitalist and anti-Zionist theories. In the magnificent Canto XXX, one of the great political poems of the century, unpardonable because it defines with such plangency his early fascism even while his contemporaries were lining up behind Stalin, he writes:

Compleynt, compleynt I hearde upon a day,
Artemis singing, Artemis, Artemis
Agaynst Pity lifted her wail:
Pity causeth the forests to fail,
Pity slayeth my nymphs,
Pity spareth so many an evil thing.
Pity befouleth April,
Pity is the root and the spring.
Now if no fayre creature followeth me
It is on account of Pity,
It is on account that Pity forbideth them slaye.
All things are made foul in this season,
This is the reason, none may seek purity
Having for foulness pity
And things growne awry;
No more do my shaftes fly
To slay. Nothing is now clean slayne
But rotteth away.

The Canto is cast in a quasi-Elizabethan mold, eluding the iambic but with a music that sounds familiar, a diction deliberately set in time, calling up the unambiguously great period of English poetry in which forms of tolerance led to the poetic and political distortions of the Jacobean and its aftermaths.

His economic theories seemed hare-brained, his anti-Semitism intolerable. Friends chose to ignore him rather than call him to account. Unchecked in his pursuit of "truth," unheeded in his Cassandra-like prophesies, he became ever more strident. The politics and economics of the later *Cantos* are increasingly crude, until the poem is broken open by the defeat of the Axis powers and Pound himself is arrested by the Americans in 1944 for treason. Was he driven mad by his theories, hatreds and defeats? The *Pisan Cantos* and the later work suggest that he was not. Certainly the poetry he wrote out of the experience of having lived through the consequences of his ideas and actions is at times mighty and resonant, at times utterly opaque. He was taken back to the United States and declared insane (otherwise he might have been executed for his actions). Fourteen years later he was released—William Carlos Williams and Frost worked hard to get him freed—and he returned to Italy to continue his long work.

He insisted that there was no "structure" to the *Cantos*, no "key" to the ways in which they fit together, no plot. His work is not to be understood through paraphrase or conventional analysis. It is the quintessence of Imagist practice, a tissue of juxtapositions of historical fact, poetry, politics, vocal registers, music, satire. The theme, Yeats said in 1936, is flux: "plot, characterisation, logical discourse, seem to him abstractions unsuitable to a man of his generation." The legacy of Hulme is fully present here, as is the legacy of Fenollosa. Pound speaks of his method as "ideogrammatic," each distinct register, quotation, voice, equivalent to an ideogram in the line of ideograms in a Chinese poem, to be read, auralized and visualized. Canto I merges Old English, Homeric and other strands; the second introduces a wholly colloquial voice in argument with Robert Browning, about *Sordello*. Each allusion invites us to read, but to read beyond, over the poet's shoulder, the texts he alludes to. There is a continual interplay between voices, cultures, registers; the reader is engaged in the poem to an unprecedented degree, not scrabbling about after footnotes but identifying (as in *The Waste Land*) the transitions from voice to voice, and responding to the modulations and metamorphoses that occur. Events inhere in place and in language. If modernism is essentially—as some critics argue—the art of anthology, of selection and collocation of material from the imaginary museum, responsible modernists will respect the integrity of what they borrow and protect it by deploying it within a system of ironies that indicate what it means in itself and what it is being used to express in the new context, about the other material gathered in that context. This is how Eliot works. This is how Pound works.

Odysseus and Confucius, Jefferson and Malatesta, the black prisoner held at Pisa alongside him and the King of Portugal, authors known and authors read, all have a part in the culture of the *Cantos*. In 1923 Pound wandered around the Italian battlefields with Ernest Hemingway, who told him the story of Sigismundo de Malatesta and his battles with the Pope, Malatesta who had the Tempio built. Malatesta becomes emblematic of power used for good, both in chastising the wickedness and greed of Pius II and in creating durable works. What in the biography begins as a casual encounter or engagement, a walking tour, an evening's conversation, finds its way into the deeper life of the *Cantos*, what Williams called "the impressive monument which Pound is building against our time." The word "against" has two senses here, the obvious sense of opposition, and the positive sense, in which a squirrel gathers nuts against winter.

After Pound we read poetry differently. If, that is, we read Pound at all. Without him, it is hard to know how we could read Basil Bunting, Louis Zukofsky, Charles Olson, Charles Reznikoff, Robert Duncan and a host of others. It is hard to know how we could read H.D., so much Pound's own creation. The diversity of his direct and indirect heirs is not division. The wealth of his own distinctive culture, with its discrete selections, sanctions in various ways their various cultures. Without Pound, much of the most innovative poetry looks like nonsense. Williams is not enough: Pound is the problematic, polyphiloprogenitive ancestor. And those who reject him, for his politics or for his poetry, build on the tradition he abandoned in 1920 when he abandoned England, the "sinking island." Returning to attend the funeral of "Possum," T. S. Eliot, he was almost entirely silent. When Stephen Spender loped up to him and reintroduced himself with the words, "I'm Stephen Spender. You don't remember me?" he replied, "No, I don't."

H.D. too came to England, and then—for personal rather than political reasons—abandoned the English. Pound's campaign for her work was almost too successful. He named her, he characterized her as the crucial Imagist, and she has never quite worked herself free of that early marketing ploy. The only woman in the first wave of major Anglo-American modernists, her work is different in kind from the others', even in its earliest and purest Imagist forms. Her major work, the *Trilogy* on war, was first published in a single volume in 1973, the three discrete parts, *The Walls Do Not Fall* (1944), *Tribute to the Angels* (1945) and *The Flowering of the Rod* (1946) having been pulped or remaindered by their publisher. Robert Lowell caricatured her vision of the war as "bombs falling on the British Museum." In 1972 *Hermetic Definition* was published. These books, with *Helen in Egypt* (1961), are the crucial ones, published long after her celebrated (or notorious) apprentice work of 1914–38.

She was born in Bethlehem, Pennsylvania, in 1886, into a devout and strict Moravian family. Her father was a learned astronomer and moved with his family to a post in Philadelphia. At Bryn Mawr she translated Latin poetry and began to write some of her own, experimenting with free verse. In England she married Richard Aldington, got to know D. H. Lawrence and many of the other writers of the day, and discovered a forceful advocate in Pound. Selling her poems to Harriet Monroe at *Poetry* he called the work "objective—no slither; direct—no excessive use of adjectives, no metaphors that won't permit examination. It's straight talk, straight as the Greek!" Talk it certainly isn't: the stilled rhythms, the utter purity of expression, leave voice out of the equation altogether. There is "no slither" because there is little movement of any kind. Still, she was the Imagist touchstone, an example of how poetry could be reclaimed from the excesses of the Georgians, where language generally seemed (to Pound) to exceed its occasion, and where the occasions themselves were merely conventional. In H.D. Pound found a concentration, an absence of sentiment, and accuracy of rhythm. The iamb was nowhere in sight. For F. S. Flint she seemed to attain "accurate mystery," a hardness without decoration (unless we take the marbly images as themselves decorative). She names things: actual flowers and trees, stones and metals. Her sand is "crisp"; "through the bronze / of shining bark and wood / run the fine threads of gold." Her most famous poem fuses the sea and the pine forest, so closely merged that each is the other:

> Whirl up, sea—
> Whirl your pointed pines,
> Splash your great pines
> On our rocks,
> Hurl your green over us,
> Cover us with your pools of fir.

It is less the images here that are potent, more the rhythm, the use of strong imperatives that are rendered gentle and suasive, an exhortation that is a description, admitting us in the word "us" of the concluding line. The poem begins at the point where two images fuse.

Her Imagist period ended with a nervous breakdown: her marriage ended, a favorite brother was killed in the war, her father died. Her friend Bryher rescued her and lovingly reassembled her. With Bryher she went to Corfu and had a vision—or a hallucination—in which she saw the Greek gods of sun and victory. In Vienna in 1933–34 she underwent psychoanalysis with Freud (her *Tribute to Freud* is a fascinating account of these experiences). He read her life as a quest that related to archetypal myths. Indeed, his reading was curiously Jungian and certainly enabling to H.D. He made what had been an instinctive quest into something more deliberate. He helped her make connections between the disparate elements in a life up to that point unsettled and emotionally chaotic, apart from the anchored and anchoring love between herself and Bryher. In 1937 she published her translation of Euripides' *Ion*, a crucial development into voices and actions. To Freud she attributed the strength she gained for renewal, the imaginative coherence that made it possible for her to begin *Trilogy* among the terrifying disruptions of the Second World War.

It is a poem that picks a way from desolation toward regeneration. The triplet and couplet stanzas are capable of delivering image *and* narrative, but are most effective in weaving connections between her own age of crisis and those ancient ages that feed her imagination: Pompeii, Egypt, Greece. Her Moravian memory becomes inclusive, her father has a symbolic place, the gods become God, eternity is a *fact*:

> Ra, Osiris, *Amen* appeared
> in a spacious bare meeting-house;

he is the world-father,
father of past aeons,

present and future equally;
beardless, not at all like Jehovah,

he was upright, slender,
impressive as the Memnon monolith,

yet he was not out of place
but perfectly at home

in the eighteenth-century
simplicity and grace;

then I woke with a start
of wonder and asked myself,

But whose eyes are those eyes? . . .

The syntax is supple and always correct; whatever the tensions there is a way to find order and connection. It is deliberate but admits surprises. In *Hermetic Definition*—her most beautiful work, beautiful in the old way of poetry—the surprise is love.

Why did you come
to trouble my decline:
I am old (I was old till you came). . .

Here is the climate of the Mediterranean, but also the climate of her childhood:

O, do not bring snow-water
but fresh snow;
I would be bathed with stars . . .

Pound and Eliot in different ways would have concurred with her quiet triumph in untangling memory, lust and desire, in the lines:

love built on dreams
of the forgotten first unsatisfied embrace,
is satisfied.

A Pause for Breath

Approaching the present, the historian runs into trouble. He enters the teeming city of the almost present and present, and as at Seven Dials in London, several plausible streets lead off in different directions. Being one traveler, long the historian stands. His chronology has been crumbling for a century already. Omissions have occurred along the way, regrettable omissions, among them William Collins and Edward Young, Arthur Hugh Clough and Robert Bridges reduced to adjuncts of Arnold and Hopkins, respectively. Where are the hymn writers—Isaac Watts in particular? And Lear and Carroll, the nonsense poets?

Chronology must be abandoned. Why do so many more poets call out for attention in the twentieth century than before? Is it demographic, the huge harvest of poetries from lands once pink on the globe? Or have the "winds of history" not yet gotten round to their winnowing? Had this account been written in 1798, would I have felt compelled to include Sir John Denham, John Pomfret, George Stepney, Richard Duke, Samuel Garth, John Hughes, Elijah Fenton, Gilbert West, David Mallet and thirty or so others? Of the fifty-two poets in Doctor Johnson's *Lives*, which deals with his century, only eight detain us here, two thirteenths of what he regarded as necessary.

Standing at Seven Dials, we could make forays down streets called Australia, Canada (a short street, that), New Zealand, India, Ireland, South Africa, the Caribbean, the United States or Great Britain. But *English* poetry is different from New Zealand or Caribbean poetry. New Zealand poetry may mean a great deal to the domestic readership but does not export. What interests us is poetry that is New Zealand poetry *and* English poetry. To follow *national* streets would go against the grain of this history.

Another strategy: Follow journalistic and academic fashions. The second half of the twentieth century has been lavishly preoccupied—when it claims to be preoccupied with poetry at all—with other things, with poetry's context, its usefulness to a cause, its "witness" and moral probity construed in the light of shifting preferences and concerns. We could follow ethnic routes, gender routes, gender-preference routes. We could follow pseudo-generic routes: performance poetry, protest poetry, concrete poetry. We could credit the rhetoric of schools, regionalisms and groupings. It would be another way. But it, too, would break the governing principle of this account—to look at the development of form, prosody, the language of poetry, connections between poems and poets, rather than record political and literary fashions.

There are earlier periods in which, like today, critical attention has focused on the orthodox and ephemeral, the eyes of critics resolutely averted from inappropriate achievement and radical imagination—if by "radical" we mean those imaginations that refine and redefine the art of poetry, paying tribute to tradition by innovation and extension, and that distrust the conventions of the age. The eighteenth century was such an age, the fin-de-siècle after the Wilde trial, and the decorums and orthodoxies of the 1930s. Political correctness is not new in anything but name. Today there are multiple orthodoxies, which might suggest a relatively larger measure of poetic freedom, but they are not—like eighteenth-century orthodoxies—governed by poetic imperatives so much as by other interests.

It is by way of inappropriate achievement and radical imagination that poetry has developed since the eighteenth century. Advocates can be found, but often made partisan by anger at perceived neglect, so that they make shrill claims. Pound is surrounded by a hectic industry, by hedges of patristics. Stevens and Ashbery are increasingly encumbered. Even Larkin begins to enjoy a polemical palisade.

The emergence of Basil Bunting, W. S. Graham and other writers who missed the boats of youth can be seen as enabling to readers and poets today, but their absence from their own period, as Hopkins's absence from his or Emily Dickinson's from hers, deprive not only the author but the literature itself of crucial relationships and potential exchanges. It is possible for half a century to look in the wrong direction, or to look for the wrong things in the right direction.

There are about two hundred poets we might attend to in the remaining pages. It will be impossible to do even two thirteenths of that number justice. The first six centuries have accommodated only 130 writers in any detail. Now I shall choose poets whose work, rooted in a locality or in a particular "speech," have had or will have the energy to cross seas and continents. Much that belongs to national literatures is excluded because its forms and the issues it raises are specific to a nation. The irruption of modernism in countries that rejected it first time round, the growth of the "postmodern" in literatures that were never shaken out by the modern: fascinating, even heroic phenomena, but their lineaments are already familiar. Poems in traditional forms that have not been brushed by the modern, that have not made their choices consciously rather than conventionally, also belong to their rather than to our culture.

Our modern culture? For me it begins with Hardy and Pound, Eliot and Yeats, Williams and Stevens. It has been an absentminded culture, mislaying H.D., Isaac Rosenberg, Charlotte Mew, Ivor Gurney, David Jones, Basil Bunting, Laura Riding, Sorley Maclean, Mina Loy, then rediscovering them. It has piously carried forward poets like Carl Sandburg and C. Day-Lewis, Rupert Brooke and Edith Sitwell—at last, regretfully, abandoning them on a very high shelf.

We can find continuities within a culture that seems riven between hostile camps. Thom Gunn in *P N Review* argues for a "spectrum" approach to modern American poetry, an approach that finds common ground between the experimental Language Poets and the radical traditionalism of Edgar Bowers, the old and new formalists. His approach—my approach—acknowledges diversity with commonality of resources. It insists on plurality as against faction and canonical closure, even if faction can be useful for poets finding their feet in a difficult "culture of reception." My approach acknowledges ethnicity, gender or gender preference, when they affect the development of poetic language and form, the extension of expression, the opening of new space. It proposes stable points of departure, even as it exemplifies difference and identifies the new.

We have arrived at André Malraux's and Donald Davie's Imaginary Museum. Davie writes: "The chief advantage of looking at modern poetry from the point of view of the Imaginary Museum is that only from this standpoint do poetic styles as various as those of Wallace Stevens and T. S. Eliot, of Ezra Pound and W. B. Yeats, appear as so many different (yet related) answers to one and the same problem— the problem of a radically changed relationship to the poetic past, a relationship which must be different from Tennyson's or Pope's." The formation of "movements" and the writing of manifestos are attempts to reconstitute what is found now only in separation. A poet may have theories, but what validates the work is the work itself. Given the twenty-four-hour open access to the Museum, a franchise now extended through the World Wide Web, any poet can trifle with what is found there, or—as was the case with Pound, Eliot, Stevens and Yeats—can choose and integrate into their work elements that answer a thematic or formal need the poet has. Pound, in taking troubadour or Provençal poetry on board, takes on board the languages in which the poems are written, the history that animates them, where possible a sense of the original poets. Responsible borrowing from the Imaginary Museum means more than "I like that": it means "I need to understand that. I *need* that."

I consider poets who add resources to poetry and may influence the future growth of the art and the language, poets who please me or who make me take stock. Taste is one function, judgment another and they do not always run in synch. It is possible (if taste is to develop) for it to be led by judgment; there are poets in this book who puzzle me in a way that I believe will turn to pleasure in due course. I was puzzled by Bunting, Davie, Ashbery and Sisson; coming to terms with this puzzlement has been an education.

I ought to declare a bias. Since Langland and Gower addressed their very different audiences in the fourteenth century, there have been two kinds of poetry and two kinds of audience. One kind of poetry seeks to elicit a collective response. Its origins are in the popular Bible tradition, its most eloquent and acclaimed modern exponents are the performance poets. Their poems are political, wedded to a community of concern and an immediate period. There is another kind of poetry, differently rooted in the Bible and the Book of Common Prayer, which elicits what one critic calls a "communal" response, a poetry to which each reader responds in an individual way and which is sufficiently capacious to accommodate a variety of needs and responses. The first kind of poetry engenders "solidarity" of a social and political kind; the second kind produces communion, an experience shared in different ways, to different degrees, to individual ends. I prefer the second kind. I am ill at ease with a poetry that has designs on me rather than on its subject and its medium. I prefer grace to compulsion.

Taking bearings from the modernists, I love Hardy and Frost; a taste for Murray, Larkin and Cope frees me from dogma. A reader who takes modernist bearings believes it is possible to find coherence in a large body of work from many corners of the world. A postmodern reader witnesses (gratefully) to incoherence, and a New Formalist reader might wish that Pound, Eliot, Lawrence and Williams had never put pen to paper.

I intend to steer the remainder of the way by the big lights of the first half of the century: Wallace Stevens, William Carlos Williams, Hugh MacDiarmid, W. H. Auden, Yvor Winters, William Empson, Robert Graves and Laura Riding. Into their orbits I hope to draw other poets and then to infer directions, or by indirection find direction out.

"Arranging, deepening, enchanting"

WALLACE STEVENS, MARIANNE MOORE, ELIZABETH BISHOP,
JOHN ASHBERY, AMY CLAMPITT, SHARON OLDS, MARK DOTY

We are unlikely to find anything so nearly carnal as H.D.'s "the forgotten first unsatisfied embrace" in Wallace Stevens's verse. Certainly no war ever shook the foundations of his world, though two world wars happened some way off, in the Europe from which his beautiful books and some of his prints and pictures came, carefully parceled, and to which, promptly, he remitted payment but which he never visited. He had writer-correspondents—it would be too much to call them friends—and when they sent him a book of theirs to read he might reply: "Reading one's friends' books is a good deal like kissing their wives, I suppose. The less said about it, the better." The friends' wives that he kissed, chastely, were generally business associates. In 1916 he joined the Hartford Accident and Indemnity Company, Hartford, Connecticut, of which he became vice president in 1934 and with which he remained until his death in 1955. The photograph of him that hangs above my desk shows a gray-suited gray-tied Stevens, gray face and gray-white hair, emerging from a gray building. Color was reserved for the poetry. He was one of Eliot's sins of omission at Faber and Faber: Why did he wait so long to publish Stevens, a poet more self-effacing than he was himself and quite obviously his peer? Perhaps there the answer lies. Asked what he thought of *Four Quartets*, Stevens with characteristic evasiveness replied, "I've read them of course, but I have to keep away from Eliot or I wouldn't have any individuality of my own."

Nine years Eliot's senior, Stevens was born in 1879 in Reading, Pennsylvania, of Dutch extraction on his mother's side. His father was a lawyer. He was at Harvard from 1897 to 1900, and then at New York Law School, and was admitted in 1904 to the bar. He started practicing law, and married in 1909. Seven years later he signed his soul over to the Hartford.

He started writing poetry, with excessive reticence, in his teens. In his high-school magazine he published two quatrains, subscribed with his initials only, and entitled "Autumn" (which remained his favorite poetic season):

> Long lines of coral light
>   And evening star,
> One shade that leads the night
>   On from afar.

The second quatrain expresses adolescent sorrow, loneliness and anticipation. It was not until he was thirty-five that Harriet Monroe published—under the pseudonym Peter Parasol—some poems. Then she included an early version of "Sunday Morning" under his own name in *Poetry* (Chicago) the next year, in November 1915. The eighth numbered stanza reads:

> She hears, upon the water without sound,
> A voice that cries, "The tomb in Palestine
> Is not the porch of spirits lingering.
> It is the grave of Jesus, where he lay."
> We live in an old chaos of the sun,
> Or old dependency of day and night,
> Or island solitude, unsponsored, free,
> Of the wide water, inescapable.
> Deer walk upon our mountains, and the quail
> Whistle about us their spontaneous cries;
> Sweet berries ripen in the wilderness;
> And, in the isolation of the sky,
> At evening, casual flocks of pigeons make
> Ambiguous undulations as they sink,
> Downward to darkness, on extended wings.

It is hard to imagine a more astonishing debut in *Poetry*. Each line and each sentence is transparently clear, each image alive, the voices that speak are heard to *speak*. The difficulty only arises if we seek to paraphrase, because the poem as a whole is a process that cannot be reduced to a single meaning or set of meanings. It has taken us from a lawn, a late breakfast, a woman beginning a languid Sunday out of doors, through meditations on meaning, to a known wilderness.

He had published a few poems less visibly before, including "Peter

Quince at the Clavier." He went on to publish some symbolist plays "without character or action." His first collection, *Harmonium,* appeared when he was forty-four (1923). His second book followed twelve years later: *Ideas of Order,* the year after he was made vice president. After that there was a veritable flood of books, culminating in *Collected Poems* in 1954. There was also a book of essays, *The Necessary Angel: Essays on Reality and Imagination,* published in 1951. Significant work appeared after his death, notably *Opus Posthumous.*

But then all of his work is significant, even the uncharacteristically crabby letters where he refuses to lend a friend money or remonstrates for some real or imagined advantage taken. His day job does not impinge on the poems, even though it enables them. Poetry is a world apart from the world of habit and dailiness: its feet are not on that earth because it has wings. In *Adagia,* his aphorisms, he goes so far as to say that poetry is "life's redemption," after belief in God is no longer possible. It is a redemption that knows itself to be the Supreme Fiction and that nonetheless elicits belief. Like Blake he is an enemy of reason, which destroys; unlike Blake he has no metaphysic but a physic in both senses, a medicine and a material world made over, made real, taken back to what it is before habits of work and rest, of play and passion, have dulled or misshapen it. To take it back to *is,* the poet must first be aware of what has happened to it. Through the distorted world of dailiness he finds the real, and that is poetry, even when he does not write the poem: "The humble are they that move more about the world with the lure of the real in their hearts."

His verse is a language apart as well as a world apart. No modern poet is more lush in his cadences, more achieved in metrical experiment or more regular. Were his language not always engaged in subtle thought, he would dissolve in sounds the way that Swinburne does. But the lateral and inferential thought serves up surprising dictions: we linger, we do not run on. The poems are woven together by repetitions and echoes, by kinds of closure. He loves the long poem, series and sequence. He repeats syntactical and metrical patterns precisely, altering the language they contain. The most arduously achieved poem is often the most imaginatively improvised.

When Stevens read his verse aloud, he tended to kill his cadences quite dead. His voice seemed to grudge the words that emerge discretely, destroying the music the reader carries in his head. The voice works against the high artifice, as though it spoke from the very world the poems have freed themselves from. The voice can't do the music.

From the French poets he learned about symbolism and made some of its elements his own. We are reminded time after time of the work of Paul Valéry, greatest of the later symbolists and a near contemporary of his, whose music too is a language apart and whom he read and learned from. But Stevens was intent on expressing where imagination lives (the real) and not *how* it lives, and this priority sets a distance between him and symbolism. He also read the Imagists and Eliot, and what he read, by his juniors as by his elders, made its not always detectable mark. *Adagia* is full of pellets of wisdom, for example: "Reality is a cliché from which we escape by metaphor." By this token, metaphor takes us *back* to the real. He says it a dozen different ways: a poem's subject is poetry. The musical images in his verse are different in kind from Eliot's. Music is a language, not beyond language; and painting is a language too, on which the poems feed hungrily. In fixing the flow of the world in rhythm, in clear imagery and argument that grows out of the imagery, he achieves a transcendence within the world of the senses.

It is possible to read Stevens for years with intense pleasure and never to care what the poems mean because the sense of sense is so strong and the movement of emotion so assured. "There is always an analogy between nature and the imagination, and possibly poetry is merely the strange rhetoric of that parallel: a rhetoric in which the feeling of one man is communicated to another in words of the exquisite appositeness that takes away all their verbality." Another poet produces this effect of compelling intimacy, so that as we experience pleasure we do not feel an urgent need to question meaning: Emily Dickinson. By contrast, within the magic of Yeats's Byzantium poems we stop, construe, interpret, ask: What is the golden bird, what are the mosaics, what has tangled the syntax here? In *Four Quartets* we allow the poet himself to ask us to pause and "make sense." Stevens gives us a different, more challenging freedom. If we do question his meanings and try to tie the poems in to them, we may be disappointed. The subtlety of his thought is less compelling than the magic of his grasp on the ear and eye, and on the "intellectual emotions." If we reversed the clock we would say that "Kubla Khan" is Coleridge's most Stevensian poem, creating a closed world where prose can gain no passage; a world in which imagination lives safely among the real.

He knew writers—William Carlos Williams, e. e. cummings, Marianne Moore. They knew him and his work. He was part of the group, but always far off; he did not meet Marianne Moore in the flesh until 1943. He drank abstemiously. He never invited a literary friend to his house. He never visited Europe but stayed in America, at home or on holiday in Florida or elsewhere, falling in love with skyscapes and placenames, reconciling the blue of imagination with the green of reality. "The Man with the Blue Guitar," "Le Monocle de Mon Oncle," "Sunday Morning," "Sea Surface Full of Clouds," "Thirteen Ways of Looking at a Blackbird," "An Ordinary Evening in New Haven," "Credences of Summer" are quite indispensible. It is as though Valéry and the mature Rainer Maria Rilke had combined in English, or rather American, and not only French and English are a single language (as Stevens declared) but German too. If Pound broke the pentameter, Stevens repaired it, incomparably, in "The Idea of Order at Key West," not as a meter to run with but as a meter that orders speech and integrates "real" images into a deep amazement, a flexible instrument of the "Blessed rage for order":

> Ramon Fernandez, tell me, if you know,
> Why, when the singing ended and we turned
> Toward the town, tell why the glassy lights,
> The lights in the fishing boats at anchor there,
> As the night descended, tilting in the air,
> Mastered the night and portioned out the sea,
> Fixing emblazoned zones and fiery poles,
> Arranging, deepening, enchanting night.

Donald Davie seems to suggest that one can more readily serve God and Mammon than admire both Pound *and* Stevens. Stevens, Davie said when at last his verse appeared in England in 1953, is after a "beauty" that Victorians would applaud, Pound after a different beauty ("the unconquered flame"). Stevens and Pound are different in kind, however, as Gower and Langland, or Smart and Johnson are. For Davie, Stevens is reaction in modern dress, "a Keatsian allegiance is the clue" to him. For Hugh Kenner his is "an Edward Lear poetic, pushed toward all limits." It is as a romantic that he has been absorbed into the tradition, yet he owes as large a debt to Whitman as Ezra Pound does, as large a debt to French poetry—and if not to Italian, then to German—as Pound and Eliot and Yeats. He is often gaudy, he is sometimes silly, his forms hold in the way that premodernist form was required to hold. Yet Stevens *chose* his forms, fully understanding what was afoot in modern verse, and he chose them because what he wanted his poetry to hold was not an historical, political, theological or contingent world but a world that was unassistedly "real." Of course the task was impossible, like all Promethean tasks, like the *Cantos* and *Four Quartets* and *Paterson*. His work is of a piece, and if there are longueurs in the later poetry, where he seems to jump up and down on more or less the same spot, or advance very slowly on his quarry, there is no point where the verse is untrue to its—and his—objectives.

For Stevens, Marianne Moore was "A Poet that Matters"—the title of his review of her. He wrote about his contemporaries sparingly

(Williams and John Crowe Ransom—"Tennessean"—were others). "The tall pages of *Selected Poems* by Marianne Moore are the papers of a scrupulous spirit," he begins, the physical book real in his hands. She is not overscrupulous but "unaffected, witty, colloquial." We can grant the second and third adjectives, but the first is disingenuous, because Moore is affected, often delightfully so, but there is a willfulness in her art, in the ways in which she chooses and develops forms, surprises and deliberately misdirects our reading by her syntax and lineation; do her subjects—or, rather, her themes—require such subtle snares or is there an element of the quiz mistress about her, challenging us to construe, making conscious those elements in our attention which other poets take for granted? Stevens delights in her dryness, her difference from him in sound organization, her uncommon view of the richly complex or (until she unwads and then refolds it) confused commonplace.

She was born in St. Louis, Missouri, four years before Eliot. Her father was a Presbyterian minister, and his impact on Moore as moralist is clear, though her morality was neither orthodox nor dogmatic. Like him she "believed in" family (though she never started one of her own) and individual social responsibility—the emphasis being on the individual. From her mother she derived, she said, her sense of phrasing, her "thought or pith." She studied at Bryn Mawr College, graduating in 1909, and then learned to be a typist.

She worked from 1921 to 1925 as an assistant in the New York Public Library, but already—indeed, since 1915—she had been contributing to the *Egoist*, *Poetry* and other journals. She knew Pound and Williams. In 1921, without her knowledge, H.D. and Bryher, with others, published her first book, *Poems*. Three years later, she added more poems and republished the volume as *Observations*. She became acting editor of the *Dial* for three years and under her it became a necessary magazine, with Thomas Mann, Eliot and Conrad Aiken among its contributors. She received a host of prizes, and in 1935 Eliot published her *Selected Poems* at Faber. Other books followed, and her *Collected Poems* in 1951. She translated La Fontaine's *Fables* inventively, if laboriously (though not so inventively and laboriously as Louis Zukofsky translated Catullus), and the final fruits of her nine years' labor appeared in 1954. "I fell prey to that surgical kind of courtesy of his." A *Complete Poems* appeared in 1968, with a curious misprint in the Faber edition: "First published in England MCMXVIII," predating her first book and rejuvenating her forever.

There is the Moore legend. First, the hats. A friend, remembering her in 1987, writes: "I remember she once began a story with 'I was leaving Boston wearing two hats . . .' I can't remember the story itself, I was too much taken up with the preamble. The hats were obviously too big to pack. I think the tricorne was the first classic hat and the big flat-brimmed one was more often worn later; she wore it when she came to tea with us in our London flat. She was about to go on a holiday in a canal boat in England, which I found difficult to believe. But one had to be ready to believe anything of Marianne." He remembers how, when he visited her in Brooklyn, "She sent me two dollars to pay for the journey from my New York hotel." When she lunched with him at his hotel, "She retrieved a couple of the clam shells and popped them inside her glove to take them home. Her apartment was full of little treasures." He also comments that, as against the judicious, measured generosity of her prose (advocating "achieved remoteness" and "aesthetic self-discipline"), her conversation was "sharp and even acerbic"; beneath the decorous exterior there was something "richer and less restricted." Yet in the literary battles between her friends she never seems to have taken sides—on paper in any case. Most of her adult life she spent in New York (a flat in Greenwich Village, then in Lower Manhattan) and Brooklyn (to be near her brother, a navy chaplain at the old Brooklyn Navy Yard). She died in 1972.

She was learned—her footnotes to the poems can be as entertaining as the poems themselves—but was modest about it and never built up a theory of literature, never issued manifestos or caveats, never shouted. Her poem "Poetry," originally five stanzas, thirty lines, she pruned down to three famous lines:

> I, too, dislike it.
>   Reading it, however, with a perfect contempt for it, one
>   discovers in
> it, after all, a place for the genuine.

To plant "real toads," the genuine, in "imaginary gardens"—another of her famous phrases. Temperamental and artistic reticence may be why she is less celebrated today than she should be. "Some feminine poets of the present day," she wrote in 1935, "seem to have grown horns and to like to be frightful and dainty by turns; but distorted propriety suggests effeteness. One would rather disguise than travesty emotion; give away a nice thing than sell it; dismember a garment of rich aesthetic construction than degrade it to the utilitarian offices of the boneyard." It is no wonder that feminist critics generally give her a wide berth: why does she stigmatize *feminine* poets as a separate category? (Her strictures apply across the board after the 1950s.) Modernists do not find her sufficiently vehement. Poets turn to her now as they always have done to learn about syllabics, about syntax (she is the *late* Henry James of verse).

Her syllabics are straightforward. Instead of the verse being "free" or governed by meter or regular stress patterns, she chooses to build a stanza in which the lines have a predetermined number of syllables. Indentation underlines the parallels. The shape of the stanza indicates the syllabic disposition. With the addition of rhyme, this is one of the most restrictive measures a poet can deploy. It is her chosen measure. Commenting on her poem "Bird-Witted," the poet Peter Jones declares that it "appears on analysis to have a ridiculous syllabic scheme: six ten-line stanzas with a firm rhyme scheme (a-b-a-b-c-a-d-e-g-c), the lines of each stanza with, respectively, nine, eight, six, four, seven, three, six, three, seven and four syllables. Yet the poem develops naturally, the form does not brake it." He might have added that often the stanza, even a long and elaborate stanza, is a single sentence, a further formal challenge. The stanza rather than the line is her "unit of sense."

Those who say that her verse did not develop may be unfamiliar with the uncollected early Imagist writing. However, once she found syllabics and worked them together with rhyme, she had her basic "grid," variable but strict in its controls. With this vehicle her verse explored every area of her broad interests—the news, animals and plants, friends, poems, paintings, dance, cinema—whatever it came up against: "We adopt a thought from a group of notes in the song of a bird, from a foreigner's way of pronouncing English, from the weave in a suit of clothes." It is in its precise phrasing and the surprise of the syntax that the poetry remains fresh, its rightness so complex that every reading seems to deliver us a new poem. In "The Steeple-Jack" we read:

> One by one in two's and three's, the seagulls keep
>   flying back and forth over the town clock,
> or sailing around the lighthouse without moving their wings—
>   rising
> steadily with a slight
>   quiver of the body—or flock
> mewing where

> a sea the purple of the peacock's neck is
>   paled to greenish azure as Dürer changed
> the pine green of the Tyrol to peacock blue and guinea gray.

The juxtaposition of Dürer and the seascape before her has much in common with the juxtapositions of Imagism, though she keeps the two worlds discrete, allowing them to touch only at illuminating points.

For Stevens it is the "real" that liberates imagination; for Moore it is "disinterested ends," a willingness to identify without identifying *with*, to draw without faking the lines for effect. Syllabics freed her from the iambic measure more completely than Pound's *vers libre* freed him: she was not in peril of a meter taking hold of her or her objects, which her language holds steadily and whole. "The Mind is an Enchanting Thing,"

> is an enchanted thing
>   like the glaze on a
> katydid wing
>   subdivided by sun
>   till the neetings are legion.
> Like Gieseking playing Scarlatti;
>
> like the apteryx-all
>   as a beak, or the
> kiwi's rain-shawl
>   of haired feathers, the mind
>   feeling its way as though blind,
> walks along with its eyes on the ground.

Her reading voice meticulously conveys the syntactical line. Randall Jarrell identified "her lack—her wonderful lack—of arbitrary intensity or violence, of sweep and overwhelmingness and size, of cant, of sociological significance." Her poems cannot be suborned to any ends but their own. "The Jerboa," "He 'Digesteth Harde Yron,' " "The Pangolin," "Elephants," "Like a Bulwark," "The Arctic Ox (or Goat)," "To Victor Hugo of My Crow Pluto"—there is an abundance of wonderful poems, one of the best being "What Are Years?" (which uncharacteristically has no footnotes):

> What is our innocence,
> what is our guilt? All are
>   naked, none is safe. And whence
> is courage: the unanswered question,
> the resolute doubt—
> dumbly calling, deafly listening—that
> in misfortune, even death,
>   encourages others
>   and in its defeat, stirs
>
>   the soul to be strong? He
> sees deep and is glad, who

accedes to mortality
and in his imprisonment rises
upon himself as
the sea in a chasm, struggling to be
free and unable to be,
     in its surrendering
     finds its continuing.

In 1946, reviewing *North & South*, Miss Moore declared: "Elizabeth Bishop is spectacular in being unspectacular." Elizabeth Bishop took her early bearings from Marianne Moore. They met, they corresponded, and Miss Moore's approbation meant a poem could be let free into the world. For Bishop it was an invaluable apprenticeship, and she kept faith with Moore as long as she could, but her reticences and those of her master were different in kind. There is a clarity that the reader has to work for and a clarity that is, at least initially, less effortful, more enchanting. It has to do with voice, dialogue and with a less consistently experimental approach to form, a greater rhythmic regularity. After Bishop went her own way, in 1955 she wrote "Invitation to Miss Marianne Moore," celebrating their intimacy with a rather Whitmanesque abandon. Auden has touched her art as well, and Miss Moore:

Mounting the sky with natural heroism,
above the accidents, above the malignant movies,
the taxicabs and injustices at large,
while horns are resounding in your beautiful ears
that simultaneously listen to
a soft uninvented music, fit for the musk deer,
     please come flying.

What Moore continued to admire in Bishop she admired at the outset: "Some authors do not muse within themselves; they 'think'—like the vegetable-shredder which cuts into the life of a thing. Miss Bishop is not one of these frettingly intensive machines. Yet the rational considering quality in her work is its strength—assisted by unwordiness, uncontorted intentionalness, the flicker of impudence, the natural unforced ending." Hers is an art that (she quotes a poem of Bishop's) "cuts its facets from within."

Bishop might have been the daughter Moore never had, twenty-four years her junior. Or Moore might have been the mother Bishop lost. In her introduction to *The Diary of "Helena Morley"* Bishop writes: "Happiness does not consist in worldly goods but in a peaceful home, in family affection,—things that fortune cannot bring and often takes away."

Born in 1911 (her father died when she was eight months old; her mother was committed to a mental institution when she was five) in Worcester, Massachusetts, she was reared by her mother's parents in Nova Scotia and by an aunt in Boston. She graduated from Vassar College in 1934. Her life was one of travel: to Florida, Europe, Mexico, and Brazil, where she lived for many years. Her final years were spent in Cambridge, Massachusetts, where she taught and where, in 1979, she died.

After Moore, her closest poetic connection was with Robert Lowell, her contemporary, to whom she dedicated "The Armadillo" and from whom she received the dedication of "Skunk Hour." They maintained a candid and affectionate exchange, willing to offer severe criticism when they felt it was required. He celebrated her—a poet so utterly different from him in technique and temperament—with fascinated love in *Notebook* (1970), where he considers her meticulous, patient method of composition:

> Have you ever seen an inchworm crawl up a leaf,
> cling to the very end, revolve in air,
> feeling for something to reach something? My dear,
> you hang your words in air, years old, imperfect,
> pasted to cardboard posters, gay lettered, gapped
> for the unimagined phrases and the wide-eyed Muse,
> uneasy caller, finds her casual friend.

This he revised later:

> Do
> you still hang words in air, ten years imperfect,
> joke-letters, glued to cardboard posters, with gaps
> and empties for the unimagined phrase,
> unerring Muse who scorn less casual friendships?

The body of her *Complete Poems* is not extensive: she published, after *North & South*, the Pulitzer Prize–winning *Poems* (incorporating *A Cold Spring* with her first book, 1955), then her first major book, *Questions of Travel* (1966), *Complete Poems* (1969) and the very small, immaculate collection of ten poems, *Geography III* (1977). In 1983 a comprehensive *Complete Poems* was published, and in 1993 *One Art: Letters*. In 1997 her paintings, a charming adjunct to her work and a record of her travels, appeared as *Exchanging Hats*.

A reader coming to Bishop for the first time might begin with the poem "Over 2,000 illustrations and a Complete Concordance," in which the poet thumbs through the old illustrated book, reflecting on the images that are given meaning, are redeemed, by the story they illustrate: the Nativity, the life, death and Resurrection of Christ. As she meditates on the images, the illustrations provoke a reverie of her own: memories occur to her, one after another, her travels, always her travels, *her* illustrations, with no resolving incident to make them cohere or mean. "Everything only connected by 'and' and 'and,' " she says, and taking up the concordance again longs for the validating Nativity, and the innocence of sense that she can never make.

> Open the book. (The gilt rubs off the edges
> of the pages and pollinates the fingertips.)
> Open the heavy book. Why couldn't we have seen
> this old Nativity while we were at it?
> —the dark ajar, the rocks breaking with light,
> an undisturbed, unbreathing flame,
> colorless, sparkless, freely fed on straw,
> and, lulled within, a family with pets,
> —and looked and looked our infant sight away.

The eye misreads the image, and in that misreading is the vulnerable candor, so oblique that we almost miss it: "a family with pets" appropriates the Nativity to fill a hunger, a human gap, in herself. The longing to find rather than forge connections between experiences, with a beloved, with the past, provides the dynamic of her poems. She looks and looks with such attention that what she sees is almost surrealized in its literalness: "glimpses of the always more successful surrealism of everyday life." Randall Jarrell says: "All her poems have written underneath, *I have seen it,*" and seen it with wry and anxious interrogation. In "The Fish" she sees into the creature she has caught:

> While his gills were breathing in
> the terrible oxygen
> —the frightening gills,
> fresh and crisp with blood,
> that can cut so badly—
> I thought of the coarse white flesh
> packed in like feathers,
> the big bones and the little bones,
> the dramatic reds and blacks
> of his shiny entrails,
> and the pink swim bladder
> like a big peony.

The voice affirms, hesitates, corrects itself; the image comes clear to us as it came clear to her, a process of adjusting perception until the thing is seen. Or the feeling is released. She can re-create innocence in a poem like "First Death in Nova Scotia," reclaim it in a major poem like "The Moose," from her last collection.

Her early poems are more or less rigorously formal, a formality that goes with their symbolic mode. But as she moved from symbolism toward the natural world, so her measure changed; she learned with instinctive precision to deploy free verse that mimes the movement of voice and thought. As with Moore, the enabling instrument is syntax, a syntax not always on its points, like Moore's, but seemingly casual, informal, barefoot or slippered. The effect is intimate, rapt, the voice always subject-defined, its repetitions and qualifications building toward a precise sense of the subject. The focus is often dreamlike in its fixedness: the dream can arrest, rewind, fast-forward. Causal contingencies are removed so that objects *are*, regardless of their histories or uses. Geographies, not histories: maps, the sea, the picture, the arresting and the setting down. The first poem in her first book is called "The Map."

Travel is a place in which to get lost (and found). Time's tyranny is loosened. In travel, connections occur, and connection is epiphany, a point of understanding that can be joyful or devastating, as in the villanelle "One Art." Experience is released, when it can be, in an action: freeing a fish, opening a book, shampooing her beloved's hair after a disagreement ("The Shampoo" is one of the most delicate love poems by a woman for a woman in the language), or simply moving on. Hers is a world of sensual rather than causal contingencies, contingencies that give a clear if brief defining stability to a wandering subjectivity.

Few poets of the century are as candid as Elizabeth Bishop. We know more about her from her poems, despite her reticence, her refusal to confess or provide circumstantial detail, than we do of Plath or Lowell or Sexton, who dramatize and partialize themselves. Bishop asks us to focus not *on* her but *with* her. Her disclosures are tactful: we can recognize them if we wish. Her reticence is "polite." Given her vulnerability, she could have "gone to the edge," as A. Alvarez likes poets to do, praising Plath and Lowell for their extremity. Instead she follows where William Cowper led, using language not to go to the edge but to find her way back from it; using poetry—in an eighteenth-century spirit—as a normative instrument. Even in her harshest poems, such an art is affirmative.

One of Elizabeth Bishop's passionate American admirers is John Ashbery, which may at first seem curious because Ashbery and Lowell are chalk and cheese, yet Bishop appealed to both. And Ashbery's work appealed to her. In his first book she could hear Auden (who meant more to her than critics generally acknowledge) and Stevens, but made over into something irregular, unpredictable—volatile. He can modulate from hilarity to heartbreak in a couple of phrases. You cannot pin him down, but as with Proteus there is something other than evasion in his droll, increasingly languid changes of key, register and volume. A poem like "The Instruction Manual" may owe a debt to Bishop herself, the early Bishop of *North & South*, with its informal symbolic allegories: Ashbery's description is an evasion; the occasion of the poem is an evasion of a boring task; the poem is about exclusions, but also about vision. What he may owe to Bishop principally is a sense of intimate, self-correcting speech and the "surrealism" of the everyday. His debts to Gertrude Stein are greater. Her notion of "cubist literature," that a writer can abandon meaning for a multidimensional, new art, appealed to him: simplify syntax and make a series of reversals and apparent inconsequentialities, hesitancies, surprises, local but numerous and cumulative. Ashbery is less programmatic but he loves the voices in Stein, and the Frenchnesses, and those subtle phrasal metamorphoses, the way she moves through sounds to a resolving sound as in "Lifting Belly," the way she encodes a private sexuality, creating a language at a distance from a shared context. He also values Laura Riding—the poet and story writer rather than the polemicist—for poems like "Nor is it Written," where the verse eludes paraphrase, the Proteus in the cave cannot be snared but changes shape and sound. Ashbery's is a deliberate and informed freedom from conventionality in all its aspects. It is not a freedom easily won: it was wrung from exile (an expression more dramatic than he would use), and from committed attention to different literatures and arts.

He is a poet of multiple voices, some spoken, some written, some borrowed or stolen, some parodied or invented to suggest period. These voices he does not juxtapose, as Pound does in the *Cantos*. It is hard to think of a poet from whom he differs more than he does from Pound. He takes and orchestrates the voices: verbal material from the world he grew up in, the world we live in, and echoes from the language of literature (often the most obscure), art, B-movies, the comics. Occasionally his own "I" speaks. We listen our way around to one of the other sides of cliché, to the "real" of Stevens's world.

His style is inimitable, which is why he has attracted many imitators. Some poets have learned their own, rather than his, lessons from him. The Language Poets declare a debt to *The Tennis Court Oath*, and he admires and is puzzled by their "deconstructions," speaking with special warmth of Clark Coolidge ("He uses language almost as if words were objects in a kind of assemblage"), Michael Palmer, Lyn Hejinian, Charles Bernstein and Leslie Scalapino, and from the fringes of the group Anne Lauterbach and Stephen Ratcliffe. There can be no doubt of the earnestness of these poets, and little doubt of their achievement as a skeptical public gradually allows itself to engage with some of their concerns.

Ashbery licenses two kinds of freedom: a positive freedom from conventional constraint, which makes new forms of movement possible, new in directions; and a negative freedom, which issues in the ludic inconsequentialities of his lesser followers and is to be found in the less accomplished of his own poems.

He was born in Rochester, New York, in 1927 and grew up on his father's farm in Sodus, New York. He didn't get on well with his father, "a plain ordinary farmer and we were rather poor." It wasn't that he was a farmer or they were poor, but his father had "a violent temper." His best days were spent with his grandparents in Rochester. His grandfather was a professor at the university and a distinguished physicist, the first person in America to experiment with X rays. He was also a classicist, well-read, with a library full of nineteenth-century classics including Dickens, Browning and Shelley. He was gentle and supportive. When Ashbery was seven his grandfather retired and with his wife moved to a village on the shores of Lake Ontario. Ashbery tasted the Fall of Man: he loved the city and disliked the country and now there was no excuse for staying in the comfortable, solemn, gloomy stability of the Victorian home. He has tried to replicate it, buying himself a Victorian house in Hudson, New York. "I always felt a great nostalgia for living in the city." Most "lost domains" are rural; his was urban. He did not visit New York City until he was seventeen.

At sixteen he was despatched to Deerfield Academy in Massachusetts to prepare for college. He was writing poems. A friend stole his work and submitted it to *Poetry*. At the same time, Ashbery sent his poems to *Poetry*, getting a harsh reply. It seemed that the doors to publication had been slammed in his face by the plagiarism of a confidante.

His next stop was Harvard, from which he graduated in 1949. His senior thesis was on Auden, with whose work he was "smitten." "I think it is always the first literary crush that is the important one," he says, expressing himself as he so often does in libidinal terms. A month before he left he made the acquaintance of Frank O'Hara. He undertook an MA in English at Columbia in 1951, worked in publishing, and with O'Hara, James Schuyler and Kenneth Koch began writing, collaborating and occasionally publishing work. This was the undeliberated birth of the so-called New York School of poets, growing up alongside the more celebrated and controversial painters whose work O'Hara was to be instrumental in curating at the Museum of Modern Art. In 1955 Ashbery left the United States, staying away with only occasional visits back until 1965. It was the Korean War and McCarthy that made else-where seem attractive.

In *A Calendar of Modern Poetry* (1994) John Ashbery chose to be represented by four poems: "He," the inexhaustible "How Much Longer Will I Be Able to Inhabit the Divine Sepulcher . . . ," "Rivers and Mountains" and "At North Farm." He reflects that the poems he wrote in his first decade of serious endeavor, from eighteen to twenty-eight, "seem to have a (for me) pleasingly surrealist shimmer." In a sense he was writing for his friends. They were all busy writing, not preserving their work. A poem may survive because Ashbery transcribed and sent it to a friend—to Koch when he spent a year abroad he sent the only surviving copy of O'Hara's "Memorial Day 1950." The four poets collaborated on poem sequences, single poems; a novel, *The Nest of Ninnies,* was written by Ashbery and Schuyler together, out of affection or boredom, or to pass the time. John Cage stimulated collaborations, and Cage looms large from time to time in Ashbery's resolutely unsystematic thinking.

The first two poems he preserved, from his undergraduate years, were "Some Trees" and "The Painter," written in his teens. *Turandot and Other Poems* appeared in 1953, but when he was twenty-seven he got his poems together again to make his official first collection, which was singled out by W. H. Auden as a Yale Younger Poet selection and was entitled *Some Trees* (1956). But "even before that book appeared in America I had gone to live in France where I would end up spending the next ten years."

To begin with he found it hard to write in France, without the sound of American speech in his ears. After a time he began to develop a style he describes as "slightly new." That "slightly" packs a reticence worthy of Moore, who, asked to write a testimonial for his second book, permitted herself four words: "I find him prepossessing." Not a very helpful sentence for his most awkward and suggestive volume, *The Tennis Court Oath* (1962).

In 1994, introducing the poems of his friend Pierre Martory, with whom he became close friends in Paris and who helped to teach him French, he says, "I have begun to find echoes of his work in mine. His dreams, his pessimistic résumés of childhood that are suddenly lanced by a joke, his surreal loves, his strangely lit landscapes with their inquisitive birds and disquieting flora, are fertile influences for me, though I hope I haven't stolen anything—well, better to steal than borrow, as Eliot more or less said." French itself, which he eventually mastered, he found "too clear a language for poetry. The exception to the rule being Rimbaud of course. I don't know how he managed to cloud the language the way he did and still keep to the rules of French."

In Paris it was not only poetry that affected him. There was the then explosive and fascinating world of pictures, and he was an art critic. He draws an analogy between his fascination with the line-break ("It has a mysterious thrill") and the painter's obsession with "the edge." Musical life featured Webern and others. The sparsity of Webern was of a piece with the breaking down of language and cadence he was working at; he thought he might achieve the "kind of timbre" he heard in the music. Other composers he has found suggestive and enabling, their concerns answering his, their strategies transposed into his own medium. But it was probably the writers who meant most to him, and especially Raymond Roussel: "He boasted that there was absolutely nothing real in his work, that everything was completely invented. I think that could perhaps be said of my work as well." He wrote poems in French "and translated them myself into English, with the idea of avoiding customary word-patterns and associations."

The poems of his French decade in *The Tennis Court Oath* he describes as fragmented: "I intended to put the pieces back together, so to speak, when I could figure out a way to do so." Some of the fragmentation was literal: he used cut-up techniques, buying American magazines and picking lines at random to make poems. The poems may not have been successful, but it was a way of curing himself of writer's block.

It's as well to remember that among all the avant-garde material with which he is associated, there is the other Ashbery, who loves Chaucer and ballads, one of whose favorite authors is Walter Pater (in *Houseboat Days* he incorporates passages by Pater into his poems), who advocates the work of Thomas De Quincey, of Thomas Lovell Beddoes, always seeking in English literature pockets of unjust exclusion and bringing passages back to our hearing.

Though Ashbery and O'Hara are often evoked together, Ashbery is different in kind from O'Hara. He admires O'Hara's effortlessness, a function perhaps of O'Hara's more unproblematic adjustment to New York and his homosexuality, his *natural* campness, his carelessness about the opinion of others unless he loves them. Ashbery is complex. Like O'Hara he is in love with French writing (O'Hara loves Pierre Reverdy particularly, Ashbery loves Roussel). He is intrigued by deliberate and systematic experiment, the OuLiPo group in particular. He wrote and writes in French, and translates. His cityscapes are not so consistently New York as O'Hara's. He tunes in to Americas and Europes and Orients, often all in the same poem. While O'Hara walks about New York and makes poems, Ashbery doesn't. He tends to stay at home. He teaches at Bard College and lives part of the week in Hudson. In short, his is a different and intellectually more varied world.

The constant element in his verse is "the dream," a template or a series of templates, and in this if in no other immediate way he resembles Philip Larkin, whose verse too has a repetitive dynamic. It is not a theory and never deliberately done: "I would prefer not to think I have any special aims in mind, as I might then be forced into a program for myself," he says.

An Ashbery poem is "a snapshot of whatever is going on in my head at the time": occasion, the process and so on are conflated, the poem becomes inseparable from its moment in time; even as the "meanings" of the moment drain away, the poem remains wedded to it, does not aspire to timelessness but insists on time, on the moment in its complexity. The serene and transcendent are continuous with the time-bound: Is the oven on? Will love survive? And where am I supposed to be for lunch? What "special aims" does he not have? There is never a consistent or coherent "plot" in his poems; if there is an argument it is unlikely to be logical; there are no consistent "image complexes"; no coherent meters, no rule about correct syntax. There are no rules. "I suppose I try to write from the point of view of the unconscious mind," he says. The "unconscious mind" can have considerable energy. In "A Wave" it washes a long way up the conscious beach, and the unstoppable rush of the enormous poem *Flow Chart*—a kind of fever chart—is uniquely ambitious, a series of surprises and pleasures that few readers have yet managed to assort into the sense of a whole. This is not "a cabinet of curios, collectables" but a veritable Harrods.

Ashbery has been immensely prolific in the years since his French exile. With *Rivers & Mountains* (1965) he began to reclaim the readership he had lost with his in-your-face experimental writing; *The Double Dream of Spring* (1970), the very difficult *Three Poems* (1972) in prose, and *Self-Portrait in a Convex Mirror* (1975), which made him the most celebrated poet in the United States, followed. Later collections include *Houseboat Days* (1977), *As We Know (1979)*, *Shadow Train* (1981), *A Wave* (1984), *April Galleons* (1988), *Flow Chart* (1991), *Hotel Lautréamont* (1992), *And the Stars Were Shining* (1994), *Can You Hear, Bird* (1996) and *Wakefulness* (1998). These are not slim volumes but substantial works.

Ashbery insists on overhearing. He seldom uses the same voice or the same formula twice. Amy Clampitt, on the other hand, whose work recalls now Moore, now Bishop, has a poetic scheme. However different the subject matter and tonality of her poems, once they are under way it is possible to foresee how they will pick their path through the language. Indeed, anticipation is one of the pleasures of her poetry.

Clampitt builds explanatory lines into the texts, or adds footnotes at the end of her books, explicating whatever may be obscure to the reader. This courtesy—or condescension—marked her first major collection, *The Kingfisher* (1983), published in her sixty-third year. There was a sense of freshness in this late debut, but *What the Light Was Like* (1985), *Archaic Figure* (1989) and *Westward* (1990), for all their sumptuousness of allusion, occupied much the same ground as *The Kingfisher*. Her *Collected Poems*, published in 1997, three years after her death, is too much of a good thing. "The exotic is everywhere," she wrote; "it comes to us / before there is a yen or a need for it." If the exotic is everywhere and in everything, it becomes commonplace. Clampitt is a wondering, eager earthling in an age of Martians (and the Martians took her up with enthusiasm). Her long poem "The Prairie" takes Bryant's wonderful poetic discovery, his new imaginative frontier, and finds it stale, baroque like Miss Havisham's wedding cake, Europeanized. Clampitt's poetry says there are no more frontiers. There is the mystery of detail. Here is the voice of a poet born and raised in Iowa, who settled in and settled for New York (where she worked, among other things, as an editor at Oxford University Press). But unlike the New York poets (Ashbery especially) she keeps a single speaking voice and a kind of Midwestern accent. This is her poverty and her wealth. Her syntax in its precision, as in "Grasses," can't but put us in mind of Marianne Moore:

> the oats grow tall,
> their pendent helmetfuls
> of mica-drift, examined stem
> by stem, disclose
>
> alloys so various, enamelings
> of a vermeil so
> craftless, I all but despair of
> ever reining in a
>
> metaphor for

And so the single sentence of the poem flows back, flows on. Claiming for herself a place in the English Romantic tradition (Wordsworth and his sister, Dorothy, are her polestars), she overlooks the fact that her own poetry begins not in a sense, or a memory, of fullness, but is made of fragments, which syntax and rhythm fuse each to each, although in the end the whole is somehow less than the sum of its parts.

Sharon Olds is, like Clampitt, an immigrant to New York, having been born in California and spent her childhood there. Though she is twenty-two years younger than Clampitt, her first book predates *The Kingfisher* by three years. *Satan Says* appeared in 1980. *The Sign of Saturn*, a substantial gathering from her first three books, appeared in 1991, and her controversial volume *The Father* (1992) was received by some readers as a brave act of extreme poetic candor, by others as an error of taste and judgment, a deliberate sensationalism. It focuses her lived and imagined abuse in a confessional rage at once complex, harrowing and appallingly literal. She reports that Galway Kinnell, by gentle questioning, made her realize that she was using the word "love" loosely, that at some points she meant "hate" or "fear," and the feat of saying these things and defining feeling was a liberation. The remedy for her is right love, and this, too, she expresses with vehemence: love for her own children, for example, her day-to-day world, merit a pared-down language of praise. The seeming nakedness of expression in *The Father*, the literal valency of the narratives and her adroit play with metaphor make us at first believe the poems as fact. We then adjust our focus onto how they are working, and working on us. Her technique recalls more that of Anne Sexton than of Sylvia Plath. At the beginning of her career, she reports, neither Plath nor Sexton much mattered to her: she wanted poems about Vietnam, the theme that obsessed her.

When she reads in public, Olds does not introduce her poems. "I want each poem to have all its body parts," she declares, "to be complete. Sometimes afterwards I like talking a little about a poem. I suppose I feel a great separation between conversation and poems." And yet her poems have a voice, less artful than Clampitt's but generally consistent and coherent. Both women reconstitute the "lyric I" which Ashbery has so assiduously and effectively dissolved.

Beyond John Ashbery, Elizabeth Bishop, Marianne Moore and Wallace Stevens, at different distances along the very uncertain road, we might come upon the work of Mark Doty, in particular his collection *My Alexandria* (1995), of which Philip Levine wrote, "If it were mine to invent the poet to complete the century of William Carlos Williams and Wallace Stevens, I would create Mark Doty just as he is, a maker of big, risky, fearless poems in which ordinary human experience becomes music." Doty's poems in a different spirit do what Bishop's do, they come back from an abyss, a thoroughly contemporary abyss of bereavement through the HIV-related illness of a lover. They are poems that offer to the dying, not as elegy but as celebration, the common world they have shared and made. The language is baroque, the syntax full of interesting risks, the subject matter and the scenes now familiar, now hauntingly strange. We might also find the brittlely elaborated work of the late Amy Clampitt, or Stephen Tapscott's nuanced lyrics of vision and rapt disclosure. Or Jorie Graham, whose sense of the "surface" is like Stevens's sense of green, and whose blue guitar is busy trying to play a new real music out of the *Region of Unlikeness* and out of the human body, sexual and alive, in its connections with and disconnections from the world.

You wake up and you don't know who is there breathing
    beside you (the world is a different place from what it
seems)
    and then you do.
The window is open, it is raining, then it has just
    ceased. What is the purpose of poetry, friend?
And you, are you one of those girls?
    The floor which is cold touching your instep now

is it more alive for those separate instances it crosses
    up through your whole stalk into your mind?

We might find a way to the Language Poets, to the English experi-
mentalists. Or we might more sensibly go back to Seven Dials and start
down another street.

"What shall I say, because talk I must?"

WILLIAM CARLOS WILLIAMS, LOUIS ZUKOFSKY, BASIL
BUNTING, CHARLES OLSON, ROBERT CREELEY, DENISE
LEVERTOV, ROBERT DUNCAN, J. H. PRYNNE, JOHN RILEY,
VERONICA FORREST-THOMSON, CHARLES TOMLINSON

Like Wallace Stevens, William Carlos Williams was at least two men in one: poet and successful doctor, a general practitioner with a leaning to pediatrics. He qualified as a doctor at the University of Pennsylvania in 1906. Already he was writing poetry. He started suddenly, around the age of eighteen, never before having contemplated an artistic vocation. In his *Autobiography* he recalls that his first poem was "a bolt from the blue" and "broke a spell of disillusion and suicidal despondence." It was four lines, and it filled him with "soul-satisfying joy" stronger than the self-criticism that followed.

A black, black cloud
flew over the sun
driven by fierce flying
rain.

The real Williams seems to have been born with most of his skills about him: the terse lineation, the free verse (which he never agreed to call "free," inventing the term "variable foot" to define his practice), the sense of clear image. About twenty years later, reviewing *Kora in Hell* (1921), Marianne Moore said: "Compression, colour, speed, accuracy and that restraint of instinctive craftsmanship which precludes anything dowdy or labored—it is essentially these qualities that we have in his work." Before Williams got to *Kora* he had to work his way through Keats—and Shelley.

He became a close friend of H.D. and Ezra Pound. In 1909 he published *Poems*, which he later stigmatized as "bad Keats" laced with bad Whitman. There was hope, then: two irreconcilable voices were struggling with his tongue. He also traveled to London, stayed with Pound and met Yeats. He divided his life only half jokingly into a B.C., before Pound, and an A.D., after their friendship commenced. By the time of his second book, *The Tempers* (1913), he had taken giant steps in what was to be his own direction.

Europe—he studied at Leipzig—seemed rather too full of stale culture for him, despite the vivid world that spun about Pound. After study and internship abroad he returned home and took up a practice outside the city of Paterson, New Jersey, in Rutherford, where he had been born in 1883, and married his longstanding (and later long-suffering) fiancée, Florence Herman, the famous Flossie, in 1912. His own antecedents were English, French Basque and Jewish, and he was pleased to be in himself a melting pot. His father was a traveling perfume salesman and Williams was raised by his mother and grandmother.

He was a natural prey for Pound's anthology *Des Imagistes*. He remained closer to the original Imagist practice than many of the other poets in Pound's book, including Pound himself. He opposed abstraction (Pound's GIFOA—go in fear of abstractions—was an article of faith for him) and romantic subjectivity staking an objectivist perspective: "no ideas but in things." He was not, however, content merely with the small Imagist poem, and time after time attempted major works. He took a strong dislike to T. S. Eliot, that "renegade American" who had thrown in his lot with the old culture. *The Waste Land* was a "catastrophe" not only because of its stylistic choices but because it was so darned negative. Frost he found too homespun and hickish, a stage American rather than the real thing.

His hostility to Eliot coarsened some of his polemics, but it drove him vigorously to advocate and create an American poetry and idiom that had few points of contact with the traditional mainstream. He combined verse and prose and broke the iamb so thoroughly that his successors would never be able to put it back together again. He took surrealism on board for a time with as much and as little understanding of it as Hart Crane was to have. It was natural that, for political and poetic reasons, his influence should grow. Important books (he published voluminously) included *Spring and All* (1923), the *Collected Earlier Poems* (1951), *Paterson* (published in four books between 1946 and 1958, with a fifth in note form), *The Desert Music* (1954), *Journey to Love* (1955) and *Pictures from Breughel* (1962). Three substantial volumes brought together his definitive work in the 1980s: *Collected Poems 1909–1939*, *Collected Poems 1939–1962* and a scholarly edition of *Paterson*.

He cast a spell not only on his contemporaries. Robert Lowell revered him, as did many of his generation. Allen Ginsberg regarded himself as a disciple (Williams wrote an introduction to Ginsberg's first book). Charles Olson believed himself to have received from the master the divine fire and perhaps the apostolic succession. Adrienne Rich found his example enabling in her difficult and decisive transition. Most of his poems and his extensive prose—fiction, criticism, autobiography—is fully and unapologetically wedded to the contingent world, the very cliché from which Stevens distances himself. And yet by going into that world, Williams at his best achieves the "real" that Williams writes of and for, and Stevens himself could hear what Williams was doing and acknowledged it in an essay introducing Williams's work. Two writers technically more ill assorted are hard to imagine, and yet both had America, both had careers as well as a poetic vocation. Both had Whitman in their blood, in different measures. "It isn't what he *says* that counts as a work of art," Williams writes, "it's what he makes, with such intensity of perception that it lives with an intrinsic movement of its own to verify its authenticity." These words, like many others of Williams's dicta, are not *quite* right for his own poems but better fit the verse of Stevens.

He returned to Europe in 1924, saw Pound and met Joyce, but for the most part he stayed in the Americas, pursuing his career and vocation and developing his enormous oeuvre. He wrote in the evenings or in his surgery between appointments, punching away at his typewriter. He tended to compose straight on the typewriter, rather than to type up poems written out by hand. Weekends he sometimes went to New York and met artists and writers. In 1931 he joined with fellow poets—his juniors—Charles Reznikoff, George Oppen and Louis Zukofsky to establish the short-lived "Objectivist" movement, the one club he helped to found (he was more of a fellow traveler with the Imagists). Their aim was to write poems that in their very form embodied the case they were making or representing: "The poem being an object (like a symphony or a cubist painting) it must be the purpose of the poet to make of his words a new form." The terms are more abstract than those Williams was accustomed to tolerating from others. More to the point, he wrote, "Being an object, [the poem] should be treated and controlled—but not as in the past. For past objects have about them past necessities—like the sonnet—which have conditioned them and from which, as a form itself, they cannot be freed." The objectivist set out "to invent . . . an object consonant with his day."

A consistent liberal during the McCarthy period, in 1948 he was deprived of the post of consultant in poetry at the Library of Congress, an affront that hurt him to the quick, given his devotion to a specifically

American literature. That was the year he suffered a heart attack. Gradually he handed over his medical practice to one of his two sons. Small strokes continued to weaken him and by 1961 he could no longer write.

Paterson remains his most difficult work, an enormous and uneven, wholly American epic. The geography is that of the Passaic River; the history—including the geological history—is that of the place, the falls, the city. Paterson is the Doctor at the heart of the poem, a kind of Williams surrogate, "a man identified with the city," and the voice of the city as well. The voice traces the city's life and the poet's; it encounters the multifarious Eternal Woman, symbolically a park in the city (woman as nature rather than nurture), but also incorporating Flossie and the numerous other women Williams had known. The first book is startling and magnificent, but each subsequent book loses energy. Marianne Moore's list of qualities—compression, color, speed, accuracy and restraint—is reduced down to simply "color" and "accuracy." The rest are only fitfully found. The combination of prose, lyric, letters, documentary, in a collage form, is ambitious, the apotheosis of the principle of juxtaposition of image, register and voice. It is an emphatically American adventure. "My whole life / has hung too long upon a partial victory."

"A poem," he wrote, "is a small (or large) machine made of words as [the poet] finds them inter-related about him and composes them—without distortion which would mar their exact significance—into an intense expression of his preoccupations and ardors that they may constitute a revelation in the speech that he uses." An enemy of orthodoxy, he did develop certain difficult theories of his own. If there was no such thing as "free verse" and he did not write in meter, what did he write in? The "variable foot," instinctively apprehended and deployed, was his measure, which he could never define in terms sufficiently clear to make it generally intelligible, though it is probably the source for Olson's "breath" theories, equally difficult to appraise and monitor. A poem's measure, he declares, is the line, regardless of accent or syllable count. Each line counts one beat, and "Over the whole poem it gives a pattern to the metre that can be felt as a new measure." Gertrude Stein might have said: *vers libre* is *vers libre* is *vers libre*. He invented the triadic verse, or three-stepped line, in effect a long line split into three and indented, a measure taken up by later poets, including Charles Tomlinson and Thom Gunn. He chose short lines, for the most part, "because of my nervous nature . . . The rhythmic pace was the pace of speech, an excited pace because I was excited when I wrote." The recordings of his public readings make him sound cheerful, rather shrill, with continual pauses when he seems to laugh nervously, quietly, with himself, with his poems. His temperament never visited the Waste Land: he is an heir of Emerson and Whitman, not of Melville and Dickinson.

His prose is often wonderful, especially in *In the American Grain* (1925), which sets itself the task of re-seeing America by means of the lives of its explorers and writers. His account of the conquest of Mexico has no parallel in American prose. He "renames the things seen" and makes America more coherent in its diversity, more American, in the process. But it is the poems that concern us here.

Marianne Moore reviewed his *Collected Poems* (1934): " 'The sense-less unarrangement of wild things,' which he imitates, makes some kinds of correct writing look rather foolish; and as illustrating that combination of energy and composure which is the expertness of the artist, he has never drawn a clearer self-portrait than 'Birds and Flowers' ":

What have I done
to drive you away? It is
winter, true enough, but

this day I love you.
This day
there is no time at all

more than in under
my ribs where anatomists
say the heart is—

What Williams does in poem after poem is, undeliberately, to achieve a particular kind of transformation. In his famous poem "This is just to say," an apology to his wife for having eaten the plums in the refrigerator, for example, the entire poem is conducted in a tone of apology and in visual terms, until at the close there is a sudden switch of senses to taste and temperature. He has, as it were, changed *key* by changing sense register. Without that simple sleight of language the poem would be inert. The poems that affect us move forward by way of these transitions, the language as it were changing focus by changing sense register. Sight can lead to taste or smell, which may trigger memory, nostalgia, an expression of love; or an expression of love may find grace in the scenes and objects to hand. Transitions: It is not unlike the "betweens" of Edward Thomas, in which sense is revealed and released, not in a way we can lay hold of with prose, but in a way the imagination grasps instantly. In "The Red Wheelbarrow" there is the language of function and the language of image, which provide a context (the "white chickens"). It too is a love poem, for love and gratitude are elicited as much by objects as by people.

And he remains, for all his love of the literal, a literary poet. A fine poem in his triadic measure comes rather late in his career, "The Spar-row," dedicated to his father; it is his attempt to reply to his once-beloved Keats's "Ode to a Nightingale"; it is also a way of writing about his own sexual desires "man to man," making peace with a father he knew too little. And how far we have come in poetry, that a language so plain should achieve such wry authority.

> Practical to the end,
>   it is the poem
>   of his existence
> that triumphed
>   finally;
>   a wisp of feathers
> flattened to the pavement,
>   wings spread symmetrically
>   as if in flight,   .
> the head gone,
>   the escutcheon of the breast
>   undecipherable,
> an effigy of a sparrow,
>   a dried wafer only,
>   left to say
> and it says it
>   without offense,
>   beautifully;
> This was I,
>   a sparrow,
>   I did my best;
> farewell.

The polysyllabic, poetical, highfallutin' diction is the poet's; the simple candid language belongs to the image, the no-longer-sparrow whose life and loves are the cheerful subject of the poem and whose after-existence as image is a source not of sadness but joy—it did exist, and in its exis-tence it had meaning.

Williams's association with the brief but sporadically influential 1930s movement of the Objectivists was a generally happy one. Zukofsky was the catalyst, himself spurred on by Pound, who persuaded Harriet Mon-roe to devote an issue of *Poetry* to the group, under Zukofsky's editor-ship. There followed the establishment of the Objectivist Press, funded by Oppen and called To Publishers—it set its cap against commercial publishing, producing work by Oppen and Reznikoff before going out of business—and the publication of *An "Objectivists" Anthology* (1932).

The anthology admitted work by Williams, "Marina" by Eliot (since Pound was in the background more forcefully than Williams), "Yittis-cher Charlston" by Pound, and work by Basil Bunting. Lorine Nie-decker, with her difficult, impacted "series" poems, and Muriel Rukeyser, with her sequences, though not included by Zukofsky, are also associ-ated with this group. Gertrude Stein might have been admitted, since much that they were promulgating already existed in her books and her desk-drawer manuscripts. Zukofsky, for a time the group's spokesman, produced a polemic, political in part (the group tended strongly, despite the presence of Eliot in the anthology, to the left and, despite the pres-ence of Pound, was largely Jewish in composition). The "individual word" had been degraded "in a culture which hardly seems to know that each word in itself is an arrangement." Getting back to *the word* (not to be confused with the Word) meant reconnecting with the world, break-ing through conditioning and prejudice, stripping away nuance and semantic weight, finding a new beginning. Such a beginning affects not only diction but syntax, not only syntax but the formal disposition of language on the page, its visual aspect.

Objectivist poetry is very much on the page, despite its insistence on sound values. Reviewing *Bottom on Shakespeare* in 1964, Marianne Moore remarked, "Louis and Celia Zukofsky are talented in the device of interruption to make text emphatic." In Objectivist terms, "interrup-tion" was visual and semantic. In effect Zukofsky prefigures and some-times preempts the activities of the Language Poets. There was the "spaced colon," a colon with space on either side of it; there were found poems, documentary poems, the poetry that is already there in language (and human narrative: it was the aftermath of the Wall Street Crash, the Depression) and only needs to be retrieved. The debts to Imagism are clear but limited. The Objectivist poem is not closed, is not arrested out of time but continues beyond even the small frames that Carl Rakosi, Oppen and Reznikoff sometimes use.

It belongs to the social and the political world. This is a poetry with-out metaphysical speculation, though many of the poets associated with it did in time explore—to recover in their own terms—religious belief. But the political forthrightness of much of the work, Kenneth Rexroth's for instance, kick-started a sensibility in American poetry that led to the political voice of the Beats. And politics has a sexual dimension, espe-cially for women, one that poets at the time, and in the decades follow-ing, affirmed, writing into the open. Science and technology have a central place in this new poetry, displacing old mythologies with the gathering verities of poverty and violence on a new scale.

Though Oppen, Reznikoff, Rukeyser and Niedecker would eventu-ally have found readers without the Objectivist program, I sometimes wonder whether Louis Zukofsky would have. He declared in 1948, "The test of poetry is the range of pleasure it affords as sight, sound, and intellection." The kinds of pleasure his poetry affords, to which Pound responded, are very slow; in an age increasingly given over to an art that has rapid impact and is disposable, his place is not assured, though he is perhaps one of the major *intelligences* of twentieth-century poetry. I say "perhaps" because his critical prose can be almost as opaque as his verse. His clearest aphorism is "The best way to find out about poetry is to read the poems." But how do we *read* his poems? One way in is through *29 Poems* and *29 Songs*, their relative conventionality alerting us to his experimental language, his music and themes. Robert Creeley comments, "It is a peculiar virtue of Zukofsky's work that it offers an extraordinary handbook for the writing of poems." But if we want to read, not to write, poems, what are we to do, moving on to his homophonous translations of Catullus, and finally to his enormous work, *A*?

His life isn't much help. He was born in 1904 in Brooklyn of Lithuanian-Jewish parents; he studied at Columbia and took his MA in 1924. He taught English at the University of Wisconsin at the beginning of the 1930s, at the time of the Objectivists, traveled to Europe, then returned and settled in Brooklyn Heights, teaching, writing and editing, with his wife, the composer Celia Thaew. Paul Zukofsky, the violinist, is their son.

Pound, that supreme objectifier, is Zukofsky's point of reference: *"His objects are musical shapes."* As Peter Jones comments, Zukofsky's sense of "objects," "music" and "shapes," and their relationship, are the crucial terms to understand if we intend to read Zukofsky's work, an art of "omission," in which sound takes precedence. We think of Swinburne, of Stein, but Zukofsky is like neither. His music is the poem as score rather than realization of score. It is a verbal score, not meant for singing but for the very different music that inheres in the voice. There is a puckish humor throughout, especially in the Catullus; but the closure of the poetry is such that by the time we get the joke it is no longer amusing. There is no imaginative center in *A*, no "panhandle," as Frost would say, to get hold of. Zukofsky represents the new poetry that made Frost's hackles rise.

Zukofsky died in 1978, the year after his work first appeared in England. The last decade of his life was not productive. Forty years earlier, in 1938—when the Objectivist exercise had foundered, Rukeyser had gone to Spain, the forces of fascism and communism were beginning to make common cause—Ezra Pound, deep in his polemics against Usura and its people, the Jews, dedicated his *Guide to Kulchur* "To Louis Zukofsky and Basil Bunting," "strugglers in the desert." Most readers will conclude that Zukofsky never got out of the desert, though many poets, like Creeley, will find in *A* and elsewhere a valuable resource.

Basil Bunting is another matter. He may have spent several years in Persia, on the edge of a real desert, yet the poetic landscapes he created are greener, often English—the England of his native Northumberland, with its history. "I hear Aneurin number the dead, his nipped voice," he writes. Voice again, and "nipped," suggesting Objectivist concision. But Bunting as an English poet could lend himself to a movement only in part. The rest of him was empirical, pragmatic; he trusted himself more than he trusted dos and don'ts. He might sit at Pound's feet, but he never merely imitates Pound. Attending to the mature mastery of another writer, he sets out to find his own.

Legend has it that in his teens Bunting, *il miglior schoolboy*, "edited down" Shakespeare's sonnets, rather as Pound was to do with Eliot's *The Waste Land*, hacking out superfluous words, adjusting sentence structure, finding an essential poem under the accretions of convention. The volume in which he performed this surgery no longer exists, though later, in the 1920s, he showed Dorothy Pound how to do it. He was a born modernist, paring down Shakespeare at about the time that the Anglo-American modernists were formulating Imagist polemics and remapping the canon in London. He did not meet Ezra Pound until 1923. When he did he was not unprepared for Pound's severe discipline.

Late in life he printed up a sheet entitled "I Suggest," a positive version of Pound's "A Few Don'ts": "I. Compose aloud: poetry is a sound." Poetry "lies dead on the page, until some voice brings it to life, just as music on the stave is no more than instruction to the player." In *Briggflatts* he announces:

> It is time to consider how Domenico Scarlatti
> condensed so much music into so few bars
> with never a crabbed turn or congested cadence,
> never a boast or a see-here . . .

He regularly draws the analogy between poetry and music: "To me it seems that history points to an origin that poetry and music share, in the dance that seems to be part of the make up of *homo sapiens*, and needs no more justification or conscious control than breathing." He adds, "The further poetry and music get from the dance and from each other, the less satisfactory they seem." The points that follow from "I Suggest" are built on this governing principle.

> 2. Vary rhythm enough to stir the emotion you want but not so as to lose impetus.

3. Use spoken words and syntax.
4. Fear adjectives; they bleed nouns. Hate the passive.
5. Jettison ornament gaily but keep shape.

He adds a Horatian injunction, "Put your poem away till you forget it," then:

6. Cut out every word you dare.
7. Do it again a week later, and again.

His final advice is of a piece with Eliot's refusal to elucidate: "Never explain—your reader is as smart as you." "Your reader" is not just any reader but the rare one with ears in his or her head.

Readers of Bunting's work were rare indeed for much of his life. After decades of neglect, caused in part by a less than happy relationship with potential publishers (including Eliot), Bunting was "discovered" for general readers in the 1960s by Stuart Montgomery of the Fulcrum Press. *Briggflatts* (1966) and the *Collected Poems* (1968) made it impossible to overlook Bunting any longer. Critics hostile to modernism tried to find in him a further manifestation of dubious rhythms, sterile severity, distracting mannerisms, imprecise forms. Had he cared to, he could have pleaded "not guilty" on all counts. Nor was he a mere disciple or imitator but a natural modernist, the only British poet of whom this can be said.

He was born into a Quaker family in Northumberland in 1900. Northumberland provided him with a dialect he did not suppress, despite long exile. Quaker schooling encouraged his independence and distrust of institution and hierarchy. He spent six months in prison as a conscientious objector to National Service in 1918, and the next year went to London to become a journalist, studying for a time at the London School of Economics. In 1923, when he met Pound in Paris, he subedited Ford Madox Ford's *Transatlantic Review*, then moved to Italy to work near Pound in Rapallo. There he met Yeats, who characterized him as "one of Ezra's more savage disciples." Pound put Zukofsky in his way and they became friends.

His life became nomadic, taking him through Europe and to America. In 1927–28 he was music critic for *The Outlook*. He first sensed that poetry might be something he could do when he recognized that the order and movement of *sound* in a poem might itself create a cohesion of the underlying emotions—a recognition he came to through music, that entirely connotative idiom.

Pound put fifty pages of Bunting's poems in his *Activist Anthology;* Zukofsky put him among the Objectivists. In so far as Objectivism attempted to rationalize and justify what was an instinctive approach to form, Bunting could go along with it. But a form that arose out of diction and was not imposed upon it? Bunting never developed the sort of diction from which form *could* follow (as Zukofsky, Pound and Williams did), and belongs at best on the fringes of the group.

In the Second World War Bunting joined the Air Force (it was a different sort of war from the First) and was sent to Persia. After the war he stayed on with the British Diplomatic Service as vice consul in Isphahan, where he married a Persian woman in 1948. He left, only to return later as a journalist for *The Times*, but was expelled by Mossadeq. Persian language and literature interested him—he had taught himself the language in Rapallo—and he used his years in Persia wisely. After his expulsion he returned to Northumberland and began to write once more. He produced his best work and emerged into a kind of celebrity, in demand on the international reading circuit and honored as the last modernist survivor, the one few had heard of before, a largely benign, occasionally curmudgeonly, dinosaur. He died in Northumberland in 1985.

Like other modernists', his work does not represent a break with tradition but a reformulation of it. Those who insist on his debt to Pound tend to overlook a prior, and more than equal, debt to Wordsworth, to Tudor and Elizabethan models, to Yeats, to the French symbolists, and despite a settled personal aversion, to Eliot. He adds to the list others "whose names are obvious": Dante, Horace; among the Persians Manuchehri and Ferdosi; Villon, Whitman, Zukofsky. His *Collected Poems*, even the revised and expanded editions of 1987 and 1994, constitute a concise oeuvre (he tended to destroy work-sheets and unsuccessful poems), but an essential one. He wrote, he declares, when he "could do nothing else."

The first collection, *Redimiculum Matellarum,* was published in Milan in 1930. *Poems 1950* was published in Texas. The sequence entitled *The Spoils* (1951) did not appear in England until fifteen years later, followed by *Loquitur* (a revision of *Poems 1950*) in the same year. There is a remarkable unity in this body of work, evident in *Briggflatts* and the *Collected Poems.* The themes are timeless: poverty, particular loves, departure, exile, return, regret, being misunderstood (that great troubadour and modernist sentiment), solitariness, social disgust, literary flyting, and so on. Innovation is rightly, with Bunting, a matter of making the familiar fresh, renewing perception and refocusing feeling by the ways in which the poetry speaks and sees. It is not a question of finding new subjects. The bias, from the outset in "Villon" (1925) through to *Briggflatts*, is antiscientific and antipositivist, that familiar modernism which is disenchanted with the modern and denies itself

many a resource (which Williams and the other Objectivists were will-
ing to employ). Antagonisms define Bunting as much as positive pas-
sions do, for he was a self-embattled poet par excellence.

In the preface to his *Collected Poems* Bunting says magisterially,
"Unabashed boys and girls may enjoy them. The book is theirs." Read-
ing the first poem, "Villon," might abash boys and girls alike. It pos-
sesses some of the asperity of Nashe in its presentation of the theme
of death, and more than a small echo of Yeats. It is not easy. Bunting
often uses series—of proper names, verbs or nouns—to create rhetorical
effects. In "Villon" he writes:

> Abelard and Eloïse,
> Henry the Fowler, Charlemagne,
> Genée, Lopokova, all these
> die, die in pain.

The resonance of the passage comes from associations already attached
to the names and from the Yeatsian rhythm ("Easter 1916") in which
they are conveyed. But Bunting uses rhyme and a variation on the eight-
syllable line with his own cunning elsewhere, not tying Celtic sound-
knots as Austin Clarke does, but achieving purity of statement, a
universal rather than a particular voice:

> The Emperor with the Golden Hands
> is still a word, a tint, a tone,
> insubstantial-glorious,
> when we ourselves are dead and gone
> and the green grass growing over us.

In such passages, with controlled but not exaggerated development of
back vowels, Bunting achieves unprecedented effects.

"Villon" is a satire, an elegy of sorts, a love poem, a "translation," an
"autobiography," a dramatic monologue. This multiplicity of genre is
something we come to expect. "Attis: Or Something Missing" is more
narrowly based, satirizing T. S. Eliot, who appears as a eunuch (the Attis
of Catullus's famous poem, who castrates himself in order to serve the
goddess Cybele). Bunting claimed his target was Lucretius and Cino de
Pistoia—in fact, it is an aging Prufrock, for Bunting's affective aversion
to Eliot was as intense as William Carlos Williams's. Eliot never
warmed to his verse, and every publisher knows that this is the unfor-
givable sin.

The Spoils, written when he had turned fifty, is Bunting's first major
poem. In the first of its three sections the four sons of Shem, Noah's son

and father of the Semitic peoples, speak from exile in Babylon, where his tribe leads a profitable, usurious life, rootless within an alien society, rich without contentment. The second section describes, with a nice historical sense, an ancient social stability darkly threatened:

Have you seen a falcon stoop
accurate, unforeseen
and absolute, between
wind-ripples over harvest? Dread
of what's to be, is and has been—
were we not better dead?

Note how the syntax holds, tense with fear and unease. In the third section, against the antique durability of the historical setting unsettled by the sons of Shem (for there are elements of Pound's politics embedded in Bunting's social vision), a modern European war is enacted in Africa and elsewhere. The juxtaposition of the sections reveals cultural incompatibilities and continuities. The war occurs against an image—only an image—of unsettled and predatory exile (Part I) and cultural permanence (Part II).

Briggflatts is subtitled *An Autobiography,* and we immediately think of Wordsworth's *Prelude.* But no, it is not to be read literally. The first part peoples a Northumbrian landscape with images and draws them into coherence. We meet Rawthey, the spirited bull, and the less spirited tombstone maker, tracing his new inscription with his fingertips. Rawthey embodies natural passion, music, life, and the mason represents death. Against or between these polar opposites two lovers come, watching "the mason meditate / on name and date," and respond to the world about them. They go home and make love before the fire in a language that combines literal detail and painful coyness: He unties "tape / of her striped flannel drawers" and at last "on the pricked rag mat / his fingers comb / thatch of his manhood's home." The rhyme and the conceit intrude an academic poise, or poison, into an otherwise compelling and erotic scene. The lovers then fall into mutual blame, regret, but (near doggerel in these verses) what's done can't be undone. The lovers emerge into a landscape altered. Rawthey is no longer "sweet" but "truculent, dingy." The carved stone is the headstone of dead love.

In Part II the poet is embattled, accusing, out to show the bogus world what he's made of. He succumbs to insincerity, degradation; he goes to sea and is forgotten. "Love is a vapour, we're soon through it." He goes to Italy, more tombstones and bulls, the bull here the Minotaur, approached in the transition of images between the music of birds and the complications of "Schoenberg's maze." Part III is tautly written documentary and description: what the poet sees and celebrates is vulnerable to exploitation, destruction. The war is approaching.

The Scarlatti passage is from Part IV, which begins with long lines. Bunting lets the cadence gradually dwindle. After a battle, after a flood, "I hear Aneurin . . ." The progression to the nipped statements of personal importance foregrounds the lines

> Where rats go go I,
> accustomed to penury,
> filth, disgust and fury . . .

The fifth part is the most personal. He describes the new year, the change of seasons, men with their dogs. The past rushes on him, "silence by silence sits / and Then is diffused in Now." Fixing his eyes on a star whose light has traveled fifty years to reach his "now," he reflects on the love scene in the first part. The light of the star is poetically from that date, that past:

> Fifty years a letter unanswered;
> a visit postponed for fifty years.
>
> She has been with me fifty years.
>
> Starlight quivers. I had day enough.
> For love uninterrupted night.

An oblique exorcism is enacted. "Starlight quivers" may be the star twinkling or a tear dilating on the poet's eye. The "Coda" with which the poem ends is too deliberately poetic and conclusive: the objective world the poem has worked toward is dissipated in a wan pageantry.

Among Bunting's other work are the "Odes"—in fact satires, love poems and meditations. His "Overdrafts" are translations of Latin, Persian and Italian, or of Zukofsky into Latin. He adapted Machiavelli in "How Duke Valentine Contrived," retelling Machiavelli's story in concentrated verse.

The most interesting exercise in this vein is "Chomei at Toyama," written in 1932. He took Pound's advice to young poets: translate, make the sense so it doesn't "wobble." "If ever I learned the trick [of writing poetry] . . . it was mostly from poets long dead whose names are obvious." He prefers, he wrote in a review in the *Criterion*, "*familiar* comprehension" to "academic lucidity." "Chomei at Toyama" is "a poem that, whatever its worth or worthlessness in itself, might have a useful influence: showing, for instance, that poetry can be intelligible and still be poetry: a fact that came to be doubted by the generation that took most of its ideas indirectly from Eliot." "Chomei" concentrates and essentializes the Japanese original, Kamono Chomei's prose *Hojoki* ("Life in a Dwelling One *Jo* [Ten Feet] Square"). He calls this "the most delicate contribution to the prose of the time" (i.e., 1153–1216), the Heian and early Kamakura period: the warrior caste held power; culture was not highly valued. A parallel with Bunting's own time is clear. Chomei describes natural calamities rather than the fighting that ravaged the country. Other Japanese art similarly figures in natural detail the large events of the day.

Bunting brings into play other works by Chomei and other Japanese poets. But the English poem belongs not to Chomei but to Bunting. Part of the art of translation is assimilation of historical and geographical context. Another part is to bring the poem home, hence the curious anachronisms: Sixth Avenue, Riverside Drive, commuters. As in *Briggflatts*, there is stylized autobiography here:

> I am out of place in the capital,
> people take me for a beggar,
> as you would be out of place in this sort of life,
> you are so—I regret it—so welded to your vulgarity.

Bunting and Chomei know themselves from "the others."

After the Objectivists—the Projectivists. The father of the movement is Charles Olson, a giant at six feet eight inches, who, in R. B. Kitaj's crayon portrait, looks like a bespectacled, magisterial tortoise, a professorial tortoise, head as far out of its shell as it will go, and not likely to retract it, whatever the perils. Olson, who like Pound wanted all history and all human thought to be at his disposal, is credited with inventing the term "postmodern," and much good and ill can be laid at his door. He was careless about himself, blundering like Doctor Johnson, leaving many projects and—in conversation—most of his sentences unfinished. At dinner parties he stuffed food in his pockets and once ate an oil rag. He was impecunious. In his later years he drank and drugged too much.

The son of working-class immigrants, Olson was born in 1910 in Worcester and grew up in Gloucester, Massachusetts, a town north of Boston, on the sea. He studied at Harvard, taking his MA in 1933, becoming a substantial scholar and teaching there for a time. He worked for the Roosevelt government during the war, retaining from that period a profound optimism. Later he taught at Black Mountain

College, North Carolina, where as rector in the early 1950s he attracted creative artists and spearheaded the campaign against the New Criticism, which he and others found reductive and impoverishing. The college closed in 1956. In its short history (from 1933) a number of important artists and writers were associated with it: De Kooning, Kline and Rauschenberg, John Cage, John Dewey. Cid Corman's *Origin* and Creeley's *Black Mountain Review* were ambitious magazines, and featured the work of Ginsberg, Kerouac, Ed Dorn, Gary Snyder, Jonathan Williams and people more directly associated with the school.

He later taught at the State University of New York at Buffalo but lived in Gloucester, his Paterson and the setting of *Maximus*. Olson is the father, Williams the grandfather of much of the radical formal experimentation of the last fifty years. He was more a theorist than Williams, more hands-on. He had no day job: teaching and poetry were for him a connected vocation, and one of the problems with the poems is the continual intrusion of the teacher into them.

At his funeral in 1970 Allen Ginsberg was of course present, chanting his Kaddish and getting in the way; carelessly (is it legend or fact?) stepping on a pedal that should have lowered Olson into the ground before the ceremony was quite ready for farewells. Ginsberg jammed the mechanism and the giant coffin hovered a little longer between worlds.

If he owes much to Williams, Olson also owes a debt to D. H. Lawrence, who impelled him to try to find an order in, or for, the "phenomenal world which is raging and yet apart." Alfred North Whitehead, too, helped Olson define what the human in humanism *might* be, rather than what it was. Robert Creeley quotes Whitehead's phrase describing the human: "ego object in field of objects," getting the proportion right by reestablishing the "object" nature of "ego." These mixed antecedents alert us to the fact that we cannot read Olson as a linear descendant of Pound or Williams, or *Maximus* as an unproblematic child of the *Cantos* and *Paterson*. They are themselves only remotely, and tetchily, related. What the three big poems have in common is that they are all unfinished and unfinishable.

Olson urges his reader to take risks, and not only in the poem. Lawrence was a moralist, and so is he; the disruptions both propose are radical. The "first fact" of our existence is space, not time. This adjustment, half completed in Williams, sets Olson in a different world from Pound, despite Pound's enormous scope, for what Pound conflates into the present poem is drawn from a hundred histories, and points to moments within those histories.

Olson's poetic material is drawn from as many sources as Pound's, though sources perhaps not so intensely possessed as Pound's were.

Pound's voices are located, and their interplay with other voices depends on the fixity, the *fact*, as he sees it, of their location. Olson, for his part, enters the poem from all sides, bringing material from various places. What matters is not where materials come from so much as what they do when they arrive (the same might, *mutatis mutandis,* be said of Eliot's approach, though to mention his name in this context is perilous).

In 1950 Olson wrote the essay "Projective Verse," the manifesto of a school that would include in its intensive, informal seminar room Robert Duncan, Denise Levertov, Robert Creeley and many other figures, under the steady eye of Olson himself. Projectivism took its bearing from the writings of Pound (at a time when even mentioning Pound was an act of courage) and Williams. Poetry, Olson declares, is an "open field" through which the poet transfers energy to the reader—but only the reader who is prepared, and preparation is a discipline as much of opening the ear as of clearing it of the conditionings of more traditional verse and the prejudices of preconception. "Yes, yes, we must, must, *must* get rid of the drama, at all costs—I mean, even get rid of narrative—the temptation, you hear?" Thus he spoke, meaning it, in a manner of speaking. Guy Davenport declares, "A good half the time in the classroom his students didn't know even remotely what in the name of God he could be talking about."

The poetic unit is no longer syllable, stress, foot, line or variable foot, but the "breath" unit of phrases spoken, and the way the poem falls on the page—its visual aspect—is central to its effect. The art of poetry becomes at once fully aural and fully visual, an integration of the senses. The source of the poem is the body and being of the poet; the poem should engage the body and being of the reader.

Olson's most important books of poetry are *In Cold Hell, In Thicket* (1953), *The Distances* (1960), the vast *Maximus Poems* (1960–68), which begin as letters and are eventually as varied as and more substantial than *Paterson* and perhaps more significant, and *Archaeologist of Morning*, published posthumously (1971). Of his prose books one is indispensible, *Call Me Ishmael* (1947), about Melville and about America, a volume in which an American critical imagination, of the kind that produced *In the American Grain*, reaches another high-water mark. Melville is Olson's deeper conscience. His poem "The Kingfishers" is the best way into his work: Guy Davenport calls it "the most energetically influential text in the last thirty-five years," composed in 1949 in response to the *Pisan Cantos*, the end of the war, the beginning of something—but what? Davenport calls it "a *canzone* that divides decisively modern from postmodern poetry, the theme states that when our attentions change, our culture changes." It would seem that the Projectivist theories grew out of practice, the experience of writing this poem in the great darkness of Pound's magnificently fragmentary "contrition," a contrition we have already seen had a hubris of its own.

What does not change / is the will to change

He woke, fully clothed, in his bed. He
remembered only one thing, the birds, how
when he came in, he had gone around the rooms
and got them back in their cage, the green one first,
she with the bad leg, and then the blue,
the one they had hoped was a male . . .

And then the voices change, there are the ruins, there is Cambodia, there is anthropology, lost cultures, lost value systems, inferred, flickering behind an alien language. A whole raft of cultures has been abandoned and new bearings are being found in continents where colonialisms almost erased the vital cultures.

    . . . if I have any taste
  it is because I have interested myself
  in what was slain in the sun . . .

The *Maximus* poems Davenport regards as "variations of Keats's nightingale ode," an interesting if not a helpful observation. What stable Chinese culture is to Pound, the fluid Mayas are to Olson; what the arts and political craftinesses of the Renaissance are to Pound, geology is to Olson. "A movement is closed" by *Maximus*, Davenport says, "a movement that began with Thoreau and Whitman, when America was opening out and possibilities were there to be stumbled over or embraced. Olson is the other term of this movement. He is our anti-Whitman (like Melville before him)."

Olson's impact had much to do with his openness to experience. He came to poetry from a wider world than many, from the political projects of the New Deal. He was a highly literate and scholarly man but not literary in the way of Pound or Stevens. He had the kind of tolerance that is intolerant of the less liberal, the authoritarianism of one who doubts the legitimacy of earlier cultural authority. So he invents his movement, and the laws are set out in capital letters. We mentioned breath. There is also "OPEN, or what can else be called COMPOSITION BY FIELD, as opposed to inherited line, stanza, over-all form." The poem has to be a continuous "energy discharge." "ONE PERCEPTION MUST IMMEDIATELY AND DIRECTLY LEAD TO A FURTHER PERCEP-TION . . . USE USE USE the process at all points," etc. This is the counsel of the modern TV cameraman who allows not more than three seconds' rest on any image. "FORM IS NEVER MORE THAN AN EXTENSION OF CONTENT." Everywhere physiology is privileged over psychology.

Readers of Olson, like readers of Pound, fragment him. He is too big for the beginner, too big for people well along the way. Even his friend and "heir," Robert Creeley (b. 1926), essentializes him in a useful *Selected Poems*. Creeley is a fine advocate of Olson; he has been a fine editor, too. His recitals of his own poems inspire his audiences. Those who purchase Creeley's books and take them home to a silent room find them very silent poems. There is a large body of work, much of it in a short measure, but the short line is not necessarily taut; the absence of semantic nuance gives a precision that requires precise and interesting objects. The plainer the language, the more short-breathed the rhythms, the more fascinating the subject matter must be. Those who learn their language from Williams and Pound set themselves a steep challenge. Much is left behind by both poets, deliberately, in the interests of going forward into new terrain with new instruments. The terrain is no longer so new. It is possible for a poet who works with the semantic richness of Pound, or Auden, or Larkin, to elicit through a play of ironies the latencies and the absences within the modern world. For Creeley, as for English-born Denise Levertov (1923–1998), who in the wake of Creeley went to Black Mountain College and was one of Olson's few distinguished woman disciples, too much has been jettisoned without enough being put in its place. An enormously capacious mind is needed to bring off with any authority the refining challenges that Olson proposes.

In the late 1960s and early 1970s Levertov's fame in Britain was high: she was an English bridge (a complex one) to the Black Mountain and to an American poetry that promised new directions. But her removal to the United States and her establishment there of a highly successful academic and poetic career meant that she was occluded. Her formative years—she was educated at home by a Russian-Jewish father who converted to Anglicanism and became a priest and a scholar—gave her many of the metaphysical interests that her later work, and her sense of the poem's mission, developed. She married an American G.I. in 1947 and moved to France, living near Robert Creeley, who became a friend and pointed her toward Black Mountain and the "great talkers," Olson and Duncan. One of her rules: "Insofar as poetry has a social function it is to awaken sleepers by other means than shock." Vietnam changed that: she became a social poet who wanted to make a difference. She published more than thirty books.

Robert Duncan (1919–88) worked with, and then in some ways against, what he learned from Olson. He gathered into his field of reference Gertrude Stein (who frees one from some of the strongest

chains, herself chaining her followers with bands of humorous steel),
Lawrence (whom he reads differently from Olson), Pound, H.D.,
Moore, Stevens, even Edith Sitwell. Everyone is invited except Frost
and Eliot. James Dickey bridled at Olson's postmodern. Dickey had a
troublesome relationship with the work of Duncan, who, he said, had
that "old pagan sense of the poem as a divine form of speech which
works intimately with the animism of nature"; but he was "one of the
most unpityingly, pretentious poets I have ever come across": pagan and
pretentious, divine and self-indulgent. What did Dickey make of "The
Torso," celebrating the male form, celebrating in a way more direct than
Ginsberg does with his sudden affronts the fact of the male homosexual:

Most beautiful! the red-flowering eucalyptus,
      the madrone, the yew

Is he . . .

So thou wouldst smile, and take me in thine arms
The sights of London to my exiled eyes
Is as Elysium to a new-come soul

If he be Truth
I would dwell in the illusion of him

His hands unlocking from chambers of my male body

such an idea in man's image

rising tides that sweep me towards him

. . . *homosexual?* . . .

In later life Duncan never stopped talking. Earlier on, judging from
the scale of his work, he never stopped writing. He is among the first
poets to introduce in a candid and erotic sense his homosexuality into
his verse, at a time when homosexuality was still illegal. As early as 1944
he wrote his important essay "The Homosexual in Society," blotting his
copy-book for two decades. Yet if the poet's body is at the heart of
poetic articulation, that body should recognize and acknowledge itself.
If the poem engages experiences of love, lust or arousal, surely part of
that experience is in the nature of the person that elicits a response, and
there are important considerations in being specific, which also entails
being truthful. Truthfulness should not be offensive: Duncan's essay is

moralizing and, in the light of the emerging work of Frank O'Hara and others, narrowing. He was didactic and severely responsible, in ways that set him apart, during the Vietnam period, from writers like Denise Levertov, with whom he had shared part of an education. He is curiously noble in his consistency and his insistence on contrary clarities.

There is something cloyingly benign about the tone of some of his verse as about his delicacies. He does not indulge in "camp," but he does at times deploy a language of effeminacy, of exaggerated delicacy, which cries out for a tincture, however slight, of irony. This is true of some of his erotic writing, where he mixes registers and tones from various periods to orchestrate a kind of universal experience. Even in the famous poems, it can sound silly. One of his great services was in helping to restore H.D. to the canon, and to do his best for Mary Butts and other writers who, in his view, had been written out of the century too casually. He was himself, in his early career, rejected not on the grounds of his poems but of his sexuality, quite explicitly, by editors including John Crowe Ransom at *Kenyon Review*. Other magazines followed suit. What did Pound make of him, Pound with his exceptionally harsh views about homosexuality?

Olson's followers in Britain have chosen to make their own spaces, as though association with the conventional machines of dissemination—commercial publishers, the BBC, the "reading circuit"—would compromise and misdirect the work. Olson's most intelligent and difficult English advocate is the Cambridge academic J. H. Prynne (b. 1936), who began in the wake of the Movement, writing tautly formal and rather "exquisite" poems, and found his way into Olson, on whom he has written. In his own poetry, with austere-seeming scrupulousness he sets out to trace the unedited, untidy ways in which the mind moves in a world of facts and ideas. Yet a certain tidying does occur, for no mind could move with the artful purity, the lateral coherences, of the poems he has written, developing a variety of formal strategies. Experience in his poems endeavors to be faithful to a source outside and a source within, to the "objective" and the "subjective" world. Without being discursive, his poems require discursive reading. An austere patristics encircles his work, yet it can be directly engaging. Some readers suggest an analogy between his poetry and that of John Ashbery, but Prynne's later poems require elaborate exegetics for the reader to make even prosodic sense of them, while Ashbery's, like the best poetry of any age, require merely imagination. Prynne is misread as a New York School poet by those unfamiliar with Pound, Williams and Olson. He is, like them, didactic, with the added austerities of the Leavisite Cambridge tradition.

Associated with his name are poets who have been his students or who have toiled in the vineyard with him. In 1987 Andrew Crozier and Tim Longville assembled an anthology of relevant work, *A Various Art.* One of the most accessible and rewarding of the seventeen poets included is John Riley.

> I have brought it to my heart to be a still point
> Of praise for the powers which move towards me as I
> To them, through the dimensions a tree opens up,
>
> Or a window, or a mirror. Creatures fell
> Silent, then returned my stare.
> Or a window, or a mirror. The shock of re-
>
> Turning to myself after a long journey,
> With music, has made me cry, cry out—angels
> And history through the heart's attention grow transparent.

By the time of his death, at the age of forty-one, Riley's poetry had achieved an importance beyond the trends of the day. Significant though his poems were in the 1960s and after, their value goes well beyond the context in which they were formed, and which they helped to shape for others. His is a poetry of integrity and vision: precise observation and wit coexist with beauty of image and rhythm, beauty in a timeless sense. Born in Leeds in 1937, Riley served in the Royal Air Force from 1956 to 1958, during which time he began to learn Russian. He read English at Pembroke College, Cambridge, and became a teacher. In 1966, with the poet Tim Longville, he helped set up the Grosseteste Press, a primary vehicle for the Cambridge poets, and in 1968 the *Grosseteste Review.* In 1978 he was attacked and murdered near his home in Leeds.

Veronica Forrest-Thomson (1947–75) was among the dazzling possibilities of a new poetry. She too died young. Her critical book, *Poetic Artifice: A Theory of Twentieth-Century Poetry* (1978), promised to draw together strands that had hitherto been distinguished by separation: Empson and Wittgenstein as well as the (in Britain) still new- and rebarbative-seeming forces of formalism and structuralism. Her mature poems, too, probe the nature of poetic statement in relation to a life lived in the world and in language. Some critics have been harsh on the awkwardness of her later formal writing, as though technical incompetence produced the rhythmic and syntactical problems. In my view the effects were intended, ways of apprehending and ways of distancing. In her early work her language of critical reading and her poetic language are close and natural; it was against this naturalness that her later verse moved, in the interests of a more rigorous and inclusive process. "With great brilliance and courage," wrote J. H. Prynne, "she set fear against irony and intelligible feeling against the formal irony of its literary anticipations."

An English poet of the generation before the Cambridge School, himself a graduate of Cambridge, belongs (a little uneasily) in this company: Charles Tomlinson. He comes from a working-class background in the Potteries—Stoke-on-Trent, "a land / Too handled to be primary— all the same / The first in feeling"—where he was born in 1927. He didn't suffer the "soft oppression of prosperity"; he remembers seeing a reproduction of van Gogh's *Sunflowers* in a dentist's waiting room as a boy—an early epiphany. He takes nothing for granted; nothing is second nature to him. The worlds of nature and of art he holds in his hands, in his mind and in his language with heightened wakefulness. Even mist and dream become crisp and sharp in a poetry that refuses to blur. This refusal is an aspect of his prosody quite as much as of his diction. "The hardness of crystals, the facets of cut glass; but also the shifting of light, the energising weather which is the result of a combination of sun and frost—these are the images for a certain mental climate, components for the moral landscape of my poetry in general." This is an early statement, but it holds true of his later, peopled and concentratedly political work. Hardness, cut, light, sun and frost; *mental* climate, *moral* landscape. Later he speaks of his poetry as being, like that of certain French poets he admires, a process of *sensuous cerebration*. In civic terms the values the poems propose are justice, balance, receptivity, a language that is moral and aesthetic at the same time.

He got to grammar school and then to Cambridge in the heyday of Leavis. Tomlinson was interested in film and the graphic arts and has made a secondary career of his graphic work. His own "presence" in his pictures, as in his poems, is often that of an editor: his paintings *occur*, the creative act is in essentializing them, in choosing which parts to cut out and preserve.

Donald Davie as a young man tutored him at Cambridge and they established a lasting friendship. Tomlinson taught Davie to see— architecture in particular; and Davie taught Tomlinson to read—syntax in particular. Tomlinson was hostile to what he saw as the narrowness of the Movement, with which Davie was associated. In poems like "No More Foreign Cities" he answers that narrowness (one of Kingsley Amis's *obiter dicta*, that we want no more poems about foreign cities, was the provocation) from the exotic actuality of the wider world, of different cultures, climates and lights. He is repelled by fashions and reductive rules and maintains a lively interest in other arts—architecture, sculpture, painting, music—and in travel. He is a peripatetic poet, leaving his cottage in Gloucestershire for Italy, America, Latin America, celebrated abroad even as he is at times neglected at home. He travels in language, too, by means of translation. His versions of the Russian of Fyodor Tyutchev, the Spanish of Antonio Machado, César Vallejo, Octavio Paz (especially), of Italian and French poets, are a significant second body of poetic work. He edited the seminal *Oxford Book of Verse in English Translation* (1980), which demonstrated the centrality of the practice throughout the history of our magpie literature, and how attitudes to translation and strategies of translation have evolved over six centuries.

Ezra Pound features in his anthology, and Tomlinson has found modern American poetry crucially enabling. Wallace Stevens was the star he initially steered by. In later work his guide has been Williams, also Oppen, Moore, Zukofsky; and he has an abiding interest in Pound over Eliot. His book *Some Americans* (1981) records personal debts to Williams, Moore, Zukofsky and others.

His verse is invariably fastidious. His images are seen not once, but at different times, from different angles; "eye" and "I" are gradually effaced by the full complexity of the thing, idea or story explored. He recognizes a romantic impulse in himself and opposes it, trying to write what *is*, not to personalize the world but to give it its own valency. Thus when he evokes in "Assassin" the scheming murderer of Trotsky in Mexico, he finds a whole voice for the man, gets inside his experience and lets a politics entirely anathema to him find articulation (ironized by the action).

In the 1970s he described his themes as being *place* and *the return*, almost in the spirit of Hardy. He quotes Lawrence: "All creative art must rise out of a specific soil and flicker with the spirit of place." He adds: "Since we live in a time when place is threatened by the violence of change, the thought of a specific soil carries tragic implications." The poems about the depredations of modern Bristol, where he was professor of English for many years, and about his own native landscape in the Potteries (poems written during the long final illnesses of his parents when his revisitings were painfully real and regular) touch on those "tragic implications." He frequently contrasts the suggestive ruins of past civilizations with the deliberately ruined cityscapes of modern Britain. "The Way In" is one such poem, in which "the avarice and callous utopianism" of the 1950s and 1960s issued in damage as severe and more lasting than that inflicted by the Luftwaffe in the War.

It is not surprising that his first readership was in the United States rather than in England. *The Necklace,* his first substantial publication, made an impact only in America. He emerged at a time when British poetry was "in denial," the austerities of the postwar reflected in a verse rebelling against the excesses of the 1940s and verbal comfort of any sort. Yet with the period he shares an English disgust with certain forms of excess, especially the confessional verse that emerged in the 1960s. In "Against Extremity" he rejects the willed extremism of poets like Sylvia Plath and Anne Sexton. His third book, *Seeing Is Believing*, was published in America in 1958 and in England two years later. In 1963 *A Peopled Landscape* appeared, a title chosen deliberately to answer those who regarded his poems as coldly inhuman. His first major collections, *The Way of a World* and *Written on Water*, appeared in 1969 and 1972. In "Prometheus," about the interplay between art and the world and the treacherous ideologies of Romanticism (his point of departure is Scriabin's elaborate symphonic work "Prometheus" and the Russian Revolution, registered in provincial Britain over the crackling airwaves), and in "Swimming Chenango Lake," Tomlinson's two characteristic voices come into their own. One is intellectual, meditative, feeling its way through ideas as embodied in individuals and in art; the other, with all the physical senses, engages specific landscapes and images from the natural world. The poems on the French Revolution, its hopes and betrayals, taken together constitute an essay on romantic illusions, political manipulation and excess. There is in his work a third voice, in the free-verse poems he calls "bagatelles"—anecdotes, generally slight and witty witnessings to things that he has seen or heard on his travels. They relate to Lawrence's more casual poems, without, as it were, imposing an "I" on the experiences.

In 1985 his first *Collected Poems* was published, and the variety of his achievement could be appraised. One would expect a poet of such meticulousness to be caustic and sparse, but there is abundance in his work—abundance of resource, thought and visual generosity. "According objects their own existence" was his purpose in the first book; the task throughout seems to have been to record the otherness of the world. Like Elizabeth Bishop, he begins in an attenuated symbolism, deploys synesthesia, draws analogies between the arts; in time, however, objects settle into being themselves. In "The Impalpabilities" he writes (in a version of Williams's triadic triplets):

> It is the sense
> > of things that we must include
> > > because we do not understand them
> the impalpabilities
> > in marine dark
> > the chords
> that will not resolve themselves

Reinvention

HUGH MACDIARMID, AUSTIN CLARKE, PATRICK KAVANAGH,
DAVID JONES, EDITH SITWELL, MINA LOY,
ROBINSON JEFFERS, E. E. CUMMINGS, LANGSTON HUGHES

A poet whose ambition is to reinvent a literature can begin by reinventing himself. That's what Christopher Murray Grieve did in 1922, at the age of thirty, becoming the brilliant, monstrous and ineradicable Hugh MacDiarmid, his "nom de plume (et de guerre)." When he died in 1978, he had redrawn the map of Scottish poetry and affected the whole configuration of English literature. Like the great modernists, he was dazzled by the resources available and profoundly discontented with the culture he had to hand.

> For ilka thing a man can be or think or dae
> Aye leaves a million mair unbeen, unthocht, undune,
> Till his puir warped performance is,
> To a' that micht ha' been, a thistle to the mune.

He is incontestably the greatest Scottish poet since Burns, if we exclude the wonderful Scots Gaelic poet Sorley MacLean, whom MacDiarmid acknowledged as his peer.

Because many of MacDiarmid's best poems are in a language heightened by his own invention (called Lallans, Synthetic Scots, or Vernacular Scots) based on the vernacular of the Borders and Scottish Lowlands, not on standard English, he seems at first as linguistically difficult as his forebears Dunbar and Douglas (he lacks the repose of Henryson). He fell into this idiom rather abruptly in 1922. Reading a scholarly volume entitled *Lowland Scotch as Spoken in the Lower Strathearn District of Perthshire*, he found himself producing a poem in something like that language. It remains one of his best-known poems. Had it been written in English, the tonalities and cadence would seem to set it comfortably among Hardy's *Poems 1912–1913*:

Ae weet forenicht i' the yow-trummle
I saw yon antrin thing,
A watergaw wi' its chitterin' licht
Ayont the on-ding;
An' I thocht o' the last wild look ye gied
Afore ye deed!

The sole novelty here is the language: it is a lovely poem in an unmodernist elegiac tradition. Most of the words in the poem come from two pages in the scholarly book he was reading, as though he challenged himself to assemble a poem from this limited if resonant lexical resource. Alan Bold quotes the original volume to unravel the obscurities: "yow-trummle" is "cold weather in July after sheering"; "watergaw" is "indistinct rainbow"; "on-ding" is "beating rain or snow"—all from a single page of Sir James Wilson's book. Heaney sees the moment in these terms: "The recorded words and expressions . . . stretch[ed] a trip wire in the path of Grieve's auditory imagination so that he was pitched headlong into his linguistic unconscious, into a network of emotional and linguistic systems that had been in place since childhood." He found *his* tongue, or rather Hugh MacDiarmid's. Other fine lyrics followed, and on these rests the unshakable, popular, "Burnsian" foundation of MacDiarmid's reputation.

The real difficulty as the work develops is less in the language, which is generally no more remote than Middle English, to which a reader can adjust, but in the huge lexicon he exploits, in English as well as Lallans. His best verse—and there is much in his vast opus, especially in the first half—is supple and various. A huge curate's egg: "My job, as I see it, has never been to lay a tit's egg, but to erupt like a volcano, emitting not only flame, but a lot of rubbish." Outside Scotland he has begun to gain an audience. It is no longer thought eccentric to mention him in the same breath with the other modern innovators.

Like them he was unwilling to compromise with the English literary and political establishments, which he evokes in *In Memoriam James Joyce*. He adhered to doubtful political causes of right and left, coming to rest upon a Marxism disfigured by an unalloyed respect for Stalin. There is too the problem of the immense, Siberian tundra of some of the later works, their dogged pursuit of themes better left to prose. He was impatient with those who dismissed him, but encouraged hostility from those he despised. In *Lucky Poet*, his autobiography, he characterizes the "whole gang of high mucky-mucks, famous fatheads, old wives of both sexes, stuffed shirts, hollow men with headpieces stuffed with straw, bird wits, lookers under beds, trained seals, creeping Jesuses, Scots

Wha Ha'ers . . . commercial Calvinists, makers of 'noises like a turnip,' and all the touts and toadies and lickspittles of the English Ascendancy." Hardly surprising that his progress south of the border has been less rapid than in Scotland itself.

He was born in 1892 and raised in Langholm, Dumfriesshire. Among his early teachers was the Scottish composer F. G. Scott, an important shaper of his imagination. From Langholm he went to Edinburgh and began teacher's training, but changed his mind and took up a career in journalism instead. He worked for the Fabian Research Department and contributed to A. R. Orage's *New Age*. He served in the Royal Artillery Medical Corps (1915–19), returning to journalism after the war and working in Montrose, Liverpool and London. He was a Scottish Nationalist and a Communist, expelled by the Nationalists for his membership in the Communist party, and vice versa.

Poverty and a breakdown in health followed his second marriage, and he withdrew (1933–41) to a croft on Whalsay in the Shetlands. During the Second World War he worked in a munitions factory on the Clyde and eventually settled in Biggar, Lanarkshire, where he lived until his death in 1978. He was awarded a Civil List pension in 1950. The experiences he gathered in his alternately retiring and hectically active life, and the breadth of his reading, make him a rare, encyclopedically informed writer like Pound and James Joyce, though they were less encumbered by their learning than MacDiarmid.

Distressed in the first decades of the century by his people's cultural submission to England and their ignorance of the distinctive heritage and common traditions that could make them a nation again, he made it his mission to revitalize Scottish culture. His program involved reviving—or reinventing—a Scottish language. He also adapted modernist techniques. Relentlessly he attacked the Scottish culture heroes of the day, in order to replace them with what he regarded as authentic models. Though he loved Burns's poetry, he saw in him the worst conceivable model for a modern Scottish literature. As Seamus Heaney has noted, "He prepared the ground for a Scottish literature that would be self-critical and experimental in relation to its own inherited forms and idioms, but one that would also be stimulated by developments elsewhere in world literature."

After the language, the most striking aspect of MacDiarmid's poetry is that his imagery draws on the industrial as well as the rural world. Accommodating this content in Scots broadened its expressiveness. An early influence on his language was John Jamieson's *Etymological Dictionary of the Scottish Language* (1808), from which he borrowed words to plant in the context of the current dialect, effecting a synthesis in an idiom no one spoke, or had ever spoken. Gregory Smith's *Scottish Lit-*

erature: Character and Influence (1919) defined for him a particular Scottish quality: establishing contrasts or contradictions between the real and the fantastic, then resolving them.

In MacDiarmid's poems the sublime and the ridiculous are next-door neighbors. He stresses thematic antinomies and apparent contradictions which are poetically, or literally, complementary and necessary to each other. Coleridge is MacDiarmid's authority for his belief in imagination as "the balance or reconciliation of opposites or discordant qualities." But MacDiarmid is less intellectually contained than Coleridge. The discordances occur in the public arena quite as much as in the stanza or the individual human heart.

John Davidson, too, showed MacDiarmid a way. Davidson, the most threadbare member of the Rhymers' Club, proposed a Darwinian and wholly materialist explanation of reality. His social concerns were transmuted through a relentless egotism into a form of "representative" autobiography. He had an almost sentimental regard for the unity of nature through the elements. His was a poetry of *fact*, of the tangible, a radicalization of the Gradgrind ideology. In his expository poems MacDiarmid, like Davidson, pretends to be accurate and full in detail. A poem grows out of fact, fact is its occasion and object; it should be a language of detection rather than imposition on its subject. This might seem, in essence, a modification of crucial modernist arguments, not least in its wariness of the metaphysical and its reliance on the concrete. As an aesthetic, however, it requires a degree of reticence and self-effacement far beyond the profoundly romantic impulse of MacDiarmid's nature.

His Scots poetry is his major achievement, but he was a considerable, if uneven, poet in English as well. His long poems, like Davidson's, are cumulative, though the motivating passion can be derailed by willful obscurity, or deadened by a freight of detail, or vitiated by propagandistic aphorism and occasional plagiarism. The *Second Hymn to Lenin* (1935) and *In Memoriam James Joyce* (1955) abound in good as well as overweight verse. His great poem—for each poem he wrote is part of a total and totalizing "work in progress"—is destined to remain open-ended, like the *Cantos*, *Paterson* and *Maximus*.

His verse devours trivial matter and important ideas, facts, images, feelings, petty resentments and large passions, thoughts, memories, insatiably. It swallows other men's words whole. MacDiarmid lacked the selectivity that makes Pound's and Eliot's erudition compelling. Prolixity and lack of concentration, those worst vices for the modernists, mark his writing; some say that they mar it, others that this approach traces an alternative aesthetic to Pound's, an aesthetic that demands a verse plain and sturdy enough to deal in depth with any subject. In a jumbled way MacDiarmid is the most patently learned poet of his age, at once

magpie and textbookish sage. The poem is not an end: it is for the use of
a newer age.

The early poems are intriguing in conception and execution. "The
Innumerable Christ" was inspired by Professor J. Y. Simpson's comment
"Other stars may have their Bethlehem, and their Calvary too." In his
poem MacDiarmid concludes:

> An' when the earth's as cauld's the mune
> An' a' its folks are lang syne deid,   long since
> On coontless stars the Babe maun cry
> An' the Crucified maun bleed.

Earth is continually set in a cosmic perspective, historical time con-
trasted with geological time. Thus a new significance emerges from
humanity's insignificance. In another poem he writes:

> The moonbeams kelter in the lift   undulate; sky
> An' Earth, the bare auld stane,
> Glitters beneath the seas o' Space,
> White as a mammoth bane.

His greatest poem—one of the great modernist poems—is *A Drunk
Man Looks at the Thistle* (1926). The speaker is resolutely Scots, highly
literate, very drunk. As he tumbles into a half-dream stupor beside the
thistle in the moonlight, a flood of thoughts, jostling one another for
precedence, tumbles out of him. The suppleness of the language is
astonishing, its abrupt changes of tone and mood, sometimes within a
single stanza or a single line, its natural fusion of reality and fantasy.
Edwin Morgan suggests that in the Scottish language, there is a rhetoric
absent from modern English, a facility to harness opposing impulses in
a balanced, single statement. He might have added that the kinds of
irony that restrain the southern English writer have never troubled an
emancipated Scot.

In parts the poem is bitingly satirical, particularly at the expense of
his pseudo-Scottish sentimental expatriates, the desecrators of Burns,
and of the small-minded bourgeoisie who "ca' their obstinacy 'Hame.'"
The satire on intellectuals and factionalists is shrewd. The poem moves
toward a defiant credo pertinent to all MacDiarmid's work:

> I'll ha'e nae hauf-way hoose, but aye be whaur
> Extremes meet—it's the only way I ken
> To dodge the curst conceit o' bein' richt
> That damns the vast majority o' men.

For I've nae faith in ocht I can explain,
And stert whaur the philosophers leave aff . . .

He stands at the point of dialectic synthesis, impossible to paraphrase.

The poem is written in quatrains, sestets, triplets, couplets and verse paragraphs, varying form with virtuosity to suit the content, incorporating in the flow translations and imitations of other work, including verse by Alexander Blok and Zinaida Hippius. It is sad that MacDiarmid did not devote more time to translations into Scots. He was not a patient man or—as translators have to be—a serving man. He takes what he wants, but he gives very little.

Platonic and physical love (the latter graphically evoked, the former given more body than one might expect) are another double theme. But the dominant theme, here and elsewhere, is the limits imposed by choice, by *having to choose*. In a later poem, "Light & Shadow," he writes, "On every thought I have the countless shadows fall / Of other thoughts as valid that I cannot have." To choose is to exclude: the person who chooses communism cannot be a nationalist, and vice versa. MacDiarmid does not willingly accept the exclusion that choice entails. He would prefer to *contain* opposites. This explains his refusal to be selective in his long English poems, his attempt to foreground everything and to make an *all*-encompassing poem, with disastrous structural strains on the poem (and many a reader's staying power).

The thistle in *A Drunk Man* modulates from meaning to meaning, altered in the bleary dream. At one moment moonlight metamorphoses it into a skeleton—his own. Then it stands, more conventionally, for Scotland. Later it sprouts a great red rose—not the Virgin Mary but the General Strike—which deflates like a balloon and the thistle stalk is left literal and poor. As the symbols transform before his eyes, the drunk man ruminates:

The vices that defeat the dream
Are in the plant itsel',
And till they're purged its virtues maun
In pain and misery dwell.

This poem comprehensively evokes life's antinomies—political, religious, emotional—but with a specific inflection and a location in space and historical time. Centered as it is on the fact of the thistle and the drunk man, the monologue works by accretion of suggestions and associations. It can in one breath lament the high price and low quality of Scotch, in the next expose the positive and negative tensions of sex, zero in on the possibility of revolution, the future of the Scottish language and nation, then range back over history. He manages to "Exteriorise things in a thistle," "The grisly form in which I'm caught." He conjures a number of ghosts, principally (and with weird appropriateness) Dostoevsky's (the poem is stalked by Russian writers and Soviet themes), but also Herman Melville's, for Melville alone in recent English-language literature achieved the scope MacDiarmid tried for, without forfeiting detailed accuracy. The thistle, like the white whale, is "A symbol o' the puzzle o' man's soul." The precision of detail is unforgettable; for example, we hear "God passin' wi a bobby's feet / Ootby in the lang coffin o' the street."

After *A Drunk Man* he wrote many more poems in Scots, though none to equal this early tour de force. He began to lament poverty and drudgery; his Scots approximated English more and more as he loaded its vocabulary with technical terms, until he began to write principally in English. One of the best Scots poems from the transition is "North of the Tweed"; another is a memorable elegy for his father:

We look upon each ither noo like hills
Across a valley, I'm nae mair your son.
It is my mind, nae son o' yours, that looks,
And the great darkness o' your death comes up
And equals it across the way.

In "The Seamless Garment," using the image of the weavers of the local textile industry, he speaks of Rilke's "seamless garment o' music and thought." This describes, in effect, the kind of poetry MacDiarmid tried to write—a poetry of inclusive wholeness, a poetry not complete in its grasp, but in its reach. "On a Raised Beach" is a fine example of his achievement, a major celebration and an examination of the pertinence of geology, the expressiveness of facts, with a rhetoric as powerful as Pablo Neruda's, yet more controlled, more insistently circumstantial. In the *Second Hymn to Lenin* he agrees with Joyce:

. . . the principal question
Aboot a work o' art is frae hoo deep
A life it springs—

and how high, from that depth, it can rise and how much it can raise with it. He sought a poetry "full of erudition, expertise, and ecstasy," as he says in "The Kind of Poetry I Want." He tried to achieve a multifaceted "fly-like vision." His was an inclusive talent like Lawrence's or Whitman's, only more austere and particular, more Presbyterian, less subjective. It is intellectual, satirical, deliberately inelegant, yet at the same time prophetic. In one poem he writes:

> So I am delivered from the microcosmic human chaos
> And given the perspective of a writer who can draw
> The wild disorder of a ship in a gale
> Against the vaster natural order of sea and sky.

Perspective, distance are essential to his inclusive vision. "Crystals like Blood," his best elegy, maybe his best short English poem, begins with the matter-of-fact, arresting lines "I remember how, long ago, I found / Crystals like blood in a broken stone." It examines the memory; the elegiac note is sounded as a celebration.

Like another great Scot, Thomas Carlyle, he knew his own arrogance and could make fun of it. Hard on others, he could be hard on himself. The romantic and mystical impulses that trip up his materialist mission are part and parcel of his achievement and his shortcomings, all of which he exposed in *In Memoriam James Joyce*, particularly in the section that in extract is called "The Task." The poem is filled with hostages to fortune. It calls his paradoxical, antinomian structures to account and finds them wonderfully wanting. Paradoxical choices are evident throughout, even in the choice of Scots, an act at once reactionary and revolutionary, articulating as it does against the broad complacent nationalism of Britain a narrow, redefining and positive nationalism of Scotland. MacDiarmid's nationalism is not triumphalist or at any point complacent. Its intention is recuperative; he is wresting something out of the past and out of the present, an area of distinct identity, independent value. He explores this theme inexhaustibly in prose, not least in his richly eccentric study *Scottish Eccentrics*. Scots is not a regional dialect but the reconstruction of a national language. The project may be doomed, but it is heroic, and in making the new—or remaking the old—language, he creates some of the greatest poetry of the century.

T. S. Eliot, no stranger to constructing a home in an alien culture, wrote: "It will eventually be admitted that he has done . . . more for English poetry by committing some of his finest verse to Scots, than if he had elected to write exclusively in the Southern dialect." In serving Scotland best, he served English literature as well.

Austin Clarke's task of reinvention in Ireland was more difficult than MacDiarmid's. Irish poetry had already been reinvented by Yeats, and his achievement eclipsed other writers and the Ireland they might write. When Robert Frost asked Clarke what sort of poetry he wrote, he replied, "I load myself with chains and then try to get out of them." The "chains" are formal and thematic; even in his simplest poems he is a *poeta doctus*. A close look at the exacting forms he devises, some based on Irish models, with *rime riche*, internal rhyme, assonantal and alliterative patterns and difficult stanza forms, shows how his poems at their best achieve resonance without showing off their formal complexities.

He loaded himself with chains; but he was loaded, too, with unchosen burdens. Yeats cast a long shadow. The endless debate about what constitutes Irishness in art and literature continued, as it had for Joyce in his self-imposed exile, and for Samuel Beckett. Readers were reluctant, given the achievement of Yeats and Patrick Kavanagh's accessibility, to accept Clarke on his own terms. It can't have been easy, as he emerged, to reconcile personal vocation, deep learning, a time of historic change, and an indifferent or hostile milieu. His great advocate, Thomas Kinsella, seems to occupy an almost analogous position in Ireland today. But Clarke is so encumbered and bound that his verse resists exporting.

John Montague called him "the first completely Irish poet to write in English." There is nothing of the stage Irish about him. In his autobiography, *Twice Round the Black Church* (1962), Clarke evokes his Irishness—subject matter, versification, way of speaking. Charles Tomlinson compares him with MacDiarmid, remarking that "a sense of nationality can deepen a comparatively narrow talent." It may be that it is *narrowed* rather than deepened and enabled by a sense of nationality. He gains much from being rooted in Ireland in ways Yeats was unable to be. Impoverishment comes from having to acknowledge and define that rootedness, to manifest it in prose and verse. History would not allow him to take his country of origin for granted. Tomlinson insists that Clarke's nationalism is not "the inertia of chauvinism, but a labour of recovery." Clarke adapted elements from a tradition alien to the English, working toward a separate Irish, not Anglo-Irish, poetry. It was for him a project, a required labor added on to his primary vocation, and it is responsible for peaks and troughs in his work. Yeats assimilates the Irish struggle into a preexistent rhetorical tradition. Clarke introduces the struggle, preserved in a language long suppressed, into the rhetoric itself, to forge a new poetic idiom.

He was born in Dublin in 1896. Educated at the Jesuit Belvedere College and the University of Dublin, where he later lectured in English, he traveled in England, worked as a journalist for a time, and returned to Dublin in 1937 to found the Dublin Verse Speaking Society and the Lyric Theatre Company for his own and others' plays. His verse dramas are, with Padraic Fallon's, as important as Yeats's. He was a founding member of the Irish Academy of Letters and acted as its president (1952–53). In his later years he traveled widely, reading and lecturing, and after a long period of eclipse, due largely to neglect in Ireland, he reemerged in the 1960s as an important voice. The publication of *The Collected Poems*, edited by Liam Miller, in 1974, weeks after the poet died, was an overlooked literary event. Darkness settled on a writer responsible for three novels, two books of memoirs, over twenty-eight verse plays, literary criticism, and some eighteen books of poetry, a darkness into which poets like Thomas Kinsella and Donald Davie shone their torches. Clarke will remain a poets' poet, a resource, giving pleasure to those of an Augustan temperament who value his inventive prosodies. He is not a poet a reader can relax with. He makes too many demands. As Kinsella remarks, "The diction of his last poems is a vivid, particular voice, rich and supple; nothing is unsayable. But it is no natural voice."

Clarke's sense of time is insistently historical, unlike Yeats's. The early poems attempt to realize legend: the story of Finn (his first book, *The Vengeance of Fionn*, 1917), the struggles between Ulster and the rest of Ireland, of Cuchulain, and the cast of characters made familiar, in a wholly different spirit, by Yeats. Clarke set out not to remember but to revive them. His approach in the early poems, romantic and in some ways conventionally rhetorical, is psychological—his characters are flimsy but more real than Yeats's—and historical, too, for Clarke sees in the early struggles analogies with the struggles of his day.

For almost two decades (1938–55) he wrote little poetry, devoting his attentions to the Lyric Theatre Company. When he returned to verse his approach, like Yeats's after the Abbey years, was more directly concerned with the daily affairs of Ireland, and he had mastered satirical modes. Later still the poems risked autobiography, becoming "confessional," not in the manner of Lowell's *Life Studies* but in ways he justified from his tradition: "The Confession poem was a recognised form in Gaelic and lasted until the eighteenth century." He made the form available once more.

"The Fires of Baal" and later narrative poems, on Celtic and biblical themes, develop plots familiar to most readers. They provide him with a dramatic shape which he develops, attending to the telling, to time perspectives and locations. They are composed with bardic impersonality. He could write in this way, he later commented, because at the time "the future of our new State seemed so hopeful . . . Irish writers could delay for a while in the past." The hope was illusory: the state soon demanded his satirical attention.

He had begun to work with short, interrelated poems, exchanging the epic panorama for something more condensed and immediate in effect, less defined in overall contour: the sequence. He retained an impersonal voice, but the poems were no longer bardic. "A Curse" exemplifies both the indignation Clarke could express outside satire and—

more important for his later work—the development of those exacting chains of rhythm, cross-rhyme, assonance and alliteration with which he loaded himself. "Assonance," Clarke said, "takes the clapper from the bell of rhyme. In simple patterns the tonic word at the end of the line is supported by a vowel rhyme in the middle of the next line." Donald Davie sees this as a manifestation of the impulse to intricate patterning that we see in Celtic carving and graphic art.

Pilgrimage and Other Poems (1929) is his first major collection. He begins to develop a favorite role, that of the erring priest. "Celibacy" proposes the image of ribs, with biblical associations; the "self" climbs upon itself. The cross-rhymes "briar"/"fire," "nettle"/"fell," "hunger/rung," are used with characteristic subtlety:

> Bedraggled in the briar
> And grey fire of the nettle,
> Three nights, I fell, I groaned
> On the flagstone of help
> To pluck her from my body;
> For servant ribbed with hunger
> May climb his rungs to God.

Each poem has its incident, rendered dramatically in "The Cardplayer" or—at its most intense—in "The Young Woman of Beare," which like many of his poems has an erotic current, even in the chaste diction and sparse imagery. "Although the clergy pray, / I triumph in a dream." What is the triumph?

> See! See, as from a lathe
> My polished body turning!
> He bares me at the waist
> And now blue clothes uncurl
> Upon white haunch. I let
> The last bright stitch fall down
> For him as I lean back,
> Straining with longer arms
> Above my head to snap
> The silver knots of sleep.

Irish models served him well, astonishingly so in the short-lined stanzas, though it must be said that his eros, like Basil Bunting's, is "hot with a cold passion."

Clarke's transition to the present, his achievement of an individual voice, is complete in *Night and Morning* (1938). Public themes—which

in the Irish context include the religious—develop, with a hankering
after eighteenth-century qualities of mind, clarity and purpose, as
though an Anglo-Irish strain is being admitted to temper and extend
the hard-earned, re-earned Irish idiom. He works toward satire, and the
echo of Yeats grows fainter, at last inaudible.

Images of the Church's power, temporal and psychological, recur.
Each Irish coin has at some stage passed through the collection.
Orgy, grim antithesis to grim repressiveness, fills dreams with a poison-
ous, denying dialectic, is whispered in confessional. Natural impulse,
guiltless sensuality, have little place. Clarke's anger intensifies: anger
against the Church in particular, its patterns of alienation. In "The
Straying Student" he characterizes Ireland:

> . . . this land, where every woman's son
> Must carry his own coffin and believe,
> In dread, all that the clergy teach the young.

Yet anger is ambivalent. If, in "The Jewels," he says, "The misery of
common faith / Was ours before the age of reason," he cannot deny an
impulse of nostalgia:

> O to think, when I was younger
> And could not tell the difference
> God lay upon my tongue.

The Eucharist he took before puberty has left him with a different
hunger, not of the body or the mind; reason and flesh lack the whole
nourishment of innocent faith.

In the years between these poems and *Ancient Lights: Poems and
Satires, First Series* (1955), the satirist came into his own. Ireland, with its
unreflective religious consensus and pressing political problems, was a
land where popular satire might have impact. The Church's attitude to
birth control was one of Clarke's butts even then. In "Three Poems
About Children" he recounts a fatal fire in an ill-equipped orphanage
and the bishop's consolatory platitudes. Such poems have aged badly:
the targets, hard as granite at the time, have become soft or vanished.

The poem "Ancient Lights" is "confessional," recalling childhood
and the anguish of religious confession. Other poems are occasioned by
newspaper articles, conversations, observations—small recollections
taking shape in a changed present, often humorously clarifying it. His
characters, though simplified, are rounded, not archetypal or emblem-
atic, nor characters in a private myth, as in Yeats.

A second and third series of *Poems and Satires, Too Great a Vine* (1957) and *The Horse Eaters* (1960), appeared. In the first of these, "The Loss of Strength" carries autobiography further than before. The rhythm, advancing in irregular, condensed phrases, and using the enjambement dramatically, catches the movement of a voice under pressure. The poet finds a stream that, unlike the others, "had never come to town"—is pure, unfished and undefiled. The rhythm follows too the eddying progression of the "lost water." The word "monklike" is especially telling:

>   . . . Now engineering
> Machinery destroys the weirs,
> Directs, monk-like, our natural flow:
> Yet it is pleasant at Castleconnell
> To watch the salmon brighten their raincoats.
> The reeds wade out for what is gone . . .

In a single statement he stigmatizes values held by the Church and the cash values of industrial society. He can reject what he perceives as expressions of analogous forces, both motivated by material profit, both preying on human vulnerability and impoverishing human life.

"Hippophagi" in *The Horse Eaters* is a satire on a corrupted Ireland, epitomized in the eager export of horse-flesh to the Continent for human consumption: "Horse-eating helps this ill-fare state." He revisits the theme in *Forget Me Not* (1962), in which he evokes with autobiographical detail the part the horse played in Irish life. Celebration, elegy and satire, it is more varied and vivid than the romantic epics. Epic gesture has resolved itself in particularity, moments of definition that make up for uncertainties of tone and the occasional absurdities or disproportions of sentiment:

>   . . . Too much historied
> Land, wrong in policies, armings, hope in prelates
> At courts abroad! Rags were your retribution,
> Hedge schools, a visionary knowledge in verse
> That hid itself.

His most original poem is "Mnemosyne Lay in Dust" (1966), praised by non-Irish critics as the culmination of his "confessional" mode. It recounts a nervous breakdown, hospitalization, and eventual return to the world. Maurice, the central character, obsessed with memories of places, past pleasures, past fulfillments, and debilitated in breakdown, lets associations flow freely, until "Terror repeals the mind." Through the eyes of madness he evokes the delusions and agonies of other inmates. His particular loss of memory is a metaphor for a cultural loss, a failure of connection with the past and therefore with the future. Maurice, having articulated the loss, emerges "rememorised," "his future in every vein."

There are further books, celebrations of writers whose work he valued, laments of the aging man suffering the indignity of failed sensuality in a manner different in tone and intensity from Yeats's. Among the later work Thomas Kinsella praises the "series of wickedly glittering narratives culminating in *Tiresias*: poetry as pure entertainment, serious and successful." His last major poem was "A Sermon on Swift," anecdotal, wry and cutting, addressing a crucial antecedent.

Irish poets with Irish inflections, subjects and themes have existed for centuries, but here is something new not in accent but in kind, a poetry drawing on Celtic modes, laden with the personal "chains" he described to Frost and the historical chains of circumstance. The uncompromising force of his best satires, the vividness of his love lyrics and visions, and the cool candor of his "confessions" set him apart. He cleared a non-Yeatsian space in which an Irish poet might build a confident poetry in English for which the term "Anglo-Irish" is meaningless.

Nevertheless many contemporary Irish poets turn back not to Clarke but to Patrick Kavanagh. The rich measured achievement of his early poems is betrayed by the prolixity and unbridled anger of his later satires. Beginning with rural poems about real peasants (he was a countryman), Kavanagh left this world for Dublin, rejected much of his early verse and prose, and in indignation and self-pity marked his exclusion from a world that at once attracted and repelled him. A heavy drinker, he concedes that his excesses marred his later career. And yet at the end of it, he produced some of his best work.

Kavanagh was born in 1905 in County Monaghan, son of a local cobbler. He pretty much educated himself and became a small farmer and a shoemaker. His first book of poems, *Ploughman and Other Poems,* appeared in 1936, and two years later *The Green Fool*, an autobiography which he later rejected with the poems as "stage-Irish rubbish."

> We are a dark people,
> Our eyes are ever turned
> Inward
> Watching the liar who twists
> The hill-paths awry

Whatever the faults of the early poems, there were virtues too. In "Tinker's Wife": "Her face had streaks of care / Like wires across it . . ." Most of the poems have distinctive rhythms, and it was on these that he was to build. Dublin beckoned and in 1939 he went, becoming a journalist, film reviewer, gossip columnist. It was a hand-to-mouth existence ("the big tragedy for the poet is poverty") until in 1955 he joined the Board of Extra-Mural Studies at University College. He had a steady income. His final years were troubled by difficulty and scandal. He died in 1967.

Yeats became his bête noire: there was jealousy that Yeats defined the space within which Irish poetry might be recognized. Yet time after time in his prose and verse there are echoes—phrases, cadences, grandiloquent attitudes—of Yeats. Satire was not to be Kavanagh's effective vehicle, as it was Clarke's. Too much the romantic, too much the countryman, the city was not properly in his blood, and satire is an urban genre. It is the ragged Muse he serves best, and against which he turned in Dublin, trying to shed his peasant identity. Yet his greatest poem—which he came to dislike—was about the peasantry, tackling a subject more serious and abiding than any the city could provide him. *The Great Hunger* appeared in 1942.

It is in fourteen sections, with remarkable variety of rhythm and pace. Some lines run to twenty syllables, others to three, with a free-playing rhyme scheme. The protagonist, Patrick Maguire, is a farmer who lives with his cruelly possessive invalid mother and his sister. The face he turns to the world is wholesome, dependable. In himself he becomes hollower and hollower—for lack of love, the great hunger of the title. His mother and his religion constrain him to unfulfillment.

> His dream changes again like the cloud-swung wind
> And he is not so sure now if his mother was right
> When she praised the man who made a field his bride.

His life story is one of the tension between impulse and inhibition, informed by a false sense of duty. The tourists who see Maguire idealize him: they too are hungry for another order of life. Few poems conjure so mercilessly and accurately a saga of unfulfillment such as this, subtly generalizing it so that it is in the end more potent than satire. The sexual hunger is the more potent for being undirected, like a storm impulse in search of clouds. The stage Irishman has vanished. God becomes difficult, but there is still a hunger for Him in the later poems.

One in particular, "The Long Garden," characterizes the virtues of Kavanagh's later writing.

> It was the garden of the golden apples,
> A long garden between a railway and a road
> In the sow's rooting where the hen scratches
> We dipped our fingers in the pockets of God.

The immanent God, perceived always in the most earthy places, in the new leaves, in the ploughed soil. His is an easier poetry to get hold of, more conventional in its forms and in what it expects of readers than Clarke's verse. It is not surprising that from Kavanagh stems much of the popular Irish poetry of recent decades. But not necessarily from *The Great Hunger*, which is inimitable, an invention, like a sturdy plough at the edge of an abandoned field.

Scotland, Ireland and—Wales, always neglected. It too needed invention, and the first substantive twentieth-century inventor was a Londoner whose task was, in some ways, to invent the country itself. David Jones was a convert to Roman Catholicism. He celebrates immanence in his poetry, the presence of Christ in a world revived by the Incarnation, its permanence celebrated in the Mass. Hopkins, whose inspiration is felt in every corner of Jones's imagination and spiritual vision, and who also celebrated Wales during his years there, described how the Christian faith transforms the way we see the world. The world suffused with the sacrifice of Christ is a world wholly meaningful, purposed, hopeful even when most bleak. Jones looks no further than that: the Incarnation and its momentous consequences. It is not heaven that commands his attention but the earth redeemed. Modernism is transposed, against itself, into a minor key. "The Mass *makes sense* of everything," he wrote.

He was born in Brockley, Kent, in 1895. His father was Welsh—and a Welsh speaker—who worked as a printer's overseer. Jones seemed to know all about typography, platemaking, and the processes of printing from birth. One lesson he forgot: the difficulty and cost of correcting monotype and linotype setting. The marked galley proofs and then the page proofs of his own poems, when he returned them to the publisher, were always extensively reworked, as though the typescript he submitted, already patched and stained with late corrections, was a further draft of a poem striving for a final form it could never achieve. He was almost as serious a nightmare for the old-fashioned compositor as the impossible Balzac, the absolute proof monster.

From his father Jones acquired a deep if twilit love of Wales, its legends and landscape. Wales gave him myths, London provided his literal world. His mother came of Cockney stock. Her father was a mast and block maker, and Jones learned about the river, the subtleties of ships and sailing, and the richly metaphorical dialect of the docks. He studied art at the Camberwell, later at the Westminster School of Art, pursuing an enthusiasm for William Blake and the English watercolorists and, one suspects, the work of El Greco with its emblematic and dramatic distortions. Drawing and painting occupied most of his time. His first book, *In Parenthesis* (1937), was not published until he was forty-two, already a mature graphic artist.

Four principal experiences shaped Jones's creative life. First and most devastating was the Great War. He enlisted in the Royal Welch Fusiliers and was involved in active service for three years. The image of war, its devastation and also the camaraderie it engendered, dominates his prose and verse. It remained terribly real to him, and he never entirely recovered from shell shock. A friend, visiting him in 1970, offered to light his cigarette and the burst of flame from the lighter sent the poet into a brief panic.

The second momentous event was his conversion to Roman Catholicism in 1921. Devotion to a faith that had at its heart a vital sign—the host—rather than a formal symbol, is significant. Jones insists that he does not deal with symbols. The signs, the "anathemata" he retrieves and displays, do not stand for something other: they contain in themselves the *nature* of the larger thing they signify.

The peculiar visionary Eric Gill (1882–1940) also changed Jones's life. Gill was a great lettering artist, typographer (designer of Perpetua and Gill typefaces), illustrator, sculptor and eccentric, the closest thing to William Blake England had to offer at the time. In a technological age he preached the value of traditional craftsmanship and individual artistry. At Ditchling he founded the Guild of St. Joseph and St. Dominic, a community of artists and craftsmen, with ideals of service and dedication that made it a kind of secular order. Later the guild moved to Wales. Discussions with Gill and the example of his work, industry and eccentric spirituality clarified Jones's thought. His artistic maturity dates from their association.

Though it seemed of little importance at the time, the final formative experience was Jones's visit to the Holy Land in 1934. Suffering from a nervous disorder, he went to Palestine a convalescent, without energy or enthusiasm. He stayed there some months and was intrigued by the historical remains, especially the inscribed stones from the time of the Passion. Remembering this years later, his response came powerfully, after the event. Much of his writing is set in Palestine, much of his imagery relates to his stay there. His delayed responses to experience were a result of the war. The relentless hardship of the trenches made it necessary for him to cultivate a surface indifference, to hold experience at a distance, in order to survive. *In Parenthesis,* the last major literary account by a combatant of the war, was published almost two decades after that war ended, and two years before the war cycle started once again.

Jones's poetry can be difficult and obscure, to a degree more pronounced than Eliot's or Pound's. Eccentricity of reference, an apparent eclecticism, is combined with formal strategies that produce a suggestive but not always functional discontinuity. The image of the Roman border guard, pacing remote battlements at the fringes of civilization, gazing into the dark marches beyond empire and faith, is a figure for the poet as well. The violence at the heart of the chief sacrament—the Crucifixion—and the violence implied in the extension of Roman civilization become the governing facts of his poetry. Continual tension exists between the functional prose of Rome and the evocative poetry of the signs. Verse and prose are mixed in a single work: different experiences and intensities of experience require different modes and registers for expression. There is tension, too, between the dialects he uses: a rustic colloquial (not unlike Kipling's Cockney), a Middle English thread (more Langland than Chaucer), an Elizabethan strain, and a more formal standard prose and verse language. There are echoes too of folk song, ballad, old saws, allusions to the work of others—Smart, Hopkins, Pound, Eliot, Joyce. Further, he introduces Latin phrases from the Church fathers, the Roman Mass and the Latin Bible. He introduces Welsh and other words into the texture of the verse, larding some passages with place names and references which he glosses at great length in entertaining but distracting footnotes.

"Nothing can permanently please," wrote Coleridge, "which does not contain in itself the reason why it is so, and not otherwise." The truth of this poetic law can be tested in much of Jones's poetry, where poetic effect is suddenly dissipated by a sequence of footnoted obscurities. It is a language of disorientation. Despite obscurities, it achieves a range of effects beyond that of a more conventional style. Because he draws on an abundance of social and historical registers, and because the rhythms are of a subtle nature, his poetry is meant to be read, as he says, aloud and "with deliberation." The footnotes can be read quietly, afterward.

Welsh elements have a special significance for him, however arbitrary they may at times appear to the reader. Wales is for him the cradle of British Christianity, and he evokes Christ and the Passion in a Welsh setting more than once. It is one of the places the Irish monks and saints chose for the "white martyrdom" of exile. And it is a place Rome never subdued. Its language still miraculously lives, its landscapes retain a ruggedness and beauty that possess the quality of a sign.

Jones is a contemplative rather than meditative writer. He does not analyze and appraise the mysteries but accepts and embodies them. He quotes Picasso: "I do not seek, I find." To understand his work, which is not descriptive or expository but evocative, a poetry *of* experience, not *after* experience, the fact of his faith and his purpose as a specifically religious writer must be accepted. Indeed, for the poetry to work at all, Jones must be believed, at least for the duration of the reading. He provides a possible way, a bridge, should we wish to cross it, to what he considered to be our cultural common ground—in history and in a shared faith whose signs can still be made vital and operative.

Readers who find the verse forbidding should not give up on Jones before reading his essays in *Epoch and Artist* (1973). Here he evokes an aesthetic so lucid and compelling that it colors one's reading not only of his work, but of much poetry this century. Art is, by its nature, "gratuitous," he tells us; it is not instrumental, it has no material purpose. If a beaver placed one gratuitous twig on its dam, the dam would become a font, the creature would enter the "sign world": "A culture is nothing but a sign, and the *anathemata* of a culture, 'the things set up,' can be set up only to the gods." Such a strict and liberating statement, if we accept it, questions the value of poetry mired in a world of contingency, what today passes for "main stream."

Jones sees himself as a contemplative craftsman, a "joiner" of song. He relates everything in a poem, as in his graphic work, to the object of contemplation, the sacrament. René Hague, an early and devoted critic, notes his preference for the past participle form (whit*ed*, dark*ed*, etc.), which implies that an actor, a creator, has been involved in imparting the quality to the object. The "whited" wave has been *made* white.

He tries to be scrupulous, though those who have handled the plates he made for his engravings comment on the careless quality of the cutting, suggesting poor preparation and maintenance of his tools. Certainly in the poetry there is accuracy in his detail. The terms of the crafts he writes of are correct—shipbuilding, soldiery or armory. When he tampers with historical fact, it is to emphasize a larger truth; he draws attention to anachronisms in footnotes. By putting Greek, Roman and Celtic soldiers anachronistically together in a single legion, for example, he expresses the universal nature of the Roman empire and universal complicity in the Crucifixion.

"Our making is dependent on a remembering of some sort." Poetry is the "song of deeds," and to Jones the two great deeds, war and Incarnation, are most worthy of poetry. His task is "making the signs available for today," providing a text to re-present the deeds as they continue to signify in this world, "at the turn of a civilisation." Remembering and revalidating the signs is the meaning of "sacrament," seeing the universal in the very nature of the particular or, as Coleridge wrote (translating Bacon), seeing "the latency of all in each." This is why Jones's precise materialism and localized imagery aspire to a self-transcending or mystical quality. "Art is the sole intransitive activity of man," he wrote. The poem is there, available.

Jones's poem often invokes prehistory, the Ice Age; "deposits" and "stratifications" recur. The geological time scale intensifies the historical, layers of alluvial time overlay one another much as the layers of history do in a *tel*, new cities built upon the old, the present rising on the rubble of its own antecedents. Time preserves, in this sense, and there is an analogy between the processes of nature and of history.

Jones regarded *Anathemata* (1952) as his most important work, and many poets agree with him. Eliot thought it required three readings before it became clear, but when it did it was rewarding (he must have sensed Jones's prosodic debt to him). For David Wright it is one of the "major poetic efforts of our era." One would not describe *Paradise Lost* or *The Prelude* in quite those terms: an "effort" it must have been, to hold it together conceptually, to make the parts, and the parts of parts, into coherent wholes without benefit of consecutive narrative or prescribed formal structure. Auden, drawn as much by the religious as the poetic project Jones undertook, pronounced it "probably the finest long poem written in English this century." That hedging "probably" implies the reservation of a man not quite able to give himself over to the kinds of demand Jones's forms make.

In his "Preface" Jones writes: "The action of the Mass was meant to be the central theme," with the implications of sacrament and representing the signs. He observes that "the workman must be dead to himself while engaged upon the work, otherwise we have the sort of 'self-expression' which is as undesirable in the painter or writer as in the carpenter, the cantor, the half-back, the cook." His admirers tend to take him at his word, yet it is difficult to imagine a writer less "dead to himself," more alive to the extremely personal nature of his quest, the material of his poem (which often draws on the particulars of his own life), and the recurrent poetic process that determines it. As he revises his poems, making them over the years denser, more allusive, they become more personal and intricately difficult. When he lets them go it is only on the understanding that they are still subject to revision, incomplete. *Anathemata* is subtitled *Fragments of an Attempted Writing*.

In eight sections, it begins and ends with the "action of the Mass." There is no center of interest, no plot, but a repeated process of representing the signs using various material. To read one section with understanding is to have read the whole work, for it proceeds by variation rather than extension. Salvaging material from oblivion, he is also "trying to make a shape out of the very things of which one is oneself made." Hardly "dead to himself," then; as the poem declares, "(For men can but proceed from what they know, nor is it / the mind of this flesh to practise poiesis, *ex nihilo*)." "What I have written has no plan," he remarked later, "or at least is not planned. If it has a shape it is chiefly that it returns to its beginning. It has themes and a theme even if it wanders far. If it has a unity it is that, what goes before conditions what

comes after and *vice versa*." This attempt to describe the poem's unity
defines the unity of Jones's vision, the interpenetration of past, present
and future through sacramental reenactment.

Early in the opening section of *Anathemata* occurs an example of
Jones at his most intense. He describes the making of a table. It becomes
the making of an altar, a ship and a cross, all at once. The act of carpen-
try and the thing made become signs for the Mass, the pilgrimage and
the sacrifice, central themes of the poem. These confluences or confla-
tions of meaning are a key to his approach, epitomized too in the ver-
tiginously shifting perspectives, which can seem almost oxymoronic
until we realize that the perspective is Christ's—"the high room" is "the
high cave," and the haunting phrase "down / among the altitudes" seems
to propose a divine cinematography.

He celebrates presence without a sense of transience, with no shadow
of elegy. Under the moraines of the Ice Age, the temporal *point de repère*
of the first section, he finds vital traces. The ice had been like the shroud-
ing of a dead body, "the sea-borne sheet." Thaw enabled the miracle of
new life. The natural process is analogous to the historical: the Incarna-
tion released the frozen inner landscape. While insisting on distance,
repeating "long, long, long before," Jones also insists on presence. The
Ice Age is wonderfully realized in a verse congealing into prose:

> As though the sea itself were sea-born
>   and under weigh
>   as if the whole Ivernian *mare*
>   directed from hyperboreal control-points by strategi of the
>   axis were
> one complex of formations in depth, moving on a frontage
>   widening with
> each lesser degree of latitude.

The second section, opening with Troy and Hector's death, moves to
the first legendary journey to England, the notion that Trojan Brutus
colonized these islands. Powerful inner rhyme, assonance, alliteration:
Jones makes verbs from nouns and adjectives, to strange effect. We read
"diaphanes" and "saliva'd," for instance. In the third section, he presents
the ship's arrival in a series of (unanswered) questions, not wishing to
assert what he cannot know. Yet the questions, without committing a
direct description, give a detailed account of the ship's arrival:

Did he shelter in the Small Downs?
Keeping close in, did he feel his way
Between the Flats and the Brake?

A series of possibilities builds out, suggesting the perils that might have prevented the arrival and stopped history before it could begin. In the grace of that survival is evidence of design (and designer).

Sections four and five center specifically on his grandparents' experiences: "Redriff" is said to evoke his maternal grandfather, speaking a slow, strange Cockney slang. He insists on his own strict craftsmanship, refusing to change his schedule or cheapen his craft for reward. The poem takes the form of an oblique dialogue and could be read as a tribute to Gill. Part V is indebted, Jones tells us, to the Anna Livia Plurabelle passage in Joyce's *Finnegans Wake*, beginning and ending with the cry of the lavender sellers in London streets. It is spoken for the most part by a woman, addressing a sea captain—the same captain who demanded in Part IV a speedy repair job on his ship and was rebuffed. The woman does not tell the story of her life; rather, she is part of the process of naming, of sacralizing—an ignorant but receptive transmitter of signs. She has belief without understanding, the most potent (and perilous) kind. In an amusing passage she recalls her lover, a man burdened with signs, continually distracted from the business of lovemaking:

> And then, as if he perceive a body—coming
> as if he hails a personage
> where was but insentience
> and baulk of stone
> he sings out clear
> REDDITOR LUCIS ÆTERNÆ
> These, captain, were his precise words—what sentiments I
> can't construe—but at which, captain, I cried: Enough!
> Let's to terrestrial flesh, or
> bid goodnight, I thought.

We can't but wonder that her patience lasted so long, for he has been patting the wall and speaking Sybilline phrases for several pages.

The woman's character combines elements of Ophelia, Molly Bloom, Mary Magdalene, woman and matriarch. A long tale of shipwreck, drawing on Coleridge's "Rime of the Ancient Mariner" (for which Jones made memorable illustrations) becomes a sign of the Passion; and as in the first section the ship (as it were in reverse) becomes a cross, an altar and a table. Finally the woman becomes Mary, and one is tempted to conjecture that, in Jones's original scheme, this was designed to be the last part of the poem, since it reaches a poetic climax, in a passage that combines allusions to Chaucer and Eliot, nursery rhyme and Anglo-Saxon custom, among other things:

On the ste'lyard on the Hill
weighed against our man-geld
                    between March and April
when bough begins to yield
                    and west wood springs new.
Such was his counting house
                    whose queen was in her silent parlour
on that same hill of dolour
                    about the virid month of Averil
that the poet will call cruel.
                    Such was her bread and honey
when with his darling body (of her body)
                    he won Tartary.

After *Anathemata* Jones published one further book, *The Sleeping Lord* (1974). This, read with *Epoch and Artist*, provides the best introduction to his work. The pieces it includes were written and revised over a period of thirty years. They are shorter than the major works and though they relate to one another they can be read separately. They are ordered so as to lead into his idiom, themes and style—a sort of primer for *Anathemata*. The first poem in the book, "A, a, a, Domine Deus," clarifies his mission as a poet. Open-minded, unprejudiced, he seeks signs of Him in "his manifold lurking places." The poems that follow, especially "The Wall," "The Dream of Private Clitus," "The Fatigue" and "The Tribune's Visitation," find signs in a kind of short-story form, and largely in the ancient world, since the modern, mechanized world seems almost devoid of signs: "it is easy to miss Him / at the turn of a civilisation."

Though he insists on craft and the seriousness of his vocation, Jones belongs to the Romantic as much as to the modernist tradition. His at times almost parodic formal debts to Pound, Eliot and Joyce do not set him quite in their league. His is a localized, contingent modernism. He's not compelled to abandon latent narrative or his instinct for organic forms. The poems are a rapt pursuit of a single theme and a similar poetic process practiced on a wide range of material. There is also his dogmatic reticence, a quality that becomes, in the letters to four correspondents collected in *Dai Greatcoat: A Self-portrait of David Jones in His Letters*, edited by René Hague (1981), agonizingly clear to the reader. Jones in his finished writings appears wise, subtle, even serene in his mission; in the letters he is by turns naïve, foolish, petulant, undecided, vulnerable to an alarming degree. In political terms, he fails to read the signs time after time: he is only truly at home in the world of images and imagination. The dailiness of life threatened, bored and disoriented him. The First World War left an unhealable wound, the source and limit of his originality.

The poems erect a palisade of rich allusion and obscurity (or opacity) that a devoted and well-armed reader can breach, though the faint-hearted will turn elsewhere. Jones is embattled—an unusual stance for a giver, as though he would like to give but at the same time to retain the gift. He unobtrusively reinvents religious poetry in a secular age, Welsh culture, the sweeping continuities of British and human history. When he died in 1974 many readers were surprised to learn he had still been alive.

In England reinvention took many forms, but none quite so eccentric as Edith Sitwell's. She exerts a fascination—not the fascination of Poe, whose wild music and tragic life are part of the birth of something substantial, but the fascination of a languid social and cultural tradition coming to an end in a falling chandelier of metrical sententiousness. The surprise here is that the social *type* she represents survived so long, that her writing can be so funny when it least means to be, so flat when humor is her intention. She might seem to embody, more than Wilde ever did, what we now know as camp. But camp involves self-conscious projection. There is no reason to believe that the heavily ringed, heavily rouged poet ever took herself anything less than seriously.

> Man must say farewells
> To parents now,
> And to William Tell
> And Mrs Cow . . .

She was born in Scarborough, Yorkshire, in 1887, the eldest child and only daughter of the eccentric Sir George Sitwell, a baronet of long pedigree, and Lady Ida. Sir George was an awkward papa, Lady Ida an unenthusiastic mama, repelled by her daughter's curious looks and unconventionality. Edith inherited her father's eccentricity. One of her sustained prose books is about *The English Eccentrics* (1933). From her mother she inherited pride and a sense of her large presence in the world. For one who flouted convention, she surrounded herself in later years with rituals that required strict observance: a monster of whim and self-importance, she also sometimes had a magical way with words.

She and her brothers Osbert and Sacheverell relished childhood holidays at Renishaw Hall in Derbyshire. "Colonel Fantock" celebrates those occasions. The poem is "beautiful" in her precious early manner, careful in sound organization, absurd in delineation of character. She confesses, "I always was a little outside life." How separate, chosen and unique she and her brothers were! "We all have the remote air of legend." Those Derbyshire holidays gave her "a taste for the grand and picturesque," though the stones and trees she writes about acquire a gauzy flimsiness.

Educated, in her words, "in secrecy," she fortunately had a governess with unconventional taste for Arthur Rimbaud and the French symbolists. She read them closely, through an excruciating accent, adopting the idea of "synesthesia" or "transmutation" in poetic imagery— presenting things seen in terms of smell or taste, sounds in terms of color, interchanging the senses. These bearings are taken—without subtlety but with energy—from Baudelaire's sonnet "Correspondances," which in Walter Martin's classic translation in part reads:

> Like echoes from infinity drawn out
> Into a dappled unison of light,
> Beyond the dawn of day or dead of night,
> All scents, all sounds and colours correlate.
>
> Some fragrances resemble infants' skin
> Sweeter than woodwinds, green as meadow grass—
> Others expand to fill the space they're in,
>
> Endlessly rich, corrupt, imperious;
> Amber and musk, incense and benjamin,
> In sense and spirit raptures sing as one.

Baudelaire uses synesthesia to explore subjects; Edith Sitwell uses it for display.

In 1914 Edith, aged twenty-seven, descended on London. There she spent much of the remainder of her life, until she died in 1964, queen of a court of admirers and aspiring writers. There, in 1916, while war distracted Europe, she edited *Wheels*, an avant-garde periodical whose aim was to startle the bourgeoisie, and more generally to prompt a reconsideration of the diction and scope of poetry. Her assault on philistinism and conservatism was implicitly revolutionary, but a revolution from the palace rather than the tenements. She had little truck with the Imagists. She was then, and she remained, a thoroughbred Bolshevik.

In 1924 *The Sleeping Beauty*, an autobiographical poem sequence, appeared. It was in this year too that Edith Sitwell's most popular work, the *Façade* sequence (1922), was set to music by William Walton. With *Gold Coast Customs* (1929) she moved away from playful aestheticism and, in satirical terms, commenced her denunciation of the corrupt, frivolous Mayfair life (not a difficult target), juxtaposing it with the savage rites of West African tribes. Her extended interweaving of polite society's and cannibals' customs, with Lady Bamburgher as her satirical butt, is impressionistic and imprecise. There are moments of near felicity, but the rhythms, reversing into rhymes, are forced. The "virtuosity" she calls attention to in her self-criticism is here in abeyance. This is poetry of large pretensions, in a grand manner, lacking technical and intellectual distinction. Anthropological naïveté is one of its more pardonable faults. The poem culminates in revolutionary prognostication:

> Yet the time will come
> To the heart's dark slum
> When the rich man's gold and the rich man's wheat
> Will grow in the street, that the starved may eat;—
> And the sea of the rich will give up its dead—
> And the last blood and fire from my side will be shed.
> For the fires of God go marching on.

John Brown's body is wrenched into servitude. The Christlike pose the speaker assumes in the penultimate line, with the banality of the last, deliver the coup de grace to the poem. Ronald Firbank hits the Mayfair target nail on the head in *Prancing Nigger* and other wily "experimental" prose works. Edith Sitwell is not in that league. This poem marks (not a minute too soon) the end of her experimental period.

It was followed by a decade's poetic silence. Financial hardship, the need to write prose and care for a dying friend, kept her off the Muse's back. She wrote a study of Pope that marked the beginning of a reappraisal of his work. Her prose is rapid, engaging, careless, and she draws unashamedly—sometimes word for word—from the work of other writers. In this and in her interest in eccentrics (if in little else) she resembles Hugh MacDiarmid.

At last she returned to verse. The later poems are not experimental. Some—notably "Invocation"—are elegant: the themes of age (a little early) and waiting are developed, and the theme of the suffering that results from "evil." The battle between good and evil is developed schematically; when the Second World War came she was poetically at the ready. She captured in "Still Falls the Rain" anguish and the recurrence of anguish, man's suffering at the hand of man, in a framework of religious images and in a solemn liturgical cadence. The poem is condensed, a quality rare in her later verse. But it is marred by mannerism. She pinches a line from Marlowe's *Doctor Faustus*: its intrusion wrecks the rhythm. In "Serenade: Any Man to Any Woman" she brings Ralegh's and Marlowe's most famous poems into play in a superficially developed Second World War setting: "Then die with me and be my love: / The grave shall be our shady grove." Literary influences show through baldly. "The Swans" and "A Bird's Song" vie with Yeats, unfortunately, as it happens, since the end of "Among School Children" knocks her into a cocked hat; "The Poet Laments the Coming of Age" leans upon Yeats's "Byzantium," without a hint of his subtlety—and without acknowledgment.

When the first atomic bomb was dropped, she became an apocalyptic poet par excellence. With "Three Poems of the Atomic Bomb," human apocalypse unites with her religious vision. She becomes prophetic, a prophecy lacking in particulars, chilly, inhuman. Dust, sun and wind, three elements in all her verse, come triumphantly into sway. What is missing from her later verse is the humor that tempered the experimental aestheticism of the early poems. Of *Façade* Louis Untermeyer says, "There has rarely been so brilliant an exhibition of verbal legerdemain."

A particularizing eye and specific emotion give the quality—if not of what they observe—of the experience of observation. And the *Façade* rhythms, based often on dance beats, are novel. In "Some Notes on My Poetry"—more defense than essay—she tells us she rebelled against the "rhythmical flaccidity, the verbal deadness, the dead and expected patterns." Rhythm was, she declared, "one of the principal translators between dream and reality." The *Façade* poems are "*abstract* poems—that is, they are patterns of sound." Using a phrase of Jean Cocteau's, she describes *Façade* as "the poetry of childhood overtaken by the technician."

Façade is made for music. It's difficult to read it without hearing Walton's settings. Some of the poems are unsentimentally tender—"Jodelling Song" is one, with a wide range of reference, about the end of childhood, heroism, fantasy. The unity of *Façade* is not logical or thematic but rhythmic, in a strict sense musical. Some poems enter the realm of irresistible nonsense:

Don Pasquito, the road is eloping
With your luggage, though heavy and large;
You must follow and leave your moping
Bride to my guidance and charge!

She came of poetic age in her thirties, a brief and intense maturity that stiffened into mannerism. She rejected what must have seemed to her the irresponsibility of her early poems. Yet their delight was not without conscience and commitment; often they have a disturbing burden, a message more ambiguous and—therefore?—durable than that of her rhetorical style.

In his remarkable essay "Three Hard Women" Thom Gunn tries to recover from the fat harvest of *Collected Poems* the early books of H.D.,

Marianne Moore and Mina Loy, to demonstrate that they were in revolt against a Victorian burden of conventions we can no longer conceive, and that their canonicity was, at the time, unthinkable. Of course they were women as well.

Who is this Mina Loy? Not a Hollywood actress, but a poet and iconoclast, born five years before Edith Sitwell, in London, to a prosperous middle-class family of middle-European Jewish and English Protestant extraction. She started as an artist, trained in Europe and England, was a natural decadent who became a fine artist and whose portraits of Joyce, Freud, Marinetti and Gertrude Stein (among others) gained their subjects' approval. She married, lived in Florence, became a Christian Scientist (and remained so for the rest of her life), had affairs with the Futurists, notably Marinetti and Papini, and divorced. Then, in 1918 she married the enigmatic and magnetic Arthur Cravan, nephew of Oscar Wilde (via Wilde's wife), a chunky boxer, an amazing independent spirit, con man and survivor. But the next year he failed to survive; he was murdered (or vanished) in Mexico in 1919. It was a loss from which she never recovered, to which her verse obliquely returns time after time, as though the poems she wrote in her increasing privacy were addressed in some way to him. When *The Little Review* subjected her to the question "What was your happiest moment?" she replied, "Every moment spent with Arthur Cravan." Unhappiest? "The rest of the time."

Loy's life was scattered. She returned to Paris, where she knew Guillaume Apollinaire, Djuna Barnes, Mabel Dodge, William Carlos Williams and many of the leading painters. The magazine *Contact* published her poem "O Hell," a declaration of intent:

> To clear the drifts of spring
> Of our forebears' excrements
> And bury the subconscious archives
> Under unaffected flowers

Not vindictive, but emphatic: adolescence and youth have their season to be divine. Her editor was publicizing her as an American. A British writer was unlikely to be radical in quite *her* ways. But she was English, which makes the emphases of her verse and the achievement of her pictures the more remarkable. And she became American, a focal figure in the wild Bohemia of New York, a key contributor to *Other* and a focus for the avant-garde. She moved to New York.

In 1923 her free-verse poems were gathered in *Lunar Baedeker*, published in Paris in an edition of 500 copies. Many were seized by American customs officers when the book was sent across: immoral. Few copies survive. It *was* an unsettling book, angry and savage in some of its compressed language, but celebrating Joyce, Wyndham Lewis, Brancusi, Stein: the modern with its new license and vision. She had flirted (and slept) with Futurism: its politics related to the vagrants and the maimed who drew her attention and to the unequal relations between men and women. For her the human body and the erotic exist and are crucial to the imagination—to the imagination *in language*. The erotic exists for a woman as for a man, but in terms that are more explosive, for cultural reasons, and that must elicit new kinds of response. "Love Songs to Joannes" is a poem unprecedented in English for its compressed eroticism and its mystical blasphemy. The second of the 34 "Songs" is:

> We might have coupled
> In the bedridden monopoly of a moment
> Or broken flesh with one another
> At the profane communion table
> Where wine is spilled on promiscuous lips
>
> We might have given birth to a butterfly
> With the daily news
> Printed in blood on its wings

Ezra Pound was no lover of adjectives, but he tolerated Loy's because they were doing important work. They brought into the objective clinic of the poem the bacillus of irony. Largely because of Loy, Pound developed a third category of poetry. He had defined *melopoeia*, a poetry that moves by rhythm and music, and *phanopoeia*, an image-based verse. There was now a new thing, *logopoeia*, which "is akin to nothing but language, which is a dance of the intelligence among words and ideas and modifications of ideas and characters." There is, in retrospect, rather more *melopoeia* in Loy than Pound registered. She is sometimes so succinct as to be telegraphic.

The volatility of her writing throughout the teens of the century, and in *Lunar Baedeker*, was indeed real; what other women have written since may diminish the shock of her poems, but not the originality of her project. Her fascination with vagrants led to several poems about them, in "Ignoramus," for example, and famously in *"Der Blinde Junge,"* about a young man blinded in the war whom she sees on the streets of Vienna. Gunn, admiring the poems' compression, observes that "pity may be evoked by the poem, and it inevitably is, but it isn't *in* it. Loy is a tough writer, and sentiment in the usual sense is seldom present in her work." Her language is invariably concentrated, not with the refinements of artifice but with the boiled-down residue of meaning. Each word is considered, each satiric inconsiderateness is barbed. Vagrants (as, before, the intractable and lucid artists that she praised) are lenses that diffract the world in ways more real than it can comfortably accept. The poet herself becomes like a vagrant in Europe and, memorably, in the Bowery, "a lurid lane / leading misfortune's monsters," where she lives for years, finds the materials for her art where the vagrants find their food and clothing—in the ash cans and gutters—and shares their presence as if they are fallen angels. The dispossessed are her people. She tries, for years, to hold the curious yapping literary world at bay, to vanish from it, almost, it seems, to extricate herself from its literature. And yet she cannot stop writing. In "The Widow's Jazz" she tries to re-conjure her ghost:

> Cravan
> colossal absentee
> the substitute dark
> rolls to the incandescent memory
>
>
> of love's survivor
> on this rich suttee . . .

She hears "your murdered laughter." He cuckolded her with death.

When in 1958 she at last allowed some of her work to be published, William Carlos Williams, invited to write a preface to a writer he had hardly heard of in thirty years, declared: "Mina Loy was endowed from birth with a first-rate intelligence and a sensibility which has plagued her all her life facing a shoddy world. When she puts a word down on paper it is clean; that forces her fellows to shy away from it because they are not clean and will be contaminated by her cleanliness. Therefore she has not been a successful writer and couldn't care less." Here is a rein-ventor indeed.

In Paris in the 1920s she was not reclusive. She introduced Americans to Dada and Surrealism, she was a presence at readings and soirées, at parties and concerts, a friend of many, desired by many. Pound and Eliot, Gertrude Stein and James Joyce admired her. She was the life of any party she attended because she was in every way, according to reports, brilliant. In America no less a critic than Yvor Winters laid upon her shoulders and Williams's the extraordinary burden of parenting a new poetry. He spoke of her "images that have been frozen into epigrams." When the small magazines became less inventive or closed their doors to radical experimentalism, she had no further use for them or they for her. Having shone brightly, she allowed her light to fade. She even pretended that it had gone out.

In 1936 she moved to New York, then eighteen years later to Aspen, Colorado, to be near one of her daughters. Her last poem is "Letters of the Unliving":

The one I was with you:
inhumed in chasms.
No creator
reconstrues scar-tissue
to shine as birth-star.

But to my sub-cerebral surprise
at last on blasé sorrow
dawns an iota of disgust
for life's intemperance:

"As once you were"

Withhold your ghostly reference
to the sweet once were we.

Leave me
my final illiteracy
of memory's languor—

my preference
to drift in lenient coma
an older Ophelia
in Lethe.

She died there in 1966. Much of her work remains unpublished. She will rise in due course from what her friend Wyndham Lewis called "the impalpable dark prison of neglect" and like him, as an artist, as a poet, help redefine our notion of modernism. In her salad days she was compared with Marianne Moore; she belongs more comfortably with Lewis, Pound and Gertrude Stein, a mold-breaking artist working in steel and stone rather than clay.

Beside the Bohemian lives of the modernists, the life of Robinson Jeffers is austere in the extreme. His reinvention is America, a vigorous, male and decidedly natural world, hostile to the softening and coarsening seductions of the city, especially the metropolitan city, and to any artistic or political stance that is not *independent*. He was born in the same year as Marianne Moore, 1887, in Pittsburgh, Pennsylvania. His father, a professor of Old Testament literature and a Presbyterian minister, set his child to learning Greek when he was five (eventually the poet magnificently translated Euripides' *Medea*). In 1903 the family moved to California, where he studied medicine, and then forestry, at Occidental College. In 1912, after receiving a legacy, he became a man of independent means, married in 1913 his "hawk-like" wife Una, and began quarrying and gathering from the beach the granite for his legendary house and tower at a rugged site at Carmel on the Monterey, California, coast. Such Emersonian efforts went beyond the call of duty. Having built his castle, he seldom left it. In a world of war, depressions and violent dislocations, it was his point of permanence and his recurrent subject. "Inhumanism" he called his approach, anticipating (rather eagerly it sometimes seemed) mankind's extinction. Whitman's hugely peopled poetry is emptied out by Jeffers, whose long lines recall Whitman and share with him certain biblical sources. The Old Testament has in Jeffers its modern Savonarola. The long narrative poems enact man's vexed and uncomprehending relationship with nature.

Jeffers has staunch partisans who present him as a prototypical eco-poet. Certainly the politics that follow from his vision accentuate some of the human risks of green ideology. Others see him as the poet of individualism and the far right. His publishers in the Second World War dissociated themselves from his spectacularly incorrect politics in the blurb to his collected poems.

Some readers admire him not for his politics or his ideas but for the compelling power of his narrative, its brisk movement and direct, unapologetic expressions of human desire. That it moves with melodramatic insistence through recurrent themes of incest, lust and cursed heredity dulls some of the Lawrentian *frisson*. The natural world of Ted Hughes is not far from Jeffers's.

"I decided not to tell lies in verse. Not to feign any emotion that I did not feel." This sounds wholesome. It is also terribly privileged. A man with a private income builds himself a handsome house and climbs his tower in order to stand above and judge his nation and his fellow men. It is arrant escapism, more repugnant than MacDiarmid's wildly engaged Stalinism and Pound's fascism because it needn't get its hands dirty; if apocalypse does not come now, it will come later. There is that assurance. It is a prophesy which may come true; the prophet can never be disproved. Jeffers's heirs—James Dickey at his most rhetorical, even Robert Bly with his very different politics—do not go as far as he does.

What is he doing here, in a history of poetry in English? Well, whatever his politics, he does have original skills and represents one of several culminations or closings down of Whitman's line; he is one of the reactionary, antimodernist poles of American poetry. "The poets lie too much," he says, which is as much as to say that he tells the truth. He doesn't, he's as much a liar as the rest of them. And he wrote some fine poems—the shorter poems, not too many of them—which evoke a primeval nature that he engages in body and mind, or which level a savage, prophetic, elegiac beam of language at America, as in his most famous poem:

> While this America settles in the mold of its vulgarity, heavily
>   thickening to empire,
> And protest, only a bubble in the molten mass, pops and sighs out,
>   and the mass hardens,
>
> I sadly smiling remember that the flower fades to make fruit, the
>   fruit rots to make earth
> Out of the mother; and through the spring exultances, ripeness and
>   decadence; and home to the mother.
>
> You making haste haste on decay: not blameworthy; life is good, be
>   it stubbornly long or suddenly
> A mortal splendor: meteors are not needed less than mountains:
>   shine, perishing republic.
>
> But for my children, I would have them keep their distance from
>   the thickening center; corruption
> Never has been compulsory, when the cities lie at the monster's feet
>   there are left the mountains.
>
> And boys, be in nothing so moderate as in love of man, a clever
>   servant, insufferable master.
> There is the trap that catches noblest spirits, that caught—they
>   say—God, when he walked on earth.

The relishing of pain, of storm, of suffering; the celebration of death and of the nature that survives it: "You and I, Cassandra," he says with his towering virtue. Had Mina Loy led him down "a lurid lane / leading misfortune's monsters," he would have looked neither left nor right: the sound of the sea and the smell of his mountains were his only elements. Like one of his hawks he had a singular nature—and a private income.

In "Reasons for Music," a tribute to Wallace Stevens, Archibald MacLeish wrote:

Hölderlin's question. Why be a poet
Now when the meanings do not mean?—
When the stone shape is shaped stone?—
Dürftiger Zeit?—time without inwardness?

Why lie upon our beds at night
Holding a mouthful of words, exhausted
Most by the absence of the adversary?

The reinventors reinvented the adversary: certainly Jeffers knew what it
was, his nation and its culture. And, in a more generous spirit, because
man is his subject and not the rugged coastline at Carmel, e. e. cum-
mings came up with the same sort of adversary, political, corrupt and
corrupting, "manunkind," the collective "busy monster" that consumes,
betrays and destroys the joyfully anarchic individual. At the time of the
Hungarian uprising cummings wrote:

so rah-rah-rah democracy
let's all be as thankful as hell
and bury the statue of liberty
(because it begins to smell)

The lyrical cummings remains the more popular, but the satirical cum-
mings may prove the more durable poet, anger traveling more confi-
dently through time than amorous-linguistic whimsy and the sometimes
appalling sentimentality it masks.

Edward Estlin Cummings was born with capital letters in 1894, in
Cambridge, Massachusetts. His father, an English teacher at Harvard,
dropped out to become a Unitarian minister in Boston, eventually at the
famous Old South Church, and through his father cummings was
rooted in New England Transcendentalism. The boy took a BA and an
MA at Harvard, served in the First World War as an ambulance driver
and soldier, and spent some months in a French detention camp on a
trumped-up charge (the censor had not liked his letters home), which
gave him material for his American-Kafkaesque memoir-novel *The
Enormous Room* (1922), where his inventiveness with language is already
evident, though the adjustments are not Joycean but of the surface only.
His first volume of poems, *Tulips and Chimneys* (1923), also played with
the surface and the lowercase "I," but the Tudor lyric was his underlying
music.

"sweet spring is your
time is my time is our

time for springtime is lovetime
and viva sweet love"

Later came the experiments with typography, learned perhaps from Apollinaire, an attempt to bring into the text the qualities of vocalization he required, by gaps, spaces, drop margins; and to indicate how many other words a word contains by laying it out in revealing ways. The mimesis is aural and visual at once, and our whole attention is required less for the flow of language than the dance and counterdance of words. The poetry is, in a very constricted sense, on the page. A small autumnal instance:

l(a

le
af
fa

ll

s)
one
l

iness

Introducing *Poems 1924–1954* he wrote, "Life, for eternal us, is now." The "eternal us" are the poet and his select readers, not "mostpeople" who don't like poetry and don't have lives. The complicity into which we are invited, the arrogance we are required to tolerate and applaud, at first beguiling, comes to seem inconsequential.

He split himself between Paris and Greenwich Village, and later in life between the Village and his New Hampshire farm. He died in 1962. Never happy in a single form, cummings dabbled in painting and drawing, based a satirical ballet on *Uncle Tom's Cabin*, wrote plays, and a travel diary about his trip to the Soviet Union, *Eimi* (1933), because he was fascinated with the human experiment of communism. Poems were his primary activity, but set against those of Moore and Loy, Williams and Stevens, his verse is soft-centered. It is often said that dialect poetry, translated into standard English, can prove standard-sentimental, the charm imparted only by the distortions of language: cummings is a dialect poet in this sense. His belief in the Individual, the sacred unit, the anarchic "I" in tension or conflict with the world and its institutions, issues in inventive distortions of language, but not the radical vision of a Loy or the bleakness of Jeffers. The experimentalist and iconoclast takes his place in the Elysian Fields among the conservatives.

> Buffalo Bill's
> defunct
>   who used to
>   ride a watersmooth-silver
>   stallion
> and break onetwothreefourfive pigeonsjustlikethat
>   Jesus
>
> he was a handsome man
>   and what i want to know is
> how do you like your blueyed boy
> Mister Death

There is a poetry of local speech, a poetry that tries to transcribe the improvisations of a dialect or accent peculiar to a place or a culture, and that finds release in the popular forms of that speech.

During the Harlem Renaissance, which centered on the vital musical culture, the novelists wrote some powerful, though conventional novels that included dialogue, but the narrative was generally in a standard form. What Langston Hughes set out to do was to use the cadences, the natural metaphors and dialect elements as the primary material for his verse and for his famous Jesse B. Semple letters. "Speak that I may see thee," said Ben Jonson. In Hughes's work a whole community is made visible.

Hughes was born in 1902 in Joplin, Missouri, and grew up with his maternal grandmother, his parents being separated. But he stayed some of the time with his mother in Detroit and Cleveland, where he completed high school and began writing verse, encouraged by her. His father, tired of racism, had gone to Mexico, and the budding poet visited him there. Theirs was not a happy relationship. Hughes attended Columbia for one year, dropped out, traveled and did a variety of jobs: merchant seaman, nightclub work in Paris, busboy in Washington. He wrote and wrote and in 1925 some of his poems were published in *The New Negro*. The writer Carl Van Vechten, instrumental in advancing the work of Mina Loy, took up his cause and arranged for his first book to be published. *The Weary Blues* appeared in 1926. Other white champions of the Harlem Renaissance also took an interest in him; he finished his studies at Lincoln University and settled in New York. By 1930 he was able to live from his writings and had been dubbed "the bard of Harlem." He became a public figure, helping to develop black theater in

Los Angeles, Chicago and in Harlem. He published in many genres. But poetry was his chief vocation, even though it did not butter bread the way his prose writings did. He works principally in two modes, one drawing rhythms from jazz and the blues, a poetry that with ironies and radical reversals generally avoids staginess; and poems of racial protest and definition. The jazz and blues poems have weathered rather less well than the protest poems. They were written with white readers as well as black in mind; there is something missing from them, tonalities withheld, a lack of candor about his sexuality, a guardedness in relation to his own as well as the white "culture of reception." The signals are there, the celebration of Whitman, "Pleasured equally / In seeking as in finding"; the sailors, the ungendered poems and poems where deliberate stereotypes and personifications displace persons.

The vignettes—"Mother to Son," for example, and "Song for a Dark Girl"—use a Harlem dialect which brings character and circumstance alive. These are protest poems, but the more general, "public" protest poems and some of the lyrics exploit a standard English when necessary, appropriate to the dignity of the occasion; there is also power in using a language associated with repression to draw attention to the repressed. "The Negro Speaks of Rivers" is a magnificent early poem, and "Mulatto," from 1927, an angry and subtly erotic piece in which a mulatto confronts the white man, its parent. But the most famous and resonant of the protest poems is the affirmative "I, too": "I, too, sing America. / I am the darker brother," in which the black speaker, sent to the kitchen to eat among the servants, sees a future:

> Tomorrow,
> I'll be at the table
> When company comes.
> Nobody'll dare
> Say to me,
> "Eat in the kitchen,"
> Then.
>
> Besides,
> They'll see how beautiful I am
> And be ashamed—
>
> I, too, am America

Time has moved on, and Hughes's poems of protest, while they are still resonant, belong, as much protest poetry does, primarily to their moment in history. What makes them durable is their voice.

"The troubles of a book"

ROBERT GRAVES, LAURA RIDING,
JOHN CROWE RANSOM, ALLEN TATE, HART CRANE

Some poets laughed at reinvention and change. In the end it found them out. Robert Graves declared, "Experimental work, as such, has no future. Last year's experimental poem is as out of date as last year's hat and there must come a time, perhaps not very many years hence, when there will be a nostalgic reaction from futurism to some sort of traditionalism, and in the end, back will come the Miltonic sonnet, the Spenserian stanza and the mock-heroic epic in the style of Pope."

When as a young man Graves called on Thomas Hardy at Max Gate, he was startled to learn that the old poet revised his poems very little, subjecting them at most to three or four drafts. Graves, even at that time, was a reviser par excellence, endlessly adjusting and altering, often years after a poem's first emergence into language. His acumen for revision extended to other works of literature. In 1933 he prepared a "condensation" of *David Copperfield*; in 1934 he wrote the novel *I, Claudius,* an historical distillation. He was also a free translator from classical, Celtic and Oriental texts, and even in his criticism he attempts to impose, if not detect, order and system. His fidgety insistence on forming and re-forming, on revision rather than vision, is central to his work, in which he seems bent on moving closer and closer to the elusive final statement. "I should define a good poem as one that makes complete sense; and says all it has to say memorably and economically; and has been written for no other than poetic reasons."

And the effect he produces? Edgell Rickword praised the poems in *The Pier-Glass*, his sixth collection, published in 1921 when the poet was only twenty-six. "The cleanness of Mr Graves's technique was from the first remarkable. His words are young and vigorous, carrying no more than their own weight of flesh. His rhythms, always apparently simple, possess those subtle variations, which a poet alone can introduce, making of a stock metre a personal instrument." Craftsmanship (he hated the word "technique," which leaves no room for "magic") gives the poems an air of classical impersonality. Their effect depends on the power of word and rhythm (generally traditional meters) to evoke experience, not on stimuli to the senses, visual or otherwise; not on qualities of "image" but on qualities of language. In his best poems, statement is inseparable from the words used: paraphrase is not an option. One critic calls him "the last pure lyric poet in English." He refused to make concessions to the spirit of his age and his poems do something different from those of his major contemporaries. This difference has led to his neglect. He is old-fashioned not like Housman or Philip Larkin or Charles Causley, but like Ben Jonson, Herrick, his beloved Rochester and, from an earlier age, Skelton. He proposes an ancient mission for poetry, an earnest and delighted engagement with language. The poems and poet are in exile, speaking from beyond our borders, as though from the past. His experience and survival of the First World War darken his imagination. War hangs over many of the poems, though it did not disfigure his psyche as it did David Jones's. He experienced an acute sense of the arbitrariness, loneliness, even the unworthiness of his survival. The memory of war is heavy with personal consequence. It does not, however, as in Edmund Blunden's case, bind him to the community of the dead: it sets him apart among the living. His comes to seem a charmed, a chosen life. He was liberated into exile: his poem "The Survivor" tells how survival altered the world into which he survived. "The Cloak" tells of a self-exiled peer, not exactly Graves and yet Graves at the same time: "This nobleman is at home anywhere, / His castle being, the valet says, his title." Poet, survivor, lover:

> Has he no friend at court to intercede?
> He wants none: exile's but another name
> For an old habit of non-residence
> In all but the recesses of his cloak.

Graves's "old habit of non-residence" was prompted by a love of the Mediterranean and by a rejection of industry and its dehumanizing technologies, the desecration of native landscape, a modern devaluing of relationships and standards. He speaks of this sometimes with contempt, more often with nostalgic concern, in poems such as "On Dwelling." Rather than stay at home and endure cultural impoverishment, or resist ironically as Betjeman did, he retired, sending back messages of his and our progress. A retrospective radical, not a reactionary, he longs for an unregainable world that went with the war, or perhaps earlier with his attaining puberty: a private battle, lost long ago. He fought on. In "The Cuirassiers of the Frontier" the guards at the outposts of empire embody that empire's values, its soul. Rome, the heart of empire, festers. The empire is in the Cuirassiers, though they are not in it.

Robert Ranke Graves was born in London in 1895, son of an Irish poet, songwriter and folklorist. He grew up in a highly literate household. He was admired in his pram by Swinburne. Before he went to Charterhouse School he was writing. An early poem on the "temptation to digress . . . This was about the mocking interruption of a poet's privacy by a star . . ." he claims was his first, written when he was thirteen:

> I sat in my chamber yesternight,
>   I lit the lamp, I drew the blind
> And I took my pen in hand to write;
>   But boisterous winds had rent the blind
>   And you were peering from behind—
> Peeping Tom in the skies afar,
> Bold, inquisitive, impudent star!

He went to St. John's College, Oxford, but the war interrupted his education. He joined the British Expeditionary Force and served in France, where he was wounded and suffered from shell shock. He was reported dead; indeed, he read his own obituary in *The Times* before his twenty-first birthday, and a few days later the recantation: "August 6th, 1916, Officer previously reported died of wounds now reported wounded, Graves, Capt. R., Royal Welch Fus."

To get on with serious creative work, he decided to write some popular books. His first success was *Good-bye to All That* (1929), a candid autobiographical account of his early years, the war, and the breakdown of his first marriage. He describes various attempts to earn a living between the end of the war and his withdrawal to Majorca, a move that the book itself facilitated. His candor was not complete, however: the book does not detail the huge change his life was undergoing.

Collections of his poems began appearing in 1916—*Over the Brazier* and *Goliath and David* contained war poems of considerable accomplishment, though not naked and politicized like those of his war friend, Siegfried Sassoon. In 1917 *Fairies and Fusiliers* appeared. He was trying to go deeper, seeking a truth that hovers between extreme alternatives, and managing to sound like Walter de la Mare. There is a blithe irony about some of the war poems. *Country Sentiments* (1919) is weary, retiring into pastoral. The early poetry, as well as using conventional forms, deploys ballads and nursery-rhyme rhythms and forms: "Allie, call the birds in, / The birds from the sky!" Their engaging, disturbing playfulness presents war in a stark, simplified form. Graves was an

Edward Marsh Georgian through and through, deploying a conventional, adjectival idiom. Later revisions tempered and tightened some poems; others he simply (and not always justifiably) discarded.

In time he came to feel the constriction of his conventional modes, as of his life in England, the limiting choices with which he had hedged himself about.

> Every choice is always the wrong choice,
> Every vote cast is always cast away—
> How can truth hover between alternatives?

He engaged in serious academic work and in fanciful researches into the creative process and the importance of the unconscious in creative activity. For a period he believed writing poetry was therapy. The firm poetic vocation he had taken into the trenches was still firm, but altered. It had lost direction. He explored what he called "poetic unreason," investigated modernism and reacted harshly against the work of H.D. and the Imagists. It was a time for saying no, no to the false gods and the lesser idols: to "sick, muddle-headed, sex-mad D. H. Lawrence who wrote sketches for poems, but nothing more"; and "poor, tortured Gerard Manley Hopkins." It was a time to pontificate, and to include himself in his censure. "Young poets tend to be either ambitious, or anxious to keep up with fashion. Both these failings—failings only where poetry is concerned, because they are advantages in the business world and in most of the professions—encourage him to have designs on the public. The attempt to keep up with fashion will lead him to borrow the style of whatever poet is most highly approved at the time . . . Now, I have known three generations of John Smiths. The type breeds true. John Smith II and III went to the same school, university and learned profession as John Smith I. Yet John Smith I wrote pseudo-Swinburne; John Smith II wrote pseudo-Brooke; and John Smith III is now writing pseudo-Eliot. But unless John Smith can write John Smith, however unfashionable the result, why does he bother to write at all? Surely one Swinburne, one Brooke, or one Eliot are enough in any age?"

How was Robert Graves to write Robert Graves? The tension in his poetry changed: the craftsman had been drawn toward aestheticism; now he was becoming metaphysician, psychologist (his Freudian *Poetic Unreason* was published in 1925) and wayward philosopher. He has wild theories. Meter originates with Irish hammers on anvils, ti-*tum*; whereas Old English stress patterns derive from rowing, and their verse was unrhymed "because the noise of rowlocks does not suggest rhyme." He speaks of Chaucer and Skelton reconciling "the anvil with the oar." "The rules of prosody apply only to anvil verse, or to sacred-dance verse, in which every syllable is evaluated and counted." Later he had wonderful theories about the ballad. He was moving from innocence to different sorts of knowledge, including false knowledge. He returned to innocence at the end—a passionate, aroused, old age of innocence, intensified and elegized by experience.

In late 1926 Graves's life abruptly altered. He had been corresponding with the American poet Laura Riding and invited her to join him and his wife on a journey to Egypt. She arrived and took him in hand, as a poet and as a man. Through her severe ministrations he at last pulled clear of the traumatized war years. What he called "the strong pulling of her bladed mind" left no area of his concerns untouched, untransformed. He even read cummings and (at last) Hopkins with pleasure.

Laura Riding, née Reichenthal, was born in New York in 1901. At Cornell University she began to write poems; she married a history instructor, and moved with him to the University of Louisville. Her "lost" early poems were rediscovered and published in 1992. One that may date from her time at Cornell reveals the talent fully formed, with a sense of phrase and pause that is breathtaking:

> A city seems between us. It is only love,
> Love like a sorrow still
> After a labor, after light.
> The crowds are one.
> Sleep is a single heart
> Filling the old avenues we used to know
> With miracles of dark and dread
> We dare not go to meet
> Save as our own dead stalking
> Or as two dreams walking
> One tread and terrible,
> One cloak of longing in the cold,
> Though we stand separate and wakeful
> Measuring death in miles between us
> Where a city seems and memories
> Sleep like a populace.

The relentless unfolding of the sentence, miming time and theme, and the curiously right variability of phrasing, would have arrested any editor. Poems begin with lines like "Come to me for truth," "I have been with the trees all day," "Your voice more than any song a song." She became involved with the Fugitive Group, having submitted poems to their magazine and caught the eye of Allen Tate and John Crowe Ransom, the prime movers and most substantial poets in the movement. Tate in particular responded to her intelligence but stood in awe of her conviction. Robert Graves admired her enigmatic poem "The Quids," which he read—perhaps as an individualist or anti-populist statement—in the year of her first book publication, *The Close Chaplet*, and they fell into correspondence. Graves invited her to England. The rest followed from there.

"Truth," she declared, was her objective in life as in language. Poetry was to be the means. For twenty years she tried to make it so. "Her finest poems," says Robert Nye, her editor, "seem to me to be those in which she makes discovery as she writes, poems in which the heart's and mind's truth comes more as something learned than something taught." This is astute; it goes as much for Riding as for Graves: their didactic mode can be hectoring. He also comments on the English quality of her voice. Her onetime friend Gertrude Stein always has an American inflection, but Riding can sound English, and indeed her spoken inflection was at once slow and clipped.

"The Troubles of a Book," "Come, Words, Away," "As Many Questions as Answers," "Nor is it written that you may not grieve" and more than a score of other poems set this poet apart and above many reputations that loom larger. But after two decades' writing she had said what she could in verse and it was not enough. In 1939 she abandoned poetry, explaining her decision at length and amplifying her explanation in the years that followed. She abandoned Graves and returned to America, where she devoted her remaining half century (she died in 1991) to *Rational Meaning: A New Foundation for the Definition of Words*, undertaken initially with Schuyler B. Jackson, whom she married in 1941 and with whom she lived until his death in 1968. Laura (Riding) Jackson, as she now styled herself, continued in her poetryless later years to insist on the truth quest; also trying to establish, against dozens of misreadings, the biographical and bibliographical truth of her relationship with Robert Graves, which continually seemed to be going out of focus.

Riding's and Graves's names were closely associated from 1925 to 1939, and Laura Riding, with her character and intellect, changed not only Graves but other, lesser writers, as she was to affect Auden, too, and Ted Hughes and John Ashbery later on. To a rudderless Graves she preached craft as a servant of truth, an instrument of revelation. The poet was not a witty entertainer, a word player, but a truth teller, or he was nothing. No true poem could be manufactured: it had to be discovered *in* the language. Michael Roberts (1902–1948), the anthologist, essayist and not inconsiderable poet, summarized her stance: "Poetry is the final residue of significance in language, freed from extrinsic decoration, superficial contemporaneity, and didactic bias." She helped Roberts draft the introduction to the definitive anthology of its time, the *Faber Book of Modern Verse*, insisting there that "the poetic use of language can cause discord as easily as it can cure it. A bad poem, a psychologically disordered poem, if it is technically effective may arouse uneasiness or nausea or anger in the reader." The poet has *actual* power over readers and must work with care. She rejected the growing prejudice in favor of "voice" in poetry, suggesting that the voice that matters is that of "a man talking to men" rather than "this particular man" talking to men. The eccentric individuation of her contemporaries repelled her: their writing put personality before language in a spirit of self-display, corrupting the valid mission of poetry. She could be a generously strict taskmaster, as I discovered over a decade of correspondence with her. She expected the best, which is something a little better than any individual could possibly deliver.

In Graves, who loved her, she had much to work on. His early style is decorated and metaphorical, and these "bad" elements had to go. She led him back from the Corinthian, even the Baroque, to the Doric, the timeless core. She had to get rid of the occasionally wooden diction and help him purge the "superficial contemporaneity and didactic bias" which infected his war poems and some of the subsequent writings.

With Laura Riding, Graves prepared *A Survey of Modernist Poetry* (1927). Percy Simpson had been a tutor of Graves's at Oxford. He was author of *Shakespeare's Punctuation*, and his kinds of analysis lay behind Riding and Graves's analysis of Shakespeare's 129th Sonnet, a reading that deeply influenced William Empson in writing *Seven Types of Ambiguity* and hence affected the critical (and creative) habits of two or more generations. One idea in the *Survey* is particularly relevant to Graves's work: "The reader should enter the life of the poem and submit himself to its conditions to know it as it really is." Adopting the impersonality—or neutrality—that the poet has adopted, the reader must accept before he can know.

The turbulent and often fruitful relationship with Laura Riding, and with the poets and artists who came to Majorca to be with this extraordinary pair, ended in 1939. By that time they had been significant publishers with the Seizin Press, which had issued *Epilogue* and work by Gertrude Stein and James Reeves as well as their own. They provided a kind of informal writing school, revised and winnowed Graves's early work, and wrote poems, stories, novels and criticism. Biographers have had a field day with their lives, but there is a degree of impertinence in their speculations. They distract attention from the writing and they sensationalize areas that can strictly never be understood. Who is "monstrous," for example, when a woman and a married man fall in love? Somehow blame always seems to attach to the woman: her actions are narrowly watched and read with cruel censure.

With the Second World War, Riding and Graves had to leave the island where they had spent ten years writing, publishing, editing, polemicizing. In 1956 Graves returned and set up permanent residence there. His most provocative book of the post-Riding years was *The White Goddess* (1946, extended and amended 1952 and 1961, corrected 1997), a "historical grammar of poetic myth." His thesis is that poetry is written in thrall to the Muse: the White Goddess. She is a figure defined in some of the poems, notably "To Juan at the Winter Solstice," which celebrates her omnipresence and her ineffable quality, and in "The White Goddess." Reviled by saints and sober men, she is the lady of extremes, vitality, imbalance: creative and destructive, she lives within and outside the individual, she burns off all but his capacity for love. She has no constant rules, she is "sister of the mirage and the echo." Through her, Graves externalizes and mythologizes his own tensions, as Yeats did in *A Vision*. The myth expresses his extremely personal vision—a constructed vision rather than an instinctive one. This goddess later on developed a dark-skinned sister. Although Graves makes much of the white and the dark goddesses, he never finally trusts himself to them, or not for long.

The power of sexual love, its fulfillment and denial, brought the goddess into being. In 1965 Graves wrote, "My theme has always been the practical impossibility, transcended only by miracle, of absolute love continuing between man and woman." The distance between "practical impossibility" and "miracle" led to the goddess with whom he could will or imagine into being a relationship. One of his most beautiful love poems, "Love without Hope," rises to celebration. Most of the poems relate to this theme.

Formal experiment in Graves's work usually occurs well within the bounds of tradition. There is no startling innovation in his verse—indeed, what startles is the authority with which he deploys the subject matter and imagery of romantic love poetry in the present age and with entirely contemporary authority—the effortless contemporaneity of the timeless. This is indeed "Love Respelt." The pared quality of the language, the weighing and placing of words replete with meaning in a well-judged context, and the management of strongly colloquial rhythms built on a traditional prosodic base make for the unostentatious brilliance of his poems, which would be as comprehensible and affecting to Jonson or Gray as they are to us. "Love is the echoing mind, as in the mirror / We stare on our dazed trunks at the block kneeling."

In his late poems he developed a precision reminiscent of the epigrammatic style of pieces in the Greek Anthology. It's a poetry that distrusts facility in language and in feeling and still, with the poet's memory failing and his body no longer obedient to desire, engages the durable joys and virtues, as in "The Green Flash":

Nightfall is no mere failure of sunlight:
Wait for the green flash, for the exact instant
That your sun plummets into sea;
And breathe no wish—wishes are born of weakness—
When green, Love's own hilarious tincture
Welcomes the sacred mystagogues of Night:
Owls, planets, dark oracular dreams.

He died in 1985.

An earlier poem, "In Broken Images," expresses the distinction between the true and the facile poet, the one who knows what he has to say before he begins and the one who discovers as he writes: "He becomes dull, trusting his clear images: / I become sharp, mistrusting my broken images." Trust is best invested in the senses: "He in a new confusion of his understanding; / I in a new understanding of my confusion." There is Socratic hubris in all this, yet the voice persuades us. The irony is that this poem, celebrating the aleatoric, fragmentary and unpredictable, is itself in a consistent, even a contrived, argumentative form. The most lucid development of the theme is in "The Cool Web," Graves's most popular poem and one of his best.

Formal skill, then, seems at times to run against his themes and critical cavils—and yet formal certainty is the only certainty he has. It overlies, or draws together, uncertainties, clarifying areas of confusion. From the tumbling uncertainties of feeling and the ephemeral epiphanies of the senses he wrests occasional compelling celebrations of love. "Counting the Beats," in a compact, repetitive form with a taut vocabulary and a tentative, experiential directness, is among his outstanding lyrics. The poems illuminate, sometimes dazzlingly, small areas in chaos made coherent, resolve contradictions, reconcile one set of alternatives. Beyond each poem darkness forms again. Or the poet comes up against a mirror and finds he's been traveling in the wrong direction, into the self. "Loving True, Flying Blind" summarizes his thematic career:

    . . . no soft "if," no "either-or,"
Can keep my obdurate male mind
From loving true and flying blind.

Reflecting on the neglect of his generation by academic critics, he remarked, "We were all equally post-Canonical." More vehemently he declares that theirs was not the "Age of Consolidation" but the "Age of Acquiescence." In the end, "The only demands that a poet can make from his public are that they treat him with consideration, and expect nothing from him; and do not make a public figure of him—but rather, if they please, a secret friend." He did not acquiesce, though—who knows—without Laura Riding he might have.

The Fugitives, to whom Laura Riding sent her early poems from Louisville, are one of the rare groups of American poets who defined a course and extended it while keeping its direction. It was not an apprenticeship like Imagism but a continuing (if altering) shared vocation. It defined itself in the magazine *The Fugitive*, which ran from 1922 to 1925 (nineteen issues) and carried little but poetry, poetry and poetry, with a brief editorial, and a small review section. In 1928, *Fugitives: An Anthology of Verse* was published in New York and the movement was technically over.

Part of its dynamic was political. It was Southern, it issued in an agrarian ideology which, depending on your perspective, can be seen as radical or terminally conservative. It had certain chips on its shoulder, not least a sense of undeserved neglect: Chicago, New York and London were the literary *bourses*, and Nashville, Tennessee, just wasn't on the map. It also had some fine poets and critics associated with it, in particular John Crowe Ransom and Allen Tate, and in Robert Penn Warren one of the most influential critic-editors of the century. Millions of schoolchildren, myself among them, learned to read poetry through his anthology *Understanding Poetry*, edited with Cleanth Brooks. With Brooks he founded the *Southern Review* and spearheaded the "New Criticism," which Ransom first articulated, devoted to close reading of texts along formal and ahistorical lines, another outgrowth of the original Fugitive enterprise. Poems are objects that exist beyond their historical context, are whole in themselves and contain their own justification. A poem proposes the terms on which we are to read and appraise it. We distinguish between structure and texture, between the grammar and the argument on the one hand and the imagery, diction and rhyme on the other. This is tenor and vehicle in a rather more rudimentary form, but serviceable for much verse, though not all. It omits elements of merely subjective assessment, which is fine, but it also excludes moral and political judgment. An achieved work has its *own* integrity. Ransom was unable to live up to the demands of his theories when he rejected the work of Robert Duncan on specifically sexual grounds.

Fugitive apologists claim that this group, and not the Imagists, more decisively shaped modern American poetic styles. This strikes impartial readers as absurd; but undeniably reading styles were affected by the very successful New Critical movement, and certainly the emergence in the late 1970s of the weary New Formalism would have been unthinkable without it.

"Fugitive" implied dissent and departure from the disorder of the modern, and a sense of being hunted by a hostile law and surviving against the odds. They were fleeing too from "the high-caste Brahmins of the Old South." They were all friends and there is a jovial sense of conspiracy in the risks they took. Ransom was the first to emerge mature, a fine if minor poet, subtle in control of form and diction, cautious and caustic. The body of poetic work he chose to preserve is small, succinct in all its parts, fine single poems rather than "poetry" in the more sweeping Romantic or modern sense. Riding was the only woman admitted to the group, and she was never really a part of it in the way the others were—or rather, it never became a part of her. Hart Crane also featured in the magazine, but only because of Tate's passionate advocacy.

Ransom was the conservative, even the reactionary; reluctant in "an unseemlier world," he always required persuading. He was also the finest, if not the most ambitious, of the poets. After attending Vanderbilt University in Nashville he was a Rhodes scholar at Christ Church, Oxford, where he came to recognize himself as "in manners aristocratic; in religion, ritualistic; in art, traditional." Most of his poems were written in the Fugitive years, between 1922 and 1926, though he was born in 1888 and already established when the movement began. He lived until 1974, one of the great teachers of his time and an important editor whose achievements include *Kenyon Review*, in which he was able to include critical writing by William Empson, R. P. Blackmur and many of the old Fugitive guard. In 1941 he wrote *The New Criticism*.

Allen Tate (1899–1979), the youngster, taken on board while still a student at Vanderbilt, was the firebrand. He liked and defended *The Waste Land* against Ransom; he stood up to the master. He was the "Easterner" among these men of the South (an "Easterner" born in Kentucky!), yet his "Ode to the Confederate Dead," "against" which Lowell later wrote "For the Union Dead," is the great Southern poem of the first half of the century, great in scope and in technical resource. It is no wonder that Robert Lowell, disaffected with Boston, his family, his heritage and his church, sought out Tate when, a literal fugitive, he fled Harvard. From Tate he learned that "a good poem had nothing to do with exalted feelings of being moved by the spirit": it was (Graves would have agreed) "a piece of craftsmanship." And that craftsmanship had to reveal itself *as* craftsmanship, not the art that conceals art.

Tate had a curious habit in his diction of using words in unexpected combinations and stripping them of their usual semantic nuances. The context gave each word a *single* meaning. This disruption of conventional syntax, this new-minting of words, had an abiding impact on Lowell and Randall Jarrell and affected Geoffrey Hill as well. Tate knew and liked Eliot; Ford Madox Ford championed him. He was close to Hart Crane, and was one of the few friends and critics who stood by Crane's reputation after his death. Tate is a complex and serious poet, often obscure—a poet's poet. In his criticism (but this is true of most Fugitive and post-Fugitive prose) there is an awkward argumentativeness and a rhetorical elevation, not like Eliot's secure patrician tone, which makes us all patricians with him, but schoolmasterly and a little over where he assumes our heads are likely to be. Like Ransom, he was a great teacher; but though his poetry is on an entirely different scale from his master's, Ransom's poems will weather time better than his, and will be loved by general readers as well as other poets.

Hart Crane was Tate's exact contemporary, born in 1899, drowned in 1932. He was born in Ohio, of contentious parents whose animosities harmed him. At sixteen he had a poem accepted by a New York magazine and the die was cast. The next year his parents separated and he went to New York, to lose himself in the artistic and unorthodox social world of Greenwich Village. He made contacts, then returned to Ohio, trying to work in his father's chocolate business and reading and writing all the time. He read Eliot and Pound. In 1923 he was back in the Village, making his way by copywriting. Alcoholic, homosexual (or homosexual, alcoholic) in 1920s America, he began to lose his way.

Thou canst read nothing except through appetite
And here we join eyes in that sanctity
Where brother passes brother without sight,
But finally knows conviviality . . .

Go then, unto thy turning and thy blame.
Seek bliss then, brother, in my moment's shame.
All this that balks delivery through words
Shall come to you through words prescribed by swords:

That hate is but the vengeance of a long caress,
And fame is pivotal to shame with every sun
That rises on eternity's long willingness . . .
So sleep, dear brother, in my fame, my shame undone.

Against the compelling pessimism of Eliot's *The Waste Land*, which he admired, he decided in a Rilkean or Whitmanesque spirit to be a celebrator. "I take Eliot as a point of departure toward an almost complete reverse of direction. His pessimism is amply justified, in his case. But I would apply as much of his erudition and technique as I can absorb and assemble towards a more positive, or (if I must put it so in a skeptical age) ecstatic goal." Behind Eliot was Whitman, but Crane could not manage the release of his fluent lines.

> Yes, Walt,
> Afoot again, and onward without halt,—
> Not soon, nor suddenly,—No, never to let go
> My hand
> in yours,
> Walt Whitman—
>
> so—

Melville was always there, too, both men who shared with him an open secret and a range of images.

He wrote the brilliant and difficult poem *The Bridge*, and his first book, *White Buildings,* was published in 1926. He traveled to Europe, meeting in London with one of his English admirers, Edgell Rickword, who remembers how brief the meeting was, Crane being keen to get down to the docks and try out the rougher nightlife. He went to Paris and touched a different and populous Bohemia. *The Bridge* appeared in 1930 and with a grant in 1931 he went to Mexico, intending to compose a major poem on the conquest. After a complicated time there, having fallen in love with a woman and trying to alter his nature, he set off on the return journey to America in 1932, committing suicide—it is assumed—in the Gulf of Mexico.

From his earliest poems, Crane takes a different direction from Tate. He uses words with the intention that they carry all their semantic baggage with them. Against the classical temper of Tate's poems, Crane's are decidedly romantic. Words slide into one another, association is the dynamic of the diction, and in the process surface clarity is lost. This is, in a sense, "feminist" writing as Hélène Cixous defines it: "libidinal," working at the level of image and inference and against the predetermined and imposed rigidities of logic. It looks willful, however. The reader who has loved the difficult clarity of the early poems finds *The Bridge* rebarbative. Crane is romantic in intention and temperament, speaking of his "organic" forms; and yet he constructs his poems, he struggles with his diction, he completes sections and even stanzas out of sequence. He is making not the river but the bridge. His whole oeuvre is a tragic and resonant contradiction in terms. He speaks of "pouring" his words out. They were eked, with pain and genius, out of him.

Yet judging from his letters justifying his practice to Harriet Monroe and others, Crane knew very precisely what he was doing, and that what he was doing was what he wanted to do. He had seen work by the Surrealists; he had watched his own mind in addled states rising into the light and making sense, a different sense perhaps, of the familiar world. His poetry wanted to occupy the kinds of space that Eliot's and Pound's did. Yet he had left home and left behind the possibility of further education; he read and read, yet without structure in his reading, without debate and without direction. A poet writing free verse about a local environment might get away with it, but Crane wanted and deserved to exist naturally on a plane with the metropolitan modernists. He should have been an American Lorca. He had the ear for it, perhaps the genius, but he lacked steady sunlight—either love or approbation. In the end his poems were ground out by will. They did not flow from his wonderful imagination. He disliked—he despised—himself. He had failed in his own and in his society's terms. For Tate and for Yvor Winters he represented genius and also folly, a romantic folly to which Winters nearly succumbed himself, and from which Tate recoiled with fascination. It is no wonder that Crane's body was never found: it did not want to be. What it left behind is a greater sufficiency than most men achieve. Yet "All this that balks delivery through words" defeated him. As he writes in the closing lines of "At Melville's Tomb,"

Compass, quadrant and sextant contrive
No farther tides . . . High in the azure steeps
Monody shall not wake the mariner.
This fabulous shadow only the sea keeps.

"A low, dishonest decade"

EDGELL RICKWORD, ROY CAMPBELL, WILLIAM EMPSON,
W. H. AUDEN, JOHN BETJEMAN, LOUIS MACNEICE,
THOMAS KINSELLA, JAMES FENTON

"It was on New Year's Day 1929, or thereabout, that I met Hart Crane for the first time," Edgell Rickword remembers. "He had been in England a couple of weeks, and had met Paul Robeson and eaten Christmas pudding with Robert Graves and Laura Riding and he was rather miserable. The damp raw London cold 'was like a knife in the throat,' he said." Rickword had published a few of Crane's "elegant, elusive poems" in the *Calendar of Modern Letters* two years earlier. He had tried to persuade the Communist publishers Wishart to distribute *White Buildings* and Crane wrote to thank him, adding that "a couple of years ago I found so much in your Rimbaud volume which was sympathetic and critically stimulating." In his quiet, vigorous way Edgell Rickword was at the center of things critical and poetic. And then, suddenly, he wasn't.

> And we, too, with as little fuss
> might thus ignore the world's dark edge,
> but those dead rays of coatless us
> augur the thin end of time's wedge.

Poetry all but abandoned him in 1930. One major satire (his most famous poem) came later, and a few frail lyrics in the 1970s, but his poetic career spans fourteen years, between the end of the First World War and the depths of the Great Depression. In that time he said what he had to say, without repetition and with singular skill. Then he turned his attention to Marxism.

He wrote savage poems from the war, love poems, symbolist work and poems in the manner of Donne. The marriage of Metaphysical and French symbolist disciplines provides a resource comparable to what Crane laboriously devised, but less opaque. Because Rickword was self-effacing, political and without personal ambition, his radical work in prose and verse has fallen into deep neglect. Graves, Blunden, Empson and many others knew his value as a poet, and the radical critics of the 1930s and 1940s valued him as a critic.

He was born in Colchester, Essex, in 1898, into a "moderate Tory," mildly literary household. In 1916 he enlisted in the Artists' Rifles. He became an officer in the Royal Berkshire Regiment, and after the Armistice was invalided out, having lost an eye and been awarded the Military Cross. He wrote his war poems after the war, not in the trenches. Having taught himself French while on active service in France, he went up to Oxford to read French at Doctor Johnson's college, Pembroke. Like Johnson, he found the place unpalatable. The Oxford course only went up to Victor Hugo, while the young Rickword's interests were in Rimbaud and Verlaine. After four terms he left, married and destitute, and began reviewing for the *Times Literary Supplement* and the *New Statesman*.

His literary criticism made a considerable if generally unacknowledged mark. It remains a touchstone for readers interested in poetry and in a critical approach that is coherent, open and "theoretical" without becoming categorical. F. R. Leavis's first published book was a selection from Rickword's magazine, *Calendar of Modern Letters*. Leavis subtitled it "Towards Standards of Criticism." David Holbrook called it "the first critical prose in English written this century, apart from the greater essays of T. S. Eliot." Unlike Eliot's essays, hungry for stability and resolution, Rickword's are all "directed towards the possibilities of creation," opening out the canon, reappraising, and bringing to bear on English poetry the contrasting rigors of the French and unassimilable voices of writers from different cultural and ethnic backgrounds.

His first critical book, *Rimbaud: The Boy and the Poet* (1924), was the seminal study of the French poet. He edited the *Calendar of Modern Letters* (1925–27) and two volumes of *Scrutinies* (1928, 1931), revising inflated reputations and revaluating underrated writers. Leavis takes up where Rickword left off, but with an academic bias and in a less generous spirit, and without creative inwardness as critic or editor.

After poetry left him, Rickword continued to review and write essays. He edited the *Left Review* (1934–38) and *Our Time* (1944–47). From a primary concern with literature, he moved to social commitments. A Marxist by 1930, he assumed the only activist role available to him in England at the time: his foes called him a propagandist for editing magazines aimed at a wide, political readership. He was more than a propagandist: serving a cause did not necessarily entail falsification of the evidence or attenuation of the critical imagination. Seeking to address the many rather than a select few is not an unnatural act.

He denied that Marxism killed his Muse. The best of the poems are latently political: there is no ideological gap between poet and critic. It is likely that poetry abandoned him, as it did others of his generation, for personal reasons, a series of crises, enthusiasms, passions and disappointments. The prolonged failure of his marriage destroyed a fundamental creative impulse. Marxism, looking away from the single self toward common ends, provided a sense of purpose and engagement.

Early on he differentiates between critical and creative intelligence: one is analytical, seeking objective judgments, the other intuitive, its associations subjective. Marxism simplified and intensified critical intelligence. In a conversation in the 1970s, with perhaps a touch of revisionism, he described himself as "a Marxist in the sense that I try to relate public happenings to the tissue of cause and effect which Marx divined in the interplay of material and economic forces." In the 1930s he expressed himself more vehemently: later, what had been a living cause becomes merely a critical approach.

In the poems Rickword writes intuitively *with* or even *as* the "common man," not didactically *for* him the way the poets of Auden's generation do. Rickword writes as one acquainted intimately with the trenches, with poverty and failure. He disliked cliques and the elitism that writers like Eliot and Wyndham Lewis came to stand for, though he was among the first critics to appreciate the quality and significance of Eliot's work. "One condemned modern civilisation," he said, "for its uniformity and mass-mediocrity. Eliot and Wyndham Lewis had a wrong sort of élitism, believing themselves cut off from common humanity." Is there, then, a right sort of elite? For a Marxist it is perhaps the party; for Rickword in his later years it is the writers who had made common cause without sacrificing their art. He was most alienated from the middle classes, those who could buy what should be provided by right: education, health care, housing. In "Ode to a Train-deluxe," subtitled "Written on a railway embankment near London and inscribed to our public idealists," his aversion is laid bare:

> Far from the city, grossly real,
> through Nature's absolute they stroll,
> and nimbly chase the untamed Ideal
> through palm-courts at the Metropole.
>
> Rapt in familiar unison
> with God, whose face must now appear,
> they show their wife and eldest son
> the fat-cheeked moon rise, from the Pier.

The "fat-cheeked moon," distantly echoing Hulme's ruddy farmer, ironizes the sentimentality of the comfortably off. It does not twit, it bites those who ignore "the world's dark edge." The moon frequents Rickword's poems, but never the usual poet's moon. She comes as a courtesan wooing over the corpse-littered battlefield, and when she emblematizes fickleness it is with precise attributes.

The satire of "Ode to a Train-deluxe" is gentle, compared with "Twittingpan" and "To the Wife of a Non-Interventionist Statesman." In the latter poem, Rickword's last major excursion into verse, written in 1938, the prophecy proved all too accurate. A poet climbs into the bedroom of a statesman's wife, evokes for her in sharp rhymed tetrameter couplets the case against the Spanish fascists, and urges her to use her power to deny her spouse sexual satisfaction until he abandons his noninterventionist stance toward Franco's Spain. He warns:

> Euzkadi's mines supply the ore
> to feed the Nazi dogs of war:
> Guernica's thermite rain transpires
> in doom on Oxford's dreaming spires:
> in Hitler's frantic mental haze
> already Hull and Cardiff blaze,
> and Paul's grey dome rocks to the blast
> of air-torpedoes screaming past.
> From small beginnings mighty ends:
> from calling rebel generals friends,
> from being taught at public schools
> to think the common people fools,
> Spain bleeds, and England wildly gambles
> to bribe the butcher in the shambles.

Beside a brilliant, rough-cast rhetoric, there is raging compassion in the poem as well:

> On Barcelona slums he rains
> German bombs from Fiat planes.
> Five hundred dead at ten a second
> is the world record so far reckoned;
> a hundred children in one street,
> their little hands and guts and feet,
> like offal round a butcher's stall,
> scattered where they were playing ball—

The satire had its occasion, yet it retains contemporary resonance, just as the great eighteenth-century satires do, because of its urgency, its tone and dark humor.

Rickword's original program was to remake poetry by a use of "negative emotions," including anger. "The poetry of my contemporaries was kind and nice and sweet," he said (Blunden being among his closest associates). But "there was no need to confine poetry to the expression of such feelings." Instead, the effect sought was "something like the cubists, perhaps, who wanted to paint all sides of an object, to show an object in full . . . to synthesise the various facets of an emotional experience." Since that time, modern poetry may, he conceded, have gone rather too far with "negative emotions." There may indeed have emerged a vein of negative sentimentality, a sentimentality of violence, as vacuous as the facile optimism of Christmas-card Georgians and imperial apologists. But at the time, the territory he was mapping was inhabited only by the Eliot of the Sweeney poems.

The attempt to "paint all sides of an object" led to a study of the "negative emotions" as revealed in literature, history, myth, science and psychology. The best examples Rickword could find were Rimbaud, Baudelaire, the English Metaphysical poets (particularly Donne), Charles Churchill and Swift. With these poets he felt a temperamental and programmatic affinity. Swift was "the most vigorous hater we've ever had in our literature."

Rickword's early love poems express a sense of reciprocity in sexual relations rare in English love poetry. The beloved is desired, evoked, addressed, respected, but not refined. He composed under the spell of Donne:

Since I have seen you do those intimate things
that other men but dream of; lull asleep
the sinister dark forest of your hair
and tie the bows that stir on your calm breast
faintly as leaves that shudder in their sleep;
since I have seen your stocking swallow up,
a swift black wind, the flame of your pale foot,
and feigned your slender limbs so meshed in silk
twin mermaid sisters drowned in their sleek hair;
I have not troubled overmuch with food,
and wine has seemed like water from a well;
pavements are built of fire, grass of thin flames;
all other girls grow dull as painted flowers
or flutter harmlessly like coloured flies
whose wings are tangled in the net of leaves
spread by thin boughs that grow behind your eyes.

The poem unfolds—a single sentence, with his always curious punctuation jolting us at semicolons, with rhythmic reversals—into a series of evolving perspectives whose progression is by inference. The nineteenth century is alive in hyperbolic figures that come steaming out of Rossetti's studio, yet they are also figures of this man's century: an actual woman, and what her presence evokes and represents in his turbulent, articulate heart. Extrovert wit, not introvert irony, fuels the poem.

Satires and love poems are opposite poles in Rickword's poetry. When he began his model was Donne; he fell silent after achieving something of the power of Swift. The early poems celebrate physical passion, but gradually revulsion overtakes the lover, who moves from celebration to a sense of the instability of relationships, uncertainty about even the most natural recurrences. "Dawn is a miracle each night debates, / which faith may prophesy but luck dictates." Unable to ignore "the world's dark edge," the poet confronts the negative emotions that leave experience raw, the heart wincing with hope and disappointment.

"Terminology," about fancy and the limits of language, shows how words, like time, engage and then disengage reality. The poet uses language to break the bounds of language, to contain meanings in an ordering of connotations, so that a sentence, verse or stanza reaches well beyond what it actually declares. In poetry the language begins to work only after the denotative meanings have "had their say." In his best poems thought is so complete and so completely contained in the images that selective quotation falsifies the statement. Thought in a poem functions consistently at various levels. This abundance of sense is remote from the limitations and chastenings that poets like Blunden and Sassoon imposed on themselves. The savage beauty of vision in "Birthday Ruminations" culminates in a stanza where man's disintegration is contrasted with the integrating world of the sea, with a diction as strange and wonderful as it is precise:

> The crepitation of the restless grains
> and the soft integration of fresh worlds
> and the vermiculation of the flesh,
> is the procession of the pastoral soul;
> a piscene epic, mammal tragedy.

The use in the fourth line of the verb "is" where one would expect "are" reverses the dynamic of the sentence.

Desire, time, pity, shame, solicitude and other Augustan abstractions regain authority in Rickword's poems. His work foreshadows—not just politically—the Auden generation. In "Divagations (ii)," for example, he experiments with Anglo-Saxon forms and finds them as sterile as Auden, at greater length, was to do. In "Incompatible Worlds," a poem dedicated to Swift, he uses a meter and indeed a diction so closely reminiscent of the third section of Auden's elegy on Yeats that we wonder if there is a direct debt. In his attempt to integrate the thought of Freud and Marx, Rickword fights in advance a 1930s battle, but where they discern a choice to be made, he sees a paradox to be confronted.

Beside the cool passion of Rickword, his early friend and eventual political foe the South African Ignatius Royston Dunnachie Campbell—Roy Campbell—is like a volcano. Born in Natal in 1902, he came to England in 1918, made himself known, then returned home to stir up literature in South Africa with an energetic assault on all things Afrikaans, working together with William Plomer and Laurens van der Post, with both of whom he later fell out. But then he fell out with everyone. He returned to Britain, where *Adamastor* was published, and then *The Georgiad*, in which he laid into Bloomsbury with a fierce contempt exacerbated by his resentment at Vita Sackville-West's interest in his wife. He wrote autobiographies, but while Rickword veered to the left (sharing Campbell's distaste for Bloomsbury), Campbell went right, became a Roman Catholic and an apologist for Franco, whom he eulogized in *Flowering Rifle* (1939). He did not, as he claimed, fight for Franco; it is possible that he did, however, engage in fisticuffs with Stephen Spender—a far less perilous undertaking. Campbell wrote some extraordinary poems and translations, including "Luis de Camões," about Portugal's national poet and adventurer, with whom he identified, and his versions of St. John of the Cross. His Baudelaire translations are less astonishing, his Lorca quite thin, though the irony of his advocacy of a homosexual Communist poet, he himself being adamantly heterosexual, Francoist and Catholic, should not surprise us: he did have a remarkably clear sense of what poetry is, as apart from politics. He is in his best poems decidedly South African, with all that this implies of Zulu, Afrikaans, Portuguese and British. His poetry and translations are marked by an unreflecting energy: like Wyndham Lewis, he was devoted to his art, generous in expectation and naïve in his response to disappointment. He died in a car accident in 1957.

A more critical player than Campbell on Rickword's side, the greatest critical imagination of the day and a man who, like Rickword, wrote brilliant poetry and then stopped, is William Empson. As a Cambridge student Empson admired Rickword, sought him out at the Fitzroy Tavern, and struggled to hear what the Sage might have to say: "He was the real one, if you happened to know." Rickword and Empson were the truest Sons of John Donne this century. Empson writes:

Imagine, then, by miracle, with me,
(Ambiguous gifts, as what gods give must be)

What could not possibly be there,
And learn a style from a despair.

Eleven years after Donne died, a neglected Spanish cleric, satirist and critic Baltasar Gracián wrote his *Agudeza y arte de ingenio*, a treatise on the Baroque elements in literature. Verbal duplicity, puns and ambiguity are at the heart of the verse he examines. With less clarity than Empson he defines sixty types of ambiguity. There is more than a casual connection between *Agudeza* and *Seven Types of Ambiguity* (1930). In his great critical book, published when he was twenty-four years old—the book that changed our way of reading—Empson transposes into our century the principles of Baroque and Metaphysical thought and technique. Empson's poems and criticism have given us an understanding of Donne, Rochester, Dryden and Pope. He has reopened a huge space that the Romantics had left soiled under dust sheets.

Born into the local gentry in Yorkshire, Empson, whose politics were to the left, retained a poise and civility one associates with his class and education. He went to Winchester and to Cambridge, where he studied mathematics and later, under I. A. Richards, literature. He was Richards's most brilliant student. Richards insisted that it was acceptable to ask what a poem meant, and therefore *how* it meant. Empson, due to someone finding condoms in his possession, was ejected from Cambridge, but he published his unexamined dissertation with Richards's blessing, and it was *Seven Types*. His later critical books are variously wonderful. *Some Versions of Pastoral* (1935) pursues ambiguity from diction and syntax into form. In some respects it is more important than his first book, but as with Einstein, whatever followed the law of relativity was rather an anticlimax to his public.

He was not a scholar and his critical work, like Graves's, is marred by willfulness and, unlike Graves's, by misquotation and inaccuracy. It is a small price to pay for the brilliance he treats us to. Five years after his critical debut he published *Poems*, in which he deployed ambiguities relentlessly, as though he had written the texts to which *Seven Types* might be the casebook. In 1940 another thin collection, *The Gathering Storm*, was published, a politically sophisticated and even prophetic volume, less obscure than the earlier book. In 1955 the *Collected Poems* appeared, and poetry was over for him. Indeed he claimed it had finished in 1941—a shorter creative span than Rickword's, and ended for much the same reason.

Are his intellectuality and obscurity the result of emotional intensity, personal and political, or are they, as his enemies have suggested, mere literary passion? Is he no more than a puzzle maker? There is a certain monotony in even so small a body of work: the language is too evenly awake to all its meanings, there is no repose, no base note, as though the language is more important than the poetry. In his erudition, Empson is an "academic poet," but not in a pejorative sense. There is in his verse the pressure of an entire individual intelligence and culture. Empson's expression is as authentic and individual as Wordsworth's very different language was to him. We would not call Donne "academic" but "witty." The same term can be applied to Empson, not least to make the historical connection.

The poems are accumulations of specific, local effects. There is a fascination with minuteness, with insect life, ants, maggots and the like, with scientific fact and speculation. The small becomes emblematic or correlative. The fruits of scientific analysis become points of synthesis. He once remarked that his poems "turned out to be love poems about boy being too afraid of girl to tell her anything." A girl receiving his coded messages would have been perplexed and might understandably have run toward the nearest rugby player. There is facetiousness in the remark, but perhaps some truth, since the poetry ground to a halt shortly after boy told her something and Empson married. After such knowledge, what forgiveness? Empson explains his drying up in another way. His experiences multiplied, the very wealth of experience dissipated the poetic impulse. In "Let It Go" he writes, "The more things happen to you the more you can't / Tell or remember even what they were."

Christopher Ricks, his outstanding critical heir, sees the "enabling tension" in the verse as that between a desire to beget life and a sense that "life is too dark and bleak a gift." *Misgiving* is central to the love poems. Images of evolution, development, building, accretion and sequence are balanced by a sense of their inherent perils. Darwin is at his elbow; fear and endurance are the fuels he burns. A casual tone, polite evasiveness and understatement: they are parts of his defenses. He protects himself by wit and the poems respect him.

In "Rolling the Lawn," one of his most famous sonnets, he writes: "You can't beat English lawns. Our final hope / Is flat despair." He draws into the poem a variety of references: Milton, contemporary advertisements, natural history, classical allusion, "true" and "false" religions, and a subliminal eroticism coexist. The word "roll" appears with, appropriately, seven meanings.

Beneath the serious current of his concerns there is playfulness. The poems can be tenderly precise, but sentimentality is excluded from his range by the very techniques he adopts. Most of his lines are end-stopped, the rhythms holding in suspension a cluster of words, holding them up in both senses. When longer cadences occur they are forcefully arrested at the end. The poems are built of finished rhythmic units, not around a dominant cadence, even in "Villanelle" ("It is the pain, it is the pain, endures"), where the units of rhythm are longer and affecting, but held parallel to one another, as in the early verse of Dylan Thomas.

Ezra Pound talks of "making it new." Empson uses the word "rebegetting" in much the same sense in "Letter II":

> Searching the cave gallery of your face
> My torch meets fresco after fresco ravishes
> Rebegets me.

The world, language and passion are full of fossil perceptions and expressions which the poet reanimates or which reanimate him. His best poems are like verse epistles. "Autumn in Nan-Yueh," for example, is intimate and public at the same time. This quality is sensed in many of the quietly spoken poems that are conscious, always, of the listener close by. His verse is civilized and yet his civility does not exclude passion.

Empson's editor and biographer John Haffenden writes, "So many of his early poems deal with what he called the 'neurotic (uncaused) fear' of individual isolation, the wish to escape that fear through love, and the wish also to transcend the oppressive facts of the known physical world, that the challenge of new knowledge about the universe puts him in a position of remarkable affinity with Donne," about whom he had said, "I imitated Donne only." He made his mark, if not on the Auden of early dialectics, then on Auden's publisher T. S. Eliot; on the Fugitive poets and Tate in particular, who admired his packing of language; on the poets of the Movement; and through his criticism on anyone educated in English in America or in Britain after the war and before theory dismantled the syllabus and the canon.

In 1937 the Marxist Rickword took the measure of the Marxist Auden in a short essay, "Auden and Politics." "The subject of his poetry is the struggle, but the struggle seen, as it were, by someone who whilst living in one camp, sympathises with the other; a struggle in fact which while existing externally is also taking place within the mind of the poet himself, who remains a bourgeois." It is the poet's aloofness and isolation which make his poem "Spain 1937" powerful and ideologically treacherous.

In 1937 W. H. Auden was thirty. He was firmly established as the great poet of his generation, as the great young poet in English, a reputation that had already spread to America. He was the voice of youth, the voice of the radical left, well traveled and universally celebrated; to such an extent that a double issue of the magazine *New Verse* was dedicated exclusively to celebrating his work. It was there that Rickword voiced his doubts. Allen Tate noted Auden's and his friends' "juvenile" and "provincial" perspectives, and the conspiratorial nature of his early canonization. And Dylan Thomas contributed an ambiguous tribute. "I think of Mr Auden's poetry as a hygiene, a knowledge and practice, based on a brilliantly prejudiced analysis of contemporary disorders, relating to the preservation and promotion of health, a sanitary science and a flusher of melancholia. I sometimes think of his poetry as a great war, admire intensely the mature, religious, and logical fighter, and deprecate the boy bushranger." Thomas is prescient: Auden was soon to abandon the party, and England, altogether.

The terms are interesting. *Hygiene:* imagery of disease and cure, the body and the body politic, a personified landscape; but a hygiene also in that the poet scrapes his language clean to use it with precision. *Brilliantly prejudiced analysis:* the prejudice is political; Auden was a Communist who wrote reviews and articles for the Communist press; but prejudice went deeper, into a sentimentalism about industrial landscape and industry, even broken industry; also, what none of Auden's group ever quite got beyond, a prejudice of education and class, expressing itself in a distinct tone of voice and in the patterning of the verse. *Contemporary disorders:* these too are political, the failure to square up to fascism and Nazism, the failure to alter the social structure after the huge reversals of the Depression, the failure to end Empire; but also, within the moral structure of his own 1930s generation, a disorder, an intolerance of things dear to him, not least his sexual nature. *Flusher of melancholia:* the undercurrent of wit and irony makes even his most serious poems witty. *The boy bushranger:* it is at this point that many part company with Auden, a public school boy who went to Christ Church, Oxford. Among friends he retained the schoolboy/undergraduate patois, the pranksterishness of it all; world events seemed in exaggerated form continuous with the struggles of the factional schoolboy: secret romances, plotting, scoring points, delicious conspiracy. The "mature, religious, and logical fighter" indulges in shadow boxing.

Like Eliot, Auden believed he could find stability, even when truth eluded his grasp. He affronts his youth, the more engaging man, with his age, the cantankerous, opinionated and revered poet. Each is an aspect of a decisive integrity—but it would be misleading to call that integrity "moral."

Wystan Hugh Auden was born in York in 1907. His father was a doctor, and the son retained cordial relations with him. His father's vocation interested Auden as a source of imagery. In "The Art of Healing" his father says, "Healing . . . / is not a science / but the intuitive art / of wooing nature." In 1908 the family removed to Birmingham. The landscape of the industrial Midlands fascinated Auden. Mining and geology (with its time scales dwarfing those of human history) provided another imaginative dimension.

His mother, meanwhile, a musical woman, encouraged her son. While his father was away at war, she and young Wystan sang together at the piano—Wagner, *Tristan und Isolde,* with the boy taking Isolde's part. In later life Auden wrote for music, notably an awful anthem for the United Nations and the incomparable libretto for Stravinsky's *The Rake's Progress.* Libretti were a form in which he could collaborate not only with the composer but, when appropriate, with other writers, including his partner Chester Kallman.

He spent the years from six to twelve fabricating "a private secondary world" of limestone landscapes, lead mines and workings. "In Praise of Limestone" touches on those structured fantasies, which, in retrospect, the poet saw as crucial formative acts. He learned from his secondary worlds "certain principles" that applied "to all artistic fabrication." Every work of art was a secondary world derived from and answerable to the primary world. Each work of art had meaning. Consistent, even if arbitrary, rules were necessary in the "game" of making. Within those rules the poet "must never make a statement simply because it sounds poetically exciting; he must also believe it to be true." A poet does not express himself but conveys "a view of reality common to all, seen from a unique perspective." That "unique perspective" becomes in his later work so eccentric as to transform the common reality into an exclusive, excluding enclave.

The "secondary world" is often expressed in images of state and city. A poem is "an attempt to present an analogy to the paradisal state in which Freedom and Law, System and Order are united." A good poem is "very nearly a utopia." Images that flow from this core include maps, networks, telegraph lines, railways, streets, strata, veins, postal routes—images of connection and pattern. The prepositions "between" and "among" gain almost the force of verbs. The modern hero is "the builder, who renews the ruined walls of the city."

He was sent to preparatory school in Surrey, and then to Holt School in Norfolk, where he studied biology. At fifteen he discovered by accident his poetic vocation: "One Sunday afternoon in March 1922, a friend suggested that I should [write poetry]: the thought had never occurred to me." How unlike Keats: instead of "vows were then made for me" it was a vague suggestion one boring afternoon. Nevertheless a seed was sown. The stable childhood determined many of his poetic concerns and prejudices. In "Profile," an unflattering self-portrait, he asks:

A childhood full of love
and good things to eat:
why should he not hate change?

Gastronomical images obsess the mature, comfortable and somewhat jaded Auden. Rather proud of his class origins later in life, he writes in one of his verse "shorts," or fragments:

> The class whose vices
> he pilloried was his own,
> now extinct, except
> for lone survivors like him
> who remember its virtues.

Wise after the event with what Roy Fuller calls "his honesty of self-characterisation," he atones for his early radicalism. Rickword was right after all. The political reversal is encapsulated in the late poem "The Garrison": "Whoever rules, our duty to the City / is loyal opposition."

The year after he started being a poet he came across Walter de la Mare's anthology *Come Hither* and found there the work of Frost and Hardy. Hardy immediately attracted him: "For more than a year I read no one else." He retained a respect for Hardy as a formal writer, as a wise poet who viewed the world with clarity and from a certain moral height.

In 1925 he went up to Christ Church, Oxford, to read English. He was drawn to Old English poetry and his early technical experiments in stress and alliterative forms developed from there. He edited a magazine, and the first booklet of his poems was hand set and printed by his friend Stephen Spender. Lennox Berkeley set some of the poems to music and Cecil Day-Lewis sang them. The group came together: Louis MacNeice and Christopher Isherwood were waiting in the wings.

Soon his books began to appear: 1930, *Poems* and *Paid on Both Sides: A Charade* (enthusiastically received); 1932, *The Orators;* 1933, *The Dance of Death;* 1936, *Look Stranger.*

> Look, stranger, on this island now
> The leaping light for your delight discovers,
> Stand stable here
> And silent be,
> That through the channels of the ear
> May wander like a river
> The swaying sound of the sea.

Also in 1936, *Letter to Lord Byron;* in 1937 *Spain* and *Letters from Iceland* (with MacNeice). It was the year of his *New Verse* double-issue apotheosis. That was not all. With Isherwood he'd collaborated in writing Brechtian topical plays with songs and choruses, including *The Dog*

Beneath the Skin (1935), *The Ascent of F6* (1936) and then, after *New Verse: On the Frontier* (1938), *Journey to a War* (with Isherwood, 1939). He had traveled all over the place: Japan, China, Iceland, Spain for the civil war, where he was (briefly) an ambulance driver trying to catch a glimpse of history being made.

In 1939 he and Isherwood emigrated to the United States, leaving their admirers and their politics behind. It was time, they decided, to find themselves. *Another Time* (1940) contained the last of Auden's English poems. In 1946 he became an American citizen. Reflecting on the two Audens, the English and the American, the radical and the conservative, Philip Larkin tries to imagine a conversation between two readers acquainted exclusively with one part of his oeuvre. "After an initial agreement by adjective—'Versatile,' 'Fluent,' 'Too smart sometimes'—a mystifying gap would open between them, as one spoke of a tremendously exciting English social poet full of energetic unliterary knock-about and unique lucidity of phrase, and the other of an engaging, bookish, American talent, too verbose to be memorable and too intellectual to be moving." The unity of his early work—its concern with technique, political commitment, didactic strains, openness to science and psychology—suggests that the poems are facets of a complex single statement of personal and social moment. The statement is not easy to isolate: it is a trajectory, Oxford Marxism giving way to Freudian concerns; attention to the collective becoming a concern with the individual. He could not connect Marx and Freud. They represented alternatives, and he plumped in the end for Freud. He elegized him in 1939, the year Freud died and Auden left England.

> When there are so many we shall have to mourn,
> when grief has been made so public, and exposed
>   To the critique of a whole epoch
>   The frailty of our conscience and anguish,
>
> Of whom shall we speak? For every day they die
> Among us, those who were doing us some good,
>   And knew it was never enough but
>   Hoped to improve a little by living.

The poem ends on a high note which is perhaps disingenuous in the use of the word "rational," a residue of the Marxism out of which Auden was wriggling with less difficulty than one might have expected:

> One rational voice is dumb; over a grave
> The household of Impulse mourns one dearly loved.

Sad is Eros, builder of cities,
And weeping anarchic Aphrodite.

His very early poems, included in *The English Auden*, skirt around themes that he was never able to address directly. The obscurity of those early poems is an eloquent and fascinating form of encodement. In 1930 he said in a letter to a friend, "Never write from your head, write from your cock." This is the man rather than the poet speaking, a gap that never closes. He masked the origins of his verse, his *different* desire, his libidinal priorities. He refused in later years to let his poems appear in gay anthologies. Thus to his main audience he remained a high priest, to his friends an impossible and wonderful queen. He needed Freud; but so too did his poetry.

Clive James writes, "The need to find an expression for his homosexuality was the first technical obstacle to check the torrential course of Auden's unprecedented facility. A born master of directness was obliged straightaway to find a language for indirection, thus becoming immediately involved with the drama that was to continue for the rest of his life—a drama in which the living presence of technique is the antagonist." A poet of the particular, of the material world, he could not finally, for political and temperamental reasons, particularize or politicize a key concern. Many of the poems answer to a gay reading, indeed seem to answer *only* to a gay reading, yet their desire, their occasion, is densely encoded in them. In each case a reader is free to say, "but *perhaps* he meant," and this is the freedom he wanted us to have. Eliot speaks of "impersonality," but Auden, informal and at your elbow, discloses less in his most seemingly candid poem than Eliot does in *The Waste Land*, in which he makes no bones about desire.

Auden's politics were "genitally coloured": class, cross tribal attractions; public school structures, repressions, passions—these remained most real to him. He had ascended from mini- to macro-logic; hero worship, subjugation, desire and its concealment: these are a big part of Auden, unstated but implied. He became his own case study; he resists affirmation because he will not accept the moral rightness of what he is. He accepts *that* he is but will not say it is right. This might steer us to the center of his work, his chief instrument of withholding and disclosure, that great English tool of obliquity: irony. What sort of irony? Stylistic, creating a didactic distance between the saying and the thing said.

I suspect that without some undertones of the comic,
genuine serious verse cannot be written today.

The first line of Auden's aphorism is not a problem, but it sets the scene for the second line, which gives pause: "genuine serious verse cannot be written today." What does he mean by *genuine*, what by *serious*? His "today" is the postwar, to which most of his American poetry belongs. Is he writing off a range of writers still active, and not noted for comedy, even undertonally: Eliot and Pound for starters, David Jones, Hugh MacDiarmid, H.D., Robert Graves and Laura Riding?

It may be true of his immediate, disillusioned generation: MacNeice, Spender, Betjeman, Roy Fuller are ironists in one way or another. But the next generation—Dylan Thomas, George Barker, C. H. Sisson, R. S. Thomas, Keith Douglas, W. S. Graham—are they preempted by his "rule"? He is a great one for rules.

His generation was disillusioned because it had had illusions. A Marxizing generation in its youth, in love with the Soviet experiment, championing from its point of privilege the English proletariat, supporting the Republican cause in Spain, believing in the possibility of social transformation: many were members of the Communist party and partook like believers of its dialectical sacraments. The pact between Stalin and Hitler was their road to Damascus, if the Communist subversion of the Republican cause in Spain had not been. They had to take measure of error, their intellectual error, or (a few of them) to think themselves into a deeper Stalinism. In Auden's case penance went to extraordinary lengths. He rewrote poems and then discarded them and refused to let them be reproduced. His sense of truth was stronger—as far as the 1930s poems are concerned—than his sense of poetry.

He helps us draw a distinction between proper and improper liberties that poets take to control their work. "The Platonic Blow" is a poem that, printed piratically from time to time, is described as "generally attributed to W. H. Auden." If he wrote this piece of compelling homosexual pornography (he never denied it), he did not intend it for general consumption but for the amusement of close friends. A writer should be free to write privately in this way. If those friends are less intimate than he imagines, or less careful, and the work escapes, it then belongs to the "secret record," along with letters, diaries and other bits and pieces that biographers eagerly stumble upon, and becomes (our good fortune) a part of the "parallel record."

The case is different with "Spain 1937." Auden in middle life, repelled by phrases and the cold delineation of its subject ("wicked doctrine," he called it), refused to allow it to be reprinted in the *Collected Shorter Poems*, though it was one of his most celebrated pieces. He revised it substantially in 1939, even before George Orwell's objections to it in *Inside the Whale*. But it still stuck in his moral craw. Revision could not make it palatable to the new Auden, who was by now rather old. He censored it along with other poems that he famously declared were "dishonest, or bad-mannered, or boring." (He never censored the appalling ballad "Miss Gee" or "Victor," both effective and bad-mannered.) "Spain 1937" could not be printed or quoted by critics. This gave the poem celebrity and cast a parodic light on the carpet-slippered poet. The lines that repelled him were about justifiable murder in the service of a cause, and from the end of the poem the lines in which, a good Marxist, he deifies history, making it into an Old Testament god.

> We are left alone with our day, and the time is short, and
> History to the defeated
> May say Alas but cannot help or pardon.

He crossed the lines out in Cyril Connolly's copy of the poem in the 1950s, scribbling in the margin, "This is a lie." The poem has been restored to the record, and in *The English Auden* we are given access to the 1937 and the 1939 versions. But for many years it was hard to get hold of.

In 1936 he wrote his celebrated *Letter to Lord Byron*. In Part III, as if talking about his own critical reception and the fatuity of critics in general, he addresses Byron, using his demanding stanza form, a way of paying tribute and saying to readers that he can stand beside even a great nineteenth-century poet and master Byronic irony, an instrument for extracting and focusing the satanic instinct:

> By all means let us touch our humble caps to
>   La poésie pure, the epic narrative;
> But comedy shall get its round of claps, too.
>   According to his powers, each may give;
>   Only on varied diet can we live.
> The pious fable and the dirty story
> Share in the total literary glory.
>
> There's every mode of singing robe in stock
>   From Shakespeare's gorgeous fur coat, Spenser's muff,
> Or Dryden's lounge suit to my cotton frock,
>   And Wordsworth's Harris tweed with leathern cuff.
>   Firbank, I think, wore just a just-enough;
> I fancy Whitman in a reach-me-down,
> But you, like Sherlock, in a dressing-gown.

Later in the poem, he says

"I hate a pupil-teacher," Milton said,
      Who also hated bureaucratic fools;
Milton may thank his stars that he is dead,
      Although he's learnt by heart in public schools,
      Along with Wordsworth and the list of rules;
For many a don while looking down his nose
Calls Pope and Dryden classics of our prose.

In Part IV he pays a compliment that does not ring quite true: T. S. Eliot at Faber and Faber was his publisher, as he was MacNeice's and Spender's.

But Eliot spoke the still unspoken word;
For gasworks and dried tubers I forsook
The clock at Grantchester, the English rook.

Yet, early and late, what marks Auden is a refusal to conform, to come down from his linguistic and cultural perch, to "trim." "What is a highbrow?" he asks in an early piece. "Someone who is not passive to his experience but who tries to organise, explain and alter it, someone in fact, who tries to influence his history: a man struggling for life in the water is for the time being a highbrow. The decisive factor is a conflict between the person and his environment; most of the people who are usually called highbrows had either an unhappy childhood and adolescence or suffer from physical defects." True or not, implicit in such vigorous "eccentric" views is the nonconforming Auden who fell out with the causes he espoused not only because they were compromised, but because they seemed to exalt coarseness and in the end had no space for the kinds of excellence he valued.

What Arnold in *Essays in Criticism* says of the poets of the first part of the nineteenth century might be applied to the poets of the English 1930s. Perhaps Auden and Spender would have agreed. Arnold speaks of the great energy of the period, but it went off prematurely: "And this prematureness comes from its having proceeded without having its proper data, without sufficient material to work with. In other words, the English poetry of the first quarter of this century, with plenty of energy, plenty of creative force, did not know enough. This makes Byron so empty of matter, Shelley so incoherent, Wordsworth even, profound as he is, yet so wanting in completeness and variety." Arnold's verdict applies to Auden's early poetry, which is his most compelling. He had the self-awareness and skill to reinvent himself in a different land. There is a continuity of technique, manner and tone between the earlier and later Auden; but also an entirely different thematics. "Poetry is not con-

cerned with telling people what to do, but with extending our knowl-
edge of good and evil, perhaps making the necessity for action more
urgent and its nature more clear, but only leading us to the point where
it is possible for us to make a rational and moral choice." Poetry is still
instrumental; and that "rational" is there, virtually synonymous with
"moral." The word "rational" subverts him every time.

New Year Letter (1941) is his first American collection. Several fur-
ther notable collections followed. Auden kept busy, dividing his life
between America and Austria, between Austria and Oxford, adjudicat-
ing, editing, translating, eating and drinking. He gave numerous public
readings, usually reciting his poems (amazingly) from memory and,
when he forgot a line, coughing into the microphone. He acted doddery
long before he had a right to, settling a little complacently into his fame.
His best account of himself, candid and precise, is "Prologue at Sixty," a
remarkable technical achievement. His ethic of "honesty" is finally sub-
jective and self-forgiving. Irony eases him out of many a crucial paradox.

In 1971 Auden published *A Certain World*, his "commonplace book"
of favorite excerpts, and it tells us a great deal about where he had got
to. The entries on "Commitment" make his early admirers despair.
There are several entries for hell, none for heaven; many for war, none
for peace; many for sin, none for virtue. The devil has all the best tunes.
He is a great elegist—of Freud, Yeats, and others—but also of himself.
Edgell Rickword characterized his change: "apostate humanitarian."

"He had become a reader rather than a writer," Larkin says; "litera-
ture was replacing experience as material for his verse." In his later years
advocacy became one of his great services: he discovered new writers
and criticized their work, befriended them and to some extent lived
through them. He was interested in translation and memorably cham-
pioned the work of Joseph Brodsky, helping to extract him from the
Soviet Union. His sense of the divided world persisted, and he did what
he could for writers behind the Iron Curtain. He acknowledged his
early debts, to Hardy, Edward Thomas, Eliot, Empson and Owen;
and his later debts to Marianne Moore, Laura Riding and others. He
learned from the poets of the New York School, as they had learned
from him. Until 1939 he was the guiding light of British poetry; until his
death in 1973 he was one of the guiding lights of American metropoli-
tan poetry, one of the pricks against which the rural, provincial and radi-
cally experimental writers were content to kick. In 1972 he published
Epistle to a Godson and it includes a poem called "A New Year Greeting,"
which exemplifies the quality of the later Auden, fusing many seri-
ous themes with a Swiftean humor. His body is at the center of the
poem, a planet on which nations of bacteria live and breed. He consid-
ers their natural calamities when he bathes, dresses and undresses, and

foretells the crisis they face when he dies. It is an expertly made secondary world:

> Then, sooner or later, will dawn
>   a day of Apocalypse,
> when my mantle suddenly turns
>   too cold, too rancid for you,
> appetising to predators
>   of a fiercer sort, and I
> am stripped of excuse and nimbus,
>   a Past, subject to Judgment.

Auden: great poet or great representative poet? A poet or a "classic of our prose"? He overshadows the poets of his generation. He is Chaucer to the Gower of Betjeman and the Langland of MacNeice.

John Betjeman was a year older than Auden. They coincided at Oxford in all sorts of ways, but Auden was setting off for the world while Betjeman was setting off for England. He was to develop in Britain (over time) a larger and more durable popular readership than Auden's: his 1958 *Collected Poems* was a runaway best-seller, published by Murray, who had experienced, a century and a quarter earlier, the runaway success of Byron's verse. But his work does not export as well as Auden's. He had a decisive political impact: his television programs describing the imperiled architectural treasures of the island, and raising awareness of heritage, adjusted attitudes to the past and present.

Though he is formally conventional, his verse is almost always recognizably *his*. It's more than the recurrent allusions to North Oxford, churches, suburbia and gym-slips. Landscape is evoked in terms of comfort, there is throughout a nice sense of class and propriety. In "Love in a Valley" there is no Lawrentian nakedness. The word "homestead" appears twice, there's "woodland," a "lieutenant," the statutory "tennis-court," cushioned rhododendrons, "summer-house," "welcome"; we hear "the tiny patter, sandalled footsteps." The poem breathes a static well-being. The satires are less accommodating but they too have his hallmark. It is a matter of irony and tone as well as detail. And the rhythm in couplets, quatrains and blank verse is *lightly* controlled. Vulgarity is chastised, traditional values are celebrated. There is a lot of humor, some of it dark, but lightly administered. This is light verse of a high order, and light verse need not be unserious. It is written to entertain, like the plays of Shakespeare.

I SIT DOWN
In St Botolph Bishopsgate Churchyard

And wait for the spirit of my grandfather
Toddling along from the Barbican.

Silly? Perhaps, but it is hard not to read on. He creates a mild suspense
in narrative and rhythm, a curiosity that we follow through. The elegies
and poems like "Before the Anaesthetic" show another poet, terrified of
death, lonely, hungry like Hardy for religious faith and sometimes
believing he has got it. But he never expresses a cogent metaphysic. He
takes Anglicanism as it comes. He abhors death and he abhors the
destruction of beautiful things, old habits of courtesy, old buildings,
the Downs, poetic discipline. Satire is as much his duty as elegy and
celebration. "Come friendly bombs, and fall on Slough."

A sense of place ("a topographical predilection") is conveyed in each
poem (he knew all of England and parts of Ireland very well). In the
love poems he sends up the speaker whose feelings of physical inferi-
ority translate his substantial women into Amazons. "Little, alas, to you
I mean, / For I am bald, and old, and green." He wants to be crushed in
smooth strong arms or pressed like a tennis racket to a glowing bosom.
"Pam, I adore you, you great big mountainous sportsgirl," he declares in
"Pot Pourri from a Surrey Garden." Going down market from Surrey to
"The Licorice Fields of Pontefract" he writes:

Red hair she had and golden skin,
Her sulky lips were shaped for sin,
Her sturdy legs were flannel-slack'd,
The strongest legs in Pontefract.

The poet is "held in brown arms strong and bare / And wound with
flaming ropes of hair." Rossetti's muscular graces have nothing on Bet-
jeman's girls. With great economy Betjeman evokes them, evokes whole
scenes and the society and value systems that underpin them. In 1969 he
was knighted and in 1973 he became poet laureate, a post he merited. He
replied generously, by hand, to every poem a member of the public sent
him. He died in 1984.

Louis MacNeice was a friend of Betjeman's at Marlborough School,
where among their contemporaries were Bernard Spencer and the art
historian and spy Anthony Blunt. Betjeman failed his divinity exams at
Oxford, where he found his tutor, C. S. Lewis, obstructive and unsym-
pathetic. He bitterly dropped out while MacNeice stayed and distin-
guished himself as a scholar and classicist, becoming an important
translator of the Greek and German classics (his is one of the few com-
pelling translations of Goethe).

The American poet Conrad Aiken admired him: "For sheer

readability, for speed, lightness, and easy intellectual range [the verse] is in a class by itself." *But*—there is always a "but" with Aiken—the poetry doesn't stick, "it is *too* topical, *too* transitory, *too* reportorial" and (a wonderful phrase) "it has very little *residual* magic." If the residual magic of poetry were the durable relevance of subject matter, Aiken would be right. Residual magic is, however, in rhythm, and in this respect Mac-Neice is better endowed even than Auden, as readers of "Happy Families," "The Hebrides," "Troll's Courtship," "Neutrality," "The Accident," and the more obvious of his rhythmic tours de force can prove. Aiken may mistake subject matter for subject, something that critics close to their subjects tend to do.

MacNeice was born in Belfast in 1907. His father was a Church of Ireland clergyman who later became a bishop. MacNeice acknowledged the impact of his Ulster background on the formation of his imagination, and Ireland could always rouse him to satire. Nostalgia and passion, the nature of his father's work, which set the boy apart, his mother's early death, his shyness, clumsiness, social ineptness, late puberty, were ineradicable elements in his past. Oxford was a release. Unlike Auden, Spender and Day-Lewis, MacNeice was not attracted to communism. From Oxford he went on to teach classics at Birmingham, Greek at the University of London, and then to the BBC, where he was a feature writer and producer. He wrote radio plays that suggested new possibilities for drama in that most exacting medium.

Temperamentally he was engaged by facts rather than programs; solving orthodoxies made no sense to him. Auden moved across the political spectrum, but MacNeice stayed politically "between," not passionately, like George Orwell, but quizzically. "Between" is a favorite word and stance in the early poems, different from Auden's connective "between." In MacNeice it signifies suspension: "In a between world, a world of amber" one poem begins. In "Epitaph for Liberal Poets" it is clear that he is not even able to conform to liberal humanism. He acknowledges the approach of the "tight-lipped technocratic Conquistadors"; his stance is Mark Antony's, lamenting in acceptance the inevitable triumph of Caesar, hoping the poems will survive to thaw out in another age.

Riddles and nursery rhymes attracted him early on. And hymns. Later, the sagas, medieval allegory and the Horatian odes. He chooses two different styles, one vivid, documentary, engagingly particular and linguistically inventive, the other argumentative and analytical. The poet he sees, like the broadcaster and journalist, as an extension of the common man, engaging his problems, renewing his language, but not necessarily offering answers. He is unusual in accepting the challenge of creating a journalistic poetry that *is* poetry, yet there is a reticence about the poems: it's never quite clear how committed he is to what he says. He is autobiographical at times but not confessional. Presenting his past in various forms—in the extended *Autumn Journal*, the transitional poem that follows the public events of Autumn 1939 and connects them with a personal world; in the disastrous *Autumn Sequel*; in "Carickfergus" and many late poems—he uses it to recreate and generalize but not to analyze himself. A Hardyesque sense of individual isolation recurs, with images of glass barriers, shells, crusts, the journey of separation. The "I" is no more continuous or consistent for him than it is for Eliot. Early on he weds himself to the "I" of the moment, and later in life, in "The Cromlech," he affirmed his governing conviction: that the fact of the moment (being in love, for instance) is in its time and space as true and durable a fact, even if it changes later, as "The cromlech in the clover field." His aesthetic is rooted in this relativistic conviction:

> For essence is not merely core
> And each event implies the world,
> A centre needs periphery.

Attention to the periphery may help in determining the location of the center. And this tendency is present even in his earliest poems, "Train to Dublin," for example:

> All over the world people are toasting the King,
> Red lozenges of light as each one lifts his glass,
> But I will not give you any idol or idea, creed or king,
> I give you the incidental things which pass
> Outward through space exactly as each was.

The second line recalls the more concentrated image, "The moment cradled like a brandy glass." The moment, not the connection between moments and things. The dialogue poem and eclogue, where voices and impulses are balanced and unresolved, were natural forms for him to choose. Indecision is powerful, and in the first half of the 1930s it produced some of his best poems, "Snow" and "The Hebrides" among them. The syntax unfolds unexpectedly, like the landscape.

> On those islands
> Where no train runs on rails and the tyrant time
> Has no clock-towers to signal people to doom
> With semaphore ultimatums tick by tick,
> There is still peace but not for me and not
> Perhaps for long—still peace on the bevel hills

> For those who still can live as their fathers lived
> On those islands.

These are the clichés critics object to, reenergized in their contexts; this is a language like Auden's but subtly different, a language not authoritatively set down but winding out like the guy-line strand of a web uncertain what it will attach to or whether it will hold. "Bagpipe Music," *"Les neiges d'antan"* and *"Dans Macabre"* each deploy a quite different kind of rhetoric, each works out from a different source, but the verse is seldom finger-waggingly didactic. It is experiential, with the sudden changes of tone and of key, which take us deep into feeling, a sense of the inviolability of individual isolation. Yeats can breach the isolation by love; MacNeice, who borrows certain energies from Yeats, cannot. "Prayer Before Birth" was written in 1944, in a spondaic-seeming evenness of rhythm, with a thematic burden bleaker than any he had expressed before.

After 1948 MacNeice went for answers in his poetry. Answers had to be contrived, and the poetry suffers from contrivance. What had been measured skill becomes facility; the poetry becomes, as Auden's later poetry does, "literary," in Larkin's damning sense. It tries too hard, it moves off from the particulars of lived experience.

> The middle stretch
> Of life is bad for poets; a sombre view
> Where neither works nor days look innocent
> And both seem now too many, now too few.

Autumn Sequel is an exemplary failure. He deploys terza rima and the verse flows and flows without resistance. Even John Drinkwater would have avoided lines like "But in a game, as in life, we are under Starter's Orders." MacNeice knew it didn't work and in his last books reverted to his earlier manner, the heartbreaking whimsy, the "between" world now complicated by advancing years. In "House on a Cliff" he moves away from "between" and surrenders to paradox, the drama worked out in the images—a poem that had its impact on the poets of the Movement and on Ted Hughes:

> Indoors the tang of a tiny oil lamp. Outdoors
> The winking signal on the waste of sea.
> Indoors the sound of the wind. Outdoors the wind.
> Indoors the locked heart and the lost key.

He died in 1963—of pneumonia, which he contracted recording a radio program in a damp cave. His admirers hardly expected that what we now read as late poems were to be his last (he himself thought he had reached only the midpoint—or just beyond). In them his poetic recovery is complete: "Dark Age Glosses," "Vistas," "The Wiper," "Selva Oscura" are direct, spoken. And the cluster of poems that includes "After the Crash," "Charm" and "The Introduction" shows the direction in which he might have gone—toward that evanescent truth, the core of the "residual magic."

Young poets might learn more from MacNeice than from Auden: he is the Kavanagh to Auden's Clarke. But in this instance it is the deliberate formal master, not the popular voice, who has the eloquent progeny, though writers in Northern Ireland reclaim MacNeice—some of them too passionately and improbably—and group him with his contemporaries John Hewitt and W. R. Rodgers as a progenitor of the Ulster school.

When I first came to Britain in the late 1960s, the best-known Irish poet of the newer generation was Thomas Kinsella, whose volume *Nightwalker and Other Poems* (1968) was widely admired, if not understood. In 1972 *Butcher's Dozen: A Lesson for the Octave of Widgery* appeared, a response to Bloody Sunday (the killings in Derry by British troops) and to the Widgery Inquiry, which tried to settle the matter. The far from conciliatory poem—eighteenth-century in its mode—began Kinsella's gradual eclipse in Britain. Besides, Seamus Heaney, a poet from the north of Ireland, had emerged in 1965 and was gathering momentum; his verse was less taxing than Kinsella's, he dealt more tactfully with explosive issues.

Kinsella knew his Auden well when he began his writing career. Even the poems he wrote in the 1950s, when in some ways he resembled the poets of the English Movement, were enlarged by his understanding of the ambitious forms and themes of the by-now American poet. It was never a question of imitation, rather of transposition. Besides, it was not only Auden who informed his work. Kinsella is an Irish poet through and through. His translations from the Irish tradition are celebrated as our chief access to an enormous, and for many years suppressed, resource. Ireland for him implies Swift and Goldsmith, Mangan, Davis and Fergusson, and preeminently Yeats. "There is an excess of performance in the earliest poems of William Butler Yeats," he writes, "a special narrative tone, with a dominant verbal melody. He quickly found a more direct poetic speech; always retaining the special tone, but giving sensual access to the facts and matching 'music' organically to content."

Kinsella swims naturally against tides of fashion. He does not go in fear of abstractions, he gives them body and valency. He is also alive to place, to character and voice, to direct and oblique narrative. Like early

Auden, but in quite a different world, and like Yeats in an equally separate realm, he is alive to politics. It is not strange that he is less read than John Montague, perhaps than Richard Murphy and others of his contemporaries: he makes larger demands of himself and consequently of his reader, in ways similar to Austin Clarke.

Donald Davie quotes "The Laundress," a relatively early poem, to demonstrate the elegance of his early lyrics:

> Her chair drawn to the door,
> A basket at her feet,
> She sat against the sun
> And stitched a linen sheet.
> Over harrowed Flanders
> August moved the wheat.
>
> Poplars sharing the wind
> With Saxony and France
> Dreamed at her gate,
> Soared in a summer trance.
> A cluck on the cobbled yard:
> A shadow changed its stance.

"Soared in a summer trance" is Yeatsian. But there is something other, an ease in making connection between the particular and the historical, a tremendous precision and thrift of image, an impersonality. Such verse puts much of early Larkin, apart from "MCMXIV," in perspective. There is also in these early poems a coarse vigor that did not appeal to the poets of the Movement but spoke instead to the writers who were emerging after them.

Kinsella moved on to allegory (or "emblematic" or "heraldic" verse, Davie suggests) in *Nightwalker*; and he had begun to read Ezra Pound. Audenesque habits of eloquent closure are fused with a prosody learned from Pound, making the mature poems of Thomas Kinsella some of the most remarkable, though still neglected, in modern English-language poetry.

Born in 1928 in modest circumstances in Dublin, Kinsella like Clarke is not a child of the fields or the suburbs but of the city. He abandoned a science degree at University College, Dublin, and was a civil servant until 1965. He became a professor at universities in the United States, a director of the Cuala and Dolmen presses, and founded his own Peppercanister Press, through which his poems and sequences are first published, before they are gathered together and issued commercially in longer volumes. The Peppercanister books build together toward a major single work, and we are put in mind, though Kinsella does not invite us to do so, of Pound's *Cantos*. The patterns we begin to discern and the geographies that build and build on Dublin in its different phases are difficult and fascinating. The poems are a gathering together, with history, personal candor, polemic, argument: a fusion of styles from strong and continuous recollections of eighteenth-century satire (the architecture of Dublin) to free and metered verse.

Kinsella describes a *Dual Tradition* in Irish literature, attempting to bring back fully into play the Irish linguistic tradition and the poets of Ireland neglected during the centuries of English rule. Austin Clarke is a linchpin in his argument. It is not a nationalist argument but something more fundamental, about recoveries of voice and resource that will speak more deeply to Irish writers than the off-the-peg forms and strategies of international modernism, postmodernism and anti-modernism. The liberating resources are not only Irish. Pound teaches us to discern our own voice through the static of convention, just as Proust helps us to uncover the lineaments of our own biographies as he traces the miasmic ebb and flow of Marcel's. The task is to recover rather than invent a language, to live rather than exist a life.

> Better is an handful with quietness
> than both hands full
> with travail and vexation of spirit.

> Better to leave now, and no more of this loving upset,
> hate staining the door-jamb from a head possessed
> —all things settled sour in their place,
> my blind fingers forsaking your face.

> Yet worst is the fool that foldeth his hands
> and eateth his own flesh.

Twenty-one years Kinsella's junior, and much more narrowly a disciple of Auden, James Fenton emerged as an undergraduate at Oxford as a potentially formidable poet, winning the Newdigate Prize with a sonnet sequence plus haikus called *Our Western Furniture*, about the opening of Japan to the West. It was a prescient poem since Fenton was to become a journalist, the last Western reporter to leave Saigon after it fell to the Viet Cong, a lively reporter from Cambodia, Korea, the Philippines (from which, when he lived there, he published his *Manila Envelope*, an A-4 envelope full of poems on cards, posters and foldouts).

Born in Lincoln in 1949, Fenton emerged from a background that was emphatically English: Church of England, Repton School, Magdalen College, Oxford, to read psychology and philosophy (friend of John Fuller, son of the poet Roy Fuller and himself a poet and interpreter of Auden). His first book, *Terminal Moraine* (1972), suggested a geological time scale in keeping with Auden's. It is full of formal experiment and invention. His restlessness translated into journalistic action.

From Auden, whom he admired along with Marianne Moore, Roy Fuller, Wallace Stevens (briefly to the point of idolatry) and (at the time) John Ashbery, he learned about the delights of form and formal invention; he also found out how to combine adjectives with abstract nouns to give valency to general ideas, and how to recite his poems from memory in public. This tells us something about the nature of his poems: they are either metrical or highly rhythmical with built-in mnemonics. That helps make them popular.

At Oxford he was a radical, but he did not put his poems to the service of the Cowley workers. He preferred to march and distribute leaflets, and to write his poems elsewhere, to engage his whole mind. He became a theater critic, then a foreign correspondent. In *A German Requiem* (1981) he made a major poem, the first to come out of my generation of British poets, from the postwar German experience of forgetting and remembering selectively. The poem, in part based on his reports from Germany, is in a kind of free verse, sparing in metaphor, powerfully repetitive, to which he has never returned. His next large-scale poem, "Children of Exile," in alternating metrical and free-verse lines, explored the condition of Vietnamese children adopted by Americans living in Italy, a complex political and human drama that he treats with tact and a degree of sentimentality. He returned to England, was elected professor of poetry at Oxford, publishing a further collection in which he plays, with skill, to the gallery: songs, wry social comment, AIDS elegies, love poems. "The Ballad of the Imam" reveals the virtues and the limitations of his specifically public voice. The puzzling candor—if it was candor—of poems like "Nest of Vampires" and "A Staffordshire Murderer," the broad and subtle wit of "The Skip" and "The Kingfisher's Boxing Gloves," give way to something thinner, more balladic and accessible. He remains *in posse* the most substantive poet of my generation, not because he has subject matter but because he has natural skills. He has a developed sense of audience, which now seems—as it did not when he composed *A German Requiem*—stronger than his sense of subject. His is a journey back, from remote lands to England, from the temptation of modernism to something alarmingly close to New Formalism.

Going West

YVOR WINTERS, ELIZABETH DARYUSH,
WENDY COPE, DONALD DAVIE, THOM GUNN

People who don't read modern poetry will tell you that they like rhyme and meter and modern poetry has abandoned both. "It's just chopped-up prose" or "It doesn't sing." In recent years, when the great and the good are asked to select poems, for the most part they turn to formal verse—what they remember from school. New Formalist polemic depends on this prejudice: traditional forms are embattled against the forces of unmetered modernism. In fact, though modernism and the postmodern have generated more critical and theoretical debate than "received" forms in recent times, it is they that have to justify themselves again and again, in practice and theory. And so they should, whether they intend to "make it new" or "make it real." Received forms should be understood afresh too, each time they are used. "I think a sonnet, for example, isn't fourteen lines that rhyme," says Seamus Heaney. "A sonnet is muscles and enjambements and eight and six, and it's got a waist and a middle—it is a form. In a lot of the writing that's going the rounds in the United States"—and throughout the English-speaking world—"there's a lot of talk about return to form—there are indeed fourteen lines [in a sonnet] and there are indeed rhyme words at the end, but the actual movement of the stanza, the movement of the sonnet isn't there. I would make a distinction between form which is an act of living principle, and shape which is discernible on the page, but inaudible, and kinetically, muscularly, unavailable. Poetry is a muscular response."

As a young man, Yvor Winters understood the "living principle" of unmetered verse, then apprehended on the quick the perils it implied for him and found the "living principle" in accentual-syllabic or metered verse. In "Time and the Garden," written in his formal maturity, he hankers after the large gesture, the Lawrentian moment, a pressure which he resists:

And this is like that other restlessness
To seize the greatness not yet fairly earned,
One which the tougher poets have discerned—
Gascoigne, Ben Jonson, Greville, Raleigh, Donne,
Poets who wrote great poems, one by one,
And spaced by many years, each line an act
Through which few labour, which no men retract.

The poet *earns* the poem, not only from language but from life. For Winters there is no poetic license, no given right. In this respect he is among the most self-demanding of the modernists. His reputation is as a strict and conservative critic and poet, most of the poems composed after 1930 being in accentual-syllabic form.

It may be useful to sketch four different kinds of formal choice a poet can make, either deliberately or intuitively, in relation to a subject. *Accentual verse* will have a regular number of stressed or accented syllables in a line, with a variable number of unaccented syllables. Much of the verse of Hopkins is accentual, as is the dominant mode in Eliot, Hughes and others. *Syllabic verse* is a product of this century, a device for eluding the tyranny of the iambic foot. The poet elects a stanza form in which equivalent lines stanza by stanza have the same number of syllables but an insistently variable number and positioning of accents. At its best the form rhymes, but it rhymes an accented with an unaccented syllable (so that rhyme, too, is "pushed back" and its emphases muted) or slant rhyme is chosen. This form was invented in the same year, unbeknownst to one another, by Marianne Moore and Elizabeth Daryush. It is used by Auden, Roy Fuller, Donald Davie, Thom Gunn and others as a way out of what has been, historically, the dominant mode in English verse since the great success of Gower and Chaucer in the fourteenth century, *accentual-syllabic verse,* in which lines have a predetermined number of syllables and a predetermined number of accents, usually deployed in a repetitive pattern, with appropriate variations. Finally, there is what we have called *vers libre* or free verse, a mode that Donald Davie prefers to call *unmetered verse* on the grounds that the word "free" has political and aesthetic implications quite inappropriate to this, the most difficult poetic mode to "earn." A poet who abandons syllabic and accentual regularity must create linguistic patterning in some other way: lineation, and that most subtle and treacherous poetic resource, enjambement, are chief instruments, but also patterning and pacing of syntax. Unmetered verse serves the poet who writes close to the subject, whose intention is to mime the very process that a poem enacts.

Winters was a teacher and his instruction was, like Leavis's, corrective; but unlike Leavis's, the secular moralist, his main concern is poetry and the dynamic of his criticism is creative: he is inward with the process, as it were. In "On Teaching the Young" he writes:

> The young are quick of speech.
> Grown middle-aged, I teach
> Corrosion and distrust.

Hostile to Romanticism and to "excess," he favors a spoken poetry, logical in development and structure, though that logic is not the linear logic of prose. He rejects "pseudo-reference" and "nuance" and has no truck with what he calls the "fallacy of imitative form." Within the work of Eliot, Stevens, Williams or Moore he discriminates sharply between the poems that work at a formal and moral level and those that blur, that reach too far or sell themselves short.

Born in 1900 in Chicago, Winters moved with his family to California in 1904. He returned to study in Chicago but withdrew after a year, suffering from tuberculosis. He received his MA from the University of Colorado. In 1926 he married the novelist Janet Lewis and moved to Stanford, California, where he was a graduate student and later professor of English, a post he held until his death in 1968. The titles of his illuminating and provocative critical books alert us to his priorities: *In Defense of Reason* (1947) incorporated *Primitivism and Decadence*, *Maule's Curse* and *Anatomy of Nonsense* and includes important essays on fiction and poetry; then came *The Function of Criticism* (1957) and *Forms of Discovery* (1968). His *Collected Poems* appeared in 1958 and 1960, with a definitive version published in 1978, incorporating his early work, which he disowned, and his later formal poems.

The early poems reveal how close he was at the outset to Williams, how he appreciated Pound and was alert to the writings of Moore, Loy and other modern writers on the East Coast. He is an Imagist arriving late at the feast, an Imagist with tendencies toward a kind of expressionism; the image put under severe pressure by his experiences as a teacher in remote villages in New Mexico, his solitude and other tensions. He insists, however, "My shift from the methods of those early poems to the methods of my later was not a shift from formlessness to form; it was a shift from certain kinds of form to others . . . Form is something that one perceives or does not perceive; theory in itself is insufficient." His unmetered poems "are rhythmical, not merely from line to line, but in total movement from beginning to end, and . . . the relations between the meanings of the parts is an element in the rhythm, along with the sound." He moved on because he felt restricted: abstract categories, moral reflection, intellectual exploration, seemed to be excluded from his strained Imagist manner. And his contemporaries—

Stevens in particular—were doing things he wanted to do, in a different way, on a different scale.

The early poems may have rhythm, but they do not move very much in either sense, perhaps because the images are strange and too pared back; the "I" speaks but will not let us know him, the voice is cold. His move to accentual-syllabic forms was as experimental as his earlier choice of Imagism. He was looking for a more complex form of discovery. In the later poems it is the syntax that moves us, a syntax that is patterned in terms of accent and syllable but earns a degree of freedom and variation in its assiduous balance. How much can a poet say and mean responsibly? *Just so much*, he seems to answer, biting the poem off with an irony or a reversal if it goes beyond its proper measure. A poem risks not only incoherence but evil, and "The basis of Evil is an emotion," while "Good rests in the power of rational selection in action." Emotion must be "eliminated, and, in so far as it cannot be eliminated, understood." In a sonnet like "The Realisation" he sets himself the hardest of tasks:

Death. Nothing is simpler. One is dead.
The set face now will fade out; the bare fact,
Related movement, regular, intact,
Is reabsorbed, the clay is on the bed.
The soul is mortal, nothing: the dim head
On the dim pillow, less. But thought clings flat
To this, since it can never follow that
Where no precision of the mind is bred.

Nothing to think of between you and All!
Screaming processionals of infinite
Logic are grinding down receding cold!
O fool! Madness again! Turn not, for it
Lurks in each paintless cranny, and you sprawl
Blurring a definition. Quick! You are old.

Mannered, rather archaizing, rather Jonsonian? No: wrested, candid, the poem does not console so much as clarify. This is a harsh discipline which poets as different in temperament as J. V. Cunningham and Edgar Bowers, his first generation of students, accepted. The best minds of his generation, Eliot and Pound and others, he believed, let their ideas go slippery with emotion. The challenge he set himself was to understand and then control: poetry as the instrument of stoicism, the language that restores balance.

Many of his mature poems are short and aphoristic. The best, including "Time and the Garden," "The Slow Pacific Swell" and "The California Oaks," deploy abstractions with a harsh precision—harsh in what they exclude. Is "On a View of Pasadena from the Hills" a kind of answer to Stevens's "The Idea of Order at Key West"? Stevens's poem moves into night, Winters's from dawn into the day.

Three poets have made substantial claims for Elizabeth Daryush: Winters, Roy Fuller and Donald Davie. Others are bemused. Winters refers to her as "one of the few distinguished poets of our century and a poet who can take her place without apology in the company of Campion and Herrick." Fuller describes her as "a pioneer technical innovator, whose work demands study by poets and readers on this account alone. Further . . . she is a poet of the highest dedication and seriousness." The poems "grapple with life's intensest issues." With such testimonials, we turn to Daryush's tight and slender oeuvre and wonder if we have come to the wrong party. The poems strike us as conventional in diction, in tight (usually rhymed) form. But the challenge they offer is "from the inside": they compel a reconsideration of prosody. It is only when we get to Geoffrey Hill that we encounter a comparable scrupulousness, and again he works from within the tradition.

Daryush was born in 1887. Her father, Robert Bridges, was later poet laureate and one of the outstanding prosodists in the English tradition, though now even less read than she is. Her first home was in the Berkshire village of Yattenden, and most of her early life was spent in rural Berkshire. In 1907 her father built Chilswell House, Boar's Hill, Oxford, where she lived until her marriage in 1923. With her father and mother (daughter of the great Victorian architect Alfred Waterhouse) she maintained a continual dialogue about poetry and poetics. She disagreed with her father's theories, and disagreements extended to his apprehension of meter and syllabic verse, as well as her own. Milton, she told me, was an especial bone of contention; her attention to Milton had a marked impact on her later innovations.

In 1923 she married a Persian and moved to Persia, where she lived for four years. She studied Persian poetry and produced a fine syllabic "translation," or imitation, of Jalàl ad Din Rùmi in "I am your mother, your mother's mother." After her return to Britain she moved in 1929 to Stockwell, Boar's Hill, near her father's house, where she lived until her death in 1977. All of her collections of verse, apart from three early volumes, which she suppressed, were written at Stockwell.

She wrote poems on three rhythmic models: accentual-syllabic, accentual and syllabic. Her experiments in the latter modes are radical. Her accentual verse is in effect "sprung rhythm" in the manner of Hopkins, her father's friend; and she imitates the actual form of Hopkins's "The Wreck of the Deutschland" in her most ambitious poem, "Air and

Variations," written over many years. She asked me to transcribe it from
her manuscript in 1970. She was virtually blind and wrote in a wide felt-
tip pen on lined paper in large letters. When the poem was typeset, she
read the proofs with the aid of a strong magnifying glass.

It was surprising to see her using Hopkins's meter but not his dense
diction nor his assonance. The rhapsodic form does not trick her into
rhapsody: there is a phrased pacing as in her tautest lyric poems. "Air
and Variations" is constructed on a mathematical and logical progres-
sion, which she explained to me without effecting comprehension on
my part. A stanza will illustrate the technique, especially in the dramatic
line endings, which underpin image content and the argument:

> I said: I have seen
> The wall of a mountainous wave
> Foam into spheres, then sink through green
> Of fields to a human grave;
> I have followed a sky-filled river, whose flickering throe
> Leapt from its actual nodes, to a moon-tide gave
> Its might . . . nor forward urged nor backward formed that flow.
> Each was the older twin . . .

The logic of line indentation is simple. In accentual poems, lines with most
accents are ranged farthest left; in syllabic poems, those with most sylla-
bles are ranged farthest left. Shorter lines are indented correspondingly.

In syllabic verse, the predetermined number of syllables is usually
odd, since an even number is more likely to fall into iambics. In 1934 she
published a classic definition of syllabic writing: "Metres governed only
by the number of syllables to the line, and in which the number and
position of stresses may be varied at will." She should have said "*must* be
varied." Her syllabic verse is printed without capital letters at the begin-
nings of lines "as a reminder to the reader to follow strictly the natural
speech-rhythms, and not to look for stresses where none are intended."
She adds, "I have long thought that on some such system as this for a
base, it should be possible to build up subtler and more freely-followed
accentual patterns than can be obtained either by stress-verse proper, or
by the traditional so-called syllabic metres. The bulk of English 'syllabic'
verse is, of course, not really syllabic in the strict sense, but more truly
accentual."

In a note to the *Collected Poems* (1976) she qualified her earlier descrip-
tion. Syllable count is "merely the lifeless shell" of "more vital require-
ments." In accentual verse, the constant is "time," or stress, the variable
is "number," or syllable count. In syllabic poems this is reversed—the
constant is number, the variable stress. Unexpectedness, a dramatic vari-

ety of rhythm can be achieved, but a far closer artistry must be observed. A syllabic poem which closely approaches speech rhythm and avoids the easier tension of metrical verse without forfeiting the discipline of rhyme is an unusual war poem:

> Plant no poppy (he said)
> no frail lily sublime,
> for in war's famine time
> thou'lt need but corn for bread.
>
> Hoard no jewel (he said)
> no dazzling laboured gem:
> thou'lt be forced to sell them
> for steel, so now decide.
>
> Set no flower in thy word
> (he besought, but none heard)
> cut no flash to thy wit,
> if thou must disown it
> when see'st thou sorrow's sword.

Archaisms of diction were purged from her later poems. Yet I doubt they mar this poem seriously: its sense is terse and precise.

For her it is as though the nineteenth century (apart from Landor) had never happened. Her work owes debts to seventeenth-century models. Her use of the first person, even in the elegies, is unencumbered by autobiography. She writes dramatic poems, but without a plot, tending toward allegory. One begins "Anger lay by me all night long, / His breath was hot upon my brow." She dramatizes ideas. Her prosody controls to an unusual degree our course through the poem. A poem's source is chancy, dark. Its execution and unexpected growth take place in the light: she is in control, but the poem brings its darkness with it.

Some poets use syllabics as a sort of sausage slicer, replacing the discipline of meter with an arbitrary discipline of counting on fingers and toes. Daryush makes of them a measure more, not less, exacting and precise than traditional modes. Syllabics lead not toward a greater but toward a different freedom, where rhythm obeys speech, form and content strive for a more complete integration.

One of her accentual-syllabic poems progresses in a single sentence through four seasons, the line endings measured, not calculated:

> I will hold out my arms
> To Spring who clothes me

(Says the beech),
To kind summer who warms
   My room and soothes me;
     I will reach
For rich Autumn's robe, red
   With pride and grieving;
     I will hold
Out my worn dress for dread
   Winter's unweaving
     In the cold.

As in an Imagist poem, woman and tree merge; yet these taut triplets are a world away from the loose, colloquial triplets of Williams, and from the watercolor intensities of the early *imagiste* H.D.

Donald Davie succeeded Yvor Winters as professor of English at Stanford. He shared Winters's interest in diction and something like his sense of poetic responsibility, but he brought with him a more capacious sense of formal possibility and very different social and cultural roots. He was born in Barnsley, Yorkshire, in 1922, and the landscapes and the accent of his formative years were audible at the back of his voice. In his autobiography, *These the Companions*, he recalls a Baptist boyhood and ingredients that went into the making of a distinct Englishness, as remote from the southern rural and patrician as from the Lawrentian, yet rich in possibilities. The formal language of the psalter and the very different formality of the hymns stayed with him. So did his sense of belonging to a radical dissenting tradition whose history and literature he explored with interested rather than disinterested scholarship. To his love of the hymns of Isaac Watts, Charles Wesley and others he kept adding understanding, even when he became an Anglican later in life. At this time the groundwork for his later aesthetic and moral character began to be defined, his sense of appropriate measure, his distrust of the disorderly and bohemian. A grammar-school boy, he earned a scholarship to Cambridge, his career interrupted by service during the war in the Royal Navy in Arctic Russia, where he roughly taught himself the language. Later he translated Pasternak and wrote on Russian, Polish and Hungarian literature, including his adaptation of Adam Mickiewicz's epic (a touch of Romanticism here), *Pan Tadeusz*, which he called *The Forests of Lithuania* (1959). Pasternak and Mickiewicz, as much as Ezra Pound, helped to broaden his sense of what poetry might do, beyond the early limited range he allowed himself as "a pasticheur of late Augustan styles."

In the last year of the war, in Devon, he married Doreen John. They returned to Cambridge together, where he read English. Dr. Leavis was one of the ingredients in those formative years, and Davie regarded himself as of the same party. He began his contacts with Yvor Winters, another severe taskmaster. His earliest poems were published alongside those of the 1940s poets in the wildly catholic Tambimuttu's *Poetry London*, but by the beginning of the 1950s, disaffected with the excesses of Dylan Thomas's generation, he had begun to define the constituents of a responsible art. He went on to lecture at Trinity College, Dublin. His early critical books, *Purity of Diction in English Verse* (1952) and *Articulate Energy: An Inquiry into the Syntax of English Poetry* (1955), and his first collection of poems, *Brides of Reason* (1955), appeared, an unnaturally orderly beginning, defining for himself and his generation a stance against the excesses of the 1940s: "There is no necessary connection between the poetic vocation on the one hand, and on the other exhibitionism, egoism, and licence," he wrote. In 1992 he declared that at the time "essay and poem were equivalent and almost interchangeable attempts to grapple with the one same reality." The reality of diction and of syntax, the essential instruments of a certain kind of poet's art, are singled out, examined and defined.

He discriminates between "the diction of verse" and "the language of poetry." Shakespeare and Hopkins use a language: one feels that any word might eventually find a place in their verse. But there is another kind of poet, "with whom I feel the other thing—that a selection has been made and is continually being made, that words are thrusting at the poem and being fended off from it, that however many poems these poets wrote certain words would never be allowed into the poems, except as a disastrous oversight." The discrimination comes from the century of strict decorum, the eighteenth, with which Davie has such a firm affinity. He traces the idea of diction and its implications through its century and appraises what is entailed and what lost when it declines, always with an eye on contemporary practice. *Purity of Diction* in hindsight came to be regarded as a manifesto of the Movement, that loose grouping of writers that emerged in the 1950s, using traditional forms and setting its cap against the verbal excesses of the 1940s and the ideological excesses of the 1930s—indeed, looking to Empson and the specifics of language which he had isolated and highlighted.

The notion of a responsible diction is nowhere better defined than in the poem "Epistle. To Enrique Caracciolo Trejo," from Davie's troubled and angry *More Essex Poems*, written when student difficulties at the new University of Essex threatened to destroy the radical experiment he had created there, in which writers from different languages, students and teachers were to live in a single intellectual community. Trejo was a writer invited to stay for a year. He proposed that Davie translate poems from the Spanish. But, Davie ruefully declares, his language is under siege; it cannot responsibly take the rhetorical risks the poems require:

A shrunken world
Stares from my pages.
What a pellet the authentic is!
My world of poetry,
Enrique, is not large.
Day by day it is smaller.
These poems that you have
Given me, I might
Have made them English once.
Now they are inessential.
The English that I feel in
Fears the inauthentic
Which invades it on all sides
Mortally. The style may die of it,
Die of the fear of it,
Confounding authenticity with essence.

Diction is a choice that, at times of political and emotional pressure, can become a hard necessity. Winters would have understood this argument; he might even have approved the unmetered verse in which it is written.

Articulate Energy is an inquiry, not a polemic. It examines several theories of syntax in poetry and finds them incomplete. It then looks closely at modern and past poetry and singles out various kinds of syntax and considers the thematic and prosodic implications of divergent strategies. "It will be apparent," Davie concludes, "that the impulse behind all this writing is conservative. But it is, I hope, a rational conservatism." It was the beginning of a step away from the Movement: it does not include Pound and Anglo-American modernism, but it leaves open the door through which, in due course, the poet and the critic was to pass. The break with the past that is modernism, Davie argues, is a break with past understandings and applications of syntax, a break that occurs with the symbolists and has to do with the conflation rather than the discrimination and arrangement of elements in experience. A modernism that closes off resources impoverishes us and itself. It is against impoverishments that result from theoretical or polemical approaches that Davie helps the poet and the reader. His book was read as antimodernist, so that when he began to write on Pound, and later on the Projectivists and experimental American writing, those who wanted to use *Articulate Energy* as part of an antimodern argument were frustrated.

The Movement's "rules" were to begin with restrictive, curtailing poetic ambition and scope. For Larkin and for Kingsley Amis, the rules became a kind of dogma. John Wain, the most Empsonian of the early Movementeers, broke with the rules and became a poet of rhetorical waffle, of the kind the Movement had pitted itself against. D. J. Enright teased out the strong ironic line and has followed it in many directions to great effect. For Elizabeth Jennings the rules were never sensed as rules: her forms she justified instinctively. Thom Gunn, like Davie, starts as he means to go on, refining and experimenting: for both, the Movement is a point of departure. The rules have been transposed into an abiding discipline, in Davie's case Augustan. His work is ranging and ambitious but always controlled and almost always, one way or another, didactic.

The Movement—such a drab name, after Imagism and Vorticism, Fugitives, Apocalyptics. Intentionally drab, antirhetorical. Davie may be its defining critic, but he became as he moved on much more, the defining poet-critic of his generation. The trajectory of his development makes him exemplary.

He returned from Dublin to Cambridge in 1958, and in 1964 was made the first professor of English at Essex, beginning in brilliant and radical experiment, ending his time there in acute disappointment. In 1968 he emigrated to America, becoming Winters's successor at Stanford and then, in 1978, moving to the birthplace of the Fugitive movement, Vanderbilt University in Nashville, where he remained until his retirement in 1987. He settled in Devon where he continued writing. He died in 1995.

The importance of his critical writing—particularly in *Ezra Pound: Poet as Sculptor* (1964) and his later books on Pound, *Thomas Hardy and British Poetry* (1972), *Czeslaw Milosz and the Insufficiency of Lyric* (1986) and *Under Briggflatts: A History of Poetry in Great Britain 1960–1988* (1989)—is inestimable. Like so much of his growth as a writer, many of the books are written against the grain. It was hard for him to come to terms with Pound, with his huge project, his numerous prosodies, his politics and his legacy. Always a skeptical admirer, in the end he conceded a higher estimation to Eliot, but Pound, whom he approached and reapproached in books and essays, was the angel with whom he was destined to wrestle and who named him. In the Hardy book (he loved Hardy with more rigor than Auden, more breadth than Ransom) he is compelled to set down a fact that troubles him: that Hardy may be responsible, in the poets whose work he has affected, for the failure of nerve in modern British poetry. "Hardy appears to have mistrusted, and certainly leads other poets to mistrust, the claims of poetry to transcend the linear unrolling of recorded time." This strength and weakness sets him at odds with Yeats, and when Philip Larkin famously abandons Yeats for Hardy he is making a commitment to the "world of contingencies" to which Hardy condemns the poets that he touches. It is a failure of transcendence: history displaces God, the poet forever "outside, prayer denied." Davie traces this legacy through a range of British writers, ruefully. Hardy's influence is "for good or ill," and in the longer term it came to seem "for ill" to Davie, though it never lessened his appreciation of Hardy's verse. Writing on Hardy, he made his distinction between thematic and stylistic irony, which is also a distinction between premodern and modernist writing.

The Milosz book is one of his most challenging to English poets. When he speaks of the "insufficiency of lyric" he has in mind the stable, lyric "I" which has dominated English poems from the time of Chaucer. He questions its authenticity and its continuing viability. Taking as a paradigm Milosz's major poems, written in a time of extreme disruption in his native Lithuania and Poland, Davie looks at the ways the poet finds to speak of experience on which he has no stable purchase, how he multiplies voices and perspectives to tell the complex truth. He contrasts this with the unaltered and apparently unaltering situation of the English poet. The lyric depends upon a stable "I," whether "actual" or a persona. In the face of complex or extreme experience it is no longer a serviceable instrument and the lyric itself is in jeopardy from history, that very contingent world into which Hardy binds poets who have neither the energy nor the formal resources to "transcend" the circumstantial. I simplify his subtle, detailed arguments. They are important if poetry is to speak to and of experience in more than anecdote and platitude.

In his own verse, writing as a troubled Christian unwilling to reside within the limits of contingency, unwilling at the same time to fly off into the circumambient gas of Dylan Thomas, Peter Redgrove and other writers for whom rhetorical gesture stands in for poetic sense, there is a deliberate and difficult development. In an unpublished interview from the 1960s he says, "It seems to me now that the eighteenth-century enthusiasms in which I started and the eighteenth-century effects that I tried to reproduce in my early poems, are in fact motivated very romantically; that is to say, for a twentieth-century person to yearn towards the rigidity of the couplet and the rigidity of the Johnsonian vocabulary and the rigidity of those steady civilisations which they held in mind, is very different from an eighteenth-century man wanting it." He "came to suspect" this romantic impulse, to qualify it, and without mitigating his disciplines shrugged off the merely Augustan affectation and its rhetorics, no longer a romantic Augustan but a modern one, with reason, receptivity, optimism and a tempering skepticism. In 1957 he confided to his journal that he was "not naturally" a poet; that hitherto his poems had used metaphor to decorate rather than to carry argument, and he *determines* (a very Davie word) deliberately to redirect his verse: in future his poems will be "if not *naturally*, at all events *truly* poems throughout." This he does, with assistance from Pasternak, and eventually Pound, "winning to the concrete through the abstract." In *A Sequence for Francis Parkman* (1961) the change decisively occurs. He makes the poem of phrases and expressions from the great historian: an Alexandrian experiment, a "cento." The juxtaposition of passages, the creation of historical figures, the drama played out against the background of a new continent and a recollected Europe: this experiment prefigures his own exile from England. Before he left he wrote the *Essex Poems* (1969) which without confessional self-importance but with appalling humility and candor ("Epistle," "July 1964," "Or, Solitude" and others) present a situation and a response.

Ireland stayed with him, a formative experience, revealing the ways in which a different literature in English handled itself, the deadening legacy of Yeats for later poets, the neglect of Clarke, Padraic Fallon and others. As an outsider he got a distinctive purchase on Irish poetry and helped through his essays to develop new critical perspectives. Later he did a similar service in English letters with his advocacies of Bunting, Ivor Gurney, Jack Clemo and, at a dangerous time, Pound.

America was a different kind of experience. All the time he was there he remained aware, in verse and prose, of England. He wrote *The Shires* (1974), his rediscovery of England part by part, in personal memory, literary history, mere topography. Shortly after his departure, in 1970, he published his six verse *Epistles to Eva Hesse* (1970). Hesse was Pound's German translator, and his tetrameter couplets attempt to explain, in Augustan tones but modern terms, an English tradition different in kind from Pound's. He imagines and seems to address a new consensus. He read the *Epistles* on BBC Radio 3: despite their complexity they were instantly comprehensible, his reading voice concentrating on syntax, prosody and tone: not works of a "performance poet" but poems written for the voice. "The main objective was to show that . . . as much variety of time, space and action can be encompassed in one of the traditional forms of English verse as in the much vaunted 'free forms' of the American tradition originating in Pound's *Cantos*." The proof of his case is not in what is said but in how it is said; this is his tour de force in traditional form. Satirical, essayistic, forthright, it is one of his most original works, incorporating into verse, directly and unapologetically, the arguments of his critical prose.

In the Stopping Train (1977) was his most vulnerable book and the one on which he built the later poems. At last he is able, in a verse that is candid, wry and stringent, to consider in depth themes he had touched upon in *Essex Poems*, but now without the inhibitions that stopped him short then. There is a correspondence of failure: within him, within his culture and his society. In *Three for Water-Music* (1981) he was able to move forward, paying homage to three landscapes, to Pound and Bunting, writers of whom he was made, and in his choice of forms to the Eliot of *Four Quartets*, whose themes and strategies he was approaching. *To Scorch or Freeze* (1988) is his most original and challenging volume. It revisits the Psalms with the concerns and in the mixed idioms of a man well on his way in life.

"In all but what seems inchoate," he wrote earlier, "we quiz the past, to see it straight / Requires a form just out of reach." He believed that he had achieved transcendence in his language, penetrating beyond irony with irony; he had overcome the heritage of Hardy, to speak in his own way, with and even as King David. In the process he had exhausted his Muse. He would write no more. But a couple of months before his death he sent me a verse meditation on "Our Father," a ten-part meditation, one of his most ambitious poems. The second section reads:

Tragedian of an Italy unborn,
He cudgelled himself for having prostituted
The buskin to the tiara; that's to say,
His play to the scrutiny of the Holy Father.

Later he learned how much more tolerant an
Unpolished pontiff was, than a godless State
That asked a theatre for Everyman,
The man first dulled, then frivolously diverted.

Later again (we look beyond him now)
The buskin throve by dirtying—the tiara
And then the Cross; which lives by seeing how
Unwearyingly the Father's sons revile him.

Clearly the Muse had not entirely abandoned him.

His impact as critic is durable; his poems live in formal diversity, intellectual rigor and candor. None of this came easy: his candor, Christian in the strictest sense, had consequences for his art. I am reminded of James Baldwin: "The questions which one asks oneself begin, at last, to illuminate the world, and become one's key to the experience of others. One can only face in others what one can face in oneself. On this confrontation depends the measure of our wisdom and compassion. This energy is all that one finds in the rubble of vanished civilisations, and the only hope for ours."

Davie is a lucid dissenter: engagement with literature and language is the crucial engagement with culture; he finds himself out of sympathy with cultural and political reaction quite as much as he does with those who think the art of writing is a doddle. He's as impatient with over-selling as with selling short. The self-conscious modesty of purpose of many of his contemporaries makes him furious. The art of poetry is ambitious, big-hearted. If our culture is infected with irony, the writer must develop strategies to transcend, to subvert it. He strives as a teacher to bring the reader close to the text, the writer close to the core experience of the poem that's being written. "Needing to know is always how to learn, / Needing to see brings sightings."

Thom Gunn resists the notion that he is a poet of the Movement, but he appeared in the *New Lines* anthology, which first defined the group, and critics like to insist his beginning was there: those strict accentual-syllabic rhymed forms of his early work, the vigorous ironies. He was roughly contemporary with Davie at Cambridge. They have rather a different inflection from the Oxford Movementeers, more astringent, didactic; for both there was Leavis, then Winters and California, then modernism. But they found very different routes through to their mature work.

Thomson William Gunn was born in 1929 in Gravesend, Kent, son of a Fleet Street journalist. He went to school in London, living in Hampstead in a home full of books. "I was mad about Keats and Marlowe when I was fourteen," he says and in Hampstead he was in Keats's landscape. His parents divorced when he was ten, and his mother (with whom he lived) died by her own hand when he was fifteen. He began reading novels voraciously, days at a time lost in books. In his late teens he started on Auden, who "seemed so available." After two years' National Service in the army, he went up to Cambridge. He had read Eliot and just after National Service read Baudelaire, whose impact was decisive. At university he discovered Yeats. Leavis's impact on the early poems is evident in their moral tone and concern. Leavis's pronounced homophobia may have retarded (if the surrounding culture was not enough to do so) Gunn's coming to terms with his homosexuality in his poems. "Tamer and Hawk" is powerful, but the conceit does not *require* to be read as gay.

The New Criticism was in the ascendant: "I really do think of Herbert as a kind of contemporary of mine. I don't think of him as being separated from me by an impossible four hundred years of history." Donne was in his mind as well. The adaptation of the forms and styles of other writers, other periods, seemed possible; he could invest in their lines and lives, but in a rigorously modern idiom. The anxiety of influence was not especially anxious. Unlike Eliot, Gunn does not use allusions to the past in order "to judge the tawdry present" (Davie's phrase). He says, "I don't regret the present." His poetry belongs in and to it. He published his first pamphlet with the legendary Fantasy Press.

He fell in love, by his own account, at Cambridge, with an American student. To stay with him he applied for American scholarships. In 1954 he went to Stanford on a writing fellowship. *Fighting Terms*, his first book, was published—it was the period of the "angry young men," and Gunn was the first poet among them. At Stanford he studied with Winters and began experimenting with syllabics in order to ease himself away from the exclusive tyranny of accentual-syllabic verse. For him the experiments were a way of finding a serviceable free verse: he had to work toward it. Poets who leap into what they think is free verse are often still under the sway of the pentameter and kid themselves into thinking they have achieved something radical when they are merely masking the underlying measure. His syllabic poems appeared in *The Sense of Movement* (1957) and *My Sad Captains* (1961). In *Touch* (1967) he achieves a serviceable unmetered verse for the first time: movement, choice, risk and—finally—touch. Possessing a new formal resource, he did not use it exclusively: certain kinds of statement (elegiac, celebratory, reflective) required a more conventional accentual-syllabic and stanzaic form; it is close-up poems, poems that don't wish to stand back from experience, poems of process, which require unmetered verse. He has grown technically by addition.

Winters provided a very definite creative as well as critical point of reference. In "To Yvor Winters, 1955" he evokes the teacher-poet, his home, his garden and the Airedale dogs he bred.

> And in the house there rest, piled shelf on shelf,
> The accumulations that compose the self—
> Poem and history: for if we use
> Words to maintain the actions that we choose,
> Our words, with slow defining influence,
> Stay to mark out our chosen lineaments.

In the same poem he summarizes Winters's exemplary aesthetic, one that Gunn transposes in his later work: "You keep both Rule and Energy in view, / Much power in each, most in the balanced two." "Rule" and "energy" Gunn later recasts as *definition* and *flow*. Rule, or definition, provides a structure or system in or through which the energy can flow, like Wordsworth's "stationary blasts of waterfalls." In the LSD poems in *Moly* (1971), the dark unsettling poems of *Jack Straw's Castle* (1976), the AIDS elegies in *The Man with Night Sweats* (1992) quite as much as in the early verse, you can't have one without the other. What is invigorating in Gunn is the inventiveness of definition and the intensity of flow. "In Santa Maria del Popolo" is an early paradigm in which the form, the image and the argument work astonishingly well together, as Gunn, who once wanted to be a novelist, builds into a single poem the lives of St. Paul, Caravaggio and the young poet, with a supporting cast of old women and shadows.

Winters pointed him toward Marianne Moore; he discovered Williams, Pound and Lawrence. The "Sartrean Existentialism" of the early poems gave people something other than the language and form to talk about: man is regarded as *self-creating*: by his choices, some of them unconscious and arbitrary, he makes himself, without foreknowledge, advancing in the belief that he may find. What he may find, how he may find, and where, are unknown. Martin Dodsworth called it a "voluntary commitment to the irrational" in a world without intrinsic meanings. Certainly in the early poems plots and symbols have an arbitrary air. From Baudelaire he had learned about obliquity.

Gunn settled in San Francisco in 1961. The relationship which transported him there, which informs his first substantial unmetered verse poem "Touch," informs too a poem in his 1992 collection, "The Hug." Underlying the flow, celebrated in various forms, there is a human stability. The unmetered form of "Touch" demonstrates certain qualities of "free verse." A poem must create a pattern of expectation, so that it can deliver whatever it has to deliver, by accumulation or variation. The unexpected will work only against a background of created expectation. Meter provides a ready-made constant; in unmetered verse the "measure" or "unit"—for Gunn—is the line: each line unit is seen as having equal weight, regardless of syllable count or number of stresses, and the line ending, punctuated or not, entails a discernible pause.

Early in Gunn's career G. S. Fraser contrasted Larkin's emotional economy and Gunn's emotional profligacy: heroisms were not out of place for Gunn, despite the scaled-down age—heroic or excessive action, expression through the body, its beauty, the risks it takes. Charles Tomlinson says Gunn "resolved to seek out the heroic in the experience of nihilism," as in "A Mirror for Poets," perhaps. The early poems express isolation: the watcher, the watched, the historically singled out and, in "Misanthropos," the survivor. Posing, acting, enacting; a sense of role-play; assuming an attitude if not a voice: these are things the subjects of the poems do. Gunn either celebrates wholeness, self-sufficiency, or laments separation. Isolation becomes a burden, as in Yeats and Hardy. The poems move, through drug experiences, through love, comradeship and community, beyond the singular self. The occasions of his poetry have become more diverse and, in his last book, more somber. "I have invented roots," he says. The fighting terms he has come to terms with. Advancing in the belief that he may find, he has found points of positive commitment and places of repose.

Winters's impact differed generation by generation. Those who studied with him toward the end of his life, and then with Donald Davie at Stanford, came away with strict disciplines but minds more open to the formal resources they might need; Robert Pinsky and Robert Hass have become significant critics, translators and poets. The most difficult and powerful poet of their generation is John Peck, who, like Thomas Kinsella, has learned from Pound *and* Auden, and who demands unusual qualities of attention from his readers. In Britain, through Gunn and Davie and tempered by them, Winters has a kind of progeny less formally radical than their American contemporaries. Notable among them are Robert Wells, whose roots run deep in the pastoral eighteenth century, in the classics (he has translated Theocritus and Virgil) and in the poetries and landscapes of the Mediterranean; Dick Davis, a Persian scholar and translator and an acerbic formalist who comes closest to Winters's poetic desiderata, even in the sometimes excessive refinement of his diction; Clive Wilmer, of the same Cambridge generation, also a translator and critic, who has built on foundations similar to Gunn's but created a very different poetry, sententious in the good sense, reflective, Ruskinian. Neil Powell, one of Gunn's best interpreters, a poet whose insistently—excessively?—English verse does not seem to register the fact of modernism at any point, belongs in this company.

It distorts the picture to set the witty and adroit Wendy Cope in the same frame, but her focus on accentual-syllabic forms and her impatience with modernism are illuminating here. Her experience has been the reverse of Gunn's. She began writing in free verse in 1972, imagining that nowadays rhyming forms are appropriate primarily for comic verse. In creative writing courses she discovered forms she knew nothing about—the villanelle for instance—and that work she liked, including "Do Not Go Gentle" by Dylan Thomas, might use them. She wrote a villanelle, began her formal career and lost touch with, or confidence in, unmetered verse. Gunn's collections in which the majority of the poems are in accentual-syllabic forms outsell his books dominated by unmetered verse; Cope's popular success has something to do with the same issue: an English readership likes a recognizable, well-made poem, Betjeman rather than Bunting. It likes everyday experiences and social tones. The influences she adduces among her contemporaries affected her more as catalysts than models. Dismissed as a writer of "light verse," she has been critically undervalued. The poems are funny at times, skillful always, and formally resourceful. If we regard Skelton and Gascoigne as "light," then she is "light," but in the sense of illumination rather than of weight. A poet who in an almost systematic way is misvalued, whatever sales her books achieve, is damaged by a literary environment that benefits from her popularity and might benefit from attention to her skills. More pertinently, a healthy critical environment would encourage growth and change in a way that an appreciative market, hungry for more of the same, never can.

Apocalypse and After

DYLAN THOMAS, DAVID GASCOYNE, W. S. GRAHAM, BURNS
SINGER, JOHN HEATH-STUBBS, GEORGE BARKER, C.H. SISSON,
STEVIE SMITH, THEODORE ROETHKE, R. S. THOMAS

It was against Dylan Marlais Thomas and his contemporaries that the Movement reacted. Davie quotes Vernon Watkins describing himself and Thomas as religious poets who "could never write a poem dominated by time, as Hardy could." Here was a way of escaping the contingent world, but into what? Larkin at Oxford was in awe of Thomas; when he discovered Hardy there was a change. Images in Thomas are connected less by syntax or narrative structure than by rhythm. Each phrase and fragment makes sense, but when the reader stands back from the poem its many meanings collapse like a house of cards. One can force from the poems a structural coherence, but only sometimes an emotional or even a sensual coherence. Like Hart Crane, Thomas writes always just beyond his own considerable but essentially instinctive understanding. He dazzles himself and, in performance certainly, conveyed the dazzle to his audience. When he writes *Under Milk Wood* (published after his death, in 1954) he has brought his medium within his understanding, and a sentimental understanding it is.

He was born in Swansea, Wales, in 1914. His father was a schoolmaster and poet who recited Shakespeare to the boy before he could read. His placid, childish mother was devoted to him. He remembers his early infatuation with the sound of nursery rhymes, the "colors" words suggested to him, the exciting rhythms. This apprenticeship to Mother Goose predisposed him to highly rhythmic poetry: the ballads, Poe, Hopkins, Yeats, Marlowe, Keats for his colors, Lawrence for his passions. He was adamant that Joyce was not in the mix, or the Bible or Freud. The poems bear witness against him.

Pampered, asthmatic, naughty, he went to the grammar school where his father was senior English master. His successes were limited to literary activities. A short boy, he was competitive and wanted to be best or worst at everything. Constantine Fitzgibbon, one biographer, speaks of his "flamboyant idleness." At seventeen he left school and became a newspaper reporter. After fifteen months he returned home and between 1932 and 1934 composed well over half the poems he published during his lifetime. He enjoyed dissolute roles in amateur theatricals: role-playing became a habit, only—as Robert Nye writes—"none of the masks quite fits."

Eighteen Poems appeared in 1934, followed two years later by *Twenty-Five Poems*, and in 1939 *The Map of Love* with prose and verse rounded off his early career. The collections are much of a piece and many regard them as the best of Thomas; they are more individually his than the more vatic, less obscure work of his most famous book, *Deaths and Entrances* (1946). During the war he did work for the BBC and published an autobiography, *Portrait of the Artist as a Young Dog*, in 1940. He died in 1953, aged thirty-nine, during an American lecture tour.

Describing his technique to a young fan, he wrote: "I make an image—though 'make' is not the right word; I let, perhaps, an image be 'made' emotionally in me and then apply to it what intellectual and critical forces I possess—let it breed another, let that image contradict the first, make, of the third image bred out of the other two together, a fourth contradictory image, and let them all, within my imposed formal limits, conflict." The formula is like Lawrence's for fiction: releasing four characters and letting them work out their own salvations. From Thomas's conflicting images, as much the product of will as of imagination, he tries to generate "that momentary peace which is a poem." Earlier, during his fruitful period (1932–34), he wrote to a friend lamenting the increasing obscurity of his work: "When the words do come, I pick them so thoroughly of their *live* associations that only the *death* in the word remains." And he adds, "I am a freak user of words, not a poet."

The struggle is with words, not rhythms. A fine poem, "Especially When the October Wind," shows him walking out, the wind "punishing" his hair "with frosty fingers." Everything he experiences turns to language. His loquacious heart "talks" and "sheds the syllabic blood and drains her words." He hears the "vowelled beeches," "oaken voices," "water's speeches," "the hour's word" and reads "the meadow's signs." Language displaces the world itself. The wind "punishes the land" too, "with fists of turnips." Poet and landscape are momentarily fused by a conceit of grammar. Both are extensions of language: nature is speech and so is he.

"He is shut in the twisted tower of his own observation," says Nye, "a tower where only words are real and can bleed." Seldom words as specific, denotative meaning, but words as peep-holes through to a world of analogies. More than Sitwell he is addicted to synesthesia. Words suggest, they don't signify. His misreading of Surrealism, which intrigued him, was like Crane's. When the language seems to be coming out under pressure, Nye says, it is a "simulated intensity, a confusion of depth with thickness." The words are forced into one another's company; the lines, too, sometimes seem arbitrarily yoked, assembled out of notebook jottings. The rhythm line by line is often firmly end-stopped.

Beyond rhythmic repetition, there is syntactical repetition, sentence after sentence in closely parallel structures, or stanzas echoing one another. In "Light breaks where no sun shines" the first, third and fifth stanzas begin "Light breaks where no sun shines"; "Dawn breaks behind the eyes"; and "Light breaks on secret lots"; the parallels continue, close enough so that we are required to glance back and forward. The poem becomes a point of stillness. With heavily end-stopped lines and runs, with so much cross-hatching, the eye constructs the poem rather than reading it. Everywhere there is a lurking and rather furtive eros: "We are the dark deniers, let us summon / Death from a summer woman." Death, waste, isolation are contained in opaque language that produces moods, the sense of sense, not sense itself.

The elegiac eroticism of Thomas's early poems is heady, adolescent stuff. The poems are often "about" masturbation; or they appear to be so, the occasion behind a hedge of repeated syntactical constructions, rhythmic repetitions, the intensive vocabulary unsustained by intense rhythm. "And time cast forth my mortal creature / To drift or drown upon the sea" means "I was born"—after five stanzas of lurid gestation—and "I shall die" after one more stanza. Not since Swinburne has such orchestration engulfed sense. Most of the early poems have an interpretable line or couplet that gives access, and once inside things sort of slot into place. He is always building away from relatively simple ideas, exploring a narrow category of experiences. Death—actual, or the death that comes in Elizabethan terms with orgasm—is omnipresent. "The Force that through the Green Fuse," among his most successful poems, is arresting conceptually: poet and flower, poet and nature, have a parallel vitality. Both are confronted by the fact of death. The poem glosses Robert Graves's "The Cool Web." The poet struggles weakly with the "cool web of language" that snares him. Were he indeed intent upon transcending it, he would disrupt syntax, expel the rigid phrasal parallelisms, in favor of a thoroughgoing surrealism (his surrealism is always of the surface); or he would strive for minute accuracy, to deliver himself into an actual world. In "From Love's First Fever to Her Plague" language is a province, a bandage, perhaps a prefigurative burial, and a preparation for death's "moonless acre," my favorite bit of magic in Thomas.

In "Light Breaks Where No Sun Shines" Thomas moves into a different gear. The rhythm becomes varied, supple, answering the weirdness of the diction: erotic, tentative, the lines no longer seem to be end-stopped. The poem flows from line to line, reaches a climax, and recedes. Rhythm is sufficiently varied so that syntactical repetitions come with the emphasis of refrain, not reiteration. Not rhetorical "fibs of vision."

The repetitive, rhetorical style serves him well in "social statements." "The Hand That Signed the Paper" has a ruminative authority. "Death Shall Have No Dominion" recalls Donne's "Death, be not proud," rigid as a dressmaker's, or shroud maker's, dummy. The poet *displays* his language. The elegies, including "After the Funeral," "Ceremony After a Fire Raid" and "Refusal to Mourn the Death, by Fire, of a Child in London" outdo Yeats in their simplifications and emblematizing. The actual human subject is swept, virtually immaterial, into Thomas's death-centered cosmos.

> Never until the mankind making
> Bird beast and flower
> Fathering and all humbling darkness
> Tells with silence the last light breaking
> And the still hour
> Is come of the sea tumbling in harness
>
> And I must enter again the round
> Zion of the water bead
> And the synagogue of the ear of corn
> Shall I let pray the shadow of a sound
> Or sow my salt seed
> In the least valley of sackcloth to mourn
>
> The majesty and burning of the child's death.

A long first sentence that inflates and inflates to the awful image—not an image but a deliberate gesture.

> Deep with the first dead lies London's daughter,
> Robed in the long friends,
> The grains beyond age, the dark veins of her mother,
> Secret by the unmourning water
> Of the riding Thames.
> After the first death, there is no other.

Wonderful, and like "Fern Hill," a fullness masking an emptiness. Not that we doubt the sincerity of Thomas's feelings: we doubt the sincerity and the probity of the poem, as we doubt poems that borrow their rhetoric from the Holocaust. It is impossible not to love "Fern Hill," but hard not to distrust the saccharine sadness that it generates. Thomas weaves spells. He engages language, rather than experience. When the spell releases us, nothing is clarified. There is a kind of authority to the word magic of the early poems; in the famous and popular late poems, the magic is all show. If they have a secret, it is the one we all share, partly erotic, partly elegiac. The later poems arise out of personality.

There are exceptions. "Poem in October," with its brilliant details, works like "Refusal to Mourn" and "Do Not Go Gentle" against the tragic grain. In "A Winter's Tale" Thomas's rhythmic achievement is at its most subtle. The later work is rhetoric of a high order.

A contemporary of Thomas's was the precocious young Surrealist David Gascoyne, who published his first book at the age of sixteen and at the age of nineteen, in 1935, wrote *A Short History of Surrealism*, one of the clearest studies of the movement. His early poems have become difficult. Michael Roberts found the work different in kind from that of the other English Surrealists, such as Hugh Sykes Davies and Philip O'Connor. Gascoyne wrote not exercises but necessary statements, generating a psychological surrealism (singularly English, rooted in a self even if that self was disrupted and unstable). Surrealism was less a release from the trammels of a tradition than a new and deeper formulation of them. He is a disciple of Lawrence rather than André Breton: an organized chaos, a scored impromptu. Hölderlin's madness is sentimentalized. Religion and politics are fused in poems such as "Ecce Homo," where he invokes "Christ of Revolution and of Poetry"; in his best poem, "De Profundis," with its echo of Wilde and the Roman Catholic liturgy; in "The Vagrant" and "Night Thoughts," which Michael Hamburger described as "the most Baudelairean exploration of an urban inferno written since the war." Interesting as an English Surrealist, his fault for readers today is that he was more English than Surrealist, he did not take the revolution deeply enough into his language, he loved its syntax too much, and he loved the sound of an attributable, own voice, the lyric "I" dressed in a fashionable French costume and, while learning to speak French, never quite becoming French in English.

Instinctively Surrealist in his early work, and more inadvertently surreal in the syntax and imagery of his maturity, is W. S. Graham, a poet who never wanted to earn the French title but wished to be a new voice with new ways of saying, a Scot, or a Celt, or just a poet. William Sydney Graham was born in 1918 in a tenement in Greenock, Scotland, "beside the sugar house quays," as he says—a rundown urban setting, open to the sea. He was clearly of humble, "unlettered" origins. The sea dominates the imagery of his poems, whether calm, in flood or frozen.

He remained a Celt, moving from Scotland, via London, to Cornwall where he found seascapes without urban clutter, just the occasional ruined tin mine with its human echo.

The apocalyptic poets whose focal voice was the Welshman Dylan Thomas's had a Celtic ingredient in their makeup and their verse. George Barker had enough Irish blood in him to make a play of it. There is a "Scots *timbre*" to Graham's voice, and he shares with MacDiarmid, who was for a time his master, a suppleness in tonal change, from raucous to tender, from elegy to anger and back again.

Graham attended Greenock High School, later spending a year at the Workers Educational Association College near Edinburgh. He acquired no further formal education though he became an academic in 1947–48, teaching at New York University. By that time he had published three collections, starting with *Cage Without Grievance* in 1942, issued by that rare patron of poetry David Archer (who also advanced George Barker's career) in Glasgow. In 1949 *The White Threshold*, his first substantial book, appeared.

All of his poems have a *location*, a plot and setting (or a narrative). It is crucial, if we are not to go off into gaseous symbolifications, to determine that location and narrative poem by poem. It becomes easier as the poet moves deeper into his language and understands the actual dynamic of his own verse rather than the admired dynamic of Thomas's. It was with *The Nightfishing* (1955) that he found his feet. This was bad planning in terms of his career: the book appeared the same year as *The Less Deceived* by Philip Larkin. He was sailing, with the remainder of his apocalyptic freight, into the decade of the Movement, and there was no place for him in it. He suffered years of hardship and neglect. In the late 1960s I wrote to his publishers and discovered that Graham was "dead." It transpired that he was not dead. He was resurrected and rehabilitated by Penguin, in the trilogies edited by Nikos Stangos in the 1970s. Faber acknowledged that he was indeed alive: it was time for his breakthrough. Which came and went. He did not lend himself naturally to self-promotion; indeed, he found it acutely difficult and repulsive. Thus he has yet to break through in a decisive way.

I was especially taken with his poem "The Thermal Stair," an elegy for his friend the painter Peter Lanyon, who died in a gliding accident in Cornwall. I wrote and asked the poet for the manuscript. He reinvented it, producing an elaborately "edited" draft, which I bought. Many of his poems were published in *P N Review*, in particular the "Quantz" sequence. Faber and Faber published *Malcolm Mooney's Land* in 1970, *Implements in Their Places* in 1977 and, posthumously (Graham died in 1986), *Aimed at Nobody*, doubtful and rejected drafts and a few substantial poems (1993).

For Graham, the first form of poetry criticism was *reading a poem aloud*. It proved whether a reader understood the basic syntax, character and plot of the poem. The words enter another mouth and are shaped and emitted by other lips with or without understanding. If you passed the reading test you were part of the tetchy and stimulating family.

Malcolm Mooney's Land includes many poems that seem troubled by the discontinuity of the "I," year by year, day by day, looking back at earlier poems and unable to make contact with them. In the end it is less the fluid identity that obsesses him than time, the time within which we all swim, and how what we write today stays written from where we wrote it, so that tomorrow or ten years later we come upon it and it speaks from where we were with all that we were and are no more. This disturbs him: he resents the "timeless" stability of the art object while the artist remains time-bound. "Dear Pen/Pal in the distance." He writes of and to past selves. Time can be spanned by addressing two "art stabilities" to one another: he seems briefly, symbolically, to defeat it.

His other themes include, in his words, "the lessons in physical phenomena; the mystery and adequacy of the aesthetic experience; the elation of being alive in the language." In *The White Threshold* he comes alive. He experiments with sudden, simple, largely monosyllabic lines. He begins using erratic but effective rhyme and slant rhyme. The movement is toward a balladic, three-stress line.

This revolution in his work takes hold with *The Nightfishing*, a largely autobiographical poem in seven sections, one of the major mid-length poems in the British tradition. The sea is the sea where herring fishing takes place. It is also language. He establishes a continual connection between literal activity and metaphor. The poem moves from uncertainty and instability of medium (sea and language) and voice into action, into physical engagement with the world where the "I" stabilizes. Then the evanescent "I" returns.

> Lie down, my recent madman, hardly
> Drawn into breath than shed to memory,
> For there you'll labour less lonely.
> The rigged ship in its walls of glass
> Still further forms its perfect seas
> Locked in its past transparences.

Graham lived through three phases. In the first he had no sense of audience, *word-drunk*, not sentence- or cadence-drunk; no voices, just the crammed word packages. He developed the sense of a single auditor or a small audience, he discovered the supple value of syntax combined with simple diction. A voice emerged, eccentric, beguiling, which we are willing to follow into areas of obscurity and incomprehension. We are willing because the rhythms are compelling. In the late poems, aware of readership at last, he begins to prattle, becoming mere voice, the whole dynamic that underpinned the miraculous "middle poems" surfacing and becoming hectic and unpersuasive, if amusing.

All his poems presuppose a *dialogue* in which communication is hard, if not impossible: dialogue as two monologues, or as speech answered by silence. Often the partner in dialogue is despised, hated, reviled, insulted.

> I know you well alas
> From where I sit behind
> The Art Barrier of ice.

This is not only a rhetorical pose. It is crucial to his language themes. He is suspended within it. There is almost always a "you." Communication occurs, but never of prose meanings. The poet becomes instructor, lecturer, punisher. Language is his subject and his master. He wants help with it, he wants help against it; but it is the instrument of his revolt. This is not the "poem about poetry" that we get in the lesser Movement poems, but something urgent.

In a letter written in 1975 he interpolated these lines about Nessie Dunsmuir, his devoted wife.

> Now Ness is back, the weather snapping her tail.
> O pray sit down and take a pinch of snuff.
> Take off your coat. I'll hang your faded blue Hat
> Here. Take off your shirt. Take off your cammer
> Band and breeches. Stand for a moment white
> In Nature's bare-buff. Now take off your eyes
> Take off your nose take off your mouth take off
> All great and little members. Remove your head
> And throw it out into the throstle's hedge.

The surrealizing impulse is alive and eloquent at a time when at last he has readers. He chooses the most hermetic terms to address, not the audience but the friend receiving the letter. In 1972 he writes, again in a letter:

> Father Mother I am falling
> Into Crete at night with words
> Trailing like bubbles above me from
> My tons of body. Why have you let
> Out of you both to land here
> On this enormous, foreign word?

A wonderful poet, his best poems are elegies—to Lanyon, to the painter Roger Hilton and other artist friends—and the monologues, "Johann Joachim Quantz's Five Lessons" (his masterpiece) and "To My Wife at Midnight," which celebrates the love of older people bound together by habit, pets and love but divided by argument. Were he a popular poet, his "Lake Isle of Innisfree" would be the poem "Imagine a Forest," playful and deadly earnest, in which he touches the rawest nerve of Romanticism with tact and subtlety. He is a largely benign monster, strictly inimitable, a little obscure, an acquired taste like all the poets who passed through the Apocalypse and were distracted by Dylan Thomas.

Burns Singer was drawn not by Thomas but by MacDiarmid, and then by Graham, who became his master and friend and with whom he stayed in Cornwall, exchanged letters and ideas, until Singer died at the age of thirty-six in 1964.

> Like the two limbs of a cross
> Your words, my answers lie
> Together in the place
> Where all our meanings die.

He achieved a limited popularity in his lifetime and since his death has been almost entirely eclipsed. In 1970 a suggestive but incomplete *Collected Poems* appeared. The poet and critic James Keery is preparing a complete edition, and it will be possible properly to evaluate this Scottish poet and assess to what degree he affected, to what degree he was affected by, Graham. A serious advocate, the poet Anne Cluysenaar, has written of "The Gentle Engineer" that Singer's "sense of being part of the universe, not lost in it, allows for a more positive formulation than does [Ted Hughes's] wodwoism."

> It is my own blood nips in every pore
> And I myself the calcified treadmark of
> Process towards me:
> All of a million delicate engines whisper
> Warm now, to go now
> Through dragnets of tunnels forwards as my life.
> I carry that which I am carried by.

It is hard to think of a more affirmative formulation than that. Singer is a scientist while Hughes is a romantic anthropologist.

James Hyman Singer (he later adopted his mother's maiden name as his middle name) was born in New York in 1928. When he was four his ne'er-do-well father and long-suffering mother returned to Scotland.

His background was unsettled; he had no native landscapes. Jewish, Scottish, American, Irish, Polish, he remained an American citizen though he never returned to live in America. After a checkered education, when he was Graham's disciple and spent two years in Europe, he became a marine biologist. He told his professor at Glasgow that he wanted to write poems about animals, but his mother's suicide and his father's poverty drew him back into the lines of duty. He wrote literary essays, scripted documentaries about the sea, wrote a popular book (*Living Silver*) about marine life. He translated poems from the Polish, married the black American psychologist and painter Marie Battle, but "the caterwauling insecurity of my belief in myself" stayed with him. He died, apparently of natural causes, in Plymouth while engaged in research. Much of his work was left unpublished. Only one book of poems, *Still and All* (1957), appeared in his lifetime.

MacDiarmid found Singer obscure, "a rootless cosmopolitan." It is more a case of his intellectual and formal agility and the intensity with which he feels ideas. He is rooted, as much as MacDiarmid, but not in a dialect, rather in a world that science has clarified and made luminously mysterious. He is also fascinated by Wittgenstein, a catalyst to his own poetic processes. Science and the disciplines of philosophy saved him from the easier practice of poets he admired. The title poem of *Still and All* develops an analogy between personal language and personal identity. Language is, too, a place in which to move. It has inherent disciplines but is flexible to a degree. It has laws of growth, like a natural organism. The voice that carries it is also carried *by* it. How well he understands the enjambement:

These words run vertical in their slim green tunnels
Without any turning away. They turn into
The first flower and speak from a silent bell.
But underneath it is always still
Truly awakening, slowly and slowly turning
About a shadow scribbled down by sunlight
And turning about my name. I am in my
Survival's hands. I am my shadow's theme.

"The Transparent Prisoner" is his most sustained poem, exploring not the empowered but those subject to power and constraint. The fifty "Sonnets for a Dying Man" and "Biography of an Idealist" are among the best poems of their time. His is the poetry of process in its purest sense: "For thought is always and only thought: / The thinking's different: thinking's in the blood." Anne Cluysenaar quotes a passage from his uncollected prose: "When a poet presents a series of logical thoughts in a poem, it is not to express the logic of his thoughts and thus to allow the reader to draw their logical corollaries and mnemonics—rather, it is to force the reader through the thinking of these thoughts, since the process of thinking them is an essential part of the experience which he wishes to re-create in the reader. It does not matter therefore if one logical sequence is placed alongside another with which it is logically irreconcilable, provided that both series properly belong to the experience in which they are involved." Such a view connects with Stevens, with O'Hara and Ashbery, with Sisson and Davie. Evoking a poem in terms of a Cornish landscape held by mist and then transformed by sunlight, he says:

> The watered air grew bright with single claws:
> So on the fine web spun from something stronger
> One man can hold, precarious, complete
> His own self's light that never is repeated
> But acts as orrery to all the lights of others:
> And that same web grows finer with its function,
> More beautiful to praise with each drop held
> In that peculiar tension once forever.

Among the poets who emerged alongside Thomas and Graham in the 1940s are several whose vast body of work constitutes, like the substantial volumes of the late Victorian poets, a huge, untamed and increasingly unvisited territory. In *Artorius* John Heath-Stubbs (b. 1918) creates a long narrative poem on an antique model and scale—out of Landor perhaps—that reveals, as does all his work, how inexhaustible and adaptable traditional formal resources can be. In 1941 he urged "the return to the classical tradition of English poetry," a mission in which he has persisted in free and formal verse. He is a substantial elegist.

Full of a much rawer energy is George Barker (1913–91). He began prodigiously in the early 1930s and blundered his way eloquently through various styles and rhetorics. Yeats was beguiled: "a lovely subtle mind"—"lovely" being a singularly inapposite epithet—"a rhythmical invention comparable to Gerard Hopkins"—which shows a limited understanding of the subtleties of Hopkins's verse. Barker was the youngest poet in Yeats's Oxford anthology. In 1937 Barker wrote his Surrealist epic *Calamiterror*, about the rise of fascism. His reputation gathered steam; his *True Confession*, when broadcast on radio, occasioned questions in the House of Commons because of its alleged "obscenity." Unvarnished candor has never been popular with politicians. As the 1950s progressed, and after Dylan Thomas's death, he came to represent what new movements and the Movement were set against. Like Graham he was swept off the stage. Nothing stopped him and the flow of verse continued. A late, long poem, *Anno Domini*, is his masterpiece. Like Yeats, he achieved quite a different sort of clarity in his final work. In one of his last sequences, "Five Poems on the Economics of the Eumenides," eroticism, satire and elegy are combined by his wayward, resourceful genius. The epigraph reads: "That the Eumenides, though superhuman, are not supernatural," and the first section begins:

> Flagellants of those guardians who attend me,
> in spite of your bile and bitterness and your wholly
> inhuman passion for needling those who feed you,
> when will you see that Venus is always the pay day
> of every uncharitable week? Acknowledging the exemplary
> emptiness of your soul the absolute zero of
> your response to the numerology of our need,
> why do you seek to prove that therefore Glastonbury
> Abbey was never rebuilt? When the solicitors come
> with their sweet-smelling secretaries and documents attesting
> that they seek only to serve our purposes, why,
> my dear female christs do you instantly take up an
> eighteen-foot sjambok? Who are you then? Moneta?
> Look down on us from the altitudes of your
> Empedoclean Aetna. Only old slippers remain.

Of all the poets roughly contemporary with Thomas, the one who stands apart as a great (nonacademic) critic, political theorist and uniquely gifted poet is C. H. Sisson. With the writers of his generation he shares what the Movement most distrusted, a changing prosody sanctioned by instinct, irreducible to rule. Some of his poems are in exacting Metaphysical forms, some in a free verse that takes its bearings from Eliot and Pound. He is in their direct line, and at the same time in the line of Donne and Hardy. Donne—and Hardy? The affinities (we cannot speak of connections since Hardy was not influenced by Donne or the Metaphysicals) go beyond formal invention and have to do with elaboration of syntax, the admission of the irrational, the unexpected, which reconfigures experience and language.

Sisson's approach to the writers he admires is to evoke their social and intellectual milieux, sketch in the native landscape and antecedents, the accidents and peculiarities that individuate them early on, and then to consider how they combine and transcend these factors. In an essay on Charles Péguy (1946) he asks, "Is not every sincere life, in a sense, a journey to the first years?" The first years of a life, of a culture, beginnings, break-points and re-beginnings, are all-important. What does art transcend, how does it transcend? This is not to confuse biography with criticism. Criticism follows from it, biography (not of the tittle-tattle sort) clears a ground, clarifies opacities, defines formative prejudices, how consciously they are entertained, what the work makes of them.

Charles Hubert Sisson was born in Bristol in 1914. His father was from Kendal in Westmorland, his mother from Wiltshire. His father became a clockmaker and, later, in Bristol, an optician. It was not a prosperous time for anyone. The landscapes that took hold of the poet were those of the West Country and of Somerset. He remembers in adolescence how he would know a poem was about to happen to him, "and I had not to think about it in case I should spoil it . . . There is probably something in the nature of poetry which makes it necessary to avoid conscious premeditation." It was on this point in particular that Sisson and Donald Davie tended to fall out. Sisson was the one poet of his generation with whom Davie entertained a warm friendship. In all likelihood it was because both men, from different perspectives, knew that Pound was at the heart of the century, and both men said so.

Sisson attended the University of Bristol, then studied in Germany and France when the forces of German militarism were gathering strength. He was much affected by what he foresaw: a francophile, he was intensely anxious for France, and for England. He entered the Civil Service in 1936. The next year he married. He enlisted in 1942 and because of his fluency in French and German was sent for two and a half years to the North West Frontier Province (Bengal). He translated Heine, read Dante and Virgil, and wrote the first of his mature poems, caustic and precise.

> I, whose imperfection
> Is evident and admitted
> Needing further assurance
> Must year-long be pitted
> Against fool and trooper
> Practising my integrity
> In awkward places,
> Walking until I walk easy
> Among uncomprehended faces.

The humility of the lines is exemplary: the faces are uncomprehend*ed*, not uncomprehend*ing*. He is not misunderstood but unable to understand. The poems are an attempt. "My beginnings were altogether without facility, and when I was forced into verse it was through having something not altogether easy to say." The utter difference of India clarified what England meant to him, and what Europe meant. His translation work later in life keeps pace with his poetry, and the radical changes in his poems can be related to his work on Catullus, Virgil's *Eclogue* and *Aeneid*, Lucretius, Dante and others. He takes up a translation task when he needs the freedom to concentrate on rhythm, without having to generate "content." He characterizes translation work as "fishing in other men's waters." "I seem to have undertaken the translations in order to rid the voice of a certain monotony."

In 1945 he resumed work in Whitehall, rising to Under Secretary and equivalent heights in the Ministry of Labour. He was a severe critic of the Civil Service and his essays caused controversy. In *The London Zoo*, his first substantial collection, he wrote this epitaph: "Here lies a civil servant. He was civil / To everyone, and servant to the devil." Yet he is rare among contemporaries in his belief that a writer serves best as a man engaged with the social machine, guarding the integrity of social institutions even as he criticizes and perfects them. He is a Tory in the Johnsonian sense: "One who adheres to the ancient constitution of the state, and the apostolic hierarchy of the Church of England." But God himself is difficult and often absent, especially latterly.

As a man of social engagement, Sisson admires writers like Marvell for his double vocation, and Barnes, and Swift. Their writing matured in a world of actual responsibilities. In 1972 he retired to Langport, Somerset. He had published seven books: two novels, three collections of poetry, a history of poetry in English of the first half of the century, and a classic tome on public administration. In the year of his retirement he published with Faber his savage appraisal of Walter Bagehot. Since his retirement he has become one of the great translators of our time and a poet whose work increasingly seems to mark the end, within English poetry, of high modernism and—at the same time—of the kinds of satire and lyricism that Hardy brought forward into the twentieth century. *In the Trojan Ditch: Collected Poems and Selected Translations* appeared in 1974. Reticently, almost out of sight, Sisson had developed through three generations, entirely along his own lines. That development has continued in his later books. Of William Barnes he says, "The avoidance of literature is indispensable for the man who wants to tell the truth." The "whole tact of the poet" is knowing when "he has a truth to tell." *Literary* emotion is for him always factitious.

His poems can seem Augustan, but his poetic logic is, like Marvell's, a language of association, not analysis (which belongs to prose). The poetry does not anatomize experience: it establishes connections on the other side of reason, communicating to the pulse through its distinctive rhythms. "Reason may convince, but it is rhythm that persuades," he quotes a French critic as saying. "The proof of a poem—any poem—is in its rhythm," he declares, "and that is why critical determination has in the end to await the unarguable perception." Rhythm is authority. In "The Usk," which Davie characterizes as "one of the great poems of our time," rhythm is at its most persuasive.

Lies on my tongue. Get up and bolt the door
For I am coming not to be believed
The messenger of anything I say.
So I am come, stand in the cold tonight
The servant of the grain upon my tongue,
Beware, I am the man, and let me in.

Rhythm integrates diverse material, performs feats of lucid fusion. In one of his best poems, the long "In Insula Avalonia," he taxes rhythm to the utmost, fusing personal, religious and patriotic themes in Arthurian legend (Malory is as present in his verse as Virgil and Dante). He has made the landscapes of Somerset his own much as Barnes and Hardy marked out Dorset. Davie speaks of the interweaving of themes "in a verse which, as it were, goes nowhere and says nothing, which is Shakespearean and at times Eliotic to just the degree that it is Virgilian." As in Sisson's theology, body and soul are one and cannot be understood except together. Donne was of the same mind. The verse defies paraphrase: it *is* the meaning:

Dark wind, dark wind that makes the river black
—Two swans upon it are the serpent's eyes—
Wind through the meadows as you twist your heart.

Twisted are trees, especially this oak
Which stands with all its leaves throughout the year;
There is no Autumn for its golden boughs

But winter always and a lowering sky
That hangs its blanket lower than the earth
Which we are under at this Advent-tide.

Not even ghosts. The banks are desolate
With shallow snow between the matted grass
Home of the dead but there is no one here . . .

When I first read his poems I found them rebarbative. It was not until I read "Metamorphoses," a sequence in unrhymed couplets, that suddenly my ear attuned itself to what he was doing. It was through hearing his verse in all its tonalities that I was able to hear the rhythms of Pound's *Cantos*, and to move from that to hearing Bunting and, from a very different part of the forest, Ashbery and O'Hara. Pound transformed Sisson's hearing, "opening up a new area in consciousness, indicating a point to which you may go from a point you now occupy"; Pound caused "one of those real adjustments of mind which even the most omnivorous reader can expect from only a few writers." Like the poets he opened up for me, his plain and his Virgilian styles are capable of suggesting various contexts in which a single idea exists and acts. Biblical and classical are not separate strands, the one ethical, the other aesthetic. In our culture they express a similar impulse, only one is redeemed, the other not.

The social urgency of Sisson's satire knows that the cause is lost. The material basis of "values," the erosion of traditional and theological views of "self," "person" and "identity," the triumph of the golden calf he will not accept. It is a sham deity, for we *possess* nothing; we cannot even be said to possess memory. We are possessed by existence, and by God; and whether we will or not, by history and our historical institutions which we do well to accept, explore and perfect. We *are* only in relation to them, in all their ramifications.

> What is the person? Is it hope?
> If so there is no I in me.
>   Is it a trope
> Or paraphrase of deity?
>   If so,
> I may be what I do not know.

"The Person" ends:

> There is one God we do not know
> Stretched on Orion for a cross
>   And we below
> In several sorts of lesser loss
>   Are we
> In number not identity.

Our concern with the dynamic surface of reality is such that we lose sight of what Coleridge called the "principles of permanence."

Clearly we are dealing here with a wholly English phenomenon, a man as English as MacDiarmid is Scottish or Austin Clarke is Irish. It is that Englishness that emerges in the satires and in the increasingly autumnal and elegiac note that the later poems strike, the note of "Burrington Combe," which goes back to his first years and beyond them, to the legendary and very English figures, northern and southern, out of which his heritage is made. All through his work there is a love of reversed chronology. The novel *Christopher Homm* is told backward; the first collected poems were placed in reverse order, a poem like "Homo Sapiens Is of No Importance" is a deliberate regression.

Throughout Sisson's work, even in disrupted free verse and irregular blank verse, there is a sense of rhyme. It is a rare effect, heard most clearly in "Metamorphoses," "Virgini Senescens" and the acerbic poems about old age. This feeling of rhyme has much to do with balanced phrasing, rhythmic equivalents suggesting firm closure, and assonances that produce a couplet effect even when we are reading unrhymed tetrameters. It is also the effect of an instinctive, accurate parceling out of content in correct contrast phrase by phase, a parceling that does not disrupt the rhythmic movement of the poems.

It is less in the poems that orchestrate ideas and more in those that harmonize disparate areas and allusions, where wholeness emerges from a juxtaposition of fragments, that his English vision is clearest. Its historical point of reference is the heart of the seventeenth century, when history abruptly defined the institutions that had seemed natural and given, in particular the monarchy. The works in which writers engaged with events, the conflict between Charles I and Cromwell, and the aftermath, are the most agonized and truthful in our literature. Sisson's last major sequence is the "Tristia," the title a tribute to Ovid, ten terse, elegiac epigrams in which he makes unconsoling sense of old age and what an older poet called "the vast shipwreck of my life's esteems." The ninth "Tristia" declares:

> Speech cannot be betrayed, for speech betrays,
> And what we say reveals the men we are.
> But, once come to a land where no-one is,
> We long for conversation, and a voice
> Which answers what we say when we succeed
> In saying for a moment that which is.
> O careless world, which covers what is there
> With what it hopes, or what best cheats and pays,
> But speech with others needs another tongue.
> For *a* to apeak to *b*, and *b* to *a*,
> A stream of commonalty must be found,
> Rippling at times, at times an even flow,
> And yet it turns to Lethe in the end.

Thus the "technique of ignorance" that a poet must cultivate leads, for a moment, to a stream of commonality that runs variously, that "for a moment" manages to say "that which is."

Sisson's modernism has a distinct genealogy. It starts with Hulme and moves through Eliot and Pound, Ford Madox Ford and Wyndham Lewis (about whom he has written brilliantly). It is not a literary tradition so much as a tradition of speech and seeing. Into this modernism he introduces the possibility, without affectation or extreme formal disruption as in David Jones, of a religious dimension. The only comparable English poet in this respect is Donald Davie. Sisson's verse moves into and then away from "liturgy," the decisive fusions and assimilations occurring in the poems he wrote around his fiftieth year. There is a falling away from that wholeness of vision. Having attained it, the gap that grows with the years between it and where the poet is now has proved vertiginous and his poetry of negative emotion and thought is some of the most vigorous of the century.

A beguiling poet now undervalued, though she was extremely popular for a time, is Stevie Smith, born in 1903, and—before her death in 1971—a celebrated performer of her work. Somehow she connected with the age. Asked whose poetry, among her contemporaries', she read, she replied, "Why *nobody*'s but my own." Mock innocence and candor combine in her work.

She was born in Hull. Florence Margaret Smith (for so she was then) recalls a childhood in suburban London, where she was taken at the age of three. The story may be her own:

It was a house of female habitation,
Two ladies fair inhabited the house,
And they were brave. For all though Fear knocked loud
Upon the door, and said he must come in,
They did not let him in.

The fairy tale behind this plot and cadence is "The Three Little Pigs," but these pigs are proof against the wolf. The father went to sea and came home only to get money "from Mrs. S. / Who gave it him at once, she thought she should." In the house were "two feeble babes," the younger being the author, and the "babes' great-aunt, Mrs Martha Hearn Clode." Mother died, great-aunt died, sister went away, leaving the younger babe to look after the mother's sister, "The noble aunt who so long tended us, / Faithful and true her name is. Tranquil. / Also sardonic." The poem ends with an authority that transforms whimsy into something great.

It is a house of female habitation
A house expecting strength as it is strong
A house of aristocratic mould that looks apart

When tears fall; counts despair
Derisory. Yet it has kept us well. For all its faults,
If they are faults, of sternness and reserve,
It is a Being of warmth I think; at heart
A house of mercy.

The patterns of an undemonstrative Edwardian childhood persisted into maturity, enforced by the ethic of duty and by a reserved love and gratitude. Her aunt died and Stevie Smith followed soon after.

She wrote three novels, the most notable being *Novel on Yellow Paper* (1936). Her poems are full of characters that have strayed in from larger narratives, or out of her own life. Her greatest anger is reserved for God, with whom she continually engages in one-way conversation. Her approach is direct, like a woman attacking a greengrocer for selling bad cabbages. She does not sidestep paradoxes. "How Do You See?" in her last collection is closely argued, a questioning of the mysteries she was approaching. It reveals that, naïve as she sometimes seems, she was well acquainted with academic theology. "Mother, Among the Dustbins" comments directly on a passage from St. Teresa of Avila. Hers is a learned mystification, no less serious for being expressed with wit and in disparate tones of voice. In the end she accepts a kind of anarchic Christianity, upholding the ethical distinctions but dispensing with the cruelty of the story and the dogma. She would aim to be good without enchantment (but instead she devises alternative enchantments).

Her verse is haunted by tributary rhythms which she incorporates into her various characters and voices. There is a formal residue in rhyme and runs of meter, but her anarchic approach will not allow her to follow a form through. There are fairy tales and actual stories seen from fairy-tale perspectives, and echoes of Poe, the Coleridge of "Christabel," "Kubla Khan" and "The Rime of the Ancient Mariner," Longfellow, the Tennyson of the *Idylls* and "The Lady of Shalott," Blake, Cowper, the hymn writers and many others sound. So do popular tunes like "Greensleeves," which provides the backing for a poem. It is a world of troubled innocence. Mother Goose, Alice, and also Struwelpeter. The way in which popular and deliberate echoes play through the poetry is unique.

Given the preponderance of Victorian and Edwardian models, a diction ruefully littered with "Oh" and "Alas," the painful rhymes, the doggerel, how does she evade banality? Not through irony but through a wit and tone that wrest sense from cliché and near nonsense. Her humor revives an outworn language. She makes a patchwork quilt of old rags of verse. It is not exactly new but it is bright, wise and silly.

Mr Over is dead
He died fighting and true
And on his tombstone they wrote
Over to You.

Beside this, the innocent artistry with which she speaks of fear, the obsessive fear of death, of other people:

Into the dark night
Resignedly I go,
I am not so afraid of the dark night
As the friends I do not know,
I do not fear the night above
As I fear the friends below.

Mother Goose gave poems to Theodore Roethke (1908–1983), too, but the lost innocence of Roethke's poetry is touched with tragedy. That tragedy is in part the failure of his later work, a failure from which many of the poets who learned from him also suffered. The compulsion to be seen to develop, the compulsion to generate a mythology or a coherent system, was strong in a generation dominated by figures as authoritative as Yeats, Eliot, Pound and Williams. One could either rebel, as Auden did in a sense; or one could achieve originality. The third course was to try to stow away in another poet's ship. This is what Roethke did, without being entirely aware of the extent of his dependence. "I take this cadence from a man named Yeats." And he did. His elegy begins, "I heard a dying man / Say to his gathered kin . . ." and the second stanza reads:

"What's done is yet to come;
The flesh deserts the bone,
But a kiss widens the rose;
I know, as the dying know,
Eternity is now."

He also walked in the footprints of Hopkins and Dylan Thomas. Earlier he took a leaf from Auden's book, and Louise Bogan's, and Stanley Kunitz's. This is not so much a matter of enabling influence as of partial ventriloquism. His larger themes can come too close to Wordsworth's, though American critics see Emerson there. Like many of his contemporaries he endured mental illness and was hospitalized several times. For him these were spiritual traumas that put him in the class of Smart and Blake. Whitman delivered him at last to another kind of derivativeness, and his free verse in his last book takes new risks. He was fifty-five when he died suddenly of a heart attack. His work in each of its phases is accessible and full-voiced, and it is hardly surprising that he had an impact on poets as different as Ted Hughes and Sylvia Plath, James Dickey and Seamus Heaney. He is an attractive shortcut to a dozen different destinations.

"To go forward (as a spiritual man)," he wrote in 1948, "it is necessary first to go back." His return is not like Sisson's, to identify the things of which he is made, but to find things lost, things overlooked. His is a romantic temperament that values the "I" more highly and credits it with more given identity than a classical poet would. The styles that follow from the "I" will rhapsodize when they find a useful fragment, a small epiphany. "Silence of water above a sunken tree." It is in his book *The Lost Son and Other Poems* (1948) that he is most himself and comes closest to his personal source. The "greenhouse poems" are about experiences far enough back in time, yet powerful enough in memory, to enable him to be "objective." The relatively open forms he adopts make it possible for poem to intersect with poem, giving a firm semantic coherence. The sequence continued in later books, and the "personal source," muddied when he tried (as he concedes that he has done) to compete with Yeats and Eliot, remains his best Muse.

> In a dark time, the eye begins to see,
> I meet my shadow in the deepening shade;
> I hear my echo in the echoing wood—
> A lord of nature weeping to a tree.

The trick was to set out the experience without emotional or interpretative language, to let the images and events be, and mean by being. It was a way of building back the past with immediacy and raptness, a way of avoiding self-pity and distorting rhetoric. To speak a whole self: Is this a form of narcissism or a psychological quest? The unresolved tensions when breakdown threatens or he imagines his own demise display integrity of spirit. Narcissism would be self-regarding, and though he had at times a high estimation of his poetic skills he was humanly uncertain and unsteady: he could not have held his own gaze long in the legendary pool. He does not confront himself; he gradually puts pieces together. He gets inside. "Beautiful my desire, and the place of my desire." But the "I" that feels that desire is not always worthy of it.

His promising beginning—Auden and Winters both praised his first book—stoked his hope and ambition. Indeed that early success was a kind of poison, because Roethke wanted to succeed not in his own terms only; he wanted to be recognized as successful. As a teacher he was undeniably successful, according to the poets who studied with him and those who studied his poems. In 1947, after teaching in various universities, he took a post at the University of Washington, where he remained until his sudden death.

In "My Papa's Waltz" he writes,

> You beat time on my head
> with a palm caked hard by dirt,
> Then waltzed me off to bed
> Still clinging to your shirt.

Experiences become vital again, so much so that they reforge a link between his past and his present and, in their potent typicality, include the experience of others, making a kind of archetypal "nature," resonant without rhetoric. This strategy goes far deeper than the "deep image" which some of his contemporaries and successors sought, abandoning traditional forms and the contingent world in favor of the seductions of the unconscious and of dream. Roethke writes: "One tulip on top, / One swaggering head / Over the dying, the newly dead." The pace is perfect, the flowers and their emblematic value equally real.

> The sun glittered on a small rapids.
> Some morning thing came, beating its wings.
> The great elm filled with birds.

The birds bring into a day newly illuminated a restless freedom. His dependence on other poets for structure, mythology and actual style shakes our trust in the poet; but no one can deny the original power of the poems that seek to make him whole.

He naturally could not hear how some of his poems derived: the language of Yeats, Eliot or Thomas was so much a part of him, of his natural hearing, he knew their work so well, that it must have seemed his. Young poets have this problem: they are made of what they read to begin with. It is when a poet reaches the age of forty or fifty and is still following other writers' leads that we sense a problem. In Roethke's case the problem may have been psychological rather than literary. Yet he is not alone: Crabbe in his later years imitated Wordsworth, who earlier had learned from Crabbe. Heaney suddenly, in his mid-forties, begins to sound like Lowell—for a time. Roethke attacked his critics in the essay "How to Write like Somebody Else." His individual voice never vanishes completely, and the loose-limbed movement he learned at last from Whitman, with a long free line, gave him in *The Far Field*, published posthumously in 1964, what might have been a new beginning but was in fact an authoritative end. Yet it is less from these poems than the earlier ones that other poets have taken their bearings.

I would unlearn the lingo of exasperation, all the distortions of
    malice and hatred;
I would believe my pain: and the eye quiet on the growing rose;
I would delight in my hands, the branch singing, altering the
    excessive bird;
I long for the imperishable quiet at the heart of form . . .

One influence Roethke did concede: the prose writings of Thomas
Traherne, as though his greenhouse and Traherne's garden occupied the
same spiritual space. A confusion Roethke never resolved was spiritual:
Did he discriminate between psychological breakdown and spiritual
crisis? Between himself as a child of Prussian antecedents and Adam
in the Garden, without antecedent? He is not the first poet to diffract
the troubles of autobiography through spiritual rhetoric. Poetry is not
spilled religion, nor is it religion spilled over autobiography. The mod-
ern writer who achieves something like a spiritual dimension is, like
Eliot, Jones, Davie, Sisson, Jennings, Hill, a writer who understands the
discipline of *self*-effacement, and the poetry of such a writer will often
explore the difficulty and failure of that discipline. It was always so, with
Traherne's contemporary Henry Vaughan, with Herbert, with Smart
and Cowper. Ah, Roethke might reply, but not with Blake. Exactly: He
may be the source of the problem. "I long for the imperishable quiet at
the heart of form" is a momentary spiritual perception, but the poem
does not stop long enough at that longing or take on board the weight
of the word "imperishable," which sets imagination outside time and its
material world.

A troubled poet of the spiritual—it would be limiting to call him a
religious poet—born in the same generation as Dylan Thomas and the
Apocalyptics—as Sisson and Smith, with their different forms of belief
and styles of address—is R. S. Thomas. Dylan put modern Welsh
poetry on the map, making stereotypes in *Under Milk Wood* that the
Welsh have to live down, and reaching an enormous audience with his
seductive rhetoric. R. S. is an antidote to that kind of Wales and that
kind of poetry. His readership has grown slowly because he has not
courted it. He has pursued a double vocation, as poet and priest: the
humility of his poems, as much as the exasperated anger that at times
sounds like hubris, are aspects of an integrity of purpose. He inhabits
the "moonless acre" that Dylan evoked. Joy is a rare commodity in the
world of his verse.

    One thing I have asked
Of the disposer of the issues

Of life: that truth should defer
To beauty. It was not granted.

Duty and faith clip the wings of desire, curb the tongue when it wishes
to sing or lament. Poetry for him, as for Davie, is considered speech, and
though he has been a prolific poet, his best poems seem to have been
wrested from a reluctant language.

Ronald Stuart Thomas was born in Cardiff and raised in Holyhead
of Welsh parents who were not Welsh speakers. Studying classics at the
University College of North Wales in Bangor, he began to learn Welsh,
pursuing it among his other studies as he prepared for ministry in the
Church of Wales at St. Michael's College, Llandaff. He was ordained in
1936. He makes important play of his Welshness, earning, as he puts it,
the hyphen in Anglo-Welsh. As his writing has developed so has his
sense of a nation, its culture and its precarious political and spiritual
situation. He has written important prose in a complex and untranslat-
able Welsh, but his verse has been in his mother tongue.

His first collection published in England, *Song at the Year's Turning*
(1956), incorporated two earlier collections, some new poems and a
radio play, *The Minister*. John Betjeman in his introduction reassured
readers: "R. S. Thomas is not at all literary." He took poetic form for
granted in his early work. Poetic and prosodic theories were of no inter-
est to him. The poems are written with assurance, but throughout there
are dozens of limp and off-the-peg phrases. In his later work he ques-
tions his language and achieves an entirely different quality of writing,
effectively a different kind. His earlier poems deal with his parishes in
rural Wales, his relations with his flock, with the landscape and with his
God. He was described as a "Christian realist," which fails to take into
account the poems based on Welsh legend, the personal lyrics, and the
later political and prophetic pieces. But much of his work, until his
retirement in 1972, was pastoral in both senses.

Collections appeared regularly. Readers accustomed to his relatively
formal and conventional poems began to experience misgivings. Things
were changing, in *Not That he Brought Flowers* (1968) and then most
markedly in *H'm* (1972). Free verse, strange line endings, new subject
matter, doubts of a more profound nature than had been expressed
before surfaced; doubt and formal change went hand in hand. The
received forms, the habitual language, could not cope with it. In *Poetry
for Supper* (1958) he had written:

Verse should be as natural
As the small tuber that feeds on muck

And grows slowly from obtuse soil
To the white flower of immortal beauty.

But verse ceased to be so natural, the soil was obtuse and the spirit grew impatient with it. The poet-clergyman of the early poems gives way to a man who writes now as a clergyman, and now as a poet: different voices.

The power of the early poems is in the fusion of the two roles, with the paradoxes it entails. They rapidly evoke background, then dwell on a particular image or incident, and a meaning or moral is released. With rustic parishioners his response veers between helpless impatience with their unthinking stolidity and passivity, and a grudging admiration for their simple, elemental lives. Iago Prytherch is a presence in his landscape, "Just an ordinary man of the bald Welsh hills, / Who pens a few sheep in a gap of cloud." We are near Wordsworth's "Michael" in such verse. When Thomas writes "There is something frightening in the vacancy of his mind," we understand: there is something equally frightening in the visionary fullness of the poet's mind, drawn to its rugged opposite.

"The natural" he defines as the unreflective, unclean, habit-governed servant of the land and of the years. The body itself is a "lean acre of ground that the years master." If this is nature, then cleanliness, reflection and indeed intelligence are not natural; and their attraction to Prytherch, as a moth is drawn to a naked flame, is the paradoxical essence of vocation. He tries to step away and in "A Priest to His People" despairs of the unreceptive and here *un*natural peasants.

For this I leave you
Alone in your harsh acres, herding pennies
Into a sock to serve you for a pillow
Through the long night that waits upon your span.

We do not find consistent vocabulary or perspective in Thomas: he is with his flock and then against it; he believes and then he doubts. He is a poet of feelings, whose feelings day by day issue in poems of thought: indignation, awe, sympathy (not empathy), love of beauty—all find the same rhythms, imagery and vocabulary. He often bids farewell to the peasants and their poor lives, but he returns directly. Each poem enacts. What is affecting and memorable is choice of metaphor—those pennies, for instance—for the poems are not innovative in form, rhythm or diction.

Increasingly, he comes to see morality in terms of political responsibility. Moral responsibility flows from faith and a love of the beautiful, a desire to find the same order and beauty in man. When he fails, a humane misanthropy comes into play, a rejection of the imperfectible. Or he turns to Welsh history to find, in the heroisms of the past, some elucidation of the inert present. In "Welsh History" he is forced to conclude:

> We were a people bred on legends,
> Warming our hands at the red past.
>
> We were a people, and are so yet.
> When we have finished quarrelling for crumbs
> Under the table, or gnawing the bones
> Of a dead culture, we will arise
> Armed, but not in the old way.

A prophecy for the collective: but this history has at best a muted issue in the present. It inspires vivid images—"the woman with the hair / That was the raven's and the rook's despair"—but they are elegiac.

> There is no present in Wales,
> And no future;
> There is only the past
> Brittle with relics . . .

and it is not enough. His exasperations are bitter and passionate. The future means depopulation. Technological improvements to farming reduce the rural community and erase the old ways. "The cold brain of the machine" develops its cruel, reductive logic. It even destroys Prytherch. In *Tares* (1964) he concludes:

> It is too late to start
> For destinations not of the heart
> I must stay here with my hurt.

He is at heart "on the old side of life." He finally becomes as one with Prytherch and speaks, if not for him, at least with Prytherch's soil and the graves of his people under his feet. Thomas registers his Welshness; from book to book he becomes more didactic. First he witnesses, then he rails and prophesies.

Though he is not experimental until his later work, he is inventive: many poems are a single unfolding sentence, not subtle in syntax but inevitable. He will rhyme three-line stanzas a-a-a b-b-b, admitting an awkwardness of which he makes skillful—Hardyesque—use. There are numerous fourteen-line poems, which first follow the dynamic of the sonnet and then play subtle variations on it. As he begins to release himself from meter and rhyme, cautiously and courageously effecting a change to a hit-or-miss art that leaves many of his readers behind (the change begins decisively with *H'm*), he admits, in place of the spirit of Yeats which has assisted him, the spirit of Hughes. He rails against God, he travels, his scope widens. Wales becomes not so much his subject as his pulpit; or he leaves it behind and tests his own emotional and libidinal nature. Has he read Pound? In "Pavane" he writes:

> Convergences
> Of the spirit! What
> Century, love? I,
> Too; you remember—
> Brescia? The sunlight reminds
> Of the brocade. I dined
> Long. And now the music
> Of darkness in your eyes
> Sounds. But Brescia,
> And the spreading foliage
> Of smoke! With Yeats' birds
> Grown hoarse . . .

Here is intimacy, a poetry overheard and belonging to a love that is more than pastoral, a poetry that addresses a woman, and Yeats (or God) as a master in whose service "I / Do not wish, I do not wish / To continue."

John Wain held Thomas up as an example of how a poet who abandons form damages himself. But Wain was wrong, and Davie points out why. What Thomas was painfully learning to use in a verse that, though still pentameter based, does attain remarkable freedom, is the enjambement as a rhythmic principle, not an arbitrary break. And even when end words don't rhyme, they fall visually and aurally into relationships that, like rhyme, produce a separate rhythm of sense. At first his new prosody depended entirely on line ending; as time has passed and the poet has become confident in the form, making it his own, he has broken ground newer and more fertile for other Welsh poets than the rhythmic blur and shimmer of Dylan Thomas.

The Other War

KEITH DOUGLAS, F. T. PRINCE, A. D. HOPE,
RANDALL JARRELL, NORMAN MACCAIG, EDWIN MORGAN

Keith Douglas is younger than the Apocalyptics. Had he lived longer, he would have altered our sense of their generation. He is an older *type* of poet, a man whose love of country and intelligent hunger for experience impelled him to enlist when the Second World War began, to fight, and to try to make sense of history from within its turbulence. Dylan Thomas, Barker, Graham and others who stayed away had reason to do so. Douglas had reason to go. Like the major British poets of the First World War, his art was tried and tempered by the experience, and then cruelly curtailed.

The poets of the Second World War are overshadowed by the Apocalyptics. They died incomplete. No Benjamin Britten set their words— Britten in the *War Requiem* used writers of the First World War. But they are substantial, comparable in authenticity to the best of the First World War poets. Sidney Keyes is only partly formed, Alun Lewis wonderful in patches, Donald Davie, Alan Ross and Roy Fuller had wars that were slow-moving and generally remote from action, and besides, they wrote most of their work after the war. War poets of this war are, like those of the First, those who died.

> So in conjecture stands
> my starlit body; the mind
> mobile as a fox sneaks round
> the sleepers waiting for their wounds.

When Douglas was killed in action in 1944, he was twenty-four, a year younger than Owen at his death. His poems have not dated: they share a quality with the work of Edward Thomas and, to a larger extent, Isaac Rosenberg. This has to do with the spoken tone of his verse, the non-programmatic nature of his vision, and his individual attitude to form, which he never uses prescriptively. Douglas, though young, had a wide range of interests and of nonmilitary experience. War and soldiering attracted him from childhood, but so did music, dance and literature. His earliest poems explore themes of war and conflict, but always in a wider context.

Keith Castellain Douglas was born in Tunbridge Wells in 1920, the only child of an English father and a mother of French extraction. When he was eight, his father sloped off, and Douglas never saw him again. His childhood was often solitary; he spent time drawing, beginning at the age of two to cover scraps of paper, floors, walls, and any flat surface with his illustrations. One of his favorite childhood books was *The History of the Boer War*.

The chief ingredients in his character were a sense of "the manly" and a love of creative activity. There was unusual variety in his activities: the rugby player, the Officer Training Corps trainee, the fine poet at the age of fourteen. He attended Christ's Hospital School in Sussex, following in the footsteps of Coleridge and Lamb, where both aspects of his character were encouraged, and went up to Oxford in 1938. His tutor there was the poet Edmund Blunden, another Christ's Hospital veteran, whose poems influenced the young Douglas. At Oxford he edited *Cherwell* and was active in amateur theatricals, usually backstage as designer. In his memoir of Douglas, Blunden describes the undergraduate's essays: "Brevity—but nothing impecunious about it . . . He did not care about novelty when he was feeling his way." The description fits his poems, for only seldom, as in "I Experiment," does Douglas strive for novelty, and even there his ambition is to achieve a greater fluency of style. What is startling is the rightness with which, in the early poems, he deploys a received idiom.

When war was declared, Douglas enlisted. He served first in England, then in North Africa, where he courted action in the Desert Campaign. His prose book, *Alamein to Zem-Zem*, is an outstanding account of his experience. He was injured by a land mine and hospitalized briefly in Palestine, but soon returned to active service. He was killed in the Allied invasion of Normandy.

Small successes came early. At the age of sixteen one of his poems was accepted for *New Verse*. Later his poems appeared in *Poetry London* and in minor anthologies. But he did little to advance his career and may have undervalued his talents. His *Collected Poems* (1951) appeared seven years after his death, but general recognition came only after Ted Hughes edited a *Selected Poems* (1964) and provided an introduction whose measured enthusiasm was well gauged. In 1966 a revised *Collected Poems* appeared, and since then Douglas's audience has grown. Hughes summarizes his achievement: "He has invented a style that seems to be able to deal poetically with whatever it comes up against . . . It is a language for the whole mind, at its most wakeful, and in all situations."

The poets of the 1930s turned to Owen as a suitable model. Douglas, involved in real war, adopted Rosenberg. His subjects are not so much the documentary aspects—the immediate physical horror—of war; these facts take their place in a larger context of concern. Both poets know the choicelessness in their situations, which determines patterns of conduct, regardless of conscience. In Douglas's "How to Kill," a sniper is reduced by the process that involves him, under orders, under coercion.

Impending death, which Douglas sensed as soon as he enlisted, is felt everywhere, but always subtly, never rhetorically. Charles Tomlinson writes, "Death may be the chief factor behind his verse, but it focuses rather than blurs the vision. Sensuous detail grows compact in its presence; life takes on an edge." Douglas's best poems envisage death as a force *within* the object. In "The Prisoner," a love poem invaded not by melancholy but by the apprehension of inherent death, the syntax is undecided until the last moment; and the enjambements add to the drama. Touching the beloved's face, he says:

But alas, Cheng, I cannot tell why,
today I touched a mask stretched on the stone

person of death. There was the urge
to break the bright flesh and emerge
of the ambitious cruel bone.

Syntax suggests that the speaker's urge will be violent; but the violence is in the object itself.

The poem "Leukothea" resembles Rosenberg too, a resemblance we also encounter in Geoffrey Hill's early work. "So all these years I have lived securely," Douglas writes of the fantasy of unperishing beauty. But the poem is decimated by the dream: "Last night I dreamed and found my trust betrayed / only the little bones and the great bones disarrayed." The same element of Rosenberg is felt in "The Creator." In "Desert Flowers" he addresses Rosenberg directly.

Unlike the other war poets, Douglas does not exploit the elegiac mode. He accommodates subject matter on its own terms, not blurring it by sentiment or forcing extreme experience into an alien framework or tempering it with a poetic predisposition. A violent experience in the foreground is placed in a time context, where it occurs but is limited as experience *by* its context. There is no facile nihilism; love and beauty are not idealized out of the context of relationship. An aspect of the balanced quality of the poems (so unlike Blunden's balance) is that Douglas identifies himself with all his characters and themes, with the poets of the First World War, with the Jews, with the European predicament, with enemies and comrades. His poetry contains, without resolving, the paradoxes of commitment. A polemical letter to J. C. Hall, written in 1943, declares: "My rhythms . . . are chosen to enable the poems to be read as significant speech: I see no reason to be either musical or sonorous about things at present . . . I suppose I reflect the cynicism and the careful absence of expectation (it is not quite the same as apathy) with which I view the world." The attitude is passive only to a degree; for in Douglas, the state of mind he describes is one of intense critical receptivity, too. "To be sentimental and emotional now is dangerous to oneself and others." An attitude of distrust, of no expectation of a better world, yet a commitment to work for one, to work without hope ("it doesn't mean working hopelessly") is the closest he comes to a program. "The soldiers have not found anything new to say. Their experience they will not forget easily and it seems to me that the whole body of English war poetry of this war, civil and military, will be created after the war is over." He seems to foresee Randall Jarrell, Edwin Morgan, Ted Hughes, Sylvia Plath, Geoffrey Hill . . .

He dismissed his early poems as "long metrical similes and galleries of images." The description is hardly fair. "Mummers," written when he was fourteen, shows a remarkable sense, in the use of "light," of the completed or circular image as practiced by Keats and Clare, and—if not with much authority—a reliance on difficult forms, two-syllable rhymes and a strong irregular rhythm. Even so early, the line endings are well turned. The image of conflict is already present. Another early poem, "Famous Men," introduces underwater images and the image of bones which the later poems develop. In "Caravan" we first encounter his desert. There is exoticism even at the outset, an unwillingness to be confined to the given English landscape. At the age of fifteen he wrote ".303," about guns and soldiers. Though the poem relies on rhetorical effects, the last two lines foreshadow "How to Kill":

Through a machine-gun's sights
I saw men curse, weep, cough, sprawl in their entrails;
You did not know the gardener in the vales,
    Only efficiency delights you.

The early achievement was considerable. His writing underwent no radical change at Oxford, though it developed sureness and variety of tone. "Forgotten the Red Leaves" catalogues things forgotten, with an echo of Hart Crane's "I can remember much forgetfulness." It would be hard to find another poet who, at the age of eighteen, could write with such unemphatic originality:

> These and the hazy tropic where I lived
> In tall seas where the bright fish go like footmen
> Down the blue corridors about their business,
> The jewelled skulls are down there.

Too many adjectives? Perhaps. But the poem develops that underwater geography where "The Marvel" and later poems are enacted. Several fine lyrics followed in the next year, and "Invaders," a poem that seems to owe an obscure debt to MacNeice (as does the later "Villanelle of Sunlight"), though the idiom is Douglas's own.

> Intelligences like black birds
> come on their dire wings from Europe. Sorrows
> fall like the rooks' clatter on house and garden.
> And who will drive them back before we harden?
> You will find, after a few tomorrows
> like this, nothing will matter but the black birds.

His black birds in this poem (written before he began active service) foreshadow the *bête noire* of the later work. He intended his first collection to be entitled *Bête Noire*, the "beast on my back," about which he wrote an unfinished poem in jazz rhythm. It was an obsessive presence he could not identify, like Edward Thomas's "The Other." The Oxford poems are about music, costume, dance, formal relationships, deceit on a literal level, enactment on a creative level, truth through disguise. He is the watcher, "in the wings" of the stage at Oxford, later "in the wings of Europe." The drama finds a wider sphere.

In the Oxford poems, punctuation and syntax, often unresolved, become ambiguous. Punctuation is used—as in "Farewell Poem"—more as a pause notation than a formal system. He retreats from conventional literary language to a clear speaking voice. His rhythms are original in the way they advance speaking and are not betrayed into singing cadences. In the best poems he seldom generalizes. The power is in particulars. In the original version of "Cairo Jag," a poem written in Egypt, he drew out the moral effectively. But in revision he cut the poem short, so that it resolved as unexplained experience. Five canceled lines describe his way of seeing. War—as in Blunden's poems—changes everything:

You do not gradually appreciate such qualities
but your mind will extend new hands. In a moment
will fall down like St Paul in a blinding light
the soul suffers a miraculous change
you become a true inheritor of this altered planet.

Though the poems written during and after service in the Western
Desert are less polished, they suggest what might have come. Variety of
subject matter and the intensity of the poet's experience made him move
further away from literary models, though the influence of "Report on
Experience" and others of Blunden's poems is felt in the organization of
poems such as "Negative Information." The world of appearances and a
real world, the betrayal inherent in experience, are expressed:

the girls who met us at one place
were not whores, but women old and young at once
whom accidents had turned to pretty stones,
to images slight with deceptive grace.

The living perceive their own and one another's ghosts, hideous inher-
ent presences. He comes to recognize not only the presence of death in
living things, but the identity of the living and the dead. In "The Sea
Bird" the terrible conclusion comes in a rare generalization: "All our
successes and failures are similar."

The love poems of this period—"I Listen to the Desert Wind," "The
Knife," "Song" and others—are by turns erotic and chilling. The influ-
ence of Rimbaud, three of whose sonnets Douglas translated, can be felt
in "Christodoulos," "Egypt" and others of the desert poems. In "Egypt"
there is a compelling dissonance, a seeming marriage between themes
from Blunden and Rimbaud. The beggar women—beggar girls, in
fact—are evoked:

And in fifteen years of living
found nothing different from death
but the difference of moving
and the nuisance of breath.

Tragic vision informs a fatalistic poem, "Behaviour of Fish in an Egyp-
tian Tea Garden." An attractive woman is like a white stone at the bot-
tom of a pool, drawing the fish down, but destined, herself, to be a
chattel.

In "Cairo Jag" the vision of two coexisting worlds, apparently dis-
similar but profoundly similar beneath appearances, broadens out fur-

ther. The sour, rank city with its violent but resolving pleasures is set beside the landscape of war: "But by a day's travelling you reach a new world / The vegetation is of iron." The world is new only in that it is recent. It expresses aspects of the same humanity as the city. It too has its resolving experiences. In "Dead Men" the "sanitary earth" cleans and neutralizes the rotting dead. The dogs dig them up, and "All that is good of them, the dog consumes." The pointedly materialistic use of "good" intensifies the theme. The poem ends, "The prudent mind resolves / on the lover's or the dog's attitude forever." Douglas is not prudent. He perceives a possible choice, but cannot make it. It is characteristic that his irony is positive, serving to expand, not to limit, the themes. It is an aspect of his caution—he is not willing to overstate, but his irony, rather than reducing the theme, leaves it open.

"Vergissmeinicht" is his set piece about war, with "How to Kill," undoubtedly the most searing of poems. Neutrality of tone makes it a more potent indictment of war than a journalistic or rhetorical effort could be. Child's play becomes sniper's play. "How easy it is to make a ghost," Douglas writes, as though killing were playfully creative. The sangfroid of "Aristocrats," too, and of the early "satire," "Russians," convinces us that here the poetry is in the *pitilessness*, accurate and chilling.

To value Douglas properly we must remind ourselves of the poets he chose to name. He revalues poetry, giving weight to writers who found new language, new forms for an experience that was in some senses unprecedented, and who gave themselves not to patriotism or pacifism but to direct witness, in which English poetry is poor. Edward Thomas, Ivor Gurney (whose work is still being "excavated" in the recesses of Gloucestershire), and more particularly Isaac Rosenberg are poets by whom we should measure him. Rosenberg's language belongs to the moment of experience: Rosenberg seldom stands at a distance or draws a moral; poems sit uneasily in a present tense that will not resolve its immediacy or release us in a concluding cadence. He won't trust poetic convention to let him, or the reader, off that hook. He does not make us weep as Owen does, or stir anger as Sassoon can do. He brings individual human situations up close, he *exposes* us by evoking his own exposure as calmly as dawn will allow. This is what Douglas does, too, different though his poems sound. Hughes speaks of the "air of improvisation" as "a vital part" of Douglas's "purity." The only serving poet comparable in magnitude to Douglas is Sorley Maclean, who fought in the Western Desert and survived, but wrote in Gaelic.

The South African poet Frank Templeton Prince survived as well. Born in 1912, he was educated in his native country and then at Oxford and Princeton. He served during the war in Army Intelligence at Bletchley Park and then in the Middle East, later becoming professor of

English at Southampton (1957–74). Subsequently he has taught in Jamaica and the United States. As a subtle scholar-critic of Milton (*The Italian Element in Milton's Verse*, 1954) and other major English—and latterly French—writers, he is unusually successful, aware of how much can be wrung from juxtaposition and transposition.

His first book, *Poems*, appeared in 1938 and opened magnificently with "An Epistle to a Patron." Here was a poet uncommonly himself, untouched by the Apocalypse, writing in a period voice with a decorous and mannerly syntax. The long, tactful lines of the epistle suggest the prosody of Pound's *Homage to Sextus Propertius*, developed without fuss. Here is a classicist without marmoreal ambitions, whose poems work with an austere efficiency, with long syntax and a diction stripped of nuance. This insistent cleanliness is both aesthetic and religious. He is a Roman Catholic of the wide-awake variety; his most famous poem, "Soldiers Bathing," as well as the meditations from the mind of Michelangelo, Edmund Burke, and Strafford, whose execution is coolly and devastatingly evoked, have a historical and spiritual dimension.

> All's pathos now. The body that was gross,
> Rank, ravenous, disgusting in the act or in repose,
> All fever, filth and sweat, its bestial strength
> And bestial decay, by pain and labour grows at length
> Fragile and luminous.

The couplets are made vague by rhythmic variation, long lines, short lines, no constant except speech checked by rhyme. When *Soldiers Bathing* appeared in 1954 the war was over, and few picked up on the brilliant, quiet talent revealed there or, in 1963, in the new and selected poems, *The Doors of Stone*. Lack of popularity has left Prince free to experiment with long poems, to explore ideas of England, of Judaism; not to polemicize but to find. His free verse is astringent, paced as if by a tightrope walker so as not to allow a single slip into ambiguity. His syllabics, too, move with a tense balance. The experience of the war and of his religion color much of what he writes. He has incompatible advocates. On the one hand, John Ashbery has singled him out because of the sounds he makes and the ways he makes complex sense with minimal means. Donald Davie praises him as a poet who has quietly learned from Pound and not found it necessary to polemicize: "From as long ago as 1938, with his 'Epistle to a Patron,' through the relatively famous war-poem 'Soldiers Bathing,' to *Walks in Rome* as recently as 1987, Prince has quietly assumed the liberties, and reached for the ambitious objectives that we associate with modernism." In his revised *Collected Poems* (1993) he adds recent work, what he calls "Senilia," poetry very much of the return journey, aphoristic, stoical, elegiac. He has written his poems one at a time and each is fully invested. A subject detains him, for however long the poem takes, and if the readers come they do so on his terms. He will insist on the Italians, on the poets of the English Renaissance, on Judaic wisdom. The poems belong with wisdom, not play. There is an ethical and spiritual dimension: the truths they try to tell are true. A few unusual poets seem to follow him: the Canadian Marius Kociejowski and, at a greater distance, Norm Sibum, another Canadian. Geoffrey Hill has worked with comparable integrity, if less calm generosity of spirit, in the wake of the same world war.

Classicist too is the Australian Alec Derwent Hope, born in Cooma, New South Wales, in 1907. He studied in Sydney and at Oxford, returned to Australia and became a practicing psychologist and lecturer in English at Canberra, where he was subsequently professor for many years. Though he wrote from his earliest years, his first book appeared in 1955, and he was probably the first substantial Australian poet heard abroad. In formal preferences he can seem to resemble Frost, Yeats or Graves, with an insistent maleness about his work, a charged sexuality. Judith Wright demonstrates how Hope imposes order on chaotic experience through rigorous traditional form. The chaos is not only in the world out there but within the poet himself: his fears, his powerful desires, his violent faith. "Easter Hymn" opens with the lines "Make no mistake; there will be no forgiveness; / No voice can harm you and no hand will save." He is cruel when he wants to be, resorting to caricature, retreating behind his anger. He plucks his narratives from the Bible, from classical legend, playing tricks on them and us. That furious wit— Wright calls it "defence-by-attack," but he created his attackers—gives way in later poems to moral vision. It may have thematic connections with Robinson Jeffers, but it regards the small creatures, it considers their suffering, it begins to dwell on natural detail, to long for stability and peace. Swift does not become Goldsmith, exactly, but he ceases to be so obsessed with the physiology of man and woman, the smells that go with mortality; he finds the open air and is finally able to praise. It is probably the earlier poems, because they are cruel like Swift's (without Swift's justice, but justice matters less in this age), that will abide. The bitterness of his "Inscription for a War" is worthy of Kipling. It ends in a translation from the Greek: "Go tell those old men, safe in bed, / We took their orders and are dead." In Australian poetry he looks a little out of place. He shouldn't: he is a late antecedent, no less rooted in Australia than Kenneth Slessor, Francis Webb and the even more severe James McAuley, but—by his choice of forms and his expert handling of famil- iar registers—a poet of the turbulent "main stream," a main stream into which the poems of Eliot and Pound have never flowed, or flowed only as effluent. Yet Mandelstam and Pasternak and Akhmatova he seems to hear, even through the static of translation, and Baudelaire, Mallarmé, Valéry. In 1959 McAuley wrote *The End of Modernity*; his friend Hope was not quite so ready, having tasted its fruits, to declare all the new currency counterfeit. What made him permanently controversial and for many years unpopular in Australia was his refusal to privilege Australian poetry, insisting that it should be appraised and valued in the same way that an Australian reader would praise and value the work of an English, an American or an Indian poet. This was not the music that literary nationalists wished to hear. And internationalists like Les Murray seem to find him rebarbative, too: Is he "academic," "traditionalist," "misogynist"? Unflattering adjectives flock to him, and some stick. In the light of the poems (and of the better essays) one can only say: So what?

Much has been made of Hope's Australian "vernacular." Is it or isn't it? Another poet whose work and life were colored by the war is Randall Jarrell, an American for whom the vernacular is air itself. Beside Hope he speaks without affectation. In "To Any Poet," Hope's contemporary McAuley wrote:

> Take salt upon your tongue.
> And do not feed the heart
> With sorrow, darkness or lies:
> These are the death of art.

By such a token Jarrell is a no-hoper ("It is terrible to be alive"), and yet in fact he is the best critic and one of the most eloquent poets of his generation, a sad "real one" along with Delmore Schwartz, John Berryman and Robert Lowell. At public readings Lowell often read poems by Jarrell, calling him "the most heartbreaking English poet of his generation." Poetry, for Lowell, strives for heartbreak: it issues not from subject matter but from tone. "Behind everything there is always / The unknown unwanted life," Jarrell says. He identified with the defeated and spoke through them, often lonely women in middle age with no strategy for growing old. Sentimental? Sometimes, maybe. At his best he is *rueful*, with only the memory of hope. Having almost completed his finest book, *The Lost World*, he died violently in 1965 in an accident. He was fifty-one.

Although born in Nashville, Tennessee, in 1914, Jarrell spent much of his childhood in California. The year he lived in Hollywood with his paternal grandparents when his parents were divorcing he evokes at length in "The Lost World." He left school during the Depression and went to work for his uncle. He attended Vanderbilt and became acquainted with the Fugitives, drawn in by Ransom and Warren. Tate became a friend. He was never really one of them, though he made common cause in his early work. He followed Ransom when he moved to Kenyon, but went on shortly to the University of Texas. In 1940 his poems were published in *Five Young American Poets*, and in 1942 his own collection, *Blood for a Stranger*, appeared: "nothing comes from nothing, / The darkness from the darkness. Pain comes from the darkness / And we call it wisdom. It is pain."

He joined the Army Air Corps and wrote his best early work there, some of the best American poetry of the Second World War, though he never saw active service. His most anthologized poem, "The Death of the Ball Turret Gunner," uses actual language heard in training in the last line, its cold matter-of-factness cruel alongside images of mother, womb, vulnerability. The innocence of the unborn contrasts with the cold innocence of the gunner, hunched in the belly of the ball turret beneath the plane: "From my mother's sleep I fell into the State, / And I hunched in its belly till my wet fur froze." The death of the gunner parodies birth: "When I died they washed me out of the turret with a hose." In "Losses" he wrote,

In bombers named for girls, we burned
The cities we had learned about in school—
Till our lives wore out; our bodies lay among
The people we had killed and never seen.

It is invention, but of the most affecting kind. He becomes the "other people" whose experiences he explores. *Little Friend, Little Friend* (1945), *Losses* (1948) and, also on the war, *The Seven-League Crutches* (1951) followed. The *Selected Poems* (1955) includes the best of the early volumes.

He became a teacher, for twenty years at the Women's College of the University of North Carolina at Greensboro, where he offered English and Imaginative Writing. Two further collections appeared, *The Woman at the Washington Zoo* (1960) and *The Lost World* (1965). His *Complete Poems* (1969) included a number of poems and translations omitted from earlier volumes.

"He had a deadly hand for killing what he despised," Lowell remarked of his criticism. He was also a firm advocate. Collections of his critical work include *Poetry and the Age* (1953) and *A Sad Heart at the Supermarket* (1962). He wrote a satirical novel, *Pictures from an Institution* (1954), about life on a minor American campus.

Innocence and its loss were his perennial subjects. "Loss," "lost," "child": words overused in titles. There is a once-upon-a-time feel, poems begin "When" and a memory is rebuilt; but no one ever lives happily ever after. His fairy tale belongs to the forces of time, which are evil.

> Listening, listening; it is never still.
> This is the forest: long ago the lives
> Edged armed into its tides (the axes were its stone
> Lashed with the skins of dwellers to its boughs);
> We felled our islands there, at last, with iron.
> The sunlight fell to them, according to our wish,
> And we believed, till nightfall, in that wish;
> And we believed, till nightfall, in our lives.

Nostalgia is no release: it puts loss in italics. War was a mighty process of loss, betrayed innocence, enforced complicity. The world is more fantastic than the fictions we use to interpret it. Experience can't be rationally understood. The poems are formal but open-ended. There is always the danger of waking up. The poet does not understand in a paraphrasable way; he understands through tone and modulation; interpreting dreams, he comes to apprehend the real:

> You look at the people who look back at you, at home,
> And it is different—you have understood
> Your world at last: you have tasted your own blood.

His strategy recalls Wordsworth, whom he loved, and Rilke, whom he loved even more, and who provides some of his last lines. Their sense of childhood is like his: innocence is embodied in the child who understands, when he must, intuitively. There are always dreams to hand: they transport us between past and present. "In the Ward: The Sacred Wood" has a dream dynamic. He suggests, then interrogates the suggestion. "All this I dreamed in my great ragged bed . . . / Or so I dreamed," he says in "The Island." The poems question but never provide an answer. Jarrell is compassionate and never clever (how clever he could be when he wanted!) at the expense of his voices, his "others." He exploits the everyday language—including brand names—to create a quotidian world that highlights authentic emotion. "What can be more tedious," he asks, "than a man whose every sentence is a balanced epigram without wit, profundity, or taste?" Schwartz, who of that generation flowered exuberantly earliest and faded fastest, meeting his tragic end the year after Jarrell, in eclipse, reviewed his friend in 1945 and noted "the motives of honesty, courage, and inconsolable love of life . . . here submitted to the conditions of poetry and fulfilled in them. If, as one poem declares, this life is a dream from which no one wakes, the dreamer has refused to deceive himself, to let himself go, and to forget what he believes and loves." Berryman outlived Jarrell and wrote in his 121st *Dream Song*:

> Peace to the bearded corpse.
> His last book was his best. His wives loved him.
> He saw in the forest something coming, grim,
> but did not change his purpose.

Few have written better than Jarrell on Frost and on Whitman, on Auden, Hardy, Stevens and Moore. The modern (though not Pound and only obliquely Eliot) is real to him, but his heart of hearts is invested in meter, rhyme and familiar forms of closure, in Frost more than Williams, whom he feels it his duty to love.

The war weighed upon the Scottish poet Norman MacCaig rather differently. It sent him to prison. Born in Edinburgh in 1910, he read classics at the University of Edinburgh. He became a primary school teacher and was already a committed pacifist in the late 1920s. Called up in 1941, he refused and was held in the guardhouse at Edinburgh Castle. He then went to Winchester Prison and Wormwood Scrubs, but only for ninety-three days. Then he found congenial land work in Edinburgh. After the war he returned to teaching, until, in 1970, he became a lecturer and then reader in poetry at the University of Stirling. It was an appropriate place for him, both Scottish and academic, with a creative bias. There is about MacCaig's verse a cleverness that prefigures the excesses of the 1970s "metaphor school" of so-called Martians. He is an heir of Dunbar rather than Henryson.

His first two books belong with Graham's, Apocalyptic, but with considerable formal inventiveness. They were taken to be riddles, and MacCaig—aware of their excess—did what Graham was doing, fought toward his own style. His first major collection, *Riding Lights*, came out in 1955, the same year as Graham's *The Nightfishing*, and fell, as that book did, on ears attuned to more continuous logic. From his *Collected Poems* (1985) he excludes all the early work.

Perhaps in response to the length of his friend Hugh MacDiarmid's poems, his are for the most part short. They are also, many of them, quite formal. In each there is a play of intelligence and wit. MacCaig is a child of the (late) sixteenth century who has also read his Stevens, Ransom, and the poets of the 1930s, against whom his early work rebelled. He frees up the later poems, but never lets them become unruly. Baroque rather than expressionist, he will arrest an image, decorate it, and then set it back in motion. There is a touch of anarchy about his vision, an intolerance of unquestioned habit and of authority; he could follow MacDiarmid into dissent, but not into alternative orthodoxies. When he died in 1997 he had become, not by design, Scotland's unofficial laureate. His relative neglect outside Scotland—like the neglect of the wonderful Edinburgh dialect poet Robert Garioch—is an impoverishment. His language is not hard like MacDiarmid's or Garioch's, but his work is bulky, the way Herrick's is, hundreds of small poems, constituting in Douglas Dunn's words "a poetry of detailed resemblances that cumulate into a glimpse of 'the whole world's shape.'" More, surely, than a *glimpse*? Dunn insists that MacCaig's later free verse, which is in fact irregularly iambic and not as free as he would have us believe, is less "literary" in feel than the crafted, rhymed and metered earlier poems. It is a doubtful observation. A poet's freedom is often a reader's constraint: each free-verse poem has to earn our confidence, while a metrical poem is innocent until proved guilty by the general reader. It is possible to find the metrical MacCaig more natural and, for all his complexity, easier than the deliberately unbuttoned poet of the later pieces. He makes of his debt to Wallace Stevens and Frost an echoing music that hangs uneasily in the air:

> First snow is never all the snows there were
> Come back again, but novel in the sun
> As though a newness had but just begun.
>
> It does not fall as rain does from nowhere
> Or from that cloud spinnakered on the blue,
> But from a place we feel we could not go to.

Such ventriloquism in a poet already into his forties is unsettling. The only word that is his in those six lines is "spinnakered." But what a good word it is, and it defines what is best about his metaphorical language, its unexpected rightness for *a single purpose*, be it shape, color, sound, taste or touch. At his best we see the sea and in it the huge structure of the human and the natural world with its lovely and aggressive reciprocities:

> The sea pursued
> Its beastlike amours, rolling in its sweat
> And beautiful under the moon; and a leaf was
> A lively architecture in the light.

It is beautifully large, expanding over a few stanzas from the small history of the observer with his erotic concerns projected on the moonlit waves to the large world that contains it, and at the end he reels the poem in by an "Or so he thought," returning home: "The door was near, the supper, the small lamplight."

MacCaig is reassuringly domestic, his closures often upbeat; his refusal to go the way of MacDiarmid and (in Davie's phrase) to "engage history" means that his work excludes more than it can include; for it cannot—or will not—*connect* except at an individual level. Davie is the one English critic to give MacCaig his due, in proportion, to understand where he comes from and the unusual purity (and scale) of his best achievements.

Poetry, Edwin Morgan says, should "acknowledge its environment," and unlike MacCaig, Morgan engages with history. He was not a prosecuted conscientious objector in the war: he served in the Royal Army Medical Corps (1940–46), he experienced Palestine; on his own terms he was part of that large moment in history. He was born in Glasgow in 1920, and the war broke his university education in two. He completed his degree in 1947, then taught in the English department of the University of Glasgow until 1980.

Morgan is hugely versatile, with a relatively sure control of traditional metrical and rhymed forms. His sonnets are the best to come out of Scotland this century, not least because of what they are compelled to carry and to dignify:

A shilpit dog fucks grimly by the close.
Late shadows lengthen slowly, slogans fade.
The YY PARTICK TOI grins from its shade
like the last strains of some lost *libera nos
a malo*. No deliverer ever rose
from these stone tombs to get the hell they made
unmade.

He writes ballads and elegies, dramatic monologues and epistles. Had he restricted himself to conventional forms he would be a considerable poet. But he has added a further dimension: he is the arch-experimenter. Eccentric and derivative talents like Ian Hamilton Finlay gain credit for having ploughed (with help from artist-collaborators) a single experimental field in which a number of related plants are grown for sale as artifacts. Morgan is his own experimental team. Translation from a dozen languages, ancient and modern, has opened his ears and eyes. He has been a concrete poet, a sound poet, a "sci-fi" and "video" poet; he has worked together with writers, artists and musicians on joint projects. Although his academic career provided him with resources, his verse is not academic. He entertains, and as he does so he extends the realm of the poetic. It is poetry written in such a way as to make it performable, but not performance poetry as such. The text rewards the reader in one way, the audience in another.

The case against him is that he is *too* versatile. The real Edwin Morgan never stands up. He is the Auden of Scotland, able to turn his hand to any challenge: but which are the challenges that matter? The documentary poems? The intense and vulnerable love poems? The oblique autobiography contained in *The New Divan* sequence? Or is the experimental voice the true one? Is his poetry merely in and about language, the strange philological experiments, the transformational poems? Such a case is based on a prejudice: that a poet has a definable center, an "I" that can be held responsible. The notion that a poet can have many identities, in response to occasions, is not quite accepted. Even theorists, finding so pure a proof of their theories, shy away: Morgan's multiplicity is too good to be true. "The Second Life" asks the question, "Is it true that we come alive / not once, but many times?" The answer in his case must be "yes"; even within a single book there are a dozen Morgans to deal with.

There is, I believe, an "I," autobiographical, candid, strong and vulnerable, who articulates those poems which seem most durable. That "I" lives in a Glasgow whose geography it has brought alive (in "Glasgow Sonnets," for example), whose dialect it has used for poetry and for translation (notably of Mayakovsky). Glasgow is to Morgan what New York is to Whitman, a world that connects with other worlds, European for the most part rather than English. He has evolved a prosody based on the verse paragraph rather than the line. He has learned certain lessons from Ginsberg, though unlike Ginsberg he does not let his poetry flow out of control.

At university before the war he read Eliot, Rimbaud (in French) and Mayakovsky (in Russian) and poetry opened before him. What he learned later from the Beats, from Williams and the Black Mountain poets was superadded, along with the work of the Brazilian Concrete Poets and the sound poems of Ernst Jandl. "The Loch Ness Monster's Song" is Morgan's best-known sound piece.

Insistently secular, at home in the present and hungry for the future, he finds occasions for poetry in the newspaper, on the radio, small incidents, "what time barely kept." He writes "instamatic" poems, video poems, to capture and explore "what actually happens." A lecturer in English, he takes the social world as a text and analyzes the clauses, structures and conceits of life as people live it. Poetry is an act of selection, epitomization, criticism. The problem with the instamatic and close-up poems is a certain semantic poverty: verse documentary and verse history are not the same. Language is not a dependable lens unless it is burnished and made utterly clear.

His first substantial book, *The Second Life,* appeared in 1968. Each poem was dated because it belonged—as Adrienne Rich's do—to a specific time. The elegies were written soon after their subjects' deaths (Hemingway, Marilyn Monroe, Edith Piaf), the love poems soon after the incidents they evoke. A poem should keep its anchor in its occasion. The most salutary development in his work is the way in which he comes to internalize his moralizing. In the early poems he draws attention to what he means; in the later work he just means. Throughout the poetry, from the first book to the most recent, there is a developing sequence of love poems (now elegies) which, teased out, would make a volume of very specific potency.

> A writer needs nothing but a table.
> His pencil races, pauses, crosses out.
> Five years ago he lost his friend, without
> him he struggles through a different fable.
> The one who died, he is the better one . . .

There has always been a directness and candor about his love poems, but integrated as they are into collections in which experiment, satire, elegy and other activities are going on, they may have been read as "merely literary." Nothing in Morgan, even the most amusing experiments, is "merely literary." Even the translations take English (or Scots) as close as it can go to the originals, getting at the creative dynamic itself.

Like MacDiarmid and MacCaig, Morgan is often upbeat, committed to this world (for all its faults) because of its promise. The poems present dialogue, they believe in the social world. It is a salutary romanticism, rooted in the urban rather than the rural. Religion becomes a secular force; the foe is whoever says no to natural feeling, to growth and positive change.

Candors

ROBERT LOWELL, JOHN BERRYMAN, TED HUGHES,
SYLVIA PLATH, ANNE SEXTON, PATRICIA BEER,
ELIZABETH JENNINGS, PHILIP LARKIN

The age of prurience, in which the public chooses its heroes and then whittles them down to size by dwelling in dubious detail on their life stories, is relatively new. There have been curious biographers such as Tacitus and Aubrey (and many biographers as naughty as they in invention and inflection); there have been shrewish and savage biographers like Strachey, and there have always been self-mythologizers among the poets. But poets who deliberately deal the paydirt on themselves are a more recent phenomenon. Poets have always complained and settled scores and licked their wounds, but have not for the most part opened their wounds and probed them before their readers. Discretion, obliquity have been the rule: the fiction, not the literal details and the untransmuted voices of the life. Not *confession* as it began to be practiced in 1959. *Life Studies* by Robert Lowell was described as "confessional verse" by the reviewer M. L. Rosenthal in *The Nation* in 1959: a new genre was born. It is important to remember that Lowell did not invent the term.

What does "confessional verse" imply? Donald Davie mischievously proposes Whitman as a "confessional poet." Why must confession always suggest negative testimony? A poet might as well confess to virtue as to other qualities. The braggart is confessing; the negative confessional selects and exaggerates like the braggart. The virtue of Lowell's poetry is in its seeming candor. "Confessional" suggests religion as well: the communicant on his way to penance and sacramental absolution. Confession would seem to imply the possibility of reparation and forgiveness. It is a sacrament Lowell understood from his Roman Catholic years, when he spent days at a time on his knees. The heart must be contrite, the posture humble. It doesn't call good deeds and impulses into the account, though they should be part of any sacrament of self-recognition. Confession is not an end in itself: it leads to communion and back to community.

In confessional poetry this has not been the pattern. Lowell is unusual in the mercilessness of his verse, but also in the way he makes his situation generally pertinent, even characteristic, of his age, his class and his gender. With lesser poets (and in Lowell's lesser poems) the hubris is overbearing. If the writer has such a firm handle on the situation, knows the details, the causes and effects, why bother to confess? The therapy precedes it. But in Lowell the details come together, a trail of cruel sparks that illuminate the past and future, yet cannot be controlled. He writes in "Night Sweat":

> . . . one life, one writing! but the downward glide
> and bias of existing wrings us dry—
> always inside me is the child who died,
> always inside me is his will to die—
> one universe, one body—in this urn
> the animal night sweats of the spirit burn.

Here he confesses to a beloved, the woman who stands by him and who would understand him if she could. Confession of this kind can only take place in the context of love; but why then are we made party to it? For the same reason that we are made party (more obliquely) to Eliot's pain in *The Waste Land*, and with greater candor to Pound's in the *Pisan Cantos*: "the downward glide / and bias of existing." When religious belief is in abeyance, whom can we turn to, in what terms can we speak? In literal details, or—the alternative strategy, which Anne Sexton and Sylvia Plath devised—in symbolic narratives.

Lowell belonged to a vulnerable generation and like Jarrell writes a poetry of symptoms: illness, false health, false hope, failure—and love. The private and the public illuminate each other; his illness in crucial ways is representative of a mind-set and of a class, but is also, in crucial ways, distinct. From the forced formal and thematic stability of his early poetry to the controlled surrender of the later, the development is courageous and inevitable. It affects the earlier work: in an unstable world what has already been made and finished or abandoned can be remade, unmade. He returns to his early work and rewrites it. Poems written in the transition between phases are consistently his best, but always vulnerable to later attentions. Nietzsche in his later years refused to revise his early work on the grounds that the older man he had become despised the young man he had been, as the young man would have despised the older. For Lowell, though clearly his "I" was unstable, growing and withering and growing again, the poem stood apart from its original occasion and was prey to his revisitings.

He was born in Boston in 1917 into an undistinguished branch of a distinguished "aristocratic" Boston family with substantial political and cultural connections. He had a strong, sentimental and snobbish mother and a cardboard cutout of a father. At his exclusive school he was nicknamed Caligula because of his unpredictability and cruelty, and the nickname "Cal" stayed with him for life. He went to Harvard and then, rebelling against his family and his privileged culture, transferred to Kenyon College to study with Ransom and Tate. In 1940 he graduated in classics and, furthering his rebellion, became a Roman Catholic. Three years later, in protest against the Allied bombing of European cities (about which Jarrell wrote so memorably), he became a conscientious objector and spent time in detention, again to the horror of his family. His first book appeared in 1944 and his second, *Lord Weary's Castle*, published in 1946 when he was twenty-nine, won a Pulitzer Prize. There was no contest: he was the major figure in American poetry.

The early verse was formally congested and opaque. Even today it has a forbiddingly bricked-in quality. There is not a moment of repose, the language is muscular and tense, intellectually and semantically overheated, metrically clenched. Elegy and anger are tightly bound. His Catholicism is not Boston Irish but has the Puritan intensity of his Pilgrim ancestors. Melville is a tutelary spirit, but where his prose is lavishly Jacobean, Lowell's verse is austerely deliberate. He is with Ahab, not Ishmael. His poems neither spoke nor sang but throbbed and growled. "Mr. Edwards and the Spider" almost makes a break, using a complex metaphysical stanza form with amazing skill; but a spiritual tension turns image into conceit.

In *The Mills of the Kavanaughs* the Roman Catholic concerns weakened, giving way to a more classical movement, with consecutive narrative. In the twenty-two-page title poem he began to detect a new direction. It was hard work and eight years passed before *Life Studies*, a definitive break for him and for American and—subsequently—the other English poetries.

A suffering mad self is his subject, with its antecedent selves and the uncomprehended other selves around it—lovers, wife, family, friends, fellow inmates in asylums, figures from history—all are fodder for *Life Studies*; the title insists on the actuality of the circumstances and characters and their language. It also insists on the nakedness of the subjects. They are transformed into rather than out of themselves.

The change in his work came about for many reasons. One of the most interesting is that he gave public readings. "By the time I came to *Life Studies* I'd been writing my autobiography and also writing poems that broke meter. I'd been doing a lot of reading aloud. I went on a trip to the West Coast and read at least once a day and sometimes twice for fourteen days, and more and more I found that I was simplifying my poems. If I had a Latin quotation I'd translate it into English. If adding a couple of syllables in a line made it clearer I'd add them, and I'd make little changes just impromptu as I read." He began to write new lines more simply and directly. On the reading circuit a sense of his audience changed him. And he heard Allen Ginsberg read, met him and admired the ways in which he made his own liberties. Lowell moved from a regularly stressed and metrical verse to looser meter, toward a free verse always ghosted by iambics. Did the loosening improve the poems? Auden declared that a poem is never finished, only abandoned. Lowell found he couldn't let go, even of the work he had written fifteen years before.

Self-expression, self-exploration, sometimes self-dramatization: this was a peril he faced, and his imitators and successors even more so. But there are substantial gains: the heavy symbolism of the earlier poems is gone, or is made organic to a larger statement. The ordinary world finds a central place, indeed it is foregrounded. Politics begin to weigh: Korea, then Vietnam, and always domestic politics.

The mixed reception that *Life Studies* received, even from friends who found the poems too exposed and vulnerable, invasive of the privacy of others, may have been one factor in the difficult years that followed its publication. He had struggled to wrest the poems from his old style, and it took time for the work to settle in the public mind. With each book critics tended to say, "Lowell has gone off," but after two or three years (always in time for the next book) the verdict was reversed, so that the next book could be seen as having "gone off." It is a measure of his stride that there is so much distance between book and book.

He fished in other men's waters with *Imitations* (1961), the translations and versions of foreign poetry, ancient and modern, which he brought within his orbit. He translated Racine as well, the *Phèdre*, and the theater seduced him (in 1965 *The Old Glory*, three plays based on stories by Hawthorne and Melville, appeared after respectfully received productions). It was, however, his 1964 volume, *For the Union Dead*, that eventually united critics around him. Here the vulnerability of relationships and values is most eloquently and *politically* explored; the good and the disabling traditions, history, politics and autobiography combine. His confession is circumstantial, full of the contingent world—not solipsism or exorcism but a going into. There is no quick fix, but candor can uncover the damaged nerves. His writing began to accelerate. In 1967 *Near the Ocean* appeared, then in 1970 the rich mess of fourteen-line poems looking like sonnets that was *Notebook*, broken down and expanded into three books in 1973: *History, For Lizzie and Harriet* and *The Dolphin*. Was Lowell in competition with Berryman's *Dream Songs*, trying to write a long poem out of short ones? He reassimilates earlier work. The fourteen-liners generally conclude in paradoxes that tip the poem into a quizzical resonance.

He broke up *Notebook*, which had mingled personal, historical and other verses in an impromptu spirit (hence the title), because he ended up disliking what one critic (whom he quotes in a poem—all part of the voracious, self-referential mix) called its "seedy grandiloquence." He had a habit of listening to critics, even when they were wrong, and he lamented that he had so few. The worst moment for a poet, he confided, is when he is so celebrated that critics (and friends like Jarrell) cease to engage his work with direct severity. He also split up *Notebook* because his life changed. He fell in love with Caroline Blackwood, divorced his (second) wife Elizabeth Hardwick and found definable phases in his life that he wanted his new sequences to reflect. *History* contains the poems that deal with the many figures from history and from the literary past he knew intimately, with their life stories and their thought. *For Lizzie and Harriet* dealt with his love for his now ex-wife and daughter and the terrible difficulties of their marriage, for which he took responsibility. And *The Dolphin* celebrated his new love.

Auden was appalled: How could a poet actually take passages from the agonized letters of a woman who loved him and whom he was divorcing and set them verbatim in a poem? Elizabeth Bishop was equally, though less vehemently, affronted. But it was the logical development of the poet who had written "To Speak of the Woe Which Is in Marriage," initially taken as a thinly veiled fiction, now revealed to have been pure candor. The focus on *self*, the confidence that self is of sufficient interest to readers that its unraveling is a sufficient subject, and the—call it—solipsism that appropriates the literal language of others' suffering to lend veracity to his own account: this is a radical approach to subject matter, a setting of poetry not within but above life, as privileged to appropriate and consume whatever it wants from the living world. Yet the radicalism is not reflected in a formal way: the shock is in what he does rather than in how he does it. The great stylistic shift that occurs in *Life Studies* here becomes reflex—eloquent but formulaic, like those relentless and endless fourteen-liners, a form that will spin out two lines' worth of occasion or boil down fifty, a kind of merciless Procrustean bed. The deliberate poet has become quite arbitrary, himself subject to the sway of a large and increasingly casual art.

In 1977 he died in a taxi from Kennedy Airport in New York, returning to Elizabeth Hardwick. Having seen all the symptoms in his society and in himself, he succumbed to them. A year later his last book, *Day by Day,* was published.

> Those blessèd structures, plot and rhyme—
> why are they no help to me now
> I want to make
> something imagined, not recalled?

Memory and imagination had become snagged together, tragically, fruitfully. That was the big paradox of the life that produced the hundreds of small paradoxes in the later poems. "All's misalliance." Hence the power of the great poems, "My Last Afternoon with Uncle Devereux Winslow," "Skunk Hour," "For the Union Dead," "Waking Early Sunday Morning" and many others, including my favorite with its tender fatalism, its loving dependence, "The Flaw."

Lowell wanted to be known as the greatest poet in America, and he was. He competed hard to get there, surpassing first Delmore Schwartz, who began before him and flowered richly before not quite enough literary success and personal failure brought him down; and then Randall Jarrell, who fascinated and frightened him and whose death, like Schwartz's, touched him deeply. He also outran John Berryman, the one poet who for a time seemed to offer real competition and whose achievement, rather eclipsed at present, should be recognized.

The style Berryman developed for *The Dream Songs,* 385 poems in "18-line sections, three six-line stanzas, each normally (for feet) 5-5-3-5-5-3, variously rhymed and not but mostly rhymed with great strictness," spoken by several voices, is more supple than Lowell's fourteen-liners but ultimately as arbitrary. Critics rightly say his work is obscure and artificial; but it is also very funny, clear (when read aloud and the voices spoken) and heartbreaking in its depiction of helplessness, of man as subject and subjected. Berryman's candor is not direct like Lowell's, it lacks his patrician assurance, but it is no less vulnerable for its wan, ingratiating ironies, its standing apart from itself. "I think *Dream Songs,* now completed, is one of the glories of the age, the single most heroic work in English poetry since the War," Lowell declared (Berryman had died by that time, having jumped off a bridge onto the frozen Mississippi). He added that Berryman "handles the language, as if he made it." The sense of a poet *making* the language—we get it in more intense form in Hopkins—is part of the fascination of Berryman. The problem with this making, as we look back on it from the experimental perspectives of later poets, is that it doesn't go far enough. The experiments with voice, form and literary allusion (there is almost as much quotation, misquotation and allusion in the sequence as in Pound) are formulaic, the poet (who taught English at university level, as Jarrell and Lowell and Roethke did) draws his resonances from the syllabus.

Yet in contrast with the inventive abundance of *The Dream Songs*, the earlier and conventional poems seem . . . conventional, even the famous early *Homage to Mistress Bradstreet*, in which he celebrates the mother of American poetry, inventing a voice for her. With dialect poetry the way to test it is to see what it would say, how it would say, adjusted into standard English. The same experiment practiced on Berryman will help the reader to discriminate between the feeble and the achieved poems.

Born in McAlester, Oklahoma, Berryman was a cradle Catholic. His banker father and schoolteacher mother moved the family to Florida, and there, when the poet was twelve, his father committed suicide in front of his window. He never escaped that image, it fueled in him a hunger for certainty and stability, a sustaining love: "All my life I will suffer from your anger," he wrote. He wanted fidelity but could not give it. He tried to love and he tried to escape through promiscuity and other forms of experiment, including drink. The sure escape was the one his father suggested and which he finally took. In "Freshman Blues" he says with an appalling gaiety in his voice,

> Thought much I then of perforated daddy,
> daddy boxed in & let down with strong straps,
> when I my friends' homes visited, with fathers
> universal & intact . . .

Berryman studied at Columbia and at Clare College, Cambridge. He taught in New York, Harvard, Princeton, and ended up at the University of Minnesota. He left no note to explain his suicide, but the poetry touches on the theme. He was persuaded that Jarrell had chosen to die, stepping deliberately out in front of the vehicle that killed him. Because of his continual hospitalizations, Lowell always seemed the most likely to die by his own hand, but he outlived them all and died of more or less natural causes. In autobiographical poems Berryman recalls suicide games at prep school. He alludes to the theme without exploring it.

Yeats was his first master, then Auden. Pound and Eliot—and Williams and Whitman—did not get to him as the Irish and English poet did. Curiously, Berryman was almost untouched by high modernism and may in the end take his place in the line of Robinson and Masters (and Stephen Crane). He has all the surface brilliance of experiment, but at heart and in his forms he remains conservative to the core. This is the irony, that Jarrell and Berryman restructured conventional resources so as to build a bridge across the troubled years of dowdy formalism and polemical experiment. They provided verse that seemed authentic and challenging, but not *too* challenging. They were bearded but not untidy like the Beats. They were reassuringly literary.

> There sat down, once, a thing on Henry's heart
> só heavy, if he had a hundred years
> & more, & weeping, sleepless, in all them time
> Henry could not make good.
> Starts again always in Henry's ears
> the little cough somewhere, an odour, a chime . . .

The accented "só" puts us in mind of Hopkins, perhaps, and what follows is a strange paraphrase of Shakespeare's Paulina, her impassioned remonstration with Leontes in *A Winter's Tale*. And the poem progresses through Yeats, and again Shakespeare. When it falls into a brutal demotic diction, the word order is deranged, not to bring it close to voice, but to run it against the natural cadences of speech. Powerful to a point, but literary. "I am not Henry, you know, I pay income tax; Henry pays no income tax." Henry is the alien, the outcast, the white Negro, the man blacked up for the minstrel show, stepping out of himself, performing. All the *Dream Songs* are performance. We are put in mind of cummings, but a cummings carrying a huge library on his back: not just the Elizabethans but, credulously, all the critics and the variorums. Where cummings gets angry with books, with politics, with habitual language, Berryman gets tragic and sad: his norm is displacement, disappointment, and all the fun in his language is out of key. Self-indulgence has a place in every poet's work, but in Berryman's, too prominent a place. It is the candor of Hoccleve, mournful and helpless, saying me, me, me.

Good teachers end up as implausible headmasters, good salesmen as uncomfortable sales directors. And difficult, brilliant outsiders are often recognized and lured inside. Creon would rather Antigone were on his side of the wall when curfew sounds. Philip Larkin and Ted Hughes are both temperamental Antigones. Hughes had his own world and his own griefs: the establishment bought a stake in them. Larkin stopped writing when he became a celebrity: his apotheosis blurred his hard, reluctant vision. Hughes kept writing: Poet Laureate, he celebrated the Queen Mother's birthday and mourned the death of Princess Diana. But whether inside or outside he remained an unstable, unsettling figure. He preserved himself better than Larkin did.

A writer of many parts, he was never content to stop with poetry. He wrote stories, children's poetry, stage pieces. He invented a "talking without words," Orghast. He translated from the poets of Eastern Europe and, triumphantly in 1996, from Ovid. He was a powerful advocate, especially of Emily Dickinson and Keith Douglas. He was drawn to manifestations of power and to those creatures (some of them human) who manage to survive the excesses of power. Singularity, the "single mind sized skull," intrigued him; in Shakespeare's tragedies how a single humor displaces the more complex elements of character and compels human action much as instinct compels animal action. His poem "Thrushes" is an alarming statement of this interest, seeming to celebrate pure instinct.

Here is another kind of candor, a poetic commitment to theme that does not reflect on morality but on essential energy, which is not "considered speech" in Davie's sense but "authentic speech" (some of it hard to speak aloud), the language of Heathcliff rather than Linton. Humanism is alluring but inadequate, the old symbols bankrupt. Yet one of the incongruities in Hughes is that, while his poetry celebrates the natural action, the direct perception, its language is often worked up and overwrought, laboriously alliterative and assonantal, larded with adjectives (especially in *Gaudete*): a Baroque imagination with a bone through its nose. Against this there is the utter elegance of "October Dawn" or the tender poise of "The Moon and Little Frieda," the subverted beauty of "Crow and the Birds."

Hughes was born in Mytholmroyd, Yorkshire, in 1930. The landscape of his poems is here, their actual settings in a place sparsely inhabited, where nature is still red in tooth and claw: an austere, craggy and—apart from the vales—treeless area with big skies and the ruins of industry: mills, pits, with some pits still working. When he was seven his family moved to Mexborough, where he attended the local grammar school. His brother hunted and fished and became a gamekeeper. Hughes learned from him and from his father, a veteran of the First World War, one of seventeen survivors of a whole regiment which fought at Gallipoli. The natural world and his father's life and losses were Hughes's determining themes. By the time he was fifteen he was writing verse.

Before he went up to Cambridge, he did his National Service as an RAF ground wireless mechanic in East Yorkshire. He spent his time reading Shakespeare and putting together the thoughts and instincts that fill his enormous and eccentric study of the poet, *Shakespeare and the Goddess of Complete Being*. The epyllia are, he believes, the key to the bard. His selection of Shakespeare's verse contains the most brilliant of his introductions. His shorter critical writings are luminously clear, and though he beams a very particular and personal light on the writers he admires, he is clarifying even when he misses the mark.

At Cambridge he came up against Leavis with his harsh anticreative disciplines. He switched from English to anthropology and archaeology, disciplines crucial to his sense of *underlying* theme. In 1956 he married the American poet Sylvia Plath. They went to America, he taught at Amherst, they spent time at the writers' community of Yaddo, and late in 1959 returned to England. Hughes's first book, which his wife placed with a publisher, appeared in 1957. It was *The Hawk in the Rain*. The Movement was over for Hughes: his poems are rooted not in urban experience, not in the Apocalypse, but in a vigorous language that owes debts more subtle than Berryman's to Hopkins, and especially to Shakespeare, though he is richly colloquial in his diction.

Was Hughes a "nature poet" or are his animals and images of nature in fact symbolic enactments of human types and aggressions? *Lupercal* (1960), his second substantial collection, raises the question more insistently. The single-mindedness of his creatures and the relishing in them of violence and survival, have—if read politically, as critics often read politically the early poems of Gunn celebrating the brutishness of young thugs—a treacherous note, as if Robinson Jeffers had been transported to the Yorkshire moors and celebrated atavistic rituals against the encroaching social world. The hawk, the thrush, the pike, the bull are not only the physical but the moral centers of their worlds; the poet, by withholding comment, seems to assent to and endorse their natures. The forms they choose are rough-hewn, conventional forms, accentual and often rhymed, stabilities within a natural world in flux, fragments of structured language within an inarticulate chaos. In the children's books *Meet My Folks* (1961) and *Earth Owl and Other Moon People* (1963), fairy tale and fancy are superadded to this natural world. If D. H. Lawrence helped Hughes find a style, the two writers could hardly be more different in their tonality and in their moral vision.

For five years his relationship with Sylvia Plath was creatively fruitful. They separated in 1962 and the formal and imaginative frame of his poetry altered. Each substantial collection that followed approached the world of the early poems from a different angle, the poet moving from the literal-seeming into the allegorical and mythological. His first major book, *Wodwo* (1967), and his most celebrated and controversial book, the sequence called *Crow* (1970), paint him into a corner from which he has escaped spectacularly in *Tales from Ovid*. *Cave Birds* (1975), the staged but sometimes beguiling *Season Songs* (1976), the appalling narrative *Gaudete* (1977), *Moortown Diary* (1989) and the laureate poems *Raincharm for the Duchy* (1992), which reinvent the poem of public occasion, often seem the work of a poet who has strayed from his natural course. *Birthday Letters* (1998), evoking his relationship with Sylvia Plath living and dead—poems that he assures us were written over a period of thirty years—attempts a new prosody and at times an understated narrative quite out of character with what has come before, and with only a fitful authority.

If natural and human violence seem to dominate his work, they do so not as violence. Calvin Bedient says, "His weakness is not violence but the absolute egotism of survival. It is the victor he loves, not war." This may be true of the first two books; in the later poems he marvels at and sometimes celebrates the survivor, and it is perhaps here that we should seek his "politics," in the celebration of individual rather than collective will. Survival and growth occur not by acquiescing to an artificial or a historical structure but often by living *against*.

Lawrence declares, "Man cannot live in chaos . . . The animals can. To the animal all is chaos, only there are a few recurring motions and aspects within the surge." The violence of the natural world is not absolute for Lawrence: he warns against exaggerated vision, he says that "the yearning for chaos becomes a nostalgia." Violence taken too far becomes sentimental, if by that we mean a blurring of issues, simplification rather than clarification, that resolving of a poem in gesture. If Lawrence wrote about thrushes, his birds might be the clockwork figures of Hughes's poem, but they would also sing. The sentimentality of violence—we meet it in Jeffers, in the Apocalyptics, in the Beats—is deceit and self-deception. In a number of Hughes's early poems the word "horizon" does overtime in concluding lines as the poem is sent out in search of resonance. Resonances can be borrowed, too: from Hopkins, Owen, Eliot, Dylan Thomas and Lawrence. We keep coming back to Lawrence: what sets both poets apart from the dominant voices of their formative years is their distrust of irony, their attempt to get back inside the language of their poems, after the deliberate distancings of modernism in Lawrence's case and the Movement in Hughes's. In abandoning the ironically circumscribed but various world of the Movement, Hughes may strike a deeper note, but his thematic range is and remains extremely narrow. Solitariness, choicelessness: his animal and human creatures are distorted in order to serve his themes. This, in effect, is his form of candor, diffracting through more or less familiar images taken from a common world an uncommon sensibility, particular passions and anxieties. Creatures become emblematic, illuminating a metaphorical, not a complex natural truth: the quintessence of the poetic fallacy. When Hughes's world and the animal's world coincide, the best poems occur, or when Hughes—recognizing this tendency in his work—invents an animal, "Wodwo," for instance, borrowed from the philological obscurity of *Gawain and the Green Knight*, to do within the natural world what Hughes is doing through it, defining a nature, an identity.

> What am I to split
> The glassy grain of water looking upward I see the bed
> Of the river above me upside down very clear
> What am I doing here in mid-air? Why do I find
> this frog so interesting as I inspect its most secret
> interior and make it my own?

Crow is another such creature. So too is "The Thought Fox," one of his earliest poems: an invention, and what matters is the process of inventing, of finding out.

Lawrence subjects us to violence and pain, "opens" us, in order to be filled and fulfilled. Hughes at times seems to want to open us to be hurt. His poems may not ironize, and yet the poet as often as not stands apart from the violence he makes in language—a witness, not a subject. When he includes himself, as in "Wind," and nature rattles against the wobbly certainties of domestic life, his poems take on a deeper life. In the war poems, too, "Bayonet Charge," for example, he recreates rather than witnesses. "Six Young Men," a better poem, falls into the sentimentality of violence by making an emblematic experience out of what masquerades as a literal narrative. In "Pike" a reciprocity is established between fish and fisherman: the *poem* is not single-minded. "View of a Pig" in its cold, largely monosyllabic witness, is powerful, too: a dead energy generates a new kind of energy in the language. Not since Wordsworth has a poet been able to use the verb "to be" with what feels like transitive force.

In *Wodwo* literal creatures give way to imaginary ones, nightmare is all about us, and in *Crow* a metaphysical, historical and individual nightmare, cast in anthropological terms, occurs. The Australian artist Leonard Baskin produced a series of engravings and Hughes wrote his poems to illustrate them. The poems of *Crow* "wrote themselves." Hughes presented them as a fragment of an unfinished epic, colored by primitive song, but also by the Bible and Shakespeare and—in fragmentary form as in *The Waste Land*, but masked and half digested— elements from the great cultures that led to the Second World War and the Holocaust. Exposure to the experimental and radical writing of Eastern Europe had an impact on his work. But whereas Vasko Popa and János Pilinszky, poets he translated collaboratively, developed a style in response to the mercilessly violent history of the century on their countries and people, Hughes devises a style that is not similarly compelled. In *Crow* the extremes of violence come to seem like the action in comic books, Tom and Jerryish, not credible and not quite funny.

His poetry proved less susceptible to development than the work of the Movement poets, Davie and Gunn in particular. He just wasn't interested in language and form in the ways that they are; he did not think but felt his way forward. In *Tales from Ovid* he stepped into quite another world, a classical world not made of marble, not ruined, but a place in which extreme action is not the only option, where the lyrical has its place and psychology is more nuanced and various than it has been before. He was not translating Ovid but adapting him, or working in fruitful collaboration. He set himself free, by an act of will, of the repetitive and narrowing world of his earlier writing. His form of candor was exorcism, working out emotions and impulses through images and complex verbal structures. Exorcism is a form of candor that sidesteps confession. The freedom of *Tales from Ovid* does not reject but incorporates in a larger pattern what has gone before. In *Birthday Letters* he took a further step, addressing a loss without self-pity and with as much precision as his memory would allow, answering with unusual quietness, and with his eyes averted from them, decades of savage and malicious critics and gossips, trying to resolve a relationship that was his and hers but has become legendary, emblematic. It is a partial triumph, lacing in intimacy, a confession that must assert and reassert its sincerity, a candor that wants to be believed. At the root of the poems is love, of course, but also a complex set of angers that, in order to keep them under control, Hughes had to convey in a largely matter-of-fact prosody, writing against his cadential instincts. It is a fascinating experiment, a candor that is cold, calculated and only marginally vulnerable, the ultimate in his poetry of survival, counting the cost and discounting (obliquely) the lies that have grown around the story of two young poets and their marriage. It may be that "Lovesong" in *Crow* tells a deeper truth than *Birthday Letters*, but readers would rather this was not so.

Yet *Birthday Letters*, with its allusive echoes and tributes to Plath's poetry, does not quite bridge the very real distances between these two poets: man and woman, British and American, rural and urban, primitive and sophisticated. In her poems, "The fountains are dry and the roses over." Fountains, not rivers and lakes; roses, not thistles and brambles. She is the deliberate poet, she devises strategies, she competes for space and attention. She is experimental, setting herself exercises. She is an ironist. If the energies of their language at times seem comparable, they flow from different sources and it was more their human proximity than a sense of common poetic objectives that makes them seem so close in their marked differences, their incompatibilities. "Hughes loved her and wanted a wife; she loved him and wanted a monster."

"I think my poems come immediately out of the sensuous and emotional experiences I have, but I must say I cannot sympathise with these cries from the heart that are informed by nothing except a needle or a knife or whatever it is." This is what Sylvia Plath *said*, vainly preempting later imitators and advocates. "I believe that one should be able to control and manipulate experiences, even the most terrifying—like madness, being tortured, this kind of experience—and one should be able to manipulate these experiences with an informed and intelligent mind. I think that personal experience shouldn't be a kind of shut box and mirror-looking narcissistic experience. I believe it should be generally relevant, to such things as Hiroshima and Dachau, and so on." That "and so on" tells us how much an artist she is, how devastating experiences of the century become a resource for the poet, how history (and autobiography) can be manipulated with aesthetic but not moral qualm. Anger, anxiety, fear and love, primary emotions, can dispose of the hard facts of existence as they wish. Intense ephemeral feeling is in control. Hughes celebrates the brutally single-minded. It is at least stable, or seemingly so. Plath places at the control panels of her art a treacherous instability licensed to do what it likes not only with language but with fact. Is there, she seems to ask, any imaginative fact *outside* language? What does she mean by *generally* relevant to Dachau and Hiroshima? Are Dachau and Hiroshima comparable historical facts in the way she suggests? Are her conflations, a casual shorthand, not treacherous to her, to the world, to her readers?

James Dickey thinks so, repelled by the slickness of her art (even at her most extreme she is artful, writing with and perhaps for effect). The poems for him are "glib"; he finds "intolerable in either literature or in the world" the "slick, knowing patter about suffering and guilt, particularly about one's own." His emphatic perspective is that of a male writer more in the mold of Hughes and Jeffers than of Eliot and Lowell. For Al Alvarez, who was instrumental after her death in promoting Plath's poems in anthology and through criticism, she is far from glib. Indeed she is a weapon in his damaging polemic against the "gentility" of the Movement poets: she goes to the edge of polite experience and beyond, to the edge itself, and this he believes is laudable. He writes, "It needed not only great intelligence and insight to handle the material . . . it also took a kind of bravery. Poetry of this order is a murderous art." His overstatement is as extreme as Dickey's. If Plath's art is "slick," it is more than that: slickness is part of a wider aesthetic. If it were true, as Alvarez says, that "the achievement of her final style is to make poetry and death inseparable," then the work is wicked, which is not the case. Plath raises moral and artistic issues that cannot be resolved by critics who want to use her for their own ends. This goes for later feminist criticism, with its tendentious hagiography and the demonization of Ted Hughes.

A poetry of extremity must first be poetry. And where Plath is concerned, getting at the poetry is complicated by the problem of biography: her relationship with her mother and father, her displacement as an American in England, her marriage to an unusual Englishman, the creation of a family, the end of their relationship, her suicide. The poems are read as oblique autobiography and explained in terms of events that biographers and legend supply. Yet no biographer has access to the human content of events. No one will ever be able to say that Sylvia Plath *intended* to die, even when the evidence points in that direction. No one, not even the participants themselves, can assign responsibility. Since the story is known, it is hard not to read the poems in the light of it; yet unlike Lowell's, Plath's confessions are symbolic rather than circumstantial. Even when she attended writing classes in Boston with Anne Sexton, and they met after class over cocktails to discuss their suicide attempts, she was an experimental writer who "manipulated" the self as much as she manipulated language: to be visible, audible, admired.

Plath was born in Boston in 1932. Her first poem was published when she was eight years old, in the *Boston Sunday Herald*. Her father, of German extraction, was an entomologist, a professor at Boston University. He betrayed and abandoned her, dying of diabetes and a gangrenous leg that finds its way into her poems. She was eight. This departure is one of the eventual occasions for the poem "Daddy."

> Daddy, you can lie back now.
>
> There's a stake in your fat black heart
> And the villagers never liked you.
> They are dancing and stamping on you.
> They always *knew* it was you.
> Daddy, daddy, you bastard, I'm through.

Daddy, in Gestapo uniform, as Dracula, as an inhumanly passionate being, is a generalized projection bearing little relation to Mr. Plath—or to Ted Hughes. But her father's death destabilized her. An early poem, written when she was sixteen, is entitled "To Ariadne"—a figure central to later poems—and subtitled "(deserted by Theseus)."

> Your cries are lost, your curses are unheard by him
> That treads his winged way above the cloud.
> The honeyed words upon your lips are brine;
> The bitter salt wind sings off-key and loud.

Her mother filled the space he left with a directive love that the young poet relished and resented. *Letters Home* tells the story of a complex relationship, the daughter's needs always clear, but the mother's needs implicit in the poet's account of her progress, her successes. She graduated from Smith College (after a severe nervous breakdown induced by overwork) in 1955, and attended Lowell's poetry course at Harvard (he was ill much of the time, and working toward *Life Studies*). She was reading Dylan Thomas (whose birthday she shared), Yeats, Moore, Roethke. Roethke's impact and that of Anne Sexton on her work should not be underestimated. Sexton started writing relatively late, in response to mental breakdowns, and some of Plath's poems draw with surprising freedom on Sexton, borrowing lines, cadences and strategies. Sexton was already further along the way to Plath's kind of dramatic confessionalism than Lowell ever went. There was W. D. Snodgrass, too, one of Sexton's elected models for handling personal material (though Snodgrass's "confessionalism" does not ventriloquize and appropriate in the ways that Sexton's does). Sexton's first book, *To Bedlam and Part Way Back,* appeared in the same year as Plath's *The Colossus* (1960), and became raw material (with other, rawer material) for Plath's major poems in *Ariel*, published two years after her death, in 1965. What Sexton suggested to Plath was the force of simple rhyme and simple rhythm, the magic of nursery rhyme darkened by time, of fairy tale where the happy ending somehow doesn't happen. Sexton showed Plath the way, and then Plath died first, stealing a march on her friend, which Sexton resented and envied. Four years Plath's senior, Anne Sexton survived her by twelve years, committing suicide in 1974. But Plath keeps hold of the laurels. There are wonderful things in the *Complete Poems* of Sexton, published in 1981, but many of them are things we associate, whatever their original source, with Plath, and Sexton's work seems but a footnote to hers.

After Smith College, after early successes—how competitive Plath was, and how jealous at times of the success of her contemporaries, Adrienne Rich, for example—she was awarded a Fulbright scholarship and traveled to the older Cambridge, in England, where she met Ted Hughes and they married in 1956. After a time in the United States they settled in England in 1960. She died in 1963, the year in which her autobiographical novel *The Bell Jar* was published. *Crossing the Water* and *Winter Trees* were interim publications. At last in 1981 Ted Hughes assembled the *Collected Poems*.

The quality that distinguishes Plath, what has made her a potent influence on impressionable writers in the wake of *Ariel*, is her use of metaphors so strong that they displace what they set out to define and qualify, great cuckoos in the formal nest. By means of such metaphors she seeks to generalize her experience, to step outside it, to render impersonal the (apparently) intensely personal. Yet it is hard to imagine a poetry more forcefully stamped with a personality and voice: American, feminine and for all its traditional powers, eccentric. It is no wonder that feminist critics have found it difficult to approach her, except in the poems where she talks about male projections on women, and preferred initially to attack the people and social prejudices that "martyred" her.

The later work has attracted most attention, suicide validating extreme statement: "She really meant it all." It is wasteful to overlook the *Colossus* poems, however. She was a busy housewife and mother as well as a poet: the verse and the life with their "complementary intensities" were kept apart (a strategy writers like Eavan Boland learned to reject, finding in poetry an integrative art). She said that her poems "have one thing in common. They were all written at about four in the morning—that still, blue, almost eternal hour before cockcrow, before the baby's cry, before the glassy music of the milkman, settling his bottles."

"Daddy" is an extreme example of her distinctive "confessional" mode. It is important for what it reveals about Plath; it tries to attach her experience to a wide realm, by means of imagery and rhetoric. Yet it is the passionate love and anger we remember, so disproportionate that they adhere uniquely to the allegorical figures she has created of "him" and of "herself," the speaker. She *alters* facts: she knows them, and what matters is the poetic experience, the ordered realization of what she knows, true to the impression, not the fact. She announces, "Here is a poem spoken by a girl with an Electra complex. Her father died while she thought he was God. Her case is complicated by the fact that her father was also a Nazi and her mother very possibly part Jewish. In the daughter the two strains marry and paralyze each other—she has to act out the awful little allegory once more before she is free of it." That is what the poems do, "act out the awful little allegory," exorcise rather than confess. If we look for candor here, it is in her truthfulness to the emotion of the moment and the theme to which it attaches. In "Lady Lazarus" she gives symbolic order to her suicide attempts—or Lady Lazarus does. Lady Lazarus is a highly specific and radical creation.

> The second time I meant
> To last it out and not come back at all.
> I rocked shut
>
> As a seashell.
> They had to call and call
> And pick the worms off me like sticky pearls.

Dying
Is an art, like everything else.
I do it exceptionally well.

I do it so it feels like hell.

Of *The Colossus* some critics complain that it is a series of exercises or "compositions" rather than poems. Her earlier work should be assessed in different terms from the later. It was written before the full impact of Sexton's book had registered, before marriage had become a place of pain. Her preoccupation with death in *Colossus* is a powerful but objective fascination. She takes different risks from those of the *Ariel* poems: prosodic risks, risks of diction and subject matter. In *Ariel* there is a radical rethinking of form, a powerfully directive "I" who is sufficiently the poet herself to give the poems an authenticity that Sexton's generally lack. The authority of voice replaces the authority of closed form. The poems are for speaking aloud. Early poems suggest later strategies. "Lorelei": "It is no night to drown in" yet there is the luring song of the fatal ladies:

Sisters, your song
Bears a burden too weighty
For the whorled ear's listening

Here, in a well-steered country,
Under a balanced ruler.

Their voices derange "by harmony" and prefigure the tones of *Ariel*, where death is no longer held at a remove by art and its habitual imposition of objectivity, its natural irony. *Ariel* brings death close—killer and victim, the subject naked or in an imposed costume, facing the music and, worse, the silence. She shifts tone and shuffles images with enormous skill. It is a skill of urgency more than deliberate art. The art of verse is second nature to her.

As a collection *Ariel* is less complete, less lucid, than *Colossus*. The speaker is more centrally part of the later poems, she cannot stand back, she is implicated. An inverted irony takes her further in. The language of hysteria and madness and the language of surrealism merge. The flowers breathe her air; the pain of sickness and of childbirth gives rise, through eyes half open or half closed, to large and alarming metaphors. Fear is always near at hand. In "A Birthday Present" the poem asks: "What is this, behind this veil, is it ugly, is it beautiful? / It is shimmering, has it breasts, has it edges?" Fear is at its most intense in the "bee" poems, especially in "The Bee Meeting," essentialized through allegory:

> Who are these people at the bridge to meet me? They are the
>   villagers—
> The rector, the midwife, the sexton, the agent for bees.
> In my sleeveless summery dress I have no protection,
> And they are all gloved and covered, why did nobody tell me?
> They are smiling and taking out veils tacked to ancient hats.
> I am nude as a chicken neck, does nobody love me?

The poem is made of questions and no answers, of assertions that she corrects with more bizarre assertions. Unlike the others, she is displaced: not of the village, singled out, patronized, the subject rather than a witness to the subject. The queen is flushed out, her society is wrecked. If Hughes is drawn to Ovid in his later work, Plath was a master of metamorphoses more than three decades before him:

> I am exhausted, I am exhausted—
> Pillar of white in a blackout of knives.
> I am the magician's girl who does not flinch.

The "pillar of white" comes first, the "magician's girl" comes second. The metaphor precedes the subject. This reversal, not uncommon in Plath, means that we see first a blur and then a clarity, a process of refocusing which is nightmarish.

> The villagers are untying their disguises, they are shaking hands.
> Whose is that long white box in the grove, what have they
>   accomplished, why am I cold.

The questions abandon the question mark. The outsider is the victim— ignorant, vulnerable, manipulated. She no longer expects an answer. Such a small and eloquent detail as an absent question mark reveals a debt not to Sexton or Hughes or Rich, but to Robert Graves.

She is the victim all right, eaten, sacrificed, a meal for others, for the man, the child. She speaks with, rather than for, other victims. When she uses Hiroshima and Dachau it is in part to borrow a horror, to increase the volume of her poem; but it also suggests that suburban pain, the pain of rejection, loss, doubt, fear, misunderstanding, are not unlike the pain of those subjected to the great brutalities of the century. The theme is choicelessness and powerlessness. Hers is the voice of the victim, rendered passive, coming alive not to resist so much as to witness—a form of resistance, perhaps. The exploitation of the Holocaust and the bombing of Japan shocked when the poems were first published; now it sometimes offends. But it is impossible not to understand, beneath the rhetorical gesture, a different and compelling reason for making the connection. Her positive legacy has been less for those who ape her rhetoric, more for those who find in her use of wildly apposite metaphor a key to seeing things in new ways, a kind of Brechtian *Verfremdung*. In this sense the poet who has taken most from her is the cool, controlled and mannered Craig Raine, the Martian, with his now exhausted metaphor school. There is no clear evidence that Plath—or Raine, for that matter—was familiar with the earlier poems of Norman MacCaig. He passed that way with his wonderful formal tact, a miniaturist and a romantic. His poems are microcosms without totalitarian ambitions. Plath's are always macrocosmic.

In the two or three months after her marriage was over, late in 1962, Plath wrote the bulk of the poems in *Ariel* at great speed and with astonishing assurance. She thought she knew how extraordinary they were, but there was nobody to tell her. She was very hungry for response, for affectionate recognition, but her human intensities, her transparent unhappiness, kept at bay those who might have responded to her that terribly cold winter of 1962. She died.

Early in the 1970s, when Robert Lowell was a fellow of All Souls College, Oxford, he met two English poets who intrigued him. The first, Elizabeth Jennings, was regarded as a "confessional poet." He admired her will and her resourcefulness: "She's tough," he said, a judgment shrewder than her friends realized at the time. And in the formidably witty presence of Patricia Beer he recognized a poet whose restraint, like Elizabeth Bishop's, though on a smaller scale, was telling in unusual ways. What she doesn't say and how she doesn't say it are a vivid lesson in an age when from so many sleeves hung psychotic hearts. Beer's "Autobiography" is succinct and says all that we need to know, perhaps all that we ought to know, about a poet.

I sailed through many waters,
Cold following warm because I moved
Though Arctic and equator were steady.

Harbours sank as I discarded them,
Landmarks melted into the sky
When I needed them no longer.

I left behind all weathers.
I passed dolphins, flying-fish and seagulls
That are ships in their own stories.

In generous if patrician tones, she seemed to put the excesses of the 1960s behind her. Hers was an unusual candor: she had herself in wry perspective.

Born into a Plymouth Brethren (Fundamentalist Christian) family in 1919, Patricia Beer is the Stanley Spencer of modern poetry: lucid, cannily innocent, she apprehends death with a secularized religious imagination; she accepts the inescapable, vivid materiality of the world. In the introduction to her *Collected Poems* she speaks of her slowness in acquainting herself with modern poetry: it was hard disengaging herself from a strict, spiritual world. She went to Exeter for her university degree and read English with a view to becoming a teacher, the one vocation open to a woman of her family's faith. But she went further, too far, and left the Brethren behind. She took a B. Litt. at St. Hugh's College, Oxford, then taught for seven years in Italy, in Padua and Rome. She became acquainted with Eugenio Montale, the great Italian poet. She began to read all the literature she had skirted round before. In 1953 she returned to England, not having written verse since her school days. She involved herself in the fashionable "loose and lush" writing of the time, laboring in the shadow of Dylan Thomas. In 1962 she became a critic and teacher at Goldsmith's College, London. She felt a certain affinity with the Movement, but hers was a different kind of irony.

Religion taught her fundamentalism, personal salvation through faith, uprightness, respectability. She sang the hymns, she came to know the nineteenth century, she feared hellfire. Her mother was a strong-willed housewife, her father a clerk on the railway. One grandfather was a coffin maker, the other a tombstone sculptor. Death became a central theme. So was "madness" or inadequacy. In her wonderful memoir, *Mrs Beer's House* (1968), she remembers a cousin who was incapable in various ways, who was loved and sent away. One critic—in the light of her poem "The Flood," perhaps—calls her "a religious poet stripped of the blurring consolations of religion." She visits churchyards, she evokes the dead of two centuries. Ghosts, witches and ancestors are her familiars. She wants to understand what she is made of. She is fascinated by believers, whether orthodox or eccentric, people who have something to live for and by. Even in the poems of landscape, it is the human figure (or a cat) that occupies center stage. And though by her choices she reveals herself, she does not take herself as subject, except in the poems that explore her illness, an illness of age which she renders in specific but not autobiographical terms. What she is becomes clear from what and how she sees.

Her native landscape is Devon: Exmouth represents security, Torquay adventure and exposure; there is the estuary, the nearby country-side, and eventually the landscape where she now lives, in Up Ottery. She loves writers associated with landscape, Hardy especially, and historical personages that belong to her corner of the world, Drake and the mariners, the sea and the colonies. Her poetic antecedents are often to be found in the prose and verse of the nineteenth century, especially in prose fiction, rather than in the Metaphysicals, about whom she has also written. The values of her verse are—duly ironized—continuous with the prose values of the Victorian writers she admires. Many of the poems grow out of writers' lives or literary texts by Jane Austen, the Brontës, Elizabeth Gaskell, George Eliot, Dickens and others.

What sets her apart from the Movement is the quality of her ironies. She takes the religious imagination, its certainties and uncertainties, seriously but without belief. With irony she defends herself from terror. It is not a distancing device nor an instrument to ingratiate herself with the reader or invite complicity. It separates her from memory and harsh subject matter. In her verse we meet prose virtues: narrative or argumentative structure, "plot" and climax, but the sense is evenly drawn out through the poem. She *seems* to believe in an objective truth in her verse. The cloth of the poems is starched: she uses meter and syllabics according to her subject, and her forms, even the experimental ones, are so subtle that we are inclined to take them for granted. What she writes is poetry because, for all their prose strategies, the poems approach truths that only poetry can essentialize. Relatively quietly, her poems condense and essentialize experiences, and they give to other lives, fictional and actual, a proper imaginative valency.

The experience of her poems, even those drawn from literature, is as vivid as "primary" experience: indeed, it *is* primary experience. Why not? The "derivative" nature of poetry is emblematized in her work not in a disabling way but as a virtue, as Bauhaus architecture acknowledges its materiality and its constituent parts by highlighting them. The real issue with Beer is the seemingly prosaic nature of her poems, a strategy as distinctive as Stevie Smith's weird spoken and sung approach. There is, too, the matter of her wide-eyed candor. She is a poet whose work has gone through a series of mature periods, each her own, each a different sort of honesty. From *The Loss of the Magyar* (1959), book by book through to the *Collected Poems* (1988), *Friend of Heraclitus* (1993) and *Autumn* (1997) she has followed her own course. In *Autumn* she writes of a serious illness:

I was born tongue-tied. Ages later
Here comes once more the suffocator

That I cannot recall but must
Have been what paralysed me most

Of all the things I could not do.
My speech is back in prison now.

Whatever silenced me when young
Has put a thimble on my tongue.

Autumn (and illness) overtake her; her eyes are more than ever awake to
ripening colors, and to the young whose season is not yet defined. She
comes to terms: with her own serious illness, the deaths of friends and
the encroachments of age. She also remembers family, with a surreal
clarity in her materialism ("Ballad of the Underpass" is in equal degrees
terrifying and affirmative). She reads characters from Shakespeare into
life. Wilfred Owen writes to his "Dearest of Mothers" full of optimism,
which the date, "1918," ironizes. "Sequence" considers her own nearly
fatal illness and its consequences, using tautened couplets that ache with
the stark necessity of rhyme. Beer does not flinch from hard subjects or
sentimentalize; she knows how grief works, how clarifying laughter can
make things less intolerable. Hers is a crucially English form of disclo-
sure: she stands outside herself, as curious as we are about what the
poems will tell.

Elizabeth Jennings, like Beer, has gone through many transforma-
tions. She is a conventional poet, despite early interest in Eliot and
Graves. Her conventionality has to do with diction and form. She is
most at home in meter and rhyme, the sonnet and the lyric, where the
challenge is diction and the accommodation of hard subject matter.

She was born in Boston, Lincolnshire, in 1926. She had a troubled
childhood and attempted suicide more than once. Unlike Plath, Jen-
nings does not allegorize the causes for her mental disturbance. Poetry
is not exorcism but sacrament, a sharing. However extreme her illness,
poetry is a way back from the edge, not over it; at her most disturbed she
witnesses other people. Without recourse to stylistic ironies, she gains a
perspective on herself. The seasons, landscapes, artifacts and people sur-
round her.

In 1961, after she had written her first three celebrated collections of
poems—*A Way of Looking*, *A Sense of the World* and *Song for a Birth or a
Death*—she published her most substantial critical work. Of *Every
Changing Shape*, a series of related essays, she writes: "I am concerned
with three things—the making of poems, the nature of mystical experi-
ence, and the relationship between them." She was thirty-five, working
as an editor at a publishing house in London, on the threshold of a reli-

gious and psychological crisis that was to beset her for twenty years. She wrote this book "at the pitch of poetry," with entire concentration.

She insists on continuities in the language of poetry, its inescapable contingencies. "Poets work upon and through each other," she declares. The natural and inevitable interdependence between poets and poems is "the real meaning of tradition and influence." This is not far from Eliot's sense of the contemporaneity of all literature, and its transcendence. For her, transcendence is not an aesthetic but a spiritual verity. The connection between Herbert, Traherne and Vaughan is more than a literary matter. It entails affinities not so much of temperament as of spirit. Her own connection with Eliot and Hopkins, with Edwin Muir and Christina Rossetti, Charlotte Mew and Rilke, is as patent as her loving inferences from St. Teresa of Avila and Julian of Norwich. "If there is . . . a connection between poetry and mysticism, then it will be found as easily in the fifth century in Italy as in the fourteenth century in England or the twentieth century in France." All her chosen poets are from the Christian era, and her poems—perhaps this is why Lowell honored them and her—invariably have a potent religious dimension.

She prefers the language of embodiment, containing rather than describing meanings: "With this ring I thee wed" rather than "I give you this ring as a sign of our marriage." Enactment in language—a function of rhythm, word order, diction—can impart a spiritual dimension to work of secular writers; poems can mean more than a poet intends, as if touched by a grace the poet inadvertently accesses and cannot deny. For a religious poet, crisis comes when grace recedes, as it does in Vaughan and Cowper, St. John of the Cross and Hart Crane, and from time to time in Jennings: the anxiety of disconnection is potent and can be fatal.

A cradle Catholic, she has not sought emancipation from the metaphysical as Beer does. She makes no bones about belief or doubt. Yet without resorting to politic and bland strategies of ecumenicism, she finds energies outside her church, even outside faith. In taking the title of her critical book from Eliot's early poem "Portrait of a Lady," she indicates the protean nature of the spirit, eluding embodiment in an age of doubt. In choosing Eliot she signals a debt (not a great one, judging from her formal strategies) to the modernists.

She seeks out mystics, religious writers and those whose approach is oblique, for whom the structures of faith are drained of meaning, but who continue to surprise—in Larkin's phrase—"a hunger in themselves to be more serious." Language is a net made by men and women, its weave too coarse or fragile to snare and hold the transcendent meanings it is after. Mystics write about the experience of mysticism, striving to express what it is and how to attain it. A poet makes a poem, and "What the poet says about how he made it is always a falling away from the experience itself; it throws a backward light. The poet's explanations are approximations at best." All criticism illuminates, if at all, in retrospect, a backward light. It is the task of theory to project into the past and future.

The concerns of *Every Changing Shape* are the concerns of her poetry. She has written philosophical poems, but they take her no further than a threshold; beyond is a pathway or a set of stairs. What matters is what happens when the "I," the insistent first person of the early poems, the conscious "mind" with its intractable definitions and flaws, which occurs with such frequency in her books, including those written during her illness, reaches the point of "communion." Like Cowper, who wrote out of distress and nightmare toward a common light where men and women walked and worshipped in the vulgar tongue, Jennings's work moves toward a norm. For her, as a Catholic, that norm has a crucial spiritual sanction.

Her poems function cumulatively, building toward understanding. They do not aspire to coherent structure but to coherent meaning. They are tentative and do not overreach, do not make claims too large. When they come up against contrary evidence they do not try to hide it. The age is secular and the concerns of the poetic imagination—as Davie argued in *Thomas Hardy and British Poetry*—have been trammeled in contingencies. Since the 1930s, for many writers, history has displaced the transcendent concerns of those poets from whom the large figures of the past took their bearings. Jennings is awkwardly out of place in her difficult adherence to a strict order, living at the same time in a daily world.

The self-effacement of her approach does not conceal the anachronistic nature of her quest, the hubris of her presumption that in 1961— or in 1999 or 2020—such concerns retain meaning for poets and readers. Postmodernism is in the ascendant and language itself beleaguered by those who deny that it possesses the nominal properties in which a religious poet's faith is grounded. Her task may seem hopeless. She is no ironist, and this too sets her apart from her generation. She speaks of "bold humility and a disinterested intelligence." No intelligence is disinterested—that much can be conceded to the postmodernist. But the quality of her interest is different in kind from that which emanates from most seminar rooms. Her beliefs are not a matter of opinion.

She attended St. Anne's College, Oxford, and became a librarian in the city. Her early distinction made her a focal figure for younger poets. They gathered about her and called themselves Elizabethans. She encouraged them. Her own work is enhanced by her advocacies of her younger contemporaries, and of Charlotte Mew and Christina Rossetti. There is formidable accomplishment in the early work. For her second book she received a Somerset Maugham Award and traveled to Italy, one of the formative experiences in her life. The year when it all changed was 1961, the year of her breakdown. She turned to Hopkins, to the dark sonnets. *The Mind Has Mountains,* her 1966 collection, reveals the force and integrity of her struggle. Her first *Collected Poems* (1967) looked for a time like a swan song, the collections that followed containing few notable new poems. At last in 1975, in *Growing Points,* she found direction again, with a substantial increase in her technical resources. Since then her work has grown more confident and occasionally achieves moments of serenity that, in the fifteen years of her struggle with madness, would have seemed impossible. Her 1986 *Collected Poems* received the W. H. Smith Award—inevitably, one is tempted to say. In it she sorted out her earlier work, purged the poems of painful transition, abandoned the terrible free-association free-verse poems of her worst years, and came to rest on affirmation.

If the Movement adopted her, it was because of her formal intelligence and her responsible statements. They took their bearings from Empson, Auden and Betjeman; she took hers from Graves. Her stance is one of trust, not distrust; her poems are always vulnerable. And she did not wish to reject the poets of the 1940s or any other resources. She was and remains singularly unpolemical. If her early (unpublished) poems were pale imitations of Eliot, she stumbled on Graves and fell in love with the well-made lyric. She is more an heir of the Georgians than of Hopkins and Herbert, whom she reveres. The greatest influence on her poetic texture is not Eliot or Graves but Edwin Muir. Her religion, her poetic antecedents, and her effective absence from the world during the defining years of feminism left her poems untouched by theory, yet she is herself an interesting case study for feminists in terms of her poetic strategies, commitments and denials.

She compares making poems to the practice of prayer: it reconciles the individual with what is outside it; self is lost in a larger stability. "Each brings an island in his heart to square / With what he finds, and all is something strange / And most expected." Prayer and poetry also risk the terrifying world of shadows. In her poem on Rembrandt's late self-portraits, in which she implicates herself, she declares, "To paint's to breathe / And all the darknesses are dared."

The paradox of Jennings's poetry is that the experiences that might have broken her style open—mental illness and its vertiginous phases— seemed to make the forms more tight. Not wishing to project or falsify, the poems about her experiences in a mental hospital are forceful by means of understatement. It is in the serener, later poems, when she revisits almost in a Fern Hill spirit her childhood in Lincolnshire, when she reflects on painters and other artists, on the bed-sit life, solitude, the solace and attrition of neighbors, the mature loves that leave so much unspoken, when she experiences bereavement or speaks in the voice of the Virgin or Christ, that form at last is challenged, as though it is no longer quite adequate for the fullness of her statements. In her later books parts of poems are the best she has written, other parts the worst. "This is my love and now it must be spoken" is an urgent line, but it introduces a tepid poem; another poem begins turgidly and rises to unprecedented heights. The unevenness is exhilarating and vexing. No poem is without a moment at least of astonishment, but few are as complete as "My Grandmother" and "Song for a Birth or a Death" from her middle books. Perhaps, though she writes discrete lyrics, she is a poet who, like another Catholic writer, David Jones, makes sense only *in extenso*, where the predictable and pedestrian exist beside the epiphanic. The world and her poetry include cliché and utter particularity, crude off-the-peg sentiment and the most bespoke of spiritual insights.

Almost every poem that Philip Larkin included in his four books was classically complete. Some pieces that Anthony Thwaite recovered from magazines and notebooks are also complete; only seldom does Larkin miss his targets; the lapses in diction are usually deliberate. He of all the Movement poets remained most true to his point of departure, and only he of his generation achieved the large readership that other poets envy. His work is controversial not in itself but in what he represents to poets and critics of different camps. He certainly did as much as Housman to turn back the clock of English poetry; like Housman, he is the modern poet most often quoted—in church, in Parliament, in the classroom—by folk who latch on to a phrase or stanza, without bothering to understand what the poem as a whole might mean. His was the characteristic voice of the 1950s and 1960s, regarded by some as the most significant English poet of the postwar.

Where does he come from? From the uptight middle class, with a father whose Little Englandism was Mosleyite, with a quiet, undemonstrative mother to whom he was devoted. Coventry, 1922. Grammar school in the city. A solitary adolescence filled with novel writing as other boys' is with onanism. The manuscripts disposed of furtively. Oxford—St. John's College. His friends included Kingsley Amis, John Wain, Robert Conquest. An infatuation with Dylan Thomas, and with Yeats up to *Words for Music Perhaps*—hence none of Yeats's later asperity rubbed off on Larkin. This is fortunate, for Larkin learned his own asperity, which owes nothing to Yeats. He wrote to Michael Hamburger that, to him, the "tradition of poetry" is "emotion and honesty of emotion, and it doesn't matter who it is written by or how, if this is conveyed." Only one adjustment of this point of view was made after, but it is all-important: "how" became crucial. Auden and Betjeman taught

him that, and finally the vaccination against Romanticism, the poetry of
Hardy, read early on spring mornings in his uncurtained bed-sit. But it
was a romantic temperament that had to content itself with disappoint-
ment as its theme.

He does not idealize the past. He does not see it, in Hardy's terms,
as unrealized, either. It is simply unrealizable. Not Wordsworth's infant
trailing clouds of glory behind whom gates of the prison-house close;
not Brownings' "Never the time and the place / And the loved one all
together" or even Hardy's "Everything glowed with a gleam; / But we
were looking away." There was no cloud-trailing infant, no all together,
no glow. Yet from these poets Larkin took crucial bearings. Death is his
abiding muse, not love or even lust, with its temporary solaces. He
essentializes childhood in "I Remember, I Remember," with its wan
allusion to Thomas Hood's lovely poem about home, its irony at Law-
rence's expense, its train journey (there are numerous train journeys in
Larkin, the university librarian traveling to committee meetings around
the country).

> "Was that," my friend smiled, "where you 'have your roots'?"
> No, only where my childhood was unspent,
> I wanted to retort, just where I started . . .

There is time betrayed, as in "Home," and opportunity wasted *passim*. It
begins even before the bleak poem "On Being 26," which he chose to
exclude from his books but his executors have stirred back into the
bleak, miraculous mix: not a good poem despite its formal deftnesses.
Here we find self-pity. How he overcomes it is one triumph of his work.

Davie contrasts Hardy's irony, which is thematic, with the irony of
the Movement, which is stylistic. It is a distinction valid for all the
Movement poets except Larkin. For Larkin irony inheres, and if it is at
times stylistic, his stance toward the world, it is also inherent in the
experiences he writes from. It is there in "Deceptions," a line of which
gives the title to his first mature collection, *The Less Deceived* (1955), and
ends with a rapist imagined bursting into "fulfilment's desolate attic."
Irony can be terrifying, even when it is funny, as in "Toads" and "Toads
Revisited." It can make a reader anxious and uncomfortable about pain,
distance, exclusion, in "An Arundel Tomb" for example.

The earlier poems speak in the first person singular, but with *The
Whitsun Weddings* (1964) and *High Windows* (1974) Larkin writes "we"
more often than "I," implicating us or inviting us into complicity, not
communion. We share in diminishment, in the gathering darkness.
What makes him distinctive? Formally, Kingsley Amis and—in differ-
ent ways—Jennings, Gunn and Davie are comparably astute. Perhaps he

understands the dynamics of living form better than they; or perhaps it is because he often chooses not the particular but the characteristic detail: "the music on the piano stool" (which music? that is for us to decide), "that vase" (again we fill in the shape and color of the noun). He wanted to be the novelist, Amis the poet, but irony dictated that they should be changelings. Yet just as Amis conceives of paragraphs and chapters as stanzas and introduces even in absurd situations unusually poetic structural elements, so that an emptied lyricism is always in his voice, so Larkin tells consistent stories and creates consistent voices in his poems. Whatever the form is doing (and mere narrative never displaces form), details are arranged so as to create a coherence in scene or emotional development. The movement of the eye in "Church Going"; the changing tones of voice, from anger, to fear, dismay and resignation in "The Old Fools"; the self-reflexive voice of "High Windows"; the scrupulous and bizarrely erotic allegory of "Next Please": over and above formal precision there is a kind of consistent psychology, that of a character who may be a persona or—as seems more likely in a poet so apparently pitched against modernism as Larkin—may be a conjuration of the poet's own voice.

Larkin's inverted romanticism means that he distrusts the subjective, his own and that of the characters he creates and the people he observes. So he evokes them through the physical objects with which they surround themselves. The prospective landlady emerges from her mode of speech, Mr. Bleaney through the articles he has left behind, the footprint into which the speaker of the poem is willing to step. The "cut price crowd" rushes from the stark new suburbs to shop, its values determined and defined by the objects it rushes to acquire. His music is jazz, but the Sidney Bechet blues, not Charlie Parker.

In his first book he "ghosted for the ghost of Yeats." *The North Ship* (1945) is full of echoes. He borrows the rhetoric of a passionate poet to express passionlessness: "The heart in its own endless silence kneeling." He was actually young, writing on mauve paper, reading by candlelight through narrowed eyes, making poems from the froth of other men's language. His two novels followed in 1946 and 1947, *Jill* and *A Girl in Winter*. Only his more serious fans value them.

The Less Deceived emanated from a small press in Hull, where Larkin had gone after time in Belfast and Leicester to be librarian at the Brynmore Jones Library at the university. It did well, and the next year he was a central exhibit in *New Lines*, Robert Conquest's anthology, which defined the Movement in its first phase. His later collections came at longer and longer intervals, with, between times, a book on jazz (*All What Jazz*, 1972), the *Oxford Book of Twentieth Century English Verse* (1973) and *Required Writing: Miscellaneous Pieces 1955–1982* (1983). His

Collected Poems appeared posthumously in 1988, and a volume of letters and a biography followed, books he explicitly instructed in his will should never appear.

"I never think of poetry or the poetry scene, only separate poems written by individuals," he says. His task as a poet is "to preserve things I have seen / thought / felt"; poems are "verbal devices," "verbal pickling." They build toward a point of "liftoff"; poems are structured, then, to a thematic or dramatic climax, which can occur in the release of an image or a change in tone of voice from the fatuous and lighthearted to deadly earnest. In his prose the irony is for the most part stylistic. In a guarded way in conversation he made concessions: about Laura Riding, whom he regarded as a charlatan but whose rhythms, he confessed, he found mysteriously irresistible; about French symbolism, even about Eliot and other modernist writing. He had a public persona to maintain, but the private man could have an open and independent judgment.

Like his beloved Hardy and Edward Thomas he is a great deployer of negative words, often positive words turned negative, but more subtly, negative words that by a prefix become very nearly affirmative: "unfakeable," "unignorable," "unpriceable." Part of his understatement is that he works from below, as it were, not cutting down a large Romantic subject by irony but, by counterirony, building a subject up. When he is being savage about the poor, the old, the uncultured, we can be sure that by the end of the poem they will have been understood and celebrated, the savagery having been redirected at himself, his attitude, his circumstances. Hardy stands—hungry for faith—outside the church, "prayer denied." Larkin stands apart from the group, excluded, observing and understanding his separateness.

His originality begins in reaction: to the naïve idealism of the 1930s poets, to the beguiling excess of the Apocalyptics. He accepted the various frustrations and defeats of life—active only in apprehending and describing, and not until the later work counseling action, in specifically social poems. If his technique did not develop after *The Less Deceived*, his perspectives broadened, and his conservatism tended toward satire.

The poems are invariably subtly made and self-contained; we respond without footnotes, without consulting any document beyond a daily paper. The poems are replete with the small dramas, losses and frustrations that add up to the large gradual tragedy of lives in a thousand furnished rooms and modest houses, in a particular country at a particular time.

Hardy taught him to look outside, to fix the eye on detail, and to leave the impulsive, private, impressionable world of *The North Ship* behind, to disembark on the terra firma of landscape, of the time that is now and the world that is the welfare state. Hardy showed him how to write as a person who stands at the edge of the crowd, prevented from joining in by a habit of mind that asks uncomfortable questions.

There are, thereafter, only *poems*, no concept of poetry, no impulse to order poems in a single "statement." A poem works cumulatively: the scene, tone or argument is set in motion, details assemble, until there is a point of liftoff, a modulation of tone or a deepening of seriousness. From the evocation of externals, the poet proceeds to release their composite meanings. When "liftoff" fails the poems can be vivid verse catalogues only, like "To the Sea" and "Show Saturday."

The themes in *The North Ship*—unwilling capitulation to the system of things, love's unsuccess, frustration, boredom, loneliness, and especially time, "the echo of an axe / Within a wood"—inform the later poems. All that is lacking is the Larkin scenario to make emotion or lack of emotion come alive, through particulars. The early problem may have been that the "I" was not a voice but a poetical persona, much as the "I" in *High Windows* is sometimes an outdated "I" who no longer sounds true.

The adjustment of style between *The North Ship* and *The Less Deceived* is complete. The first poem in the second collection, "Lines on a Young Lady's Photograph Album," is Betjemanesque, though more sinewy than Betjeman, with an Edwardian archness. The poet's attraction to the young lady is strongly sexual. Images are not symbolic but evocative particulars. A subtler change came in *The Whitsun Weddings*. The perspective widens, images derive from broader experience, the vision becomes social. In a world heavy with late capitalism, a world of transactions and relationships which time renders senseless, the tragedy of unfulfillment moves out from the "I." The first poem in the book, "Here," progresses panoramically through details of landscape that reveal a community, its history and ambitions, much as the details in "Church Going" reveal a faith. The panorama is urban, then—moving out—rural, "where removed lives / Loneliness clarifies." The juxtaposition of two isolations—individuals isolated in the crowd and the individual isolated in the landscape—is heightened by the speaker's isolation from both, a middleman undertaking a verbal transaction. In "Wants," the world divides between those who find despair incomprehensible and those who find it unspeakable.

In *High Windows* there are more Larkins at work than at any time before; each Larkin is skillful and suggestive but none quite so centered as the Larkin of the previous books. The poet of "Here" reappears—without his earlier power—in "To the Sea" and "Show Saturday." His attempt to celebrate social customs and rites is hampered by his temperament. He knows that rites, too, have their date. Browning impinges on "Livings (iii)": perhaps Larkin wanted to try dramatic monologues as a way out of the self. There are notable successes in essentially new tones. "High Windows" itself has assurance, candor, and an unresolved suggestiveness seldom found in the earlier work. The same quality, but a different tone, informs "The Explosion," about a pit disaster. "The Old Fools" has an asperity tempered by tenderness. Age was nearer at hand. The last eleven years of his life included no further books of poems. Only one major poem, "Aubade," was added to the body of work, a poem that, like so many before it but with unprecedented urgency, considered death: "Not to be here, / Not to be anywhere / And soon." The wry, socially lacerating and self-lacerating tone of "Vers de Société" has given way to a genuine terror: not panic, but the fear of a man excluded from all consolation, approaching the summit of extinction's alp, which he reached in 1985.

Why is a poet of such unoptimistic temperament so popular? Perhaps most of all because of the insidiousness of his verse, the way that after one or two readings it lodges in memory. It has, with its characteristic details, its spoken tones, its formal assurance, the sound of truth, and a poet who speaks bleak truths is probably more valuable than one who gives us airy and empty consolations. The candor of Larkin is different in kind from the candor of Lowell and Plath, not more English, precisely, but more democratic. His truths (if they are true) carry at least the consolation of clarity, unfuzzed by darkly autobiographical resentments. No doubt they are there behind the poems, but the poet has had the tact to push them very nearly out of sight.

Language and the Body

ALLEN GINSBERG, ADRIENNE RICH, EAVAN BOLAND,
LOUISE GLÜCK, JORIE GRAHAM, JUDITH WRIGHT,
GWEN HARWOOD, ALLEN CURNOW, JAMES K. BAXTER,
W. S. MERWIN

Theodore Roethke numbered among his "more tedious contemporaries" in America the "roaring asses, hysterics, sweet-myself beatniks, earless wonders happy with effects a child of two could improve on." The loudest poetry voices of the second half of the twentieth century were the Beats, preeminent among them Allen Ginsberg, who made noises about the American system and way of life, about sexual and spiritual liberation, about war and repression. "I want to be known as the most brilliant man in America," he says in "Ego Confession."

He also wrote poems. "His poetry made things happen," said one obituary. That's not quite right. His performances, his polemics, his affronting or affirming presence made things happen. His example as a performer touched poets remote from him in temperament, like Lowell and Bob Dylan. But the poems, the ones that are regarded as "great": Do they exist apart from his voice, apart from their aurality, on the page as poems? With Robert Duncan and Paul Goodman, we are told, he "invented gay liberation": "It was Ginsberg, perhaps more than any other individual, who helped turn marginal forms of behaviour into norms: psychedelic drugs, distrust of government institutions, sexual explicitness, guiltless hedonism, fear of nuclear energy." His political and social impact was considerable; I remember his smoky, thronged performances in the 1960s as experiences in which nine tenths of my fellow undergraduates underwent temporary conversions, gratefully surrendering to the power of an event from which few of us stood back in disbelief. There was something medieval in the hysteria that the "sweet-myself" leader (he was a leader) evoked, emancipating us from the American dream into an alternative order. Rejection implies a system; anarchy is the most exacting political form and seldom lasts for long.

Apart from the congregation's suspension of intelligence during those performance events, I most remember the homespun textures, the voluminous hair and the smells—smoke of several varieties, sweat, scents. Ginsberg was a body and his mission seemed to be to deliver us back to a sense of our bodies as a place of grace and an instrument of praise.

> Everything is holy! everybody's holy! everywhere is holy! everyday
>   is in eternity! Everyman's an angel!

But after the priest and prophet has departed and we are left clutching his book, what do the poems *do*?

There are three Allen Ginsbergs. First and most arresting is the young poet struggling under the constraining patronage of Williams, but with the soulful spirit already bubbling away in him:

> The warm bodies
>   shine together
> in the darkness,
>   the hand moves
> to the center
>   of the flesh,
> the skin trembles
>   in happiness
> and the soul comes
>   joyful to the eye . . .

Then there is the second Ginsberg (already a friend of Burroughs and Kerouac), visited by William Blake in the privacy of his room, Ginsberg being in the last throes of masturbation. Blake brushed him with angel dust and gave him wings—or filled him with helium, as well as social anger—and in the wake of these visitations came the poems *Howl* and later *Kaddish*. Then, traveling on a Japanese train, he became Allen Ginsberg III: a Buddhist no longer burning toward death but celebrating life (through his own) in all its muzzy "wholeness." A gentler poet, American still, ambitious and—when need be—unscrupulous, playing to the gallery.

Ginsberg is not Blake, lacking the craft, the formal and spiritual skills of that master. Nor is he Whitman, though he's often presented as Whitman's heir. "I saw you, Walt Whitman, childless, lonely old grubber, poking among the meats in the refrigerator and eying the grocery boys." This is Ginsberg's appropriation, simplified and sentimentalized. Whitman's "I" was indeed inclusive. It is not that he "spoke for

America" but his voice included everyone. Whitman's poetry is full of characteristic detail rather than specific imagery. He is the poem's vehicle but not systematically its subject. He honors the body politic and its wounds hurt him; his own wounds he regards as trivial, beneath the dignity of the larger poem. America is registered through him. By Ginsberg's day, perhaps the body politic was too old and raddled to draw from the poet the passion it commanded from Whitman. If Ginsberg gets anything from his predecessor, it is a rhetoric, a long line (but, in *Howl* crammed full of chaotic specifics, rather than representative shapes). Ginsberg's passion is for the marginal, the other societies which the empowered society excludes. Wounding the whole America of Whitman is his mission—perhaps to force into it, through those wounds, the Americas that America excluded. Like an anti-Savonarola, he loves to polarize the damned and the saved, the beat and the square, the "heads" and the gays over the straights, men over women. It is the female *body* he cannot get his imagination around: he observes it with horror and awe. His "I" is himself.

Ginsberg could be the priest of holy madness, anti-authoritarian, a man of generosity, a voice of the future; but he signed the papers to have his mother lobotomized, supported authoritarian individuals and regimes as long as they were ranged against his primary foe, the United States, was ungenerous to fellow poets if they were not of his camp and promoted himself at the expense of those around him, even after he had shaved off his beard and assumed the quiet demeanor of an almost dapper professor. The big days were in the 1950s, and his last four decades fed off the fat of the huge and unexpected pop-star success of his setting out. He remained a compelling performer, even of the awful later poems. Self-projection was his incomparable skill and it proved fatal to the work in the end: the voice could imbue a shopping list with transcendent significance.

It is to his first three books that future readers will attend, *Howl and Other Poems* (1956), *Kaddish and Other Poems* (1960) and *Reality Sandwiches* (1963). In 1963 Buddhism claimed him on the Kyoto-Tokyo Express. Nothing he subsequently wrote was wholly without interest, but, subdued by his new beliefs, the later work is after-echo.

Ginsberg was born in Paterson, New Jersey, his father a poet and teacher, his mother a woman who suffered from mental illness. It was the presence of his father that at once inspired and inhibited his development. When he wrote *Howl* he dreaded not the censor but his father's response to the lines "who let themselves be fucked in the ass by saintly motorcyclists, and screamed with joy, / who blew and were blown by those human seraphim, the sailors, caresses of Atlantic and Caribbean love, / who balled in the morning in the evenings in rosegardens and the grass of public parks and cemeteries scattering their semen freely to whomever come who may" and so on. Once he had got these facts down on paper and into print, he had broken a personal taboo and could say anything he liked in the future. The radical element in his work is not his politics, his homosexuality, his drug-taking, so much as the purging of inhibition, personal reserve, self-pity, the abandonment of the "bourgeois first person singular." Egocentric he remains, but his is not the suffering lyrical "ego" of most of his contemporaries, even of some of his contemporaries among the Beats.

Paterson: William Carlos Williams. It is not surprising that Williams—who admired the early Ginsberg—should have written the preface to *Howl and Other Poems*. "Hold back the edges of your gowns, Ladies, we are going through hell." Ladies are in particular peril from the poem. Hell must be defined before "Holiness" can get to work. Another Beat poet, Gregory Corso, said, "I am the substance of my poetry." Ginsberg is substance too: he pours all the verbal jewelry and garbage in his mind into the poem, and then performs it in those long, hectic, racing lines where the best we can do is snatch at the sense. Reading it on the page, do we try to "construe" it as we do other poetry? Do we try to read quickly so as to replicate the poet's vocalities? Do we take the long lines as single aphoristic units? It is a poem to be heard. On the page it is like a complex musical score. Not only does it need to be performed, it should be heard by a group. It is not a poetry for the private reader. The performance poets who have learned from Ginsberg say that they will alter their poems in response to a specific audience, to immediate public events, to the city in which they are performing. *Textuality* is beside the point. When you slow it down every assertion (it is a poem of assertions) becomes questionable, even the opening lines:

> I saw the best minds of my generation destroyed by madness,
>   starving hysterical naked
> dragging themselves through the negro streets at dawn looking for
>   an angry fix,
> angelheaded hipsters burning for the ancient heavenly connection
>   to the starry dynamo in the machinery of night,
> who poverty and tatters and hollow-eyed and high sat up smoking
>   in the supernatural darkness of cold-water flats floating across
>   the tops of cities contemplating jazz . . .

The sentence runs on and on, syntax not so much abandoned as dissipated. Were these indeed the *best* minds of his generation? What had happened to their intelligence? "Minds" is wrong—"spirit," "soul" or "imagination" might have served better. But points of diction are beside the point. If we strip away the more rhetorical adjectives and adjectival phrases the poem says as much:

> I saw the minds destroyed by madness,
> dragging themselves through the streets at dawn looking for a fix,
> hipsters burning for the connection to the dynamo in the
>   machinery of night,
> who sat up smoking in the darkness of cold-water flats floating
>   across the tops of cities contemplating jazz . . .

The poet's mouth needs to cram itself full of words: half a mouthful won't do.

Williams had never seen anything quite like Ginsberg before. He was astonished by the way the poet let himself say anything: he "experiences it to the hilt." This is not quite right: the language goes to places the poet would not and could not go. Rising on his own enthusiasm, Williams declares: "We are blind and live our blind lives out in blindness. Poets are damned but they are not blind, they see with the eyes of angels." Nonsense, but good sales copy. "4 Sniffs & I'm High."

Ginsberg studied at Columbia University, knew Burroughs, whose prose electrified him, and Jack Kerouac. He fell miserably in love with Neal Cassady, whose full-voiced letters to Kerouac affected the style of the author of *On the Road* and *The Dharma Bums* quite as much as it did Ginsberg's own. Conversation and the intimate epistle that let rip with rage, fantasy, affection, description—language that allowed itself maximum liberty—were the crucial elements that formed Ginsberg's style.

He dropped out of college for a year, traveling and doing odd jobs. Wandering became a vocation. The reading tour was a way of life, a heroic progress around the globe again and again. He was the guru of the Beats, and he spread the word, so that throughout Europe he became an icon and fathered dozens of would-be Beats. His most celebrated stopover was in Prague, where, in 1965, students elected him king of the May and he was immediately deported. He wrote *"Kral Majales"* to commemorate this heroic martyrdom at the hands of "the Marxists" who "have beat me upon the street."

In interviews he told how his poems came to him, what combinations of drugs helped him to release the language of *Howl* (Part II was "composed during a peyote vision") and other poems, including his most important, *Kaddish* (written after "an injection of amphetamine plus a little bit of morphine, plus some Dexedrine later on to keep me going, because it was all in one long sitting"). "First thought, best thought," he declared.

Kaddish is a long lament, following a Hebrew form, for his mother.

The pain is real, and with grief, guilt and anger he evokes the world of which she was made and by which she was unmade.

> Strange now to think of you, gone without corsets and eyes, while I
> walk on the sunny pavement of Greenwich Village
> downtown Manhattan, clear winter noon, and I've been up all
> night, talking, talking, reading the Kaddish aloud, listening to
> Ray Charles blues shout blind on the phonograph
> the rhythm the rhythm—and your memory in my head three years
> after—And read Adonais' last triumphant stanzas aloud—wept,
> realizing how we suffer

This poem in particular belongs to Ginsberg; the other poems belong to his generation. It was Kerouac who described his friends as the "beat generation." He might have been alluding to the jazz beat, or to the sense of being "beat"—tired out with things as they were, dropouts. Or is there a connection with "beatitude"? That is the spin Ginsberg would have given it. By that token, writers remote from the druggy subculture aspects of the Beats in the 1950s and 1960s might be gathered into its fold.

Ginsberg dropped on American poetry like a bomb; his generation outgrew him and American poetry has outgrown him. Adrienne Rich, a more profound and consistent radical, redefines the spaces that English-language poetry can occupy. Ginsberg's is a poetry of powerful but local revolt; Rich's is a criticism and a revolution.

Hazlitt remembers how Wordsworth and Coleridge were passionate for liberty; but after the French Revolution "failed," love of liberty was displaced by a hunger for legitimacy and the security that goes with it. Time alters many poets in this way. Adrienne Rich breaks the pattern. Her (increasingly green) radicalism has grown, changing in complexity as events change and she herself grows older. She will not allow herself to be marginalized again, as she was, inadvertently, in her first world. She sets her cap against "degradation," a term that has a different sense in different contexts. In the arts, she contrasts the movie on the big screen with the movie on television, an image of technological and critical reductiveness, consumerism, passivity. She speaks in her prose of the 1970s of re-visioning, a function her poetry sets out to perform. How did she come to terms with feminism and with her own sexuality? Unlike Ginsberg, changed by a single moment of apprehension, for Rich the process is long and difficult: "the awakening of consciousness is not like the crossing of a frontier," it is not like religious conversion, no divine "grace" descends: it is a becoming conscious, a deliberate, rigorous reconstruction of self. What is she working with? We can begin by giving her labels, like a well-traveled suitcase: American, half Jew on her father's side, liberal-socialist, disabled; woman, daughter, wife, mother; lesbian, lover; feminist, radical-feminist. All and none of these sobriquets—used selectively by one faction or another—characterize her as a writer or explain why she has been to some extent responsible for changing the reading, writing and teaching of poetry by women, gay men and others.

We can place her in space and time: Adrienne Cecile Rich. Born in Baltimore, Maryland, 1929. The Depression, Roosevelt, the New Deal, idealism. Her Jewish father was a pathologist at Johns Hopkins University, her mother a southern Gentile. During her childhood, the Second World War ran its course. In 1951 she graduated from Radcliffe College (Harvard). McCarthy was hunting witches, there was Eisenhower, Korea, Hungary. In the period after her graduation she published two books of poems, enjoyed a Guggenheim Fellowship, married and had three sons. Her first book, *A Change of World* (1951), was selected by Auden for the Yale Younger Poets series. He patronized her in his complacently schoolmarmy foreword: the poems "are neatly and modestly dressed, speak quietly but do not mumble, respect their elders but are not cowed by them and do not tell fibs." It does not take a feminist reading to sense the sexual distaste. Auden had a neat skill for infantilizing the other, when he wasn't Aunt Sallying it as in "Miss Gee." Auden's manner and tone express the urbane disdain for the woman poet that was commonplace at the time. Sylvia Plath, roughly Rich's contemporary, was jealous of her spectacular early success. She saw Rich one night: "Short black hair, great sparking black eyes and a tulip-red umbrella: honest, frank, forthright and even opinionated."

In the 1960s there was Black Power, the rise of feminism and the gay movement. There was Vietnam. It is necessary to set her in these contexts because they provide occasions first for her formal strategies and tentativenesses, then for the emerging assurance that has made her a figure central to the American women's movement and to the liberalization of American poetry.

Auden was, of course, one of the elders she respected, and her early verse belongs with the New Criticism and the conventional closures of the early Movement. American and British poetry were briefly in phase. Her work was assured from the outset. In retrospect the radical seeds were already sown in the first poems, but it was with *Snapshots of a Daughter-in-Law* (1962) that the important changes began, continuing through her next three collections with their "political" titles *Necessities of Life* (1966), *Leaflets* (1969), *The Will to Change* (1971). She was teaching open admissions at City College, New York, in touch with aspiring writers from every ethnic and social background. The suburban world receded. In that year her father and her husband died. These losses and new experiences led to her highly controversial volume *Diving into the Wreck* (1973), where she combines her voices—mother, lesbian, teacher, wife, woman. In "At a Bach Concert" she wrote:

> A too-compassionate art is only half an art.
> Only such proud restraining purity
> Restores the else-betrayed, too-human heart.

To make a whole art, it was necessary first to fill in the other half, which might mean, for a time, that compassion will give way to a harsh truth-telling, telling the truth not only to the world but to the self. To tell the truth in poetry there have to be the forms, the words and the will to use them.

There is an almost too tidy pattern in her development, not that she set out to grow as she has done but that when the truth of an idea becomes clear to her, she will act upon it even if that action is against the grain of her instincts. Thus from the tight and efficient conventional forms of her early work she has, step by step, learned to abandon resources and create new ones in their place. The old forms bear a weight of previous attitudes, values and expectations. To speak clearly of the things she wishes to speak of she needs a *singular* style, not eccentric or idiosyncratic but one that, when it needs to do so, can incorporate prose, the speaking voices of others, a poetry that is open and belongs (she dates her poems scrupulously) to a time in her life and in history, an occasion. The truth always has a context, is always particular. The words "bomb," "woman," "peace," "love," mean one thing in 1951, something different in 2001—different not only for the poet who uses them but for the society in which the language lives. Dating poems is not a way of confining them to their occasions in time but a gloss on where they come from, part of the process of reading the occasion back into them. This is true even of the early poems. In *The Diamond Cutters* (1955) she visits Europe, still bruised by war damage, and declares:

> We come like dreamers searching for an answer,
> Passionately in need to reconstruct
> The columned roofs under the blazing sky,
> The courts so open, so forever locked.
>
> And some of us, as dreamers, excavate
> Under the blanching light of sleep's high noon,
> The artifacts of thought, the site of love,
> Whose Hadrian has given the slip, and gone.

The little metrical rush of the last line reveals what skill she leaves behind when she abandons meter. Here already, inadvertently, is the manifesto of the poet who will write *Diving into the Wreck* and the feminist and radical-feminist poetry that will excavate and reinterpret the ruins. She is the new custodian, cherishing and changing. In "Diving into the Wreck" she writes,

> I came to explore the wreck.
> The words are purposes.
> The words are maps.
> I came to see the damage that was done
> and the treasures that prevail.

Compassion and commitment do not always go together; or rather, compassion must know when it should turn to anger and action if it is not to become complicit in the ills it compassionates. "Art" gives way to a greater immediate intensity; balance goes in favor of a different kind of truth-telling. In the title poem of *Snapshots of a Daughter-in-Law* she becomes restless. Her art and her sense of what a poet ought to be and how a poet ought to speak have restrained her too long. A different note enters her voice; she implicates herself.

> A thinking woman sleeps with monsters.
> The beak that grips her, she becomes. And Nature,
> that sprung-lidded, still commodious
> steamer-trunk of *tempora* and *mores*
> gets stuffed with it all: the mildewed orange-flowers,
> the female pills, the terrible breasts
> of Boadicea beneath flat foxes' heads and orchids.

The poems show women—Emily Dickinson among them—as figures of strength in action or achievement, as forms of Woman:

> Reading while waiting
> for the iron to heat,
> writing, *My Life had stood—a Loaded Gun—*
> in that Amherst pantry while the jellies boil and scum,
> or, more often,
> iron-eyed and beaked and purposed as a bird,
> dusting everything on the whatnot every day of life.

With this volume Adrienne Rich forgets her manners and turns from a concern with style to a responsibility to voice. Eavan Boland records, "For the first time, we hear a distinctive note: the sound of a silenced woman suddenly able to voice a conventional suppression in terms of an imaginative one."

Adrienne Rich knew something fundamental had occurred. "I find that I can no longer go to write a poem with a neat handful of materials and express those materials according to a prior plan." It was 1964. "The poem itself engenders new sensations, new awareness in me as it progresses. Without for one moment turning my back on conscious choice and selection, I have been increasingly willing to let the unconscious offer its materials, to listen to more than the one voice of a single idea. Perhaps a simpler way of putting it would be to say that instead of poems about experience I am getting poems that are experiences, that contribute to my knowledge and my emotional life even while they reflect and assimilate it." It was a change that many of her contemporaries, male and female, went through, leaving behind the acceptable and sanctioned world of the closed lyric in search of the "deep image." Unlike her contemporaries, Rich had some idea of what she would like to find, so that when—in the unconscious, on the television screen, in the street—she happened upon it she would recognize it. Where they as often as not dredged up ghostly forms and false gods, she had a shareable shape to look for. Conventional forms will not be of use here. The line, unpunctuated, becomes a rhythmic unit, matter-of-fact and firm. The music is vertical, not horizontal, a sequence of alert phrases rather than an integrating flow. In *Diving into the Wreck* she says

> . . . the mirror of the fire
> of my mind, burning as if it could go on
> burning itself, burning down
> feeding on everything
> till there is nothing in life
> that has not fed that fire . . .

Eavan Boland writes of her poems: "They contest the structure of the poetic tradition. They interrogate language itself. In all of this, they describe a struggle and record a moment which was not my struggle and would never be my moment . . . And yet these poems came to the very edge of the rooms I worked in, dreamed in, listened for a child's cry in . . . I felt that the life I lived was not the one these poems commended. It was too far from the tumult, too deep in the past. And yet these poems helped me live it . . . Truly important poets change two things and never one without the other: the interior of the poem and external perceptions of the identity of the poet."

The later books are variously polemical. In 1997 Eavan Boland introduced *Selected Poems*, which includes work from before and after *Wreck* that had appeared in *The Dream of a Common Language* (1978), *A Wild Patience Has Taken Me This Far* (1981), *Your Native Land, Your Life* (1986), *Time's Power* (1989), *An Atlas of the Difficult World* (1991) and *Dark Fields of the Republic* (1995). Changes between 1951 and 1997 are large. Feminism, lesbianism, political affection and disaffection spoiled her good manners. So too did a sense of the internal alterations of poetry necessary if she was to find, and then tell, the "truth" of experience as a woman—not confessional strategies that would individuate and bourgeoisify her, but comradely strategies that would be serviceable as *processes* for her readers, enabling them to enact for themselves the adjustments her poems proposed.

In the foreword to her first substantial book of essays, *Lies, Secrets and Silence* (1979), Rich wrote, "The entire history of women's struggle for self-determination has been muffled in silence over and over. One serious cultural obstacle encountered by any feminist writer is that each feminist work has tended to be received as if it emerged from nowhere; as if each of us had lived, thought, and worked without any historical past or contextual present. This is one of the ways in which women's work and thinking has been made to seem sporadic, errant, orphaned of any tradition of its own." If for Octavio Paz modernism is a tradition of discontinuity, for women writers it is "the phenomenon of interruption." I keep thinking of Charlotte Smith and Charlotte Mew. Rich has been one of the important writers busy drawing out and drawing together a relatively coherent tradition of women's writing, international and multicultural, whose beginnings are grasped and understood.

Her second major prose collection seems to rebel against the radical feminist separatism implied in the first. *What Is Found There: Notebooks on Poetry and Politics* (1993) suggests that separatism may have done its work and that the writing can again become inclusive. "The oppressor's language" has been to some extent made over. Because her poems insist on their occasions, their place in history, they do not invite imitation, but their processes and concerns can be transposed. She is formally the most enabling of poets, though in terms of texture we might feel she has deliberately impoverished herself.

Eavan Boland was not influenced by Rich, "And yet," she says, "these poems came to the very edge of the rooms I worked in, dreamed in, listened for a child's cry in," and perhaps in her ambitious poem "Anna Liffey" the refrains and cadence pay a kind of tribute to Rich. Boland's own life and moment are remote from Rich's, however; her mission and her poetry quite different.

Boland was born in Dublin in 1944. Her father was a senior diplomat: Irish ambassador during her childhood to the Court of St. James and then to the United Nations ("My father had a superb intelligence, but it was a rational one"). Her mother was a painter, trained in France, her work on view at the National Gallery, Dublin. Orphaned early, her mother had a foster mother who was a fine storyteller, and into the young poet's childhood her mother introduced "this wonderful fragrance of the unrational, the inexplicable, the eloquent fragment." "What We Lost," from the sequence "Outside History," evokes the broken narratives between women. A countrywoman is sewing, evening gathers, the candles are lit, a child waits. Tea is poured, and in the quiet domestic interior, where so many of Boland's poems are set,

> The child grows still, sensing something of importance.
> The woman settles and begins her story.
>
> Believe it, what we lost is here in this room
> on this veiled evening.
> The woman finishes. The story ends.
> The child, who is my mother, gets up, moves away.
>
> In the winter air, unheard, unshared,
> the moment happens, hangs fire, leads nowhere.
> The light will fall and the room darken,
> the child fall asleep and the story be forgotten.
>
> The fields are dark already.
> The frail connections have been made and are broken.
> The dumb-show of legend has become language,
> is becoming silence and who will know that once
>
> words were possibilities and disappointments,
> were scented closets filled with love-letters
> and memories and lavender hemmed into muslin,
> stored in sachets, aired in bed-linen;
>
> and travelled silks and the tones of cotton
> tautened into bodices, subtly shaped by breathing;
> were the rooms of childhood with their griefless peace,
> their hands and whispers, their candles weeping brightly?

The last ten lines are a single sentence making the connections between objects though the connections between words are lost. When the stories are forgotten the artifacts, the made and cherished things, are the only text the woman has to work with in making her connections, discovering the active verbs and running syntax of a sentence she could call *her* own. It was her mother—and her husband, the novelist Kevin Casey, whom she married in 1969—who gave her "a sense of the geography of the imagination."

She lived in London from the age of six to twelve, in a large residence, rather displaced by her accent and her culture from other children. "Some of the feelings I recognise as having migrated into themes I keep going back to—exile, types of estrangement, a relation to objects—began there." Boland lived in New York for a time, returning to Ireland in her midteens to school. Before going up to university she took a job and saved to print her first pamphlet of poems in 1963. She attended Trinity College, Dublin. Hers is the generation of Seamus Heaney, Derek Mahon, Michael Longley, Brendan Kennelly. Patrick Kavanagh was as important to her as he was to them. But apart from the intellectual stimulus of that environment, there were deprivations she began to feel. The "genderless poem" is what was expected of her. There was the danger of becoming an honorary male poet or, in the cruel terminology of some feminist critics, a "male-identified female poet." In "The Achill Woman," the poet, a student preparing for finals, retires to a rural croft to revise "the Court poets of the Silver Age" and one evening encounters a countrywoman, speaks with her and begins to find herself. It is an incident to which Boland has referred in prose essays and interviews, the point at which she began to apprehend her Irishness and her womanhood as something given, positive and in the broadest sense political:

> but nothing now can change the way I went
> indoors, chilled by the wind
> and made a fire
> and took down my book
> and opened it and failed to comprehend
>
> the harmonies of servitude,
> the grace music gives to flattery
> and language borrows from ambition—

The poets she could no longer comprehend were those who, like Spenser and Ralegh, had fought to control the ancestors of that Achill woman.

Boland attended the Iowa Writers' Workshop. Her first book, *New Territory*, appeared in 1967. She had already begun to break away physically and imaginatively from the Dublin scene, to create a gendered space and insist on its different boundaries and its very distinct dynamic. "I went to the suburbs. I married. I had two children." Here she discovered, as she wrote, "that what went into the Irish poem and what stayed outside it was both tense and hazardous for an Irish woman poet." Irish women have had to negotiate from being *objects* in the Irish poem to being authors of it. In earlier poems, "You could have a political murder but not a baby." It was a time of cautious adjustment—like Rich, she knew that change in life as in art has to be worked for and cannot be effected in a moment. "I began to know that I had to bring the poem I'd learned to write near to the life I was starting to live. And that if anything had to yield in that process, it was the poem not the life." In 1975 *The War Horse* appeared, an uneasy collection, followed by two books that mark a radical departure for her, *In Her Own Image* (1980) and *Night Feed* (1982), poems that confront the subject matter of love, womanhood, motherhood—the physiology, the tensions and emotions of the complex domestic vocation. "*Night Feed* is the book I could have been argued out of, if I had let myself listen to what was around me." But she listened to poems, to Plath's poetry, for instance, which took her closer to her experience and through natural reticences about bringing into a poem the facts of menstruation and childbirth, breast-feeding and the dailiness of a woman's life. It was a case of "the visionary risk of the life I lived becoming the poems I wrote." Kavanagh, Clarke and Padraic Fallon had to work out from the great poem of Yeats; they had to "write a whole psychic terrain back into it." Indeed, the overshadowed Irish poet, the poet who isn't Yeats, or Heaney, has always to clear a space in the shadow of these presences. Boland was writing "a whole psychic terrain" into the Irish poem as well, not again but for the first time.

After *Night Feed* and some poems in *The Journey* (1986) she was labeled a "domestic poet." She accepted the label and saw herself as a subversive, "an indoor nature poet," having memorably described what nature poets do—"someone like Frost, or the best of John Clare, for example. Their lexicon is the overlooked and the disregarded. They are revelatory poets. They single out the devalued and make a deep, metaphorical relation between it and some devalued parts of perception . . . What happens is that the poet becomes the agent in the poem for a different way of seeing." Frost and Clare: Theirs is not formal innovation but an extension of the lexicon, a new "diction" accommodating experience and voice.

At every point it is the *poetry* that registers her intentions, that alters and develops in response to what is no longer available, what is newly perceived. But the poem *is not instrumental*, though the prose that surrounds it may be. Rich uses her poems to make declarations; her poems can be useful, use may even be their primary intention. Boland respects her art in a different way. Truthfulness is not, as in Rich, primarily to the moment. Language is more stable for her than for Rich. Of her feminism, she says it is "an enabling perception but it's not an aesthetic one. The poem is a place—at least for me—where all kinds of certainties stop. All sorts of beliefs, convictions, certainties get left on that threshold. I couldn't be a feminist poet. Simply because the poem is a place of experience and not a place of convictions." Such clarity challenges her generation and is an example to the next.

Like Rich, she acknowledges the importance of workshops. In 1982 she started one in Kilkenny, where those who attended experienced "the freedom to speak with other women of hard things; speaking from shared experience of womanhood" and writing out of it. She remains an active teacher, now in the United States, where she is director of the writing program at Stanford University.

Her own work of the 1980s was marked by a sharpening interest not so much in form and genre—traditional, lyric, unmetered or whatever—as in *the line*. Her first major book, *The Journey*, understands as part of her radical transition a necessary stylization to bring line and voice into accord, then line, voice and stanza. She began to risk again the long line, taking her bearings and some of her narrative and imagery from Virgil. She is the most classical woman poet since H.D.

Outside History (1990) is her most popular book. "Here I was in a different ethical area. Writing about the lost, the voiceless, the silent. And exploring my relation to them. And—more dangerous still—feeling my ways into the powerlessness of an experience through the power of expressing it. This wasn't an area of artistic experiment. It was an area of ethical imagination, where you had to be sure, every step of the way— every word and every line—that it was good faith and good poetry. And it couldn't be one without the other."

Boland is a poet who understands what she is up to with uncanny clarity. Her major sequences often appear alongside a substantial essay, telling herself and her readers what she intends, discussing the difficulties of composition and defining the space the poem occupies. *In a Time of Violence* (1994) was no exception: "I want a poem I can grow old in. I want a poem I can die in. That's a very different undertaking for a woman poet than for a poet like Yeats . . . A woman poet has to grow old in poems in which she has been fixed in youth and passivity: in beauty and ornament. The sexual has to be separated from the erotic . . . The woman poet has to write her poem free of any resonance of the object she once was in it." "Anna Liffey" is her most ambitious poem to date, a highly rhythmical fusion of self, woman, mother, river. It is rapt, repetitive, the song of a kind of Liffey-maiden, not a meditation but a forward vision. There are uncharacteristic echoes in it—of "Diving into the

Wreck," perhaps; of the Eliot of "Ash Wednesday" and maybe of *Four Quartets*. Surely not! But I think there are. Her misgivings about modernism have much to do with the fact that the experimentation and the solutions proposed were aesthetic. The aesthetic solution excludes; *Object Lessons,* her substantial prose work, considers some of those exclusions, and the 1995 *Collected Poems* reveals how rapidly a poet who takes risks one at a time can move, and how far she can go. The progression, book to book, is part of the fascination of her work.

The American poet Louise Glück provides the same fascination in her trajectory, different though that trajectory is. In an essay she writes, "One of the revelations of art is the discovery of a tone or perspective at once wholly unexpected and wholly true to a set of materials." This truth to materials—language, occasion, antecedent—is the proof of a poem. For the poet the question of truth (variously conceived) outweighs all others. In "The Silver Lily" she says:

> White over white, the moon rose over the birch tree.
> And in the crook, where the tree divides,
> leaves of the first daffodils, in moonlight
> soft greenish-silver.
>
> We have come too far together toward the end now
> to fear the end. These nights, I am no longer even certain
> I know what the end means. And you, who've been with a
>   man—
>
> after the first cries,
> doesn't joy, like fear, make no sound?

This, from her Pulitzer Prize collection *The Wild Iris* (1993), embodies the tact for truth that opens possibilities without affirming anything. Helen Vendler wrote of the connections such a poetry makes: "Her poems . . . have achieved the unusual distinction of being neither 'confessional' nor 'intellectual' in the usual senses of those words, which are often thought to represent two camps in the life of poetry . . . What a strange book *The Wild Iris* is, appearing in this *fin-de-siècle*, written in the language of flowers. It is a *lieder* cycle, with all the mournful cadences of that form. It wagers everything on the poetic energy remaining in the old troubadour image of the spring, the Biblical lilies of the field, natural resurrection."

Glück's earlier books include *Firstborn* (1968), *The House on Marshland* (1975), *Descending Figure* (1980), *the Triumph of Achilles* (1985) and *Ararat* (1990). She teaches at Williams College and lives in Vermont. Her firm reticence and her mercilessness with herself and her own experience, in prose and verse, make her an unusually powerful witness. "Hawk's Shadow" is terrifyingly prescient, as though Yeats's Leda answered back.

> Embracing in the road
> for some reason I no longer remember
> and then drawing apart, seeing
> that shape ahead—how close was it?
> We looked up to where the hawk
> hovered with its kill; I watched them
> veering toward West Hill, casting
> their one shadow in the dirt, the all-inclusive
> shape of the predator—
> Then they disappeared. And I thought:
> one shadow. Like the one we made,
> you holding me.

Every end of a book is for her a "conscious diagnostic act, a swearing off," in which she discerns the themes, habits and preoccupations of the just-finished volume as defining the tasks of the next. It is a conscious but not a predetermined evolution, marking time in changes. Readers hear specifics of sequence: the ferocious tension of her first book moves toward the finely spun lyricism of the second. The nouns of that book acquire intimate weight and become the icons of her third collection, then rise to an archetypal, mythic scale in the fourth. The fifth, *Ararat*, is perhaps her least successful, its place in the sequence less certain. But the poems are as various as the force of the poet's intelligence is constant. The austerely beautiful voice that has become her keynote speaks of a life lived in unflinching awareness.

There is a similar sense of connected development, book by book, in the more expansive, less certain work of Jorie Graham. She explores the erotic with unusual clarity and assurance. In "The Strangers," from her book *The Errancy* (1996), she writes:

> The hand I placed on you, what if it
> didn't exist, where it began, the declension
> of your opening shirt, dusk postponed in each glazed and arctic
> button, pale reddish shirt—what if it doesn't
> exist—these fingers browsing the cotton surface, swimming in the
>   steadfast surface—
> what if there's no place it can exist

this looking for a place to lie down in,
to make a tiny civilization . . .

It is a pensive, erotic book and follows on the substantial selection—
from *Hybrids of Plants and of Ghosts* (1980), *Erosion* (1983), *The End of
Beauty* (1987), *Region of Unlikeness* (1991) and *Materialism* (1993)—in her
Pulitzer Prize–winning *The Dream of the Unified Field* (1995). Graham
approaches a number of numinous characters, each an embodiment of
sexual, emotional, political or spiritual desire—desire seeking its place
in an age of betrayed values, where dreaming is rubbed thin by reason,
frayed by the speed of facts. Error she explores as a heroic form of find-
ing one's way—a purposeful wandering toward truth, a pilgrimage in
which the heart's longing is guide. Lovers celebrate the body; angels
deliver celestial warnings. Here are Pascal and his wager, Akhmatova
and her refusal; a few soldiers sleep before a sepulcher while something
inexplicable happens behind their backs. In its abundance, the poetry is
remote from Glück's and Boland's; in its refusal to *clarify* it has little in
common with Rich's, either; yet these three poets in one way and
another have helped clear a space for this questing work, in which
sacred and spiritual, celestial and corporeal, attempt to coexist. Graham
writes in "The Visible World":

I dig my hands into the absolute. The surface breaks
into shingled, grassed clusters; lifts.
If I press, pick-in with fingers, pluck,
I can unfold the loam. It is tender. It is a tender
manoeuvre, hands making and unmaking promises.
Diggers, forgetters . . . A series of successive single instances . . .
Frames of reference moving . . .
The speed of light, down here, upthrown, in my hands:
bacteria, milky roots, pilgrimages of spores, deranged and rippling
mosses.

Her poetry insists that "the visible world" exists: but what is its exis-
tence? Beyond the merely subjective or lyrical, she ventures with philo-
sophical rigor into an area "saturated with phenomena," in Helen
Vendler's phrase, a place of shifting perspectives and abrupt changes,
sometimes vertiginous in their reversals. Poetry and science collaborate
in her work, finding a tense equilibrium. History, too, has a place. Hers
is a new kind of narrative, offering open forms full of possibility. Her
inclusive art takes big risks. Ashbery describes her "utterance that
swings with the conviction of Blake's, that one does not want to stop lis-
tening to." Her Blake has little in common with Ginsberg's. Blake

insisted that he wrote the Prophetic Books "from immediate dictation and even against my will." He doesn't *always* know what he's saying. Graham is that sort of poet, finding what she has to say less in the process of saying than in reflecting on the finished work.

On the other side of the world, Judith Wright never lets her poetry "out of her hands." One feels she could vouch for and justify every syllable she sets down, even those from the weak middle books, where she tried to swallow too much philosophy. Yet she does in Australia, and with fewer literary resources, some of the things that Boland and Rich do in Ireland and the United States. She marks out a space, not only for the experience of woman in poetry, but for the experience of other voices that the tradition and history of Australia have silenced or driven (until latterly) to the margins. Was her celebrated "Lament for Passenger Pigeons" influenced by Eliot? Stevens? Dante? Its themes are ecological, feminist *avant la lettre*. Its generic nature is not quite satire, or elegy: Is there a new genre, material celebration? Could it be that the poem is largely her own, as the later poems undoubtedly are, and in their themes the early poems as well?

Wright was born in 1915, the year of Gallipoli, in New South Wales. The First World War overshadowed her early years: her history seemed to be happening in another world. Then came a harsh Depression, the Second World War (when Australia was genuinely threatened, Darwin was bombed and history was nearer at hand). These facts overarch the early and middle work.

Wright's antecedents were English, French, Scots, "pastoralists rather than farmers"—owners of shire-sized lands on which sheep were raised. Her father was an enlightened landholder interested in native Australian things and even in the people. Early on she was aware of Aboriginal dispossession and the brutal inequity of the *terra nullius* position (the legal position that the land was previously unpossessed) of the national government. "Niggers Leap," "Bora Ring" and other poems touch on the theme, and on the "clearances," which in the interests of creating pasture altered the ecology of the country forever.

She was brought up thirty miles from the nearest town and started school at thirteen. Before that she did "correspondence lessons," supervised by her mother, who died when Wright was eleven, and whose pedagogic role was filled by an aunt and then governesses. She hated her Anglican boarding school: its arbitrary rules and disciplines strengthened the individual and rebel in her. Serious education for women was not considered important at the time. Her paternal grandmother, who possessed an excellent library, encouraged her to go to university; she was the first woman in her family to do so. She did clerical work for a time, associated herself with the journal *Meanjin Papers* and lived modestly and creatively. Her early books caused a small stir: she was doing something unusual and from the outset her themes were not those of the male writers of the day. They doffed their caps to her (which kept her in her place without robbing her of her self-respect). *The Moving Image* appeared in 1946. Her chief model appears to have been the King James Version of the Bible. In 1949 a more original and radical volume followed, *Woman to Man,* and in 1953, *The Gateway.* She married Jack McKinney, a nonacademic philosopher with whom she collaborated in works that her admirers did not admire.

Her poems changed direction. They became deliberately philosophical, centering on ideas that no longer came with the embodied wholeness, the psychological completeness of the earlier poems. Her later books do not stay at this point, however: she grows through the ruminative period, so that from book to book, widely spaced (*The Two Fires,* of 1955, *The Other Half,* of 1966, *Alive,* of 1973 and *Phantom Dwelling,* of 1986), she recovered her own skills, much enhanced by what she had learned during the collaborative period. In 1986 she announced that she would write no more poems, dedicating her remaining years to the issues of land rights. In 1991 she assembled *A Human Pattern,* her definitive selected poems, ending with the astonishing sequence of ghazals, a poetic form like the couplet, "The Shadow of Fire," which in their condensed brevity owe a debt to Oriental verse, and in formal choice to Persian. She deliberately aligned herself, after the decades of working in European forms, with the cultures nearer at hand: she became an Asian. So in "Notes from the Edge" she declares

> I used to love Keats, Blake;
> now I try haiku
> for its honed brevities,
> its inclusive silences.
>
> Issa. Shiki. Buson. Bashō.
> Few words and with no rhetoric.
> Enclosed by silence
> as is the thrush's call.

The main verb disappears, the poems seek stasis. In "Dust," a ghazal from the sequence, she puts her new approach to the test:

> In my sixty-eighth year drought stopped the song of the rivers,
> sent ghosts of wheatfield blowing over the sky.

In the swimming-hole the water's dropped so low
I bruise my knees on rocks which are new acquaintances.

The daybreak moon is blurred in a gauze of dust.
Long ago my mother's face looked through a grey motor-veil.

Fallen leaves on the current scarcely move.
But the azure kingfisher flashes upriver still.

Poems written in age confuse the years.
We all live, said Bashō, in a phantom dwelling.

The rift between her "European vision" and the "non-European reality" in which she lived had begun to trouble her in her middle years.

The blue crane fishing on Cooloolah's twilight
has fished there longer than our centuries.
He is the certain heir of lake and evening,
and he will wear their colour till he dies;

but I'm a stranger, come of a conquering people.
I cannot share his calm, who watch his lake,
being unloved by all my eyes delight in
and made uneasy, for an old murder's sake.

Between the "construct" of European nature and the "reality" of the Aboriginal sense of and contact with nature was a vast gulf. How could a poet of the privileged classes negotiate it? Being a woman helped, being a woman of liberal temperament and strong character. The women she wished to reach—writers in particular—welcomed her, especially Oodgeroo (Kath Walker), whose work Wright has championed.

There is in the middle work an oversimple set of dualities which the poems play between: man and woman, outdoors and indoors, labor and love—raw and cooked, as Lévi-Strauss puts it. It was more complex cultural dichotomies that led to the great poems in *Phantom Dwelling*: they were not susceptible to easy polarizations, and besides, Wright did not want to become native but to understand what it meant, and what her ancestors had done to it and its meanings. Her prose books *The Generations of Men* (in semifictional form) and *The Cry for the Dead* (a more literal narrative) explored this area.

Though Wright belongs chronologically to the generation of A. D. Hope and James McAuley, she seems to belong equally to the two generations that followed, her own work changing and leading the changes in Australian writing and opening a way for the new poetry of the older people. Like them she has a sense of good and of evil; the latter is not metaphysical so much as a sense of good wasted. Moral rather than metaphysical, her poems are didactic, moving between personal, social and ethical concerns. Man is continually touched by a grace he repeatedly denies. It is almost too late, she says; but like Cassandra she keeps talking—now in prose.

Gwen Harwood, five years Wright's junior, brings different priorities to Australian poetry. Born in Brisbane in 1920, she had a radiant childhood. She spent much of her life in Tasmania. A musician by training, she combined two vocations. She was deeply familiar with Wittgenstein, whose words "Not how the world is, is the mystical, but that it is" set her on her way to becoming a poet. Raising her family, she kept her poetry private until the 1950s, when she began letting the work out. Her reputation has grown steadily: a wide public responds to her generally upbeat and positive vision. The poems are scrupulously crafted, rhymed, lyrical (and sometimes very funny). Beside the open, large-scale and "answerable" poems of Wright, Harwood's work is more "social" in an eighteenth-century way, "polite" even when it is being boldly erotic, satirical and self-parodying. There is nothing insistently of her country in the poems—a detail, a place name—but for her the sole challenge is being human, not being human and Australian. In "Carnal Knowledge II" she writes:

> Roses knocked on the glass.
> Wine like a running stream
> no evil spell could cross
> flowed round the house of touch.
> God grant me drunkenness
> if this is sober knowledge,
>
> song to melt sea and sky
> apart, and lift these hills
> from the dark shadow of what was,
> and roll them back, and lie
> in naked ignorance
> in the hollow of your thigh.

This is the obverse of A. D. Hope's vehement, disgusted eroticism and Ginsberg's misogyny. Here is a poet who wrote from the body simply, without the wild complications of Jorie Graham. In elegy, lyric and satire she celebrated the facts of being, making poems out of what the flesh in love, in childbirth, motherhood, aging and loss, taught her. She died in 1995.

Allen Curnow also celebrates, but in a language that has made necessary choices, engaged with modernism and learned to make new forms. He was born in Timaru, New Zealand, in 1911. Educated at Canterbury and Auckland universities, after a period of study for the Anglican ministry he turned to journalism, working as far afield as Fleet Street. In 1951 he joined the English Department at the University of Auckland, where he taught until 1976. He has published poetry, plays and criticism and edited two books of New Zealand verse. With James K. Baxter and C. K. Stead he stands at the head of a distinctive New Zealand poetry. In 1939 he published his first book, *Not in Narrow Seas*, which was entirely excluded from his highly selective *Early Days Yet: New and Collected Poems 1941–1997*. It was, despite his later view of it, an important volume, setting out to add to "the anti-myth about New Zealand." From such deliberate, even essayistic intent and formal conventionality his work has moved far. The distilled *Early Days Yet* reduces the volume of his oeuvre to 240 carefully chosen pages, about a third of his actual output.

Curnow is a poet who remembers his journalistic training. There is great particularity about the poems and there are journalistic subjects, too: the kidnapping and murder of the Italian politician Aldo Moro and urgent news stories that emerge from history with all the freshness of a morning headline. He also remembers what language must do and what it can do in verse. The various musicality of his writing is unique in New Zealand poetry; against Baxter's Jacobean consonantal rhetoric, Curnow generally seems to be close to song, even when the language of the poem seems closest to speech. The changes of key can be sudden and effective—he is by turns funny, coarse, commonplace, scabrous, impassioned. The late poems spend their time in retrospection, a kind of return journey looking at the first years not with nostalgia but as places that *are* because they *were*, and are real still, only fading. They never lose hold on the present. This is the summation of the themes in "Continuum," the title poem of his 1988 collection:

The moon rolls over the roof and falls behind
my house, and the moon does neither of these things,
I am talking about myself.

It's not possible to get off to sleep or
the subject or the planet, nor to think thoughts.
Better barefoot it out the front

door and lean from the porch across the privets
and the palms into the washed-out creation,
a dark place with two particular

bright clouds dusted (query) by the moon, one's mine
the other's an adversary, which may depend
on the wind, or something.

A long moment stretches, the next one is not
on time. Not unaccountably the chill of
the planking underfoot rises

in the throat, for its part the night sky empties
the whole of its contents down. Turn on a bare
heel, close the door behind

on the author, cringing demiurge, who picks up
his litter and his tools and paces me back
to bed, stealthily in step.

Curnow is described by Peter Porter as "this modern master." "He has been a major voice at every stage of his career," writes C. K. Stead, "knowing what he is about, moving at his own pace, inventive, unpredictable, writing poetry which strikes me, as it has done serially over the years, as unsurpassed by the work of any other poet at present writing in English."

Curnow survived; James K. Baxter died at the age of forty-six, with over 600 pages of *Collected Poems* (1979) in a volume that excluded his more scabrous and ephemeral writings. He was one of the most precocious poets of the century, whose neglect outside New Zealand baffles me. He is certainly uneven. The poetry that was damaged by his serious alcoholism and much of the later work written with the assistance of drugs but without an articulate supporting culture of the kind that sustained Ginsberg is poor, but the best writing, some of it from the darkest periods, is "major," if that word retains any useful sense today.

In a lecture he recalls how he wrote his first poem. "I climbed up to a hole in a bank in a hill above the sea, and there fell into the attitude of *listening* out of which poems may rise—not to the sound of the sea, but to the unheard sound of which poems are translations—it was then that I first endured that intense effort of *listening*, like a man chained to the ground trying to stand upright and walk—and from this intensity of *listening* the words emerged—

'O Ocean, in thy rocky bed
The starry fishes swim about—
There coral rocks are strewn around
Like some great temple on the ground . . .'

I was then seven years old. I don't think my methods of composition
have changed much since that time. The daimon has always to be
invoked; and there is no certainty that he will answer the invitation."
His first book was published when he was eighteen. It was called *Beyond
the Palisade* and included a number of elegies. Allen Curnow spotted
him and included his work the next year in the first of his key antholo-
gies of New Zealand poetry. Later Baxter turned on Curnow, on his
poetry and his politics.

Baxter embodies contradictions: a patriot who could be savage about
his native land; a Roman Catholic who insisted on a kind of indepen-
dence within the Church that broke its rules and institutions; a mis-
sionary to the Maoris whose culture he sentimentalized and, in a way,
adopted; a father who watched his children inject drugs. One could go
on, but such facts do not tell us much about how he got there or what
the poems do with his experience.

Baxter's father, an Otago farmer who educated himself, was a pacifist
during the First World War. His mother, the daughter of a professor of
English and classics, herself educated at Newnham College, Cam-
bridge, encouraged her son to write. He was born in 1926. When he was
eleven the family went to Europe for two years, and he returned ill at
ease with the New Zealand world. His father's pacifism set the family
apart, and this exclusion told on the boy. When he went to university in
Otago at the age of seventeen, he soon fell into alcoholism. He dropped
out, took odd jobs, tried again at university. "In Christchurch I associ-
ated with Denis Glover and Allen Curnow and became a member of the
Church of England." After many struggles he became a BA. In 1958 he
traveled to India and Japan, saw the poor, and began the long march of
conscience toward his conversion to Catholicism and Jerusalem, the
religious community he established in 1968 and where he became the
wild guru. He wrote in "Tokyo 1958":

The wind has a wrestler's legs. The sun's bonfire
Blazes at dawn on flooded streets.
Typhoon Ida is hungry over Tokaido.
Houses are smashed like kites.

Bring ladders for the poor. They fall
Like scraps of clay from the potter's wheel.

In 1958 Oxford University Press took him on and he began to find read-
ers abroad.

He certainly found models abroad. He drew on Dylan Thomas and
Yeats; then on MacNeice among the 1930s poets, and on some of his
American contemporaries, notably Lowell, whose *Life Studies* made an
impact. The *Jerusalem Sonnets* (1970) mark a high point of candor and
originality, in his language, his forms and his human vision.

In 1943 he was seventeen. He wrote "Prelude N. Z.," which begins,

> No dream, no old enchantment chains this land;
>   Its ice and dripping forests know
> one spell alone deeper than spell of snow:
>   The life that knows not life. There stand
> nor megaliths nor tombs upon our plains;
>   Torrential rains
> on man-unmastered mountains flow; our valleys
> waken to thunder-volleys . . .

It is less the sense of the poem, which is an amalgam of Hopkins,
Thomas and native atavisms, than the prosody which is astonishing; the
control of the diminishing rhymed line, the way in which syntax and
meter work in counterpoint to generate the shape of the stanza, are
unusual at any time of day. It is only rhetoric, but of a high order,
and the rhetorically less ambitious poems of the same period are, several
of them, excellent. "The Bay," written when he was twenty, finds lan-
guage for a landscape that as it is created in the mind's eye becomes
imaginary—and more real. "Songs of the Desert," also an early work
(fourteen poems in a sequence) is his first attempt at extended form and
an exercise in oblique confession. His first major sequence is "Pig Island
Letters," informal and emphatic, intemperate.

The *Jerusalem Sonnets* are written in couplets, rhyme wandering in
and out at will. The community is a place where people and animals also
wander in and out, lost in their spiritual or psychic thoughts. The thirty-
sixth sonnet, "Brother Ass, Brother Ass," characteristically begins in
humor and goodwill, then leads toward the Crucifixion. Throughout
the sequence there are wonderful similes: "Like an old horse turned to
grass I lift my head / Biting at the blossoms of the thorn tree." The
thirty-nine sonnets are his best single achievement, and his last sequence,
Autumn Testament, retains some of its virtues, but the verse is tired, the
syntax short of breath, the poet become so much the guru that the
poems aspire to the status of homily and parable.

Why did Baxter write so much? His is not the casual copiousness of
the Beats or Frank O'Hara; he is not effusive or "spontaneous." He

revised his poems. He worked hard at them and there is progression, and yet a final thinness of subject, as though the language exceeds its occasions two to one. And Baxter repeats himself, not always saying it better the second time round. Elements in his lifestyle in his last years recall the world of the Beats, but he believed—he had Christ even if he did address Lenin as "Brother"; he had a ritual, a communion based on a revealed God. He carried on his back the weight of the Fall, and neither drink nor drugs lightened that burden. Indeed, it grew heavier with each escape and return, even to the dusty pared-down world of Jerusalem. His is not Ginsberg's Blake of liberation but the Blake who writes, in his very different *Jerusalem*, how "all the tortures of repentance are tortures of self-reproach on account of our leaving the divine harvest to the enemy, the struggles of entanglement with incoherent roots." The Gospel and the faith should free mind and body to make, to work the imagination, but they remain, outside the act of creating, the trammeled mind and body he describes.

Though Baxter was not a "sweet-myself" Beatnik, in a sense he deserved to be; a society with men of Burroughs's and Kerouac's vertiginous anarchy might have sustained and directed his talent and energy into formal innovation. The pain of his huge talent, the spilling of so much of it over conventional stones, leaves the reader bemused. Baxter does not quite make it new; he does not make it consistently real. The success is huge and rhetorical, the failure intimate and formal.

William Stanley Merwin, a year Baxter's junior, took some of the same lifestyle byways that led the New Zealander into a life of fatal vision. But he was not so cruelly driven as Baxter, nor has he made such strenuous demands on himself in service of his art. He was a precocious youngster, writing—he reports—hymns for his father, a Presbyterian minister, when he was a boy, and then illustrating them. Such close proximity to a living religious vocation seems both to have inspired and repelled him. At Princeton he discovered poetry of a more modern and less monitory kind and, urged along by John Berryman and R. P. Blackmur, he found his other vocation, studying foreign literatures and becoming a formidable translator, of *El Cid* and the *Song of Roland* as well as the French Symbolists and Octavio Paz. His own poetry has now led, now followed, his work as a translator. There are some fifteen volumes of translation and a similar number of original collections.

There was a time in the late 1960s when translation seemed to have destroyed the texture of his verse. He discovered (indeed, he may have helped to invent) the "international style" of translation, without semantic depth and rhythmically undemanding, a fact he recognized and described in his poem "Losing a Language." He develops in an intriguing pattern, from the deliberated, archaizing formalism of his first book, *A Masque for Janus* (1952), the title itself alluding to a ceremonial and courtly mode long exhausted, to his recent books designed to be read *as* books and including a vision rooted in the threatened ecology of Hawaii, where he leads a life more deliberately "primal" than that he lived in New Jersey and Pennsylvania, where he spent his formative years.

He is a persuasive essayist and prose writer: his own work is subjected to his shrewd critical investigations. The 1988 *Selected Poems* reveals how the poet was falling to pieces in *The Carrier of Ladders* (1970), for which he won the Pulitzer Prize and which unaccountably remains his most celebrated volume. Since that time he has reinvented himself, on this side of Vietnam, and with a devotion to the planet which has moved from the baroque to the Doric, a style that has consciously simplified itself even as its themes have become more demanding. Detail gives way, sometimes fatally, to type and archetype. His use of rhymed form, as in "Lament for the Makers" with its very distant allusion to Dunbar, is awkward: now beguiling, now appalling. Elegy itself, as a form, falters and—given how copious a poet he has been—ends in a ghostly irony. The "clear note" the dead poets were hearing

> never promised anything
> > but the true sound of brevity
> > that will go on after me.

In his prose writings, especially in *Unframed Originals* (1994), the world of lived particulars is real in ways the poetry at times forgets to be.

Inventing and Reinventing the Wheel

GEOFFREY HILL, DEREK MAHON, CHARLES CAUSLEY,
RICHARD WILBUR, BILL MANHIRE, CRAIG RAINE,
CAROL ANN DUFFY, SIMON ARMITAGE

In the rare public readings Geoffrey Hill has given since he semi-emigrated from England, he speaks his poems clearly, attending to syntactical movement, diction, pause, without superadding "feeling" by variation in pace or tonal emphasis. A poem is complete in itself and requires of the reader only fidelity. *Only* fidelity: the hardest thing for the reading voice to do, to withhold subjectivity, to efface all but receptive intelligence and the sound of voice, in service of the poem. The poem contains all that is required, no more, no less (although readers may find less than they need to understand, not what the poem is saying, but what it is doing, especially in his 1996 collection, *Canaan*). The kind of discipline the poems require of the reader they require all the more intensely of the poet. A poem is not a meditation but a making: of a voice struggling in a historical context, for example, for spiritual clarity, or enduring pain to survive. Such a making must be true to the experience it creates, often across languages, across time: the poems has to *know* the world from which the voice is speaking so that the voice can speak; it must know that world and voice as well as the poet knows his own world and voice. The research that goes into a sequence like "Four Poems Regarding the Endurance of Poets" or *The Mystery of the Charity of Charles Péguy* is not scholarly: the investment is more intense, more self-effacing than a scholar's or novelist's would be. The establishment of appropriate dictions in English for a French, Italian or Spanish voice is a further complicating challenge. A man belongs to his age and culture by virtue of language, institutions, objects, landscapes. To understand him well enough to use his voice is the poet's tact, a tact he will use, too, in constructing his *own* voice.

It is revealing that in the poem "Canaan," Hill, evoking the ways in which his people, in losing faith, are failing in their mission to reach a promised land, are inadvertently serving Moloch, the god who oversees the second part of Ginsberg's *Howl*. Against Ginsberg's apocalyptic vision, Hill's, written forty years later, is hard and true; a too-late astringent corrective to one of the voices that most savagely and decisively traduced (by appropriation) Blake's hard vision.

Blake has been with Hill from the beginning. In 1952 the Fantasy Press issued a pamphlet of five early poems, two of which remain uncollected ("To William Dunbar" and "For Isaac Rosenberg"). From the outset Hill chose to learn from poets who "knew the clear / Fullness of vision." The poems in *Canaan* come closer than the earlier poems have done to particular events of the age in which they were written, to the extent of relating to Maastricht, privatization and some of the appropriative cultural products of the late twentieth century. The poems contain not only anger but its causes, in ways that will eventually require footnotes and explications as his earlier poems seem to do for many readers unequal to the coherent past worlds he draws together in all their otherness. It is as though he has taken on the role of an oblique Jeremiah. He gazes down, as Melville says of the preacher in *Moby Dick*, from "the Pisgah of his pulpit." Canaan recedes: a past not recognized as Canaan when he had it, when we had it, or the possibility of it.

Hill was born in 1932 in Bromsgrove, Worcestershire. It is the landscape of the Malverns, of the opening of Langland's poem *Piers Plowman*, of Edward Elgar and Ivor Gurney. Woven into *Mercian Hymns* is as much as we need to know about his childhood: the intelligent child humored if not understood by his family (his father was in the police), studying and writing alone into the night. He went from grammar school to Keble College, Oxford, Butterfield's patterned brick masterpiece which so offended Ruskin with its pseudo-Gothic lines and colors. It was a construction to feed Hill's interest in architecture.

There he wrote his first major poem at the age of twenty. "Genesis" is a poem of creation and of origins. Originally subtitled "A Ballad for Christopher Smart," it is not a conventional ballad, but there is in the persistent rhyme and progressive, lengthening rhythm a sense of the cruelly ordered world embodied in form. The poem is in five sections and follows a seven-day development. On the first day "the waves flourished at my prayer, / The rivers spawned their sand." His vision of the fecundity of nature is then colored by a sense of its cruelty. In the second section he witnesses "The osprey plunge with triggered claw / . . . To lay the living sinew bare." The third day the cry is one of fear. On the fourth day he attempts renunciation, by imagination, to elude the cruel processes of nature and create something stable and apart. The poem falls into archaism: the ideal set in a past of language, impermeable to the actuality of the present. But on the fifth day (in the fourth part of the poem) he is compelled to acknowledge and accept "flesh and blood and the blood's pain." He becomes in the last section part of the scheme, "in haste about the works of God." To make sense of the cruelty of the world he must not withdraw but engage, and engage on the side of the maker. The seventh day is left unspoken: a day of judgment. The "Genesis" is not only the emergence of the world in the individual consciousness and imagination; it is the genesis of consciousness and the conscience that inevitably accompanies it, but the "I" is not characterized or differentiated: like the speaker of a ballad it is witness, even though the subject is self.

Hill started graduate work, began teaching at Leeds, where he became professor, then went to Emmanuel College, Cambridge, as a fellow in the wake of Christopher Ricks, for many years Hill's subtlest champion. He went to Boston University in 1988, thereafter spending two thirds of each year in the United States. *For the Unfallen* (1959) was his first book; it has been followed at irregular intervals by *King Log* (1968), *Mercian Hymns* (1971), *Tenebrae* (1978), *The Mystery of the Charity of Charles Péguy* (1983), *The Lords of Limit: Essays on Literature and Ideas* (1984), *Collected Poems* (1985) and *Canaan* (1996). He translated Ibsen's *Brand* for the National Theatre.

In "Genesis" and other poems, up through *King Log*, the poet's occasions are unusual. When he, or the subject he is writing for, cannot feel or cannot act (feeling is a form of action) the poem happens: in the wake of battle, of torture, of unfulfillment in love. The compulsion, the pressure behind the poem, is *frustrated* sense, a need to articulate, combined with an intense reticence that limits the area in which he will allow the language to work. What is unfinished or unjudged is for Hill generative and haunting. Unlike many poets of his generation, he was drawn to the modernists, to their principles of juxtaposition, fragmentation in the interests of wholeness, the original integrity of form. Eliot in particular is crucial to his formation, and it is not only the Eliot of *The Waste Land* but the later Anglican Eliot that he unfashionably learns from. One critic referred to Hill's "Imagism"—an imagism of a new kind, which is alive to dictions and tones in such a way as to make juxtapositions not of images but "voice images," phrases which draw in, momentarily and with a weight of association, resonances from different registers: a flash of prose in quotation marks breaks across a poem, a false aphorism disrupts or occasions a contrary reflection, an archaism summons a ghost, or—as with Eliot—a quotation (or translated phrase) is embedded in the poem.

He does not write dramatic monologues but soliloquies. His voices speak from within their experience, not about it. Even "To the (supposed) patron" does more than imagine an interlocutor. The monologue is made, but the monologist creates a sense of his audience and world, a world of relationships with clear gradations of power and subjection, hierarchical and often brutally unjust.

There is an imbalance, the poems suggest, in all relations: in love, family, politics, religion. The language by its reticence evokes extremes of experience. Elegy is Hill's dominant mode, but not mellifluous elegy: he is for the most part harshly consonantal, a poet of phrases rather than cadences. Vocalic values are foregrounded only occasionally, and to wonderful effect in "The Pentecost Castle," a series of twelve-line fragments in a Spanish ballad mode in which secular and spiritual love and loss are fused and Lope de Vega's measure sounds for the first time, with authority, in English.

The language and terms of liturgy and of church and secular music recur not only in titles—hymns, canticles, song-book, requiem, "Funeral Music," fantasia—but in the structuring of the poems. Until *Canaan* his religious position seemed to be like Hardy's, outside the fold, wishing to communicate but unable to say and mean the creed. Latterly he has described himself as an Anglican, as if the long discipline of the poems has made belief tenable.

Anglican: England. His vision of his country, which Donald Davie described as patriotism—and no weaker word will do—is far from sentimental. He understands the great divisions, not least that between the north and south, Robin Hood versus King Arthur. His own landscape is the Midlands, which has always been—even in the time of Gower—the mediating landscape, where a poet can talk in both directions, negotiating between the hierarchical south and the democratic-anarchic north. In *Mercian Hymns*, those short poems in long, psalmlike but spoken lines, plainsong, anthologies of phrases and registers, he proposes as the ambivalent tutelary spirit of his West Midlands King Offa, a great builder, a great tyrant. Into his landscape Hill draws his own and other tributary histories. Boethius reappears for the first time in three centuries, as alive for Hill as he was for Chaucer and Elizabeth I. Offa's kingdom includes Shakespeare's birthplace. Hill is a different kind of Shakespearean from Hughes. He turns to *The Tempest*: water, treachery, injustice, cruel judgment, regeneration, redemption, a magickable or magicked reality where the magic is the moral and potentially the spiritual solvent.

Hill's contemporaries rejected the social ironies and tones of the Movement. Hill was not so absolute as they, learning useful lessons, in his quest for deeper integrities, from their ironies of disengagement. Used differently the same ironies might serve, as in "September Song" and "Ovid in the Third Reich," to go to the center rather than hold it at a distance. He learned what Donald Davie was to find in *To Scorch or Freeze*, that by foregrounding language and tone, recognizing different and differently valenced registers, a poem can work through to social and spiritual truths.

Despite his attraction in his later poetry and prose to Ruskin, Pater, Pugin and the great figures of the nineteenth century, his fascination with times of violence and what that violence does to individuals and to the imagination has not abated. "Funeral Music," the delicate approach to Paul Celan, the large imagining of Charles Péguy, the interest in Spain and the Counterreformation, the High Baroque, persist. In the Baroque the paradigms of the Reformation and then the Enlightenment are unfelt, the tension between medieval and Renaissance persists in allegory, in figuration. Hill, it sometimes seems, perilously hankers for Jesuit subtleties, precisions, logics and disciplines. His Baroque doesn't put us in mind of Donne and Herbert but of the Spanish poets. His attraction to the work of Allen Tate may be an aspect of this: Tate's *single* rhetoric, using words that come into the poem heavy with nuance, but within the poem, because of their very specific usage, shed nuance and revert to a single meaning.

Because of the integrity of Hill's achieved poems, they build a unique space in imagination. Events for him remain implicit in the places where they occurred. It is a Bergsonian notion, which Sartre paraphrases in these terms: "On going into the past an event does not cease to be; it merely ceases to act and remains 'in its place' at its date for eternity. In this way, being has been restored to the past, and it is very well done. We even affirm that duration is a multiplicity of interpenetration, and that the past is continually organised with the present." "Funeral Music" and *Mercian Hymns* are not feats of imaginative integration so much as acts of belief. Hill's antagonism to "modernizing" the texts of the past—Tyndall's Bible, Hooker's *Ecclesiastical Polity*—is more comprehensible in this light: modernization falsifies the *facts*, falsifies the language.

In his essay "The Tongue's Atrocities" he explores how far language can go—not, like Plath, probing the psyche, the subjective—but how far it can go in history, a language inevitably attached to and cultured in the individual. How far, with the Bergsonian past in mind, can a voice speak, speak of, speak to (it cannot hope to speak for); how far can it contain and judge the unspeakable and counterweigh Adorno's notorious dictum that there can be no poems after Auschwitz. What can poetry do? It can effect a "felt change of consciousness." It can make something happen within the individual, and through the individual within the wider communities to which that individual belongs. It is at this level that the unique *value* of Hill's vocation needs to be understood. The poetry, because it is so hedged about by necessary integrity and restraint, requires an unusually resolute commitment from the reader. Hill's poems aspire to exist in a public sphere. There, they compete with other vulgar tongue discourses—from liturgy to journalism—and compete with precision, though the unequal contest becomes more unequal year by year, as Canaan recedes.

Few modern poets are so completely scrupulous, so considered, as Hill. At his best the Belfast-born Irish poet Derek Mahon (b. 1941) can seem to be, but his investment in "something larger" is not so great as Hill's: his imagination has been released from the demands of an informing culture. As a result he turns rather too readily toward his reader, wry, shrugging his shoulders, as though it is too late to find the big theme his skills might be equal to. And so—Boethius again, but only distantly—he concludes "Consolations of Philosophy," about death and physical decomposition (there is no redemption), with an inclusive helplessness:

> There will be time to live through in the mind
> The lives we might have led, and get them right;
> To lie in silence listening to the wind
> Call for the living through the livelong night.

His celebrated "A Disused Shed in County Wexford" takes its epigraph from the Greek poet George Seferis: "Let them not forget us, the weak souls among the asphodels." Weak soul and strong satirist: the combination is a doubly vulnerable one. A number of his poems end in question marks, and he travels, rootless, in search of answers that only rootedness could provide—rootedness, or a new approach to form, a break with the tidyings that his stanzas make in the mess of experience.

The tidy stanza—hymn, ballad—serves best the innocent poet, and there are few of them about. Indeed, after Stevie Smith, only one, Charles Causley, comes to mind. His work has been consistently undervalued for fifty years, not that neglect has seemed to bother or inhibit him. The word "innocent" used of a poet sounds pejorative. It needn't. Causley's innocence is formal. He knows about modernism, but what he has to say requires not fragmentation but narrative, often balladic in character. He writes poems for children and about them. He turns to the Spanish poet Federico García Lorca—not the Surrealist, but the maker of ballads and popular songs. He turns to John Clare.

> O Clare! Your poetry, clear, translucent
> As your lovely name,
> I salute you with tears.

It is still just possible to write in these ways if your history allows: it is a perspective that cannot be simulated, a skill that cannot be faked. Innocence is Causley's main theme (he was a schoolmaster for most of his life, and knew the bright and dark sides of Blake's child), innocence and its betrayal.

He was born in 1917 in Launceston, Cornwall, with the round castle and the vividly decorated church; he stayed there, apart from his years in the navy (1940–46), which enriched his diction with odd colloquial metaphors and expressions. It also gave him themes and subjects: "separation, loss, death in alien places, extraordinary characters, a perpetual sense of unease about how things might end." He played the piano in a four-piece band before the war, and the rhythms of his poems sometimes follow song and dance beats. He wrote plays. In 1940 he began to write verse. *Farewell, Aggie Weston* (1951) was his first substantial book, in the vulgar tongue and the vulgar forms of popular verse. Every five or six years he has added a further slim volume, with a *Collected Poems* in 1975 and another in 1992.

Sassoon was the first poet he deliberately committed to memory. Sassoon, Housman and the Georgians made him proof against Pound and Eliot, whose work he read with respect but took little from. Causley is at home in Housman's meters, though his lads and lasses have Cornish blood in their veins and he never classicizes his locations or his plots. De la Mare, Betjeman and MacNeice have been of use to him, though none has overmastered him. His strong themes—the sea on the one hand, and a core of religious concerns and ambivalences on the other—he shares with the people he lives among. He is naturally, not by design, their poet. He and they together hear the ballad and the hymn. The poet does not foreground himself.

He calls his poems "entertainments," which, among the more serious intentions of his contemporaries, is refreshing. They are that, and often more. He blurs the lines of a sketched plot, adding more than descriptive words, providing moral and allegorical dimensions. The plot itself may be susceptible to various readings. The poems entertain as ballads and hymns do, involving the audience. And it is often audience rather than reader that the poems envisage.

Causley does not "develop" as a poet. Like Betjeman he knows his area of activity well. His experiments with Surrealism were brief, and he came home to his landscape and his vocation. A folk and popular tradition survives in his work, which belongs too among the more deliberately literary writing of the time: he comes as close as a poet can to the sentimental without falling over into mawkishness. Like Clare, like Lorca, like de la Mare.

There is no danger of mawkishness in the formalism of Richard Wilbur. His attitude to form is not unlike Wordsworth's, to which Coleridge took exception: "The strength of the genie comes of his being confined in a bottle." Form is seen as restraint; molten forces within the poet need restraining. This view does not square with Wilbur's declared mission: "Every poem of mine is autonomous"—(how Larkin would agree)—"and consists of an effort to exhaust my personal sense of the subject. It is for this reason that a poem sometimes takes me years to finish." Not a very powerful genie, then: what enables (rather than restrains) the poem is the bottle, the form.

Born in New York in 1921, Wilbur studied at Amherst College (where he heard, and sometimes learned to sound like, Frost) and served in the American infantry in Italy in the Second World War, returning to further studies at Harvard. In those years he wrote *The Beautiful Changes and Other Poems* (1947), realizing that he could make sense of experience only by giving it form. The play of wit begins in this work. These are "war poems" even if their subject matter is not war. There is common ground with Lowell's *Lord Weary's Castle*, published a year before, but Wilbur's verse is the more accessible, his themes the more widely pertinent. He went on to more dramatic approaches to subject matter and subject, finding experience through poems. He translated Molière as he has never before been translated into English, with remarkable tact and wit. He wrote the libretto out of Voltaire for Leonard Bernstein's *Candide*. His few translations from the poems of the Russian Joseph Brodsky are the only ones in English to suggest that poet's substantial qualities.

He is temperamentally more of the school of Moore than of Ransom, whose formal strategies he admired and emulated. "There is no straight / way of approaching it," he says, and his animals in their fragile, artificial-seeming (because other) worlds, into which the human world breaks with violence, are held with Moorelike care and even tenderness. "The tall camels of the spirit" could have been borrowed from one of Miss Moore's caravans. Does nature wish to express itself as well as be? "There is something they mean," he says of the "Water Walker," whose world hovers tantalizingly near the core of our spiritual world, if only metaphorically. Wilbur is aware of what he is doing. His excursions and quests are schematized, focused in a form that makes them elegant, controllable, and falsifies or violates their nature as concrete, vital and unstable things: "Such violence. And such repose." The classicist will not let him go, with his "There where" and "Then when" constructions. Yet in his forms the living antlers, the living trees, live differently. His most arresting early poem is "Castles and Distances":

> Oh, it is hunters alone
> Regret the beastly pain, it is they who love the foe
> That quarries out their force, and every arrow
> Is feathered soft with wishes to atone;
> Even the surest sword in sorrow
> Bleeds for its spoiling blow.

It is not true, we say, but for the poem and the system that the poem becomes, it can be read as true. The poem has come up against reality, making an order which does not violate the given world. Wilbur's insistent formalism, his stance against the romantic excesses and formal divagations of the age, make him a figure who might be central to the New Formalism, were it not for the demands he places on form and the complexity of themes he manages to combine in a single exhaustive poem. Wilbur is as odd in his way as Causley: not alienated, a "poet-citizen" with a sense of an audience to address, students to teach. An Augustan harbinger—or an eloquent anachronism? One suspects—given the Howard Nemerovs, Anthony Hechts, Donald Halls, John Hollanders and, on an entirely different scale, the glittering James Merrills—the former, but an Augustanism less acerbic, more celebratory and sometimes hedonistic, than the last, over which Ovid rather than Virgil presides and transformations which reveal the truth will be permitted. Polished old bottles, new water into wine.

Into the formal poetry of New Zealand, only mildly disrupted by the experiments of Allen Curnow, a disruptive force rumbled in the magazines and then burst forth with a book in 1970: *Malady*. This was the eminently civilized revolution of Bill Manhire, born in 1946, reared in the far south of New Zealand, where his parents were publicans. He began thriftily, with tautly Imagistic poems whose calm voices were out of place among the ego rant of his romantic and unbuttoned (not experimental) contemporaries. In the 1970s Manhire was in Britain studying Norse sagas, for he is a scholar by vocation, as well as a poet. He is drawn to sparsely peopled landscapes, preferably very cold. The last postcard I had from him was sent from Antarctica, where he is poet in residence, it would seem. He was making his first day trip to the South Pole on the weekend, "three hours each way." He is like the Everyperson character in his do-it-yourself-novel game, *The Brain of Katherine Mansfield* (1988), except in the question of languages: "You are just an ordinary New Zealander. You have strength, intelligence and luck, though you are not particularly good at languages. Your family and friends like you, and there is one special friend who really thinks you're swell. Yours is a well-rounded personality; your horoscope is usually good; your school report says 'satisfactory.' But somehow you are restless. Your life is missing challenge and excitement. You want to make things happen. Go to 2." It is time for reinvention, because Manhire is, like Causley and Mahon and Wilbur, a poet who knows about the wheel, but it's too round. He doesn't want to make the square, triangular and spherical wheels that take Hill on his difficult journey over the rubble of centuries, but a new-world wheel with the best properties of the old and some new features. The fullest selection of his work is *Sheet Music: Poems 1967–1982*, to which he has added *Milky Way Bar* (1991), and *My Sunshine* (1996).

So he keeps for the most part to stanzas and to syntax, but his stanzas can be very arbitrary in what they impose, and his syntax can unfold like an Ashberyian Mobius strip. He is a scholar, he is naturally conservative and wants to communicate, to make fun of the excesses of his discipline and of the dialects that attach to literary criticism and theory; he is also an explorer in language, and he doesn't like to go back to the museum every day but much of the time goes to work in the field bringing back new objects and collections. In the briefest of moments he will establish his theme (rhythmic, imagistic, syntactical) and immediately start playing variations. He is a comic rather than an ironic writer. Like other postmodernists (as we must regard him), he enjoys collaborative work, with artists and musicians. There is collaboration and there is mugging. He is generally frank about his muggings, as in "On Originality," which describes in metaphor what happens in imagination.

> Poets, I want to follow them all,
> out of the forest into the city
> or out of the city into the forest.
>
> The first one I throttle.
> I remove his dagger
> and tape it to my ankle in a shop doorway.
> Then I step into the street
> picking my nails.

Manhire has a range of wheels and spares. He honors Charles Causley, he honors etymology. In "Milton" he honors the human impulse (not the hubris, but the hunger for love) behind the most ambitious and impersonal of poems.

It is this human impulse that is missing in the "ludic" first two books of Craig Raine, *The Onion, Memory* (1978) and *A Martian Sends a Postcard Home* (1979). With what rapidity his verse burst upon the scene, and how quickly it transformed itself, so that by 1981, in *A Free Translation*, though all four wheels of his vehicle were still simile and metaphor, he had found the force of anecdote and was preparing to translate it into narrative. And narrative is what he gave us in *History: The Home Movie* (1994), a saga with two family trees like a Russian novel, and with Russian characters, and a time scale long enough to snare thousands of similes: Russian revolutionary history (we begin in 1905), the Second World War (especially rich in similes), and the after-tremors right down to 1984. With "brilliant, minute intensity," Richard Holmes declares, the family saga unfolds: the Pasternaks and the Raines.

Empson suggested that the problem with Imagism was that it had lost the use of its legs: stilled in time, the image lost context and without context, significance drains away. The constant use of strong simile deprives a poem of movement in quite another way. The points of comparison displace the subject. Narrative cannot be conducted by such means. The home movie flickers, each frame demanding attention but passing so quickly that we cannot attend; or if we stop the film and look, then we lose the flow of the poem. Ginsberg in *Howl* heaped language in and did not expect the reader to do more than get a sense of sense, a sense of anger and confusion. Raine wants us in his 334-page narrative quite as much as in his short poems to *read*.

James Fenton named the Martian School after Raine's second book appeared. In recommending *A Free Translation* he declared: "Craig Raine has set a new style and standard for his contemporaries. He has taught us to become strangers in our familiar world, to release the faculty of perception and allow it to graze at liberty in the field of experience." Fenton's bovine metaphors are suspect, since "perception," even on Mars, is hardly a cow, and experience is not a field. Metaphor has "made strange" as systematically as Raine does before: it has done so in MacCaig's work, in some of Dylan Thomas's, and notably in Sylvia Plath's. In each case the poets have done something new with prosody at the same time. It has not been a matter of dropping everything else and setting metaphor down in a prose staccato. Raine's experimentation with one poetic resource proved easy to imitate. At writing workshops students were told to "do a Raine." Impatience with the exaggerated claims that accompanied his work did not detract from his originality, but the excitement has subsided, and the "new style and standard" stayed in the 1980s. It is worth remembering that Raine is not always defamiliarizing the world. Sometimes he takes an alien world—the zoo in winter, for example, or missionaries lost in the Kalahari desert— and "familiarizes" the experience, applying familiar metaphorical templates to bring the strange within the zone of our visual perception, at the same time falsifying the nature of what is being seen in a crude appropriation. What makes "The Kalahari Desert" powerful is that the metaphorical process of perception is invested in characters in a strange and cruel environment: to liken the extreme experiences to the recognizable and domestic tames them, until those experiences assert their own nature and take their toll. In "Nature Study" Raine writes of the zoo, "In winter time, the zoo reverts to metaphor, / God's poetry of boredom," and about his verse, even extended beyond endurance in *History*, this is what it can be, the product of leisure and tedium, with— occasionally—an astonishing poem that understands that the abandonment of metaphor can produce the most powerful effects, working against expectation as the best poetry will.

Two voices, Carol Ann Duffy's and Simon Armitage's, give a "new style and standard" to British poetry in the 1990s, both acclaimed with the same overemphasis as Raine was in the 1980s, as though commercial and educational interests need to identify market leaders and set texts, to simplify the task of marketing and of educational provision. Both poets are excellent performers and workshop leaders. Both are more generous to their fellow poets than their fellow poets generally are to them, perceived popular success being poison to the yet-to-acquire-perceived-popular-success poet. Duffy and Armitage (along with Glyn Maxwell and Sean O'Brien) have outrun the pack and are already subjects of undergraduate, M.A. and Ph.D. attention: canonical not only in their lifetime but in their youth. Accessibility is the keynote. When Geoffrey Hill read his poems in Manchester in 1997, Simon Armitage, who admires Hill's work, was in the audience, yet a chasm gaped between them. It was as though they practiced quite different forms of art, more remote from one another than Skelton and Sidney, or Jonson and Clough.

Carol Ann Duffy was born in Glasgow in 1955, studied philosophy at the University of Liverpool and graduated in 1977. She began as a play-wright, and her poems often concentrate on character and voice—tones of voice, tones of feeling, rather than differentiated dictions, dramatic monologues and not soliloquies. She is a satirist who understands her foils and sympathizes with the ways in which people must behave in order to earn a living and survive in a modern world. Her Aunt Sallys have nothing in common with Auden's: she gives them a fighting chance. Except when it comes to Auden in "Alphabet for Auden," a cruel and accurate cleverly slant-rhymed doggerel indictment of the poet of this century with the greatest skills, who sold himself and his readers short.

Her books, *Standing Female Nude* (1985), *Selling Manhattan* (1987), *The Other Country* (1992) and *Mean Time* (1993), have been poetry best-sellers. Her most popular vein—dramatic monologues in the voices of wives of famous men (Mrs. Midas, Mrs. Aesop)—she develops with an eye to the audience, taking elements in the menfolk and their stories and exaggerating them for effect, an experiment she might carry further if she took the characterization into the syntax and diction of her "wives," but the actual subjects sometimes remain the menfolk and their unreasonable ambitions and demands.

It is in relatively conventional poems like "Prayer," "Miles Away," "Small Female Skull," "The Grammar of Light," that an unusual directness and transparent passion for the human emerge: desire, aloneness, love, the physicality of existence, the hungry libido of imagination. These poems do what James Fenton praised Raine's for doing through metaphor, but Duffy works with voice, meter and rhyme, with metaphor to make "strangers in our familiar world," finding in the experience of the poems' voices new experience in ourselves. Like Causley, Duffy goes to the brink of the sentimental. The process at work is one of inclusion, bringing marginal experiences into focus, aligning them with the larger structures of feeling to which they properly belong. From book to book there has been a double progression: some of the work seems more determined than ever to play to the audience, manipulating response, while the best poems are of a different order, finding new resources rather than new subject matter, and this is how a poet grows.

The poems of Simon Armitage are less grounded in human lives, more deliberately literary in their effects and concerns, though his themes too are often social and political. He has been too narrowly associated with the north of England and with Huddersfield, as if some virtue attaches to the connection; but even in his first book, *Zoom* (1989), the "demotic" of Yorkshire, used in uneasy combination with "standard" and literary English, had a staged feel about it. He found the work of Paul Muldoon enabling at the outset, and the outstanding comic and performance poet Ian McMillan, but he outgrew both and developed his own strategies, now commanding his own imitators. He has tried collaborations: with other media (*Xanadu*, written for television, 1992) and with other writers. Armitage, like Tony Harrison (who does not seem to have affected his verse, though he may have influenced his sense of objectives), finds the poem on the page only part of what a poem can be and do. The humor and pathos of his collections *Kid* (1992) and *Book of Matches* (1993) depend in part on voice and accents. *The Dead Sea Poems* move away from the safe northern base: he gathers subject matter and sets himself technical challenges with each poet he takes on board. Early admirers were sorry to see him move off from the assurance of *Zoom* and begin a more experimental progress. The peril for him, as for Duffy, is not the praise of critics but the seduction of audience. Its impact on substantial talents since the war, in the United

States, Britain, Australia and elsewhere, has been marked. Local audiences make local "entertainment demands" of diction, syntax and form. At their best both Duffy and Armitage respond but issue serious counterdemands. It is not impossible that they may raise the audience with them (they have the technical means), but it is an English or at best a British audience, a reassuring and comfortable nest no doubt, but . . .

Beyond Stylistic Irony

IAIN CRICHTON SMITH, GARY SNYDER, ELAINE FEINSTEIN,
MIMI KHALVATI, SUJATA BHATT, GILLIAN CLARKE,
ROBERT MINHINNICK, GWYNETH LEWIS,
ANDREW MOTION, DAVID CONSTANTINE

But *irony*. It is what British audiences require even of full-blooded performance poets, the poem rising to a point of witty . . . liftoff. It is what critics require, something they can identify and talk about, something that keeps the poem from running too far ahead with the ball. Irony is a crucial element in the "gentility principle" that Al Alvarez stigmatized, the element that sets the reader or the audience and the poet both on the same side of the poem: outside, the poem as closed artifact. A language of complicity, binding reader and poet to the contingencies of an agreed social tone. The victory of the kind of stylistic irony that creates a safe distance between what is said and sayer can seem complete. It is not the irony of Hardy and Housman, the cosmic irony with which reality confronts man; it is smaller, strategic, the stance with which the poet confronts the world, preserving him- or herself from deep engagement, overstatement and responsibility for what is said. In a culture capable of sustaining satire, such ironic poetry would be a sign of health; in a post-Palgrave culture still hungry for the lyric, the inversion has in the end diminished the art of poetry itself, and perhaps the art of fiction, too.

This is especially clear in translation. *English* English (as opposed to Scottish, Irish or American) translations of the ballads and *coplas* of Antonio Machado, of Federico García Lorca, or the passionate sad poetry of Luis Cernuda do not exist. The idiom is hostile to them, as it is to the expression of direct feeling and sentiment. Charles Tomlinson translates the intellectual, ironic verse of Jorge Guillén skillfully, but he comes a cropper with Machado, whom he makes into a dry, incomplete voice, not the full-throated popular poet he is in Spain. It is possible to imagine Charles Causley translating the popular poems of Lorca, but among the English no one else since Lawrence. The Surrealist Lorca might just about work—sounding like David Gascoyne on a rare good day; but continental Surrealism is generally rendered silly-sounding in English English. Whole registers of feeling have been drained out of the language, which has its unspoken decorums.

In the United States the poet Stephen Tapscott assembled a brilliant anthology of the poetry of Latin America, largely translated by American writers and best of all by Tapscott himself. Reginald Gibbons's Luis Cernuda, Robert Bly's sometimes dazzling Spanish poets, W. S. Merwin's versions work: readers are ready to make allowances for the American idiom. The Irish poet Michael Hartnett's Lorca and the Scot Edwin Morgan's are further examples. Irony is a resource, almost a decorum, for many, perhaps the majority of poets writing today. Its absence has become a resource as well.

For Iain Crichton Smith, the Scottish poet, ironies inhere in experience. He was unusual in his ability to play the whole poetic instrument unapologetically and unself-consciously. Perhaps it is because he was reared bilingual and is a significant poet in Scots Gaelic as well as English. The Gaelic tradition colored his English, as it did for Sorley MacLean, though MacLean did not write in English directly but translated his work. Smith's most famous long poem appeared in 1962: *Deer on the High Hills*. It begins with an image that soon explodes into consistent metaphors and figures—wonderful, large-scale, the doomed aristocracy of nature, the doomed aristocracy of France. But the poem exists to give language back a literal valency.

> They wore the inhuman look of aristocrats
> before a revolution comes, and the people
> blaspheme the holy bells in the high steeple.
>
> Before the ice breaks, and heroes in spring
> come up like trees with bursting wrongs in their arms
> and feed the nobles to the uniform worms.

More brilliant than the Apocalyptics' work of the 1940s, it is still within romantic earshot of it. The poem moves grandly and steadily through nature, politics and history, until at the end the poet gives the deer back to their own "language," and his language back to the objects that it names:

> There is no metaphor. The stone is stony.
> The deer step out in isolated air.
> We move at random on an innocent journey.

The rain is rainy and the sun is sunny.
The flower is flowery and the sea is salty.
My friend himself, himself my enemy.

The deer step out in isolated air.
Not nobles now but of a further journey.
Their flesh is distant as the air is airy . . .

The line of decisive transformation is "We move at random on an inno-
cent journey." Innocence is a condition that stylistic irony destroys, set-
ting the speaker outside the experience, effecting a fall from the grace of
direct experience. But that prelapsarian grace can be achieved, if irony is
avoided or somehow circumvented.

Smith was born in 1928 on the island of Lewis in the Outer Heb-
rides, where "an austere inflexible sabbatical Presbyterianism holds sway,"
providing many of his characters and themes. The religion raised "inter-
esting questions of order and spontaneity" and "singleness (on the part
of religion) and the marvellous multifariousness of the world." What is
simple becomes treacherous, tyrannical; what is complex accommodates
more of experience and more of an unsanctioned truth. His poems are
insistently against the tyrannies of singleness. "One-eyed Polyphemus is
gaining on rational eternally mobile Ulysses." In that "eternally" rests all
the hope that Smith can muster, real but vulnerable in "this world of
untheological plenitude and sometimes terror."

He was educated at Aberdeen University and after National Service
became a teacher. In 1977 he resigned to write full time. His *Selected
Poems* (1985) and *Collected Poems* (1992) contain the crucial work, and he
added two books, a collection, *Ends and Beginnings* (1994), and a long
poem, *The Human Face* (1996). He died in 1998.

Ends and Beginnings begins in elegy, with the exiles and human losses
that characterize many of his collections. It progresses through place,
history and imagined change, with an optimism particular and credible.
The poet steps out of Scotland, out of Europe. After a trip to the Golan
Heights he conceived an extended poem on the Israeli-Palestinian con-
flict, finding an unaccustomed idiom, biblical in cast.

No, it's not a question of waiting for a voice from the sky as in
　　ancient days,
or sitting at a desk like Virgil while the empire prospered around
　　him.

There is no such voice, objective and distant and impartial,
There are no Muses dressed in imperial blue.

The poet is compelled into the action he can undertake, which is to write not out of security and safety but out of risk. It is in this spirit that he considers the isolated people of his native Lewis, and those isolated in a wider culture—scholars, writers, lovers, the old—whose hunger for communion is thwarted by estranging disciplines or by the depredations of history. Douglas Dunn has commented on "that purity, that touch of originality, which marks poetry at the limits of intuition and imagining." An innocence committed to the given world takes one risk that irony avoids: it is hit or miss. Irony has the good sense to dispose of the faulty poem in the circular file, but Smith will keep a poem if he feels it tells, however marred it may be, a valuable part of a truth. When there are technical problems in a poem they tend to remain there: an awkward rhyme, a strange inversion in the syntax. It is in his extended experiments, in the prose poem for example, that he comes closest to the irony that invents strategies of distancing, except that in Smith's prose poem, the prose form is *natural* to the subjects he tackles.

The Human Face is an impassioned poem-essay in Burns's most celebrated poetic form.

> Man's inhumanity to man:
> his legacy of grief and pain,
> worse than the tiger or the lion,
>   constricts the heart
> and makes us often "howling" run
>   to our safe art . . .
>
> O see Man as he really is
> in all his frightened nakedness . . .

It is not Burns but innocence that licenses the vocative. Smith conjures up the democratic spirit of Burns in an age starved of tolerance and clarity. This is his most ambitious long poem to date. It risks the scope and sweep of the major poems of MacDiarmid and MacLean, and it is by their measure that he must be judged. Of course there are points of irony and moments of play, but as in all Smith's poems, what arrests us is a credible, impassioned sincerity. It would never occur to Smith to set himself up as a guru.

If the innocent can evade irony, so too can a prophet or a priest. The priest, that is, who speaks *as* a priest rather than as a man wrestling with faith. But didactic art is perilous: we must believe not in the truth of what we are told (we can read Dante and Herbert without being Christians) but in the truth of the telling. We are drawn up short by Jeffers, and often by Olson and (differently) by Ginsberg, by Rich, by Baxter.

Their approach is at times expository, hectoring, deliberately suasive. Despite his less hectoring didacticism, Gary Synder's unironic voice assumes a superiority of perception, of value system, of *value*, which his later poems cannot substantiate.

Snyder was born in San Francisco in 1930 and grew up in Washington State and Oregon, a West Coast phenomenon. Like Hughes he studied anthropology—in Portland, rather than Cambridge—and his life subsequently has been as varied, if not as dramatic, as Hughes's. He has worked as a logger, a seaman on a tanker, a member of a trail crew; at Berkeley he studied Oriental languages, associated with the Beats (though his language is quite different from theirs), studied Buddhism in Japan, and teaches "wilderness thought" at the University of California, Davis. Nature (the Sierra Club variety, largely unpeopled) and contemplation are the cornerstones of his verse. His first book, *Riprap*, was published in Kyoto. He is the poet Bunting's Chomei might have become with a few travel grants, access to spiritual stimulants, and a spell at Walden pond.

There is a great Oriental-seeming simplicity about his poems, as though his imagination has managed to put all the conventional furniture in storage and let itself go in a remote and clear atmosphere. Informal, provisional, the poems take in what the disencumbered eye sees in the Orient, in the unexploited corners of America. The native American wisdom of his verse exists alongside (rather incongruously) the teachings of Zen Buddhism. His "I" is Gary Snyder. He avoids metaphor and symbol, as they distance him from the world he wants to bring closer. "No ideas but in things," says the Imagist; "No ideas but in *these particular* things," Snyder replies. There is a difference: poetry for him is not literary. The strong early poems have given way, after the middle years, to a Green poetry whose politics are as tendentious as Jeffers's. The natural world outweighs the human world. *Left Out in the Rain: New Poems 1947–1985* gives a clear impression of his trajectory. Famously he declares, "I try to hold both history and wildness in my mind, that my poems may approach the true measure of things and stand against the unbalance and ignorance of our time." Nevertheless, what is lacking in his poems is history, and he is complicit in the ignorance he stigmatizes. His world is the great circle of the Pacific. "What use, Milton, a silly story / Of our lost general parents, / eaters of fruit?" The old religion and the old poetry no longer speak. He celebrates the archaic as the most richly enabling. His is an absolute challenge to the ruling values of the age, but his engagement is confrontational, beginning in what is, in the end, an indiscriminate rejection that lives off the very tolerance he will not in imagination tolerate. He is an eloquent victim of the politics of a repressive tolerance that, by tolerating the radical critic, domesticates and neutralizes him. "The comfort of the U.S. For its own." In "The Blue Sky" and other poems he produces holy writ. It would be churlish to suggest that it is not poetry, but equally churlish to suggest that it is good poetry, or even good Buddhism. Of the latter only the Buddhist can judge, of the former anyone can. The language does not allude to or create a world. It is derivative, a series of footnotes, and the poet is priest; that, or it is private meditation that we overhear; we puzzle less at the content than the purpose of such opaque obliquities. The semantic poverty of the later work, the arbitrary forms, reveal how a poet of substantial talent can go so far along the road less traveled that he is lost—or lost to us. A young reader encountering Snyder— especially the early Snyder—may be dazzled. The older reader is incredulous. Surely this is not the freedom that the struggles of modernism brought us?

With the anti–Vietnam War movement an American counterculture emerged, with which many poets associated. Some of their work reached Britain, not by the established New York or Boston route but from small presses, through alternative magazines, on the international reading circuit. Thus Olson, Niedecker, Edward Dorn and Robert Creeley appeared; thus too Snyder arrived. The imported counterculture, which for a time was almost popular in Britain among poets and audiences, met an emerging British counterculture, with some similar bearings: Williams rather than Eliot as touchstone, and a hostility to the Movement values comparable to the Americans' hostility to the New Criticism and "academic" poetry (though many counterculturalists were or became academics).

English counterculture began in the academy. Elaine Feinstein says, "When I began to write I was very well aware I didn't have the right voice for current English poetry . . . It was partly because I was so influenced by Americans . . . I started my own magazine, *Prospect,* not to publish my own poems, but to introduce Olson, Paul Blackburn and others who weren't yet known in this country. That's how I came to meet [J. H.] Prynne. In fact, I sold *Prospect* to Prynne." By "sold" she meant, "I gave him my overdraft and the title, and on that he built his connections, using my addresses . . . He made something much more out of them than anything I had." The addresses she handed on had, many of them (including Olson's), been suggested to her by Ginsberg, to whom she first wrote.

Not having the right voice: from the 1960s onward, few did have "the right voice": it had become something of an anathema; the age of Wordsworth's "voice" as a *common* language was over, displaced by voice as a particular inflection bearing the traces of cultural origin and individual "character."

Feinstein was born in 1930, in Bootle, Lancashire, into a second-generation Russian-Jewish family, and grew up in Leicester. She read English at Newnham College, Cambridge, a contemporary of Hughes and Plath. She lectured at a training college and then at the University of Essex (1967–70), appointed by Donald Davie. Since 1971 she has been a full-time writer. Her work is fully represented in *Selected Poems* (1994) and *Daylight* (1997).

Alive to her family origins in the Russian-Jewish diaspora, she developed a close affinity with the Russian poets of this and the last century. Crucial are her translations of the Russian Marina Tsvetayeva, first published in 1971, in which she develops a "gapped" technique to choreograph voice pauses and lengths, and instinctive-seeming but deliberated modernism. She was also drawn to the "new" Americans who were proof against reductive irony. Davie pointed to the Americans, Hughes to Eastern Europe.

The Black Mountain poets intrigued her. She was affected by Objectivists and Projectivists: Williams, Reznikoff. Olson sent her his famous letter defining breath "prosody." Davie admired her second book, where the stilled deliberate syntax and monotonous phrasing of the first give way to suppler syntax and something like meter. The poems are domestic, but not comfortable, manifesting instabilities of relationship, of habitation itself. There is a tension between "recapturing lost territory" and escaping into imagined territory. Fantasy "encourages a steely rejection of humanism, a fashionable resistance to compassion, which I believe is as much a luxury of an English innocence as the euphoria of the affluent flower generation." So much for the shortcut mysticisms of Snyder and Ginsberg. Epiphanies are hard-won.

Her "feminism" is diffracted through a sense of her *other* othernesses: being a Jew, even a liberal, integrated Jew. *At the Edge* (1972) explores an experiential edge unlike Alvarez's; by means of montage, bringing together disparate experiences and finding their relation, she makes a space for herself. "If you have escaped the holocaust entirely by the serendipitous chance of your family deciding not to settle in Germany, and if you are conscious of that—as I was from about age nine onwards—you don't look for suicidal risks much. That's not exciting. Death is not exciting."

> In water nothing is mean. The fugitive
> enters the river, she is washed free;
> her thoughts unravel like weeds of
> green silk: she moves downstream
> as easily as any cold-water creature

can swim between furred stones, brown
fronds, boots and tins the river holds equally.
The trees hiss overhead. She feels their shadows.
She imagines herself clean as a fish,
evasive, solitary, dumb. Her prayer:
to make peace with her own monstrous nature.

Hughes's Wodwo and Feinstein's "Patience" have much in common. But
she depicts, at the heart of things, conscience. She is increasingly a *moral*
(if not moralizing) writer. She asserts her humanism against a world in
which the arcana are valued at the expense of the empirical and human.
She fuses mind and body within the mind-and-body of the world;
her metonomies are not literary gestures, her images are literal *and*
laden. She is a poet of lyric directness. The passionate voice she brought
to the English translation of Tsvetayeva becomes her own. She writes
about love, loss, jealousy, the fear of abandonment, and in each book
her style becomes more assured. There is merciless vulnerability in
"Companionship":

It was Wordsworth's clear line I wanted,
nothing to do with mountains, only the quiet
sunshine and silence, but I hated being alone.
The lonely cannot love solitude.

I wanted a garden outside tall windows,
winter sun in leafless branches, a cold spring
with crocus in the grass and the first blossom,
and you at work in the same apartment,

my dearest friend. Today I was watching
a grey squirrel fly in the beech trees when
your words reached into me: "You know,
a poet isn't much of a companion."

Ted Hughes said: "Her simple, clean language follows the track of
the nerves. There is nothing hit or miss, nothing for effect, nothing
false. Reading her poems one feels cleansed and sharpened." She
eluded, though she read English, the chief creative blight of Cambridge
at the time. "Newnham undergraduates were not exactly encouraged to
attend Leavis's lectures, but of course we did . . . I guess we were, all,
under his influence. We all read his books. And in my third year I went

along to his seminars for practical criticism." During her years at Cambridge there was no alternative culture. In time she and friends began to provide one. "I edited an issue of the undergraduate magazine *Cambridge Opinion*; an issue called 'Writer out of Society,' based on my enthusiasm for Ezra Pound, Samuel Beckett and Allen Ginsberg. Not fashionable preoccupations at the time."

Tsvetayeva, Feinstein says, "enabled me to write without embarrassment. Because she doesn't feel embarrassed about sounding undignified." It was another, crucial step away from irony, toward the candor that has become her keynote. Irony has its place in her novels, not at the level of style so much as in the plotting. The poems are a zone of relative freedom where the "I" is strictly licensed. The rules are inferred: "I listen to [the poem] as I write. And I know it's finished when it sounds right in my head. But I never can tell which poems are the ones that are going to read well."

Marked differences of background that, in earlier decades, poets would have reflected in imagery, perhaps in diction, are now expressed in more complex inflections and formal choices. It isn't easy. The Iranian-born poet Mimi Khalvati in her first book, *In White Ink* (1991), taking the title from Hélène Cixous, who says that women in the past have written "in white ink," writes a series of poems in strict metrical forms handled brilliantly. She was forty-seven when the book appeared, and in the years since her task has been to free her voice in an equally formal but less prescriptive verse. As the language becomes freer, the "exotic" details—Iran, Farsi, politics, family—recede. Her interest in drama becomes a focused interest in voice. Her long sequence *Entries on Light* (1997) is a series of meditations on light, on what it is and does, how—as it changes—it invents and reinvents the things we see, are and were, inscribing our shadows and feelings. The sea- and skyscapes are vivid: dawn, storm, dusk, a pewtery or bright midday. Each demands a different syntax, a distinctive rhythm and rhyme. Khalvati has a well-trained eye: she is also formally a most resourceful poet, able to close her lyrical movements resonantly or, when necessary, to leave a stanza open to changes of weather. At times we think of Constable in the billowing, full stanzas, but also—in short-phrased sections—of the flat skies of Hokusai. Both are resources for her.

> One is the glory of the yet-to-be, one
> of a past that reminds us
> how we've seen it in our own lives exactly
> as it used to be but were
> blinded by those lives, distracted from our own
> perfections.

This is not merely painterly or imagistic. It engages the woman and her world in which children have grown up and gone away, and the business of living and repose needs to be reinvented for the life ahead.

Khalvati studied in Switzerland and England, gaining a purchase on her culture by means of acquired languages and cultures. The same process occurs, at a more radical level, in the poetry of Sujata Bhatt. She was born in Ahmedabad, India, in 1956, and spent her early years in Pune. But she lived, studied and worked in the United States and is a graduate of the Iowa Writers' Workshop. She now lives in Germany. *Point No Point: Selected Poems* represents the best of her first three collections, the work of a decade.

How many Indian women writers are married to Indian men? The question of cultural difference is sharply raised. For Bhatt there is always a problem of translation, from Gujarati into English, one culture into another (she has several adoptive cultures), and even from one English (that of her childhood) into another English (American, or British). In her early poem "Udaylee" she evokes the room into which women withdraw during their periods. This custom of monthly exile from the routine of women's lives has a positive aspect, the consolidation of a "sisterhood" apart, turning a condition to advantage. But this is a release from, not a release into. Bhatt's poems explore the partial and the whole releases, especially the release into the erotic, with unironic, though often witty, candor.

"Search for my Tongue" is partly a bilingual poem, with Gujarati script, transliteration and translation. Each language, the poem demonstrates, reflects a different reality; translation is at best partial and sometimes entirely inadequate. The word in Gujarati for "sun" carries a burden of associations quite different from the English word. Many Indian poets write separate bodies of work in English and their first or other language. Bhatt, in suspension between the two, combines them and places herself between, enriched and impoverished by what they give and withhold of memory and experience. Here is Indian-English rather than Anglo-Indian poetry.

The modern tradition of Indian poetry from which Bhatt emerges includes some substantial practitioners: Keki Daruwalla, Jayanta Mahapatra, A. K. Ramanujan, Nissim Ezekiel, G. S. Sharat Chandra, Arvind Krishna Mehrota, Dom Moraes and—best known, though primarily for his fiction—Vikram Seth. No substantial critical literature has emerged in India to clarify and consolidate developments: it is only when exported that Indian writers seem to be "affirmed" within a critical context. Criticism clears a space for poet and for reader. Without it there is a kind of void. In Zimbabwe such a critical context is just emerging; in South Africa and elsewhere it has been slow to develop. The essays of

Emerson and of Poe did as much for American literature as some of the better poets did, and we might sometimes wish that some of the energy and resources invested in encouraging creativity in Britain, the United States and India (among others) were invested in encouraging reading and (nonacademic) critical activity.

The neglect of Indian-English poetry may be due in part to the compromised place of English in India. There are more than two hundred languages that English stands between, beside or over. There is no coherent publishing base for English-language poets. And if modernism has had a rough ride in Australia, it sometimes seems that it has not touched India at all, except in the academy. The Indian writer is accepted at home once he or she has been accepted abroad.

Bhatt has been accepted abroad and on the terms she herself proposes, though her work—exposed as it has been to American and British poetry—is very resourceful. Each of her three separate collections has been substantial; each has had a different shape and purpose. Each has included sequences, narratives, love poems and political pieces. She is not entirely at home with the lyric and not at all at home with English tonalities. Her free verse is fast-moving, urgent with narratives, softly spoken. Her cadence is natural, her diction undecorated. Her sense of the body in the poems is unusually strong: the body rather than the five discrete senses seems to register experience.

> But the soul will be the colour of turmeric
>   spilt on white stone.
> And the creature who lives in the soul
> will count with her thumb
> on the joints of her fingers.
>
> Time will be slow
> and Time will be concrete
> and Time will be stuck
> like a wet crow peering down
> from a tree, broken and black . . .

The Stinking Rose, her third book, takes its title from one of the names for garlic. No one is neutral about it. She explores the mythologies and the magical and practical aspects of garlic in a sequence of poems. The book is also haunted by places, especially Vancouver Island (where she lived and worked for six months), and by India. Europe is present, caught in the middle as it were. There is a persistent dialogue between new worlds and old, the dialogue always intensifying in the linguistically experimental, "bilingual" poems that oppose Gujarati and English, then integrate them.

> with my home intact
>   but always changing
> so the windows don't match
> the doors anymore—the colours
> clash in the garden—
> And the ocean lives in the bedroom.
>
> I am the one
> who always goes
> away with my home
> which can only stay inside
> in my blood—my home which does not fit
>   with any geography.

In a short space of time Bhatt has been recognized as a distinctive voice. She has much to say about India and her native tongue, about America, Britain and Germany. She is, the *New Statesman* declared, "one of the finest poets alive"; alive in an unusual way to language, to issues of politics and gender, to place and history. She is generous and also unsparingly severe in her quest for the truths of experience.

As generous but less severe in her truth-telling, more conventional in her forms, is the Welsh poet Gillian Clarke (b. 1937). The undervaluing of her work, with that of Robert Minhinnick, Gwyneth Lewis and other substantial writers, is in part due to the pressures of cultural nationalism. Wales has developed an efficient national publishing industry. Many Welsh poets writing in English are handsomely published in Wales but only fitfully exported.

> The lane narrows and turns between sunburnt fields.
> Two hundred miles behind me, you at the door
> rising for breakfast, a late dream in your eyes.
> The slate's already hot. The bees are in the fuchsia.
> A rug of sunlight on the bedroom floor, ours
> and the widower's bed spread cool for homecoming.

Gillian Clarke in "Coming Home" displays a quite unusual voice. What at first appears to be in blank verse is an almost casual and wholly assured free verse, effortlessly spoken, effortlessly "musical." One need not even impose a Welsh lilt upon it. The quality of Clarke's poems, sometimes written off as merely rural or late pastoral, is rhythmic. Without fuss the poems speak. She can write with metrical regularity but her quietly urgent voice prefers to speak in this way, intimate and precisely modulated. Her *Collected Poems* (1997) trace her development to a rare prosodic originality.

The Welsh publishing house Gwasg Gomer published her first full collection of poems, *The Sundial,* in 1978. In the decades since then she has become one of the best-loved and most widely read writers of Wales. "Gillian Clarke's poems ring with lucidity and power . . . Her work is both personal and archetypal, built out of language as concrete as it is musical," the *Times Literary Supplement* said. Her history includes the unwritten stories of Welsh women. "Her language has a quality both casual and intense, mundane and visionary," wrote Dick Davis. "There is no gaudiness in her poetry; instead, the reader is aware of a generosity of spirit which allows the poems' subjects their own unbullied reality." Her subjects include a landscape that is beautiful and wounded by industry and exploitation. For Clarke, as for Iain Crichton Smith, the rural landscape is peopled, there are villages and isolated farms; landscape makes sense through the people who tend it, and their culture, enriching or impoverishing, becomes part of her culture. It is especially, as in Eavan Boland, the unwritten histories that detain her: regained languages are the most eloquent.

Robert Minhinnick (b. 1952) is alive to his environment: indeed he works for Friends of the Earth. He is more directly political than Clarke and in his later work less Welsh-centered, fascinated by New York and its people in an environment utterly transformed by technology. In Wales he visits various pasts, using the images of archaeology, of mining, and his own biography to uncover less what is lost than what might be reclaimed. He has a vulnerable native ground which terror and violation make him apprehend, as Wordsworth does in *The Prelude.* As well as nature there are the miners, the dockworkers, the men whose labor made and unmade the land- and cityscapes. Minhinnick's world is unsentimental. He understands the inevitable materialism of mere survival, the luxury of reticence. He does not allow himself that luxury: the first-person singular is himself, vulnerable and direct; if it is a question of telling a truth or perfecting a poem, he prefers to tell the truth. The voices he sometimes adopts are heard rather than invented. Jarrell said that Elizabeth Bishop's poems had written underneath them, "I have seen it." Minhinnick's have the same caption, from Cardiff to Rio, or perhaps, "I have heard it."

Sujata Bhatt's Gujarati is more or less vestigial: she does not write her poems in it, it is a fading part of her linguistic and cultural makeup. Gwyneth Lewis's Welsh, on the other hand, is a creative instrument that she exercises alongside English. She writes poems directly in English (*Parables and Faxes*, 1995), but her first language is Welsh and I was first drawn to her poems in translation by Richard Poole. Yet the English poems bring into Anglo-Welsh poetry a subtle harshness that Minhinnick has in narrative but not in diction, and an iconoclastic wit. In her Welsh poems there is a sense of the sacred and the culturally sanctioned; her English allows for anarchy, disrespect. It is as though in Welsh she is (fruitfully) constrained to given themes, as in the magnificent "Ceridwen's Country," where in English, as the title of her collection suggests, she can occupy, unconstrained, the modern world. In her Welsh poems she has tried to take "the great strengths of the Welsh tradition and push them on. These would be musicality, precision, wit and the joy of formality." There is again and very deliberately a flight from irony—in Welsh. "The kind of realism I'm after—spiritual realism—can't be written about in the mode of dry, ironic social observation." In her English poems, however, irony flickers like a neon tube. Her "parables" and "faxes," the poems about foreign parts in particular (English is the language of travel, Welsh the language of home) can't quite do without it.

It is ironic that Philip Larkin's biographer and one of the executors of his will should be one of the least stylistically ironic English poets of his generation. Andrew Motion has Larkin's sense of endings, but instead of fear and despair his speakers express regret, sadness, a stoical acceptance. He has voices and narrative; and he has a subtle ear for speech so that the poems seldom settle into meter but play the elusive double music of imagined speech (with imagined period and social inflection where necessary) and residual meter, a muted iambic: a free verse haunted by memories. Before he wrote his life of Larkin (and later of his beloved Keats), he wrote a revealing account of Edward Thomas. From each of his subjects he has learned different ways of being his own poet in the distinctive sounds the poems make, and the way in which they move from reflection (tonal definition) into sharp visual definition. His is a romantic temperament, defining itself by defining the world in which it moves.

Born in London in 1952, Motion attended University College, Oxford, where he won the Newdigate prize. His first book, *The Pleasure Steamers* (1978), was more political than it might appear. The sequence "Inland," evoking the lives of a fenland village nipped at by floods and eroded by enclosure, is a paradigmatic poem of the early 1970s, escaping the "bourgeois I" by speaking through and for other experiences, remote in time but pertinent to the issues of the day. The early 1970s were marked by such experiments in impersonality, in emptying out the "lyric I," which for a time seemed untenable, a kind of cop-out. Plurality of voice within a single poem or sequence is not a characteristic of his work. More in character are the poems that touch on his slow, agonizing personal losses. *The Pleasure Steamers* opens in several directions and his subsequent books have followed now a lyrical, now an elegiac-political line. Narrative is his favored mode, and his best sustained poem, *Independence* (1981), embeds its story in the faltering days of the Raj, the English narrator recalling a brief marriage ending in the death in childbirth of his young wife: different scales of loss and of change. The consolation—empty at that—is time.

> I woke at five to a bare house,
> luggage already half way home.
> My last morning: a delicate stripe
> of sky strengthening under my door
>
> and the chowkidar's shadowy steps
> backwards and forwards, his cough,
> and the phlegm with its soft scatter.
> When I looked out he was gone—
>
> his charpoy tipped to the wall,
> and a torn-off tooth-brush stick
> thrown on the balcony steps.
> *Sahib*. A voice loud in the hall.
>
> *The driver's come.*
> I was bowed in the cold yard
> as the servants draped their garlands on.

All remembered, all the ironies of experience, life's ironies, in a voice that those ironies have refined to witness.

Narrative itself can be a snare, and Motion's *Secret Narratives* (1983) are "secret" in the sense that they withhold the larger governing narrative. He comes closest to Larkin here in the movement of the different poems, their building toward an often plangent "liftoff." The development of his poetry has been quiet and decisive, retaining his inimitable prosody but subtilizing narrative, experimenting with fragmentation, with limiting detail; finding essentializing strategies in Geoffrey Hill and (more insistently) expansive patterns in Seamus Heaney, but keeping to his own pace and subject matters, his Englishness of voice, unfashionable, economical, naturally eloquent except when it occasionally (disastrously) tries to be.

Narrative has also partly emancipated David Constantine, like Motion a poet who took shape in the 1970s with the political concerns of the time. Born in Salford in 1944, he read German at the University of Durham and has translated and written authoritatively about Friedrich Hölderlin, whose life and "madness" and whose prosodies help to define the tensions in his own work. Constantine is formally more classical than Motion, his foursquare sense of a poem and of poetic closure (against which he sometimes struggles) reflected too in the closure of his narratives—in terms of the story told, his imaginative investment being in the different perspectives and meanings a single story can have, and the instability that "facts" contain. His long *Caspar Hauser* sequence (1994) subtly frames, in the mysterious life and death of Hauser, a tale of innocence confronting an unfamiliar world, and that world manipulating, idealizing, corrupting and destroying innocence.

The poems contain extremes: classical intention subverted by romantic temperament, the poem of praise undermined by anxiety, the political vision run aground on social reality. The present is in danger of slipping away between memory, or loss, and longing, that greatest peril for the radical imagination. Yet the past is powerful, accessed initially through the lives and deaths of his grandfather, killed on the Somme, and his grandmother, surviving for fifty years with that memory alive daily in her head. "I don't mind my poetry being thought of as 'self-expression' so long as it is understood that the self being expressed is a large and not merely biographical thing, more a state or condition than a person." It is the *lives* of other people, especially their suffering, that draw him forward. The word "condition" suggests that for him each life is a type of other lives, that his characters have not so much psychologies as circumstances and even as they stand, stand for something larger: "Through the successful poem we glimpse the life of myth, of recurrence, archetype, pattern; and the association with myth can act unsettlingly, or like a solvent, upon the biographical and individual life." Yet that particular individual life, the solid, contingent truth of it, must be respected and included in the poem, must be returned to and accepted. What Motion does with his subtle prosodies Constantine achieves through a syntax that, while correct, is the source of his powerful ambiguities, the tonal plangencies and the "solvent" that eases meanings together and apart:

> Once since he died I saw him in a dream
> Wherever the dead are, he was jovial,
> He clapped me hard between his hands and said:
> Stay, but I would not and I came back here
> Where the living are. Now it is April

And kneeling on the warm earth in a sort of shame,
Dumb, fearful, not fit for company
For anything opening I begin again
Pulling the ground elder . . .

Image becomes symbol, the dream of the dead—out of Homer, Virgil, Dante—feeds into an actual world and an activity that delivers release and releases meanings. Classical legend and literary memory: the movement of the poem is very like that of Edward Thomas's, part of the "self" that Constantine expresses. The "I" can erase itself by borrowing voices, or it can speak with all the voices that it contains, emancipated by poetry's memory, by antecedent and continuity, from the mere contingencies of "I." He has an Augustan sense of what voice is (the sense that Wordsworth had), with a romantic instinct for appropriate diction. His very rootedness in complex traditions which he recognizes and accepts enables him to speak naturally, in a whole voice, which is his and more than his.

"An instance of itself"

FRANK O'HARA, JOHN ASH, JAMES SCHUYLER,
KENNETH KOCH, MARK STRAND, CHRISTOPHER MIDDLETON,
ROY FISHER, MICHAEL HOFMANN, JEFFREY WAINWRIGHT

At Harvard, John Ashbery says, Frank O'Hara "had a very sort of pugnacious and pugilistic look. He had a broken nose. He didn't look like a very cordial person." Ashbery got to know him properly a month before graduation. They became friends in New York.

Many people get O'Hara wrong, as a man, as a poet. His biographer Brad Gooch seems more interested in O'Hara's libido than in the poet himself, and does little to bring the poetry alive *in* the life. O'Hara was born in Baltimore, Maryland, in 1926 and raised in Grafton, Massachusetts. He served in the navy for two years, then went to Harvard, where he took a degree in music. After graduate school, in 1951 he settled in New York and took a job with the Museum of Modern Art. His life became New York and the art scene of the time: Willem De Kooning, Franz Kline and Jackson ("Jack the Dripper") Pollock, the Abstract Expressionists. He was an editorial associate of *Art News*, to which Ashbery and James Schuyler contributed—his friends and "members" of the informal grouping of poets called in retrospect the New York School. In 1960 he became assistant curator of the Museum of Modern Art. He was killed on Fire Island in an accident with a beach buggy, struck down in the early morning of 24 July 1966 in the dark on the dunes.

His casual attitude to his poems tells us much about him and them: it's not that he didn't value them, but he didn't worry much about them after they were written. He was not especially interested in a final permanent text. Donald Allen, editing the posthumous *Collected Poems*, found more than five hundred (others have been added since), many previously unpublished. Some survived not in O'Hara's manuscripts but in transcriptions sent by Ashbery to Kenneth Koch when Koch was abroad and Ashbery was trying to bring him round to liking O'Hara's work. Chance survivals, like the poems jotted down and put in a drawer—the wrong drawer. What mattered was the writing of them. He published only four collections, *A City Winter* (1952), *Meditations in an Emergency* (1956), *Second Avenue* (1960) and *Lunch Poems* (1964), none of them with "leading" publishing houses. He preferred to work with galleries, as though the poems were entries in an exhibition catalogue, an exhibition made of his daily life.

In "Notes on *Second Avenue*," appended to his longest and most ambitious poem, he rejects theories of poetry: "I have a feeling that the philosophical reduction of reality to a dealable-with system so distorts life that one's 'reward' for the endeavour (a minor one at that) is illness both from inside and from outside." Ashbery is of the same mind: "I would prefer not to think I have any special aims in mind, as I might then be forced into a program for myself," he says.

In the five-hundred-odd pages of the *Collected Poems* O'Hara begins with a rather witty, spoken simplicity, the poems in the language he used with his friends, wry, light, a little naughty, but without the scatological grittiness of the Beats. Ginsberg may have affected some of his poems, "Second Avenue" in particular, but while Ginsberg is always comfortably unwashed and hairy of face, O'Hara is cleanshaven and unobtrusive, keeping his own rather than everyone else's counsel. There is a reticence about the man and the poems. In many ways he is closer to Whitman than Ginsberg ever gets; and to Lorca and Mayakovsky because he understands Futurism and Surrealism, and when his poetry surrealizes it is with a knowledge of what he wants the surreal to do for the poem. He doesn't blunder and risk like Crane, or rant like Ginsberg. His poems are busy in the world; they haven't the time to stand back and preach or invent monstrous forms. He is the most New York of the New York poets.

There are experiments with prose poems, mixtures of prose and verse, and a complication of formal choices, with Williamsesque lineation here, a touch of Auden there, where he experiments with sonnets or (lovingly?) ridicules Wyatt, or apostrophizes friends, or celebrates. There is Jane Freilicher, the woman he loves asexually, whom he watches as a painter would watch his models and portrays in a hundred postures and gestures. He's the Big Apple Bonnard. Other women, too, feature repeatedly. At no point does he disguise his sexual imagination. He doesn't foreground it, either. His camp is a natural manner, less refined than Firbank's, less crafted, more off-the-cuff.

The characters in his city are poets, painters, editors, arts administrators, delicatessen people, booksellers. He calls God "The Finger" and has dubious and riotous thoughts about him. As he develops, the poems experiment with "painterly" approaches, the cubism of language. He reifies language. Words *fit* things and periods and attitudes, and it is getting that fit, for descriptive or ironic purposes, that interests O'Hara. Hofmannsthal said in the famous *Chandos Letter* that we find the depths on the surface. That is certainly O'Hara's depth. This is a debt to painters he knew and with whom he collaborated, whose persons and work he celebrated in many poems. There are also celebrations of Pasternak, Mayakovsky (whose Brooklyn Bridge poem, along with Lorca's and Hart Crane's, was part of O'Hara's intimate anthology). He has a love/hate relationship in the poems with the wild excesses of Rachmaninoff, whom he apostrophizes time after time; also with the miniaturism of Satie. Crane may have left a mark on some of the increasing precisions, ambitions and obliquities of O'Hara's language. He sends Emerson up, but never Whitman. "Second Avenue" is dedicated "In memory of Vladimir Mayakovsky" and Pasternak is never far from his thoughts. But his love of the Russians stops with Yevtushenko and Voznesensky, whom he sees as reductivists and opportunists, unworthy dwarfs inheriting the language of giants. He did not live long enough to form an opinion of Joseph Brodsky.

There are grand poems about big and little themes, lightly ironized, and then the larger ironies of the mature work, where heartbreak and laughter hold hands (as in "The Day Lady Died"). The poems to James Dean are passionate and adolescent, and his address "To the Film Industry in Crisis" joyfully eloquent:

Not you, lean quarterlies and swarthy periodicals
with your studious incursions toward the pomposity of ants,
nor you, experimental theatre in which Emotive Fruition
is wedding Poetic Insight perpetually, nor you,
promenading Grand Opera, obvious as an ear (though you
are close to my heart), but you, Motion Picture Industry,
it's you I love!

He describes the different constituent experiences of the poem "Second Avenue," then says: "I don't know if this method is of any interest in taking little pieces of it. You see how it makes it seem very jumbled, while actually everything in it either happened to me or I felt happening (saw, imagined) on Second Avenue." There is a warning to the close-reading critic: "The verbal elements are not too interesting to discuss although they are intended consciously to keep the surface of the poem high and dry, not wet, reflective and self-conscious. Perhaps the obscurity comes in here, in the relationship between the surface and the meaning, but I like it that way since the one is the other (you have to use words) and I hope the poem to *be* a subject, not just about it." This is one of the most important sentences, throwaway though it is, in the poetry of our time, confirmed by Ashbery in another formulation: "The poem is the chronicle of the creative act that produces it." It is not a question of "poetry about poetry" but "poetry as poetry." "Process" and "product" are one.

"Pain always produces logic, which is very bad for you," O'Hara warns us. Authority produces logic, too, perhaps because it produces pain. Legitimacy produces logic. And logic is invariably reductive and constraining, leading to rules and programs and building the prison house. "I'm not saying that I don't have practically the most lofty ideas of anyone writing today, but what difference does that make? They're just ideas."

He hardly revised his later poems. They are part of a process of living, the acts of thinking and feeling slowed down just long enough to get them on paper, a quick sketch, but not held still and worked on or worked up to a mighty semantic canvas. Authenticity is in the avoidance of finish, as in Abstract Expressionism, but with a less serious, more spirited *sprezzatura*. There are postcard and letter poems, jottings, odes, each bound up in its occasion, some of the occasions of a seemingly trivial dailiness. The city is the center—not even Baudelaire was so citified a poet as O'Hara. And it's not just any city, but New York, its specific streets, buildings, cafés, rooms and persons, present as "living facts." A poem does not seek to translate or refine them. What matters is the fit of the language to its occasion, its time, and the sequence time gives it. He jokingly calls his technique *personism*. He could if he'd wished have telephoned his beloved, but he wrote a poem instead: it exists between two persons, not between two covers.

The English poet John Ash first introduced me to O'Hara's work. His own poetry is indebted to the New York poets, but also to the writers, music and art that affected them. He shares sources with them, his poems like theirs are synesthetic, mixing senses, and allusively mixing media. Cinema is a crucial ingredient for all the poets of this kidney, cinema with its exaggerated feelings, its giant images, the passion and the kitsch. Born in Manchester in 1948, Ash built New York for himself well before he emigrated. Imagination disposes of parents and replaces them with a benign grandmother; the poet is freed into an undistorted infancy of wonder and curiosity, though there are also nightmares that intensify with time.

Ash's technique is not to transform the image or the occasion by metaphor but to extend and distort it, the variations taking us into progressive keys of implication, complicity: the whole burden carried by an image or plot modulated by voice or voices, the interplay of voices: "You do not need to understand, / You do not understand." In a writer like

Ash poetry reaches an awkward cultural puberty, stimulated by film, Surrealism, Expressionism in art, opera, the classics coming alive out of the marble ruins. Memory is treacherous, and this "puberty" does strange things. The past is at once enchanted and terrible, the future at best a Chekhovian adumbration. The poems are "about" points of change, regret, partial recognition. Ash is a wonderful elegist, very funny and very sad.

The drive to understand leads to questions rather than answers. Each question has a specific voice, not Socratic (there are no right answers, every answer is wrong) but curious, childish in perspective if not in language. The questions are about use and connection, but never about truth; Ash avoids moral generalization despite his social satire.

> The morning was clear
> And I could have wished the taxi ride
> From the airport longer, a week
> Of that comfort and postponement
> Would not have been too much.
> I did not know what to do
> When my mother opened the door.
> She was a worn curtain.
> She was a Trojan heroine.
> The sky resembled a still lake surface.
> The roses were bright but ended early.
> This is the ending of the year.
> Cities surround us, they shimmer
> Under different names.
> My mother's hair has not turned white.
> The roses were bright but ended early.

His *Selected Poems* draws on his four collections. "A little querulous, perhaps?" Carolyn Kizer asked in the *New York Times Book Review*. "Never mind. This may be the most auspicious debut of its kind since Auden's." Richard Tillinghast describes how he "moves easily from the hieratic to the demotic." The language is not unstable: it is going about its playful, powerful business of saying and seeing. Ashbery commends the poetry as "resonant with gorgeous imagery that distracts one from the super-lucid, rational argument that quietly continues to assert itself. It seems both familiar and strange, noble and funny, romantic and level-headed." There is more traceable plot and paraphrasable content in Ash than in Ashbery, but then their missions are rather different, their worlds distinct. Ash now lives in Turkey. *A Byzantine Journey,* his remarkable prose engagement with his favorite subject, Turkey, was published in 1995.

James Schuyler (1923–91), like Ashbery and O'Hara, owed a large debt to Auden, with whom he stayed for a time on Ischia and whose poems in *Nones* he typed (as Lowell had typed for Roethke). His elegy for Auden is matter-of-fact in the way O'Hara is, but the moments are in the past, as so often with him: the things not done, the love not quite spoken, the things not to be done again.

> On Ischia he claimed to take
> St. Restituta seriously, and
> sat at Maria's café in the cobbled
> square saying, "Poets should
> dress like businessmen," while
> he wore an incredible peach-
> colored nylon shirt. And on
> Fire Island his telling someone
> "You must write each book as
> though it were your last." And
> when he learned that in Florence
> I and my friend Bill Aalto had
> fished his drafts of poems
> out of the wastepaper basket,
> he took to burning them, saying,
> "I feel like an ambassador burning
> secret papers."

"So much / to remember, so little / to say," he chides himself, and says with gratitude too late, a poem too small, "Goodbye." Auden felt at home in the relatively relaxed company of the poems and persons of the New York School; to some extent (because he could not really *change*) they helped make his later work too comfortable with itself and with his sometimes monstrous attitudes—monstrous because of what he had been and because his retuned, rekeyed rhetoric was still intact.

Schuyler chose New York, but not with O'Hara's absolute and exclusive devotion. He too worked at the Museum of Modern Art for a time, and at *Art News*. He was affected by painting, but not in the fundamental way that O'Hara was. "The Morning of the Poem" and "Hymn to Life" are not as urban, or as brisk or brittle as O'Hara's poems. He is a city pastoralist, rambling through seasons that affect stone and brick quite as much as trees and fields. O'Hara in love is overwhelmed, hyperbolic, preening or contemplative; Schuyler is weakened and sentimentalized by desire. One of his best poems, "Buried at Springs," opens with a hornet and the poet in the same room, passes in brilliantly painterly detail through landscape and timescape to elegize O'Hara, the imagery understated to the point of heartbreak.

Kenneth Koch is the maverick among the mavericks of the New York School. Born in 1925 in Cincinnati, Ohio, he saw action during the Second World War in the Pacific. He graduated from Harvard and was drawn to the poets (O'Hara and Ashbery especially) and the painters of New York. He spent three years in France and Italy. In 1962 he published *Thank You*, a work that—like Ashbery's *The Tennis Court Oath*— remains a benchmark for his later experiments and developments. Here are the wild, strange inventories, the humor that in Koch becomes a chain of hilarity, a Rabelaisian sensuality and reveling in exclamation marks. He is a parodist, a fine formalist when he wants to be, a mini-dramatist, a writer of urban eclogues. In "A New Guide: 13" (*One Train*, 1995) he says,

> Look at the clouds.
> They may be what I look at most of all
> Without seeing anything.
> It may be that many other things are the same way
> But with clouds it's obvious.
>
> The motorboat runs through the sky reflected in the river.
> Look at the long trail of clouds behind.

Beneath the bright surface run serious currents; the poems "maintain power," writes Denis Donoghue, "by rarely choosing to exert it." He is "a masterly innovator," writes David Lehman, "who has used his extravagant powers of wit and invention to enlarge the sphere of the poetic." He has collaborated with other writers and with painters. He has an insatiable hunger for new forms, new directions, new *kinds* of writing, for example, the themes and variations of "One Train May Hide Another," and the "poems by ships at sea," the post-Apollinaire couplets of "A Time Zone," the orientalizing quatrains of "The First Step," and the hundred or so little poems that constitute the big poem "On Aesthetics." "He is above all a love poet, therefore a serious one," Frank Kermode said. "The Art of Poetry" paints us out of a corner.

> It is true that good poetry is difficult to write.
> Poetry is an escape from anxiety and a source of it as well.
> On the whole, it seems to me worthwhile. At the end of a poem
> One may be tempted to grow too universal, philosophical and
> vague

Or to bring in History, or the Sea, but one should not do that
If one can possibly help it, since it makes
Each thing one writes sound like everything else,
And poetry and life are not like that. Now I have said enough.

Mark Strand begins "almost as a painter would": the spirit of
Edward Hopper (on whom he has written) hovers over the large clari-
ties of a poetry that gathers its energies widely, from the visible world
and the world of languages (he is an eminent translator and has taught
and traveled widely).

"This is my Main Street," he said as he started off
That morning, leaving the town to the others,
Entering the high-woods tipped in pink

By the rising sun but still dark where he walked.
"This is the way," he continued as he watched
For the great space that he felt sure
Would open before him, a stark sea over which
The turbulent sky would drop the shadowy shapes
Of its song, and he would move his arms

And begin to mark, almost as a painter would,
The passages of greater and lesser worth, the silken
Tropes and calls to this or that, coarsely conceived . . .

The visible world includes the unprovable reality of dream, assembled to
read like allegory, but uprooted from any system or theology, making
oblique truths against the waking world.

Strand was born on Prince Edward Island, Canada, and studied and
taught in the United States (Yale, Columbia, Princeton, Harvard, Iowa,
Utah, Wesleyan), Italy and Brazil. His first book was *Sleeping with One
Eye Open* (1964). The surrealism of his early writing, learned from the
Latin American rather than the European Surrealists, gives way to more
defined and profound intentions. Octavio Paz says that he "has chosen
the negative path, with loss as the first step towards fullness: it is also the
opening to a transparent verbal perfection." He writes poems of auto-
biography, remarkable elegies and love poems. Yet he can seem—in his
humor, his positive ironies—a first cousin of New York poets, one of
those who did not end up in New York.

New York in the 1960s was a bright nursery of invention and experi-
ment. London wasn't. English poets who didn't like what English
poetry was doing—the Group, the easy politenesses and tepid satire of

the center—stayed in the provinces or went abroad. For over thirty years Christopher Middleton has been "easily the most intelligent and serious of our innovators, a poet with a disconcerting knack of making it new in almost every poem," according to John Lucas, and with something like disbelief Douglas Dunn agrees: "an avant-garde poet we can actually *read*." Middleton is also an astonishing essayist whose most challenging piece, "Reflections on a Viking Prow," throws down a gauntlet: "To recapture poetic reality in a tottering world, we may have to revise, once more, the idea of a poem as an expression of the 'contents' of a subjectivity. Some poems, at least, and some types of poetic language, constitute structures of a singularly radiant kind, where 'self-expression' has undergone a profound change of function. We experience these structures, if not as revelations of being, then as apertures upon being. We experience them as we experience nothing else." He turns his attention, first, to the "intrinsic virtues of preindustrial artifacts, not only ones that had explicitly sacred value."

The roots of such an approach are clearly in the nineteenth century and in the great modernists within the European tradition, German and French as well as English-speaking. But they go deeper, and the argument is hortatory rather than polemical, pulling back the corner on a creative possibility which looks new but is in fact the *fons et origo*. There are the confessionals, the volcanic forces of Whitman and Artaud, there are the "milieu writers," and then there are those who "are connected with specific places, solid scenes: they are the 'artificer poets.' " "Never frontal reportage about apparent localities, their writings are formal creations which enshrine and radiate poetic space." Middleton adduces the Rome of Propertius, the Swabia of Mörike, and he mentions Lorca, Kafka, Baudelaire and others, none of them English until we come to Hopkins, and then to Kipling, not the poet but the writer of travel letters. The best way of moving forward is moving away, following the right lights. Middleton is a man of long traditions. He wrote in a letter about an anthology of English poetry in which all the poems were "dilated anecdotes": "Whatever can have happened to the understanding that poetry—and not only at outer limits—universalises words, or works and plays words up to a condition of clearest starlight?"

If Middleton's analysis of the state of the British and American imagination is correct and if poets had the respect for him he deserves, plus the subtlety and tenacity of mind to take his arguments on board, even if only to reject them consciously, it would be the beginning of a change in the creative environment. Middleton has much in common, in terms of outlook, with the New York School poets, but there is a severity in him. He is a trained philologist, a scholar and translator, and a luminous critic. A poet-critic who deserves to be read alongside him is the American Guy Davenport, whose *The Geography of the Imagination* is a postwar critical classic.

Middleton was born in Truro, Cornwall, in 1926. He studied at Merton College, Oxford, and then taught at the University of Zürich and at King's College, London, and finally as professor of Germanic languages at the University of Texas, Austin. He has published translations of Robert Walser, Friedrich Nietzsche, Friedrich Hölderlin, Goethe, Gert Hofmann and many others.

In his poems various historical periods are sighted through a personal lens and in a shifting perspective: those of a man now captive, now free. Transformation is his theme, one kind of moment or thing changing into another. His poems are like miniatures refracting, waking the imagination to larger, gradual, encompassing transformations. There is no heavy Germanic solemnity in the poems, despite the fact that Middleton has for many years been a professional Germanist. His touch is light in both senses. Goethe made his Italian journey, but Middleton has taken the road to Turkey, which is both a modern country and an echo of Byzantium.

> If someone barefoot stood in a saloon,
> His dromedary might be chomping outside,
> That majestic meal. High olive notes
> Plucked from a mandolin. Fumes. Leafgreen.
>
> A dark descends. There, with banana palm,
> Consorts forbidden music. Ugly. Ocean.
> Delay it . . .

"I seek to interdict the code, so that a true message may be generated." And, again, "Poems have become experiences which did not exist before the poem." He has no time for the Movement. "The owls / have built a stinking nest in the Eighteenth Century." Along the road he tries to take there are stale puddles, and there is fear: fear of the forces lurking in the shadows, fear of taking the wrong turn. The destination is worth the risk.

In Roy Fisher, Middleton may have the poet he is looking for. Born in Birmingham in 1930 and educated at Birmingham University, Fisher made Birmingham, not the most promising of places, it might seem, his "locality." He also retains a freedom to use whatever form he feels his subject needs, from rhymed and metered verse (which he handles with mixed success at best) to quite ambitious forms of experiment, a versatility like F. T. Prince's, though Fisher is more copious and more wedded to the contingent world than Prince. His long poem "City" meditates on

Birmingham, using prose and verse and learning tonal and technical tips from Williams and Olson. If the imagination makes the world, the best way to understand its power and its flaws is by examining the world it made, the snares and surfaces, the streets and sounds. In proposing "a fresh Matter of Britain" (after all, we have the Matter of Ireland) he recognizes, as Middleton does, the need for some serious engagement with ideas and places, with ways of seeing and connecting that might "enshrine and radiate poetic space." The title of the poem in which he makes this proposal takes us back to painting: "On the Neglect of Figure Composition." Fisher is directly political in his poetry, as any writer dealing seriously with place must be.

Fisher and Middleton have published many of their books and pamphlets with small provincial presses, yet both have gained if not acceptance at least tolerance from the "main stream." They span the dangerous gulf between the "poetry establishment" and the generative, discontented antiestablishments. Their real affinities are with the "counterculture" and their presence in the other camp is too tactful, too late: from Derbyshire and Texas respectively, they cannot constitute a center, and change seems to come in British and American poetry largely from a concentration of voices in a place, the availability of publishing resources, and the consolidation of a critical literature which makes a space with access roads and finger-posts for the general public. The diaspora of the avant-garde or its institutionalization in universities ensures that—even in an electronic age—metropolitan interests and values, which are quantifiable and commercial, will call the tune.

Michael Hofmann writes, "I hope to bring with me my own intensity, an almost abstract thing, from the words, like Montale. That's the only value." Is this perhaps the new English poet Middleton envisages? There is the mention of Montale, for starters. Here is a man who reads Italian writers. Then, he was born in Freiburg, Germany. His father was a distinguished German novelist. He is bilingual. He came to Britain at the age of seven, studied in Edinburgh, Bristol, Winchester, Cambridge, Regensburg. He translates from the German. He travels.

But Hofmann was doing his research on Robert Lowell, and the ironies and paradoxes of his earlier poems in *Nights in the Iron Hotel* were only partly paid for. The relationships and underlying themes were his, and by his second book he was moving on, exploring his relations with his father. "Everything for me meets there: German, writing, feeling, sex, self-disgust, the future, the rudder of my life." It's at this point that Hofmann might seem to disappoint Middleton's hopes: "my life." It is a very singular and distinct life. The poems interest us, as many of Lowell's do, first for what they tell, not how they tell.

Yet the how is interesting, and in some of the early poems ("Kleist in

Paris," for example, in its curious half-blank, half-free verse, an epistle in the voice of the young poet-dramatist, with a lived sense of place and a living sense of desire) the imprint of Lowell is invisible. When he begins, in his first book, to write in images, whole figurative poems, reporting on experience in a staccato voice without inflection, the self withheld from the first-person experience, there is a sense of willed impoverishment. These poems, of the early 1980s, were fashionable. In "A gymnast swings like a hooked fish" the Martian note sounds, except that Hofmann is better than a Martian, there is a wandering prosody, cunningly irregular. The poems do not flow, they are phrased and full of pauses, and where the pauses come the reader supplies the emotional inflection. The poems about his father do indeed unpack a life, a pair of lives, the theme more deeply and tactfully treated than Tony Harrison's explorations of himself and his father. For Hofmann there are no easy categories: he is implicated in his father's world, culture and class. There is no resolution, even in his father's sudden death a few years later, commemorated in his place and absence in "For Gert Hofmann, died 1 July."

Michael Hofmann goes to Mexico. In a handful of poems whose accuracy is precise and surreal like Elizabeth Bishop's (though his tone is not so certain), he takes the measure of places, tying Mexico in via Lawrence to his own literary culture and by Maximilian to his Continental culture. Both are refracted through Mexico's emphatic otherness; his verse is free with a lingering iambic beat. He is able to see with clarity through his languages and with his language.

In his first book, *Heart's Desire* (1978), Jeffrey Wainwright sets off from a territory very much his own. In "Thomas Müntzer," a poem in the voice of a Protestant reformer who believed that God was so immanent that he would protect him from his foes and led his peasant army to defeat at Frankenhausen, he brings together the sense of political defeat that came in the wake of 1968 with an historical defeat resulting from analogous ideological naïveté. Into Müntzer he also feeds elements of his own life, not speaking in his own voice but incorporating his own experience as a father, an activist and a teacher. The poem synthesizes several urgent concerns in a single voice, generous, severe, fantastical. The fantasy is in Müntzer's dream of flying, the severity in his attitude to the empowered, his generosity in his sense of grace and of natural abundance. The poem is a sequence in twelve sections, each a separate "movement" in the speaker's progress. The epigraph from Antonio Machado also relates the poem to the miasma of commitments in the Spanish Civil War: "I have seen in my solitude / very clear things / that are not true." This is political writing of a high order because of the "very clear things" it sees which history has made true: not vision but witness.

Wainwright was born in Stoke-on-Trent in 1944. He read English at Leeds University and now teaches at the Manchester Metropolitan University. He studied with Geoffrey Hill, and though his verse does not sound like Hill's he continues to learn from him. Hill incorporated autobiographical elements into *Mercian Hymns* and other poems. Wainwright in 1994 wrote, "The strength that poetry—having absorbed the discursiveness of neo-classicism, the subjectivity of romanticism and the fragmentation of modernism—now possesses is the opportunity to combine so many different aspects of experience, knowledge and ways of speaking, and to mix them in a way that is richer, more linguistically—that is to say humanly—diverse than any of the argufying discourses it might feed from. Descartes, a child's bedtime memories, geology and evolution (popularly apprehended), a bit of argot and verbal playfulness can co-exist here as in no other form outside the literary." He is not talking about interior monologues or loose associationism, but of the syntheses a poet can effect with voices that transcend individual voice. This is what Hill does, diction, dialect and register conveying images and having the force of images in themselves—of period, class, relation. Wainwright starts with the varieties of language and sets himself apart from poets who, like Hofmann and most of his contemporaries, use poetry to unlock the themes that constitute the self, apprehending through his father "German, writing, feeling, sex, self-disgust, the future, the rudder of my life." Wainwright's meticulous and entirely deliberate approach has more in common with the spontaneities of O'Hara and Ashbery and the radiances of Middleton, than with the "milieu writers" who crowd the center stage.

Wainwright's early poems, which seemed difficult at the time, are now readily accessible: readers have grown with him into his later work, "The Mad Talk of George III and a Hymn to Liberty," "The Swimming Body" and other sequences and single poems. He is especially fond of the sequence, and in his *Selected Poems* he disrupts chronology in order to make a larger sequence out of his sequences, suggesting that "development" is beside the point, that "self," too, is irrelevant: what matters is the poetry, in its integrity, "an instance of itself." The body of work is small but not cautious: in "getting it right" Wainwright gives no hostages to fortune. His vocation is utterly serious, and even if it takes five years, he will wait (as Elizabeth Bishop, a similarly careful poet did) until it is ready.

The Red-Headed Pupil and Other Poems (1994) includes poems that are difficult but resonant. "The red-headed pupil is worried he is / not following." But as in "Müntzer," there's a lot to follow. What is his body, what is his brain, and what is his mind? How can he be him? What is real, and can he look for it? Is he only a different version of a brick wall?

Studiously, peering closer, as though at an anatomy lesson, "he tries hard." Autobiography again, but tautly controlled. The pupil is the red-headed poet in his youth, or his son.

The earlier themes are there despite the passage of time, the Thatcher years, the wear and tear of growing older. In the poem the imagination is young and puzzled. "There is the idea of mattering, even as against Empires. And of Freedom." Being free of thirst, hunger, disease, could the red-headed pupil be free of everything—of love, of belief, of the dead? How can he talk of these things? How can all these bits of history, dreams, quotations, family, different voices as well as what he tries to think of for himself, fit together? It is trying to make them fit, combining and recombining, that gives us this extraordinary poem, or rather sequence of twelve-line poems in batches of twenty-four, like the times table. They look tidy, boxed up, as neat as cause and effect—"the click / the this because of that." Can everything be understood and interpreted? "He looks perplexed." He tries harder.

"Free Rein" is a companion sequence, in different terms and tone, with broad political and human perspectives and a unique prosody. It is the "Thomas Müntzer" sequence two decades on. The issues are still unresolved despite history. The hunger for justice does not die down, it grows more intense with the passage of years.

Speaking and Speaking For

SEAMUS HEANEY, PAUL MULDOON, DEREK WALCOTT, LORNA
GOODISON, EDWARD KAMAU BRATHWAITE, TONY HARRISON,
JOSEPH BRODSKY, LES MURRAY

Once he sensed a thematic link between George Herbert's poem
"The Pulley" and one of his own, "Squarings," Seamus Heaney
believed. His belief as he reports it to us is that "a reliable criti-
cal course could be plotted by following a poetic sixth sense." It is not a
matter of a critical intelligence and a poetic imagination being at odds:
there is a critical imagination and a poetic intelligence as well. Intro-
ducing the volume of his Oxford lectures, *The Redress of Poetry* (1995), he
was declaring, at the heart of an academic institution, that analytical
criticism and literary theory are secondary, that serious readers navigate
by ear and imagination. He goes further, calling Robert Pinsky as a
witness (Heaney and Pinsky are both professors). In Pinsky's essay
"Responsibilities of the Poet," in a language overballasted with meta-
phor, he proclaims a splendid truth. The poet "needs not so much an
audience, as to feel a need to answer, a promise to respond. The prom-
ise may be a contradiction, it may be unwanted, it may go unheeded . . .
but it is owed, and the sense that it is owed is a basic requirement for the
poet's good feeling about the art. This need to answer, as firm as a bor-
rowed object or a cash debt, is the ground where the centaur walks."
That the poet is answerable—to his subject, his audience, or, more
properly, to his language—is unexceptionable. What gives pause is the
insistence on "the poet's good feeling about his art." Heaney pushes it:
his notion of redress is that the poem takes the reader, even if only in a
glimpse, "beyond confusion"; it is "a glimpse that has to be its own
reward," though he adds that it "fills the reader with a momentary sense
of freedom and wholeness." It is, in short, necessarily affirmative. Words-
worth becomes a prime witness; Heaney also calls Frost, Hardy and
Rilke to the stand.

These arguments seem to me remote from *poems*. They can get in the
way of poems and, as they become dogma, steer the art in directions it

doesn't necessarily want to go. In a poet of Heaney's skills the art is generally stronger than the rhetoric that tries to enlarge it. Making poems is one thing, being a poet quite another. Being a poet comes after the event of the poem; poets can interpose themselves between the poem and the audience, the poem and its "redress" or "responsibility." In Pinsky as in Heaney it is the poem that must answer, and it needs no special pleading. The kind of critical magniloquence that mars the often penetrating essays of Joseph Brodsky, who meant a great deal to Heaney, has rubbed off on many successful poets. It is nothing new; it is part of the legacy of Romanticism. When Wordsworth learned to talk in the large categories that Heaney admires, his poetry was in trouble. Poems hate such afflatus, such ambition at their expense.

Heaney was born in Mossbawn, County Derry, Northern Ireland, in 1939. His father was a Roman Catholic farmer. The eldest of nine children, Heaney won a scholarship, after attending Anahorish School, to St. Columb's College, Derry, where he boarded. "My sensibility," he told John Haffenden, "was formed by the dolorous murmurings of the rosary, and the generally Marian quality of devotion. The reality that was addressed was maternal, and the posture was one of supplication." He learned patience, "the best virtue," and the "Hail Mary" struck him as a "better poem" than the "Our Father," because it is "faintly amorous." Already—or is it retrospect adjusting history?—poetry was coloring, or displacing, faith.

He attended Queen's University, Belfast, became a schoolteacher, then returned to his university as a lecturer in 1965. The next year he published his first collection, *Death of a Naturalist*. He taught at Queen's University (with a year in California) until 1972, and during that time his second and third collections appeared, *Door into the Dark* (1969) and *Wintering Out* (1972). He spent four years in County Wicklow (*North* was published in 1975), then moved to Dublin. *Field Work* appeared in 1979, with his first *Selected Poems*. In 1984 he was appointed Boylston Professor of Rhetoric and Oratory at Harvard and in 1989 Professor of Poetry at Oxford. He has been prolific: *Station Island* and *Sweeney Astray* (1984), *The Haw Lantern* and *New and Selected Poems 1966–1987* (1987), *Seeing Things* (1991), *The Spirit Level* (1996) after receiving the Nobel Prize for Literature in 1995, in addition to anthologies, introductions, essays, and three prose collections, *Preoccupations: Selected Prose 1968–1978* (1979), *The Government of the Tongue* (1988) and *The Redress of Poetry* (1995).

For all his travels, Heaney remains a poet with a locality and landscape, though he is displaced from it as he was once displaced in it. His early displacement was due to the fact that he did not have a rural vocation—an estrangement like Tony Harrison's from his class and community—but Heaney is neither bitter nor enraged: he expresses through his evocations a warm solidarity with what he left behind, a nostalgia for the past that becomes a nostalgia for the present, which he can watch but cannot in conscience fully engage. This failure of engagement is one of the most powerful themes of his poetry and a testament to its political and social integrity.

In *Wintering Out* he brings politics into his verse directly. Politics had been latent, he claims, before, and perhaps he is right. He began writing when he began teaching: an urge to compete with R. S. Thomas, with Hughes, classroom poets. Like Thomas he becomes political when his environment is politicized, when the pull of history becomes too hard to resist. Would he have achieved his public eminence without the Troubles? To what extent do external factors here, as in Plath and Hughes (and latterly Gunn), determine his reputation? The question, posed by those who resent his success, is fatuous. The Troubles are not external to one whose community is riven by them, nor do they become external when he leaves. We have to connect where he came from with where he has gone, what he was with what he now is, the uses made of him and his resistance to or complicity in those uses.

Brodsky used him (and Walcott and Murray) to develop his polemic about the decline of British and American poetry, the rotten center and the healthy periphery. Brodsky had a purpose: to empower the historically marginalized at the expense of the traditionally empowered. His chosen poets, with the full authority of the English tradition (a tradition rather lacking in the eighteenth century, rather poor in the Enlightenment, but then Brodsky was a child of Counterreformation), spoke and *spoke for*. Brodsky's strategy was expedient, political and timely. But he came to believe in it himself. Fortunately, Heaney, Walcott and Murray, while they learned about the poetry of Eastern Europe from Brodsky and gained much from his wide learning, are less credulous. Having seen how writers and literatures can be marginalized, they have not lent their weight to the polemic. With Brodsky, however, they share a wariness of modernism and of the postmodern. (Critics speak of the influence of Williams on Heaney's short-lined poems: the diction as much as the underlying iambic tell against this judgment.) Their prosodies are seldom radically experimental, whatever risks they take with diction and the larger forms. They align themselves with the Romantics, with notions of organic form. Their first-person singular, their "I," is remarkably secure against the instabilities through which it is buffeted.

There seems to be a close kinship between the mature poems of Heaney and of Walcott, the ways in which they read back into their early lives and landscapes, making connections; the ways in which their language itself fans out like a place full of histories and losses. Their quatrain poems advance, in an oblique and condensed language, on their childhoods, Irish and Caribbean, restoring them in heightened hues. But Walcott never speaks, as Heaney does, of the "exclusive civilities" of English. In this Heaney sounds more like another poet of the Caribbean, Edward Kamau Brathwaite.

English, the argument runs, is a language *imposed* on Ireland; it is historically and semantically inimical to Heaney's Irish Catholic experience. It is colored by Protestantism, it excludes whole registers of feeling, it ironizes attitudes that are close to Heaney's heart. What are the "exclusive civilities"? What hegemony can a language exercise through literature? To what extent is a language we are born to, which our parents and grandparents and great-grandparents were born to, imposed, to what extent is it given? Imposition is on the first and sometimes the second generation: then the people get hold of their language; they alter it, infiltrate it, make spaces in it, possess it. Stephen Dedalus in the famous "tundish" scene in Joyce's *Portrait of the Artist as a Young Man* is a witness to the difference of dialect between the English mentor and the Irish youth. He doesn't wish he spoke Irish instead of English. He is stating a fact: that languages in different usage develop different valencies. He resents hearing his form of the language patronized by one who imagines his version is superior. Heaney's and Brathwaite's stance is now a commonplace, a form of rhetoric that can be adapted to various causes. Language is subvertible, however, and poetry has been and remains a means of subversion. But only if, as in Hill, it is reified, only if the poem is in and against its language. The subtle redress of such poetry is for the reader rather than the audience.

Is it not the various radicalisms of poetry which have ensured that in the area of literature at least language cannot tyrannize? The examples of Marlowe and Rochester, Milton and Blake, Shelley and Auden, Smart and Cowper; the hard models of Pound and MacDiarmid, within whose work we can discriminate both the radicalism and its signal failure: they affirm a more complex reality.

Opposition to *literary* hegemony is a notion that, if taken seriously into composition (as in the work of Brathwaite), impoverishes the poet's expressive resources and works against the possibility of transcendence. Walcott is right to affirm that Herbert and Herrick belong as much to him as they do to Larkin, though he speaks from a more "problematic" background than Heaney's. These are positive continuities; to break them is to impoverish self and art, and an impoverished art does not provide "redress."

Fortunately Heaney does not take the argument deep into his poetry.

He hears different dialects and accents and they mean different things. "The Guttural Muse" in *Field Work*, the book he struggled hardest for, brings together two experiences: the image of the "doctor fish" and the sound of people talking a "redemptive" dialect outside the poet's hotel window, sounds that assuaged his sense of isolation and aloneness and let him see "beyond confusion." The poem, however, talks about the issue, it does not embody it. In his essay "Englands of the Mind" he schematically teases out three models of diction, a Latinate, an Anglo-Saxon and a Norman, and characterizes Hill, Hughes and Larkin according to his plan. Too tidy, but suggestive.

Heaney's model is not Joyce and not the great Irish *Táin*. It is Auden, who teaches that the poet's tasks are making, judging and knowing. The making starts for Heaney in inadvertent politics. In 1974 he spoke of the Republican street rhymes he learned at Anahorish school, full of resistance and Irish patriotism. He was forced to memorize Byron and Keats. He loved to *hear* Wodehouse's characters but he could not *speak* their accents aloud. He got over his schooling. He was touched deeply by Hopkins, by Frost and Roethke, by Patrick Kavanagh. Later he was knocked rather off course by the power of Lowell's poems and by Lowell's presence in Ireland.

His approach to the present and its recurrences is generally through analogues—ghosts, bog people, childhood—the past lighting and alighting on the present. It is a deeply conservative aesthetic. "Beware of 'literary emotion,' " he says, and it is of Wordsworth, the poet of *The Prelude*, that he reminds us. The particularity of the early poems with their dependence on mimetic sound, their attempt to get close to the rural world, ensured his popularity. The world he created was authentically rural, and his rural world was closer to that of the Georgians than to the factory farming that had destroyed the wells and hedges of England.

He moves from that landscape to a wider sense of Ireland, the shape that it is in a map, the roads that intersect it, the histories that divide it. The development of his early writing is vivid, culminating in the historical and then the autobiographical poems in *North*. The struggle of *Field Work* is exhilarating: the poet has made a choice, has left the north of Ireland, has withdrawn from his great literary success into a place where he tries to rethink and remake his art. His most harrowing, quietly spoken political poem, "Casualty," is embedded in a sequence that gives it depth and context. The best poems in *The Haw Lantern, Seeing Things* and *The Spirit Level* are the results of the ongoing reinvention of self that begins in *Field Work*. Other poets—Czeslaw Milosz, Zbigniew Herbert, Robert Lowell, Joseph Brodsky—are catalysts; the classics invite his complicity so that he takes Dante and Homer on board. There is a tentativeness in his growth, a willingness to be blown off course, a self-knowledge sufficient to right the rudder and go on, following that sixth sense he speaks of. In the last of his "Squarings," the forty-eight twelve-line triplet poems that are the "invention" of *Seeing Things*, he says:

> Strange how things in the offing, once they're sensed,
> Convert to things foreknown;
> And how what's come upon is manifest
>
> Only in light of what has been gone through.

Like Heaney, Paul Muldoon was brought up in rural Ulster. He was born in Portadown, County Armagh, in 1951 and brought up near the Moy, a village to which his poems return. Muldoon's mother was a teacher with strong literary interests, his father a farm laborer friendly to the Republican cause, a Lawrentian formula that resulted not in *Sons and Lovers* but in poems about complementarities and incompatibilities. Fruitful and tragic misalliances are a recurrent theme in his poems, wired and triggered by ironies that can be unexpectedly savage or heart-breaking. Seamus Heaney was one of his teachers at Queen's University, and there, encouraged by Heaney and his own contemporaries, including Michael Longley, he became the most precocious poet of the Belfast "Group." He read Frost with special attention, though the American's impact on his prosody and narrative strategies is limited, except when he is producing, as in "The Mountain," ironic connections. "Frost was important to me early on because his line, his tone of voice, was so much a bare canvas." *New Weather,* his first book, came only three years after Heaney's debut, in 1972. Muldoon was twenty-one. He went on to work as a BBC producer, then went freelance and, in 1980, took the academic route to the United States. He now teaches at Princeton.

Muldoon often builds with baroque delicacy a trellis of ironies over rather rudimentary themes and subjects. He likes the Metaphysicals, he likes conceits. Eclectic in his range of reference and allusion, very funny much of the time, without the sense of displacement that we hear in Heaney, he is always seriously at play, but never twice at the same game. *Mules* (1977), *Why Brownlee Left* (1980), *Quoof* (1983), *Meeting the British* (1987), *Madoc: A Mystery* (1990) and *The Annals of Chile* (1994) disrupt the strategies of the Martians and play fast and loose with the "narrative" or "anecdotal" school that displaced them, reminding readers (and poets, including his Irish contemporaries) of the enormous resources of modernism. Editors who had tired of pale imitations of Martian verse began to find their submission trays filling with Muldoon imitations.

His formal and verbal inventiveness leads away from self. In *Madoc* he risks rewriting the lives of Coleridge and Southey, as if they had fulfilled the ambition of Pantisocracy and set up their community on the banks of the Susquehanna. Philosophers from the ancient Greeks to Stephen Hawking comment tersely and in character on the enterprise. It is very funny, very learned, a high-table game. He speaks for a whole history of thought, talked down, as it were, but not trivialized. "I'm interested in ventriloquism, in speaking through other people, other voices." *The Annals of Chile,* on the other hand, is in voices that must be close to the poet's own, exploring losses and a birth. The poet's voice comes equivocally from his own lips. It won't stay there for long, distrustful of the eloquence it finds. "I'm very much against expressing a categorical view of the world. I hope I can continue to discover something, and not to underline or bolster up what I already think I know."

A poet's first need, Heaney says, is "to make works that seem all his own work." The second need is harder, "to go beyond himself and take on the otherness of the world in works that remain his own yet offer rights-of-way to everybody else." This is Derek Walcott's achievement in "The Schooner *Flight.*" "I imagine he has done for the Caribbean," says Heaney, "what Synge did for Ireland, found a language woven out of dialect and literature, neither folksy nor condescending, a singular idiom evolved out of one man's inherited divisions and obsessions, an idiom which allows an older life to exult in itself and yet at the same time keeps the cool of 'the new.' " Synge: like Walcott, a dramatist. But Walcott is first a poet, and his language is less inventive than Synge's, though no less compelling. Walcott was born in Castries, St. Lucia, in 1930. His father, a civil servant, died when he was one. His mother was a respected schoolteacher. His was a relatively prosperous family, part of the "high-brown bourgeoisie," distant from poor blacks and from whites. Both his grandfathers were white Europeans, both his grandmothers were of African origin. His early world was scarred by a fire: Castries burned down in his childhood, and was rebuilt. He has two memories of the town, the first immutable.

Walcott attended local schools. With his brother he published his first two books, *25 Poems* (Port-of-Spain, Trinidad, Guardian Commercial Printer, 1948) and *Epitaph for the Young: XII Cantos* (Barbados, Advocate, 1949). He had begun to paint, and he remains an accomplished watercolorist. A poet he perhaps encountered in Jamaica, Lorna Goodison (born in 1943), is a forceful artist and a substantial poet who touches on many of the issues that Walcott does but in a less formal verse, halfway between Walcott and Brathwaite. In "Guinea Woman" she says:

Great grandmother
was a guinea woman
wide eyes turning
the corners of her face
could see behind her . . .
It seems her fate was anchored
in the unfathomable sea
for great grandmother caught the eye of a sailor
whose ship sailed without him from Lucea harbour.
Great grandmother's royal scent of
cinnamon and escallions
drew the sailor up the straits of Africa,
the evidence of blue-eyed grandmother
the first Mulatta
taken into backra's household
and covered with his name.
They forbade great grandmother's
guinea woman presence
they washed away her scent of
cinnamon and escallions
controlled the child's antelope walk
and called her uprisings rebellions.

But, great grandmother
I see your features blood dark
appearing
in the children of each new
breeding
the high yellow brown
is darkening down.
Listen, children
it's great grandmother's turn.

Walcott went to the University of the West Indies in Kingston,
Jamaica, long before Goodison attended the Jamaica School of Art. He
graduated in 1953. In 1959 he helped to found the Trinidad Theatre
Workshop, which he directed until 1977. Then he got onto the teaching
circuit and went to the United States.

In the year of his graduation he published *Poems* (Jamaica, City
Printery, 1951). His "real books" began to appear a decade later: *In a
Green Night: Poems 1948–1960* (London, 1962) and *Selected Poems* (New
York, 1964). Robert Graves declared, "Derek Walcott handles English
with a closer understanding of its inner magic than most (if not any) of

his contemporaries." Then followed *The Castaway and Other Poems* (1965), *The Gulf and Other Poems* (1969), *Another Life* (1973), *Sea Grapes* (1976), *The Star-Apple Kingdom* (1979), *The Fortunate Traveller* (1981), *Midsummer* (1984), *Collected Poems 1948–1984* (1986), *The Arkansas Testament* (1987) and the epic *Omeros* (1990). He received the Nobel Prize in 1992, and published *The Bounty* in 1997.

Brodsky deprives Walcott of some essential roots and fundamental politics. Half of Walcott's and Goodison's ancestors were forced to come to the New World. The poets now compel the elements of European culture—language, genre, tropes, narratives—to come after, and force them to confront and then contain the very experiences which their original privilege compelled. If we believe that culture can be "owned," it can also be "taken" or expropriated. An "owned language" cannot be disowned but it can be reformed and owned differently. A church building can become a stable or a theater, the epic of ancient heroes can be used to draw into heroic lineaments the experiences of fishermen and small traders (like the originals of the Homeric heroes).

It's worth using a technical linguistic term: *diglossia*. It means that two identifiable, different varieties of language coexist in a single culture, one for formal occasions and literature, the other spoken in a variety of dialects. In the case of the West Indies, the "higher" language is the received or imposed one, whether French or Spanish or English. The task for the writer is to bring up, as in Leeds Tony Harrison does, the lower into the higher, to leaven and subvert it. To possess it. To scrape some of the colonial history off it, or put some of the written-out history back in. An alternative is to formalize the "lower language" and make a *diglossia* between a deliberately formalized dialect and a variety of spoken forms (which is Hugh MacDiarmid's approach to Scots).

Our literary sense of the West Indies is largely shaped by V. S. Naipaul, the *Biswas* vision (1961). He is called "Old Misery" by some in the Caribbean; he's of East Indian rather than African extraction, and there are shades of resentment in his attitudes as in attitudes toward him. *The Middle Passage* (1962) speaks of the people of Coronie in Surinam: "A derelict man in a derelict land; a man discovering himself, with surprise and resignation, lost in a landscape which had never ceased to be unreal because the scene of an enforced and always temporary residence; the slaves kidnapped from one continent and abandoned on the unprofitable plantations of another, from which there could never more be escape: I was glad to leave Coronie, for, more than lazy Negroes, it held the full desolation that came to those who made the middle passage." Later he adds, "The history of the islands can never be satisfactorily told. Brutality is not the only difficulty. History is built around achievement and creation; and nothing was created in the West Indies." Derek

Walcott writes in 1973, in response: "Nothing will always be created in the West Indies for quite a long time, because whatever will come out of there is like nothing one has ever seen before."

Naipaul's critics take issue with this: creation can begin in resistance and struggle. What are the images to be, however? Borrowed images or images generated at home? If borrowed, the authentication is borrowed. If forged at home, what will legitimize them? To Naipaul's *The Middle Passage* Brathwaite responds with *Rights [sic] of Passage*: "Where then is the nigger's home?" And in 1979 Walcott's "The Schooner *Flight*" in *The Star-Apple Kingdom* proposes a new West Indian identity.

The poem is spoken by the mulatto Shabine. He begins in the colonial confusion, leaving Trinidad on his wanderings: "and either I'm nobody, or I'm a nation" expresses the crucial European-sourced paradox. Naipaul's "nobody," Toussaint's "nation," yet a nation of *synthesis* and, in Shabine's travels, a nation without frontiers, and a nation *by choice*. The racial categories are complex, not "monolithic," especially in areas with substantial East Indian rooted communities. Race and region, race and religion, race and nation are not "congruent categories."

In the Caribbean it is necessary to acknowledge the emblematic centrality of Aimé Césaire, whose *Cahier d'un retour au pays natal* is the first significant "text" from the West Indies, written in French and from exile in France in the 1930s, the first work using the word *négritude*, an essentializing idea that resulted in a series of "theories," all in "a single category." It was a reaction to the "them and us," but also a necessary recognition. It helped to define, from a distinct and native perspective, facts about colonialism and its aftermath. It made it harder for historians of any race to ignore those perspectives and perceptions.

For Césaire's anthology in 1948 Jean-Paul Sartre wrote *Black Orpheus*. Sartre prescribes *négritude* as a necessary part of black liberation and underlines the crucial importance of the new black writers in the process. French intellectuals welcomed writing in French by black people from the Caribbean and North Africa. But essentially African ideologies have only recently—in the 1980s and 1990s—begun to interpret what had previously been historicized in European terms, by way of ideologies of capitalism and socialism. Kamau Brathwaite and Wilson Harris, the novelist, poet and critic from Guyana, have long argued for different historical models to be applied to Caribbean culture.

Sartre declared that black writers "have no language common to them all; to incite the oppressed to unite they must have recourse to the language of the oppressor . . . Only through it can they communicate; like the scholars of the sixteenth century who understood each other only in Latin, the blacks rediscover themselves only on the terrain full of traps which white men have set for them. The colonist rises between the colonials to be the eternal mediator; he is there, always there, even though absent, in the most secret councils." In the language. As Brathwaite says, "It was in language that the slave was perhaps most successfully imprisoned by his master, and it was in his (mis-)use of it that he most effectively rebelled."

In the 1950s a necessary reaction against notions of *négritude* sets in among black writers themselves: Sartre's argument, necessary at the time perhaps, had become reductive and homogenizing. Césaire himself began to warn against the anticolonial force of American rhetoric and what it implied for new patterns of dependence—on aid, capitalist patterns of exploitation and so on. The debate began among French writers. It was then taken up by the Spanish speakers (especially Cubans—Martì, Alejo Carpentier, Nicolás Guillén) and finally the English speakers.

For English-language Caribbean writers the struggle for self-definition has affinities with the emergence of black identity and power in the United States. It began to gather steam in the 1960s. It is important to remember that before that time much of the force for reform (rather than revolution) came from religious groups. This continues. The Rastafarians started in the 1930s but came to the fore in the 1950s in Jamaica. Now it is impossible to separate West Indian, American and colonial experiences: they are part of a single nexus of interests, actions and reactions.

Walcott remembers an earlier time. In "Sainte Lucie" (1976) he says, "Come back to me my language"—the language of youth and innocence; also of "tribe" and "community." But he had begun to change his language, and a comparison between two versions of the same poem demonstrates how, without too much adjustment, his verse could adapt to a new politics, a changing mission, best explored in "The Schooner *Flight*," but also in exhaustive detail in *Omeros*. In 1958 he wrote the sonnet (Sonnet VI) with the epigraph *"my country 'tis of thee"*:

> Garçon, that was a fête . . . I mean they had
> Free whiskey and they had some fellows beating
> Steel from one of the bands in Trinidad,
> And everywhere you turn people was eating
> And drinking and so on and I think
> They catch two guys with his wife on the beach,
> But "there will be nothing like Keats, each
> Generation has its angst, and we have none,"
> And he wouldn't let a comma in edgewise
> (Black writer, you know, one of them Oxford guys),
> And it was next day in the papers that the heart
> Of a young child was torn from it alive

By two practitioners of the native art.
But that was far away from all the jump and jive.

Ten years later the poem was included in *In a Green Night*:

Poppa, da' was a fête! I mean it had
Free rum free whiskey and some fellars beating
Pan from one of them band in Trinidad
And everywhere you turn was people eating
And drinking and don't name me but I think
They catch his wife with two tests up the beach
While he drunk quoting Shelley with "Each
Generation has its *angst*, but we has none"
And wouldn't let a comma in edgewise.
(Black writer chap, one of them Oxbridge guys.)
And it was round this part once that the heart
Of a young child was torn from it alive
By two practitioners of native art,
But that was long before this jump and jive.

In *The Arkansas Testament* Walcott is writing largely in standard English, and the poems about his childhood in particular revisit it through English, through Latin, and by highlighting how the French words and the native words for different things and creatures give them a different force and identity. So when he brings Homeric themes and techniques into the American Mediterranean and the thousands of islands of the Caribbean, Homer is altered, and all that Homer has meant to English literature is subtly altered, by the new content, the new politics, which do not replicate but extend the old. Joyce used the *Odyssey* in analogous ways, but in a less answerable geography. It is a matter of making connections in terms that distort neither the classical nor the neoclassical culture. Walcott's resistance to political imperatives and ideologies is heroic in just the ways Brodsky suggests, yet he is as open as Muldoon is to the charge of "failing to declare himself." That failure is surely the crucial declaration a poet must make.

Not according to Edward Kamau Brathwaite. Brathwaite was born in Barbados in 1930 into a middle-class family. He was educated there and at Pembroke College, Cambridge, where he read history. From 1955 to 1962 he taught in Ghana and started a children's theater there. It was a difficult time for him, but later he revised his view of it—a time of growing solidarity and self-discovery. His doctoral thesis at the University of Sussex was on the Jamaican slave trade and Creole society in the eighteenth century. He returned to the West Indies and taught history at the University of the West Indies until his retirement.

He published plays and several major collections of poetry, beginning with *Rights of Passage* (1967), then *Masks* (1968) and *Islands* (1969), which constituted his first trilogy, *The Arrivants: A New World Trilogy* (1973). This was followed by *Other Exiles* (1975), *Mother Poem* (1977), *Sun Poem* (1982), *Third World Poems* (1983), *X/Self* (1987) and *Middle Passages* (1992). For Brathwaite English is a colonial, "owned" language. He rebels in various ways against it, and against his own early poetry and poetic strategies, resembling in this the American poet Leroi Jones (Amiri Baraka), whose later work involves the complete unweaving of his powerful early poems and their replacement by quite a different kind of power, fueled less by compassion than by anger.

Brathwaite perceived in prosody what he took to be a crucial tyranny, and his analysis is vehement and subtle, though reductive. The crucial tyranny is in the iambic pentameter, which is hostile to native speech rhythms (which contain more "stress"), and in English poetic diction, which does not admit Caribbean reality or words. For centuries an English curriculum has been imposed in which Caribbean students are asked to read poems about snow and daffodils rather than their own weather, their own plants and creatures. The English tradition is less a resource than a form of impoverishment and constraint. Brathwaite tries to create a new poetry based on Jamaican speech patterns, unmetered, aurally emphatic and, on the page, using a range of types, sizes and densities, visually eloquent as well.

Like Walcott's, his "landscape" is a seascape of islands and oceans in various states of weather. His Shakespeare is *The Tempest* and his hero Caliban. "Ah, brave third world!" as Walcott exclaims, devoted to the same play for other reasons. Like Walcott, Brathwaite tries to provide his culture with an epic. His trilogies are Homeric in scope. While Walcott attempts to create an accessible high culture, Brathwaite tries for a culture grown from and for the "grass roots," which he identifies, defines and speaks for.

Tony Harrison identifies with the Caribbean poets in all of their languages, with the Central Americans, with the Africans engaged in liberation movements against Portugal, with anyone who is speaking out against historical injustices. The working classes at home in Britain are as much victims of colonial tyranny as the subject peoples of the Empire. They are ghettoized, their labor exploited, their rights expendable. In his Marxizing years, Harrison busily connected with his travels and his poems dozens of points of injustice on the globe—those points where articulate resistance occurred.

He was born in Leeds in 1937, into a working-class family. Leeds gives him his "mother tongue": not English but a dialect of it. His father was a baker. He has commented on the "disintegrative effect" of the 1944 Education Act. At eleven he won a working-class boy's scholarship to Leeds Grammar School, where by his account he suffered for his accent and his class. He proceeded to the University of Leeds, where he read classics, followed by a postgraduate diploma in linguistics. He was at Leeds with Geoffrey Hill, the editor and poet Jon Silkin and the Nigerian writer Wole Soyinka, who won the Nobel Prize in 1986.

Harrison presents himself as half missionary, half comic: Livingston and George Formby, Africa and Leeds. He is a missionary without metaphysics, but with a political dogma. He is a comic busking the wrong class. His first job was as a schoolmaster in Dewsbury. In 1962 he went to the new Ahmadu Bello University, Northern Nigeria, to lecture in English. He spent four years in Africa and here his sense of drama began to develop. He produces not readable but actable versions of plays: he generally writes with his eye on truth to the medium rather than the page. He speaks of Sophocles, of wrestling with the original, tapping "the political assumptions." "You don't have to batter the original into submission; you use the weight of its political assumptions." *Aikin Mata* was more than a glimmer, it was the first evidence of his dramatic techniques. He adapted the *Lysistrata* of Aristophanes, pitting standard against pidgin English in a modern setting. He gave standard English to the dominant tribe. He included women.

After Africa, he spent 1966 teaching at Charles University, Prague, where he wrote two essays on Virgil, brilliant examples of his Marxist style. He was an Arts Fellow in 1967, shuffling between Newcastle-on-Tyne and Durham. Newcastle became home: the place from which one sets out on travels and adventures. He traveled: to North and South America (Cuba, Nicaragua and elsewhere, looking at revolutions and resistances). Between 1969 and 1970 he embarked on a UNESCO fellowship to Cuba, Brazil, Senegal, Gambia. *Newcastle Is Peru* had appeared. In 1970 he published his first controversial book, *Loiners*. It used bad language, it talked ill of the Commonwealth service, it shocked. His linguistic skills soon took him away from poetic to dramatic controversy. In 1977 he was made resident dramatist at the National Theatre, having already become a successful translator of opera libretti, with a strong sense of equivalences between the sound values of different languages and the dynamics of singing. In 1985 he hit real controversy, when his poem *V* was screened on national television, with its four-letter words (which caused the furor) and its gloves-off examination of adolescent hooliganism and racism. This is his most painful and candid work: as a Marxist, he sees the other side on a number of crucial issues. It was a point of political crisis for him. *V* signified "victory" (Churchill), "versus" and "fuck you" (Thatcher). Written in rough quatrains verging at times on doggerel, with a demotic entirely unalloyed, it was the first inclusion in verse of skinhead language, the rhetoric of racism, class and sexual division. It was also an elegy for the poet's parents.

There are several models for modern political poetry. First is Yeats's, intimate and engaged (or rather, implicated), the powerful statement of "Easter 1916." Then there is Kinsella's *Butcher's Dozen*, Rickword's "To the Wife of a Non-Interventionist Statesman," Augustan satire that establishes cause, consequence and cure, "the doggerel Route." Third is the Muldoonesque, in which the formal elements are foregrounded: doubt, indecision and inconclusion are the keynotes. Finally there is Harrison's "Looking in on conflict"—the camera, the refusal to appropriate (or so he says) what the camera sees to a specific political end.

Harrison is always a dramatist poet, his poems are spoken outward to the audience, with designs on that audience. He creates a more or less credible, more or less consistent persona. He refers in his poetry to Milton and Keats as his models, but when one reads his work *in extenso* one is put in mind of Kipling. The use of dialect, the orchestration of voices, and the obsessively insistent iambic drub us into submission or alienation. In his later work George Formby and Keats are in retreat, the somber tones of Livingstone and Milton in the ascendant. With Marxism licking its wounds after the changes in Eastern Europe, Harrison has become rather an apocalyptic; the solving dogmas are dead. Revolution is no longer anticipated, and without it there is only the end of things. History now includes nature. Politics for the writer of radical instincts now includes ecology and little else. As he says in "Initial Illumination," it is "doubtful in these dark days what poems can do."

No longer do the reclamations of his early poems occur. Language brings with it a culture. The language may be Greek, or Latin, or Cornish, or Middle English, or Leeds dialect. The mixture of languages is a play of political ironies, but that play is played out. It is in *Earthworks* (1964) and *Newcastle Is Peru* (1967)—with its allusion to the poet Cleveland as the drunken protagonist (a tribute to MacDiarmid?)—the poems and Meredithian sonnets of *Loiners* (1970), *From the School of Eloquence* (1978) and *Continuous* (1980) that the essential Harrison is to be found. A few fine later poems, in particular *A Kumquat for John Keats* (1981), precede the television work, which is deliberately controversial, a poetry of painful simplifications of history, politics and culture. Whatever their power on the screen (variable at best), they represent an alarming intentionality. In *The Blasphemers' Banquet* (1989) he joins the company of Byron, Voltaire, Rushdie and others as the champion of free speech. Giving voice to the voiceless, which he does so committedly in his earlier poems, is one thing; giving voice to those who speak perfectly well for themselves is something quite different. The poet is in danger of colonizing territories of infinitely greater wealth or power than he possesses: the German poet Heinrich Heine, for example, in *The Gaze of the Gorgon*: "If art can't cope / it's just another form of dope, / and leaves the Gorgon in control / of all the freedoms of the soul." Harrison's eye is keenly political. The Gulf War provoked *A Cold Coming* (1990), eloquent, incomplete, like *The Shadow of Hiroshima* (1995).

Harrison insists on his own life story. It is the heart of his best sonnets. From Robert Lowell he learns the surface lessons of confessionalism, the *fiction* of the self. Poems like "National Trust" and "On Not Being Milton" are powerful, and the poems to his parents moving and compassionate. The experiments with television have extended the medium of television, but not of poetry. Poetry that collaborates with the camera grows lax in its precisions, and journalistic. The eye takes over from the ear, and language becomes caption to image. It is different in the theater, where his mighty translations have made a durable impact. As a poet he speaks for others, even in their voices, but not in their terms nor in the terms of their culture. "Others" are translated for his needs, his program.

The Russian poet Joseph Brodsky (1940–1996) deliberately mythologized himself. In the world of literal fact he was expelled from the Soviet Union in 1972 as a "parasite," became an American citizen and a celebrated academic and speaker, and was awarded the Nobel Prize for Literature in 1987. He grew powerful in the intellectual world of New York. It is more as an impresario and critic than as a poet that Brodsky has already figured in this history. He brought together Heaney, Walcott and Murray; he traced a new map of Parnassus, setting its various summits on the peripheries and showing a center grown hollow.

His Russian poems were advocated by W. H. Auden, who introduced a Penguin selection in 1973. The translator was George L. Kline, who tried to keep close to Brodsky's forms. Brodsky was a stickler for formal equivalences between original poems and translations—not only his own. His second major volume in English, *A Part of Speech*, included a few of Richard Wilbur's translations, "The Funeral of Bobo" being the single best translation of Brodsky. Auden's claims for the Russian seemed to be sustainable in the light of such versions. But already Brodsky was dissatisfied with translators.

He began to collaborate with his translators, and then to crowd them out. Trying to compose in metered and rhymed English, he created a centipede with many elbows and very few wrists. What grace is to be found is not natural, though some of the striven-for effects actually work. The poems often express emphatic opinions, but their authority is not earned. Brodsky's posthumous collection *So Forth* (1996) is either deliberately awkward in subtle ways which elude his critics, or bad. Take, for instance, these lines from "Flourish":

> O if the birds sang while the clouds felt bored by singing,
> and the eye gaining blue as it traced their trill
> could make out the keys in the door and, beyond, a ceiling
> and those whose address at present begins with nil.

The emperor is not stark naked, but he wears rags of an archaic rhetoric, without even the belt of closed syntax to gird him. In *On Grief and Reason,* his posthumous collection of essays, he has lost the vigor of his earlier (translated) prose. These are polite essays, sententious and ingratiating. The rewards of exile in a country that stood in awe of his life story and his erudition, and was reluctant to withdraw the hand that fed him even when he bit, were considerable, but—to his writing— treacherous.

Les Murray is heard as "the Australian voice," but an eccentric one: a rural poet speaking for an urban culture, a Roman Catholic speaking for a largely secular people. I doubt that he sees himself as speaking for "a people." For persons, perhaps, for creatures (in *Translations from the Natural World*). His favorite polemic is that every form of expression is poetry: some people do it with language, others with dance, or skating, or chopping timber. Poetry, a universal making, a universal *kind* of engagement, is not, in his view, confined to language, though (fortunately) his own is. Neglect of writers who are not from the "central cultures," neglect of the eccentric, the misfit, he will not tolerate. In the wake of the long neglect of Australian writing in Britain and America, he is a sharp critic and a warm advocate, calling attention to merit not only in the field of verse. But it is *merit* he calls attention to—there are no double standards. And the absence of a double standard makes him enemies at home.

It is worth remembering that Australia is a coastal culture, a necklace of habitation around a largely "dead heart." The first Australian poet was the son of transported convicts—Charles Harpur, whom Murray celebrates, a nineteenth-century presence embodying the Europe/Australia split; hostile at once to England and to his cloddish society. In his anthology *Fivefathers: Five Australian Poets of the Pre-academic Era* Murray celebrates Kenneth Slessor, Roland Robinson, David Campbell, James McAuley and Francis Webb as establishing the traditions within which he writes. "This book," writes Les Murray, "presents to British and European readers selections from the work of five leading Australian poets of the generation before mine." They are, with Judith

Wright, A. D. Hope and Gwen Harwood, key figures in "a Golden Age of Australian poetry which paradoxically coincided with its greatest marginalisation."

Murray's characteristically emphatic introductory essays to the poets, of whom he is in a real sense himself made, and his "essential" selections from their work, are personal. He evokes the writers' circumstances, the trajectories of their very different work, and he suggests why their accomplishment has been eclipsed in the wider *bourse* of English-language literary reputations. The academy has much to answer for, he says, yet the freedom the poets enjoyed was partly a result of their very neglect by institutions. Murray strikes effectively against "that imperial trap of exclusion," making the map of the century's poetry larger. He also writes within a tradition described by Scottish writers, Hugh Mac-Diarmid and Sorley MacLean; by Frost and Jeffers; by a host of poets he has read attentively and celebrated in essays or in tributes. Only, not the modernists. His impatience with Pound, Eliot and the rest is resolute.

He celebrates the environment of his childhood, the farm and its creatures, which he loved because he did not feel comfortable at school. He evokes the poetry of gossip, the "bush balladry." His father was at the heart of things, and his voice, his stories are behind many of the poems. It is from this background that Murray learns the intimacy of his address, direct, subtle but always including. "An Absolutely Ordinary Rainbow," one of his most moving poems, exhibits his main qualities. It tells a story. It is cadential rather than metrical. It is *democratic*, about how people respond, and the urban world is presented sympathetically. It is religious but not doctrinaire, about a man weeping publicly and his effect on others, about the grace of acknowledged grief. It is an emotive poem, designed to be read aloud, but not a performance poem and not written on any audience's terms. Most important, its antimodernist drift means that Murray's intention is to "make it present" rather than "make it new."

Murray's collections begin in 1965 with *The Ilex Tree*. His verse novel *The Boys who Stole the Funeral* (1980) is 140 sonnets, a modest precursor to his massive verse novel *Fredy Neptune* (1998), a story that takes its protagonist through the history of the twentieth century in a series of adventures and reflections. His first substantial book to be published outside Australia was *The Vernacular Republic: Poems 1961–1981* (1982). It put his poems not only on the map but at the center of it. Later books include *The Daylight Moon* (1987), *Dog Fox Field* (1990), the large *Collected Poems* (1991), *Translations from the Natural World* (1993) and *Subhuman Redneck Poems* (1996), awarded—ironically, in view of his attitude to modernism—the T. S. Eliot Prize of 1996.

Written in the wake of his father's death, the book is full of the memories that, at whatever age, finding oneself an orphan elicit. In his case it was not only his father's death but his own vexed childhood that came back in all its anxious detail. In "Burning Want" he writes,

> From just on puberty, I lived in funeral:
> mother dead of miscarriage, father trying to be dead,
> we'd boil sweat-brown cloth; cows repossessed the garden.
> Lovemaking brought death, was the unuttered principle.
>
> I met a tall adopted girl some kids thought aloof,
> but she was intelligent. Her poise of white-blonde hair
> proved her no kin to the squat tanned couple who loved her.
> Only now do I realise she was my first love.
>
> But all my names were fat-names, at my new town school.
> Between classes, kids did erocide: destruction of sexual morale.
> Mass refusal of unasked love; that works . . .

"It would be as myopic to regard Mr. Murray as an Australian poet as to call Yeats an Irishman," Joseph Brodsky said in his overemphatic generosity. "He is, quite simply, the one by whom the language lives." And Derek Walcott: "There is no poetry in the English language so rooted in its sacredness, so broad-leafed in its pleasures, and yet so intimate and conversational." Murray is a poet of the sacred, but a sacredness that rises out of this, our material world. The world of our language.

> Lotus leaves, standing feet above the water,
> collect at their centre a perfect lens of rain
> and heel, and tip it back into the water.
>
> Their baby leaves are feet again, or slant lips
> scrolled in declaration; pointed at toe and heel
> they echo an unwalked sole in their pale green crinkles
>
> and under blown and picket blooms, the floor
> of floating leaves rolls light rainwater marbles
> back and forth on sharkskins of anchored rippling.

Loose Ends

Beside earlier centuries, the twentieth in this account is overcrowded with poets. And yet it is not crowded enough. There are significant absences, as in the earlier centuries, for which amends will have to be made another time.

Or is the account too full, the approach too tolerant? Breaks in transmission have thinned out the poetry of the fourteenth and fifteenth centuries. Time and fashion have winnowed the poets in Doctor Johnson's *Lives*. The late Victorians have sunk under the weight of their collected works. Should a historian not do the winnowing of time and fashion for readers today? There are certainly a dozen poets of this century whose work will be taken off the shelves or accessed on the flickering screens of the twenty-third century. It's almost clear who those poets will be. But as soon as one tries to give them context, that context consists of other poets who have claims on our attention.

Books about poetry either limit the period they cover or concentrate on a theme. My history is peculiar in that it is written by a reader who—though he teaches in a university—distrusts critical specialism. The real academic work, that of the scholar, is necessarily specialized and of great value in establishing and recovering texts, but many academic *critics* only feel confident in judgment in a specific period, or drive a theoretical skewer through poetry, investing their faith not in a poem but in a predetermined approach to poetry.

It is an act of folly, I now know, to undertake so large a task as this. What fueled it from the outset was a fierce and sometimes partisan enthusiasm for specific poems. I like the way that poems connect with one another and weave a larger pattern. A living poem can energize another poem at five hundred years' distance, or across the other side of the world. For the most part I follow chronology in this history, knowing how unfashionable in academic circles it now is to plot such a course. But it is only against a sense of chronology, of developing styles, that the surprise of what was once genuinely new can be understood, its abiding value inferred.

What cannot be inferred, however, is future direction. The twentieth century is so diverse, the new technologies so volatile, that the historian is wary of becoming a prophet. No one could have predicted the enormous achievement of Chaucer, Spenser or Ben Jonson. After Jonson, certain definable lines emerge and there is for a time a progressive logic in chronology, which breaks down in the second half of the eighteenth century and is never restored. A historian can be a prophet after the event, making the case for neglected writers. Swinburne and then T. S. Eliot restored Donne, for instance, and Laura Riding is not alone in having tried to restore Charles Doughty, whose time may yet come. But "may yet come" begins to sound like prophesy; for his time to come it will take a poet rather than a critical advocate to resurrect him.

We can predict that the questions that arise out of religious belief or doubt, out of history, politics, economics, out of anxiety, sexual desire or frustration, love or hate, will continue to exercise poets to come. So too will the nature of language, what can and cannot be said and formed. Answers will come, if at all, not in poetic theories and poets' essays, grand statements or aphorisms—things that occur after the crisis and the creative event. Answers will come in poems, not as argument but as form. Even in those poems that contain argument, what matters as poetry is form, how words work together, the sounds and silences their combination makes, the ordered effects they produce in the attentive hearer. This is what survives when argument goes stale, when the rules of play change, when the poem's occasion is lost.

Acknowledgments

I am indebted to several people for their assistance with *Lives of the Poets*. My agent, David Godwin, entertained the idea of a book I had wanted to write for many years. Rebecca Wilson of Weidenfeld commissioned and inspired it, and Ian Pindar patiently and tactfully translated it into English. The incomparable Robyn Marsack corrected and prepared it for press. Penny Jones helped assemble the text. For the American edition the textual assiduity of Rita Madrigal and Katherine Scott, and the care of Stephanie Katz were invaluable. And it is a special pleasure and privilege to have as my editor at Knopf Carol Janeway. My colleagues at Carcanet Press, Pamela Heaton and Joyce Nield, and my colleagues at the University of Manchester, in particular Professor Richard Francis, Shelagh Aston, Mary Syner and Chris Gribble, helped in various ways. At the John Rylands University Library the archivist Stella Halkyard and at the Manchester City Art Gallery Mary Griffiths provided valuable support. Sophie Hannah monitored the work. My friend Angel García-Gómez endured a year of writing. Always present were the defining voices of C. H. Sisson and Donald Davie, and also of Edgell Rickword, I. A. Richards, Octavio Paz, Laura (Riding) Jackson, Elizabeth Daryush, Elizabeth Bishop, W. S. Graham, David Arkell and others who down the years have meant a great deal to me through their writings, example and friendship.

Some passages in this book draw on material included in *50 British Poets, 1300–1900* (1980) and *50 Modern British Poets* (1979), and on various essays and reviews I have written over the last thirty years.

Brief Bibliography

A full bibliography for a book of this nature would be as long as the book itself. This is a summary list of editions of poetry and poets' prose I have used, most of them available in libraries, bookshops or on the Internet. Other editions exist. The dates I give are generally of the volumes I have consulted. I provide a merely preliminary list of anthologies and secondary works, critical and contextual. I omit most monographs and biographies. Readers will discover that in the cases of some significant poets, critical volumes and biographies are in print while no edition of the work is currently available.

Oxford, Penguin, Faber and W. W. Norton anthologies are useful starting points, those that concentrate on a period, a nation and those with a generic concern. Everyman, Penguin, Oxford, Carcanet and other imprints publish inexpensive single-author selections. Those who want critical direction can consult the multi-volume guides from Penguin, Sphere, Oxford, Cambridge and others.

I have a marked preference for critical writing by practicing poets, from Dryden through Johnson, Coleridge, Arnold, Pound, Ford, Eliot, Rickword and Graves to the present day. In the bibliography, prose by poets is listed after the poetry. I include volumes by some authors not discussed in *Lives of the Poets*; their omission (for reasons of length) I regret and their work I value. That list of "esteemed omissions" might have been much extended.

EDITIONS AND SELECTIONS (VERSE AND PROSE)

Aiken, Conrad. *Collected Poems* (London, 1971)

Ammons, A. R. *Selected Longer Poems* (New York, 1980)

———. *Selected Poems* (New York, 1987)

Armitage, Simon. *Book of Matches* (London, 1993)

———. *Cloudcuckooland* (London, 1997)

———. *The Dead Sea Poems* (London, 1995)

———. *Kid* (London, 1992)

———. *Zoom* (Newcastle-upon-Tyne, 1989)

Arnold, Matthew. *Poems* (London, 1965)

———. *Selected Criticism* (London, 1972)

Ash, John. *Selected Poems* (Manchester, 1997)

Ashbery, John. *And the Stars Were Shining* (Manchester, 1994)

———. *Can You Hear, Bird* (Manchester, 1996)

———. *Flow Chart* (Manchester, 1991)

———. *Girls on the Run* (Manchester, 1999)

———. *Hotel Lautréamont* (Manchester, 1992)

———. *The Mooring of Starting Out: The First Five Books of Poetry* (Manchester, 1997)

———. *Selected Poems* (Manchester, 1986)

———. *Self-Portrait in a Convex Mirror* (Manchester, 1977)

———. *Wakefulness* (Manchester, 1998)

———. *A Wave* (Manchester, 1984)

Auden, W. H. *Collected Poems* (London, 1991)

———. *The Dyer's Hand* (London, 1963)

———. *The Enchaféd Flood* (London, 1951)

———. *The English Auden: Poems, Essays and Dramatic Writings 1921–1939* (London, 1977)

———. *Forewords and Afterwords* (London, 1973)

———. *Selected Poems* (London, 1979)

Bacon, Sir Francis. *Works* (seven volumes, London, 1890)

Baraka, Amiri [Leroy Jones]. *Selected Poems* (New York, 1979)

Barbour, John. *The Bruce* (Edinburgh, 1997)

Barker, George. *Collected Poems* (London, 1987)

Barnes, William. *The Poems of William Barnes* (London, 1962)

———. *Selected Poems* (ed. Thomas Hardy, London, 1908)

Baxter, James K. *Collected Poems* (Wellington, 1979)

Beddoes, Thomas Lovell. *Plays and Poems* (London, 1950)

Beer, Patricia. *Autumn* (Manchester, 1997)

———. *Collected Poems* (Manchester, 1988)

———. *Friend of Heraclitus* (Manchester, 1993)

Behn, Aphra. *The Works of Aphra Behn* (London, 1915)

Berryman, John. *Collected Poems 1937–1971* (London, 1990)

———. *The Dream Songs* (London, 1990)

———. *The Freedom of the Poet* (New York, 1976)

Betjeman, Sir John. *Collected Poems* (London, 1979)

———. *Summoned by Bells* (London, 1969)

Bhatt, Sujata. *Point No Point: Selected Poems* (Manchester, 1997)

Bishop, Elizabeth. *Exchanging Hats: Paintings* (Manchester, 1997)

———. *The Collected Prose* (New York, 1984)

———. *The Complete Poems 1927–1979* (New York, 1983)

Blake, William. *Complete Writings* (Oxford, 1969)

Blunden, Edmund. *Selected Poems* (Manchester, 1982)

———. *A Selection of His Poetry and Prose* (London, 1950)

Boland, Eavan. *Collected Poems* (Manchester, 1996)

———. *The Lost Land* (Manchester, 1998)

———. *Object Lessons* (Manchester, 1995)

Brackenbury, Alison. *Selected Poems* (Manchester, 1991)

———. *1829* (Manchester, 1995)

Bradstreet, Anne. *Poems* (New York, 1970)

———. *The Works of Anne Bradstreet in Verse and Prose* (Chesterton, Mass., 1867)

Brathwaite, Edward Kamau. *The Arrivants* (Oxford, 1973)

———. *History of the Voice: The Development of Nation Language in Anglophone Caribbean Poetry* (Port-of-Spain, Trinidad and Tobago, 1984)

———. *Middle Passages* (Newcastle-upon-Tyne, 1991)

———. *Third World Poems* (Harlow, 1983)

Brodsky, Joseph. *Less Than One: Selected Essays* (London, 1986)

———. *A Part of Speech* (London, 1980)

———. *So Forth* (New York, 1996)

———. *To Urania: Selected Poems* (New York, 1988)

Brontë, Anne. *The Poems of Anne Brontë* (London, 1979)

Brontë, Charlotte. *Selected Brontë Poems* (Oxford, 1985)

Brontë, Emily. *The Complete Poems of Emily Brontë* (New York, 1941)

Brooke, Rupert. *Collected Poems* (London, 1918)

Browning, Elizabeth Barrett. *The Poetical Works* (Oxford, 1910)

Browning, Robert. *The Poems and Plays* (New York, 1934)

Bryant, William Cullen. *The Poetical Works* (New York, 1903)

Bunting, Basil. *Collected Poems* (Oxford, 1978)

———. *The Complete White Oxen: Collected Shorter Fiction* (Berkeley, 1968)

Burns, Robert. *Poems and Songs* (Oxford, 1971)

Byron, George Gordon, Lord. *Poetical Works* (Oxford, 1970)

Campbell, Roy. *Collected Works* (two volumes, Johannesburg, 1985)

Campion, Thomas. *Observations on the Art of English Poesie* (London, 1969)

———. *Works* (London, 1970)

Carew, Thomas. *The Poems of Thomas Carew* (Oxford, 1970)

———. *Cavalier Poets: Selected Poems* (ed. Thomas Clayton, Oxford, 1978)

Causley, Charles. *Collected Poems* (London, 1992)

Cavendish, Margaret, *Natures Pictures* (London, 1656)

———. Duchess of Newcastle. *Poems, and Fancies* (London, 1653)

Chapman, George. *Chapman's Homer* (Princeton, 1956)

———. *The Poems* (New York, 1962)

Chatterton, Thomas. *Complete Works* (Oxford, 1971)

Chaucer, Geoffrey. *Complete Poetry and Prose* (ed. Fisher, London, 1977)

———. *Works* (ed. Robinson, Cambridge, Mass., 1974)

Clampitt, Amy. *Collected Poems* (New York, 1997)

Clare, John. *John Clare by Himself* (Manchester, 1996)

———. *Selected Poems and Prose* (Oxford, 1967)

Clarke, Austin. *Collected Plays* (Dublin, 1963)

———. *Collected Poems* (Dublin, 1974)

Clarke, Gillian. *Collected Poems* (Manchester, 1997)

———. *Five Fields* (Manchester, 1998)

Clough, Arthur Hugh. *Poetical Works* (Oxford, 1968)

Coleridge, Samuel Taylor. *Biographia Literaria* (London, 1975)

———. *Collected Letters* (Oxford, 1971)

———. *Poetical Works* (Oxford, 1969)

———. *Table Talk* (London, 1884)

Collins, William. *The Poems of Gray, Collins and Goldsmith* (ed. Roger Lonsdale, London, 1976)

Constantine, David. *Caspar Hauser* (Newcastle-upon-Tyne, 1994)

———. *Selected Poems* (Newcastle-upon-Tyne, 1991)

Cope, Wendy. *Making Cocoa for Kingsley Amis* (London, 1986)

———. *Serious Concerns* (London, 1991)

Cowley, Abraham. *Poetry and Prose* (London, 1949)

Cowper, William. *Complete Poetical Works* (London, 1905)

Crabbe, George. *The Life and Complete Poetical Works* (London, 1851)

Crane, Hart. *The Poems of Hart Crane* (New York, 1986)

Crane, Stephen. *Complete Poems* (New York, 1972)

Crashaw, Richard. *The Poems, English, Latin and Greek* (London, 1957)

Creeley, Robert. *Selected Poems* (Berkeley, 1991)

cummings, e e. *Complete Poems* (London, 1981)

———. *The Enormous Room* (1922; Harmondsworth, 1971)

Curnow, Allen. *Early Days Yet: New and Collected Poems 1941–1997* (Manchester, 1997)

Daniel, Samuel. *Poems and a Defence of Ryme* (Cambridge, Mass., 1930)

———. *A Selection from the Poetry of Samuel Daniel and Michael Drayton* (London, 1899)

Daryush, Elizabeth. *Collected Poems* (Manchester, 1976)

Davenant, Sir William. *The Shorter Poems and Songs from the Plays and Masques* (Oxford, 1972)

Davie, Donald. *Collected Poems* (Manchester, 1999)

———. *Czeslaw Milosz and the Insufficiency of Lyric* (Knoxville, 1986)

———. *Older Masters* (Manchester, 1992)

———. *Purity of Diction in English Verse* and *Articulate Energy* (Manchester, 1994)

———. *Studies in Ezra Pound* (Manchester, 1991)

———. *Thomas Hardy and British Poetry* (London, 1972)

———. *Under Briggflatts: A History of Poetry in Great Britain 1960–1988* (Manchester, 1989)

Davis, Dick. *Devices and Desires: New and Selected Poems 1967–1987* (London, 1988)

———. *Touchwood* (London, 1996)

De la Mare, Walter. *Complete Poems* (London, 1969)

De Vere, Edward, Earl of Oxford. *Poems* (London, 1904)

Dickinson, Emily. *The Complete Poems of Emily Dickinson* (London, 1970)

———. *Selected Letters* (Cambridge, Mass., 1985)

Donne, John. *Complete English Poems* (Harmondsworth, 1971)

———. *No Man Is an Island: A Selection from the Prose of John Donne* (London, 1997)

———. *Poetical Works* (Oxford, 1971)

Doolittle, Hilda (H.D.). *Collected Poems 1912–1944* (Manchester, 1984)

———. *End to Torment: A Memoir of Ezra Pound* (Manchester, 1980)

———. *Helen in Egypt* (Manchester, 1974)

———. *Hermetic Definition* (Manchester, 1972)

———. *Selected Poems* (Manchester, 1989)

———. *Trilogy* (Manchester, 1973)

Douglas, Gavin. *Selections from Gavin Douglas* (Oxford, 1964)

Douglas, Keith. *Complete Poems* (Oxford, 1987)

———. *A Prose Miscellany* (Manchester, 1985)

Drayton, Michael. *A Selection from the Poetry of Samuel Daniel and Michael Drayton* (London, 1899)

———. *Works* (five volumes, Oxford, 1932–33)

Drummond of Hawthornden, William. *Poems and Prose* (Edinburgh, 1976)

Dryden, John. *Poetical Works* (Oxford, 1967)

———. *Of Dramatic Poesy and Other Critical Essays* (London, 1971)

Duffy, Carol-Ann. *Selected Poems* (Harmondsworth, 1994)

Dunbar, William. *Poems* (Oxford, 1970)

Duncan, Robert. *Selected Poems* (Manchester, 1993)

Dunn, Douglas. *Selected Poems 1964–1983* (London, 1986)

Eliot, T. S. *Complete Poems and Plays* (London, 1969)

———. *Inventions of the March Hare: Poems 1909–1917* (London, 1996)

———. *The Letters of T. S. Eliot 1898–1922* (London, 1971)

———. *Notes Towards the Definition of Culture* (London, 1948)

———. *The Sacred Wood: Essays on Poetry and Criticism* (London, 1920)

———. *Selected Essays* (London, 1975)

———. *"To Criticize the Critic" and Other Writings* (London, 1965)

———. *The Waste Land: Facsimile and Transcript of the Original Draft* (London, 1974)

Elizabeth I. *Poems of Queen Elizabeth I* (Providence, R. I., 1964)

Emerson, Ralph Waldo. *Selected Prose and Poetry* (New York, 1950)

Empson, William. *Collected Poems* (London, 1962)

———. *Milton's God* (London, 1961)

———. *Seven Types of Ambiguity* (1930; Harmondsworth, 1973)

———. *Some Versions of Pastoral* (1935; Harmondsworth, 1966)

Enright, D. J. *The Alluring Problem: An Essay on Irony* (Oxford, 1968)

———. *The Apothecary's Shop* (London, 1957)

———. *Collected Poems* (1998)

———. *Conspirators and Poets* (London, 1966)

———. *A Mania for Sentences* (London, 1983)

Feinstein, Elaine. *Daylight* (Manchester, 1996)

———. *Selected Poems* (Manchester, 1994)

Fenton, James. *The Memory of War and Children in Exile* (Harmondsworth, 1992)

———. *Out of Danger* (Harmondsworth, 1993)

Finch, Anne, Countess of Winchilsea. *The Poems of Anne, Countess of Winchilsea* (Chicago, 1903)

Fisher, Roy. *Poems 1955–1987* (Oxford, 1988)

Ford, Ford Madox. *The March of Litera-ture* (1938; London, 1947)

———. *Selected Poems* (Manchester, 1997)

Frost, Robert. *The Poetry of Robert Frost* (London, 1969)

———. *Selected Letters* (New York, 1965)

Fuller, Roy. *Collected Poems 1934–1984* (London, 1985)

———. *Owls and Artificers* (London, 1974)

———. *Professors and Gods* (London, 1977)

Garioch, Robert. *Complete Poetical Works* (Edinburgh, 1983)

Gascoigne, George. *Complete Works* (two volumes, London, 1907–10)

———. *The Green Knight: Selected Poetry and Prose* (Manchester, 1982)

Gascoyne, David Emery. *Selected Poems* (London, 1994)

———. *A Short Survey of Surrealism* (1935; London, 1970)

Gawain Poet. *Pearl* (Oxford, 1953)

———. *Sir Gawain and the Green Knight* (Oxford, 1967)

Gay, John. *Poetry and Prose* (Oxford, 1975)

Ginsberg, Allen. *Collected Poems 1947–1980* (New York, 1984)

Glück, Louise. *The First Five Books of Poems* (Manchester, 1997)

———. *Meadowlands* (Manchester, 1998)

———. *Proofs and Theories* (Manchester, 1999)

———. *The Wild Iris* (Manchester, 1996)

Goldsmith, Oliver. *Poems and Plays* (London, 1977)

———. *The Poems of Gray, Collins and Goldsmith* (ed. Roger Lonsdale, London, 1976)

Goodison, Lorna. *Heartease* (London, 1989)

———. *I Am Becoming My Mother* (London, 1986)

———. *Tamarind Season* (Kingston, 1980)

Gower, John. *Confessio Amantis* (New York, 1968)

———. *English Works* (Oxford, 1957)

Graham, Jorie. *The Dream of the Unified Field: Selected Poems* (Manchester, 1996)

———. *The Errancy* (Manchester, 1998)

Graham, W. S. *Collected Poems 1942–1975* (London, 1979)

———. *Selected Poems* (London, 1996)

Graves, Robert. *Centenary Selected Poems* (Manchester, 1995)

———. *Collected Writings on Poetry* (Manchester, 1995)

———. *Complete Poems I* (Manchester, 1995)

———. *Complete Poems II* (Manchester, 1997)

———. *Complete Poems III* (Manchester, 1999)

———. *Goodbye to All That* (1929, rev. ed. 1957; Harmondsworth, 1969)

Gray, Thomas. *Complete Poems* (Oxford, 1966)

———. *The Poems of Gray, Collins and Goldsmith* (ed. Roger Lonsdale, London, 1976)

Grieve, Christopher Murray. *See* Mac-Diarmid, Hugh.

Gunn, Thom. *Collected Poems* (London, 1993)

———. *The Occasions of Poetry, Essays in Criticism and Autobiography* (London, 1985)

———. *Shelf Life: Essays, Memoirs and an Interview* (London, 1994)

Gurney, Ivor. *Collected Poems* (Oxford, 1982)

———. *Severn and Somme* and *War's Embers* (Manchester, 1997)

———. *80 Poems or So* (Manchester, 1997)

Hamburger, Michael. *Collected Poems* (London, 1995)

———. *The Truth of Poetry* (London, 1969)

Hardy, Thomas. *Complete Poems* (London, 1978)

———. *The Dynasts* (London, 1965)

———. *The Life of Thomas Hardy* (1930; London, 1962)

Harrison, Tony. *A Cold Coming* (Newcastle-upon-Tyne, 1992)

———. *The Gaze of the Gorgon* (Newcastle-upon-Tyne, 1992)

———. *Selected Poems* (Harmondsworth, 1987)

——. *Theatre Works 1973–1985* (Harmondsworth, 1986)

Harwood, Gwen. *Collected Poems* (Oxford, 1991)

Hass, Robert. *Twentieth Century Pleasures* (New York, 1984)

Hawes, Stephen. In *English Verse Between Chaucer and Surrey* (ed. Hammond, Oxford, 1927)

H.D. *See* Doolittle, Hilda.

Heaney, Seamus. *The Government of the Tongue* (London, 1988)

——. *Opened Ground: Poems 1966–1996* (London, 1998)

——. *Preoccupations: Selected Prose 1968–1978* (London, 1980)

——. *The Redress of Poetry: Oxford Lectures* (London, 1995)

Heath-Stubbs, John. *Collected Poems 1943–1987* (Manchester, 1988)

——. *The Literary Essays* (Manchester, 1998)

——. *Sweetapple Earth* (Manchester, 1993)

Hemans, Felicia Dorothea. *Works* (seven volumes, London, 1839)

Henryson, Robert. *Poems* (Oxford, 1975)

——. *Poems and Fables* (London, 1958)

Herbert, George. *Poems* (Oxford, 1961)

Herrick, Robert. *Poetical Works* (Oxford, 1956)

——. *Cavalier Poets: Selected Poems* (ed. Thomas Clayton, Oxford, 1978)

Hill, Geoffrey. *Canaan* (Harmondsworth, 1997)

——. *Collected Poems* (London, 1985)

——. *The Lords of Limit* (London, 1984)

Hoccleve, Thomas. *Selected Poems* (Manchester, 1982)

Hofmann, Michael. *Acrimony* (London, 1986)

——. *Corona, Corona* (London, 1993)

——. *Night in the Iron Hotel* (London, 1983)

Hood, Thomas. *Selected Poems* (Manchester, 1992)

Hope, A. D. *Collected Poems* (Sydney, 1972)

——. *Selected Poems* (Manchester, 1986)

Hopkins, Gerard Manley. *Letters to Robert Bridges* (Oxford, 1955)

——. *Poems and Prose* (London, 1984)

Housman, A. E. *Collected Poems* (London, 1967)

——. *The Name and Nature of Poetry* (Cambridge, 1933)

Hughes, Langston. *The Panther and the Lash* (New York, 1969)

——. *Selected Poems* (New York, 1990)

Hughes, Ted. *Birthday Letters* (London, 1998)

——. *New Selected Poems 1957–1994* (London, 1995)

——. *Shakespeare and the Goddess of Complete Being* (London, 1992)

——. *Winter Pollen: Occasional Prose* (London, 1994)

Hulme, T. E. *Selected Writings* (Manchester, 1998)

Jackson, Laura (Riding). *First Awakenings* (Manchester, 1992)

——. *The Poems of Laura Riding* (Manchester, 1980)

——. *A Selection of the Poems* (Manchester, 1994)

——. *The Telling* (London, 1972)

Jarrell, Randall. *The Complete Poems* (London, 1971)

——. *Kipling, Auden & Co: Essays and Reviews 1935–1964* (Manchester, 1982)

——. *Poetry and the Age* (New York, 1953)

——. *The Third Book of Criticism* (New York, 1969)

Jeffers, Robinson. *The Double Axe* (New York, 1977)

——. *Selected Poems* (Manchester, 1987)

Jennings, Elizabeth. *Collected Poems* (Manchester, 1987)

——. *Every Changing Shape* (1961; Manchester, 1996)

——. *Familiar Spirits* (Manchester, 1994)

——. *In the Meantime* (Manchester, 1996)

——. *Praises* (Manchester, 1998)

——. *Times and Seasons* (Manchester, 1992)

Johnson, Samuel. *Complete English Poems* (Harmondsworth, 1971)

——. *Lives of the English Poets* (London, 1975)

——. *The Works of the English Poets, with Prefaces, Biographical and Critical* (seventy-five volumes, London, 1790)

Jones, David. *Anathemata* (London, 1972)

——. *The Dying Gaul* (London, 1978)

——. *Epoch and Artist* (London, 1973)

——. *In Parenthesis* (London, 1969)

——. *The Sleeping Lord and Other Fragments* (London, 1974)

Jonson, Ben. *The Complete Poems* (Harmondsworth, 1975)

Justice, Donald. *Selected Poems* (London, 1980)

Kavanagh, Patrick. *Collected Poems* (London, 1972)

Kavanagh, P. J. *Collected Poems* (Manchester, 1992)

Keats, John. *The Complete Poems* (Harmondsworth, 1977)

Keyes, Sidney. *The Collected Poems* (London, 1988)

Khalvati, Mimi. *Entries on Light* (Manchester, 1998)

——. *In White Ink* (Manchester, 1991)

——. *Mirrorwork* (Manchester, 1995)

Kinsella, Thomas. *An Duanaire, 1600–1900: Poems of the Dispossessed* (Dublin, 1981)

——. *Blood and Family* (Oxford, 1988)

——. *The Dual Tradition* (Manchester, 1995)

——. *From Centre City* (Oxford, 1994)

——. *Poems 1972–1978* (Oxford, 1980)

——. *Selected Poems 1956–1973* (Dublin, 1980)

——. *The Táin* (Dublin, 1969)

Kipling, Rudyard. *Verse: definitive edition* (London, 1940)

——. *A Choice of Kipling's Verse* (ed. T. S. Eliot, London, 1941)

Koch, Kenneth. *Making Your Own Days: The Pleasures of Reading and Writing Poetry* (New York, 1998)

——. *One Train* (Manchester, 1997)

——. *Selected Poems* (Manchester, 1991)

Landor, Walter Savage. *Poems* (London, 1971)

Langland, William. *Piers Plowman: "B" Version* (London, 1975)

Lanyer, Emilia. *The Poems of Shakespeare's Dark Lady* (London, 1978)

Larkin, Philip. *Collected Poems* (London, 1988)

——. *Required Writing* (London, 1983)

——. *Selected Letters* (London, 1992)

Lawrence, D. H. *Complete Poems* (London, 1957)

——. *Studies in Classic American Literature* (London, 1923)

Leonard, Tom. *Intimate Voices: selected work 1965–1983* (Newcastle-upon-Tyne, 1984)

Levertov, Denise. *Breathing the Water* (New York, 1987)

——. *Collected Earlier Poems 1940–1960* (New York, 1979)

——. *A Door in the Hive* (New York, 1989)

——. *Evening Train* (New York, 1992)

——. *New and Selected Essays* (New York, 1992)

——. *Selected Poems* (Newcastle-upon-Tyne, 1986)

Lewis, Alun. *A Miscellany of His Writings* (Bridgend, 1982)

——. *Selected Poetry and Prose* (London, 1966)

Lewis, Gwyneth. *Parables and Faxes* (Newcastle-upon-Tyne, 1994)

——. *Zero Gravity* (Newcastle-upon-Tyne, 1998)

Lewis, Wyndham. *Collected Poems and Plays* (Manchester, 1979)

Longfellow, Henry Wadsworth. *Poems* (London, 1970)

Lovelace, Richard. *Poems* (Oxford, 1930)

——. *Cavalier Poets: Selected Poems* (ed. Thomas Clayton, Oxford, 1978)

Lowell, Amy. *Complete Poetical Works* (Boston, 1955)

Lowell, Robert. *Collected Prose* (New York, 1987)

——. *Day by Day* (London, 1978)

——. *The Dolphin* (London, 1973)

——. *For Lizzie and Harriet* (London, 1973)

———. *For the Union Dead* (New York, 1964)

———. *History* (London, 1973)

———. *Life Studies* (London, 1959)

———. *Near the Ocean* (London, 1967)

———. *Notebook 1967–8* (New York, 1969)

———. *The Old Glory* (New York, 1964)

———. *Poems 1938–1949* (London, 1950)

———. *Selected Poems* (New York, 1977)

Loy, Mina. *The Lost Lunar Baedeker* (Manchester, 1997)

Lydgate, John. *Poems* (London, 1966)

MacCaig, Norman. *Collected Poems* (London, 1990)

MacDiarmid, Hugh (Christopher Murray Grieve). *Complete Poems I* (Manchester, 1993)

———. *Complete Poems II* (Manchester, 1994)

———. *Contemporary Scottish Studies* (Manchester, 1995)

———. *Lucky Poet* (1943; Manchester, 1994)

———. *The Raucle Tongue I* (Manchester, 1996)

———. *The Raucle Tongue II* (Manchester, 1997)

———. *The Raucle Tongue III* (Manchester, 1998)

———. *Selected Poetry* (Manchester, 1992)

MacLean, Sorley. *From Wood to Ridge: Collected Poems in Gaelic and English* (Manchester, 1989)

MacNeice, Louis. *Collected Poems* (London, 1966)

———. *Modern Poetry: A Personal Essay* (1938; London, 1969)

———. *The Poetry of W. B. Yeats* (1941; London, 1967)

MacPherson, James. *Mark Akenside, James MacPherson and Edward Young: Selected Poems* (ed. Clark, Manchester, 1994)

McAuley, James. *Collected Poems* (Sydney, 1993)

Mahon, Derek. *Selected Poems* (Harmondsworth, 1993)

Manhire, Bill. *Milky Way Bar* (Manchester, 1991)

———. *My Sunshine* (Wellington, 1996)

———. *Sheet Music: Poems 1967–1982* (Wellington, 1996)

———. *Zoetropes: Poems 1972–1982* (Manchester, 1984)

Marlowe, Christopher. *Complete Poems and Translations* (Harmondsworth, 1971)

Marvell, Andrew. *Complete Poems* (Harmondsworth, 1972)

Masefield, John. *Selected Poems* (Manchester, 1984)

Masters, Edgar Lee. *Poems* (London, 1972)

———. *Spoon River Anthology* (1915; London, 1962)

Maxwell, Glyn. *Out of the Rain* (Newcastle-upon-Tyne, 1992)

———. *Rest for the Wicked* (Newcastle-upon-Tyne, 1995)

———. *Tale of the Mayor's Son* (Newcastle-upon-Tyne, 1990)

Melville, Herman. *Selected Tales and Poems* (New York, 1950)

———. *Selected Poems* (New York, 1964)

Merrill, James. *Selected Poems 1946–1985* (New York, 1992)

Merwin, W. S. *The River Sound* (New York, 1999)

———. *Selected Poems* (New York, 1988)

———. *Unframed Originals* (New York, 1994)

Mew, Charlotte. *Collected Poems and Selected Prose* (Manchester, 1997)

Middleton, Christopher. *The Balcony Tree* (Manchester, 1992)

———. *Intimate Chronicles* (Manchester, 1996)

———. *Jackdaw Jiving: Selected Essays on Poetry and Translation* (Manchester, 1998)

———. *Selected Writings* (Manchester, 1989)

Millay, Edna St. Vincent. *Selected Poems* (Manchester, 1992)

Milton, John. *Poetical Works* (Oxford, 1966)

———. *Poems* (ed. Carey and Fowler, London, 1968)

Minhinnick, Robert. *Selected Poems* (Manchester, 1999)

Moore, Marianne. *Complete Poems* (London, 1984)

Moore, Nicholas. *Longings of the Acrobats: Selected Poems* (Manchester, 1990)

More, Sir Thomas. *The English Works* (volumes 1 and 2, London, 1931)

Morgan, Edwin. *Collected Poems* (Manchester, 1990)

———. *Collected Translations* (Manchester, 1996)

———. *Crossing the Border* (Manchester, 1990)

———. *Essays* (Manchester, 1974)

———. *Sweeping Out the Dark* (Manchester, 1994)

———. *Virtual and Other Realities* (Manchester, 1997)

Motion, Andrew. *Dangerous Play: Poems 1974–1984* (Harmondsworth, 1984)

———. *Love in a Life* (London, 1991)

———. *Natural Causes* (London, 1987)

———. *Salt Water* (London, 1997)

Muir, Edwin. *Collected Poems* (London, 1964)

———. *Essays in Literature and Society* (London, 1965)

Muldoon, Paul. *New Selected Poems 1968–1994* (London, 1996)

Murray, Les. *The Boys Who Stole the Funeral* (Manchester, 1989)

———. *Collected Poems* (Manchester, 1998)

———. *Fredy Neptune* (Manchester, 1998)

———. *The Paperbark Tree* (Manchester, 1992)

Nashe, Thomas. *The Works* (London, 1958)

Niedecker, Lorine. *From This Condensery: The Complete Writing* (North Carolina, 1985)

O'Hara, Frank. *Collected Poems* (New York, 1971)

———. *Selected Poems* (Manchester, 1991)

Olds, Sharon. *The Father* (New York, 1992)

———. *The Sign of Saturn* (New York, 1991)

Olson, Charles. *Call Me Ishmael* (San Francisco, 1967)

———. *Collected Poems* (Berkeley, 1987)

———. *Human Universe and Other Essays* (New York, 1967)

———. *Mayan Letters* (London, 1968)

———. *The Maximus Poems* (Berkeley, 1983)

———. *Selected Poems* (Berkeley, 1993)

Oppen, George. *Collected Poems* (New York, 1975)

Orleans, Charles of. *English Poems* (Oxford, 1941)

Owen, Wilfred. *Collected Letters* (London, 1967)

———. *The Poems* (London, 1990)

Palmer, Michael. *The Lion Bridge: Selected Poems 1972–1995* (New York, 1998)

Peck, John. *Argura* (Manchester, 1993)

———. *The Broken Blockhouse Wall* (Manchester, 1979)

———. *"M" and Other Poems* (Evanston, Ill., 1996)

———. *Poems and Translations of Hi Lo* (Manchester, 1991)

———. *Selva Morale* (Manchester, 1995)

Percy, Thomas. *Reliques of Ancient English Poetry* (London, 1765)

Philips, Katherine. *Poems, By the Most Deservedly Admired Mrs Katherine Philips, The Matchless Orinda* (London, 1667)

Pinsky, Robert. *The Figured Wheel: New and Collected Poems 1966–1996* (Manchester, 1997)

———. *Landor's Poetry* (Chicago, 1968)

Plath, Sylvia. *Collected Poems* (London, 1981)

———. *Johnny Panic and the Bible of Dreams* (London, 1977; 1979)

Poe, Edgar Allan. *Poems and Essays* (London, 1969)

———. *Selected Writings* (Harmondsworth, 1970)

Pope, Alexander. *Poetical Works* (Oxford, 1966)

Porter, Peter. *Collected Poems* (Oxford, 1984)

Pound, Ezra. *The ABC of Reading* (1934; London, 1991)
———. *The Cantos of Ezra Pound* (New York, 1972)
———. *Collected Shorter Poems* (London, 1984)
———. *Ernest Fenollosa: The Chinese Written Character as a Medium for Poetry* (Washington, D.C., 1951)
———. *A Guide to Kulchur* (New York, 1952)
———. *The Literary Essays of Ezra Pound* (London, 1954)
———. *Selected Prose 1909–1965* (London, 1973)
———. *The Translations of Ezra Pound* (New York, 1953)
Powell, Neil. *Selected Poems* (Manchester, 1998)
Prince, F. T. *Collected Poems 1935–1992* (Manchester, 1993)
———. *The Italian Element in Milton's Verse* (Oxford, 1962)
Prynne, J. H. *Poems* (Edinburgh, 1982)
Quarles, Francis. *The Complete Works* (three volumes, 1880–81)
Raine, Craig. *Haydn and the Valve Trumpet* (London, 1990)
———. *History: The Home Movie* (Harmondsworth, 1994)
———. *A Martian Sends a Postcard Home* (Oxford, 1979)
———. *The Onion, Memory* (Oxford, 1978)
———. *Rich* (London, 1984)
Ralegh, Sir Walter. *Selected Writings* (Manchester, 1984)
Ransom, John Crowe. *Poems* (Manchester, 1991)
———. *Poems and Essays* (New York, 1955)
Redgrove, Peter. *Moon Disposes: Poems 1954–1987* (London, 1987)
Reed, Henry. *Collected Poems* (Oxford, 1991)
Rexroth, Kenneth. *Selected Poems* (New York, 1984)
Reznikoff, Charles. *Poems 1918–1975: The Complete Poems* (Santa Barbara, 1989)
Rich, Adrienne. *An Atlas of the Difficult World: Poems 1988–1991* (New York, 1991)
———. *Blood, Bread, and Poetry: Selected Prose 1979–1986* (New York, 1987)
———. *Collected Early Poems 1950–1970* (New York, 1970)
———. *Dark Fields of the Republic: Poems 1991–1995* (New York, 1995)
———. *The Fact of a Doorframe: Poems Selected and New 1950–1984* (New York, 1984)
———. *On Lies, Secrets and Silence* (New York, 1979)
———. *Time's Power: Poems 1985–1988* (New York, 1988)
Rickword, Edgell. *Collected Poems* (Manchester, 1991)
———. *Essays and Opinions 1921–1931* (Manchester, 1974)
———. *Literature in Society* (Manchester, 1978)
Riding, Laura. *See* Jackson, Laura (Riding).
Ridler, Anne. *Collected Poems* (Manchester, 1994)
Riley, John. *Selected Poems* (Manchester, 1995)
Robinson, Edwin Arlington. *Selected Poems* (New York, 1953)
Rochester, John Wilmot, Earl of. *Complete Works* (Harmondsworth, 1994)
Roethke, Theodore. *Collected Poems* (London, 1985)
———. *On the Poet and his Craft: Selected Prose* (Seattle, 1965)
Romer, Stephen. *Idols* (Oxford, 1986)
———. *Plato's Ladder* (Oxford, 1992)
Rosenberg, Isaac. *The Collected Works of Isaac Rosenberg* (London, 1979)
Rossetti, Christina. *The Poetical Works of Christina Georgina Rossetti* (London, 1904)
Rossetti, Dante Gabriel. *Poetical Works* (1903)
Sackville, Thomas (Earl of Dorset). *Poetical Works of Surrey and Sackville* (Oxford, 1854)
Sandburg, Carl. *Complete Poems* (New York, 1970)

Sassoon, Siegfried. *Collected Poems 1908–1956* (London, 1984)

Schuyler, James. *Selected Poems* (Manchester, 1990)

Schwartz, Delmore. *What Is to Be Given: Selected Poems* (Manchester, 1976)

Scott, Sir Walter. *Selected Poems* (Manchester, 1992)

Scovell, E. J. *Collected Poems* (Manchester, 1988)

Scupham, Peter. *Selected Poems* (Oxford, 1990)

Sedley, Sir Charles. *Poetical and Dramatic Works* (London, 1928)

Seth, Vikram. *The Golden Gate* (New York, 1986)

——. *The Humble Administrator's Garden* (Manchester, 1985)

Shakespeare, William. *New Variorum* (Philadelphia, 1944)

——. *Poems and Sonnets* (London, 1898)

Shelley, Percy Bysshe. *Poetical Works* (Oxford, 1970)

Sibum, Norm. *In Laban's Field* (Manchester, 1993)

Sidney, Mary (Countess of Pembroke). *The Psalms of Sir Philip Sidney and the Countess of Pembroke* (New York, 1963)

Sidney, Sir Philip. *An Apology for Poetry* (Manchester, 1964)

——. *Arcadia* (Harmondsworth, 1977)

——. *Poems* (Oxford, 1962)

Singer, James Burns. *Selected Poems* (Manchester, 1977)

Sisson, C. H. *The Avoidance of Literature: Collected Essays* (Manchester, 1979)

——. *Collected Poems* (Manchester, 1998)

——. *Collected Translations* (Manchester, 1997)

——. *English Perspectives* (Manchester, 1992)

——. *English Poetry 1900–1950* (London, 1971)

——. *In Two Minds* (Manchester, 1990)

Sitwell, Edith. *"Façade" and Other Poems 1920–1935* (London, 1971)

——. *Selected Poems* (London, 1965).

Skelton, John. *Poems* (Oxford, 1969)

Slessor, Kenneth. *Selected Poems* (Sydney, 1975)

Smart, Christopher. *Selected Poems* (Harmondsworth, 1990)

Smith, Charlotte. *Beachy Head, with Other Poems* (London, 1807)

——. *Elegiac Sonnets* (London, 1784)

Smith, Iain Crichton. *Collected Poems* (Manchester, 1992)

——. *Ends and Beginnings* (Manchester, 1994)

——. *The Human Face* (Manchester, 1996)

——. *The Leaf and the Marble* (Manchester, 1998)

——. *Towards the Human: Selected Essays* (Edinburgh, 1986)

Smith, Stevie. *Collected Poems* (Harmondsworth, 1975)

Snyder, Gary. *No Nature: New and Selected Poems* (New York, 1992)

Southey, Robert. *The Poems* (Oxford, 1909)

Spender, Stephen. *Selected Poems* (London, 1965)

Spenser, Edmund. *Poetical Works* (Oxford, 1970)

Stein, Gertrude. *Look at Me and Here I Am* (London, 1967)

——. *Stanzas in Meditation and Other Poems 1929–1933* (New York, 1956)

Stevens, Wallace. *Collected Poems* (London, 1955)

——. *The Necessary Angel* (New York, 1952)

——. *Opus Posthumous* (London, 1959)

Strand, Mark. *Blizzard of One* (New York, 1998)

——. *Selected Poems* (Manchester, 1995)

Suckling, Sir John. *The Works* (Oxford, 1971)

——. *Cavalier Poets: Selected Poems* (ed. Thomas Clayton, Oxford, 1978)

Surrey, Henry Howard, Earl of. *Poems* (Oxford, 1964)

Swift, Jonathan. *Poetical Works* (Oxford, 1967)

Swinburne, Algernon Charles. *George Chapman: A Critical Essay* (New York, 1977)

——. *Selected Poetry and Prose* (New York, 1968)

Tate, Allen. *Collected Poems 1919–1976* (London, 1978)

——. *Essays of Four Decades* (London, 1970)

Tate, James. *Selected Poems* (Manchester, 1997)

Taylor, Edward. *Poems* (New Haven, 1960)

——. *Poetical Works* (Princeton, 1967)

Tennyson, Alfred, Lord. *Poems* (three volumes, London, 1969)

Thomas, Dylan. *Collected Poems 1934–1953* (London, 1966)

——. *Portrait of the Artist as a Young Dog* (London, 1940)

——. *Under Milk Wood* (London, 1954)

Thomas, Edward. *Collected Poems* (London, 1949)

——. *A Language Not to Be Betrayed* (Manchester, 1981)

——. *Poems and Last Poems* (London, 1973)

Thomas, R. S. *Complete Poems* (London, 1993)

——. *Selected Prose* (Bridgend, 1986)

Thompson, Francis. *The Works* (three volumes, London, 1913)

Thomson, James. *The Complete Poetical Works of James Thomson* (London, 1951)

——. *Poems and Some Letters* (London, 1963)

Thoreau, Henry David. *Collected Poems* (New York, 1966)

——. *Walden* (Harmondsworth, 1973)

Tomlinson, Charles. *Annunciations* (Oxford, 1989)

——. *Collected Poems* (Oxford, 1985)

——. *The Door in the Wall* (Oxford, 1992)

——. *Jubilation* (Oxford, 1995)

——. *The Return* (Oxford, 1987)

——. *Some Americans: A Personal Record* (Berkeley, 1981)

Traherne, Thomas. *Selected Poems and Prose* (Harmondsworth, 1991)

Turberville, George. *English Poets II* (Oxford, 1810)

Tusser, Thomas. *Five Hundred Points of Good Husbandry* (Oxford, 1984)

Vaughan, Henry. *Complete Poems* (Harmondsworth, 1976)

Vaux, Thomas, Lord. In *Songes and Sonettes: Tottel's Miscellany* (Cambridge, Mass., 1924–37)

Wainwright, Jeffrey. *The Apparent Colonnades* (Manchester, 1999)

——. *The Red-Headed Pupil* (Manchester, 1994)

——. *Selected Poems* (Manchester, 1985)

Walcott, Derek. *The Bounty* (London, 1997)

——. *Collected Poems 1948–1984* (London, 1990)

——. *Omeros* (London, 1990)

Waller, Edmund. *The Poems of Edmund Waller* (London, 1893)

Warner, Sylvia Townsend. *Collected Poems* (Manchester, 1982)

Watkins, Vernon. *Collected Poems* (Ipswich, 1986)

Wells, Robert. *Lusus* (Manchester, 1999)

——. *Selected Poems* (Manchester, 1986)

Wheatley, Phillis. *The Poems of Phillis Wheatley* (New York, 1989)

Whitman, Walt. *Complete Poetry, Selected Prose and Letters* (London, 1938)

——. *Leaves of Grass* (London, 1965)

——. *Portable Walt Whitman* (London, 1971)

Whitney, Isabella. *The Copy of a letter, lately written in meeter, by a yonge Gentilwoman: to her unconstant lover* (London, 1567)

——. *A sweet nosegay or pleasant posye* (London, 15..)

Wickham, Anna. *The Writings of Anna Wickham: Free Woman and Poet* (London, 1984)

Wilbur, Richard. *New and Collected Poems* (London, 1989)

——. *Responses: Prose Pieces 1953–1976* (New York, 1976)

Wilde, Oscar. *The Complete Works* (London, 1966)

Williams, William Carlos. *Collected Poems 1909–1939* (Manchester, 1986)

——. *Collected Poems 1939–1962* (Manchester, 1988)

——. *I Wanted to Write a Poem: The Autobiography of the Works of a Poet* (1958; New York, 1978)

——. *In the American Grain* (1925; New York, 1956)

——. *Paterson* (Manchester, 1992)

——. *Selected Essays* (New York, 1969)

Wilmer, Clive. *Poets Talking* (Manchester, 1994)

——. *Selected Poems* (Manchester, 1995)

Winters, Yvor. *Collected Poems* (Manchester, 1978)

——. *The Function of Criticism* (Chicago, 1957)

——. *In Defense of Reason* (Chicago, 1947)

——. *The Uncollected Essays and Reviews* (Chicago, 1973)

Woods, Gregory. *Articulate Flesh: Male Homo-Eroticism and Modern Poetry* (New Haven, 1987)

——. *A History of Gay Literature: The Male Tradition* (New Haven, 1998)

——. *We Have the Melon* (Manchester, 1992)

Wordsworth, William. *Poetical Works* (Oxford, 1969)

——. *Selected Prose* (Harmondsworth, 1988)

Wright, David. *Metrical Observations* (Manchester, 1980)

——. *Poems and Versions* (Manchester, 1992)

——. *To the Gods the Shades: New and Collected Poems* (Manchester, 1976)

Wright, James, *Collected Poems* (Middletown, Conn., 1972)

Wright, Judith. *Collected Poems* (Manchester, 1994)

——. *Preoccupations in Australian Poetry* (London, 1965)

Wroth, Mary. *The Poems of Lady Mary Wroth* (Baton Rouge, 1983)

Wyatt, Sir Thomas. *The Complete Poems* (New Haven, 1978)

Yeats, William Butler. *Autobiographies* (1926; London, 1955)

——. *Collected Poems* (London, 1982)

——. *Essays and Introductions* (London, 1961)

——. *Memoirs* (London, 1973)

——. *Mythologies* (London, 1959)

Young, Andrew. *Selected Poems* (Manchester, 1998)

Young. Edward. *Mark Akenside, James MacPherson and Edward Young: Selected Poems* (ed. Clark, Manchester, 1994)

Zukofsky, Louis. *"A"* (Berkeley, 1978)

——. *Complete Short Poetry* (Baltimore, 1991)

ANTHOLOGIES

Adcock, Fleur. *Faber Book of Twentieth Century Women's Poetry* (London, 1987)

Allen, Donald M. *The New American Poetry* (London, 1960)

Allison, A. W. et al. *The Norton Anthology of Poetry* (New York, 1983)

Alvarez, A. *The New Poetry* (Harmondsworth, 1962)

Atwood, Margaret. *The New Oxford Book of Canadian Verse* (Oxford, 1985)

Baker, Kenneth. *The Faber Book of War Poetry* (London, 1996)

Bennett, J. A. W., and G. V. Smithers. *Early Middle English Verse and Prose* (Oxford, 1968)

Bornholdt, J., G. O'Brien and M. Williams. *An Anthology of New Zealand Poetry in English* (Auckland, 1997)

Breen, Jennifer. *Women Romantic Poets* (London, 1992)

Buckley, Vincent. *The Faber Book of Modern Australian Verse* (London, 1991)

Burnett, Paula. *Penguin Book of Caribbean Verse in English* (Harmondsworth, 1986)

Chambers, E. K. *The Oxford Book of Sixteenth Century Verse* (Oxford, 1966)

Clayton, Thomas. *Cavalier Poets: Selected Poems* (Oxford, 1978)

Conran, Anthony. *The Penguin Book of Welsh Verse* (Harmondsworth, 1967)

Couzyn, Jeni. *The Bloodaxe Book of Contemporary Women Poets* (Newcastle-upon-Tyne, 1985)

Crozier, Andrew, and Tim Longville. *A Various Art* (Manchester, 1987)

Curnow, Alan. *The Penguin Book of New Zealand Verse* (Harmondsworth, 1960)

Davie, Donald. *The New Oxford Book of Christian Verse* (Oxford, 1981)

Davison, Dennis. *The Penguin Book of Eighteenth-Century Verse* (Harmondsworth, 1973)

Deane, Seamus. *The Field Day Anthology of Irish Writing* (three volumes, Derry, 1991)

Dunn, Douglas. *The Faber Book of Twentieth-Century Scottish Poetry* (London, 1992)

Enright, D. J. *The Oxford Book of Contemporary Verse* (Oxford, 1980)

Fifteen Poets from Gower to Arnold (Oxford, 1940)

Fowler, Alastair. *The New Oxford Book of Seventeenth Century Verse* (Oxford, 1991)

France, Linda. *Sixty Women Poets* (Newcastle-upon-Tyne, 1993)

Gardner, Helen. *The Metaphysical Poets* (Harmondsworth, 1966)

Gilbert, Sandra M., and Susan Gubar. *The Norton Anthology of Literature by Women: The Traditions in English* (New York, 1996)

Graves, Robert. *English and Scottish Ballads* (London, 1957)

Gray, Stephen. *The Penguin Book of Southern African Verse* (Harmondsworth, 1989)

Greer, G. et al. *Kissing the Rod: An Anthology of Seventeenth-Century Women's Verse* (London, 1988)

Gustafson, Ralph. *The Penguin Book of Canadian Verse* (Harmondsworth, 1967)

Hall, Donald. *American Poetry: An Introductory Anthology* (London, 1969)

Hall, Joseph. *Selections from Early Middle English 1130–1250* (Oxford, 1920)

Hamilton, Ian. *The Poetry of War 1939–1945* (London, 1965)

Heath-Stubbs, J., and David Wright. *Faber Book of Twentieth-Century Verse* (London, 1965)

Heseltine, Harry. *The Penguin Book of Australian Verse* (Harmondsworth, 1972)

Hulse, M., D. Kennedy and D. Morley. *The New Poetry* (Newcastle-upon-Tyne, 1993)

Hymns Ancient and Modern (London, 1916)

Johnson, Samuel. *The Works of the English Poets, with Prefaces, Biographical and Critical* (seventy-five volumes, London, 1790)

Jones, Peter. *Imagist Poetry* (Harmondsworth, 1972)

Kinsella, Thomas. *The New Oxford Book of Irish Verse* (Oxford, 1986)

Larkin, Philip. *The Oxford Book of Twentieth-Century English Verse* (Oxford, 1973)

Lonsdale, Roger. *Eighteenth-Century Women Poets* (Oxford, 1989)

———. *The New Oxford Book of Eighteenth-Century Verse* (Oxford, 1985)

Moore, Geoffrey. *American Literature: A Representative Anthology of American Writing from Colonial Times to the Present* (London, 1964)

———. *Penguin Book of American Verse* (Harmondsworth, revised edition, 1977)

Morrison, Blake, and Andrew Motion. *The Penguin Book of Contemporary British Poetry* (Harmondsworth, 1982)

Muldoon, Paul. *The Faber Book of Contemporary Irish Poetry* (London, 1992)

Murray, Les. *Fivefathers: Five Australian Poets of the Pre-academic Era* (Manchester, 1994)

Parfitt, George. *Silver Poets of the Seventeenth Century* (London, 1974)

Pratt, William. *The Fugitive Poets: Modern Southern Poetry in Perspective* (Nashville, Tenn., 1991)

Pritchard, R. E. *Poetry by English Women: Elizabethan to Victorian* (Manchester, 1990)

Reese, M. A. *Elizabethan Verse Romances* (London, 1968)

Reeves, James. *Georgian Poetry* (Harmondsworth, 1962)

Rennison, Nick, and Michael Schmidt. *Poets on Poets* (Manchester, 1997)

Ricks, Christopher. *The New Oxford Book of Victorian Verse* (Oxford, 1987)

Roberts, Michael. *The Faber Book of Modern Verse* (London, 1951)

Sands, Donald B. *Middle English Verse Romances* (Oxford, 1988)

Schmidt, Michael. *A Calendar of Modern Poetry* (Manchester, 1994)

Scott, Tom. *The Penguin Book of Scottish Verse* (Harmondsworth, 1970)

Sisam, Kenneth. *Fourteenth Century Verse and Prose* (Oxford, 1921)

Skelton, Robin. *Poetry of the Forties* (Harmondsworth, 1968)

——. *Poetry of the Thirties* (Harmondsworth, 1964)

Smith, David Nichol. *The Oxford Book of Eighteenth Century Verse* (Oxford, 1926)

Soyinka, Wole. *Poems of Black Africa* (London, 1975)

Stallworthy, Jon. *The Oxford Book of War Poetry* (Oxford, 1894)

Thornton, R. K. R. *Poetry of the 'Nineties* (Harmondsworth, 1970)

Tomlinson, Charles. *The Oxford Book of Verse in English Translation* (1980)

Tottel, Richard. *The Paradyse of Daynty Devises* (Cambridge, Mass., 1924–37)

——. *Songes and Sonettes: Tottel's Miscellany* (Cambridge, Mass., 1924–37)

Vendler, Helen. *The Faber Book of Contemporary American Poetry* (London, 1994)

Watson, Roderick. *The Poetry of Scotland* (Edinburgh, 1995)

Williams, John. *English Renaissance Poetry: A Collection of Shorter Poems from Skelton to Jonson* (Fayetteville, Ark., 1990)

Woudhuysen, H. R. *The Penguin Book of Renaissance Verse* (Harmondsworth, 1993)

Wright, David. *Longer Contemporary Poems* (Harmondsworth, 1966)

——. *The Mid-Century: English Poetry 1940–1960* (Harmondsworth, 1965)

Yeats, William Butler. *Oxford Book of Modern Verse* (Oxford, 1936)

HISTORY AND SECONDARY

Abrams, M. H. *The Mirror and the Lamp: Romantic Theory and the Critical Tradition* (Oxford, 1953)

Addison, Joseph. *Critical Essays from the Spectator* (Oxford, 1970)

Alvarez, A. *Beyond All This Fiddle* (London, 1968)

——. *The Savage God* (London, 1971)

——. *The Shaping Spirit* (London, 1958)

——. *Under Pressure: The Writer in Society* (London, 1965)

Armstrong, Isobel. *Victorian Poetry: Poetry, Poetics and Politics* (London, 1991)

Attridge, Derek. *Poetic Rhythm* (Cambridge, 1995)

Aubrey, John. *Brief Lives* (London, 1949)

Bate, Walter Jackson. *The Burden of the Past and the English Poet* (London, 1971)

Bedient, Calvin. *Eight Contemporary Poets* (London, 1974)

Bennett, Joan. *Five Metaphysical Poets* (Cambridge, 1966)

Bergonzi, Bernard. *Heroes' Twilight* (Manchester, 1996)

——. *The Twentieth Century* (London, 1970)

Bloom, Harold. *The Anxiety of Influence* (Oxford, 1973)
——. *Figures of Capable Imagination* (New York, 1976)
——. *Ruin the Sacred Truths: Poetry and Belief from the Bible to the Present* (Cambridge, Mass., 1989)
Bradford, Richard. *A Linguistic History of English Poetry* (London, 1993)
Brogan, T. V. F., ed. *The New Princeton Handbook of Poetic Terms* (Princeton, 1994)
Brooks, Cleanth. *The Well Wrought Urn* (London, 1968)
Brooks, Cleanth, and Robert Penn Warren. *Understanding Poetry* (New York, 1938)
Burrow, J. A. *Essays in Mediaeval Literature* (Oxford, 1984)
——. *Mediaeval Writers and Their Work: Middle English Literature 1100–1500* (Oxford, 1982)
——. *Ricardian Poetry: Chaucer, Gower, Langland and the "Gawain" poet* (London, 1971)
Bush, Douglas. *English Literature in the Earlier Seventeenth Century 1600–1660* (Oxford, 1946)
Buxton, John. *Elizabethan Taste* (London, 1963)
Corcoran, Neil. *English Poetry Since 1940* (London, 1993)
Craig, Cairns, ed. *History of Scottish Literature* (four volumes, Aberdeen, 1987–89)
Crawford, Robert. *Devolving English Literature* (Oxford, 1993)
Crawford, Robert, et. al. *Talking Verse: Interviews with Poets* (St. Andrews, 1995)
Croft, P. J. *Autograph Poetry in the English Language* (two volumes, London, 1973)
Cunliffe, Marcus. *The Literature of the United States* (Harmondsworth, 1970)
Daiches, David, ed. *A Critical History of English Literature* (four volumes, London, 1969)
Davenport, Guy. *The Geography of the Imagination* (San Francisco, 1981)

De Quincey, Thomas. *Recollections of the Lakes and the Lake Poets* (Harmondsworth, 1970)
Edwards, Michael. *Towards a Christian Poetics* (London, 1984)
Elliott, E., et al. *Columbia Literary History of the United States* (New York, 1988)
Everett, Barbara. *Poets in their Time: Essays on English Poetry from Donne to Larkin* (London, 1986)
Ford, Boris. ed. *New Pelican Guide to English Literature* (nine volumes, Harmondsworth, 1988)
Fowler, Alastair. *A History of English Literature: Forms and Kinds from the Middle Ages to the Present* (Oxford, 1987)
Fussell, Paul. *The Great War and Modern Memory* (Oxford, 1975)
——. *Poetic Metre and Poetic Form* (New York, 1979)
Gray, Richard. *American Poetry of the Twentieth Century* (London, 1990)
Haffenden, John. *Viewpoints: poets in conversation* (London, 1981)
Hammond, Gerald. *Fleeting Things: English Poets and Poems, 1616–1660* (Cambridge, Mass., 1990)
Hart, James. *Oxford Companion to American Literature* (New York, 1975)
Hazlitt, William. *Selected Writings* (Harmondsworth, 1970)
Hill, Christopher. *Milton and the English Revolution* (Oxford, 1977)
Hollander, John. *Rhyme's Reason: A Guide to English Verse* (New Haven, 1981)
Howard, Richard. *Alone with America* (New York, 1980)
Jones, John. *William Wordsworth: The Egotistical Sublime* (London, 1964)
Jones, Peter. *50 American Poets* (London, 1980)
Kalstone, David. *Becoming a Poet: Elizabeth Bishop with Marianne Moore and Robert Lowell* (New York, 1989)
Kennedy, David. *New Relations: The*

Refashioning of British poetry 1980–94 (Bridgend, 1996)

Kenner, Hugh. *The Pound Era: The Age of Ezra Pound, T. S. Eliot, James Joyce and Wyndham Lewis* (London, 1975)

——. *A Sinking Island: The Modern English Writers* (London, 1988)

Kermode, Frank. *An Appetite for Poetry* (London, 1989)

——. *The Classic* (London, 1975)

——. *Forms of Attention* (London, 1985)

——. *The Genesis of Secrecy* (London, 1979)

——. *History and Value* (Oxford, 1988)

——. *Living Milton* (London, 1960)

——. *Poetry, Narrative, History* (1990)

——. *Romantic Image* (London, 1957)

——. *The Sense of an Ending* (London, 1967)

——. *The Uses of Error* (London, 1991)

Leavis, F. R. *The Common Pursuit* (London, 1952)

——. *New Bearings in English Poetry* (London, 1961)

——. *Revaluation: Tradition and Development in English Poetry* (Harmondsworth, 1964)

Lever, J. W. *The Elizabethan Love Sonnet* (London, 1956)

Lewis, C. S. *The Allegory of Love: A Study in Mediaeval Tradition* (Oxford, 1936)

——. *The Discarded Image: An Introduction to Mediaeval and Renaissance Literature* (Cambridge, 1964)

——. *English Literature in the Sixteenth Century* (Oxford, 1953)

Lucas, John. *England and Englishness: Ideas of Nationhood in English Poetry 1688–1900* (London, 1990)

Maycock, Alan. *Chronicles of Little Gidding* (London, 1954)

Martz, Louis. *The Poetry of Meditation* (New Haven, 1954)

Morrison, Blake. *The Movement: English Poetry and Fiction of the 1950s* (Oxford, 1980)

Nowottny, Winifred. *The Language Poets Use* (London, 1962)

Perkins, David. *A History of Modern Poetry: Modernism and After* (New Haven, 1987)

Plimpton, George, ed. *Poets at Work: The Paris Review Interviews* (Harmondsworth, 1989)

Plant, Marjorie. *The English Book Trade: An Economic History of the Making and Sale of Books* (London, 1939)

Praz, Mario. *The Romantic Agony* (London, 1966)

Richards, I. A. *Principles of Literary Criticism* (London, 1967)

Ricks, Christopher. *The Force of Poetry* (Oxford, 1984)

——. *Keats and Embarrassment* (Oxford, 1974)

——. *Milton's Grand Style* (Oxford, 1963)

——. *Tennyson* (London, 1972)

Scully, James. *Modern Poets on Modern Poetry* (London, 1970)

Smith, Bruce. *Homosexual Desire in Shakespeare's England: A Cultural Poetics* (Chicago, 1991)

Spiller, Robert, et al., eds. *Literary History of the United States* (London, 1975)

Spingarn, J. E. *A History of Literary Criticism in the Renaissance* (New York, 1908)

Stead, C. K. *The New Poetic* (Harmondsworth, 1967)

Steele, Timothy. *Missing Measures: Modern Poetry and the Revolt Against Meter* (Arkansas, 1990)

Strachey, Lytton. *Eminent Victorians* (London, 1908)

Tuve, Rosemond. *Elizabethan and Metaphysical Imagery* (Chicago, 1947)

Vendler, Helen. *The Music of What Happens: Poems, Poets, Critics* (New York, 1988)

——. *Part of Nature, Part of Us: Modern American Poets* (New York, 1980)

Ward, Sir A. W. and A. R. Waller, eds. *Cambridge History of English Literature* (fifteen volumes, 1907)

Warton, Thomas. *The History of English Poetry: From the Close of the Eleventh* to the Commencement of the Eighteenth Century (four volumes, 1824)

Willey, Basil. *The Eighteenth Century Background* (London, 1939)

———. *Nineteenth Century Studies: Coleridge to Matthew Arnold* (London, 1949)

———. *The Seventeenth Century Background* (London, 1934)

Wilson, Edmund. *Axel's Castle: A Study in the Imaginative Literature of 1870–1930* (New York, 1931)

———. *From the Uncollected Edmund Wilson* (Athens, Ohio, 1995)

Index

OSCAR WILDE
by Richard Ellmann

The writing of *Oscar Wilde* took nearly twenty years of research, and it will stand as the definitive biography. The book's emotional resonance, its riches of color and conversation, and the subtlety of its critical illuminations give life to this portrait of the complex man, the charmer, the great playwright, the daring champion of the primacy of art.

Biography/0-394-75984-2

SILENT WOMAN
Sylvia Plath and Ted Hughes
by Janet Malcolm

From the moment it was first published in *The New Yorker,* this brilliant work of literary criticism aroused great attention. Janet Malcolm brings her shrewd intelligence to bear on the legend of Sylvia Plath and the wildly productive industry of Plath biographies. Features a new afterword by Malcolm.

Biography/Literary Criticism/0-679-75140-8

VIRGINIA WOOLF
by Hermione Lee

While Virginia Woolf has had no shortage of biographers, none has seemed as naturally suited to the task as Hermione Lee. Subscribing to Virginia Woolf's own belief in the fluidity and elusiveness of identity, Lee comes at her subject from a multitude of perspectives, producing a richly layered portrait of the writer and the woman that leaves all of her complexities and contradictions intact.

Biography/0-375-70136-2

WALT WHITMAN'S AMERICA
by David S. Reynolds

David Reynolds shows how Whitman gathered inspiration from nineteenth-century American life: the convulsions of slavery and depression; the dandyism of the Bowery "b'hoys"; the rhetoric of actors, orators, and divines. We see how he reconciled his own homosexuality with contemporary mores and how his courtship of the public presaged the vogues of advertising and celebrity.

Biography/History/0-679-76709-6

Available at your local bookstore, or call toll-free to order:
1-800-793-2665 (credit cards only).